KT-368-219

COLIN DRURY

MANAGEMENT AND COST ACCOUNTING

7TH EDITION

Colin Drury is Emeritus Professor at the
University of Huddersfield, UK

NORWICH CITY COLLEGE LIBRARY

Stock No	229937	
Class	658.1511 DRU	
Cat.		Proc.

SOUTH-WESTERN
CENGAGE Learning

Australia • Brazil • Japan • Korea • Mexico • Singapore • Spain • United Kingdom • United States

Management and Cost Accounting, 7th Edition
Colin Drury

Publisher: Pat Bond
Development editor: James Clark
Production manager: Alissa Chappell
Manufacturing manager: Helen Mason
Marketing manager: Anne-Marie Scoones
Typesetter: Saxon Graphics, Derby, UK
Cover design: Jackie Wrout
Text design: Design Deluxe, Bath, UK

© 2008, Colin Drury

All rights reserved by Cengage Learning 2008. The text of this publication, or any part thereof, may not be reproduced or transmitted in any form or by any means, electronic or mechanical, including photocopying, recording, storage in an information retrieval system, or otherwise, without prior permission of the publisher.

While the publisher has taken all reasonable care in the preparation of this book, the publisher makes no representation, express or implied, with regard to the accuracy of the information contained in this book and cannot accept any legal responsibility or liability for any errors or omissions from the book or the consequences thereof.

For product information and technology assistance, contact emea.info@cengage.com.

For permission to use material from this text or product, and for permission queries, email Clsuk.permissions@cengage.com

Products and services that are referred to in this book may be either trademarks and/or registered trademarks of their respective owners. The publishers and author/s make no claim to these trademarks.

British Library Cataloguing-in-Publication Data
A catalogue record for this book is available from the British Library

ISBN: 978–1–84480–566–2

Cengage Learning EMEA
High Holborn House, 50–51 Bedford Row
London WC1R 4LR

Cengage Learning products are represented in Canada by Nelson Education Ltd.

For your lifelong learning solutions, visit www.cengage.co.uk
Purchase e-books or e-chapters at: http://estore.bized.co.uk

Printed by G Canale & C, Italy

arner

COLIN DRURY Management and Cost Accounting, 7th edition

Visit the Management and Cost Accounting website at www.drury-online.com to find further teaching and learning material including:

- Learning notes
- Case studies
- Examview® Interactive Self-Test Questions
- Weblinks
- PowerPoint slides
- Guide to Excel
- Definitions of accounting and finance terms
- Extra question and answer material
- Student's Manual sample chapter

For Lecturers

All of the student web resources listed above plus:

- Instructor's manual – including answers to IM Review problems in the text
- Case study teaching notes to accompany the case studies on the website
- Downloadable figures and tables from the book for use in your teaching
- Overhead transparencies – available to download as pdf files
- Spreadsheet exercises

Supplementary Resources

ExamView ® (ISBN 978-1-84480-572-3)

This testbank and test generator provides a huge amount of different types of questions, allowing lecturers to create online, paper and local area network (LAN) tests. This CD-based product is only available from your Cengage Learning sales representative.

Online courses

All of the web material is available in a format that is compatible with virtual learning environments such as Blackboard and WebCT. This version of the product is only available from your Cengage Learning sales representative.

229 937

BRIEF CONTENTS

CONTENTS

PART ONE
Introduction to Management and Cost Accounting 2

1 Introduction to management accounting 5

2 An introduction to cost terms and concepts 27

PART TWO
Cost Accumulation for Inventory Valuation and Profit Measurement 44

3 Cost assignment 47

4 Accounting entries for a job costing system 79

PREFACE

The aim of the seventh edition of this book is to explain the principles involved in designing and evaluating management and cost accounting information systems. Management accounting systems accumulate, classify, summarize and report information that will assist employees within an organization in their decision making, planning, control and performance measurement activities. A cost accounting system is concerned with accumulating costs for inventory valuation to meet external financial accounting and internal monthly or quarterly profit measurement requirements. As the title suggests, this book is concerned with both management and cost accounting but emphasis is placed on the former.

A large number of cost and management accounting textbooks have been published. Many of these books contain a detailed description of accounting techniques without any discussion of the principles involved in evaluating management and cost accounting systems. Such books often lack a conceptual framework, and ignore the considerable amount of research conducted in management accounting in the past three decades. At the other extreme some books focus entirely on a conceptual framework of management accounting with an emphasis on developing normative models of what ought to be. These books pay little attention to accounting techniques. My objective has been to produce a book which falls within these two extremes.

This book is intended primarily for undergraduate students who are pursuing a one- or two-year management accounting course, and for students who are preparing for the cost and management accounting examinations of the professional accountancy bodies at an intermediate or advanced professional level. It should also be of use to postgraduate and higher national diploma students who are studying cost and management accounting for the first time. An introductory course in financial accounting is not a prerequisite, although many students will have undertaken such a course.

STRUCTURE AND PLAN OF THE BOOK

A major theme of this book is that different financial information is required for different purposes, but my experience indicates that this approach can confuse students. In one chapter of a typical book students are told that costs should be allocated to products including a fair share of overhead costs; in another chapter they are told that some of the allocated costs are irrelevant and should be disregarded. In yet another chapter they are told that costs should be related to people (responsibility centres) and not products, whereas elsewhere no mention is made of responsibility centres.

In writing this book I have devised a framework that is intended to overcome these difficulties. The framework is based on the principle that there are three ways of constructing accounting information. The first is cost accounting with its emphasis on producing product costs for allocating costs between cost of goods sold and inventories to meet external and internal financial accounting inventory valuation and profit measurement requirements. The second is the notion of decision relevant costs with the emphasis on providing information to help managers to make good decisions. The third is responsibility accounting and performance measurement which focuses on both financial and non-financial information; in particular the assignment of costs and revenues to responsibility centres.

This book is divided into six parts. The first part (Part One) consists of two chapters and provides an introduction to management and cost accounting and a framework for studying the remaining chapters. The following three parts reflect the three different ways of constructing accounting information. Part Two consists of five chapters and is entitled 'Cost Accumulation for Inventory Valuation and Profit Measurement'. This section focuses mainly on assigning costs to products to separate the costs incurred during a period between costs of goods sold and the closing inventory valuation for internal and external profit measurement. The extent to which product costs accumulated for inventory valuation and profit measurement should be adjusted for meeting decision-making, cost control and performance measurement requirements is also briefly considered. Part Three consists of seven chapters and is entitled 'Information for Decision-making'. Here the focus is on measuring and identifying those costs which are relevant for different types of decisions.

The title of Part Four is 'Information for Planning, Control and Performance Measurement'. It consists of six chapters and concentrates on the process of translating goals and objectives into specific activities and the resources that are required, via the short-term (budgeting) and long-term planning processes, to achieve the goals and objectives. In addition, the management control systems that organizations use are described and the role that management accounting control systems play within the overall control process is examined. The emphasis here is on the accounting process as a means of providing information to help managers control the activities for which they are responsible. Performance measurement and evaluation within different segments of the organization is also examined.

Part Five consists of two chapters and is entitled 'Cost Management and Strategic Management Accounting.' The first chapter focuses on cost management and the second on strategic management accounting. Part Six consists of three chapters and is entitled 'The Application of Quantitative Methods to Management Accounting'.

In devising a framework around the three methods of constructing financial information there is a risk that the student will not appreciate that the three categories use many common elements, that they overlap, and that they constitute a single overall management accounting system, rather than three independent systems. I have taken steps to minimize this risk in each section by emphasizing why financial information for one purpose should or should not be adjusted for another purpose. In short, each section of the book is not presented in isolation and an integrative approach has been taken.

When I wrote this book an important consideration was the extent to which the application of quantitative techniques should be integrated with the appropriate topics or considered separately. I have chosen to integrate quantitative techniques whenever they are an essential part of a chapter. For example, the use of probability statistics are essential to Chapter 12 (Decision making under conditions of risk and uncertainty) but my objective has been to confine them, where possible, to Part Six.

This approach allows for maximum flexibility. Lecturers wishing to integrate quantitative techniques with earlier chapters may do so but those who wish to concentrate on other matters will not be hampered by having to exclude the relevant quantitative portions of chapters.

MAJOR CHANGES IN THE CONTENT OF THE SEVENTH EDITION

The most noticeable change to the seventh edition is the large reduction in the size of the book. Recent editions have incorporated the enormous changes that have occurred in the theory and practice of management accounting over the past two decades but still retained those traditional topics that are now diminishing in importance. This approach has resulted in an expansion in the size of each new edition culminating in the sixth edition containing 1280 pages. It was apparent from the visual appearance and feedback from the lecturers that there was a need to reduce the size of the book. Compared with the sixth edition the page count of the seventh edition has been reduced by approximately 40 per cent. This reduction has been achieved by reducing the content and condensing the space allocated to the assessment material.

Feedback from a lecturers' survey from users of the sixth edition indicated that a significant majority of the respondents identified specific topics contained in the text that were not included in their teaching programmes whereas a minority of respondents indicated that the same topics were included in their teaching programmes. In order to meet the different requirements of lecturers, and also reduce the size of the book, various topics from the sixth edition have been transferred from the text to learning notes that can be accessed by students and lecturers on the companion website. Examples of topics that are now incorporated as learning notes within the seventh edition include contract costing, selecting the cost driver denominator level for use with ABC systems, the contingency approach to management accounting and statistical variance investigation models. The learning notes tend to include the more complex issues that often do not feature as part of the content of other management accounting textbooks. All learning notes are appropriately referenced within the text. For example, at appropriate points within specific chapters the reader's attention is drawn to the fact that, for a particular topic, more complex issues exist and that a discussion of these issues can be found by referring to a specific learning note on the companion website. In addition, several non-essential traditional topics (e.g. CVP analysis under conditions of uncertainty) have been deleted from the text and not included as website learning notes.

The quantity of the assessment material in the seventh edition is not significantly different from that contained in the sixth edition. However, the material in the seventh edition is presented in double column format and this has enabled the number of pages allocated to assessment material to be substantially reduced. The lecturers' survey also indicated that, even though questions that were included in the *Instructor's Manual* could be accessed by students from the student side of the website, there was a strong preference for these questions to be included in the main text. Those questions that were included in the sixth edition of the *Instructor's Manual* have therefore been transferred to the main text. To provide the space for these questions the Student's Manual questions that were contained in the white boxes in the main text of the sixth edition have been transferred to the seventh edition of the Student's Manual. The review problems in the seventh edition therefore include questions with fully worked solutions in a separate section at the end of the book and questions where solutions are only available to lecturers in the accompanying *Instructor's Manual*.

A major feature of the seventh edition is that the transfer of more complex material from the text to learning notes on the student and lecturer sides of the website has enabled the content to be simplified in order to make it more readable and understandable. The content of the sixth edition has been thoroughly reviewed and where appropriate the opportunity has been taken to rewrite, simplify and improve the presentation of the existing material. For example, the material relating to losses in process in Chapter 5 and cost estimation in Chapter 23 has been rewritten and simplified. New material has been added to Chapter 13 (Capital Investment Decisions) and Chapter 15 (the Budgeting Process) relating, respectively, to discounting monthly cash flows and the recent criticisms of budgeting as reflected in the beyond budgeting approach. The material relating to the balanced scorecard in Chapter 22 has been extensively rewritten. Substantial changes have been made to the end-of-chapter assessment material that contains the solutions in a separate section at the end of the book. Also the two category classification of the assessment material review problems by intermediate and advanced levels has been replaced by a three category classification (basic, intermediate and advanced). Finally, many of the 'Real World Views' that provide examples of the practical application of management accounting have been replaced by more recent examples that provide better illustrations of the practical applications. In addition, questions have been added to the 'Real World Views' to encourage readers to think about the issues involved.

CASE STUDIES

The final section of this book includes a list of over 30 case studies that are available on the dedicated website for this book. Both lecturers and students can download these case studies from the companion website. Teaching notes for the case studies can be downloaded only by lecturers from the password protected lecturer's section of the website. The cases generally cover the content of several chapters and contain questions to which there is no ideal answer. They are intended to encourage independent thought and initiative and to relate and apply your understanding of the content of this book in more uncertain situations. They are also intended to develop your critical thinking and analytical skills.

HIGHLIGHTING OF ADVANCED READING SECTIONS

Feedback relating to previous editions has indicated that one of the major advantages of this book has been the comprehensive treatment of management accounting. Some readers, however, will not require a comprehensive treatment of all of the topics that are contained in the book. To meet the different requirements of the readers, the more advanced material that is not essential for those readers not requiring an in-depth knowledge of a particular topic has been highlighted using a vertical green line. If you do require an in-depth knowledge of a topic you may find it helpful to initially omit the advanced reading sections, or skim them, on your first reading. You should read them in detail only when you fully understand the content of the remaining parts of the chapter. The advanced reading sections are more appropriate for an advanced course and may normally be omitted if you are pursuing an introductory course. For some chapters all of the content represents advanced reading. Where this situation occurs readers are informed at the beginning of the relevant chapters and the highlighting mechanism is not used.

INTERNATIONAL FOCUS

The book has now become an established text in many different countries throughout the world. Because of this a more international focus has been adopted. A major feature is the presentation of boxed exhibits of surveys and practical applications of management accounting in companies in many different countries, particularly the European mainland. Most of the assessment material has incorporated questions set by the UK professional accountancy bodies. These questions are appropriate for worldwide use and users who are not familiar with the requirements of the UK professional accountancy bodies should note that many of the advanced level questions also contain the beneficial features described above for case study assignments.

RECOMMENDED READING

A separate section is included at the end of most chapters providing advice on key articles or books which you are recommended to read if you wish to pursue topics and issues in more depth. Many of the references are the original work of writers who have played a major role in the development of management accounting. The contribution of such writers is often reflected in this book but there is frequently no substitute for original work of the authors. The detailed references are presented in the Bibliography towards the end of the book.

ASSESSMENT MATERIAL

Throughout this book I have kept the illustrations simple. You can check your understanding of each chapter by answering the review questions. Each question is followed by page numbers within parentheses that indicate where in the text the answers to specific questions can be found. More complex review problems are also set at the end of each chapter to enable students to pursue certain topics in more depth. Each question is graded according to the level of difficulty. Questions graded 'Basic' are appropriate for a first year course and normally take less than 20 minutes to complete. Questions graded 'Intermediate' are also normally appropriate for a first year course but take about 30-45 minutes to complete whereas questions graded 'Advanced' are normally appropriate for a second year course or the final stages of the professional accountancy examinations. Fully worked solutions to the review problems not prefixed by the term 'IM' (Instructor's Manual) are provided in a separate section at the end of the book.

This book is part of an integrated educational package. A *Student's Manual* provides additional review problems with fully worked solutions. Students are strongly recommended to purchase the *Student's Manual*, which complements this book. In addition, the *Instructor's Manual* provides suggested solutions to the questions at the end of each chapter that are prefixed by the term 'IM.' The solutions to these questions are not available to students. The *Instructor's Manual* can be downloaded free from the lecturers' section of the website. Case studies are also available for students and lecturers to access on the accompanying website www.drury-online.com. Case study teaching notes are only available to lecturers on the lecturer's password protected section of the website.

Also available on request for adopting lecturers is an Examview® testbank CD-ROM offering the 1800+ questions tailored to the content of the book, for use in classroom assessment. Please contact your local Cengage Learning sales representative for this resource

SUPPLEMENTARY MATERIAL

DEDICATED WEBSITE

The dedicated website can be found at www.drury-online.com. The lecturer section is password protected and the password is available free to lecturers who confirm their adoption of the seventh edition – lecturers should complete the registration form on the website to apply for their password, which will then be sent to them by e-mail. The student resources section is accessed by using the unique personal access code bound inside the front cover of this edition. Please follow the guidelines on the attached card to access the material

The following range of material is available:

FOR STUDENTS AND LECTURERS:

LEARNING NOTES

The learning notes relate to either specific topics that may be only be applicable to the curriculum for a minority of the readers, or a discussion of topics where more complex issues are involved that not all readers may wish to pursue. All learning notes are appropriately cross-referenced within the text to the website. For example, at appropriate points within specific chapters the reader's attention is drawn to the fact that, for a particular topic, more complex issues exist and that a discussion of these issues can be found by referring to a specific learning note on the student resources section of the website.

CASE STUDIES

Internationally focused case studies. (NB Teaching notes to accompany the cases are available in the password protected lecturer area of the site).

EXAMVIEW® INTERACTIVE SELF-TEST QUESTIONS
(compiled by Wayne Fiddler of Huddersfield University)

Interactive multiple choice questions to accompany each chapter. The student takes the test online to check their grasp of the key points in each chapter. Feedback is provided where the student chooses the wrong answer.

POWERPOINT SLIDES

PowerPoint presentations to accompany each chapter.

GUIDE TO EXCEL (written by Steve Rickaby)

A PDF guide to Microsoft Excel giving you all the information you need to train yourself in basic Excel skills.

LINKS TO ACCOUNTING AND FINANCE SITES ON THE WEB

Including links to the main accounting firms, accounting magazines and journals and careers and job search pages.

DEFINITIONS OF ACCOUNTING AND FINANCE TERMS

Handy introductions to Accounting and Finance techniques, disciplines and concepts

FOR LECTURERS ONLY (PASSWORD PROTECTED)

INSTRUCTOR'S MANUAL

Available to download free from the site in PDF (Portable Document Format), the manual includes answers to the questions at the end of each chapter prefixed by the term 'IM.'

TEACHING NOTES TO THE CASE STUDIES

To accompany the case studies available in the student area of the website.

SPREADSHEET EXERCISES
(compiled and designed by Alicia Gazely of Nottingham Trent University)

Created in Excel to accompany the self assessment exercises in the book, the exercises can be saved by the lecturer to their own directories and distributed to students as each topic is covered. Each exercise explains a basic spreadsheet technique which illustrates, and allows the student to explore, examples in the main text.

POWERPOINT SLIDES AND OHP TRANSPARENCIES

PowerPoint presentations and OHP transparencies to accompany each chapter.

ADDITIONAL REAL WORLD VIEWS
(written by Jako Volschenk, University of Stellenbosch)

An additional set of Real World Views exploring Management Accounting concepts in a South African perspective, but equally applicable for use on teaching in UK and Europe.

SUPPLEMENTARY RESOURCES FOR LECTURERS

Lecturers who adopt this text are provided with the following comprehensive package of additional materials to assist in the preparation and delivery of courses:

Student's Manual (ISBN 978-1-84480-568-6)

ExamView ® (ISBN 978-1-84480-572-3)

This testbank and test generator provides a huge amount of different types of questions, allowing lecturers to create online, paper and local area network (LAN) tests. This CD-based product is only available from your Cengage Learning sales representative.

SUPPLEMENTARY RESOURCES FOR STUDENTS

A Student's Manual to help you work through the text is available from all good bookshops. Order it by quoting **ISBN 978-1-84480-568-6**

ALTERNATIVE COURSE SEQUENCES

Although conceived and developed as a unified whole, the book can be tailored to the individual requirements of a course, and so the preferences of the individual reader. For a discussion of the alternative sequencing of the chapters see Guidelines to Using the Book in Chapter 1. The following are suggested programmes for various courses:

A two year management accounting course for undergraduates:
The content of all of the book should be relevant but if the aim is to exclude some of the technical aspects relating to cost accumulation for inventory valuation and profit measurement then Part One, Chapter 3 (Part Two) and Parts Three to Six are recommended.

A one year degree or post experience course in management accounting:
Part One, Chapter 3 (Part Two), Part Three (the non-advanced reading sections within Chapters 8 -13) and Part Four (non-advanced reading sections within Chapters 15, 16, 17, 19 and 20)

Non-advanced professional accountancy examinations with a major emphasis on cost accounting:
All of Parts One and Two, Chapters 8 and 9 of Part Three plus the non-advanced reading sections of Chapters 15, 16, 17 and 18 of Part Four.

Professional accountancy examinations at the advanced level:
The content of the entire book.

ACKNOWLEDGEMENTS

I am indebted to many individuals for their ideas and assistance in preparing this and previous editions of the book. In particular, I would like to thank the following who have provided material for inclusion in the text and the dedicated website or who have commented on this and earlier editions of the book:

Anthony Atkinson, University of Waterloo
Stan Brignall, Aston Business School
Jose Manuel de Matos Carvalho, ISCA de Coimbra, Portugal
Peter Clarke, University College Dublin
Jayne Ducker, Sheffield Hallam University
Wayne Fiddler, University of Huddersfield
Ian G Fisher, John Moores University
Lin Fitzgerald, Loughborough University
Alicia Gazely, Nottingham Trent University

Lewis Gordon, Liverpool John Moores University
Richard Grey, University of Strathclyde
Antony Head, Sheffield Hallam University
Ian Herbert, Loughborough University
John Innes, University of Dundee
Mike Johnson, University of Dundee
Cathy Knowles, Oxford Brookes University
Michel Lebas, Groupe HEC
Falconer Mitchell, University of Edinburgh
Jodie Moll, University of Manchester
Peter Nordgaard, Copenhagen Business School
Deryl Northcott, Auckland University of Technology
Dan Otzen, Copenhagen Business School
Rona O'Brien , Sheffield Hallam University
Gary Owen, University of Greenwich
Graham Parker, Kingston University
Jukka Pellinen, University of Jyväskylä
John Perrin, University of Exeter
Martin Quinn, Dublin City University
Tony Rayman, University of Bradford
James S. Reece, University of Michigan
Carsten Rohde, Copenhagen Business School
Jonathan Rooks, Southbank University
Robin Roslender, Heriot-Watt University
David Russell, De Montfort University
John Shank, The Amos Tuck School of Business, Dartmouth College
Julia Smith, University of Wales Cardiff
Mike Tayles, University of Hull
Ben Ukaegbu, London Metropolitan University
Richard M.S. Wilson, Loughborough University Business School

I am also indebted to Martin Quinn for providing the new real world views that have been added to the seventh edition and Patrick Bond, Anna Carter, James Clark and Alissa Chappell at Cengage Learning for their valuable publishing advice, support and assistance. My appreciation goes also to the Chartered Institute of Management Accountants, the Chartered Association of Certified Accountants, the Institute of Chartered Accountants in England and Wales, and the Association of Accounting Technicians for permission to reproduce examination questions. Questions from the Chartered Institute of Management Accountants' examinations are designated CIMA; questions from the Chartered Association of Certified Accountants are designated CACA or ACCA; questions from the Institute of Chartered Accountants in England and Wales are designated ICAEW; and questions from the Association of Accounting Technicians are designated AAT. The answers in the text and accompanying Student's and Instructor's Manuals to this book are my own and are in no way the approved solutions of the above professional bodies. Finally, and most importantly I would like to thank my wife, Bronwen, for converting the original manuscript of the earlier editions into final type-written form and for her continued help and support throughout the six editions of this book.

Walk Through Tour

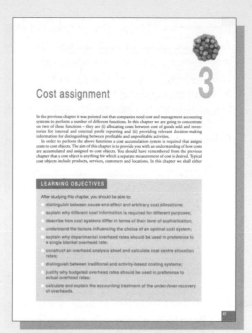

Learning objectives Listed at the start of each chapter highlighting the core coverage contained within.

Real world views Real world cases are provided throughout the text, helping to demonstrate theory in practice and the practical application of accounting in real companies around the world.

Key terms and concepts Highlighted throughout the text where they first appear alerting students to the core concepts and techniques. These are also listed at the end of each chapter with page references.

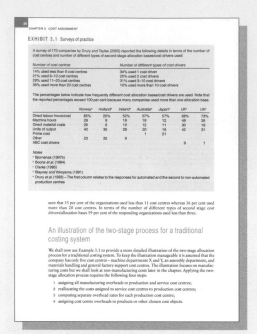

Exhibits Illustrations of accounting techniques and information are presented throughout the text.

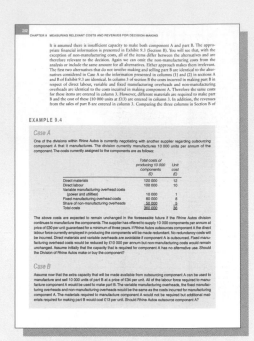

Examples Worked accounting examples are shown throughout the text.

Advanced reading More advanced material has been highlighted, this is not essential for a basic understanding of each chapter. These sections should be read when you have fully understood the remaining chapter content.

Recommended readings Further reading lists to supplement key topics.

Summary Bulleted lists at the end of each chapter review and recap key points and how they relate to the Learning Objectives.

Key examination points Important examination tips are present at the end of each chapter. They demonstrate how to approach important chapter-specific issues when studying for your examinations.

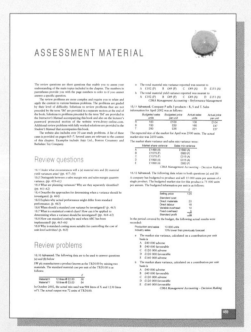

Review questions Short questions that enable you to assess your understanding of the main topics included in the chapter.

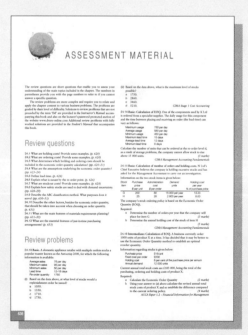

Review problems Graded by difficulty level, these more complex questions have worked solutions either at the back of the book, or in the accompanying Instructor's Manual.

MANAGEMENT AND COST ACCOUNTING

PART ONE

Introduction to Management and Cost Accounting

The objective of this section is to provide an introduction to management and cost accounting.

In Chapter 1 we define accounting and distinguish between financial, management and cost accounting. This is followed by an examination of the role of management accounting in providing information to managers for decision-making, planning, control and performance measurement. In addition, the important changes that are taking place in the business environment are considered. Progression through the book will reveal how these changes are influencing management accounting systems. In Chapter 2 the basic cost terms and concepts that are used in the management accounting literature are described.

Introduction to management accounting

1

There are many definitions of accounting, but the one that captures the theme of this book is the definition formulated by the American Accounting Association. It describes accounting as

> the process of identifying, measuring and communicating economic information to permit informed judgements and decisions by users of the information.

In other words, accounting is concerned with providing both financial and non-financial information that will help decision-makers to make good decisions. An understanding of accounting therefore requires an understanding of the decision-making process and an awareness of the users of accounting information.

During the past two decades many organizations in both the manufacturing and service sectors have faced dramatic changes in their business environment. Deregulation combined with extensive competition from overseas companies in domestic markets has resulted in a situation

LEARNING OBJECTIVES

After studying this chapter, you should be able to:

- distinguish between management accounting and financial accounting;
- identify and describe the elements involved in the decision-making, planning and control process;
- justify the view that a major objective of commercial organizations is to broadly seek to maximize the present value of future cash flows;
- explain the factors that have influenced the changes in the competitive environment;
- outline and describe the key success factors that directly affect customer satisfaction;
- identify and describe the functions of a cost and management accounting system;
- provide a brief historical description of management accounting.

where most companies are now competing in a highly competitive global market. At the same time there has been a significant reduction in product life cycles arising from technological innovations and the need to meet increasingly discriminating customer demands. To compete successfully in today's highly competitive global environment companies have made customer satisfaction an overriding priority. They have also adopted new management approaches and manufacturing companies have changed their manufacturing systems and invested in new technologies. These changes have had a significant influence on management accounting systems. Progression through the book will reveal how these changes have influenced management accounting systems, but first of all it is important that you have a good background knowledge of some of the important changes that have occurred in the business environment. This chapter aims to provide such knowledge.

The objective of this first chapter is to provide the background knowledge that will enable you to achieve a more meaningful insight into the issues and problems of management accounting that are discussed in the book. We begin by looking at the users of accounting information and identifying their requirements. This is followed by a description of the decision-making process and the changing business environment. Finally, the different functions of management accounting are described.

The users of accounting information

Accounting is a language that communicates economic information to people who have an interest in an organization – managers, shareholders and potential investors, employees, creditors and the government. Managers require information that will assist them in their decision-making and control activities; for example, information is needed on the estimated selling prices, costs, demand, competitive position and profitability of various products and services that are provided by the organization. Shareholders require information on the value of their investment and the income that is derived from their shareholding. Employees require information on the ability of the firm to meet wage demands and avoid redundancies. Creditors and the providers of loan capital require information on a firm's ability to meet its financial obligations. Government agencies like the Central Statistical Office collect accounting information and require such information as the details of sales activity, profits, investments, stocks, dividends paid, the proportion of profits absorbed by taxation and so on. In addition the Inland Revenue needs information on the amount of profits that are subject to taxation. All this information is important for determining policies to manage the economy.

Accounting information is not confined to business organizations. Accounting information about individuals is also important and is used by other individuals; for example, credit may only be extended to an individual after the prospective borrower has furnished a reasonable accounting of his private financial affairs. Non-profit-making organizations such as churches, charitable organizations, clubs and government units such as local authorities, also require accounting information for decision-making, and for reporting the results of their activities. For example, a tennis club will require information on the cost of undertaking its various activities so that a decision can be made as to the amount of the annual subscription that it will charge to its members. Similarly, local authorities need information on the costs of undertaking specific activities so that decisions can be made as to which activities will be undertaken and the resources that must be raised to finance them.

The foregoing discussion has indicated that there are many users of accounting information who require information for decision-making. The objective of accounting is to provide sufficient information to meet the needs of the various users at the lowest possible cost. Obviously, the benefit derived from using an information system for decision-making must be greater than the cost of operating the system.

An examination of the various users of accounting information indicates that they can be divided into two categories:

1 internal parties within the organization;

2 external parties such as shareholders, creditors and regulatory agencies, outside the organization.

It is possible to distinguish between two branches of accounting, that reflect the internal and external users of accounting information. Management accounting is concerned with the provision of information to people within the organization to help them make better decisions and improve the efficiency and effectiveness of existing operations, whereas financial accounting is concerned with the provision of information to external parties outside the organization. Thus, management accounting could be called internal reporting and financial accounting could be called external reporting. This book concentrates on management accounting.

Differences between management accounting and financial accounting

The major differences between these two branches of accounting are:

- *Legal requirements.* There is a statutory requirement for public limited companies to produce annual financial accounts regardless of whether or not management regards this information as useful. Management accounting, by contrast, is entirely optional and information should be produced only if it is considered that the benefits from the use of the information by management exceed the cost of collecting it.

- *Focus on individual parts or segments of the business.* Financial accounting reports describe the whole of the business whereas management accounting focuses on small parts of the organization, for example the cost and profitability of products, services, customers and activities. In addition, management accounting information measures the economic performance of decentralized operating units, such as divisions and departments.

- *Generally accepted accounting principles.* Financial accounting statements must be prepared to conform with the legal requirements and the generally accepted accounting principles established by the regulatory bodies such as the Financial Accounting Standards Board (FASB) in the USA the Accounting Standards Board (ASB) in the UK and the International Accounting Standards Board. These requirements are essential to ensure the uniformity and consistency that is needed for external financial statements. Outside users need assurance that external statements are prepared in accordance with generally accepted accounting principles so that the inter-company and historical comparisons are possible. Thus financial accounting data should be objective and verifiable. In contrast, management accountants are not required to adhere to generally accepted accounting principles when providing managerial information for internal purposes. Instead, the focus is on the serving management's needs and providing information that is useful to managers relating to their decision-making, planning and control functions.

- *Time dimension.* Financial accounting reports what has happened in the past in an organization, whereas management accounting is concerned with *future* information as well as past information. Decisions are concerned with *future* events and management therefore requires details of expected *future* costs and revenues.

- *Report frequency.* A detailed set of financial accounts is published annually and less detailed accounts are published semi-annually. Management requires information quickly if it is to act on it. Consequently management accounting reports on various activities may be prepared at daily, weekly or monthly intervals.

The decision-making process

The decision-making process encompasses planning and control activities. Because information produced by management accountants must be judged in the light of its ultimate effect on the outcome of decisions, a necessary precedent to an understanding of management accounting is an understanding of the *decision-making process*.

Figure 1.1 presents a diagram of a decision-making model (The decision-making planning and control process). The first five stages represent the decision-making or the planning process. Planning involves making choices between alternatives and is primarily a decision-making activity. The final two stages represent the *control process*, which is the process of measuring and correcting actual performance to ensure that the alternatives that are chosen and the plans for implementing them are carried out. You should note that the decision-making model specified in Figure 1.1 is a theoretical model based on the assumption of rational economic behaviour. This assumption has been challenged on the grounds that such behaviour does not always reflect actual real world behaviour (Burchell *et al.*, 1980).

Identifying objectives

Before good decisions can be made there must be some guiding aim or direction that will enable the decision-makers to assess the desirability of favouring one course of action over another. Hence, the first stage in the decision-making process should be to specify the goals or objectives of the organization.

Considerable controversy exists as to what the objectives of firms are or should be. Economic theory normally assumes that firms seek to maximize profits for the owners of the firm (the ordinary shareholders in a limited company) or, more precisely, the maximization of shareholders' wealth. Various arguments have been used to support the profit maximization objective. There is the legal argument that the ordinary shareholders are the owners of the firm, which therefore should be run for their benefit by trustee managers. Another argument supporting the profit objective is that profit maximization leads to the maximization of overall economic welfare. That is, by doing the best for yourself, you are unconsciously doing the best for society. Moreover, it seems a reasonable belief that the interests of firms will be better served by a larger profit than by a smaller profit, so that maximization is at least a useful approximation.

Some writers (e.g. Simon, 1959) believe that businessmen are content to find a plan that provides satisfactory profits rather than to maximize profits. Because people have limited powers

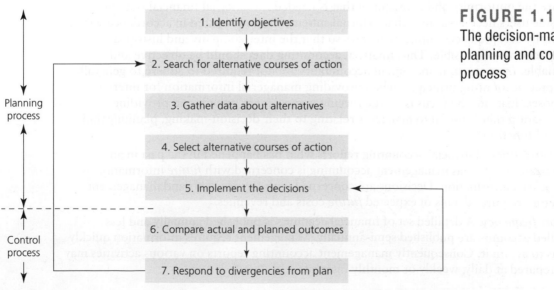

FIGURE 1.1
The decision-making, planning and control process

of understanding and can deal with only a limited amount of information at a time (Simon uses the term bounded rationality to describe these constraints), they tend to search for solutions only until the first acceptable solution is found. No further attempt is made to find an even better solution or to continue the search until the best solution is discovered. Such behaviour, where the search is terminated on finding a satisfactory, rather than optimal solution, is known as satisficing.

Cyert and March (1969) have argued that the firm is a coalition of various different groups – shareholders, employees, customers, suppliers and the government – each of whom must be paid a minimum to participate in the coalition. Any excess benefits after meeting these minimum constraints are seen as being the object of bargaining between the various groups. In addition, a firm is subject to constraints of a societal nature. Maintaining a clean environment, employing disabled workers and providing social and recreation facilities are all examples of social goals that a firm may pursue.

Clearly it is too simplistic to say that the only objective of a business firm is to maximize profits. Some managers seek to establish a power base and build an empire; another goal is security; the removal of uncertainty regarding the future may override the pure profit motive. Nevertheless, the view adopted in this book is that, broadly, firms seek to maximize the value of future net cash inflows (that is, future cash receipts less cash payments) or to be more precise the present value of future net cash inflows.[1] This is equivalent to maximizing shareholder value. (The concept of present value is explained in Chapter 13.) Organizations may also pursue more specific objectives but maximizing the present value of future net cash inflows represents a broad core objective for most firms. The reasons for choosing this objective are as follows:

1 It is unlikely that any other objective is as widely applicable in measuring the ability of the organization to survive in the future.

2 It is unlikely that maximizing the present value of future cash flows can be realized in practice, but by establishing the principles necessary to achieve this objective you will learn how to increase the present value of future cash flows.

3 It enables shareholders as a group in the bargaining coalition to know how much the pursuit of other goals is costing them by indicating the amount of cash distributed among the members of the coalition.

The search for alternative courses of action

The second stage in the decision-making model is a search for a range of possible courses of action (or strategies) that might enable the objectives to be achieved. If the management of a company concentrates entirely on its present product range and markets, and market shares and cash flows are allowed to decline, there is a danger that the company will be unable to generate sufficient cash flows to survive in the future. To maximize future cash flows, it is essential that management identifies potential opportunities and threats in its current environment and takes specific steps immediately so that the organization will not be taken by surprise by any developments which may occur in the future. In particular, the company should consider one or more of the following courses of action:

1 developing *new* products for sale in *existing* markets;

2 developing *new* products for *new* markets;

3 developing *new* markets for *existing* products.

The search for alternative courses of action involves the acquisition of information concerning future opportunities and environments; it is the most difficult and important stage of the decision-making process. Ideally, firms should consider all alternative courses of action, but, in practice they consider only a few alternatives, with the search process being localized initially. If this type of routine search activity fails to produce satisfactory solutions, the search will become more widespread (Cyert and March, 1969). We shall examine the search process in more detail in Chapter 15.

Gather data about alternatives

When potential areas of activity are identified, management should assess the potential growth rate of the activities, the ability of the company to establish adequate market shares, and the cash flows for each alternative activity for various states of nature. Because decision problems exist in an uncertain environment, it is necessary to consider certain factors that are outside the decision-maker's control, which may occur for each alternative course of action. These uncontrollable factors are called states of nature. Some examples of possible states of nature are economic boom, high inflation, recession, the strength of competition and so on.

The course of action selected by a firm using the information presented above will commit its resources for a lengthy period of time, and how the overall place of the firm will be affected within its environment that is, the products it makes, the markets it operates in and its ability to meet future changes. Such decisions dictate the firm's long-run possibilities and hence the type of decisions it can make in the future. These decisions are normally referred to as long-run or strategic decisions. Strategic decisions have a profound effect on the firm's future position, and it is therefore essential that adequate data are gathered about the firm's capabilities and the environment in which it operates. We shall discuss this topic in Chapters 13–15. Because of their importance, strategic decisions should be the concern of top management.

Besides strategic or long-term decisions, management must also make decisions that do not commit the firm's resources for a lengthy period of time. Such decisions are known as short-term or operating decisions and are normally the concern of lower-level managers. Short-term decisions are based on the environment of today, and the physical, human and financial resources presently available to the firm. These are, to a considerable extent, determined by the quality of the firm's long-term decisions. Examples of short-term decisions include the following:

1 What selling prices should be set for the firm's products?
2 How many units should be produced of each product?
3 What media shall we use for advertising the firm's products?
4 What level of service shall we offer customers in terms of the number of days required to deliver an order and the after-sales service?

Data must also be gathered for short-term decisions; for example, data on the selling prices of competitors' products and services, estimated demand at alternative selling prices, and predicted costs for different activity levels must be assembled for pricing and output decisions. When the data have been gathered, management must decide which courses of action to take.

Select appropriate alternative courses of action

In practice, decision-making involves choosing between competing alternative courses of action and selecting the alternative that best satisfies the objectives of an organization. Assuming that our objective is to maximize future net cash inflows, the alternative selected should be based on a comparison of the differences between the cash flows. Consequently, an incremental analysis of the net cash benefits for each alternative should be applied. The alternatives are ranked in terms of net cash benefits, and those showing the greatest benefits are chosen subject to taking into account any qualitative factors. We shall discuss how incremental cash flows are measured for short-term and long-term decisions and the impact of qualitative factors in Chapters 8–14.

Implementation of the decisions

Once alternative courses of action have been selected, they should be implemented as part of the budgeting process. The budget is a financial plan for implementing the various decisions that management has made. The budgets for all of the various decisions are expressed in terms of cash inflows and outflows, and sales revenues and expenses. These budgets are merged together into a single unifying statement of the organization's expectations for future periods. This statement is known as a **master budget**. The master budget consists of a budgeted profit and loss account, cash flow statement and balance sheet. The budgeting process communicates to everyone in the organization the part that they are expected to play in implementing management's decisions. Chapter 15 focuses on the budgeting process.

Comparing actual and planned outcomes and responding to divergencies from plan

The final stages in the process outlined in Figure 1.1 of comparing actual and planned outcomes and responses to divergencies from plan represent the firm's control process. The managerial function of **control** consists of the measurement, reporting and subsequent correction of performance in an attempt to ensure that the firm's objectives and plans are achieved. In other words, the objective of the control process is to ensure that the work is done so as to fulfil the original intentions.

To monitor performance, the accountant produces **performance reports** and presents them to the appropriate managers who are responsible for implementing the various decisions. Performance reports consisting of a comparison of actual outcomes (actual costs and revenues) and planned outcomes (budgeted costs and revenues) should be issued at regular intervals. Performance reports provide **feedback** information by comparing planned and actual outcomes. Such reports should highlight those activities that do not conform to plans, so that managers can devote their scarce time to focusing mainly on these items. This process represents the application of **management by exception**. Effective control requires that corrective action is taken so that actual outcomes conform to planned outcomes. Alternatively, the plans may require modification if the comparisons indicate that the plans are no longer attainable.

The process of taking corrective action so that actual outcomes conform to planned outcomes, or the modification of the plans if the comparisons indicate that actual outcomes do not conform to planned outcomes, is indicated by the arrowed lines in Figure 1.1 linking stages 7 and 5 and 7 and 2. These arrowed lines represent 'feedback loops'. They signify that the process is dynamic and stress the interdependencies between the various stages in the process. The feedback loop between stages 7 and 2 indicates that the plans should be regularly reviewed, and if they are no longer attainable then alternative courses of action must be considered for achieving the organization's objectives. The second loop stresses the corrective action taken so that actual outcomes conform to planned outcomes. Chapters 15–18 focus on the planning and control process.

Changing competitive environment

Prior to the 1980s many organizations in Western countries operated in a protected competitive environment. Barriers of communication and geographical distance, and sometimes protected markets, limited the ability of overseas companies to compete in domestic markets. There was little incentive for firms to maximize efficiency and improve management practices, or to minimize costs, as cost increases could often be passed on to customers. During the 1980s, however, organizations began to encounter severe competition from overseas competitors that offered high-quality products at low prices. By establishing global networks for acquiring raw materials and distributing goods overseas, competitors were able to gain access to domestic markets throughout the world. To be successful companies now have to compete not only against domestic competitors but also against the best companies in the world.

Excellence in manufacturing can provide a competitive weapon to compete in sophisticated world-wide markets. In order to compete effectively companies must be capable of manufacturing innovative products of high quality at a low cost, and also provide a first-class customer service. At the same time, they must have the flexibility to cope with short product life cycles, demands for greater product variety from more discriminating customers and increasing international competition. World-class manufacturing companies have responded to these competitive demands by replacing traditional production systems with new just-in-time production systems and investing in advanced manufacturing technologies (AMTs). The major features of these new systems and their implications for management accounting will be described throughout the book.

Virtually all types of service organization have also faced major changes in their competitive environment. Before the 1980s many service organizations, such as those operating in the airlines, utilities and financial service industries, were either government-owned monopolies or operated in a highly regulated, protected and non-competitive environment. These organizations were not subject to any great pressure to improve the quality and efficiency of their operations or to improve profitability by eliminating services or products that were making losses. Furthermore, more efficient competitors were often prevented from entering the markets in which the regulated companies operated. Prices were set to cover operating costs and provide a predetermined return on capital. Hence cost increases could often be absorbed by increasing the prices of the services. Little attention was therefore given to developing cost systems that accurately measured the costs and profitability of individual services.

Privatization of government-controlled companies and deregulation in the 1980s completely changed the competitive environment in which service companies operated. Pricing and competitive restrictions were virtually eliminated. Deregulation, intensive competition and an expanding product range created the need for service organizations to focus on cost management and develop management accounting information systems that enabled them to understand their cost base and determine the sources of profitability for their products, customers and markets. Many service organizations have only recently turned their attention to management accounting. One of the major features of the business environment in recent decades has been the growth in the service industry and the growth of the management accounting function within service organizations.

Changing product life cycles

A product's life cycle is the period of time from initial expenditure on research and development to the time at which support to customers is withdrawn. Intensive global competition and technological innovation combined with increasingly discriminating and sophisticated customer demands have resulted in a dramatic decline in product life cycles. To be successful companies must now speed up the rate at which they introduce new products to the market. Being later to the market than the competitors can have a dramatic effect on product profitability.

In many industries a large fraction of a product's life-cycle costs are determined by decisions made early in its life cycle. This has created a need for management accounting to place greater emphasis on providing information at the design stage because many of the costs are committed or locked in at this time. Therefore to compete successfully companies must be able to manage their costs effectively at the design stage, have the capability to adapt to new, different and changing customer requirements and reduce the time to market of new and modified products.

Focus on customer satisfaction and new management approaches

In order to compete in today's competitive environment companies have had to become more customer-driven and make customer satisfaction an overriding priority. Customers are demanding ever-improving levels of service in cost, quality, reliability, delivery, and the choice of innovative new products. Figure 1.2 illustrates this focus on customer satisfaction as the overriding priority. In order to provide customer satisfaction organizations must concentrate on those key success factors that directly affect it. Figure 1.2 identifies cost efficiency, quality, time and innovation as the key success factors. In addition to concentrating on these factors organizations are adopting new management approaches in their quest to achieve customer satisfaction. These new approaches are illustrated in Figure 1.2. They are continuous improvement, employee empowerment and total value-chain analysis. Let us now examine each of the items shown in Figure 1.2 in more detail.

The first item listed in Figure 1.2 refers to cost efficiency. Since customers will buy the product with the lowest price, all other things being equal, keeping costs low and being cost efficient provides an organization with a strong competitive advantage. Increased competition has also made decision errors due to poor cost information more probable and more costly. If the cost system results in distorted product costs being reported, then overcosted products or services will lead to higher bid prices and business lost to those competitors who are able to quote lower prices purely because their cost systems produce more accurate cost information. Alternatively, there is a danger that undercosted products or services will result in the acceptance of unprofitable business.

These developments have made many companies aware of the need to improve their cost systems so that they can produce more accurate cost information to determine the cost of their products and services, pinpoint loss-making activities and analyze profits by products, sales outlets, customers and markets.

In addition to demanding low cost product customers are demanding high quality products and services. Most companies are responding to this by focusing on total quality management (TQM). The goal of TQM is customer satisfaction. TQM is a term used to describe a situation where *all* business functions are involved in a process of continuous quality improvement. TQM has broadened from its early concentration on the statistical monitoring of manufacturing processes, to a customer-oriented process of continuous improvement that focuses on delivering products or services of consistently high quality in a timely fashion. The emphasis on TQM has created fresh demands on the management accounting function to expand its role by becoming involved in measuring and evaluating the quality of products and services and the activities that produce them.

Organizations are also seeking to increase customer satisfaction by providing a speedier response to customer requests, ensuring 100 per cent on-time delivery and reducing the time taken to develop and bring new products to market. For these reasons management accounting

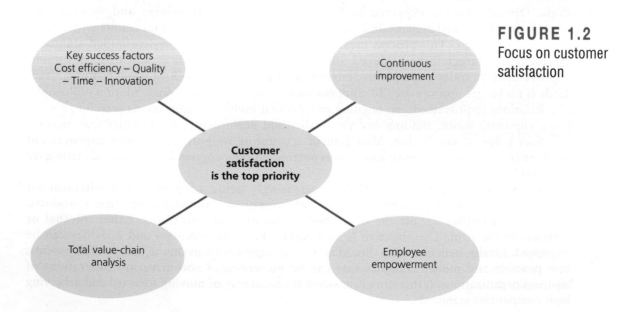

FIGURE 1.2
Focus on customer satisfaction

Key success factors
Cost efficiency – Quality
– Time – Innovation

Continuous
improvement

**Customer
satisfaction
is the top priority**

Total value-chain
analysis

Employee
empowerment

systems now place more emphasis on time-based measures, which have beome an important competitive variable. Cycle time is one measure that management accounting systems have begun to focus on. It is the length of time from start to completion of a product or service. It consists of the sum of processing time, move time, wait time and inspection time. Move time is the amount of time it takes to transfer the product during the production process from one location to another. Wait time is the amount of time that the product sits around waiting for processing, moving, inspecting, reworking or the amount of time it spends in finished goods stock waiting to be sold and despatched. Inspection time is the amount of time making sure that the product is defect free or the amount of time actually spent reworking the product to remedy identified defects in quality. Only processing time adds value to the product, and the remaining activities are non-value added activities in the sense that they can be reduced or eliminated without altering the product's service potential to the customer. Organizations are therefore focusing on minimizing cycle time by reducing the time spent on such activities. The management accounting system has an important role to play in this process by identifying and reporting on the time devoted to value added and non-value added activities. Cycle time measures have also become important for service organizations. For example, the time taken to process mortgage loan applications by financial organizations can be considerable involving substantial non-value added waiting time. Thus, reducing the time to process the applications enhances customer satisfaction and creates the potential for increasing sales revenue.

The final key success factor shown in Figure 1.2 relates to innovation. To be successful companies must develop a steady stream of innovative new products and services and have the capability to adapt to changing customer requirements. It has already been stressed earlier in this chapter that being later to the market than competitors can have a dramatic effect on product profitability. Companies have therefore begun to incorporate performance measures that focus on flexibility and innovation in their management accounting systems. Flexibility relates to the responsiveness in meeting customer requirements. Flexibility measures include the total launch time for new products, the length of development cycles and the ability to change the production mix quickly. Innovation measures include an assessment of the key characteristics of new products relative to those of competitors, feedback on customer satisfaction with the new features and characteristics of newly introduced products, and the number of new products launched and their launch times.

You can see by referring to Figure 1.2 that organizations are attempting to achieve customer satisfaction by adopting a philosophy of continuous improvement. Traditionally, organizations have sought to study activities and establish standard operating procedures and materials requirements based on observing and establishing optimum input/output relationships. Operators were expected to follow the standard procedures and management accountants developed systems and measurements that compared actual results with predetermined standards. This process created a climate whereby the predetermined standards represented a target to be achieved and maintained rather than a policy of continuous improvement. In today's competitive environment performance against static historical standards is no longer appropriate. To compete successfully companies must adopt a philosophy of continuous improvement, an ongoing process that involves a continuous search to reduce costs, eliminate waste, and improve the quality and performance of activities that increase customer value or satisfaction. Management accounting supports continuous improvement by identifying ways to improve and then reporting on the progress of the methods that have been implemented.

Benchmarking is a technique that is increasingly being adopted as a mechanism for achieving continuous improvement. It is a continuous process of measuring a firm's products, services or activities against the other best performing organizations, either internal or external to the firm. The objective is to ascertain how the processes and activities can be improved. Ideally, benchmarking should involve an external focus on the latest developments, best practice and model examples that can be incorporated within various operations of business organizations. It therefore represents the ideal way of moving forward and achieving high competitive standards.

In their quest for the continuous improvement of organizational activities managers have found that they have had to rely more on the people closest to the operating processes and customers to develop new approaches to performing activities. This has led to employees being provided with relevant information to enable them to make continuous improvements to the output of processes. Allowing employees to take such actions without the authorization by superiors has come to be known as employee empowerment. It is argued that by empowering employees and giving them relevant information they will be able to respond faster to customers, increase process flexibility, reduce cycle time and improve morale. Management accounting is therefore moving from its traditional emphasis on providing information to managers to monitor the activities of employees to providing information to employees to empower them to focus on the continuous improvement of activities.

Increasing attention is now being given to value-chain analysis as a means of increasing customer satisfaction and managing costs more effectively. The value chain is illustrated in Figure 1.3. It is the linked set of value-creating activities all the way from basic raw material sources for component suppliers through to the ultimate end-use product or service delivered to the customer. Coordinating the individual parts of the value chain together to work as a team creates the conditions to improve customer satisfaction, particularly in terms of cost efficiency, quality and delivery. It is also appropriate to view the value chain from the customer's perspective, with each link being seen as the customer of the previous link. If each link in the value chain is designed to meet the needs of its customers, then end-customer satisfaction should ensue. Furthermore, by viewing each link in the value chain as a supplier–customer relationship, the opinions of the customers can be used to provide useful feedback information on assessing the quality of service provided by the supplier. Opportunities are thus identified for improving activities throughout the entire value chain. The aim is to manage the linkages in the value chain better than competitors and thus create a competitive advantage. Management accounting plays a major role in providing information to help managers administer linkages in the value chain.

Finally, there are other aspects of customer satisfaction that are not specified in Figure 1.2 – namely, social responsibility and corporate ethics. Customers are no longer satisfied if companies simply comply with the legal requirements of undertaking their activities. They expect company managers to be more proactive in terms of their social responsibility. Company stakeholders are now giving high priority to social responsibility, safety and environmental issues, besides corporate ethics. In response to these pressures many companies are now introducing mechanisms for measuring, reporting and monitoring their environmental costs and activities. A code of ethics has also become an essential part of corporate culture. In addition, professional accounting organizations play an important role in promoting a high standard of ethical behaviour by their members. Both of the professional bodies representing management accountants in the UK (Chartered Institute of Management Accountants) and the USA (Institute of Management Accountants) have issued a code of ethical guidelines for their members and established mechanisms for monitoring and enforcing professional ethics. The guidelines are concerned with ensuring that accountants follow fundamental principles relating to integrity (not being a party to any falsification), objectivity (not being biased or prejudiced), confidentiality and professional competence and due care (maintaining the skills required to ensure a competent professional service).

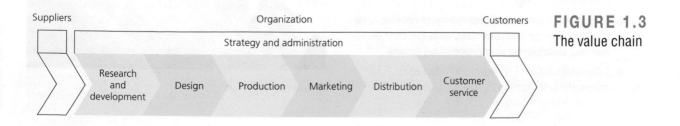

Suppliers   Organization   Customers

Strategy and administration

Research and development   Design   Production   Marketing   Distribution   Customer service

FIGURE 1.3
The value chain

The impact of information technology

During the past decade the use of information technology (IT) to support business activities has increased dramatically with the development of electronic business communication technologies known as e-business, e-commerce or internet commerce. These developments are having a big impact on businesses. For example, consumers are becoming more discerning when purchasing products or services because they are able to derive more information from the internet on the relative merits of the different product offerings. E-commerce has provided the potential to develop new ways of doing things that have enabled considerable cost savings to be made from streamlining business processes and generating extra revenues from the adept use of on-line sales facilities (e.g. ticketless airline bookings and internet banking). The ability to use e-commerce more proficiently than competitors provides the potential for companies to establish a competitive advantage.

One advanced IT application that has had a considerable impact on business information systems is enterprise resource planning systems (ERPS). The number of adopters of ERPS has increased rapidly throughout the world since they were first introduced in the mid-1990s. An ERPS comprises a set of integrated software applications modules that aim to control all information flows within a company. They cover most business functions (including accounting). Standard ERPS accounting modules incorporate many menus including bookkeeping, product profitability analysis and budgeting. All the modules are fully integrated in a common database and users can access real-time information on all aspects of the business. Using real time data thus enables managers to continually improve the efficiencies of processes. A major feature of ERPS systems is that all data are entered only once, typically where the data originate. There are a number of ERPS packages on the market provided by companies such as SAP, Baan, Oracle and J.D. Edwards. SAP is the market leader with more than 7500 users in 90 countries (Scapens *et al.*, 1998).

The introduction of ERPS has the potential to have a significant impact on the work of management accountants. In particular, ERPS substantially reduce routine information gathering

REAL WORLD VIEWS 1.1

A look at a key feature of easyJet's business

As one of the pioneers in the low cost airline market, easyJet bases its business on a number of principles:

- Minimize distribution costs by using the internet to take bookings. About 90 per cent of all easyJet tickets are sold via the Web. This makes the company one of Europe's largest internet retailers.

- Maximize efficient use of assets, by increasing turn-around time at airports.

- A 'simple-service model' means the end of free on-board catering.

- Ticketless travel, where passengers receive an e-mail confirming their booking, cuts the cost of issuing, distributing and processing tickets.

- Intensive use of IT in administration and management, aiming to run a paperless office.

Discussion point

How can the management accounting function provide information to support a low cost strategy?

© THE FLIGHT COLLECTION/ALAMY

SOURCE: EASYJET WEBSITE (WWW.EASYJET.COM)

and the processing of information by management accountants. Instead of managers asking management accountants for information, they can access the system to derive the information they require directly by PC and do their own analyzes. Because ERPS integrate separate business functions in one system for the whole company coordination is usually undertaken centrally by information specialists who are responsible for both the implementation and operation of the system. In multinational companies this has standardized the global flow of information, but it has also limited the ability to generate locally relevant information.

Because ERPS perform the routine tasks that were once part of the accountants' daily routines, accountants have had to expand their roles or risk possible redundancy. ERPS has provided the potential for accountants to use the time freed up from routine information gathering to adopt the role of advisers and internal consultants to the business. Management accountants have now become more involved in interpreting the information generated from the ERPS and providing business support for managers.

International convergence of management accounting practices

This book has become an established text in many different countries throughout the world. It is therefore assumed that the content is appropriate for use in different countries. This assumption is based on the premise that management accounting practices generally do not differ across countries. Granlund and Lukka (1998) provide support for this assumption. They argue that there is a strong current tendency towards global homogenization of management accounting practices within the industrialized parts of the world.

Granlund and Lukka distinguish between management accounting practices at the macro and micro levels. The macro level relates to concepts and techniques; in other words, it relates mainly

---

SOURCE: WWW.SAP.COM

REAL WORLD VIEWS 1.2

The effect on enterprise resource planning systems on management accounting practice

Enterprise resource planning systems (ERPS) such as SAP, Oracle and Peoplesoft are utilized by most global firms. For example, according to the SAP Business community website:

'Almost all the chemical, high-tech, and pharmaceutical companies on the Fortune 500 in 2003 are SAP customers. SAP also serves eight of the world's top 10 banks, 33 of Europe's 50 leading financial institutions, and nine of the 10 most successful insurance companies in the world.'

An ERPS is defined by Davenport (2000, p2) as an integrated enterprise-wide system which supports all key functional areas of an organization, linking front and back office systems. They are designed to solve the problem of information fragmentation in large organizations via the use of a single integrated database and generic best practice business processes. They typically automate the majority of business transactions, provide real time reporting and integrate the planning and production systems.

What effect has this had on management accounting practice? Granlund and Malmi (2002) examined if ERPS can have direct and indirect effects on management accounting control systems and on the work of management accountants. Little evidence was found to support major change in control systems. However, ERPS was found to have a direct impact on the work of management accountants. Many processes and transactions were automated or eliminated, enabling management accountants to spend more time analyzing data.

Discussion point

Other than technical competence, what other skills might be required of a management accountant?

to the content of this book. In contrast, the micro level is concerned with the behavioural patterns relating to how management accounting information is actually used. Granlund and Lukka argue that, at the macro level, the forces of convergence have started to dominate those of divergence. They identify various drivers of convergence but the most important relate to the intensified global competition, developments in information technology, the increasing tendency of transnational companies to standardize their practices, the global consultancy industry and the use of globally applied textbooks and teaching.

Firms throughout the world are adopting similar integrated enterprise resource planning systems or standardized software packages that have resulted in the standardization of data collection formats and reporting patterns of accounting information. In multinational companies this process has resulted in the standardization of the global flow of information, but it has also limited the ability to generate locally relevant information. Besides the impact of integrated IT systems, it is common for the headquarters/parent company of a transnational enterprise to force foreign divisions to adopt similar accounting practices to those of the headquarters/parent company. A large global consultancy industry has recently emerged that tends to promote the same standard solutions globally. The consultancy industry also enthusiastically supports mimetic processes. Granlund and Lukka describe mimetic processes as processes by which companies, under conditions of uncertainty, copy publicly known and appreciated models of operation from each other, especially from successful companies that have a good reputation. Finally, the same textbooks are used globally and university and professional accounting syllabuses tend to be similar in different countries.

At the micro level Granlund and Lukka acknowledge that differences in national and corporate culture can result in management accounting practices differing across countries. For example, national cultures have been categorized as the extent to which:

1 the inequality between people is considered to be normal and acceptable;

2 the culture is assertive and competitive as opposed to being modest and caring;

3 the culture feels comfortable with uncertainty and ambiguity; and

4 the culture focuses on long-term or short-term outcomes.

There is evidence to suggest that accounting information is used in different ways in different national cultures, such as being used in a rigorous/rigid manner for managerial performance evaluation in cultures exhibiting certain national traits and in a more flexible way in cultures exhibiting different national traits. At the macro level Granlund and Lukka argue that the impact of national culture is diminishing because of the increasing emerging pressures to follow national trends to secure national competitiveness.

Functions of management accounting

A cost and management accounting system should generate information to meet the following requirements. It should:

1 allocate costs between cost of goods sold and inventories for internal and external profit reporting;

2 provide relevant information to help managers make better decisions;

3 provide information for planning, control, performance measurement and continuous improvement.

Financial accounting rules require that we match costs with revenues to calculate profit. Consequently any unsold finished goods stock or partly completed stock (work in progress) will *not* be included in the cost of goods sold, which is matched against sales revenue during a given period. In an organization that produces a wide range of different products it will be necessary, for stock (inventory) valuation purposes, to charge the costs to each individual product. The total value of the stocks of completed products and work in progress plus any unused raw materials forms the basis for determining the inventory valuation to be deducted from the current period's costs when calculating profit. This total is also the basis for determining the stock valuation for inclusion in the balance sheet. Costs are therefore traced to each individual job or product for financial accounting requirements in order to allocate the costs incurred during a period between cost of goods sold and inventories. This information is required for meeting *external* financial accounting requirements, but most organizations also produce *internal* profit reports at monthly intervals. Thus product costs are also required for periodic internal profit reporting. Many service organizations, however, do not carry any stocks and product costs are therefore not required by these organizations for valuing inventories.

The second requirement of a cost and management accounting system is to provide relevant financial information to managers to help them make better decisions. This involves both routine and non-routine reporting. Routine information is required relating to the profitability of various segments of the business such as products, services, customers and distribution channels in order to ensure that only profitable activities are undertaken. Information is also required for making resource allocation and product/service mix and discontinuation decisions. In some situations cost information extracted from the costing system also plays a crucial role in determining selling prices, particularly in markets where customized products and services are provided that do not have readily available market prices. Non-routine information is required for strategic decisions. These decisions are made at infrequent intervals and include decisions relating to the development and introduction of new products and services, investment in new plant and equipment and the negotiation of long-term contracts with customers and suppliers.

Accurate cost information is required in decision-making for distinguishing between profitable and unprofitable activities. If the cost system does not capture accurately enough the consumption of resources by products, the reported product (or service) costs will be distorted, and there is a danger that managers may drop profitable products or continue the production of unprofitable products. Where cost information is used to determine selling prices the under-costing of products or services can result in the acceptance of unprofitable business whereas over-costing can result in bids being rejected and the loss of profitable business.

Management accounting systems should also provide information for planning, control, performance measurement and continuous improvement. Planning involves translating goals and objectives into the specific activities and resources that are required to achieve the goals and objectives. Companies develop both long-term and short-term plans and the management accounting function plays a critical role in this process. Short-term plans, in the form of the budgeting process, are prepared in more detail than the longer-term plans and are one of the mechanisms used by managers as a basis for control and performance evaluation. Control is the process of ensuring that the actual outcomes conform with the planned outcomes. The control process involves the setting of targets or standards (often derived from the budgeting process) against which actual results are measured. Performance is then measured and compared with the targets on a periodic basis. The management accountant's role is to provide managers with feedback information in the form of periodic reports, suitably analyzed, to enable them to determine if operations for which they are responsible are proceeding according to plan and identify those activities where corrective action is necessary. In particular, the management accounting function should provide economic feedback to managers to assist them in controlling costs and improving the efficiency and effectiveness of operations.

It is appropriate at this point to distinguish between cost accounting and management accounting. Cost accounting is concerned with cost accumulation for inventory valuation to meet the requirements of external reporting and internal profit measurement, whereas management accounting relates to the provision of appropriate information for decision-making, planning, control and performance evaluation. It is apparent from an examination of the literature that the distinction between cost accounting and management accounting is extremely vague with some writers referring to the decision-making aspects in terms of cost accounting and other writers using the term management accounting; the two terms are often used synonymously. In this book no attempt will be made to distinguish between these two terms.

You should now be aware from the above discussion that a management accounting system serves multiple purposes. The emphasis throughout the book is that costs must be assembled in different ways for different purposes. A firm can choose to have multiple accounting systems (i.e. a separate system for each purpose) or one basic accounting system and set of accounts that serve inventory valuation and profit measurement, decision-making and performance evaluation requirements. Most firms choose, on the basis of costs versus benefits criteria, to operate a single accounting system. A single database is maintained with costs appropriately coded and classified so that relevant cost information can be extracted to meet each of the above requirements. Where future cost information is required the database may be maintained at target (standard) costs, or if actual costs are recorded, they are adjusted for anticipated price changes. We shall examine in the next chapter how relevant cost information can be extracted from a single database and adjusted to meet different user requirements. You should note, however, that in many organizations the database was originally established to support financial accounting reporting requirements. Many organizations have only recently redesigned their database in order to more fully satisfy the requirements of management accounting. Unfortunately, some organizations still continue to use the same database that was originally designed to meet financial accounting requirements.

A brief historical review of management accounting

The origins of today's management accounting can be traced back to the Industrial Revolution of the nineteenth century. According to Johnson and Kaplan (1987), most of the of the management accounting practices that were in use in the mid-1980s had been developed by 1925, and for the next 60 years there was a slow-down, or even a halt, in management accounting innovation. They argue that this stagnation can be attributed mainly to the demand for product cost information for external financial accounting reports. The separation of the ownership and management of organizations created a need for the owners of a business to monitor the effective stewardship of their investment. This need led to the development of financial accounting, which generated a published report for investors and creditors summarizing the financial position of the company. Statutory obligations were established requiring companies to publish audited annual financial statements. In addition, there was a requirement for these published statements to conform to a set of rules known as Generally Accepted Accounting Principles (GAAP), which were developed by regulators.

The preparation of published external financial accounting statements required that costs be allocated between cost of goods sold and inventories. Cost accounting emerged to meet this requirement. Simple procedures were established to allocate costs to products that were objective and verifiable for financial accounting purposes. Such costs, however, were not sufficiently accurate for decision-making purposes and for distinguishing between profitable and unprofitable products and services. Johnson and Kaplan argue that the product costs derived for financial accounting purposes were also being used for management accounting purposes. They conclude that managers did not have to yield the design of management accounting systems to financial accountants and auditors. Separate systems could have been maintained for managerial and financial accounting purposes, but the high cost of information collection meant that the costs of maintaining two systems exceeded the additional benefits. Thus, companies relied primarily on the same information as that used for external financial reporting to manage their internal operations.

Johnson and Kaplan claim that, over the years, organizations had become fixated on the cost systems of the 1920s. Furthermore, when the information systems were automated in the 1960s, the system designers merely automated the manual systems that were developed in the 1920s. Johnson and Kaplan conclude that the lack of management accounting innovation over the decades and the failure to respond to its changing environment resulted in a situation in the mid-1980s where firms were using management accounting systems that were obsolete and no longer relevant to the changing competitive and manufacturing environment.

During the late 1980s, criticisms of current management accounting practices were widely publicized in the professional and academic accounting literature. In 1987 Johnson and Kaplan's book entitled *Relevance Lost: The Rise and Fall of Management Accounting*, was published. An enormous amount of publicity was generated by this book as a result of the authors' criticisms of management accounting. Many other commentators also concluded that management accounting was in a crisis and that fundamental changes in practice were required.

Since the mid-1980s management accounting practitioners and academics have sought to modify and implement new techniques that are relevant to today's environment and that will ensure that management accounting regains its relevance. By the mid-1990s Kaplan (1994) stated that:

> The past 10 years have seen a revolution in management accounting theory and practice. The seeds of the revolution can be seen in publications in the early to mid 1980s that identified the failings and obsolescence of existing cost and performance measurement systems. Since that time we have seen remarkable innovations in management accounting; even more remarkable has been the speed with which the new concepts have become widely known, accepted and implemented in practice and integrated into a large number of educational programmes.

Summary of the contents of this book

This book is divided into six parts. The first part (Part One) consists of two chapters and provides an introduction to management and cost accounting and a framework for studying the remaining chapters. Part Two consists of five chapters and is entitled 'Cost Accumulation for Inventory Valuation and Profit Measurement'. This section focuses mainly on cost accounting. It is concerned with assigning costs to products to separate costs incurred during a period between costs of goods sold and the closing inventory valuation. The extent to which product costs accumulated for inventory valuation and profit measurement should be adjusted for meeting decision-making, cost control and performance measurement requirements is also briefly considered. Part Three consists of seven chapters and is entitled 'Information for Decision-making'. Here the focus is on measuring and identifying those costs which are relevant for different types of decisions.

The title of Part Four is 'Information for Planning, Control and Performance Measurement'. It consists of six chapters and concentrates on the process of translating goals and objectives into specific activities and the resources that are required, via the short-term (budgeting) and long-term planning processes, to achieve the goals and objectives. In addition, the management control systems that organizations use are described and the role that management accounting control systems play within the overall control process is examined. The emphasis here is on the accounting process as a means of providing information to help managers control the activities for which they are responsible. Performance measurement and evaluation within different segments of the organization is also examined.

Part Five consists of two chapters and is entitled 'Cost Management and Strategic Management Accounting'. The first chapter focuses on cost management and the second on strategic management accounting. The sixth part consists of three chapters and is entitled 'The Application of Quantitative Methods to Management Accounting'.

Guidelines for using this book

If you are pursuing a course of management accounting, without cost accumulation for inventory valuation and profit measurement, Chapters 4–7 in Part Two can be omitted, since the rest of this book does not rely heavily on these chapters. Alternatively, you could delay your reading of Chapters 4–7 in Part Two until you have studied Parts Three and Four. Chapter 18 in Part Four is only appropriate if your curriculum requires a detailed knowledge of the technical aspects of variance analysis. If you wish to gain an insight into cost accumulation for inventory valuation and profit measurement but do not wish to study it in depth, you may prefer to read only Chapters 3 and 7 of Part Two. It is important that you read Chapter 3, which focuses on traditional methods of tracing overheads to cost objects prior to reading Chapter 10 on activity-based costing.

The chapters on the application of quantitative techniques to management accounting have been delayed until Part Five. An alternative approach would be to read Chapter 23 immediately after reading Chapter 8 on cost–volume–profit analysis. Chapter 24 is self-contained and may be assigned to follow any of the chapters in Part Four. Chapter 25 should be read only after you have studied Chapter 9.

ADVANCED READING

A comprehensive treatment of all of the topics that are contained in this book will not be essential for all readers. To meet the different requirements of the readers, the more advanced material that is not essential for those readers not requiring an in-depth knowledge of a particular topic has been highlighted. The start of each advanced reading section has a clearly identifiable heading and a vertical green line is used to highlight the full section. If you do require an in-depth knowledge of a topic you may find it helpful initially to omit the advanced reading sections, or skim them, on your first reading. You should read them in detail only when you fully understand the content of the remaining parts of the chapter. The advanced reading sections are more appropriate for an advanced course and may normally be omitted if you are pursuing an introductory course.

SUMMARY

The following items relate to the learning objectives listed at the beginning of the chapter.

● **Distinguish between management accounting and financial accounting.**

Management accounting differs from financial accounting in several different ways. Management accounting is concerned with the provision of information to internal users to help them make better decisions and improve the efficiency and effectiveness of operations. Financial accounting is concerned with the provision of information to external parties outside the organization. Unlike financial accounting there is no statutory requirement for management accounting to produce financial statements or follow externally imposed rules. Furthermore, management accounting provides information relating to different parts of the business whereas financial accounting reports focus on the whole business. Management accounting also tends to be more future oriented and reports are often published on a daily basis whereas financial accounting reports are published semi-annually.

● **Identify and describe the elements involved in the decision-making, planning and control process.**

The following elements are involved in the decision-making, planning and control process: (a) identify the objectives that will guide the business; (b) search for a range of possible courses of action that might enable the objectives to be achieved; (c) gather data about the alternatives; (d) select appropriate alternative courses of action that will enable the objectives to be achieved; (e) implement the decisions as part of the planning and budgeting process; (f) compare actual and planned outcomes; and (g) respond to divergencies from plan by taking corrective action so that actual outcomes conform to planned outcomes or modify the plans if the comparisons indicate that the plans are no longer attainable.

● **Justify the view that a major objective of commercial organizations is to broadly seek to maximize the present value of future cash flows.**

The reasons for identifying maximizing the present value of future cash flows as a major objective are: (a) it is equivalent to maximizing shareholder value; (b) it is unlikely that any other objective is as widely applicable in measuring the ability of the organization to survive in the future; (c) although it is unlikely that maximizing the present value of future cash flows can be realized in practice it is still important to establish the principles necessary to achieve this objective; and (d) it enables shareholders as a group in the bargaining coalition to know how much the pursuit of other goals is costing them by indicating the amount of cash distributed among the members of the coalition.

● **Explain the factors that have influenced the changes in the competitive environment.**

The factors influencing the change in the competitive environment are (a) globalization of world trade; (b) privatization of government-controlled companies and deregulation in various industries; (c) changing product life cycles; (d) changing customer tastes that demand ever-improving levels of service in cost, quality, reliability, delivery and the choice of new products; and (e) the emergence of e-business.

● **Outline and describe the key success factors that directly affect customer satisfaction.**

The key success factors are cost efficiency, quality, time and innovation. Since customers will generally prefer to buy the product or service at the lowest price, all other things being equal, keeping costs low and being cost efficient provides an organization with a strong competitive advantage. Customers also demand high quality products and services and this has resulted in companies making quality a key competitive variable. Organizations are also seeking to increase customer satisfaction by providing a speedier response to customer requests, ensuring 100 per cent on-time delivery and reducing the time taken to bring new products to the market. To be successful companies must be innovative and develop a steady stream of new products and services and have the capability to rapidly adapt to changing customer requirements.

● **Identify and describe the functions of a cost and management accounting system.**

A cost and management accounting system should generate information to meet the following requirements:

(a) allocate costs between cost of goods sold and inventories for internal and external profit reporting and inventory valuation; (b) provide relevant information to help managers make better decisions; and (c) provide information for planning, control, performance measurement and continuous improvement.

● **Provide a brief historical description of management accounting.**

Most of the management accounting practices that were in use in the mid-1980s had been developed by 1925, and for the next 60 years there was virtually a halt in management accounting innovation. By the mid-1980s firms were using management accounting systems that were obsolete and no longer relevant to the changing competitive and manufacturing environment. During the late 1980s, criticisms of current management accounting practices were widely publicized in the professional and academic accounting literature. In response to the criticisms considerable progress has been made in modifying and implementing new techniques that are relevant to today's environment and that will ensure that management accounting regains its relevance.

Note

1 The total profits over the life of a business are identical with total net cash inflows. However, the profits calculated for a particular accounting period will be different from the net cash flows for that period. The difference arises because of the accruals concept in financial accounting. For most situations in this book, decisions that will lead to changes in profits are also assumed to lead to identical changes in net cash flows.

Key terms and concepts

Each chapter includes a section like this. You should make sure that you understand each of the terms listed below before you proceed to the next chapter. Their meanings are explained on the page numbers indicated.

benchmarking (p. 14)
bounded rationality (p. 9)
budget (p. 10)
continuous improvement (p. 14)
control (p. 11)
corporate ethics (p. 15)
cost accounting (p. 19)
cost efficient (p. 13)
cycle time (p. 14)
e-business (p. 16)
e-commerce (p. 16)
employee empowerment (p. 15)
enterprise resource planning systems (p. 16)

feedback (p. 11)
feedback loop (p. 11)
financial accounting (pp. 7, 18)
innovation (p. 14)
internet commerce (p. 16)
long-run decisions (p. 10)
management accounting (pp. 7, 19)
management by exception (p. 11)
master budget (p. 11)
non-value added activities (p. 14)
objectives of the organization (p. 8)
operating decisions (p. 10)
performance reports (p. 11)
planning (p. 8)

product life cycle (p. 12)
satisficing (p. 9)
short-term decisions (p. 10)
social responsibility (p. 15)
states of nature (p. 10)
strategic decisions (p. 10)
strategies (p. 9)
time-based measures (p. 14)
total quality management (p. 13)
value-chain analysis (p. 15)

Key examination points

Chapter 1 has provided an introduction to the scope of management accounting. It is unlikely that examination questions will be set that refer to the content of an introductory chapter. However, questions are sometimes set requiring you to outline how a costing system can assist the management of an organization. Note that the examiner may not distinguish between cost accounting and management accounting. Cost accounting is often used to also embrace management accounting. Your discussion of a cost accounting system should therefore include a description (with illustrations) of how the system provides information for decision-making, planning and control. Make sure that you draw off your experience from the whole of a first-year course and not just this introductory chapter.

ASSESSMENT MATERIAL

The review questions are short questions that enable you to assess your understanding of the main topics included in the chapter. The numbers in parentheses provide you with the page numbers to refer to if you cannot answer a specific question.

The remaining chapters also contain review problems. These are more complex and require you to relate and apply the chapter content to various business problems. Fully worked solutions to many of the review problems are provided in a separate section at the end of the book.

The website also includes over 30 case study problems. A list of these cases is provided on pages 665–7. The Electronic Boards case is a case study that is relevant to the introductory stages of a management accounting course.

Review questions

1.1 Identify and describe the different users of accounting information. *(pp. 6–7)*

1.2 Describe the differences between management accounting and financial accounting. *(p. 7)*

1.3 Explain each of the elements of the decision-making, planning and control process. *(pp. 8–11)*

1.4 Describe what is meant by management by exception. *(p. 11)*

1.5 What is a product's life cycle? *(p. 12)*

1.6 Describe what is meant by continuous improvement, benchmarking and employee empowerment. *(pp. 14–15)*

1.7 Describe the different activities in the value chain. *(p. 15)*

1.8 Explain why firms are beginning to concentrate on social responsibility and corporate ethics. *(p. 15)*

1.9 Describe the different functions of management accounting. *(pp. 18–20)*

1.10 Describe enterprise resource planning systems and their impact on management accountants. *(pp. 16–17)*

1.11 Provide a brief historical description of management accounting. *(pp. 20–21)*

An introduction to cost terms and concepts

2

In Chapter 1 it was pointed out that accounting systems measure costs which are used for profit measurement and inventory valuation, decision-making, performance measurement and control. The term cost is a frequently used word that reflects a monetary measure of the resources sacrificed or forgone to achieve a specific objective, such as acquiring a good or service. However, the term must be defined more precisely before the 'cost' can be determined. You will find that the word *cost* is rarely used without a preceding adjective to specify the type of cost being considered.

To understand how accounting systems calculate costs and to communicate accounting information effectively to others requires a thorough understanding of what cost means. Unfortunately, the term has multiple meanings and different types of costs are used in different situations. Therefore a preceding term must be added to clarify the assumptions that underlie a cost measurement. A large terminology has emerged to indicate more clearly which cost meaning is being conveyed. Examples include variable cost, fixed cost, opportunity cost and sunk cost. The aim of this chapter is to provide you with an understanding of the basic cost terms and concepts that are used in the management accounting literature.

LEARNING OBJECTIVES

After studying this chapter, you should be able to:

- explain why it is necessary to understand the meaning of different cost terms;

- define and illustrate a cost object;

- explain the meaning of each of the key terms listed at the end of this chapter;

- explain why in the short term some costs and revenues are not relevant for decision-making;

- distinguish between job costing and process costing;

- describe the three purposes for which cost information is required.

Cost objects

A cost object is any activity for which a separate measurement of costs is desired. In other words, if the users of accounting information want to know the cost of something, this something is called a cost object. Examples of cost objects include the cost of a product, the cost of rendering a service to a bank customer or hospital patient, the cost of operating a particular department or sales territory, or indeed anything for which one wants to measure the cost of resources used.

We shall see that the cost collection system typically accounts for costs in two broad stages:

1 It accumulates costs by classifying them into certain categories such as labour, materials and overhead costs (or by cost behaviour such as fixed and variable).

2 It then assigns these costs to cost objects.

In this chapter we shall focus on the following cost terms and concepts:

- direct and indirect costs;
- period and product costs;
- cost behaviour in relation to volume of activity;
- relevant and irrelevant costs;
- avoidable and unavoidable costs;
- sunk costs;
- opportunity costs;
- incremental and marginal costs.

Direct and indirect costs

Costs that are assigned to cost objects can be divided into two categories: direct costs and indirect costs. Direct costs are those costs that can be specifically and exclusively identified with a particular cost object. In contrast, indirect costs cannot be identified specifically and exclusively with a given cost object. Let us assume that our cost object is a product, or to be more specific a particular type of desk that is manufactured by an organization. In this situation the wood that is used to manufacture the desk can be specifically and exclusively identified with a particular desk and can thus be classified as a direct cost. Similarly, the wages of operatives whose time can be traced to the specific desk are a direct cost. In contrast, the salaries of factory supervisors or the rent of the factory cannot be specifically and exclusively traced to a particular desk and these costs are therefore classified as indirect.

Sometimes, however, direct costs are treated as indirect because tracing costs directly to the cost object is not cost effective. For example, the nails used to manufacture a particular desk can be identified specifically with the desk, but, because the cost is likely to be insignificant, the expense of tracing such items does not justify the possible benefits from calculating more accurate product costs.

Direct costs can be accurately traced because they can be physically identified with a particular object whereas indirect costs cannot. An estimate must be made of resources consumed by cost objects for indirect costs. Therefore, the more direct costs that can be traced to a cost object, the more accurate is the cost assignment.

The distinction between direct and indirect costs also depends on the cost object. A cost can be treated as direct for one cost object but indirect in respect of another. If the cost object is the cost of using different distribution channels, then the rental of warehouses and the salaries of storekeepers will be regarded as direct for each distribution channel. Also consider a supervisor's salary in a maintenance department of a manufacturing company. If the cost object is the maintenance department, then the salary is a direct cost. However, if the cost object is the product, both the warehouse rental and the salaries of the storekeepers and the supervisor will be an indirect cost because these costs cannot be specifically identified with the product.

Categories of manufacturing costs

In manufacturing organizations products are frequently the cost object. Traditionally, cost accounting systems in manufacturing organizations have reflected the need to assign costs to products to value stocks and measure profits based on imposed external financial accounting requirements. Traditional cost accounting systems accumulate product costs as follows:

Direct materials	xxx
Direct labour	xxx
Prime cost	xxx
Manufacturing overhead	xxx
Total manufacturing cost	xxx

Direct materials consist of all those materials that can be identified with a specific product. For example, wood that is used to manufacture a desk can easily be identified as part of the product, and can thus be classified as direct materials. Alternatively, materials used for the repair of a machine that is used for the manufacture of many different desks are classified as indirect materials. These items of materials cannot be identified with any one product, because they are used for the benefit of all products rather than for any one specific product. Note that indirect materials form part of the manufacturing overhead cost.

Direct labour consists of those labour costs that can be specifically traced to or identified with a particular product. Examples of direct labour costs include the wages of operatives who assemble parts into the finished product, or machine operatives engaged in the production process. By contrast, the salaries of factory supervisors or the wages paid to the staff in the stores department cannot be specifically identified with the product, and thus form part of the indirect labour costs. The wages of all employees who do not work on the product itself but who assist in the manufacturing operation are thus classified as part of the indirect labour costs. As with indirect materials, indirect labour is classified as part of the manufacturing overhead cost.

Prime cost refers to the direct costs of the product and consists of direct labour costs plus direct material costs plus any direct expenses. The cost of hiring a machine for producing a specific product is an example of a direct expense.

Manufacturing overhead consists of all manufacturing costs other than direct labour, direct materials and direct expenses. It therefore includes all indirect manufacturing labour and materials costs plus indirect manufacturing expenses. Examples of indirect manufacturing expenses in a multi-product company include rent of the factory and depreciation of machinery.

To ascertain the total manufacturing cost of a product, all that is required for the direct cost items is to record the amount of resources used on the appropriate documents. The specific product or order (i.e. the cost object) to which the costs should be assigned should be entered on the document. For example, the units of materials used in making a particular product are recorded on a stores requisition, and the hours of direct labour used are recorded on job cards. Having obtained the quantity of resources used for the direct items, it is necessary to ascertain the price paid for these resources. The total of the resources used multiplied by the price paid per unit of resources used provides us with the total of the direct costs or the prime cost for a product.

Manufacturing overheads cannot be directly traced to products. Instead they are assigned to products using cost allocations. A cost allocation is the process of estimating the cost of resources consumed by products that involves the use of surrogate, rather than direct measures. The process of assigning indirect costs (overheads) to cost objects will be explained in the next chapter.

Period and product costs

External financial accounting rules in most countries require that for inventory valuation, only manufacturing costs should be included in the calculation of product costs (for the United Kingdom see Statement of Standard Accounting Practice (SSAP 9), published by the Accounting Standards Committee). Accountants therefore classify costs as product costs and period costs. Product costs are those costs that are identified with goods purchased or produced for resale. In a manufacturing organization they are costs that the accountant attaches to the product and that are included in the inventory valuation for finished goods, or for partly completed goods (work in progress), until they are sold; they are then recorded as expenses and matched against sales for calculating profit. Period costs are those costs that are not included in the inventory valuation and as a result are treated as expenses in the period in which they are incurred. *Hence no attempt is made to attach period costs to products for inventory valuation purposes.*

In a manufacturing organization all manufacturing costs are regarded as product costs and non-manufacturing costs are regarded as period costs. Companies operating in the merchandising sector, such as retailing or wholesaling organizations, purchase goods for resale without changing their basic form. The cost of the goods purchased is regarded as a product cost and all other costs such as administration and selling and distribution expenses are considered to be period costs. The treatment of period and product costs for a manufacturing organization is illustrated in Figure 2.1. You will see that both product and period costs are eventually classified as expenses. The major difference is the point in time at which they are so classified.

Why are non-manufacturing costs treated as period costs and not included in the inventory valuation? There are two reasons. First, inventories are assets (unsold production) and assets represent resources that have been acquired that are expected to contribute to future revenue. Manufacturing costs incurred in making a product can be expected to generate future revenues to cover the cost of production. There is no guarantee, however, that non-manufacturing costs will generate future revenue, because they do not represent value added to any specific product. Therefore, they are not included in the inventory valuation. Second, many non-manufacturing costs (e.g. distribution costs) are not incurred when the product is being stored. Hence it is inappropriate to include such costs within the inventory valuation.

An illustration of the accounting treatment of period and product costs for income (profit) measurement purposes is presented in Example 2.1.

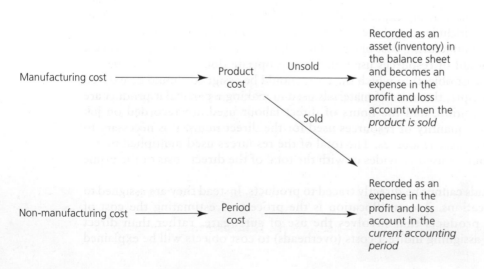

FIGURE 2.1
Treatment of period and product costs

EXAMPLE 2.1

The Flanders company produces 100 000 identical units of a product during period 1. The costs for the period are as follows:

	(£)	(£)
Manufacturing costs:		
Direct labour	400 000	
Direct materials	200 000	
Manufacturing overheads	200 000	800 000
Non-manufacturing costs		300 000

During period 1, the company sold 50 000 units for £750 000, and the remaining 50 000 units were unsold at the end of the period. There was no opening stock at the start of the period. The profit and loss account for period 1 will be as follows:

	(£)	(£)
Sales (50 000)		750 000
Manufacturing costs (*product costs*):		
Direct labour	400 000	
Direct materials	200 000	
Manufacturing overheads	200 000	
	800 000	
Less closing stock (50% or 50 000 units)	400 000	
Cost of goods sold (50% or 50 000 units)		400 000
Gross profit		350 000
Less non-manufacturing costs (*period costs*)		300 000
Net profit		50 000

Fifty per cent of the production was sold during the period and the remaining 50 per cent was produced for inventories. Half of the product costs are therefore identified as an expense for the period and the remainder are included in the closing inventory valuation. If we assume that the closing inventory is sold in the next accounting period, the remaining 50 per cent of the product costs will become expenses in the next accounting period. However, all the period costs became an expense in this accounting period, because this is the period to which they relate. Note that only product costs form the basis for the calculation of cost of goods sold, and that period costs do not form part of this calculation.

Cost behaviour

A knowledge of how costs and revenues will vary with different levels of activity (or volume) is essential for decision-making. Activity or volume may be measured in terms of units of production or sales, hours worked, miles travelled, patients seen, students enrolled or any other appropriate measure of the activity of an organization. Examples of decisions that require information on how costs and revenues vary with different levels of activity include the following:

1 What should the planned level of activity be for the next year?
2 Should we reduce the selling price to sell more units?
3 Would it be wiser to pay our sales staff by a straight commission, a straight salary, or by some combination of the two?
4 How do the costs and revenues of a hospital change if one more patient is admitted for a seven-day stay?

5 How do the costs and revenues of a hotel change if a room and meals are provided for two guests for a seven-day stay?

6 How will costs and revenues change if output is increased (or decreased) by 15 per cent?

For each of the above decisions management requires estimates of costs and revenues at different levels of activity for the alternative courses of action.

The terms 'variable', 'fixed', 'semi-variable' and 'semi-fixed' have been traditionally used in the management accounting literature to describe how a cost reacts to changes in activity. Variable costs vary in direct proportion to the volume of activity; that is, doubling the level of activity will double the total variable cost. Consequently, *total* variable costs are linear and *unit* variable cost is constant. Figure 2.2 illustrates a variable cost where the variable cost per unit of activity is £10. It is unlikely that variable cost per unit will be constant for all levels of activity. We shall discuss the reasons why accountants normally assume that variable costs are constant per unit of activity in Chapter 8. Examples of variable manufacturing costs include piecework labour, direct materials and energy to operate the machines. These costs are assumed to fluctuate directly in proportion to operating activity within a certain range of activity. Examples of non-manufacturing variable costs include sales commissions, which fluctuate with sales value, and petrol, which fluctuates with the number of miles travelled.

Fixed costs remain constant over wide ranges of activity for a specified time period. Examples of fixed costs include depreciation of the factory building, supervisors' salaries and leasing charges for cars used by the salesforce. Figure 2.3 illustrates fixed costs.

You will see that the *total* fixed costs are constant for all levels of activity whereas *unit* fixed costs decrease proportionally with the level of activity. For example, if the total of the fixed costs is £5000 for a month the fixed costs per unit will be as follows:

Units produced	Fixed cost per unit (£)
1	5000
10	500
100	50
1000	5

Because unit fixed costs are not constant per unit they must be interpreted with caution. For decision-making, it is better to work with total fixed costs rather than unit costs.

In practice it is unlikely that fixed costs will be constant over the full range of activity. They may increase in steps in the manner depicted in Figure 2.4. We shall discuss the justification for assuming that fixed costs are constant over a wide range of activity in Chapter 8.

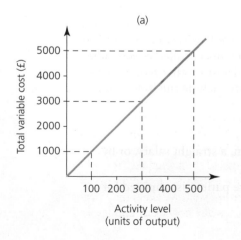
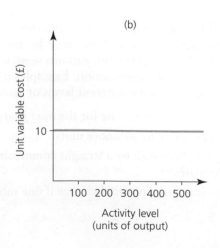

FIGURE 2.2
Variable costs: (a) total; (b) unit

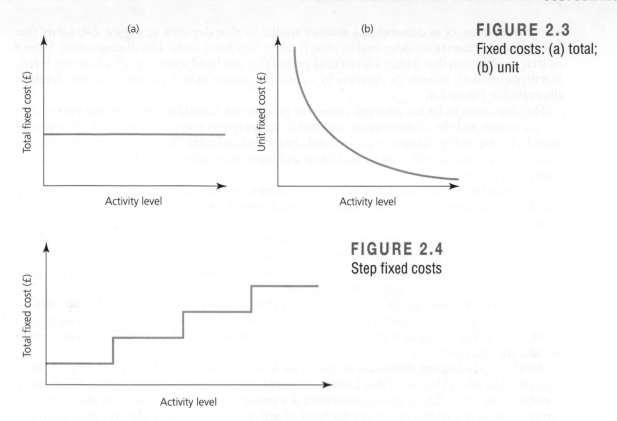

FIGURE 2.3
Fixed costs: (a) total;
(b) unit

FIGURE 2.4
Step fixed costs

The distinction between fixed and variable costs must be made relative to the time period under consideration. Over a sufficiently long time period of several years, virtually all costs are variable. During such a long period of time, contraction in demand will be accompanied by reductions in virtually all categories of costs. For example, senior managers can be released, machinery need not be replaced and even buildings and land can be sold. Similarly, large expansions in activity will eventually cause all categories of costs to increase.

Within shorter time periods, costs will be fixed or variable in relation to changes in activity. The shorter the time period, the greater the probability that a particular cost will be fixed. Consider a time period of one year. The costs of providing the firm's operating capacity such as depreciation and the salaries of senior plant managers are likely to be fixed in relation to changes in activity. Decisions on the firm's intended future potential level of operating capacity will determine the amount of capacity costs to be incurred. These decisions will have been made previously as part of the capital budgeting and long-term planning process. Once these decisions have been made, they cannot easily be reversed in the short term. Plant investment and abandonment decisions should not be based on short-term fluctuations in demand within a particular year. Instead, they should be reviewed periodically as part of the long-term planning process and decisions made based on long-run demand over several years. Thus capacity costs will tend to be fixed in relation to changes of activity within short-term periods such as one year. However, over long-term periods of several years, significant changes in demand will cause capacity costs to change.

Spending on some fixed costs, such as direct labour and supervisory salaries, can be adjusted in the short term to reflect changes in activity. For example, if production activity declines significantly then direct workers and supervisors might continue to be employed in the hope that the decline in demand will be temporary; but if there is no upsurge in demand then staff might eventually be made redundant. If, on the other hand, production capacity expands to some critical level, additional workers might be employed, but the process of recruiting such workers may take several months. Thus within a short-term period, such as one year, labour costs can change in response to changes in demand in a manner similar to that depicted in Figure 2.4. Costs that behave in this manner are described as semi-fixed or step fixed costs. The distinguishing feature of step fixed costs is that within a given time period they are fixed within specified activity levels, but they eventually increase or decrease by a constant amount at various critical activity levels as illustrated in Figure 2.4.

Our discussion so far has assumed a one-year time period. Consider a shorter time period such as one month and the circumstances outlined in the previous paragraph where it takes several months to respond to changes in activity and alter spending levels. Over very short-term periods such as one month, spending on direct labour and supervisory salaries will be fixed in relation to changes in activity.

You should now understand that over a given short-term period, such as one year, costs will be variable, fixed or semi-fixed. Over longer-term time periods of several years, all costs will tend to change in response to large changes in activity (or to changes in the range and variety of products or services marketed), and fixed costs will become semi-fixed and change in the manner depicted in Figure 2.4. Because fixed costs do not remain fixed in the long-term, some writers prefer to describe them as long-term variable costs, but we shall continue to use the term fixed costs since this is the term most widely used in the literature.

Note, however, that in the short term, even though fixed costs are normally assumed to remain unchanged in response to changes in the level of activity, they may change in response to other factors. For example, if price levels increase then some fixed costs such as management salaries will increase.

Before concluding our discussion of cost behaviour in relation to volume of activity, we must consider semi-variable costs (also known as mixed costs). These include both a fixed and a variable component. The cost of maintenance is a semi-variable cost consisting of planned maintenance that is undertaken whatever the level of activity, and a variable element that is directly related to the level of activity. A further example of a semi-variable cost is where sales representatives are paid a fixed salary plus a commission on sales.

Relevant and irrelevant costs and revenues

For decision-making, costs and revenues can be classified according to whether they are relevant to a particular decision. Relevant costs and revenues are those *future* costs and revenues that will be changed by a decision, whereas irrelevant costs and revenues are those that will not be affected by the decision. For example, if you are faced with a choice of making a journey using your own car or by public transport, the car tax and insurance costs are irrelevant, since they will remain the same whatever alternative is chosen. However, petrol costs for the car will differ depending on which alternative is chosen, and this cost will be relevant for decision-making.

Let us now consider a further illustration of the classification of relevant and irrelevant costs. Assume a company purchased raw materials a few years ago for £100 and that there appears to be no possibility of selling these materials or using them in future production apart from in connection with an enquiry from a former customer. This customer is prepared to purchase a product that will require the use of all these materials, but he is not prepared to pay more than £250 per unit. The additional costs of converting these materials into the required product are £200. Should the company accept the order for £250? It appears that the cost of the order is £300, consisting of £100 material cost and £200 conversion cost, but this is incorrect because the £100 material cost will remain the same whether the order is accepted or rejected. The material cost is therefore irrelevant for the decision, but if the order is accepted the conversion costs will change by £200, and this conversion cost is a relevant cost. If we compare the revenue of £250 with the relevant cost for the order of £200, it means that the order should be accepted, assuming of course that no higher-priced orders can be obtained elsewhere. The following calculation shows that this is the correct decision.

	Do not accept order (£)	Accept order (£)
Materials	100	100
Conversion costs	—	200
Revenue	—	(250)
Net costs	100	50

The net costs of the company are £50 less, or alternatively the company is £50 better off as a result of accepting the order. This agrees with the £50 advantage which was suggested by the relevant cost method.

In this illustration the sales revenue was relevant to the decision because future revenue changed depending on which alternative was selected; but sales revenue may also be irrelevant for decision-making. Consider a situation where a company can meet its sales demand by purchasing either machine A or machine B. The output of both machines is identical, but the operating costs and purchase costs of the machines are different. In this situation the sales revenue will remain unchanged irrespective of which machine is purchased (assuming of course that the quality of output is identical for both machines). Consequently, sales revenue is irrelevant for this decision; the relevant items are the operating costs and the cost of the machines. We have now established an important principle regarding the classification of cost and

Cost focus in low-cost airlines

An appreciation of the cost structure of a business is critical to its strategic and operational success. Even in hard times, managing and protecting a cost base can deliver superior performance. A case in point is that of low-cost airline companies like Ryanair. Despite largely uncontrollable events like terrorist threats and high oil prices, Ryanair continues to deliver high profit and growth figures while mainstream airlines struggle. Such growth and profit can only be maintained through a continuous focus on all costs of the company. Such a focus requires a complete understanding of operations and associated costs. For the 2006 financial year, Ryanair reported a 26 per cent increase in passenger traffic, a 28 per cent increase in turnover and a 12 per cent increase in after tax profit. Costs were reduced by 6 per cent, fuel excluded.

Examples of cost saving initiatives at Ryanair during 2006 were web based check-in and aircraft winglet modification. Web based check-in, with associated baggage charges, has encouraged passengers to travel with fewer bags thereby reducing handling costs and improving fuel efficiency. A small modification to its standard Boeing 737 aircraft – a winglet at the end of each wing – has reduced fuel consumption by 2 per cent.

Michael O'Leary, CEO, comments that the low cost model adopted by Ryanair will allow continued growth when many competitors are reporting losses.

Discussion points

1 Can you identify fixed and variable costs which might be incurred at a company like Ryanair?

2 Having read the above, would you agree that a business can do nothing about costs which are beyond its internal control?

REAL WORLD VIEWS 2.1

© GEOGPHOTOS/ALAMY

SOURCE: PRESS RELEASE 06/06/2006, WWW.RYANAIR.COM

revenues for decision-making; namely, that in the short term not all costs and revenues are relevant for decision-making.

Avoidable and unavoidable costs

Sometimes the terms avoidable and unavoidable costs are used instead of relevant and irrelevant cost. Avoidable costs are those costs that may be saved by not adopting a given alternative, whereas unavoidable costs cannot be saved. Therefore, only avoidable costs are relevant for decision-making purposes. Consider the example that we used to illustrate relevant and irrelevant costs. The material costs of £100 are unavoidable and irrelevant, but the conversion costs of £200 are avoidable and hence relevant. The decision rule is to accept those alternatives that generate revenues in excess of the avoidable costs.

Sunk costs

These costs are the cost of resources already acquired where the total will be unaffected by the choice between various alternatives. They are costs that have been created by a decision made in the past and that cannot be changed by any decision that will be made in the future. The expenditure of £100 on materials that were no longer required, referred to in the preceding section, is an example of a sunk cost. Similarly, the written down values of assets previously purchased are sunk costs. For example, if a machine was purchased four years ago for £100 000 with an expected life of five years and nil scrap value then the written down value will be £20 000 if straight line depreciation is used. This written down value will have to be written off, no matter what possible alternative future action might be chosen. If the machine was scrapped, the £20 000 would be written off; if the machine was used for productive purposes, the £20 000 would still have to be written off. This cost cannot be changed by any future decision and is therefore classified as a sunk cost.

Sunk costs are irrelevant for decision-making, but they are distinguished from irrelevant costs because not all irrelevant costs are sunk costs. For example, a comparison of two alternative production methods may result in identical direct material expenditure for both alternatives, so the direct material cost is irrelevant because it will remain the same whichever alternative is chosen, but the material cost is not sunk cost since it will be incurred in the future.

Opportunity costs

Some costs for decision-making cannot normally be collected within the accounting system. Costs that are collected within the accounting system are based on past payments or commitments to pay at some time in the future. Sometimes it is necessary for decision-making to impute costs that will not require cash outlays, and these imputed costs are called opportunity costs. An opportunity cost is a cost that measures the opportunity that is lost or sacrificed when the choice of one course of action requires that an alternative course of action be given up. Consider the information presented in Example 2.2.

It is important to note that opportunity costs only apply to the use of scarce resources. Where resources are not scarce, no sacrifice exists from using these resources. In Example 2.2 if machine X was operating at 80 per cent of its potential capacity and the decision to accept the contract would not have resulted in reduced production of product A there would have been no loss of revenue, and the opportunity cost would be zero.

You should now be aware that opportunity costs are of vital importance for decision-making. If no alternative use of resources exist then the opportunity cost is zero, but if resources have an alternative use, and are scarce, then an opportunity cost does exist.

EXAMPLE 2.2

A company has an opportunity to obtain a contract for the production of a special component. This component will require 100 hours of processing on machine X. Machine X is working at full capacity on the production of product A, and the only way in which the contract can be fulfilled is by reducing the output of product A. This will result in a lost profit contribution of £200. The contract will also result in *additional* variable costs of £1000.

If the company takes on the contract, it will sacrifice a profit contribution of £200 from the lost output of product A. This represents an opportunity cost, and should be included as part of the cost when negotiating for the contract. The contract price should at least cover the additional costs of £1000 plus the £200 opportunity cost to ensure that the company will be better off in the short term by accepting the contract.

Incremental and marginal costs

Incremental (also called differential) costs and revenues are the difference between costs and revenues for the corresponding items under each alternative being considered. For example, the incremental costs of increasing output from 1000 to 1100 units per week are the additional costs of producing an extra 100 units per week. Incremental costs may or may not include fixed costs. If fixed costs change as a result of a decision, the increase in costs represents an incremental cost. If fixed costs do not change as a result of a decision, the incremental costs will be zero.

Incremental costs and revenues are similar in principle to the economist's concept of marginal cost and marginal revenue. The main difference is that marginal cost/revenue represents the additional cost/revenue of one extra unit of output whereas incremental cost/revenue represents the additional cost/revenue resulting from a group of additional units of output. The economist normally represents the theoretical relationship between cost/revenue and output in terms of the marginal cost/revenue of single additional units of output. We shall see that the accountant is normally more interested in the incremental cost/revenue of increasing production and sales to whatever extent is contemplated, and this is most unlikely to be a single unit of output.

Job costing and process costing systems

There are two basic types of systems that companies can adopt – job costing and process costing systems. Job costing relates to a costing system that is required in organizations where each unit or batch of output of a product or service is unique. This creates the need for the cost of each unit to be calculated separately. The term 'job' thus relates to each unique unit or batch of output. Job costing systems are used in industries that provide customized products or services. For example, accounting firms provide customized services to clients with each client requiring services that consume different quantities of resources. Engineering companies often make machines to meet individual customer specifications. The contracts undertaken by construction and civil engineering companies differ greatly for each customer. In all of these organizations costs must be traced to each individual customer's order.

In contrast, process costing relates to those situations where masses of identical units are produced and it is unnecessary to assign costs to individual units of output. Products are produced in the same manner and consume the same amount of direct costs and overheads. It is therefore unnecessary to assign costs to individual units of output. Instead, the average cost per unit of output is calculated by dividing the total costs assigned to a product or service for a period by the number of units of output for that period. Industries where process costing is widely used include chemical processing, oil refining, food processing and brewing.

In practice these two costing systems represent extreme ends of a continuum. The output of many organizations requires a combination of the elements of both job costing and process costing.

Maintaining a cost database

In the previous chapter we noted that a cost and management accounting system should generate information to meet the following requirements:

1 to allocate costs between cost of goods sold and inventories for internal and external profit measurement and inventory valuation;
2 to provide relevant information to help managers make better decisions;
3 to provide information for planning, control and performance measurement.

A database should be maintained, with costs appropriately coded and classified, so that relevant cost information can be extracted to meet each of the above requirements.

A suitable coding system enables costs to be accumulated by the required cost objects (such as products or services, departments, responsibility centres, distribution channels, etc.) and also to be classified by appropriate categories. Typical cost classifications within the database are by categories of expense (direct materials, direct labour and overheads) and by cost behaviour (fixed and variable). In practice, direct materials will be accumulated by each individual type of material, direct labour by different grades of labour and overhead costs by different categories of indirect expenses (e.g. rent, depreciation, supervision, etc.).

For *inventory valuation* the costs of all partly completed products (work in progress) and unsold finished products can be extracted from the database to ascertain the total cost assigned to inventories. The cost of goods sold that is deducted from sales revenues to compute the profit for the period can also be extracted by summing the manufacturing costs of all those products that have been sold during the period.

The allocation of costs to products is inappropriate for *cost control and performance measurement*, as the manufacture of the product may consist of several different operations, all of which are the responsibility of different individuals. To overcome this problem, costs and revenues must be traced to the individuals who are responsible for incurring them. This system is known as responsibility accounting.

Responsibility accounting involves the creation of responsibility centres. A responsibility centre may be defined as an organization unit or part of a business for whose performance a manager is held accountable. Responsibility accounting enables accountability for financial results and outcomes to be allocated to individuals throughout the organization. The objective of responsibility accounting is to measure the results of each responsibility centre. It involves accumulating costs and revenues for each responsibility centre so that deviations from a performance target (typically the budget) can be attributed to the individual who is accountable for the responsibility centre.

For *cost control and performance measurement* the accountant produces performance reports at regular intervals for each responsibility centre. The reports are generated by extracting from the database costs analyzed by responsibility centres and categories of expenses. Actual costs for each item of expense listed on the performance report should be compared with budgeted costs so that those costs that do not conform to plan can be pinpointed and investigated.

Future costs, rather than past costs, are required for *decision-making*. Therefore costs extracted from the database should be adjusted for anticipated price changes. We have noted that classification of costs by cost behaviour is important for evaluating the financial impact of expansion or contraction decisions. Costs, however, are not classified as relevant or irrelevant within the database because relevance depends on the circumstances. Consider a situation where a company is negotiating a contract for the sale of one of its products with a customer in an overseas country which is not part of its normal market. If the company has temporary excess capacity and the contract is for 100 units for one month only, then the direct labour cost will remain the same irrespective of whether or not the contract is undertaken. The direct labour cost will therefore be irrelevant. Let us now assume that the contract is for 100 units per month for three years and the company has excess capacity. For long-term decisions direct labour will be a relevant cost because if the contract is not undertaken direct labour can be redeployed or made redundant. Undertaking the contract will result in additional direct labour costs.

The above example shows that the classification of costs as relevant or irrelevant depends on the circumstances. In one situation a cost may be relevant, but in another the same cost may not be relevant. Costs can only be classified as relevant or irrelevant when the circumstances have been identified relating to a particular decision.

Where a company sells many products or services their profitability should be monitored at regular intervals so that potentially unprofitable products can be highlighted for a more detailed study of their future viability. This information is extracted from the database with costs reported by categories of expenses and divided into their fixed and variable elements. In Chapter 9 we shall focus in more detail on product/segmented profitability analysis. Finally, you should note that when the activities of an organization consist of a series of common or repetitive operations, targets or standard product costs, rather than actual costs, may be recorded in the database. Standard costs are predetermined costs; they are target costs that should be incurred under efficient operating conditions. They should be reviewed and updated at periodic intervals. If product standard costs are recorded in the database there is no need continuously to trace costs to products and therefore a considerable amount of data processing time can be saved. Actual costs, however, will still be traced to responsibility centres for cost control and performance evaluation.

SUMMARY

The following items relate to the learning objectives listed at the beginning of the chapter.

● **Explain why it is necessary to understand the meaning of different cost terms.**

The term 'cost' has multiple meanings and different types of costs are used in different situations. Therefore, a preceding term must be added to clarify the assumptions that underlie a measurement.

● **Define and illustrate a cost object.**

A cost object is any activity for which a separate measurement of cost is required. In other words managers often want to know the cost of something and the 'thing' that they want to know the cost of is a cost object. Examples of cost objects include the cost of a new product, the cost of operating a sales outlet and the cost of operating a specific machine.

● **Explain the meaning of each of the key terms listed at the end of this chapter.**

You should check your understanding of each of the terms listed in the key terms and concepts section below by referring to the page numbers that are shown in the parentheses following each key term.

● **Explain why in the short term some costs and revenues are not relevant for decision-making.**

In the short term some costs and revenues may remain unchanged for all alternatives under consideration. For example, if you wish to determine the costs of driving to work in your own car or using public transport, the cost of the road fund taxation licence and insurance will remain the same for both alternatives, assuming that you intend to keep your car for leisure purposes. Therefore the costs of these items are not relevant for assisting you in your decision to travel to work by public transport or using your own car. Costs that remain unchanged for all alternatives under consideration are not relevant for decision-making.

● **Distinguish between job costing and process costing.**

A job costing system relates to a costing system where each unit or batch of output of product(s) or service(s) is unique. This creates the need for the cost of each unit or batch to be calculated separately. In contrast a process costing system relates to situations where masses of identical units or batches are produced thus making it unnecessary to assign costs to individual units or batches of output. Instead, the average cost per unit or batch of output is calculated by dividing the total costs assigned to a product or service for the period by the number of units or batches of output for that period.

● **Describe the three purposes for which cost information is required.**

A cost and management accounting system should generate information to meet the following requirements:

(a) to allocate costs between cost of goods sold and inventories for internal and external profit reporting and inventory valuation;
(b) to provide relevant information to help managers make better decisions;
(c) to provide information for planning, control and performance measurement.

A database should be maintained with costs appropriately coded or classified, so that relevant information can be extracted for meeting each of the above requirements.

Key terms and concepts

avoidable costs (p. 36)
cost allocations (p. 29)
cost object (p. 28)
differential costs (p. 37)
direct costs (p. 28)
direct labour (p. 29)
direct materials (p. 29)
fixed costs (p. 32)
incremental costs (p. 37)
indirect cost (p. 28)
indirect labour costs (p. 29)

indirect materials (p. 29)
irrelevant costs and revenues (p. 34)
job costing (p. 37)
long-term variable costs (p. 34)
manufacturing overhead (p. 29)
marginal cost/revenue (p. 37)
mixed costs (p. 34)
opportunity cost (p. 36)
period costs (p. 30)
prime cost (p. 29)
process costing (p. 37)

product costs (p. 30)
relevant costs and revenues (p. 34)
responsibility accounting (p. 37)
responsibility centre (p. 37)
semi-fixed costs (p. 34)
semi-variable costs (p. 34)
step fixed costs (p. 34)
sunk cost (p. 36)
unavoidable costs (p. 36)
variable costs (p. 32)

Recommended reading

This chapter has explained the meaning of the important terms that you will encounter when reading this book. For a more comprehensive description and detailed explanation of various

cost terms you should refer to the Chartered Institute of Management Accountants' Official Terminology (2005).

Key examination points

First year management accounting course examinations frequently involve short essay questions requiring you to describe various cost terms or to discuss the concept that different costs are required for different purposes (see Review problems 2.19–2.25 for examples). It is therefore important that you understand all of the cost terms that have been described in this chapter. In particular, you should be able to explain the context within which a cost term is normally used. For example, a cost such as wages paid to casual labourers will be classified as indirect for inventory valuation purposes but as

a direct charge to a responsibility centre or department for cost control purposes. A common error is for students to produce a very short answer, but you must be prepared to expand your answer and to include various situations within which the use of a cost term is appropriate. Always make sure your answer includes illustrations of cost terms. Multiple choice questions are also often set on topics included in this chapter. Review problems 2.16–2.18 are typical examples of such questions. You should now attempt these and compare your answers with the solutions.

ASSESSMENT MATERIAL

The review questions are short questions that enable you to assess your understanding of the main topics included in the chapter. The numbers in parentheses provide you with the page numbers to refer to if you cannot answer a specific question.

The review problems are more complex and require you to relate and apply the content to various business problems. The problems are graded by their level of difficulty. Solutions to review problems that are not preceded by the term 'IM' are provided in a separate section at the end of the book. Solutions to problems preceded by the term 'IM' are provided in the *Instructor's Manual* accompanying this book and also on the lecturer's password protected section of the website www.drury-online.com. Additional review problems with fully worked solutions are provided in the *Student's Manual* that accompanies this book.

The website also includes over 30 case study problems. A list of these cases is provided on pages 665–7. The Electronic Boards case is a case study that is relevant to the introductory stages of a management accounting course.

Review questions

2.1 Define the meaning of the term 'cost object' and provide three examples of cost objects. *(p. 28)*
2.2 Distinguish between a direct and indirect cost. *(p. 28)*
2.3 Describe how a given direct cost item can be both a direct and indirect cost. *(p. 28)*
2.4 Provide examples of each of the following: (a) direct labour, (b) indirect labour, (c) direct materials, (d) indirect materials, and (e) indirect expenses. *(p. 29)*
2.5 Explain the meaning of the terms: (a) prime cost, (b) overheads, and (c) cost allocations. *(p. 29)*
2.6 Distinguish between product costs and period costs. *(p. 30)*
2.7 Provide examples of decisions that require knowledge of how costs and revenues vary with different levels of activity. *(pp. 31–32)*
2.8 Explain the meaning of each of the following terms: (a) variable costs, (b) fixed costs, (c) semi-fixed costs, and (d) semi-variable costs. Provide examples of costs for each of the four categories. *(pp. 32–34)*
2.9 Distinguish between relevant (avoidable) and irrelevant (unavoidable) costs and provide examples of each type of cost. *(pp. 34–36)*
2.10 Explain the meaning of the term 'sunk cost'. *(p. 36)*
2.11 Distinguish between incremental and marginal costs. *(p. 37)*
2.12 What is an opportunity cost? Give some examples. *(p. 36)*
2.13 Distinguish between job costing and process costing. *(p. 37)*
2.14 Explain responsibility accounting. *(p. 38)*

Review problems

2.15 Basic. Classify each of the following as being usually fixed (F), variable (V), semi-fixed (SF) or semi-variable (SV):

  a direct labour;
  b depreciation of machinery;
  c factory rental;
  d supplies and other indirect materials;
  e advertising;
  f maintenance of machinery;
  g factory manager's salary;
  h supervisory personnel;
  i royalty payments.

2.16 Basic. Which ONE of the following costs could NOT be classified as a production overhead cost in a food processing company?

  a The cost of renting the factory building.
  b The salary of the factory manager.
  c The depreciation of equipment located in the materials store.
  d The cost of ingredients.

CIMA Management Accounting Fundamentals

2.17 Basic. Which one of the following would be classified as indirect labour?

  a Assembly workers on a car production line
  b Bricklayers in a house building company
  c Machinists in a factory producing clothes
  d Forklift truck drivers in the stores of an engineering company

ACCA 1.2: Financial Information for Management

2.18 Basic. Fixed costs are conventionally deemed to be:

  a constant per unit of output;
  b constant in total when production volume changes;
  c outside the control of management;
  d those unaffected by inflation.

CIMA Stage 1 Cost Accounting

2.19 Intermediate. Prepare a report for the Managing Director of your company explaining how costs may be classified by their behaviour, with particular reference to the effects both on total and on unit costs. Your report should:

  (i) say why it is necessary to classify costs by their behaviour, and
  (ii) be illustrated by sketch graphs within the body of the report.

(15 marks)
CIMA Stage 1 Accounting

2.20 Intermediate. Cost classifications used in costing include:

  (i) period costs
  (ii) product costs
  (iii) variable costs
  (iv) opportunity costs

Required:
Explain each of these classifications, with examples of the types of costs that may be included.

(17 marks)
ACCA Level 1 Costing

2.21 Intermediate.

  a Describe the role of the cost accountant in a manufacturing organization. *(8 marks)*
  b Explain whether you agree with each of the following statements:
      (i) 'All direct costs are variable.'
      (ii) 'Variable costs are controllable and fixed costs are not.'
      (iii) 'Sunk costs are irrelevant when providing decision making information.' *(9 marks)*

ACCA Level 1 Costing

2.22 Intermediate. 'Cost may be classified in a variety of ways according to their nature and the information needs of management.' Explain and discuss this statement, illustrating with examples of the classifications required for different purposes.

(22 marks)
ICSA Management Accounting

2.23 Intermediate. It is commonly suggested that a management accounting system should be capable of supplying different measures of cost for different purposes. You are required to set out the main types of purpose for which cost information may be required in a business organization, and to discuss the alternative measures of cost which might be appropriate for each purpose.

ICAEW Management Accounting

2.24 Intermediate. *Opportunity cost* and *sunk cost* are among the concepts of cost commonly discussed.

You are required:

(i) to define these terms precisely;   *(4 marks)*
(ii) to suggest for each of them situations in which the concept might be applied;   *(4 marks)*
(iii) to assess briefly the significance of each of the concepts.

(4 marks)

ICAEW P2 Management Accounting

2.25 Intermediate. Distinguish between, and provide an illustration of:

(i) 'avoidable' and 'unavoidable' costs;
(ii) 'cost centres' and 'cost units'.   *(8 marks)*

ACCA Foundation Paper 3

2.26 Intermediate: Cost behaviour.

Data	(£)
Cost of motor car	5500
Trade-in price after 2 years or 60 000 miles is expected to be	1500
Maintenance – 6-monthly service costing	60
Spares/replacement parts, per 1000 miles	20
Vehicle licence, per annum	80
Insurance, per annum	150
Tyre replacements after 25 000 miles, four at £37.50 each	
Petrol, per gallon	1.90
Average mileage from one gallon is 25 miles.	

a   From the above data you are required:
   (i) to prepare a schedule to be presented to management showing for the mileages of 5000, 10 000, 15 000 and 30 000 miles per annum:
       (1) total variable cost
       (2) total fixed cost
       (3) total cost
       (4) variable cost per mile (in pence to nearest penny)
       (5) fixed cost per mile (in pence to nearest penny)
       (6) total cost per mile (in pence to nearest penny)
       If, in classifying the costs, you consider that some can be treated as either variable or fixed, state the assumption(s) on which your answer is based together with brief supporting reason(s).
   (ii) on graph paper plot the information given in your answer to (i) above for the costs listed against (1), (2), (3) and (6).
   (iii) to read off from your graph(s) in (ii) and state the approximate total costs applicable to 18 000 miles and 25 000 miles and the total cost per mile at these two mileages.
b   'The more miles you travel, the cheaper it becomes.' Comment briefly on this statement.   *(25 marks)*

CIMA Cost Accounting 1

2.27 Intermediate: Sunk and opportunity costs for decision-making. Mrs Johnston has taken out a lease on a shop for a down payment of £5000. Additionally, the rent under the lease amounts to £5000 per annum. If the lease is cancelled, the initial payment of £5000 is forfeit. Mrs Johnston plans to use the shop for the sale of clothing, and has estimated operations for the next twelve months as follows:

	(£)	(£)
Sales	115 000	
Less Value-added tax (VAT)	15 000	
Sales Less VAT		100 000
Cost of goods sold	50 000	
Wages and wage related costs	12 000	
Rent including the down payment	10 000	
Rates, heating, lighting and insurance	13 000	
Audit, legal and general expenses	2 000	
		87 000
Net profit before tax		13 000

In the figures no provision has been made for the cost of Mrs Johnston but it is estimated that one half of her time will be devoted to the business. She is undecided whether to continue with her plans, because she knows that she can sublet the shop to a friend for a monthly rent of £550 if she does not use the shop herself.

You are required to:

a   (i) explain and identify the 'sunk' and 'opportunity' costs in the situation depicted above;
    (ii) state what decision Mrs Johnston should make according to the information given, supporting your conclusion with a financial statement;   *(11 marks)*
b   explain the meaning and use of 'notional' (or 'imputed') costs and quote two supporting examples.   *(4 marks)*

CIMA Foundation Cost Accounting 1

IM2.1 Basic: Cost classification. For the relevant cost data in items (1)–(7), indicate which of the following is the best classification.

a   sunk cost
b   incremental cost
c   variable cost
d   fixed cost
e   semi-variable cost
f   semi-fixed cost
g   controllable cost
h   non-controllable cost
i   opportunity cost

(1) A company is considering selling an old machine. The machine has a book value of £20 000. In evaluating the decision to sell the machine, the £20 000 is a …
(2) As an alternative to the old machine, the company can rent a new one. It will cost £3000 a year. In analysing the cost–volume behaviour the rental is a …
(3) To run the firm's machines, here are two alternative courses of action. One is to pay the operator a base salary plus a small amount per unit produced. This makes the total cost of the operators a …
(4) As an alternative, the firm can pay the operators a flat salary. It would then use one machine when volume is low, two when it expands, and three during peak periods. This means that the total operator cost would now be a …
(5) The machine mentioned in (1) could be sold for £8000. If the firm considers retaining and using it, the £8000 is a …
(6) If the firm wishes to use the machine any longer, it must be repaired. For the decision to retain the machine, the repair cost is a …
(7) The machine is charged to the foreman of each department at a rate of £3000 a year. In evaluating the foreman, the charge is a …

IM2.2 Basic: Cost classification. A company manufactures and retails clothing. You are required to group the costs which are listed below and numbered (1)–(20) into the following classifications (each cost is intended to belong to only one classification):

(i)   direct materials
(ii)   direct labour
(iii) direct expenses
(iv)   indirect production overhead
(v)   research and development costs
(vi)   selling and distribution costs
(vii) administration costs
(viii) finance costs

(1)   Lubricant for sewing machines
(2)   Floppy disks for general office computer
(3)   Maintenance contract for general office photocopying machine
(4)   Telephone rental plus metered calls
(5)   Interest on bank overdraft
(6)   Performing Rights Society charge for music broadcast throughout the factory
(7)   Market research undertaken prior to a new product launch
(8)   Wages of security guards for factory
(9)   Carriage on purchase of basic raw material

(10) Royalty payable on number of units of product XY produced
(11) Road fund licences for delivery vehicles
(12) Parcels sent to customers
(13) Cost of advertising products on television
(14) Audit fees
(15) Chief accountant's salary
(16) Wages of operatives in the cutting department
(17) Cost of painting advertising slogans on delivery vans
(18) Wages of storekeepers in materials store
(19) Wages of fork lift truck drivers who handle raw materials
(20) Developing a new product in the laboratory

(10 marks)
CIMA Cost Accounting 1

IM2.3 Intermediate: Analysis of costs by behaviour for decision-making.
The Northshire Hospital Trust operates two types of specialist X-ray scanning machines, XR1 and XR50. Details for the next period are estimated as follows:

Machine	XR1	XR50
Running hours	1100	2000
	(£)	(£)
Variable running costs (excluding plates)	27 500	64 000
Fixed costs	20 000	97 500

A brain scan is normally carried out on machine type XR1: this task uses special X-ray plates costing £40 each and takes four hours of machine time. Because of the nature of the process, around 10 per cent of the scans produce blurred and therefore useless results.

Required:

a Calculate the cost of a satisfactory brain scan on machine type XR1. *(7 marks)*
b Brain scans can also be done on machine type XR50 and would take only 1.8 hours per scan with a reduced reject rate of 6 per cent. However, the cost of the X-ray plates would be £55 per scan.

Required:
Advise which type should be used, assuming sufficient capacity is available on both types of machine. *(8 marks)*
CIMA Stage 1 Cost Accounting

IM2.4 Intermediate: Product cost calculation. From the information given below you are required to:

a prepare a standard cost sheet for one unit and enter on the standard cost sheet the costs to show sub-totals for:
(i) prime cost
(ii) variable production cost
(iii) total production cost
(iv) total cost
b calculate the selling price per unit allowing for a profit of 15 per cent of the selling price.

The following data are given:

Budgeted output for the year 9800 units
Standard details for one unit:
Direct materials 40 square metres at £5.30 per square metre

Direct wages:
 Bonding department 48 hours at £2.50 per hour
 Finishing department 30 hours at £1.90 per hour
 Budgeted costs and hours per annum:

Variable overhead:

	(£)	(hours)
Bonding department	375 000	500 000
Finishing department	150 000	300 000

Fixed overhead:

	(£)	(hours)
Production	392 000	
Selling and distribution	196 000	
Administration	98 000	

(15 marks)
CIMA Cost Accounting 1

PART TWO

Cost Accumulation for Inventory Valuation and Profit Measurement

This section focuses mainly on assigning costs to products to separate costs incurred during a period between costs of goods sold and the closing inventory valuation. The extent to which product costs accumulated for inventory valuation and profit measurement should be adjusted for meeting decision-making, cost control and performance measurement requirements is also briefly considered.

Chapter 3 aims to provide you with an understanding of how costs are assigned to cost objects. In particular the chapter focuses on the assignment of indirect costs using traditional and activity-based systems. In Chapter 4 the emphasis is on the accounting entries necessary to record transactions within a job costing system. The issues relating to a cost accumulation procedure for a process costing system are described in Chapter 5. This is a system that is applicable to industries that produce many units of the same product during a particular period. In Chapter 6 the problems associated with calculating product costs in those industries that produce joint and by-products are discussed. The final chapter in this section is concerned with the alternative accounting methods of assigning fixed manufacturing overheads to products and their implications for profit measurement and inventory valuation.

Cost assignment

3

In the previous chapter it was pointed out that companies need cost and management accounting systems to perform a number of different functions. In this chapter we are going to concentrate on two of these functions – they are (i) allocating costs between cost of goods sold and inventories for internal and external profit reporting and (ii) providing relevant decision-making information for distinguishing between profitable and unprofitable activities.

In order to perform the above functions a cost accumulation system is required that assigns costs to cost objects. The aim of this chapter is to provide you with an understanding of how costs are accumulated and assigned to cost objects. You should have remembered from the previous chapter that a cost object is anything for which a separate measurement of cost is desired. Typical cost objects include products, services, customers and locations. In this chapter we shall either

LEARNING OBJECTIVES

After studying this chapter, you should be able to:

● **distinguish between cause-and-effect and arbitrary cost allocations;**

● **explain why different cost information is required for different purposes;**

● **describe how cost systems differ in terms of their level of sophistication;**

● **understand the factors influencing the choice of an optimal cost system;**

● **explain why departmental overhead rates should be used in preference to a single blanket overhead rate;**

● **construct an overhead analysis sheet and calculate cost centre allocation rates;**

● **distinguish between traditional and activity-based costing systems;**

● **justify why budgeted overhead rates should be used in preference to actual overhead rates;**

● **calculate and explain the accounting treatment of the under-/over-recovery of overheads.**

use the term cost object as a generic term or assume that products are the cost object. However, the same cost assignment principles can be applied to all cost objects.

We begin by explaining how the cost assignment process differs for direct and indirect costs.

Assignment of direct and indirect costs

Costs that are assigned to cost objects can be divided into two categories – direct costs and indirect costs. Sometimes the term overheads is used instead of indirect costs. Direct costs can be accurately traced to cost objects because they can be specifically and exclusively traced to a particular cost object whereas indirect costs cannot. Where a cost can be directly assigned to a cost object the term cost tracing is used. In contrast, indirect costs cannot be traced directly to a cost object because they are usually common to several cost objects. Indirect costs are therefore assigned to cost objects using cost allocations.

A cost allocation is the process of assigning costs when a direct measure does not exist for the quantity of resources consumed by a particular cost object. Cost allocations involve the use of surrogate rather than direct measures. For example, consider an activity such as receiving incoming materials. Assuming that the cost of receiving materials is strongly influenced by the number of receipts then costs can be allocated to products (i.e. the cost object) based on the number of material receipts each product requires. The basis that is used to allocate costs to cost objects (i.e. the number of material receipts in our example) is called an allocation base or cost driver. If 20 per cent of the total number of receipts for a period were required for a particular product then 20 per cent of the total costs of receiving incoming materials would be allocated to that product. Assuming that the product was discontinued, and not replaced, we would expect action to be taken to reduce the resources required for receiving materials by 20 per cent.

In the above illustration the allocation base is assumed to be a significant determinant of the cost of receiving incoming materials. Where allocation bases are significant determinants of the costs we shall describe them as cause-and-effect allocations. Where a cost allocation base is used that is not a significant determinant of its cost the term arbitrary allocation will be used. An example of an arbitrary allocation would be if direct labour hours were used as the allocation base to allocate the costs of materials receiving. If a labour intensive product required a large proportion of direct labour hours (say 30 per cent) but few material receipts it would be allocated with a large proportion of the costs of material receiving. The allocation would be an inaccurate assignment of the resources consumed by the product. Furthermore, if the product were discontinued, and not replaced, the cost of the material receiving activity would not decline by 30 per cent because the allocation base is not a significant determinant of the costs of the materials receiving activity. Arbitrary allocations are therefore likely to result in inaccurate allocations of indirect costs to cost objects.

Figure 3.1 provides a summary of the assignment process. You can see that direct costs are assigned to cost objects using cost tracing whereas indirect cost are assigned using cost allocations. For accurate assignment of indirect costs to cost objects cause-and-effect allocations should

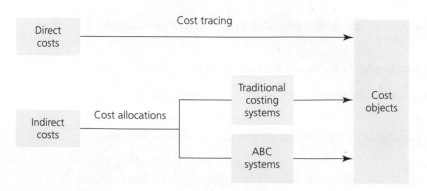

FIGURE 3.1
Cost allocations and cost tracing

be used. Two types of systems can be used to assign indirect costs to cost objects. They are traditional costing systems and activity-based-costing (ABC) systems. Traditional costing systems were developed in the early 1900s and are still widely used today. They rely extensively on arbitrary cost allocations. ABC systems only emerged in the late 1980s. One of the major aims of ABC systems is to use only cause-and-effect cost allocations. Both cost systems adopt identical approaches to assigning direct costs to cost objects. We shall look at traditional and ABC systems in more detail later in the chapter.

Different costs for different purposes

Manufacturing organizations assign costs to products for two purposes: first, for internal profit measurement and external financial accounting requirements in order to allocate the manufacturing costs incurred during a period between cost of goods sold and inventories; secondly, to provide useful information for managerial decision-making requirements. In order to meet financial accounting requirements, it may not be necessary to accurately trace costs to *individual* products. Consider a situation where a firm produces 1000 different products and the costs incurred during a period are £10 million. A well-designed product costing system should accurately analyze the £10 million costs incurred between cost of sales and inventories. Let us assume the true figures are £7 million and £3 million. Approximate but inaccurate *individual* product costs may provide a reasonable approximation of how much of the £10 million should be attributed to cost of sales and inventories. Some product costs may be overstated and others may be understated, but this would not matter for financial accounting purposes as long as the *total* of the individual product costs assigned to cost of sales and inventories was approximately £7 million and £3 million.

For decision-making purposes, however, more accurate product costs are required so that we can distinguish between profitable and unprofitable products. By more accurately measuring the resources consumed by products, or other cost objects, a firm can identify its sources of profits and losses. If the cost system does not capture sufficiently accurately the consumption of resources by products, the reported product costs will be distorted, and there is a danger that managers may drop profitable products or continue production of unprofitable products.

Besides different levels of accuracy, different cost information is required for different purposes. For meeting external financial accounting requirements, financial accounting regulations and legal requirements in most countries require that inventories should be valued at manufacturing cost. Therefore only manufacturing costs are assigned to products for meeting external financial accounting requirements. For decision-making non-manufacturing costs must be taken into account and assigned to products. Not all costs, however may be relevant for decision-making. For example, depreciation of plant and machinery will not be affected by a decision to discontinue a product. Such costs were described in the previous chapter as irrelevant and sunk for decision-making. Thus depreciation of plant must be assigned to products for inventory valuation but it should not be assigned for discontinuation decisions.

Maintaining a single or separate databases

Because different costs and different levels of accuracy are required for different purposes some organizations maintain two separate costing systems, one for decision-making and the other for inventory valuation and profit measurement. In a survey of 187 UK companies Drury and Tayles (2000) reported that 9 per cent of the companies maintained two cost accumulation systems, one for decision-making and the other for inventory valuation. The remaining 91 per cent of organizations maintained a costing system on a single database from which appropriate cost information was extracted to provide the required information for both decision-making and inventory valuation. When a single database is maintained only costs that must be assigned for inventory valuation are extracted for meeting financial accounting requirements, whereas for decision-making only costs which are relevant for the decision are extracted. Inventory valuation is not an issue for many service organizations. They do not carry inventories and therefore a costing system is not required for meeting inventory valuation requirements.

Where a single database is maintained cost assignments cannot be at different levels of accuracy for different purposes. In the late 1980s, according to Johnson and Kaplan (1987), most organizations were relying on costing systems that had been designed primarily for meeting external financial accounting requirements. These systems were designed decades ago when information processing costs were high and precluded the use of more sophisticated methods of assigning indirect costs to products. Such systems are still widely used today. They rely extensively on arbitrary cost allocations which may be sufficiently accurate for meeting external financial accounting requirements but not for meeting decision-making requirements. Johnson and Kaplan concluded that until recently management accounting practices have followed and become subservient to meeting financial accounting requirements.

Cost–benefit issues and cost systems design

These criticisms resulted in the emergence of ABC in the late 1980s. Surveys in many countries suggest that between 20 and 30 per cent of the surveyed organizations have implemented ABC systems. The majority of organizations therefore continue to operate traditional systems. Both traditional and ABC systems vary in their level of sophistication but, as a general rule, traditional systems tend to be simplistic whereas ABC systems tend to be sophisticated. What determines the chosen level of sophistication of a costing system? The answer is that the choice should be made on costs versus benefits criteria. Simplistic systems are inexpensive to operate, but they are likely to result in inaccurate cost assignments and the reporting of inaccurate costs. Managers using cost information extracted from simplistic systems are more likely to make important mistakes arising from using inaccurate cost information. The end result may be a high cost of errors. Conversely, sophisticated systems are more expensive to operate but they minimize the cost of errors. However, the aim should not be to have the most accurate cost system. Improvements should be made in the level of sophistication of the costing system up to the point where the marginal cost of improvement equals the marginal benefit from the improvement.

Figure 3.2 illustrates the above points with costing systems ranging from simplistic to sophisticated. Highly simplistic costing systems are located on the extreme left. Common features of such systems are that they are inexpensive to operate, make extensive use of arbitrary allocations of indirect costs and normally result in low levels of accuracy and a high cost of errors. On the extreme right are highly sophisticated systems. These systems use only cause-and-effect allocations, are more expensive to operate, have high levels of accuracy and minimize the cost of errors. Cost systems in most organizations are not located at either of these extreme points. Instead, they are located at different points within the range shown in Figure 3.2.

The optimal cost system is different for different organizations. For example, the optimal costing system will be located towards the extreme left for an organization whose indirect costs are a low percentage of total costs and which also has a fairly standardized product range, all

Simplistic systems		Highly sophisticated systems
• Inexpensive to operate	Level of sophistication	• Expensive to operate
• Extensive use of arbitrary cost allocations	⟷	• Extensive use of cause-and-effect cost allocations
• Low levels of accuracy		• High levels of accuracy
• High cost of errors		• Low cost of errors

FIGURE 3.2
Cost systems – varying levels of sophistication for cost assignment

consuming organizational resources in similar proportions. In these circumstances simplistic systems may not result in the reporting of inaccurate costs. In contrast, the optimal costing system for organizations with a high proportion of indirect costs, whose products consume organizational resources in different proportions, will be located towards the extreme right. More sophisticated costing systems are required to capture the diversity of consumption of organizational resources and accurately assign the high level of indirect costs to different cost objects.

Assigning direct costs to cost objects

Both simplistic and sophisticated systems accurately assign direct costs to cost objects. Cost assignment merely involves the implementation of suitable data processing procedures to identify and record the resources consumed by cost objects. Consider direct labour. The time spent on providing a service to a specific customer, or manufacturing a specific product, is recorded on source documents, such as time sheets or job cards. Details of the customer's account number, job number or the product's code are also entered on these documents. The employee's hourly rate of pay is then entered so that the direct labour cost for the employee can be assigned to the appropriate cost object.

For direct materials the source document is a materials requisition. Details of the materials issued for manufacturing a product, or providing a specific service, are recorded on the materials requisition. The customer's account number, job number or product code is also entered and the items listed on the requisition are priced at their cost of acquisition. The details on the material requisition thus represent the source information for assigning the cost of the materials to the appropriate cost object. A more detailed explanation of this procedure is provided in the next chapter.

In many organizations the recording procedure for direct costs is computerized using bar coding and other forms of on-line information recording. The source documents only exist in the form of computer records. Because direct costs can be accurately assigned to cost objects whereas many indirect costs cannot, the remainder of this chapter will focus on indirect cost assignment.

Plant-wide (blanket) overhead rates

The most simplistic traditional costing system assigns indirect costs to cost objects using a single overhead rate for the organization as a whole. You will recall at the start of this chapter that it was pointed out that indirect costs are also called overheads. The terms blanket overhead rate or plant-wide rate are used to describe a single overhead rate that is established for the organization as a whole. Let us assume that the total manufacturing overheads for the manufacturing plant of Arcadia are £900 000 and that the company has selected direct labour hours as the allocation base for assigning overheads to products. Assuming that the total number of direct labour hours are 60 000 for the period the plant-wide overhead rate for Arcadia is £15 per direct labour hour (£900 000/60 000 direct labour hours). This calculation consists of two stages. First, overheads are accumulated in one single plant-wide pool for a period. Second, a plant-wide rate is computed by dividing the total amount of overheads accumulated (£900 000) by the selected allocation base (60 000 direct labour hours). The overhead costs are assigned to products by multiplying the plant-wide rate by the units of the selected allocation base (direct labour hours) used by each product.

Assume now that Arcadia is considering establishing separate overheads for each of its three production departments. Further investigations reveal that the products made by the company require different operations and some products do not pass through all three departments. These investigations also indicate that the £900 000 total manufacturing overheads and 60 000 direct labour hours can be analyzed as follows:

	Department A	Department B	Department C	Total
Overheads	£200 000	£600 000	£100 000	£900 000
Direct labour hours	20 000	20 000	20 000	60 000
Overhead rate per direct labour hour	£10	£30	£5	£15

Consider now a situation where product Z requires 20 direct labour hours in department C but does not pass through departments A and B. If a plant-wide overhead rate is used then overheads of £300 (20 hours at £15 per hour) will be allocated to product Z. On the other hand, if a departmental overhead rate is used, only £100 (20 hours at £5 per hour) would be allocated to product Z. Which method should be used? The logical answer must be to establish separate departmental overhead rates, since product Z only consumes overheads in department C. If the plant-wide overhead rate were applied, all the factory overhead rates would be averaged out and product Z would be indirectly allocated with some of the overheads of department B. This would not be satisfactory, since product Z does not consume any of the resources and this department incurs a large amount of the overhead expenditure.

Where some departments are more 'overhead-intensive' than others, products spending more time in the overhead-intensive departments should be assigned more overhead costs than those spending less time. Departmental rates capture these possible effects but plant-wide rates do not, because of the averaging process. We can conclude that a plant-wide rate will generally result in the reporting of inaccurate product costs. A plant-wide rate can only be justified when all products consume departmental overheads in approximately the same proportions. In the above illustration each department accounts for one-third of the total direct labour hours. If all products spend approximately one-third of their time in each department, a plant-wide overhead rate can be used. Consider a situation where product X spends one hour in each department and product Y spends five hours in each department. Overheads of £45 and £225 respectively would be allocated to products X and Y using either a plant-wide rate (3 hours at £15 and 15 hours at £15) or separate departmental overhead rates. If a diverse product range is produced with products spending different proportions of time in each department, separate departmental overhead rates should be established.

Recent surveys indicate that less than 5 per cent of the surveyed organizations use a single plant-wide overhead rate. In Scandinavia only 5 per cent of the Finnish companies (Lukka and Granlund, 1996), one Norwegian company (Bjornenak, 1997b) and none of the Swedish companies sampled (Ask et al., 1996) used a single plant-wide rate. Zero usage of plant-wide rates was also reported from a survey of Greek companies (Ballas and Venieris, 1996). In a more recent study of UK organizations Al-Omiri and Drury (2007) reported that a plant-wide rate was used by 4 per cent of the surveyed organizations.

The two-stage allocation process

It is apparent from the previous section that separate departmental overhead rates should normally be established. To establish departmental overhead rates an approach, known as the two-stage allocation process, is used. This process applies to assigning costs to other cost objects, besides products, and is applicable to all organizations that assign indirect costs to cost objects. The approach applies to both traditional and ABC systems.

The two-stage allocation process is illustrated in Figure 3.3. You can see that in the first stage overheads are assigned to cost centres (also called cost pools). The terms cost centres or cost pools are used to describe a location to which overhead costs are initially assigned. Normally cost centres consist of departments, but in some cases they consist of smaller segments such as separate work centres within a department. In the second stage the costs accumulated in the cost centres are allocated to cost objects using selected allocation bases (you should remember from our discussion earlier that allocation bases are also called cost drivers). Traditional costing systems tend to use a small number of second stage allocation bases, typically direct labour hours or machine hours. In other words, traditional systems assume that direct labour or machine hours have a significant influence in the long term on the level of overhead expenditure. Other allocation bases used to a lesser extent by traditional systems are direct labour cost, direct materials cost and units of output. These methods are described and illustrated in Learning Note 3.1 on the dedicated open access website (see Preface for details).

Within the two-stage allocation process ABC systems differ from traditional systems by having a greater number of cost centres in the first stage and a greater number, and variety, of cost drivers or allocation bases in the second stage. Both systems will be described in more detail later in the chapter.

How many cost centres should a firm establish? If only a small number of cost centres are established it is likely that activities within a cost centre will not be homogeneous and, if the consumption of the activities by products/services within the cost centres varies, activity resource consumption will not be accurately measured. Therefore, in most situations, increasing the number of cost centres increases the accuracy of measuring the indirect costs consumed by cost objects. The choice of the number of cost centres should be based on cost–benefit criteria using the principles described on pages 50–51. Exhibit 3.1 (first section) shows the number of cost centres and second stage cost allocation bases reported by Drury and Tayles (2005) in a survey of 170 UK organizations. It can be

(a) Traditional costing systems

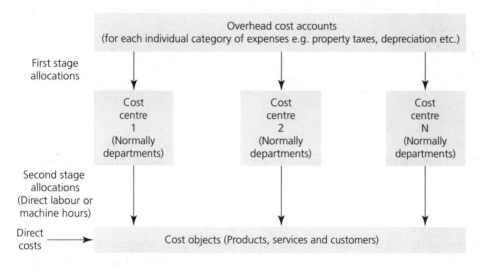

(b) Activity-based costing systems

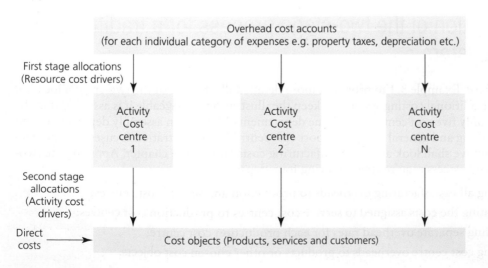

FIGURE 3.3

An illustration of the two-stage allocation process for traditional and activity-based costing systems

EXHIBIT 3.1 Surveys of practice

A survey of 170 companies by Drury and Tayles (2005) reported the following details in terms of the number of cost centres and number of different types of second stage allocation bases/cost drivers used:

Number of cost centres	Number of different types of cost drivers
14% used less than 6 cost centres	34% used 1 cost driver
21% used 6–10 cost centres	25% used 2 cost drivers
29% used 11–20 cost centres	31% used 3–10 cost drivers
36% used more than 20 cost centres	10% used more than 10 cost drivers

The percentages below indicate how frequently different cost allocation bases/cost drivers are used. Note that the reported percentages exceed 100 per cent because many companies used more than one allocation base.

	Norway[a]	Holland[b]	Ireland[c]	Australia[d]	Japan[d]	UK[e]	UK[e]
Direct labour hours/cost	65%	20%	52%	57%	57%	68%	73%
Machine hours	29	9	19	19	12	49	26
Direct material costs	26	6	10	12	11	30	19
Units of output	40	30	28	20	16	42	31
Prime cost				1	21		
Other	23	35	9				
ABC cost drivers						9	7

Notes
[a] Bjornenak (1997b)
[b] Boons *et al.* (1994)
[c] Clarke (1995)
[d] Blayney and Yokoyama (1991)
[e] Drury *et al.* (1993) – The first column relates to the responses for automated and the second to non-automated production centres

seen that 35 per cent of the organizations used less than 11 cost centres whereas 36 per cent used more than 20 cost centres. In terms of the number of different types of second stage cost drivers/allocation bases 59 per cent of the responding organizations used less than three.

An illustration of the two-stage process for a traditional costing system

We shall now use Example 3.1 to provide a more detailed illustration of the two-stage allocation process for a traditional costing system. To keep the illustration manageable it is assumed that the company has only five cost centres – machine departments X and Y, an assembly department, and materials handling and general factory support cost centres. The illustration focuses on manufacturing costs but we shall look at non-manufacturing costs later in the chapter. Applying the two-stage allocation process requires the following four steps:

1 assigning all manufacturing overheads to production and service cost centres;
2 reallocating the costs assigned to service cost centres to production cost centres;
3 computing separate overhead rates for each production cost centre;
4 assigning cost centre overheads to products or other chosen cost objects.

Steps 1 and 2 comprise stage one and steps 3 and 4 relate to the second stage of the two-stage allocation process. Let us now consider each of these steps in detail.

EXAMPLE 3.1

The annual overhead costs for the Enterprise Company which has three production centres (two machine centres and one assembly centre) and two service centres (materials procurement and general factory support) are as follows:

	(£)	(£)
Indirect wages and supervision		
Machine centres: X	1 000 000	
Y	1 000 000	
Assembly	1 500 000	
Materials procurement	1 100 000	
General factory support	1 480 000	6 080 000
Indirect materials		
Machine centres: X	500 000	
Y	805 000	
Assembly	105 000	
Materials procurement	0	
General factory support	10 000	1 420 000
Lighting and heating	500 000	
Property taxes	1 000 000	
Insurance of machinery	150 000	
Depreciation of machinery	1 500 000	
Insurance of buildings	250 000	
Salaries of works management	800 000	4 200 000
		11 700 000

The following information is also available:

	Book value of machinery (£)	Area occupied (sq. metres)	Number of employees	Direct labour hours	Machine hours
Machine shop: X	8 000 000	10 000	300	1 000 000	2 000 000
Y	5 000 000	5 000	200	1 000 000	1 000 000
Assembly	1 000 000	15 000	300	2 000 000	
Stores	500 000	15 000	100		
Maintenance	500 000	5 000	100		
	15 000 000	50 000	1000		

Details of total materials issues (i.e. direct and indirect materials) to the production centres are as follows:

	£
Machine shop X	4 000 000
Machine shop Y	3 000 000
Assembly	1 000 000
	8 000 000

To allocate the overheads listed above to the production and service centres we must prepare an overhead analysis sheet, as shown in Exhibit 3.2.

Step 1 – Assigning all manufacturing overheads to production and service cost centres

Using the information given in Example 3.1 our initial objective is to assign all manufacturing overheads to production and service cost centres. To do this requires the preparation of an overhead analysis sheet. This document is shown in Exhibit 3.2. In many organizations it will consist only in computer form.

If you look at Example 3.1 you will see that the indirect labour and indirect material costs have been directly traced to cost centres. Although these items cannot be directly assigned to products they can be directly assigned to the cost centres. In other words, they are indirect costs when products are the cost objects and direct costs when cost centres are the cost object. Therefore they are traced directly to the cost centres shown in the overhead analysis sheet in Exhibit 3.2. The remaining costs shown in Example 3.1 cannot be traced directly to the cost

EXHIBIT 3.2 Overhead analysis sheet

| Item of expenditure | Basis of allocation | Total (£) | Production centres | | | Service centres | |
			Machine centre X (£)	Machine centre Y (£)	Assembly (£)	Materials procurement (£)	General factory support (£)
Indirect wage and supervision	Direct	6 080 000	1 000 000	1 000 000	1 500 000	1 100 000	1 480 000
Indirect materials	Direct	1 420 000	500 000	805 000	105 000		10 000
Lighting and heating	Area	500 000	100 000	50 000	150 000	150 000	50 000
Property taxes	Area	1 000 000	200 000	100 000	300 000	300 000	100 000
Insurance of machinery	Book value of machinery	150 000	80 000	50 000	10 000	5 000	5 000
Depreciation of machinery	Book value of machinery	1 500 000	800 000	500 000	100 000	50 000	50 000
Insurance of buildings	Area	250 000	50 000	25 000	75 000	75 000	25 000
Salaries of works management	Number of employees	800 000	240 000	160 000	240 000	80 000	80 000
	(1)	11 700 000	2 970 000	2 690 000	2 480 000	1 760 000	1 800 000
Reallocation of service centre costs							
Materials procurement	Value of materials issued	—	880 000	660 000	220 000	1 760 000	
General factory support	Direct labour hours	—	450 000	450 000	900 000		1 800 000
	(2)	11 700 000	4 300 000	3 800 000	3 600 000	—	—
Machine hours and direct labour hours			2 000 000	1 000 000	2 000 000		
Machine hour overhead rate			£2.15	£3.80			
Direct labour hour overhead rate					£1.80		

centres and must be allocated to the cost centre using appropriate allocation bases. The term first stage allocation bases is used to describe allocations at this point. The following list summarizes commonly used first stage allocation bases:

Cost	Basis of allocation
Property taxes, lighting and heating	Area
Employee-related expenditure:	
works management, works canteen, payroll office	Number of employees
Depreciation and insurance of plant and machinery	Value of items of plant and machinery

Applying the allocation bases to the data given in respect of the Enterprise Company in Example 3.1 it is assumed that property taxes, lighting and heating, and insurance of buildings are related to the total floor area of the buildings, and the benefit obtained by each cost centre can therefore be ascertained according to the proportion of floor area which it occupies. The total floor area of the factory shown in Example 3.1 is 50 000 square metres; machine centre X occupies 20 per cent of this and machine centre Y a further 10 per cent. Therefore, if you refer to the overhead analysis sheet in Exhibit 3.2 you will see that 20 per cent of property taxes, lighting and heating and insurance of buildings are allocated to machine centre X, and 10 per cent are allocated to machine centre Y.

The insurance premium paid and depreciation of machinery are generally regarded as being related to the book value of the machinery. Because the book value of machinery for machine centre X is 8/15 of the total book value and machine centre Y is 5/15 of the total book value then 8/15 and 5/15 of the insurance and depreciation of machinery is allocated to machine centres X and Y.

It is assumed that the amount of time that works management devotes to each cost centre is related to the number of employees in each centre; since 30 per cent of the total employees are employed in machine centre X, 30 per cent of the salaries of works management will be allocated to this centre.

If you now look at the overhead analysis sheet shown in Exhibit 3.2, you will see in the row labelled '(1)' that all manufacturing overheads for the Enterprise Company have been assigned to the three production and two service cost centres.

Step 2 – Reallocating the costs assigned to service cost centres to production cost centres

The next step is to reallocate the costs that have been assigned to service cost centres to production cost centres. Service departments (i.e. service cost centres) are those departments that exist to provide services of various kinds to other units within the organization. They are sometimes called support departments. The Enterprise Company has two service centres. They are materials procurement and general factory support which includes activities such as production scheduling and machine maintenance. These service centres render essential services that support the production process, but they do not deal directly with the products. Therefore it is not possible to allocate service centre costs to products passing through these centres. To assign costs to products traditional costing systems reallocate service centre costs to production centres that actually work on the product. The method that is chosen to allocate service centre costs to production centre should be related to the benefits that the production centres derive from the service rendered.

We shall assume that the value of materials issued (shown in Example 3.1) provides a suitable approximation of the benefit that each of the production centres receives from materials procurement. Therefore 50 per cent of the value of materials is issued to machine centre X, resulting in 50 per cent of the total costs of materials procurement being allocated to this centre. If you refer to Exhibit 3.2 you will see that £880 000 (50 per cent of material procurement costs of

£1 760 000) has been reallocated to machine centre X. It is also assumed that direct labour hours provides an approximation of the benefits received by the production centres from general factory support resulting in the total costs for this centre being reallocated to the production centres proportionate to direct labour hours. Therefore since machine centre X consumes 25 per cent of the direct labour hours £450 000 (25 per cent of the total costs of £1 800 000 assigned to general factory support) has been reallocated to machine centre X. You will see in the row labelled '(2)' in Exhibit 3.2 that all manufacturing costs have now been assigned to the three production centres. This completes the first stage of the two-stage allocation process.

Step 3 – Computing separate overhead rates for each production cost centre

The second stage of the two-stage process is to allocate overheads of each production centre to overheads passing through that centre. The most frequently used allocation bases used by traditional costing systems are based on the amount of time products spend in each production centre – for example direct labour hours, machine hours and direct wages. In respect of non-machine centres, direct labour hours is the most frequently used allocation base. This implies that the overheads incurred by a production centre are closely related to direct labour hours worked. In the case of machine centres a machine hour overhead rate is preferable since most of the overheads (e.g. depreciation) are likely to be more closely related to machine hours. We shall assume that the Enterprise Company uses a machine hour rate for the machine production centres and a direct labour hour rate for the assembly centre. The overhead rates are calculated by applying the following formula:

$$\frac{\text{cost centre overheads}}{\text{cost centre direct labour hours or machine hours}}$$

The calculations using the information given in Exhibit 3.2 are as follows:

$$\text{Machine centre X} = \frac{£4\,300\,000}{2\,000\,000 \text{ machine hours}} = £2.15 \text{ per machine hour}$$

$$\text{Machine centre Y} = \frac{£3\,800\,000}{1\,000\,000 \text{ machine hours}} = £3.80 \text{ per machine hour}$$

$$\text{Assembly department} = \frac{£3\,600\,000}{2\,000\,000 \text{ direct labour hours}} = £1.80 \text{ per direct labour hour}$$

Step 4 – Assigning cost centre overheads to products or other chosen cost objects

The final step is to allocate the overheads to products passing through the production centres. Therefore if a product spends 10 hours in machine cost centre A overheads of £21.50 (10 × £2.15) will be allocated to the product. We shall compute the manufacturing costs of two products. Product A is a low sales volume product with direct costs of £100. It is manufactured in batches of 100 units and each unit requires 5 hours in machine centre A, 10 hours in machine centre B and 10 hours in the assembly centre. Product B is a high sales volume product thus enabling it to be manufactured in larger batches. It is manufactured in batches of 200 units and each unit requires 10 hours in machine centre A, 20 hours in machine centre B and 20 hours in the assembly centre. Direct costs of £200 have been assigned to product B. The calculations of the manufacturing costs assigned to the products are as follows:

Product A	£
Direct costs (100 units × £100)	10 000
Overhead allocations	
Machine centre A (100 units × 5 machine hours × £2.15)	1 075
Machine centre B (100 units × 10 machine hours × £3.80)	3 800
Assembly (100 units × 10 direct labour hours × £1.80)	1 800
Total cost	16 675
Cost per unit (£16 675/100 units) = £166.75	

Product B	£
Direct costs (200 units × £200)	40 000
Overhead allocations	
Machine centre A (200 units × 10 machine hours × £2.15)	4 300
Machine centre B (200 units × 20 machine hours × £3.80)	15 200
Assembly (200 units × 20 direct labour hours × £1.80)	7 200
Total cost	66 700
Cost per unit (£66 700/200 units) = £333.50	

The overhead allocation procedure is more complicated where service cost centres serve each other. In Example 3.1 it was assumed that materials procurement does not provide any services for general factory support and that general factory support does not provide any services for materials procurement. An understanding of situations where service cost centres do serve each other is not, however, necessary for a general understanding of the overhead procedure, and the problem of service centre reciprocal cost allocations is therefore dealt with in Appendix 3.1.

An illustration of the two-stage process for an ABC system

ADVANCED READING

Earlier in this chapter Figure 3.3 was used to contrast the general features of ABC systems with traditional costing systems. It was pointed out that ABC systems differ from traditional systems by having a greater number of cost centres in the first stage, and a greater number, and variety, of cost drivers/allocation bases in the second stage of the two-stage allocation process. We shall now look at ABC systems in more detail.

You will see from Figure 3.3 that another major distinguishing feature of ABC is that overheads are assigned to each major activity, rather than departments, which normally represent cost centres with traditional systems. Activities consist of the aggregation of many different tasks and are described by verbs associated with objects. Typical support activities include schedule production, set-up machines, move materials, purchase materials, inspect items, and process supplier records. When costs are accumulated by activities they are known as activity cost centres. Production process activities include machine products and assemble products. Thus within the production process, activity cost centres are often identical to the cost centres used by traditional cost systems.

A further distinguishing feature is that traditional systems normally assign service/support costs by reallocating their costs to production cost centres so that they are assigned to products within the production centre cost driver rates. In contrast, ABC systems tend to establish separate cost driver rates for support centres, and assign the cost of support activities directly to cost objects without any reallocation to production centres.

We shall now use Example 3.1 for the Enterprise Company to illustrate ABC in more detail. It is assumed that the activity cost centres for machining and assembling products are identical to the production cost centres used by the traditional costing system. We shall also assume that three activity cost centres have been established for each of the support functions. They are purchasing components, receiving components and disbursing materials for materials procurement and production scheduling, setting-up machines and a quality inspection of the completed products for general factory support. Both ABC and traditional systems use the same approach to assign costs to cost centres in the first stage of the two-stage allocation process. If you refer to column 2 in the upper section of Exhibit 3.3 you will see that the costs assigned to the production activities have been extracted from row 1 in the overhead analysis sheet shown in Exhibit 3.2, which was used for the traditional costing system. In the overhead analysis sheet we only assigned costs with the traditional costing system to materials procurement (i.e. £1 760 000) and general factory support (i.e. £1 800 000), and not to the activities within these support functions. However, the costs for the activities within these functions would be derived adopting the same approach as that used in Exhibit 3.2, but to simplify the presentation the cost assignments to the materials procurement and general factory support activity cost centres are not shown.

Exhibit 3.3 shows the product cost calculations for an ABC system. By referring to the second column in the upper section of this exhibit you will see that the costs assigned to the purchasing, receiving and disbursement of materials activities total £1 760 000, the same as the total allocated to the materials procurement function by the traditional system shown in Exhibit 3.2. Similarly, the total costs assigned to the production scheduling, set-up and quality inspection activities in column 2 of the upper section of Exhibit 3.3 total £1 800 000, the same as the total costs allocated to the general factory support function in Exhibit 3.2.

Now look at columns 1 and 3 in the upper section of Exhibit 3.3. You will see that with the ABC system The Enterprise Company has established nine activity cost centres and seven different second-stage cost drivers. Note also that the cost drivers for the production activities are the same of those used for the traditional costing system. Based on their observations of ABC systems Kaplan and Cooper (1998) suggest that relatively simple ABC systems having 30–50 activity cost centres and many cost drivers ought to report reasonably accurate costs.

To emphasize the point that ABC systems use cause-and-effect second stage allocations the term cost driver tends to be used instead of allocation base. Cost drivers should be significant determinants of the cost of activities. For example, if the cost of processing purchase orders is determined by the number of purchase orders that each product generates, then the number of purchase orders would represent the cost driver for the cost of processing purchase orders. Other cost drivers used by the Enterprise Company are shown in column 3 of Exhibit 3.3. They are the number of receipts for receiving components, number of production runs for disbursing materials and scheduling production, number of set-up hours for setting up the machines and the number of first item inspections for quality inspection of a batch of completed products. You will see from column 5 in the first section of Exhibit 3.3 that cost driver rates are computed by dividing the activity centre cost by the quantity of the cost driver used.

Activity centre costs are assigned to products by multiplying the cost driver rate by the quantity of the cost driver used by products. These calculations are shown in the second section of Exhibit 3.3. You will see from the first section in Exhibit 3.3 that the costs assigned to the purchasing activity are £960 000 for processing 10 000 purchasing orders resulting in a cost driver rate of £96 per purchasing order. The second section shows that a batch of 100 units of product A, and 200 units of product B, each require one purchased component and thus one purchase order. Therefore purchase order costs of £96 are allocated to each batch. The same approach is used to allocate the costs of the remaining activities shown in Exhibit 3.3. You should now work through Exhibit 3.3 and study the product cost calculations.

The costs assigned to products using each costing system are as follows:

	Traditional costing system £	ABC system £
Product A	166.75	205.88
Product B	333.50	301.03

Compared with the ABC system the traditional system undercosts product A and overcosts product B. By reallocating the service centre costs to the production centres and allocating the costs to products on the basis of either machine hours or direct labour hours the traditional system incorrectly assumes that these allocation bases are the cause of the costs of the support activities. Compared with product A, product B consumes twice as many machine and direct labour hours per unit of output. Therefore, relative to Product A, the traditional costing system allocates twice the amount of support costs to product B.

In contrast, ABC systems create separate cost centres for each major support activity and allocate costs to products using cost drivers that are the significant determinants of the cost of the activities. The ABC system recognizes that a batch of both products consume the same quantity of purchasing, receiving and inspection activities and, for these activities, allocates the same costs to both products. Because product B is manufactured in batches of 200 units, and product A in batches of 100 units, the cost per unit of output for product B is half the amount of Product A for these activities. Product A also has five unique machined components, whereas product B has

EXHIBIT 3.3 An illustration of cost assignment with an ABC system

(1) Activity	(2) Activity cost £	(3) Activity cost driver	(4) Quantity of activity cost driver	(5) Activity cost driver rate (Col. 2/Col.4)
Production activities:				
Machining: activity centre A	2 970 000	Number of machine hours	2 000 000 machine hours	£1.485 per hour
Machining: activity centre B	2 690 000	Number of machine hours	1 000 000 machine hours	£2.69 per hour
Assembly	2 480 000	Number of direct labour hours	2 000 000 direct lab. hours	£1.24 per hour
	8 140 000			
Materials procurement activities:				
Purchasing components	960 000	Number of purchase orders	10 000 purchase orders	£96 per order
Receiving components	600 000	Number of material receipts	5 000 receipts	£120 per receipt
Disburse materials	200 000	Number of production runs	2 000 production runs	£100 per production run
	1 760 000			
General factory support activities:				
Production scheduling	1 000 000	Number of production runs	2 000 production runs	£500 per production run
Set-up machines	600 000	Number of set-up hours	12 000 set-up hours	£50 per set-up hour
Quality inspection	200 000	Number of first item inspections	1 000 inspections	£200 per inspection
	1 800 000			
Total cost of all manufacturing activities	11 700 000			

Computation of product costs

(1) Activity	(2) Activity cost driver rate (derived from Col. 5 above)	(3) Quantity of cost driver used by 100 units of product A	(4) Quantity of cost driver used by 200 units of product B	(5) Activity cost assigned to product A (Col. 2 × Col. 3)	(6) Activity cost assigned to product B (Col. 2 × Col. 4)
Machining: activity centre A	£1.485 per hour	500 hours	2 000 hours	742.50	2 970.00
Machining: activity centre B	£2.69 per hour	1 000 hours	4 000 hours	2 690.00	10 760.00
Assembly	£1.24 per hour	1 000 hours	4 000 hours	1 240.00	4 960.00
Purchasing components	£96 per order	1 component	1 component	96.00	96.00
Receiving components	£120 per receipt	1 component	1 component	120.00	120.00
Disburse materials	£100 per production run	5 production runs[a]	1 production run	500.00	100.00
Production scheduling	£500 per production run	5 production runs[a]	1 production run	2 500.00	500.00
Set-up machines	£50 per set-up hour	50 set-up hours	10 set-up hours	2 500.00	500.00
Quality inspection	£200 per inspection	1 inspection	1 inspection	200.00	200.00
Total overhead cost				10 588.50	20 206.00
Units produced				100 units	200 units
Overhead cost per unit				£105.88	£101.03
Direct costs per unit				100.00	200.00
Total cost per unit of output				205.88	301.03

Note
[a] Five production runs are required to machine several unique components before they can be assembled into a final product.

only one, resulting in a batch of Product A requiring five production runs whereas a batch of Product B only requires one. Therefore, relative to product B, the ABC system assigns five times more costs to product A for the production scheduling and disbursement of materials activities (see columns 5 and 6 in the lower part of Exhibit 3.3). Because product A is a more complex product it requires relatively more support activity resources and the cost of this complexity is captured by the ABC system.

The unit costs derived from traditional and ABC systems must be used with care. For example, if a customer requested a batch of 400 units of product B the cost would not be twice the amount of a batch of 200 units. Assuming that for a batch of 400 units the number of purchase orders, material receipts, production runs, set-up hours and inspections remained the same as that required for a batch of 200 units the cost of the support activities would remain unchanged, but the direct costs would increase by a factor of two to reflect the fact that twice the amount of resources would be required.

Extracting relevant costs for decision-making

The cost computations relating to the Enterprise Company for products A and B represent the costs that should be generated for meeting stock valuation and profit measurement requirements. For decision-making non-manufacturing costs should also be taken into account. In addition, some of the costs that have been assigned to the products may not be relevant for certain decisions. For example, if you look at the overhead analysis sheet in Exhibit 3.2 you will see that property taxes, depreciation of machinery and insurance of buildings and machinery have been assigned to cost centres, and thus included in the costs assigned to products, for both traditional and ABC systems. If these costs are unaffected by a decision to discontinue a product they should not be assigned to products when undertaking product discontinuation reviews. However, if cost information is used to determine selling prices such costs may need to be assigned to products to ensure that the selling price of a customer's order covers a fair share of all organizational costs. It is therefore necessary to ensure that the costs incorporated in the overhead analysis are suitably coded so that different overhead rates can be extracted for different combinations of costs. This will enable relevant cost information to be extracted from the database for meeting different requirements. For an illustration of this approach you should refer to the answer to Review problem 3.22.

Our objective in this chapter has not been to focus on the cost information that should be extracted from the costing system for meeting decision-making requirements. Instead, it is to provide you with an understanding of how cost systems assign costs to cost objects. In Chapter 9 we shall concentrate on the cost information that should be extracted for decision-making. Also, only the basic principles of ABC have been introduced. A more theoretical approach to ABC will be presented in Chapter 10 with an emphasis being given to how cost information generated from an ABC system can be used for decision-making.

Budgeted overhead rates

Our discussion in this chapter has assumed that the *actual* overheads for an accounting period have been allocated to the products. However, the calculation of overhead rates based on the *actual* overheads incurred during an accounting period causes a number of problems. First, the product cost calculations have to be delayed until the end of the accounting period, since the overhead rate calculations cannot be obtained before this date, but information on product costs is required quickly if it is to be used for monthly profit calculations and inventory valuations or as a basis for setting selling prices. Secondly, one may argue that the timing problem can be resolved by calculating actual overhead rates at more frequent intervals, say on a monthly basis, but the objection to this proposal is that a large amount of overhead expenditure is fixed in the short term whereas activity will vary from month to month, giving large fluctuations in the overhead rates. Consider Example 3.2.

Such fluctuating overhead rates are not representative of typical, normal production conditions. Management has committed itself to a specific level of fixed costs in the light of foreseeable needs for beyond one month. Thus, where production fluctuates, monthly overhead rates may be volatile. Furthermore, some costs such as repairs, maintenance and heating are not incurred evenly throughout the year. Therefore, if monthly overhead rates are used, these costs will not be allocated fairly to units of output. For example, heating costs would be charged only to winter production so that products produced in winter would be more expensive than those produced in summer.

An average, annualized rate based on the relationship of total annual overhead to total annual activity is more representative of typical relationships between total costs and volume than a monthly rate. What is required is a normal product cost based on average long-term production rather than an actual product cost, which is affected by month-to-month fluctuations in production volume. Taking these factors into consideration, it is preferable to establish a budgeted overhead rate based on annual *estimated* overhead expenditure and activity.

SOURCE: ADAPTED FROM ABERNETHY, M.A. *ET AL.*, PRODUCT DIVERSITY AND COSTING SYSTEM DESIGN CHOICE: FIELD STUDY EVIDENCE, *MANAGEMENT ACCOUNTING RESEARCH*, 2001, 12, PP261–279. WITH PERMISSION FROM ELSEVIER

Product diversity and costing system design choice

Two Australian firms, one with three divisions (HC1, HC2 and HC3), and the second with two divisions (FT1 and FT2) were studied. HC1 and FT1 had the simplest costing systems with all of the overheads accumulated into a single cost pool. In other words, a plant-wide overhead rate was used. HC2 and HC3 established separate 'work centre cost pools' that reflect manufacturing processes (e.g. HC2 had three cost pools and HC3 two cost pools). Overheads such as power were directly traced to the work centres. The remaining overheads were allocated to the work centres based on their levels of direct labour hours (DLHs) usage. The work centre overhead was then determined by dividing the work centre cost pool by the number of DLHs and allocating the costs to the product according to the consumption of DLHs in each of the work centres.

FT2 was the only research site that had a highly sophisticated costing system consisting of many different cost pools. The overheads for each cost pool were allocated to products on the basis of two cost drivers, namely direct labour hours and machine hours. The overheads allocated based on DLHs included indirect labour associated with materials handling, packers and factory foremen. Overheads allocated on the basis of machine hours include costs that vary with machine hours (e.g. power and electricity) as well as fixed costs such as factory management and depreciation.

HC1, HC2 and FT1 all had low product diversity (i.e. products consumed organizational resources in similar proportions) and users were satisfied with the information provided by the costing system. Both HC3 and FT2 had high levels of product diversity. FT2 had a relatively sophisticated costing system while HC3 maintained a simplistic system.

The users of the costing system at FT2 were very satisfied with the system whereas there was much dissatisfaction with HC3's system. Costing information at HC3 was particularly important for determining product costs. However, management believed that the costs were highly inaccurate and were inadequate for setting prices. Overheads were large and product diversity was high creating the need for a relatively sophisticated costing system. However, a simplistic costing system was implemented. This absence of 'fit' was a major dissatisfaction with the existing costing system. In contrast, there was a 'fit' between the costing systems and the level of product diversity in the four other business units and a general satisfaction with the costing systems.

REAL WORLD VIEWS 3.1

Discussion points

1   Why might increasing the number of cost centres (pools) result in the reporting of more accurate product costs?

2   What other factors, besides product diversity, might enable a simplistic product costing system to report reasonably accurate product costs?

EXAMPLE 3.2

The fixed overheads for Euro are £24 million per annum, and monthly production varies from 400 000 to 1 million hours. The monthly overhead rate for fixed overhead will therefore fluctuate as follows:

Monthly overhead	£2 000 000	£2 000 000
Monthly production	400 000 hours	1 000 000 hours
Monthly overhead rate	£5 per hour	£2 per hour

Overhead expenditure that is fixed in the short term remains constant each month, but monthly production fluctuates because of holiday periods and seasonal variations in demand. Consequently the overhead rate varies from £2 to £5 per hour. It would be unreasonable for a product worked on in one month to be allocated overheads at a rate of £5 per hour and an identical product worked on in another month allocated at a rate of only £2 per hour.

Consequently the procedure outlined in the previous sections for calculating cost centre overhead rates for traditional and ABC systems should be based on *standard* activity levels and not *actual* activity levels. We shall consider how we might determine standard activity in Chapter 7. Surveys of product costing practices indicate that most organizations use annual budgeted activity as a measure of standard activity.

Under- and over-recovery of overheads

The effect of calculating overhead rates based on budgeted annual overhead expenditure and activity is that it will be most unlikely that the overhead allocated to products manufactured during the period will be the same as the actual overhead incurred. Consider a situation where the estimated annual fixed overheads are £2 000 000 and the estimated annual activity is 1 000 000 direct labour hours. The estimated fixed overhead rate will be £2 per hour. Assume that actual overheads are £2 000 000 and are therefore identical with the estimate, but that actual activity is 900 000 direct labour hours instead of the estimated 1 000 000 hours. In this situation only £1 800 000 will be charged to production. This calculation is based on 900 000 direct labour hours at £2 per hour, giving an under-recovery of overheads of £200 000.

Consider an alternative situation where the actual overheads are £1 950 000 instead of the estimated £2 000 000, and actual activity is 1 000 000 direct labour hours, which is identical to the original estimate. In this situation 1 000 000 direct labour hours at £2 per hour will be charged to production giving an over-recovery of £50 000. This example illustrates that there will be an under- or over-recovery of overheads whenever actual activity or overhead expenditure is different from the budgeted overheads and activity used to estimate the budgeted overhead rate. This under- or over-recovery of fixed overheads is also called a volume variance.

Accounting regulations in most countries recommend that the under- or over-recovery of overheads should be regarded as a period cost adjustment. For example, the UK Statement of Standard Accounting Practice on Stocks and Work in Progress (SSAP 9) and the international accounting standard on inventories (IAS2) recommend that the allocation of overheads in the valuation of inventories and work in progress needs to be based on the company's normal level of activity and that any under- or over-recovery should be written off in the current year. This procedure is illustrated in Figure 3.4. Note that any under- or over-recovery of overhead is not allocated to products. Also note that the under-recovery is recorded as an expense in the current accounting period whereas an over-recovery is recorded as a reduction in the expenses for the period. Finally you should note that our discussion here is concerned with how to treat any under- or over-recovery for the purpose of financial accounting and its impact on inventory valuation and profit measurement.

Maintaining the database at standard costs

Most organizations whose activities consist of a series of common or repetitive operations maintain their database at standard, rather than actual cost, for both traditional and ABC systems. Standard costs are pre-determined target costs that should be incurred under efficient operating conditions. For example, assume that the standard direct labour cost for performing a particular operation is £40 (consisting of 5 hours at £8 per hour) and the standard cost of a purchased component (say component Z) is £50. The direct costs for a product requiring only this operation and the purchased component Z would be recorded in the database at a standard cost of £90. Assuming that the product only passed through a single cost centre with a budgeted overhead rate of £20 per direct labour hour the overhead cost for the product would be recorded in the database at £100 standard cost (5 standard direct labour hours at £20 per hour). Instead of a product being recorded in the database at its standard *unit* cost the database may consist of the standard costs of a batch of output, such as normal batch sizes of say 100 or 200 units output of the product.

When a standard costing system is used the database is maintained at standard cost and actual output is costed at the standard cost. Actual costs are recorded, but not at the individual product level, and an adjustment is made at the end of the accounting period by recording as a period cost the difference between standard cost and actual cost for the actual output. This adjustment ensures that the standard costs are converted to actual costs in the profit statement for meeting external financial accounting reporting requirements.

It is not important at this point that you have a detailed understanding of a standard costing system. However, it is important that you are aware that a database may consist of standard (estimated) costs rather than actual costs. We shall look at standard costing in detail in Chapter 17.

Non-manufacturing overheads

In respect of financial accounting, only manufacturing costs are allocated to products. Non-manufacturing overheads are regarded as period costs and are disposed of in exactly the same way as the under- or over-recovery of manufacturing overheads outlined in Figure 3.4. For external reporting it is therefore unnecessary to allocate non-manufacturing overheads to products. However, for decision-making non-manufacturing costs should be assigned to products. For example, in many organizations it is not uncommon for selling prices to be based on estimates of total cost or even actual cost. Housing contractors and garages often charge for their services by adding a percentage profit margin to actual cost.

Some non-manufacturing costs may be a direct cost of the product. Delivery costs, salesmen's salaries and travelling expenses may be directly identifiable with the product, but it is likely that

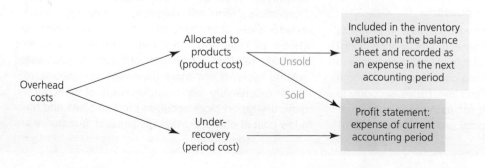

FIGURE 3.4

Illustration of under-recovery of factory overheads

many non-manufacturing overheads cannot be allocated directly to specific products. On what basis should we allocate non-manufacturing overheads? The answer is that we should select an allocation base/cost driver that corresponds most closely to non-manufacturing overheads. The problem is that allocation bases that are widely used by traditional costing systems, such as direct labour hours, machine hours and direct labour cost are not necessarily those that are closely related to non-manufacturing overheads. Therefore traditional systems tend to use arbitrary, rather than cause-and-effect allocation bases, to allocate non-manufacturing overheads to products. The most widely used approach is to allocate non-manufacturing overheads on the ability of the products to bear such costs. This approach can be implemented by allocating non-manufacturing costs to products on the basis of their manufacturing costs. This procedure is illustrated in Example 3.3.

EXAMPLE 3.3

The estimated non-manufacturing and manufacturing costs of a company for the year ending 31 December are £500 000 and £1 million respectively. The non-manufacturing overhead absorption rate is calculated as follows:

$$\frac{\text{estimated non-manufacturing overhead}}{\text{estimated manufacturing cost}}$$

In percentage terms each product will be allocated with non-manufacturing overheads at a rate of 50 per cent of its total manufacturing cost.

SUMMARY

The following items relate to the learning objectives listed at the beginning of the chapter.

● **Distinguish between cause-and-effect and arbitrary allocations.**

Allocation bases which are significant determinants of costs that are being allocated are described as cause-and-effect allocations whereas arbitrary allocations refer to allocation bases that are not the significant determinants of the costs. To accurately measure the cost of resources used by cost objects cause-and-effect allocations should be used.

● **Explain why different cost information is required for different purposes.**

Manufacturing organizations assign costs to products for two purposes: first for external (financial accounting) profit measurement and inventory valuation purposes in order to allocate manufacturing costs incurred during a period to cost of goods sold and inventories; secondly to provide useful information for managerial decision-making requirements. Financial accounting regulations

specify that only manufacturing costs should be assigned to products for meeting inventory and profit measurement requirements. Both manufacturing and non-manufacturing costs, however, may be relevant for decision-making. In addition, not all costs that are assigned to products for inventory valuation and profit measurement are relevant for decision-making. For example, costs that will not be affected by a decision (e.g. depreciation) are normally not relevant for decision-making.

● **Describe how cost systems differ in terms of their level of sophistication.**

Cost systems range from simplistic to sophisticated. Simplistic systems are inexpensive to operate, involve extensive use of arbitrary allocations, have a high likelihood of reporting inaccurate product costs and generally result in a high cost of errors. Sophisticated costing systems are more expensive to operate, rely more extensively on cause-and-effect allocations, generally report more accurate product costs and have a low cost of errors. Further distinguishing features are that simplistic costing systems have a small number of first-stage cost centres/pools and use a single second-stage cost driver. In contrast, sophisticated costing systems use many first-stage cost centres/pools and many different types of second-stage drivers.

● Understand the factors influencing the choice of an optimal costing system.

The optimal costing system is different for different organizations and should be determined on a costs versus benefits basis. Simplistic costing systems are appropriate in organizations whose indirect costs are a low percentage of total costs and which also have a fairly standardized product range, all consuming organizational resources in similar proportions. Under these circumstances simplistic costing systems may report costs that are sufficiently accurate for decision-making purposes. Conversely, organizations with a high proportion of indirect costs, whose products consume organizational resources in different proportions are likely to require sophisticated costing systems.

● Explain why departmental overhead rates should be used in preference to a single blanket overhead rate.

A blanket (also known as plant-wide) overhead rate establishes a single overhead rate for the organization as a whole whereas departmental rates involve indirect costs being accumulated by different departments and a separate overhead rate being established for each department. A blanket overhead rate can only be justified when all products or services consume departmental overheads in approximately the same proportions. Such circumstances are unlikely to be applicable to most organizations resulting in blanket overheads generally reporting inaccurate product/service costs.

● Construct an overhead analysis sheet and calculate cost centre allocation rates.

Cost centre overhead allocation rates are established and assigned to cost objects using the two-stage allocation overhead procedure. In the first stage, an overhead analysis sheet is used to (a) allocate overheads to production and service centres or departments and (b) to reallocate the total service department overheads to production departments. The second stage involves (a) the calculation of appropriate departmental overhead rates and (b) the allocation of overheads to products passing through each department. These steps were illustrated using data presented in Example 3.1.

● Distinguish between traditional and activity-based costing systems.

The major distinguishing features of ABC compared with traditional costing systems are that ABC systems assign costs to activity cost centres rather than departments. ABC systems thus tend to use a greater number of cost centres in the first-stage of the allocation process. In the second-stage they also use a greater number, and variety, of second-stage allocation bases that mostly rely on cause-and-effect allocation bases. In contrast, traditional systems use second-stage allocation bases that rely on arbitrary allocations.

● Justify why budgeted overhead rates should be used in preference to actual overhead rates.

Because the uses of actual overhead rates causes a delay in the calculation of product or service costs, and the use of monthly rates causes fluctuations in the overhead rates throughout the year, it is recommended that annual budgeted overhead rates should be used.

● Calculate and explain the treatment of the under-/over-recovery of overheads.

The use of annual budgeted overhead rates gives an under- or over-recovery of overheads whenever actual overhead expenditure or activity is different from budget. Any under- or over-recovery is generally regarded as a period cost adjustment and written off to the profit and loss statement and thus not allocated to products.

● Additional learning objectives presented in Appendix 3.1.

The appendix to this chapter includes the following additional learning objective: to be able to reallocate service department costs to production departments when service departments provide services for other service departments as well as production departments. This topic tends to be included in the syllabus requirements of the examinations set by professional accountancy bodies but may not be part of the course curriculum for other courses. You can omit Appendix 3.1 if this topic is not part of your course curriculum.

Appendix 3.1: Inter-service department reallocations

Service departments provide services for other service departments as well as for production departments. For example, a personnel department provides services for other service departments such as the power generating plant, maintenance department and stores. The power generating department also provides heat and light for other service departments, including the personnel department, and so on. When such interactions occur, the allocation process can become complicated. Difficulties arise because each service department begins to accumulate charges from other service departments from which it receives services, and these must be reallocated back to the user department. Once it has begun, this allocation and reallocation process can continue for a long time before a solution is found. The problem is illustrated in Example 3A.1. We shall use the example to illustrate four different methods of allocating the service department costs:

1 repeated distribution method;

2 simultaneous equation method;

3 specified order of closing method;

4 direct allocation method.

1. Repeated distribution method

Where this method is adopted, the service department costs are repeatedly allocated in the specified percentages until the figures become too small to be significant. You can see from line 2 of Exhibit 3A.1 that the overheads of service department 1 are allocated according to the prescribed percentages. As a result, some of the overheads of service department 1 are transferred to service department 2. In line 3 the overheads of service department 2 are allocated, which means that service department 1 receives some further costs. The costs of service department 1 are again allocated, and service department 2 receives some further costs. This process continues until line 7, by which time the costs have become so small that any further

EXAMPLE 3A.1

A company has three production departments and two service departments. The overhead analysis sheet provides the following totals of the overheads analyzed to production and service departments:

		(£)
Production department	X	48 000
	Y	42 000
	Z	30 000
Service department	1	14 040
	2	18 000
		152 040

The expenses of the service departments are apportioned as follows:

	Production departments			Service departments	
	X	Y	Z	1	2
Service department 1	20%	40%	30%	—	10%
Service department 2	40%	20%	20%	20%	—

EXHIBIT 3A.1 Repeated distribution method

| Line | Production departments | | | Service departments | | Total |
	X	Y	Z	1	2	
1 Allocation as per overhead analysis	48 000	42 000	30 000	14 040	18 000	152 040
2 Allocation of service department 1	2 808 (20%)	5 616 (40%)	4 212 (30%)	(14 040)	1 404 (10%) 19 404	
3 Allocation of service department 2	7 762 (40%)	3 881 (20%)	3 880 (20%)	3 881 (20%)	(19 404)	
4 Allocation of service department 1	776 (20%)	1 552 (40%)	1 165 (30%)	(3 881)	388 (10%)	
5 Allocation of service department 2	154 (40%)	78 (20%)	78 (20%)	78 (20%)	(388)	
6 Allocation of service department 1	16 (20%)	31 (40%)	23 (30%)	(78)	8 (10%)	
7 Allocation of service department 2	4 (40%)	2 (20%)	2 (20%)	—	(8)	
8 Total overheads	59 520	53 160	39 360	—	—	152 040

detailed apportionments are unnecessary. As a result, the total overheads in line 8 of £152 040 are allocated to production departments only.

2. Simultaneous equation method

When this method is used simultaneous equations are initially established as follows: Let

$$x = \text{total overhead of service department 1}$$
$$y = \text{total overhead of service department 2}$$

The total overhead transferred into service departments 1 and 2 can be expressed as

$$x = 14\ 040 + 0.2y$$
$$y = 18\ 000 + 0.1x$$

Rearranging the above equations:

$$x - 0.2y = 14\ 040 \qquad (1)$$
$$-0.1x + y = 18\ 000 \qquad (2)$$

We can now multiply equation (1) by 5 and equation (2) by 1, giving

$$5x - y = 70\ 200$$
$$-0.1x + y = 18\ 000$$

Adding the above equations together we have

$$4.9x = 88\ 200$$

Therefore

$$x = 18\ 000\ (= 88\ 200/4.9)$$

Substituting this value for x in equation (1), we have

$$18\ 000 - 0.2y = 14\ 040$$

Therefore $\qquad -0.2y = -3\ 960$

Therefore $\qquad y = 19\ 800$

We now apportion the values for x and y to the production departments in the agreed percentages.

Line	X	Y	Z	Total
1 Allocation as per overhead analysis	48 000	42 000	30 000	120 000
2 Allocation of service department 1	3 600 (20%)	7 200 (40%)	5 400 (30%)	16 200
3 Allocation of service department 2	7 920 (40%)	3 960 (20%)	3 960 (20%)	15 840
4	59 520	53 160	39 360	152 040

You will see from line 2 that the value for X (service department 1) of £18 000 is allocated in the specified percentages. Similarly, in line 3 the value for Y (service department 2) of £19 800 is apportioned in the specified percentages. As a result the totals in line 4 are in agreement with the totals in line 8 of the repeated distribution method (Exhibit 3A.1).

3. Specified order of closing

If this method is used the service departments' overheads are allocated to the production departments in a certain order. The service department that does the largest proportion of work for other service departments is closed first; the service department that does the second largest proportion of work for other service departments is closed second; and so on. Return charges are not made to service departments whose costs have previously been allocated. Let us now apply this method to the information contained in Example 3A.1. The results are given in Exhibit 3A.2.

The costs of service department 2 are allocated first (line 2) because 20 per cent of its work is related to service department 1, whereas only 10 per cent of the work of service department 1 is related to service department 2. In line 3 we allocate the costs of service department 1, but the return charges are not made to department 2. This means that the proportions allocated have changed as 10 per cent of the costs of service department 1 have not been allocated to service

EXHIBIT 3A.2 Specified order of closing method

	Production departments			Service departments		
Line	X	Y	Z	1	2	Total
1 Allocation as per overhead analysis	48 000	42 000	30 000	14 040	18 000	152 040
2 Allocate service department 2	7 200 (40%)	3 600 (20%)	3 600 (20%)	3 600 (20%)	(18 000)	
3 Allocate service department 1	3 920 (2/9)	7 840 (4/9)	5 880 (3/9)	(17 640)	—	
4	59 120	53 440	39 480	—	—	152 040

department 2. Therefore 20 per cent out of a 90 per cent total or 2/9 of the costs of service department 1 are allocated to department X.

You will see that the totals allocated in line 4 do not agree with the totals allocated under the repeated distribution or simultaneous equation methods. This is because the specified order of closing method sacrifices accuracy for clerical convenience. However, if this method provides a close approximation to an alternative accurate calculation then there are strong arguments for its use.

4. Direct allocation method

This method is illustrated in Exhibit 3A.3. It ignores inter-service department service reallocations. Therefore service department costs are reallocated only to production departments. This means that the proportions allocated have changed as 10 per cent of the costs of service department 1 have not been allocated to service department 2. Therefore 20 per cent out of a 90 per cent total, or 2/9 of the costs of service department 1, are allocated to department X, 4/9 are allocated to department Y and 3/9 are allocated to department Z. Similarly the proportions allocated for service department 2 have changed with 4/8 (40 per cent out of 80 per cent) of the costs of service department 2 being allocated to department X, 2/8 to department Y and 2/8 to department Z. The only justification for using the direct allocation method is its simplicity. The method is recommended when inter-service reallocations are relatively insignificant.

EXHIBIT 3A.3 Direct allocation method

Line		Production departments			Service departments		Total
		X	Y	Z	1	2	
1	Allocation as per overhead analysis	48 000	42 000	30 000	14 040	18 000	152 040
2	Allocate service department 1	3 120 (2/9)	6 240 (4/9)	4 680 (3/9)	(14 040)		
3	Allocate service department 2	9 000 (4/8)	4 500 (2/8)	4 500 (2/8)	—	(18 000)	
4		60 120	52 740	39 180	—	—	152 040

Key terms and concepts

Recommended readings

If your course requires a detailed understanding of accounting for direct labour and materials you should refer to Learning Note 3.2 on the website supporting this book. For an explanation of how you can access the website you should refer to the preface. For a more detailed review of cost allocations for different purposes see Ahmed and Scapens (1991, 2000). You should refer to Brierley et al. (2001) for a review of European product costing practices. See also Drury and Tayles (2005) for a description of overhead absorption procedures in UK organizations.

Key examination points

A typical question (e.g. Review problem 3.20) will require you to analyze overheads by departments and calculate appropriate overhead allocation rates. These questions may require a large number of calculations, and it is possible that you will make calculation errors. Do make sure that your answer is clearly presented, since marks tend to be allocated according to whether you have adopted the correct method. You are recommended to present your answer in a format similar to Exhibit 3.2. For a traditional costing system you should normally recommend a direct labour hour rate if a department is non-mechanized and a machine hour rate if machine hours are the dominant activity. You should only recommend the direct wages percentage method when the rates within a non-mechanized department are uniform.

Where a question requires you to present information for decision-making, do not include apportioned fixed overheads in the calculations. Remember the total manufacturing costs should be calculated for stock valuation, but incremental costs should be calculated for decision-making purposes (see answer to Review problem 3.22).

Finally, ensure that you can calculate under- or over-recoveries of overheads. To check your understanding of this topic you should refer to the solution to Review problem 3.15.

ASSESSMENT MATERIAL

The review questions are short questions that enable you to assess your understanding of the main topics included in the chapter. The numbers in parentheses provide you with the page numbers to refer to if you cannot answer a specific question.

The review problems are more complex and require you to relate and apply the content to various business problems. The problems are graded by their level of difficulty. Solutions to review problems that are not preceded by the term 'IM' are provided in a separate section at the end of the book. Solutions to problems preceded by the term 'IM' are provided in the *Instructor's Manual* accompanying this book and also on the lecturer's password protected section of the website www.drury-online.com. Additional review problems with fully worked solutions are provided in the *Student's Manual* that accompanies this book.

The website also includes over 30 case study problems. A list of these cases is provided on pages 665–7. Cases that are relevant to the content of this chapter include Electronics Boards plc.

Review questions

3.1 Why are indirect costs not directly traced to cost objects in the same way as direct costs? *(p. 48)*
3.2 Define cost tracing, cost allocation, allocation base and cost driver. *(p. 48)*
3.3 Distinguish between arbitrary and cause-and-effect allocations. *(p. 48)*
3.4 Explain how cost information differs for profit measurement/inventory valuation requirements compared with decision-making requirements. *(p. 49)*
3.5 Explain why cost systems should differ in terms of their level of sophistication. *(pp. 50–51)*
3.6 Describe the process of assigning direct labour and direct materials to cost objects. *(p. 51)*
3.7 Why are separate departmental or cost centre overhead rates preferred to a plant-wide (blanket) overhead rate? *(pp. 51–52)*
3.8 Describe the two-stage overhead allocation procedure. *(pp. 52–53)*
3.9 Define the term 'activities'. *(p. 59)*
3.10 Describe two important features that distinguish between activity-based costing and traditional costing systems. *(p. 59)*
3.11 Why are some overhead costs sometimes not relevant for decision-making purposes? *(p. 62)*
3.12 Why are budgeted overhead rates preferred to actual overhead rates? *(pp. 62–63)*
3.13 Give two reasons for the under or over-recovery of overheads at the end of the accounting period. *(p. 64)*

Review problems

3.14 Basic. A company uses a predetermined overhead recovery rate based on machine hours. Budgeted factory overhead for a year amounted to £720 000, but actual factory overhead incurred was £738 000. During the year, the company absorbed £714 000 of factory overhead on 119 000 actual machine hours.

What was the company's budgeted level of machine hours for the year?

  a 116 098
  b 119 000
  c 120 000
  d 123 000   *ACCA Foundation Paper 3*

3.15 Basic. J Ltd uses standard absorption costing and absorbs production overheads on the basis of standard machine hours. The following budgeted and actual information applied in its last accounting period:

	Budget	Actual
Production overhead	$180 000	$178 080
Machine hours	50 000	48 260
Units produced	40 000	38 760

At the end of the period, production overhead will be reported as

  a under-absorbed by $4344.
  b under-absorbed by $3660.
  c over-absorbed by $4344.
  d over-absorbed by $3660.
           CIMA Management Accounting Fundamentals

3.16 Basic. A company has over-absorbed fixed production overheads for the period by £6000. The fixed production overhead absorption rate was £8 per unit and is based on the normal level of activity of 5000 units. Actual production was 4500 units.

What was the actual fixed production overheads incurred for the period?

  a £30 000
  b £36 000
  c £40 000
  d £42 000
           ACCA Paper 1.2 – Financial Information for Management

3.17 Basic. A company absorbs overheads on machine hours. In a period, actual machine hours were 17 285, actual overheads were £496 500 and there was under-absorption of £12 520.

What was the budgeted level of overheads?

  a £483 980
  b £496 500
  c £509 020
  d It cannot be calculated from the information provided.
           CIMA Stage 1 Cost Accounting

3.18 Basic. Canberra has established the following information regarding fixed overheads for the coming month:

Budgeted information:

Fixed overheads	£180 000
Labour hours	3 000
Machine hours	10 000
Units of production	5 000

Actual fixed costs for the last month were £160 000.

Canberra produces many different products using highly automated manufacturing processes and absorbs overheads on the most appropriate basis.

What will be the pre-determined overhead absorption rate?

  a £16
  b £18
  c £36
  d £60   *ACCA Paper 1.2 – Financial Information for Management*

3.19 Basic. An engineering firm operates a job costing system. Production overhead is absorbed at the rate of $8.50 per machine hour. In order to allow for non-production overhead costs and profit, a mark-up of 60 per cent of prime cost is added to the production cost when preparing price estimates.

The estimated requirements of job number 808 are as follows:

Direct materials	$10 650
Direct labour	$3 260
Machine hours	140

The estimated price notified to the customer for job number 808 will be

a $22 256

b $22 851

c $23 446

d $24 160   *CIMA – Management Accounting Fundamentals*

3.20 Intermediate: Overhead analysis and calculation of product costs. A furniture-making business manufactures quality furniture to customers' orders. It has three production departments and two service departments. Budgeted overhead costs for the coming year are as follows:

	Total (£)
Rent and Rates	12 800
Machine insurance	6 000
Telephone charges	3 200
Depreciation	18 000
Production Supervisor's salaries	24 000
Heating and Lighting	6 400
	70 400

The three production departments – A, B and C, and the two service departments – X and Y, are housed in the new premises, the details of which, together with other statistics and information, are given below.

	Departments				
	A	B	C	X	Y
Floor area occupied (sq.metres)	3000	1800	600	600	400
Machine value (£000)	24	10	8	4	2
Direct labour hrs budgeted	3200	1800	1000		
Labour rates per hour	£3.80	£3.50	£3.40	£3.00	£3.00
Allocated Overheads:					
Specific to each department (£000)	2.8	1.7	1.2	0.8	0.6
Service Department X's costs apportioned	50%	25%	25%		
Service Department Y's costs apportioned	20%	30%	50%		

Required:

a Prepare a statement showing the overhead cost budgeted for each department, showing the basis of apportionment used. Also calculate suitable overhead absorption rates. *(9 marks)*

b Two pieces of furniture are to be manufactured for customers. Direct costs are as follows:

	Job 123	Job 124
Direct Material	£154	£108
Direct Labour	20 hours Dept A	16 hours Dept A
	12 hours Dept B	10 hours Dept B
	10 hours Dept C	14 hours Dept C

Calculate the total costs of each job. *(5 marks)*

c If the firm quotes prices to customers that reflect a required profit of 25 per cent on selling price, calculate the quoted selling price for each job. *(2 marks)*

d If material costs are a significant part of total costs in a manufacturing company, describe a system of material control that might be used in order to effectively control costs, paying particular attention to the stock control aspect. *(9 marks)*
AAT Stage 3 Cost Accounting and Budgeting

3.21 Intermediate: Calculation of product overhead costs. Bookdon Public Limited Company manufactures three products in two production departments, a machine shop and a fitting section; it also has two service departments, a canteen and a machine maintenance section. Shown below are next year's budgeted production data and manufacturing costs for the company.

	Product X	Product Y	Product Z
Production	4200 units	6900 units	1700 units
Prime cost:			
Direct materials	£11 per unit	£14 per unit	£17 per unit
Direct labour:			
Machine shop	£6 per unit	£4 per unit	£2 per unit
Fitting section	£12 per unit	£3 per unit	£21 per unit
Machine hours per unit	6 hours per unit	3 hours per unit	4 hours per unit

	Machine shop	Fitting section	Canteen	Machine maintenance section	Total
Budgeted overheads (£):					
Allocated overheads	27 660	19 470	16 600	26 650	90 380
Rent, rates, heat and light					17 000
Depreciation and insurance of equipment					25 000
Additional data:					
Gross book value of equipment (£)	150 000	75 000	30 000	45 000	
Number of employees	18	14	4	4	
Floor space occupied (square metres)	3 600	1 400	1 000	800	

It has been estimated that approximately 70 per cent of the machine maintenance section's costs are incurred servicing the machine shop and the remainder incurred servicing the fitting section.

Required:

a (i) Calculate the following budgeted overhead absorption rates:
A machine hour rate for the machine shop.
A rate expressed as a percentage of direct wages for the fitting section.
All workings and assumptions should be clearly shown.
(12 marks)

(ii) Calculate the budgeted manufacturing overhead cost per unit of product X. *(2 marks)*

b The production director of Bookdon PLC has suggested that 'as the actual overheads incurred and units produced are usually different from the budgeted and as a consequence profits of each month end are distorted by over/under absorbed overheads, it would be more accurate to calculate the actual overhead cost per unit each month end by dividing the total number of all units actually produced during the month into the actual overheads incurred.'

Critically examine the production director's suggestion.
(8 marks)
ACCA Level 1 Costing

3.22 Intermediate: Make or buy decision. Shown below is next year's budget for the forming and finishing departments of Tooton Ltd. The departments manufacture three different types of component, which are incorporated into the output of the firm's finished products.

	Component		
	A	B	C
Production (units)	14 000	10 000	6 000
Prime cost (£ per unit):			
Direct materials			
Forming dept	8	7	9
Direct labour			
Forming dept	6	9	12
Finishing dept	10	15	8
	24	31	29
Manufacturing times (hours per unit):			
Machining			
Forming dept	4	3	2
Direct labour			
Forming dept	2	3	4
Finishing dept	3	10	2

	Forming department (£)	Finishing department (£)
Variable overheads	200 900	115 500
Fixed overheads	401 800	231 000
	£602 700	£346 500
Machine time required and available	98 000 hours	—
Labour hours required and available	82 000 hours	154 000 hours

The forming department is mechanized and employs only one grade of labour, the finishing department employs several grades of labour with differing hourly rates of pay.

Required:

a Calculate suitable overhead absorption rates for the forming and finishing departments for next year and include a brief explanation for your choice of rates. *(6 marks)*

b Another firm has offered to supply next years budgeted quantities of the above components at the following prices:

Component A	£30
Component B	£65
Component C	£60

Advise management whether it would be more economical to purchase any of the above components from the outside supplier. You must show your workings and, considering cost criteria only, clearly state any assumptions made or any aspects that may require further investigation.

(8 marks)

c Critically consider the purpose of calculating production overheads absorption rates. *(8 marks)*

ACCA Foundation Costing

3.23 Intermediate: Reapportionment of service department costs.

A company reapportions the costs incurred by two service cost centres, materials handling and inspection, to the three production cost centres of machining, finishing and assembly.

The following are the overhead costs which have been allocated and apportioned to the five cost centres:

	(£000)
Machining	400
Finishing	200
Assembly	100
Materials handling	100
Inspection	50

Estimates of the benefits received by each cost centre are as follows:

	Machining %	Finishing %	Assembly %	Materials handling %	Inspection %
Materials handling	30	25	35	—	10
Inspection	20	30	45	5	—

You are required to:

a calculate the charge for overhead to *each* of the *three* production cost centres, including the amounts reapportioned from the two service centres, using:
(i) the continuous allotment (or repeated distribution) method;
(ii) an algebraic method; *(15 marks)*

b comment on whether reapportioning service cost centre costs is generally worthwhile and suggest an alternative treatment for such costs; *(4 marks)*

c discuss the following statement: 'Some writers advocate that an under- or over-absorption of overhead should be apportioned between the cost of goods sold in the period to which it relates and to closing stocks. However, the United Kingdom practice is to treat under- or over-absorption of overhead as a period cost. *(6 marks)*

CIMA Stage 2 Cost Accounting 3

IM3.1 Intermediate.

a Explain why predetermined overhead absorption rates are preferred to overhead absorption rates calculated from factual information after the end of a financial period.

b The production overhead absorption rates of factories X and Y are calculated using similar methods. However, the rate used by factory X is lower than that used by factory Y. Both factories produce the same type of product. You are required to discuss whether or not this can be taken to be a sign that factory X is more efficient than factory Y. *(20 marks)*

CIMA Cost Accounting 1

IM3.2 Intermediate. Critically consider the purpose of calculating production overhead absorption rates.

IM3.3 Intermediate.

a Specify and explain the factors to be considered in determining whether to utilize a single factory-wide recovery rate for all production overheads or a separate rate for each cost centre, production or service department. *(12 marks)*

b Describe three methods of determining fixed overhead recovery rates and specify the circumstances under which each method is superior to the other methods mentioned. *(8 marks)*

ACCA P2 Management Accounting

IM3.4 Intermediate: Overhead analysis, calculation of overhead rate and overhead charged to a unit of output. A company makes a range of products with total budgeted manufacturing overheads of £973 560 incurred in three production departments (A, B and C) and one service department.

Department A has 10 direct employees, who each work 37 hours per week.

Department B has five machines, each or which is operated for 24 hours per week.

Department C is expected to produce 148 000 units of final product in the budget period.

The company will operate for 48 weeks in the budget period.

Budgeted overheads incurred directly by each department are:

Production department A	£261 745
Production department B	£226 120
Production department C	£93 890
Service department	£53 305

The balance of budgeted overheads are apportioned to departments as follows:

Production department A	40%
Production department B	35%
Production department C	20%
Service department	5%

Service department overheads are apportioned equally to each production department. You are required to:

a Calculate an appropriate predetermined overhead absorption rate in each production department. *(9 marks)*

b Calculate the manufacturing overhead cost per unit of finished product in a batch of 100 units which take 9 direct labour hours in department A and three machine hours in department B to produce. *(3 marks)*

(12 marks)

ACCA Foundation Paper 3

IM3.5 Intermediate: Overhead analysis sheet and calculation of overhead rates. Dunstan Ltd manufactures tents and sleeping bags in three separate production departments. The principal manufacturing processes consist of cutting material in the pattern cutting room, and sewing the material in either the tent or the sleeping bag departments. For the year to 31 July cost centre expenses and other relevant information are budgeted as follows:

	Total (£)	Cutting room (£)	Tents (£)	Sleeping bags (£)	Raw material stores (£)	Canteen (£)	Main- tenance (£)
Indirect wages	147 200	6 400	19 500	20 100	41 200	15 000	45 000
Consumable materials	54 600	5 300	4 100	2 300	—	18 700	24 200
Plant depreciation	84 200	31 200	17 500	24 600	2 500	3 400	5 000
Power	31 700						
Heat and light	13 800						
Rent and rates	14 400						
Building insurance	13 500						
Floor area (sq. ft)	30 000	8 000	10 000	7 000	1 500	2 500	1 000
Estimated power usage (%)	100	17	38	32	3	8	2
Direct labour (hours)	112 000	7 000	48 000	57 000	—	—	—
Machine usage (hours)	87 000	2 000	40 000	45 000	—	—	—
Value of raw material issues (%)	100	62.5	12.5	12.5	—	—	12.5

Requirements:

a Prepare in columnar form a statement calculating the overhead absorption rates for each machine hour and each direct labour hour for each of the three production units. You should use bases of apportionment and absorption which you consider most appropriate, and the bases used should be clearly indicated in your statement. *(16 marks)* b 'The use of pre-determined overhead absorption rates based on budgets is preferable to the use of absorption rates calculated from historical data available after the end of a financial period.'

Discuss this statement insofar as it relates to the financial management of a business. *(5 marks)*

ICAEW PI AC Techniques

IM3.6 Intermediate: Computation of three different overhead absorption rates and a cost-plus selling price. A manufacturing company has prepared the following budgeted information for the forthcoming year:

	£
Direct material	800 000
Direct labour	200 000
Direct expenses	40 000
Production overhead	600 000
Administrative overhead	328 000
Budgeted activity levels include:	
Budgeted production units	600 000
Machine hours	50 000
Labour hours	40 000

It has recently spent heavily upon advanced technological machinery and reduced its workforce. As a consequence it is thinking about changing its basis for overhead absorption from a percentage of direct labour cost to either a machine hour or labour hour basis. The administrative overhead is to be absorbed as a percentage of factory cost.

Required:

a Prepare pre-determined overhead absorption rates for production overheads based upon the three different bases for absorption mentioned above. *(6 marks)*

b Outline the reasons for calculating a pre-determined overhead absorption rate. *(2 marks)*

c Select the overhead absorption rate that you think the organization should use giving reasons for your decision. *(3 marks)*

d The company has been asked to price job AX, this job requires the following:

Direct material	£3788
Direct labour	£1100
Direct expenses	£422
Machine hours	120
Labour hours	220

Compute the price for this job using the absorption rate selected in (c) above, given that the company profit margin is equal to 10 per cent of the price. *(6 marks)*

e The company previously paid its direct labour workers upon a time basis but is now contemplating moving over to an incentive scheme.

Required:

Draft a memo to the Chief Accountant outlining the general characteristics and advantages of employing a successful incentive scheme. *(8 marks)*

AAT Cost Accounting and Budgeting

IM3.7 Intermediate: Calculation of overhead absorption rates and under/over-recovery of overheads. BEC Limited operates an absorption costing system. Its budget for the year ended 31 December shows that it expects its production overhead expenditure to be as follows:

	Fixed £	Variable £
Machining department	600 000	480 000
Hand finishing department	360 000	400 000

During the year it expects to make 200 000 units of its product. This is expected to take 80 000 machine hours in the machining department and 120 000 labour hours in the hand finishing department.

The costs and activity are expected to arise evenly throughout the year, and the budget has been used as the basis of calculating the company's absorption rates.

During March the monthly profit statement reported:

(i) that the actual hours worked in each department were

Machining	6000 hours
Hand finishing	9600 hours

(ii) that the actual overhead costs incurred were

	Fixed £	Variable £
Machining	48 500	36 000
Hand finishing	33 600	33 500

(iii) that the actual production was 15 000 units.

Required:

a Calculate appropriate pre-determined absorption rates for the year ended 31 December *(4 marks)*

b (i) Calculate the under/over absorption of overhead for each department of the company for March; *(4 marks)*

(ii) Comment on the problems of using predetermined absorption rates based on the arbitrary apportionment of overhead costs, with regard to comparisons of actual/target performance; *(4 marks)*

c State the reasons why absorption costing is used by companies. *(3 marks)*

(Total 15 marks)

CIMA Stage 1 Accounting

IM3.8 Intermediate: Calculation of under/over recovery of overheads. A company produces several products which pass through the two production departments in its factory. These two departments are concerned with filling and sealing operations. There are two service departments, maintenance and canteen, in the factory.

Predetermined overhead absorption rates, based on direct labour hours, are established for the two production departments. The budgeted expenditure for these departments for the period just ended, including the apportionment of service department overheads, was £110 040 for filling, and £53 300 for sealing. Budgeted direct labour hours were 13 100 for filling and 10 250 for sealing.

Service department overheads are apportioned as follows:

Maintenance	–	Filling	70%
Maintenance	–	Sealing	27%
Maintenance	–	Canteen	3%
Canteen	–	Filling	60%
	–	Sealing	32%
	–	Maintenance	8%

During the period just ended, actual overhead costs and activity were as follows:

	(£)	Direct labour hours
Filling	74 260	12 820
Sealing	38 115	10 075
Maintenance	25 050	
Canteen	24 375	

Required:

a Calculate the overheads absorbed in the period and the extent of the under/over absorption in each of the two production departments. *(14 marks)*

b State, and critically assess, the objectives of overhead apportionment and absorption. *(11 marks)*

ACCA Level 1 Cost and Management Accounting 1

IM3.9 Intermediate: Under- and over-absorption of overheads and calculation of budgeted expenditure and activity. A large firm of solicitors uses a job costing system to identify costs with individual clients. Hours worked by professional staff are used as the basis for charging overhead costs to client services. A predetermined rate is used, derived from budgets drawn up at the beginning of each year commencing on 1 April.

In the year to 31 March 2000 the overheads of the solicitors' practice, which were absorbed at a rate of £7.50 per hour of professional staff, were over-absorbed by £4760. Actual overheads incurred were £742 600. Professional hours worked were 1360 over budget.

The solicitors' practice has decided to refine its overhead charging system by differentiating between the hours of senior and junior professional staff, respectively. A premium of 40 per cent is to be applied to the hourly overhead rate for senior staff compared with junior staff.

Budgets for the year to 31 March 2001 are as follows:

Senior professional staff hours	21 600
Junior professional staff hours	79 300
Practice overheads	£784 000

Required

a Calculate for the year ended 31 March 2000:
   (i) budgeted professional staff hours;
   (ii) budgeted overhead expenditure.   (5 marks)

b Calculate, for the year ended 31 March 2001, the overhead absorption rates (to three decimal places of a £) to be applied to:
   (i) senior professional staff hours;
   (ii) junior professional staff hours.   (4 marks)

c How is the change in method of charging overheads likely to improve the firm's job costing system?   (3 marks)

d Explain briefly why overhead absorbed using predetermined rates may differ from actual overhead incurred for the same period.
                                                  (2 marks)
                          ACCA Foundation Paper 3

IM3.10 Intermediate: Reapportionment of service department costs. JR Co. Ltd's budgeted overheads for the forthcoming period applicable to its production departments, are as follows:

	(£000)
1	870
2	690

The budgeted total costs for the forthcoming period for the service departments, are as follows:

	(£000)
G	160
H	82

The use made of each of the services has been estimated as follows.

	Production department		Service department	
	1	2	G	H
G(%)	60	30	—	10
H(%)	50	30	20	—

Required:

Apportion the service department costs to production departments:

   (i)   using the step-wise (elimination) method, starting with G;
   (ii) using the reciprocal (simultaneous equation) method;
   (iii) commenting briefly on your figures.   (8 marks)
                          ACCA Paper 8 Managerial Finance

IM3.11 Advanced: Reapportionment of service department costs and comments on apportionment and absorption calculation. The Isis Engineering Company operates a job order costing system which includes the use of predetermined overhead absorption rates. The company has two service cost centres and two production cost centres. The production cost centre overheads are charged to jobs via direct labour hour rates which are currently £3.10 per hour in production cost centre A and £11.00 per hour in production cost centre B. The calculations involved in determining these rates have excluded any consideration of the services that are provided by each service cost centre to the other.

The bases used to charge general factory overhead and service cost centre expenses to the production cost centres are as follows:

   (i)   general factory overhead is apportioned on the basis of the floor area used by each of the production and service cost centres,
   (ii) the expenses of service cost centre 1 are charged out on the basis of the number of personnel in each production cost centre,
   (iii) the expenses of service cost centre 2 are charged out on the basis of the usage of its services by each production cost centre.

The company's overhead absorption rates are revised annually prior to the beginning of each year, using an analysis of the outcome of the current year and the draft plans and forecasts for the forthcoming year. The revised rates for next year are to be based on the following data:

	General factory overhead	Service cost centres 1	Service cost centres 2	Product cost centres A	Product cost centres B
Budgeted overhead for next year (before any reallocation) (£)	210 000	93 800	38 600	182 800	124 800
% of factory floor area	—	5	10	15	70
% of factory personnel	—	10	18	63	9
Estimated usage of services of service cost centre 2 in forthcoming year (hours)	—	1 000	—	4 000	25 000
Budgeted direct labour hours for next year (to be used to calculate next year's absorption rates)	—	—	—	120 000	20 000
Budgeted direct labour hours for current year (these figures were used in the calculation of this year's absorption rates)	—	—	—	100 000	30 000

a Ignoring the question of reciprocal charges between the service cost centres, you are required to calculate the revised overhead absorption rates for the two production cost centres. Use the company's established procedures.   (6 marks)

b Comment on the extent of the differences between the current overhead absorption rates and those you have calculated in your answer to (a). Set out the likely reasons for these differences.
                                                  (4 marks)

c Each service cost centre provides services to the other. Recalculate next year's overhead absorption rates, recognizing the existence of such reciprocal services and assuming that they can be measured on the same bases as those used to allocate costs to the production cost centres.   (6 marks)

d Assume that:
   (i)   General factory overhead is a fixed cost.
   (ii) Service cost centre 1 is concerned with inspection and quality control, with its budgeted expenses (before any reallocations) being 10 per cent fixed and 90 per cent variable.
   (iii) Service cost centre 2 is the company's plant maintenance section, with its budgeted expenses (before any reallocations) being 90 per cent fixed and 10 per cent variable.
   (iv) Production cost centre A is labour-intensive, with its budgeted overhead (before any reallocation) being 90 per cent fixed and 10 per cent variable.
   (v)   Production cost centre B is highly mechanized, with its budgeted overhead (before any reallocations) being 20 per cent fixed and 80 per cent variable.
       In the light of these assumptions, comment on the cost apportionment and absorption calculations made in parts (a) and (c) and suggest any improvements that you would consider appropriate.   (6 marks)
                          ACCA Level 2 Management Accounting

IM3.12 Advanced: Product cost calculation and costs for decision-making. Kaminsky Ltd manufactures belts and braces. The firm is organized into five departments. These are belt-making, braces-making, and three service departments (maintenance, warehousing, and administration).

Direct costs are accumulated for each department. Factory-wide indirect costs (which are fixed for all production levels within the present capacity limits) are apportioned to departments on the basis of the percentage of floorspace occupied. Service department costs are apportioned on the basis of estimated usage, measured as the percentage of the labour hours operated in the service department utilized by the user department.

Each service department also services at least one other service department.

Budgeted data for the forthcoming year are shown below:

	Belts	Braces	Admin-istration dept	Main-tenance dept	Ware-housing	Company total
(1) Output and sales (units):						
Output capacity	150 000	60 000				
Output budgeted	100 000	50 000				
Sales budgeted	100 000	50 000				
(2) Direct variable costs (£000):						
Materials	120	130	—	20	30	300
Labour	80	70	50	80	20	300
Total	200	200	50	100	50	600
(3) Factory-wide fixed indirect costs (£000)						1000
(4) Floor-space (%)	40	40	5	10	5	100
(5) Usage of service department labour hours (%)						
Administration	40	40	—	10	10	100
Warehousing	50	25	—	25	—	100
Maintenance	30	30	—	—	40	100

a   You are required to calculate the total cost per unit of belts and braces respectively, in accordance with the system operated by Kaminsky Ltd.
(12 marks)

b   In addition to the above data, it has been decided that the selling prices of the products are to be determined on a cost-plus basis, as the unit total cost plus 20 per cent.

Two special orders have been received, outside the normal run of business, and not provided for in the budget.

They are as follows:

(i) an order for 1000 belts from Camfam, an international relief organization, offering to pay £5000 for them.

(ii) a contract to supply 2000 belts a week for 50 weeks to Mixon Spenders, a chainstore, at a price per belt of 'unit total cost plus 10 per cent'.

You are required to set out the considerations which the management of Kaminsky Ltd should take into account in deciding whether to accept each of these orders, and to advise them as far as you are able on the basis of the information given.
(8 marks)

c   'Normalized overhead rates largely eliminate from inventories, from cost of goods sold, and from gross margin any unfavourable impact of having production out of balance with the long-run demand for a company's products.'

You are required to explain and comment upon the above statement.
(5 marks)
ICAEW Management Accounting

Accounting entries for a job costing system

4

This chapter is concerned with the accounting entries necessary to record transactions within a job costing system. In Chapter 2 it was pointed out that job costing relates to a costing system that is required in organizations where each unit or batch of output of a product or service is unique. This creates the need for the cost of each unit to be calculated separately. The term 'job' thus relates to each unique unit or batch of output. In contrast, process costing relates to those situations where masses of identical units are produced and it is unnecessary to assign costs to individual units of output. Instead, the cost of a single unit of output can be obtained by merely dividing the total costs assigned to the cost object for a period by the units of output for that period. In practice these two costing systems represent extreme ends of a continuum. The output of many organizations requires a combination of the elements of both job costing and process costing. However, the accounting methods described in this chapter can be applied to all types of costing systems ranging from purely job to process, or a combination of both. In the next chapter we shall look at process costing in detail. You should also note that the term contract costing is used to describe a job costing system that is applied to relatively large cost units that take a considerable amount of time to complete (e.g. building and civil engineering work). If your course curriculum requires an understanding of contract costing you will find that this topic is covered in Learning Note 4.1 on the open access website (see Preface for details).

LEARNING OBJECTIVES

After studying this chapter, you should be able to:

- describe the materials recording procedure;
- distinguish between first in, first out (FIFO), last in, first out (LIFO) and average cost methods of stores pricing;
- record the accounting entries for an integrated and interlocking accounting system;
- distinguish between an integrated and an interlocking accounting system;
- describe backflush costing.

The accounting system on which we shall concentrate our attention is one in which the cost and financial accounts are combined in one set of accounts; this is known as an integrated cost accounting system. An alternative system, where the cost and financial accounts are maintained independently, is known as an interlocking cost accounting system. The integrated cost accounting system is generally considered to be preferable to the interlocking system, since the latter involves a duplication of accounting entries.

A knowledge of the materials recording procedure will enable you to have a better understanding of the accounting entries. Therefore we shall begin by looking at this procedure.

Materials recording procedure

When goods are received they are inspected and details of the quantity of each type of goods received are listed on a goods received note. The goods received note is the source document for entering details of the items received in the receipts column of the appropriate stores ledger account. An illustration of a stores ledger account is provided in Exhibit 4.1. This document is merely a record of the quantity and value of each individual item of material stored by the organization. In most organizations this document will only consist in the form of a computer record.

The formal authorization for the issue of materials is a stores requisition. The type and quantity of materials issued are listed on the requisition. This document also contains details of the job number, product code or overhead account for which the materials are required. Exhibit 4.2 provides an illustration of a typical stores requisition. Each of the items listed on the materials requisition are priced from the information recorded in the receipts column of the appropriate stores ledger account. The information on the stores requisition is then recorded in the issues column of the appropriate stores ledger account and a balance of the quantity and value for each of the specific items of materials is calculated. The cost of each item of material listed on the stores requisition is assigned to the appropriate job number or overhead account. In practice this clerical process is likely to be computerized.

Pricing the issues of materials

A difficulty that arises with material issues is the cost to associate with each issue. This is because the same type of material may have been purchased at several different prices. Actual cost can

EXHIBIT 4.1 A stores ledger account

\multicolumn{12}{c}{**Stores ledger account**}
\multicolumn{5}{l}{Material: .... Code: ....}				\multicolumn{4}{r}{Maximum quantity: .... Minimum quantity: ....}
	Receipts				Issues				Stock		
Date	GRN no.	Quantity	Unit price (£)	Amount (£)	Stores req. no.	Quantity	Unit price (£)	Amount (£)	Quantity	Unit price (£)	Amount (£)

take on several different values, and some method of pricing material issues must be selected. Consider the situation presented in Example 4.1.

There are three alternative methods that you might consider for calculating the cost of materials issued to job Z which will impact on both the cost of sales and the inventory valuation that is incorporated in the April monthly profit statement and balance sheet. First, you can assume that the first item received was the first item to be issued, that is first in, first out (FIFO). In the example the 5000 units issued to job Z would be priced at £1 and the closing inventory would be valued at £6000 (5000 units at £1.20 per unit).

Secondly, you could assume that the last item to be received was the first item to be issued, that is, last in, first out (LIFO). Here a material cost of £6000 (5000 units at £1.20 per unit) would be recorded against the cost of job Z and the closing inventory would be valued at £5000 (5000 units at £1 per unit).

Thirdly there may be a strong case for issuing the items at the average cost of the materials in stock (i.e. £1.10 per unit). With an average cost system the job cost would be recorded at £5500 and the closing inventory would also be valued at £5500. The following is a summary of the three different materials pricing methods relating to Example 4.1:

	Cost of sales (i.e. charge to job Z) (£)	Closing inventory (£)	Total costs (£)
First in first out (FIFO)	5000 (5000 × £1)	6000 (5000 × £1.20)	11 000
Last in, first out (LIFO)	6000 (5000 × £1.20)	5000 (5000 × £1)	11 000
Average cost	5500 (5000 × £1.10)	5500 (5000 × £1.10)	11 000

FIFO appears to be the most logical method in the sense that it makes the same assumption as the physical flow of materials through an organization; that is, it is assumed that items received first

EXHIBIT 4.2 A stores requisition

Stores requisition					No.		
Material required for: (job or overhead account) Department:						Date:	
[Quantity]	Description	Code no.	Weight	Rate	£	[Notes]	
Foreman							

EXAMPLE 4.1

On 5 March Nordic purchased 5000 units of materials at £1 each. A further 5000 units were purchased on 30 March at £1.20 each. During April 5000 units were issued to job Z. No further issues were made during April and you are now preparing the monthly accounts for April.

will be issued first. During periods of inflation, the earliest materials that have the lowest purchase price will be issued first. This assumption leads to a lower cost of sales calculation, and therefore a higher profit than would be obtained by using either of the other methods. Note also that the closing inventory will be at the latest and therefore higher prices. With the LIFO method the latest and higher prices are assigned to the cost of sales and therefore lower profits will be reported compared with using either FIFO or average cost. The value of the closing inventory will be at the earliest and therefore lower prices. Under the average cost method, the cost of sales and the closing inventory will fall somewhere between the values recorded for the FIFO and LIFO methods.

LIFO is not an acceptable method of pricing for taxation purposes in the UK, although this does not preclude its use provided that the accounts are adjusted for taxation purposes. The UK Statement of Standard Accounting Practice on Stocks and Work in Progress (SSAP 9) and the International Accounting Standard (IAS2) on inventory valuation, however, states that LIFO does not bear a reasonable relationship to actual costs obtained during the period, and implies that this method is inappropriate for external reporting. In view of these comments, the FIFO or the average cost method should be used for external financial accounting purposes.

The above discussion relates to pricing the issue of materials for internal and external profit measurement and inventory valuation. For decision-making the focus is on future costs, rather than the allocation of past costs, and therefore using different methods of pricing materials is not an issue.

Control accounts

The recording system is based on a system of control accounts. A control account is a summary account, where entries are made from totals of transactions for a period. For example, the balance in the stores ledger control account will be supported by a voluminous file of stores ledger accounts, which will add up to agree with the total in the stores ledger control account. Assuming 1000 items of materials were received for a period that totalled £200 000, an entry of the total of £200 000 would be recorded on the debit (receipts side) of the stores ledger *control* account. This will be supported by 1000 separate entries in each of the individual stores ledger accounts. The total of all these *individual* entries will add up to £200 000. A system of control accounts enables one to check the accuracy of the various accounting entries, since the total of all the *individual* entries in the various stores ledger accounts should agree with the control account, which will have received the *totals* of the various transactions. The file of all the individual accounts (for example the individual stores ledger accounts) supporting the total control account is called the subsidiary ledger.

We shall now examine the accounting entries necessary to record the transaction outlined in Example 4.2. A manual system is described so that the accounting entries can be followed, but the normal practice is now for these accounts to be maintained on a computer. You will find a summary of the accounting entries set out in Exhibit 4.3, where each transaction is prefixed by the appropriate number to give a clearer understanding of the necessary entries relating to each transaction. In addition, the appropriate journal entry is shown for each transaction together with a supporting explanation.

Recording the purchase of raw materials

The entry to record the purchase of materials in transaction 1 is

Dr Stores ledger control account	182 000	
Cr Creditors control account		182 000

EXAMPLE 4.2

The following are the transactions of AB Ltd for the month of April.

1 Raw materials of £182 000 were purchases on credit.

2 Raw materials of £2000 were returned to the supplier because of defects.

3 The total of stores requisitions for direct materials issued for the period was £165 000.

4 The total issues for indirect materials for the period was £10 000.

5 Gross wages of £185 000 were incurred during the period
consisting of wages paid to employees £105 000
Tax deductions payable to the Government (i.e. Inland Revenue) £60 000
National Insurance contributions due £20 000

6 All the amounts due in transaction 5 were settled by cash during the period.

7 The allocation of the gross wages for the period was as follows:
Direct wages £145 000
Indirect wages £40 000

8 The employer's contribution for National Insurance deductions was £25 000.

9 Indirect factory expenses of £41 000 were incurred during the period.

10 Depreciation of factory machinery was £30 000.

11 Overhead expenses allocated to jobs by means of overhead allocation rates was £140 000 for the period.

12 Non-manufacturing overhead incurred during the period was £40 000.

13 The cost of jobs completed and transferred to finished goods stock was £300 000.

14 The sales value of goods withdrawn from stock and delivered to customers was £400 000 for the period.

15 The cost of goods withdrawn from stock and delivered to customers was
£240 000 for the period.

This accounting entry reflects the fact that the company has incurred a short-term liability to acquire a current asset consisting of raw material stock. Each purchase is also entered in the receipts column of an individual stores ledger account (a separate record is used for each item of materials purchases) for the quantity received, a unit price and amount. In addition, a separate credit entry is made in each individual creditor's account. Note that the entries in the control accounts form part of the system of double entry, whereas the separate entries in the individual accounts are detailed subsidiary records, which do not form part of the double entry system.

The entry for transaction 2 for materials returned to suppliers is:

Dr Creditors control account 2000
Cr Stores ledger control account 2000

An entry for the returned materials is also made in the appropriate stores ledger records and in the individual creditors' accounts.

Recording the issue of materials

The storekeeper issues materials from store in exchange for a duly authorized stores requisition. For direct materials the job number will be recorded on the stores requisition, while for indirect materials the overhead account number will be entered on the requisition. The issue of direct

EXHIBIT 4.3 Summary of accounting transactions for AB Ltd

Stores ledger control account

1. Creditors a/c	182 000	2. Creditors a/c		2 000
		3. Work in progress a/c		165 000
		4. Factory overhead a/c		10 000
		Balance c/d		5 000
	182 000			182 000
Balance b/d	5 000			

Factory overhead control account

4. Stores ledger a/c	10 000	11. Work in progress a/c	140 000
7. Wages control a/c	40 000	Balance – under-recovery	
8. National Insurance		transferred to costing	
contributions a/c	25 000	P&L a/c	6 000
9. Expense creditors a/c	41 000		
10. Provision for depreciation a/c	30 000		
	146 000		146 000

Non-manufacturing overhead control account

12. Expense creditor a/c	40 000	Transferred to costing	
		P&L a/c	40 000

Creditors account

2. Stores ledger a/c	2 000	1. Stores ledger a/c	182 000

Wages accrued account

6. Cash/bank	105 000	5. Wages control a/c	105 000

Tax payable account

6. Cash/bank	60 000	5. Wages control a/c	60 000

National Insurance contributions account

6. Cash/bank	20 000	5. Wage control a/c	20 000
8. Cash/bank	25 000	8. Factory overhead a/c	25 000
	45 000		45 000

Expense creditors account

		9. Factory overhead a/c	41 000
		12. Non-manufacturing overhead	40 000

Work in progress control account

3. Stores ledger a/c	165 000	13. Finished goods	
7. Wages control a/c	145 000	stock a/c	300 000
11. Factory overhead a/c	140 000	Balance c/d	150 000
	450 000		450 000
Balanced b/d	150 000		

Finished goods stock account

13. Work in progress a/c	300 000		15. Cost of sales a/c		240 000
			Balance c/d		60 000
	300 000				300 000
Balance b/d	60 000				

Cost of sales account

15. Finished goods stock a/c	240 000	Transferred to costing		
		P&L a/c		240 000

Provision for depreciation account

	10. Factory overhead	30 000

Wages control account

5. Wages accrued a/c	105 000	7. Work in progress a/c		145 000
5. Tax payable a/c	60 000	7. Factory overhead a/c		40 000
5. National Insurance a/c	20 000			
	185 000			185 000

Sales account

Transferred to costing P&L	400 000	14. Debtors	400 000

Debtors account

14. Sales a/c	400 000

Costing profit and loss account

Sales a/c		400 000
Less cost of sales a/c		240 000
Gross profit		160 000
Less under-recovery of factory overhead	6 000	
Non-manufacturing overhead	40 000	46 000
Net profit		114 000

materials involves a transfer of the materials from stores to production. For transaction 3, material requisitions will have been summarized and the resulting totals will be recorded as follows:

Dr Work in progress account	165 000	
Cr Stores ledger control account		165 000

This accounting entry reflects the fact that raw material stock is being converted into work in progress (WIP) stock. In addition to the above entries in the control accounts, the individual jobs will be charged with the cost of the material issued so that job costs can be calculated. Each issue is also entered in the issues column on the appropriate stores ledger record.

The entry for transaction 4 for the issue of indirect materials is:

Dr Factory overhead control account	10 000	
Cr Stores ledger control account		10 000

In addition to the entry in the factory overhead account, the cost of material issued will be entered in the individual overhead accounts. These separate overhead accounts will normally consist of individual indirect material accounts for each responsibility centre. Periodically, the totals of each responsibility centre account for indirect materials will be entered in performance reports for comparison with the budgeted indirect material cost.

After transactions 1–4 have been recorded, the stores ledger control account would look like this:

Stores ledger control account

1. Creditors a/c	182 000	2. Creditors a/c	2 000
		3. Work in progress a/c	165 000
		4. Factory overhead a/c	10 000
		Balance c/d	5 000
	182 000		182 000
Balance b/d	5 000		

Accounting procedure for labour costs

Accounting for labour costs can be divided into the following two distinct phases:

1 Computations of the gross pay for each employee and calculation of payments to be made to employees, government, pension funds, etc. (payroll accounting).

2 Allocation of labour costs to jobs, overhead account and capital accounts (labour cost accounting).

An entry is then made in the payroll for each employee, showing the gross pay, tax deductions and other authorized deductions. The gross pay less the deductions gives the net pay, and this is the amount of cash paid to each employee. The payroll gives details of the total amount of cash due to employees and the amounts due to the Government (i.e. Inland Revenue), Pension Funds and Savings Funds, etc. To keep the illustration simple at this stage, transaction 5 includes only deductions in respect of taxes and National Insurance. The accounting entries for transaction 5 are:

Dr Wages control account	185 000	
Cr Tax payable account		60 000
Cr National Insurance contributions account		20 000
Cr Wages accrued account		105 000

The credit entries in transaction 5 will be cleared by a payment of cash. The payment of wages will involve an immediate cash payment, but some slight delay may occur with the payment of tax and National Insurance since the final date for payment of these items is normally a few weeks after the payment of wages. The entries for the cash payments for these items (transaction 6) are:

Dr Tax payable account	60 000	
Dr National Insurance contributions account	20 000	
Dr Wages accrued account	105 000	
Cr Cash/bank		185 000

Note that the credit entries for transaction 5 merely represent the recording of amounts due for future payments. The wages control account, however, represents the gross wages for the period, and it is the amount in this account that must be allocated to the job, overhead and capital accounts. Transaction 7 gives details of the allocation of the gross wages. The accounting entries are:

```
Dr Work in progress control account          145 000
Dr Factory overhead control account           40 000
    Cr Wages control account                          185 000
```

In addition to the total entry in the work in progress control account, the labour cost will be charged to the individual job accounts. Similarly, the total entry in the factory overhead control account will be supported by an entry in each individual overhead account for the indirect labour cost incurred.

Transaction 8 represents the employer's contribution for National Insurance payments. The National Insurance deductions in transaction 5 represent the employees' contributions where the company acts merely as an agent, paying these contributions on behalf of the employee. The employer is also responsible for making a contribution in respect of each employee. To keep the accounting entries simple here, the employer's contributions will be charged to the factory overhead account. The accounting entry for transaction 8 is therefore:

```
Dr Factory overhead control account                25 000
    Cr National Insurance contributions account            25 000
```

The National Insurance contributions account will be closed with the following entry when the cash payment is made:

```
Dr National Insurance contributions account        25 000
    Cr Cash/bank                                           25 000
```

After recording these transactions, the wages control account would look like this:

Wages control account

5. Wages accrued a/c	105 000	7. Work in progress a/c	145 000
5. Tax payable a/c	60 000	7. Factory overhead a/c	40 000
5. National Insurance a/c	20 000		
	185 000		185 000

Accounting procedure for manufacturing overheads

Accounting for manufacturing overheads involves entering details of the actual amount of manufacturing overhead incurred on the debit side of the factory overhead control account. The total amount of overheads charged to production is recorded on the credit side of the factory overhead account. In the previous chapter we established that manufacturing overheads are charged to production using budgeted overhead rates. It is most unlikely, however, that the actual amount of overhead incurred, which is recorded on the debit side of the account, will be in agreement with the amount of overhead allocated to jobs, which is recorded on the credit side of the account. The difference represents the under- or over-recovery of factory overheads, which is transferred to the profit and loss account, in accordance with the requirements of the UK Statement of Standard Accounting Practice on Stocks and Work in Progress (SSAP 9) and the International Accounting Standard (IAS2) on inventory valuation.

Transaction 9 represents various indirect expenses that have been incurred and that will eventually have to be paid in cash, for example property taxes and lighting and heating. Transaction 10 includes other indirect expenses that do not involve a cash commitment. For simplicity it is assumed that depreciation of factory machinery is the only item that falls into this category. The accounting entries for transactions 9 and 10 are:

```
Dr Factory overhead control account              71 000
    Cr Expense creditors control account                      41 000
    Cr Provision of depreciation account                      30 000
```

In addition, subsidiary entries, not forming part of the double entry system, will be made in individual overhead accounts. These accounts will be headed by the title of the cost centre followed by the object of expenditure. For example, it may be possible to assign indirect materials directly to specific cost centres, and separate records can then be kept of the indirect materials charge for each centre. It will not, however, be possible to allocate property taxes, lighting and heating directly to cost centres, and entries should be made in individual overhead accounts for these items. These expenses should then be apportioned to cost centres as described in Chapter 3 to compute product costs for meeting financial accounting inventory valuation requirements.

Transaction 11 refers to the total overheads that have been charged to jobs using the estimated overhead absorption rates. The accounting entry in the control accounts for allocating overheads to jobs is:

```
Dr Work in progress control account              140 000
    Cr Factory overhead control account                      140 000
```

In addition to this entry, the individual jobs are charged so that job costs can be calculated. When these entries have been made the factory overhead control account would look like this:

	Factory overhead control account		
4. Stores ledger control a/c	10 000	11. Work in progress	
7. Wages control a/c	40 000	control a/c	140 000
8. Employer's National		Balance – Under-recovery	
Insurance contributions a/c	25 000	of overhead transferred to	
		costing profit and loss a/c	6 000
9. Expense creditors a/c	41 000		
10. Provision for			
depreciation a/c	30 000		
	146 000		146 000

The debit side of this account indicates that £146 000 overhead has been incurred, but examination of the credit side indicates that only £140 000 has been allocated to jobs via overhead allocation rates. The balance of £6000 represents an under-recovery of factory overhead, which is regarded as a period cost to be charged to the costing profit and loss account in the current accounting period. The reasons for this were explained in the previous chapter.

Non-manufacturing overheads

You will have noted in the previous chapter that non-manufacturing overhead costs are regarded as period costs and not product costs, and non-manufacturing overheads are not therefore charged to the work in progress control account. The accounting entry for transaction 12 is:

```
Dr Non-manufacturing overheads account           40 000
    Cr Expense creditors account                             40 000
```

At the end of the period the non-manufacturing overheads will be transferred to the profit and loss account as a period cost by means of the following accounting entry:

```
Dr Profit and loss account                    40 000
    Cr Non-manufacturing overheads account              40 000
```

In practice, separate control accounts are maintained for administrative, marketing and financial overheads, but, to simplify this example, all the non-manufacturing overheads are included in one control account. In addition, subsidiary records will be kept that analyze the total non-manufacturing overheads by individual accounts, for example office stationery account, sales person's travelling expenses account, etc.

Accounting procedures for jobs completed and products sold

When jobs have been completed, they are transferred from the factory floor to the finished goods store. The total of the job accounts for the completed jobs for the period is recorded as a transfer from the work in progress control account to the finished goods stock account. The accounting entry for transaction 13 is:

```
Dr Finished goods stock account               300 000
    Cr Work in progress control account                 300 000
```

When the goods are removed from the finished goods stock and delivered to the customers, the revenue is recognized. It is a fundamental principle of financial accounting that only costs associated with earning the revenue are included as expenses. The cost of those goods that have been delivered to customers must therefore be matched against the revenue due from delivery of the goods so that the gross profit can be calculated. Any goods that have not been delivered to customers will be included as part of the finished stock valuation. The accounting entries to reflect these transactions are:

```
Transaction 14
Dr Debtors control account                    400 000
    Cr Sales account                                    400 000

Transaction 15
Dr Cost of sales account                      240 000
    Cr Finished goods stock account                     240 000
```

Costing profit and loss account

At frequent intervals management may wish to ascertain the profit to date for the particular period. The accounting procedure outlined in this chapter provides a data base from which a costing profit and loss account may easily be prepared. The costing profit and loss account for AB Ltd based on the information given in Example 4.2 is set out in Exhibit 4.3 shown on pages 84–5. Alternatively, management may prefer the profit statement to be presented in a format similar to that which is necessary for external reporting. Such information can easily be extracted from the subsidiary records.

Interlocking accounting

Interlocking accounting is a system where the cost and financial accounts are maintained independently of each other, and in the cost accounts no attempt is made to keep a separate record of the financial accounting transactions. Examples of financial accounting transactions include entries in the various creditors, debtors and capital accounts. To maintain the double entry records, an account must be maintained in the cost accounts to record the corresponding entry that, in an integrated accounting system, would normally be made in one of the financial accounts (creditors, debtors accounts, etc.). This account is called a cost control or general ledger adjustment account.

Using an interlocking accounting system to record the transactions listed in Example 4.2, the entries in the creditors, wages accrued, taxation payable, National Insurance contributions, expense creditors, provision for depreciation and debtors accounts would be replaced by the entries shown below in the cost control account. Note that the entries in the remaining accounts will be unchanged.

Cost control account

2.	Stores ledger control a/c	2 000	1.	Stores ledger control a/c	182 000
14.	Sales a/c	400 000	5.	Wages control a/c	185 000
	Balance c/d	215 000	8.	Factory overhead control a/c	25 000
			9.	Expense creditors a/c	41 000
			12.	Non-manufacturing overhead a/c	40 000
			10.	Factory overhead a/c	30 000
				Profit and loss a/c (profit for period)	114 000
		617 000			617 000
				Balance b/d	215 000

Accounting entries for a JIT manufacturing system

During the late 1980s and early 1990s many organizations adopted a just-in-time (JIT) manufacturing philosophy. The major features of a JIT philosophy will be explained in Chapter 21 but at this point it is appropriate to note that implementing a JIT philosophy is normally accompanied by a cellular production layout whereby each cell produces similar products. Consequently, a form of process costing environment emerges. There is also a high velocity of WIP movement throughout the cell, and so it is extremely difficult to trace actual costs to *individual* products. Adopting a JIT philosophy also results in a substantial reduction in inventories so that inventory valuation becomes less relevant. Therefore simplified accounting procedures can be adopted for allocating costs between cost of sales and inventories. This simplified procedure is known as backflush costing.

Backflush costing aims to eliminate detailed accounting transactions. Rather than tracking the movement of materials through the production process, a backflush costing system focuses first on the output of the organization and then works backwards when allocating cost between costs of goods sold and inventories, with no separate accounting for WIP. In contrast, conventional product costing systems track costs in synchronization with the movement of the products from direct materials, through WIP to finished goods. We shall now use Example 4.3 to illustrate two variants of backflush costing. Trigger points determine when the entries are made in the accounting system.

Actual conversion costs are recorded as incurred, just the same as conventional recording systems. Conversion costs are then applied to products at various trigger points. It is assumed

EXAMPLE 4.3

The transactions for the month of May for JIT plc are as follows:

Purchase of raw materials	£1 515 000
Conversion costs incurred during the period	£1 010 000
Finished goods manufactured during the period	100 000 units
Sales for the period	98 000 units

There are no opening stocks of raw materials, WIP or finished goods. The standard and actual cost per unit of output is £25 (£15 materials and £10 conversion cost). The company uses an integrated cost accounting system.

that any conversion costs not applied to products are carried forward and disposed of at the year end. The accounting entries are as follows:

Method 1

Trigger point

1 – The purchase of raw materials and components

2 – The manufacture of finished goods

	(£)	(£)
1. Dr Raw material inventory account	1 515 000	
Cr Creditors		1 515 000
2. Dr Conversion costs	1 010 000	
Cr Expense creditors		1 010 000
3. Dr Finished goods inventory (100 000 × £25)	2 500 000	
Cr Raw material inventory (100 000 × £15)		1 500 000
Cr Conversion costs (100 000 × £10)		1 000 000
4. Dr Cost of goods sold (98 000 × £25)	2 450 000	
Cr Finished goods inventory		2 450 000

The ledger accounts in respect of the above transactions are shown in Exhibit 4.4.

Method 2

This is the simplest variant of backflush costing. There is only one trigger point. We shall assume that the trigger point is the manufacture of a finished unit. Conversion costs are debited as the actual costs are incurred. The accounting entries are:

	(£)	(£)
1. Dr Finished goods inventory (100 000 × £25)	2 500 000	
Cr Creditors		1 500 000
Cr Conversion costs		1 000 000
2. Dr Cost of goods sold (98 000 × £25)	2 450 000	
Cr Finished goods inventory		2 450 000

The end of month inventory balance is £50 000 finished goods. At the end of the period the £15 000 of raw materials purchased but not yet manufactured into finished goods will not have been recorded in the internal product costing system. It is therefore not included in the closing stock valuation.

You will see that the WIP account is eliminated with both the variants that are illustrated. If inventories are low, the vast majority of manufacturing costs will form part of cost of goods sold and will not be deferred in inventory. In this situation the volume of work involved in tracking costs through WIP, cost of goods sold and finished goods is unlikely to be justified. This considerably reduces the volume of transactions recorded in the internal accounting system. Note, however, that it may be necessary to track the progress of units on the production line, but there will be no attempt to trace costs to units progressing through the system.

The second variant is suitable only for JIT systems with minimum raw materials and WIP inventories. Note that both methods allocate identical amounts to the cost of goods sold for the period. The second method may yield significantly different inventory valuations from conventional product costing systems. It is therefore claimed that this method of backflush costing may not be acceptable for external financial reporting. However, if inventories are low or not subject to significant change from one accounting period to the next, operating income and inventory valuations derived from backflush costing will not be materially different from the results reported by the conventional system. In these circumstances backflush costing is acceptable for external financial reporting.

EXHIBIT 4.4 Ledger accounts for a backflush costing system (Method 1)

Raw materials inventory

1. Creditors	£1 515 000		3. Finished goods	£1 500 000

Finished goods inventory

3. Raw materials	£1 500 000		4. COGS	£2 450 000
3. Conversion costs	£1 000 000			

Conversion costs

2. Creditors	£1 010 000		3. Finished goods	£1 000 000

Cost of goods sold (COGS)

4. Finished goods	£2 450 000

The end of month inventory balances are

	(£)
Raw materials	15 000
Finished goods	50 000
	65 000

SUMMARY

The following items relate to the learning objectives listed at the beginning of the chapter.

● **Describe the materials recording procedure.**

When the materials are received the quantities and values are recorded in a separate stores ledger account for each item of material. The issues of materials are recorded on a stores requisition, which contains details of the job number product code or overhead account for which the materials are required. The information on the stores requisition is then recorded in the issues column of the appropriate stores ledger account and after each issue a balance of the quantity and value for each of the specific items of materials is calculated. The cost of each item of material listed on the stores requisition is assigned to the appropriate job number, product or overhead account. In practice this clerical process is likely to be computerized.

● **Distinguish between first in, first out (FIFO), last in, first out (LIFO) and average cost methods of stores pricing.**

Because the same type of materials may have been purchased at several different prices actual cost can take on several different values. Therefore an assumption must be made when pricing the materials used. FIFO assumes that the first item that was received in stock was the first item issued so the earlier purchase prices are used. LIFO assumes

that the last item to be received is the first item to be issued resulting in the later purchase prices being used. The average cost method assumes that materials are issued at the average cost of materials in stock.

● **Record the accounting entries for an integrated and interlocking accounting system.**

A summary of the accounting entries for an integrated accounting system, where all purchases and expenses are settled in cash, is shown diagrammatically in Figure 4.1.

● **Distinguish between an integrated and an interlocking cost accounting system.**

With an integrated costing accounting system, the cost and financial accounts are combined in one set of accounts whereas the cost and financial accounts are maintained independently with an interlocking accounting system. An integrated accounting system is recommended since it avoids the duplication of accounting entries.

FIGURE 4.1
Flow of accounting entries in an integrated accounting system

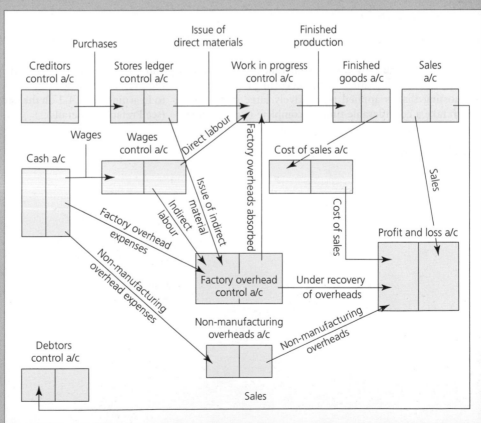

● **Describe backflush costing.**

Backflush costing is a simplified costing system that aims to eliminate detailed accounting transactions. It is applied when a just-in-time production philosophy is adopted. Instead of tracking the movement of materials through the production process, a backflush costing system focuses first on the output of the organization and then works backwards when allocating cost between cost of goods sold and inventories, with no separate accounting for work-in-progress. In contrast, a conventional integrated accounting system tracks costs in synchronization with the movement of the products from direct materials, through work-in-progress to finished goods.

Key terms and concepts

average cost (p. 81)
backflush costing (p. 90)
contract costing (p. 79)
control account (p. 82)
first in, first out (FIFO) (p. 81)

integrated cost accounting system (p. 80)
interlocking cost accounting system (pp. 80, 90)
labour cost accounting (p. 86)

last in, first out (LIFO) (p. 81)
payroll accounting (p. 86)
stores ledger account (p. 80)
stores requisition (p. 80)

Recommended reading

To illustrate the principles of stores pricing a simplistic illustration was presented. For a more complex illustration you should refer to Drury (2003). Alternatively, you can look at this chapter on the website. For an explanation of how you can access the website you should refer to the Preface of this book. For a more detailed illustration of backflush costing you should refer to Foster and Horngren (1988).

Key examination points

Professional accounting bodies sometimes set questions relating to contract costing. Contract costing is a system of job costing that is applied to relatively large cost units, which take a considerable time to complete (e.g. building and construction work). If your course curriculum requires a knowledge of contract costing you should refer to Learning Note 4.1 on the dedicated open access website (see Preface for details).

ASSESSMENT MATERIAL

The review questions are short questions that enable you to assess your understanding of the main topics included in the chapter. The numbers in parentheses provide you with the page numbers to refer to if you cannot answer a specific question.

The review problems are more complex and require you to relate and apply the content to various business problems. The problems are graded by their level of difficulty. Solutions to review problems that are not preceded by the term 'IM' are provided in a separate section at the end of the book. Solutions to problems preceded by the term 'IM' are provided in the *Instructor's Manual* accompanying this book and also on the lecturer's password protected section of the website www.drury-online.com. Additional review problems with fully worked solutions are provided in the *Student's Manual* that accompanies this book.

Review questions

4.1 Distinguish between an integrated and interlocking accounting system. (p. 80)

4.2 Describe the first in, first out (FIFO), last in, first out and average cost methods of stores pricing. (p. 81)

4.3 Explain the purpose of a stores ledger account. (p. 80)

4.4 Explain the purpose of control accounts. (p. 82)

4.5 List the accounting entries for the purchase and issues of direct and indirect materials. (pp. 82–83, p. 85)

4.6 List the accounting entries for the payment and the allocation of gross wages. (pp. 86–87)

4.7 List the accounting entries for the payment and allocation of overheads. (pp. 87–88)

4.8 Explain the circumstances when backflush costing is used. (pp. 90–92)

4.9 Describe the major aims of backflush costing. (p. 90)

Review problems

4.10 Basic. The effect of using the last in, first out (LIFO) method of stock valuation rather than first in, first out (FIFO) method in a period of rising prices is:

  a to report lower profits and a lower value of closing stock
  b to report higher profits and a higher value of closing stock
  c to report lower profits and a higher value of closing stock
  d to report higher profits and a lower value of closing stock
CIMA Management Accounting Fundamentals

4.11 Basic. E Ltd's stock purchases during a recent week were as follows:

Day	Price per unit ($)	Units purchased
1	1.45	55
2	1.60	80
3	1.75	120
4	1.80	75
5	1.90	130

There was no stock at the beginning of the week. 420 units were issued to production during the week. The company updates its stock records after every transaction.

  a Using a first in, first out (FIFO) method of costing stock issues, the value of closing stock would be:
    A $58.00 B $70.00 C $72.00 D $76.00

  b If E Ltd changes to the weighted average method of stock valuation, the effect on closing stock value and on profit compared with the FIFO method will be:

    A Higher closing stock value and higher gross profit
    B Lower closing stock value and higher gross profit
    C Lower closing stock value and lower gross profit
    D Higher closing stock value and lower gross profit
CIMA Management Accounting Fundamentals

4.12 Basic. At the end of a period, in an integrated cost and financial accounting system, the accounting entries for overhead over-absorbed would be:

  a DR Profit and loss account
      CR Work-in-progress control account
  b DR Profit and loss account
      CR Overhead control account
  c DR Work-in-progress control account
      CR Overhead control account
  d DR Overhead control account
      CR Profit and loss account
CIMA Stage 1 – Cost Accounting and Quantitative Methods

4.13 Basic. The following data have been taken from the books of CB plc, which uses a non-integrated accounting system:

	Financial accounts £	Cost accounts £
Opening stock of materials	5000	6400
Closing stock of materials	4000	5200
Opening stock of finished goods	9800	9600
Closing stock of finished goods	7900	7600

The effect of these stock valuation differences on the profit reported by the financial and cost accounting ledgers is that

  a the financial accounting profit is £300 greater than the cost accounting profit.
  b the financial accounting profit is £2100 greater than the cost accounting profit.
  c the cost accounting profit is £300 greater than the financial accounting profit.
  d the cost accounting profit is £900 greater than the financial accounting profit.
  e the cost accounting profit is £2100 greater than the financial accounting profit.
CIMA Stage 2 – Operational Cost Accounting

4.14 Intermediate. MN plc uses a JIT system and backflush accounting. It does not use a raw material stock control account. During April, 1000 units were produced and sold. The standard cost per unit is £100: this includes materials of £45. During April, £60 000 of conversion costs were incurred. The debit balance on the cost of goods sold account for April was

  a £90 000
  b £95 000
  c £105 000
  d £110 000
  e £115 000
(2 marks)
CIMA Management Accounting – Decision Making

4.15 Basic: Stores pricing. Z Ltd had the following transactions in one of its raw materials during April

Opening stock		40 units	@£10 each
April 4	Bought	140 units	@£11 each
10	Used	90 units	
12	Bought	60 units	@£12 each
13	Used	100 units	
16	Bought	200 units	@£10 each
21	Used	70 units	
23	Used	80 units	
26	Bought	50 units	@£12 each
29	Used	60 units	

You are required to:

a write up the stores ledger card using
   (i) FIFO and
   (ii) LIFO
   methods of stock valuation; *(8 marks)*

b state the cost of material used for each system during April; *(2 marks)*

c describe the weighted-average method of valuing stocks and explain how the use of this method would affect the cost of materials used and the balance sheet of Z Ltd compared to FIFO and LIFO in times of consistently rising prices. (Do NOT restate the stores ledger card for the above transactions using this method.) *(5 marks)*
   CIMA Stage 1 Accounting

4.16 Intermediate: Integrated accounts. In the absence of the accountant you have been asked to prepare a months cost accounts for a company which operates a batch costing system fully integrated with the financial accounts. The cost clerk has provided you with the following information, which he thinks is relevant:

	(£)
Balances at beginning of month:	
Stores ledger control account	24 175
Work in progress control account	19 210
Finished Goods control account	34 164
Prepayments of production overheads	
brought forward from previous month	2 100

	(£)
Transactions during the month:	
Materials purchased	76 150
Materials issued: to production	26 350
for factory maintenance	3 280
Materials transferred between batches	1 450

	Direct workers (£)	Indirect workers (£)
Total wages paid:		
Net	17 646	3 342
Employees deductions	4 364	890
Direct wages charged to batches from work tickets	15 236	
Recorded non-productive time of direct workers	5 230	
Direct wages incurred on production of capital equipment, for use in the factory	2 670	
Selling and distribution overheads incurred	5 240	
Other production overheads incurred	12 200	
Sales	75 400	
Cost of finished goods sold	59 830	
Cost of goods completed and transferred into finished goods store during the month	62 130	
Physical stock value of work in progress at end of month	24 360	

The production overhead absorption rate is 150 per cent of direct wages, and it is the policy of the company to include a share of production overheads in the cost of capital equipment constructed in the factory.

Required:

a Prepare the following accounts for the month:
   stores ledger control account
   wages control account
   work in progress control account
   finished goods control account
   production overhead control account
   profit/loss account. *(12 marks)*

b Identify any aspects of the accounts which you consider should be investigated. *(4 marks)*

c Explain why it is necessary to value a company's stocks at the end of each period and also why, in a manufacturing company, expense items such as factory rent, wages of direct operatives, power costs, etc. are included in the value of work in progress and finished goods stocks. *(6 marks)*
   ACCA Level 1 Costing

4.17 Intermediate: Backflush costing.

a Explain the term 'backflush accounting' and the circumstances in which its use would be appropriate. *(6 marks)*

b CSIX Ltd manufactures fuel pumps using a just-in-time manufacturing system which is supported by a backflush accounting system. The backflush accounting system has two trigger points for the creation of journal entries. These trigger points are:
   the purchase of raw materials
   the manufacture of finished goods
   The transactions during the month of November 2005 were as follows:

Purchase of raw materials	£5 575 000
Conversion costs incurred:	
Labour	£1 735 000
Overheads	£3 148 000
Finished goods completed (units)	210 000
Sales for the month (units)	206 000

There were no opening inventories of raw materials, work-in-progress or finished goods at 1 November. The standard cost per unit of output is £48. This is made up of £26 for materials and £22 for conversion costs (of which labour comprises £8.20).

Required:

(i) Prepare ledger accounts to record the above transactions for November 2005. *(6 marks)*

(ii) Briefly explain whether the just-in-time system operated by CSIX Ltd can be regarded as 'perfect'. *(3 marks)*
   ACCA Performance Measurement Paper 3.3

IM4.1 Intermediate: Integrated cost accounting. XY Limited commenced trading on 1 February with fully paid issued share capital of £500 000, Fixed Assets of £275 000 and Cash at Bank of £225 000. By the end of April, the following transactions had taken place:

1. Purchases on credit from suppliers amounted to £572 500 of which £525 000 was raw materials and £47 500 was for items classified as production overhead.
2. Wages incurred for all staff were £675 000, represented by cash paid £500 000 and wage deductions of £175 000 in respect of income tax etc.
3. Payments were made by cheque for the following overhead costs:

	£
Production	20 000
Selling	40 000
Administration	25 000

4. Issues of raw materials were £180 000 to Department A, £192 500 to Department B and £65 000 for production overhead items.
5. Wages incurred were analyzed to functions as follows:

	£
Work in progress – Department A	300 000
Work in progress – Department B	260 000
Production overhead	42 500
Selling overhead	47 500
Administration overhead	25 000
	675 000

6. Production overhead absorbed in the period by Department A was £110 000 and by Department B £120 000.
7. The production facilities, when not in use, were patrolled by guards from a security firm and £26 000 was owing for this service. £39 000 was also owed to a firm of management consultants which advises on production procedures; invoices for these two services are to be entered into the accounts.

8. The cost of finished goods completed was

	Department A £	Department B £
Direct labour	290 000	255 000
Direct materials	175 000	185 000
Production overhead	105 000	115 000
	570 000	555 000

9. Sales on credit were £870 000 and the cost of those sales was £700 000.
10. Depreciation of productive plant and equipment was £15 000.
11. Cash received from debtors totalled £520 000.
12. Payments to creditors were £150 000.

You are required

a to open the ledger accounts at the commencement of the trading period;
b using integrated accounting, to record the transactions for the three months ended 30 April;
c to prepare, in vertical format, for presentation to management,
  (i) a profit statement for the period;
  (ii) the balance sheet at 30 April. (20 marks)
  CIMA Stage 2 Cost Accounting

IM4.2 Intermediate: Preparation of interlocking accounts from incomplete information.

a Describe briefly *three* major differences between:
  (i) financial accounting, and
  (ii) cost and management accounting. (6 marks)

b Below are incomplete cost accounts for a period:

Stores ledger control account (£000)	
Opening balance	176.0
Financial ledger control a/c	224.2

Production wages control account (£000)	
Financial ledger control a/c	196.0

Production overhead control account (£000)	
Financial ledger control a/c	119.3

Job ledger control account (£000)	
Opening balance	114.9

The balances at the end of the period were:

	(£000)
Stores ledger	169.5
Jobs ledger	153.0

During the period 64 500 kilos of direct material were issued from stores at a weighted average price of £3.20 per kilo. The balance of materials issued from stores represented indirect materials.

75 per cent of the production wages are classified as 'direct'. Average gross wages of direct workers was £5.00 per hour. Production overheads are absorbed at a predetermined rate of £6.50 per direct labour hour.

Required:

Complete the cost accounts for the period. (8 marks)
ACCA Foundation Paper 3

IM4.3 Integrated accounts and stores pricing. On 30 October 2002 the following were among the balances in the cost ledger of a company manufacturing a single product (Product X) in a single process operation:

	Dr	Cr
Raw Material Control Account	£87 460	
Manufacturing Overhead Control Account		£5 123
Finished Goods Account	£148 352	

The raw material ledger comprised the following balances at 30 October 2002:

Direct materials:
Material A:	18 760 kg	£52 715
Material B:	4 242 kg	£29 994
Indirect materials:		£4 751

12 160 kg of Product X were in finished goods stock on 30 October 2002.

During November 1999 the following occurred:

(i) Raw materials purchased on credit:
Material A:	34 220 kg at £2.85/kg
Material B:	34 520 kg at £7.10/kg
Indirect:	£7221

(ii) Raw materials issued from stock:
Material A:	35 176 kg
Material B:	13 364 kg
Indirect:	£6917

Direct materials are issued at weighted average prices (calculated at the end of each month to three decimal places of £).

(iii) Wages incurred:
Direct	£186 743 (23 900 hours)
Indirect	£74 887

(iv) Other manufacturing overhead costs totalled £112 194. Manufacturing overheads are absorbed at a predetermined rate of £8.00 per direct labour hour. Any over/under absorbed overhead at the end of November should be left as a balance on the manufacturing overhead control account.

(v) 45 937 kg of Product X were manufactured. There was no work-in-progress at the beginning or end of the period. A normal loss of 5 per cent of input is expected.

(vi) 43 210 kg of Product X were sold. A monthly weighted average cost per kg (to three decimal places of £) is used to determine the production cost of sales.

Required:

a Prepare the following cost accounts for the month of November 2002.

  Raw Material Control Account
  Manufacturing Overhead Control Account
  Work-in-Progress Account
  Finished Goods Account

  All entries to the accounts should be rounded to the nearest whole £. Clearly show any workings supporting your answer. (16 marks)

b Explain the concept of equivalent units and its relevance in a process costing system. (4 marks)
  ACCA Management Information Paper 3

IM4.4 Intermediate: Labour cost accounting and recording of journal entries.

a Identify the costs to a business arising from labour turnover. (5 marks)

b A company operates a factory which employed 40 direct workers throughout the four-week period just ended. Direct employees were paid at a basic rate of £4.00 per hour for a 38-hour week. Total hours of the direct workers in the four-week period were 6528. Overtime, which is paid at a premium of 35 per cent, is worked in order to meet general production requirements. Employee deductions total 30 per cent of gross wages. 188 hours of direct workers' time were registered as idle.

Required:
Prepare journal entries to account for the labour costs of direct workers for the period. (7 marks)
  ACCA Foundation Stage Paper 3

IM4.5 Intermediate: Preparation of the wages control account plus an evaluation of the impact of a proposed piecework system. One of the production departments in A Ltd's factory employs 52 direct operatives and 9 indirect operatives. Basic hourly rates of pay are £4.80 and £3.90 respectively. Overtime, which is worked regularly to meet general production requirements, is paid at a premium of 30 per cent over basic rate.

The following further information is provided for the period just ended:

Hours worked:	
Direct operatives:	
Total hours worked	25 520 hours
Overtime hours worked	2 120 hours
Indirect operatives:	
Total hours worked	4 430 hours
Overtime hours worked	380 hours
Production:	
Product 1, 36 000 units in 7 200 hours	
Product 2, 116 000 units in 11 600 hours	
Product 3, 52 800 units in 4 400 hours	
Non-productive time:	2 320 hours
Wages paid (net of tax and employees' National Insurance):	
Direct operatives	£97 955
Indirect operatives	£13 859

The senior management of A Ltd are considering the introduction of a piecework payment scheme into the factory. Following work study analysis, expected productivities and proposed piecework rates for the direct operatives, in the production department referred to above, have been determined as follows:

	Productivity (output per hour)	Piecework rate (per unit)
Product 1	66 units	£1.00
Product 2	12 units	£0.50
Product 3	14.4 units	£0.40

Non-productive time is expected to remain at 10 per cent of productive time, and would be paid at £3.50 per hour.

Required:

a Prepare the production department's wages control account for the period in A Ltd's integrated accounting system. (Ignore employers' National Insurance.) *(9 marks)*

b Examine the effect of the proposed piecework payment scheme on direct labour and overhead costs. *(11 marks)*

ACCA Cost and Management Accounting 1

Process costing

5

A process costing system is used in those industries where masses of similar products or services are produced. Products are produced in the same manner and consume the same amount of direct costs and overheads. It is therefore unnecessary to assign costs to individual units of output. Instead, the average cost per unit of output is calculated by dividing the total costs assigned to a product or service for a period by the number of units of output for that period. Industries where process costing is widely used include chemical processing, oil refining, food processing and brewing. In contrast, job costing relates to a costing system where each unit or batch of output is unique. This creates the need for the cost of each unit to be calculated separately.

Our objective in this chapter is to examine the cost accumulation procedure that is required for inventory valuation and profit measurement for a process costing system. We begin with a description of the flow of production and costs in a process costing environment. We shall then focus on the cost accumulation system. To provide a structured presentation three different scenarios will be presented. First, all output is fully complete. Second, ending work in progress exists, but no beginning work in progress, and some of the units started during the period are incomplete at the end of the period. Our third scenario is the existence of both beginning and ending work in progress of uncompleted units. One of the most complex areas in process costing is accounting for losses when units within the process are both fully and partially complete. Because some courses omit this topic it will be discussed in Appendix 5.1.

LEARNING OBJECTIVES

After studying this chapter you should be able to:

- explain when process costing systems are appropriate;
- explain the accounting treatment of normal and abnormal losses;
- prepare process, normal loss, abnormal loss and abnormal gain accounts when there is no ending work in progress;
- explain and calculate equivalent units;
- compute the value of closing work in progress and completed production using the weighted average and first in, first out methods of valuing work in progress.

Flow of production and costs in a process costing system

The flow of production and costs in a process costing system is illustrated in Exhibit 5.1. The major differences between process and job costing are also highlighted. You will see that production moves from one process (or department) to the next until final completion occurs. Each production process performs some part of the total operation and transfers its completed production to the next process, where it becomes the input for further processing. The completed production of the last process is transferred to the finished goods inventory.

The cost accumulation procedure follows this production flow. Control accounts are established for each process (or department) and direct and indirect costs are assigned to each process. A process costing system is easier to operate than a job costing system because the detailed work of allocating costs to many individual cost units is unnecessary. Also, many of the costs that are indirect in a job costing system may be regarded as direct in a process costing system. For example, supervision and depreciation that is confined to one process would be treated as part of the direct costs of that process in a process costing system, since these costs are directly attributable to the cost object (i.e. the department or process). However, such costs are normally regarded as indirect in a job costing system because they are not directly attributable to a specific job.

As production moves from process to process costs are transferred with it. For example, in Exhibit 5.1 the costs of process A would be transferred to process B; process B costs would then be added to this cost and the resulting total cost transferred to process C; process C costs would then added to this cost. Therefore the cost becomes cumulative as production proceeds and the

EXHIBIT 5.1 A comparison of job and process costing

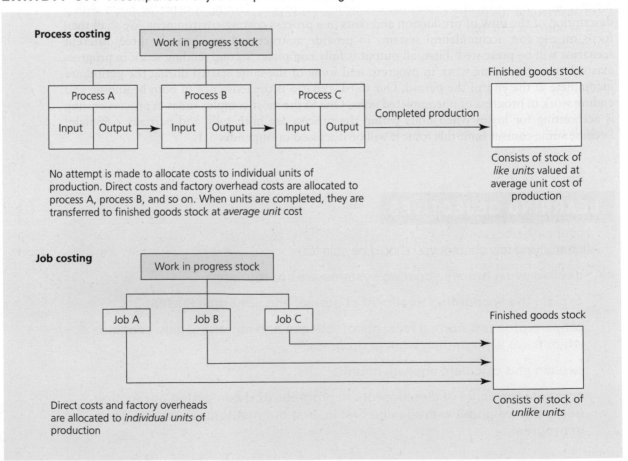

addition of the costs from the last department's cost determines the total cost. The cost per unit of the completed product thus consists of the total cost accumulated in process C for the period divided by the output for that period.

Process costing when all output is fully complete

Throughout this section it is assumed that all output within each process is fully complete. We shall examine the following situations:

1. no losses within a process;
2. normal losses with no scrap value;
3. abnormal losses with no scrap value;
4. normal losses with a scrap value;
5. abnormal losses with a scrap value;
6. abnormal gains with a scrap value.

You should now look at Example 5.1. The information shown in this example will be used to illustrate the accounting entries. To simplify the presentation it is assumed that the product is produced within a single process.

No losses within the process

To calculate the cost per unit (i.e. litre) of output for case 1 in Example 5.1 we merely divide the total cost incurred for the period of £120 000 by the output for the period (12 000 litres). The cost per unit of output is £10. In practice the cost per unit is analyzed by the different cost categories such as direct materials and conversion cost which consists of the sum of direct labour and overhead costs.

Normal losses in process with no scrap value

Certain losses are inherent in the production process and cannot be eliminated. For example, liquids may evaporate, part of the cloth required to make a suit may be lost and losses occur in

EXAMPLE 5.1

Dartmouth Company produces a liquid fertilizer within a single production process. During the month of May the input into the process was 12 000 litres at a cost of £120 000. There were no opening or closing inventories and all output was fully complete. We shall prepare the process account and calculate the cost per litre of output for the single process for each of the following six cases:

Case	Input (litres)	Output (litres)	Normal loss (litres)	Abnormal loss (litres)	Abnormal gain (litres)	Scrap value of spoilt output (£ per litre)
1	12 000	12 000	0	0	0	0
2	12 000	10 000	2000 (1/6)	0	0	0
3	12 000	9 000	2000 (1/6)	1 000	0	0
4	12 000	10 000	2000 (1/6)	0	0	5
5	12 000	9 000	2000 (1/6)	1 000	0	5
6	12 000	11 000	2000 (1/6)	0	1 000	5

cutting wood to make furniture. These losses occur under efficient operating conditions and are unavoidable. They are referred to as normal or uncontrollable losses. Because they are an inherent part of the production process normal losses are absorbed by the good production. Where normal losses apply the cost per unit of output is calculated by dividing the costs incurred for a period by the *expected* output from the actual input for that period. Looking at case 2 in Example 5.1 you will see that the normal loss is one sixth of the input. Therefore for an input of 12 000 litres the *expected* output is 10 000 litres so that the cost per unit of output is £12 (£120 000/10 000 litres). Actual output is equal to expected output so there is neither an abnormal loss nor gain. Compared with case 1 the unit cost has increased by £2 per unit because the cost of the normal loss has been absorbed by the good production. Our objective is to calculate the cost of normal production under normal efficient operating conditions.

Abnormal losses in process with no scrap value

In addition to losses that cannot be avoided, there are some losses that are not expected to occur under efficient operating conditions, for example the improper mixing of ingredients, the use of inferior materials and the incorrect cutting of cloth. These losses are not an inherent part of the production process, and are referred to as abnormal or controllable losses. Because they are not an inherent part of the production process and arise from inefficiencies they are not included in the process costs. Instead, they are removed from the appropriate process account and reported separately as an abnormal loss. The abnormal loss is treated as a period cost and written off in the profit statement at the end of the accounting period. This ensures that abnormal losses are not incorporated in any inventory valuations.

For case 3 in Example 5.1 the expected output is 10 000 litres but the actual output was 9000 litres, resulting in an abnormal loss of 1000 litres. Our objective is the same as that for normal losses. That is to calculate the cost per litre of the *expected* output (i.e. normal production), which is:

$$\frac{\text{input cost (£120 000)}}{\text{expected output (10 000 litres)}} = £12$$

Note that the unit cost is the same for an output of 10 000 or 9000 litres since our objective is to calculate the cost per unit of normal output. The distribution of the input costs is as follows:

	(£)
Completed production transferred to the next process (or finished goods inventory) 9000 litres at £12	108 000
Abnormal loss: 1000 litres at £12	12 000
	120 000

The abnormal loss is valued at the cost per unit of normal production. Abnormal losses can only be controlled in the future by establishing the cause of the abnormal loss and taking appropriate remedial action to ensure that it does not reoccur. The entries in the process account will look like this:

Process account

	Litres	Unit cost (£)	(£)		Litres	Unit cost (£)	(£)
Input cost	12 000	10	120 000	Normal loss	2 000	—	—
				Output to finished goods inventory	9 000	12	108 000
				Abnormal loss	1 000	12	12 000
			120 000				120 000

Process accounts represent work in progress (WIP) accounts. Input costs are debited to the process account and the output from the process is entered on the credit side. You will see from the process account that no entry is made in the account for the normal loss (except for an entry made in the units column). The transfer to the finished goods inventory (or the next process) is at the cost of normal production. The abnormal loss is removed from the process costs and reported separately as a loss in the abnormal loss account. This draws the attention of management to those losses that may be controllable. At the end of the accounting period the abnormal loss account is written off in the profit statement as a period cost. The inventory valuation will not therefore include any abnormal expenses. The overall effect is that the abnormal losses are correctly allocated to the period in which they arise and are not carried forward as a future expense in the closing inventory valuation.

Normal losses in process with a scrap value

In case 4 actual output is equal to the expected output of 10 000 litres so there is neither an abnormal gain nor loss. All of the units lost represent a normal loss in process. However, the units

SOURCE: WWW.BUSHMILLS.COM

Producing a world-famous whiskey

Bushmills Irish Whiskey, a world renowned brand of Diageo plc, is distilled in county Antrim in Northern Ireland. The Old Bushmills distillery has been in operation since 1608 and currently markets five distinct whiskeys under the Bushmills brand.

Whiskey production is essentially a five part process. The basic raw materials are barley and natural water. The first process, malting, allows barley corns to germinate for four days. An enzyme called diastase is formed inside each grain, which converts the starch in the grain to sugar. The corns are then dried in an oven.

The second process, mashing, takes the dried barley and grinds it a flour called 'grist'. Hot water is added to the grist to produce a sugary liquid called 'wort'. The wort is now ready to be transformed in to alcohol by fermentation.

The third process, fermentation, is a simple natural process which occurs when yeast and sugar are mixed. The wort is pumped in to a large vessel, where yeast is added. Fermentation is allowed to proceed for two days. The result liquid, called the 'wash' is now ready for transfer to the Still house for distillation, the fourth process.

Distillation involves heating the wash gradually in a large copper kettle called the Pot Still. As alcohol has a lower boiling point than water, the alcohol vapours condense first, run off and cool down to a liquid. Two further distillations are performed to ensure purity. The resulting liquid, called spirit, is a clear liquid with a high alcohol content.

The final step, maturation, sees the spirit placed in seasoned oak casks for a number of years – ranging from three to 21 years. The casks tend to be former American bourbon or Spanish sherry casks. The spirit acquires its colour and flavour from the casks. Once matured for the required period, the whiskies are bottled in the bottling plant at Bushmills, typically in 750ml bottles.

REAL WORLD VIEWS 5.1

Discussion points

1 Why is job costing not appropriate to a process such as whiskey production?

2 Do you think losses of spirit might occur during the maturation process?

Barrels await delivery in the warehouse of the Old Bushmills Distillery Co
© AA WORLD TRAVEL LIBRARY/ALAMY

lost now have a scrap value of £5 per litre. The sales value of the spoiled units should be offset against the costs of the appropriate process where the loss occurred. Therefore the sales value of the normal loss is credited to the process account and a corresponding debit entry will be made in the cash or accounts receivable (debtors) account. The calculation of the cost per unit of output is as follows:

$$\frac{\text{Input cost less scrap value of normal loss}}{\text{Expected output}} = \frac{£120\,000 - (2000 \times £5)}{10\,000 \text{ litres}} = £11$$

Compared with cases 2 and 3 the cost per unit has declined from £12 per litre to £11 per litre to reflect the fact that the normal spoilage has a scrap value which has been offset against the process costs.

The entries in the process account will look like this:

Process account

	Litres	Unit cost (£)	(£)		Litres	Unit cost (£)	(£)
Input cost	12 000	10	120 000	Normal loss	2 000	—	10 000
				Output to finished goods inventory	10 000	11	110 000
			120 000				120 000

Note that the scrap value of the normal loss is credited against the normal loss entry in the process account.

Abnormal losses in process with a scrap value

In case 5 expected output is 10 000 litres for an input of 12 000 litres and actual output is 9000 litres resulting in a normal loss of 2000 litres and an abnormal loss of 1000 litres. The lost units have a scrap value of £5 per litre. Since our objective is to calculate the cost per unit for the expected (normal) output only the scrap value of the normal loss of 2000 litres should be deducted in ascertaining the cost per unit. Therefore the cost per unit calculation is the same as that for case 4 (i.e. £11). The sales value of the additional 1000 litres lost represents revenue of an abnormal nature and should not be used to reduce the process unit cost. This revenue is offset against the cost of the abnormal loss which is of interest to management. The net cost incurred in the process is £105 000 (£120 000 input cost less 3000 litres lost with a scrap value of £5 per litre), and the distribution of this cost is:

	(£)	(£)
Completed production transferred to the next process (or finished goods inventory) (9000 litres at £11 per litre)		99 000
Abnormal loss:		
1000 litres at £11 per litre	11 000	
Less scrap value (1000 litres at £5)	5 000	6 000
		105 000

The entries in the process account will be as follows:

Process account

	Litres	Unit cost (£)	(£)		Litres	Unit cost (£)	(£)
Input cost	12 000	10	120 000	Normal loss	2 000	—	10 000
				Output to finished			
				goods inventory	9 000	11	99 000
				Abnormal loss	1 000	11	11 000
			120 000				120 000

Abnormal loss account

	(£)		(£)
Process account	11 000	Cash sale for units scrapped	5 000
		Balance transferred to profit statement	6 000
	11 000		11 000

Abnormal gains with a scrap value

On occasions the actual loss in process may be less than expected, in which case an **abnormal gain** occurs (see Case 6 in Example 5.1). As in the previous cases it is necessary with Case 6 to begin with calculating the cost per unit of normal output. For normal output our assumptions are the same as those for cases 4 and 5 (i.e. a normal loss of one sixth and a scrap value of £5 per litre) so the cost per unit of output is the same (i.e. £11 per litre). The calculation is as follows:

$$\frac{\text{Input cost less scrap value of normal loss}}{\text{Expected output}} = \frac{£120\ 000 - (2000 \times £5)}{10\ 000\ \text{litres}} = £11$$

The net cost incurred in the process is £115 000 (£120 000 input cost less 1000 litres spoilt with a sales value of £5 per litre), and the distribution of this cost is as follows:

		(£)
Transferred to finished goods inventory		
(11 000 litres at £11 per litre)		121 000
Less abnormal gain (1000 litres at £11 per litre)	11 000	
lost sales of spoiled units (1000 litres at £5 per litre)	5 000	6 000
		115 000

Note that the cost per unit is based on the normal production cost per unit and is not affected by the fact that an abnormal gain occurred or that sales of the spoiled units with a sales value of £5000 did not materialize. Our objective is to produce a cost per unit based on normal operating efficiency.

The accounting entries are as follows:

Process account

	Litres	Unit cost (£)	(£)		Litres	Unit cost (£)	(£)
Input cost	12 000	10	120 000	Normal loss	2 000	—	10 000
Abnormal				Output to finished			
gain	1 000	11	11 000	goods inventory	11 000	11	121 000
			131 000				131 000

Abnormal gain account

	(£)		(£)
Normal loss account	5 000	Process account	11 000
Profit and loss statement (Balance)	6 000		
	11 000		11 000

Income due from normal losses

	(£)		(£)
Process account	10 000	Abnormal gain account	5 000
		Cash from spoiled units	
		(1000 litres at £5)	5 000
	10 000		10 000

You will see that the abnormal gain has been removed from the process account and that it is valued at the cost per unit of normal production (£11). However, as 1000 litres were gained, there was a loss of sales revenue of £5000, and this lost revenue is offset against the abnormal gain. The net gain is therefore £6000, and this is the amount that should be credited to the profit statement.

The process account is credited with the expected sales revenue from the normal loss (2000 litres at £5), since the objective is to record in the process account normal net costs of production. Because the normal loss of 2000 litres does not occur, the company will not obtain the sales value of £10 000 from the expected lost output. This problem is resolved by making a corresponding debit entry in a normal loss account, which represents the amount due from the sale proceeds from the expected normal loss. The amount due (£10 000) is then reduced by £5000 to reflect the fact that only 1000 litres were lost. This is achieved by crediting the normal loss account (income due) and debiting the abnormal gain account with £5000, so that the balance of the normal loss account shows the actual amount of cash received for the income due from the spoiled units (i.e. £5000, which consists of 1000 litres at £5 per litre).

Process costing with ending work in progress partially complete

So far we have assumed that all output within a process is fully complete. We shall now consider situations where output started during a period is partially complete at the end of the period. In other words, ending work in progress exists within a process. When some of the output started during a period is partially complete at the end of the period, unit costs cannot be computed by simply dividing the total costs for a period by the output for that period. For example, if 8000 units were started and completed during a period and another 2000 units were partly completed then these two items cannot be added together to ascertain their unit cost. We must convert the work in progress into finished equivalents (also referred to as equivalent production) so that the unit cost can be obtained.

To do this we must estimate the percentage degree of completion of the work in progress and multiply this by the number of units in progress at the end of the accounting period. If the 2000 partly completed units were 50 per cent complete, we could express this as an equivalent production of 1000 fully completed units. This would then be added to the completed production of 8000 units to give a total equivalent production of 9000 units. The cost per unit would then be calculated in the normal way. For example, if the costs for the period were £180 000 then the cost per unit completed would be £20 (£180 000/9000 units) and the distribution of this cost would be as follows:

	(£)
Completed units transferred to the next process (8000 units at £20)	160 000
Work in progress (1000 equivalent units at £20)	20 000
	180 000

Elements of costs with different degrees of completion

A complication that may arise concerning equivalent units is that in any given stock of work in progress not all of the elements that make up the total cost may have reached the same degree of completion. For example, materials may be added at the start of the process, and are thus fully complete, whereas labour and manufacturing overhead (i.e. the conversion costs) may be added uniformly throughout the process. Hence, the ending work in progress may consist of materials that are 100 per cent complete and conversion costs that are only partially complete. Where this situation arises, separate equivalent production calculations must be made for each element of cost. The calculation of unit costs and the allocation of costs to work in progress and completed production when different elements of costs are subject to different degrees of completion will now be illustrated using the data given in Example 5.2.

The following statement shows the calculation of the cost per unit for process A:

Calculation of cost per unit for process A

Cost element	Total cost (£)	Completed units	WIP equivalent units	Total equivalent units	Cost per unit (£)
Materials	210 000	10 000	4 000	14 000	15.00
Conversion cost	144 000	10 000	2 000	12 000	12.00
	354 000				27.00

	(£)	(£)
Value of work in progress:		
Materials (4000 units at £15)	60 000	
Conversion cost (2000 units at £12)	24 000	84 000
Completed units (10 000) units at £27)		270 000
		354 000

EXAMPLE 5.2

The Fontenbleau Company manufactures a product that passes through two processes. The following information relates to the two processes:

	Process A	Process B
Opening work in progress	—	—
Units introduced into the process	14 000	10 000
Units completed and transferred to the next process or finished goods inventory	10 000	9 000
Closing work in progress	4 000	1 000
Costs of production transferred from process A[a]		£270 000
Material costs added	£210 000	£108 000
Conversion costs	£144 000	£171 000

Materials are added at the start of process A and at the end of process B and conversion costs are added uniformly throughout both processes. The closing work in progress is estimated to be 50 per cent complete for both processes.

Note
[a]This information is derived from the preparation of process A accounts.

The process account will look like this:

Process A account

Materials	210 000	Completed units transferred	
		to process B	270 000
Conversion cost	144 000	Closing WIP c/fwd	84 000
	354 000		354 000
Opening WIP b/fwd	84 000		

You will see from the above statement that details are collected relating to the equivalent production for completed units and work in progress by materials and conversion costs. This information is required to calculate the cost per unit of equivalent production for each element of cost. The work in progress of 4000 units is considered to be fully complete regarding materials. As materials are issued at the start of the process any partly completed units in ending work in progress must be fully complete as far as materials are concerned. Therefore an entry of 4000 units is made in the work in progress equivalent units column in the above statement for materials. Regarding conversion cost, the 4000 units in progress are only 50 per cent complete and therefore the entry in the work in progress column for this element of cost is 2000 units. To compute the value of work in progress, the unit costs are multiplied separately by the materials and conversion cost work in progress equivalent production figures. Only one calculation is required to ascertain the value of completed production. This is obtained by multiplying the total cost per unit of £27 by the completed production. Note that the cost of the output of £354 000 in the above statement is in agreement with the cost of input of £354 000.

Previous process cost

As production moves through processing, the output of one process becomes the input of the next process. The next process will carry out additional conversion work, and may add further materials. It is important to distinguish between these different cost items; this is achieved by labelling the transferred cost from the previous process 'previous process cost'. Note that this element of cost will always be fully complete as far as closing work in progress is concerned. Let us now calculate the unit costs and the value of work in progress and completed production for process B. To do this we prepare a statement similar to the one we prepared for process A.

Calculation of cost per unit for process B

Cost element	Total cost (£)	Completed units	WIP equivalent units	Total equivalent units	Cost per unit (£)
Previous process cost	270 000	9 000	1000	10 000	27.00
Materials	108 000	9 000	—	9 000	12.00
Conversion cost	171 000	9 000	500	9 500	18.00
	549 000				57.00

		(£)	(£)
Value of work in progress:			
Previous process cost (1000 units at £27)		27 000	
Materials		—	
Conversion cost (500 units at £18)		9 000	36 000
Completed units (9000 units at £57)			513 000
			549 000

Process B account

Previous process cost	270 000	Completed production		
Materials	108 000	transferred to finished stock	513 000	
Conversions cost	171 000	Closing work in progress c/fwd	36 000	
	549 000		549 000	
Opening WIP b/fwd	36 000			

You will see that the previous process cost is treated as a separate process cost, and, since this element of cost will not be added to in process B, the closing work in progress must be fully complete as far as previous process cost is concerned. Note that, after the first process, materials may be issued at different stages of production. In process B materials are not issued until the end of the process, and the closing work in progress will not have reached this point; the equivalent production for the closing work in progress will therefore be zero for materials.

Normally, material costs are introduced at one stage in the process and not uniformly throughout the process. If the work in progress has passed the point at which the materials are added then the materials will be 100 per cent complete. If this point has not been reached then the equivalent production for materials will be zero.

Beginning and ending work in progress of uncompleted units

When opening stocks of work in progress exist, an assumption must be made regarding the allocation of this opening stock to the current accounting period to determine the unit cost for the period. Two alternative assumptions are possible. First, one may assume that opening work in progress is inextricably merged with the units introduced in the current period and can no longer be identified separately – the weighted average method. Secondly, one may assume that the opening work in progress is the first group of units to be processed and completed during the current month – the first in, first out method. Let us now compare these methods using the information contained in Example 5.3.

EXAMPLE 5.3

The Baltic Company has two processes, X and Y. Material is introduced at the start of process X, and additional material is added to process Y when the process is 70 per cent complete. Conversion costs are applied uniformly throughout both processes. The completed units of process X are immediately transferred to process Y, and the completed production of process Y is transferred to finished goods stock. Data for the period include the following:

	Process X	Process Y
Opening work in progress	6000 units 60% converted, consisting of materials £72 000 and conversion cost £45 900	2000 units 80% converted, consisting of previous process cost of £91 800, materials £12 000 and conversion costs £38 400
Units started during the period	16 000 units	18 000 units
Closing work in progress	4000 units 3/4 complete	8000 units 1/2 complete
Material costs added during the period	£192 000	£60 000
Conversion costs added during the period	£225 000	£259 200

For more complex problems it is always a good idea to start by calculating the number of units completed during the period. The calculations are as follows:

	Process X	Process Y
Opening work in progress	6 000	2 000
Units introduced during period	16 000	18 000
Total input for period	22 000	20 000
Less closing work in progress	4 000	8 000
Balance – completed production	18 000	12 000

Weighted average method

The calculation of the unit cost for process X using the weighted average method is as follows:

Process X – weighted average method

Cost element	Opening WIP (£)	Current cost (£)	Total cost (£)	Completed units	WIP equiv. units	Total equiv. units	Cost per [unit] (£)
Materials	72 000	192 000	264 000	18 000	4000	22 000	12.00
Conversion cost	45 900	225 000	270 900	18 000	3000	21 000	12.90
	117 900		534 900				24.90

	(£)	(£)
Work in progress:		
Materials (4000 units at £12)	48 000	
Conversion (3000 units at £12.90)	38 700	86 700
Completed units (18 000 units at £24.90)		448 200
		534 900

Process X account

Opening work in progress b/fwd	117 900	Completed production	
Materials	192 000	transferred to process Y	448 200
Conversion cost	225 000	Closing work in progress c/fwd	86 700
	534 900		534 900
Opening work in progress b/fwd	86 700		

You can see from the statement of unit cost calculations that the opening work in progress is assumed to be completed in the current period. The current period's costs will include the cost of finishing off the opening work in progress, and the cost of the work in progress will be included in the total cost figure. The completed units will include the 6000 units in progress that will have been completed during the period. The statement therefore includes all the costs of the opening work in progress and the resulting units, fully completed. In other words, we have assumed that the opening work in progress is intermingled with the production of the current period to form one homogeneous batch of production. The equivalent number of units for this batch of production is divided into the costs of the current period, plus the value of the opening work in progress, to calculate the cost per unit.

Let us now calculate the unit cost for process Y using the weighted average method. From the calculation of the unit costs you can see the previous process cost is fully complete as far as the closing work in progress is concerned. Note that materials are added when the process is 70 per cent complete, but the closing work in progress is only 50 per cent complete. At the stage in question no materials will have been added to the closing work in progress, and the equivalent production will be zero. As with process X, it is necessary to add the opening work in progress cost to the current cost. The equivalent production of opening work in progress is ignored since this is included as being fully complete in the completed units column. Note also that the completed production cost of process X is included in the current cost column for 'the previous process cost' in the unit cost calculation for process Y.

Process Y – Weighted average method

Cost element	Opening WIP value (£)	Current period cost (£)	Total cost (£)	Completed units	WIP equiv. units	Total equiv. units	Cost per unit (£)
Previous process cost	91 800	448 200	540 000	12 000	8000	20 000	27.00
Materials	12 000	60 000	72 000	12 000	—	12 000	6.00
Conversion cost	38 400	259 200	297 600	12 000	4000	16 000	18.60
	142 200		909 600				51.60

	(£)	(£)
Value of work in progress:		
Previous process cost (8000 units at £27)	216 000	
Materials	—	
Conversion cost (4000 units at £18.60)	74 400	290 400
Completed units (12 000 units at £51.60)		619 200
		909 600

Process Y account

Opening work in progress	142 200	Completed production	
Transferred from process X	448 200	transferred to finished stock	619 200
Materials	60 000	Closing work in progress c/fwd	290 400
Conversion cost	259 200		
	909 600		909 600
Opening work in progress b/fwd	290 400		

First in first out (FIFO) method

Many courses focus only on the weighted average method of process costing. You should therefore check your course curriculum to ascertain whether or not you need to read this section relating to the FIFO method. The FIFO method of process costing assumes that the opening work in progress is the first group of units to be processed and completed during the current period. The opening work in progress is charged separately to completed production, and the cost per unit is based only on the *current period* costs and production for the current period. The closing work in progress is assumed to come from the new units started during the period. Let us now use Example 5.3 to illustrate the FIFO method for process X and Y.

Process X – FIFO method

Cost element	Current period costs (£)	Completed units less opening WIP equiv. units	Closing WIP equiv. units	Current total equiv. units	Cost per unit (£)
Materials	192 000	12 000 (18 000 – 6000)	4000	16 000	12.00
Conversion cost	225 000	14 400 (18 000 – 3600)	3000	17 400	12.93
	417 000				24.93

		(£)	(£)
Completed production:			
Opening WIP		117 900	
Materials (12 000 units at £12)		144 000	
Conversion cost (14 400 units at £12.93)		186 207	448 107
Closing WIP:			
Materials (4000 units at £12)		48 000	
Conversion cost (3000 units at £12.93)		38 793	86 793
			534 900

From this calculation you can see that the average cost per unit is based on current period costs divided by the current total equivalent units for the period. The latter figure excludes the equivalent production for opening work in progress since this was performed in the previous period. Note that the closing work in progress is multiplied by the current period average cost per unit. The closing work in progress includes only the current costs and does not include any of the opening work in progress, which is carried forward from the previous period. The objective is to ensure that the opening work in progress is kept separate and is identified as part of the cost of the completed production. The opening work in progress of £117 900 is not therefore included in the unit cost calculations, but is added directly to the completed production.

Let us now calculate the units costs for process Y:

Process Y – FIFO method

Cost element	Current costs (£)	Completed units less opening WIP equiv. units	Closing WIP equiv. units	Current total equiv. units	Cost per unit (£)
Previous process cost	448 107	10 000 (12 000 – 2000)	8000	18 000	24.8948
Materials	60 000	10 000 (12 000 – 2000)	–	10 000	6.0
Conversion cost	259 200	10 400 (12 000 – 1600)	4000	14 400	18.0
	767 307				48.8948

		(£)	(£)
Cost of completed production:			
Opening WIP		142 200	
Previous process cost (10 000 units at £24.8948)		248 948	
Materials (10 000 units at £6)		60 000	
Conversion cost (10 400 units at £18)		187 200	638 348
Cost of closing work in progress:			
Previous process cost (8000 units at £24.8948)		199 159	
Materials		–	
Conversion cost (4000 units at £18)		72 000	271 159
			909 507

Note that in this calculation the *opening* work in progress is 80 per cent completed, and that the materials are added when the process is 70 per cent complete. Hence, materials will be fully complete. Remember also that previous process cost is always 100 per cent complete. Therefore in the third column of the above statement 2000 units opening work in progress is deducted for these two elements of cost from the 12 000 units of completed production. Conversion cost will be 80 per cent complete so 1600 equivalent units are deducted from the completed production. Our objective in the third column is to extract the equivalent completed units that were derived from the units started during the current period. You should also note that the previous process cost of £448 107 represents the cost of completed production of process X, which has been transferred to process Y.

The closing work in progress valuations and the charges to completed production are fairly similar for both methods. The difference in the calculations between FIFO and the weighted average method is likely to be insignificant where the quantity of inventories and the input prices do not fluctuate significantly from month to month. Both methods are acceptable for product costing, but it appears that the FIFO method is not widely used in practice (Horngren, 1967).

Partially completed output and losses in process

Earlier in this chapter we looked at how to deal with losses in process when all of the output in a process was fully complete. We also need to look at the treatment of losses when all of the output is not fully complete. When this situation occurs the computations can become complex. Accounting for losses when all of the output is not fully complete does not form part of the curriculum for many courses. However, most professional management accounting courses do require you to have a knowledge of this topic. Because of these different requirements this topic is dealt with in Appendix 5.1. You should therefore check the requirements of your curriculum to ascertain whether you can omit Appendix 5.1.

Batch/operating costing

It is not always possible to classify cost accumulation systems into job costing and process costing systems. Where manufactured goods have some common characteristics and also some individual characteristics, the cost accumulation system may be a combination of both the job costing and process costing systems. For example, the production of footwear, clothing and furniture often involves the production of batches, which are variations of a single design and require a sequence of standardized operations. Let us consider a company that makes kitchen units. Each unit may have the same basic frame, and require the same operation, but the remaining operations may differ: some frames may require sinks, others may require to be fitted with work tops; different types of doors may be fitted to each unit, some may be low-quality doors while others may be of a higher quality. The cost of a kitchen unit will therefore consist of the basic frame plus the conversion costs of the appropriate operations. The principles of the cost accumulation system are illustrated in Exhibit 5.2.

The cost of each product consists of the cost of operation 1 plus a combination of the conversion costs for operations 2–5. The cost per unit produced for a particular operation consists of the average unit cost of each batch produced for each operation. It may well be that some products may be subject to a final operation that is unique to the product. The production cost will then consist of the average cost of a combination of operations 1–5 plus the specific cost of the final unique operation. The cost of the final operation will be traced specifically to the product using a job costing system. The final product cost therefore consists of a combination of process costing techniques and job costing techniques. This system of costing is referred to as operation costing or batch costing.

EXHIBIT 5.2 A batch costing system

| | Operations | | | | | |
Product	1	2	3	4	5	Product cost
A	✓	✓	✓			A = cost of operations 1, 2, 3
B	✓			✓	✓	B = cost of operations 1, 4, 5
C	✓	✓		✓		C = cost of operations 1, 2, 4
D	✓		✓		✓	D = cost of operations 1, 3, 5
E	✓	✓			✓	E = cost of operations 1, 2, 5

SUMMARY

The following items relate to the learning objectives listed at the beginning of the chapter.

● **Explain when process costing systems are appropriate.**

A process costing system is appropriate in those situations where masses of identical units or batches are produced thus making it unnecessary to assign costs to individual units or batches of output. Instead, the average cost per unit or batch of output is calculated by dividing the total costs assigned to a product or service for the period by the number of units or batches of output for that period. Industries using process costing systems include chemicals, textiles and oil refining.

● **Explain the accounting treatment of normal and abnormal losses.**

Normal losses are inherent in the production process and cannot be eliminated: their cost should be borne by the good production. This is achieved by dividing the costs incurred for a period by the expected output rather than the actual output. Abnormal losses are avoidable, and the cost of these losses should not be assigned to products but recorded separately as an abnormal loss and written off as a period cost in the profit statement. Scrap sales (if any) that result from the losses should be allocated to the appropriate process account (for normal losses) and the abnormal loss account (for abnormal losses).

● **Prepare process, normal loss, abnormal loss and abnormal gain accounts when there is no ending work in progress.**

The cost accumulation procedure follows the production flow. Control accounts are established for each process

(or department) and costs are assigned (debited) to each process. Abnormal losses are credited to the process where they were incurred and debited to an abnormal loss account. Scrap sales arising from normal losses are credited to the process account and any sales of scrap arising from abnormal losses are credited to the abnormal losses account. The accounting entries were illustrated using Example 5.1.

● **Explain and calculate equivalent units.**

Where stocks of work in progress are in existence, it is necessary in order to create homogeneous units of output to convert the work in progress into finished equivalent units of output. To do this we must estimate the percentage degree of completion of the work in progress and multiply this by the number of units in progress at the end of the accounting period. For example, if there are 5000 completed units estimated to be 40 per cent complete this represents an equivalent production of 2000 completed units.

● **Compute the value of closing work in progress and completed production using the weighted average method and first in, first out methods of valuing work in progress.**

There are two alternative methods of allocating opening work in progress costs to production: the weighted average and first in, first out methods. If the weighted average method is used, both the units and the value of opening work in progress are merged with the current period costs and production to calculate the average cost per unit. Using the first in, first out method, the opening work in progress is assumed to be the first group of units to be processed and completed during the current period. The opening work in progress is therefore assigned separately to completed production and the cost per unit is based only on current costs and production for the period. The closing work in progress is assumed to come from the new units that have been started during the period.

● **Additional learning objectives specified in Appendix 5.1.**

The appendix to this chapter includes one additional objective: to compute the value of normal and abnormal losses when there is ending work in progress. Because accounting for losses when all of the output is not fully complete is a complex topic that does not form part of the curriculum for many courses, this topic is dealt with in Appendix 5.1. You should check your course curriculum to ascertain if you need to read Appendix 5.1.

ADVANCED READING

Appendix 5.1: Losses in process and partially completed units

Normal losses

Losses can occur at different stages within a process. Where losses are assumed to occur at the final stage of completion only units that have reached this stage should be allocated with the cost of the loss. Therefore none of the cost should be allocated to closing work in progress (WIP), since they represent incomplete units. Consider Example 5A.1.

The cost per unit is calculated as follows:

Element of cost	Total cost (£)	Completed units	Normal loss	WIP equiv. units	Total equiv. units	Cost per unit (£)
Materials	5000	600	100	300	1000	5.0
Conversion cost	3400	600	100	150	850	4.0
	8400					9.0

	(£)	(£)
Value of work in progress:		
Materials (300 units at £5)	1500	
Conversion cost (150 units at £4)	600	2100
Completed units (600 units at £9)	5400	
Normal loss (100 units at £9)	900	6300
		8400

EXAMPLE 5A.1

A department with no opening work in progress introduces 1000 units into the process; 600 are completed, 300 are half-completed and 100 units are lost (all normal). *Losses occur upon completion.* Material costs are £5000 (all introduced at the start of the process) and conversion costs are £3400.

You can see from the unit cost calculation that an additional column is added for the equivalent units of normal loss. Note also that the cost of the normal loss is added to the cost of completed production, since it is detected at the final stage of completion. The closing WIP has not reached this stage, and therefore does not bear any of the loss. The cost per unit completed after the allocation of the normal loss is £10.50 (£6300/600 units).

Most examination questions, however, are normally based on the assumption that you will adopt an alternative method known as the short-cut method. With this method no entry is made in the unit cost statement for normal losses. The calculations adopting the short-cut method are as follows:

	Total cost (£)	Completed units	WIP equiv. units	Total equiv. units	Cost per unit (£)	WIP (£)
Materials	5000	600	300	900	5.5555	1666.65
Conversion cost	3400	600	150	750	4.5333	680.00
					10.0888	2346.65
			Completed units (600 × £10.0888)			6053.35
						8400.00

With the short cut method the costs allocated to WIP and completed units differs from the allocations based on assigning all of the cost of the normal loss to completed production. This is because the short cut method allocates the cost of the normal loss to both closing WIP and completed units based on the ratio of WIP and completed units equivalent production. The short cut method is only theoretically correct where losses occur at an earlier stage in the production process and the WIP has reached this stage. In these circumstances it is appropriate to allocate the cost of the normal loss between WIP and completed units. Let us now assume for Example 5A.1 that the loss is detected when the process has reached the 50 per cent stage of completion. In our revised example the WIP has been processed beyond the point where the loss occurs (the 50 per cent stage of completion) so it is appropriate to allocate a share of the cost of normal loss to WIP. The revised cost per unit, if the short cut method is not adopted is as follows:

Element of cost	Total cost (£)	Completed units	Normal loss	WIP equiv. units	Total equiv. units	Cost per unit
Materials	5000	600	100	300	1000	5.00
Conversion cost	3400	600	50	150	800	4.25
	8400					9.25

The 100 lost units will not be processed any further once the loss is detected at the 50 per cent completion stage. Therefore 50 units equivalent production (100 units × 50 per cent) is entered in the normal loss column for conversion cost equivalent production. Note that materials are introduced at the start of the process and are fully complete when the loss is detected. The cost of the normal loss is

	£
Materials (100 × £5)	500.00
Conversion cost (50 × £4.25)	212.50
	712.50

How should we allocate the normal loss between completed production and work in progress? Several different approaches are advocated, but the most common approach is to apportion the normal loss in the ratio of completed units and WIP equivalent units as follows:

Completed units		*WIP*	
	(£)		*(£)*
Materials 600/900 × £500	333.33	300/900 × £500	166.67
Conversion cost 600/750 × £212.50	170.00	150/750 × £212.50	42.50
	503.33		209.17

The cost of completed units and WIP is:

	(£)	*(£)*
Completed units:		
(600 × £9.25)	5550.00	
Share of normal loss	503.33	6053.33
WIP:		
Materials (300 × £5)	1500.00	
Conversion cost (150 × £4.25)	637.50	
Share of normal loss	209.17	2346.67
		8400.00

The costs allocated to completed unit and WIP are now identical to the costs that have been allocated with the short cut method. For the revised circumstances where the WIP has reached the stage where the losses are assumed to occur the short cut method is theoretically correct. However, even when circumstances exist where the short cut method is not theoretically correct examination questions are normally based on the assumption that you will adopt this method because of its simplicity.

Abnormal losses

Where abnormal losses occur the normal unit cost statement should be prepared but with an additional column for abnormal loss equivalent units. Consider the information presented in Example 5A.2. You can see from this example that losses are detected when production has reached the 50 per cent stage of completion and that WIP has been processed beyond this point. Therefore it is appropriate to use the short cut method. The unit cost calculations are as follows:

Element of cost	*Total cost* *(£)*	*Completed units*	*Abnormal loss*	*WIP equiv. units*	*Total equiv. units*	*Cost per unit* *(£)*
Previous						
process cost	10 000	600	50	250	900	11.111
Materials	8 000	600	50	250	900	8.888
Conversion						
cost	2 900	600	25	150	775	3.742
	20 900					23.741

From this calculation you can see that materials and the previous process cost are 100 per cent complete when the loss is discovered. However, spoilt units will not be processed any further once the loss is detected, and the lost units will be 50 per cent complete in respect of conversion costs.

EXAMPLE 5A.2

> A department with no opening work in progress introduces 1000 units into the process: 600 are completed, 250 are 60 per cent complete and 150 units are lost, consisting of 100 units normal loss and 50 units abnormal loss. Losses are detected *when production is 50 per cent complete*. Material costs are £8000 (all introduced at the start of the process), conversion costs are £2900 and the previous process cost is £10 000.

The costs are accounted for as follows:

	£	£
Value of work in progress		
Previous process cost (250 units at £11.111)	2 777	
Materials (250 units at £8.888)	2 222	
Conversion cost (150 units at £3.742)	561	5 560
Completed units:		
600 units at £23.741		14 246
Abnormal loss:		
Previous process cost (50 units at £11.111)	556	
Materials (50 units at £8.888)	444	
Conversion cost (25 units at £3.742)	94	1 094
		20 900

Key terms and concepts

abnormal gain (p. 105)
abnormal or controllable losses
   (p. 102)
batch costing (p. 114)
conversion cost (p. 101)

equivalent production (p. 106)
first in, first out method (p. 109)
normal or uncontrollable losses
   (p. 102)
operation costing (p. 114)

previous process cost (p. 108)
weighted average method (p. 109)

Key examination points

Process costing questions require many calculations and there is a possibility that you will make calculation errors. Make sure that your answer is clearly presented so that the examiner can ascertain whether or not you are using correct methods to calculate the cost per unit. Questions can generally be classified by three categories. First, all output is fully complete and the problem of equivalent production does not arise (see answer to Review problem 5.18 for an example). Second, work in progress (WIP) output is partially complete and there are no losses in process. Third, losses in

process apply when WIP is partially complete. Review problems 5.19 and 5.20 fall within the third category with the former assuming the weighted average and the latter FIFO method of (stock) valuation. Because of its simplicity you should adopt the short cut method for questions involving losses in process and equivalent production. You should, however, point out that the short cut method is not theoretically correct if losses are assumed to occur at the end of the process. Examination questions generally assume that you will adopt the short cut method.

ASSESSMENT MATERIAL

The review questions are short questions that enable you to assess your understanding of the main topics included in the chapter. The numbers in parentheses provide you with the page numbers to refer to if you cannot answer a specific question.

The review problems are more complex and require you to relate and apply the content to various business problems. The problems are graded by their level of difficulty. Solutions to review problems that are not preceded by the term 'IM' are provided in a separate section at the end of the book. Solutions to problems preceded by the term 'IM' are provided in the *Instructor's Manual* accompanying this book and also on the lecturer's password protected section of the website www.drury-online.com. Additional review problems with fully worked solutions are provided in the *Student's Manual* that accompanies this book.

Review questions

5.1 Describe the differences between process costing and job costing. *(p. 100)*

5.2 Provide examples of industries that use process costing. *(p. 99)*

5.3 Why is cost accumulation easier with a process costing system compared with a job costing system? *(p. 100)*

5.4 Distinguish between normal and abnormal losses and explain how their accounting treatment differs. *(p. 102)*

5.5 What are equivalent units? Why are they needed with a process costing system? *(p. 106)*

5.6 Why is it necessarily to treat 'previous process cost' as a separate element of cost in a process costing system? *(p. 108)*

5.7 How is the equivalent unit cost calculation affected when materials are added at the beginning or at a later stage of the process rather than uniformly throughout the process? *(p. 109)*

5.8 Describe how the weighted average and FIFO methods differ in assigning costs to units completed and closing work in progress. *(pp. 111–13)*

5.9 Under what conditions will the weighted average and FIFO methods give similar results? *(p. 113)*

5.10 Explain the distinguishing features of a batch/operating costing system. *(pp. 113–14)*

5.11 What are the implications for the accounting treatment of normal and abnormal losses if losses are assumed to be detected (a) at the end of the process, and (b) before the end of the process? *(pp. 115–17)*

Review problems

5.12 Basic. A company uses process costing to value its output and all materials are input at the start of the process. The following information relates to the process for one month:

Input	3000 units
Opening stock	400 units
Losses	10% of input is expected to be lost
Closing stock	200 units

How many good units were output from the process if actual losses were 400 units?

a 2800 units
b 2900 units
c 3000 units
d 3200 units *ACCA 1.2: Financial Information for Management*

5.13 Basic. A company uses process costing to value its output. The following was recorded for the period:

Input materials	2000 units at £4.50 per unit
Conversion costs	£13 340
Normal loss	5% of input valued at £3 per unit
Actual loss	150 units

There were no opening or closing stocks.

What was the valuation of one unit of output to one decimal place?

a £11.8
b £11.6
c £11.2
d £11.0 *ACCA 1.2: Financial Information for Management*

5.14 Basic. The following details relate to the main process of W Limited, a chemical manufacturer:

Opening work in progress	2000 litres, fully complete as to materials and 40% complete as to conversion
Material input	24 000 litres
Normal loss is 10% of input	
Output to process 2	19 500 litres
Closing work in progress	3000 litres, fully complete as to materials and 45% complete as to conversion

The number of equivalent units to be included in W Limited's calculation of the cost per equivalent unit using a FIFO basis of valuation are:

	Materials	Conversion
a	19 400	18 950
b	20 500	20 050
c	21 600	21 150
d	23 600	20 750
e	23 600	21 950

CIMA Stage 2

5.15 Basic. The following information is required for sub-questions (a) to (c)

The incomplete process account relating to period 4 for a company which manufactures paper is shown below:

Process account					
	Units	$		Units	$
Material	4000	16 000	Finished goods	2750	
Labour		8 125	Normal loss	400	700
Production overhead		3 498	Work in progress	700	

There was no opening work in process (WIP). Closing WIP, consisting of 700 units, was complete as shown:

Material	100%
Labour	50%
Production overhead	40%

Losses are recognised at the end of the production process and are sold for $1.75 per unit.

(a) Given the outcome of the process, which ONE of the following accounting entries is needed to complete the double entry to the process account?

	Debit	Credit
a	Abnormal Loss account	Process account
b	Process account	Abnormal Loss account
c	Abnormal Gain account	Process account
d	Process account	Abnormal Gain account

(b) The value of the closing WIP was

   a $3868
   b $4158
   c $4678
   d $5288

(c) The total value of the units transferred to finished goods was

   a $21 052.50
   b $21 587.50
   c $22 122.50
   d $22 656.50   *CIMA – Management Accounting Fundamentals*

5.16 Intermediate. The following process account has been drawn up for the last month:

Process account

	Units	£		Units	£
Opening WP	250	3 000	Normal loss	225	450
Input:			Output	4100	
Materials	4500	22 500	Abnormal Loss	275	
Labour		37 500	Closing WIP	150	
	4750			4750	

Work in progress has the following level of completion:

	Material	Labour
Opening WIP	100%	40%
Closing WIP	100%	30%

The company uses the FIFO method for valuing the output from the process and all losses occurred at the end of the process.

What were the equivalent units for labour?

   a   4380 units
   b   4270 units
   c   4320 units
   d   4420 units.
   ACCA Paper 1.2 – Financial Information for Management

5.17 Intermediate. CW Ltd makes one product in a single process. The details of the process for period 2 were as follows:

There were 800 units of opening work in progress valued as follows:
   Material £98,000
   Labour £46,000
   Production overheads £7,600

During the period 1,800 units were added to the process and the following costs were incurred:
   Material £387,800
   Labour £276,320
   Production overheads £149,280

There were 500 units of closing work in progress, which were 100 per cent complete for material, 90 per cent complete for labour and 40 per cent complete for production overheads.

A normal loss equal to 10 per cent of new material input during the period was expected. The actual loss amounted to 180 units. Each unit of loss was sold for £10 per unit.

CW Ltd uses weighted average costing.

Calculate the cost of the output for the period.
   CIMA P1 Management Accounting: Performance Evaluation

5.18 Intermediate: Preparation of process accounts with all output fully complete. 'No Friction' is an industrial lubricant, which is formed by subjecting certain crude chemicals to two successive processes. The output of process 1 is passed to process 2, where it is blended with other chemicals. The process costs for period 3 were as follows:

Process 1
   Material: 3000 kg @ £0.25 per kg
   Labour: £120
   Process plant time: 12 hours @ £20 per hour

Process 2
   Material: 2000 kg @ £0.40 per kg
   Labour: £84
   Process plant time: 20 hours @ £13.50 per hour

General overhead for period 3 amounted to £357 and is absorbed into process costs on a process labour basis.

The normal output of process 1 is 80 per cent of input, while that of process 2 is 90 per cent of input.

Waste matter from process 1 is sold for £0.20 per kg, while that from process 2 is sold for £0.30 per kg.

The output for period 3 was as follows:
   Process 1   2300 kg
   Process 2   4000 kg

There was no stock or work in process at either the beginning or the end of the period, and it may be assumed that all available waste matter had been sold at the prices indicated.

You are required to show how the foregoing data would be recorded in a system of cost accounts.

5.19 Intermediate: Losses in process (weighted average). Chemical Processors manufacture Wonderchem using two processes, mixing and distillation. The following details relate to the distillation process for a period

No opening work in progress (WIP)		
Input from mixing	36 000 kg at a cost of	£166 000
Labour for period		£43 800
Overheads for period		£29 200

Closing WIP of 8000 kg, which was 100 per cent complete for materials and 50 per cent complete for labour and overheads.

The normal loss in distillation is 10 per cent of fully complete production. Actual loss in the period was 3600 kg, fully complete, which were scrapped.

Required:
   a   Calculate whether there was a normal or abnormal loss or abnormal gain for the period.   *(2 marks)*
   b   Prepare the distillation process account for the period, showing clearly weights and values.   *(10 marks)*
   c   Explain what changes would be required in the accounts if the scrapped production had a resale value, and give the accounting entries.   *(3 marks)*
   CIMA Stage 1 Cost Accounting

5.20 Intermediate: FIFO method and losses in process. A company operates several production processes involving the mixing of ingredients to produce bulk animal feedstuffs. One such product is mixed in two separate process operations. The information below is of the costs incurred in, and output from, Process 2 during the period just completed.

Costs incurred:	£
Transfers from Process 1	187 704
Raw materials costs	47 972
Conversion costs	63 176
Opening work in process	3 009
Production:	Units
Opening work in process	1 200
(100% complete, apart from	
Process 2 conversion costs which	
were 50% complete)	
Transfers from Process 1	112 000
Completed output	105 400
Closing work in process	1 600
(100% complete, apart from	
Process 2 conversion costs which	
were 75% complete)	

Normal wastage of materials (including product transferred from Process 1), which occurs in the early stages of Process 2 (after all materials have been added), is expected to be 5 per cent of input. Process 2 conversion costs are all apportioned to units of good output. Wastage materials have no saleable value.

Required:

a Prepare the Process 2 account for the period, using FIFO principles. *(15 marks)*

b Explain how, and why, your calculations would have been different if wastage occurred at the end of the process.

(5 marks)

ACCA Cost and Management Accounting

IM5.1 Intermediate.

a Describe the distinguishing characteristics of production systems where

(i) job costing techniques would be used, and

(ii) process costing techniques would be used. *(3 marks)*

b Job costing produces more accurate product costs than process costing. Critically examine the above statement by contrasting the information requirements, procedures and problems associated with each costing method. *(14 marks)*

ACCA Level 1 Costing

IM5.2 Intermediate: Preparation of process accounts with all output fully completed.

A product is manufactured by passing through three processes: A, B and C. In process C a by-product is also produced which is then transferred to process D where it is completed. For the first week in October, actual data included:

	Process A	Process B	Process C	Process D
Normal loss of input (%)	5	10	5	10
Scrap value (£ per unit)	1.50	2.00	4.00	2.00
Estimated sales value of by-product (£ per unit)	–	–	8.00	–
Output (units)	5760	5100	4370	–
Output of by-product (units)	–	–	510	450
	(£)	(£)	(£)	(£)
Direct materials (6000 units)	12 000	–	–	–
Direct materials added in process	5 000	9000	4000	220
Direct wages	4 000	6000	2000	200
Direct expenses	800	1680	2260	151

Budgeted production overhead for the week is £30 500.

Budgeted direct wages for the week are £12 200.

You are required to prepare:

a accounts for process A, B, C and D. *(20 marks)*

b abnormal loss account and abnormal gain account. *(5 marks)*

CIMA P1 Cost Accounting 2

IM5.3 Intermediate: Discussion question on methods of apportioning joint costs and the preparation of process accounts with all output fully completed.

a 'While the ascertainment of product costs could be said to be one of the objectives of cost accounting, where joint products are produced and joint costs incurred, the total cost computed for the product may depend upon the method selected for the apportionment of joint costs, thus making it difficult for management to make decisions about the future of products.'

You are required to discuss the above statement and to state *two* different methods of apportioning joint costs to joint products.

(8 marks)

b A company using process costing manufactures a single product which passes through two processes, the output of process 1 becoming the input to process 2. Normal losses and abnormal losses are defective units having a scrap value and cash is received at the end of the period for all such units.

The following information relates to the four-week period of accounting period number 7.

Raw material issued to process 1 was 3000 units at a cost of £5 per unit.

There was no opening or closing work-in-progress but opening and closing stocks of finished goods were £20 000 and £23 000 respectively.

	Process 1	Process 2
Normal loss as a percentage of input	10%	5%
Output in units	2800	2600
Scrap value per unit	£2	£5
Additional components	£1000	£780
Direct wages incurred	£4000	£6000
Direct expenses incurred	£10 000	£14 000
Production overhead as a percentage of direct wages	75%	125%

You are required to present the accounts for

Process 1
Process 2
Finished goods
Normal loss
Abnormal loss
Abnormal gain
Profit and loss (so far as it relates to any of the accounts listed above).

(17 marks)

CIMA Stage 2 Cost Accounting

IM5.4 Intermediate: Equivalent production and losses in process.

Industrial Solvents Limited mixes together three chemicals – A, B and C – in the ratio 3:2:1 to produce Allklean, a specialised anti-static fluid. The chemicals cost £8, £6 and £3.90 per litre respectively.

In a period, 12 000 litres in total were input to the mixing process. The normal process loss is 5 per cent of input and in the period there was an abnormal loss of 100 litres whilst the completed production was 9500 litres.

There was no opening work-in-progress (WIP) and the closing WIP was 100 per cent complete for materials and 40 per cent complete for labour and overheads. Labour and overheads were £41 280 in total for the period. Materials lost in production are scrapped.

Required:

a Calculate the volume of closing WIP. *(3 marks)*

b Prepare the mixing process account for the period, showing clearly volumes and values. *(9 marks)*

c Briefly explain what changes would be necessary in your account if an abnormal gain were achieved in a period. *(3 marks)*

CIMA Stage 1 Cost Accounting

IM5.5 Intermediate: Losses in process (weighted average).

a A company uses a process costing system in which the following terms arise:

conversion costs
work-in-process
equivalent units
normal loss
abnormal loss.

Required:

Provide a definition of each of these terms. *(5 marks)*

b Explain how you would treat normal and abnormal losses in process costs accounts. *(4 marks)*

c One of the products manufactured by the company passes through two separate processes. In each process losses, arising from rejected material, occur. In Process 1, normal losses are 20 per cent of input. In Process 2, normal losses are 10 per cent of input. The losses arise at the end of each of the processes. Reject material can be sold. Process 1 reject material can be sold for £1.20 per kilo, and Process 2 reject material for £1.42 per kilo.

Information for a period is as follows:

Process 1:

Material input 9000 kilos, cost £14 964.
Direct labour 2450 hours at £3.40 per hour.
Production overhead £2.60 per direct labour hour.
Material output 7300 kilos.

Process 2:

Material input 7300 kilos.
Direct labour 1000 hours at £3.40 per hour.
Production overhead £2.90 per direct labour hour.
Material output 4700 kilos.

122

CHAPTER 5 PROCESS COSTING

At the end of the period 2000 kilos of material were incomplete in Process 2. These were 50 per cent complete as regards direct labour and production overhead. There was no opening work-in-process in either process, and no closing work-in-process in Process 1.

Required:

Prepare the relevant cost accounts for the period. *(16 marks)*

ACCA Level 1 Costing

IM5.6 Intermediate: Losses in process and weighted averages method. ABC plc operates an integrated cost accounting system and has a financial year which ends on 30 September. It operates in a processing industry in which a single product is produced by passing inputs through two sequential processes. A normal loss of 10 per cent of input is expected in each process.

The following account balances have been extracted from its ledger at 31 August:

	Debit (£)	Credit (£)
Process 1 (Materials £4400; Conversion costs £3744)	8144	
Process 2 (Process 1 £4431; Conversion costs £5250)	9681	
Abnormal loss	1400	
Abnormal gain		300
Overhead control account		250
Sales		585 000
Cost of sales	442 500	
Finished goods stock	65 000	

ABC plc uses the weighted average method of accounting for work in process.

During September the following transactions occurred:

Process 1

materials input	4000 kg costing £22 000
labour cost	£12 000
transfer to process 2	2400 kg

Process 2

transfer from process 1	2400 kg
labour cost	£15 000
transfer to finished goods	2500 kg
Overhead costs incurred amounted to	£54 000
Sales to customers were	£52 000

Overhead costs are absorbed into process costs on the basis of 150 per cent of labour cost.

The losses which arise in process 1 have no scrap value: those arising in process 2 can be sold for £2 per kg.

Details of opening and closing work in process for the month of September are as follows:

	Opening	Closing
Process 1	3000 kg	3400 kg
Process 2	2250 kg	2600 kg

In both processes closing work in process is fully complete as to material cost and 40 per cent complete as to conversion cost.

Stocks of finished goods at 30 September were valued at cost of £60 000.

Required:

Prepare the ledger accounts for September and the annual profit and loss account of ABC plc. (Commence with the balances given above, balance off and transfer any balances as appropriate.) *(25 marks)*

CIMA Stage 2 Operational Cost Accounting

IM5.7 Intermediate: Process accounts involving an abnormal gain and equivalent production. The following information relates to a manufacturing process for a period:

Materials costs	£16 445
Labour and overhead costs	£28 596

10 000 units of output were produced by the process in the period, of which 420 failed testing and were scrapped. Scrapped units normally represent 5 per cent of total production output. Testing takes place when production units are 60 per cent complete in terms of labour and overheads. Materials are input at the beginning of the process. All scrapped units were sold in the period for £0.40 per unit.

Required:

Prepare the process accounts for the period, including those for process scrap and abnormal losses/gains. *(12 marks)*

ACCA Foundation Stage Paper 3

IM5.8 Intermediate: Losses in process (FIFO and weighted average methods). A company produces a single product from one of its manufacturing processes. The following information of process inputs, outputs and work in process relates to the most recently completed period:

	kg
Opening work in process	21 700
Materials input	105 600
Output completed	92 400
Closing work in process	28 200

The opening and closing work in process are respectively 60 per cent and 50 per cent complete as to conversion costs. Losses occur at the beginning of the process and have a scrap value of £0.45 per kg.

The opening work in process included raw material costs of £56 420 and conversion costs of £30 597. Costs incurred during the period were:

Materials input	£276 672
Conversion costs	£226 195

Required:

a Calculate the unit costs of production (£ per kg to four decimal places) using:
   (i) the weighted average method of valuation and assuming that all losses are treated as normal;
   (ii) the FIFO method of valuation and assuming that normal losses are 5 per cent of materials input. *(13 marks)*

b Prepare the process account for situation (a) (ii) above. *(6 marks)*

c Distinguish between:
   (i) joint products, and
   (ii) by-products and contrast their treatment in process accounts. *(6 marks)*

ACCA Cost and Management Accounting 1

IM5.9 Advanced: FIFO method and losses in process.

a You are required to explain and discuss the alternative methods of accounting for normal and abnormal spoilage. *(8 marks)*

b Weston Harvey Ltd assembles and finishes trapfoils from bought-in components which are utilized at the beginning of the assembly process. The other assembly costs are incurred evenly throughout that process. When the assembly process is complete, the finishing process is undertaken. Overhead is absorbed into assembly, but not finishing, at the rate of 100 per cent of direct assembly cost.

It is considered normal for some trapfoils to be spoiled during assembly and finishing. Quality control inspection is applied at the conclusion of the finishing process to determine whether units are spoiled.

It is accepted that the spoilage is normal if spoiled units are no more than one-eighteenth of the completed good units produced. Normal spoilage is treated as a product cost, and incorporated into the cost of good production. Any spoilage in excess of this limit is classed as abnormal, and written off as a loss of the period in which it occurs.

Trapfoils are valuable in relation to their weight and size. Despite vigilant security precautions it is common that some units are lost, probably by pilferage. The cost of lost units is written off as a loss of the period in which it occurs. This cost is measured as the cost of the bought-in components plus the assembly process, but no finishing cost is charged.

Weston Harvey uses a FIFO system of costing.

The following data summarize the firm's activities during November:

Opening work in process:	
Bought-in components	£60 000
Direct assembly cost to 31 October	£25 000
No. of units (on average one-half assembled)	50 000
Direct costs incurred during November	
Bought-in components received	£120 000
Direct assembly cost	£40 000
Direct finishing cost	£30 000
Production data for November:	Trapfoils
Components received into assembly	112 000
Good units completed	90 000
Spoiled units	10 000
Lost units	2 000

None of the opening work in process had at that stage entered the finishing process. Similarly, nor had any of the closing work in process at the end of the month. The units in the closing work in process were, on average, one-third complete as to assembly; none had entered the finishing process.

You are required:

i to calculate the number of units in the closing work in process;
(3 marks)

ii to calculate the number of equivalent units processed in November, distinguishing between bought-in components, assembly and finishing;
(6 marks)

iii to calculate the number of equivalent units processed in November, subdivided into the amounts for good units produced, spoilage, lost units and closing work in process.
(8 marks)

ICAEW Management Accounting

IM5.10 Advanced: Comparison of FIFO and weighted average, stock valuation methods. On 1 October Bland Ltd opened a plant for making verniers. Data for the first two months' operations are shown below:

	October (units)	November (units)
Units started in month	3900	2700
Units completed (all sold)	2400	2400
Closing work in progress	1500	1800
	(£)	(£)
Variable costs:		
Materials	58 500	48 600
Labour	36 000	21 000
Fixed costs	63 000	63 000
Sales revenue	112 800	120 000

At 31 October the units in closing work in progress were 100 per cent complete for materials and 80 per cent complete for labour. At 30 November the units in closing work in progress were 100 per cent complete for materials and 50 per cent complete for labour.

The company's policy for valuation of work in progress is under review. The board of directors decided that two alternative profit and loss statements should be prepared for October and November. One statement would value work in progress on a weighted average cost basis and the other would adopt a first-in, first-out basis. Fixed costs would be absorbed in proportion to actual labour costs in both cases.

For October both bases gave a closing work in progress valuation of £55 500 and a profit of £10 800. When the statements for November were presented to the board the following suggestions were made:

1 'We wouldn't have a problem over the valuation basis if we used standard costs.'

2 'Standard cost valuation could be misleading for an operation facing volatile costs; all data should be on a current cost basis for management purposes.'

3 'It would be simpler and more informative to go to a direct cost valuation basis for management use.'

4 'All that management needs is a cash flow report; leave the work in progress valuation to the year-end financial accounts.'

Requirements:

a Prepare profit and loss statements for November on the two alternative bases decided by the board of directors, showing workings.
(9 marks)

b Explain, with supporting calculations, the differences between the results shown by each statement you have prepared.
(6 marks)

c Assess the main strengths and weaknesses of each of the suggestions made by the directors, confining your assessment to matters relating to the effects of work in progress valuation on performance measurement.
(10 marks)

ICAEW P2 Management Accounting

Joint and by-product costing

6

A distinguishing feature of the production of joint and by-products is that the products are not identifiable as different products until a specific point in the production process is reached. Before this point joint costs are incurred on the production of all products emerging from the joint production process. It is therefore not possible to trace joint costs to individual products.

To meet internal and external profit measurement and inventory valuation requirements, it is necessary to assign all product-related costs (including joint costs) to products so that costs can be allocated to inventories and cost of goods sold. The assignment of joint costs to products, however, is of little use for decision-making. We shall begin by distinguishing between joint and by-products. This will be followed by an examination of the different methods that can be used to allocate joint costs to products for inventory valuation. We shall then go on to discuss which costs are relevant for decision-making.

Distinguishing between joint products and by-products

Joint products and by-products arise in situations where the production of one product makes inevitable the production of other products. When a group of individual products is simultaneously

LEARNING OBJECTIVES

After studying this chapter, you should be able to:

● **distinguish between joint products and by-products;**

● **explain and identify the split-off point in a joint-cost situation;**

● **explain the alternative methods of allocating joint costs to products;**

● **discuss the arguments for and against each of the methods of allocating joint costs to products;**

● **present relevant financial information for a decision as to whether a product should be sold at a particular stage or further processed;**

● **describe the accounting treatment of by-products.**

produced, and each product has a significant relative sales value, the outputs are usually called joint products. Those products that are part of the simultaneous production process and have a minor sales value when compared with the joint products are called by-products.

As their name implies, by-products are those products that result incidentally from the main joint products. By-products may have a considerable absolute value, but the crucial classification test is that the sales value is small when compared with the values of the joint products. Joint products are crucial to the commercial viability of an organization, whereas by-products are incidental. In other words, by-products do not usually influence the decision as to whether or not to produce the main product, and they normally have little effect on the prices set for the main (joint) products. Examples of industries that produce both joint and by-products include chemicals, oil refining, mining, flour milling and gas manufacturing.

A distinguishing feature of the production of joint and by-products, is that the products are not identifiable as different individual products until a specific point in the production process is reached, known as the split-off point. All products may separate at one time, or different products may emerge at intervals. Before the split-off point, costs cannot be traced to particular products. For example, it is not possible to determine what part of the cost of processing a barrel of crude oil should be allocated to petrol, kerosene or paraffin. After the split-off point, joint products may be sold or subjected to further processing. If the latter is the case, any further processing costs can be traced to the specific products involved.

Figure 6.1 illustrates a simplified production process for joint and by-products. You will notice from this illustration that, at the split-off point, joint products A and B and by-product C all emerge, and that it is not possible to allocate costs of the joint process directly to the joint products or by-products. After the split-off point, further processing costs are added to the joint products before sale, and these costs can be specifically attributed to the joint products. By-product C in this instance is sold at the split-off point without further processing, although sometimes by-products may be further processed after the split-off point before they are sold on the outside market.

Methods of allocating joint costs

If all the production for a particular period was sold, the problem of allocating joint costs to products for inventory valuation and profit measurement would not exist. Inventory valuations would not be necessary, and the calculation of profit would merely require the deduction of total cost from total sales. However, if inventories are in existence at the end of the period, cost allocation to products are necessary. As any such allocations are bound to be subjective and arbitrary, this area will involve the accountant in making decisions which are among the most

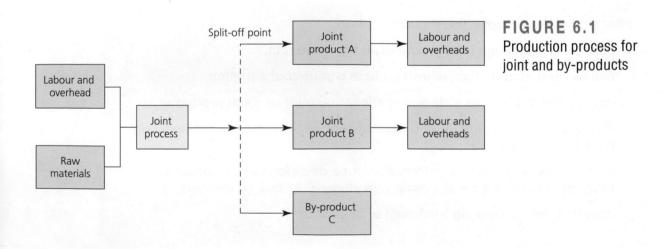

FIGURE 6.1
Production process for joint and by-products

difficult to defend. All one can do is to attempt to choose an allocation method that seems to provide a rational and reasonable method of cost distribution. The most frequently used methods that are used to allocate joint costs up to split-off point can be divided into the following two categories:

1 Methods based on physical measures such as weight, volume, etc.
2 Methods assumed to measure the ability to absorb joint costs based on allocating joint costs relative to the market values of the products.

We shall now look at four methods that are used for allocating joint costs using the information given in Example 6.1. In Example 6.1 products X, Y and Z all become finished products at the split-off point. The problem arises as to how much of the £600 000 joint costs should be allocated to each individual product? The £600 000 cannot be specifically identified with any of the individual products, since the products themselves were not separated before the split-off point, but some method must be used to split the £600 000 among the three products so that inventories can be valued and the profit for the period calculated. The first method we shall look at is called the physical measures method.

Physical measures method

Using the physical measures method, the cost allocation is a simple allocation of joint costs in proportion to volume. Each product is assumed to receive similar benefits from the joint cost, and is therefore charged with its proportionate share of the total cost. The cost allocations using this method are as follows:

Product	Units produced	Proportion to total	Joint costs allocated (£)	Cost per unit (£)
X	40 000	$\frac{1}{3}$	200 000	5
Y	20 000	$\frac{1}{6}$	100 000	5
Z	60 000	$\frac{1}{2}$	300 000	5
	120 000		600 000	

Note that this method assumes that the cost per unit is the same for each of the products. Therefore an alternative method of allocating joint costs is as follows:

$$\text{cost per unit} = £5 \ (£600\ 000/120\ 000)$$

EXAMPLE 6.1

During the month of July the Van Nostrand Company processes a basic raw material through a manufacturing process that yields three products – products X, Y and Z. There were no opening inventories and the products are sold at the split-off point without further processing. We shall initially assume that all of the output is sold during the period. Details of the production process and the sales revenues are given in the following diagram.

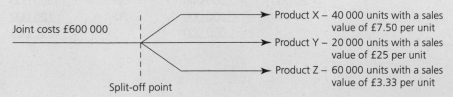

Joint costs £600 000

Split-off point

Product X – 40 000 units with a sales value of £7.50 per unit

Product Y – 20 000 units with a sales value of £25 per unit

Product Z – 60 000 units with a sales value of £3.33 per unit

Thus the joint cost allocations are:

$$Product X: 40\ 000 \times £5 = £200\ 000$$
$$Product Y: 20\ 000 \times £5 = £100\ 000$$
$$Product Z: 60\ 000 \times £5 = £300\ 000$$

Where market prices of the joint products differ, the assumptions of identical costs per unit for each joint product will result in some products showing high profits while others may show losses. This can give misleading profit calculations. Let us look at the product profit calculations using the information given in Example 6.1.

Product	Sales revenue (£)	Total cost (£)	Profit (loss) (£)	Profit/sales (%)
X	300 000	200 000	100 000	33⅓
Y	500 000	100 000	400 000	80
Z	200 000	300 000	(100 000)	(50)
	1 000 000	600 000	400 000	40

You will see from these figures that the allocation of the joint costs bears no relationship to the revenue-producing power of the individual products. Product Z is allocated with the largest share of the joint costs but has the lowest total sales revenue; product Y is allocated with the lowest share of the joint costs but has the highest total sales revenue. A further problem is that the joint products must be measurable by the same unit of measurement. Difficult measurement problems arise in respect of products emerging from the joint process consisting of solids, liquids and gases, and it is necessary to find some common base. For example, in the case of coke, allocations can be made on the basis of theoretical yields extracted from a ton of coke. The main advantage of using the physical measures method is simplicity, but this is outweighed by its many disadvantages.

Sales value at split-off point method

When the **sales value at split-off point method** is used, joint costs are allocated to joint products in proportion to the estimated sales value of production on the assumption that higher selling prices indicate higher costs. To a certain extent, this method could better be described as a means of apportioning profits or losses, according to sales value, rather than a method for allocating costs. Using the information in Example 6.1, the allocations under the sales value method would be as follows:

Product	Units produced	Sales value (£)	Proportion of sales value to total (%)	Joint costs allocated (£)
X	40 000	300 000	30	180 000
Y	20 000	500 000	50	300 000
Z	60 000	200 000	20	120 000
		1 000 000		600 000

The revised product profit calculations would be as follows:

Product	Sales revenue (£)	Total cost (£)	Profit (loss) (£)	Profit/sales (%)
X	300 000	180 000	120 000	40
Y	500 000	300 000	200 000	40
Z	200 000	120 000	80 000	40
	1 000 000	600 000	400 000	

The sales value method ensures that joint costs are allocated based on their ability to absorb joint costs but can be criticized since it is based on the assumption that sales revenue determines prior costs. For example, an unprofitable product with low sales revenue will be allocated with a small share of joint cost, thus giving the impression that it is generating profits.

Net realizable value method

In Example 6.1 we have assumed that all products are sold at the split-off point and that no additional costs are incurred beyond that point. In practice, however, it is likely that joint products will be processed individually beyond the split-off point, and market values may not exist for the products at this stage. To estimate the sales value at the split-off point, it is therefore necessary to use the estimated sales value at the point of sale and work backwards. This method is called the **net realizable value method**. The net realizable value at split-off point can be estimated by deducting from the sales revenues the further processing costs at the point of sale. This approach is illustrated with the data given in Example 6.2 which is the same as Example 6.1 except that further processing costs beyond split-off point are now assumed to exist. You should now refer to Example 6.2.

The calculation of the net realizable value and the allocation of joint costs using this method is as follows:

Product	Sales value (£)	Costs beyond split-off point (£)	Estimated net realizable value at split-off point (£)	Proportion to total (%)	Joint costs allocated (£)	Profit (£)	Gross profit (%)
X	300 000	80 000	220 000	27.5	165 000	55 000	18.33
Y	500 000	100 000	400 000	50.0	300 000	100 000	20.00
Z	200 000	20 000	180 000	22.5	135 000	45 000	22.50
	1 000 000	200 000	800 000		600 000	200 000	20.00

Note that the joint costs are allocated in proportion to each product's net realizable value at split-off point.

Constant gross profit percentage method

When the products are subject to further processing after split-off point and the net realizable method is used, the gross profit percentages are different for each product. In the above illustration they are 18.33 per cent for product X, 20 per cent for Y and 22.5 per cent for Z. It could be argued that, since the three products arise from a single productive process, they should earn identical gross profit percentages. The **constant gross profit percentage method** allocates joint costs so that the overall gross profit percentage is identical for each individual product. From the information contained in Example 6.2 the joint costs would be allocated in such a way that the

EXAMPLE 6.2

Assume the same situation as Example 6.1 except that further processing costs now apply. Details of the production process and sales revenues are given in the following diagram:

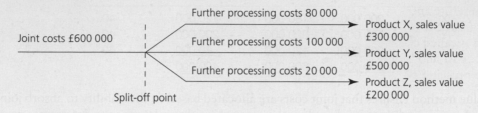

resulting gross profit percentage for each of the three products is equal to the overall gross profit percentage of 20 per cent. Note that the gross profit percentage is calculated by deducting the *total* costs of the three products (£800 000) from the *total* sales (£1 000 000) and expressing the profit (£200 000) as a percentage of sales. The calculations are as follows:

	Product X (£)	Product Y (£)	Product Z (£)	Total (£)
Sales value	300 000	500 000	200 000	1 000 000
Gross profit (20%)	60 000	100 000	40 000	200 000
Cost of goods sold	240 000	400 000	160 000	800 000
Less separable further processing costs	80 000	100 000	20 000	200 000
Allocated joint costs	160 000	300 000	140 000	600 000

You can see that the required gross profit percentage of 20 per cent is computed for each product. The additional further processing costs for each product are then deducted, and the balance represents the allocated joint costs.

The **constant gross profit percentage method** implicitly assumes that there is a uniform relationship between cost and sales value for each individual product. However, such an assumption is questionable, since we do not observe identical gross profit percentages for individual products in multi-product companies that do not involve joint costs.

Comparison of methods

What factors should be considered in selecting the most appropriate method of allocating joint costs? The cause-and-effect criterion, described in Chapter 3, cannot be used because there is no cause-and-effect relationship between the *individual* products and the incurrence of joint costs. Joint costs are caused by *all* products and not by individual products. Where cause-and-effect relationships cannot be established allocations ought to based on the benefits received criterion. If benefits received cannot be measured costs should be allocated based on the principle of equity or fairness. The net realizable method or the sales value at split-off point are the methods that best meet the benefits received criterion. The latter also has the added advantage of simplicity if sales values at the split-off point exists. It is also difficult to estimate the net realizable value in industries where there are numerous subsequent further processing stages and multiple split-off points. Similar measurement problems can also apply with the physical measures methods. In some industries a common denominator for physical measures for each product does not exist. For example, the output of the joint process may consist of a combination of solids, liquids and gases.

The purpose for which joint-cost allocations are used is also important. Besides being required for inventory valuation and profit measurement joint-cost allocations may be used as a mechanism for setting selling prices. For example, some utilities recharge their customers for usage of joint facilities. If market prices do not exist selling prices are likely to be determined by adding a suitable profit margin to the costs allocated to the products. The method used to allocate joint costs will therefore influence product costs, and in turn, the selling price. If external market prices do not exist it is illogical to use sales value methods to allocate joint costs. This would involve what is called circular reasoning because cost allocations determine selling prices, which in turn affect cost allocations, which will also lead to further changes in selling prices and sales revenues. For pricing purposes a physical measures method should be used if external market prices do not exist. What methods do companies actually use? Little empirical evidence exists apart from a UK survey by Slater and Wootton (1984). Their survey findings are presented in Exhibit 6.1. You will see that a physical measures method is most widely used. In practice firms are likely to use a method where the output from the joint process can be measured without too much difficulty. Establishing a common output measure is extremely difficult in some organizations. To overcome this problem they value inventories at their estimated net realizable value minus a normal profit margin.

Irrelevance of joint cost allocations for decision-making

Our previous discussion has concentrated on the allocation of joint costs for inventory valuation and profit measurement. Joint product costs that have been computed for inventory valuation are normally inappropriate for decision-making. For decision-making relevant costs should be used – these represent the incremental costs relating to a decision. Therefore costs that will be unaffected by a decision are classed as irrelevant. Joint-cost allocations are thus irrelevant for decision-making. Consider the information presented in Example 6.3.

EXHIBIT 6.1 Surveys of company practice

A survey of UK chemical and oil refining companies by Slater and Wootton (1984) reported the following methods of allocating joint costs:

	%
Physical measures method	76
Sales value method	5
Negotiated basis	19
Other	14

Note
The percentages add up to more than 100% because some companies used more than one method.

The analysis by industry indicated that the following methods were used:

Type of company	Predominant cost allocation method used
Petrochemicals	Sales value at split-off point or estimated net realizable method
Coal processing	Physical measures method
Coal chemicals	Physical measures method
Oil refining	No allocation of joint costs

The joint cost of £1 000 000 will be incurred irrespective of which decision is taken, and is not relevant for this decision. The information which is required for the decision is a comparison of the additional costs with the additional revenues from converting product Y into product Z. The following information should therefore be provided:

Additional revenue and costs from converting product Y into product Z	(£)
Additional revenues (50 000 × £2)	100 000
Additional conversion costs	60 000
Additional profit from conversion	40 000

REAL WORLD VIEWS 6.1

Joint product costing in the semiconductor industry

In the semiconductor industry, the production of memory chips may be viewed as a joint processing situation because the output consists of different quality chips from a common production run. The manufacturing operation is composed of three phases: fabrication, assembly, and a 'stress test'. The first and second steps are mandatory. The third is optional and necessary to produce memory with a longer life expectancy. Of the three cases, only fabrication represents a joint production process; assembly and stress testing are separable steps.

The input to the fabrication phase is raw silicon wafers, which are first photolithographed and then baked at high temperatures. Each wafer will yield multiple chips of identical design. Upon completion of the fabrication process, the finished wafer is tested to identify usable and unusable chips. The test also classifies usable chips according to density (the number of good memory bits) and speed (the time required to access those bits.)

The input to the assembly process is usable chips, which are encapsulated in ceramic and wired for use on a memory board. The encapsulation process varies according to the number of chips, which constitute a finished module. Modules of a given density may be composed of one all-good chip or multiple partially-good chips. The finished modules are subjected to a nondestructive functional test to identify defective output.

If an extended life expectancy is not required, the good modules are not processed any further. A small sample of the good modules is subjected to the destructive reliability test before the finished product is considered salable. This destructive reliability test is a traditional quality control step designed to establish the 'time-to-failure' distribution of the output. The profile of this distribution will depend, in part, upon whether the modules were subjected to the optional stress test.

If a longer life expectancy is desired, the modules are stressed before being tested for reliability. This optional step exposes the modules to extreme conditions and those that survive are labelled extended-life modules. The proportion of the modules selected to undergo the stress test is under management control and can be varied with market conditions.

The final output of the process differs in quality according to a variety of dimensions. These include number of chips per module, speed, life expectancy, and temperature tolerance.

Discussion point

Which costs are relevant for determining whether an extended life expectancy is required for the good modules?

© KRZYSZTOF ZMIJ/ISTOCKPHOTO.COM

SOURCE: ADAPTED FROM CATS-BARIL ET AL., JOINT PRODUCT COSTING IN THE SEMICONDUCTOR INDUSTRY, MANAGEMENT ACCOUNTING (USA), PP. 28–35.

EXAMPLE 6.3

The Adriatic Company incurs joint product costs of £1 000 000 for the production of two joint products, X and Y. Both products can be sold at split-off point. However, if additional costs of £60 000 are incurred on product Y then it can be converted into product Z and sold for £10 per unit. The joint costs and the sales revenue at split-off point are illustrated in the following diagram:

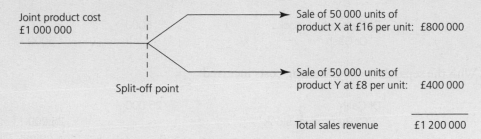

You are requested to advise management whether or not product Y should be converted in product Z.

The proof that profits will increase by £40 000 if conversion takes place is as follows:

	Convert to product Z (£)	Do not convert (£)
Sales	1 300 000	1 200 000
Total costs	1 060 000	1 000 000
Profits	240 000	200 000

The general rule is that it will be profitable to extend the processing of a joint product so long as the additional revenues exceed the additional costs, but note that the variable portion of the joint costs will be relevant for some decisions. For an illustration of a situation where joint variable costs are relevant for decision-making. You should refer to Learning Note 6.1 on the open access website (see Preface for details).

Accounting for by-products

By-products are products that have a minor sales value and that emerge incidentally from the production of the major product. As the major objective of the company is to produce the joint products, it can justifiably be argued that the joint costs should be allocated only to the joint products and that the by-products should not be allocated with any portion of the joint cost that are incurred before the split-off point. Any costs that are incurred in producing by-products after the split-off point can justifiably be charged to the by-product, since such costs are incurred for the benefit of the by-product only.

By-product revenues or by-product net revenues (the sales revenue of the by-product less the additional further processing costs after the split-off point) should be deducted from the cost of the joint products or the main product from which it emerges. Consider Example 6.4.

None of the joint costs shown in Example 6.4 is allocated to the by-product but the further processing costs of £5000 (5000 kg × £1) are charged to the by-product. The net revenues from the by-product of £20 000 (sales revenue of £25 000 less further processing costs of £5000) are deducted from the costs of the joint process (£3 020 000). Thus joint costs of £3 000 000 will be allocated to joint products A and B using one of the allocation methods described in this chapter. The accounting entries for the by-product will be as follows:

Dr By-product stock (5000 × £4)	20 000	
Cr Joint process WIP account		20 000

With the net revenue due from the production of the by-product:

Dr By-product stock	5000	
Cr Cash		5000

With the separable manufacturing costs incurred:

Dr Cash	25 000	
Cr By-product stock		25 000

With the value of by-products sales for the period.

EXAMPLE 6.4

The Neopolitan Company operates a manufacturing process which produces joint products A and B and by-product C. The joint costs of the manufacturing process are £3 020 000, incurred in the manufacture of:

Product A	30 000 kg
Product B	50 000 kg
Product C	5 000 kg

By-product C requires further processing at a cost of £1 per kg, after which it can be sold at £5 per kg.

SOURCE: WWW.KADANTGRANTEK.COM.

REAL WORLD VIEWS 6.2

Environmentally friendly products from paper-mill sludge

Each year, the paper and pulp industry produce millions of tons of sludge in the production of paper. This sludge is typically disposed of in landfill sites or incinerated. Both disposal methods are costly and environmentally undesirable. However, some firms are now transforming undesirable by-products in to commercially viable consumer and industrial products.

One such firm is Kadant Grantek Inc, based in Wisconsin, USA. Kadant Grantek process paper mill sludge from local paper mills at a rate of approximately 250 tons per day. The sludge is dried and granulated to make a number of products – an agricultural seed carrier called Biodac, an industrial absorbent called Gran-sorb and a cat litter called PaPurr. The process is clean, releasing only steam in to the atmosphere. No waste or further by-products are produced.

Kadant Grantek collect the paper mill sludge free of charge from the paper mills. The paper mills in turn do not incur landfill or incineration costs and can portray a greener image. A win-win situation for both parties.

Discussion point

Assuming paper mills decide to sell their sludge for a small fee, how might they account for the revenue generated?

SUMMARY

The following items relate to the learning objectives listed at the beginning of the chapter.

● **Distinguish between joint products and by-products.**

Both joint products and by-products arise from a joint production process whereby the products are not separately identifiable until after they have emerged from this joint process. Joint products have relatively high sales value whereas by-products have a low sales value compared with the sales value of a joint product. Joint products are also crucial to the commercial viability of an organization, whereas by-products are incidental.

● **Explain and identify the split-off point in a joint cost situation.**

The split-off point is the point in the process when products become separately identifiable.

● **Explain the alternative methods of allocating joint costs to products.**

Four different methods of allocating joint costs to products were described – physical measures, sales value at split-off point, net realizable value and gross profit percentage methods. The physical measures method simply allocates joint costs to individual products in proportion to their production volumes. The second method allocates joint costs to individual products based on their sales value at split-off point. If market prices of products at the split-off point do not exist, the sales value can be estimated using the net realizable method. With this method the net realizable values of the joint products at split-off point are estimated by deducting the further processing costs from the sales value at the point of sale. The gross profit percentage method allocates joint costs so that the overall gross profit percentage is identical for each product.

● **Discuss the arguments for and against each of the methods of allocating joint costs to products.**

Cost should be allocated based on cause-and-effect relationships. Such relationships cannot be observed with joint products. When this situation occurs it is recommended that joint costs should be allocated based on the benefits received criterion. The advantage of the physical measures method is its simplicity but it suffers from the disadvantage that it can lead to a situation where the recorded joint cost inventory valuation for a product is in excess of its net realizable value. The sales value at split-off point suffers from the disadvantage that sales values for many joint products do not exist at the split-off point. The gross profit percentage method assumes that there is a uniform relationship between cost and sales value for each product. However, such a relationship is questionable since identical gross profit percentages for individual products in multi-product companies that do not have joint costs are not observed. Both the sales value at split-off point and the net realizable value methods most closely meet the benefits received criterion but the latter is likely to be the preferred method if sales values at the split-off point do not exist.

● **Present relevant financial information for a decision as to whether a product should be sold at a particular stage or further processed.**

The joint costs allocated to products are irrelevant for decisions relating to further processing. Such decisions should be based on a comparison of the incremental costs with the incremental revenues arising from further processing. The presentation of relevant financial information for further processing decisions was illustrated using the data presented in Example 6.3.

● **Describe the accounting treatment of by-products.**

By-product net-revenues should be deducted from the cost of the joint production process prior to allocating the costs to the individual joint products. The accounting treatment of by-products was illustrated with the data presented in Example 6.4.

Key terms and concepts

by-products (p. 126, p. 133)
constant gross profit percentage
    method (p. 129, p. 130)
further processing costs (p. 126)

joint products (p. 126)
net realizable value method (p. 129)
physical measures method (p. 127)

sales value at split-off point method
    (p. 128)
split-off point (p. 126)

Recommended readings

For a description of a system of joint product costing involving the production of memory chips of differing quality in the semiconductor industry in the USA you should refer to Cats-Baril *et al.* (1986). Research publications relating to the costs and joint products of English teaching hospitals and joint blood product costs are reported respectively in Perrin (1987) and Trenchard and Dixon (2003). For a more detailed discussion of cost allocations in general you should refer to Ahmed and Scapens (1991) and Young (1985).

Key examination points

It is necessary to apportion joint costs to joint products for inventory valuation and profit measurement purposes. Remember that the costs calculated for inventory valuation purposes should not be used for decision-making purposes. Examination questions normally require joint product cost calculations and the presentation of information as to whether a product should be sold at split-off point or further processed (see the answers to Review problems 6.12 and 6.13). A common mistake with the latter requirement is to include joint cost apportionments. You should compare incremental revenues with incremental costs and indicate that, in the short term, joint costs are not relevant to the decision to sell at the split-off point or process further.

ASSESSMENT MATERIAL

The review questions are short questions that enable you to assess your understanding of the main topics included in the chapter. The numbers in parentheses provide you with the page numbers to refer to if you cannot answer a specific question.

The review problems are more complex and require you to relate and apply the content to various business problems. The problems are graded by their level of difficulty. Solutions to review problems that are not preceded by the term 'IM' are provided in a separate section at the end of the book. Solutions to problems preceded by the term 'IM' are provided in the *Instructor's Manual* accompanying this book and also on the lecturer's password protected section of the website www.drury-online.com. Additional review problems with fully worked solutions are provided in the *Student's Manual* that accompanies this book.

Review questions

6.1 Define joint costs, split-off point and further processing costs. (*p. 126*)
6.2 Distinguish between joint products and by-products. (*p. 126*)
6.3 Provide examples of industries that produce both joint products and by-products. (*p. 126*)
6.4 Explain why it is necessary to allocate joint costs to products. (*p. 126*)
6.5 Describe the four different methods of allocating joint costs to products. (*pp. 127–30*)
6.6 Why is the physical measure method considered to be an unsatisfactory joint-cost allocation method? (*p. 128*)
6.7 Explain the factors that should influence the choice of method when allocating joint costs to products. (*pp. 130–31*)
6.8 Explain the financial information that should be included in a decision as to whether a product should be sold at the split-off point or further processed. (*pp. 131–33*)
6.9 Describe the accounting treatment of by-products. (*pp. 133–34*)

Review problems

6.10 Basic. A company simultaneously produces three products (X, Y and Z) from a single process. X and Y are processed further before they can be sold; Z is a by-product that is sold immediately for $6 per unit without incurring any further costs. The sales prices of X and Y after further processing are $50 per unit and $60 per unit respectively.

Data for October are as follows:

	$
Joint production costs that produced 2500 units of X, 3500 units of Y and 3000 units of Z	140 000
Further processing costs for 2500 units of X	24 000
Further processing costs for 3500 units of Y	46 000

Joint costs are apportioned using the final sales value method.

Calculate the total cost of the production of X for October.

(*3 marks*)

CIMA P1 Management Accounting, Performance Evaluation

6.11 Intermediate: Apportionment of joint costs. The marketing director of your company has expressed concern about product X, which for some time has shown a loss, and has stated that some action will have to be taken.

Product X is produced from material A which is one of two raw materials jointly produced by passing chemicals through a process.

Representative data for the process is as follows:

Output (kg):	
Material A	10 000
Material B	30 000
Process B (£):	
Raw material	83 600
Conversion costs	58 000

Joint costs are apportioned to the two raw materials according to the weight of output.

Production costs incurred in converting material A into product X are £1.80 per kg of material A used. A yield of 90 per cent is achieved. Product X is sold for £5.60 per kg. Material B is sold without further processing for £6.00 per kg.

Required:

a   Calculate the profit/loss per kg of product X and material B, respectively.   (*7 marks*)
b   Comment upon the marketing director's concern, advising him whether you consider any action should be taken.   (*7 marks*)
c   Demonstrate an alternative joint cost apportionment for product X and comment briefly upon this alternative method of apportionment.   (*8 marks*)

ACCA Level 1 Costing

6.12 Intermediate: Preparation of profit statements and decision on further processing.

a   Polimur Ltd operates a process that produces three joint products, all in an unrefined condition. The operating results of the process for October 2000 are shown below.

Output from process:	
Product A	100 tonnes
Product B	80 tonnes
Product C	80 tonnes

The month's operating costs were £1 300 000. The closing stocks were 20 tonnes of A, 15 tonnes of B and 5 tonnes of C. The value of the closing stock is calculated by apportioning costs according to weight of output. There were no opening stocks and the balance of the output was sold to a refining company at the following prices:

Product A	£5 per kg
Product B	£4 per kg
Product C	£9 per kg

Required:
Prepare an operating statement showing the relevant trading results for October 2000.   (*6 marks*)

b   The management of Polimur Ltd have been considering a proposal to establish their own refining operations.

The current market prices of the refined products are:

Product A	£17 per kg
Product B	£14 per kg
Product C	£20.50 per kg

The estimated unit costs of the refining operation are:

	Product A (£ per kg)	Product B (£ per kg)	Product C (£ per kg)
Direct materials	0.50	0.75	2.50
Direct labour	2.00	3.00	4.00
Variable overheads	1.50	2.25	5.50

Prime costs would be variable. Fixed overheads, which would be £700 000 monthly, would be direct to the refining operation. Special equipment is required for refining product B and this would be rented at a cost, not included in the above figures, of £360 000 per month.

It may be assumed that there would be no weight loss in the refining process and that the quantity refined each month would be similar to October's output shown in (a) above.

Required:

Prepare a statement that will assist management to evaluate the proposal to commence refining operations. Include any further comments or observations you consider relevant.

(16 marks)
ACCA Foundation Costing

6.13 Advanced: Calculation of joint product costs and the evaluation of an incremental order. Rayman Company produces three chemical products, J1X, J2Y and B1Z. Raw materials are processed in a single plant to produce two intermediate products, J1 and J2, in fixed proportions. There is no market for these two intermediate products. J1 is processed further through process X to yield the product J1X, product J2 is converted into J2Y by a separate finishing process Y. The Y finishing process produces both J2Y and a waste material, B1, which has no market value. The Rayman Company can convert B1, after additional processing through process Z, into a saleable by-product, B1Z. The company can sell as much B1Z as it can produce at a price of £1.50 per kg.

At normal levels of production and sales, 600 000 kg of the common input material are processed each month. There are 440 000 kg and 110 000 kg respectively, of the intermediate products J1 and J2, produced from this level of input. After the separate finishing processes, fixed proportions of J1X, J2Y and B1Z emerge, as shown below with current market prices (all losses are normal losses).

Product	Quantity kg	Market Price per kg
J1X	400 000	£2.425
J2Y	100 000	£4.50
B1Z	10 000	£1.50

At these normal volumes, materials and processing costs are as follows:

	Common Plant Facility (£000)	Separate Finishing Processes X (£000)	Separate Finishing Processes Y (£000)	Separate Finishing Processes Z (£000)
Direct materials	320	110	15	1.0
Direct labour	150	225	90	5.5
Variable overhead	30	50	25	0.5
Fixed overhead	50	25	5	3.0
Total	550	410	135	10.0

Selling and administrative costs are entirely fixed and cannot be traced to any of the three products.

Required:

a Draw a diagram which shows the flow of these products, through the processes, label the diagram and show the quantities involved in normal operation. *(2 marks)*

b Calculate the *cost per unit* of the finished products J1X and J2Y and the *total manufacturing profit*, for the month, attributed to each product assuming all joint costs are allocated based on:
  (i)   physical units *(3 marks)*
  (ii) net realizable value *(4 marks)*
  and comment briefly on the two methods. *(3 marks)*
  NB All losses are normal losses.

c A new customer has approached Rayman wishing to purchase 10 000 kg of J2Y for £4.00 per kg. This is extra to the present level of business indicated above.

Advise the management how they may respond to this approach by:
(i)   Developing a financial evaluation of the offer. *(4 marks)*
(ii) Clarifying any assumptions and further questions which may apply. *(4 marks)*
ACCA Paper 8 Managerial Finance

IM6.1 Intermediate.

a Explain briefly the term 'joint products' in the context of process costing. *(2 marks)*

b Discuss whether, and if so how, joint process costs should be shared among joint products. (Assume that no further processing is required after the split-off point.) *(11 marks)*

c Explain briefly the concept of 'equivalent units' in process costing. *(4 marks)*
ACCA Level 1 Costing

IM6.2 Intermediate.

a Discuss the problems which joint products and by-products pose the management accountant, especially in his attempts to produce useful product profitability reports. Outline the usual accounting treatments of joint and by-products and indicate the extent to which these treatments are effective in overcoming the problems you have discussed. In your answer clearly describe the differences between joint and by-products and provide an example of each. *(14 marks)*

b A common process produces several joint products. After the common process has been completed each product requires further specific, and directly attributable, expenditure in order to 'finish off' the product and put it in a saleable condition. Specify the conditions under which it is rational to undertake:
(i)   the common process, and
(ii) the final 'finishing off' of each of the products which are the output from the common process.
Illustrate your answer with a single numerical example. *(6 marks)*
ACCA P2 Management Accounting

IM6.3 Intermediate. Explain how the apportionment of those costs incurred up to the separation point of two or more joint products could give information which is unacceptable for (i) stock valuation and (ii) decision-making. Use figures of your own choice to illustrate your answer. *(9 marks)*
ACCA Level 2 Management Accounting

IM6.4 Intermediate: Preparation of joint and by-product process account. XYZ plc, a paint manufacturer, operates a process costing system. The following details related to process 2 for the month of October:

Opening work in progress	5000 litres fully complete as to transfers from process 1 and 40% complete as to labour and overhead, valued at £60 000
Transfer from process 1	65 000 litres valued at cost of £578 500
Direct labour	£101 400
Variable overhead	£80 000
Fixed overhead	£40 000
Normal loss	5% of volume transferred from process 1, scrap value £2.00 per litre
Actual output	30 000 litres of paint X (a joint product) 25 000 litres of paint Y (a joint product) 7000 litres of by-product Z
Closing work in progress	6000 litres fully complete as to transfers from process 1 and 60% complete as to labour and overhead.

The final selling price of products X, Y and Z are:

Paint X	£15.00 per litre
Paint Y	£18.00 per litre
Product Z	£4.00 per litre

There are no further processing costs associated with either paint X or the by-product, but paint Y requires further processing at a cost of £1.50 per litre.

All three products incur packaging costs of £0.50 per litre before they can be sold.

Required:

a Prepare the process 2 account for the month of October, apportioning the common costs between the joint products, based upon their values at the point of separation   (20 marks)

b Prepare the abnormal loss/gain account, showing clearly the amount to be transferred to the profit and loss account. (4 marks)

c Describe one other method of apportioning the common costs between the joint products, *and* explain why it is necessary to make such apportionments, and their usefulness when measuring product profitability.   (6 marks)

CIMA Stage 2 Operational Cost Accounting

IM6.5 Intermediate: Joint cost apportionment and a decision on further processing. QR Limited operates a chemical process which produces four different products Q, R, S and T from the input of one raw material plus water. Budget information for the forthcoming financial year is as follows:

	(£000)
Raw materials cost	268
Initial processing cost	464

Product	Output in litres	Sales (£1000)	Additional processing cost (£000
Q	400 000	768	160
R	90 000	232	128
S	5 000	32	–
T	9 000	240	8

The company policy is to apportion the costs prior to the split-off point on a method based on net sales value.

Currently, the intention is to sell product S without further processing but to process the other three products after the split-off point. However, it has been proposed that an alternative strategy would be to sell all four products at the split-off point without further processing. If this were done the selling prices obtainable would be as follows:

	Per litre (£)
Q	1.28
R	1.60
S	6.40
T	20.00

You are required:

a to prepare budgeted profit statement showing the profit or loss for each product, and in total, if the current intention is proceeded with;   (10 marks)

b to show the profit or loss by product, and in total, if the alternative strategy were to be adopted;   (6 marks)

c to recommend what should be done and why, assuming that there is no more profitable alternative use for the plant.   (4 marks)

CIMA Stage 2 Cost Accounting

IM6.6 Intermediate: Joint cost apportionment and decision on further processing. A company manufactures four products from an input of a raw material to process 1. Following this process, product A is processed in process 2, product B in process 3, product C in process 4 and product D in process 5.

The normal loss in process 1 is 10 per cent of input, and there are no expected losses in the other processes. Scrap value in process 1 is £0.50 per litre. The costs incurred in process 1 are apportioned to each product according to the volume of output of each product. Production overhead is absorbed as a percentage of direct wages.

Data in respect of the month of October:

	Process					
	1 (£000)	2 (£000)	3 (£000)	4 (£000)	5 (£000)	Total (£000)
Direct materials at £1.25 per litre	100					100
Direct wages	48	12	8	4	16	88
Production overhead						66

	Product			
	A	B	C	D
Output (litres)	22 000	20 000	10 000	18 000
Selling price (£)	4.00	3.00	2.00	5.00
Estimated sales value at end of Process 1 (£)	2.50	2.80	1.20	3.00

You are required to:

a calculate the profit or loss for each product for the month, assuming all output is sold at the normal selling price;   (4 marks)

b suggest and evaluate an alternative production strategy which would optimize profit for the month. It should not be assumed that the output of process 1 can be changed;   (12 marks)

c suggest to what management should devote its attention, if it is to achieve the potential benefit indicated in (b).   (4 marks)

CIMA P1 Cost Accounting 2

IM6.7 Advanced: Joint cost stock valuation and decision-making. Milo plc has a number of chemical processing plants in the UK. At one of these plants it takes an annual input of 400 000 gallons of raw material A and converts it into two liquid products, B and C.

The standard yield from one gallon of material A is 0.65 gallons of B and 0.3 gallons of C. Product B is processed further, without volume loss, and then sold as product D. Product C has hitherto been sold without further processing. In the year ended 31 July 2000, the cost of material A was £20 per gallon. The selling price of product C was £5 per gallon and transport costs from plant to customer were £74 000.

Negotiations are taking place with Takeup Ltd who would purchase the total production of product C for the years ending 31 July 2001 and 2002 provided it was converted to product E by further processing. It is unlikely that the contract would be renewed after 31 July 2002. New specialized transport costing £120 000 and special vats costing £80 000 will have to be acquired if the contract is to be undertaken. The vats will be installed in part of the existing factory that is presently unused and for which no use has been forecast for the next three years. Both transport and vats will have no residual value at the end of the contract. The company uses straight line depreciation.

Projected data for 2001 and 2002 are as follows:

	Liquid A	Liquid D	Liquid E
Amount processed (gallons)	400 000		
Processing costs (£):			
Cost of liquid A per gallon	20		
Wages to split-off	400 000 p.a.		
Overheads to split-off	250 000 p.a.		
Further processing			
Materials per gallon		3.50	3.30
Wages per gallon		2.50	1.70
Overheads		52 000 p.a.	37 000 p.a.
Selling costs (£):			
Total expenses	–	125 000 p.a.	–
Selling price per gallon (£)		40.00	15.50
Total plant administration costs are £95 000 p.a.			

You are required to:

a Show whether or not Milo plc should accept the contract and produce liquid E in 2001 and 2002.   (5 marks)

b Prepare a pro forma income statement which can be used to evaluate the performance of the individual products sold, assuming all liquid processed is sold, in the financial year to 31 July 2001,
(i) assuming liquids D and C are sold,
(ii) assuming liquids D and E are sold.
Give reasons for the layout adopted and comment on the apportionment of pre-separation costs.   (12 marks)

c Calculate, assuming that 10 000 gallons of liquid C remain unsold at 31 July 2000, and using the FIFO basis for inventory valuation, what would be the valuation of:
(i) the stock of liquid C, and
(ii) 10 000 gallons of liquid E after conversion from liquid C.   (4 marks)

d Calculate an inventory valuation at replacement cost of 10 000 gallons of liquid E in stock at 31 July 2001, assuming that the cost of material A is to be increased by 25 per cent from that date; and comment on the advisability of using replacement cost for inventory valuation purposes in the monthly management accounts.   (4 marks)

Note: Ignore taxation.

ICAEW P2 Management Accounting

IM6.8 Advanced: Cost per unit calculation and decision-making. A chemical company has a contract to supply annually 3600 tonnes of product A at £24 a tonne and 4000 tonnes of product B at £14.50 a tonne. The basic components for these products are obtained from a joint initial distillation process. From this joint distillation a residue is produced which is processed to yield 380 tonnes of by-product Z. By-product Z is sold locally at £5 a tonne and the net income is credited to the joint distillation process.

The budget for the year ending 30 June 2001 includes the following data:

| | Joint Process | Separable cost | | By-product Z |
		Product A	Product B	
Variable cost per tonne of input (£)	5	11	2	1
Fixed costs for year (£)	5000	4000	8000	500
Evaporation loss in process (% of input)	6	10	20	5

Since the budget was compiled it has been decided that an extensive five-week overhaul of the joint distillation plant will be necessary during the year. This will cost an additional £17 000 in repair costs and reduce all production in the year by 10 per cent. Supplies of the products can be imported to meet the contract commitment at a cost of £25 a tonne for A and £15 a tonne for B.

Experiments have also shown that the joint distillation plant operations could be changed during the year such that either:

(i) The output of distillate for product A would increase by 200 tonnes with a corresponding reduction in product B distillate. This change would increase the joint distillation variable costs for the whole of that operation by 2 per cent, or

(ii) The residue for by-product Z could be mixed with distillate for products A and B proportionate to the present output of these products. By intensifying the subsequent processing for products A and B acceptable quality could be obtained. The intensified operation would increase product A and B separable fixed costs by 5 per cent and increase the evaporation loss for the whole operation to 11 per cent and 21 per cent respectively.

You are required to:

a calculate on the basis of the original budget:
   (i) the unit costs of products A and B; and
   (ii) the total profit for the year;

b calculate the change in the unit costs of products A and B based on the reduced production;

c calculate the profit for the year if the shortfall of production is made up by imported products;

d advise management whether either of the alternative distillation operations would improve the profitability calculated under (c) and whether you recommend the use of either.   (30 marks)

CIMA P3 Management Accounting

IM6.9 Advanced: Calculation of cost per unit, break-even point and a recommended selling price. A chemical company produces amongst its product range two industrial cleaning fluids, A and B. These products are manufactured jointly. In 2001 total sales are expected to be restricted because home trade outlets for fluid B are limited to 54 000 gallons for the year. At this level plant capacity will be under-utilized by 25 per cent.

From the information given below you are required to:

a draw a flow diagram of the operations;

b calculate separately for fluids A and B for the year:
   (i) total manufacturing cost;
   (ii) manufacturing cost per gallon;
   (iii) list price per gallon;
   (iv) profit for the year.

c calculate the break-even price per gallon to manufacture an extra 3000 gallons of fluid B for export and which would incur selling, distribution and administration costs of £1260;

d state the price you would recommend the company should quote per gallon for this export business, with a brief explanation for your decision.

The following data are given:

1. Description of processes

Process 1: Raw materials L and M are mixed together and filtered. There is an evaporation loss of 10 per cent.

Process 2: The mixture from Process 1 is boiled and this reduces the volume by 20 per cent. The remaining liquid distils into 50 per cent extract A, 25 per cent extract B, and 25 per cent by-product C.

Process 3: Two parts of extract A are blended with one part of raw material N, and one part of extract B with one part of raw material N, to form respectively fluids A and B.

Process 4: Fluid A is filled into one-gallon labelled bottles and fluid B into six-gallon preprinted drums and they are then both ready for sale. One percent wastage in labels occurs in this process.

2. Costs

Cost per gallon (£)	
Raw material L	0.20
Raw material M	0.50
Raw material N	2.00

	Cost (£)
Containers: 1-gallon bottles	0.27 each
Containers: 6-gallon drums	5.80 each
Bottle labels, per thousand	2.20

Direct wages:	Per gallon of input processed (£)
Process 1	0.11
Process 2	0.15
Process 3	0.20
Process 4	0.30

Manufacturing overhead:

Process	Fixed per annum (£)	Variable, per gallon of input processed (£)
1	6 000	0.04
2	20 250	0.20
3	19 500	0.10
4	14 250	0.10

By-product C is collected in bulk by a local company which pays £0.50 per gallon for it and the income is credited to process 2.

Process costs are apportioned entirely to the two main products on the basis of their output from each process.

No inventories of part-finished materials are held at any time.

Fluid A is sold through agents on the basis of list price less 20 per cent and fluid B at list price less 33 1/3 per cent.

Of the net selling price, profit amounts to 8 per cent, selling and distribution costs to 12 per cent and administration costs to 5 per cent. Taxation should be ignored.

CIMA P3 Management Accounting

Income effects of alternative cost accumulation systems

7

In the previous chapters we looked at the procedures necessary to ascertain product or job costs for inventory valuation to meet the requirements of external reporting. The approach that we adopted was to allocate all manufacturing cost to products, and to value unsold stocks at their total cost of manufacture. Non-manufacturing costs were not allocated to the products but were charged directly to the profit statement and excluded from the inventory valuation. A costing system based on these principles is known as an absorption or full costing system.

In this chapter we are going to look at an alternative costing system known as variable costing, marginal costing or direct costing. Under this alternative system, only variable manufacturing costs are assigned to products and included in the inventory valuation. Fixed manufacturing costs are not allocated to the product, but are considered as period costs and charged directly to the profit statement. Both absorption costing and variable costing systems are in complete agreement regarding the treatment of non-manufacturing costs as period costs. The disagreement between the proponents of absorption costing and the proponents of variable costing is concerned with whether or not manufacturing fixed overhead should be regarded as a period cost or a product cost. An illustration of the different treatment of fixed manufacturing overhead for both

LEARNING OBJECTIVES

After studying this chapter, you should be able to:

- explain the differences between an absorption costing and a variable costing system;

- prepare profit statements based on a variable costing and absorption costing system;

- explain the difference in profits between variable and absorption costing profit calculations;

- explain the arguments for and against variable and absorption costing;

- describe the various denominator levels that can be used with an absorption costing system;

- explain why the choice of an appropriate denominator level is important.

absorption and variable costing systems is shown in Exhibit 7.1. You should note that in Exhibit 7.1 direct labour is assumed to be a variable cost. Generally direct labour is not a short term variable cost that varies in direct proportion to the volume of activity. It is a step fixed cost (see Chapter 2) that varies in the longer term. In other words, it is a longer term variable cost. Because of this, variable costing systems generally assume that direct labour is a variable cost.

External and internal reporting

Many writers have argued the cases for and against variable costing for inventory valuation for external reporting. One important requirement for external reporting is consistency. It would be

EXHIBIT 7.1 Absorption and variable costing systems

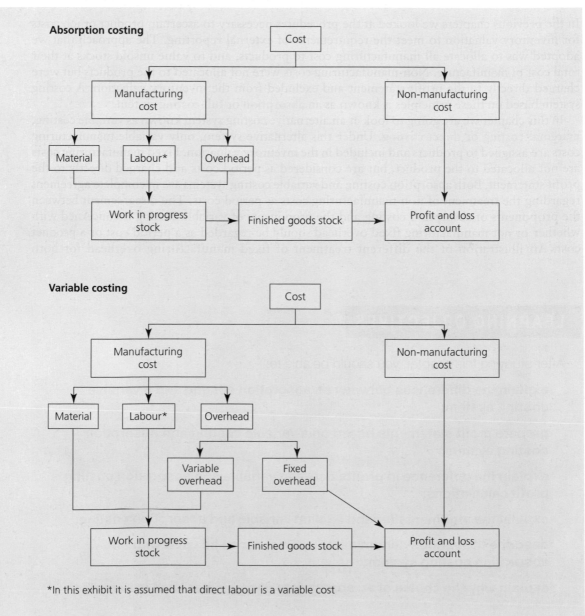

*In this exhibit it is assumed that direct labour is a variable cost

unacceptable if companies changed their methods of inventory valuation from year to year. In addition, inter-company comparison would be difficult if some companies valued their stocks on an absorption cost basis while others did so on a variable cost basis. Furthermore, the users of external accounting reports need reassurance that the published financial statements have been prepared in accordance with generally accepted standards of good accounting practice. Therefore there is a strong case for the acceptance of one method of stock valuation for external reporting. In the UK a Statement of Standard Accounting Practice on Stocks and Work in Progress was published by the Accounting Standards Committee (SSAP 9). This states:

> In order to match costs and revenue, cost of stocks and work in progress should comprise that expenditure which has been incurred in the normal course of business in bringing the product or service to its present location and condition. Such costs will include all related production overheads, even though these may accrue on a time basis.

The effect of this statement in SSAP 9 was to require absorption costing for external reporting and for non-manufacturing costs to be treated as period costs. The International Accounting Standard on Inventories (IAS2) also requires that companies in other countries adopt absorption costing.

In spite of the fact that absorption costing is required for external reporting, the variable costing versus absorption costing debate is still of considerable importance for internal reporting. Management normally require profit statements at monthly or quarterly intervals, and will no doubt wish to receive separate profit statements for each major product group or segment of the business. This information is particularly useful in evaluating the performance of divisional managers. Management must therefore decide whether absorption costing or variable costing provides the more meaningful information in assessing the economic and managerial performance of the different segments of the business.

However, before discussing the arguments for and against absorption and variable costing, let us look at a simple illustration of both methods using Example 7.1. To keep things simple we shall assume that the company in this example produces only one product using a single overhead rate for the company as a whole, with units of output being used as the allocation base. These assumptions are very simplistic, but the same general principles apply to both simplistic and complex product settings relating to the impact that variable and absorption costing have on profit measurement and inventory valuation. A more complex example would not enhance your understanding of the issues involved. You should now refer to Example 7.1.

EXAMPLE 7.1

The following information is available for periods 1 6 for the Samuelson Company:

	(£)
Unit selling price	10
Unit variable cost	6
Fixed costs per each period	300 000

The company produces only one product. Budgeted activity is expected to average 150 000 units per period, and production and sales for each period are as follows:

	Period 1	Period 2	Period 3	Period 4	Period 5	Period 6
Units sold (000's)	150	120	180	150	140	160
Units produced (000's)	150	150	150	150	170	140

There were no opening stocks at the start of period 1, and the actual manufacturing fixed overhead incurred was £300 000 per period. We shall also assume that non-manufacturing overheads are £100 000 per period.

Variable costing

The variable costing profit statements are shown in Exhibit 7.2. You will see that when a system of variable costing is used, the product cost is £6 per unit, and includes variable costs only since variable costs are assigned to the product. In period 1 production is 150 000 units at a variable cost of £6 per unit. The total fixed costs are then added separately to produce a total manufacturing cost of £1 200 000. Note that the fixed costs of £300 000 are assigned to the period in which they are incurred.

In period 2, 150 000 units are produced but only 120 000 are sold. Therefore 30 000 units remain in stock at the end of the period. In order to match costs with revenues, the sales of 120 000 units should be matched with costs for 120 000. As 150 000 units were produced, we need to value the 30 000 units in stock and deduct this sum from the production cost. Using the variable costing system, the 30 000 units in stock are valued at £6 per unit. A closing inventory of £180 000 will then be deducted from the production costs, giving a cost of sales figure of £720 000. Note that the closing inventory valuation does not include any fixed overheads.

The 30 000 units of closing inventory in period 2 becomes the opening inventory for period 3 and therefore an expense for this period. The production cost for the 150 000 units made in period 3 is added to this opening inventory valuation. The overall effect is that costs for 180 000 units are matched against sales for 180 000 units. The profits for periods 4–6 are calculated in the same way.

Absorption costing

Let us now consider in Exhibit 7.3 the profit calculations when closing stocks are valued on an absorption costing basis. With the absorption costing method, a share of the fixed production overheads are allocated to individual products and are included in the products' production cost. Fixed overheads are assigned to products by establishing overhead absorption rates as described in Chapter 3. To establish the overhead rate we must divide the fixed overheads of £300 000 for the period by an appropriate denominator level. Most companies use an annual budgeted activity measure of the overhead allocation base as the denominator level (we shall discuss the different approaches that can be used for determining denominator levels later in the chapter). Our allocation base in Example 7.1 is units of output and we shall assume that the annual budgeted

EXHIBIT 7.2 Variable costing statements

	Period 1 (£000s)	Period 2 (£000s)	Period 3 (£000s)	Period 4 (£000s)	Period 5 (£000s)	Period 6 (£000s)
Opening stock	—	—	180	—	—	180
Production cost	900	900	900	900	1020	840
Closing stock	—	(180)	—	—	(180)	(60)
Cost of sales	900	720	1080	900	840	960
Fixed costs	300	300	300	300	300	300
Total costs	1200	1020	1380	1200	1140	1260
Sales	1500	1200	1800	1500	1400	1600
Gross profit	300	180	420	300	260	340
Less non-manufacturing costs	100	100	100	100	100	100
Net profit	200	80	320	200	160	240

output is 1 800 000 units giving an average for each monthly period of 150 000 units. Therefore the budgeted fixed overhead rate is £2 per unit (£300 000/150 000 units). The product cost now consists of a variable cost (£6) plus a fixed manufacturing cost (£2), making a total of £8 per unit. Hence, the production cost for period 1 is £1 200 000 (150 000 units at £8).

Now compare the absorption costing statement (Exhibit 7.3) with the variable costing statement (Exhibit 7.2) for period 1. With absorption costing, the fixed cost is included in the production cost figure, whereas with variable costing only the variable cost is included. With variable costing, the fixed cost is allocated separately as a lump sum and is not included in the cost of sales figure. Note also that the closing inventory of 30 000 units for period 2 is valued at £8 per unit in the absorption costing statement, whereas the closing inventory is valued at only £6 in the variable costing statement.

In calculating profits, the matching principle that has been applied in the absorption costing statement in the same way as that described for variable costing. However, complications arise in periods 5 and 6; in period 5, 170 000 units were produced, so the production cost of £1 360 000 includes fixed overheads of £340 000 (170 000 units at £2). The total fixed overheads incurred for the period are only £300 000, so £40 000 too much has been allocated. This over-recovery of fixed overhead is recorded as a period cost adjustment. (A full explanation of under- and over-recoveries of overheads and the reasons for period cost adjustments was presented in Chapter 3; if you are unsure of this concept, please refer back now to the section headed 'Under- and over-recovery of overheads'.) Note also that the under- or over-recovery of fixed overheads is also called volume variance.

In period 6, 140 000 units were produced at a cost of £1 120 000, which included only £280 000 (140 000 units at £2) for fixed overheads. As a result, there is an under-recovery of £20 000, which is written off as a period cost. You can see that an under- or over-recovery of fixed overhead occurs whenever actual production differs from the budged average level of activity of 150 000 units, since the calculation of the fixed overhead rate of £2 per unit was based on the assumption that actual production would be 150 000 units per period. Note that both variable and absorption costing systems do not assign non-manufacturing costs to products for stock valuation.

EXHIBIT 7.3 Absorption costing statements

	Period 1 (£000s)	Period 2 (£000s)	Period 3 (£000s)	Period 4 (£000s)	Period 5 (£000s)	Period 6 (£000s)
Opening stock	—	—	240	—	—	240
Production cost	1200	1200	1200	1200	1360	1120
Closing stock	—	(240)	—	—	(240)	(80)
Cost of sales	1200	960	1440	1200	1120	1280
Adjustments for under/(over) recovery of overhead	—	—	—	—	(40)	20
Total costs	1200	960	1440	1200	1080	1300
Sales	1500	1200	1800	1500	1400	1600
Gross profit	300	240	360	300	320	300
Less non-manufacturing costs	100	100	100	100	100	100
Net profit	200	140	260	200	220	200

Variable costing and absorption costing: a comparison of their impact on profit

A comparison of the variable costing and absorption costing statements produced from the information contained in Example 7.1 reveals the following differences in profit calculations:

a The profits calculated under the absorption costing and variable costing systems are identical for periods 1 and 4.

b The absorption costing profits are higher than the variable costing profits in periods 2 and 5.

c The variable costing profits are higher than the absorption costing profits in periods 3 and 6.

Let us now consider each of these in a little more detail.

Production equals sales

In periods 1 and 4 the profits are the same for both methods of costing; in both periods production is equal to sales, and inventories will neither increase nor decrease. Therefore if opening inventories exist, the same amount of fixed overhead will be carried forward as an expense to be included in the current period in the opening inventory valuation as will be deducted in the closing inventory valuation from the production cost figure. The overall effect is that, with an absorption costing system, the only fixed overhead that will be included as an expense for the period will be the amount of fixed overhead that is incurred for the period. Thus, whenever sales are equal to production the profits will be the same for both the absorption costing and variable costing systems.

Production exceeds sales

In periods 2 and 5 the absorption costing system produces higher profits; in both periods production exceeds sales. Profits are higher for absorption costing when production is in excess of sales, because inventories are increasing. The effect of this is that a greater amount of fixed overheads in the closing inventory is being deducted from the expenses of the period than is being brought forward in the opening inventory for the period. For example, in period 2 the opening inventory is zero and no fixed overheads are brought forward from the previous period. However, a closing inventory of 30 000 units means that £60 000 fixed overhead has to be deducted from the production cost for the period. In other words, only £240 000 is being allocated for fixed overhead with the absorption costing system, whereas the variable costing system allocates the £300 000 fixed overhead incurred for the period. The effect of this is that profits are £60 000 greater with the absorption costing system. As a general rule, if production is in excess of sales, the absorption costing system will show a higher profit than the variable costing system.

Sales exceed production

In periods 3 and 6 the variable costing system produces higher profits; in both periods sales exceed production. When this situation occurs, inventories decline and a greater amount of fixed overheads will need to be brought forward as an expense in the opening inventory than is being deducted in the closing inventory adjustment. For example, with the absorption costing system, in period 6, 30 000 units of opening inventory are brought forward, so that fixed costs of £60 000 are included in the inventory valuation. However, a closing inventory of 10 000 units requires a deduction of £20 000 fixed overheads from the production costs. The overall effect is that an additional £40 000 fixed overheads is included as an expense within the stock movements, and a total of £340 000 fixed overheads is allocated for the period. The variable costing system, on the other hand, would allocate fixed overheads for the period of only £300 000. As a result, profits are £40 000 greater with the variable costing system. As a general rule, if sales are in excess of production, the variable costing system will show a higher profit than the absorption costing system.

Impact of sales fluctuations

The profit calculations for an absorption costing system can produce some strange results. For example, in period 6 the sales volume has increased but profits have declined, in spite of the fact that both the selling price and the cost structure have remained unchanged. A manager whose performance is being judged in period 6 is likely to have little confidence in an accounting system that shows a decline in profits when sales volume has increased and the cost structure and selling price have not changed. The opposite occurs in period 5. In this period the sales volume declines but profit increases. The situations in periods 5 and 6 arise because the under- or over-recovery of fixed overhead is treated as a period cost, and such adjustments can at times give a misleading picture of profits.

In contrast, the variable costing profit calculations show that when sales volume increases profit also increases. Alternatively, when sales volume decreases, profit also decreases. These relationships continue as long as the selling price and cost structure remain unchanged. Looking again at the variable costing profit calculations, you will note that profit declines in period 5 when the sales volume declines, and increases in period 6 when the sales volume also increases. The reasons for these changes are that, with a system of variable costing, profit is a function of sales volume only, when the selling price and cost structure remain unchanged. However, with absorption costing, profit is a function of both sales volume and production volume.

A mathematical model of the profit functions

In Appendix 7.1 the following formula is developed to model the profit function for an absorption costing system when unit costs remain unchanged throughout the period:

$$\text{OPBT}_{AC} = (\text{ucm} - \text{ufmc})Q_s + (\text{ufmc} \times Q_p) - \text{FC} \qquad (7.1)$$

where

ucm	= Contribution margin per unit (i.e. selling price per unit – variable cost per unit)
ufmc	= Pre-determined fixed manufacturing overhead per unit of output
Q_p	= Number of units produced
Q_s	= Number of units sold
FC	= Total fixed costs (manufacturing and non-manufacturing)
OPBT_{AC}	= Operating profit before taxes for the period (Absorption costing)
OPBT_{VC}	= Operating profit before taxes for the period (Variable costing)

Applying formula 7.1 to the data given in Example 7.1 gives the following profit function:

$$(£4 - £2)Q_s + (£2 \times Q_p) - £400\,000 = £2Q_s + £2Q_p - £400\,000$$

Applying the above profit function to periods 4–6 we get:

$$\text{Period 4} = £2(150\,000) + £2(150\,000) - £400\,000 = £200\,000$$
$$\text{Period 5} = £2(140\,000) + £2(170\,000) - £400\,000 = £220\,000$$
$$\text{Period 6} = £2(160\,000) + £2(140\,000) - £400\,000 = £200\,000$$

When production equals sales identical profits with an absorption and variable costing system are reported. Therefore formula 7.1 converts to the following variable costing profit function if we let $Q_s = Q_p$:

$$\text{Variable costing operating profit} = \text{ucm} \cdot \text{Qs} - \text{FC} \qquad (7.2)$$

Using the data given in Example 7.1 the profit function is:

$$£4Q_s - £400\ 000$$

Applying the above profit function to periods 4–6 we get:

$$\text{Period } 4 = £4(150\ 000) - £400\ 000 = £200\ 000$$
$$\text{Period } 5 = £4(140\ 000) - £400\ 000 = £160\ 000$$
$$\text{Period } 6 = £4(160\ 000) - £400\ 000 = £240\ 000$$

The difference between the reported operating profits for an absorption costing and a variable costing system can be derived by deducting formulae 7.2 from 7.1 giving:

$$\text{ufmc}(Q_p - Q_s) \qquad (7.3)$$

If you look closely at the above term you will see that it represents the inventory change (in units) multiplied by the fixed manufacturing overhead rate. Applying formula 7.3 to period 5 the inventory change $(Q_p - Q_s)$ is 30 000 units (positive) so that absorption costing profits exceed variable costing profits by £60 000 (30 000 units at £2 overhead rate). For an explanation of how formulae (7.1) and (7.2) are derived you should refer to Appendix 7.1.

Some arguments in support of variable costing

Variable costing provides more useful information for decision-making

The separation of fixed and variable costs helps to provide relevant information about costs for making decisions. Relevant costs are required for a variety of short-term decisions, for example whether to make a component internally or to purchase externally, as well as problems relating to product-mix. These decisions will be discussed in Chapter 9. In addition, the estimation of costs for different levels of activities requires that costs be split into their fixed and variable elements. The assumption is that only with a variable costing system will such an analysis of costs be available. It is therefore assumed that projection of future costs and revenues for different activity levels, and the use of relevant cost decision-making techniques, are possible only if a variable costing system is adopted. There is no reason, however, why an absorption costing system cannot be used for profit measurement and inventory valuation and costs can be analyzed into their fixed and variable elements for decision-making. The advantage of variable costing is that the analysis of variable and fixed costs is highlighted. (Such an analysis is not a required feature of an absorption costing system.)

Variable costing removes from profit the effect of inventory changes

We have seen that, with variable costing, profit is a function of sales volume, whereas, with absorption costing, profit is a function of both sales and production. We have also learned, using absorption costing principles, that it is possible for profit to decline when sales volumes increase. Where stock levels are likely to fluctuate significantly, profits may be distorted when they are calculated on an absorption costing basis, since the stock changes will significantly affect the amount of fixed overheads allocated to an accounting period.

Fluctuating stock levels are less likely to occur when one measures profits on an annual basis, but on a monthly or quarterly basis seasonal variations in sales may cause significant fluctuations. As profits are likely to be distorted by an absorption costing system, there are strong arguments for using variable costing methods when profits are measured at frequent intervals and stock levels fluctuate from month to month. Because frequent profit statements are presented only for management, the argument for variable costing is stronger for management accounting. A survey by Drury and Tayles (2006) relating to 187 UK companies reported that 84 per cent of the companies prepared profit statements at monthly or quarterly intervals. Financial accounts are presented for public release annually or at half-yearly intervals; because significant changes in stock levels are less likely on an annual basis, the argument for the use of variable costing in financial accounting is not as strong.

A further argument for using variable costing for internal reporting is that the internal profit statements may be used as a basis for measuring managerial performance. Managers may deliberately alter their inventory levels to influence profit when an absorption costing system is used; for example, it is possible for a manager to defer deliberately some of the fixed overhead allocation by unnecessarily increasing stocks over successive periods.

There is a limit, to how long managers can continue to increase stocks, and eventually the situation will arise when it is necessary to reduce them, and the deferred fixed overheads will eventually be allocated to the periods when the inventories are reduced. Nevertheless, there is likely to remain some scope for manipulating profits in the short term. Also senior management can implement control performance measures to guard against such behaviour. For example, the reporting of performance measures that monitor changes in inventory volumes will highlight those situations where managers are manipulating profits by unnecessarily increasing inventory levels.

Variable costing avoids fixed overheads being capitalized in unsaleable stocks

In a period when sales demand decreases, a company can end up with surplus stocks on hand. With an absorption costing system, only a portion of the fixed overheads incurred during the period will be allocated as an expense because the remainder of the fixed overhead will be included in the valuation of the surplus stocks. If these surplus stocks cannot be disposed of, the profit calculation for the current period will be misleading, since fixed overheads will have been deferred to later accounting periods. However, there may be some delay before management concludes that the stocks cannot be sold without a very large reduction in the selling price. The stocks will therefore be over-valued, and a stock write-off will be necessary in a later accounting period. The overall effect may be that the current period's profits will be overstated.

Some arguments in support of absorption costing

Absorption costing does not understate the importance of fixed costs

Some people argue that decisions based on a variable costing system may concentrate only on sales revenues and variable costs and ignore the fact that fixed costs must be met in the long run. For example, if a pricing decision is based on variable costs only, then sales revenue may be insufficient to cover all the costs. It is also argued that the use of an absorption costing system, by allocating fixed costs to a product, ensures that fixed costs will be covered. These arguments are incorrect. Absorption costing will not ensure that fixed costs will be recovered if actual sales volume is less than the estimate used to calculate the fixed overhead rate. For example, consider a situation where fixed costs are £100 000 and an estimated normal activity of 10 000 units is used to calculate the overhead rate. Fixed costs are recovered at £10 per unit. Assume that variable cost is £5 per unit and selling price is set at £20 (total cost plus one-third). If actual sales volume is 5000 units then total sales revenue will be £100 000 and total costs will be £125 000. Total costs therefore exceed total sales revenue. The argument that a variable costing system will cause managers to ignore fixed costs is based on the assumption that such managers are not very bright! A failure to consider fixed costs is due to faulty management and not to a faulty accounting system. Furthermore, using variable costing for inventory valuation and profit measurement still enables full cost information to be extracted for pricing decisions.

Absorption costing avoids fictitious losses being reported

In a business that relies on seasonal sales and in which production is built up outside the sales season to meet demand the full amount of fixed overheads incurred will be charged, in a variable costing system, against sales. However, in those periods where production is being built up for sales in a later season, sales revenue will be low but fixed costs will be recorded as an expense. The result is that losses will be reported during out-of-season periods, and large profits will be reported in the periods when the goods are sold.

By contrast, in an absorption costing system fixed overheads will be deferred and included in the closing inventory valuation, and will be recorded as an expense only in the period in which the goods are sold. Losses are therefore unlikely to be reported in the periods when stocks are being built up. In these circumstances absorption costing appears to provide the more logical profit calculation.

Fixed overheads are essential for production

The proponents of absorption costing argue that the production of goods is not possible if fixed manufacturing costs are not incurred. Consequently, fixed manufacturing overheads should be allocated to units produced and included in the inventory valuation.

Consistency with external reporting

Top management may prefer their internal profit reporting systems to be consistent with the external financial accounting absorption costing systems so that they will be congruent with the measures used by financial markets to appraise overall company performance. In a pilot study of six UK companies Hopper *et al.* (1992) observed that senior managers are primarily interested in financial accounting information because it is perceived as having a major influence on how financial markets evaluate companies and their management. If top management believe that financial accounting information does influence share prices then they are likely to use the same rules and procedures for both internal and external profit measurement and inventory valuation so that managers will focus on the same measures as those used by financial markets. Also the fact that managerial rewards are often linked to external financial measures provides a further motivation to ensure that internal accounting systems do not conflict with external financial accounting reporting requirements.

Alternative denominator level measures

When absorption costing systems are used estimated fixed overhead rates must be calculated. These rates will be significantly influenced by the choice of the activity level; that is the denominator activity level that is used to calculate the overhead rate. This problem applies only to fixed overheads, and the greater the proportion of fixed overheads in an organization's cost structure the more acute is the problem. Fixed costs arise from situations where resources must be acquired in discrete, not continuous, amounts in such a way that the supply of resources cannot be continuously adjusted to match the usage of resources. For example, a machine might be purchased that provides an annual capacity of 5000 machine hours but changes in sales demand may cause the annual usage to vary from 2500 to 5000 hours. It is not possible to match the supply and usage of the resource and unused capacity will arise in those periods where the resources used are less than the 5000 hours of capacity supplied.

In contrast, variable costs arise in those situations where the supply of resources can be continually adjusted to match the usage of resources. For example, the spending on energy costs associated with running machinery (i.e. the supply and resources) can be immediately reduced by 50 per cent if resources used decline by 50 per cent say, from 5000 hours to 2500 hours. There is no unused capacity in respect of variable costs. Consequently with variable cost the cost per unit of resource used will be constant.

With fixed overheads the cost per unit of resource used will fluctuate with changes in estimates of activity usage because fixed overhead spending remains constant over a wide range of activity. For example, if the estimated annual fixed overheads associated with the machine referred to above are £192 000 and annual activity is estimated to be 5000 hours then the machine hour rate will be £38.40 (£192 000/5000 hours). Alternatively if annual activity is estimated to be 2500 hours then the rate will be £76.80 (£192 000/2500 hours). Therefore the choice of the denominator capacity level can have a profound effect on product cost calculations.

Several choices are available for determining the denominator activity level when calculating overhead rates. Consider the situation described in Example 7.2.

There are four different denominator activity levels that can be used in Example 7.2. They are:

1 Theoretical maximum capacity of 6000 hours = £32 per hour (£192 000/6000 hours);

2 Practical capacity of 5000 hours = £38.40 per hour (£192 000/5000 hours);

3 Normal average long-run activity of 4800 hours = £40 per hour (£192 000/4800 hours);

4 Budgeted activity of 4000 hours = £48 per hour (£192 000/4000 hours).

Theoretical maximum capacity is a measure of maximum operating capacity based on 100 per cent efficiency with no interruptions for maintenance or other factors. We can reject this measure on the grounds that it represents an activity level that is most unlikely to be achieved. The capacity was acquired with the expectation of supplying a maximum of 5000 hours rather than a theoretical maximum of 6000 hours. This former measure is called practical capacity. Practical capacity represents the maximum capacity that is likely to be supplied by the machine after taking into account unavoidable interruptions arising from machine maintenance and plant holiday closures. In other words, practical capacity is defined as theoretical capacity less activity lost arising from unavoidable interruptions. Normal activity is a measure of capacity required to satisfy average customer demand over a longer term period of, say, approximately three years after taking into account seasonal and cyclical fluctuations. Finally, budgeted activity is the activity level based on the capacity utilization required for the next budget period.

Assuming in Example 7.2 that actual activity and expenditure are identical to budget then, for each of the above denominator activity levels, the annual costs of £192 000 will be allocated as follows:

	Allocated to products	Volume variance (i.e. cost of unused capacity)	Total
Practical capacity	4000 hours × £38.40 = £153 600	1000 hours × £38.40 = £38 400	£192 000
Normal activity	4000 hours × £40 = £160 000	800 hours × £40 = £32 000	£192 000
Budgeted activity	4000 hours × £48 = £192 000	Nil	£192 000

EXAMPLE 7.2

The Green Company has established a separate cost centre for one of its machines. The annual budgeted fixed overheads assigned to the cost centre are £192 000. Green operates three shifts per day of 8 hours, five days per week for 50 weeks per year (the company closes down for holiday periods for two weeks per year). The maximum machine operating hours are 6000 hours per annum (50 weeks × 24 hrs × 5 days) but because of preventive maintenance the maximum practical operating usage is 5000 hours per annum. It is estimated that normal sales demand over the next three years will result in the machine being required for 4800 hours per annum. However, because of current adverse economic conditions budgeted usage for the coming year is 4000 hours. Assume that actual fixed overheads incurred are identical to the estimated fixed overheads and that there are no opening stocks at the start of the budget period.

Note that the overheads allocated to products consist of 4000 hours worked on products during the year multiplied by the appropriate overhead rate. The cost of unused capacity is the under-recovery of overheads arising from actual activity being different from the activity level used to calculate the overhead rate. If practical capacity is used the cost highlights that part of total capacity supplied (5000 hours) that has not been utilized. With normal activity the under-recovery of £32 000 represents the cost of failing to utilize the normal activity of 4800 hours. In Example 7.2 we assumed that actual activity was equivalent to budgeted activity. However, if actual activity is less than budgeted activity then the under-recovery can be interpreted as the cost of failing to achieve budgeted activity.

Impact on inventory valuation of profit computations

The choice of an appropriate activity level can have a significant effect on the inventory valuation and profit computation. Assume in Example 7.2 that 90 per cent of the output was sold and the remaining 10 per cent unsold and that there were no inventories at the start of the period. Thus 90 per cent of the overheads allocated to products will be allocated to cost of sales, and 10 per cent will be allocated to inventories. The volume variance arising from the under- or over-recovery of fixed overheads (i.e. the cost of unused capacity) is recorded as a period cost and therefore charged as an expense against the current period. It is not included in the inventory valuation. The computations are as follows:

	Expenses recorded for the period[a] (£)	Allocated to inventories[b] (£)	Total (£)
Practical capacity	176 640	15 360	192 000
Normal activity	176 000	16 000	192 000
Budgeted activity	172 800	19 200	192 000

[a]90% of overhead allocated to products plus cost of unused capacity.
[b]10% of overhead allocated to products.

In the above illustration the choice of the denominator level has not had an important impact on the inventory valuation and the cost of sales (and therefore the profit computation). Nevertheless, the impact can be material when inventories are of significant value. Many service organizations, however, do not hold inventories and just-in-time manufacturing firms aim to maintain minimal inventory levels. In these situations virtually all of the expenses incurred during a period will be recorded as a period expense whatever denominator activity level is selected to calculate the overhead rate. We can therefore conclude that for many organizations the choice of the denominator activity level has little impact on profit measurement and inventory valuation. Therefore the impact of the chosen denominator level depends on the circumstances.

Even where the choice of the denominator level is not of significant importance for profit measurement and inventory valuation it can be of crucial importance for other purposes, such as pricing decisions and managing the cost of unused capacity. Since our objective in this chapter is to focus on the impact of the choice of denominator level on profit measurement and inventory measurement we shall defer a discussion of these other issues until Chapter 10.

Finally, what denominator levels do firms actually use? A study of UK organizations by Drury and Tayles (2000) reported that 86 per cent of the respondents used budgeted annual activity. The popularity of this method is that budgeted annual activity is readily available, being determined as part of the annual budgeting process.

SUMMARY

The following items relate to the learning objectives listed at the beginning of the chapter.

● **Explain the differences between an absorption costing and a variable costing system.**

With an absorption costing system, fixed manufacturing overheads are allocated to the products and these are included in the inventory valuations. With a variable costing system, only variable manufacturing costs are assigned to the product; fixed manufacturing costs are regarded as period costs and written off as a lump sum to the profit and loss account. Both variable and absorption costing systems treat non-manufacturing overheads as period costs.

● **Prepare profit statements based on a variable costing and absorption costing system.**

With a variable costing system manufacturing fixed costs are added to the variable manufacturing cost of sales to determine total manufacturing costs to be deducted from sales revenues. Manufacturing fixed costs are assigned to products with an absorption costing system. Therefore, manufacturing cost of sales is valued at full cost (manufacturing variable costs plus manufacturing fixed costs). With an absorption costing system fixed manufacturing costs are unitized by dividing the total manufacturing costs by estimated output. If actual output differs from estimated output an under- or over-recovery of overheads arises. This is recorded as a period cost adjustment in the current accounting period.

● **Explain the difference in profits between variable and absorption costing profit calculations.**

When production exceeds sales, absorption costing systems report higher profits. Variable costing systems yield higher profits when sales exceed production. Nevertheless, total profits over the life of the business will be the same for both systems. Differences arise merely in the profits attributed to each accounting period.

● **Explain the arguments for and against variable and absorption costing.**

The proponents of variable costing claim that it enables more useful information to be presented for decision-making but such claims are questionable since similar relevant cost information can easily be extracted from an absorption costing system. The major advantage of variable costing is that profit is reflected as a function of sales, whereas, with an absorption costing system, profit is a function of both sales and production. It is possible with absorption costing, when all other factors remain unchanged, for sales to increase and profit to decline. In contrast, with a variable costing system, when sales increase, profits also increase. A further advantage of variable costing is that fixed overheads are not capitalized in unsaleable stocks. The arguments that have been made supporting absorption costing include:

(a) absorption costing does not understate the importance of fixed costs;
(b) absorption costing avoids the possibility of fictitious losses being reported;
(c) fixed manufacturing overheads are essential to production and therefore should be incorporated in the product costs; and
(d) internal profit measurement should be consistent with absorption costing profit measurement that is used for external reporting requirements.

● **Describe the various denominator levels that can be used with an absorption costing system.**

Four different denominator levels were described. Theoretical maximum capacity is a measure of maximum operating capacity based on 100 per cent efficiency with no interruptions for maintenance or machine breakdowns. Practical capacity represents the maximum capacity that is likely to be supplied after taking into account unavoidable interruptions such as machine maintenance and plant holiday closures. Normal capacity is a measure of capacity required to satisfy average demand over a long-term period (e.g. 3–5 years). Budgeted activity is the activity based on capacity utilization required for the next budget period.

● **Explain why the choice of an appropriate denominator level is important.**

The use of each alternative measure results in the computation of a different overhead rate. This can result in significantly different reported product costs, profit levels and inventory valuations.

Appendix 7.1: Derivation of the profit function for an absorption costing system

Using the formulae listed in Exhibit 7A.1 the variable costing profit function can be expressed in equation form as follows:

$$
\begin{aligned}
OPBT_{VC} &= \text{Sales} - \text{Variable manufacturing costs of goods sold} \\
&\quad - \text{non-manufacturing variable costs} - \text{All fixed costs} \\
&= usp \cdot Q_s - uvmc \cdot Q_s - uvnmc \cdot Q_s - FC \qquad (7.A1) \\
&= ucm \cdot Q_s - FC \text{ (Note that the term contribution margin is used to} \\
&\quad \text{describe unit selling price less unit variable cost)}
\end{aligned}
$$

The distinguishable feature between absorption costing and variable costing relates to the timing of the recognition of fixed manufacturing overheads (FC_m) as an expense. Variable and absorption costing reported profits differ by the amount of fixed manufacturing overheads that are included in the change in opening and closing inventories. This is equivalent to the difference between production and sales volumes multiplied by the manufacturing fixed overhead absorption rate.

EXHIBIT 7.A1 Summary of notation used

ucm	= Contribution margin per unit (i.e. selling price per unit – variable cost per unit)
usp	= Selling price per unit
uvmc	= Variable manufacturing cost per unit
uvnmc	= Variable non-manufacturing cost per unit
ufmc	= Pre-determined fixed manufacturing overhead per unit of output
Q_p	= Number of units produced
Q_s	= Number of units sold
FC	= Total fixed costs (manufacturing and non-manufacturing)
FC_m	= Total fixed manufacturing costs
FCnmc	= Total fixed manufacturing costs
$OPBT_{AC}$	= Operating profit before taxes for the period (Absorption costing)
$OPBT_{VC}$	= Operating profit before taxes for the period (Variable costing)

We can therefore use equation (7.A1) as the basis for establishing the equation for the absorption costing profit function:

$$
\begin{aligned}
OPBT_{AC} &= ucm \cdot Q_s - FC + (Q_p - Q_s)ufmc \\
&= ucm \cdot Q_s - FC + (Q_p \times ufmc) - (Q_s \times ufmc) \qquad (7.A2) \\
&= (ucm - ufmc)Q_s + (ufmc \times Q_p) - FC
\end{aligned}
$$

Key terms and concepts

absorption costing (p. 141)
budgeted activity (p. 151)
direct costing (p. 141)
full costing (p. 141)

marginal costing (p. 141)
normal activity (p. 151)
period cost adjustment (p. 145)
practical capacity (p. 151)

theoretical maximum capacity
(p. 151)
variable costing (p. 141)
volume variance (p. 145)

Key examination points

A common mistake is for students to calculate *actual* overhead rates when preparing absorption costing profit statements. Normal or budgeted activity should be used to calculate overhead absorption rates, and this rate should be used to calculate the production overhead cost for all periods given in the question. Do not calculate different actual overhead rates for each accounting period.

Remember not to include non-manufacturing overheads in the inventory valuations for both variable and absorption costing. Also note that variable selling overheads will vary with sales and not production. Another common mistake is not to include an adjustment for under-/over-recovery of fixed overheads when actual production deviates from the normal or budgeted production. You should note that under-/over-recovery of overhead arises only with fixed overheads and when an absorption costing system is used.

ASSESSMENT MATERIAL

The review questions are short questions that enable you to assess your understanding of the main topics included in the chapter. The numbers in parentheses provide you with the page numbers to refer to if you cannot answer a specific question.

The review problems are more complex and require you to relate and apply the content to various business problems. The problems are graded by their level of difficulty. Solutions to review problems that are not preceded by the term 'IM' are provided in a separate section at the end of the book. Solutions to problems preceded by the term 'IM' are provided in the *Instructor's Manual* accompanying this book and also on the lecturer's password protected section of the website www.drury-online.com. Additional review problems with fully worked solutions are provided in the *Student's Manual* that accompanies this book.

Review questions

7.1 Distinguish between variable costing and absorption costing. *(pp. 141–42)*
7.2 How are non-manufacturing fixed costs treated under absorption and variable costing systems? *(p. 141)*
7.3 Describe the circumstances when variable and absorption costing systems will report identical profits. *(p. 146)*
7.4 Under what circumstances will absorption costing report higher profits than variable costing? *(p. 146)*
7.5 Under what circumstances will variable costing report higher profits than absorption costing? *(p. 146)*
7.6 What arguments can be advanced in favour of variable costing? *(pp. 148–49)*
7.7 What arguments can be advanced in favour of absorption costing? *(pp. 149–50)*
7.8 Explain how absorption costing can encourage managers to engage in behaviour that is harmful to the organization. *(p. 149)*
7.9 Why is it necessary to select an appropriate denominator level measure only with absorption costing systems? *(pp. 150–51)*
7.10 Identify and describe the four different denominator level measures that can be used to estimate fixed overhead rates. *(p. 151)*
7.11 Explain why the choice of an appropriate denominator level is important. *(p. 152)*
7.12 Why is budgeted activity the most widely used denominator measure? *(p. 153)*

Review problems

7.13 Basic. WTD Ltd produces a single product. The management currently uses marginal costing but is considering using absorption costing in the future.

The budgeted fixed production overheads for the period are £500 000. The budgeted output for the period is 2000 units. There were 800 units of opening inventory at the beginning of the period and 500 units of closing inventory at the end of the period.

If absorption costing principles were applied, the profit for the period compared to the marginal costing profit would be
a £75 000 higher
b £75 000 lower
c £125 000 higher
d £125 000 lower
CIMA P1 Management Accounting: Performance Evaluation

7.14 Basic. In a period, opening stocks were 12 600 units and closing stocks 14 100 units. The profit based on marginal costing was £50 400 and profit using absorption costing was £60 150. The fixed overhead absorption rate per unit (to the nearest penny) is
a £4.00
b £4.27
c £4.77
d £6.50
CIMA Stage 1 Cost Accounting

7.15 Basic. A newly formed company has drawn up the following budgets for its first two accounting periods:

	Period 1	Period 2
Sales units	9 500	10 300
Production units (equivalent to normal capacity)	10 000	10 000

The following budgeted information applies to both periods:

	$
Selling price per unit	6.40
Variable cost per unit	3.60
Fixed production overhead per period	15 000

a In period 1, the budgeted profit will be
  i the same under both absorption costing and marginal costing.
  ii $750 higher under marginal costing.
  iii $750 higher under absorption costing.
  iv $1400 higher under absorption costing.

b In period 2, everything was as budgeted, except for the fixed production overhead, which was $15 700.

  The reported profit, using absorption costing in period 2, would be
  i $12 300
  ii $12 690
  iii $13 140
  iv $13 840 *CIMA – Management Accounting Fundamentals*

7.16 Intermediate: Preparation of variable and absorption costing statements and an explanation of the differences in profits. Bittern Ltd manufactures and sells a single product at a unit selling price of £25. In constant-price-level terms its cost structure is as follows:

Variable costs:	
Production materials	£10 per unit produced
Distribution	£1 per unit sold
Semi-variable costs:	
Labour	£5000 per annum, plus £2 per unit produced
Fixed costs:	
Overheads	£5000 per annum

For several years Bittern has operated a system of variable costing for management accounting purposes. It has been decided to review the system and to compare it for management accounting purposes with an absorption costing system.

As part of the review, you have been asked to prepare estimates of Bittern's profits in constant-price-level terms over a three-year period in

three different hypothetical situations, and to compare the two types of system generally for management accounting purposes.

a In each of the following three sets of hypothetical circumstances, calculate Bittern's profit in each of years t_1, t_2 and t_3, and also in total over the three year period t_1 to t_3, using first a variable costing system and then a full-cost absorption costing system with fixed cost recovery based on a normal production level of 1000 units per annum:

i Stable unit levels of production, sales and inventory

	t_1	t_2	t_3
Opening stock	100	100	100
Production	1000	1000	1000
Sales	1000	1000	1000
Closing stock	100	100	100

(5 marks)

ii Stable unit level of sales, but fluctuating unit levels of production and inventory

	t_1	t_2	t_3
Opening stock	100	600	400
Production	1500	800	700
Sales	1000	1000	1000
Closing stock	600	400	100

(5 marks)

iii Stable unit level of production, but fluctuating unit levels of sales and inventory

	t_1	t_2	t_3
Opening stock	100	600	400
Production	1000	1000	1000
Sales	500	1200	1300
Closing stock	600	400	100

(5 marks)

(Note that all the data in i–iii are volumes, not values.)

b Write a short comparative evaluation of variable and absorption costing systems for management accounting purposes, paying particular attention to profit measurement, and using your answer to (a) to illustrate your arguments if you wish.

(10 marks)
ICAEW Management Accounting

IM7.1 Intermediate. In product costing the costs attributed to each unit of production may be calculated by using either

i absorption costing, or
ii marginal (or direct or variable) costing.

Similarly, in departmental cost or profit reports the fixed costs of overhead or service departments may be allocated to production departments as an integral part of the production departments' costs or else segregated in some form.

Required:
Describe absorption and marginal (or direct or variable) costing and outline the strengths and weaknesses of each method. *(11 marks)*
ACCA P2 Management Accounting

IM7.2 Intermediate. Discuss the arguments for and against the inclusion of fixed overheads in stock valuation for the purpose of internal profit measurement.

IM7.3 Intermediate: Preparation of variable and absorption costing statements. Solo Limited makes and sells a single product. The following data relate to periods 1 to 4.

	(£)
Variable cost per unit	30
Selling price per unit	55
Fixed costs per period	6000

Normal activity is 500 units and production and sales for the four periods are as follows:

	Period 1 units	Period 2 units	Period 3 units	Period 4 units
Sales	500	400	550	450
Production	500	500	450	500

There were no opening stocks at the start of period 1.

Required:
a Prepare operating statements for EACH of the periods 1 to 4, based on marginal costing principles. *(4 marks)*
b Prepare operating statements for EACH of the periods 1 to 4, based on absorption costing principles. *(6 marks)*
c Comment briefly on the results obtained in each period AND in total by the two systems. *(5 marks)*
CIMA Stage 1 Cost Accounting

IM7.4 Intermediate: Preparation of variable and absorption costing profit statements and comments in support of a variable costing system.
A manufacturer of glass bottles has been affected by competition from plastic bottles and is currently operating at between 65 and 70 per cent of maximum capacity.

The company at present reports profits on an absorption costing basis but with the high fixed costs associated with the glass container industry and a substantial difference between sales volumes and production in some months, the accountant has been criticized for reporting widely different profits from month to month. To counteract this criticism, he is proposing in future to report profits based on marginal costing and in his proposal to management lists the following reasons for wishing to change:

1. Marginal costing provides for the complete segregation of fixed costs, thus facilitating closer control of production costs.
2. It eliminates the distortion of interim profit statements which occur when there are seasonal fluctuations in sales volume although production is at a fairly constant level.
3. It results in cost information which is more helpful in determining the sales policy necessary to maximise profits.

From the accounting records the following figures were extracted:
Standard cost per gross (a gross is 144 bottles and is the cost unit used within the business):

	(£)
Direct materials	8.00
Direct labour	7.20
Variable production overhead	3.36
Total variable production cost	18.56
Fixed production overhead	7.52*
Total production standard cost	26.08

*The fixed production overhead rate was based on the following computations:
Total annual fixed production overhead was budgeted at £7 584 000 or £632 000 per month. Production volume was set at 1 008 000 gross bottles or 70 per cent of maximum capacity.

There is a slight difference in budgeted fixed production overhead at different levels of operating:

Activity level (per cent of maximum capacity)	Amount per month (£000)
50–75	632
76–90	648
91–100	656

You may assume that actual fixed production overhead incurred was as budgeted.

Additional information:

	September	October
Gross sold	87 000	101 000
Gross produced	115 000	78 000
Sales price, per gross	£32	£32
Fixed selling costs	£120 000	£120 000
Fixed administrative costs	£80 000	£80 000

There were no finished goods in stock at 1 September.

You are required
a to prepare monthly profit statements for September and October using
i absorption costing; and
ii marginal costing; *(16 marks)*
b to comment briefly on the accountant's three reasons which he listed to support his proposal. *(9 marks)*
CIMA Stage 2 Cost Accounting

IM7.5 Intermediate: Calculation of overhead absorption rates and an explanation of the differences in profits. A company manufactures a single product with the following variable costs per unit

Direct materials	£7.00
Direct labour	£5.50
Manufacturing overhead	£2.00

The selling price of the product is £36.00 per unit. Fixed manufacturing costs are expected to be £1 340 000 for a period. Fixed non-manufacturing costs are expected to be £875 000. Fixed manufacturing costs can be analyzed as follows:

Production 1	Department 2	Service Department	General Factory
£380 000	£465 000	£265 000	£230 000

'General Factory' costs represent space costs, for example rates, lighting and heating. Space utilization is as follows:

Production department 1	40%
Production department 2	50%
Service department	10%

60 per cent of service department costs are labour related and the remaining 40 per cent machine related.

Normal production department activity is:

	Direct labour hours	Machine hours	Production units
Department 1	80 000	2400	120 000
Department 2	100 000	2400	120 000

Fixed manufacturing overheads are absorbed at a predetermined rate per unit of production for each production department, based upon normal activity.

Required:

a Prepare a profit statement for a period using the full absorption costing system described above and showing each element of cost separately. Costs for the period were as per expectation, except for additional expenditure of £20 000 on fixed manufacturing overhead in Production Department 1. Production and sales were 116 000 and 114 000 units respectively for the period. *(14 marks)*

b Prepare a profit statement for the period using marginal costing principles instead. *(5 marks)*

c Contrast the general effect on profit of using absorption and marginal costing systems respectively. (Use the figures calculated in (a) and (b) above to illustrate your answer.) *(6 marks)*

ACCA Cost and Management Accounting 1

IM7.6 Advanced: Preparation and comments on variable and absorption costing profit statements. Synchrodot Ltd manufactures two standard products, product 1 selling at £15 and product 2 selling at £18. A standard absorption costing system is in operation and summarised details of the unit cost standards are as follows:

	Standard Cost Data – Summary	
	Product 1 (£)	Product 2 (£)
Direct Material Cost	2	3
Direct Labour Cost	1	2
Overhead (Fixed and Variable)	7	9
	£10	£14

The budgeted fixed factory overhead for Synchrodot Ltd is £180 000 (per quarter) for product 1 and £480 000 (per quarter) for product 2. This apportionment to product lines is achieved by using a variety of 'appropriate' bases for individual expense categories, e.g. floor space for rates, number of workstaff for supervisory salaries etc. The fixed overhead is absorbed into production using practical capacity as the basis and any volume variance is written off (or credited) to the Profit and Loss Account in the quarter in which it occurs. Any planned volume variance in the quarterly budgets is dealt with similarly. The practical capacity per quarter is 30 000 units for product 1 and 60 000 units for product 2.

At the March board meeting the draft budgeted income statement for the April/May/June quarter is presented for consideration. This shows the following:

Budgeted Income Statement for April, May and June

		Product 1		Product 2
Budgeted Sales Quantity		30 000 units		57 000 units
Budgeted Production Quantity		24 000 units		60 000 units
Budgeted Sales Revenue		£450 000		£1 026 000
Budgeted Production Costs				
Direct Material		£48 000		£180 000
Direct Labour		24 000		120 000
Factory Overhead		204 000		540 000
		£276 000		£840 000
Add:				
Budgeted opening Finished Goods				
Stock at 1 April	(8000 units)	80 000	(3000 units)	42 000
		356 000		£882 000
Less:				
Budgeted closing Finished Goods				
Stock at 30 June	(2000 units)	20 000	(6000 units)	84 000
Budgeted Manufacturing Cost of Budgeted Sales		£336 000		£798 000
Budgeted Manufacturing Profit		£114 000		£228 000
Budgeted Administrative and Selling Costs (fixed)		30 000		48 000
Budgeted Profit		£84 000		£180 000

The statement causes consternation at the board meeting because it seems to show that product 2 contributes much more profit than product 1 and yet this has not previously been apparent.

The Sales Director is perplexed and he points out that the budgeted sales programme for the forthcoming quarter is identical with that accepted for the current quarter (January/February/March) and yet the budget for the current quarter shows a budgeted profit of £120 000 for each product line and the actual results seem to be in line with the budget.

The Production Director emphasises that identical assumptions, as to unit variable costs, selling prices and manufacturing efficiency, underlie both budgets but there has been a change in the budgeted production pattern. He produces the following table:

Budgeted Production	Product 1	Product 2
January/February/March	30 000 units	52 500 units
April/May/June	24 000 units	60 000 units

He urges that the company's budgeting procedures be overhauled as he can see no reason why the quarter's profit should be £24 000 up on the previous quarter and why the net profit for product 1 should fall from £4.00 to £2.80 per unit sold, whereas, for product 2 it should rise from £2.11 to £3.16.

You are required:

a To reconstruct the company's budget for the January/February/March quarter. *(6 marks)*

b To restate the budgets (for both quarters) using standard marginal cost as the stock valuation basis. *(8 marks)*

c To comment on the queries raised by the Sales Director and the Production Director and on the varying profit figures disclosed by the alternative budgets. *(8 marks)*

ACCA Level 2 Management Accounting

IM7.7 Advanced: Explanation of difference between absorption and variable costing profit statements. The accountant of Minerva Ltd, a small company manufacturing only one product, wishes to decide how to present the company's monthly management accounts. To date only actual information has been presented on an historic cost basis, with stocks valued at average cost. Standard costs have now been derived for the costs of production. The practical capacity (also known as full capacity) for annual production is 160 000 units, and this has been used as the basis for the allocation of production overheads. Selling and administration fixed overheads have been allocated assuming all 160 000 units are sold. The expected production capacity for 2001 is 140 000 units. It is anticipated now that, for the 12 months to 31 December 2001, production and sales volume will equal 120 000 units, compared to the forecast sales and production volumes of 140 000 units. The standard cost and standard profit per unit based on practical capacity is:

	(£ per unit)	(£ per unit)
Selling price		25.00
Production costs:		
Variable	8.00	
Fixed	6.00	
	14.00	
Variable selling costs	1.00	15.00
		10.00
Other fixed costs:		
Administration	2.10	
Selling	1.20	3.30
Standard profit per unit		6.70

The accountant has prepared the following three drafts (see below) of Minerva Ltd's profit and loss account for the month of November 2000 using three different accounting methods. The drafts are based on data relating to production, sales and stock for November 2000 which are given below.

Production and sales quantities November 2000

	(units)
Opening stock	20 000
Production	8 000
	28 000
Less Sales	10 000
Closing stock	18 000

The accountant is trying to choose the best method of presenting the financial information to the directors. The present method is shown under the Actual costs column; the two other methods are based on the standard costs derived above.

The following estimated figures for the month of December 2000 have just come to hand:

Sales 12 000 units at £25
Production costs:
  variable £116 000
  fixed £90 000

Production 14 000 units
Administration costs £24 500
Selling costs:
  variable £12 000
  fixed £15 000

Draft profit and loss accounts for the month ended 30 November 2000

	Actual costs		Absorption cost method		Variable cost method	
	(£000)	(£000)	(£000)	(£000)	(£000)	(£000)
Sales (10 000 units at £25)		250		250		250
Opening stock	280		280		160	
Production costs:						
variable	60		112[a]		64	
fixed	66		—		—	
	406		392		224	
Closing stock	261	145	252	140	144	80
		105		110		170
Variable selling costs		—		—		10
Gross profit/contribution		105		110		160
Other expenses:						
Production – fixed	—		—		80	
Administration – fixed	23		21		28	
Selling:						
variable	11		10		—	
fixed	14	48	12	43	16	124
		57		67		36
Variances						
Production						
variable – expenditure			(4)		(4)	
fixed – volume			32		—	
– expenditure			(14)		(14)	
Administration – volume			7		—	
– expenditure			(5)		(5)	
Selling:						
variable – expenditure			1		1	
fixed – volume			4		—	
– expenditure		—	(2)	19	(2)	(24)
Net profit		57		48		60

Note
[a] Sum of variable and fixed costs.

Requirements
a Prepare a schedule explaining the main difference(s) between the net profit figures for November 2000 under the three different allocation methods. *(8 marks)*
b Discuss the relative merits of the two suggested alternative methods as a means of providing useful information to the company's senior management. *(8 marks)*
c Draw up a short report for senior management presenting your recommendations for the choice of method of preparing the monthly accounts, incorporating in your report the profit and loss account for November and the projected profit and loss account for December 2000 as examples of your recommendations.
(9 marks)
ICAEW P2 Management Accounting

PART THREE

Information for Decision-making

The objective of this Part, which contains seven chapters, is to consider the provision of financial information that will help managers to make better decisions. Chapter 8–12 are concerned mainly with short-term decisions based on the environment of today, and the physical, human and financial resources that are presently available to a firm; these decisions are determined to a considerable extent by the quality of the firm's long-term decisions. An important distinction between the long-term and short-term decisions is that the former cannot easily be reversed whereas the latter can often be changed. The actions that follow short-term decisions are frequently repeated, and it is possible for different actions to be taken in the future. For example, the setting of a particular selling price or product mix can often be changed fairly quickly. With regard to long-term decisions, such as capital investment, which involves, for example, the purchase of new plant and machinery, it is not easy to change a decision in the short term. Resources may only be available for major investments in plant and machinery at lengthy intervals, and it is unlikely that plant replacement decisions will be repeated in the short term.

Chapters 8–12 concentrate mainly on how accounting information can be applied to different forms of short-term decisions. Chapter 8 focuses on what will happen to the financial results if a specific level of activity or volume fluctuates. This information is required for making optimal short-term output decisions. Chapter 9 examines how costs and revenues should be measured for a range of non-routine short-term and long-term decisions. Chapter 10 focuses on an alternative approach for measuring resources consumed by cost objects. This approach is called activity-based costing. Chapter 11 is concerned with profitability analysis and the provision of financial information for pricing decisions. Chapters 8–11 assume a world of certainty, whereas Chapter 12 introduces methods of incorporating uncertainty into the analysis, and the topics covered in Chapters 8–11 are re-examined under conditions of uncertainty.

The final two chapters in this part are concerned with long-term decisions. Chapter 13 looks at the appraisal methods that are used for evaluating capital investment decisions, and introduces the concept of the time value of money. Chapter 14 examines more complex issues relating to capital investment decisions. In particular, the impact of capital rationing, taxation, inflation and risk is examined.

Cost–volume–profit analysis

In the previous chapters we have considered how costs should be accumulated for inventory valuation and profit measurement, and we have stressed that costs should be accumulated in a different way for decision-making and cost control. In the next seven chapters we shall look at the presentation of financial information for decision-making. We begin by considering how management accounting information can be of assistance in providing answers to questions about the consequences of following particular courses of action. Such questions might include 'How many units must be sold to break-even?' 'What would be the effect on profits if we reduce our selling price and sell more units?' 'What sales volume is required to meet the additional fixed charges arising from an advertising campaign?' 'Should we pay our sales people on the basis of a salary only, or on the basis of a commission only, or by a combination of the two?' These and other questions can be answered using cost–volume–profit (CVP) analysis.

This is a systematic method of examining the relationship between changes in activity (i.e. output) and changes in total sales revenue, expenses and net profit. As a model of these relationships CVP analysis simplifies the real-world conditions that a firm will face. Like most models, which are abstractions from reality, CVP analysis is subject to a number of underlying assumptions

LEARNING OBJECTIVES

After studying this chapter, you should be able to:

● describe the differences between the accountant's and the economist's model of cost–volume–profit analysis;

● justify the use of linear cost and revenue functions in the accountant's model;

● apply the mathematical approach to answer questions similar to those listed in Example 8.1;

● construct break-even, contribution and profit–volume graphs;

● apply cost–volume–profit analysis in a multi-product setting;

● identify and explain the assumptions on which cost–volume–profit analysis is based.

and limitations, which will be discussed later in this chapter; nevertheless, it is a powerful tool for decision-making in certain situations.

This objective of CVP analysis is to establish what will happen to the financial results if a specified level of activity or volume fluctuates. This information is vital to management, since one of the most important variables influencing total sales revenue, total costs and profits is output or volume. For this reason output is given special attention, since knowledge of this relationship will enable management to identify the critical output levels, such as the level at which neither a profit nor a loss will occur (i.e. the break-even point).

CVP analysis is based on the relationship between volume and sales revenue, costs and profit in the short run, the short run normally being a period of one year, or less, in which the output of a firm is restricted to that available from the current operating capacity. In the short run, some inputs can be increased, but others cannot. For example, additional supplies of materials and unskilled labour may be obtained at short notice, but it takes time to expand the capacity of plant and machinery. Thus output is limited in the short run because plant facilities cannot be expanded. It also takes time to reduce capacity, and therefore in the short run a firm must operate on a relatively constant stock of production resources. Furthermore, most of the costs and prices of a firm's products will have already been determined, and the major area of uncertainty will be sales volume. Short-run profitability will therefore be most sensitive to sales volume. CVP analysis thus highlights the effects of changes in sales volume on the level of profits in the short run.

The theoretical relationship between total sales revenue, costs and profits with volume has been developed by economists. In order to provide a theoretical basis for examining the accountant's approach to CVP analysis this chapter begins by describing the economist's model of CVP analysis.

The economist's model

An economist's model of CVP behaviour is presented in Figure 8.1. You will see that the total-revenue line is assumed to be curvilinear, which indicates that the firm is only able to sell increasing quantities of output by reducing the selling price per unit; thus the total revenue line does not increase proportionately with output. To increase the quantity of sales, it is necessary to reduce the unit selling price, which results in the total revenue line rising less steeply, and eventually beginning to decline. This is because the adverse effect of price reductions outweighs the benefits of increased sales volume.

The total cost line AD shows that, between points A and B, total costs rise steeply at first as the firm operates at the lower levels of the volume range. This reflects the difficulties of efficiently operating a plant designed for much larger volume levels. Between points B and C, the total cost line begins to level out and rise less steeply because the firm is now able to operate the plant within the efficient operating range and can take advantage of specialization of labour, and

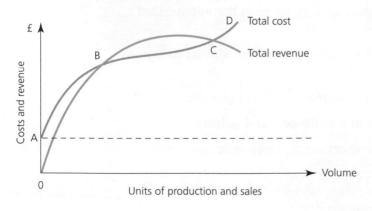

FIGURE 8.1
Economist's cost–volume graph

smooth production schedules. In the upper portion of the volume range the total cost line between points C and D rises more and more steeply as the cost per unit increases. This is because the output per direct labour hour declines when the plant is operated beyond the activity level for which it was designed: bottlenecks develop, production schedules become more complex, and plant breakdowns begin to occur. The overall effect is that the cost per unit of output increases and causes the total cost line to rise steeply.

The dashed horizontal line from point A represents the cost of providing the basic operating capacity, and is the economist's interpretation of the total fixed costs of the firm. Note also from Figure 8.1 that the shape of the total revenue line is such that it crosses the total cost line at two points. In other words, there are two output levels at which the total costs are equal to the total revenues; or more simply, there are two break-even points.

It is the shape of the variable cost function in the economist's model that has the most significant influence on the total cost function; this is illustrated in Figure 8.2. The economist assumes that the average *unit* variable cost declines initially, reflecting the fact that, as output expands, a firm is able to obtain bulk discounts on the purchase of raw materials and can benefit from the division of labour; this results in the labour cost per unit being reduced. The economist refers to this situation as increasing returns to scale. The fact that *unit* variable cost is higher at lower levels of activity causes the total cost line between points A and B in Figure 8.1 to rise steeply. From Figure 8.2 you can see that the *unit* variable cost levels out between output levels Q_1 and Q_2 and then gradually begins to rise. This is because the firm is operating at its most efficient output level, and further economies of scale are not possible in the short term. However, beyond output level Q_2, the plant is being operated at a higher level than that for which it was intended, and bottlenecks and plant breakdowns occur. The effect of this is that output per direct labour hour declines, and causes the variable cost per unit to increase. The economist describes this situation as decreasing returns to scale.

It is the shape of the variable cost function that causes the total cost line to behave in the manner indicated in Figure 8.1. Between points B and C, the total cost line rises less steeply, indicating that the firm is operating in the range where unit variable cost is at its lowest. Between points C and D, the total cost line rises more steeply, since the variable cost per unit is increasing owing to decreasing returns to scale.

The accountant's cost–volume–profit model

The diagram for the accountant's model is presented in Figure 8.3. Note that the dashed line represents the economist's total cost function, which enables a comparison to be made with the accountant's total cost function. The accountant's diagram assumes a variable cost and a selling price that are constant per unit; this results in a linear relationship (i.e. a straight line) for total revenue and total cost as volume changes. The effect is that there is only one break-even point in the diagram, and the profit area widens as volume increases. The most profitable output is therefore at maximum practical capacity. Clearly, the economist's model appears to be more realistic, since it assumes that the total cost curve is non-linear.

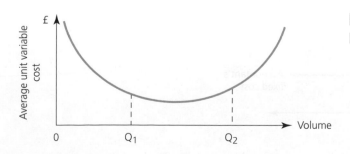

FIGURE 8.2
Economist's variable cost function

Relevant range

How can we justify the accountant's assumption of linear cost and linear revenue functions? The answer is that the accountants' diagram is not intended to provide an accurate representation of total cost and total revenue throughout all ranges of output. The objective is to represent the behaviour of total cost and revenue over the range of output at which a firm expects to be operating within a short-term planning horizon. This range of output is represented by the output range between points X and Y in Figure 8.3. The term relevant range is used to refer to the output range at which the firm expects to be operating within a short-term planning horizon. This relevant range also broadly represents the output levels which the firm has had experience of operating in the past and for which cost information is available.

You can see from Figure 8.3 that, between points X and Y, the shape of the accountant's total cost line is very similar to that of the economist's. This is because the total cost line is only intended to provide a good approximation within the relevant range. Within this range, the accountant assumes that the variable cost per unit is the same throughout the entire range of output, and the total cost line is therefore linear. Note that the cost function is approximately linear within this range. It would be unwise, however, to make this assumption for production levels outside the relevant range. It would be more appropriate if the accountant's total cost line was presented for the relevant range of output only, and not extended to the vertical axis or to the output levels beyond Y in Figure 8.3.

Fixed cost function

Note also that the accountant's fixed cost function in Figure 8.3 meets the vertical axis at a different point to that at which the economist's total cost line meets the vertical axis. The reason for this can be explained from Figure 8.4. The fixed cost level of 0A may be applicable to, say, activity level Q_2 to Q_3, but if there were to be a prolonged economic recession then output might fall below Q_1, and this could result in redundancies and shutdowns. Therefore fixed costs may be reduced to 0B if there is a prolonged and a significant decline in sales demand. Alternatively, additional fixed costs will be incurred if long-term sales volume is expected to be greater than Q_3. Over a longer-term time horizon, the fixed cost line will consist of a series of step functions rather than the horizontal straight line depicted in Figure 8.3. However, since within its short-term planning horizon the firm expects to be operating between output levels Q_2 and Q_3, it will be committed, in the short term, to fixed costs of 0A; but you should remember that if there was a prolonged economic recession then in the longer term fixed costs may be reduced to 0B.

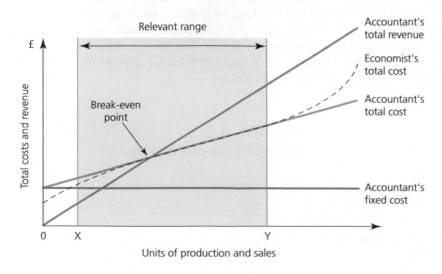

FIGURE 8.3
Accountant's cost–volume–profit diagram

The fixed cost line for output levels below Q_1 (i.e. 0B) represents the cost of providing the basic operating capacity, and this line is the equivalent to the point where the economist's total cost line meets the vertical axis in Figure 8.3. Because the accountant assumes that in the short term the firm will operate in the relevant range between Q_2 and Q_3, the accountant's fixed cost line 0A in Figure 8.4 represents the fixed costs for the relevant output range only, which the firm is committed to in the current period and does not represent the fixed costs that would be incurred at the extreme levels of output beyond the shaded area in Figure 8.4.

Total revenue function

Let us now compare the total revenue line for the accountant and the economist. We have seen that the accountant assumes that selling price is constant over the relevant range of output, and therefore the total revenue line is a straight line. The accountant's assumption about the revenue line is a realistic one in those firms that operate in industries where selling prices tend to be fixed in the short term. A further factor reinforcing the assumption of a fixed selling price is that competition may take the form of non-price rather than price competition. Moreover, beyond the relevant range, increases in output may only be possible by offering substantial reductions in price. As it is not the intention of firms to operate outside the relevant range, the accountant makes no attempt to produce accurate revenue functions outside this range. It might be more meaningful in Figure 8.3 if the total revenue line was presented for output levels X and Y within the relevant range, instead of being extended to the left and right of these points.

A mathematical approach to cost–volume–profit analysis

Instead of using a diagram to present CVP information, we can use mathematical relationships. The mathematical approach is a quicker and more flexible method of producing the appropriate information than the graphical approach, and is a particularly appropriate form of input to a computer financial model.

When developing a mathematical formula for producing CVP information, you should note that one is assuming that selling price and costs remain constant per unit of output. Such an assumption may be valid for unit selling price and variable cost, but remember that in Chapter 2 we noted that in the short run fixed costs are a constant *total* amount whereas *unit* cost changes with output levels. As a result, profit per *unit* also changes with volume. For example, if fixed costs are £10 000 for a period and output is 10 000 units, the fixed cost will be £1 per unit. Alternatively, if output is 5000 units, the fixed cost will be £2 per unit. Profit per unit will not therefore be constant over varying output levels and it is incorrect to unitize fixed costs for CVP decisions.

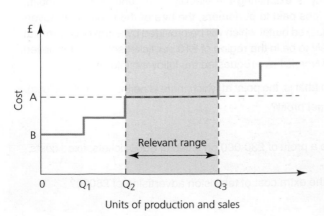

FIGURE 8.4
Accountant's fixed costs

We can develop a mathematical formula from the following relationship:

$$\text{net profit} = (\text{units sold} \times \text{unit selling price})$$
$$- [(\text{units sold} \times \text{unit variable cost}) + \text{total fixed costs}]$$

The following symbols can be used to represent the various items in the above equation:

NP = net profit

x = units sold

P = selling price

b = unit variable cost

a = total fixed costs

The equation can now be expressed in mathematical terms as

$$NP = Px - (a + bx) \tag{8.1}$$

You should now refer to Example 8.1. This example will be used to illustrate the application of the mathematical approach to CVP analysis.

Let us now provide the information requested in Example 8.1.

1 Break-even point in units (i.e. number of tickets sold)

Since $NP = Px - (a + bx)$, the break-even point is at a level of output (x) where

$$a + bx = Px - NP$$

Substituting the information in Example 8.1, we have

$$60\,000 + 10x = 20x - 0$$
$$60\,000 = 10x$$

and so $x = 6000$ tickets (or £120 000 total sales at £20 per ticket).

EXAMPLE 8.1

Norvik Enterprises operate in the leisure and entertainment industry and one of its activities is to promote concerts at locations throughout Europe. The company is examining the viability of a concert in Stockholm. Estimated fixed costs are £60 000. These include the fees paid to perfomers, the hire of the venue and advertising costs. Variable costs consist of the cost of a pre-packed buffet which will be provided by a firm of caterers at a price, which is currently being negotiated, but it is likely to be in the region of £10 per ticket sold. The proposed price for the sale of a ticket is £20. The management of Norvic have requested the following information:

1 The number of tickets that must be sold to break-even (that is, the point at which there is neither a profit nor loss).

2 How many tickets must be sold to earn £30 000 target profit?

3 What profit would result if 8000 tickets were sold?

4 What selling price would have to be charged to give a profit of £30 000 on sales of 8000 tickets, fixed costs of £60 000 and variable costs of £10 per ticket?

5 How many additional tickets must be sold to cover the extra cost of television advertising of £8000?

An alternative non-mathematical method, called the contribution margin approach, can also be used. Contribution margin is equal to sales minus variable expenses. Because the variable cost per unit and the selling price per unit are assumed to be constant the contribution margin per unit is also assumed to be constant. In Example 8.1 note that each ticket sold generates a contribution of £10, which is available to cover fixed costs and, after they are covered, to contribute to profit. When we have obtained sufficient total contribution to cover fixed costs, the break-even point is achieved, and the alternative formula is

$$\text{break-even point in units} = \frac{\text{fixed costs}}{\text{contribution per unit}}$$

The contribution margin approach can be related to the mathematical formula approach. Consider the penultimate line of the formula approach; it reads

$$£60\,000 = 10x$$

and so

$$x = \frac{£60\,000}{£10}$$

giving the contribution margin formula

$$\frac{\text{fixed costs}}{\text{contribution per unit}}$$

The contribution margin approach is therefore a restatement of the mathematical formula, and either technique can be used; it is a matter of personal preference.

2 Units to be sold to obtain a £30 000 profit

Using the equation $NP = Px - (a + bx)$ and substituting the information in Example 8.1, we have

$$£30\,000 = £20x - (£60\,000 + £10x)$$
$$£90\,000 = £10x$$

and so

$$x = 9000 \text{ tickets}$$

If we apply the contribution margin approach and wish to achieve the desired profit, we must obtain sufficient contribution to cover the fixed costs (i.e. the break-even point) plus a further contribution to cover the target profit. Hence we simply add the target profit to the fixed costs so that the equation using the contribution margin approach is

$$\text{units sold for target profit} = \frac{\text{fixed costs} + \text{target profit}}{\text{contribution per unit}}$$

This is merely a restatement of the penultimate line of the mathematical formula, which reads

$$£90\,000 = £10x$$

and so

$$x = \frac{£90\,000}{£10}$$

3 Profit from the sale of 8000 tickets

Substituting in the equation $NP = Px - (a + bx)$, we have

$$NP = £20 \times 8000 - (£60\,000 + £10 \times 8000)$$
$$= £160\,000 - (£60\,000 + £80\,000)$$

and so $\qquad NP = £20\,000$

Alternatively, we can apply the contribution margin approach. The total contribution from the sale of 8000 tickets is £80 000 (8000 × £10). To ascertain the profit we deduct the fixed costs of £60 000 giving a net profit of £20 000.

Let us now assume that we wish to ascertain the impact on profit if a further 1000 tickets are sold so that sales volume increases from 8000 to 9000 tickets. Assuming that fixed costs remain unchanged, the impact on a firm's profits resulting from a change in the number of units sold can be determined by multiplying the unit contribution margin by the change in units sold. Therefore the increase in profits will be £10 000 (1000 units times a unit contribution margin of £10).

4 Selling price to be charged to show a profit of £30 000 on sales of 8000 units

Applying the formula for net profit (i.e. Equation 8.1)

$$£30\,000 = 8000P - (60\,000 + (£10 \times 8000))$$
$$= 8000P - £140\,000$$

giving $\qquad 8000P = £170\,000$

and $\qquad P = £21.25$ (i.e. an increase of £1.25 per ticket)

An alternative approach is to determine the total required revenue to obtain a profit of £30 000. This is £170 000, which is derived from the sum of the fixed costs (£60 000), variable costs (8000 × £10) and the target profit (£30 000). Dividing the required sales revenues of £170 000 by the sales volume (8000 tickets) gives a selling price of £21.25.

5 Additional sales volume to meet £8000 additional fixed advertising charges

The contribution per unit is £10 and fixed costs will increase by £8000. Therefore an extra 800 tickets must be sold to cover the additional fixed costs of £8000.

The profit–volume ratio

The **profit–volume ratio** (also known as the contribution margin ratio) is the contribution divided by sales. It represents the proportion of each £1 sales available to cover fixed costs and provide for profit. In Example 8.1 the contribution is £10 per unit and the selling price is £20 per unit; the profit–volume ratio is 0.5. This means that for each £1 sale a contribution of £0.50 is earned. Because we assume that selling price and contribution per unit are constant, the profit–volume ratio is also assumed to be constant. Therefore the profit–volume ratio can be computed using either unit figures or total figures. Given an estimate of total sales revenue, it is possible to use the profit–volume ratio to estimate total contribution. For example, if total sales revenue is estimated to be £200 000, the total contribution will be £100 000 (£200 000 × 0.5). To calculate the profit, we deduct fixed costs of £60 000; thus a profit of £40 000 will be obtained from total sales revenue of £200 000.

Expressing the above computations in mathematical terms:

$$NP = (\text{Sales revenue} \times \text{PV ratio}) - \text{Fixed costs}$$

$$NP + \text{Fixed costs} = \text{Sales revenue} \times \text{PV ratio}$$

Therefore the break-even sales revenue (where $NP = 0$) = Fixed costs/PV ratio.

Relevant range

It is vital to remember that, CVP analysis can only be used for decisions that result in outcomes within the relevant range. Outside this range the unit selling price and the variable cost are no longer deemed to be constant per unit, and any results obtained from the formulae that fall outside the relevant range will be incorrect. The concept of the relevant range is more appropriate for production settings but it can apply within non-production settings. Returning to Norvic Enterprises in Example 8.1, let us assume that the caterers' charges will be higher per ticket if ticket sales are below 4000 but lower if sales exceed 12 000 tickets. Thus, the £10 variable cost relates only to a sales volume within a range of 4000–12 000 tickets. Outside this range other costs apply. Also the number of seats made available at the venue is flexible and the hire cost will be reduced for sales of less than 4000 tickets and increased for sales beyond 12 000 tickets. In other words, we will assume that the relevant range is a sales volume of 4000–12 000 tickets and outside this range the results of our CVP analysis do not apply.

Margin of safety

The margin of safety indicates by how much sales may decrease before a loss occurs. Using Example 8.1, where unit selling price and variable cost were £20 and £10 respectively and fixed costs were

---

REAL WORLD VIEWS 8.1

Starting a business

For any person starting a business, determining whether the business is a profitable venture or otherwise is often problematic. However, the business idea should be a financially sound idea to be viable.

Quite often, the first point of contact for a fledgling entrepreneur is a bank, business association or government agency. For the typical start-up business, it is more important to ensure that ongoing operating costs are covered by sales revenue in the short to medium term. It would of course be the intention to make a profit in the medium to long term.

The United States Small Business Administration (SBA)[1] was set up in 1953. It provides advice and finance to small business. Over 20 million US businesses have benefited from SBA loans, advice and counselling. One basic tool recommended by the SBA is break-even analysis. Break-even means a business makes neither profit nor loss. If a start up business can identify its costs and revenues it can establish the level of sales required to at least break-even. If the level of break-even sales cannot be achieved, then the business idea may not be sound financially.

In order to identify the break-even point, a business must be able to identify its fixed and variable costs. Fixed costs must be paid regardless of sales volume. Therefore the sales revenue less the variable costs must be enough to cover fixed costs. The calculation of the break-even point requires no more than simple arithmetic – providing a simple tool for the entrepreneur to make a quick decision to abandon or revise the business plan.

Discussion points

1 Are fixed and variable costs always readily identifiable?

2 In what other business scenarios might break-even calculations prove useful?

[1] www.sba.gov.

£60 000, we noted that the break-even point was 6000 tickets or £120 000 sales value. If sales are expected to be 8000 tickets or £160 000, the margin of safety will be 2000 tickets or £40 000. Alternatively, we can express the margin of safety in a percentage form based on the following ratio:

$$\text{percentage margin of safety} = \frac{\text{expected sales} - \text{break-even sales}}{\text{expected sales}}$$

$$= \frac{£160\,000 - £120\,000}{£160\,000} = 25\%$$

Constructing the break-even chart

Managers may obtain a clearer understanding of CVP behaviour if the information is presented in graphical format. Using the data in Example 8.1, we can construct the break-even chart for Norvik Enterprises (Figure 8.5). In constructing the graph, the fixed costs are plotted as a single horizontal line at the £60 000 level. Variable costs at the rate of £10 per unit of volume are added to the fixed costs to enable the total cost line to be plotted. Two points are required to insert the total cost line. At zero sales volume total cost will be equal to the fixed costs of £60 000. At 12 000 units sales volume total costs will be £180 000 consisting of £120 000 variable cost plus £60 000 fixed costs. The total revenue line is plotted at the rate of £20 per unit of volume. The constraints of the relevant range consisting of two vertical lines are then added to the graph: beyond these lines we have little assurance that the CVP relationships are valid.

The point at which the total sales revenue line cuts the total cost line is the point where the concert makes neither a profit nor a loss. This is the break-even point and is 6000 tickets or £120 000 total sales revenue. The distance between the total sales revenue line and the total cost line at a volume below the break-even point represents losses that will occur for various sales

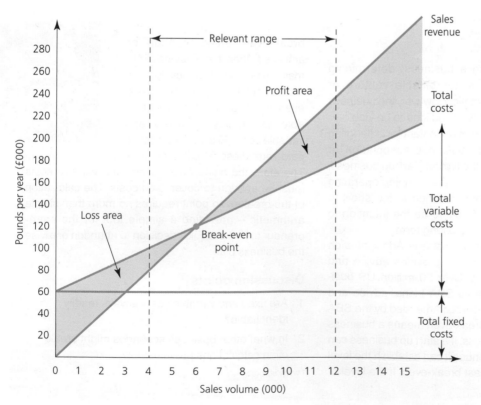

FIGURE 8.5
Break-even chart for Example 8.1

levels below 6000 tickets. Similarly, if the company operates at a sales volume above the break-even point, the difference between the total revenue and the total cost lines represents the profit that results from sales levels above 6000 tickets.

Alternative presentation of cost–volume–profit analysis

Contribution graph

In Figure 8.5 the fixed cost line is drawn parallel to the horizontal axis, and the variable cost is the difference between the total cost line and the fixed cost line. An alternative to Figure 8.5 for the data contained in Example 8.1 is illustrated in Figure 8.6. This alternative presentation is called a contribution graph. In Figure 8.6 the variable cost line is drawn first at £10 per unit of volume. The fixed costs are represented by the difference between the total cost line and the variable cost line. Because fixed costs are assumed to be a constant sum throughout the entire output range, a constant sum of £60 000 for fixed costs is added to the variable cost line, which results in the total cost line being drawn parallel to the variable cost line. The advantage of this form of presentation is that the total contribution is emphasized in the graph, and is represented by the difference between the total sales revenue line and the total variable cost line.

Profit–volume graph

The break-even and contribution charts do not highlight the profit or loss at different volume levels. To ascertain the profit or loss figures from a break-even chart, it is necessary to determine the difference between the total-cost and total-revenue lines. The profit–volume graph is a more convenient method of showing the impact of changes in volume on profit. Such a graph is illustrated in Figure 8.7. The horizontal axis represents the various levels of sales volume, and the profits

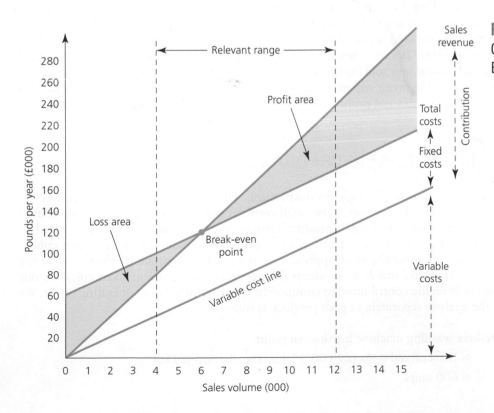

FIGURE 8.6
Contribution chart for Example 8.1

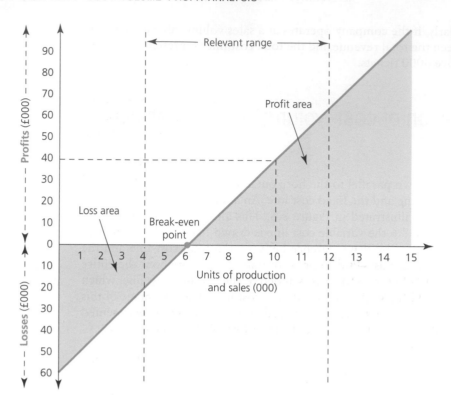

FIGURE 8.7
Profit–volume graph for Example 8.1

and losses for the period are recorded on the vertical scale. You will see from Figure 8.7 that profits or losses are plotted for each of the various sales levels, and these points are connected by a profit line. Two points are required to plot the profit line. When units sold are zero a loss equal to the amount of fixed costs (£60 000) will be reported. At the break-even point (zero profits) sales volume is 6000 units. Therefore the break-even point is plotted at the point where the profit line intersects the horizontal line at a sales volume of 6000 tickets. The profit line is drawn between the two points. With each unit sold, a contribution of £10 is obtained towards the fixed costs, and the break-even point is at 6000 tickets, when the total contribution exactly equals the total of the fixed costs. With each additional unit sold beyond 6000 tickets, a surplus of £10 per ticket is obtained. If 10 000 tickets are sold, the profit will be £40 000 (4000 tickets at £10 contribution). You can see this relationship between sales and profit at 10 000 tickets from the dotted lines in Figure 8.7.

Multi-product cost–volume–profit analysis

Our analysis so far has assumed a single-product setting. However, most firms produce and sell many products or services. In this section we shall consider how we can adapt the analysis used for a single-product setting to a multi-product setting. Consider the situation presented in Example 8.2. You will see that the company sells two products so that there are two unit contribution margins. We can apply the same approach as that used for a single product if all of the fixed costs are directly attributable to products (i.e. there are no common fixed costs) or our analysis focuses only on the contribution to common fixed costs, rather than operating profit. We simply apply the analysis separately to each product as follows:

De-luxe washing machine break-even point
= Direct fixed costs (£90 000)/Unit contribution (£150)
= 600 units

Standard washing machine break-even point

= Direct fixed costs (£27 000)/Unit contribution (£90)

= 300 units

However, selling 600 de-luxe and 300 standard washing machines will generate a contribution that only covers direct fixed costs; the common fixed costs will not be covered. A loss equal to the common fixed costs will be reported. The break-even point for the firm as a whole has not been ascertained.

You may think that the break-even point for the firm as a whole can be derived if we allocate the common fixed costs to each individual product but this approach is inappropriate because the allocation will be arbitrary. The common fixed costs cannot be specifically identified with either of the products since they can only be avoided if *both* products are not sold. The solution to our problem is to convert the sales volume measure of the individual products into standard batches of products based on the planned sales mix. You will from see from Example 8.2 that Super Bright plans to sell 1200 de-luxe and 600 standard machines giving a sales mix of 1200:600. Reducing this sales mix to the smallest whole number gives a mix of 2:1. In other words, for the sale of every two de-luxe machines one standard machine is expected to be sold. We therefore define our standard batch of products as comprising two de-luxe and one standard machine giving a contribution of £390 per batch (two de-luxe machines at a contribution of £150 per unit sold plus and one standard machine at a contribution of £90).

The break-even point in standard batches can be calculated by using the same break-even equation that we used for a single product so that:

Break-even number of batches = Total fixed costs (£156 000)/Contribution margin per batch (£390)

= 400 batches

SOURCE: AEPPEL, T. (1993), 'VW CHIEF DECLARES A CRISIS AND PRESCRIBES BOLD ACTION', THE WALL STREET JOURNAL, 1 APRIL, P.B4.

The impact of Volkswagen's high break-even point on profitability

REAL WORLD VIEWS 8.2

In the early 1990s Volkswagen AG of Germany reported a large continuing decline in earnings even though in 1992 it sold a record 3.5 million vehicles world-wide. One of the reasons for the declining profitability was that its break-even point was above 90 per cent. Consequently, sales had to exceed 90 per cent capacity before profits were reported. The company had to run its factory on overtime just to make a small profit. In contrast, European competitors already had break-even points below 70 per cent of capacity. To overcome this problem, steps were taken to reduce fixed capacity costs that would enable it in the short-term to head rapidly to a break-even below 90 per cent.

Discussion points

1 Why does the company have a higher break-even point than its competitors?

2 How does a high break-even point influence the profitability of a company?

Wolfsburg Autostadt, car city of Volkswagen AG
© TRAVELSTOCK44/ALAMY

The sales mix used to define a standard batch (2:1) can be now be used to convert the break-even point (measured in standard batches) into a break-even point expressed in terms of the required combination of individual products sold. Thus, 800 de-luxe machines (2 × 400) and 400 (1 × 400) standard machines must be sold to break-even. The following profit statement verifies this outcome:

Units sold	De-luxe machine 800 (£)	Standard machine 400 (£)	Total (£)
Unit contribution margin	150	90	
Contribution to direct and common fixed costs	120 000	36 000	156 000
Less: Direct fixed costs	90 000	27 000	117 000
Contribution to common fixed costs	30 000	9 000	39 000
Less: Common fixed costs			39 000
Operating profit			0

Let us now assume that the actual sales volume for the period was 1200 units, the same total volume as the break-even volume, but consisting of a sales mix of 600 units of each machine. Thus, the actual sales mix is 1:1 compared with a planned sales mix of 2:1. The total contribution to direct and common fixed costs will be £144 000 ([£150 × 600] + [£90 × 600]) and

EXAMPLE 8.2

The Super Bright Company sells two types of washing machines – a de-luxe model and a standard model. The financial controller has prepared the following information based on the sales forecast for the period:

Sales volume (units)	De-luxe machine 1200 (£)	Standard machine 600 (£)	Total (£)
Unit selling price	300	200	
Unit variable cost	150	110	
Unit contribution	150	90	
Total sales revenues	360 000	120 000	480 000
Less: Total variable cost	180 000	66 000	246 000
Contribution to direct and common fixed costs[a]	180 000	54 000	234 000
Less: Direct avoidable fixed costs	90 000	27 000	117 000
Contribution to common fixed costs[a]	90 000	27 000	117 000
Less common (indirect) fixed costs			39 000
Operating profit			78 000

The common fixed costs relate to the costs of common facilities and can only be avoided if neither of the products is sold. The managing director is concerned that sales may be less than forecast and has requested information relating to the break-even point for the activities for the period.

Note

[a]Contribution was defined earlier in this chapter as sales less variable costs. Where fixed costs are divided into direct and common (indirect) fixed costs it is possible to identify two separate contribution categories. The first is described as contribution to direct and common fixed costs and this is identical to the conventional definition, being equivalent to sales less variable costs. The second is after a further deduction of direct fixed costs and is described as 'Contribution to common or indirect fixed costs'.

a loss of £12 000 (£144 000 contribution – £156 000 total fixed costs) will occur. It should now be apparent to you that the break-even point (or the sales volumes required to achieve a target profit) is not a unique number: it varies depending upon the composition of the sales mix. Because the actual sales mix differs from the planned sales mix, the sales mix used to define a standard batch has changed from 2:1 to 1:1 so that the contribution per batch changes from £390 to £240 ([1 × £150] + [1 × £90]). Therefore the revised break-even point will be 650 batches (£156 000 total fixed costs/£240 contribution per batch) which converts to a sales volume of 650 units of each machine based on a 1:1 sales mix. Generally, an increase in the proportion of sales of higher contribution margin products will decrease the break-even point whereas increases in sales of the lower margin products will increase the break-even point.

Cost–volume–profit analysis assumptions

It is essential that anyone preparing or interpreting CVP information is aware of the underlying assumptions on which the information has been prepared. If these assumptions are not recognized, or the analysis modified, errors may result and incorrect conclusions may be drawn from the analysis. We shall now consider these important assumptions. They are as follows:

1 All other variables remain constant.
2 A single product or constant sales mix.
3 Total costs and total revenue are linear functions of output.
4 Profits are calculated on a variable costing basis.
5 The analysis applies to the relevant range only.
6 Costs can be accurately divided into their fixed and variable elements.
7 The analysis applies only to a short-term time horizon.

1 All other variables remain constant

It has been assumed that all variables other than the particular one under consideration have remained constant throughout the analysis. In other words, it is assumed that volume is the only factor that will cause costs and revenues to change. However, changes in other variables such as production efficiency, sales mix, price levels and production methods can have an important influence on sales revenue and costs. If significant changes in these other variables occur the CVP analysis presentation will be incorrect.

2 Single product or constant sales mix

CVP analysis assumes that either a single product is sold or, if a range of products is sold, that sales will be in accordance with a predetermined sales mix. When a predetermined sales mix is used, it can be depicted in the CVP analysis by measuring sales volume using standard batch sizes based on a planned sales mix. Any CVP analysis must be interpreted carefully if the initial product mix assumptions do not hold.

3 Total costs and total revenue are linear functions of output

The analysis assumes that unit variable cost and selling price are constant. This assumption is only likely to be valid within the relevant range of production described earlier in this chapter.

4 Profits are calculated on a variable costing basis

The analysis assumes that the fixed costs incurred during the period are charged as an expense for that period. Therefore variable-costing profit calculations are assumed. If absorption-costing profit calculations are used, it is necessary to assume that production is equal to sales for the analysis to predict absorption costing profits. If this situation does not occur, the inventory levels will change and the fixed overheads allocated for the period will be different from the amount actually incurred during the period. Under absorption costing, only when production equals sales will the amount of fixed overhead incurred be equal to the amount of fixed overhead charged as an expense. For the application of CVP analysis with an absorption costing system you should refer to Learning Note 8.1 on the dedicated open access website (see Preface for details).

5 Analysis applies to relevant range only

Earlier in this chapter we noted that CVP analysis is appropriate only for decisions taken within the relevant production range, and that it is incorrect to project cost and revenue figures beyond the relevant range.

6 Costs can be accurately divided into their fixed and variable elements

CVP analysis assumes that costs can be accurately analyzed into their fixed and variable elements. The separation of semi-variable costs into their fixed and variable elements is extremely difficult in practice. Nevertheless a reasonably accurate analysis is necessary if CVP analysis is to provide relevant information for decision-making.

7 The analysis applies only to a short-term time horizon

At the beginning of this chapter we noted that CVP analysis is based on the relationship between volume and sales revenue, costs and profits in the short-term, the short-term being typically a period of one year. In the short-term the costs of providing a firm's operating capacity, such as property taxes and the salaries of senior managers, are likely to be fixed in relation to changes in activity. It is therefore assumed that in the short term some costs will be fixed and unaffected by changes in volume whereas other (variable) costs will vary with changes in volume. In the short-run volume is the most important variable influencing total revenue, costs and profit. For this reason volume is given special attention in the form of CVP analysis. You should note, however, that in the long-term other variables, besides volume, will cause costs to change.

Cost–volume–profit analysis and computer applications

The output from a CVP model is only as good as the input. The analysis will include assumptions about sales mix, production efficiency, price levels, total fixed costs, variable costs and selling price per unit. Obviously, estimates regarding these variables will be subject to varying degrees of uncertainty.

Sensitivity analysis is one approach for coping with changes in the values of the variables. Sensitivity analysis focuses on how a result will be changed if the original estimates or the underlying assumptions change. With regard to CVP analysis, sensitivity analysis answers questions such as the following:

1 What will the profit be if the sales mix changes from that originally predicted?
2 What will the profit be if fixed costs increase by 10 per cent and variable costs decline by 5 per cent?

The widespread use of spreadsheet packages has enabled management accountants to develop CVP computerized models. Managers can now consider alternative plans by keying the information into a computer, which can quickly show changes both graphically and numerically. Thus managers can study various combinations of changes in selling prices, fixed costs, variable costs and product mix, and can react quickly without waiting for formal reports from the management accountant.

Separation of semi-variable costs

CVP analysis assumes that costs can be accurately analyzed into their fixed and variable elements. Direct material is generally presumed to be a variable cost, whereas depreciation, which is related to time and not usage, is a fixed cost. Semi-variable costs, however, include both a fixed and variable component. The cost of maintenance is a semi-variable cost consisting of planned maintenance which is undertaken whatever the level of activity, and a variable element which is directly related to activity. The separation of semi-variable costs into their fixed and variable elements is extremely difficult in practice, but an accurate analysis is necessary for CVP analysis.

Mathematical techniques should be used to separate costs accurately into fixed and variable elements. For a discussion of these techniques you should refer to Chapter 23. However, first-year cost and management accounting examinations sometimes require you to separate fixed and variable costs using a more simplistic non-mathematical technique called the high–low method.

The high–low method consists of examining past costs and activity, selecting the highest and lowest activity levels and comparing the changes in costs which result from the two levels. Assume that the following activity levels and costs are extracted:

	Volume of production (units)	Indirect costs (£)
Lowest activity	5 000	22 000
Highest activity	10 000	32 000

If variable costs are constant per unit and the fixed costs remain unchanged the increase in costs will be due entirely to an increase in variable costs. The variable cost per unit is therefore calculated as follows:

$$\frac{\text{Difference in cost}}{\text{Difference in activity}} = \frac{£10\,000}{5000 \text{ units}}$$

$$= £2 \text{ variable cost per unit of activity}$$

The fixed cost can be estimated at any level of activity by subtracting the variable cost portion from the total cost. At an activity level of 5000 units the total cost is £22 000 and the total variable cost is £10 000 (5000 units at 2 per unit). The balance of £12 000 is assumed to represent the fixed cost.

SUMMARY

The following items relate to the learning objectives listed at the beginning of the chapter.

● **Describe the differences between the accountant's and the economist's model of cost–volume–profit analysis.**

The major differences are that the total cost and total revenue functions are curvilinear in the economist's model whereas the accountant's model assumes linear relationships. However, the accountant's model is intended to predict CVP behaviour only within the relevant range, where a firm is likely to be operating on constant returns to scale. A comparison of the two models suggested that, within the relevant range of activity, the total costs and revenue functions are fairly similar.

● **Justify the use of linear cost and revenue functions in the accountant's model.**

Within the relevant range it is generally assumed that cost and revenue functions are approximately linear. Outside the relevant range linearity is unlikely to apply. Care is therefore required in interpreting CVP relationships outside the relevant range.

● **Apply the mathematical approach to answer questions similar to those listed in Example 8.1.**

In Example 8.1, the break-even point was derived by dividing fixed costs by the contribution per unit. To ascertain the number of units sold to achieve a target profit the sum of the fixed costs and the target profit is divided by the contribution per unit.

● **Construct break-even, contribution and profit–volume graphs.**

Managers may obtain a clearer understanding of CVP behaviour if the information is presented in graphical format. With the break-even chart the fixed costs are plotted as a single horizontal line. The total cost line is plotted by adding variable costs to fixed costs. The reverse situation applies with a contribution graph. The variable costs are plotted first and the fixed costs are added to variable costs to plot the total cost line. Because fixed costs are assumed to be a constant sum throughout the output range, the total cost line is drawn parallel to the variable cost line. The break-even and contribution graphs do not highlight the profit or loss at different output levels and must be ascertained by comparing the differences between the total cost and total revenue lines. The profit–volume graph shows the impact of changes in volume on profits. The profits and losses are plotted for each of the various sales levels and these are connected by a profit line. You should refer to Figures 8.5–8.7 for an illustration of the graphs.

● **Apply cost–volume–profit analysis in a multi-product setting.**

Multi-product CVP analysis requires that an assumption is made concerning the expected sales mix. The approach that is used is to convert the multi-product CVP analysis into a single product analysis based on the assumption that output consists of standard batches of the multiple products based on the expected sales mix. However, you should note that the answers change as the sales mix changes.

● **Identify and explain the assumptions on which cost–volume–profit analysis is based.**

Cost–volume–profit analysis is based on the following assumptions: (a) all variables, other than volume, remain constant; (b) the sales mix remains constant; (c) total costs and revenues are linear functions of output; (d) profits are calculated on a variable costing basis; (e) the analysis applies only to the relevant range; (f) costs can be accurately divided into their fixed and variable elements; and (g) the analysis applies only to a short-term horizon.

Key terms and concepts

break-even chart (p. 174)
break-even point (p. 167)
contribution graph (p. 175)
contribution margin (p. 171)
contribution margin ratio (p. 172)

decreasing returns to scale (p. 167)
high–low method (p. 181)
increasing returns to scale (p. 167)
margin of safety (p. 173)
profit–volume graph (p. 175)

profit–volume ratio (p. 172)
relevant range (p. 168)
sensitivity analysis (p. 180)

Key examination points

Students tend to experience little difficulty in preparing break-even charts, but many cannot construct profit–volume charts. Remember that the horizontal axis represents the level of activity, while profit/losses are shown on the vertical axis. The maximum loss is at zero activity, and is equal to fixed costs. For practice on preparing a profit–volume chart you should attempt Review problem 8.18 and compare your answer with the solution. Students also experience difficulty with the following:

1 coping with multi-product situations;
2 calculating the break-even point when total sales and costs are given but no information is given on the unit costs;
3 explaining the assumptions of CVP analysis.

For multi-product situations you should base your answer on the average contribution per unit, using the approach shown in Example 8.2 Review problem 8.21 requires the computation of a break-even point in a multi-product setting. When unit costs are not given the break-even point in sales value can be calculated as follows:

$$\text{Fixed costs} \times \frac{\text{total estimated sales}}{\text{total estimated contribution}}$$

or

$$\frac{\text{Fixed costs}}{\text{profit} - \text{volume ratio}}$$

You should refer to the solutions to Review problem 8.19 for an illustration of the application of the above approach. Sometimes questions will give details of costs but not the split into the fixed and variable elements. You can separate the total costs into their fixed and variable elements using the high–low method described in the chapter. This approach is required for Review problem 8.19.

ASSESSMENT MATERIAL

The review questions are short questions that enable you to assess your understanding of the main topics included in the chapter. The numbers in parentheses provide you with the page numbers to refer to if you cannot answer a specific question.

The review problems are more complex and require you to relate and apply the content to various business problems. The problems are graded by their level of difficulty. Solutions to review problems that are not preceded by the term 'IM' are provided in a separate section at the end of the book. Solutions to problems preceded by the term 'IM' are provided in the *Instructor's Manual* accompanying this book and also on the lecturer's password protected section of the website www.drury-online.com. Additional review problems with fully worked solutions are provided in the *Student's Manual* that accompanies this book.

The website also includes over 30 case study problems. A list of these cases is provided on pages 665–7. Several cases are relevant to the content of this chapter. Examples include Dumbellow Ltd., Hardhat Ltd. and Merrion Products Ltd.

Review questions

8.1 Provide examples of how cost–volume–profit analysis can be used for decision-making. *(p. 165)*

8.2 Distinguish between the economist's and the accountant's approach to cost–volume–profit analysis. *(pp. 166–69)*

8.3 Explain what is meant by the term 'relevant range'. *(p. 168)*

8.4 Define the term 'contribution margin'. *(p. 171)*

8.5 Define the term 'profit–volume ratio' and explain how it can be used for cost–volume–profit analysis. *(p. 172)*

8.6 Describe and distinguish between the three different approaches of presenting cost–volume–profit relationships in graphical format. *(pp. 174–76)*

8.7 Describe the assumptions underlying cost–volume–profit analysis. *(pp. 179–80)*

8.8 How can a company with multiple products use cost–volume–profit analysis? *(pp. 176–79)*

8.9 Explain why the break-even point changes when there is a change in sales mix. *(p. 179)*

8.10 How can sensitivity analysis be used in conjunction with cost–volume–profit analysis? *(pp. 180–81)*

Review problems

8.11 Basic. A company has established a budgeted sales revenue for the forthcoming period of £500 000 with an associated contribution of £275 000. Fixed production costs are £137 500 and fixed selling costs are £27 500.

What is the break-even sales revenue?

- a £75 625
- b £90 750
- c £250 000
- d £300 000

ACCA Paper 1.2 – Financial Information for Management

8.12 Basic. Z plc currently sells products Aye, Bee and Cee in equal quantities and at the same selling price per unit. The contribution to sales ratio for product Aye is 40 per cent; for product Bee it is 50 per cent and the total is 48 per cent. If fixed costs are unaffected by mix and are currently 20 per cent of sales, the effect of changing the product mix to:

Aye	40%
Bee	25%
Cee	35%

is that the total contribution/total sales ratio changes to:

- a 27.4%
- b 45.3%
- c 47.4%
- d 48.4%
- e 68.4% *CIMA Stage 2*

8.13 Basic. The following information is required for sub-questions (a) and (b)

W Ltd makes leather purses. It has drawn up the following budget for its next financial period:

Selling price per unit	$11.60
Variable production cost per unit	$3.40
Sales commission	5% of selling price
Fixed production costs	$430 500
Fixed selling and administration costs	$198 150
Sales	90 000 units

(a) The margin of safety represents
- a 5.6% of budgeted sales
- b 8.3% of budgeted sales
- c 11.6% of budgeted sales
- d 14.8% of budgeted sales

(b) The marketing manager has indicated that an increase in the selling price to $12.25 per unit would not affect the number of units sold, provided that the sales commission is increased to 8 per cent of the selling price.

These changes will cause the break-even point (to the nearest whole number) to be
- a 71 033 units
- b 76 016 units
- c 79 879 units
- d 87 070 units *CIMA – Management Accounting Fundamentals*

8.14 Intermediate. Z plc provides a single service to its customers. An analysis of its budget for the year ending 31 December 2002 shows that in period 4, when the budgeted activity was 5220 service units with a sales value of £42 each, the margin of safety was 19.575 per cent.

The budgeted contribution to sales ratio of the service is 40 per cent.

Budgeted fixed costs in period 4 were nearest to
- a £1700
- b £71 000
- c £88 000
- d £176 000
  CIMA Management Accounting – Performance Management

8.15 Intermediate. RT plc sells three products.

Product R has a contribution to sales ratio of 30 per cent.
Product S has a contribution to sales ratio of 20 per cent.
Product T has a contribution to sales ratio of 25 per cent.

Monthly fixed costs are £100 000.

If the products are sold in the ratio:

   R: 2   S: 5   T: 3

the monthly break-even sales revenue, to the nearest £1, is

  a   £400 000
  b   £411 107
  c   £425 532
  d   impossible to calculate without further information.   *(2 marks)*
        CIMA Management Accounting – Performance Management

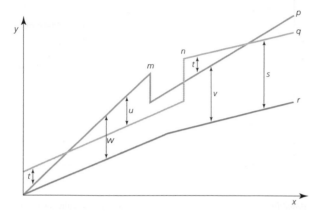

8.16 Intermediate. A break-even chart is shown below for Windhurst Ltd. You are required:

  i   to identify the components of the break-even chart labelled *p, q, r, s, t, u, v, w, x* and *y*;   *(5 marks)*
  ii   to suggest what events are represented at the values of *x* that are labelled *m* and *n* on the chart;   *(3 marks)*
  iii   to assess the usefulness of break-even analysis to senior management of a small company.   *(7 marks)*
        ICAEW Management Accounting

8.17 Intermediate. S plc produces and sells three products, X, Y and Z. It has contracts to supply products X and Y, which will utilise all of the specific materials that are available to make these two products during the next period. The revenue these contracts will generate and the contribution to sales (c/s) ratios of products X and Y are as follows:

	Product X	Product Y
Revenue	£10 million	£20 million
C/S ratio	15%	10%

Product Z has a c/s ratio of 25 per cent.

The total fixed costs of S plc are £5.5 million during the next period and management have budgeted to earn a profit of £1 million.

Calculate the revenue that needs to be generated by Product Z for S plc to achieve the budgeted profit.   *(3 marks)*
        CIMA P1 Management Accounting: Performance Evaluation

8.18 Intermediate: Preparation of break-even and profit–volume graphs. ZED plc manufactures one standard product, which sells at £10. You are required to:

  a   prepare from the data given below, a break-even and profit–volume graph showing the results for the six months ending 30 April and to determine:
    (i) the fixed costs;
    (ii) the variable cost per unit;
    (iii) the profit–volume ratio;
    (iv) the break-even point;
    (v) the margin of safety;

Month	Sales (units)	Profit/(loss) (£)
November	30 000	40 000
December	35 000	60 000
January	15 000	(20 000)
February	24 000	16 000

March	26 000	24 000
April	18 000	(8 000)

  b   discuss the limitations of such a graph;
  c   explain the use of the relevant range in such a graph.
        (20 marks)
        CIMA Cost Accounting 2

8.19 Intermediate: Preparation of a contribution graph. Z plc operates a single retail outlet selling direct to the public. Profit statements for August and September are as follows:

	August	September
Sales	80 000	90 000
Cost of sales	50 000	55 000
Gross profit	30 000	35 000
Less:		
Selling and distribution	8 000	9 000
Administration	15 000	15 000
Net profit	7 000	11 000

Required:

  a   Use the high- and low-points technique to identify the behaviour of:
    (i) cost of sales;
    (ii) selling and distribution costs;
    (iii) administration costs.   *(4 marks)*
  b   Draw a contribution break-even chart and identify the monthly break-even sales value and area of contribution.
        (10 marks)
  c   Assuming a margin of safety equal to 30 per cent of the break-even value, calculate Z plc's annual profit.   *(2 marks)*
  d   Z plc is now considering opening another retail outlet selling the same products. Z plc plans to use the same profit margins in both outlets and has estimated that the specific fixed costs of the second outlet will be £100 000 per annum.
    Z plc also expects that 10 per cent of its annual sales from its existing outlet would transfer to this second outlet if it were to be opened.
    Calculate the annual value of sales required from the new outlet in order to achieve the same annual profit as previously obtained from the single outlet.   *(5 marks)*
  e   Briefly describe the cost accounting requirements of organizations of this type.   *(4 marks)*
        Chartered Institute of Management Accountants Operational Cost Accounting Stage 2

8.20 Intermediate: Preparation of a break-even chart with step fixed costs. Toowomba manufactures various products and uses CVP analysis to establish the minimum level of production to ensure profitability.

Fixed costs of £50 000 have been allocated to a specific product but are expected to increase to £100 000 once production exceeds 30 000 units, as a new factory will need to be rented in order to produce the extra units. Variable costs per unit are stable at £5 per unit over all levels of activity. Revenue from this product will be £7.50 per unit.

Required:

  a   Formulate the equations for the total cost at:
    (i) less than or equal to 30 000 units;
    (ii) more than 30 000 units.   *(2 marks)*
  b   Prepare a break-even chart and clearly identify the break-even point or points.   *(6 marks)*
  c   Discuss the implications of the results from your graph in (b) with regard to Toowomba's production plans.   *(2 marks)*
        ACCA Paper 1.2 – Financial Information for Management

8.21 Intermediate: Changes in sales mix. XYZ Ltd produces two products and the following budget applies for 20 × 2:

	Product X (£)	Product Y (£)
Selling price	6	12
Variable costs	2	4
Contribution margin	4	8
Fixed costs apportioned	£100 000	£200 000
Units sold	70 000	30 000

You are required to calculate the break-even points for each product and the company as a whole and comment on your findings.

8.22 Advanced: Non-graphical CVP behaviour. Tweed Ltd is a company engaged solely in the manufacture of jumpers, which are bought mainly for sporting activities. Present sales are direct to retailers, but in recent years there has been a steady decline in output because of increased foreign competition. In the last trading year (2001) the accounting report indicated that the company produced the lowest profit for 10 years. The forecast for 2002 indicates that the present deterioration in profits is likely to continue. The company considers that a profit of £80 000 should be achieved to provide an adequate return on capital. The managing director has asked that a review be made of the present pricing and marketing policies. The marketing director has completed this review, and passes the proposals on to you for evaluation and recommendation, together with the profit and loss account for year ending 31 December 2001.

Tweed Ltd profit and loss account for year ending 31 December 2001

	(£)	(£)	(£)
Sales revenue			
(100 000 jumpers at £10)			1 000 000
Factory cost of goods sold:			
Direct materials	100 000		
Direct labour	350 000		
Variable factory overheads	60 000		
Fixed factory overheads	220 000	730 000	
Administration overhead		140 000	
Selling and distribution overhead			
Sales commission (2% of sales)	20 000		
Delivery costs (variable per unit sold)	50 000		
Fixed costs	40 000	110 000	980 000
Profit			20 000

The information to be submitted to the managing director includes the following three proposals:

i   To proceed on the basis of analyzes of market research studies which indicate that the demand for the jumpers is such that 10 per cent reduction in selling price would increase demand by 40 per cent.

ii   To proceed with an enquiry that the marketing director has had from a mail order company about the possibility of purchasing 50 000 units annually if the selling price is right. The mail order company would transport the jumpers from Tweed Ltd to its own warehouse, and no sales commission would be paid on these sales by Tweed Ltd. However, if an acceptable price can be negotiated, Tweed Ltd would be expected to contribute £60 000 per annum towards the cost of producing the mail order catalogue. It would also be necessary for Tweed Ltd to provide special additional packaging at a cost of £0.50 per jumper. The marketing director considers that in 2002 the sales from existing business would remain unchanged at 100 000 units, based on a selling price of £10 if the mail order contract is undertaken.

iii   To proceed on the basis of a view by the marketing director that a 10 per cent price reduction, together with a national advertising campaign costing £30 000 may increase sales to the maximum capacity of 160 000 jumpers.

Required:

a   The calculation of break-even sales value based on the 2001 accounts.

b   A financial evaluation of proposal (i) and a calculation of the number of units Tweed Ltd would require to sell at £9 each to earn the target profit of £80 000.

c   A calculation of the minimum prices that would have to be quoted to the mail order company, first, to ensure that Tweed Ltd would, at least, break even on the mail order contract, secondly, to ensure that the same overall profit is earned as proposal (i) and, thirdly, to ensure that the overall target profit is earned.

d   A financial evaluation of proposal (iii).

IM8.1 Intermediate. Shown below is a typical cost–volume–profit chart:

Required:

a   Explain to a colleague who is not an accountant the reasons for the change in result on this cost–volume–profit chart from a loss at point (a) to a profit at point (b).   *(3 marks)*

b   Identify and critically examine the underlying assumptions of this type of cost–volume–profit analysis and consider whether such analyzes are useful to the management of an organization.
(14 marks)
(Total 17 marks)
ACCA Level 1 Costing

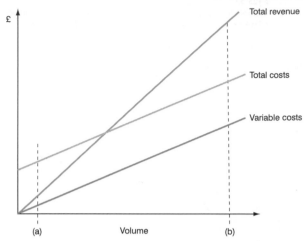

IM8.2 Intermediate. The graphs shown below show cost–volume–profit relationships as they are typically represented in (i) management accounting and (ii) economic theory. In each graph TR=total revenue, TC=total cost, and P=profit. You are required to compare these different representations of cost–volume–profit relationships, identifying, explaining and commenting on points of similarity and also differences.
(15 marks)
ICAEW Management Accounting

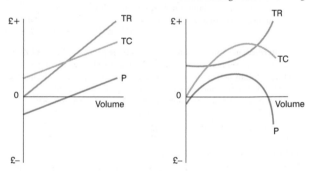

IM8.3 Intermediate. 'A break-even chart must be interpreted in the light of the limitations of its underlying assumptions …' (From *Cost Accounting: A Managerial Emphasis*, by C.T. Horngren.)

Required:

a   Discuss the extent to which the above statement is valid and both describe and briefly appraise the reasons for five of the most important underlying assumptions of break-even analysis.
(14 marks)

b   For any *three* of the underlying assumptions provided in answer to (a) above, give an example of circumstances in which that assumption is violated. Indicate the nature of the violation and the extent to which the break-even chart can be adapted to allow for this violation.   *(6 marks)*
ACCA P2 Management Accounting

IM8.4 Advanced. The accountant's approach to cost–volume–profit analysis has been criticized in that, among other matters, it does not deal with the following:

a   situations where sales volume differs radically from production volume;

b   situations where the sales revenue and the total cost functions are markedly non-linear;

c changes in product mix;

d risk and uncertainty.

Explain these objections to the accountant's conventional cost–volume–profit model and suggest how they can be overcome or ameliorated.

(17 marks)

ACCA Level 2 Management Accounting

IM8.5 Intermediate: Multi-product profit–volume graph. JK Limited has prepared a budget for the next 12 months when it intends to make and sell four products, details of which are shown below:

Product	Sales in units (thousands)	Selling price per unit (£)	Variable cost per unit (£)
J	10	20	14.00
K	10	40	8.00
L	50	4	4.20
M	20	10	7.00

Budgeted fixed costs are £240 000 per annum and total assets employed are £570 000.

You are required

a to calculate the total contribution earned by each product and their combined total contributions; *(2 marks)*

b to plot the data of your answer to (a) above in the form of a contribution to sales graph (sometimes referred to as a profit–volume graph) *on the graph paper provided*; *(6 marks)*

c to explain your graph to management, to comment on the results shown and to state the break-even point; *(4 marks)*

d to describe briefly three ways in which the overall contribution to sales ratio could be improved. *(3 marks)*

CIMA Stage 2 Cost Accounting

IM8.6 Intermediate: Break-even chart with increases in fixed costs.

a Identify and discuss briefly *five* assumptions underlying cost–volume–profit analysis. *(10 marks)*

b A local authority, whose area includes a holiday resort situated on the east coast, operates, for 30 weeks each year, a holiday home which is let to visiting parties of children in care from other authorities. The children are accompanied by their own house mothers who supervise them throughout their holiday. From six to fifteen guests are accepted on terms of £100 per person per week. No differential charges exist for adults and children.

Weekly costs incurred by the host authority are:

	(£ per guest)
Food	25
Electricity for heating and cooking	3
Domestic (laundry, cleaning etc.) expenses	5
Use of minibus	10

Seasonal staff supervise and carry out the necessary duties at the home at a cost of £11 000 for the 30-week period. This provides staffing sufficient for six to ten guests per week but if eleven or more guests are to be accommodated, additional staff at a total cost of £200 per week are engaged for the whole of the 30-week period.

Rent, including rates for the property, is £4000 per annum and the garden of the home is maintained by the council's recreation department which charges a nominal fee of £1000 per annum.

You are required to:

(i) tabulate the appropriate figures in such a way as to show the break-even point(s) and to comment on your figures; *(8 marks)*

(ii) draw, on the graph paper provided, a chart to illustrate your answer to (b)(i) above. *(7 marks)*

CIMA Cost Accounting Stage 2

IM8.7 Intermediate: Analysis of costs into fixed and variable elements and break-even point calculation.

a 'The analysis of total cost into its behavioural elements is essential for effective cost and management accounting.'

Required

Comment on the statement above, illustrating your answer with examples of cost behaviour patterns. *(5 marks)*

b The total costs incurred at various output levels, for a process operation in a factory, have been measured as follows:

Output (units)	Total cost (£)
11 500	102 476
12 000	104 730
12 500	106 263
13 000	108 021
13 500	110 727
14 000	113 201

Required:

Using the high–low method, analyze the costs of the process operation into fixed and variable components. *(4 marks)*

c Calculate, and comment upon, the break-even output level of the process operation in (b) above, based upon the fixed and variable costs identified and assuming a selling price of £10.60 per unit.

(5 marks)

ACCA Foundation Paper 3

IM8.8 Intermediate: Non-graphical CVP analysis and the acceptance of a special order. Video Technology Plc was established in 1987 to assemble video cassette recorders (VCRs). There is now increased competition in its markets and the company expects to find it difficult to make an acceptable profit next year. You have been appointed as an accounting technician at the company, and have been given a copy of the draft budget for the next financial year.

Draft budget for 12 months to 30 November 2001

	(£m)	(£m)
Sales income		960.0
Cost of sales:		
Variable assembly materials	374.4	
Variable labour	192.0	
Factory overheads – variable	172.8	
– fixed	43.0	(782.2)
Gross profit		177.8
Selling overheads – commission	38.4	
– fixed	108.0	
Administration overheads – fixed	20.0	(166.4)
Net profit		11.4

The following information is also supplied to you by the company's financial controller, Edward Davies:

1 planned sales for the draft budget in the year to 30 November 2001 are expected to be 25 per cent less than the total of 3.2 million VCR units sold in the year to 30 November 2000;

2 the company operates a Just-In-Time stock control system, which means it holds no stocks of any kind;

3 if more than 3 million VCR units are made and sold, the unit cost of material falls by £4 per unit;

4 sales commission is based on the number of units sold and not on turnover;

5 the draft budget assumes that the factory will only be working at two-thirds of maximum capacity;

6 sales above maximum capacity are not possible.

Edward Davies explains that the Board is not happy with the profit projected in the draft budget, and that the sales director, Anne Williams, has produced three proposals to try and improve matters.

1 Proposal A involves launching an aggressive marketing campaign:
(i) this would involve a single additional fixed cost of £14 million for advertising;
(ii) there would be a revised commission payment of £18 per unit sold;
(iii) sales volume would be expected to increase by 10 per cent above the level projected in the draft budget, with no change in the unit selling price.

2 Proposal B involves a 5 per cent reduction in the unit selling price:
(i) this is estimated to bring the sales volume back to the level in the year to 30 November 2000.

3 Proposal C involves a 10 per cent reduction in the unit selling price:
(i) fixed selling overheads would also be reduced by £45 million;
(ii) if proposal C is accepted, the sales director believes sales volume will be 3.8 million units.

Task 1

    a For each of the three proposals, calculate the:
        (i) change in profits compared with the draft budget;
        (ii) break-even point in units and turnover.
    b Recommend which proposal, if any, should be accepted on financial grounds.
    c Identify *three* non-financial issues to be considered before a final decision is made.

Edward Davies now tells you that the company is considering a new export order with a proposed selling price of £3 million. He provides you with the following information:

1 The order will require two types of material:
    (i) material A is in regular use by the company. The amount in stock originally cost £0.85 million, but its standard cost is £0.9 million. The amount in stock is sufficient for the order. The current market price of material A to be used in the order is £0.8 million;
    (ii) material B is no longer used by the company and cannot be used elsewhere if not used on the order. The amount in stock originally cost £0.2 million although its current purchase price is £0.3 million. The amount of material B in stock is only half the amount required on the order. If not used on the order, the amount in stock could be sold for £0.1 million;
2 direct labour of £1.0 million will be charged to the order. This includes £0.2 million for idle time, as a result of insufficient orders to keep the workforce fully employed. The company has a policy of no redundancies, and spreads the resulting cost of idle time across all orders;
3 variable factory overheads are expected to be £0.9 million;
4 fixed factory overheads are apportioned against the order at the rate of 50 per cent of variable factory overheads;
5 no sales commission will be paid.

Task 2

Prepare a memo for Edward Davies:

    a showing whether or not the order should be accepted at the proposed selling price;
    b identifying the technique(s) you have used in reaching this conclusion.   *AAT Technicians Stage*

IM8.9 Intermediate: Decision-making and non-graphical CVP analysis. York plc was formed three years ago by a group of research scientists to market a new medicine that they had invented. The technology involved in the medicine's manufacture is both complex and expensive. Because of this, the company is faced with a high level of fixed costs.

This is of particular concern to Dr Harper, the company's chief executive. She recently arranged a conference of all management staff to discuss company profitability. Dr Harper showed the managers how average unit cost fell as production volume increased and explained that this was due to the company's heavy fixed cost base. 'It is clear,' she said, 'that as we produce closer to the plant's maximum capacity of 70 000 packs the average cost per pack falls. Producing and selling as close to that limit as possible must be good for company profitability.' The data she used are reproduced below:

Production volume (packs)	40 000	50 000	60 000	70 000
Average cost per unit[a]	£430	£388	£360	£340
Current sales and production				
volume:	65 000 packs			
Selling price per pack:	£420			

[a]Defined as the total of fixed and variable costs, divided by the production volume

You are a member of York plc's management accounting team and shortly after the conference you are called to a meeting with Ben Cooper, the company's marketing director. He is interested in knowing how profitability changes with production.

Task 1

Ben Cooper asks you to calculate:

    a the amount of York plc's fixed costs;
    b the profit of the company at its current sales volume of 65 000 packs;
    c the break-even point in units;
    d the margin of safety expressed as a percentage.

Ben Cooper now tells you of a discussion he has recently had with Dr Harper. Dr Harper had once more emphasized the need to produce as

close as possible to the maximum capacity of 70 000 packs. Ben Cooper has the possibility of obtaining an export order for an extra 5000 packs but, because the competition is strong, the selling price would only be £330. Dr Harper has suggested that this order should be rejected as it is below cost and so will reduce company profitability. However, she would be prepared, on this occasion, to sell the packs on a cost basis for £340 each, provided the order was increased to 15 000 packs.

Task 2

Write a memo to Ben Cooper. Your memo should:

    a calculate the change in profits from accepting the order for 5000 packs at £330;
    b calculate the change in profits from accepting an order for 15 000 packs at £340;
    c briefly explain and justify which proposal, if either, should be accepted;
    d identify *two* non-financial factors which should be taken into account before making a final decision.

AAT Technicians Stage

IM8.10 Intermediate: Marginal costing and absorption costing profit computations and calculation of break-even point for a given sales mix. A company has two products with the following unit costs for a period:

	Product A (£/unit)	Product B (£/unit)
Direct materials	1.20	2.03
Direct labour	1.40	1.50
Variable production overheads	0.70	0.80
Fixed production overheads	1.10	1.10
Variable other overheads	0.15	0.20
Fixed other overheads	0.50	0.50

Production and sales of the two products for the period were:

	Product A (000 units)	Product B (000 units)
Production	250	100
Sales	225	110

Production was at normal levels. Unit costs in opening stock were the same as those for the period listed above.

Required:

    a State whether, and why, absorption or marginal costing would show a higher company profit for the period, and calculate the difference in profit depending upon which method is used.

        (4 marks)

    b Calculate the break-even sales revenue for the period (to the nearest £000) based on the above mix of sales. The selling prices of products A and B were £5.70 and £6.90 per unit, respectively.

        (7 marks)

ACCA Foundation Stage Paper 3

IM8.11 Advanced: CVP analysis based on capacity usage in a leisure centre. A local government authority owns and operates a leisure centre with numerous sporting facilities, residential accommodation, a cafeteria and a sports shop. The summer season lasts for 20 weeks including a peak period of six weeks corresponding to the school holidays. The following budgets have been prepared for the next summer season:

Accommodation
60 single rooms let on a daily basis.
35 double rooms let on a daily basis at 160 per cent of the single room rate.
Fixed costs £29 900
Variable costs £4 per single room per day and £6.40 per double room per day.

Sports Centre
Residential guests each pay £2 per day and casual visitors £3 per day for the use of facilities.
Fixed costs £15 500

Sports Shop
Estimated contribution £1 per person per day.
Fixed costs £8250

Cafeteria
Estimated contribution £1.50 per person per day.
Fixed costs £12 750

During the summer season the centre is open seven days a week and the following activity levels are anticipated:

Double rooms fully booked for the whole season.

Single rooms fully booked for the peak period but at only 80 per cent of capacity during the rest of the season.

30 casual visitors per day on average.

You are required to

a   calculate the charges for single and double rooms assuming that the authority wishes to make a £10 000 profit on accommodation;   (6 marks)

b   calculate the anticipated total profit for the leisure centre as a whole for the season;   (10 marks)

c   advise the authority whether an offer of £250 000 from a private leisure company to operate the centre for five years is worthwhile, assuming that the authority uses a 10 per cent cost of capital and operations continue as outlined above.   (4 marks)

CIMA Stage 3 Management Accounting Techniques

Measuring relevant costs and revenues for decision-making

9

In this chapter we are going to focus on measuring costs and benefits for non-routine decisions. The term 'special studies' is sometimes used to refer to decisions that are not routinely made at frequent intervals. In other words, special studies are undertaken whenever a decision needs to be taken; such as discontinuing a product or a channel of distribution, making a component within the company or buying from an outside supplier, introducing a new product and replacing existing equipment. Special studies require only those costs and revenues that are relevant to the specific alternative courses of action to be reported. The term 'decision-relevant approach' is used to describe the specific costs and benefits that should be reported for special studies. We shall assume that the objective when examining alternative courses of action is to maximize the present value of future net cash inflows. The calculations of present values will be explained in Chapter 13. We also assume for this chapter that future costs and benefits are known with certainty; decision-making under conditions of uncertainty will be considered in Chapter 12. In Chapters 13 and 14 we shall concentrate on the special studies required for capital investment decisions.

LEARNING OBJECTIVES

After studying this chapter, you should be able to:

- distinguish between relevant and irrelevant costs and revenues;

- explain the importance of qualitative factors;

- distinguish between the relevant and irrelevant costs and revenues for the five decision-making problems described;

- describe the key concept that should be applied for presenting information for product-mix decisions when capacity constraints apply;

- explain why the book value of equipment is irrelevant when making equipment replacement decisions;

- describe the opportunity cost concept;

- explain the misconceptions relating to relevant costs and revenues.

It is important that you note at this stage that a decision-relevant approach adopts whichever planning time horizon the decision maker considers appropriate for a given situation. However, it is important not to focus excessively on the short term, since the objective is to maximize long-term net cash inflows. We begin by introducing the concept of relevant cost and applying this principle to special studies relating to the following:

1 special selling price decisions;

2 product-mix decisions when capacity constraints exist;

3 decisions on replacement of equipment;

4 outsourcing (make or buy) decisions;

5 discontinuation decisions.

We shall then consider in more detail the specific problems that arise in assessing the relevant costs of materials and labour.

The aim of this chapter is to provide you with an understanding of the principles that should be used to identify relevant costs and revenues. It is assumed that relevant costs can be easily measured but, in reality, some indirect relevant costs can be difficult to measure. The measurement of indirect relevant costs for decision-making using activity-based-costing techniques will be examined in the next chapter.

The meaning of relevance

The relevant costs and benefits required for decision-making are only those that will be affected by the decision. Costs and benefits that are independent of a decision are obviously not relevant and need not be considered when making that decision. The relevant financial inputs for decision-making purposes are therefore *future* cash flows, which will differ between the various alternatives being considered. In other words, only differential (or incremental) cash flows should be taken into account, and cash flows that will be the same for all alternatives are irrelevant. Since decision-making is concerned with choosing between future alternative courses of action, and nothing can be done to alter the past, then past costs (also known as sunk costs) are not relevant for decision-making. Consider a situation where an individual is uncertain as to whether he or she should purchase a monthly rail ticket to travel to work or use their car. Assuming that the individual will keep the car, whether or not he or she travels to work by train, the cost of the road fund licence and insurance will be irrelevant, since these costs remain the same irrespective of the mode of travel. The cost of petrol will, however, be relevant, since this cost will vary depending on which method of transport is chosen.

You will see that both depreciation and the allocation of common fixed costs are irrelevant for decision-making. Both are sunk costs. Depreciation represents the allocation of past costs to future periods. The original cost is unavoidable and common to all alternatives. Therefore it is irrelevant. Similarly, any allocation of common fixed costs will be irrelevant for decision-making since the choice of allocation method does not affect the level of cost to the company. It merely results in a redistribution of the same sunk cost between cost objects (e.g. products or locations within the organization).

Importance of qualitative factors

In many situations it is difficult to quantify in monetary terms all the important elements of a decision. Those factors that cannot be expressed in monetary terms are classified as qualitative factors. A decline in employee morale that results from redundancies arising from a closure decision is an example of a qualitative factor. It is essential that qualitative factors be brought to the attention of management during the decision-making process, since otherwise there may be a danger that a wrong decision will be made. For example, the cost of manufacturing a component internally may be more expensive than purchasing from an outside supplier. However, the decision to purchase from an outside supplier could result in the closing down of the company's facilities for manufacturing the component. The effect of such a decision might lead to redundancies and a decline in employees' morale, which could affect future output. In addition, the company will now be at the mercy of the supplier who might seek to increase prices on subsequent contracts and/or may not always deliver on time. The company may not then be in a position to meet customers' requirements. In turn, this could result in a loss of customer goodwill and a decline in future sales.

It may not be possible to quantify in monetary terms the effect of a decline in employees' morale or loss of customer goodwill, but the accountant in such circumstances should present the relevant quantifiable financial information and draw attention to those qualitative items that may have an impact on future profitability. In circumstances such as those given in the above example management must estimate the likelihood of the supplier failing to meet the company's demand for future supplies and the likely effect on customer goodwill if there is a delay in meeting orders. If the component can be obtained from many suppliers and repeat orders for the company's products are unlikely then the company may give little weighting to these qualitative factors. Alternatively, if the component can be obtained from only one supplier and the company relies heavily on repeat sales to existing customers then the qualitative factors will be of considerable importance. In the latter situation the company may consider that the quantifiable cost savings from purchasing the component from an outside supplier are insufficient to cover the risk of the qualitative factors occurring.

If it is possible qualitative factors should be expressed in quantitative non-financial terms. For example, the increase in percentage of on-time deliveries from a new production process, the reduction in customer waiting time from a decision to invest in additional cash dispensing machines and the reduction in the number of units of defective output delivered to customers arising from an investment in quality inspection are all examples of qualitative factors that can be expressed in non-financial numerical terms.

Let us now move on to apply the relevant cost approach to a variety of decision-making problems. We shall concentrate on measuring the financial outcomes but do remember that they do not always provide the full story. Qualitative factors should also be taken into account in the decision-making process.

Special pricing decisions

Special pricing decisions relate to pricing decisions outside the main market. Typically they involve one-time only orders or orders at a price below the prevailing market price. Consider the information presented in Example 9.1.

At first glance it looks as if the order should be rejected since the proposed selling price is less than the total cost of £33. A study of the cost estimates, however, indicates that during the next quarter, the direct labour, manufacturing (i.e. non-variable) fixed overheads and the marketing and distribution costs will remain the same irrespective of whether or not the order is accepted. These costs are therefore irrelevant for this decision. The direct material costs, variable manufacturing overheads and the cost of adding the leisure company's logo will be different if the order is accepted. Hence they are relevant for making the decision. The financial information required for the decision is shown in Exhibit 9.1.

You can see from Exhibit 9.1 that different approaches can be used for presenting relevant cost and revenue information. Information can be presented that includes both relevant and irrelevant costs or revenues for all alternatives under consideration. If this approach is adopted the *same* amount for the irrelevant items (i.e. those items that remain unchanged as a result of the decision which are direct labour, manufacturing non-variable overheads and the marketing and

EXAMPLE 9.1

The Caledonian Company is a manufacturer of clothing that sells its output directly to clothing retailers. One of its departments manufactures sweaters. The department has a production capacity of 50 000 sweaters per month. Because of the liquidation of one of its major customers the company has excess capacity. For the next quarter current monthly production and sales volume is expected to be 35 000 sweaters at a selling price of £40 per sweater. Expected costs and revenues for the next month at an activity level of 35 000 sweaters are as follows:

	(£)	(£)
Direct labour	420 000	12
Direct materials	280 000	8
Variable manufacturing overheads	70 000	2
Manufacturing non-variable overheads	280 000	8
Marketing and distribution costs	105 000	3
Total costs	1 155 000	33
Sales	1 400 000	40
Profit	245 000	7

Caledonian is expecting an upsurge in demand and considers that the excess capacity is temporary. A company in the leisure industry has offered to buy for its staff 3000 sweaters each month for the next three months at a price of £20 per sweater. The company would collect the sweaters from Caledonian's factory and thus no marketing and distribution costs will be incurred. No subsequent sales to this customer are anticipated. The company would require its company logo inserting on the sweater and Caledonian has predicted that this will cost £1 per sweater. Should Caledonian accept the offer from the company?

EXHIBIT 9.1 Evaluation of three month order from the company in the leisure industry

	(1) Do not accept order (£ per month)	(2) Accept order (£ per month)	(3) Difference (relevant costs) (£ per month)
Direct labour	420 000	420 000	
Direct materials	280 000	304 000	24 000
Variable manufacturing overheads	70 000	76 000	6 000
Manufacturing non-variable overheads	280 000	280 000	
Inserting company logo		3 000	3 000
Marketing and distribution costs	105 000	105 000	
Total costs	1 155 000	1 188 000	33 000
Sales	1 400 000	1 460 000	60 000
Profit per month	245 000	272 000	27 000

distribution costs in our example) are included for all alternatives, thus making them irrelevant to the decision. This information is presented in columns (1) and (2) in Exhibit 9.1. Alternatively, you can present cost information in columns (1) and (2) that excludes the irrelevant costs and revenues because they are identical for both alternatives. A third alternative is to present only the relevant (differential) costs. This approach is shown in column (3) of Exhibit 9.1. Note that column (3) represents the difference between columns (1) and (2). All of the methods show that the company is better off by £27 000 *per month* if the order is accepted.

Four important factors must be considered before recommending acceptance of the order. Most of these relate to the assumption that there are no long-run implications from accepting the offer at a selling price of £20 per sweater. First, it is assumed that the future selling price will not be affected by selling some of the output at a price below the going market price. If this assumption is incorrect then competitors may engage in similar practices of reducing their selling prices in an attempt to unload spare capacity. This may lead to a fall in the market price, which in turn would lead to a fall in profits from future sales. The loss of future profits may be greater than the short-term gain obtained from accepting special orders at prices below the existing market price. Given that Caledonian has found a customer in a different market from its normal market it is unlikely that the market price would be affected. However, if the customer had been within Caledonian's normal retail market there would be a real danger that the market price would be affected. Secondly, the decision to accept the order prevents the company from accepting other orders that may be obtained during the period at the going price. In other words, it is assumed that no better opportunities will present themselves during the period. Thirdly, it is assumed that the company has unused resources that have no alternative uses that will yield a contribution to profits in excess of £27 000 *per month*. Finally, it is assumed that the fixed costs are unavoidable for the period under consideration. In other words, we assume that the direct labour force and the fixed overheads cannot be reduced in the short term, or that they are to be retained for an upsurge in demand, which is expected to occur in the longer term.

It is important that great care is taken in presenting financial information for decision-making. For stock valuation, external financial regulations require that the sweaters must be valued at their manufacturing cost of £30. Using this cost would lead to the incorrect decision being taken. For decision-making purposes only future costs that will be relevant to the decision should be included. Costs that have been computed for meeting stock valuation requirements must not therefore be used for decision-making purposes.

When you are trying to establish which costs are relevant to a particular decision you may find that some costs will be relevant in one situation but irrelevant in another. In Example 9.1 we assumed that direct labour was not a relevant cost. The company wishes to retain the direct labour for an expected upsurge in demand and therefore the direct labour cost will be same whether or not the offer is accepted. Alternatively, Caledonian may have had an agreement with its workforce that entitled them to at least three months' notice in the event of any redundancies. Therefore, even if Caledonian was not expecting an upsurge in demand direct labour would have been a fixed cost within the three month time horizon. But now let us consider what the relevant cost would be if direct labour consisted of casual labour who are hired on a daily basis. In this situation direct labour will be a relevant cost, since the labour costs will not be incurred if the order is not accepted.

The identification of relevant costs depends on the circumstances. In one situation a cost may be relevant, but in another the same cost may not be relevant. It is not therefore possible to provide a list of costs that would be relevant in particular situations. In each situation you should follow the principle that the relevant costs are future costs that differ among alternatives. The important question to ask when determining the relevant cost is: What difference will it make? The accountant must be aware of all the issues relating to a decision and ascertain full details of the changes that will result, and then proceed to select the relevant financial information to present to management.

Evaluation of a longer-term order

In Example 9.1 we focused on a short-term time horizon of three months. Capacity cannot easily be altered in the short term and therefore direct labour and fixed costs are likely to be irrelevant costs with respect to short-term decisions. In the longer-term, however, it may be possible to reduce capacity and spending on fixed costs and direct labour. Let us now assume that for Example 9.1 that Caledonian's assumption about an expected upsurge in the market proved to be incorrect and that it estimates that demand in the foreseeable future will remain at 35 000 sweaters *per month*. Given that it has a productive capacity of 50 000 sweaters it has sought to develop a long-term market for the unutilized capacity of 15 000 sweaters. As a result of its experience with the one-time special order with the company in the leisure industry, Caledonian has sought to develop a market with other companies operating in the leisure industry. Assume that this process has resulted in potential customers that are prepared to enter into a contractual agreement for a three year period for a supply of 15 000 sweaters *per month* at an agreed price of £25 per sweater. The cost of inserting the insignia required by each customer would remain unchanged at £1 per sweater. No marketing and distribution costs would be incurred with any of the orders. Caledonian considers that it has investigated all other possibilities to develop a market for the excess capacity. Should it enter into contractual agreements with the suppliers at £25 per sweater?

If Caledonian does not enter into contractual agreement with the suppliers the direct labour required will be made redundant. No redundancy costs will be involved. Further investigations indicate that manufacturing non-variable costs of £70 000 *per month* could be saved if a decision was made to reduce capacity by 15 000 sweaters per month. For example, the rental contracts for some of the machinery will not be renewed. Also some savings will be made in supervisory labour and support costs. Savings in marketing and distribution costs would be £20 000 *per month*. Assume also that if the capacity was reduced factory rearrangements would result in part of the facilities being rented out at £25 000 *per month*. Note that because variable costs vary directly with changes in volume, direct materials and variable manufacturing overheads will decline by 30 per cent if capacity is reduced by 30 per cent from 50 000 to 35 000 sweaters.

We are now faced with a longer-term decision where some of the costs that were fixed in the short term can be changed in the longer term. The appropriate financial data for the analysis is shown in Exhibit 9.2. Note that in Exhibit 9.2 the information for an activity of 35 000 sweaters incorporates the changes arising from the capacity reduction whereas the information presented for the same activity level in Exhibit 9.1 is based on the assumption that capacity will be maintained at 50 000 sweaters. Therefore the direct labour cost in Exhibit 9.1 is £420 000 because it represents the labour required to meet demand at full capacity. If capacity is permanently reduced from 50 000 to 35 000 sweaters (i.e. a 30 per cent reduction) it is assumed that direct labour costs will be reduced by 30 per cent from £420 000 to £294 000. This is the amount shown in Exhibit 9.2.

A comparison of the monthly outcomes reported in columns (1) and (2) of Exhibit 9.2 indicates that the company is better off by £31 000 *per month* if it reduces capacity to 35 000 sweaters, assuming that there are no qualitative factors. Instead of presenting the data in columns (1) and (2) you can present only the differential (relevant) costs and revenues shown in column (3). This approach also indicates that the company is better off by £31 000 per month. Note that

EXHIBIT 9.2 Evaluation of orders for the unutilized capacity over a three year time horizon

Monthly sales and production in units	(1) Do not accept orders 35 000 (£)	(2) Accept the orders 50 000 (£)	(3) Difference (relevant costs) 15 000 (£)
Direct labour	294 000	420 000	126 000
Direct materials	280 000	400 000	120 000
Variable manufacturing overheads	70 000	100 000	30 000
Manufacturing non-variable overheads	210 000	280 000	70 000
Inserting company logo		15 000	15 000
Marketing and distribution costs	85 000	105 000	20 000
Total costs	939 000	1 320 000	381 000
Revenues from rental of facilities	25 000		25 000
Sales revenues	1 400 000	1 775 000	(375 000)
Profit per month	486 000	455 000	31 000

the entry in column (3) of £25 000 is the lost revenues from the rent of the unutilized capacity if the company accepts the orders. This represents the opportunity cost of accepting the orders. We shall discuss opportunity costs later in the chapter.

Where the choice of one course of action requires that an alternative course of action is given up, the financial benefits that are forgone or sacrificed are known as opportunity costs. In other words, opportunity costs represent the lost contribution to profits arising from the best use of the alternative forgone. Opportunity costs only arise when resources are scarce and have alternative uses. Thus, in our illustration the capacity allocated to producing 15 000 sweaters results in an opportunity cost (i.e. the lost revenues from the rent of the capacity) of £25 000 per month.

In Exhibit 9.2 all of the costs and revenues are relevant to the decision because some of the costs that were fixed in the short term could be changed in the longer term. Therefore whether or not a cost is relevant often depends on the time horizon under consideration. Thus it is important that the information presented for decision-making relates to the appropriate time horizon. If inappropriate time horizons are selected there is a danger that misleading information will be presented. Remember that our aim should always be to maximize *long-term* net cash inflows.

Dangers of focusing excessively on a short-run time horizon

The problems arising from not taking into account the long-term consequences of accepting business that covers short-term incremental costs have been discussed by Kaplan (1990). He illustrates a situation where a company that makes pens has excess capacity, and a salesperson negotiates an order for 20 000 purple pens (a variation to the pens that are currently being made) at a price in excess of the incremental cost. In response to the question 'Should the order be accepted?' Kaplan states:

> take the order. The economics of making the purple pen with the excess capacity are overwhelming. There's no question that if you have excess capacity, the workers are all hired, the technology exists, and you have the product designed, and someone says, let's get an order for 20 000 purple pens, then the relevant consideration is price less the material cost of the purple pens. Don't even worry about the labour cost because you're going to pay them anyway. The second thing we tell them, however, is that they are never to ask us this question again ... Suppose that every month managers see that they have excess capacity to make 20 000 more pens, and salespeople are calling in special orders for turquoise pens, for purple pens with red caps, and other such customised products. Why not accept all these orders based on short-run contribution margin? The answer is that if they do, then costs that appear fixed in the short-term will start to increase, or expenses currently being incurred will be incapable of being reduced (p. 14).

Kaplan stresses that by utilizing the unused capacity to increase the range of products produced (i.e. different variations of pens in the above example), the production process becomes more complex and consequently the fixed costs of managing the additional complexity will eventually increase. Long-term considerations should therefore always be taken into account when special pricing decisions are being evaluated. In particular, there is a danger that a series of special orders will be evaluated independently as short-term decisions. Consequently, those resources that cannot be adjusted in the short term will be treated as irrelevant for each decision. However, the effect of accepting a series of consecutive special orders over several periods constitutes a long-term decision. If special orders are always evaluated as short-term decisions a situation can arise whereby the decision to reduce capacity is continually deferred.

Product-mix decisions when capacity constraints exist

In the short term sales demand may be in excess of current productivity capacity. For example, output may be restricted by a shortage of skilled labour, materials, equipment or space. When sales demand is in excess of a company's productive capacity, the resources responsible for limiting the output should be identified. These scarce resources are known as limiting factors. Within a short-term time period it is unlikely that production constraints can be removed and additional resources acquired. Where limiting factors apply, profit is maximized when the greatest possible contribution to profit is obtained each time the scarce or limiting factor is used. Consider Example 9.2.

In this situation the company's ability to increase its output and profits/net cash inflows is limited in the short term by the availability of machine capacity. You may think, when first looking at the available information, that the company should give top priority to producing component X, since this yields the highest contribution per unit sold, but this assumption would be incorrect. To produce each unit of component X, 6 scarce machine hours are required, whereas components Y and Z use only 2 hours and 1 hour respectively of scarce machine hours. By concentrating on producing components Y and Z, the company can sell 2000 units of each component and still have some machine capacity left to make component X. If the company concentrates on producing component X it will only be able to meet the maximum sales demand of component X, and will have no machine capacity left to make components Y or Z. The way in which you should determine the optimum production plan is to calculate the contribution per limiting factor for each component and then to rank the components in order of profitability based on this calculation.

Using the figures in the present example the result would be as follows:

	Component X	Component Y	Component Z
Contribution per unit	£12	£10	£6
Machine hours required	6 hours	2 hours	1 hour
Contribution per machine hour	£2	£5	£6
Ranking	3	2	1

The company can now allocate the 12 000 scarce machine hours in accordance with the above rankings. The first choice should be to produce as much as possible of component Z. The maximum sales are 2000 units, and production of this quantity will result in the use of 2000 machine hours, thus leaving 10 000 unused hours. The second choice should be to produce as much of component Y as possible. The maximum sales of 2000 units will result in the use of 4000

EXAMPLE 9.2

Rhine Autos is a major European producer of automobiles. A department within one of its divisions supplies component parts to firms operating within the automobile industry. The following information is provided relating to the anticipated demand and the productive capacity for the next quarter in respect of three components that are manufactured within the department:

	Component X	Component Y	Component Z
Contribution per unit of output	£12	£10	£6
Machine hours required per unit of output	6 hours	2 hours	1 hour
Estimated sales demand	2 000 units	2000 units	2000 units
Required machine hours for the quarter	12 000 hours	4000 hours	2000 hours

Because of the breakdown of one of its special purpose machines capacity is limited to 12 000 machine hours for the period, and this is insufficient to meet total sales demand. You have been asked to advise on the mix of products that should be produced during the period.

machine hours. Production of both components Z and Y require 6000 machine hours, leaving a balance of 6000 hours for the production of component X, which will enable 1000 units of component X to be produced.

We can now summarize the allocation of the scarce machine hours:

Production	Machine hours used	Balance of machine hours available
2000 units of Z	2000	10 000
2000 units of Y	4000	6 000
1000 units of X	6000	—

This production programme results in the following total contribution:

	(£)
2000 units of Z at £6 per unit contribution	12 000
2000 units of Y at £10 per unit contribution	20 000
1000 units of X at £12 per unit contribution	12 000
Total contribution	44 000

Always remember that it is necessary to consider other qualitative factors before the production programme is determined. For example, customer goodwill may be lost causing a fall in future sales if the company is unable to supply all three products to, say, 150 of its regular customers. Difficulties may arise in applying this procedure when there is more than one scarce resource. It could not be applied if, for example, labour hours were also scarce and the contribution per labour hour resulted in component Y being ranked first, followed by components X and Z. In this type of situation, where more than one resource is scarce, it is necessary to resort to linear programming methods in order to determine the optimal production programme. The application of linear programming to decision-making when there are several scarce resources will be examined in Chapter 25.

The approach described above can also be applied in non-manufacturing organizations. For example, in a major UK retail store display space is the limiting factor. The store maximizes its short-term profits by allocating shelving space on the basis of contribution per metre of shelving space. For an illustration of a product-mix decision with a capacity constraint within an agricultural setting you should refer to the solution to Review problem 9.24.

Finally, it is important that you remember that the approach outlined in this section applies only to those situations where capacity constraints cannot be removed in the short term. In the longer term additional resources should be acquired if the contribution from the extra capacity exceeds the cost of acquisition. You should note that the principles described in this section have also been applied to a new approach to production management known as the theory of constraints and throughput accounting. This approach is described in the appendix of this chapter.

Replacement of equipment – the irrelevance of past costs

Replacement of equipment is a capital investment or long-term decision that requires the use of discounted cash flow procedures. These procedures are discussed in detail in Chapter 13, but one aspect of asset replacement decisions which we will consider at this stage is how to deal with the book value (i.e. the written-down value) of old equipment. This is a problem that has been known to cause difficulty, but the correct approach is to apply relevant cost principles (i.e. past or sunk costs are irrelevant for decision-making). We shall now use Example 9.3 to illustrate the irrelevance of the book value of old equipment in a replacement decision. To avoid any possible confusion, it will be assumed here that £1 of cash inflow or outflow in year 1 is equivalent to £1 of cash inflow or outflow in, say, year 3. Such an assumption would in reality be incorrect and you will see why this is so in Chapter 13, but by adopting this assumption at this stage, the replacement problem can be simplified and we can focus our attention on the treatment of the book value of the old equipment in the replacement decision.

You can see from an examination of Example 9.3 that the total costs over a period of three years for each of the alternatives are as follows:

	(1) Retain present machine (£)	(2) Buy replacement machine (£)	(3) Difference (relevant costs/ revenues) (£)
Variable/incremental operating costs:			
20 000 units at £3 per unit for 3 years	180 000		
20 000 units at £2 per unit for 3 years		120 000	(60 000)
Old machine book value:			
3-year annual depreciation charge	90 000		
Lump sum write-off		90 000	
Old machine disposal value		(40 000)	(40 000)
Initial purchase price of new machine		70 000	70 000
Total cost	270 000	240 000	30 000

You can see from the above analysis that the £90 000 book value of the old machine is irrelevant to the decision. Book values are not relevant costs because they are past or sunk costs and are therefore the same for all potential courses of action. If the present machine is retained, three years' depreciation at £30 000 per annum will be written off annually whereas if the new machine is purchased the £90 000 will be written off as a lump sum if it is replaced. Note that depreciation charges for the new machine are not included in the analysis since the cost of purchasing the machine is already included in the analysis. The sum of the annual depreciation charges are equivalent to the purchase cost. Thus, including both items would amount to double counting.

The above analysis shows that the costs of operating the replacement machine are £30 000 less than the costs of operating the existing machine over the three year period. Again there are several different methods of presenting the information. They all show a £30 000 advantage in favour of replacing the machine. You can present the information shown in columns (1) and (2) above, as long as you ensure that the same amount for the irrelevant items is included for all alternatives. Instead, you can present columns (1) and (2) with the irrelevant item (i.e. the £90 000) omitted or you can present the differential items listed in column (3). However, if

EXAMPLE 9.3

A division within Rhine Autos purchased a machine three years ago for £180 000. Depreciation using the straight line basis, assuming a life of six years and with no salvage value, has been recorded each year in the financial accounts. The present written-down value of the equipment is £90 000 and it has a remaining life of three years. Management is considering replacing this machine with a new machine that will reduce the variable operating costs. The new machine will cost £70 000 and will have an expected life of three years with no scrap value. The variable operating costs are £3 per unit of output for the old machine and £2 per unit for the new machine. It is expected that both machines will be operated at a capacity of 20 000 units per annum. The sales revenues from the output of both machines will therefore be identical. The current disposal or sale value of the old machine is £40 000 and it will be zero in three years time.

you adopt the latter approach you will probably find it more meaningful to restate column (3) as follows:

	(£)
Savings on variable operating costs (3 years)	60 000
Sale proceeds of existing machine	40 000
	100 000
Less purchase cost of replacement machine	70 000
Savings on purchasing replacement machine	30 000

Outsourcing and make or buy decisions

Outsourcing is the process of obtaining goods or services from outside suppliers instead of producing the same goods or providing the same services within the organization. Decisions on whether to produce components or provide services within the organization or to acquire them from outside suppliers are called outsourcing or make or buy decisions. Many organizations outsource some of their activities such as their payroll and purchasing functions or the purchase of speciality components. Increasingly municipal local services such as waste disposal, highways and property maintenance are being outsourced. Consider the information presented in Example 9.4 (Case A).

At first glance it appears that the component should be outsourced since the purchase price of £30 is less than the current total unit cost of manufacturing. However, the unit costs include some costs that will be unchanged whether or not the components are outsourced. These costs are therefore not relevant to the decision. Assume also that there are no alternative uses of the released capacity if the components are outsourced. The appropriate cost information is presented in Exhibit 9.3 (Section A). Alternative approaches to presenting relevant cost and revenue information are presented. In columns (1) and (2) of Exhibit 9.3 cost information is presented that includes both relevant and irrelevant costs for both alternatives under consideration. The same amount for non-manufacturing overheads, which are irrelevant, is included for both alternatives. By including the same amount in both columns the cost is made irrelevant. Alternatively, you can present cost information in columns (1) and (2) that excludes any irrelevant costs and revenues because they are identical for both alternatives. Adopting either approach will result in a difference of £60 000 in favour of making component A.

The third approach is to list only the relevant costs, cost savings and any relevant revenues. This approach is shown in column (3) of Exhibit 9.3 (Section A). This column represents the differential costs or revenues and it is derived from the differences between columns (1) and (2). In column (3) only the information that is relevant to the decision is presented. You will see that this approach compares the relevant costs of making directly against outsourcing. It indicates that the additional costs of making component A are £240 000 but this enables purchasing costs of £300 000 to be saved. Therefore the company makes a net saving of £60 000 from making the components compared with outsourcing.

However, you will probably find column (3) easier to interpret if it is restated as two separate alternatives as shown in Exhibit 9.3. All of the approaches described in this and the preceding paragraph yield identical results. You can adopt any of them. It is a matter of personal preference.

Let us now re-examine the situation when the extra capacity created from not producing component A has an alternative use. Consider the information presented in Example 9.4 (Case B). The management of Rhine Autos now have three alternatives. They are:

1 Make component A and do not make part B.

2 Outsource component A and do not make part B.

3 Outsource component A and make and sell part B.

It is assumed there is insufficient capacity to make both component A and part B. The appropriate financial information is presented in Exhibit 9.3 (Section B). You will see that, with the exception of non-manufacturing costs, all of the items differ between the alternatives and are therefore relevant to the decision. Again we can omit the non-manufacturing costs from the analysis or include the same amount for all alternatives. Either approach makes them irrelevant. The first two alternatives that do not involve making and selling part B are identical to the alternatives considered in Case A so the information presented in columns (1) and (2) in sections A and B of Exhibit 9.3 are identical. In column 3 of section B the costs incurred in making part B in respect of direct labour, variable and fixed manufacturing overheads and non-manufacturing overheads are identical to the costs incurred in making component A. Therefore the same costs for these items are entered in column 3. However, different materials are required to make part B and the cost of these (10 000 units at £13) are entered in column 3. In addition, the revenues from the sales of part B are entered in column 3. Comparing the three columns in Section B of

EXAMPLE 9.4

Case A

One of the divisions within Rhine Autos is currently negotiating with another supplier regarding outsourcing component A that it manufactures. The division currently manufactures 10 000 units per annum of the component. The costs currently assigned to the components are as follows:

	Total costs of producing 10 000 components (£)	Unit cost (£)
Direct materials	120 000	12
Direct labour	100 000	10
Variable manufacturing overhead costs (power and utilities)	10 000	1
Fixed manufacturing overhead costs	80 000	8
Share of non-manufacturing overheads	50 000	5
Total costs	360 000	36

The above costs are expected to remain unchanged in the foreseeable future if the Rhine Autos division continues to manufacture the components. The supplier has offered to supply 10 000 components per annum at price of £30 per unit guaranteed for a minimum of three years. If Rhine Autos outsources component A the direct labour force currently employed in producing the components will be made redundant. No redundancy costs will be incurred. Direct materials and variable overheads are avoidable if component A is outsourced. Fixed manufacturing overhead costs would be reduced by £10 000 per annum but non-manufacturing costs would remain unchanged. Assume initially that the capacity that is required for component A has no alternative use. Should the Division of Rhine Autos make or buy the component?

Case B

Assume now that the extra capacity that will be made available from outsourcing component A can be used to manufacture and sell 10 000 units of part B at a price of £34 per unit. All of the labour force required to manufacture component A would be used to make part B. The variable manufacturing overheads, the fixed manufacturing overheads and non-manufacturing overheads would be the same as the costs incurred for manufacturing component A. The materials required to manufacture component A would not be required but additional materials required for making part B would cost £13 per unit. Should Rhine Autos outsource component A?

EXHIBIT 9.3 Evaluating a make or buy decision

Section A – Assuming there is no alternative use of the released capacity

	Total cost of continuing to make 10 000 components (1) (£ per annum)	Total cost of buying 10 000 components (2) (£ per annum)	Difference (relevant) (cost) (3) (£ per annum)
Direct materials	120 000		120 000
Direct labour	100 000		100 000
Variable manufacturing overhead costs (power and utilities)	10 000		10 000
Fixed manufacturing overhead costs	80 000	70 000	10 000
Non-manufacturing overheads	50 000	50 000	
Outside purchase cost incurred/(saved)	_____	300 000	(300 000)
Total costs incurred/(saved) per annum	360 000	420 000	(60 000)

Column 3 is easier to interpret if it is restated as two separate alternatives as follows:

	Relevant cost of making component A (£ per annum)	Relevant cost of outsourcing component A (£ per annum)
Direct materials	120 000	
Direct labour	100 000	
Variable manufacturing overhead costs	10 000	
Fixed manufacturing overhead costs	10 000	
Outside purchase cost incurred	_____	300 000
	240 000	300 000

Section B – Assuming the released capacity has alternative uses

	(1) Make component A and do not make part B (£ per annum)	(2) Buy component A and do not make part B (£ per annum)	(3) Buy component A and make part B (£ per annum)
Direct materials	120 000		130 000
Direct labour	100 000		100 000
Variable manufacturing overhead costs	10 000		10 000
Fixed manufacturing overhead costs	80 000	70 000	80 000
Non-manufacturing overheads	50 000	50 000	50 000
Outside purchase cost incurred		300 000	300 000
Revenues from sales of part B	_____	_____	(340 000)
Total net costs	360 000	420 000	330 000

Exhibit 9.3 indicates that buying component A and using the extra capacity that is created to make part B is the preferred alternative.

The incremental costs of outsourcing are £60 000 more than making component B (see Section A of Exhibit 9.3) but the extra capacity released from outsourcing component A enables Rhine Autos to obtain a profit contribution of £90 000 (£340 000 incremental sales from part B less £250 000 incremental/relevant costs of making part B). The overall outcome is a £30 000 net benefit from outsourcing. Note that the relevant costs of making part B are the same as those of making component A, apart from direct materials, which cost £130 000. In other words, the relevant (incremental) costs of making part B (compared with outsourcing) are as follows:

	(£)
Direct materials	130 000
Direct labour	100 000
Variable manufacturing overhead costs	10 000
Fixed manufacturing overhead costs	10 000
	250 000

REAL WORLD VIEWS 9.1

Measures of product attractiveness in retail operations

Shelf space limits the quantity and variety of products offered by a retail operation. The visibility of a particular stock-keeping unit (SKU) and probability of a stock-out are related to the space allocated to the SKU. Total contribution for the retail operation is influenced by how shelf space is allocated to the SKUs. For retailers, shelf space 'is their life blood – and it's very limited and expensive'. Shelf space, accordingly, can be treated as a constraint in retailing operations. The most attractive SKU is the SKU that generates the greatest contribution per unit of space (square foot or cubic foot). To calculate contribution, all incremental expenses are deducted from incremental revenue. Incremental revenues include retail price and other direct revenue such as deals, allowances, forward-buy and prompt-payment discounts. Incremental expenses include any money paid out as a result of selling one unit of a particular item. Included in the incremental expenses would be the invoice unit cost and other invoiced amounts (shipping charges, for example) that can be traced directly to the sale of the particular item. Incremental revenues and expenses are found by dividing case values by the number of units per case.

If capacity is not changed, then the relevant costs are the incremental costs rather than full costs. The choice of low direct product cost items (i.e. a full product cost including a share of the fixed warehouse, transport and storage costs) over high direct product cost items is essentially a choice to use less of the capacity that has already been paid for. If the costs of capacity are fixed, then using less capacity will not save money. Like the product mix problem, the answer to the space management problem is how to allocate existing capacity so that profit is maximized. To maximize profits where profits are constrained by space limitations, capacity should be allocated on the basis of the SKU that generates the greatest contribution per unit of space.

Discussion point

What are the relevant costs and revenues applicable to retail operations?

© GIANNI MURATORE/ALAMY

SOURCE: ADAPTED FROM GARDINER, S.C. MEASURES OF PRODUCT ATTRACTIVENESS AND THE THEORY OF CONSTRAINTS, INTERNATIONAL JOURNAL OF RETAIL AND DISTRIBUTION, 1993, VOL. 21, NO. 7, PP. 37–40.
EMERALD PUBLISHERS WWW.EMERALDINSIGHT.COM/IJRD.HTML.

Discontinuation decisions

Most organizations periodically analyze profits by one or more cost objects, such as products or services, customers and locations. Periodic profitability analysis provides attention-directing information that highlights those unprofitable activities that require a more detailed appraisal (sometimes referred to as a special study) to ascertain whether or not they should be discontinued. In this section we shall illustrate how the principle of relevant costs can be applied to discontinuation decisions. Consider Example 9.5. You will see that it focuses on a decision whether to discontinue operating a sales territory, but the same principles can also be applied to discontinuing products, services or customers.

In Example 9.5 Euro Company analyzes profits by locations. Profits are analyzed by regions which are then further analyzed by sales territories within each region. It is apparent from Example 9.5 that the Scandinavian region is profitable but the profitability analysis suggests that the Helsinki sales territory is unprofitable. A more detailed study is required to ascertain whether it should be discontinued. Let us assume that this study indicates that:

1 Discontinuing the Helsinki sales territory will eliminate cost of goods sold, salespersons' salaries, sales office rent and regional and headquarters expenses arising from cause-and-effect cost allocations.

2 Discontinuing the Helsinki sales territory will have no effect on depreciation of sales office equipment, warehouse rent, depreciation of warehouse equipment and regional and headquarters expenses arising from arbitrary cost allocations. The same costs will be incurred by the company for all of these items even if the sales territory is discontinued.

EXAMPLE 9.5

The Euro Company is a wholesaler who sells its products to retailers throughout Europe. Euro's headquarters is in Brussels. The company has adopted a regional structure with each region consisting of 3–5 sales territories. Each region has its own regional office and a warehouse which distributes the goods directly to the customers. Each sales territory also has an office where the marketing staff are located. The Scandinavian region consists of three sales territories with offices located in Stockholm, Oslo and Helsinki. The budgeted results for the next quarter are as follows:

	Stockholm (£000s)	Oslo (£000s)	Helsinki (£000s)	Total (£000s)
Cost of goods sold	800	850	1000	2650
Salespersons' salaries	160	200	240	600
Sales office rent	60	90	120	270
Depreciation of sales office equipment	20	30	40	90
Apportionment of warehouse rent	24	24	24	72
Depreciation of warehouse equipment	20	16	22	58
Regional and headquarters costs				
Cause-and-effect allocations	120	152	186	458
Arbitrary apportionments	360	400	340	1100
Total costs assigned to each location	1564	1762	1972	5298
Reported profit/(loss)	236	238	(272)	202
Sales	1800	2000	1700	5500

Assuming that the above results are likely to be typical of future quarterly performance should the Helsinki territory be discontinued?

Note that in the event of discontinuation the sales office will not be required and the rental will be eliminated whereas the warehouse rent relates to the warehouse for the region as a whole and, unless the company moves to a smaller warehouse, the rental will remain unchanged. It is therefore not a relevant cost. Discontinuation will result in the creation of additional space and if the extra space remains unused there are no financial consequences to take into account. However, if the additional space can be sub-let to generate rental income the income would be incorporated as an opportunity cost for the alternative of keeping the Helsinki territory.

Exhibit 9.4 shows the relevant cost computations. Column (1) shows the costs incurred by the company if the sales territory is kept open and column (2) shows the costs that would be incurred if a decision was taken to drop the sales territory. Therefore in column (2) only those costs that would be eliminated (i.e. those items listed in item (1) above) are deducted from column (1). You can see that the company will continue to incur some of the costs (i.e. those items listed in item (2) above) even if the Helsinki territory is closed and these costs are therefore irrelevant to the decision. Again you can either include, or exclude, the irrelevant costs in columns (1) and (2) as long as you ensure that the same amount of irrelevant costs is included for both alternatives if you adopt the first approach. Both approaches will show that future profits will decline by £154 000 if the Helsinki territory is closed. Alternatively, you can present just the relevant costs and revenues shown in column (3). This approach indicates that keeping the sales territory open results in additional sales revenues of £1 700 000 but additional costs of £1 546 000 are incurred giving a contribution of £154 000 towards fixed costs and profits.

You will have noted that we have assumed that the regional and headquarters costs assigned to the sales territories on the basis of cause-and-effect allocations can be eliminated if the Helsinki territory is discontinued. These are indirect costs that fluctuate in the longer-term according to the demand for them and it is assumed that the selected allocation base, or cost driver, provides a reasonably accurate measure of resources consumed by the sales territories. Cause-and-effect allocation bases assume that if the cause is eliminated or reduced, the effect (i.e. the costs) will be eliminated or reduced. If cost drivers are selected that result in allocations that are inaccurate measures of resources consumed by cost objects (i.e. sales territories)

EXHIBIT 9.4 Relevant cost analysis relating to the discontinuation of the Helsinki territory

	Total costs and revenues to be assigned		
	(1) Keep Helsinki territory open (£000s)	(2) Discontinue Helsinki territory (£000s)	(3) Difference incremental costs and revenues (£000s)
Cost of goods sold	2650	1650	1000
Salespersons' salaries	600	360	240
Sales office rent	270	150	120
Depreciation of sales office equipment	90	90	
Apportionment of warehouse rent	72	72	
Depreciation of warehouse equipment	58	58	
Regional and headquarters costs			
Cause-and-effect allocations	458	272	186
Arbitrary apportionments	1100	1100	
Total costs to be assigned	5298	3752	1546
Reported profit	202	48	154
Sales	5500	3800	1700

the relevant costs derived from these allocations will be incorrect and incorrect decisions may be made. We shall explore this issue in some detail in the next chapter when we look at activity-based costing.

Determining the relevant costs of direct materials

So far in this chapter we have assumed, when considering various decisions, that any materials required would not be taken from existing stocks but would be purchased at a later date, and so the estimated purchase price would be the relevant material cost. Where materials are taken from existing stock do remember that the original purchase price represents a past or sunk cost and is therefore irrelevant for decision-making. If the materials are to be replaced then using the materials for a particular activity will necessitate their replacement. Thus, the decision to use the materials on an activity will result in additional acquisition costs compared with the situation if the materials were not used on that particular activity. Therefore the future replacement cost represents the relevant cost of the materials.

Consider now the situation where the materials have no further use apart from being used on a particular activity. If the materials have some realizable value, the use of the materials will result in lost sales revenues, and this lost sales revenue will represent an opportunity cost that must be assigned to the activity. Alternatively, if the materials have no realizable value the relevant cost of the materials will be zero.

Determining the relevant costs of direct labour

Determining the direct labour costs that are relevant to short-term decisions depends on the circumstances. Where a company has temporary spare capacity and the labour force is to be maintained in the short term, the direct labour cost incurred will remain the same for all alternative decisions. The direct labour cost will therefore be irrelevant for short-term decision-making purposes. Consider now a situation where casual labour is used and where workers can be hired on a daily basis; a company may then adjust the employment of labour to exactly the amount required to meet the production requirements. The labour cost will increase if the company accepts additional work, and will decrease if production is reduced. In this situation the labour cost will be a relevant cost for decision-making purposes.

In a situation where full capacity exists and additional labour supplies are unavailable in the short term, and where no further overtime working is possible, the only way that labour resources could then be obtained for a specific order would be to reduce existing production. This would release labour for the order, but the reduced production would result in a lost contribution, and this lost contribution must be taken into account when ascertaining the relevant cost for the specific order. The relevant labour cost per hour where full capacity exists is therefore the hourly labour rate plus an opportunity cost consisting of the contribution per hour that is lost by accepting the order. For a more detailed illustration explaining why this is the appropriate cost you should refer to Learning Note 9.1 on the open access website (see Preface for details).

SUMMARY

The following items relate to the learning objectives listed at the beginning of the chapter.

● **Distinguish between relevant and irrelevant costs and revenues.**

Relevant costs/revenues represent those future costs/revenues that will be changed by a particular decision, whereas irrelevant costs/revenues will not be affected by that decision. In the short-term total profits will be increased (or total losses decreased) if a course of action is chosen where relevant revenues are in excess of relevant costs.

● **Explain the importance of qualitative factors.**

Quantitative factors refer to outcomes that can be measured in numerical terms. In many situations it is difficult to quantify all the important elements of a decision. Those factors that cannot be expressed in numerical terms are called qualitative factors. Examples of qualitative factors include changes in employee morale and the impact of being at the mercy of a supplier when a decision is made to close a company's facilities and sub-contract components. Although qualitative factors cannot be quantified it is essential that they are taken into account in the decision-making process.

● **Distinguish between the relevant and irrelevant costs and revenues for the five decision-making problems described.**

The five decision-making problems described were: (a) special selling price decisions; (b) product-mix decisions when capacity constraints apply; (c) decisions on the replacement of equipment; (d) outsourcing (make or buy) decisions; and (e) discontinuation decisions. Different approaches can be used for presenting relevant cost and revenue information. Information can be presented that includes both relevant and irrelevant items for all alternatives under consideration. If this approach is adopted the same amount for the irrelevant items (i.e. those items that remain unchanged as a result of the decision) are included for all alternatives thus making them irrelevant for the decision. Alternatively, information can be presented that lists only the relevant costs for the alternatives under consideration. Where only two alternatives are being considered a third approach is to present only the relevant (differential) items. You can adopt either

approach. It is a matter of personal preference. All three approaches were illustrated for the five decision-making problems.

● **Describe the key concept that should be applied for presenting information for product-mix decisions when capacity constraints apply.**

The information presented should rank the products by the contribution per unit of the constraining or limiting factor (i.e. the scarce resource). The capacity of the scarce resource should allocated according to this ranking.

● **Explain why the book value of equipment is irrelevant when making equipment replacement decisions.**

The book value of equipment is a past (sunk) cost that cannot be changed for any alternative under consideration. Only future costs or revenues that will differ between alternatives are relevant for replacement decisions.

● **Describe the opportunity cost concept.**

Where the choice of one course of action requires that an alternative course of action be given up the financial benefits that are forgone or sacrificed are known as opportunity costs. Opportunity costs thus represent the lost contribution to profits arising from the best alternative forgone. They arise only when the resources are scarce and have alternative uses. Opportunity costs must therefore be included in the analysis when presenting relevant information for decision-making.

● **Explain the misconceptions relating to relevant costs and revenues.**

The main misconception relates to the assumption that only sales revenues and variable costs are relevant and that fixed costs are irrelevant for decision-making. Sometimes variable costs are irrelevant. For example, they are irrelevant when they are the same for all alternatives under consideration. Fixed costs are also relevant when they differ among the alternatives. For a more detailed discussion explaining the misconceptions relating to relevant costs and revenues you should refer to Learning Note 9.2 on the open access website (see Preface for details).

● **Additional learning objective presented in Appendix 9.1.**

The appendix to this chapter includes the following additional learning objective: describe the theory of constraints and throughput accounting. This topic has been presented in the appendix because it is not vital to understanding the principles of measuring relevant costs and revenues for decision-making. The topic also tends to be covered on more advanced courses and may not form part of your course curriculum. You should therefore check with your course curriculum to ascertain whether you need to study this topic.

Appendix 9.1: The theory of constraints and throughput accounting

During the 1980s Goldratt and Cox (1984) advocated a new approach to production management called optimized production technology (OPT). OPT is based on the principle that profits are expanded by increasing the throughput of the plant. The OPT approach determines what prevents throughput being higher by distinguishing between bottleneck and non-bottleneck resources. A bottleneck might be a machine whose capacity limits the throughput of the whole production process. The aim is to identify bottlenecks and remove them or, if this is not possible, ensure that they are fully utilized at all times. Non-bottleneck resources should be scheduled and operated based on constraints within the system, and should not be used to produce more than the bottlenecks can absorb. The OPT philosophy therefore advocates that non-bottleneck resources should not be utilized to 100 per cent of their capacity, since this would merely result in an increase in inventory. Thus idle time in non-bottleneck areas is not considered detrimental to the efficiency of the organization. If it were utilized, it would result in increased inventory without a corresponding increase in throughput for the plant.

Goldratt and Cox (1992) describe the process of maximizing operating profit when faced with bottleneck and non-bottleneck operations as the theory of constraints (TOC). The process involves five steps:

1 identify the system's bottlenecks;
2 decide how to exploit the bottlenecks;
3 subordinate everything else to the decision in step 2;
4 elevate the system's bottlenecks;
5 if, in the previous steps, a bottleneck has been broken go back to step 1.

The first step involves identifying the constraint which restricts output from being expanded. Having identified the bottleneck it becomes the focus of attention since only the bottleneck can restrict or enhance the flow of products. It is therefore essential to ensure that the bottleneck activity is fully utilized. Decisions regarding the optimum mix of products to be produced by the bottleneck activity must be made. Step 3 requires that the optimum production of the bottleneck activity determines the production schedule of the non-bottleneck activities. In other words, the output of the non-bottleneck operations are linked to the needs of the bottleneck activity. There is no point in a non-bottleneck activity supplying more than the bottleneck activity can consume. This would merely result in an increase in WIP inventories and no increase in sales volume. The TOC is a process of continuous improvement to clear the throughput chain of all constraints. Thus, step 4 involves taking action to remove (that is, elevate) the constraint. This might involve replacing a bottleneck machine with a faster one, increasing the bottleneck efficiency or changing the design of the product to reduce the processing time required by the activity. When a bottleneck activity has been elevated and replaced by a new bottleneck it is necessary to return to step 1 and repeat the process.

To apply TOC ideas Goldratt and Cox advocate the use of three key measures.

1 *Throughput contribution* which is the rate at which the system generates profit through sales. It is defined as sales less direct materials.

2 *Investments* (inventory) which is the sum of inventories, research and development costs and the costs of equipment and buildings.

3 *Other operational expenses* which include all operating costs (other than direct materials) incurred to earn throughput contribution.

The TOC aims to increase throughput contribution while simultaneously reducing inventory and operational expenses. However, the scope for reducing the latter is limited since they must be maintained at some minimum level for production to take place at all. In other words, operational expenses are assumed to be fixed costs. Goldratt and Cox argue that traditional management accounting is obsessed by the need to reduce operational expenses, which results in a declining spiral of cost-cutting, followed by falling production and a further round of cost-cutting. Instead, they advocate a throughput orientation whereby throughput must be given first priority, inventories second and operational expenses last.

REAL WORLD VIEWS 9A.1

Throughput accounting: The Garrett Automative experience

Garrett Automative Ltd (GAL) is a UK subsidiary of an American parent company that manufactures turbochargers for the automative industry. GAL decided to begin its profit improvement programme by examining its factory throughput. Throughput was defined as the rate at which raw materials were turned into sales. In other words, throughput was defined as sales less material costs per period of time. All operating costs, other than direct materials were considered to be fixed in the short run. In conjunction with its new OPT scheduling system factory bottlenecks, defined as an activity within the organization where demand for the resource outstrips the capacity to supply, were identified. The bottlenecks became certain machines in the factory. The mechanism to improve profitability was to maximize throughput contribution by optimizing the use of bottleneck resources.

Management sought to alleviate the bottlenecks by making additional investments to improve bottleneck capacity and by shifting some of the operations from bottleneck to non-bottleneck machines. New investments to improve efficiency at non-bottleneck machines were rejected because this greater efficiency did nothing to improve throughput contribution. Priority was given to investments in bottlenecks. To motivate the employees to increase throughput the performance reporting system was changed. Less emphasis was given to labour efficiency and schedule adherence was introduced as a key performance measure. Employees at non-bottleneck operations were requested not to produce more than the scheduled quantity and use any surplus time on training and TQM initiatives.

GAL has found throughput accounting to be extremely helpful in its particular situation. By concentrating on managing its bottlenecks, GAL has been able to increase its production to meet its sales demand of many different types of turbochargers in relatively small batch sizes.

Discussion point

How could the approach described above be applied in a service organization, such as the National Health Service?

© WESTEND 61/ALAMY

SOURCE: ADAPTED FROM DARLINGTON, J. ET AL. (1992), THROUGHPUT ACCOUNTING: THE GARRETT AUTOMATIVE EXPERIENCE, MANAGEMENT ACCOUNTING (UK), APRIL 1992, PP. 32–35, 38 AND COUGHLAN, P. AND DARLINGTON, J. (1993), AS FAST AS THE SLOWEST OPERATIONS: THE THEORY OF CONSTRAINTS, MANAGEMENT ACCOUNTING (UK), JUNE 1993, PP. 14–17.

The TOC adopts a short-run time horizon and treats all operating expenses (including direct labour but excluding direct materials) as fixed, thus implying that variable costing should be used for decision-making, profit measurement and inventory valuation. It emphasizes the management of bottleneck activities as the key to improving performance by focusing on the short-run maximization of throughput contribution. Adopting the throughput approach to implement the TOC, however, appears to be merely a restatement of the contribution per limiting factor that was described in this chapter. Consider the situation outlined in Example 9A.1.

You can see from Example 9A.1 that the required machine utilization is as follows:

Machine	1	112%	(1800/1600 × 100)
	2	169%	(2700/1600 × 100)
	3	56%	(900/1600 × 100)

Machine 2 represents the bottleneck activity because it has the highest machine utilization. To ascertain the optimum use of the bottleneck activity we calculate the throughput contribution per hour for machine 2 for each product and rank the products in order of profitability based on this calculation. Using the figures in the present example the result would be as follows:

	Product X	Product Y	Product Z
Contribution per unit	£12	£10	£6
Machine 2 hours required	9	3	1.5
Contribution per machine hour	£1.33	£3.33	£4
Ranking	3	2	1

The allocation of the 1600 hours for the bottleneck activity is:

	Machine hours used	Balance of hours available
Production		
200 units of Z	300	1300
200 units of Y	600	700
77 units of X	700	—

EXAMPLE 9A.1

A company produces three products using three different machines. The following information is available for a period.

Product	X	Y	Z	Total
Throughput contribution (Sales – direct materials)	£12	£10	£6	
Machine hours required per unit:				
Machine 1	6	2	1	
Machine 2	9	3	1.5	
Machine 3	3	1	0.5	
Estimated sales demand	200	200	200	
Required machine hours				
Machine 1	1200	400	200	1800
Machine 2	1800	600	300	2700
Machine 3	600	200	100	900

Machine capacity is limited to 1600 hours for each machine.

Following the five step TOC process outlined earlier, action should be taken to remove the constraint. Let us assume that a financial analysis indicates that the purchase of a second 'Type 2' machine is justified. Machine capacity will now be increased by 1600 hours to 3200 hours and Machine 2 will no longer be a constraint. In other words, the bottleneck will have been elevated and Machine 1 will now become the constraint. The above process must now be repeated to determine the optimum output for Machine 1.

Galloway and Waldron (1988) advocate an approach called throughput accounting to apply the TOC philosophy. To ascertain the optimum use of the bottleneck activity they rank the products according to a measure they have devised called the throughput accounting (TA) ratio. They define the TA ratio as:

$$\text{TA Ratio} = \frac{\text{Return per factory hour}}{\text{Cost per factory hour}}$$

$$\text{where Return per factory hour} = \frac{\text{Sales price} - \text{Material cost}}{\text{Time on key resource}}$$

$$\text{and Cost per factory hour} = \frac{\text{Total factory cost}}{\text{Total time available on key resource}}$$

Note that sales less direct material cost is equal to throughput contribution, total factory cost is defined in exactly the same way as other operational expenses (see TOC measures described earlier) and return per factory hour is identical to the throughput contribution per hour of the bottleneck activity. Let us assume for Example 9A.1 that the total factory cost for the period is £3200. The TA ratios and product rankings for the bottleneck activity (Machine 2), using the data shown in Example 9A.1, are as follows:

	Product X	Product Y	Product Z
1. Return per factory hour	£1.33	£3.33	£4
2. Cost per factory hour (£3200/1600 hours)	£2	£2	£2
3. TA ratio (Row 1/Row 2)	0.665	1.665	2
4. Ranking	3	2	1

The rankings are identical to the contribution per bottleneck hour calculated earlier. Given that the TA ratio is calculated by dividing the contribution per bottleneck hour (described as return per factory hour) by a constant amount (cost per factory hour) the TA ratio appears merely to represent a restatement of the contribution per limiting factor described in the main body of this chapter. However, it is possible to distinguish between throughput accounting and the contribution approach. Contribution and throughput accounting differ in terms of their definition of variable cost. Contribution treats direct materials, direct labour and variable overheads as variable costs whereas throughput accounting assumes that only direct materials represent variable costs. Throughput accounting is thus more short-term oriented and assumes that direct labour and variable overheads cannot be avoided within a very short-term period. In contrast, contribution assumes that the short-term represents a longer period than that assumed with throughput accounting and thus classifies direct labour and variable overheads as variable costs that vary with output in the longer term.

Goldratt (1992) does not advocate any specific accounting practices. Instead, accountants are encouraged to learn TOC ideas and apply them to accounting in ways that suit their own circumstances. However, traditional techniques that have been described in management accounting textbooks for many years, such as how product mix decisions should be made when capacity constraints apply, can be viewed as an attempt to apply TOC ideas. Thus, applying TOC ideas to accounting does not represent a radical innovation in accounting but a move towards the widespread adoption of short-run variable costing techniques. Hence, the same criticisms that have been applied to variable costing can also be made to the application of TOC ideas. That is, all expenses other than direct materials are assumed to be fixed and unavoidable. For a more detailed discussion of the TOC and throughput accounting you should refer to Dugdale and Jones (1998), Jones and Dugdale (1998) and the solution to Review problem 9.25.

Key terms and concepts

decision-relevant approach (p. 191)
differential cash flow (p. 192)
incremental cash flow (p. 192)
limiting factor (p. 198)
opportunity cost (p. 197)

optimized production technology (p. 209)
outsourcing (p. 201)
qualitative factors (p. 192)
relevant cost (p. 192)

replacement cost (p. 207)
special studies (p. 191)
theory of constraints (pp. 199, 209)
throughput accounting (pp. 199, 212)
written-down value (p. 199)

Recommended reading

For a discussion of the arguments for and against using the contribution analysis approach you should refer to the *Journal of Management Accounting Research* (USA) Fall 1990, 1–32, 'Contribution margin analysis: no longer relevant. Strategic cost management: the new paradigm', which reproduces the contributions from a panel of speakers at the American Accounting Association Annual Meeting: Ferrara (pp. 1–2) Kaplan (pp. 2–15), Shank (pp. 15–21), Horngren (pp. 21–4), Boer (pp. 24–7), together with concluding remarks (pp. 27–32). For a detailed discussion of the theory of constraints and throughput accounting you should refer to Jones and Dugdale (1998) and Dugdale and Jones (1998).

Key examination points

A common mistake that students make when presenting information for decision-making is to compare *unit* costs. With this approach, there is a danger that fixed costs will be unitized and treated as variable costs. In most cases you should compare total amounts of costs and revenues rather than unit amounts. Many students do not present the information clearly and concisely. There are many alternative ways of presenting the information, but the simplest approach is to list future costs and revenues for each alternative in a format similar to Exhibit 9.1. You should exclude irrelevant items or ensure that the same amount for irrelevant items is included for each alternative. To determine the amount to be entered for each alternative, you should ask yourself what difference it will make if the alternative is selected.

Never allocate common fixed costs to the alternatives. You should focus on how each alternative will affect future cash flows of the organization. Changes in the apportionment of fixed costs will not alter future cash flows of the company. Remember that if a resource is scarce, your analysis should recommend the alternative that yields the largest contribution per limiting factor. You should now attempt the Review problems and compare your answers with the solutions that are provided. These problems will test your understanding of a variety of decision problems that have been covered in Chapter 9. Pay particular attention to Review problem 9.23 since this includes many of the aspects that were discussed in the chapter.

ASSESSMENT MATERIAL

The review questions are short questions that enable you to assess your understanding of the main topics included in the chapter. The numbers in parentheses provide you with the page numbers to refer to if you cannot answer a specific question.

The review problems are more complex and require you to relate and apply the content to various business problems. The problems are graded by their level of difficulty. Solutions to review problems that are not preceded by the term 'IM' are provided in a separate section at the end of the book. Solutions to problems preceded by the term 'IM' are provided in the *Instructor's Manual* accompanying this book and also on the lecturer's password protected section of the website www.drury-online.com. Additional review problems with fully worked solutions are provided in the *Student's Manual* that accompanies this book.

The website also includes over 30 case study problems. A list of these cases is provided on pages 665–7. Several cases are relevant to the content of this chapter. Examples include Fleet Ltd. and High Street Reproduction Furniture Ltd.

Review questions

9.1 What is a relevant cost? *(p. 192)*

9.2 Why is it important to recognize qualitative factors when presenting information for decision-making? Provide examples of qualitative factors. *(pp. 192–93)*

9.3 What underlying principle should be followed in determining relevant costs for decision-making? *(p. 195)*

9.4 Explain what is meant by special pricing decisions. *(p. 193)*

9.5 Describe the important factors that must be taken into account when making special pricing decisions. *(p. 194)*

9.6 Describe the dangers involved in focusing excessively on a short-run decision-making time horizon. *(p. 197)*

9.7 Define limiting factors. *(p. 198)*

9.8 How should a company determine its optimal product mix when a limiting factor exists? *(p. 198)*

9.9 Why is the written down value and depreciation of an asset being considered for replacement irrelevant when making replacement decisions? *(p. 000)*

9.10 Explain the importance of opportunity costs for decision-making. *(p. 197)*

9.11 Explain the circumstances when the original purchase price of materials are irrelevant for decision-making. *(p. 207)*

9.12 Why does the relevant cost of labour differ depending upon the circumstances? *(p. 207)*

9.13 Describe the five steps involved in applying the theory of constraints. *(p. 209)*

9.14 Describe throughput accounting and explain how it can be used to determine the optimum use of a bottleneck activity. *(pp. 212–13)*

Review problems

9.15 Basic. A company produces three products which have the following details:

	I Per unit	II Per unit	III Per unit
Direct materials (at £5/kg)	8 kg	5 kg	6 kg
Contribution per unit	£35	£25	£48
Contribution per kg of material	$4.375	£5	£8
Demand (excluding special contract) (units)	3000	5000	2000

The company must produce 1000 units of Product I for a special contract before meeting normal demand. Unfortunately there are only 35 000 kg of material available.

What is the optimal production plan?

	I	II	III
A	1000	4600	2000
B	1000	3000	2000
C	2875	—	2000
D	3000	2200	—

ACCA – Financial Information for Management

9.16 Basic. A company has just secured a new contract which requires 500 hours of labour.

There are 400 hours of spare labour capacity. The remaining hours could be worked as overtime at time and a half or labour could be diverted from the production of product X. Product X currently earns a contribution of £4 in two labour hours and direct labour is currently paid at a rate of £12 per normal hour.

What is the relevant cost of labour for the contract?

   a   £200
   b   £1200
   c   £1400
   d   £1800   *ACCA – Financial Information for Management*

9.17 Basic. X plc intends to use relevant costs as the basis of the selling price for a special order: the printing of a brochure. The brochure requires a particular type of paper that is not regularly used by X plc although a limited amount is in X plc's inventory which was left over from a previous job. The cost when X plc bought this paper last year was $15 per ream and there are 100 reams in inventory. The brochure requires 250 reams. The current market price of the paper is $26 per ream, and the resale value of the paper in inventory is $10 per ream.

The relevant cost of the paper to be used in printing the brochure is

   a $2,500
   b $4,900
   c $5,400
   d $6,500

CIMA P2 Management Accounting: Decision Management

9.18 Basic. A company is considering accepting a one-year contract which will require four skilled employees. The four skilled employees could be recruited on a one-year contract at a cost of £40 000, per employee. The employees would be supervised by an existing manager who earns £60 000 per annum. It is expected that supervision of the contract would take 10 per cent of the manager's time.

Instead of recruiting new employees, the company could retrain some existing employees who currently earn £30 000 per year. The training would cost £15 000 in total. If these employees were used they would need to be replaced at a total cost of £100 000.

The relevant labour cost of the contract is:

a   £100 000
b   £115 000
c   £135 000
d   £141 000
e   £166 000   *CIMA Stage 2*

9.19 Basic. Camden has three divisions. Information for the year ended 30 September is as follows:

	Division A £'000	Division B £'000	Division C £'000	Total £'000
Sales	350	420	150	920
Variable costs	280	210	120	610
Contribution	70	210	30	310
Fixed costs				262.5
Net profit				47.5

General fixed overheads are allocated to each division on the basis of sales revenue; 60 per cent of the total fixed costs incurred by the company are specific to each division being split equally between them.

Using relevant costing techniques, which divisions should remain open if Camden wishes to maximise profits?

a   A, B and C
b   A and B only
c   B only
d   B and C only.

ACCA Paper 1.2 – Financial Information for Management

9.20 Intermediate. JJ Ltd manufactures three products: W, X and Y. The products use a series of different machines but there is a common machine that is a bottleneck.

The standard selling price and standard cost per unit for each product for the forthcoming period are as follows:

	W £	X £	Y £
Selling price	200	150	150
Cost			
Direct material	41	20	30
Labour	30	20	36
Overheads	60	40	50
Profit	69	70	34
Bottleneck machine – minutes per unit	9	10	7

40 per cent of the overhead cost is classified as variable

Using a throughput accounting approach, what would be the ranking of the products for best use of the bottleneck?   *(3 marks)*

CIMA P1 Management Accounting: Performance Evaluation

9.21 Intermediate: Decision on which of two mutually exclusive contracts to accept. A company in the civil engineering industry with headquarters located 22 miles from London undertakes contracts anywhere in the United Kingdom.

The company has had its tender for a job in north-east England accepted at £288 000 and work is due to begin in March. However, the company has also been asked to undertake a contract on the south coast of England. The price offered for this contract is £352 000. Both of the contracts cannot be taken simultaneously because of constraints on staff site management personnel and on plant available. An escape clause enables the company to withdraw from the contract in the north-east, provided notice is given before the end of November and an agreed penalty of £28 000 is paid.

The following estimates have been submitted by the company's quantity surveyor:

Cost estimates	North-east (£)	South coast (£)
Materials:		
In stock at original cost, Material X	21 600	
In stock at original cost, Material Y		24 800
Firm orders placed at original cost, Material X	30 400	
Not yet ordered – current cost, Material X	60 000	
Not yet ordered – current cost, Material Z		71 200
Labour – hired locally	86 000	110 000
Site management	34 000	34 000
Staff accommodation and travel for site management	6 800	5 600
Plant on site – depreciation	9 600	12 800
Interest on capital, 8%	5 120	6 400
Total local contract costs	253 520	264 800
Headquarters costs allocated at rate of 5% on total contract costs	12 676	13 240
	266 196	278 040
Contract price	288 000	352 000
Estimated profit	21 804	73 960

Notes:

1. X, Y and Z are three building materials. Material X is not in common use and would not realize much money if re-sold; however, it could be used on other contracts but only as a substitute for another material currently quoted at 10 per cent less than the original cost of X. The price of Y, a material in common use, has doubled since it was purchased; its net realizable value if re-sold would be its new price less 15 per cent to cover disposal costs. Alternatively it could be kept for use on other contracts in the following financial year.

2. With the construction industry not yet recovered from the recent recession, the company is confident that manual labour, both skilled and unskilled, could be hired locally on a subcontracting basis to meet the needs of each of the contracts.

3. The plant which would be needed for the south coast contract has been owned for some years and £12 800 is the year's depreciation on a straight-line basis. If the north-east contract is undertaken, less plant will be required but the surplus plant will be hired out for the period of the contract at a rental of £6000.

4. It is the company's policy to charge all contracts with notional interest at 8 per cent on estimated working capital involved in contracts. Progress payments would be receivable from the contractee.

5. Salaries and general costs of operating the small headquarters amount to about £108 000 each year. There are usually ten contracts being supervised at the same time.

6. Each of the two contracts is expected to last from March to February which, coincidentally, is the company's financial year.

7. Site management is treated as a fixed cost.

You are required, as the management accountant to the company,

a   to present comparative statements to show the net benefit to the company of undertaking the more advantageous of the two contracts;   *(12 marks)*

b   to explain the reasoning behind the inclusion in (or omission from) your comparative financial statements, of each item given in the cost estimates and the notes relating thereto.   *(13 marks)*

CIMA Stage 2 Cost Accounting

9.22 Intermediate: Deletion of a product. Blackarm Ltd makes three products and is reviewing the profitability of its product line. You are given the following budgeted data about the firm for the coming year.

Product	A	B	C
Sales (in units)	100 000	120 000	80 000
	(£)	(£)	(£)
Revenue	1 500 000	1 440 000	880 000
Costs:			
Material	500 000	480 000	240 000
Labour	400 000	320 000	160 000
Overhead	650 000	600 000	360 000
	1 550 000	1 400 000	760 000
Profit/(Loss)	(50 000)	40 000	120 000

The company is concerned about the loss on product A. It is considering ceasing production of it and switching the spare capacity of 100 000 units to Product C.

You are told:

(i)   All production is sold.

(ii)   25 per cent of the labour cost for each product is fixed in nature.

(iii) Fixed administration overheads of £900 000 in total have been apportioned to each product on the basis of units sold and are included in the overhead costs above. All other overhead costs are variable in nature.

(iv) Ceasing production of product A would eliminate the fixed labour charge associated with it and one-sixth of the fixed administration overhead apportioned to product A.

(v) Increasing the production of product C by 100 000 units would mean that the fixed labour cost associated with product C would double, the variable labour cost would rise by 20 per cent and its selling price would have to be decreased by £1.50 in order to achieve the increased sales.

Required:

a Prepare a marginal cost statement for a unit of each product on the basis of:
   (i) the original budget;
   (ii) if product A is deleted. (12 marks)

b Prepare a statement showing the total contribution and profit for each product group on the basis of:
   (i) the original budget;
   (ii) if product A is deleted. (8 marks)

c Using your results from (a) and (b) advise whether product A should be deleted from the product range, giving reasons for your decision. (5 marks)

AAT Cost Accounting and Budgeting

9.23 Advanced: Alternative uses of obsolete materials. Brown Ltd is a company that has in stock some materials of type XY that cost £75 000 but that are now obsolete and have a scrap value of only £21 000. Other than selling the material for scrap, there are only two alternative uses for them.

Alternative 1: Converting the obsolete materials into a specialized product, which would require the following additional work and materials:

Material A	600 units
Material B	1 000 units
Direct labour:	
5000 hours unskilled	
5000 hours semi-skilled	
5000 hours highly skilled	15 000 hours
Extra selling and delivery expenses	£27 000
Extra advertising	£18 000

The conversion would produce 900 units of saleable product, and these could be sold for £400 per unit.

Material A is already in stock and is widely used within the firm. Although present stocks together with orders already planned will be sufficient to facilitate normal activity, any extra material used by adopting this alternative will necessitate such materials being replaced immediately. Material B is also in stock, but it is unlikely that any additional supplies can be obtained for some considerable time because of an industrial dispute. At the present time material B is normally used in the production of product Z, which sells at £390 per unit and incurs total variable cost (excluding material B) of £210 per unit. Each unit of product Z uses four units of material B.

The details of materials A and B are as follows:

	Material A (£)	Material B (£)
Acquisition cost at time of purchase	100 per unit	10 per unit
Net realizable value	85 per unit	18 per unit
Replacement cost	90 per unit	—

Alternative 2: Adapting the obsolete materials for use as a substitute for a sub-assembly that is regularly used within the firm. Details of the extra work and materials required are as follows:

Material C	1000 units
Direct labour:	
4000 hours unskilled	
1000 hours semi-skilled	
4000 hours highly skilled	9000 hours

1200 units of the sub-assembly are regularly used per quarter, at a cost of £900 per unit. The adaptation of material XY would reduce the quantity of the sub-assembly purchased from outside the firm to 900 units for the next quarter only. However, since the volume purchased would be reduced, some discount would be lost, and the price of those purchased from outside would increase to £950 per unit for that quarter.

Material C is not available externally, but is manufactured by Brown Ltd. The 1000 units required would be available from stocks, but would be produced as extra production. The standard cost per unit of material C would be as follows:

	(£)
Direct labour, 6 hours unskilled labour	36
Raw materials	13
Variable overhead, 6 hours at £1	6
Fixed overhead, 6 hours at £3	18
	73

The wage rates and overhead recovery rates for Brown Ltd are:

Variable overhead	£1 per direct labour hour
Fixed overhead	£3 per direct labour hour
Unskilled labour	£6 per direct labour hour
Semi-skilled labour	£8 per direct labour hour
Highly skilled labour	£10 per direct labour hour

The unskilled labour is employed on a casual basis and sufficient labour can be acquired to exactly meet the production requirements. Semi-skilled labour is part of the permanent labour force, but the company has temporary excess supply of this type of labour at the present time. Highly skilled labour is in short supply and cannot be increased significantly in the short term; this labour is presently engaged in meeting the demand for product L, which requires four hours of highly skilled labour. The contribution (sales less direct labour and material costs and variable overheads) from the sale of one unit of product L is £24.

Given this information, you are required to present cost information advising whether the stocks of material XY should be sold, converted into a specialized product (alternative 1) or adapted for use as a substitute for a sub-assembly (alternative 2).

9.24 Advanced: Limiting factors and optimal production programme. A market gardener is planning his production for next season, and he has asked you as a cost accountant, to recommend the optimal mix of vegetable production for the coming year. He has given you the following data relating to the current year.

	Potatoes	Turnips	Parsnips	Carrots
Area occupied (acres)	25	20	30	25
Yield per acre (tonnes)	10	8	9	12
Selling price per tonne (£)	100	125	150	135
Variable cost per acre (£):				
Fertilizers	30	25	45	40
Seeds	15	20	30	25
Pesticides	25	15	20	25
Direct wages	400	450	500	570
Fixed overhead per annum £54 000				

The land that is being used for the production of carrots and parsnips can be used for either crop, but not for potatoes or turnips. The land being used for potatoes and turnips can be used for either crop, but not for carrots or parsnips. In order to provide an adequate market service, the gardener must produce each year at least 40 tonnes each of potatoes and turnips and 36 tonnes each of parsnips and carrots.

a You are required to present a statement to show:
   (i) the profit for the current year;
   (ii) the profit for the production mix that you would recommend.

b Assuming that the land could be cultivated in such a way that any of the above crops could be produced and there was no market commitment, you are required to:
   (i) advise the market gardener on which crop he should concentrate his production;
   (ii) calculate the profit if he were to do so;
   (iii) calculate in sterling the break-even point of sales.

(25 marks)
CIMA Cost Accounting 2

9.25 Advanced: Throughput accounting. Ride Ltd is engaged in the manufacturing and marketing of bicycles. Two bicycles are produced. These are the 'Roadster' which is designed for use on roads and the 'Everest' which is a bicycle designed for use in mountainous areas. The following information relates to the year ending 31 December 2005.

1   Unit selling price and cost data is as follows:

	Roadster £	Everest £
Selling price	200	280
Material cost	80	100
Variable production conversion costs	20	60

2   Fixed production overheads attributable to the manufacture of the bicycles will amount to £4 050 000.

3   Expected demand is as follows:

Roadster	150 000 units
Everest	70 000 units

4   Each bicycle is completed in the finishing department. The number of each type of bicycle that can be completed in one hour in the finishing department is as follows:

Roadster	6.25
Everest	5.00

There are a total of 30 000 hours available within the finishing department.

5   Ride Ltd operates a just in time (JIT) manufacturing system with regard to the manufacture of bicycles and aims to hold very little work-in-progress and no finished goods stocks whatsoever.

Required:

a   Using marginal costing principles, calculate the mix (units) of each type of bicycle which will maximise net profit and state the value of that profit.
(6 marks)

b   Calculate the throughput accounting ratio for each type of bicycle and briefly discuss when it is worth producing a product where throughput accounting principles are in operation. Your answer should assume that the variable overhead cost amounting to £4 800 000 incurred as a result of the chosen product mix in part (a) is fixed in the short-term.
(5 marks)

c   Using throughput accounting principles, advise management of the quantities of each type of bicycle that should be manufactured which will maximise net profit and prepare a projection of the net profit that would be earned by Ride Ltd in the year ending 31 December 2005.
(5 marks)

d   Explain two aspects in which the concept of 'contribution' in throughput accounting differs from its use in marginal costing.
(4 marks)

ACCA 3.3: Performance Management

IM9.1 Advanced. 'I remember being told about the useful decision-making technique of limiting factor analysis (also known as "contribution per unit of the key factor"). If an organisation is prepared to believe that, in the short run, all costs other than direct materials are fixed costs, is this not the same thing that throughput accounting is talking about? Why rename limiting factor analysis as throughput accounting?'

Requirements:

a   Explain what a limiting (or 'key') factor is and what sort of things can become limiting factors in a business situation. Which of the factors in the scenario could become a limiting factor?   (8 marks)

b   Explain the techniques that have been developed to assist in business decision-making when single or multiple limiting factors are encountered.
(7 marks)

c   Explain the management idea known as throughput accounting. State and justify your opinion on whether or not throughput accounting and limiting factor analysis are the same thing. Briefly comment on whether throughput accounting is likely to be of relevance to a company.
(10 marks)

CIMA Stage 3 Management Accounting Applications

IM9.2 Intermediate: Acceptance of a contract. JB Limited is a small specialist manufacturer of electronic components and much of its output is used by the makers of aircraft for both civil and military purposes. One of the few aircraft manufacturers has offered a contract to JB Limited for the supply, over the next twelve months, of 400 identical components.

The data relating to the production of each component is as follows:

(i)   Material requirements:
      3 kg material M1 – see note 1 below
      2 kg material P2 – see note 2 below
      1 Part No. 678 – see note 3 below

Note 1. Material M1 is in continuous use by the company. 1000 kg are currently held in stock at a book value of £4.70 per kg but it is known that future purchases will cost £5.50 per kg.

Note 2. 1200 kg of material P2 are held in stock. The original cost of this material was £4.30 per kg but as the material has not been required for the last two years it has been written down to £1.50 per kg scrap value. The only foreseeable alternative use is as a substitute for material P4 (in current use) but this would involve further processing costs of £1.60 per kg. The current cost of material P4 is £3.60 per kg.

Note 3. It is estimated that the Part No. 678 could be bought for £50 each.

(ii)   Labour requirements: Each component would require five hours of skilled labour and five hours of semi-skilled. An employee possessing the necessary skills is available and is currently paid £5 per hour. A replacement would, however, have to be obtained at a rate of £4 per hour for the work which would otherwise be done by the skilled employee. The current rate for semi-skilled work is £3 per hour and an additional employee could be appointed for this work.

(iii)   Overhead: JB Limited absorbs overhead by a machine hour rate, currently £20 per hour of which £7 is for variable overhead and £13 for fixed overhead. If this contract is undertaken it is estimated that fixed costs will increase for the duration of the contract by £3200. Spare machine capacity is available and each component would require four machine hours.

A price of £145 per component has been suggested by the large company which makes aircraft.

You are required to:

a   State whether or not the contract should be accepted and support your conclusion with appropriate figures for presentation to management;
(16 marks)

b   comment briefly on *three* factors which management ought to consider and which may influence their decision.
(9 marks)

CIMA Cost Accounting Stage 2

IM9.3 Intermediate: Preparation of a cost estimate involving the identification of relevant costs. You are the management accountant of a publishing and printing company which has been asked to quote for the production of a programme for the local village fair. The work would be carried out in addition to the normal work of the company. Because of existing commitments, some weekend working would be required to complete the printing of the programme. A trainee accountant has produced the following cost estimate based upon the resources as specified by the production manager:

	(£)
Direct materials:	
paper (book value)	5 000
inks (purchase price)	2 400
Direct labour:	
skilled 250 hours at £4.00	1 000
unskilled 100 hours at £3.50	350
Variable overhead 350 hours at £4.00	1400
Printing press depreciation 200 hours at £2.50	500
Fixed production costs 350 hours at £6.00	2 100
Estimating department costs	400
	13 150

You are aware that considerable publicity could be obtained for the company if you are able to win this order and the price quoted must be very competitive.

The following are relevant to the cost estimate above:

1.   The paper to be used is currently in stock at a value of £5000. It is of an unusual colour which has not been used for some time. The replacement price of the paper is £8000, while the scrap value of that in stock is £2500. The production manager does not foresee any alternative use for the paper if it is not used for the village fair programmes.

2.   The inks required are not held in stock. They would have to be purchased in bulk at a cost of £3000. 80 per cent of the ink purchased would be used in printing the programme. No other use is foreseen for the remainder.

3. Skilled direct labour is in short supply, and to accommodate the printing of the programmes, 50 per cent of the time required would be worked at weekends, for which a premium of 25 per cent above the normal hourly rate is paid. The normal hourly rate is £4.00 per hour.

4. Unskilled labour is presently under-utilized, and at present 200 hours per week are recorded as idle time. If the printing work is carried out at a weekend, 25 unskilled hours would have to occur at this time, but the employees concerned would be given two hours' time off (for which they would be paid) in lieu of each hour worked.

5. Variable overhead represents the cost of operating the printing press and binding machines.

6. When not being used by the company, the printing press is hired to outside companies for £6.00 per hour. This earns a contribution of £3.00 per hour. There is unlimited demand for this facility.

7. Fixed production costs are those incurred by and absorbed into production, using an hourly rate based on budgeted activity.

8. The cost of the estimating department represents time spent in discussion with the village fair committee concerning the printing of its programme.

Required:

a Prepare a revised cost estimate using the opportunity cost approach, showing clearly the minimum price that the company should accept for the order. Give reasons for each resource valuation in your cost estimate. *(16 marks)*

b Explain why contribution theory is used as a basis for providing information relevant to decision-making. *(4 marks)*

c Explain the relevance of opportunity costs in decision-making. *(5 marks)*

CIMA Stage 2 Operational Costs Accounting

IM9.4 Intermediate: Decision on whether to launch a new product. A company is currently manufacturing at only 60 per cent of full practical capacity, in each of its two production departments, due to a reduction in market share. The company is seeking to launch a new product which it is hoped will recover some lost sales.

The estimated direct costs of the new product, Product X, are to be established from the following information:

Direct materials:

Every 100 units of the product will require 30 kilos net of Material A. Losses of 10 per cent of materials input are to be expected. Material A costs £5.40 per kilo before discount. A quantity discount of 5 per cent is given on all purchases if the monthly purchase quantity exceeds 25 000 kilos. Other materials are expected to cost £1.34 per unit of Product X.

Direct labour (per hundred units):

Department 1: 40 hours at £4.00 per hour.
Department 2: 15 hours at £4.50 per hour.

Separate overhead absorption rates are established for each production department. Department 1 overheads are absorbed at 130 per cent of direct wages, which is based upon the expected overhead costs and usage of capacity if Product X is launched. The rate in Department 2 is to be established as a rate per direct labour hour also based on expected usage of capacity. The following annual figures for Department 2 are based on full practical capacity:

Overhead, £5 424 000:

Direct labour hours, 2 200 000.

Variable overheads in Department 1 are assessed at 40 per cent of direct wages and in Department 2 are £1 980 000 (at full practical capacity).

Non-production overheads are estimated as follows (per unit of Product X):

Variable, £0.70
Fixed, £1.95

The selling price for Product X is expected to be £9.95 per unit, with annual sales of 2 400 000 units.

Required:

a Determine the estimated cost per unit of Product X. *(13 marks)*

b Comment on the viability of Product X. *(7 marks)*

c Market research indicates that an alternative selling price for Product X could be £9.45 per unit, at which price annual sales would be expected to be 2 900 000 units. Determine, and comment briefly upon, the optimum selling price. *(5 marks)*

ACCA Cost and Management Accounting 1

IM9.5 Intermediate: Limiting key factors. PDR plc manufactures four products using the same machinery. The following details relate to its products:

	Product A £ per unit	Product B £ per unit	Product C £ per unit	Product D £ per unit
Selling price	28	30	45	42
Direct material	5	6	8	6
Direct labour	4	4	8	8
Variable overhead	3	3	6	6
Fixed overhead*	8	8	16	16
Profit	8	9	7	6
Labour hours	1	1	2	2
Machine hours	4	3	4	5
	Units	Units	Units	Units
Maximum demand per week	200	180	250	100

*Absorbed based on budgeted labour hours of 1000 per week.

There is a maximum of 2000 machine hours available per week.

Requirement:

a Determine the production plan which will maximise the weekly profit of PDR plc and prepare a profit statement showing the profit your plan will yield. *(10 marks)*

b The marketing director of PDR plc is concerned at the company's inability to meet the quantity demanded by its customers.

Two alternative strategies are being considered to overcome this:

(i) to increase the number of hours worked using the existing machinery by working overtime. Such overtime would be paid at a premium of 50 per cent above normal labour rates, and variable overhead costs would be expected to increase in proportion to labour costs.

(ii) to buy product B from an overseas supplier at a cost of £19 per unit including carriage. This would need to be repackaged at a cost of £1 per unit before it could be sold.

Requirement:

Evaluate each of the two alternative strategies and, as management accountant, prepare a report to the marketing director, stating your reasons (quantitative and qualitative) as to which, if either, should be adopted. *(15 marks)*

CIMA Stage 2 Operational Cost Accounting

IM9.6 Intermediate: Allocation of scarce capacity and make or buy decision where scarce capacity exists. PQR Limited is an engineering company engaged in the manufacture of components and finished products.

The company is highly mechanised and each of the components and finished products requires the use of one or more types of machine in its machining department. The following costs and revenues (where appropriate) relate to a single component or unit of the finished product:

	Components A £	B £	Finished products C £	D £
Selling price			127	161
Direct materials	8	29	33	38
Direct wages	10	30	20	25
Variable overhead:				
Drilling	6	3	9	12
Grinding	8	16	4	12
Fixed overhead:				
Drilling	12	6	18	24
Grinding	10	20	5	15
Total cost	54	104	89	126

Notes

1. The labour hour rate is £5 per hour.

2. Overhead absorption rates per machine hour are as follows:

	Variable £	Fixed £
Drilling (per hour)	3	6
Grinding (per hour)	4	5

3. Components A and B are NOT used in finished products C and D. They are used in the company's other products, none of which use the drilling or grinding machines. The company does not manufacture any other components.

4. The number of machine drilling hours available is limited to 1650 per week. There are 2500 machine grinding hours available per week. These numbers of hours have been used to calculate the absorption rates stated above.

5. The maximum demand in units per week for each of the finished products has been estimated by the marketing director as:

Product C   250 units
Product D   500 units

6. The internal demand for components A and B each week is as follows:

Component A   50 units
Component B   100 units

7. There is no external market for components A and B.

8. PQR Limited has a contract to supply 50 units of each of its finished products to a major customer each week. These quantities are included in the maximum units of demand given in note 5 above.

Requirement:

a Calculate the number of units of *each* finished product that PQR Limited should produce in order to maximise its profits, and the profit per week that this should yield. *(12 marks)*

b (i) The production director has now discovered that he can obtain unlimited quantities of components identical to A and B for £50 and £96 per unit respectively. State whether this information changes the production plan of the company if it wishes to continue to maximise its profits per week. If appropriate, state the revised production plan and the net benefit per week caused by the change to the production plan. *(7 marks)*

(ii) The solution of problems involving more than one limiting factor requires the use of linear programming.

Explain why this technique must be used in such circumstances, and the steps used to solve such a problem when using the graphical linear programming technique.

(6 marks)

CIMA Stage 2 Operational Cost Accounting

IM9.7 Intermediate: Limiting/key factors and a decision whether it is profitable to expand output by overtime. B Ltd manufactures a range of products which are sold to a limited number of wholesale outlets. Four of these products are manufactured in a particular department on common equipment. No other facilities are available for the manufacture of these products.

Owing to greater than expected increases in demand, normal single shift working is rapidly becoming insufficient to meet sales requirements. Overtime and, in the longer term, expansion of facilities are being considered.

Selling prices and product costs, based on single shift working utilizing practical capacity to the full, are as follows:

	Product (£/unit)			
	W	X	Y	Z
Selling price	3.650	3.900	2.250	2.950
Product costs:				
Direct materials	0.805	0.996	0.450	0.647
Direct labour	0.604	0.651	0.405	0.509
Variable manufacturing overhead	0.240	0.247	0.201	0.217
Fixed manufacturing overhead	0.855	0.950	0.475	0.760
Variable selling and admin overhead	0.216	0.216	0.216	0.216
Fixed selling and admin overhead	0.365	0.390	0.225	0.295

Fixed manufacturing overheads are absorbed on the basis of machine hours which, at practical capacity, are 2250 per period. Total fixed manufacturing overhead per period is £427 500. Fixed selling and administration overhead, which totals £190 000 per period, is shared amongst products at a rate of 10 per cent of sales.

The sales forecast for the following period (in thousands of units) is:

Product W   190
Product X   125
Product Y   144
Product Z   142

Overtime could be worked to make up any production shortfall in normal time. Direct labour would be paid at a premium of 50 per cent above basic rate. Other variable costs would be expected to remain unchanged per unit of output. Fixed costs would increase by £24 570 per period.

Required:

a If overtime is not worked in the following period, recommend the quantity of each product that should be manufactured in order to maximize profit. *(12 marks)*

b Calculate the expected profit in the following period if overtime is worked as necessary to meet sales requirements. *(7 marks)*

c Consider the factors which should influence the decision whether or not to work overtime in such a situation. *(6 marks)*

ACCA Cost and Management Accounting 1

IM9.8 Advanced: Allocation of land to four different types of vegetables based on key factor principles. A South American farms 960 hectares of land on which he grows squash, kale, lettuce and beans. Of the total, 680 hectares are suitable for all four vegetables, but the remaining 280 hectares are suitable only for kale and lettuce. Labour for all kinds of farm work is plentiful.

The market requires that all four types of vegetable must be produced with a minimum of 10 000 boxes of any one line. The farmer has decided that the area devoted to any crop should be in terms of complete hectares and not in fractions of a hectare. The only other limitation is that not more than 227 500 boxes of any one crop should be produced.

Data concerning production, market prices and costs are as follows:

	Squash	Kale	Lettuce	Beans
Annual yield				
(boxes per hectare)	350	100	70	180
	(Pesos)	(Pesos)	(Pesos)	(Pesos)
Costs				
Direct:				
Materials per hectare	476	216	192	312
Labour:				
Growing, per hectare	896	608	372	528
Harvesting and packing,				
per box	3.60	3.28	4.40	5.20
Transport, per box	5.20	5.20	4.00	9.60
Market price, per box	15.38	15.87	18.38	22.27

Fixed overhead per annum:

	(Pesos)
Growing	122 000
Harvesting	74 000
Transport	74 000
General administration	100 000
Notional rent	74 000

It is possible to make the entire farm viable for all four vegetables if certain drainage work is undertaken. This would involve capital investment and it would have the following effects on direct harvesting costs of some of the vegetables:

| | Capital cost | Change from normal harvesting costs | |
| | | Squash | Beans |
	(Pesos)	(Pesos per box)	
First lot of 10 hectares	19 000 total	+1.2	−1.2
Next lot of 10 hectares	17 500 total	+1.3	−1.3
Next lot of 10 hectares	15 000 total	+1.4	−1.4
Remaining land (per hectare)	1850	+1.5	−1.5

The farmer is willing to undertake such investment only if he can obtain a return of 15 per cent DCF for a four-year period.

You are required to

a advise the farmer, within the given constraints,
(i) the area to be cultivated with each crop if he is to achieve the largest total profit, *(13 marks)*
(ii) the amount of this total profit, *(3 marks)*
(iii) the number of hectares it is worth draining and the use to which they would be put; *(10 marks)*

b comment briefly on four of the financial dangers of going ahead with the drainage work. *(4 marks)*

Notes: Show all relevant calculations in arriving at your answer. Ignore tax and inflation.

CIMA Stage 4 Management Accounting – Decision Making

IM9.9 Advanced: Relevant costs for a pricing decision. Johnson trades as a chandler at the Savoy Marina. His profit in this business during the year to 30 June was £12 000. Johnson also undertakes occasional contracts to build pleasure cruisers, and is considering the price at which to bid for the contract to build the *Blue Blood* for Mr B.W. Dunn, delivery to be in one year's time. He has no other contract in hand, or under consideration, for at least the next few months.

Johnson expects that if he undertakes the contract he would devote one-quarter of his time to it. To facilitate this he would employ G. Harrison, an unqualified practitioner, to undertake his book-keeping and other paperwork, at a cost of £2000.

He would also have to employ on the contract one supervisor at a cost of £11 000 and two craftsmen at a cost of £8800 each; these costs include Johnson's normal apportionment of the fixed overheads of his business at the rate of 10 per cent of labour cost.

During spells of bad weather one of the craftsmen could be employed for the equivalent of up to three months full-time during the winter in maintenance and painting work in the chandler's business. He would use materials costing £1000. Johnson already has two inclusive quotations from jobbing builders for this maintenance and painting work, one for £2500 and the other for £3500, the work to start immediately.

The equipment which would be used on the *Blue Blood* contract was bought nine years ago for £21 000. Depreciation has been written off on a straight-line basis, assuming a ten-year life and a scrap value of £1000. The current replacement cost of similar new equipment is £60 000, and is expected to be £66 000 in one year's time. Johnson has recently been offered £6000 for the equipment, and considers that in a year's time he would have little difficulty in obtaining £3000 for it. The plant is useful to Johnson only for contract work.

In order to build the *Blue Blood* Johnson will need six types of material, as follows:

Material code	In stock	Needed for contract	Purchase price of stock items	Current purchase price	Current resale price
A	100	1000	1.10	3.00	2.00
B	1 100	1000	2.00	0.90	1.00
C	—	100	—	6.00	—
D	100	200	4.00	3.00	2.00
E	50 000	5000	0.18	0.20	0.25
F	1 000	3000	0.90	2.00	1.00

No. of units — *Price per unit (£)*

Materials B and E are sold regularly in the chandler's business. Material A could be sold to a local sculptor, if not used for the contract. Materials A and E can be used for other purposes, such as property maintenance. Johnson has no other use for materials D and F, the stocks of which are obsolete.

The *Blue Blood* would be built in a yard held on a lease with four years remaining at a fixed annual rental of £5000. It would occupy half of this yard, which is useful to Johnson only for contract work.

Johnson anticipates that the direct expenses of the contract, other than those noted above, would be £6500.

Johnson has recently been offered a one-year appointment at a fee of £15 000 to manage a boat-building firm on the Isle of Wight. If he accepted the offer he would be unable to take on the contract to build *Blue Blood*, or any other contract. He would have to employ a manager to run the chandler's business at an annual cost (including fidelity insurance) of £10 000, and would incur additional personal living costs of £2000.

You are required:

a to calculate the price at which Johnson should be willing to take on the contract in order to break even, based exclusively on the information given above;   *(15 marks)*

b to set out any further considerations which you think that Johnson should take into account in setting the price at which he would tender for the contract.   *(10 marks)*

Ignore taxation.

ICAEW Management Accounting

IM9.10 Advanced: Decision on whether a department should be closed. Shortflower Ltd currently publish, print and distribute a range of catalogues and instruction manuals. The management have now decided to discontinue printing and distribution and concentrate solely on publishing. Longplant Ltd will print and distribute the range of catalogues and instruction manuals on behalf of Shortflower Ltd commencing either at 30 June or 30 November. Longplant Ltd will receive £65 000 per month for a contract which will commence either at 30 June or 30 November.

The results of Shortflower Ltd for a typical month are as follows:

	Publishing (£000)	Printing (£000)	Distribution (£000)
Salaries and wages	28	18	4
Materials and supplies	5.5	31	1.1
Occupancy costs	7	8.5	1.2
Depreciation	0.8	4.2	0.7

Other information has been gathered relating to the possible closure proposals:

(i) Two specialist staff from printing will be retained at their present salary of £1500 each per month in order to fulfil a link function with Longplant Ltd. One further staff member will be transferred to publishing to fill a staff vacancy through staff turnover, anticipated in July. This staff member will be paid at his present salary of £1400 per month which is £100 more than that of the staff member who is expected to leave. On closure all other printing and distribution staff will be made redundant and paid an average of two months redundancy pay.

(ii) The printing department has a supply of materials (already paid for) which cost £18 000 and which will be sold to Longplant Ltd for £10 000 if closure takes place on 30 June. Otherwise the material will be used as part of the July printing requirements. The distribution department has a contract to purchase pallets at a cost of £500 per month for July and August. A cancellation clause allows for non-delivery of the pallets for July and August for a one-off payment of £300. Non-delivery for August only will require a payment of £100. If the pallets are taken from the supplier Longplant Ltd has agreed to purchase them at a price of £380 for each month's supply which is available. Pallet costs are included in the distribution material and supplies cost stated for a typical month.

(iii) Company expenditure on apportioned occupancy costs to printing and distribution will be reduced by 15 per cent per month if printing and distribution departments are closed. At present, 30 per cent of printing and 25 per cent of distribution occupancy costs are directly attributable costs which are avoidable on closure, whilst the remainder are apportioned costs.

(iv) Closure of the printing and distribution departments will make it possible to sub-let part of the building for a monthly fee of £2500 when space is available.

(v) Printing plant and machinery has an estimated net book value of £48 000 at 30 June. It is anticipated that it will be sold at a loss of £21 000 on 30 June. If sold on 30 November the prospective buyer will pay £25 000.

(vi) The net book value of distribution vehicles at 30 June is estimated as £80 000. They could be sold to the original supplier at £48 000 on 30 June. The original supplier would purchase the vehicles on 30 November for a price of £44 000.

Required:
Using the above information, prepare a summary to show whether Shortflower Ltd should close the printing and distribution departments on financial grounds on 30 June or on 30 November. Explanatory notes and calculations should be shown. Ignore taxation.

(22 marks)
ACCA Level 2 Cost and Management Accounting II

Activity-based costing

10

The aim of the previous chapter was to provide you with an understanding of the principles that should be used to identify relevant costs and revenues for various types of decisions. It was assumed that relevant costs could easily be measured but, in reality, it was pointed out that indirect relevant costs can be difficult to identify and measure. The measurement of indirect relevant costs for decision-making using activity-based costing (ABC) techniques will be examined in this chapter. The aim of this chapter is to provide you with a conceptual under-standing of ABC. Some of the issues explored are complex and therefore much of the content of this chapter is appropriate for a second year management accounting course. If you are pursuing a first year course the content relating to ABC that was presented in Chapter 3 should meet your requirements. In addition, you may wish to read this chapter and omit those sections that are labelled advanced reading. Because this chapter extends the material covered in Chapter 3 you are recommended to refresh your memory by reading pages 59–62 prior to reading this chapter.

LEARNING OBJECTIVES

After studying this chapter you should be able to:

- explain why a cost accumulation system is required for generating relevant cost information for decision-making;

- describe the differences between activity-based and traditional costing systems;

- explain why traditional costing systems can provide misleading information for decision-making;

- identify and explain each of the four stages involved in designing ABC systems;

- describe the ABC cost hierarchy;

- describe the ABC profitability analysis hierarchy;

- describe the ABC resource consumption model.

Our focus will be on an organization's *existing* products or services. There is also a need to manage *future* activities to ensure that only profitable products and services are launched. Here the emphasis is on providing cost information using techniques such as target costing, life cycle costing and value engineering. These issues will be explored in Chapter 21 and the mechanisms for appraising investments in new products, services or locations will be described in Chapters 13 and 14. We shall also defer our discussion of the relevant cost information that is required for pricing decisions until the next chapter.

Unless otherwise stated we shall assume that products are the cost objects but the techniques used, and the principles established, can also be applied to other cost objects such as customers, services and locations. We begin with an examination of the role that a cost accumulation system plays in generating relevant cost information for decision-making.

The need for a cost accumulation system in generating relevant cost information for decision-making

There are three main reasons why a cost accumulation system is required to generate relevant cost information for decision-making. They are:

1 many indirect costs are relevant for decision-making;

2 an attention-directing information system is required that periodically identifies those potentially unprofitable products that require more detailed special studies;

3 product decisions are not independent.

There is a danger that only those incremental costs that are uniquely attributable to individual products will be classified as relevant and indirect costs will be classified as irrelevant for decision-making. Direct costs are transparent and how they will be affected by decisions is clearly observable. In contrast, how indirect costs will be affected by decisions is not clearly observable.

The costs of many joint resources are indirect but fluctuate in the long term according to the demand for them. The cost of support functions fall within this category. They include activities such as materials procurement, materials handling, production scheduling, warehousing, expediting and customer order processing. Product introduction, discontinuation, redesign and mix decisions determine the demand for support function resources. For example, if a decision results in a 10 per cent reduction in the demand for the resources of a support activity then we would expect, in the long term, for some of the costs of that support activity to decline by 10 per cent. Therefore, to estimate the impact that decisions will have on the support activities (and their future costs) a cost accumulation system is required that assigns those indirect costs, using cause-and-effect allocations, to products.

The second reason relates to the need for a periodic attention-directing reporting system. Periodic product profitability analysis meets this requirement. A cost accumulation system is therefore required to assign costs to products for periodic profitability analysis to identify those potentially unprofitable products/services that require more detailed special studies to ascertain if they are likely to be profitable in the future.

The third reason for using a cost accumulation system is that many product related decisions are not independent. Consider again those joint resources shared by most products and that fluctuate in the longer term according to the demand for them. If we focus only on individual products and assume that they are independent, decisions will be taken in isolation of decisions made on other products. For joint resources the incremental/avoidable costs relating to a decision to add or drop a *single* product may be zero. Assuming that 20 products are viewed in this manner then the sum of the incremental costs will be zero. However, if the 20 products are viewed as a *whole* there may be a significant change in resource usage and incremental costs for those joint resources that fluctuate according to the demand for them.

Cooper (1990b) also argues that decisions should not be viewed independently. He states:

The decision to drop one product will typically not change 'fixed' overhead spending. In contrast, dropping 50 products might allow considerable changes to be made. Stated somewhat tritely, the sum of the parts (the decision to drop individual products) is not equal to the sum of the whole (the realisable savings from having dropped 50 products). To help them make effective decisions, managers require cost systems that provide insights into the whole, not just isolated individual parts (p. 58).

Types of cost systems

Costing systems can vary in terms of which costs are assigned to cost objects and their level of sophistication. Typically cost systems are classified as follows:

1 direct costing systems;
2 traditional absorption costing systems;
3 activity-based costing systems.

Direct costing systems only assign direct costs to cost objects. Because they do not assign indirect costs to cost objects they report contributions to indirect costs. Periodic profitability analysis would thus be used to highlight negative or low contribution products. An estimate of those indirect costs that are relevant to the decision should be incorporated within the analysis at the special study stage. The disadvantage of direct costing systems is that systems are not in place to measure and assign indirect costs to cost objects. Direct costing systems can only be recommended where indirect costs are a low proportion of an organization's total costs.

Both traditional and ABC systems assign indirect costs to cost objects. The major features of these systems were described in Chapter 3 and the assignment of costs to products was illustrated for both systems. In the next section the major features that were described in Chapter 3 are briefly summarized but the assignment of costs to products will not be repeated. If you wish to renew your understanding of the detailed cost assignment process you should refer back to Chapter 3 for an illustration of the application of the two-stage allocation process for both traditional and ABC systems.

A comparison of traditional and ABC systems

Figure 3.3 was used in Chapter 3 to illustrate the major differences between traditional costing and ABC systems. This diagram is repeated in the form of Figure 10.1 to provide you with an overview of both systems. Both use a two-stage allocation process. In the first stage a traditional system allocates overheads to production and service departments and then reallocates service department costs to the production departments. An ABC system assigns overheads to each major activity (rather than departments). With ABC systems, many activity-based cost centres (alternatively known as activity cost pools) are established, whereas with traditional systems overheads tend to be pooled by departments, although they are normally described as cost centres.

Activities consist of the aggregation of many different tasks and are described by verbs associated with objects. Typical support activities include: schedule production, set-up machines, move materials, purchase materials, inspect items, process supplier records, expedite and process customer orders. Production process activities include machine products and assemble products. Within the production process, activity cost centres are often identical to the cost centres used by traditional cost systems. Support activities are also sometimes identical to cost centres used by traditional systems, such as when the purchasing department and activity are both treated as cost centres. Overall, however, ABC systems will normally have a greater number of cost centres.

The second stage of the two-stage allocation process allocates costs from cost centres (pools) to products or other chosen cost objects. Traditional costing systems trace overheads to products using a small number of second stage allocation bases (normally described as overhead allocation rates), which vary directly with the volume produced. Instead of using the terms 'allocation bases' or 'overhead allocation rates' the term 'cost driver' is used by ABC systems. Direct labour and machine hours are the allocation bases that are normally used by traditional costing systems. In contrast, ABC systems use many different types of second-stage cost drivers, including non-volume-based drivers, such as the number of production runs for production scheduling and the number of purchase orders for the purchasing activity.

Therefore the major distinguishing features of ABC systems are that within the two-stage allocation process they rely on:

1 a greater number of cost centres;

2 a greater number and variety of second stage cost drivers.

By using a greater number of cost centres and different types of cost drivers that cause activity resource consumption, and assigning activity costs to cost objects on the basis of cost driver usage, ABC systems can more accurately measure the resources consumed by cost objects.

(a) Traditional costing systems

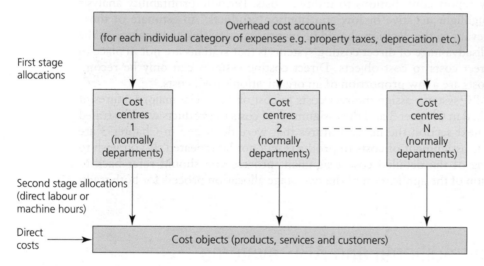

(b) Activity-based costing systems

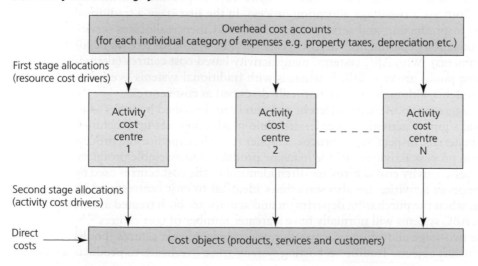

FIGURE 10.1

An illustration of the two-stage allocation process for traditional and activity-based costing systems

Traditional cost systems tend to report less accurate costs because they use cost drivers where no cause-and-effect relationships exist to assign support costs to cost objects.

The emergence of ABC systems

During the 1980s the limitations of traditional product costing systems began to be widely publicized. These systems were designed decades ago when most companies manufactured a narrow range of products, and direct labour and materials were the dominant factory costs. Overhead costs were relatively small, and the distortions arising from inappropriate overhead allocations were not significant. Information processing costs were high, and it was therefore difficult to justify more sophisticated overhead allocation methods.

Today companies produce a wide range of products; direct labour represents only a small fraction of total costs, and overhead costs are of considerable importance. Simplistic overhead allocations using a declining direct labour base cannot be justified, particularly when information processing costs are no longer a barrier to introducing more sophisticated cost systems. Furthermore, the intense global competition of the 1980s has made decision errors due to poor cost information more probable and more costly.

During the 1980s a few firms in the USA and Europe implemented ABC type systems. In a series of articles based on observations of innovative ABC type systems Cooper and Kaplan conceptualized the ideas underpinning these systems and coined the term ABC. These articles were first published in 1988. They generated a considerable amount of publicity and consultants began to market and implement ABC systems before the end of the decade. In a survey of UK companies Innes and Mitchell (1991) reported that approximately 10 per cent of the surveyed companies had implemented, or were in the process of implementing ABC. Based on their experience of working with early US adopters, Cooper and Kaplan articulated their ideas and reported further theoretical advances in articles published between 1990 and 1992. These ideas and the theoretical advances are described in the remainder of this chapter. ABC ideas have now become firmly embedded in the management accounting literature and educational courses.

Volume-based and non-volume-based cost drivers

Our comparison of ABC systems with traditional costing systems indicated that ABC systems rely on a greater number and variety of second stage cost drivers. The term 'variety of cost drivers' refers to the fact that ABC systems use both volume-based and non-volume-based cost drivers. In contrast, traditional systems use only volume-based cost drivers. Volume-based cost drivers assume that a product's consumption of overhead resources is directly related to units produced. In other words, they assume that the overhead consumed by products is highly correlated with the number of units produced. Typical volume-based cost drivers used by traditional systems are units of output, direct labour hours and machine hours. These cost drivers are appropriate for measuring the consumption of expenses such as machine energy costs, depreciation related to machine usage, indirect labour employed in production centres and inspection costs where each item produced is subject to final inspection. For example, machine hours are an appropriate cost driver for energy costs since if volume is increased by 10 per cent, machine hours are likely to increase by 10 per cent, thus causing 10 per cent more energy costs to be consumed. Similarly, an increase in volume of 10 per cent is likely to increase the consumption of direct labour hours by 10 per cent and, assuming that indirect labour hours are correlated with direct labour hours, 10 per cent more indirect labour costs will be consumed.

Volume-based drivers are appropriate in the above circumstances because activities are performed each time a unit of the product or service is produced. In contrast, non-volume related activities are not performed each time a unit of the product or service is produced. Consider, for example, two activities – setting up a machine and re-engineering products. Set-up resources are consumed each time a machine is changed from one product to another. It costs the same to set-up a machine for 10 or 5000 items. As more set-ups are done more set-up resources are consumed. The number of set-ups, rather than the number of units produced, is a more appropriate measure of the consumption of the set-up activity. Similarly, product re-engineering costs may depend upon the number of different engineering works orders and not the number of units produced. For both of these activities, non-volume-based cost drivers such as number of set-ups and engineering orders are needed for the accurate assignment of the costs of these activities.

Using only volume-based cost drivers to assign non-volume related overhead costs can result in the reporting of distorted product costs. The extent of distortion depends on what proportion of total overhead costs the non-volume based overheads represent and the level of product diversity. If a large proportion of an organization's costs are unrelated to volume there is danger that inaccurate product costs will be reported. Conversely, if non-volume related overhead costs are only a small proportion of total overhead costs, the distortion of product costs will not be significant. In these circumstances traditional product costing systems are likely to be acceptable.

Product diversity applies when products consume different overhead activities in dissimilar proportions. Differences in product size, product complexity, sizes of batches and set-up times cause product diversity. If all products consume overhead resources in similar proportions product diversity will be low and products will consume non-volume related activities in the same proportion as volume-related activities. Hence, product cost distortion will not occur with traditional product costing systems. Two conditions are therefore necessary for product cost distortion – non-volume-related overhead costs are a large proportion of total overhead costs and product diversity applies. Where these two conditions exist traditional product costing systems can result in the overcosting of high volume products and undercosting of low volume products. Consider the information presented in Example 10.1.

The reported product costs and profits for the two products are as follows:

	Traditional system		ABC system	
	Product HV (£)	Product LV (£)	Product HV (£)	Product LV (£)
Direct costs	310 000	40 000	310 000	40 000
Overheads allocated[a]	300 000 (30%)	50 000 (5%)	150 000 (15%)	150 000 (15%)
Reported profits/(losses)	(10 000)	60 000	140 000	(40 000)
Sales revenues	600 000	150 000	600 000	150 000

Note
[a]Allocation of £1 million overheads using direct labour hours as the allocation base for the traditional system and number of batches processed as the cost driver for the ABC system.

Because product HV is a high volume product that consumes 30 per cent of the direct labour hours whereas product LV, the low volume product consumes only 5 per cent, the traditional system that uses direct labour hours as the allocation base allocates six times more overheads to product HV. However, ABC systems recognize that overheads are caused by other factors, besides volume. In our example, all of the overheads are assumed to be volume unrelated. They are caused by the number of batches processed and the ABC system establishes a cause-and-effect allocation relationship by using the number of batches processed as the cost driver. Both products require 15 per cent of the total number of batches so they are allocated with an equal amount of overheads.

It is apparent from the consumption ratios of the two products that the traditional system based on direct labour hours will overcost high volume products and undercost low volume products. Consumption ratios represent the proportion of each activity consumed by a product. The consumption ratios if direct labour hours are used as the cost driver are 0.30 for product HV and 0.05 for product LV so that six times more overheads will be assigned to product HV. When the number of batches processed are used as the cost driver the consumption ratios are 0.15 for each product and an equal amount of overhead will be assigned to each product. Distorted product costs are reported with the traditional costing system that uses the volume-based cost driver because the two conditions specified above apply. First, non-volume related overheads are a large proportion of total overheads, being 100 per cent in our example. Second, product diversity exists because the product consumption ratios for the two identified cost drivers are significantly different. Our illustration shows that if the consumption ratios for batches processed had been the same as the ratios for direct labour the traditional and ABC systems would report identical product costs.

With the traditional costing system misleading information is reported. A small loss is reported for product HV and if it were discontinued the costing system mistakenly gives the impression that overheads will decline in the longer term by £300 000. Furthermore, the message from the costing system is to concentrate on the more profitable speciality products like product LV. In reality this strategy would be disastrous because low volume products like product LV are made in small batches and require more people for scheduling production, performing set-ups, inspection of the batches and handling a large number of customer requests for small orders. The long-term effect would be escalating overhead costs.

In contrast, the ABC system allocates overheads on a cause-and-effect basis and more accurately measures the relatively high level of overhead resources consumed by product LV. The message from the profitability analysis is the opposite from the traditional system; that is, product HV is profitable and product LV is unprofitable. If product LV is discontinued, and assuming that the cost driver is the cause of all the overheads then a decision to discontinue product LV should result in the reduction in resource spending on overheads by £150 000.

Example 10.1 is very simplistic. It is assumed that the organization has established only a single cost centre or cost pool, when in reality many will be established with a traditional system, and even more with an ABC system. Furthermore, the data have been deliberately biased to show the superiority of ABC. The aim of the illustration has been to highlight the potential cost of errors that can occur when information extracted from simplistic and inaccurate cost systems is used for decision-making.

EXAMPLE 10.1

Assume that the Balearic company has only one overhead cost centre or cost pool. It currently operates a traditional costing system using direct labour hours to allocate overheads to products. The company produces several products, two of which are products HV and LV. Product HV is made in high volumes whereas product LV is made in low volumes. Product HV consumes 30 per cent of the direct labour hours and product LV consumes only 5 per cent. Because of the high volume production product HV can be made in large production batches but the irregular and low level of demand for product LV requires it to be made in small batches. A detailed investigation indicates that the number of batches processed causes the demand for overhead resources. The traditional system is therefore replaced with an ABC system using the number of batches processed as the cost driver. You ascertain that each product accounts for 15 per cent of the batches processed during the period and the overheads assigned to the cost centre that fluctuate in the long term according to the demand for them amount to £1 million. The direct costs and sales revenues assigned to the products are as follows:

	Product HV (£)	Product LV (£)
Direct costs	310 000	40 000
Sales revenues	600 000	150 000

Show the product profitability analysis for products HV and LV using the traditional and ABC systems.

Designing ABC systems

The discussion so far has provided a broad overview of ABC. We shall now examine ABC in more detail by looking at the design of ABC systems. Four steps are involved. They are:

1 identifying the major activities that take place in an organization;

2 assigning costs to cost pools/cost centres for each activity;

3 determining the cost driver for each major activity;

4 assigning the cost of activities to products according to the product's demand for activities.

The first two steps relate to the first stage, and the final two steps to the second stage, of the two-stage allocation process shown in Figure 10.1. Let us now consider each of these stages in more detail.

Step 1: Identifying activities

Activities are composed of the aggregation of units of work or tasks and are described by verbs associated with tasks. For example, purchasing of materials might be identified as a separate activity. This activity consists of the aggregation of many different tasks, such as receiving a purchase request, identifying suppliers, preparing purchase orders, mailing purchase orders and performing follow-ups.

REAL WORLD VIEWS 10.1

The shift in the assignment of overhead costs at Hewlett-Packard

A division of Hewlett-Packard that manufactures electronic circuit boards faced an environment that conformed closely to the conditions for which ABC is recommended:

● diverse products;

● relatively high overhead costs and for some products, higher than the direct costs;

● production volumes that vary significantly among products;

● the belief by the operating managers that the old traditional system did not give meaningful product costs.

An ABC system was introduced consisting of ten different cost pools and drivers. The composition of the cost pools and selection of the most appropriate drivers resulted from an intense analysis of the production process and cost behaviour patterns. When the company implemented ABC the costs of the old and new system were compared. One circuit board that would have been assigned with overheads of $5 with the old system had a reported total cost of $25 with ABC – an increase of 400 per cent. Another circuit board that would have been assigned an overhead of $123 with the old system was assigned $45 with ABC.

During a six-month forecast and budget cycle, the ABC system resulted in shifting millions of dollars of costs between customers and products and thus had a dramatic impact on product design and pricing decisions.

Discussion points

1 Why do you think the cost of the circuit boards differed between the old and the new costing system?

2 What benefits are likely to be obtained from introducing the ABC system?

© VISIONS OF AMERICA, LLC/ALAMY

SOURCE: MERZ, M. AND HARDY, A. (1993), ABC PUTS ACCOUNTANTS ON THE DESIGN TEAM AT HP, MANAGEMENT ACCOUNTING (USA), SEPTEMBER, PP. 24–6.

Activities are identified by carrying out an activity analysis. Innes and Mitchell (1995b) suggest that a useful starting point is to examine a physical plan of the workplace (to identify how all work space is being used) and the payroll listings (to ensure all relevant personnel have been taken into account). This examination normally has to be supplemented by a series of interviews with the staff involved, or having staff complete a time sheet for a specific time period explaining how their time is spent. Interviewers will ask managers and employees questions such as what staff work at the location and what tasks are performed by the persons employed at the location.

Many detailed tasks are likely to be identified in the first instance, but after further interviews, the main activities will emerge. The activities chosen should be at a reasonable level of aggregation based on costs versus benefits criteria. For example, rather than classifying purchasing of materials as an activity, each of its constituent tasks could be classified as separate activities. However, this level of decomposition would involve the collection of a vast amount of data and is likely to be too costly for product costing purposes. Alternatively, the purchasing activity might be merged with the materials receiving, storage and issuing activities to form a single materials procurement and handling activity. This is likely to represent too high a level of aggregation because a single cost driver is unlikely to provide a satisfactory determinant of the cost of the activity. For example, selecting the number of purchase orders as a cost driver may provide a good explanation of purchasing costs but may be entirely inappropriate for explaining costs relating to receiving and issuing. Therefore, instead of establishing materials procurement and handling as a single activity it may be preferable to decompose it into three separate activities; namely purchasing, receiving and issuing activities, and establish separate cost drivers for each activity.

Recent studies suggest that between twenty and thirty activity centres tend to be the norm. The final choice of activities must be a matter of judgement but it is likely to be influenced by factors such as the total cost of the activity centre (it must be of significance to justify separate treatment) and the ability of a single driver to provide a satisfactory determinant of the cost of the activity. Where the latter is not possible further decomposition of the activity will be necessary. Activities with the same product consumption ratios can use the same cost driver to assign costs to products. Thus, all activities that have the same cost driver can be merged to form a single activity cost centre.

Step 2: Assigning costs to activity cost centres

After the activities have been identified the cost of resources consumed over a specified period must be assigned to each activity. The aim is to determine how much the organization is spending on each of its activities. Many of the resources will be directly attributable to specific activity centres but others (such as labour and lighting and heating costs) may be indirect and jointly shared by several activities. These costs should be assigned to activities on the basis of cause-and-effect cost drivers, or interviews with staff who can provide reasonable estimates of the resources consumed by different activities. Arbitrary allocations should not be used. The greater the amount of costs traced to activity centres by cost apportionments at this stage the more arbitrary and less reliable will be the product cost information generated by ABC systems. Cause-and-effect cost drivers used at this stage to allocate shared resources to individual activities are called resource cost drivers.

Step 3: Selecting appropriate cost drivers for assigning the cost of activities to cost objects

In order to assign the costs attached to each activity cost centre to products a cost driver must be selected for each activity centre. Cost drivers used at this stage are called activity cost drivers. Several factors must be borne in mind when selecting a suitable cost driver. First, it should provide a good explanation of costs in each activity cost pool. Second, a cost driver should be easily measurable, the data should be relatively easy to obtain and be identifiable with products. The costs of measurement should therefore be taken into account.

Activity cost drivers consist of transaction and duration drivers. Transaction drivers, such as the number of purchase orders processed, number of customer orders processed, number of inspections performed and the number of set-ups undertaken, all count the number of times an activity is performed. Transaction drivers are the least expensive type of cost driver but they are also likely to be the least accurate because they assume that the same quantity of resources is required every time an activity is performed. However, if the variation in the amount of resources required by individual cost objects is not great transaction drivers will provide a reasonably accurate measurement of activity resources consumed. If this condition does not apply then duration cost drivers should be used.

Duration drivers represent the amount of time required to perform an activity. Examples of duration drivers include set-up hours and inspection hours. For example, if one product requires a short set-up time and another requires a long time then using set-up hours as the cost driver will more accurately measure activity resource consumption than the transaction driver (number of set-ups) which assumes that an equal amount of activity resources are consumed by both products. Using the number of set-ups will result in the product that requires a long set-up time being undercosted whereas the product that requires a short set-up will be overcosted. This problem can be overcome by using set-up hours as the cost driver, but this will increase the measurement costs.

In most situations data will not initially be available relating to the past costs of activities or potential cost driver volumes. To ascertain potential cost drivers interviews will be required with the personnel involved with the specific activities. The interviews will seek to ascertain what causes the particular activity to consume resources and incur costs. The final choice of a cost driver is likely to be based on managerial judgement after taking into account the factors outlined above.

Step 4: Assigning the cost of the activities to products

The final stage involves applying the cost driver rates to products. Therefore the cost driver must be measurable in a way that enables it to be identified with individual products. Thus, if set-up hours are selected as a cost driver, there must be a mechanism for measuring the set-up hours consumed by each product. Alternatively, if the number of set-ups is selected as the cost driver measurements by products are not required since all products that require a set-up are charged with a constant set-up cost. The ease and cost of obtaining data on cost driver consumption by products is therefore a factor that must be considered during the third stage when an appropriate cost driver is being selected.

Activity hierarchies

Manufacturing activities can be classified along a cost hierarchy dimension consisting of:

1 unit-level activities;
2 batch-level activities;
3 product-sustaining activities;
4 facility-sustaining activities.

Unit-level activities (also known as volume-related activities) are performed each time a unit of the product or service is produced. Expenses in this category include direct labour, direct materials, energy costs and expenses that are consumed in proportion to machine processing time (such as maintenance). Unit-level activities consume resources in proportion to the number of units of production and sales volume. For example, if a firm produces 10 per cent more units it will consume 10 per cent more labour cost, 10 per cent more machine hours and 10 per cent more energy costs. Typical cost drivers for unit level activities include labour hours, machine hours and the quantity of materials processed. These cost drivers are also used by traditional costing systems. Traditional systems are therefore also appropriate for assigning the costs of unit-level activities to cost objects.

Batch-related activities, such as setting up a machine or processing a purchase order, are performed each time a batch of goods is produced. The cost of batch-related activities varies with the number of batches made, but is common (or fixed) for all units within the batch. For example, set-up resources are consumed when a machine is changed from one product to another. As more batches are produced, more set-up resources are consumed. It costs the same to set-up a machine for 10 or 5000 items. Thus the demands for the set-up resources are independent of the number of units produced after completing the set-up. Similarly, purchasing resources are consumed each time a purchasing order is processed, but the resources consumed are independent of the number of units included in the purchase order. Other examples of batch-related costs include resources devoted to production scheduling, first-item inspection and materials movement. Traditional costing systems treat batch-related expenses as fixed costs, whereas ABC systems assume that batch-related expenses vary with the number of batches processed.

Product-sustaining activities or service-sustaining activities are performed to enable the production and sale of individual products (or services). Examples of product-sustaining activities provided by Kaplan and Cooper (1998) include maintaining and updating product specifications and the technical support provided for individual products and services. Other examples are the resources to prepare and implement engineering change notices (ECNs), to design processes and test routines for individual products, and to perform product enhancements. The costs of product-sustaining activities are incurred irrespective of the number of units of output or the number of batches processed and their expenses will tend to increase as the number of products manufactured is increased. ABC uses product-level bases such as number of active part numbers and number of ECNs to assign these costs to products. Kaplan and Cooper (1998) have extended their ideas to situations where customers are the cost objects with the equivalent term for product-sustaining being customer-sustaining activities. Customer market research and support for an individual customer, or groups of customers if they represent the cost object, are examples of customer-sustaining activities.

The final activity category is facility-sustaining (or business-sustaining) activities. They are performed to support the facility's general manufacturing process and include general administrative staff, plant management and property costs. They are incurred to support the organization as a whole and are common and joint to all products manufactured in the plant. There would have to be a dramatic change in activity, resulting in an expansion or contraction in the size of the plant, for facility-sustaining costs to change. Such events are most unlikely in most organizations. Therefore the ABC literature advocates that these costs should not be assigned to products since they are unavoidable and irrelevant for most decisions. Instead, they are regarded as common costs to *all* products made in the plant and deducted as a lump sum from the total of the operating margins from *all* products.

Activity-based costing profitability analysis

ADVANCED READING

Cooper and Kaplan (1991) applied the ABC hierarchical activity classification to profitability analysis. The general principles of activity profitability analysis applied to different cost objects is illustrated in Figure 10.2. This approach categorizes costs according to the causes of their variability at different hierarchical levels. Hierarchies identify the lowest level to which cost can meaningfully be assigned without relying on arbitrary allocations. In Figure 10.2 the lowest hierarchical levels (shown at the top of the diagram) are product, customer and facility contributions and, ignoring the business unit level the highest levels (shown at the bottom of the diagram) are product lines, distribution channels and country profits.

Let us initially focus on products as the cost object. Look at the column for products as the cost object in Figure 10.2. You will see that a unit-level contribution margin is calculated for each *individual* product. This is derived by deducting the cost of unit-level activities from sales revenues. From this unit-level contribution expenses relating to batch-related activities are deducted. Next the cost of product-sustaining activities are deducted. Thus, three different contribution levels are reported at the *individual* product level. Differentiating contributions at these levels provides a better understanding of the implications of product-mix and discontinuation decisions in terms of cost and profit behaviour.

In Figure 10.2 there are two further levels within the product hierarchy. They are the product brand level and the product line level. Some organizations do not market their products by brands and therefore have only one further level within the product hierarchy. A product line consists of a group of similar products. For example, banks have product lines such as savings accounts, lending services, currency services, insurance services and brokering services. Each product line contains individual product variants. The savings product line would include low balance/low interest savings accounts, high balance/high interest accounts, postal and internet savings accounts and other product variants. The lending services product line would include personal loans, house mortgage loans, business loans and other product variants within the product line.

Some organizations market groupings of products within their product lines as separate brands. A typical example of the difference between product brands and product lines is Procter & Gamble who market some of their products within their detergent product line under the Tide label and others without this label.

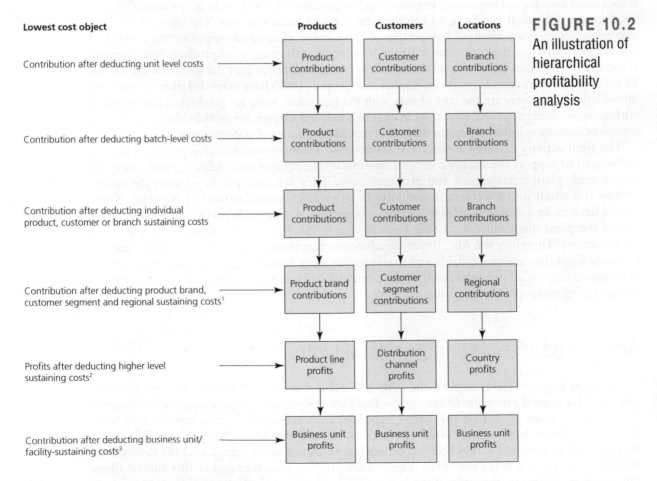

FIGURE 10.2
An illustration of hierarchical profitability analysis

Notes

[1] Consists of expenses dedicated to sustaining specific product brands or customer segments or regions but which cannot be attributed to individual products, customers or branches.

[2] Consists of expenses dedicated to sustaining the product lines or distribution channels or countries but which cannot be attributed to lower items within the hierarchy.

[3] Consists of expenses dedicated to the business as a whole and not attributable to any lower items within the hierarchy.

Where products are marketed by brands, all expenditure relating to a brand, such as management and brand marketing is for the benefit of all products within the brand and not for any specific individual product. Therefore, such brand-sustaining expenses should be attributed to the brand and not to individual products within the brand.

The same reasoning can be applied to the next level in the hierarchy. For example, marketing, research and development and distribution expenses might be incurred for the benefit of the whole product line and not for any specific brands or products within the line. Therefore these product line-sustaining expenses should be attributed to the product line but no attempt should be made to allocate them to individual products or brands. Finally, the profit for the organizational unit as a whole can be determined by deducting facility-sustaining expenses from the sum of the individual product line contributions.

A similar approach to the one described above for products can also be applied to other cost objects. The two final columns shown in Figure 10.2 illustrate how the approach can be applied to customers and locations. The aim of ABC hierarchical profitability analysis is to assign all organizational expenses to a particular hierarchical or organizational level where cause-and-effect cost assignments can be established so that arbitrary allocations are non-existent. The hierarchical approach helps to identify the impact on resource consumption by adding or dropping items at each level of the hierarchy. For example, if a brand is dropped activities at the brand level and below (i.e. above the brand profits row in Figure 10.2) which are uniquely associated with the brand will be affected, but higher level activities (i.e. at the product line level) will be unaffected. Similarly, if a product within a particular brand is dropped then all unit, batch and product-sustaining activities uniquely associated with that product will be affected but higher level brand and product-level activities will be unaffected.

Resource consumption models

Cooper and Kaplan (1992) emphasize that ABC systems are models of resource consumption. ABC systems measure the cost of using resources and not the cost of supplying resources and highlight the critical role played by unused capacity. To have a good conceptual grasp of ABC it is essential that you understand the content of this section.

Kaplan (1994) used the following equation to formalize the relationship between activity resources supplied and activity resources used for each activity:

$$\text{Cost of resources supplied} = \text{Cost of resources used} + \text{Cost of unused capacity} \qquad (10.1)$$

To illustrate the application of the above formula we shall use Example 10.2. The left-hand side of the above equation indicates that the amount of expenditure on an activity depends on the cost of resources supplied rather than the cost of resources used. Example 10.2 contains data relating to the processing of purchase orders activity in which the equivalent of ten full-time staff are committed to the activity. You will see that the estimated annual cost is £300 000. This represents the cost of resources supplied. This expenditure provides the capacity to process 15 000 purchase orders (i.e. the quantity of resources supplied of the cost driver) per annum. Therefore the estimated cost of processing each purchase order is £20 (£300 000/15 000 orders that can be processed).

ABC systems measure the cost of resources used by individual products, services or customers. During any particular period the number of orders processed will vary. In Example 10.2 it is assumed that the Etna Company expects to process 13 000 purchase orders (i.e. the quantity of resources used). The ABC system will therefore assign £260 000 (13 000 orders at £20 per order) to the parts and materials ordered during the year. This represents the cost of resources used.

The cost of unused capacity represents the difference between the cost of resources supplied and the cost of resources used. Resources have been acquired to enable 15 000 purchase orders to be processed but during the year only 13 000 orders will be processed giving an unused capacity of 2000 purchase orders. Hence the predicted cost of the unused capacity will be £40 000 (2000 orders at £20 per order).

Unused capacity arises because the supply of some resources has to be acquired in discrete amounts in advance of usage such that the supply cannot be continually adjusted in the short run to match exactly the usage of resources. Typical expenses in this category include the acquisition of equipment or the employment of non-piecework employees. The expenses of supplying these resources are incurred independently of usage in the short run and this independence has led to them being categorized as fixed costs. Kaplan and Cooper (1998) describe such resources as committed resources. In contrast, there are other types of resources whose supply can be continually adjusted to match exactly the usage of resources. For example, materials, casual labour and the supply of energy for running machinery can be continually adjusted to match the exact demand. Thus the cost of supplying these resources will generally equal the cost of resources used and the resources will have no unused capacity. Kaplan and Cooper classify these resources as 'flexible resources' although they have traditionally been categorized as variable costs.

The problem of adjusting the supply of resources to match the usage of resources and eliminating unused capacity therefore applies only to committed resources. Where the cost of supplying resources in the short run is fixed, the quantity used will fluctuate each period based on the activities performed for the output produced. Activity-based systems measure the cost of *using* these resources, even though the cost of supplying them will not vary with short-run usage.

Managers make decisions (for example, changes in output volume and mix, process changes and improvements and changes in product and process design) that result in changes in activity resource usage. Assuming that such decisions result in a decline in the demand for activity resources then the first term on the right-hand side of equation 10.1 will decline (the cost of resources used) but the cost of unused capacity (the second term on the right-hand side of the equation) will increase to offset exactly the lower resource usage cost. To translate the benefits of reduced activity demands into cash flow savings management action is

EXAMPLE 10.2

The following information relates to the purchasing activity in a division of the Etna Company for the next year:

(1) Resources supplied

10 full-time staff at £30 000 per year (including
employment costs) = £300 000 annual activity cost

Cost driver = Number of purchase orders processed

Quantity of cost driver supplied per year:
(Each member of staff can process
1500 orders per year) = 15 000 purchase orders

Estimated cost driver rate = £20 per purchase order
(£300 000/15 000 orders)

(2) Resources used

Estimated number of purchase orders to be
processed during the year = 13 000

Estimated cost of resources used assigned
to parts and materials = £260 000 (13 000 × £20)

(3) Cost of unused capacity

Resources supplied (15 000) – Resources
used (13 000) at £20 per order = £40 000 (2000 × £20)

required. They must permanently remove the unused capacity by reducing spending on the supply of the resources. Thus to make a resource variable in the downward direction requires two management decisions first to reduce the demand for the resource and, second, to lower the spending on the resource.

Demands for activity resources can also increase because of decisions to introduce new products, expand output and create greater product variety. Such decisions can lead to situations where activity resource usage exceeds the supply of resources. In the short term the excess demand might be absorbed by people working longer or faster or delaying production. Eventually, however, additional spending will be required to increase the supply of activity resources. Thus, even if permanent changes in activity resource consumption occur that result in either unused or excess capacity there may be a significant time lag before the supply of activity resources is adjusted to match the revised predicted activity usage. Indeed, there is always a danger that managers may not act to reduce the spending on the supply of resources to match a reduction in demand. They may keep existing resources in place even when there has been a substantial decline in demands for the activities consuming the resources. Consequently, there will be no benefits arising from actions to reduce activity usage. However, if decisions are made based on reported ABC costs it is implicitly assumed that predicted changes in activity resource usage will be translated into equivalent cash flow changes for the resources supplied.

A major feature of ABC systems is therefore that reported product, service or customer costs represent estimates of the cost of resources used. In a period, many decisions are made that affect the usage of resources. It is not feasible to link the required changes in the supply of resources with the change in usage predicted by each *individual* decision. The periodic reporting of both the predicted quantity and the cost of unused capacity for each activity signals the need for management to investigate the potential for reducing the activity resources supplied. In the case of flexible resources cash flow changes will soon follow decisions to reduce activity usage, such as dropping a product, but for committed resources performing one less set-up, ordering one less batch of materials or undertaking one fewer engineering change notice will not result in an automatic reduction in spending. It will create additional capacity and changes in spending on the supply of resources will often be the outcome of the totality of many decisions rather than focusing on a one-off product decision. Such ideas are considered to be of such vital importance by Kaplan and Cooper that they conclude that managing used and unused capacity is the central focus of ABC.

You should note that support activity costs are caused by the level of activity that is made available (i.e. the capacity supplied) rather than the budgeted level of actual usage. Therefore the correct denominator activity level to use for calculating activity cost driver rates is practical capacity (ie. the capacity supplied) and not the anticipated activity usage. For a more detailed discussion relating to selecting the denominator activity level you should refer to Learning Note 10.1 on the open access website (see Preface for details).

Cost versus benefits considerations

In Chapter 3 it was pointed out that the design of a cost system should be based on cost versus benefit considerations. A sophisticated ABC system should generate the most accurate product costs. However, the cost of implementing and operating an ABC system is significantly more expensive than operating a direct costing or a traditional costing system. In particular, the training and software requirements may prohibit its adoption by small organizations. The partial costs reported by direct costing systems, and the distorted costs reported by traditional systems, may result in significant mistakes in decisions (such as selling unprofitable products or dropping profitable products) arising from the use of this information. If the cost of errors arising from using partial or distorted information generated from using these systems exceeds the additional costs of implementing and operating an ABC system then an ABC system ought to be implemented.

The optimal costing system is different for different organizations. A simplistic traditional costing system may report reasonably accurate product costs in organizations that have the following characteristics:

1 low levels of competition;

2 non-volume related indirect costs that are a low proportion of total indirect costs;

3 a fairly standardized product range all consuming organizational resources in similar proportions (i.e. low product diversity).

In contrast, a sophisticated ABC system may be optimal for organizations having following characteristics:

1 intensive competition;

2 non-volume related indirect costs that are a high proportion of total indirect costs;

3 a diverse range of products, all consuming organizational resources in significantly different proportions (i.e. high product diversity).

Periodic review of an ABC database

The detailed tracking of costs is unnecessary when ABC information is used for decision-making. A data base should be maintained that is reviewed periodically, say once or twice a year. In addition periodic cost and profitability audits (similar to that illustrated in Figure 10.2) should be undertaken to provide a strategic review of the costs and profitability of a firm's products, customers and sales outlets. Rather than focusing on the past it is preferable to concentrate on the future profitability of products and customers using estimated activity-based costs. It is therefore recommended that an activity-cost data base is maintained at estimated standard costs that are updated on an annual or semi-annual basis.

ABC in service organizations

Kaplan and Cooper (1998) suggest that service companies are ideal candidates for ABC, even more than manufacturing companies. Their justification for this statement is that most of the costs in service organizations are indirect. In contrast, manufacturing companies can trace important components (such as direct materials and direct labour) of costs to individual products. Therefore indirect costs are likely to be a much smaller proportion of total costs. Service organizations must also supply most of their resources in advance and fluctuations in the usage of activity resources by individual services and customers does not influence short-term spending to supply the resources. Such costs are treated by traditional costing systems as fixed and irrelevant for most decisions. This resulted in a situation where profitability analysis was not considered helpful for decision-making. Furthermore, until recently many service organizations were either government owned monopolies or operated in a highly regulated, protected and non-competitive environment. These organizations were not subject to any great pressures to improve profitability by identifying and eliminating non-profit making activities. Cost increases could also be absorbed by increasing the prices of services to customers. Little attention was therefore given to developing cost systems that accurately measured the costs and profitability of individual services.

A UK survey by Drury and Tayles (2005) suggests that service organizations are more likely to implement ABC systems. They reported that 51 per cent of the financial and service organizations surveyed, compared with 15 per cent of manufacturing organizations, had implemented ABC. Kaplan and Cooper (1998) illustrate how ABC was applied in The Co-operative Bank, a medium sized UK bank. ABC was used for product and customer profitability analysis. The following are some of the activities and cost drivers that were identified:

Activity	Cost driver
Provide ATM services	Number of ATM transactions
Clear debit items	Number of debits processed
Clear credit items	Number of credits processed
Issue chequebooks	Number of chequebooks issued
Computer processing	Number of computer transactions
Prepare statements of account transactions	Number of statements issued
Administer mortgages	Number of mortgages maintained

Activity costs were allocated to the different savings and loans products based on their demand for the activities using the cost drivers as a measure of resource consumption. Some expenses, such as finance and human resource management, were not assigned to products because they were considered to be for the benefit of the organization as a whole and not attributable to individual products. These business sustaining costs represented approximately 15 per cent of total operating expenses. Profitability analysis was extended to customer segments within product groups. The study revealed that approximately half of the current accounts, particularly those with low balances and high transactions were unprofitable. By identifying the profitable

ABC within a service organization

On face value, product costing at British Telecom (BT) should be both simple and uncontroversial. This is not so for two reasons:

- Most products share the use of the same network or support structure and costs do not vary with volume usage. This means that relatively few costs can be directly allocated to individual products and even apportionment poses practical problems.

- Different product costs are subject to different levels of competition. There are few natural markets in which prices can be established; therefore prices tend to be cost-based and subject to the approval of the regulator. BT's cost allocation processes must be open to detailed scrutiny to prove there is no unfair cross-subsidization between competitive and monopoly activities.

The fundamental principle underlying BT's methods, cost causation, states that costs should be apportioned on the basis of what caused them to be incurred. BT's cost apportionments use a variety of non-financial data taken from all parts of the business. For marketing and sales costs, traditional techniques would probably treat these costs as fixed or allocate them based on turnover. The BT approach is to analyze by activity and to seek a cost driver for each. In other words, ABC techniques are used to allocate costs to products via activity analysis.

There has been an increasing drive from the government to break up monopolies and introduce further privatization. This is likely to leave a general network provider who will provide a fixed-cost asset base used jointly by other parties. Problems of how to charge equitably for this usage are likely to result in an even greater pressure for accurate fixed cost analysis. One answer may be a more extended use of ABC techniques in the way that BT has adopted them.

Discussion points

1 Can you identify another type of service organization that might find ABC useful?

2 Do you think many businesses utilize ABC techniques? Why or why not?

REAL WORLD VIEWS 10.2

REPRODUCED COURTESY OF BTPLC

SOURCE: BUSSEY, B.A. (1993), ABC WITHIN A SERVICE ORGANIZATION, *MANAGEMENT ACCOUNTING* (UK), PP. 40–1, 65.

customer segments the marketing function was able to direct its effort to attracting more new customers, and enhancing relationships with those existing customers, whose behaviour would be profitable to the bank.

ABC cost management applications

Our aim in this chapter has been to look at how ABC can be used to provide information for decision-making by more accurately assigning costs to cost objects, such as products, customers and locations. In addition, ABC can be used for a range of cost management applications. They include cost reduction, activity-based budgeting, performance measurement, benchmarking of activities, process management and business process re-engineering.

The decision to implement ABC should not, therefore, be based only on its ability to produce more accurate and relevant decision-making information. Indeed, surveys by Innes and Mitchell (1995a) and Innes *et al.* (2000) on ABC applications suggests that the cost management applications tend to outweigh the product costing applications which were central to ABC's initial development. We shall examine ABC applications to cost management in Chapter 21. Finally, you should note that care should be exercised when using unit costs derived from ABC systems. For a discussion of the limitations of ABC unit costs you should refer to Learning Note 10.2 on the open access website.

EXHIBIT 10.1 Surveys of company practice

Surveys of UK companies indicate that approximately 15 per cent of the surveyed companies had implemented ABC (Drury and Tayles, 2005; Innes *et al.*, 2000). Similar adoption rates of 10 per cent were found in Ireland (Clarke, 1992) and 14 per cent in Canada (Armitage and Nicholson, 1993). Reported usage rates for mainland Europe are 19 per cent in Belgium (Bruggerman *et al.*, 1996) and 6 per cent in Finland in 1992, 11 per cent in 1993 and 24 per cent in 1995 (Virtanen *et al.*, 1996). Low usage rates have been reported in Denmark (Israelsen *et al.*, 1996), Sweden (Ask *et al.*, 1996) and Germany (Scherrer, 1996). Activity-based techniques do not appear to have been adopted in Greece (Ballas and Vanieris, 1996), Italy (Barbato *et al.*, 1996) or Spain (Saez-Torrecilla *et al.*, 1996).

The UK study by Drury and Tayles indicated that company size and business sector had a significant impact on ABC adoption rates. The adoption rates were 45 per cent for the largest organizations (annual sales in excess of £300m) and 51 per cent for financial and service organizations. Although the ABC adopters used significantly more cost pools and cost drivers than the non-adopters most adopters used fewer cost pools and drivers compared with what is recommended in the literature. Approximately 50 per cent of the ABC adopters used less than 50 cost centres and less than ten separate types of cost driver rates. Other studies have examined the applications of ABC. Innes and Mitchell (1995) found that cost reduction was the most widely used application. Other widely used applications included product/service pricing, cost modelling and performance measurement/improvement.

Friedman and Lynne's (1995, 1999) case study research of 12 UK companies cited top management support as a significant factor influencing the success or failure of ABC systems. Implementation problems identified included the amount of work in setting up the system and data collection, difficulties in identifying activities and selecting cost drivers, lack of resources and inadequate computer software. The benefits reported included more accurate cost information for product pricing, more accurate profitability analysis, improved cost control and a better understanding of cost causation.

SUMMARY

The following items relate to the learning objectives listed at the beginning of the chapter.

● **Explain why a cost accumulation system is required for generating relevant cost information for decision-making.**

There are three main reasons why a cost accumulation system is required for generating relevant cost information. First, many indirect costs are relevant for decision-making and a costing system is therefore required that provides an estimate of resources consumed by cost objects using cause-and-effect allocations to allocate indirect costs. Second, an attention-directing information system is required that periodically identifies those potentially unprofitable products that require more detailed special studies. Third, many product decisions are not independent and to capture product interdependencies those joint resources that fluctuate in the longer-term according to the demand for them should be assigned to products.

● **Describe the differences between activity-based and traditional costing systems.**

The major differences relate to the two-stage allocation process. In the first-stage, traditional systems allocate indirect costs to cost centres (normally departments) whereas activity-based systems allocate indirect costs to cost centres based on activities rather than departments. Since there are many more activities than departments a distinguishing feature is that activity-based systems will have a greater number of cost centres in the first stage of the allocation process. In the second stage, traditional systems use a limited number of different types of second stage volume-based allocation bases (cost drivers) whereas activity-based systems use many different types of volume-based and non-volume-based cause-and-effect second stage drivers.

● **Explain why traditional costing systems can provide misleading information for decision-making.**

Traditional systems often tend to rely on arbitrary allocations of indirect costs. In particular, they rely extensively on volume-based allocations. Many indirect costs are not volume-based but, if volume-based allocation bases are used, high volume products are likely to be assigned with a greater proportion of indirect costs than they have consumed whereas low volume products will be assigned a lower proportion. In these circumstances traditional systems will overcost high volume products and undercost low volume products. In contrast, ABC systems recognize that many indirect costs vary in proportion to changes other than production volume. By identifying the cost drivers that cause the costs to change and assigning costs to cost objects on the basis of cost driver usage, costs can be more accurately traced. It is claimed that this cause-and-effect relationship provides a superior way of determining relevant costs.

● **Identify and explain each of the four stages involved in designing ABC systems.**

The design of ABC systems involves the following four stages: (a) identify the major activities that take place in the organization; (b) create a cost centre/cost pool for each activity; (c) determine the cost driver for each major activity; and (d) trace the cost of activities to the product according to a product's demand (using cost drivers as a measure of demand) for activities.

● **Describe the ABC cost hierarchy.**

ABC systems classify activities along a cost hierarchy consisting of unit-level, batch-level, product-sustaining and facility-sustaining activities. Unit-level activities are performed each time a unit of the product or service is produced. Examples include direct labour and energy costs. Batch-level activities are performed each time a batch is produced. Examples include setting up a machine or processing a purchase order. Product-sustaining activities are performed to enable the production and sale of individual products. Examples include the technical support provided for individual products and the resources required performing product enhancements. Facility-sustaining activities are performed to support the facility's general manufacturing process. They include general administrative staff and property support costs.

● **Describe the ABC profitability analysis hierarchy.**

The ABC profitability analysis hierarchy categorizes costs according to their variability at different hierarchical levels to report different hierarchical contribution levels. At the final level, facility or business-sustaining costs are deducted from the sum of the product contributions to derive a profit at the business unit level. In other words, facility/business sustaining costs are not allocated to individual products. The aim of hierarchical profitability analysis is to assign all organizational expenses to a particular hierarchical or organizational level where cause-and-effect cost assignments can be established so that arbitrary apportionments are non-existent.

● **Describe the ABC resource consumption model.**

ABC systems are models of resource consumption. They measure the cost of using resources and not the cost of supplying resources. The difference between the cost of resources supplied and the cost of resources used represents the cost of unused capacity. The cost of unused capacity for each activity is the reporting mechanism for identifying the need to adjust the supply of resources to match the usage of resources. However, to translate the benefits of reduced activity demands into cash flow savings, management action is required to remove the unused capacity by reducing the spending on the supply of resources.

Key terms and concepts

activities (p. 223)
activity cost drivers (p. 229)
batch-related activities (p. 231)
brand-sustaining expenses (p. 233)
business-sustaining activities (p. 231)
committed resources (p. 234)
consumption ratios (p. 226)
cost drivers (p. 224)
cost of resources supplied (p. 233)
cost of resources used (p. 233)

cost of unused capacity (p. 233)
customer-sustaining activities
  (p. 231)
duration drivers (p. 230)
facility-sustaining activities (p. 231)
flexible resources (p. 234)
models of resource consumption
  (p. 233)
non-volume based cost drivers
  (p. 226)

product line-sustaining expenses
  (p. 233)
product-sustaining activities (p. 231)
resource cost drivers (p. 229)
service-sustaining activities (p. 231)
transaction drivers (p. 230)
unit-level activities (p. 230)
volume-based cost drivers (p. 225)

Recommended reading

Kaplan and Cooper have been the major contributors to the development of activity-based costing. Much of this chapter has therefore drawn off their ideas. For a detailed description of activity-based costing which incorporates all of Kaplan and Cooper's ideas you should consult their book *Cost and Effect:*

Using Integrated Systems to Drive Profitability and Performance (1998). You should refer to the bibliography at the end of this book for the detailed reference. Other interesting articles that comment on developments in the ABC literature are Jones and Dugdale (2002) and Lukka and Granlund (2002).

Key examination points

Questions often require you to compute product costs for a traditional system and an activity-based system and explain the difference between the product costs. Questions also often require you to outline the circumstances where ABC systems are likely to prove most beneficial.

ASSESSMENT MATERIAL

The review questions are short questions that enable you to assess your understanding of the main topics included in the chapter. The numbers in parentheses provide you with the page numbers to refer to if you cannot answer a specific question.

The review problems are more complex and require you to relate and apply the content to various business problems. The problems are graded by their level of difficulty. Solutions to review problems that are not preceded by the term 'IM' are provided in a separate section at the end of the book. Solutions to problems preceded by the term 'IM' are provided in the *Instructor's Manual* accompanying this book and also on the lecturer's password protected section of the website www.drury-online.com. Additional review problems with fully worked solutions are provided in the *Student's Manual* that accompanies this book.

Review questions

10.1 Explain why a cost accumulation system is required for generating relevant cost information for decision-making. *(pp. 222–23)*

10.2 Describe the three different types of cost systems that can be used to assign costs to cost objects. *(p. 223)*

10.3 What are the fundamental differences between a traditional and an ABC system? *(pp. 223–24)*

10.4 Define activities and cost drivers. *(pp. 223–24)*

10.5 What factors led to the emergence of ABC systems? *(p. 225)*

10.6 Distinguish between volume-based and non-volume-based cost drivers. *(pp. 225–27)*

10.7 Describe the circumstances when traditional costing systems are likely to report distorted costs. *(p. 226, p. 236)*

10.8 Explain how low volume products can be undercosted and high volume products overcosted when traditional costing systems are used. *(pp. 226–27)*

10.9 What is meant by 'product diversity' and why is it important for product costing? *(p. 226)*

10.10 Describe each of the four stages involved in designing ABC systems. *(pp. 228–30)*

10.11 Distinguish between resource cost drivers and activity cost drivers. *(p. 229)*

10.12 Distinguish between transaction and duration cost drivers. *(p. 230)*

10.13 Describe the ABC manufacturing cost hierarchy. *(pp. 230–31)*

10.14 Describe the ABC profitability analysis hierarchy. *(pp. 231-33)*

10.15 What is an ABC resource consumption model? *(pp. 233–35)*

10.16 Distinguish between the cost of resources supplied, the cost of resources used and the cost of unused capacity. *(pp. 233–35)*

10.17 Explain the circumstances when ABC is likely to be preferred to traditional costing systems. *(p. 236)*

10.18 Provide examples of how ABC can be used in service organizations. *(p. 237)*

Review problems

10.19 Intermediate. CJD Ltd manufactures plastic components for the car industry. The following budgeted information is available for three of their key plastic components:

	W £ per unit	X £ per unit	Y £ per unit
Selling price	200	183	175
Direct material	50	40	35
Direct labour	30	35	30
Units produced and sold	10 000	15 000	18 000

The total number of activities for each of the three products for the period is as follows:

Number of purchase requisitions	1200	1800	2000
Number of set ups	240	260	300

Overhead costs have been analyzed as follows:

Receiving/inspecting quality assurance	£1 400 000
Production scheduling/machine set up	£1 200 000

Calculate the budgeted profit per unit for each of the three products using activity based budgeting. *(4 marks)*

CIMA P1 Management Accounting: Performance Evaluation

10.20 Intermediate. DRP Limited has recently introduced an Activity Based Costing system. It manufactures three products, details of which are set out below:

	Product D	Product R	Product P
Budgeted annual production (units)	100 000	100 000	50 000
Batch size (units)	100	50	25
Machine set-ups per batch	3	4	6
Purchase orders per batch	2	1	1
Processing time per unit (minutes)	2	3	3

Three cost pools have been identified. Their budgeted costs for the year ending 30 June 2003 are as follows:

Machine set-up costs	£150 000
Purchasing of materials	£70 000
Processing	£80 000

The budgeted machine set-up cost per unit of product R is nearest to

a £0.52
b £0.60
c £6.52
d £26.09

(3 marks)

CIMA Management Accounting – Performance Management

10.21 Intermediate. *It is now fairly widely accepted that conventional cost accounting distorts management's view of business through unrepresentative overhead allocation and inappropriate product costing.*

This is because the traditional approach usually absorbs overhead costs across products and orders solely on the basis of the direct labour involved in their manufacture. And as direct labour as a proportion of total manufacturing cost continues to fall, this leads to more and more distortion and misrepresentation of the impact of particular products on total overhead costs.

(From an article in *The Financial Times*)

You are required to discuss the above and to suggest what approaches are being adopted by management accountants to overcome such criticism.

(15 marks)

CIMA Stage 2 Cost Accounting

10.22 Advanced. Large service organizations, such as banks and hospitals, used to be noted for their lack of standard costing systems, and their relatively unsophisticated budgeting and control systems compared with large manufacturing organizations. But this is changing and many large service organizations are now revising their use of management accounting techniques.

Requirements:

a   Explain which features of large-scale service organizations encourage the application of activity-based approaches to the analysis of cost information.   *(6 marks)*

b   Explain which features of service organizations may create problems for the application of activity-based costing.   *(4 marks)*

c   Explain the uses for activity-based cost information in service industries.   *(4 marks)*

d   Many large service organizations were at one time state-owned, but have been privatised. Examples in some countries include electricity supply and telecommunications. They are often regulated. Similar systems of regulation of prices by an independent authority exist in many countries, and are designed to act as a surrogate for market competition in industries where it is difficult to ensure a genuinely competitive market.

Explain which aspects of cost information and systems in service organisations would particularly interest a regulator, and why these features would be of interest.   *(6 marks)*
CIMA Stage 4 Management Accounting Control Systems

10.23 Intermediate: Comparison of traditional product costing with ABC. Having attended a CIMA course on activity-based costing (ABC) you decide to experiment by applying the principles of ABC to the four products currently made and sold by your company. Details of the four products and relevant information are given below for one period:

Product	A	B	C	D
Output in units	120	100	80	120
Costs per unit:	(£)	(£)	(£)	(£)
Direct material	40	50	30	60
Direct labour	28	21	14	21
Machine hours (per unit)	4	3	2	3

The four products are similar and are usually produced in production runs of 20 units and sold in batches of 10 units.

The production overhead is currently absorbed by using a machine hour rate, and the total of the production overhead for the period has been analysed as follows:

	(£)
Machine department costs (rent, business rates, depreciation and supervision)	10 430
Set-up costs	5 250
Stores receiving	3 600
Inspection/Quality control	2 100
Materials handling and despatch	4 620

You have ascertained that the 'cost drivers' to be used are as listed below for the overhead costs shown:

Cost	Cost Driver
Set up costs	Number of production runs
Stores receiving	Requisitions raised
Inspection/Quality control	Number of production runs
Materials handling and despatch	Orders executed

The number of requisitions raised on the stores was 20 for each product and the number of orders executed was 42, each order being for a batch of 10 of a product. You are required

a   to calculate the total costs for each product if all overhead costs are absorbed on a machine hour basis;   *(4 marks)*

b   to calculate the total costs for each product, using activity-based costing;   *(7 marks)*

c   to calculate and list the unit product costs from your figures in (a) and (b) above, to show the differences and to comment briefly on any conclusions which may be drawn which could have pricing and profit implications.   *(4 marks)*
CIMA Stage 2 Cost Accounting

10.24 Advanced: Computation of product costs for traditional and ABC systems. The following information provides details of the costs, volume and cost drivers for a particular period in respect of ABC plc, a hypothetical company:

	Product X	Product Y	Product Z	Total
1. Production and sales (units)	30 000	20 000	8 000	
2. Raw material usage (units)	5	5	11	
3. Direct material cost	£25	£20	£11	£1 238 000
4. Direct labour hours	1⅓	2	1	88 000
5. Machine hours	1⅓	1	2	76 000
6. Direct labour cost	8	£12	£6	
7. Number of production runs	3	7	20	30
8. Number of deliveries	9	3	20	32
9. Number of receipts (2 × 7)ᵃ	15	35	220	270
10. Number of production orders	15	10	25	50
11. Overhead costs:				
Set-up	30 000			
Machines	760 000			
Receiving	435 000			
Packing	250 000			
Engineering	373 000			
	£1 848 000			

ᵃThe company operates a just-in-time inventory policy, and receives each component once per production run.

In the past the company has allocated overheads to products on the basis of direct labour hours.

However, the majority of overheads are more closely related to machine hours than direct labour hours.

The company has recently redesigned its cost system by recovering overheads using two volume-related bases: machine hours and a materials handling overhead rate for recovering overheads of the receiving department. Both the current and the previous cost system reported low profit margins for product X, which is the company's highest-selling product. The management accountant has recently attended a conference on activity-based costing, and the overhead costs for the last period have been analyzed by the major activities in order to compute activity-based costs.

From the above information you are required to:

a   Compute the product costs using a traditional volume-related costing system based on the assumptions that:
   (i)   all overheads are recovered on the basis of direct labour hours (i.e. the company's past product costing system);
   (ii) the overheads of the receiving department are recovered by a materials handling overhead rate and the remaining overheads are recovered using a machine hour rate (i.e. the company's current costing system).

b   Compute product costs using an activity-based costing system.

c   Briefly explain the differences between the product cost computations in (a) and (b).

10.25 Advanced: ABC product cost calculation. Linacre Co operates an activity-based costing system and has forecast the following information for next year.

Cost Pool	Cost	Cost Driver	Number of Drivers
Production set-ups	£105 000	Set-ups	300
Product testing	£300 000	Tests	1500
Component supply and storage	£25 000	Component orders	500
Customer orders and delivery	£112 500	Customer orders	1000

General fixed overheads such as lighting and heating, which cannot be linked to any specific activity, are expected to be £900 000 and these overheads are absorbed on a direct labour hour basis. Total direct labour hours for next year are expected to be 300 000 hours.

Linacre Co expects orders for Product ZT3 next year to be 100 orders of 60 units per order and 60 orders of 50 units per order. The company holds no stocks of Product ZT3 and will need to produce the order requirement in production runs of 900 units. One order for components is placed prior to each production run. Four tests are made during each production run to ensure that quality standards are maintained. The following additional cost and profit information relates to product ZT3:

Component cost:	£1.00 per unit
Direct labour:	10 minutes per unit at £7.80 per hour
Profit mark up:	40% of total unit cost

Required:

a Calculate the activity-based recovery rates for each cost pool.

(4 marks)

b Calculate the total unit cost and selling price of Product ZT3.

(9 marks)

c Discuss the reasons why activity-based costing may be preferred to traditional absorption costing in the modern manufacturing environment.

(12 marks)

ACCA 2.4 Financial Management and Control

10.26 Advanced: Traditional and ABC profitability analysis. Abkaber plc assembles three types of motorcycle at the same factory: the 50cc Sunshine; the 250cc Roadster and the 1000cc Fireball. It sells the motorcycles throughout the world. In response to market pressures Abkaber plc has invested heavily in new manufacturing technology in recent years and, as a result, has significantly reduced the size of its workforce.

Historically, the company has allocated all overhead costs using total direct labour hours, but is now considering introducing Activity Based Costing (ABC). Abkaber plc's accountant has produced the following analysis.

	Annual Output (units)	Annual Direct Labour Hours	Selling Price (£ per unit)	Raw material cost (£ per unit)
Sunshine	2000	200 000	4000	400
Roadster	1600	220 000	6000	600
Fireball	400	80 000	8000	900

The three cost drivers that generate overheads are:

Deliveries to retailers	–	the number of deliveries of motorcycles to retail showrooms
Set-ups	–	the number of times the assembly line process is re-set to accommodate a production run of a different type of motorcycle
Purchase orders	–	the number of purchase orders.

The annual cost driver volumes relating to each activity and for each type of motorcycle are as follows:

	Number of deliveries to retailers	Number of set-ups	Number of purchase orders
Sunshine	100	35	400
Roadster	80	40	300
Fireball	70	25	100

The annual overhead costs relating to these activities are as follows:

	£
Deliveries to retailers	2 400 000
Set-up costs	6 000 000
Purchase orders	3 600 000

All direct labour is paid at £5 per hour. The company holds no stocks. At a board meeting there was some concern over the introduction of activity based costing.

The finance director argued: 'I very much doubt whether selling the Fireball is viable but I am not convinced that activity based costing would tell us any more than the use of labour hours in assessing the viability of each product.'

The marketing director argued: 'I am in the process of negotiating a major new contract with a motorcycle rental company for the Sunshine model. For such a big order they will not pay our normal prices but we need to at least cover our incremental costs. I am not convinced that activity based costing would achieve this as it merely averages costs for our entire production'.

The managing director argued: 'I believe that activity based costing would be an improvement but it still has its problems. For instance, if we carry out an activity many times surely we get better at it and costs fall rather than remain constant. Similarly, some costs are fixed and do not vary either with labour hours or any other cost driver.'

The chairman argued: 'I cannot see the problem. The overall profit for the company is the same no matter which method of allocating overheads we use. It seems to make no difference to me.'

Required:

a Calculate the total profit on each of Abkaber plc's three types of product using each of the following methods to attribute overheads:

(i) the existing method based upon labour hours; and

(ii) activity-based costing.

(13 marks)

b Write a report to the directors of Abkaber plc, as its management accountant. The report should:

(i) evaluate the labour hours and the activity-based costing methods in the circumstances of Abkaber plc; and

(ii) examine the implications of activity-based costing for Abkaber plc, and in so doing evaluate the issues raised by each of the directors.

Refer to your calculations in requirement (a) above where appropriate.

(12 marks)

ACCA 2.4 Financial Management and Control

IM10.1 Intermediate. The traditional methods of cost allocation, cost apportionment and absorption into products are being challenged by some writers who claim that much information given to management is misleading when these methods of dealing with fixed overheads are used to determine product costs.

You are required to explain what is meant by *cost allocation, cost apportionment* and *absorption* and to describe briefly the alternative approach of *activity-based costing* in order to ascertain total product costs.

(15 marks)

CIMA Stage 2 Cost Accounting

IM10.2 Intermediate. 'Attributing direct costs and absorbing overhead costs to the product/service through an activity-based costing approach will result in a better understanding of the true cost of the final output.'

(*Source:* a recent CIMA publication on costing in a service environment.)

You are required to explain and comment on the above statement.

(15 marks)

CIMA Stage 2 Cost Accounting

IM10.3 Advanced. The basic ideas justifying the use of Activity-Based Costing (ABC) and Activity Based Budgeting (ABB) are well publicised, and the number of applications has increased. However, there are apparently still significant problems in changing from existing systems.

Requirements:

a Explain which characteristics of an organization, such as its structure, product range, or environment, may make the use of activity based techniques particularly useful. (5 marks)

b Explain the problems that may cause an organization to decide not to use, or to abandon use of, activity based techniques.

(8 marks)

c Some categorizations of cost drivers provide hierarchical models:

(i) unit-level activities,

(ii) batch activities,

(iii) product sustaining activities,

(iv) facility sustaining activities.

Other analyzes focus on 'value adding' and 'non-value adding' activities.

Requirement:

Explain what is meant by 'non-value adding activities', and discuss the usefulness of this form of analysis. (7 marks)

CIMA Stage 4 Management Accounting Control Systems

IM10.4 Intermediate: Calculation of ABC product costs and a discussion of the usefulness of ABC. Trimake Limited makes three main products, using broadly the same production methods and equipment for each. A conventional product costing system is used at present, although an activity-based costing (ABC) system is being considered. Details of the three products for a typical period are:

	Hours per unit		Materials per unit £	Volumes Units
	Labour hours	Machine unit		
Product X	½	1½	20	750
Product Y	1½	1	12	1250
Product Z	1	3	25	7000

Direct labour costs £6 per hour and production overheads are absorbed on a machine hour basis. The rate for the period is £28 per machine hour.

a You are required to calculate the cost per unit for each product using conventional methods.

(4 marks)

Further analysis shows that the total of production overheads can be divided as follows:

	(%)
Costs relating to set-ups	35
Costs relating to machinery	20
Costs relating to materials handling	15
Costs relating to inspection	30
Total production overhead	100%

The following activity volumes are associated with the product line for the period as a whole.

Total activities for the period:

	Number of set-ups	Number of movements of materials	Number of inspections
Product X	75	12	150
Product Y	115	21	180
Product Z	480	87	670
	670	120	1000

You are required

b   to calculate the cost per unit for each product using ABC principles; *(15 marks)*

c   to comment on the reasons for any differences in the costs in your answers to (a) and (b). *(3 marks)*

CIMA Stage 3 Management Accounting Techniques

IM10.5 Advanced: Comparison of traditional product costing with ABC. Duo plc produces two products A and B. Each has two components specified as sequentially numbered parts i.e. product A (parts 1 and 2) and product B (parts 3 and 4). Two production departments (machinery and fitting) are supported by five service activities (material procurement, material handling, maintenance, quality control and set up). Product A is a uniform product manufactured each year in 12 monthly high volume production runs. Product B is manufactured in low volume customised batches involving 25 separate production runs each month. Additional information is as follows:

	Product A	Product B
Production details:		
Components	Parts 1, 2	Parts 3, 4
Annual volume produced	300 000 units	300 000 units
Annual direct labour hours:		
Machinery department	500 000 DLH	600 000 DLH
Fitting department	150 000 DLH	200 000 DLH

Overhead Cost Analysis[a]

	(£000s)
Material handling	1 500
Material procurement	2 000
Set-up	1 500
Maintenance	2 500
Quality control	3 000
Machinery (machinery power, depreciation etc.)[b]	2 500
Fitting (machine, depreciation, power etc.)[b]	2 000
	15 000

[a]It may be assumed that these represent fairly homogeneous activity-based cost pools.
[b]It is assumed these costs (depreciation, power etc.) are primarily production volume driven and that direct labour hours are an appropriate surrogate measure of this.

Cost Driver Analysis

	Annual Cost Driver Volume per Component			
Cost Driver	Part 1	Part 2	Part 3	Part 4
Material movements	180	160	1 000	1 200
Number of orders	200	300	2 000	4 000
Number of set-ups	12	12	300	300
Maintenance hours	7 000	5 000	10 000	8 000
Number of inspections	360	360	2 400	1 000
Direct labour hours	150 000	350 000	200 000	400 000
Direct labour hours	50 000	100 000	60 000	140 000

You are required to compute the unit costs for products A and B using (i) a traditional volume-based product costing system and (ii) an activity-based costing system.

(Adapted from Innes, J. and Mitchell, F., *Activity Based Costing: A Review with Case Studies*, Chartered Institute of Management Accountants, 1990)

IM10.6 Advanced: Profitability analysis using ABC as traditional cost allocation bases. ABC plc, a group operating retail stores, is compiling its budget statements for the next year. In this exercise revenues and costs at each store A, B and C are predicted. Additionally, all central costs of warehousing and a head office are allocated across the three stores in order to arrive at a total cost and net profit of each store operation.

In earlier years the central costs were allocated in total based on the total sales value of each store. But as a result of dissatisfaction expressed by some store managers alternative methods are to be evaluated.

The predicted results before any re-allocation of central costs are as follows:

	A (£000)	B (£000)	C (000)
Sales	5000	4000	3000
Costs of sales	2800	2300	1900
Gross margin	2200	1700	1100
Local operating expenses			
Variable	660	730	310
Fixed	700	600	500
Operating profit	840	370	290

The central costs which are to be allocated are:

	(£000)
Warehouse costs:	
Depreciation	100
Storage	80
Operating and despatch	120
Delivery	300
Head office:	
Salaries	200
Advertising	80
Establishment	120
Total	1000

The management accountant has carried out discussions with staff at all locations in order to identify more suitable 'cost drivers' of some of the central costs. So far the following has been revealed.

	A	B	C
Number of despatches	550	450	520
Total delivery distances (thousand miles)	70	50	90
Storage space occupied (%)	40	30	30

1. An analysis of senior management time revealed that 10 per cent of their time was devoted to warehouse issues with the remainder shared equally between the three stores.
2. It was agreed that the only basis on which to allocate the advertising costs was sales revenue.
3. Establishment costs were mainly occupancy costs of senior management.

This analysis has been carried out against a background of developments in the company, for example, automated warehousing and greater integration with suppliers.

Required:

a   As the management accountant prepare a report for the management of the group which:

(i)   Computes the budgeted net profit of each store based on the *sales value* allocation base originally adopted and explains 'cost driver', 'volume' and 'complexity' issues in relation to cost allocation commenting on the possible implications of the dissatisfaction expressed. *(6 marks)*

(ii) Computes the budgeted net profit of each store using the additional information provided, discusses the extent to which an improvement has been achieved in the information on the costs and profitability of running the stores and comments on the results. *(11 marks)*

b   Explain briefly how regression analysis and coefficient of determination (r^2) could be used in confirming the delivery mileage allocation method used in (a) above. *(3 marks)*

ACCA Paper 8 Managerial Finance

IM10.7 Advanced: Unit cost computation based on traditional and ABC systems. Excel Ltd make and sell two products, VG4U and VG2. Both products are manufactured through two consecutive processes – making and packing. Raw material is input at the commencement of the making process. The following estimated information is available for the period ending 31 March:

(i)

	Making (£000)	Packing (£000)
Conversion costs:		
Variable	350	280
Fixed	210	140

40 per cent of fixed costs are product specific, the remainder are company fixed costs. Fixed costs will remain unchanged throughout a wide activity range.

(ii) **Product information:**

	VG4U	VG2
Production time per unit:		
Making (minutes)	5.25	5.25
Packing (minutes)	6	4
Production sales (units)	5000	3000
Selling price per unit (£)	150	180
Direct material cost per unit (£)	30	30

(iii) **Conversion costs are absorbed by products using estimated time based rates.**

Required:

a Using the above information,

    (i) calculate unit costs for each product, analyzed as relevant.

                                                   (10 marks)

    (ii) comment on a management suggestion that the production and sale of one of the products should not proceed in the period ending 31 March.   *(4 marks)*

b Additional information is gathered for the period ending 31 March as follows:

    (i) The making process consists of two consecutive activities, moulding and trimming. The moulding variable conversion costs are incurred in proportion to the temperature required in the moulds. The variable trimming conversion costs are incurred in proportion to the consistency of the material when it emerges from the moulds. The variable packing process conversion costs are incurred in proportion to the time required for each product. Packing materials (which are part of the variable packing cost) requirement depends on the complexity of packing specified for each product.

    (ii) The proportions of product specific conversion costs (variable and fixed) are analyzed as follows:
Making process: moulding (60 per cent); trimming (40 per cent)
Packing process: conversion (70 per cent); packing material (30 per cent)

    (iii) An investigation into the effect of the cost drivers on costs has indicated that the proportions in which the total product specific conversion costs are attributable to VG4U and VG2 are as follows:

	VG4U	VG2
Temperature (moulding)	2	1
Material consistency (trimming)	2	5
Time (packing)	3	2
Packing (complexity)	1	3

    (iv) Company fixed costs are apportioned to products at an overall average rate per product unit based on the estimated figures.

Required:

Calculate amended unit costs for each product where activity based costing is used and company fixed costs are apportioned as detailed above.

                                                   (12 marks)

c Comment on the relevance of the amended unit costs in evaluating the management suggestion that one of the products be discontinued in the period ending 31 March.   *(4 marks)*

d Management wish to achieve an overall net profit margin of 15 per cent on sales in the period ending 31 March in order to meet return on capital targets.

Required:

Explain how target costing may be used in achieving the required return and suggest specific areas of investigation.   *(5 marks)*

ACCA Paper 9 Information for Control and Decision Making

Pricing decisions and profitability analysis

11

Accounting information is often an important input to pricing decisions. Organizations that sell products or services that are highly customized or differentiated from each other by special features, or who are market leaders, have some discretion in setting selling prices. In these organizations the pricing decision will be influenced by the cost of the product. The cost information that is accumulated and presented is therefore important for pricing decisions. In other organizations prices are set by overall market and supply forces and they have little influence over the selling prices of their products and services. Nevertheless, cost information is still of considerable importance in these organizations for determining the relative profitability of different products and services so that management can determine the target product mix to which its marketing effort should be directed.

In this chapter we shall focus on both of the above situations. We shall consider the role that accounting information plays in determining the selling price by a price setting firm. Where prices are set by the market our emphasis will be on examining the cost information that is required for product-mix decisions. In particular, we shall focus on both product and customer profitability analysis. The content of this chapter is normally applicable only to second year management accounting courses.

LEARNING OBJECTIVES

After studying this chapter, you should be able to:

● explain the relevant cost information that should be presented in price setting firms for both short-term and long-term decisions;

● describe product and customer profitability analysis and the information that should be included for managing the product and customer mix;

● describe the target costing approach to pricing;

● describe the different cost-plus pricing methods for deriving selling prices;

● explain the limitations of cost-plus pricing;

● justify why cost-plus pricing is widely used;

● identify and describe the different pricing policies.

The theoretical solution to pricing decisions is derived from economic theory, which explains how the optimal selling price is determined. A knowledge of economic theory is not essential for understanding the content of this chapter but it does provide a theoretical background for the principles influencing pricing decisions. For a discussion of economic theory relating to pricing decisions you should refer to Learning Note 11.1 on the dedicated open access website (see Preface for details).

The role of cost information in pricing decisions

Most organizations need to make decisions about setting or accepting selling prices for their products or services. In some firms prices are set by overall market supply and demand forces and the firm has little or no influence over the selling prices of its products or services. This situation is likely to occur where there are many firms in an industry and there is little to distinguish their products from each other. No one firm can influence prices significantly by its own actions. For example, in commodity markets such as wheat, coffee, rice and sugar prices are set for the market as a whole based on the forces of supply and demand. Also, small firms operating in an industry where prices are set by the dominant market leaders will have little influence over the price of their products or services. Firms that have little or no influence over the prices of their products or services are described as price takers.

In contrast firms selling products or services which are highly customized or differentiated from each other by special features, or who are market leaders, have some discretion in setting prices. Here the pricing decision will be influenced by the cost of the product, the actions of competitors and the extent to which customers value the product. We shall describe those firms that have some discretion over setting the selling price of their products or services as price setters. In practice, firms may be price setters for some of their products and price takers for others.

Where firms are price setters cost information is often an important input into the pricing decision. Cost information is also of vital importance to price takers in deciding on the output and mix of products and services to which their marketing effort should be directed, given their market prices. For both price takers and price setters the decision time horizon determines the cost information that is relevant for product pricing or output-mix decisions. We shall therefore consider the following four different situations:

1   a price setting firm facing short-run pricing decisions;
2   a price setting firm facing long-run pricing decisions;
3   a price taker firm facing short-run product-mix decisions;
4   a price taker firm facing long-run product-mix decisions.

A price setting firm facing short-run pricing decisions

Companies can encounter situations where they are faced with the opportunity of bidding for a one-time special order in competition with other suppliers. In this situation only the incremental costs of undertaking the order should be taken into account. It is likely that most of the resources required to fill the order will have already been acquired and the cost of these resources will be incurred whether or not the bid is accepted by the customer. Typically, the incremental costs are likely to consist of:

● extra materials that are required to fulfil the order;
● any extra part-time labour, overtime or other labour costs;
● the extra energy and maintenance costs for the machinery and equipment required to complete the order.

The incremental costs of one-off special orders in service companies are likely to be minimal. For example, the incremental cost of accepting one-off special business for a hotel may consist of only the cost of additional meals, laundering and bathroom facilities. In most cases, incremental costs are likely to be confined to items within unit-level activities. Resources for batch, product and service-sustaining activities are likely to have already been acquired and in most cases no extra costs on the supply of activities are likely to be incurred.

Bids should be made at prices that exceed incremental costs. Any excess of revenues over incremental costs will provide a contribution to committed fixed costs which would not otherwise have been obtained. Given the short-term nature of the decision long-term considerations are likely to be non-existent and, apart from the consideration of bids by competitors, cost data are likely to be the dominant factor in determining the bid price.

Any bid for one-time special orders that is based on covering only short-term incremental costs must meet all of the following conditions:

- Sufficient capacity is available for all resources that are required to fulfil the order. If some resources are fully utilized, opportunity costs (see Chapter 9 for an illustration) of the scarce resources must be covered by the bid price.

- The bid price will not affect the future selling prices and the customer will not expect repeat business to be priced to cover short-term incremental costs.

- The order will utilize unused capacity for only a short period and capacity will be released for use on more profitable opportunities. If more profitable opportunities do not exist and a short-term focus is always adopted to utilize unused capacity then the effect of pricing a series of special orders over several periods to cover incremental costs constitutes a long-term decision. Thus, the situation arises whereby the decision to reduce capacity is continually deferred and short-term incremental costs are used for long-term decisions.

A price setting firm facing long-run pricing decisions

In this section we shall focus on three approaches that are relevant to a price setting firm facing long-run pricing decisions. They are:

1 Pricing customized products
2 Pricing non-customized products
3 Target costing for pricing non-customized products

Pricing customized products

In the long run firms can adjust the supply of virtually all of their activity resources. Therefore a product or service should be priced to cover all of the resources that are committed to it. If a firm is unable to generate sufficient revenues to cover the long-run costs of all its products, and its business sustaining costs, then it will make losses and will not be able to survive. Setting prices to cover all of the resources that are committed to each individual product (or service) requires a costing system that accurately measures resources consumed by each product. If inaccurate costs are used undercosting or overcosting will occur. In the former situation there is a danger that prices will be set that fail to cover the long-run resources committed to a product. Conversely, with the latter situation profitable business may be lost because over-stated product costs have resulted in excessive prices being set that adversely affect sales volumes and revenues. Where firms are price setters there are stronger grounds for justifying the adoption of ABC systems.

The terms full cost or long-run cost are used to represent the sum of the cost of all those resources that are committed to a product in the long-term. The term is not precisely defined and may include or exclude facility/business sustaining costs. Let us now consider a full cost computation for a product pricing decision using an ABC system. You should now refer to the data presented in Example 11.1.

The estimate of the cost of the resources required to fulfil the order is as follows:

Unit-level expenses		
Direct materials (500 × £22)	11 000	
Direct labour (500 × 2 hours × £10)	10 000	
Machining (500 × 1 hour × £30)	15 000	36 000
Batch-level expenses		
Purchasing and receiving materials and components (6 × £100)	600	
Scheduling production (4 production runs × £250)	1 000	
Setting-up machines (4 production runs × 3 hours × £120)	1 440	
Packaging and delivering (1 delivery at £400)	400	3 440
Product-sustaining expenses		
Engineering design and support (50 hours × £80)		4 000
Customer-sustaining expenses		
Marketing and order negotiation (2 visits × £300 per visit)	600	
Customer support (50 support hours × £50)	2 500	3 100
Total cost of resources (excluding facility-sustaining costs)		46 540

EXAMPLE 11.1

The Kalahari Company has received a request for a price quotation from one of its regular customers for an order of 500 units with the following characteristics:

Direct labour per unit produced	2 hours
Direct materials per unit produced	£22
Machine hours per unit produced	1 hour
Number of component and material purchases	6
Number of production runs for the components prior to assembly	4
Average set-up time per production run	3 hours
Number of deliveries	1
Number of customer visits	2
Engineering design and support	50 hours
Customer support	50 hours

Details of the activities required for the order are as follows:

Activity	Activity cost driver rate
Direct labour processing and assembly activities	£10 per labour hour
Machine processing	£30 per machine hour
Purchasing and receiving materials and components	£100 per purchase order
Scheduling production	£250 per production run
Setting-up machines	£120 per set-up hour
Packaging and delivering orders to customers	£400 per delivery
Invoicing and accounts administration	£120 per customer order
Marketing and order negotiation	£300 per customer visit
Customer support activities including after sales service	£50 per customer service hour
Engineering design and support	£80 per engineering hour

The full cost (excluding facility-sustaining costs) of the order is £46 540. It was pointed out in the previous chapter that facility-sustaining costs are incurred to support the organization as a whole and not for individual products. Therefore they should not be allocated to products for most decisions. Any allocation will be arbitrary. However, such costs must be covered by sales revenues, and for pricing purposes their allocation can be justified as long as they are separately reported.

What allocation base should be used for facility-sustaining costs? The answer is a base that will influence behaviour that the organization wishes to encourage. For example, if the organization has adopted a strategy of standardizing and reducing the number of separate parts maintained it could choose the number of parts as the allocation base. Thus, the facility-sustaining costs allocated to a product would increase with the number of parts used for an order and product designers would be motivated to use standard parts. If a behaviourally desirable allocation base cannot be established then a base should be selected that has a neutral effect and which does not encourage undesirable behaviour. Reporting facility-sustaining costs as a separate category should reduce, or eliminate, the behavioural impact of the chosen allocation base since this provides a clear signal to management that it is an arbitrary allocation, and not a cause-and-effect allocation. We shall look at the behavioural impact of cost drivers in more detail in Chapter 21.

To determine a proposed selling price an appropriate percentage mark-up is added to the estimated cost. In our example facility-sustaining costs have not been allocated to the order. Thus the mark-up that is added should be sufficient to cover a fair share of facility-sustaining costs and provide a profit contribution. Where facility-sustaining costs are allocated a smaller percentage mark-up would be added since the mark-up is required to provide only a profit contribution. Let us assume that the Kalahari Company adds a mark-up of 20 per cent. This would result in a mark-up of £9308 (20 per cent × £46 540) being added to the cost estimate of £46 540, giving a proposed selling price of £55 848. The approach that we have adopted here is called cost-plus pricing. We shall discuss cost-plus pricing and the factors influencing the determination of the profit mark-ups later in the chapter.

Note that the activity-based cost information provides a better understanding of cost behaviour. The batch, product and customer-sustaining costs are unrelated to quantity ordered whereas the unit-level costs are volume related. This provides useful information for salespersons in negotiations with the customer relating to the price and size of the order. Assume that the customer considers purchasing 3000 units, instead of the 500 units originally quoted. If the larger order will enable the company to order 3000 components, instead of 500, and each production run for a component processes 3000 units instead of 500, the batch-level expenses will remain unchanged. Also the cost of the product and customer-sustaining activities will be the same for the larger order but the cost of the unit-level activity resources required will increase by a factor of six because six times the amount of resources will be required for the larger order. Thus the cost of the resources used for an order of 3000 units will be:

	(£)
Unit-level expenses (6 × £36 000[a])	216 000
Batch-level expenses	3 440
Product-sustaining expenses	4 000
Customer-sustaining expenses	3 100
Total cost of resources (excluding facility-sustaining costs)	226 540

Note
[a]Unit-level expenses for an order of 500 units multiplied by a factor of 6.

The cost per unit for a 500 unit order size is £93.08 (£46 540/500) compared with £75.51 (£226 540/3000) for a 3000 unit order size and the resulting proposed unit selling prices are £111.70 (£93.08 × 120 per cent) and £90.61 (£75.51 × 120 per cent) respectively.

Pricing non-customized products

In Example 11.1 the Kalahari Company was faced with a pricing decision for the sale of a highly customized product to a single customer. The pricing decision would have been based on direct negotiations with the customer for a known quantity. In contrast, a market leader must make a pricing decision, normally for large and unknown volumes, of a single product that is sold to thousands of different customers. To apply cost-plus pricing in this situation an estimate is required of sales volume to determine a unit cost which will determine the cost-plus selling price. This circular process occurs because we are now faced with two unknowns which have a cause-and-effect relationship, namely selling price and sales volume. In this situation it is recommended that cost-plus selling prices are estimated for a range of potential sales volumes. Consider the information presented in Example 11.2 (Case A).

You will see that the Auckland Company has produced estimates of total costs for a range of activity levels. Ideally, the cost estimates should be built up in a manner similar to the activity-based cost estimates that were used by the Kalahari Company in Example 11.1. However, for brevity the cost build-up is not shown. Instead of adding a percentage profit margin the Auckland Company has added a fixed lump sum target profit contribution of £2 million.

EXAMPLE 11.2

Case A

The Auckland Company is launching a new product. Sales volume will be dependent on the selling price and customer acceptance but because the product differs substantially from other products within the same product category it has not been possible to obtain any meaningful estimates of price/demand relationships. The best estimate is that demand is likely to range between 100 000 and 200 000 units provided that the selling price is less than £100. Based on this information the company has produced the following cost estimates and selling prices required to generate a target profit contribution of £2 million from the product.

Sales volume (000's)	100	120	140	160	180	200
Total cost (£000's)	10 000	10 800	11 200	11 600	12 600	13 000
Required profit contribution (£000's)	2 000	2 000	2 000	2 000	2 000	2 000
Required sales revenues (£000's)	12 000	12 800	13 200	13 600	14 600	15 000
Required selling price to achieve target profit contribution (£)	120.00	106.67	94.29	85.00	81.11	75.00
Unit cost (£)	100.00	90.00	80.00	72.50	70.00	65.00

Case B

Assume now an alternative scenario for the product in Case A. The same cost schedule applies but the £2 million minimum contribution no longer applies. In addition, Auckland now undertakes market research. Based on this research, and comparisons with similar product types and their current selling prices and sales volumes, estimates of sales demand at different selling prices have been made. These estimates, together with the estimates of total costs obtained in Case A are shown below:

Potential selling price	£100	£90	£80	£70	£60
Estimated sales volume at the potential selling price (000's)	120	140	180	190	200
Estimated total sales revenue (£000's)	12 000	12 600	14 400	13 300	12 000
Estimated total cost (£000's)	10 800	11 200	12 600	12 800	13 000
Estimated profit (loss) contribution (£000's)	1 200	1 400	1 800	500	(1 000)

The information presented indicates to management the sales volumes, and their accompanying selling prices, that are required to generate the required profit contribution. The unit cost calculation indicates the break-even selling price at each sales volume that is required to cover the cost of the resources committed at that particular volume. Management must assess the likelihood of selling the specified volumes at the designated prices and choose the price which they consider has the highest probability of generating at least the specified sales volume. If none of the sales volumes are likely to be achieved at the designated selling prices management must consider how demand can be stimulated and/or costs reduced to make the product viable. If neither of these, or other strategies, are successful the product should not be launched. The final decision must be based on management judgement and knowledge of the market.

The situation presented in Example 11.2 represents the most extreme example of the lack of market data for making a pricing decision. If we reconsider the pricing decision faced by the company it is likely that similar products are already marketed and information may be available relating to their market shares and sales volumes. Assuming that Auckland's product is differentiated from other similar products a relative comparison should be possible of its strengths and weaknesses and whether customers would be prepared to pay a price in excess of the prices of similar products. It is therefore possible that Auckland may be able to undertake market research to obtain rough approximations of demand levels at a range of potential selling prices. Let us assume that Auckland adopts this approach, and apart from this, the facts are the same as those given in Example 11.2 (Case A).

Now look at Case B in Example 11.2. The demand estimates are given for a range of selling prices. In addition the projected costs, sales revenues and profit contribution are shown. You can see that profits are maximized at a selling price of £80. The information also shows the effect of pursuing other pricing policies. For example, a lower selling price of £70 might be selected to discourage competition and ensure that a larger share of the market is obtained in the future. Where demand estimates are available ABC cost information should be presented for different potential volume levels and compared with projected sales revenues derived from estimated price/output relationships. Ideally, the cost projections should be based on a life-cycle costing approach to ensure that costs incurred over the whole of a product's life cycle are taken into account in the pricing decision. We shall look at life-cycle costing in Chapter 21.

Pricing non-customized products using target costing

Instead of using cost-plus pricing approach described in Exhibit 11.3 (Case A) whereby cost is used as the starting point to determine the selling price, target costing is the reverse of this process. With target costing the starting point is the determination of the target selling price. Next a standard or desired profit margin is deducted to get a target cost for the product. The aim is to ensure that the future cost will not be higher than the target cost. The stages involved in target costing can be summarized as follows:

Stage 1: determine the target price which customers will be prepared to pay for the product;

Stage 2: deduct a target profit margin from the target price to determine the target cost;

Stage 3: estimate the actual cost of the product;

Stage 4: if estimated actual cost exceeds the target cost investigate ways of driving down the actual cost to the target cost.

The first stage requires market research to determine the customers' perceived value of the product, its differentiation value relative to competing products and the price of competing products. The target profit margin depends on the planned return on investment for the organization as a whole and profit as a percentage of sales. This is then decomposed into a target profit for each product which is then deducted from the target price to give the target cost. The target cost is compared with the predicted actual cost. If the predicted actual cost is above the target cost intensive efforts are made to close the gap. Product designers focus on modifying the design of the product so that it becomes cheaper to produce. Manufacturing engineers also concentrate on methods of improving production processes and efficiencies.

The aim is to drive the predicted actual cost down to the target cost but if the target cost cannot be achieved at the pre-production stage the product may still be launched if management are confident that the process of continuous improvement and learning curve effects (see Chapter 23) will enable the target cost to be achieved early in the product's life. If this is not possible the product will not be launched.

The major attraction of target costing is that marketing factors and customer research provide the basis for determining selling price whereas cost tends to be the dominant factor with cost-plus pricing. A further attraction is that the approach requires the collaboration of product designers, production engineers, marketing and finance staff whose focus is on managing costs at the product design stage. At this stage costs can be most effectively managed because a decision committing the firm to incur costs will not have been made.

Target costing is most suited for setting prices for non-customized and high sales volume products. It is also an important mechanism for managing the cost of future products. We shall therefore look at target costing in more detail when we focus on cost management in Chapter 21.

A price taker firm facing short-run product-mix decisions

Price taking firms may be faced with opportunities of taking on short-term business at a market determined selling price. In this situation the cost information that is required is no different from that of a price setting firm making a short-run pricing decision. In other words, accepting short-term business where the incremental sales revenues exceed incremental short-run costs will provide a contribution towards committed fixed costs which would not otherwise have been obtained. However, such business is acceptable only if the same conditions as those specified for a price setting firm apply. You should remember that these conditions are:

- sufficient capacity is available for all resources that are required from undertaking the business (if some resources are fully utilized, opportunity costs of the scarce resources must be covered by the selling price);
- the company will not commit itself to repeat longer-term business that is priced to cover only short-term incremental costs;
- the order will utilize unused capacity for only a short period and capacity will be released for use on more profitable opportunities.

Besides considering new short-term opportunities organizations may, in certain situations, review their existing product-mix over a short-term time horizon. Consider a situation where a firm has excess capacity which is being retained for an expected upsurge in demand. If committed resources are to be maintained then the product profitability analysis of existing products should be based on a comparison of incremental revenues with short-term incremental costs. The same principle applies as that which applied for accepting new short-term business where spare capacity exists. That is, in the short term products should be retained if their incremental revenues exceed their incremental short-term costs.

Where short-term capacity constraints apply, such that the firm has profitable products whose sales demand exceeds its productive capacity, the product-mix should be based on maximizing contribution per limiting production factor as described in Chapter 9. You may wish to refer back to Example 9.2 for an illustration of this approach. Do note, however, that in the longer-term capacity constraints can be removed.

A price taker firm facing long-run product-mix decisions

ADVANCED READING

When prices are set by the market a firm has to decide which products to sell given their market prices. In the longer-term a firm can adjust the supply of resources committed to a product. Therefore the sales revenue from a service or product should exceed the cost of all the resources that are committed to it. Hence there is a need to undertake periodic profitability analysis to distinguish between profitable and unprofitable products in order to ensure that only profitable products are sold. Activity-based profitability analysis should be used to evaluate each product's long-run profitability. In the previous chapter Figure 10.2 was used to illustrate ABC hierarchical profitability analysis. This diagram is repeated in the form of Figure 11.1. You will see that where products are the cost object four different hierarchical levels have been identified – the individual products, the product brand groupings, the product line and finally the whole business unit. At the individual product level all of the resources required for undertaking the unit, batch and product-sustaining activities that are associated with a product would no longer be required if that product were discontinued. Thus, if the product's sales revenues do not exceed the cost of the resources of these activities it should be subject to a special study for a discontinuation decision.

If product groups are marketed as separate brands the next level within the profitability hierarchy is brand profitability. The sum of the individual product profit contributions (that is, sales revenues less

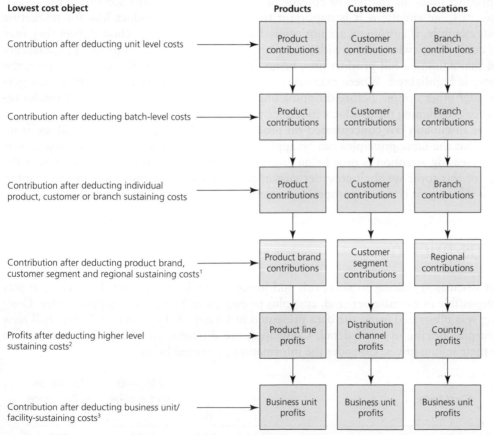

Lowest cost object

Contribution after deducting unit level costs

Contribution after deducting batch-level costs

Contribution after deducting individual product, customer or branch sustaining costs

Contribution after deducting product brand, customer segment and regional sustaining costs[1]

Profits after deducting higher level sustaining costs[2]

Contribution after deducting business unit/ facility-sustaining costs[3]

Products | **Customers** | **Locations**

Product contributions | Customer contributions | Branch contributions

Product contributions | Customer contributions | Branch contributions

Product contributions | Customer contributions | Branch contributions

Product brand contributions | Customer segment contributions | Regional contributions

Product line profits | Distribution channel profits | Country profits

Business unit profits | Business unit profits | Business unit profits

FIGURE 11.1
An illustration of hierarchical profitability analysis

Notes

[1] Consists of expenses dedicated to sustaining specific product brands or customer segments or regions but which cannot be attributed to individual products, customers or branches.

[2] Consists of expenses dedicated to sustaining the product lines or distribution channels or countries but which cannot be attributed to lower items within the hierarchy.

[3] Consists of expenses dedicated to the business as a whole and not attributable to any lower items within the hierarchy.

the cost of the unit, batch and product-sustaining activities) within a brand must be sufficient to cover those brand-sustaining expenses that can be attributed to the brand but not the individual products within the brand. Thus it is possible for each individual product within the product brand to generate positive contributions but for the brand grouping to be unprofitable because the brand-sustaining expenses exceed the sum of individual product contributions. In these circumstances a special study is required to consider alternative courses of action that can be undertaken to make the brand profitable.

Product line profitability is the next level in the hierarchy in Figure 11.1. The same principle applies. That is, if the product line consists of a number of separate groupings of branded and non-branded products the sum of their contributions (that is, sales revenues less the cost of the unit, batch, product-sustaining and brand-sustaining activities) should exceed those product-line sustaining expenses that are attributable to the product line as a whole but not the individual groupings of branded and non-branded products within the product line. Here a negative profit contribution would signal the need to undertake a major special study to investigate alternative courses of action relating to how the product line can be made profitable.

The final level in the profitability hierarchy shown in Figure 11.1 relates to the profitability of the business unit as a whole. Here the profit for the business unit can be determined by deducting the facility or business-sustaining expenses that are attributable to the business unit as a whole, but not to lower levels within the hierarchy, from the sum of the product line contributions. Clearly a business must generate profits in the long term if it is to survive.

Most of the decisions are likely to be made at the individual product level. Before discontinuing a product other alternatives or considerations must be taken into account at the special study stage. In some situations it is important to maintain a full product line for marketing reasons. For example, if customers are not offered a full product line to choose from they may migrate to competitors who offer a wider choice. By reporting individual product profitability the cost of maintaining a full product line, being the sum of unprofitable products within the product line, is highlighted. Where maintaining a full product line is not required managers should consider other options before dropping unprofitable products. They should consider re-engineering or redesigning the products to reduce their resource consumption.

The above discussion has concentrated on product profitability analysis. You will see from Figure 11.1 that the same principles can be applied to other cost objects, such as customers or locations. Increasing attention is now being given to customer profitability analysis. Given the importance of this topic we shall consider customer profitability analysis later in the chapter. However, at this stage it is more appropriate to examine cost-plus pricing in more detail.

Cost-plus pricing

Our earlier discussion relating to short-run and long-run pricing suggested that, where it was virtually impossible to estimate demand, cost-plus pricing should be used by a price-setter. Cost-plus pricing was illustrated using the data presented in Examples 11.1 and 11.2. We shall now look at cost-plus pricing in more detail. Companies use different cost bases and mark-ups to determine their selling prices. Consider the information presented below:

Cost base	(£)	Mark-up percentage	Cost-plus selling price (£)
(1) Direct variable costs	200	150	500
(2) Direct non-variable costs	100		
(3) Total direct costs	300	70	510
(4) Indirect costs	80		
(5) Total cost (excluding higher level sustaining costs)	380	40	532
(6) Higher level sustaining costs	60		
(7) Total cost	440	20	528

In the above illustration four different cost bases are used resulting in four different selling prices. In row (1) only direct variable costs are assigned to products for cost-plus pricing and a high percentage mark-up (150 per cent) is added to cover direct non-variable costs, indirect costs and higher level sustaining costs (e.g. facility sustaining costs) and also to provide a contribution towards profit. Where products are the cost object higher level sustaining costs would include brand, product line and business-sustaining costs. This approach is best suited to short-term pricing decisions.

The second cost base is row (3). Here a smaller percentage margin (70 per cent) is added to cover indirect costs, the higher level sustaining costs and to provide a contribution to profit. Indirect costs are not therefore assigned to products for cost-plus pricing. This cost base is appropriate if indirect costs are a small percentage of an organization's total costs. The disadvantage of adopting this approach is that the consumption of joint resources by products is not measured. By adding a percentage mark-up to direct costs indirect costs are effectively allocated to products using direct costs as the allocation base. Hence, the approach implicitly uses arbitrary apportionments.

The third cost base is 'Total cost' (excluding higher level sustaining costs). With this base a lower profit margin (40 per cent) is added to cover higher level sustaining costs and a profit contribution. This cost base is recommended for long-run pricing and was the approach illustrated in Examples 11.1 and 11.2. Ideally, ABC systems should be used to compute total (full) costs.

SOURCE: OFFICIAL EUROPEAN PLAYSTATION WEBSITE – HTTP://EU.PLAYSTATION.COM/PS3/

Pricing the next generation Sony PlayStation

When pricing a new product, the price set by the product manufacturer will reflect not only the cost of production, but also reflect the products features and a clear understanding of the target consumer group. Consumer electronics is one sector where this is particularly evident.

Take for example the Sony PlayStation. The latest revision of the ever popular games console, the PS3, is available in Europe from March 2007. The new edition promises many new features such as increased storage (using Blu-Ray discs which store six times more data than a double-sided DVD) and the clearest images yet using HDTV technology. New technology comes at a price – €499 for a 20GB and €599 for a 60GB model. The PS3's predecessor, the PS2 launched at approximately €300–350 in late 2000.

A consumer electronics product such as the PS3 is assembled from a definitive number of components and sub-components, all of which should readily have a cost attached. Add to this, costs of labour, marketing and other overheads costs and a final product cost can be derived. To this the producer will add a profit margin to aid the setting of a retail price for the product. The final price of products such as the PS3 also reflect the products 'value' relative to competing games consoles – particularly in relation to the features offered to the user.

Discussion points

1 Do you think the price of a games console such as the PS3 is determined more by what consumers will pay (a price taking case) or by what the manufacturer wishes to sell the product for (a price setting case)?

2 In comparison to other personal computing products, do you feel the price of the PS3 is high or low? Give reasons for your answer.

REAL WORLD VIEWS 11.1

REPRODUCED COURTESY OF SONY
"⚙" AND "PLAYSTATION" ARE REGISTERED TRADEMARKS OF SONY COMPUTER ENTERTAINMENT INC.

The final cost base is row (7) which includes an allocation of all costs but do remember that higher level sustaining costs cannot be allocated to products on a cause-and-effect basis. Some organizations, however, may wish to allocate all costs to products to ensure that all costs are covered in the cost base. The lowest percentage mark-up (20 per cent) is therefore added since the aim is to provide only a profit contribution.

Establishing target mark-up percentages

Mark-ups are related to the demand for a product. A firm is able to command a higher mark-up for a product that has a high demand. Mark-ups are also likely to decrease when competition is intensive. Target mark-up percentages tend to vary from product line to product line to correspond with well-established differences in custom, competitive position and likely demand. For example, luxury goods with a low sales turnover may attract high profit margins whereas non-luxury goods with a high sales turnover may attract low profit margins.

Another approach is to choose a mark-up to earn a target rate of return on invested capital. This approach seeks to estimate the amount of investment attributable to a product and then set a price that ensures a satisfactory return on investment for a given volume. For example, assume that cost per unit for a product is £100 and that the annual volume is 10 000 units. If the product requires an investment of £1 million and the target rate of return is 15 per cent, the target mark-up will be:

$$\frac{15\% \times £1\,000\,000}{10\,000 \text{ units}} = £15 \text{ per unit}$$

The target price will be £100 plus £15, or £115 per unit. The major problem of applying this approach is that it is difficult to determine the capital invested to support a product. Assets are normally used for many different products and therefore it is necessary to allocate investments in assets to different products. This process is likely to involve arbitrary allocations.

Note that once the target selling price has been calculated, it is rarely adopted without amendment. The price is adjusted upwards or downwards depending on such factors as the future capacity that is available, the extent of competition from other firms, and management's general knowledge of the market. For example, if the price calculation is much lower than that which management considers the customer will be prepared to pay, the price may be increased.

We may ask ourselves the question 'Why should cost-based pricing formulae be used when the final price is likely to be altered by management?' The answer is that cost based pricing formulae provide an initial approximation of the selling price. It is a target price and is important information, although by no means the only information that should be used when the final pricing decision is made. Management should use this information, together with their knowledge of the market and their intended pricing strategies, before the final price is set.

Limitations of cost-plus pricing

The main criticism that has been made against cost-plus pricing is that demand is ignored. The price is set by adding a mark-up to cost, and this may bear no relationship to the price-demand relationship. It is assumed that prices should depend solely on costs. For example, a cost-plus formula may suggest a price of £20 for a product where the demand is 100 000 units, whereas at a price of £25 the demand might be 80 000 units. Assuming that the variable cost for each unit sold is £15, the total contribution will be £500 000 at a selling price of £20, compared with a total contribution of £800 000 at a selling price of £25. Thus cost-plus pricing formulae might lead to incorrect decisions.

It is often claimed that cost-based pricing formulae serve as a pricing 'floor' shielding the seller from a loss. This argument, however, is incorrect since it is quite possible for a firm to lose money even though every product is priced higher than the estimated unit cost. The reason for this is that if sales demand falls below the activity level that was used to calculate the fixed cost per unit, the total sales revenue may be insufficient to cover the total fixed costs. Cost-plus pricing will only ensure that all the costs will be met, and the target profits earned, if the sales volume is equal to, or more than, the activity level that was used to estimate total unit costs.

Consider a hypothetical situation where all of the costs attributable to a product are fixed in the short-term and amount to £1 million. Assume that the cost per unit is £100 derived from an estimated volume of 10 000 units. The selling price is set at £130 using the cost-plus method and a mark-up of 30 per cent. If actual sales volume is 7000 units, sales revenues will be £910 000 compared with total costs of £1 million. Therefore the product will incur a loss of £90 000 even though it is priced above full cost.

Reasons for using cost-plus pricing

Considering the limitations of cost-plus pricing, why is it that these techniques are frequently used in practice? Baxter and Oxenfeldt (1961) suggest the following reasons:

> They offer a means by which plausible prices can be found with ease and speed, no matter how many products the firm handles. Moreover, its imposing computations look factual and precise, and its prices may well seem more defensible on moral grounds than prices established by other means. Thus a monopolist threatened by a public inquiry might reasonably feel that he is safeguarding his case by cost-plus pricing.

Another major reason for the widespread use of cost-plus pricing methods is that they may help a firm to predict the prices of other firms. For example, if a firm has been operating in an industry where average mark-ups have been 40 per cent in the past, it may be possible to predict that competitors will be adding a 40 per cent mark-up to their costs. Assuming that all the firms in the industry have similar cost structures, it will be possible to predict the price range within which competitors may price their products. If all the firms in an industry price their products in this way, it may encourage price stability.

In response to the main objection that cost-based pricing formulae ignore demand, we have noted that the actual price that is calculated by the formula is rarely adopted without amendments. The price is adjusted upwards or downwards after taking account of the number of sales orders on hand, the extent of competition from other firms, the importance of the customer in terms of future sales, and the policy relating to customer relations. Therefore it is argued that management attempts to adjust the mark-up based on the state of sales demand and other factors which are of vital importance in the pricing decision.

Pricing policies

Cost information is only one of many variables that must be considered in the pricing decision. The final price that is selected will depend upon the pricing policy of the company. A price-skimming or pricing penetration policy might be selected.

A price-skimming policy is an attempt to exploit those sections of the market that are relatively insensitive to price changes. For example, high initial prices may be charged to take advantage of the novelty appeal of a new product when demand is initially inelastic. A skimming pricing policy offers a safeguard against unexpected future increases in costs, or a large fall in demand after the novelty appeal has declined. Once the market becomes saturated, the price can be reduced to attract that part of the market that has not yet been exploited. A skimming pricing policy should not be adopted when a number of close substitutes are already being marketed. Here the demand curve is likely to be elastic, and any price in excess of that being charged for a substitute product by a competitor is likely to lead to a large reduction in sales.

A penetration pricing policy is based on the concept of charging low prices initially with the intention of gaining rapid acceptance of the product. Such a policy is appropriate when close substitutes are available or when the market is easy to enter. The low price discourages potential competitors from entering the market and enables a company to establish a large share of the market. This can be achieved more easily when the product is new, than later on when buying habits have become established.

Many products have a product life cycle consisting of four stages: introductory, growth, maturity and decline. At the introductory stage the product is launched and there is minimal awareness and acceptance of it. Sales begin to expand rapidly at the growth stage because of introductory promotions and greater customer awareness, but this begins to taper off at the maturity stage as potential new customers are exhausted. At the decline stage sales diminish as the product is gradually replaced with new and better versions.

Sizer (1989) suggests that in the introductory stage it may be appropriate to shade upwards or downwards the price found by normal analysis to create a more favourable demand in future years. For example, he suggests that limited production capacity may rule out low prices. Therefore a higher initial price than that suggested by normal analysis may be set and progressively reduced, if and when (a) price elasticity of demand increases or (b) additional capacity becomes available. Alternatively if there is no production capacity constraint, a lower price than that suggested by normal analysis may be preferred. Such a price may result in a higher sales volume and a slow competitive reaction, which will enable the company to establish a large market share and to earn higher profits in the long term.

At the maturity stage a firm will be less concerned with the future effects of current selling prices and should adopt a selling price that maximizes short-run profits.

Customer profitability analysis

In the past, management accounting reports have tended to concentrate on analysing profits by products. Increasing attention is now being given to analysing profits by customers using an activity-based costing approach. Customer profitability analysis provides important information that can be used to determine which classes of customers should be emphasized or de-emphasized and the price to charge for customer services. Let us now look at an illustration of customer profitability analysis. Consider the information presented in Example 11.3. The profitability analysis in respect of the four customers is as follows:

	A	B	Y	Z
Customer attributable costs:				
Sales order processing	60 000	30 000	15 000	9 000
Sales visits	4 000	2 000	1 000	1 000
Normal deliveries	30 000	10 000	2 500	1 250
Special (urgent) deliveries	10 000	2 500	0	0
Credit collection[a]	24 658	8 220	1 370	5 480
	128 658	52 720	19 870	16 730
Operating profit contribution	90 000	120 000	70 000	200 000
Contribution to higher level sustaining expenses	(38 658)	67 280	50 130	183 270

Note
[a](Annual sales revenue × 10%) × (Average collection period/365)

You can see from the above analysis that A and B are high cost to serve whereas Y and Z are low cost to serve customers. Customer A provides a positive operating profit contribution but is unprofitable when customer attributable costs are taken into account. This is because customer A requires more sales orders, sales visits and normal and urgent deliveries than the other customers. In addition, the customer is slow to pay and has higher delivery costs than the other customers. Customer profitability analysis identifies the characteristics of high cost and low cost to serve customers and shows how customer profitability can be increased. The information should be used to persuade high cost to serve customers to modify their buying behaviour away from placing numerous small orders and/or purchasing non-standard items that are costly to make. For example, customer A can be made profitable if action is taken to persuade the customer to place a smaller number of larger quantity orders, avoid special deliveries and reduce the credit period. If unprofitable customers cannot be persuaded to change their buying behaviour selling prices should be increased (or discounts on list prices reduced) to cover the extra resources consumed. Thus ABC is required for customer profitability analysis so that the resources consumed by customers can be accurately measured.

The customer profitability analysis can also be used to rank customers by order of profitability based on Pareto analysis. This type of analysis is based on observations by Pareto that a very small proportion of items usually account for the majority of the value. For example, the Darwin Company might find that 20 per cent of the customers account for 80 per cent of the profits. Special attention can then be given to enhancing the relationships with the most profitable customers to ensure that they do not migrate to other competitors. In addition greater emphasis can be given to attracting new customers that have the same attributes as the most profitable customers.

Organizations, such as banks, often with a large customer base in excess of one million customers cannot apply customer profitability analysis at the individual customer level. Instead, they concentrate on customer segment profitability analysis by combining groups of customers into meaningful segments. This enables profitable segments to be highlighted where customer retention is particularly important and provides an input for determining the appropriate marketing strategies for attracting the new customers that have the most profit potential. Segment groupings that are used by banks include income classes, age bands, socio-economic categories and family units.

EXAMPLE 11.3

The Darwin Company has recently adopted customer profitability analysis. It has undertaken a customer profitability review for the past 12 months. Details of the activities and the cost driver rates relating to those expenses that can be attributed to customers are as follows:

Activity	Cost driver rate
Sales order processing	£300 per sales order
Sales visits	£200 per sales visit
Normal delivery costs	£1 per delivery kilometre travelled
Special (urgent) deliveries	£500 per special delivery
Credit collection costs	10% per annum on average payment time

Details relating to four of the firm's customers are as follows:

Customer	A	B	Y	Z
Number of sales orders	200	100	50	30
Number of sales visits	20	10	5	5
Kilometres per delivery	300	200	100	50
Number of deliveries	100	50	25	25
Total delivery kilometres	30 000	10 000	2 500	1 250
Special (urgent deliveries)	20	5	0	0
Average collection period (days)	90	30	10	10
Annual sales	£1 million	£1 million	£0.5 million	£2 million
Annual operating profit contribution[a]	£90 000	£120 000	£70 000	£200 000

Note
[a] Consists of sales revenues less cost of unit-level and batch-related activities

SUMMARY

The following items relate to the learning objectives listed at the beginning of the chapter.

● **Explain the relevant cost information that should be presented in price setting firms for both short-term and long-term decisions.**

For short-term decisions the incremental costs of accepting an order should be presented. Bids should then be made at prices that exceed incremental costs. For short-term decisions many costs are likely to be fixed and irrelevant. Short-term pricing decisions should meet the following conditions: (a) spare capacity should be available for all of the resources that are required to fulfil an order; (b) the bid price should represent a one-off price that will not be repeated for future orders; and (c) the order will utilize unused capacity for only a short period and capacity will be released for use on more profitable opportunities. For long-term decisions a firm can adjust the supply of virtually all of the resources. Therefore, cost information should be presented providing details of all of the resources that are committed to a product or service. Since facility-sustaining costs should be covered in the long-term by sales revenues there are strong arguments for allocating such costs for long-run pricing decisions. To determine an appropriate selling price a mark-up is added to the total cost of the resources assigned to the product/service to provide a contribution to profits. If facility-sustaining costs are not allocated the mark-up must be sufficient to provide a contribution to covering facility-sustaining costs and a contribution to profit.

● **Describe product and customer profitability analysis and the information that should be included for managing the product and customer mix.**

Price-taking firms have to decide which products to sell, given their market prices. A mechanism is therefore required that ascertains whether or not the sales revenues from a product/service (or customer) exceeds the cost of resources that are committed to it. Periodic profitability analysis meets this requirement. Ideally, ABC hierarchical profitability analysis should be used that categorizes costs according to their variability at different hierarchical levels to report different hierarchical contribution levels. The aim of the hierarchical analysis should be to assign all organizational expenses to a particular hierarchical or organizational level where cause-and-effect cost assignments can be established so that arbitrary apportionments are avoided. The approach is illustrated in Figure 11.1.

● **Describe the target costing approach to pricing.**

Target costing is the reverse of cost-plus pricing. With target costing the starting point is the determination of the target selling price – the price that customers are willing to pay for the product (or service). Next a target profit margin is deducted to derive a target cost. The target cost represents the estimated long-run cost of the product (or service) that enables the target profit to be achieved. Predicted actual costs are compared with the target cost and, where the predicted actual cost exceeds the target cost, intensive efforts are made through value engineering methods to achieve the target cost. If the target cost is not achieved the product/service is unlikely to be launched.

● **Describe the different cost-plus pricing methods for deriving selling prices.**

Different cost bases can be used for cost-plus pricing. Bases include direct variable costs, total direct costs, total direct and indirect costs (excluding higher level facility/business sustaining costs) and total cost based on an assignment of a share of all organizational costs to the product or service. Different percentage profit margins are added depending on the cost base that is used. If direct variable cost is used as the cost base, a high percentage margin will be added to provide a contribution to cover a share of all of those costs that are not included in the cost base plus profits. Alternatively if total cost is used as the cost base a lower percentage margin will be added to provide only a contribution to profits.

● **Explain the limitations of cost-plus pricing.**

Cost-plus pricing has three major limitations. First, demand is ignored. Secondly, the approach requires that some assumption be made about future volume prior to ascertaining the cost and calculating the cost-plus selling prices. This can lead to an increase in the derived cost-plus selling price when demand is falling and vice-versa. Thirdly, there is no guarantee that total sales revenue will be in excess of total costs even when each product is priced above 'cost'.

● **Justify why cost-plus pricing is widely used.**

There are several reasons why cost-plus pricing is widely used. First, it offers a means by which prices can be determined with ease and speed in organizations that produce hundreds of products. Cost-plus pricing is likely to be particularly applicable to those products that generate relatively minor revenues that are not critical to an organization's success. A second justification is that cost-based pricing methods may encourage price stability by enabling firms to predict the prices of their competitors. Also, target mark-ups can be adjusted upwards or downwards according to expected demand, thus ensuring that demand is indirectly taken into account.

● **Identify and describe the different pricing policies.**

Cost information is only one of the many variables that must be considered in the pricing decision. The final price that is selected will depend upon the pricing policy of a company. A price-skimming policy or a pricing penetration policy might be selected. A price-skimming policy attempts to charge high initial prices to exploit those sections of the market where demand is initially insensitive to pricing changes. In contrast, a penetration pricing policy is based on the concept of charging low prices initially with the intention of gaining rapid acceptance of the product (or service).

● **Additional learning objective presented in Appendix 11.1**

The appendix to this chapter includes an additional learning objective: to calculate the optimal selling price using differential calculus. This topic is included in the appendix because it is not included in the syllabus requirements of many courses. However, the examinations set by some professional accountancy bodies do require a knowledge of this topic. You should therefore check your course curriculum to ascertain whether you need to read Appendix 11.1

EXHIBIT 11.1 Surveys of practice

A survey of 187 UK organizations by Drury and Tayles (2006) indicated that 60 per cent used cost-plus pricing. Most of the organizations that used cost-plus pricing indicated that it was applied selectively. It accounted for less than 10 per cent of total sales revenues for 26 per cent of the respondents and more than 50 per cent for 39 per cent of the organizations. Most of the firms (85 per cent) used full cost and the remaining 15 per cent used direct cost as the pricing base. The survey also indicated that 74 per cent analyzed profits either by customers or customer categories. In terms of factors influencing the importance of cost-plus pricing a survey of UK and Australian companies by Guilding *et al.* (2005) reported that the intensity of competition was positively related to the importance of cost-plus pricing.

An earlier UK study by Innes and Mitchell (1995a) reported that 50 per cent of the respondents had used customer profitability analysis and a further 12 per cent planned to do so in the future. Of those respondents that ranked customer profitability 60 per cent indicated that the Pareto 80/20 rule broadly applied (that, is 20 per cent of the customers were generating 80 per cent of the profits).

Dekker and Smidt (2003) undertook a survey of 32 Dutch firms on the use of costing practices that resembled the Japanese target costing concept. They reported that 19 out of the 32 firms used these practices, although they used different names for them. Adoption was highest among assembling firms and was related to a competitive and unpredictable environment.

Appendix 11.1: Calculating optimal selling prices using differential calculus

The optimal output is determined at the point where marginal revenue equals marginal cost (see Chapter 2). The highest selling price at which the optimum output can be sold determines the optimal selling price. If demand and cost schedules are known, it is possible to derive simultaneously the optimum output level and selling price using differential calculus. Consider Example 11A.1.

The first step when calculating the optimum selling price is to calculate total cost and revenue functions. The total cost (TC) function is

$$TC = £700\ 000 + £70x$$

where x is the annual level of demand and output.

At present the selling price is £160 and demand is 10 000 units. Each increase or decrease in price of £2 results in a corresponding decrease or increase in demand of 500 units. Therefore, if the selling price were increased to £200, demand would be zero. To increase demand by one unit, selling price must be reduced by £0.004 (£2/500 units). Thus the maximum selling price (SP) for an output of x units is

$$SP = £200 - £0.004x$$

Assuming that the output demanded is 10 000 units SP = £200 − £0.004 (10 000) = £160. Therefore if demand is 10 000 units, the maximum selling price is £160, the same selling price given in Example 11A.1. We shall now use differential calculus to derive the optimal selling price:

$$TC = £700\ 000 + £70x$$
$$SP = £200 - £0.004x$$

Therefore total revenue (TR) for an output of x units $= £200x - £0.004x^2$

$$\text{marginal cost (MC)} = \frac{dTC}{dx} = £70$$

$$\text{marginal revenue (MR)} = \frac{dTR}{dx} = £200 - £0.008x$$

EXAMPLE 11A.1

A division within the Caspian Company sells a single product. Divisional fixed costs are £700 000 per annum and a variable cost of £70 is incurred for each additional unit produced and sold over a very large range of outputs. The current selling price for the product is £160, and at this price 10 000 units are demanded per annum. It is estimated that for each successive increase in price of £2 annual demand will be reduced by 500 units. Alternatively, for each £2 reduction in price demand will increase by 500 units.

Calculate the optimum output and price for the product assuming that if prices are set within each £2 range there will be a proportionate change in demand.

At the optimum output level

$$\frac{dTC}{dx} = \frac{dTR}{dx}$$

And so

$$£70 = £200 - £0.008x$$
$$x = 162\ 500 \text{ units}$$

The highest selling price at which this output can be sold is

$$SP = £200 - £0.004\ (16\ 250)$$

so

$$SP = £135$$

Thus optimum selling price and output are £135 and 162 500 units respectively.

For a more detailed example of setting optimal selling prices using differential calculus you should refer to Review problem 11.17 at the end of this chapter and to its solution.

Key terms and concepts

cost-plus pricing (p. 251)
customer profitability analysis
  (p. 260)
full cost (p. 249)
long-run cost (p. 249)

Pareto analysis (p. 261)
penetration pricing policy (p. 259)
price setters (p. 248)
price-skimming policy (p. 259)
price takers (p. 248)

product life cycle (p. 260)
target costing (p. 253)
target rate of return on invested
  capital (p. 258)

Recommended reading

Sizer (1989) has written extensively on pricing. His writings on this topic are still relevant today. You are recommended to read Chapters 11 and 12 of his book. These chapters focus on different pricing policies and the information that management requires to make sound pricing decisions. Few empirical studies have been undertaken on pricing decisions but one such study is that by Mills (1988). For an historical analysis of the allocation of common costs in pricing decisions you should refer to Burrows (1994). You should refer to Lucas (2003) for an evaluation of research supporting the accountants' and economists' respective positions to pricing. A more detailed description of target costing can be found in an article by Kato (1993) and a book written by Yoshikawa et al. (1993). For a survey of target costing in Dutch firms you should refer to Dekker and Smidt (2003).

Key examination points

Questions requiring the use of differential calculus are sometimes set by the professional accountancy examination bodies. You should refer to Review problems 11.17. Where demand information is given you should avoid calculating and recommending cost-plus selling prices. Wherever possible, incorporate estimated revenues and costs for different demand levels and recommend the saving price that yields the maximum profit. You should also be prepared to discuss the limitations of cost-plus pricing and indicate why it is widely used in spite of these limitations.

ASSESSMENT MATERIAL

The review questions are short questions that enable you to assess your understanding of the main topics included in the chapter. The numbers in parentheses provide you with the page numbers to refer to if you cannot answer a specific question.

The review problems are more complex and require you to relate and apply the content to various business problems. The problems are graded by their level of difficulty. Solutions to review problems that are not preceded by the term 'IM' are provided in a separate section at the end of the book. Solutions to problems preceded by the term 'IM' are provided in the *Instructor's Manual* accompanying this book and also on the lecturer's password protected section of the website www.drury-online.com. Additional review problems with fully worked solutions are provided in the *Student's Manual* that accompanies this book.

The website also includes over 30 case problems. A list of these cases is provided on pages 665–7. Several cases are relevant to the content of this chapter. Examples include Lynch Printers and Reichard Maschinen.

Review questions

11.1 Distinguish between a price taker and a price setter. *(p. 248)*
11.2 What costs are likely to be relevant for (a) a short-run pricing decision, and (b) a long-run pricing decision? *(pp. 248–51)*
11.3 What is meant by the term 'full cost'? *(p. 249)*
11.4 What is meant by cost-plus pricing? *(p. 251, p. 256)*
11.5 Distinguish between cost-plus pricing and target costing. *(p. 253)*
11.6 Describe the four stages involved with target costing. *(p. 253)*
11.7 What role does cost information play in price taking firms? *(p. 254)*
11.8 Describe the alternative cost bases that can be used with cost-plus pricing. *(pp. 257–58)*
11.9 What are the limitations of cost-plus pricing? *(pp. 258–59)*
11.10 Why is cost-plus pricing frequently used in practice? *(p. 259)*
11.11 Describe the different kinds of pricing policies that an organization can apply. *(pp. 259–60)*
11.12 Why is customer profitability analysis important? *(pp. 260–61)*

Review problems

11.13 Intermediate: Calculation of an optimal selling price. A company manufactures a single product, product Y. It has documented levels of demand at certain selling prices for this product as follows:

Demand	Selling price per unit	Cost per unit
Units	£	£
1100	48	24
1200	46	21
1300	45	20
1400	42	19

Required:
Using a tabular approach, calculate the marginal revenues and marginal costs for product Y at the different levels of demand, and so determine the selling price at which the company profits are maximized. *(10 marks)*
ACCA – Financial Information for Management

11.14 Intermediate: Calculation of different cost-plus prices. Albany has recently spent some time on researching and developing a new product for which they are trying to establish a suitable price. Previously they have used cost plus 20 per cent to set the selling price.

The standard cost per unit has been estimated as follows:

	£	
Direct materials		
Material 1	10	(4 kg at £2.50/kg)
Material 2	7	(1 kg at £7/kg)
Direct labour	13	(2 hours at £6.50/hour)
Fixed overheads	7	(2 hours at £3.50/hour)
	37	

Required:
a Using the standard costs calculate two different cost plus prices using two different bases and explain an advantage and disadvantage of each method. *(6 marks)*
b Give two other possible pricing strategies that could be adopted and describe the impact of each one on the price of the product. *(4 marks)*
ACCA Paper 1.2 – Financial Information for Management

11.15 Advanced: Limiting factor resource allocation and comparison of marginal revenue to determine optimum output and price.

a A manufacturer has three products, A, B, and C. Currently sales, cost and selling price details and processing time requirements are as follows:

	Product A	Product B	Product C
Annual sales (units)	6000	6000	750
Selling price (£)	20.00	31.00	39.00
Unit cost (£)	18.00	24.00	30.00
Processing time required per unit (hours)	1	1	2

The firm is working at full capacity (13 500 processing hours per year). Fixed manufacturing overheads are absorbed into unit costs by a charge of 200 per cent of variable cost. This procedure fully absorbs the fixed manufacturing overhead. Assuming that:

(i) processing time can be switched from one product line to another,
(ii) the demand at current selling prices is:

Product A	Product B	Product C
11 000	8 000	2 000

and

(iii) the selling prices are not to be altered. You are required to calculate the best production programme for the next operating period and to indicate the increase in net profit that this should yield. In addition identify the shadow price of a processing hour. *(11 marks)*

b A review of the selling prices is in progress and it has been estimated that, for each product, an increase in the selling price would result in a fall in demand at the rate of 2000 units for an increase of £1 and similarly, that a decrease of £1 would increase demand by 2000 units. Specifically the following price/demand relationships would apply:

Product A		Product B		Product C	
Selling price (£)	Estimated demand	Selling price (£)	Estimated demand	Selling price (£)	Estimated demand
24.50	2 000	34.00	2 000	39.00	2 000
23.50	4 000	33.00	4 000	38.00	4 000
22.50	6 000	32.00	6 000	37.00	6 000
21.50	8 000	31.00	8 000	36.00	8 000
20.50	10 000	30.00	10 000	35.00	10 000
19.50	12 000	29.00	12 000	34.00	12 000
18.50	14 000	28.00	14 000	33.00	14 000

From this information you are required to calculate the best selling prices, the revised best production plan and the net profit that this plan should produce.

(11 marks)

ACCA Level 2 Management Accounting

11.16 Advanced: Discussion of cost and revenue models. An essential aspect of financial and business planning is concerned with estimating costs and revenues and deciding the optimum output and price levels. A company produces a single product and operates in a market where it has to lower the sale price of all its units if it wishes to sell more. The company's costing and marketing departments currently use the following cost and revenue model (all output is sold in the current period):

Current Model:

Total Costs $= 5000 + 0.6x$
Total Revenue $= 20x - 0.01x^2$

Where $x =$ the number of units sold

The company has recently updated its cost and revenue model:

Revised model:

Total Costs $= 4750 + 0.8x$
Total Revenue $= 19x - 0.009x^2$

The acceptability of the current model and the proposed changes as a basis for profit planning and for monitoring performance is to be reviewed.

Required:

a Explain the structure of the current and the revised model.

(4 marks)

b It has been estimated that the revised model will result in an optimal output of 1011 units being produced and sold.
(i) Suggest two alternative ways of determining this optimal level of output. *(3 marks)*
(ii) Discuss the extent to which adherence to this output target is a satisfactory indicator of managerial performance. *(3 marks)*

c Name and comment on cost and revenue factors which should be considered in order to improve the validity of the model as a profit forecasting model. *(10 marks)*

ACCA P3 Performance Measurement

11.17 Advanced: Calculation of optimum selling price using differential calculus.

a Scott St Cyr wishes to decide whether to lease a new machine to assist in the manufacture of his single product for the coming quarter, and also to decide what price to charge for his product in order to maximize his profit (or minimize his loss).
In the quarter just ended his results were as follows:

	(£000)	(£000)
Sales (200 000 units)		600
Less: Cost of goods sold		
Production wages: fixed	20	
piecework	90	
	110	
Materials	400	
		510
Gross profit		90
Less royalties (£0.50 per unit sold)	100	
Less administration (fixed cost)	30	
		130
Loss		(40)

St Cyr expects that, during the coming quarter,
(i) fixed basic wages (£20 000), fixed administration costs (£30 000) and the royalty rate will not change;
(ii) the piecework rate will increase to £0.50 per unit.

Quality control is very difficult and a high proportion of material is spoiled. A new machine has become available that can be delivered immediately. Tests have shown that it will eliminate the quality control problems, resulting in a halving of the usage of materials. It cannot be bought but can be leased for £115 000 per quarter.

The product has a very short shelf life, and is produced only to order. St Cyr estimates that if he were to change the unit selling price, demand for the product would increase by 1000 units per quarter for each one penny (£0.01) decrease in the selling price (so that he would receive orders for 500 000 units if he were to offer them free of charge), and would decrease by 1000 units per quarter for each one penny (£0.01) increase in the unit selling price (so that at a price of £5 his sales would be zero).

You are required to advise Scott St Cyr whether, in the coming quarter, he should lease the new machine and also the price that he should charge for his product, in order to maximize his profit.

(15 marks)

b Christian Pass Ltd operates in an entirely different industry. However, it also produces to order, and carries no inventory.

Its demand function is estimated to be $P = 100 - 2Q$ (where P is the unit selling price in £ and Q is the quantity demanded in thousands of units).

Its total costs function is estimated to be $C = Q^2 + 10Q + 500$ (where C is the total cost in £000 and Q is as above).

You are required in respect of Christian Pass Ltd to
(i) calculate the output in units that will maximize total profit, and to calculate the corresponding unit selling price, total profit, and total sales revenue. *(5 marks)*
(ii) calculate the output in units that will maximize total revenues, and to calculate the corresponding unit selling price, total loss, and total sales revenue. *(5 marks)*

ICAEW Management Accounting

11.18 Intermediate: Discussion of marginal and absorption cost approaches to pricing. ML is an engineering company that specialises in providing engineering facilities to businesses that cannot justify operating their own facilities in-house. ML employs a number of engineers who are skilled in different engineering techniques that enable ML to provide a full range of engineering facilities to its customers. Most of the work undertaken by ML is unique to each of its customers, often requiring the manufacture of spare parts for its customers' equipment, or the building of new equipment from customer drawings. As a result most of ML's work is short-term, with some jobs being completed within hours while others may take a few days.

To date ML has adopted a cost plus approach to setting its prices. This is based upon an absorption costing system that uses machine hours as the basis of absorbing overhead costs into individual job costs. The Managing Director is concerned that over recent months ML has been unsuccessful when quoting for work with the consequence that there has been an increase in the level of unused capacity. It has been suggested that ML should adopt an alternative approach to its pricing based on marginal costing since *any price that exceeds variable costs is better than no work*.

Required:

With reference to the above scenario
(i) briefly explain absorption and marginal cost approaches to pricing;
(ii) discuss the validity of the comment *any price that exceeds variable costs is better than no work*. *(10 marks)*

CIMA P2 Management Accounting: Decision Management

11.19 Advanced. At one of its regular monthly meetings the board of Giant Steps Ltd was discussing its pricing and output policies. Giant Steps Ltd is a multi-product firm, operating in several distinct but related competitive markets. It aims to maximize profits.

You are required to comment critically and concisely on any four of the following six statements which were included in the taped record of the meeting:

a Profit is maximized by charging the highest possible price.

b The product manager's pricing policy should be to set a price which will maximize demand, by ensuring that contribution per unit is maximized.

c   Allocation of overheads and joint costs enables management to compare performance between products, projects, or divisions.

d   Allocation of overheads and joint costs is a way of accountants grabbing power and influence from marketing and production people.

e   Our management accounts must be consistent with our published external accounts, so we must follow SSAP 9 on overhead allocation.

f   Expenditure on Research and Development would be a past or sunk cost, and no matter what decision about output or price was eventually made it would have no bearing on the recovery of that expenditure.   *(12 marks)*

ICAEW Management Accounting

IM11.1 Advanced. A company supplying capital equipment to the engineering industry is part of a large group of diverse companies. It determines its tender prices by adding a standard profit margin as a percentage of its prime cost.

Although it is working at full capacity the group managing director considers the company's annual return on capital employed as inadequate.

You are required, as the group assistant management accountant, to provide him with the following information:

a   why the return-on-prime-cost (ROPC) approach to tendering would be likely to yield an inadequate return on capital employed;   *(7 marks)*

b   the steps involved in calculating a return on capital employed (ROCE) tendering rate for a particular contract;   *(7 marks)*

c   three problems likely to be encountered in meeting a pre-set profit target on a ROCE basis.   *(6 marks)*

CIMA P3 Management Accounting

IM11.2 Advanced. It has been stated that companies do not have profitable products, only profitable customers. Many companies have placed emphasis on the concept of Customer Account Profitability (CAP) analysis in order to increase their earnings and returns to shareholders. Much of the theory of CAP draws from the view that the main strategic thrust operated by many companies is to encourage the development and sale of new products to existing customers.

Requirements:

a   Briefly explain the concept of CAP analysis.   *(5 marks)*

b   Critically appraise the value of CAP analysis as a means of increasing earnings per share and returns to shareholders.   *(15 marks)*

CIMA Stage 4 Strategic Management Accounting and Marketing

IM11.3 Advanced: Discussion of pricing strategies. A producer of high quality executive motor cars has developed a new model which it knows to be very advanced both technically and in style by comparison with the competition in its market segment.

The company's reputation for high quality is well-established and its servicing network in its major markets is excellent. However, its record in timely delivery has not been so good in previous years, though this has been improving considerably.

In the past few years it has introduced annual variations/improvements in its major models. When it launched a major new vehicle some six years ago the recommended retail price was so low in relation to the excellent specification of the car that a tremendous demand built up quickly and a two-year queue for the car developed within six months. Within three months a second-hand model had been sold at an auction for nearly 50 per cent more than the list price and even after a year of production a sizeable premium above list price was being obtained.

The company considers that, in relation to the competition, the proposed new model will be as attractive as was its predecessor six years ago. Control of costs is very good so that accurate cost data for the new model are to hand. For the previous model, the company assessed the long-term targeted annual production level and calculated its prices on that basis. In the first year, production was 30 per cent of that total.

For the present model the company expects that the relationship between first-year production and longer-term annual production will also be about 30 per cent, though the absolute levels in both cases are expected to be higher than previously.

The senior management committee, of which you are a member, has been asked to recommend the pricing approach that the company should adopt for the new model.

You are required

a   to list the major pricing approaches available in this situation and discuss in some detail the relative merits and disadvantages to the company of each approach in the context of the new model;   *(15 marks)*

b   to recommend which approach you would propose, giving your reasons;   *(5 marks)*

c   to outline briefly in which ways, if any, your answers to (a) and (b) above would differ if, instead of a high quality executive car, you were pricing a new family model of car with some unusual features that the company might introduce.

(5 marks)

CIMA Stage 4 Management Accounting Decision Making

IM11.4 Advanced: Cost-plus and relevant cost information for pricing decisions. Josun plc manufactures cereal based foods, including various breakfast cereals under private brand labels. In March the company had been approached by Cohin plc, a large national supermarket chain, to tender for the manufacture and supply of a crunchy style breakfast cereal made from oats, nuts, raisins, etc. The tender required Josun to quote prices for a 1.5 kg packet at three different weekly volumes: 50 000, 60 000 and 70 000. Josun plc had, at present, excess capacity on some of its machines and could make a maximum of 80 000 packets of cereal a week.

Josun's management accountant is asked to prepare a costing for the Cohin tender. The company prepares its tender prices on the basis of full cost plus 15 per cent of cost as a profit margin. The full cost is made up of five elements: raw materials per packet of £0.30; operating wages £0.12 per packet; manufacturing overheads costed at 200 per cent of operating wages; administration and other corporate overheads at 100 per cent of operating wages; and packaging and transport costing £0.10 per packet. The sales manager has suggested that as an incentive to Cohin, the profit margin be cut on the 60 000 and 70 000 tenders by ½ per cent and 1 per cent to 14½ per cent and 14 per cent respectively. The manufacturing and administration overheads are forecast as fixed at £12 500 per week, unless output drops to 50 000 units or below per week, when a saving of £1000 per week can be made. If no contract is undertaken then all the manufacturing and administration overheads will be saved except for £600 per week. If the tender is accepted the volume produced and sold will be determined by the sales achieved by Cohin.

A week before the Cohin tender is to be presented for negotiation, Josun receives an enquiry from Stamford plc, a rival supermarket chain, to produce, weekly, 60 000 packets of a similar type of breakfast cereal of slightly superior quality at a price of £1.20 per 1.5 kg packet, the quality and mix of the cereal constituents being laid down by Stamford. This product will fill a gap in Stamford's private label range of cereals. The estimated variable costs for this contract would be: raw materials £0.40p per packet, operating labour £0.15 per packet and packaging and transport £0.12 per packet. None of the 80 000 weekly capacity could be used for another product if either of these contracts were taken up.

You are required to:

a   compute the three selling prices per packet for the Cohin tender using Josun's normal pricing method;   *(3 marks)*

b   advise Josun, giving your financial reasons, on the relative merits of the two contracts;   *(6 marks)*

c   discuss the merits of full-cost pricing as a method of arriving at selling prices;   *(5 marks)*

d   make recommendations to Josun as to the method it might use to derive its selling prices in future;   *(3 marks)*

e   calculate the expected value of each tender given the following information and recommend which potential customer should receive the greater sales effort. It is estimated that there is a 70 per cent chance of Stamford signing the contract for the weekly production of 60 000 packets, while there is a 20 per cent chance of Cohin not accepting the tender. It is also estimated that the probabilities of Cohin achieving weekly sales volumes of 50 000, 60 000 or 70 000 are 0.3, 0.5 and 0.2 respectively. The two sets of negotiations are completely independent of each other;

(4 marks)

f   provide, with reasons, for each of the two contracts under negotiation, a minimum and a recommended price that Josun could ask for the extra quantity that could be produced under each contract and which would ensure the full utilization of Josun's weekly capacity of 80 000 packets.   *(4 marks)*

ICAEW P2 Management Accounting

IM11.5 Advanced: Selection of optimal selling price based on demand and cost schedules. Sniwe plc intend to launch a commemorative product for the 2004 Olympic games onto the UK market commencing 1 August 2002. The product will have variable costs of £16 per unit.

Production capacity available for the product is sufficient for 2000 units per annum. Sniwe plc has made a policy decision to produce to the maximum available capacity during the year to 31 July 2003.

Demand for the product during the year to 31 July 2003 is expected to be price dependent, as follows:

Selling price per unit (£)	Annual sales (units)
20	2000
30	1600
40	1200
50	1100
60	1000
70	700
80	400

It is anticipated that in the year to 31 July 2004 the availability of similar competitor products will lead to a market price of £40 per unit for the product during that year.

During the year to 31 July 2004, Sniwe plc intend to produce only at the activity level required to enable them to satisfy demand, with stocks being run down to zero if possible. This policy is intended as a precaution against a sudden collapse of the market for the product by 31 July 2004.

Required:

(Ignoring tax and the time value of money.)

a   Determine the launch price at 1 August 2002 which will maximize the net benefit to Sniwe plc during the two year period to 31 July 2004 where the demand potential for the year to 31 July 2004 is estimated as (i) 3600 units and (ii) 1000 units.   *(12 marks)*

b   Identify which of the launch strategies detailed in (a)(i) and (a)(ii) above will result in unsold stock remaining at 31 July 2004. Advise management of the minimum price at which such unsold stock should be able to be sold in order to alter the initial launch price strategy which will maximize the net benefit to Sniwe plc over the life of the product.   *(6 marks)*

c   Comment on any other factors which might influence the initial launch price strategy where the demand in the year to 31 July 2004 is estimated at 1000 units.   *(4 marks)*

ACCA Level 2 Management Accounting

IM11.6 Advanced: Calculation of unit costs and optimum selling price. French Ltd is about to commence operations utilizing a simple production process to produce two products X and Y. It is the policy of French to operate the new factory at its maximum output in the first year of operations. Cost and production details estimated for the first year's operations are:

Product	Production resources per unit — Labour hours	Production resources per unit — Machine hours	Variable cost per unit — Direct labour (£)	Variable cost per unit — Direct materials (£)	Fixed production overheads directly attributable to product (£000)	Maximum production (000 units)
X	1	4	5	6	120	40
Y	8	2	28	16	280	10

There are also general fixed production overheads concerned in the manufacture of both products but which cannot be directly attributed to either. This general fixed production overhead is estimated at £720 000 for the first year of operations. It is thought that the cost structure of the first year will also be operative in the second year.

Both products are new and French is one of the first firms to produce them. Hence in the first year of operations the sales price can be set by French. In the second and subsequent years it is felt that the market for X

and Y will have become more settled and French will largely conform to the competitive market prices that will become established. The sales manager has researched the first year's market potential and has estimated sales volumes for various ranges of selling price. The details are:

Product X — Range of per unit sales prices (£) (£)	Product X — Sales volume (000)	Product Y — Range of per unit sales prices (£) (£)	Product Y — Sales volume (000)
Up to 24.00	36	Up to 96.00	11
24.01 to 30.00	32	96.01 to 108.00	10
30.01 to 36.00	18	108.01 to 120.00	9
36.01 to 42.00*	8	120.01 to 132.00	8
		132.01 to 144.00	7
		144.01 to 156.00*	5

*Maximum price.

The managing director of French wishes to ascertain the total production cost of X and Y as, he says, 'Until we know the per unit cost of production we cannot properly determine the first year's sales price. Price must always ensure that total cost is covered and there is an element of profit – therefore I feel that the price should be total cost plus 20 per cent. The determination of cost is fairly simple as most costs are clearly attributable to either X or Y. The general factory overhead will probably be allocated to the products in accordance with some measure of usage of factory resources such as labour or machine hours. The choice between labour and machine hours is the only problem in determining the cost of each product – but the problem is minor and so, therefore, is the problem of pricing.'

Required:

a   Produce statements showing the effect the cost allocation and pricing methods mentioned by the managing director will have on
(i)   unit costs,
(ii) closing stock values, and
(iii) disclosed profit for the first year of operation.   *(8 marks)*

b   Briefly comment on the results in (a) above and advise the managing director on the validity of using the per unit cost figures produced for pricing decisions.   *(4 marks)*

c   Provide appropriate statements to the management of French Ltd which will be of direct relevance in assisting the determination of the optimum prices of X and Y for the first year of operations. The statements should be designed to provide assistance in each of the following, separate, cases:
(i)   year II demand will be below productive capacity;
(ii) year II demand will be substantially in excess of productive capacity.

In both cases the competitive market sales prices per unit for year II are expected to be

X – £30 per unit
Y – £130 per unit

Clearly specify, and explain, your advice to French for each of the cases described.

(Ignore taxation and the time value of money.)   *(8 marks)*

ACCA P2 Management Accounting

IM11.7 Advanced: Calculation of optimal output level adopting a limiting factor approach and the computation of optimum selling prices using differential calculus. AB plc. makes two products, Alpha and Beta. The company made a £500 000 profit last year and proposes an identical plan for the coming year. The relevant data for last year are summarized in Table 1.

Table 1: Actuals for last year

	Product Alpha	Product Beta
Actual production and sales (units)	20 000	40 000
Total costs per unit	£20	£40
Selling prices per unit (25% on cost)	£25	£50
Machining time per unit (hours)	2	1
Potential demand at above selling prices (units)	30 000	50 000

Fixed costs were £480 000 for the year, absorbed on machining hours which were fully utilized for the production achieved.

A new Managing Director has been appointed and he is somewhat sceptical about the plan being proposed. Furthermore, he thinks that additional machining capacity should be installed to remove any production bottlenecks and wonders whether a more flexible pricing policy should be adopted.

Table 2 summarizes the changes in costs involved for the extra capacity and gives price/demand data, supplied by the Marketing Department, applicable to the conditions expected in the next period.

Table 2: Costs

Extra machining capacity would increase fixed costs by 10 per cent in total. Variable costs and machining times per unit would remain unchanged.

	Product Alpha	Product Beta
Price/demand data		
Price range (per unit)	£20–30	£45–55
Expected demand (000 units)	45–15	70–30

You are required to

a calculate the plan to maximize profits for the coming year based on the data and selling prices in Table 1; *(7 marks)*

b comment on the pricing system for the existing plan used in Table 1; *(3 marks)*

c calculate the best selling prices and production plan based on the data in Table 2; *(7 marks)*

d comment on the methods you have used in part (c) to find the optimum prices and production levels. *(3 marks)*

Any assumptions made must be clearly stated.

CIMA Stage 3 Management Accounting Techniques

IM11.8 Advanced: Calculation of optimum quantity and prices for joint products using differential calculus plus a discussion of joint cost allocations. Nuts plc produces alpha and beta in two stages. The separation process produces crude alpha and beta from a raw material costing £170 per tonne. The cost of the separation process is £100 per tonne of raw material. Each tonne of raw material generates 0.4 tonne of crude alpha and 0.6 tonne of crude beta. Neither product can be sold in its crude state.

The refining process costs £125 per tonne for alpha and £50 per tonne for beta; no weight is lost in refining. The demand functions for refined alpha and refined beta are independent of each other, and the corresponding price equations are:

$$P_A = 1250 - \frac{100Q_A}{32}$$

$$P_B = 666\frac{2}{3} - \frac{100Q_B}{18}$$

where P_A = price per tonne of refined alpha
P_B = price per tonne of refined beta
Q_A = quantity of refined alpha
Q_B = quantity of refined beta

The company is considering whether any part of the production of crude alpha or crude beta should be treated as a by-product. The by-product would be taken away free of charge by a large-scale pig farming enterprise.

Requirements

a If all the output of the separation process is refined and sold:
  (i) calculate the optimal quantity of raw material to be processed and the quantities and prices of the refined products, and
  (ii) determine the 'major' product which is worth refining and the 'minor' product which deserves consideration as a potential by-product, but do not attempt to calculate at this stage how much of the 'minor' product would be refined. *(10 marks)*

b Calculate:
  (i) the optimal quantity of the 'major' product which would be worth producing regardless of the value of the 'minor' product, and
  (ii) the quantity of the resulting 'minor' product that would be worth refining. *(6 marks)*

c Evaluate the principal methods and problems of joint-cost allocation for stock valuation, referring to Nuts plc where appropriate. *(9 marks)*

ICAEW P2 Management Accounting

IM11.9 Advanced: Calculation of optimum selling prices using differential calculus. Cassidy Computers plc sells one of its products, a plug-in card for personal computer systems, in both the UK and Ruritania. The relationship between price and demand is different in the two markets, and can be represented as follows:

Home market: Price (in £) = $68 - 8Q1$
Export market: Price (in $) = $110 - 10Q2$

where $Q1$ is the quantity demanded (in 000) in the home market and $Q2$ is the quantity demanded (in 000) in the export market. The current exchange rate is 2 Ruritanian dollars to the pound.

The variable cost of producing the cards is subject to economies of scale, and can be represented as:

Unit variable cost (in £) = $19 - Q$ (where $Q = Q1 + Q2$).

Requirements

a Calculate the optimum selling price and total contribution made by the product if it can be sold
  (i) only in the home market
  (ii) only in the export market
  (iii) in both markets. *(10 marks)*

b Calculate the optimum selling prices and total contribution made by the product if it can be sold in both markets, but subject to a constraint imposed by the Ruritanian government that the company can sell no more cards in Ruritania than it sells in its home market. How sensitive are the prices to be charged in each market and the total contribution, to changes in the exchange rate over the range $1 = £0.25 to $1 = £1.00? *(8 marks)*

c How does the volatility of foreign exchange rates affect the ways in which export sales are priced in practice? *(7 marks)*

ICAEW P2 Management Accounting

Decision-making under conditions of risk and uncertainty

12

In Chapters 8–11 we considered the use of a single representative set of estimates for predicting future costs and revenues when alternative courses of action are followed. For example, in Chapter 11 we used a single representative estimate of demand for each selling price. However, the outcome of a particular decision may be affected by an uncertain environment that cannot be predicted, and a single representative estimate does not therefore convey all the information that might reasonably influence a decision.

Let us now look at a more complicated example; consider a situation where a company has two mutually exclusive potential alternatives, A and B, which each yield receipts of £50 000. The estimated costs of alternative A can be predicted with considerable confidence, and are expected to fall in the range of £40 000–£42 000; £41 000 might be considered a reasonable estimate of cost. The estimate for alternative B is subject to much greater uncertainty, since this alternative requires high-precision work involving operations that are unfamiliar to the company's labour force. The estimated costs are between £35 000 and £45 000, but £40 000 is selected as a representative estimate. If we consider single representative estimates alternative B appears preferable, since the estimated profit is £10 000 compared with an estimated profit of £9000 for alternative A; but a different picture may emerge if we take into account the range of possible outcomes.

LEARNING OBJECTIVES

After studying this chapter, you should be able to:

- calculate and explain the meaning of expected values;

- explain the meaning of the terms standard deviation and coefficient of variation as measures of risk and outline their limitations;

- construct a decision tree when there is a range of alternatives and possible outcomes;

- describe and calculate the value of perfect and imperfect information;

- explain and apply the maximin, maximax and regret criteria;

- explain the implications of pursuing a diversification strategy.

Alternative A is expected to yield a profit of between £8000 and £10 000 whereas the range of profits for alternative B is between £5000 and £15 000. Management may consider it preferable to opt for a fairly certain profit of between £8000 and £10 000 for alternative A rather than take the chance of earning a profit of £5000 from alternative B (even though there is the possibility of earning a profit of £15 000 at the other extreme).

This example demonstrates that there is a need to incorporate the uncertainty relating to each alternative into the decision-making process, and in this chapter we shall consider the various methods of doing this.

Risk and uncertainty

A distinction is often drawn by decision theorists between risk and uncertainty. Risk is applied to a situation where there are several possible outcomes and there is relevant past experience to enable statistical evidence to be produced for predicting the possible outcomes. Uncertainty exists where there are several possible outcomes, but there is little previous statistical evidence to enable the possible outcomes to be predicted. Most business decisions can be classified in the uncertainty category, but the distinction between risk and uncertainty is not essential for our analysis and we shall use the terms interchangeably.

Probabilities

Because decision problems exist in an uncertain environment, it is necessary to consider those uncontrollable factors that are outside the decision-maker's control and that may occur for alternative courses of action. These uncontrollable factors are called events or states of nature. For example, in a product launch situation possible states of nature could consist of events such as a similar product being launched by a competitor at a lower price, at the same price, at a higher price or no similar product being launched.

The likelihood that an event or state of nature will occur is known as its probability, and this is normally expressed in decimal form with a value between 0 and 1. A value of 0 denotes a nil likelihood of occurrence whereas a value of 1 signifies absolute certainty – a definite occurrence. A probability of 0.4 means that the event is expected to occur four times out of ten. The total of the probabilities for events that can possibly occur must sum to 1.0. For example, if a tutor indicates that the probability of a student passing an examination is 0.7 then this means that the student has a 70 per cent chance of passing the examination. Given that the pass/fail alternatives represent an exhaustive listing of all possible outcomes of the event, the probability of not passing the examination is 0.3.

The information can be presented in a probability distribution. A probability distribution is a list of all possible outcomes for an event and the probability that each will occur. The probability distribution for the above illustration is as follows:

Outcome	Probability
Pass examination	0.7
Do not pass examination	0.3
Total	1.0

Some probabilities are known as objective probabilities because they can be established mathematically or compiled from historical data. Tossing a coin and throwing a die are examples of objective probabilities. For example, the probability of heads occurring when tossing a coin logically must be 0.5. This can be proved by tossing the coin many times and observing the results. Similarly, the probability of obtaining number 1 when a die is thrown is 0.166 (i.e. one-sixth).

This again can be ascertained from logical reasoning or recording the results obtained from repeated throws of the dice.

It is unlikely that objective probabilities can be established for business decisions, since many past observations or repeated experiments for particular decisions are not possible; the probabilities will have to be estimated based on managerial judgement. Probabilities established in this way are known as subjective probabilities because no two individuals will necessarily assign the same probabilities to a particular outcome. Subjective probabilities are based on an individual's expert knowledge, past experience, and observations of current variables which are likely to have an impact on future events. Such probabilities are unlikely to be estimated correctly, but any estimate of a future uncertain event is bound to be subject to error.

The advantage of this approach is that it provides more meaningful information than stating the most likely outcome. Consider, for example, a situation where a tutor is asked to state whether student A and student B will pass an examination. The tutor may reply that both students are expected to pass the examination. This is the tutor's estimate of the most likely outcome. However, the following probability distributions are preferable:

Outcome	Student A probability	Student B probability
Pass examination	0.9	0.6
Do not pass examination	0.1	0.4
Total	1.0	1.0

Such a probability distribution requires the tutor to specify the degree of confidence in his or her estimate of the likely outcome of a future event. This information is clearly more meaningful than a mere estimate of the most likely outcome that both students are expected to pass the examination, because it indicates that it is most unlikely that A will fail, whereas there is a possibility that B will fail. Let us now apply the principles of probability theory to business decision-making.

Probability distributions and expected value

The presentation of a probability distribution for each alternative course of action can provide useful additional information to management, since the distribution indicates the degree of uncertainty that exists for each alternative course of action. Probability distributions enable management to consider not only the possible profits (i.e. the payoff) from each alternative course of action but also the amount of uncertainty that applies to each alternative. Let us now consider the situation presented in Example 12.1.

From the probability distributions shown in Example 12.1 you will see that there is a 1 in 10 chance that profits will be £6000 for product A, but there is also a 4 in 10 chance that profits will be £8000. A more useful way of reading the probability distribution is to state that there is a 7 in 10 chance that profits will be £8000 or less. This is obtained by adding together the probabilities for profits of £6000, £7000 and £8000. Similarly, there is a 3 in 10 chance that profits will be £9000 or more.

Expected values

The expected value (sometimes called expected payoff) is calculated by weighting each of the profit levels (i.e. possible outcomes) in Example 12.1 by its associated probability. The sum of these weighted amounts is called the expected value of the probability distribution. In other words, the expected value is the weighted arithmetic mean of the possible outcomes. The expected values of £8000 and £8900 calculated for products A and B take into account a range of possible outcomes rather than using a *single most likely estimate*. For example, the single most likely estimate is the profit level with the highest probability attached to it. For both products A and B in Example 12.1 the single most likely estimate is £8000, which appears to indicate that we may be indifferent as to which product should be made. However the expected value calculation takes into account the possibility that a range of different profits are possible and weights these profits by the probability of their occurrence. The weighted calculation indicates that product B is expected to produce the highest average profits in the future.

The expected value of a decision represents the long-run average outcome that is expected to occur if a particular course of action is undertaken many times. For example, if the decision to make products A and B is repeated on, say, 100 occasions in the future then product A will be expected to give an average profit of £8000 whereas product B would be expected to give an average profit of £8900. The expected values are the averages of the possible outcomes based on management estimates. There is no guarantee that the actual outcome will equal the expected value. Indeed, the expected value for product B does not appear in the probability distribution.

EXAMPLE 12.1

A manager is considering whether to make product A or product B, but only one can be produced. The estimated sales demand for each product is uncertain. A detailed investigation of the possible sales demand for each product gives the following probability distribution of the profits for each product.

Product A probability distribution

(1)	(2)	(3)
	Estimated	Weighted
Outcome	probability	(col. 1 amount × col. 2)
		(£)
Profits of £6000	0.10	600
Profits of £7000	0.20	1400
Profits of £8000	0.40	3200
Profits of £9000	0.20	1800
Profits of £10 000	0.10	1000
	1.00	
	Expected value	8000

Product B probability distribution

(1)	(2)	(3)
	Estimated	Weighted
Outcome	probability	(col. 1 amount × col. 2)
		(£)
Profits of £4000	0.05	200
Profits of £6000	0.10	600
Profits of £8000	0.40	3200
Profits of £10 000	0.25	2500
Profits of £12 000	0.20	2400
	1.00	
	Expected value	8900

Which product should the company make?

Measuring the amount of uncertainty

In addition to the expected values of the profits for the various alternatives, management is also interested in the degree of uncertainty of the expected future profits. For example, let us assume that another alternative course of action, say, product C, is added to the alternatives in Example 12.1 and that the probability distribution is as follows:

Product C probability distribution

Outcome	Estimated probability	Weighted amount (£)
Loss of £4000	0.5	(2 000)
Profit of £22 000	0.5	11 000
	Expected value	9 000

Product C has a higher expected value than either product A or product B, but it is unlikely that management will prefer product C to product B, because of the greater variability of the possible outcomes. In other words, there is a greater degree of uncertainty attached to product C.

The conventional measure of the dispersion of a probability distribution is the standard deviation. The standard deviation (σ) is the square root of the mean of the squared deviations from the expected value and is calculated from the following formula:

$$\sigma = \sqrt{\sum_{x=1}^{n}(A_x - \overline{A})^2 P_x}\qquad(12.1)$$

where A_x are the profit-level observations, $\overline{A}$ is the expected or mean value, P_x is the probability of each outcome, and the summation is over all possible observations, where n is the total number of possibilities.

The calculations of the standard deviations for products A and B in Example 12.1 are set out in Exhibit 12.1. If we are comparing the standard deviations of two probability distributions with different expected values, we cannot make a direct comparison. Can you see why this should be so? Consider the following probability distribution for another product, say product D.

Product D probability distribution

Outcome	Estimated probability	Weighted amount (£)
Profits of £40 000	0.05	2 000
Profits of £60 000	0.10	6 000
Profits of £80 000	0.40	32 000
Profits of £100 000	0.25	25 000
Profits of £120 000	0.20	24 000
	Expected value	89 000

The standard deviation for product D is £21 424, but all of the possible outcomes are ten times as large as the corresponding outcomes for product B. The outcomes for product D also have the same pattern of probabilities as product B, and we might conclude that the two projects are equally risky. Nevertheless, the standard deviation for product D is ten times as large as that for product B. This scale effect can be removed be replacing the standard deviation with a relative measure of dispersion. The relative amount of dispersion can be expressed by the coefficient of variation, which is simply the standard deviation divided by the expected value. The coefficient of variation for product B is 2142.40/8900 = 0.241 (or 24.1 per cent), and for product D it is also 0.241 (21 424/89 000), thus indicating that the relative amount of dispersion is the same for both products.

Measures such as expected values, standard deviations or coefficient of variations are used to summarize the characteristics of alternative courses of action, but they are poor substitutes for representing the probability distributions, since they do not provide the decision-maker with all the relevant information. There is an argument for presenting the entire probability distribution directly to the decision-maker. Such an approach is appropriate when management must select one from a small number of alternatives, but in situations where many alternatives need to be considered the examination of many probability distributions is likely to be difficult and time-consuming. In such situations management may have no alternative but to compare the expected values and coefficients of variation.

EXHIBIT 12.1 Calculation of standard deviations

Product A

(1) Profit (£)	(2) Deviation from expected value, $A_x - \bar{A}$ (£)	(3) Squared deviation $(A_x - \bar{A})^2$ (£)	(4) Probability	(5) Weighted amount (col. 3 × col. 4) (£)
6 000	−2000	4 000 000	0.1	400 000
7 000	−1000	1 000 000	0.2	200 000
8 000	0	–	0.4	–
9 000	+1000	1 000 000	0.2	200 000
10 000	+2000	4 000 000	0.1	400 000
			Sum of squared deviations	1 200 000
			Standard deviation	£1 095.40
			Expected value	£8 000

Product B

(1) Profit (£)	(2) Deviation $A_x - \bar{A}$ (£)	(3) Squared deviation $(A_x - \bar{A})^2$ (£)	(4) Probability	(5) Weighted amount (col. 3 × col. 4) (£)
4 000	−4900	24 010 000	0.05	1 200 500
6 000	−2900	8 410 000	0.10	841 000
8 000	−900	810 000	0.40	324 000
10 000	1100	1 210 000	0.25	302 500
12 000	3100	9 610 000	0.20	1 922 000
			Sum of squared deviations	4 590 000
			Standard deviation	£2 142.40
			Expected value	£8 900

Attitudes to risk by individuals

How do we determine whether or not a risky course of action should be undertaken? The answer to this question depends on the decision-maker's attitude to risk. We can identify three possible attitudes: an aversion to risk, a desire for risk and an indifference to risk. Consider two alternatives, A and B, which have the following possible outcomes, depending on the state of the economy (i.e. the state of nature):

Possible returns

State of the economy	A (£)	B (£)
Recession	90	0
Normal	100	100
Boom	110	200

If we assume that the three states of the economy are equally likely then the expected value for each alternative is £100. A risk-seeker is one who, given a choice between more or less risky alternatives with identical expected values, prefers the riskier alternative (alternative B). Faced with the same choice, a risk-averter would select the less risky alternative (alternative A). The person who is indifferent to risk (risk neutral) would be indifferent to both alternatives because they have the same expected values. With regard to investors in general, studies of the securities markets provide convincing evidence that the majority of investors are risk-averse.

Let us now reconsider how useful expected value calculations are for choosing between alternative courses of action. Expected values represent a long-run average solution, but decisions should not be made on the basis of expected values alone, since they do not enable the decision-maker's attitude towards risk to be taken into account. Consider for example, a situation where two individuals play a coin-tossing game, with the loser giving the winner £5000. The expected value to the player who calls heads is as follows:

Outcome	Cash flow (£)	Probability	Weighted amount (£)
Heads	+5000	0.5	+2500
Tails	−5000	0.5	−2500
		Expected value	0

The expected value is zero, but this will not be the actual outcome if only one game is played. The expected-value calculation represents the average outcome only if the game is repeated on many occasions. However, because the game is to be played only once, it is unlikely that each player will find the expected value calculation on its own to be a useful calculation for decision-making. In fact, the expected value calculation implies that each player is indifferent to playing the game, but this indifference will only apply if the two players are neutral to risk. However, a risk-averter will find the game most unattractive. As most business managers are unlikely to be neutral towards risk, and business decisions are rarely repeated, it is unwise for decisions to be made solely on the basis of expected values. At the very least, expected values should be supplemented with measures of dispersion and, where possible, decisions should be made after comparing the probability distributions of the various alternative courses of action.

Decision tree analysis

In the examples earlier in this chapter we have assumed that profits were uncertain because of the uncertainty of sales demand. In practice, more than one variable may be uncertain (e.g. sales and costs), and also the value of some variables may be dependent on the values of other variables. Many outcomes may therefore be possible, and some outcomes may be dependent on previous outcomes. A useful analytical tool for clarifying the range of alternative courses of action and their possible outcomes is a decision tree.

A decision tree is a diagram showing several possible courses of action and possible events (i.e. states of nature) and the potential outcomes for each course of action. Each alternative course of action or event is represented by a branch, which leads to subsidiary branches for further courses of action or possible events. Decision trees are designed to illustrate the full range of alternatives and events that can occur, under all envisaged conditions. The value of a decision tree is that its logical analysis of a problem enables a complete strategy to be drawn up to cover all eventualities before a firm becomes committed to a scheme. Let us now consider Example 12.2. This will be used to illustrate how decision trees can be applied to decision-making under conditions of uncertainty.

The decision tree for Example 12.2 is set out in Figure 12.1. The boxes indicate the point at which decisions have to be taken, and the branches emanating from it indicate the available alternative courses of action. The circles indicate the points at which there are environmental changes that affect the consequences of prior decisions. The branches from these points indicate the possible types of environment (states of nature) that may occur.

Note that the joint probability of two events occurring together is the probability of one event times the probability of the other event. For example, the probability of the development effort succeeding and the product being very successful consists of the products of the probabilities of these two events, i.e. 0.75 times 0.4, giving a probability of 0.30. Similarly, the probability of the development effort being successful and the product being moderately successful is 0.225 (0.75 × 0.3). The total expected value for the decision to develop the product consists of the sum of all the items in the expected value column on the 'Develop product' branch of the decision tree, i.e. £49 500. If we assume that there are no other alternatives available, other than the decision not to develop, the expected value of £49 500 for developing the product can be compared with the expected value of zero for not developing the product. Decision theory would suggest that the product should be developed because a positive expected value occurs. However, this does not mean that an outcome of £49 500 profit is guaranteed. The expected-value calculation indicates

EXAMPLE 12.2

A company is considering whether to develop and market a new product. Development costs are estimated to be £180 000, and there is a 0.75 probability that the development effort will be successful and a 0.25 probability that the development effort will be unsuccessful. If the development is successful, the product will be marketed, and it is estimated that:

1 if the product is very successful profits will be £540 000;
2 if the product is moderately successful profits will be £100 000;
3 if the product is a failure, there will be a loss of £400 000.

Each of the above profit and loss calculations is after taking into account the development costs of £180 000. The estimated probabilities of each of the above events are as follows:

1 Very successful   0.4
2 Moderately successful 0.3
3 Failure   0.3

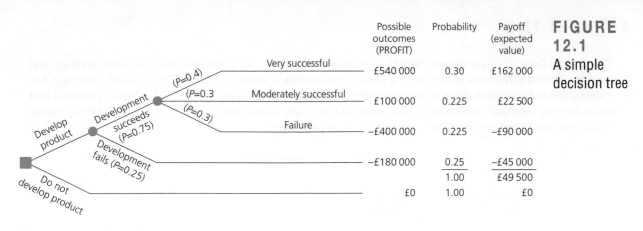

FIGURE
12.1
A simple
decision tree

■ Decision point ● Possible events

that if the probabilities are correct and this decision was repeated on many occasions an average profit of £49 500 would result.

Unfortunately, the decision will not be repeated on many occasions, and a run of repeated losses could force a company out of business before it has the chance to repeat similar decisions. Management may therefore prefer to examine the following probability distribution for developing the product shown in Figure 12.1:

Outcome	Probability
Loss of £400 000	0.225
Loss of £180 000	0.25
Profit of £100 000	0.225
Profit of £540 000	0.30

Management may decide that the project is too risky, since there is nearly a 0.5 probability of a loss occurring.

The decision tree provides a convenient means of identifying all the possible alternative courses of action and their interdependencies. This approach is particularly useful for assisting in the construction of probability distributions when many combinations of events are possible.

Buying perfect and imperfect information

When a decision-maker is faced with a series of uncertain events that might occur, he or she should consider the possibility of obtaining additional information about which event is likely to occur. This section considers how we can calculate the maximum amount it would be worth paying to acquire additional information from a particular source. The approach we shall take is to compare the expected value of a decision if the information is acquired against the expected value with the absence of the information. The difference represents the maximum amount it is worth paying for the additional information. Consider Example 12.3.

Without the additional information, machine A will be purchased using the expected-value decision rule. If the additional information is obtained then this will give a perfect prediction of the level of demand, and the size of the machine can be matched with the level of demand. Therefore if demand is predicted to be low, machine A will be purchased, whereas if demand is predicted to be high, machine B will be purchased. The revised expected value is

$$(0.5 \times £100\ 000) + (0.5 \times £200\ 000) = £150\ 000$$

EXAMPLE 12.3

The Boston Company must choose between one of two machines – machine A has low fixed costs and high unit variable costs whereas machine B has high fixed costs and low unit variable costs. Consequently, machine A is most suited to low-level demand whereas machine B is suited to high-level demand. For simplicity assume that there are only two possible demand levels – low and high – and the estimated probability of each of these events is 0.5. The estimated profits for each demand level are as follows:

	Low demand (£)	High demand (£)	Expected value (£)
Machine A	100 000	160 000	130 000
Machine B	10 000	200 000	105 000

There is a possibility of employing a firm of market consultants who would be able to provide a perfect prediction of the actual demand. What is the maximum amount the company should be prepared to pay the consultants for the additional information?

You can see that the expected value is calculated by taking the highest profit in the case of low and high demand. When the decision to employ the market consultants is being taken, it is not known which level of demand will be predicted. Therefore the best estimate of the outcome from obtaining the additional information is a 0.5 probability that it will predict a low demand and a 0.5 probability that it will predict a high demand. (These are the probabilities that are currently associated with low and high demand.)

The value of the additional information is ascertained by deducting the expected value without the market survey (£130 000) from the expected value with the survey (£150 000). Thus the additional information increases expected value from £130 000 to £150 000 and the expected value of perfect information is £20 000. As long as the cost of obtaining the information is less than £20 000, the firm of market consultants should be employed.

In the above illustration it was assumed that the additional information would give a 100 per cent accurate prediction of the expected demand. In practice, it is unlikely that *perfect* information is obtainable, but *imperfect* information (for example, predictions of future demand may be only 80 per cent reliable) may still be worth obtaining. However, the value of imperfect information will always be less than the value of perfect information except when both equal zero. This would occur where the additional information would not change the decision. Note that the principles that are applied for calculating the value of imperfect information are the same as those we applied for calculating the value of perfect information, but the calculations are more complex. For an illustration see Scapens (1991).

Maximin, maximax and regret criteria

In some situations it might not be possible to assign meaningful estimates of probabilities to possible outcomes. Where this situation occurs managers might use any of the following criteria to make decisions: maximin, maximax or the criterion of regret.

The assumption underlying the maximin criterion is that the worst possible outcome will always occur and the decision-maker should therefore select the largest payoff under this assumption. Consider the Boston Company in Example 12.3. You can see that the worst outcomes are £100 000 for machine A and £10 000 for machine B. Consequently, machine A should be purchased using the maximin decision rule.

The maximax criterion is the opposite of maximin, and is based on the assumption that the best payoff will occur. Referring again to Example 12.3, the highest payoffs are £160 000 for machine A and £200 000 for machine B. Therefore machine B will be selected under the maximax criterion.

The regret criterion is based on the fact that, having selected an alternative that does not turn out to be the best, the decision-maker will regret not having chosen another alternative when he or she had the opportunity. Thus if in Example 12.3 machine B has been selected on the assumption that the high level of demand would occur, and the high level of demand actually did occur, there would be no regret. However, if machine A has been selected, the company would lose £40 000 (£200 000 – £160 000). This measures the amount of the regret. Similarly, if machine A was selected on the assumption that demand would be low, and the low level of demand actually did occur, there would be no regret; but if machine B was selected, the amount of the regret would be £90 000 (£100 000 – £10 000). This information is summarized in the following regret matrix:

	State of nature	
	Low demand (£)	High demand (£)
Choose machine A	0	40 000
Choose machine B	90 000	0

The aim of the regret criterion is to minimize the maximum possible regret. The maximum regret for machine A is £40 000 while that for Machine B is £90 000. Machine A would therefore be selected using the regret criterion.

Risk reduction and diversification

It is unwise for a firm to invest all its funds in a single project, since an unfavourable event may occur that will affect this project and have a dramatic effect on the firm's total financial position. A better approach would be for the firm to adopt a diversification strategy and invest in a number of different projects. If this diversification strategy is followed, an unfavourable event that affects one project may have relatively less effect on the remaining projects and thus have only a small impact on the firm's overall financial position. That is, a firm should not put all of its eggs in one basket, but should try to minimize risk by spreading its investments over a variety of projects.

The objective in pursuing a diversification strategy is to achieve certain desirable characteristics regarding risk and expected return. Let us now consider Example 12.4. From Example 12.4 it can be seen that both the existing activities (umbrella manufacturing) and the proposed new project (ice-cream manufacturing) are risky when considered on their own, but when they are combined, the risk is eliminated because whatever the outcome the cash inflow will be £20 000. Example 12.4 tells us that we should not only consider the risk of individual projects but should also take into account how the risks of potential new projects and existing activities co-vary with each other. Risk is eliminated completely in Example 12.4 because perfect negative correlation (i.e. where the correlation coefficient is –1) exists between the cash flows of the proposed project and the cash flows of the existing activities. When the cash flows are perfectly positively correlated (where the correlation is +1), risk reduction cannot be achieved when the projects are combined. For all other correlation values risk reduction advantages can be obtained by investing in projects that are not perfectly correlated with existing activities.

The important point that emerges from the above discussion is that it is not the risk of individual projects in isolation that is of interest but rather the incremental risk that each project will contribute to the overall risk of the firm.

EXAMPLE 12.4

A firm which currently manufactures umbrellas is considering diversifying and investing in the manufacture of ice-cream. The predicted cash flows for the existing activities and the new project are shown below.

States of nature	Existing activities (Umbrella manufacturing) (£)	Proposed project (Ice-cream manufacturing) (£)	Combination of existing activities and the proposed project (£)
Sunshine	−40 000	+60 000	+20 000
Rain	+60 000	−40 000	+20 000

To simplify the illustration it is assumed that only two states of nature exist (rain or sunshine) and each has a probability of 0.5.

SUMMARY

The following items relate to the learning objectives listed at the beginning of the chapter.

● **Calculate and explain the meaning of expected values.**

The expected value is calculated by weighting each of the possible outcomes by its associated probability. The sum of these weighted outcomes is called the expected value of the probability distribution. In other words, the expected value is the weighted arithmetic mean of the possible outcomes.

● **Explain the meaning of the terms standard deviation and coefficient of variation as measures of risk and outline their limitations.**

Standard deviation measures the dispersion of the possible outcomes. It is an absolute measure. In contrast, the coefficient of variation is a relative measure derived from dividing the standard deviation by the expected value. Both measures attempt to summarize the risk associated with a probability distribution. They assume that risk is measured in terms of the spread of possible outcomes. Decision-makers are probably more interested in a downside measure of risk that measures the possibility of risk being less than the expected value. Because of this there are strong arguments for presenting the entire probability distribution to the decision-maker.

● **Construct a decision tree when there is a range of alternatives and possible outcomes.**

Where there are many possible outcomes for various alternatives, and some outcomes are dependent on previous outcomes, a decision tree is a useful analytical tool for clarifying the range of alternative courses of actions and their possible outcomes. A decision tree is a diagram that shows the possible courses of actions, the potential events (states of nature for each outcome) together with their potential outcomes and associated probabilities. A decision tree thus represents an analytical tool for deriving expected values and a probability distribution in more complex situations.

● **Describe and calculate the value of perfect and imperfect information.**

The value of perfect and imperfect information relates to determining the value of the maximum amount it is worth paying for additional information. The approach involves comparing the expected value of a decision if the information is acquired against the expected value with the absence of the information. The difference represents the maximum value that it is worth paying for the additional information. You should refer to the section in the chapter on buying perfect and imperfect information for an illustration of the calculation of the value of perfect information.

● **Explain and apply the maximin, maximax and regret criteria.**

In some situations it might not be possible to assign meaningful estimates of probabilities to possible outcomes. When this situation occurs either the maximin, maximax or regret criteria may be used. The maximin criterion assumes that the worst possible outcome will occur and that the decision should be based on the largest payoff under this assumption. The maximax is the opposite to maximin, and is based on the assumption that the best possible payoff will occur. The regret criterion is based on the fact that, having selected an alternative that does not turn out to be the best, the decision-maker will regret not having chosen another alternative when he or she had the opportunity. The aim is to minimize the maximum possible regret. The application of the criteria was illustrated using Example 12.3.

● **Explain the implication of pursuing a diversification strategy.**

The implication of diversification is that the degree of uncertainty attached to various alternatives should not be considered in isolation. Instead, how an alternative interacts with existing activities should be considered. The aim should be to measure incremental, rather than the total risk, of a project.

Key terms and concepts

coefficient of variation (p. 276)
decision tree (p. 278)
diversification strategy (p. 281)
events (p. 272)
expected value (p. 273)
expected value of perfect
    information (p. 280)
maximax criterion (p. 281)

maximin criterion (p. 280)
objective probabilities (p. 272)
probability (p. 272)
probability distribution (p. 272)
regret criterion (p. 281)
risk (p. 272)
risk-averter (p. 277)
risk neutral (p. 277)

risk-seeker (p. 277)
single most likely estimate (p. 274)
standard deviation (p. 274)
states of nature (p. 272)
subjective probabilities (p. 273)
uncertainty (p. 272)

Recommended reading

A more detailed treatment of decision trees can be found in Chapter 4 of Moore and Thomas (1991). For an explanation and illustration of how imperfect information can be valued you should refer to Chapter 7 of Scapens (1991).

Key examination points

When you are faced with problems requiring an evaluation of alternatives with uncertain outcomes, you should calculate expected values and present probability distributions.

Note that expected values on their own are unlikely to be particularly useful and there is a need to supplement this measure with a probability distribution. Avoid calculating standard deviations, since they are rarely required and are a poor substitute for probability distributions.

It is particularly important with this topic that you plan your answer carefully. Once you have started your answer, it is difficult to remedy the situation if you initially adopt the wrong approach. A rough sketch of a decision tree at the start of your answer will force you to analyze the problem and identify all the alternatives and possible outcomes.

Examination questions on this topic sometimes also include a requirement as to whether additional perfect information should be purchased. Do make sure that you understand how to calculate the value of perfect information.

ASSESSMENT MATERIAL

The review questions are short questions that enable you to assess your understanding of the main topics included in the chapter. The numbers in parentheses provide you with the page numbers to refer to if you cannot answer a specific question.

The review problems are more complex and require you to relate and apply the content to various business problems. The problems are graded by their level of difficulty. Solutions to review problems that are not preceded by the term 'IM' are provided in a separate section at the end of the book. Solutions to problems preceded by the term 'IM' are provided in the *Instructor's Manual* accompanying this book and also on the lecturer's password protected section of the website www.drury-online.com. Additional review problems with fully worked solutions are provided in the *Student's Manual* that accompanies this book.

Review questions

12.1 Distinguish between risk and uncertainty. *(p. 272)*
12.2 What is a probability distribution? *(p. 272)*
12.3 How do subjective probabilities differ from objective probabilities? *(pp. 272–73)*
12.4 Distinguish between expected value and the single most likely estimate. *(pp. 273–74)*
12.5 Distinguish between the standard deviation and the coefficient of variation. *(pp. 275–76)*
12.6 What are the disadvantages of the standard deviation as a measure of risk? *(p. 276)*
12.7 What is a decision tree and what purpose does it serve? *(pp. 278–79)*
12.8 What is the expected value of perfect information and how can it be determined? *(pp. 279–80)*
12.9 Distinguish between maximin, maximax and regret criteria. When might it be appropriate to apply these criteria? *(pp. 280–81)*
12.10 How does diversification impact on measuring risk? *(pp. 281–82)*

Review problems

12.11 Intermediate. Darwin uses decision tree analysis in order to evaluate potential projects. The company has been looking at the launch of a new product which it believes has a 70 per cent probability of success. The company is, however, considering undertaking an advertising campaign costing £50 000, which would increase the probability of success to 95 per cent.

If successful the product would generate income of £200 000 otherwise £70 000 would be received.

What is the maximum that the company would be prepared to pay for the advertising?

a £32 500
b £29 000
c £17 500
d £50 000.

ACCA Paper 1.2 – Financial Information for Management

12.12 Intermediate. A company uses decision tree analysis to evaluate potential options. The management accountant for the company has established the following:

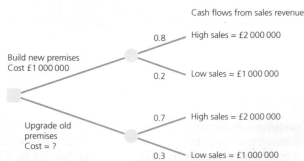

What would be the cost of the upgrade that would make the company financially indifferent between building new premises and upgrading the old one?

a £100 000
b £900 000
c £1 000 000
d £1 700 000

ACCA Paper 1.2 – Financial Information for Management

12.13 Intermediate. A company expects to sell 1000 units per month of a new product but there is uncertainty as to both the unit selling price and the unit variable cost of the product. The following estimates of selling price, variable costs and their related probabilities have been made:

Selling Price		Unit Variance Cost	
£ per unit	Probability	£ per unit	Probability
20	25%	8	20%
25	40%	10	50%
30	35%	12	30%

There are specific fixed costs of £5000 per month expected for the new product.

The expected value of monthly contribution is:

a £5,890
b £10,300
c £10,890
d £15,300

12.14 Intermediate. Use the data presented in 12.13. The probability of the monthly contribution from the new product exceeding £13,500 is:

a 24.5%
b 30.5%
c 63.0%
d 92.5%

CIMA P2 Management Accounting: Decision Management

12.15 Intermediate. A baker is trying to decide the number of batches of a particular type of bread that he should bake each day. Daily demand ranges from 10 batches to 12 batched. Each batch of bread that is baked and sold yields a positive contribution of £50, but each batch of bread baked that is not sold yields a negative contribution of £20.

Assuming the baker adopts the *minimax regret* decision rule, calculate the number of batches of bread that he should bake each day. You must justify your answer. *(4 marks)*

CIMA P2 Management Accounting: Decision Management

12.16 Advanced: Expected values, probability distributions and regret criterion. Central Ltd has developed a new product, and is currently considering the marketing and pricing policy it should employ for this. Specifically, it is considering whether the sales price should be set at £15 per unit or at the higher level of £24 per unit. Sales volumes at these two prices are shown in the following table:

Sales price £15 per unit		Sales price £24 per unit	
Forecast sales volume (000)	Probability	Forecast sales volume (000)	Probability
20	0.1	8	0.1
30	0.6	16	0.3
40	0.3	20	0.3
		24	0.3

The fixed production costs of the venture will be £38 000.

The level of the advertising and publicity costs will depend on the sales price and the market aimed for. With a sales price of £15 per unit, the advertising and publicity costs will amount to £12 000. With a sales price of £24 per unit, these costs will total £122 000.

Labour and variable overhead costs will amount to £5 per unit produced. Each unit produced requires 2 kg of raw material and the basic cost is expected to be £4 per kg. However, the suppliers of the raw materials are prepared to lower the price in return for a firm agreement to purchase a guaranteed minimum quantity. If Central Ltd contracts to purchase at least 40 000 kg then the price will be reduced to £3.75 per kg for *all* purchases. If Central contracts to purchase a minimum of 60 000 kg then the price will be reduced to £3.50 per kg for all purchases. It is only if Central Ltd guarantees either of the above minimum levels of purchases in advance that the appropriate reduced prices will be operative.

If Central Ltd were to enter into one of the agreements for the supply of raw material and was to find that it did not require to utilize the entire quantity of materials purchased then the excess could be sold. The sales price will depend upon the quantity that is offered for sale. If 16 000 kg or more are sold, the sales price will be £2.90 per kg for all sales. If less than 16 000 kg are offered, the sales price will be only £2.40 per kg.

Irrespective of amount sold, the costs incurred in selling the excess raw materials will be, per kg, as follows:

Packaging	£0.30
Delivery	£0.45
Insurance	£0.15

Central's management team feels that losses are undesirable, while high expected money values are desirable. Therefore it is considering the utilization of a formula that incorporated both aspects of the outcome to measure the desirability of each strategy. The formula to be used to measure the desirability is:

$$desirability = L + 3E$$

where L is the lowest outcome of the strategy and E is the expected monetary value of the strategy. The higher this measures, the more desirable the strategy.

The marketing manager seeks the advice of you, the management accountant, to assist in deciding the appropriate strategy. He says 'we need to make two decisions now:

(i) Which price per unit should be charged: £15 or £24?

(ii) Should all purchases of raw materials be at the price of £4 per kg, or should we enter into an agreement for a basic minimum quantity? If we enter into an agreement then what minimum level of purchases should we guarantee?

As you are the management accountant, I expect you to provide me with some useful relevant figures.'

Required:

  a   Provide statements that show the various expected outcomes of each of the choices open to Central Ltd. *(10 marks)*

  b   Advise on its best choice of strategies if Central Ltd's objective is

    (i)   to maximize the expected monetary value of the outcomes;

    (ii)   to minimize the harm done to the firm if the worst outcome of each choice were to eventuate;

    (iii)   to maximize the score on the above mentioned measure of desirability. *(6 marks)*

  c   Briefly comment on either

    (i)   two other factors that may be relevant in reaching a decision; OR

    (ii)   the decision criteria utilized in (b) above. *(4 marks)*

ACCA P2 Management Accounting

12.17 Advanced: Expected values, maximin criterion and value of perfect information. Recyc plc is a company which reprocesses factory waste in order to extract good quality aluminium. Information concerning its operations is as follows:

(i) Recyc plc places an advance order each year for chemical X for use in the aluminium extraction process. It will enter into an advance contract for the coming year for chemical X at one of three levels – high, medium or low, which correspond to the requirements of a high, medium or low level of waste available for reprocessing.

(ii) The level of waste available will not be known when the advance order for chemical X is entered into. A set of probabilities have been estimated by management as to the likelihood of the quantity of waste being at a high, medium or low level.

(iii) Where the advance order entered into for chemical X is lower than that required for the level of waste for processing actually received, a discount from the original demand price is allowed by the supplier for the total quantity of chemical X actually required.

(iv) Where the advance order entered into for chemical X is in excess of that required to satisfy the actual level of waste for reprocessing, a penalty payment in excess of the original demand price is payable for the total quantity of chemical X actually required.

A summary of the information relating to the above points is as follows:

Level of reprocessing	Waste available (000 kg)	Probability	Chemical X costs per kg		
			Advance order (£)	Conversion discount (£)	Conversion premium (£)
High	50 000	0.30	1.00		
Medium	38 000	0.50	1.20		
Low	30 000	0.20	1.40		
Chemical X: order conversion:					
Low to medium				0.10	
Medium to high				0.10	
Low to high				0.15	
Medium to low					0.25
High to medium					0.25
High to low					0.60

Aluminium is sold at £0.65 per kg. Variable costs (excluding chemical X costs) are 70 per cent of sales revenue.

Aluminium extracted from the waste is 15 per cent of the waste input. Chemical X is added to the reprocessing at the rate of 1 kg per 100 kg of waste.

Required:

  a   Prepare a summary which shows the budgeted contribution earned by Recyc plc for the coming year for each of nine possible outcomes. *(14 marks)*

  b   On the basis of maximizing expected value, advise Recyc plc whether the advance order for chemical X should be at low, medium or high level. *(3 marks)*

  c   State the contribution for the coming year which corresponds to the use of (i) maximax and (ii) maximin decision criteria, and comment on the risk preference of management which is indicated by each. *(6 marks)*

  d   Recyc plc are considering employing a consultant who will be able to say with certainty in advance of the placing of the order for chemical X, which level of waste will be available for reprocessing.

On the basis of expected value, determine the maximum sum which Recyc plc should be willing to pay the consultant for this information. *(6 marks)* e   Explain and comment on the steps involved in evaluating the purchase of imperfect information from the consultant in respect of the quantity of waste which will be available for reprocessing.

(6 marks)

ACCA Paper 9 Information for Control and Decision Making

12.18 Advanced: Decision tree, expected value and maximin criterion.

a   The Alternative Sustenance Company is considering introducing a new franchised product, Wholefood Waffles.

Existing ovens now used for making some of the present 'Half-Baked' range of products could be used instead for baking the Wholefood Waffles. However, new special batch mixing equipment would be needed. This cannot be purchased, but can be hired from the franchiser in three alternative specifications, for batch sizes of 200, 300 and 600 units respectively. The annual cost of hiring the mixing equipment would be £5000, £15 000 and £21 500 respectively.

The 'Half-Baked' product which would be dropped from the range currently earns a contribution of £90 000 per annum, which it is confidently expected could be continued if the product were retained in the range.

The company's marketing manager considers that, at the market price for Wholefood Waffles of £0.40 per unit, it is equally probable that the demand for this product would be 600 000 or 1 000 000 units per annum.

The company's production manager has estimated the variable costs per unit of making Wholefood Waffles and the probabilities of those costs being incurred, as follows:

Batch size: Cost per unit (pence)	200 units Probability if annual sales are either 600 000 or 1 000 000 units	300 units Probability if annual sales are either 600 000 or 1 000 000 units	600 units Probability if annual sales are 600 000 units	600 units Probability if annual sales are 1 000 000
£0.20	0.1	0.2	0.3	0.5
£0.25	0.1	0.5	0.1	0.2
£0.30	0.8	0.3	0.6	0.3

You are required:

(i) to draw a decision tree setting out the problem faced by the company,   *(12 marks)*

(ii) to show in each of the following three independent situations which size of mixing machine, if any, the company should hire:

(1) to satisfy a 'maximin' (or 'minimax' criterion),

(2) to maximize the expected value of contribution per annum,

(3) to minimize the probability of earning an annual contribution of less than £100 000.   *(7 marks)*

b   You are required to outline briefly the strengths and limitations of the methods of analysis which you have used in part (a) above.

(6 marks)

ICAEW Management Accounting

IM12.1 Advanced: Preparation of project statements for different demand levels and calculations of expected profit. Seeprint Limited is negotiating an initial one year contract with an important customer for the supply of a specialized printed colour catalogue at a fixed contract price of £16 per catalogue. Seeprint's normal capacity for producing such catalogues is 50 000 per annum.

Last year Seeprint Limited earned £11 000 profit per month from a number of small accounts requiring specialized colour catalogues. If the contract under negotiation is not undertaken, then a similar profit might be obtained from these customers next year, but, if it is undertaken, there will be no profit from such customers.

The estimated costs of producing colour catalogues of a specialized nature are given below.

The costs below are considered certain with the exception of the direct materials price.

Cost data:

	(£)
Variable costs per catalogue	
Direct materials	4.50
Direct wages	3.00
Direct expenses	1.30

	Output levels (capacity utilization)		
Semi-variable costs	80% (£)	100% (£)	120% (£)
Indirect materials	46 800	47 000	74 400
Indirect wages	51 200	55 000	72 000
Indirect expenses	6 000	8 000	9 600

Estimated fixed costs per annum:

Depreciation of specialist equipment	£8 000
Supervisory and management salaries	£20 000
Other fixed costs allocated to specialist colour catalogues production	£32 000

You are required to:

a   Tabulate the costs and profits per unit and in total and the annual profits, assuming that the contract orders in the year are: (i) 40 000, (ii) 50 000 and (iii) 60 000 catalogues, at a direct material cost of £4.50 per catalogue. Comment on the tabulation you have prepared.   *(10 marks)*

b   Calculate the expected profit for the year if it is assumed that the probability of the total order is:

0.4 for 40 000 catalogues
0.5 for 50 000 catalogues
0.1 for 60 000 catalogues

and that the probability of direct material cost is:

0.5 at £4.50 per catalogue
0.3 at £5.00 per catalogue
0.2 at £5.50 per catalogue.   *(6 marks)*

c   Discuss the implications for Seeprint Limited of the acceptance or otherwise of the contract with the important customer.

(6 marks)

ACCA Level 2 Management Accounting

IM12.2 Advanced: CVP analysis and uncertainty. The accountant of Laburnum Ltd is preparing documents for a forthcoming meeting of the budget committee. Currently, variable cost is 40 per cent of selling price and total fixed costs are £40 000 per year.

The company uses an historical cost accounting system. There is concern that the level of costs may rise during the ensuing year and the chairman of the budget committee has expressed interest in a probabilistic approach to an investigation of the effect that this will have on historic cost profits. The accountant is attempting to prepare the documents in a way which will be most helpful to the committee members. He has obtained the following estimates from his colleagues:

	Average inflation rate over ensuing year	Probability
Pessimistic	10%	0.4
Most likely	5%	0.5
Optimistic	1%	0.1
		1.0

	Demand at current selling prices	Probability
Pessimistic	£50 000	0.3
Most likely	£75 000	0.6
Optimistic	£100 000	0.1
		1.0

The demand figures are given in terms of sales value at the current level of selling prices but it is considered that the company could adjust its selling prices in line with the inflation rate without affecting customer demand in real terms.

Some of the company's fixed costs are contractually fixed and some are apportionments of past costs; of the total fixed costs, an estimated 85 per cent will remain constant irrespective of the inflation rate.

You are required to analyze the foregoing information in a way which you consider will assist management with its budgeting problem. Although you should assume that the directors of Laburnum Ltd are solely interested in the effect of inflation on historic cost profits, you should comment on the validity of the accountant's intended approach. As part of your analysis you are required to calculate:

(i) the probability of at least breaking even, and

(ii) the probability of achieving a profit of at least £20 000.

(16 marks)
ACCA Level 2 Management Accounting

IM12.3 Advanced: Output decision based on expected values. A ticket agent has an arrangement with a concert hall that holds pop concerts on 60 nights a year whereby he receives discounts as follows per concert:

For purchase of:	He receives a discount of:
200 tickets	20%
300 tickets	25%
400 tickets	30%
500 tickets or more	40%

Purchases must be in full hundreds. The average price per ticket is £3.

He must decide in advance each year the number of tickets he will purchase. If he has any tickets unsold by the afternoon of the concert he must return them to the box office. If the box office sells any of these he receives 60 per cent of their price.

His sales records over a few years show that for a concert with extremely popular artistes he can be confident of selling 500 tickets, for one with lesser known artistes 350 tickets, and for one with relatively unknown artistes 200 tickets.

His records also show that 10 per cent of tickets he returns are sold by the box office.

His administration costs incurred in selling tickets are the same per concert irrespective of the popularity of the artistes.

There are two possible scenarios in which his sales records can be viewed:

Scenario 1: that, on average, he can expect concerts with lesser known artistes

Scenario 2: that the frequency of concerts will be:

	(%)
with popular artistes	45
with lesser known artistes	30
with unknown artistes	25
	100

You are required to calculate:

a   separately for each of Scenarios 1 and 2:
   (a) the expected demand for tickets per concert;
   (b) (i)   the level of his purchases of tickets per concert that will give him the largest profit over a long period of time;
       (ii) the profit per concert that this level of purchases of tickets will yield;

b   for Scenario 2 only: the maximum sum per annum that the ticket agent should pay to a pop concert specialist for 100 per cent correct predictions as to the likely success of each concert.

(25 marks)
CIMA P3 Management Accounting

IM12.4 Advanced: Contracting hotel accommodation based on uncertain demand. Crabbe, the owner of the Ocean Hotel, is concerned about the hotel's finances and has asked your advice. He gives you the following information:

We have rooms for 80 guests. When the hotel is open, whatever the level of business, we have to meet the following each month:

	(£)
Staff wages and benefits	12 500
General overheads (rates, electricity, etc)	8 000
Depreciation	2 200
Interest on mortgage and bank loan	1 800
Repayments on mortgage and bank loan	2 500
Drawings for my own needs	1 000
	28 000

'For our normal business we charge an average of £20 per night for each guest. Each guest-night involves variable costs of £4 for laundry and cleaning. Guests also spend money in the restaurant, which on average brings us another £5 per guest-night after meeting variable costs.

'I need advice on two problems; one concerns the month of September and the other relates to the winter.

(1) 'Normal business in September will depend on weather conditions, and the probabilities of occupancy from normal business are:

	For month of September		
Weather condition	A	B	C
Probability	0.3	0.4	0.3
Occupancy (total guest-nights)	1440	1680	1920

'Airtravel Tours has enquired about a block booking at a discount in September. I intend to quote a discount of 40 per cent on our normal guest-night charge. In the restaurant Airtravels package tourists will only bring us £3 per guest-night after variable costs. Airtravel could take all our capacity, but I have to decide how many guest-nights to offer. The contract will mean that I agree in advance to take the same number of Airtravel tourists every night throughout September. If they won't accept my price, I would be prepared to go as far as a 60 per cent discount.

(2) 'When we come to the winter, trade is usually so bad that we close for three months. We retain only a skeleton staff, costing £1500 per month, and general overheads are reduced from £8000 to £2000. I am trying to find ways of keeping open this winter, but staying open will incur the full monthly outgoings.

'If we remained open for all three months I estimate our basic winter trade at reduced prices, together with income from conferences, would be as follows:

	Average number of guests per night	Charge per guest-night (£)	Restaurant revenue per guest-night net of variable costs (£)
Basic winter trade	12	14	5
Conferences, etc.	30	13	4

'Alternatively, I am considering offering a series of language courses. We could not take any other guests, and I estimate the total demand for the three months as follows:

Market condition	X	Y	Z
Probability	0.3	0.4	0.3
Occupancy (total guest-nights)	2160	4320	6480

'If the courses are offered we shall have to run them for the full three months irrespective of the take-up. The charge per night would be £24, and the revenue from the restaurant net of variable cost would only be £1 per guest-night.

We would have to spend about £5000 per month on tutors, and the courses would also have to be advertised beforehand at a cost of £1500.'

Assume 30-day months throughout.

Requirements:

a   Calculate the number of guest-nights Crabbe should contract to Airtravel Tours at the quoted 40 per cent discount. *(6 marks)*

b   Determine the minimum price per guest-night at which it would be worthwhile for Crabbe to do business with Airtravel, and the maximum number of guest-nights it would be worthwhile to contract at this price. *(4 marks)*

c   Assess which of the winter options Crabbe should undertake and state any reservation you may have about your assessment. *(9 marks)*

d   Briefly explain the criteria on which you have identified costs to assess Crabbe's business options in requirements (a) to (c). *(6 marks)*

ICAEW P2 Management Accounting

IM12.5 Advanced: Pricing and purchase conract decisions based on uncertain demand and calculation of maximum price to pay for perfect information. Z Ltd is considering various product pricing and material purchasing options with regard to a new product it has in development. Estimates of demand and costs are as follows:

If selling price per unit is		£15 per unit	£20 per unit
Forecasts	Probability	Sales volume (000 units)	Sales volume (000 units)
Optimistic	0.3	36	28
Most likely	0.5	28	23
Pessimistic	0.2	18	13
Variable manufacturing costs (excluding materials) per unit		£3	£3
Advertising and selling costs		£25 000	£96 000
General fixed costs		£40 000	£40 000

Each unit requires 3kg of material and because of storage problems any unused material must be sold at £1 per kg. The sole suppliers of the material offer three purchase options, which must be decided at the outset, as follows:

(i) any quantity at £3 per kg, or
(ii) a price of £2.75 per kg for a minimum quantity of 50 000 kg, or
(iii) a price of £2.50 per kg for a minimum quantity of 70 000 kg.

You are required, assuming that the company is risk neutral, to

a prepare calculations to show what pricing and purchasing decisions the company should make, clearly indicating the recommended decisions;   *(15 marks)*

b calculate the maximum price you would pay for perfect information as to whether the demand would be optimistic or most likely pessimistic.   *(5 marks)*

CIMA Stage 3 Management Accounting Techniques

IM12.6 Advanced: Selling price decision based on expected values and value of additional information. Warren Ltd is to produce a new product in a short-term venture which will utilize some obsolete materials and expected spare capacity. The new product will be advertised in quarter I with production and sales taking price in quarter II. No further production or sales are anticipated.

Sales volumes are uncertain but will, to some extent, be a function of sales price. The possible sales volumes and the advertising costs associated with each potential sales price are as follows:

Sales price £20 per unit		Sales price £25 per unit		Sales price £40 per unit	
Sales volume units (000)	Probability	Sales volume units (000)	Probability	Sales volume units (000)	Probability
4	0.1	2	0.1	0	0.2
6	0.4	5	0.2	3	0.5
8	0.5	6	0.2	10	0.2
		8	0.5	15	0.1

Advertising costs	£20 000	£50 000	£100 000

The resources used in the production of each unit of the product are:

Production labour:	grade 1	2 hours
	grade 2	1 hour
Materials: X	1 unit	
Y	2 units	

The normal cost per hour of labour is

grade 1	£2
grade 2	£3

However, before considering the effects of the current venture, there is expected to be 4000 hours of idle time for each grade of labour in quarter II. Idle time is paid at the normal rates.

Material X is in stock at a book value of £8 per unit, but is widely used within the firm and any usage for the purposes of this venture will require replacing. Replacement cost is £9 per unit.

Material Y is obsolete stock. There are 16 000 units in stock at a book value of £3.50 per unit and any stock not used will have to be disposed of at a cost, to Warren, of £2 per unit. Further quantities of Y can be purchased for £4 per unit.

Overhead recovery rates are
Variable overhead   £2 per direct labour hour worked
Fixed overhead   £3 per direct labour hour worked

Total fixed overheads will not alter as a result of the current venture.

Feedback from advertising will enable the exact demand to be determined at the end of quarter I and production in quarter II will be set to equal that demand. However, it is necessary to decide now on the sales price in order that it can be incorporated into the advertising campaign.

Required:
a Calculate the expected money value of the venture at each sales price and on the basis of this advise Warren of its best course of action.   *(12 marks)*
b Briefly explain why the management of Warren might rationally reject the sales price leading to the highest expected money value and prefer one of the other sales prices.   *(4 marks)*

c It will be possible, for the sales price of £40 per unit only, to ascertain which of the four levels of demand will eventuate. If the indications are that the demand will be low then the advertising campaign can be cancelled at a cost of £10 000 but it would then not be possible to continue the venture at another sales price. This accurate information concerning demand will cost £5000 to obtain.

Indicate whether it is worthwhile obtaining the information and ascertain whether it would alter the advice given in (a) above.   *(4 marks)*

ACCA Level 2 Management Accounting

IM12.7 Advanced: Hire of machine based on uncertain demand and value of perfect information. The Ruddle Co. Ltd had planned to install and, with effect from next April, commence operating sophisticated machinery for the production of a new product – product Zed. However, the supplier of the machinery has just announced that delivery of the machinery will be delayed by six months and this will mean that Ruddle will not now be able to undertake production using that machinery until October.

'The first six months of production' stated the commercial manager of Ruddle 'is particularly crucial as we have already contracted to supply several national supermarket groups with whatever quantities of Zed they require during that period at a price of £40 per unit. Their demand is, at this stage, uncertain but would have been well within the capacity of the permanent machinery we were to have installed. The best estimates of the total demand for the first period are thought to be:

Estimated demand – first six months	
Quantity (000 units)	Probability
10	0.5
14	0.3
16	0.2

'Whatever the level of demand, we are going to meet it in full even if it means operating at a loss for the first half year. Therefore I suggest we consider the possibility of hiring equipment on which temporary production can take place'. Details of the only machines which could be hired are:

	Machine A	Machine B	Machine C
Productive capacity per six month period (units)	10 000	12 000	16 000
Variable production cost for each unit produced	£6.5	£6	£5
Other 'fixed' costs total for six months	£320 000	£350 000	£400 000

In addition to the above costs there will be a variable material cost of £5 per unit. For purchases greater than 10 000 units a discount of 20 per cent per unit will be given, but this only applies to the excess over 10 000 units.

Should production capacity be less than demand then Ruddle could subcontract production of up to 6000 units but would be required to supply raw materials. Subcontracting costs are:
up to 4000 units subcontracted £30 per unit
any excess over 4000 units subcontracted £35 per unit.

These subcontracting costs relate only to the work carried out by the subcontractor and exclude the costs of raw materials.

The commercial manager makes the following further points, 'Due to the lead time required for setting up production, the choice of which machine to hire must be made before the precise demand is known. However, demand will be known in time for production to be scheduled so that an equal number of units can be produced each month. We will, of course, only produce sufficient to meet demand.'

'We need to decide which machine to hire. However, I wonder whether it would be worthwhile seeking the assistance of a firm of market researchers? Their reputation suggests that they are very accurate and they may be able to inform us whether demand is to be 10, 14 or 16 thousand units.'

Required:
a For each of the three machines which could be hired show the possible monetary outcomes and, using expected values, advise Ruddle on its best course of action.   *(12 marks)*

b (i) Calculate the maximum amount which it would be worthwhile to pay to the firm of market researchers to ascertain details of demand. (You are required to assume that the market researchers will produce an absolutely accurate forecast and that demand will be exactly equal to one of the three demand figures given.) *(4 marks)*

(ii) Comment on the view that as perfect information is never obtainable the calculation of the expected value of perfect information is not worthwhile. Briefly explain any uses such a calculation may have. *(4 marks)*

Ignore taxation and the time value of money.

ACCA P2 Management Accounting

IM12.8 Advanced: Calculation of expected value of perfect and imperfect information. Butterfield Ltd manufactures a single brand of dog-food called 'Lots O Grissle' (LOG). Sales have stabilized for several years at a level of £20 million per annum at current prices. This level is not expected to change in the foreseeable future (except as indicated below). It is well below the capacity of the plant. The managing director, Mr Rover, is considering how to stimulate growth in the company's turnover and profits. After rejecting all of the alternative possibilities that he can imagine, or that have been suggested to him, he is reviewing a proposal to introduce a new luxury dog-food product. It would be called 'Before Eight Mince' (BEM), and would have a recommended retail price of £0.50 per tin. It would require no new investment, and would incur no additional fixed costs.

Mr Rover has decided that he will undertake this new development only if he can anticipate that it will at least break even in the first year of operation.

a Mr Rover estimates that BEM has a 75 per cent chance of gaining acceptance in the marketplace. His best estimate is that if the product gains acceptance it will have sales in the forthcoming year of £3.2 million at retail prices, given a contribution of £1 million after meeting the variable costs of manufacture and distribution. If, on the other hand, the product fails to gain acceptance, sales for the year will, he thinks, be only £800 000 at retail prices, and for various reasons there would be a negative contribution of £400 000 in that year.

You are required to show whether, on the basis of these preliminary estimates, Mr Rover should give the BEM project further consideration. *(4 marks)*

b Mr Rover discusses the new project informally with his sales director, Mr Khoo Chee Khoo, who suggests that some of the sales achieved for the new product would cause lost sales of LOG. In terms of retail values he estimates the likelihood of this as follows:

There is a 50 per cent chance that sales of LOG will fall by half of the sales of BEM.
There is a 25 per cent chance that sales of LOG will fall by one-quarter of the sales of BEM.
There is a 25 per cent chance that sales of LOG will fall by three-quarters of the sales of BEM.

The contribution margin ratio of LOG is 25 per cent at all relevant levels of sales and output. You are required to show whether, after accepting these further estimates, Mr Rover should give the BEM project further consideration. *(5 marks)*

c Mr Rover wonders also whether, before attempting to proceed any further, he should have some market research undertaken. He approaches Delphi Associates, a firm of market research consultants for whom he has a high regard. On previous occasions he has found them to be always right in their forecasts, and he considers that their advice will give him as near perfect information as it is possible to get. He decides to ask Delphi to advise him only on whether or not BEM will gain acceptance in the marketplace in the sense in which he has defined it; he will back Mr Khoo Chee Khoo's judgement about the effects of the introduction of BEM on the sales of LOG. If Delphi advise him that the product will not be accepted he will not proceed further. Delphi have told him that their fee for this work would be £100 000.

You are required to show whether Mr Rover should instruct Delphi Associates to carry out the market research proposals. *(5 marks)*

d Preliminary discussions with Delphi suggest that Delphi's forecast will not be entirely reliable. They believe that, if they indicate that BEM will gain acceptance, there is only a 90 per cent chance that they will be right; and, if they indicate failure to gain acceptance, there is only a 70 per cent chance that they will be right. This implies a 75 per cent chance overall that Delphi will indicate acceptance, in line with Mr Rover's estimate.

You are required to show the maximum amount that Mr Rover should be prepared to pay Delphi to undertake the market research, given the new estimates of the reliability of their advice. *(5 marks)*

e You are required to outline briefly the strengths and limitations of your methods of analysis in (a)–(d) above. *(6 marks)*

ICAEW Management Accounting

Capital investment decisions: appraisal methods

13

Capital investment decisions are those decisions that involve current outlays in return for a stream of benefits in future years. It is true to say that all of the firm's expenditures are made in expectation of realizing future benefits. The distinguishing feature between short-term decisions and capital investment (long-term) decisions is time. Generally, we can classify short-term decisions as those that involve a relatively short time horizon, say one year, from the commitment of funds to the receipt of the benefits. On the other hand, capital investment decisions are those decisions where a significant period of time elapses between the outlay and the recoupment of the investment. We shall see that this commitment of funds for a significant period of time involves an interest cost, which must be brought into the analysis. With short-term decisions, funds are committed only for short periods of time, and the interest cost is normally so small that it can be ignored.

Capital investment decisions normally represent the most important decisions that an organization makes, since they commit a substantial proportion of a firm's resources to actions that are likely to be irreversible. Such decisions are applicable to all sectors of society. Business

---

LEARNING OBJECTIVES

After studying this chapter, you should be able to:

- explain the opportunity cost of an investment;

- distinguish between compounding and discounting;

- explain the concepts of net present value (NPV), internal rate of return (IRR), payback method and accounting rate of return (ARR);

- calculate NPV, IRR, the payback period and ARR;

- justify the superiority of NPV over the IRR;

- explain the limitations of payback and ARR;

- justify why the payback and ARR methods are widely used in practice;

- describe the effect of performance measurement on capital investment decisions.

firms' investment decisions include investments in plant and machinery, research and development, advertising and warehouse facilities. Investment decisions in the public sector include new roads, schools and airports. Individuals' investment decisions include house-buying and the purchase of consumer durables. In this and the following chapter we shall examine the economic evaluation of the desirability of investment proposals. We shall concentrate on the investment decisions of business firms, but the same principles, with modifications, apply to individuals, and the public sector.

To simplify the introduction to capital investment decision, we shall assume initially that all cash inflows and outflows are known with certainty, and that sufficient funds are available to undertake all profitable investments. We will also assume a world where there are no taxes and where there is an absence of inflation. These factors will be brought into the analysis in the next chapter.

The opportunity cost of an investment

Investors can invest in securities traded in financial markets. If you prefer to avoid risk, you can invest in government securities, which will yield a *fixed* return. On the other hand, you may prefer to invest in *risky* securities such as the ordinary shares of companies quoted on the stock exchange. If you invest in the ordinary shares of a company, you will find that the return will vary from year to year, depending on the performance of the company and its future expectations. Investors normally prefer to avoid risk if possible, and will generally invest in risky securities only if they believe that they will obtain a greater return for the increased risk. Suppose that risk-free gilt-edged securities issued by the government yield a return of 10 per cent. You will therefore be prepared to invest in ordinary shares only if you expect the return to be greater than 10 per cent; let us assume that you require an *expected* return of 15 per cent to induce you to invest in ordinary shares in preference to a risk-free security. Note that expected return means the estimated average future return. You would expect to earn, on average, 15 per cent, but in some years you might earn more and in others considerably less.

Suppose you invest in company X ordinary shares. Would you want company X to invest your money in a capital project that gives less than 15 per cent? Surely not, assuming the project has the same risk as the alternative investments in shares of other companies that are yielding a return of 15 per cent. You would prefer company X to invest in other companies' ordinary shares at 15 per cent or, alternatively, to repay your investment so that you could invest yourself at 15 per cent.

The rates of return that are available from investments in securities in financial markets such as ordinary shares and government gilt-edged securities represent the opportunity cost of an investment in capital projects; that is, if cash is invested in the capital project, it cannot be invested elsewhere to earn a return. A firm should therefore invest in capital projects only if they yield a return in excess of the opportunity cost of the investment. The opportunity cost of the investment is also known as the minimum required rate of return, cost of capital, discount rate or interest rate.

The return on securities traded in financial markets provides us with the opportunity costs, that is the required rates of return available on securities. The expected returns that investors require from the ordinary shares of different companies vary because some companies' shares are more risky than others. The greater the risk, the greater the expected returns. Consider Figure 13.1. You can see that as the risk of a security increases the return that investors require to compensate for the extra risk increases. Consequently, investors will expect to receive a return in excess of 15 per cent if they invest in securities that have a higher risk than company X ordinary shares. If this return was not forthcoming, investors would not purchase high-risk securities. It is therefore important that companies investing in high-risk capital projects earn higher returns to compensate investors for this risk. You can also see that a risk-free security such as a gilt-edged government security yields the lowest return, i.e. 10 per cent. Consequently, if a firm invests in a

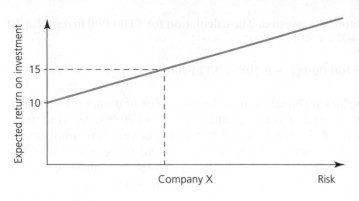

FIGURE 13.1
Risk–return trade-off

project with zero risk, it should earn a return in excess of 10 per cent. If the project does not yield this return and no other projects are available then the funds earmarked for the project should be repaid to the shareholders as dividends. The shareholders could then invest the funds themselves at 10 per cent.

Compounding and discounting

Our objective is to calculate and compare returns on an investment in a capital project with an alternative equal risk investment in securities traded in the financial markets. This comparison is made using a technique called discounted cash flow (DCF) analysis. Because a DCF analysis is the opposite of the concept of compounding interest, we shall initially focus on compound interest calculations.

Suppose you are investing £100 000 in a risk-free security yielding a return of 10 per cent payable at the end of each year. Exhibit 13.1 shows that if the interest is reinvested, your investment will accumulate to £146 410 by the end of year 4. Period 0 in the first column of Exhibit 13.1 means that no time has elapsed or the time is *now*, period 1 means one year later, and so on. The values in Exhibit 13.1 can also be obtained by using the formula:

$$FV_n = V_0 (1 + K)^n \tag{13.1}$$

where FV_n denotes the future value of an investment in n years, V_0 denotes the amount invested at the beginning of the period (year 0), K denotes the rate of return on the investment and n denotes

EXHIBIT 13.1 The value of £100 000 invested at 10%, compounded annually, for four years

End of year	Interest earned (£)	Total investment (£)
0		100 000
	0.10 × 100 000	10 000
1		110 000
	0.10 × 110 000	11 000
2		121 000
	0.10 × 121 000	12 100
3		133 100
	0.10 × 133 100	13 310
4		146 410

the number of years for which the money is invested. The calculation for £100 000 invested at 10 per cent for two years is

$$FV_2 = £100\ 000\ (1 + 0.10)^2 = £121\ 000$$

In Exhibit 13.1 all of the year-end values are equal as far as the time value of money is concerned. For example, £121 000 received at the end of year 2 is equivalent to £100 000 received today and invested at 10 per cent. Similarly, £133 100 received at the end of year 3 is equivalent to £121 000 received at the end of year 2, since £121 000 can be invested at the end of year 2 to accumulate to £133 100. Unfortunately, none of the amounts are directly comparable at any single moment in time, because each amount is expressed at a different point in time.

When making capital investment decisions, we must convert cash inflows and outflows for different years into a common value. This is achieved by converting the cash flows into their respective values at the same point in time. Mathematically, any point in time can be chosen, since all four figures in Exhibit 13.1 are equal to £100 000 at year 0, £110 000 at year 1, £121 000 at year 2, and so on. However, it is preferable to choose the point in time at which the decision is taken, and this is the present time or year 0. All of the values in Exhibit 13.1 can therefore be expressed in values at the present time (i.e. 'present value') of £100 000.

The process of converting cash to be received in the future into a value at the present time by the use of an interest rate is termed **discounting** and the resulting present value is the **discounted present value**. Compounding is the opposite of discounting, since it is the future value of present value cash flows. Equation (13.1) for calculating future values can be rearranged to produce the present value formula:

$$V_0 \text{ (present value)} = \frac{FV_n}{(1+K)^n} \tag{13.2}$$

By applying this equation, the calculation for £121 000 received at the end of year 2 can be expressed as

$$\text{present value} = \frac{£121\ 000}{(1+0.10)^2} = £100\ 000$$

You should now be aware that £1 received today is not equal to £1 received one year from today. No rational person will be equally satisfied with receiving £1 a year from now as opposed to receiving it today, because money received today can be used to earn interest over the ensuing year. Thus one year from now an investor can have the original £1 plus one year's interest on it. For example, if the interest rate is 10 per cent each £1 invested now will yield £1.10 one year from now. That is, £1 received today is equal to £1.10 one year from today at 10 per cent interest. Alternatively, £1 one year from today is equal to £0.9091 today, its present value because £0.9091, plus 10 per cent interest for one year amounts to £1. The concept that £1 received in the future is not equal to £1 received today is known as the **time value of money**.

We shall now consider four different methods of appraising capital investments: the net present value, internal rate of return, accounting rate of return and payback methods. We shall see that the first two methods take into account the time value of money whereas the accounting rate of return and payback methods ignore this factor.

The concept of net present value

By using discounted cash flow techniques and calculating present values, we can compare the return on an investment in capital projects with an alternative equal risk investment in securities traded in the financial market. Suppose a firm is considering four projects (all of which are risk-free) shown in Exhibit 13.2. You can see that each of the projects is identical with the investment in the risk-free security shown in Exhibit 13.1 because you can cash in this investment for £110 000 in year 1, £121 000 in year 2, £133 100 in year 3 and £146 410 in year 4. In other words your potential cash receipts from the risk-free security are identical to the net cash flows for projects A, B, C and D shown in Exhibit 13.2. Consequently, the firm should be indifferent as to whether it uses the funds to invest in the projects or invests the funds in securities of identical risk traded in the financial markets.

The most straightforward way of determining whether a project yields a return in excess of the alternative equal risk investment in traded securities is to calculate the net present value (NPV). This is the present value of the net cash inflows less the project's initial investment outlay. If the rate of return from the project is greater than the return from an equivalent risk investment in securities traded in the financial market, the NPV will be positive. Alternatively, if the rate of return is lower, the NPV will be negative. A positive NPV therefore indicates that an investment should be accepted, while a negative value indicates that it should be rejected. A zero NPV calculation indicates that the firm should be indifferent to whether the project is accepted or rejected.

You can see that the present value of each of the projects shown in Exhibit 13.2 is £100 000. You should now deduct the investment cost of £100 000 to calculate the project's NPV. The NPV for each project is zero. The firm should therefore be indifferent to whether it accepts any of the projects or invests the funds in an equivalent risk-free security. This was our conclusion when we compared the cash flows of the projects with the investments in a risk-free security shown in Exhibit 13.1.

You can see that it is better for the firm to invest in any of the projects shown in Exhibit 13.2 if their initial investment outlays are less than £100 000. This is because we have to pay £100 000 to obtain an equivalent stream of cash flows from a security traded in the financial markets. Conversely, we should reject the investment in the projects if their initial investment outlays are greater than £100 000. You should now see that the NPV rule leads to a direct comparison of a project with an equivalent risk security traded in the financial market. Given that the present value of the net cash inflows for each project is £100 000, their NPVs will be positive (thus signifying acceptance) if the initial investment outlay is less than £100 000 and negative (thus signifying rejection) if the initial outlay is greater than £100 000.

EXHIBIT 13.2 Evaluation of four risk-free projects

	A (£)	B (£)	C (£)	D (£)
Project investment outlay	100 000	100 000	100 000	100 000
End of year cash flows:				
Year 1	110 000	0	0	0
2	0	121 000	0	0
3	0	0	133 100	0
4	0	0	0	146 410
present value =	$\frac{110\ 000}{1.10}$	$\frac{121\ 000}{(1.10)^2}$	$\frac{133\ 000}{(1.10)^3}$	$\frac{146\ 410}{(1.10)^4}$
	= 100 000	= 100 000	= 100 000	= 100 000

Calculating net present values

You should now have an intuitive understanding of the NPV rule. We shall now learn how to calculate NPVs. The NPV can be expressed as:

$$NPV = \frac{FV_1}{1+K} + \frac{FV_2}{(1+K)^2} + \frac{FV_3}{(1+K)^3} + \cdots + \frac{FV_n}{(1+K)^n} - I_0 \qquad (13.3)$$

where I_0 represents the investment outlay and FV represents the future values received in years 1 to n. The rate of return K used is the return available on an equivalent risk security in the financial market. Consider the situation in Example 13.1.

The net present value calculation for Project A is:

$$NPV = \frac{£300\,000}{(1.10)} + \frac{£1\,000\,000}{(1.10)^2} + \frac{£400\,000}{(1.10)^3} - £1\,000\,000 = +£399\,700$$

Alternatively, the net present value can be calculated by referring to a published table of present values. You will find examples of such a table if you refer to Appendix A (see page 692). To use the table, simply find the discount factors by referring to each year of the cash flows and the appropriate interest rate.

For example, if you refer to year 1 in Appendix A, and the 10 per cent column, this will show a discount factor of 0.909. For years 2 and 3 the discount factors are 0.826 and 0.751. You then multiply the cash flows by the discount factors to find the present value of the cash flows. The calculation is as follows:

Year	Amount (£000's)	Discount factor	Present value (£)
1	300	0.9091	272 730
2	1000	0.8264	826 400
3	400	0.7513	300 520
			1 399 650
		Less initial outlay	1 000 000
		Net present value	399 650

In order to reconcile the NPV calculations derived from formula 13.3 and the discount tables the discount factors used in this chapter are based on four decimal places. Normally the factors given

EXAMPLE 13.1

The Bothnia Company is evaluating two projects with an expected life of three years and an investment outlay of £1 million. The estimated net cash inflows for each project are as follows:

	Project A (£)	Project B (£)
Year 1	300 000	600 000
Year 2	1 000 000	600 000
Year 3	400 000	600 000

The opportunity cost of capital for both projects is 10 per cent. You are required to calculate the net present value for each project.

in Appendix A based on three decimal places will suffice. The difference between the two calcu-lations shown above is due to rounding differences.

Note that the discount factors in the present value table are based on £1 received in *n* years time calculated according to the present value formula (equation 13.2). For example, £1 received in years 1, 2 and 3 when the interest rate is 10 per cent is calculated (based on four decimal places) as follows:

$$\text{Year 1} = £1/1.10 = 0.9091$$
$$\text{Year 2} = £1(1.10)^2 = 0.8264$$
$$\text{Year 3} = £1(1.10)^3 = 0.7513$$

The positive net present value from the investment indicates the increase in the market value of the shareholders' funds which should occur once the stock market becomes aware of the acceptance of the project. The net present value also represents the potential increase in present consumption that the project makes available to the ordinary shareholders, after any funds used have been repaid with interest. For example, assume that the firm finances the investment of £1 million in Example 13.1 by borrowing £1 399 700 at 10 per cent and repays the loan and interest out of the project's proceeds as they occur. You can see from the repayment schedule in Exhibit 13.3 that £399 700 received from the loan is available for current consumption, and the remaining £1 000 000 can be invested in the project. The cash flows from the project are just sufficient to repay the loan. Therefore acceptance of the project enables the ordinary shareholders' present consumption to be increased by the net present value of £399 700. Hence the acceptance of all available projects with a positive net present value should lead to the maximization of shareholders' wealth.

Let us now calculate the net present value for Project B shown in Example 13.1. The cash flows for project B represent an annuity. An annuity is an asset that pays a fixed sum each period for a specific number of periods. You can see for project B that the cash flows are £600,000 per annum for three years. When the annual cash flows are equivalent to an annuity, the calculation of net present value is simplified. The discount factors for an annuity are set out in Appendix B (see page 694). We need to find the discount factor for 10 per cent for three years. If you refer to Appendix B, you will see that it is 2.487. The NPV is calculated as follows:

Annual cash inflow	Discount factor	Present value (£)
£600 000	2.487	1 492 200
	Less investment cost	1 000 000
	Net present value	492 200

You will see that the total present value for the period is calculated by multiplying the cash inflow by the discount factor. It is important to note that the annuity tables shown in Appendix B can only be applied when the annual cash flows are the same each year. Annuities are also based on the assumption that cash flows for the first period are received at the end of the period, and not at the

EXHIBIT 13.3 The pattern of cash flows assuming that the loan is repaid out of the proceeds of the project

Year	Loan outstanding at start of year (1) (£)	Interest at 10% (2) (£)	Total amount owed before repayment (3) = (1) + (2) (£)	Proceeds from project (4) (£)	Loan outstanding at year end (5) = (3) – (4) (£)
1	1 399 700	139 970	1 539 670	300 000	1 239 670
2	1 239 670	123 967	1 363 637	1 000 000	363 637
3	363 637	36 363	400 000	400 000	0

start of the period, and that all subsequent cash flows are received at the end of each period. Note that the discount factors shown in Appendix B are derived from the following formula for an annuity:

$$\text{Present value} = \frac{A}{r}\left(1 - \frac{1}{(1+r)^n}\right) \tag{13.4}$$

where A is the annuity amount and r (also denoted by K) is the interest/discount rate per period.

Therefore the annuity factor for the present value for £1 received in each of three periods at a cost of capital (discount rate) of 10 per cent is:

$$PV = \frac{£1}{0.10}\left(1 - \frac{1}{(1+0.10)^3}\right) = 10 \, (0.24868) = 2.487$$

Sometimes, to simplify the calculations, examination questions are set based on the assumption that constant cash flows occur into perpetuity. In this situation the present value is determined by dividing the cash flow by the discount rate. For example, the present value of a cash flow of £100 per annum into perpetuity at a discount rate of 10 per cent is £1000 (£100/0.10). Again the present value calculation is based on the assumption that the first cash flow is received one period hence.

The internal rate of return

The **internal rate of return (IRR)** is an alternative technique for use in making capital investment decisions that also takes into account the time value of money. The internal rate of return represents the true interest rate earned on an investment over the course of its economic life. This measure is sometimes referred to as the **discounted rate of return**. The internal rate of return is the interest rate K that when used to discount all cash flows resulting from an investment, will equate the present value of the cash receipts to the present value of the cash outlays. In other words, it is the discount rate that will cause the net present value of an investment to be zero. Alternatively, the internal rate of return can be described as the maximum cost of capital that can be applied to finance a project without causing harm to the shareholders. The internal rate of return is found by solving for the value of K from the following formula:

$$I_0 = \frac{FV_1}{1+K} + \frac{FV_2}{(1+K)^2} + \frac{FV_3}{(1+K)^3} + \cdots + \frac{FV_n}{(1+K)^n} \tag{13.5}$$

It is easier, however, to use the discount tables. Let us now calculate the internal rate of return (using discount factors based on four decimal places) for Project A in Example 13.1.

The IRR can be found by trial and error by using a number of discount factors until the NPV equals zero. For example, if we use a 25 per cent discount factor, we get a positive NPV of £84 800. We must therefore try a higher figure. Applying 35 per cent gives a negative NPV of £66 530. We know then that the NPV will be zero somewhere between 25 per cent and 35 per cent. In fact, the IRR is between 30 per cent and 31 per cent but closest to 30 per cent, as indicated by the following calculation:

Year	Net cash flow (£)	Discount factor (30%)	Present value of cash flow (£)
1	300 000	0.7692	230 760
2	1 000 000	0.5917	591 700
3	400 000	0.4552	182 080
		Net present value	1 004 540
		Less initial outlay	1 000 000
		Net present value	4 540

It is claimed that the calculation of the IRR does not require the prior specification of the cost of capital. The decision rule is that if the IRR is greater than the opportunity cost of capital, the investment is profitable and will yield a positive NPV. Alternatively, if the IRR is less than the cost of capital, the investment is unprofitable and will result in a negative NPV. Therefore any interpretation of the significance of the IRR will still require that we estimate the cost of capital. The calculation of the IRR is illustrated in Figure 13.2.

The dots in the graph represent the NPV at different discount rates. The point where the line joining the dots cuts the horizontal axis indicates the IRR (the point at which the NPV is zero). Figure 13.2 indicates that the IRR is approximately 30 per cent, and you can see from this diagram that the interpolation method can be used to calculate the IRR without carrying out trial and error calculations. When we use interpolation, we infer the missing term (in this case the discount rate at which NPV is zero) from a known series of numbers. For example, at a discount rate of 25 per cent the NPV is +£84 800 and for a discount rate of 35 per cent the NPV is –£66 530. The total distance between these points is £151 330 (+£84 800 and –£66 530). The calculation for the approximate IRR is therefore

$$25\% + \frac{84\ 800}{151\ 330} \times (35\% - 25\%) = 30.60\%$$

In other words, if you move down line A in Figure 13.2 from a discount rate of 25 per cent by £84 800, you will reach the point at which NPV is zero. The distance between the two points on line A is £151 330, and we are given the discount rates of 25 per cent and 35 per cent for these points. Therefore 84 800/151 330 represents the distance that we must move between these two points for the NPV to be zero. This distance in terms of the discount rate is 5.60 per cent [(84 800/151 330) × 10 per cent], which, when added to the starting point of 25 per cent, produces an IRR of 30.60 per cent. The formula using the interpolation method is as follows:

$$A + \frac{C}{C - D}(B - A) \qquad (13.6)$$

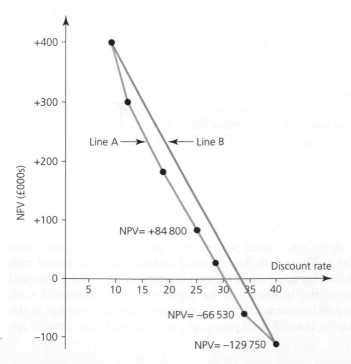

FIGURE 13.2

Interpretation of the internal rate of return

where A is the discount rate of the low trial, B is the discount rate of the high trial, C is the NPV of cash inflow of the low trial and D is the NPV of cash inflow of the high trial. Thus

$$25\% + \left[\frac{84\,800}{84\,800 - (-66\,530)} \times 10\% \right]$$

$$= 25\% + \left[\frac{84\,800}{151\,330} \times 10\% \right]$$

$$= 30.60\%$$

Note that the interpolation method only gives an approximation of the IRR. The greater the distance between any two points that have a positive and a negative NPV, the less accurate is the IRR calculation. Consider line B in Figure 13.2. The point where it cuts the horizontal axis is approximately 33 per cent, whereas the actual IRR is 30.60 per cent.

The calculation of the IRR is easier when the cash flows are of a constant amount each year. Let us now calculate the internal rate of return for project B in Example 13.1. Because the cash flows are equal each year, we can use the annuity table in Appendix B. When the cash flows are discounted at the IRR, the NPV will be zero. The IRR will therefore be at the point where

$$[\text{annual cash flow}] \times \left[\begin{array}{c} \text{discount factor for number of years} \\ \text{for which cash flow is received} \end{array} \right] - \left[\begin{array}{c} \text{investment} \\ \text{cost} \end{array} \right] = 0$$

Rearranging this formula, the internal rate of return will be at the point where

$$\text{discount factor} = \frac{\text{investment cost}}{\text{annual cash flow}}$$

Substituting the figures for project B in Example 13.1,

$$\text{discount factor} = \frac{£1\,000\,000}{£600\,000} = 1.666$$

We now examine the entries for the year 3 row in Appendix B to find the figures closest to 1.666. They are 1.673 (entered in the 36 per cent column) and 1.652 (entered in the 37 per cent column). We can therefore conclude that the IRR is between 36 per cent and 37 per cent. However, because the cost of capital is 10 per cent, an accurate calculation is unnecessary; the IRR is far in excess of the cost of capital.

The calculation of the IRR can be rather tedious (as the cited examples show), but the trial-and-error approach can be programmed for fast and accurate solution by a computer or calculator. The calculation problems are no longer a justification for preferring the NPV method of investment appraisal. Nevertheless, there are theoretical justifications, which we shall discuss later in this chapter, that support the NPV method.

Relevant cash flows

Investment decisions, like all other decisions, should be analyzed in terms of the cash flows that can be directly attributable to them. These cash flows should include the incremental cash flows that will occur in the future following acceptance of the investment. The cash flows will include cash inflows and outflows, or the inflows may be represented by savings in cash outflows. For example, a decision to purchase new machinery may generate cash savings in the form of reduced out-of-pocket operating costs. For all practical purposes such cost savings are equivalent to cash receipts.

It is important to note that depreciation is not included in the cash flow estimates for capital investment decisions, since it is a non-cash expense. This is because the capital investment cost of the asset to be depreciated is included as a cash outflow at the start of the project, and depreciation is merely a financial accounting method for allocating past capital costs to future accounting periods. Any inclusion of depreciation will lead to double counting.

Timing of cash flows

To simplify the presentation our calculations have been based on the assumption that any cash flows in future years will occur in one lump sum at the year end. Obviously, this is an unrealistic assumption, since cash flows are likely to occur at various times throughout the year, and a more realistic assumption is to assume that cash flows occur at the end of each month and use monthly discount rates. Typically, discount and interest rates are quoted as rates per annum using the term annual percentage rate (APR). If you wish to use monthly discount rates it is necessary to convert annual discount rates to monthly rates. An approximation of the monthly discount rate can be obtained by dividing the annual rate by 12. However, this simplified calculation ignores the compounding effect whereby each monthly interest payment is reinvested to earn more interest each month. To convert the annual discount rate to a monthly discount rate that takes into account the compounding effect we must use the following formula:

$$\text{Monthly discount rate} = (_{12}\sqrt{1 + \text{APR}}) - 1 \tag{13.7}$$

Assume that the annual percentage discount rate is 12.68 per cent. Applying formula 13.7 gives a monthly discount rate of:

$$(_{12}\sqrt{1.1268}) - 1 = 1.01 - 1 = .01 \text{ (i.e. 1 per cent per month).}$$

Therefore the monthly cash flows would be discounted at 1 per cent. In other words, 1 per cent compounded monthly is equivalent to 12.68 per cent compounded annually. Note that the monthly discount rates can also be converted to annual percentage rates using the formula:

$$(1 + k)^{12} - 1 \text{ (where } k = \text{the monthly discount rate)} \tag{13.8}$$

Assuming a monthly rate of 1 per cent the annual rate is $(1.01)^{12} - 1 = 0.1268$ (i.e. 12.68 per cent per annum).

Comparison of net present value and internal rate of return

In many situations the internal rate of return method will result in the same decision as the net present value method. In the case of conventional projects (in which an initial cash outflow is followed by a series of cash inflows) that are independent of each other (i.e. where the selection of a particular project does not preclude the choice of the other), both NPV and IRR rules will lead to the same accept/reject decisions. However, there are also situations where the IRR method may lead to different decisions being made from those that would follow the adoption of the NPV procedure.

Mutually exclusive projects

Where projects are mutually exclusive, it is possible for the NPV and the IRR methods to suggest different rankings as to which project should be given priority. Mutually exclusive projects exist where the acceptance of one project excludes the acceptance of another project, for example the choice of one of several possible factory locations, or the choice of one of many different possible machines. When evaluating mutually exclusive projects, the IRR method can incorrectly rank projects, because of its reinvestment assumptions, and in these circumstances it is recommended that the NPV method is used.

Percentage returns

Another problem with the IRR rule is that it expresses the result as a percentage rather than in monetary terms. Comparison of percentage returns can be misleading; for example, compare an investment of £10 000 that yields a return of 50 per cent with an investment of £100 000 that yields a return of 25 per cent. If only one of the investments can be undertaken, the first investment will yield £5000 but the second will yield £25 000. If we assume that the cost of capital is 10 per cent, and that no other suitable investments are available, any surplus funds will be invested at the cost of capital (i.e. the returns available from equal risk securities traded in financial markets). Choosing the first investment will leave a further £90 000 to be invested, but this can only be invested at 10 per cent, yielding a return of £9000. Adding this to the return of £5000 from the £10 000 investment gives a total return of £14 000. Clearly, the second investment, which yields a return of £25 000, is preferable. Thus, if the objective is to maximize the shareholders' wealth then NPV provides the correct measure.

Reinvestment assumptions

The assumption concerning the reinvestment of interim cash flows from the acceptance of projects provides another reason for supporting the superiority of the NPV method. The implicit assumption if the NPV method is adopted is that the cash flows generated from an investment will be reinvested immediately at the cost of capital (i.e. the returns available from equal risk securities traded in financial markets). However, the IRR method makes a different implicit assumption about the reinvestment of the cash flows. It assumes that all the proceeds from a project can be reinvested immediately to earn a return equal to the IRR of the original project. This assumption is likely to be unrealistic because a firm should have accepted all projects which offer a return in excess of the cost of capital, and any other funds that become available can only be reinvested at the cost of capital. This is the assumption that is implicit in the NPV rule.

Unconventional cash flows

Where a project has unconventional cash flows, the IRR has a technical shortcoming. Most projects have conventional cash flows that consist of an initial negative cash flow followed by positive cash inflows in later years. In this situation the algebraic sign changes, being negative at the start and positive in all future periods. If the sign of the net cash flows changes in successive periods, it is possible for the calculations to produce as many internal rates of return as there are sign changes. While multiple rates of return are mathematically possible, only one rate of return is economically significant in determining whether or not the investment is profitable.

Fortunately, the majority of investment decisions consist of conventional cash flows that produce a single IRR calculation. However, the problem cannot be ignored, since unconventional cash flows are possible and, if the decision-maker is unaware of the situation, serious errors may occur at the decision-making stage. Example 13.2 illustrates a situation where two internal rates of return occur.

You will find that the cash flows in Example 13.2 give internal rates of return of 5 per cent and 50 per cent. The effect of multiple rates of return on the NPV calculations is illustrated in Figure 13.3.

When the cost of capital is between 5 per cent and 50 per cent, the NPV is positive and, following the NPV rule, the project should be accepted. However, if the IRR calculation of 5 per

EXAMPLE 13.2

The Bothnia Company has the following series of cash flows for a specific project:

Year 0	−£400 000 (Investment outlay)
Year 1	+£1 020 000 (Net cash inflows)
Year 2	−£630 000 (Environmental and disposal costs)

You are required to calculate the internal rate of return.

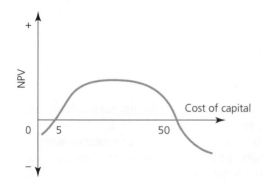

FIGURE 13.3
Net present values for unconventional cash flows

cent is used, the project may be incorrectly rejected if the cost of capital is in excess of 5 per cent. You can see that the graph of the NPV in Figure 13.3 indicates that this is an incorrect decision when the cost of capital is between 5 per cent and 50 per cent. Alternatively, if the IRR of 50 per cent is used, this will lead to the same decision being made as if the NPV rule were adopted, provided that the cost of capital is greater than 5 per cent. Note that the NPV is negative if the cost of capital is less than 5 per cent.

Techniques that ignore the time value of money

In addition to those methods that take into account the time value of money two other methods that ignore this factor are frequently used in practice. These are the payback method and the accounting rate of return method. Methods that ignore the time value of money are theoretically weak, and they will not necessarily lead to the maximization of the market value of ordinary shares. Nevertheless, the fact that they are frequently used in practice means that we should be aware of these techniques and their limitations.

Payback method

The **payback method** is one of the simplest and most frequently used methods of capital investment appraisal. It is defined as the length of time that is required for a stream of cash proceeds from an investment to recover the original cash outlay required by the investment. If the stream of cash flows from the investment is constant each year, the payback period can be calculated by dividing the total initial cash outlay by the amount of the expected annual cash proceeds. Therefore if an investment requires an initial outlay of £60 000 and is expected to produce annual cash inflows of

£20 000 per year for five years, the payback period will be £60 000 divided by £20 000, or three years. If the stream of expected proceeds is not constant from year to year, the payback period is determined by adding up the cash inflows expected in successive years until the total is equal to the original outlay. Example 13.3 illustrates two projects, A and B, that require the same initial outlay of £50 000 but that display different time profiles of benefits.

In Example 13.3 project A pays back its initial investment cost in three years, whereas project B pays back its initial cost in four years. Therefore project A would be ranked in preference to project B because it has the fastest payback period. However, project B has a higher NPV, and the payback method incorrectly ranks project A in preference to project B. Two obvious deficiencies are apparent from these calculations. First, the payback method does not take into account cash flows that are earned after the payback period and, secondly, it fails to take into account the differences in the timing of the proceeds which are earned before the payback period. Payback computations ignore the important fact that future cash receipts cannot be validly compared with an initial outlay until they are discounted to their present values.

REAL WORLD VIEWS 13.1

Payback on new technology

Typically, a firm deciding to invest in new technology will face many problems. From a monetary viewpoint, investing in technology must provide some form of payback. Cost reductions and/or increased revenues should be great enough to recoup funds invested within a reasonable time frame. With new technologies, the payback can be quite fast as the cost of new technology tends to decrease in the short-term.

Radio Frequency Identification (RFID) is a relatively new technology which is of interest to major retailers such as Tesco. RFID is essentially a bar-code which can be scanned by a radio scanner, without human input. With an RFID tag attached to a product, it can be tracked throughout stores and warehouses, enabling real time traceability of product. Tesco began its RFID investment project, called Secure Supply Chain, in late 2004. The initial goal of the project was to track high-value non-food items such as razor blades, mobile phones and computer accessories in all UK stores. The ultimate project goal is to use RFID in all 1400 UK stores and 30 distribution centres on high and low value products.

As of mid-2006, Tesco had encountered some problems. For example, the company has been accused of 'spying' on customers by using RFID and problems have occurred with EU regulators on radio frequency usages. While the project time-frame has been longer than expected, Tesco is continuing with the project. It has formed alliances with suppliers like Robert Wiseman Dairies to automatically record incoming stock in stores.

The RFID tags themselves are constantly falling in price, making the investment more attractive and providing a faster payback. Chicago based Diamond Management & Technology consultants predict RFID tag costs will fall to 5 cents per tag by 2010, with hardware costs remaining stable or decreasing. This would provide an expected payback of approximately one year.

Discussion points

1 Can you think of examples of how RFID technology could reduce costs for retailers like Tesco?

2 If comparing investment alternatives, would you always choose that with the shortest payback period?

RFID technology
© RA-PHOTOS/ISTOCKPHOTO.COM

SOURCES: WWW.RFIDJOURNAL.COM 'ACHIEVING RFID'S FULL POTENTIAL' BY DARIN YUG, BILL GILLILAND, AND STEVEN LEGNINE, DIAMOND MANAGEMENT & TECHNOLOGY CONSULTANTS, CHICAGO ILLINOIS. WWW.DIAMONDCONSULTANTS.COM

Not only does the payback period incorrectly rank project A in preference to project B, but the method can also result in the acceptance of projects that have a negative NPV. Consider the cash flows for project C in Example 13.4.

The payback period for project C is three years, and if this was within the time limit set by management, the project would be accepted in spite of its negative NPV. Note also that the payback method would rank project C in preference to project B in Example 13.3, despite the fact that B would yield a positive NPV.

The payback period can only be a valid indicator of the time that an investment requires to pay for itself, if all cash flows are first discounted to their present values and the discounted values are then used to calculate the payback period. This adjustment gives rise to what is known as the adjusted or discounted payback method. Even when such an adjustment is made, the adjusted payback method cannot be a complete measure of an investment's profitability. It can estimate whether an investment is likely to be profitable, but it cannot estimate how profitable the investment will be.

Despite the theoretical limitations of the payback method it is the method most widely used in practice (see Exhibit 13.4). Why, then, is payback the most widely applied formal investment

EXAMPLE 13.3

The cash flows and NPV calculations for two projects are as follows:

	Project A		Project B	
	(£)	(£)	(£)	(£)
Initial cost				
Net cash inflows		50 000		50 000
Year 1	10 000		10 000	
Year 2	20 000		10 000	
Year 3	20 000		10 000	
Year 4	20 000		20 000	
Year 5	10 000		30 000	
Year 6	–		30 000	
Year 7	–	80 000	30 000	140 000
NPV at a 10% cost capital		10 500		39 460

EXAMPLE 13.4

The cash flows and NPV calculation for project C are as follows:

	(£)	(£)
Initial cost		
Net cash inflows		50 000
Year 1	10 000	
Year 2	20 000	
Year 3	20 000	
Year 4	3 500	
Year 5	3 500	
Year 6	3 500	
Year 7	3 500	64 000
NPV (at 10% cost of capital)		(−1 036)

appraisal technique? It is a particularly useful approach for ranking projects where a firm faces liquidity constraints and requires a fast repayment of investments. The payback method may also be appropriate in situations where risky investments are made in uncertain markets that are subject to fast design and product changes or where future cash flows are extremely difficult to predict. The payback method assumes that risk is time-related: the longer the period, the greater the chance of failure. By concentrating on the early cash flows, payback uses data in which managers have greater confidence. Thus, the payback period can be used as a rough measure of risk, based on the assumption that the longer it takes for a project to pay for itself, the riskier it is. Managers may also choose projects with quick payback periods because of self-interest. If a manager's performance is measured using short-term criteria, such as net profits, there is a danger that he or she may choose projects with quick paybacks to show improved net profits as soon as possible. The payback method is also frequently used in conjunction with the NPV or IRR methods. It serves as a simple first-level screening device that identifies those projects that should be subject to more rigorous investigation. A further attraction of payback is that it is easily understood by all levels of management and provides an important summary measure: how quickly will the project

EXHIBIT 13.4 Surveys of practice

Surveys conducted by Pike relating to the investment appraisal techniques by 100 large UK companies between 1975 and 1992 provide an indication of the changing trends in practice in large UK companies. Pike's findings relating to the percentage of firms using different appraisal methods are as follows:

	1975 %	1981 %	1986 %	1992 %
Payback	73	81	92	94
Accounting rate of return	51	49	56	50
DCF methods (IRR or NPV)	58	68	84	88
Internal rate of return (IRR)	44	57	75	81
Net present value (NPV)	32	39	68	74

Source: Pike (1996)

A study of 300 UK manufacturing organizations by Drury *et al.* (1993) sought to ascertain the extent to which particular techniques were used. The figures below indicate the percentage of firms that often or always used a particular technique:

	All organizations %	Smallest organizations %	Largest organizations %
Payback (unadjusted)	63	56	55
Discounted payback	42	30	48
Accounting rate of return	41	35	53
Internal rate of return	57	30	85
Net present value	43	23	80

More recently a UK study by Arnold and Hatzopoulos (2000) reported that NPV has overtaken IRR as the most widely used method by larger firms. They reported that 97 per cent of large firms use NPV compared with 84 per cent which employ IRR.

A survey by Brounen *et al.* (2004) in mainland Europe reported that the usage of the payback method was 65 per cent in the Netherlands, 50 per cent in Germany and 51 per cent in France. NPV was used by 70 per cent of the German respondents compared with 56 per cent using IRR. Usage of IRR exceeded that of NPV in the Netherlands and France.

recover its initial outlay? Ideally, the payback method should be used in conjunction with the NPV method, and the cash flows discounted before the payback period is calculated.

It is apparent from the surveys shown in Exhibit 13.4 that firms use a combination of appraisal methods. The studies by Pike indicate a trend in the increasing usage of discount rates. The Drury *et al.* study suggests that larger organizations use net present value and internal rate of return to a greater extent than the smaller organizations. The Drury *et al.* study also asked the respondents to rank the appraisal methods in order of importance for evaluating major projects. The larger organizations ranked internal rate of return first, followed by payback and net present value whereas the smaller organizations ranked payback first, internal rate of return second and intuitive management judgement third.

Accounting rate of return

The accounting rate of return (also known as the return on investment and return on capital employed) is calculated by dividing the average annual profits from a project into the average investment cost. It differs from other methods in that profits rather than cash flows are used. Note that profits are not equal to cash flows because financial accounting profit measurement is based on the accruals concept. Assuming that depreciation represents the only non-cash expense, profit is equivalent to cash flows less depreciation. The use of accounting rate of return can be attributed to the wide use of the return on investment measure in financial statement analysis.

When the average annual net profits are calculated, only additional revenues and costs that follow from the investment are included in the calculation. The average annual net profit is therefore calculated by dividing the difference between incremental revenues and costs by the estimated life of the investment. The incremental costs include either the *net* investment cost or the total depreciation charges, these figures being identical. The average investment figure that is used in the calculation depends on the method employed to calculate depreciation. If straight-line depreciation is used, it is presumed that investment will decline in a linear fashion as the asset ages. The average investment under this assumption is one-half of the amount of the initial investment plus one-half of the scrap value at the end of the project's life.[1]

For example, the three projects described in Examples 13.3 and 13.4 for which the payback period was computed required an initial outlay of £50 000. If we assume that the projects have no scrap values and that straight-line depreciation is used, the average investment for each project will be £25 000. The calculation of the accounting rate of return for each of these projects is as follows:

$$\text{accounting rate of return} = \frac{\text{average annual profits}}{\text{average investment}}$$

$$\text{project A} = \frac{6\ 000}{25\ 000} = 24\%$$

$$\text{project B} = \frac{12\ 857}{25\ 000} = 51\%$$

$$\text{project C} = \frac{2\ 000}{25\ 000} = 8\%$$

For project A the total profit over its five-year life is £30 000 (£80 000 − £50 000), giving an average annual profit of £6000. The average annual profits for projects B and C are calculated in a similar manner.

It follows that the accounting rate of return is superior to the payback method in one respect; that is, it allows for differences in the useful lives of the assets being compared. For example, the calculations set out above reflect the high earnings of project B over the whole life of the project, and consequently it is ranked in preference to project A. Also, projects A and C have the same payback periods, but the accounting rate of return correctly indicates that project A is preferable to project C.

However, the accounting rate of return suffers from the serious defect that it ignores the time value of money. When the method is used in relation to a project where the cash inflows do not occur until near the end of its life, it will show the same accounting rate of return as it would for a project where the cash inflows occur early in its life, providing that the average cash inflows are the same. For this reason the accounting rate of return cannot be recommended. Nevertheless, the accounting rate of return is widely used in practice (see Exhibit 13.4). This is probably due to the fact that the annual accounting rate of return is frequently used to measure the managerial performance of different business units within a company. Therefore, managers are likely to be interested in how any new investment contributes to the business unit's overall accounting rate of return.

The effect of performance measurement on capital investment decisions

The way that the performance of a manager is measured is likely to have a profound effect on the decisions he or she will make. There is a danger that, because of the way performance is measured, a manager may be motivated to take the wrong decision and not follow the NPV rule. Consider the information presented in Exhibit 13.5 in respect of the net cash inflows and the annual reported profits or losses for projects J and K. The figures without the parentheses refer to the cash inflows whereas the figures within the parentheses refer to annual reported profit. You will see that the total cash inflows over the five year lives for projects J and K are £11 million and £5 million respectively. Both projects require an initial outlay of £5 million. Assuming a cost of capital of 10 per cent, without undertaking any calculations it is clear that project J will have a positive NPV and project K will have a negative NPV.

EXHIBIT 13.5 Annual net cash inflows (profits/losses) for two projects each with an initial outlay of £5 million

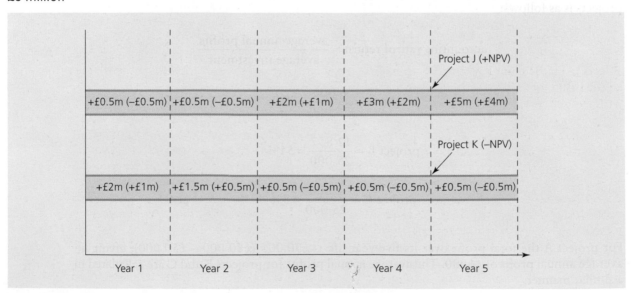

If the straight line method of depreciation is used the annual depreciation for both projects will be £1 million (£5 million investment cost/5 years). Therefore the reported profits (shown in parentheses) are derived from deducting the annual depreciation charge from the annual net cash inflows. For decision-making the focus is on the entire life of the projects. Our objective is to ascertain whether the present value of the cash inflows exceeds the present value of the cash outflows over the entire life of a project, and not allocate the NPV to different accounting periods as indicated by the dashed vertical lines in Exhibit 13.5. In other words we require an answer to the question will the project add value?

In contrast, a company is required to report on its performance externally at annual intervals and managerial performance is also often evaluated on an annual or more frequent basis. Evaluating managerial performance at the end of the five year project lives is clearly too long a time scale since managers are unlikely to remain in the same job for such lengthy periods. Therefore, if a manager's performance is measured using short-term criteria, such as annual profits, he or she may choose projects that have a favourable impact on short-term financial performance. Because Project J will have a negative impact on performance in its early years (i.e. it contributes losses) there is a danger that a manager who is anxious to improve his or her short-term performance might reject project J even though it has a positive impact on the performance measure in the long-term.

The reverse may happen with project K. This has a favourable impact on the short-term profit performance measure in years one and two but a negative impact in the longer-term so the manager might accept the project to improve his or her short-term performance measure.

It is thus important to avoid an excessive focus on short-term profitability measures since this can have a negative impact on long-term profitability. Emphasis should also be given to measuring a manager's contribution to an organization's long-term objectives. These issues are discussed in Chapter 19 when we shall look at performance measurement in more detail. However, at this point you should note that the way in which managerial performance is measured will influence their decisions and may motivate them to work in their own best interests, even when this is not in the best interest of the organization.

Qualitative factors

Not all investment projects can be described completely in terms of monetary costs and benefits (e.g. a new cafeteria for the employees or the installation of safety equipment). Nevertheless, the procedures described in this chapter may be useful by making the value placed by management on quantitative factors explicit. For example, if the present value of the cash outlays for a project is £100 000 and the benefits from the project are difficult to quantify, management must make a value judgement as to whether or not the benefits are in excess of £100 000. In the case of capital expenditure on facilities for employees, or expenditure to avoid unpleasant environmental effects from the company's manufacturing process, one can take the view that the present value of the cash outlays represents the cost to shareholders of the pursuit of goals other than the maximization of shareholders' funds. In other words, ordinary shareholders, as a group in the bargaining coalition, should know how much the pursuit of other goals is costing them.

There is also a danger that those aspects of a new investment that are difficult to quantify may be omitted from the financial appraisal. This applies particularly to investments in advanced manufacturing technologies that yield benefits such as improved quality and delivery times and a greater flexibility that provides the potential for low cost production of high-variety, low-volume goods. Various commentators have criticized financial appraisal techniques because they fail to take such qualitative aspects into account. They claim that an over-emphasis on the quantitative aspects has inhibited investment in advanced manufacturing technologies.

The difficulty in quantifying the cash flows is no excuse for omitting them from the analysis. A bad estimate is better than no estimate at all. One approach that has been suggested for overcoming these difficulties is not to attempt to place a value on those benefits that are difficult to quantify. Instead, the process can be reversed by estimating how large these benefits must be in order to justify the proposed investment. Assume that a project with an estimated life of ten years and a cost of capital of 20 per cent has a negative NPV of £1 million. To achieve a positive NPV, or in other words to obtain the required rate of return of 20 per cent, additional cash flows would need to be achieved that when discounted at 20 per cent, would amount to at least £1 million. The project lasts for ten years, and the discount factor for an annuity over ten years at 20 per cent is 4.192. Therefore the additional cash flows from the benefits that have not been quantified must be greater than £238 550 per annum (note that £1 million divided by an annuity factor (Appendix B) for ten years at 20 per cent (4.192) equals £238 550) in order to justify the proposed investment. Discussions should then take place to consider whether benefits that have not been quantified, such as improved flexibility, rapid customer service and market adaptability, are worth more than £238 550 per year.

SUMMARY

The following items relate to the learning objectives listed at the beginning of the chapter.

● **Explain the opportunity cost of an investment.**

The rates of return that are available from investments in financial markets in securities with different levels of risk (e.g. company shares, company and government bonds) represent the opportunity cost of an investment. In other words, if cash is invested in a capital project it cannot be invested elsewhere to earn a return. A firm should therefore only invest in projects that yield a return in excess of the opportunity cost of investment.

● **Distinguish between compounding and discounting.**

The process of converting cash invested today at a specific interest rate into a future value is known as compounding. Discounting is the opposite of compounding and refers to the process of converting cash to be received in the future into the value at the present time. The resulting present value is called the discounted present value.

● **Explain the concepts of net present value (NPV), internal rate of return (IRR), payback method and accounting rate of return (ARR).**

Both NPV and IRR are methods of determining whether a project yields a return in excess of an equal risk investment in traded financial securities. A positive NPV provides an absolute value of the amount by which an investment exceeds the return available from an alternative investment in financial securities of equal risk. Conversely, a negative value indicates the amount by which an investment fails to match an equal risk

investment in financial securities. In contrast, the IRR indicates the true percentage return from an investment after taking into account the time value of money. To ascertain whether an investment should be undertaken, the percentage internal rate of return on investment should be compared with the returns available from investing in equal risk in financial securities. Investing in all projects that have positive NPVs or IRRs in excess of the opportunity cost of capital should maximize shareholder value. The payback method is the length of time that is required for a stream of cash proceeds from an investment to recover the original cash outflow required by the investment. The ARR expresses the annual average profits arising from a project as a percentage return on the average investment required for the project.

● **Calculate NPV, IRR, the payback period and ARR.**

The NPV is calculated by discounting the net cash inflows from a project and deducting the investment outlay. The IRR is calculated by ascertaining the discount rate that will cause the NPV of a project to be zero. The payback period is calculated by adding up the cash flows expected in successive years until the total is equal to the original outlay. The ARR is calculated by dividing the average annual profits estimated from a project by the average investment cost. The calculation of NPV and IRR was illustrated using Example 13.1 and Examples 13.3 and 13.4 were used to illustrate the calculations of the payback period and the ARR.

● **Justify the superiority of NPV over the IRR.**

NPV is considered to be theoretically superior to IRR because: (a) unlike the NPV method the IRR method cannot be guaranteed to rank mutually exclusive projects correctly; (b) the percentage returns generated by the IRR method can be misleading when choosing between alternatives; (c) the IRR method makes incorrect reinvestment assumptions by assuming that the interim cash flows can be reinvested at the IRR rather than the cost of capital; and (d) where unconventional cash flows occur multiple IRRs are possible.

Explain the limitations of payback and ARR.

The major limitations of the payback method are that it ignores the time value of money and it does not take into account the cash flows that are earned after the payback period. The ARR also fails to take into account the time value of money and relies on a percentage return rather than an absolute value.

Justify why the payback and ARR methods are widely used in practice.

The payback method is frequently used in practice because (a) it is considered useful when firms face liquidity constraints and require a fast repayment of their investments; (b) it serves as a simple first-level screening device that identifies those projects that should be subject to more rigorous investigations; and (c) it provides a rough measure of risk, based on the assumption that the longer it takes for a project to pay for itself, the riskier it is. The ARR is a widely-used financial accounting measure of managerial and company performance. Therefore, managers are likely to be interested in how any new investment contributes to the business unit's overall accounting rate of return.

Describe the effect of performance measurement on capital investment decisions.

Managerial and company performance is normally evaluated using short-term financial criteria whereas investment appraisal decisions should be based on the cash flows over the whole life of the projects. Thus, the way that performance is evaluated can have a profound influence on investment decisions and there is a danger that managers will make decisions on the basis of an investment's impact on the short-term financial performance evaluation criteria rather than using the NPV decision rule.

Note

1 Consider a project that costs £10 000 and has a life of four years and an estimated scrap value of £2000. The following diagram (using straight line depreciation to calculate the written down values) illustrates why the project's scrap value is added to the initial outlay to calculate the average capital employed. You can see that at the mid-point of the project's life the capital employed is equal to £6000 (i.e. ½ (10 000 + £2000)).

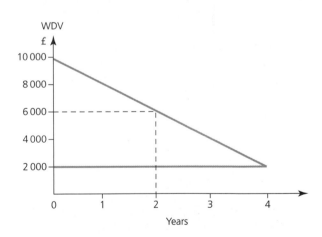

Key terms and concepts

accounting rate of return (p. 307)
annual percentage rate (APR) (p. 301)
annuity (p. 297)
compounding interest (p. 293)
cost of capital (p. 292)
discounted rate of return (p. 298)
discounted cash flow (p. 293)
discounted payback method (p. 305)

discounted present value (p. 294)
discount rate (p. 292)
discounting (p. 294)
interest rate (p. 292)
internal rate of return (p. 298)
minimum required rate of return (p. 292)
mutually exclusive projects (p. 301)
net present value (p. 295)

opportunity cost of an investment (p. 292)
payback method (p. 303)
present value (p. 294)
return on capital employed (p. 307)
return on investment (p. 307)
risk-free gilt-edged securities (p. 292)
time value of money (p. 294)

Recommended reading

The financing of capital projects is normally part of a corporate finance course. If you wish to undertake further reading relating to the financing of capital investments you should refer to Pike and Neale (2005) or Brealey and Myers (2006). For a discussion of the issues relating to appraising investments in advanced manufacturing technologies you should read the publications by Currie (1990, 1991a,b) and Sizer and Motteram, Chapter 15 (1996).

Key examination points

A common mistake is a failure to distinguish between relevant and irrelevant cash flows. Remember to include only incremental cash flows in a DCF analysis. Depreciation and reapportionments of overheads should not be included. If you are required to evaluate mutually exclusive projects, use NPV, since IRR can give incorrect rankings. Where IRR calculations are required, check that the cash flows are conventional. For unconventional cash flows it is necessary to calculate more than one IRR. Normally, very accurate calculations of the IRR will not be required, and an approximate answer using the interpolation method should be appropriate.

Note that the examination questions set by the professional accountancy examining bodies normally provide you with the formulae for annuities for both present and future values. Sometimes examination questions require you to use formula 13.4, shown within the chapter, to determine the constant cash flow per period (i.e. the annuity amount) required to produce a given *present* value. You should refer to the answer to Review problem 13.17 for an illustration of how the annuity value is calculated. Examinations questions may also require you to use the annuity formula for *future* values, rather than the present value formula presented in the text. The following future value annuity formula is normally provided:

$$\text{Future value} = A\left(\frac{(1+r)^n - 1}{r}\right)$$

where r (also denoted by k) is the rate of interest per period and A is the annuity amount.

Typical examination questions require you to calculate the future value of an annuity or the annuity value where the future value is given.

ASSESSMENT MATERIAL

The review questions are short questions that enable you to assess your understanding of the main topics included in the chapter. The numbers in parentheses provide you with the page numbers to refer to if you cannot answer a specific question.

The review problems are more complex and require you to relate and apply the content to various business problems. The problems are graded by their level of difficulty. Solutions to review problems that are not preceded by the term 'IM' are provided in a separate section at the end of the book. Solutions to problems preceded by the term 'IM' are provided in the *Instructor's Manual* accompanying this book and also on the lecturer's password protected section of the website www.drury-online.com. Additional review problems with fully worked solutions are provided in the *Student's Manual* that accompanies this book.

The website also includes over 30 case problems. A list of these cases is provided on pages 665–7. The Rawhide Development Company is a case study that is relevant to the content of this chapter.

Review questions

13.1 What is meant by the opportunity cost of an investment? What role does it play in capital investment decisions? *(pp. 292–93)*
13.2 Distinguish between compounding and discounting. *(pp. 293–94)*
13.3 Explain what is meant by the term 'time value of money'. *(p. 294)*
13.4 Describe the concept of net present value (NPV). *(p. 298)*
13.5 Explain what is meant by the internal rate of return (IRR). *(p. 298)*
13.6 Distinguish between independent and mutually exclusive projects. *(pp. 301–02)*
13.7 Explain the theoretical arguments for preferring NPV to IRR when choosing among mutually exclusive projects. *(pp. 301–02)*
13.8 Why might managers choose to use IRR in preference to NPV? *(p. 299)*
13.9 Describe the payback method. What are its main strengths and weaknesses? *(pp. 303–06)*
13.10 Describe the accounting rate of return. What are its main strengths and weaknesses? *(pp. 307–08)*
13.11 Distinguish between the payback method and discounted payback method. *(pp. 303–05)*
13.12 What impact can the way in which a manager's performance is measured have on capital investment decisions? *(pp. 308–09)*

Review problems

13.13 Basic. An investment has the following cash inflows and cash outflows:

Time	Cash flow per annum
	£000
0	(20 000)
1–4	3 000
5–8	7 000
10	(10 000)

What is the net present value of the investment at a discount rate of 8 per cent?

  a (£2416)
  b (£7046)
  c £6981
  d £2351

ACCA Paper 1.2 – Financial Information for Management

13.14 Basic. An investment gives the following results:

Net present value	Discount rate
£000	
383	10%
(246)	15%

What is the estimated internal rate of return to the nearest whole percentage?

  a 12%
  b 13%
  c 14%
  d 17%

ACCA Paper 1.2 – Financial Information for Management

13.15 Intermediate. Sydney is considering making a monthly investment for her son who will be five years old on his next birthday. She wishes to make payments until his 18th birthday and intends to pay £50 per month into an account yielding an APR of 12.68 per cent. She plans to start making payments into the account the month after her son's fifth birthday.

How much will be in the account immediately after the final payment has been made?

  a £18 847
  b £18 377
  c £17 606
  d £18 610.

ACCA Paper 1.2 – Financial Information for Management

13.16 Intermediate. Sydney wishes to make an investment on a monthly basis starting next month for five years. The payments into the fund would be made on the first day of each month.

The interest rate will be 0.5 per cent per month. Sydney needs a terminal value of £7000.

What should be the monthly payments into the fund to the nearest £?

  a £75
  b £86
  c £100
  d £117

ACCA Paper 1.2 – Financial Information for Management

13.17 Intermediate. Augustine wishes to take out a loan for £2000. The interest rate on this loan would be 10 per cent per annum and Augustine wishes to make equal monthly repayments, comprising interest and principal, over three years starting one month after the loan is taken out.

What would be the monthly repayment on the loan (to the nearest £)?

  a £56
  b £64
  c £66
  d £67

ACCA Paper 1.2 – Financial Information for Management

13.18 Intermediate: Calculation of terminal values and monthly repayments.

a James is considering paying £50 into a fund on a monthly basis for ten years starting in one year's time. The interest earned will be 1 per cent per month. Once all of these payments have been made the investment will be transferred immediately to an account that will earn interest at 15 per cent per annum until maturity. The fund matures five years after the last payment is made into the fund.

Required:

Calculate the terminal value of the fund in 15 years' time to the nearest £. *(3 marks)*

b Doug wishes to take out a loan for £2000. He has the choice of two loans:

Loan 1: monthly payments for 36 months at an APR of 9.38 per cent

Loan 2: monthly payments for 24 months at an APR of 12.68 per cent

Required:

(i) Calculate the monthly repayments for loans 1 and 2 to two decimal places. *(5 marks)*

(ii) Calculate the total amount repaid under each loan and purely on the basis of this information recommend which loan Doug should choose. *(2 marks)*

ACCA Paper 1.2 – Financial Information for Management

13.19 Intermediate: Calculation of payback, ARR and NPV. The following data are supplied relating to two investment projects, only one of which may be selected:

	Project A (£)	Project B (£)
Initial capital expenditure	50 000	50 000
Profit (loss) year 1	25 000	10 000
2	20 000	10 000
3	15 000	14 000
4	10 000	26 000
Estimated resale value at end of year 4	10 000	10 000

Notes

1 Profit is calculated after deducting straight-line depreciation.
2 The cost of capital is 10 per cent.

Required:

a Calculate for each project:
(i) average annual rate of return on average capital invested;
(ii) payback period;
(iii) net present value. *(12 marks)*

b Briefly discuss the relative merits of the three methods of evaluation mentioned in (a) above. *(10 marks)*

c Explain which project you would recommend for acceptance. *(3 marks)*

AAT

13.20 Advanced: Calculation of payback, ARR and NPV. Stadler is an ambitious young executive who has recently been appointed to the position of financial director of Paradis plc, a small listed company. Stadler regards this appointment as a temporary one, enabling him to gain experience before moving to a larger organization. His intention is to leave Paradis plc in three years' time, with its share price standing high. As a consequence, he is particularly concerned that the reported profits of Paradis plc should be as high as possible in his third and final year with the company.

Paradis plc has recently raised £350 000 from a rights issue, and the directors are considering three ways of using these funds. Three projects (A, B and C) are being considered, each involving the immediate purchase of equipment costing £350 000. One project only can be undertaken, and the equipment for each project will have a useful life equal to that of the project, with no scrap value. Stadler favours project C because it is expected to show the highest accounting profit in the third year. However, he does not wish to reveal his real reasons for favouring project C, and so, in his report to the chairman, he recommends project

C because it shows the highest internal rate of return. The following summary is taken from his report:

Project	Net cash flows (£000) Years									Internal rate of return (%)
	0	1	2	3	4	5	6	7	8	
A	−350	100	110	104	112	138	160	180	–	27.5
B	−350	40	100	210	260	160	–	–	–	26.4
C	−350	200	150	240	40	–	–	–	–	33.0

The chairman of the company is accustomed to projects being appraised in terms of payback and accounting rate of return, and he is consequently suspicious of the use of internal rate of return as a method of project selection. Accordingly, the chairman has asked for an independent report on the choice of project. The company's cost of capital is 20 per cent and a policy of straight-line depreciation is used to write off the cost of equipment in the financial statements.

Requirements:

a Calculate the payback period for each project. *(3 marks)*

b Calculate the accounting rate of return for each project. *(5 marks)*

c Prepare a report for the chairman with supporting calculations indicating which project should be preferred by the ordinary shareholders of Paradis plc. *(12 marks)*

d Discuss the assumptions about the reactions of the stock market that are implicit in Stadler's choice of project C. *(5 marks)*

Note: ignore taxation.

ICAEW P2 Financial Management

13.21 Advanced: Calculation of NPV and IRR, a discussion of the inconsistency in ranking and a calculation of the cost of capital at which the ranking changes. A company is considering which of two mutually exclusive projects it should undertake. The finance director thinks that the project with the higher NPV should be chosen whereas the managing director thinks that the one with the higher IRR should be undertaken especially as both projects have the same initial outlay and length of life. The company anticipates a cost of capital of 10 per cent and the net after tax cash flows of the projects are as follows:

	Project X (£000)	Project Y (£000)
Year 0	−200	−200
1	35	218
2	80	10
3	90	10
4	75	4
5	20	3

You are required to:

a calculate the NPV and IRR of each project; *(6 marks)*

b recommend, with reasons, which project you would undertake (if either); *(4 marks)*

c explain the inconsistency in ranking of the two projects in view of the remarks of the directors; *(4 marks)*

d identify the cost of capital at which your recommendation in (b) would be reversed. *(6 marks)*

CIMA Stage 3 Management Accounting Techniques

IM13.1 Advanced. The evidence of many recent studies suggests that there are major differences between current theories of investment appraisal and the methods which firms actually use in evaluating long-term investments.

You are required to:

a present theoretical arguments for the choice of net present value as the best method of investment appraisal;

b explain why in practice other methods of evaluating investment projects have proved to be more popular with decision-makers than the net present value method.

IM13.2 Intermediate: Payback, accounting rate of return and NPV calculations plus a discussion of qualitative factors. The following information relates to three possible capital expenditure projects. Because of capital rationing only one project can be accepted.

		Project	
	A	B	C
Initial Cost	£200 000	£230 000	£180 000
Expected Life	5 years	5 years	4 years
Scrap value expected	£10 000	£15 000	£8000
Expected Cash Inflows	(£)	(£)	(£)
End Year 1	80 000	100 000	55 000
2	70 000	70 000	65 000
3	65 000	50 000	95 000
4	60 000	50 000	100 000
5	55 000	50 000	

The company estimates its cost of capital is 18 per cent.

Calculate

a   The pay back period for each project. (4 marks)
b   The Accounting Rate of Return for each project. (4 marks)
c   The Net present value of each project. (8 marks)
d   Which project should be accepted – give reasons. (5 marks)
e   Explain the factors management would need to consider: in addition to the financial factors before making a final decision on a project. (4 marks)

AAT Stage 3 Cost Accounting and Budgeting

IM13.3 Intermediate: Calculation of payback, NPV and ARR for mutually exclusive projects. Your company is considering investing in its own transport fleet. The present position is that carriage is contracted to an outside organization. The life of the transport fleet would be five years, after which time the vehicles would have to be disposed of.

The cost to your company of using the outside organization for its carriage needs is £250 000 for this year. This cost, it is projected, will rise 10 per cent per annum over the life of the project. The initial cost of the transport fleet would be £750 000 and it is estimated that the following costs would be incurred over the next five years:

	Drivers' Costs (£)	Repairs & Maintenance (£)	Other Costs (£)
Year 1	33 000	8 000	130 000
Year 2	35 000	13 000	135 000
Year 3	36 000	15 000	140 000
Year 4	38 000	16 000	136 000
Year 5	40 000	18 000	142 000

Other costs include depreciation. It is projected that the fleet would be sold for £150 000 at the end of year 5. It has been agreed to depreciate the fleet on a straight line basis.

To raise funds for the project your company is proposing to raise a long-term loan at 12 per cent interest rate per annum.

You are told that there is an alternative project that could be invested in using the funds raised, which has the following projected results:

Payback = 3 years
Accounting rate of return = 30%
Net present value = £140 000.

As funds are limited, investment can only be made in one project.

Note: The transport fleet would be purchased at the beginning of the project and all other expenditure would be incurred at the end of each relevant year.

Required:

a   Prepare a table showing the net cash savings to be made by the firm over the life of the transport fleet project. (5 marks)
b   Calculate the following for the transport fleet project:
    (i)   Payback period
    (ii) Accounting rate of return
    (iii) Net present value (13 marks)
c   Write a short report to the Investment Manager in your company outlining whether investment should be committed to the transport fleet or the alternative project outlined. Clearly state the reasons for your decision. (7 marks)

AAT Cost Accounting and Budgeting

IM13.4 Intermediate: NPV and payback calculations. You are employed as the assistant accountant in your company and you are currently working on an appraisal of a project to purchase a new machine. The machine will cost £55 000 and will have a useful life of three years. You have already estimated the cash flows from the project and their taxation effect, and the results of your estimates can be summarized as follows:

	Year 1	Year 2	Year 3
Post-tax cash inflow	£18 000	£29 000	£31 000

Your company uses a post-tax cost of capital of 8 per cent to appraise all projects of this type.

Task 1

a   Calculate the net present value of the proposal to purchase the machine. Ignore the effects of inflation and assume that all cash flows occur at the end of the year.
b   Calculate the payback period for the investment in the machine.

Task 2

The marketing director has asked you to let her know as soon as you have completed your appraisal of the project. She has asked you to provide her with some explanation of your calculations and of how taxation affects the proposal.

Prepare a memorandum to the marketing director which answers her queries. Your memorandum should contain the following:

a   your recommendation concerning the proposal;
b   an explanation of the meaning of the net present value and the payback period;
c   an explanation of the effects of taxation on the cash flows arising from capital expenditure. *AAT Technicians Stage*

IM13.5 Intermediate: Present value of purchasing or renting machinery. The Portsmere Hospital operates its own laundry. Last year the laundry processed 120 000 kilograms of washing and this year the total is forecast to grow to 132 000 kilograms. This growth in laundry processed is forecast to continue at the same percentage rate for the next seven years. Because of this, the hospital must immediately replace its existing laundry equipment. Currently, it is considering two options, the purchase of machine A or the rental of machine B. Information on both options is given below:

Machine A – purchase	
Annual capacity (kilograms)	£180 000
Material cost per kilogram	£2.00
Labour cost per kilogram	£3.00
Fixed costs per annum	£20 000
Life of machine	3 years
Capital cost	£60 000
Depreciation per annum	£20 000

Machine B – rent	
Annual capacity (kilograms)	£170 000
Material cost per kilogram	£1.80
Labour cost per kilogram	£3.40
Fixed costs per annum	£18 000
Rental per annum	£20 000
Rental agreement	3 years
Depreciation per annum	nil

Other information:
1.   The hospital is able to call on an outside laundry if there is either a breakdown or any other reason why the washing cannot be undertaken in-house. The charge would be £10 per kilogram of washing.
2.   Machine A, if purchased, would have to be paid for immediately. All other cash flows can be assumed to occur at the end of the year.
3.   Machine A will have no residual value at any time.
4.   The existing laundry equipment could be sold for £10 000 cash.
5.   The fixed costs are a direct cost of operating the laundry.
6.   The hospital's discount rate for projects of this nature is 15 per cent.

You are an accounting technician employed by the Portsmere Hospital and you are asked to write a brief report to its chief executive. Your report should:

a   evaluate the two options for operating the laundry, using discounted cash flow techniques;
b   recommend the preferred option and identify *one* possible non-financial benefit;
c   justify your treatment of the £10 000 cash value of the existing equipment;
d   explain what is meant by discounted cashflow.

Note: Inflation can be ignored.

AAT Technicians Stage

IM13.6 Advanced: Comparison of NPV and IRR. Using the discounted cash flow yield (internal rate of return) for evaluating investment opportunities has the basic weakness that it does not give attention to the amount of the capital investment, in that a return of 20 per cent on an investment of £1000 may be given a higher ranking than a return of 15 per cent on an investment of £10 000.

Comment in general on the above statement and refer in particular to the problem of giving priorities to (ranking) investment proposals.

Your answers should make use of the following information.

	Project A cash flow (£)	Project B cash flow (£)
Year 0 (Capital investments)	1000	10 000
1 Cash flows	240	2 300
2 Cash flows	288	2 640
3 Cash flows	346	3 040
4 Cash flows	414	3 500
5 Cash flows	498	4 020
Cost of capital	10%	10%

Taxation can be ignored.

(20 marks)
ACCA P3 Financial Management

IM13.7 Advanced: Calculation of NPV and additional cash flows which will result in a zero NPV. Losrock Housing Association is considering the implementation of a refurbishment programme on one of its housing estates which would reduce maintenance and heating costs and enable a rent increase to be made.

Relevant data are as follows:
(i) Number of houses: 300.
(ii) Annual maintenance cost per house: £300. This will be reduced by 25 per cent on completion of the refurbishment of each house.
(iii) Annual heating cost per house: £500. This will be reduced by 30 per cent on completion of the refurbishment of each house.
(iv) Annual rental income per house: £2100. This will be increased by 15 per cent on completion of the refurbishment of each house.
(v) Two contractors A and B have each quoted a price of £2000 per house to implement the refurbishment work.
(vi) The quoted completion profiles for each contractor are as follows:

	Number of houses refurbished		
	Year 1	Year 2	Year 3
Contractor A	90	90	120
Contractor B	150	90	60

(vii) Contractor A requires £100 000 at the commencement of the work and the balance of the contract price in proportion to the number of houses completed in each of years 1 to 3. Contractor B requires £300 000 at the commencement of the work and the balance of the contract price in proportion to the number of houses completed in each of years 1 to 3.
(viii) An eight year period from the commencement of the work should be used as the time horizon for the evaluation of the viability of the refurbishment programme.

Assume that all events and cash flows arise at year end points. Savings and rent increases will commence in the year following refurbishment.

Ignore taxation.

Required:
a Prepare financial summaries and hence advise management whether to accept the quote from contractor A or contractor B in each of the following situations:
(i) ignoring the discounting of cash flows; and
(ii) where the cost of capital is determined as 14 per cent.
(14 marks)
b For contractor A only, calculate the maximum refurbishment price per house at which the work would be acceptable to Losrock Housing Association on financial grounds using discounted cash flows as the decision base, where the initial payment remains at £100 000 and the balance is paid in proportion to the houses completed in each of years 1 to 3. *(5 marks)*
c Suggest additional information relating to maintenance and heating costs which might affect the acceptability of the existing quotes per house where discounted cash flows are used as the decision base. *(3 marks)*
ACCA Level 2 Management Accounting

IM13.8 Advanced: Replacement decision and the conflict between decision-making and performance evaluation models. Paragon Products plc has a factory which manufactures a wide range of plastic household utensils. One of these is a plastic brush which is made from a special raw material used only for this purpose. The brush is moulded on a purpose-built machine which was installed in January 1997 at a cost of £210 000 with an expected useful life of seven years. This machine was assumed to have zero scrap value at the end of its life and was depreciated on the same straight line basis that the company used for all equipment.

Recently an improved machine has become available, at a price of £130 000, which requires two men to operate it rather than the five men required by the existing machine. It also uses a coarser grade of raw material costing £70 per tonne (1000 kg), compared with £75 per tonne for the present material. Further, it would use only 60 per cent of the power consumed by the existing machine. However, it has an expected life of only three years and an expected scrap value of £10 000.

The factory manager is considering replacing the existing machine immediately with the new one as the suppliers have offered him £40 000 for the existing machine, which is substantially more than could be obtained on the second hand market, provided the new machine is installed by 1 January 2001. Unfortunately this would leave stocks of the old raw material sufficient to make 40 000 brushes which could not be used and which would fetch only £25 per tonne on resale.

The brush department is treated as a profit centre. Current production amounts to 200 000 brushes a year which are sold at a wholesale price of £1 each. The production of each brush uses 2 kg of the raw material, consumes 1 kW hour of electricity costing £0.05, and incurs direct labour costs amounting to £0.25 per brush. Overhead costs amount to £60 000 per annum and include £10 000 relating to supervision costs which vary according to the number of employees. The men no longer required to operate the new machine could be found employment elsewhere in the factory and would be paid their current wage although they would be performing less skilled work normally paid at 80 per cent of their current rate.

Requirements:
a Evaluate the proposal to replace the existing machine with the new model, ignoring the time value of money in your analysis.
(10 marks)
b Construct brush department profit and loss accounts for each alternative for 2001, 2002 and 2003. Indicate how the factory manager's decision might be influenced by these figures.
(8 marks)
c Explain how your analysis would be affected if the new machine had a longer expected life and the time value of money was to be taken into account. *(7 marks)*
Note: Ignore taxation.

ICAEW P2 Management Accounting

IM13.9 Advanced: Calculation of a contract price involving monthly discounting and compounding. Franzl is a contract engineer working for a division of a large construction company. He is responsible for the negotiation of contract prices and the subsequent collection of instalment monies from customers. It is company policy to achieve a mark-up of at least 10 per cent on the direct production costs of a contract, but there is no company policy on the speed of customer payment. Franzl usually attempts to persuade customers to pay in six-monthly instalments in arrears.

Franzl is presently engaged in deciding upon the minimum acceptable price for contract K491, which will last for 24 months. He has estimated that the following direct production costs will be incurred:

	(£)
Raw material	168 000
Labour	120 000
Plant depreciation	18 400
Equipment rental	30 000
	336 400

On the basis of these costs Franzl estimates that the minimum contract price should be £370 000. The raw material and labour costs are expected to arise evenly over the period of the contract and to be paid monthly in arrears. Plant depreciation has been calculated as the difference between the cost of the new plant (£32 400) which will be purchased for the contract and its realizable value (£14 000) at the end of contract. Special equipment will be rented for the first year of the contract, the rent being paid in two six-monthly instalments in advance. The contract will be financed from head office funds, on which interest of 1 per cent per month is charged or credited according to whether the construction division is a net borrower or net lender.

Requirements:

a Calculate the net present value of contract K491 assuming that Franzl's minimum price and normal payment terms are accepted.

(5 marks)

b Assuming that the customer agrees to pay the instalments in advance rather than arrears, calculate the new contract price and mark-up that Franzl could accept so as to leave the net present value of the contract unchanged.

(5 marks)

c Prepare two statements to show that the eventual cash surpluses generated in (a) and (b) are identical. The statements need show *only* the total cash received and paid for each category of revenue and expense.

(6 marks)

d Discuss the factors that should influence the tender price for a long-term contract.

(9 marks)

Note: Ignore taxation.

ICAEW Financial Management

Capital investment decisions: the impact of capital rationing, taxation, inflation and risk

14

In the previous chapter the major techniques that can be used for appraising capital investment decisions were introduced and their relative merits were assessed. To simplify the discussion, we made a number of assumptions: first, that cash inflows and outflows were known with certainty; secondly that sufficient funds were available to enable acceptance of all those projects with positive net present values; thirdly, that firms operated in an environment where there was no taxation and no inflation; and finally, that the cost of capital was the risk-free rate.

In this chapter we shall relax these assumptions and discuss how capital investment techniques can be applied to more complicated situations. In addition, we shall look at the procedures that should be in place for initiating, authorizing and reviewing project investments. Many of the topics included in this chapter are complex and more appropriate to a second year management accounting course. Also some of the topics may be incorporated in a corporate finance course rather than a management accounting course. Therefore, you should check whether the topics are included in your course curriculum prior to reading this chapter.

LEARNING OBJECTIVES

After studying this chapter, you should be able to:

● explain capital rationing and select the optimum combination of investments when capital is rationed for a single period;

● calculate the incremental taxation payments arising from a proposed investment;

● describe the two approaches for adjusting for inflation when appraising capital projects;

● explain how risk-adjusted discount rates are calculated;

● explain how sensitivity analysis can be applied to investment appraisal;

● describe the initiation, authorization and review procedures for the investment process.

Capital rationing

In our previous discussions it has been suggested that all investments with positive net present values should be undertaken. For mutually exclusive projects the project with the highest net present value should be chosen. However, situations may occur where there are insufficient funds available to enable a firm to undertake all those projects that yield a positive net present value. The situation is described as capital rationing. Capital rationing occurs whenever there is a budget ceiling, or a market constraint on the amount of funds that can be invested during a specific period of time. For various reasons top management may pursue a policy of limiting the amount of funds available for investment in any one period. Such policies may apply to firms that finance all their capital investment with internal funds. Alternatively, in a large decentralized organization top management may limit the funds available to the divisional managers for investment.

The term 'soft capital rationing' is often used to refer to situations where, for various reasons the firm *internally* imposes a budget ceiling on the amount of capital expenditure. On the other hand, where the amount of capital investment is restricted because of *external* constraints such as the inability to obtain funds from the financial markets, the term 'hard capital rationing' is used.

Whenever capital rationing exists, management should allocate the limited available capital in a way that maximizes the NPVs of the firm. Thus it is necessary to rank all investment opportunities so that the NPV can be maximized from the use of the available funds. Ranking in terms of absolute NPVs will normally give incorrect results, since this method leads to the selection of large projects, each of which has a high individual NPV but that have in total a lower NPV than a large number of smaller projects with lower individual NPVs. For example, the ranking of projects by NPV will favour a project that yields an NPV of £1000, for an investment of £10 000, over two projects of £5000 that each yield an individual NPV of £800. Clearly, if funds are restricted to £10 000, it is better to accept the two smaller projects, which will yield a total NPV of £1600. Consider the situation presented in Example 14.1.

Our aim is to select the projects in descending order of profitability until the investment funds of £20 million have been exhausted. If we use the net present value method of ranking, the following projects will be selected:

EXAMPLE 14.1

A division of the Bothnia Company that operates under the constraint of capital rationing has identified seven independent investments from which to choose. The company has £20 million available for capital investment during the current period. Which projects should the company choose? The net present values and profitability index ratios for each of the projects are as follows:

Projects	Investment required (£m)	Present value, PV (£m)	Net present value (£m)	Profitability index (PV/ investment cost)	Ranking as per NPVs	Ranking as per profitability index
A	2.5	3.25	0.75	1.30	6	2
B	10.0	10.825	0.825	1.08	5	6
C	5.0	7.575	2.575	1.51	1	1
D	10.0	12.35	2.35	1.23	2	3
E	12.5	13.35	0.85	1.07	4	7
F	2.5	3.0	0.5	1.20	7	4
G	5.0	5.9	0.9	1.18	3	5

Projects selected in order of ranking	Investment cost (£m)	New present value (£m)
C	5	2.575
D	10	2.350
G	5	0.900
	Total net present value	5.825

Instead of ranking by NPVs projects should be ranked by their profitability index. The prof-itability index is defined as the present value of a project divided by its investment outlay. The profitability index represents the application of the approach outlined in Chapter 9 for allo-cating scarce resources (i.e. with investment funds being the scarce resource in Example 14.1). Only projects with a profitability index in excess of 1.0 are acceptable since they have positive NPVs. For ranking purposes projects should be accepted in descending order based on their profitability index. Therefore, if we adopt the rankings by the profitability index, the selected projects will be as follows:

Projects selected in order of ranking	Investment cost (£m)	Net present value (£)
C	5.0	2.575
A	2.5	0.750
D	10.0	2.350
F	2.5	0.500
	Total net present value	6.175

You can see that the ranking of projects by the profitability index gives the highest NPV. Our discussion so far has assumed that investment funds are restricted for one period only. To extend the analysis to multi-period capital rationing it is necessary to adopt the mathematical programming techniques described in Chapter 25.

Taxation and investment decisions

In our discussions so far we have ignored the impact of taxation. Taxation rules differ between countries but in most countries similar principles tend to apply relating to the taxation allowances available on capital investment expenditure. Companies rarely pay taxes on the profits that are disclosed in their annual published accounts, since certain expenses that are deducted in the published accounts are not allowable deductions for taxation purposes. For example, depreciation is not an allowable deduction; instead, taxation legislation enables capital allowances (also known as writing-down allowances or depreciation tax shields) to be claimed on capital expenditure that is incurred on plant and machinery and other fixed assets. Capital allowances represent standardized depreciation allowances granted by the tax authorities. These allowances vary from country to country but their common aim is to enable the *net* cost of assets to be deducted as an allowable expense, either throughout their economic life or on an accel-erated basis which is shorter than an asset's economic life.

Taxation laws in different countries typically specify the amount of capital expenditure that is allowable (sometimes this exceeds the cost of the asset where a government wishes to stimulate investment), the time period over which the capital allowances can be claimed and the depreci-ation method to be employed. Currently in the UK, larger companies can claim annual capital allowances of 25 per cent on the written-down value of plant and equipment based on the reducing balance method of depreciation. Different percentage capital allowances are also available on other assets such as industrial buildings where an allowance of 4 per cent per annum based on straight line depreciation can be claimed.[1]

Let us now consider how taxation affects the NPV calculations. You will see that the calculation must include the incremental tax cash flows arising from the investment. Consider the information presented in Example 14.2.

The first stage is to calculate the annual writing down allowances (i.e. the capital allowances). The calculations are as follows:

End of year	Annual writing-down allowance (£)	Written-down value (£)
0	0	1 000 000
1	250 000 (25% × £1 000 000)	750 000
2	187 500 (25% × £750 000)	562 500
3	140 630 (25% × £562 500)	421 870
4	105 470 (25% × £421 870)	316 400
	683 600	

Next we calculate the additional taxable profits arising from the project. The calculations are as follows:

	Year 1 (£)	Year 2 (£)	Year 3 (£)	Year 4 (£)
Incremental annual profits	500 000	500 000	500 000	500 000
Less annual writing-down allowance	250 000	187 500	140 630	105 470
Incremental taxable profits	250 000	312 500	359 370	394 530
Incremental tax at 35%	87 500	109 370	125 780	138 090

You can see that for each year the incremental tax payment is calculated as follows:

corporate tax rate × (incremental profits – capital allowance)

Note that depreciation charges should not be included in the calculation of incremental cash flows or taxable profits. We must now consider the timing of the taxation payments. In the UK taxation payments vary depending on the end of the accounting year, but they are generally paid approximately one year after the end of the company's accounting year. We shall apply this rule to our example. This means that the tax payment of £87 500 for year 1 will be paid at the end of year 2, £109 370 tax will be paid at the end of year 3 and so on.

The incremental tax payments are now included in the NPV calculation:

Year	Cash flow (£)	Taxation	Net cash flow (£)	Discount factor	Present value (£)
0	–1 000 000	0	–1 000 000	1.0000	–1 000 000
1	+500 000	0	+500 000	0.9091	+454 550
2	+500 000	–87 500	+412 500	0.8264	+340 890
3	+500 000	–109 370	+390 630	0.7513	+293 480
4	+500 000 }+316 400[a]	–125 780	+690 620	0.6830	+471 690
5	0	–138 090	–138 090	0.6209	–85 740
				Net present value	+474 870

[a]Sale of machinery for written down value of £316 400.

EXAMPLE 14.2

The Sentosa Company operates in Ruratania where investments in plant and machinery are eligible for 25 per cent annual writing-down allowances on the written-down value using the reducing balance method of depreciation. The corporate tax rate is 35 per cent. The company is considering whether to purchase some machinery which will cost £1 million and which is expected to result in additional net cash inflows and profits of £500 000 per annum for four years. It is anticipated that the machinery will be sold at the end of year 4 for its written-down value for taxation purposes. Assume a one year lag in the payment of taxes. Calculate the net present value.

The taxation rules in most countries allow capital allowances to be claimed on the *net* cost of the asset. In our example the machine will be purchased for £1 million and the estimated realizable value at the end of its life is its written-down value of £316 400. Therefore the estimated net cost of the machine is £683 600. You will see from the calculation of the writing down allowances at the start of this section that the total of the allowances amounts to the net cost. How would the analysis change if the estimated realizable value for the machine was different from its written-down value, say £450 000? The company will have claimed allowances of £683 600 but the estimated net cost of the machine is £550 000 (£1 million – £450 000 estimated net realizable value). Therefore excess allowances of £133 600 (£683 600 – £550 000) will have been claimed and an adjustment must be made at the end of year 4 so that the tax authorities can claim back the excess allowance. This adjustment is called a balancing charge.

Note that the above calculation of taxable profits for year 4 will now be as follows:

Incremental annual profits	500 000
Less annual writing-down allowance	(105 470)
Add balancing charge	133 600
Incremental taxable profits	528 130
Incremental taxation at 35%	184 845

An alternative calculation is to assume that a writing-down allowance will not be claimed in year 4. The balancing charge is now calculated by deducting the written-down value at the end of year 3 of £421 870 from the *actual* sales value at the time of sale (i.e. £450 000 sale proceeds). The balancing charge is now £28 130. This is the same as the net charge incorporated in the above calculation (£133 600 – £105 470 = £28 130). You can adopt either method. It is a matter of personal preference.

Let us now assume that the estimated disposal value is less than the written-down value for tax purposes, say £250 000. The net investment cost is £750 000 (£1 000 000 – £250 000), but you will see that our calculations at the start of this section indicate that estimated taxation capital allowances of £683 600 will have been claimed by the end of year 4. Therefore an adjustment of £66 400 (£750 000 – £683 600) must be made at the end of year 4 to reflect the fact that insufficient capital allowances have been claimed. This adjustment is called a balancing allowance.

Thus in year 4 the total capital allowance will consist of an annual writing-down allowance of £105 470 plus a balancing allowance of £66 400, giving a total of £171 870. Taxable profits for year 4 are now £328 130 (500 000 – £171 870), and tax at the rate of 35 per cent on these profits will be paid at the end of year 5.

Do note that in the UK, and some other countries, it is possible to combine similar types of assets into asset pools and purchases and sales of assets are added to the pool so that balancing allowances and charges on individual assets do not arise. However, similar outcomes are likely to occur. Accordingly, it is essential when appraising investment proposals to be fully aware of the specific taxation legislation that applies so that you can precisely determine the taxation impact. In most cases taxation is likely to have an important effect on the NPV calculation. For an illustration of the treatment of asset acquisitions and disposals when asset are incorporated into a general pool you should refer to the article by Franklin (1998).

The effect of inflation on capital investment appraisal

ADVANCED READING

What impact does inflation have on capital investment decisions? We shall see that inflation affects future cash flows and the return that shareholders require on the investment (i.e. the discount rate). How does inflation affect the required rate of return on an investment? According to Fisher (1930), the rates quoted on financial securities such as treasury bills fully reflect anticipated inflation. Note that the rates quoted on securities are known as nominal or money rates of return, whereas the real rate of return represents the rate that would be required in the absence of inflation. Fisher proposed the following equation relating to the nominal rate of return to the real rate of return and the rate of inflation:

$$\left(1 + \frac{\text{nominal rate}}{\text{of return}}\right) = \left(1 + \frac{\text{real rate}}{\text{of return}}\right) \times \left(1 + \frac{\text{expected rate}}{\text{of inflation}}\right) \tag{14.1}$$

Suppose that the real rate of return is expected to be 2 per cent and the anticipated rate of inflation 8 per cent. Applying Fisher's equation, the nominal or money rate of return would be

$$(1 + 0.02)(1 + 0.08) = 1.1016$$

The nominal rate of return would therefore be 10.16 per cent (i.e. 1.1016 − 1). In the absence of inflation, an individual who invests £100 in a risk-free security will require a 2 per cent return of £102 to compensate for the time value of money. Assuming that the expected rate of inflation is 8 per cent, then to maintain the return of £102 in real terms this return will have to grow by 8 per cent to £110.16 (i.e. £102 + 8 per cent). Therefore a real rate of return of 2 per cent requires a nominal rate of return of 10.16 per cent when the expected rate of inflation is 8 per cent.

Inflation also affects future cash flows. For example, assume that you expect a cash flow of £100 in one year's time when there is no inflation. Now assume that that the predicted annual inflation rate is 10 per cent. Your expected cash flow at the end of the year will now be £110, instead of £100. However, you will be no better off as a result of the 10 per cent increase in cash flows. Assume that you can buy physical goods, say widgets, at £1 each when there is no inflation so that at the end of the year you can buy 100 widgets. With an annual inflation rate of 10 per cent the cost of a widget will increase to £1.10 and your cash flow will be £110, but your purchasing power will remain unchanged because you will still only be able to buy 100 widgets.

The increase in cash flows from £100 to £110 is an illusion because it is offset by a decline in the purchasing power of the monetary unit. Rather than expressing cash flows in year one monetary units it is more meaningful to express the cash flows in today's purchasing power or monetary unit (that is, in real cash flows). Thus, £110 receivable at the end of year one is equivalent to £100 in today's purchasing power. When cash flows are expressed in monetary units at the time when they are received they are described as nominal cash flows whereas cash flows expressed in today's (that is, time zero) purchasing power are known as real cash flows. Therefore the £110 cash flow is a nominal cash flow but if it is expressed in today's purchasing power it will be equivalent to a real cash flow of £100.

Real cash flows can be converted to nominal cash flows using the following formula:

$$\text{Nominal cash flow} = \text{Real cash flow } (1 + \text{the anticipated rate of inflation})^n \tag{14.2}$$

where n = the number of periods that the cash flows are subject to inflation.

Alternatively, we can rearrange formula (14.2) to restate it in terms of real cash flows:

Real cash flow = Nominal cash flow/(1 + the anticipated rate of inflation)^n (14.3)

Therefore if a real cash flow expressed in today's purchasing power is £100 and the anticipated annual rate of inflation is 10 per cent then the nominal value at the end of year 2 will be:

$$£100(1 + 0.10)^2 = £121$$

or a nominal cash flow of £121 receivable at the end of year 2 will be equivalent to a real cash flow of:

$$£121/(1 + 0.10)^2 = £100$$

The average rate of inflation for all goods and services traded in an economy is known as the general rate of inflation. Assume that your cash flow of £100 has increased at exactly the same rate as the general rate of inflation (in other words, the general rate of inflation is 10 per cent). Therefore your purchasing power has remained unchanged and you will be no better or worse off if all your cash flows increase at the general rate of inflation. Indeed, we would expect the same result to apply when we calculate NPVs. If project cash flows increase at exactly the same rate as the general rate of inflation we would expect NPV to be identical to what the NPV would be if there was no inflation. Consider Example 14.3.

You should recall from Chapter 13 that the NPV can be expressed in formula terms as:

$$\frac{FV_1}{1+K} + \frac{FV_2}{(1+K)^2} + \frac{FV_3}{(1+K)^3} + \cdots + \frac{FV_n}{(1+K)^n} - I_0$$

where FV_n are future values, K is the cost of capital and I_0 is the initial investment cost. The NPV calculation is

$$\frac{£600\ 000}{1.10} + \frac{£400\ 000}{(1.10)^2} + \frac{£1\ 000\ 000}{(1.10)^3} - £1\ 000\ 000 = £627\ 347$$

Let us now adjust Example 14.3 and incorporate the effects of inflation. Suppose that an annual inflation rate of 8 per cent is expected during the three years of the project. In this situation the stock market data that are used to calculate the rate of return required by investors will include a premium for anticipated inflation. Hence this premium will be incorporated in the required rate

EXAMPLE 14.3

A division within the Bothnia Company is considering whether to undertake a project that will cost £1 million and will have the following cash inflows:

Year 1	£600 000
Year 2	£400 000
Year 3	£1 000 000

The cost of capital (i.e. the required rate of return) is 10 per cent and the expected rate of inflation is zero. Ignore taxation. Calculate the net present value. Initially assume zero inflation.

of return on the project (i.e. the applicable cost of capital for the project). The revised required rate of return (RRR) is calculated using Fisher's formula:

$$1 + \text{nominal RRR} = [1 + \text{real RRR }(0.10)] \times [1 + \text{rate of inflation}(0.08)]$$
$$= (1 + 0.10)(1 + 0.08)$$
$$= 1.188$$

Therefore the RRR is now 18.8 per cent (i.e. $1.188 - 1$). It is also necessary to adjust the cash flows for inflation. The revised NPV calculation is

$$\frac{£600\,000(1.08)}{(1.10)(1.08)} + \frac{£400\,000(1.08)^2}{(1.10)^2(1.08)^2} + \frac{£1\,000\,000(1.08)^3}{(1.10)^3(1.08)^3} - £1\,000\,000 = £627\,347$$

You can see in the numerator of the NPV calculation that the real cash flows are adjusted at the compound rate of inflation of 8 per cent. In the denominators of the calculation Fisher's equation is shown to calculate the discount rate assuming an expected inflation rate of 8 per cent. Consequently, the inflation factors of 1.08 cancel out. Therefore if the cash flows and the required rate of return are subject to the same rate of inflation then the project's NPV will be unaffected by expected changes in the level of inflation. For example, if inflation is now expected to be 5 per cent instead of 8 per cent then the inflation factor of 1.08 in the numerator and denominator of the NPV calculation would be replaced by 1.05. However, the revised inflation factors would still cancel out, and NPV would remain unchanged.

Looking at the NPV calculation, you should see that there are two correct approaches for adjusting for inflation which will lead to the same answer. They are:

Method 1: Predict *nominal cash flows* (i.e. adjust the cash flows for inflation) and use a *nominal discount rate*.

Method 2: Predict *real cash flows* at today's prices and use a *real discount rate*.

You will have noted that the approach outlined above used Method 1. Can you see that if we use Method 2 the inflation factors of 1.08 will be omitted from the numerator and denominator in the above NPV calculation but the NPV will remain unchanged? The NPV calculation will thus be identical to the calculation shown earlier, which assumed zero inflation.

The correct treatment of inflation therefore requires that the assumptions about inflation that enter the cash flow forecasts are consistent with those that enter into the discount rate calculation. You must avoid the mistakes that are commonly made of discounting real cash flows at nominal discount rates or the discounting of nominal cash flows at real discount rates.

Calculating risk-adjusted discount rates

In Chapter 13 we noted that a company should only invest in new projects if the returns are greater than those that the shareholders could obtain from investing in securities of the same risk traded in the financial markets. If we can measure the returns that investors require for different levels of risk, we can use these rates of return as the discount rates for calculating net present values and thus incorporate risk into investment appraisal.

Studies of average past average returns from investing in securities listed on the UK and USA stock exchanges indicate returns of approximately 4 per cent for treasury bills and 13 per cent for ordinary shares (i.e. common stocks). Investing in treasury bills is nearly risk free, but investing in ordinary shares is risky.[2] There is a possibility that you could earn very low or very high returns if you invest in ordinary shares. The studies of past returns indicate that the safest investment has yielded the lowest average rate of return. The evidence indicates that investors require higher expected returns for investing in risky securities.

The average return from investing in ordinary shares represents the average return you would have obtained from investing in all shares listed on the UK or USA stock exchange. A portfolio containing all shares, or a representative sample, listed on a national stock exchange is termed the market portfolio. It is possible for investors to invest in a portfolio of shares (or a unit trust) that in terms of risk and return is virtually identical to the market portfolio.

The extra average return in the past from investing in the market portfolio compared with the risk free investment has been 9 per cent (13 per cent–4 per cent). This extra return is called the risk premium. Suppose a firm has a project that in terms of risk is identical with the market portfolio. What is the *current* required rate of return on this project? We calculate this by taking the current interest rate on treasury bill securities (called the risk-free rate) and adding the average past risk premium of 9 per cent. Assume that the current interest rate is 4 per cent. The required rate of return (RRR) is calculated as follows:

$$\text{RRR on an equivalent investment to the market portfolio} = \text{risk-free rate (4\%)} + \text{average past risk premium (9\%)} \qquad (14.4)$$

Therefore the project's cash flows should be discounted at 13 per cent and a project that is risk free should be discounted at the same rate as that available from investing in treasury bills (i.e. 4 per cent).

We have now established two benchmarks: the discount rate for risk-free projects and the discount rate for investments that have a risk equivalent to the market portfolio. However, we have not established how discount rates can be estimated for projects that do not fall into these categories. To do this, we must consider the relationship between risk and return.

Let us consider the risk and return from holding the market portfolio. Assume that the expected return from holding the market portfolio is 13 per cent and the risk-free rate of interest is 4 per cent. Therefore the risk premium required for holding the market portfolio is 9 per cent. We shall also assume that the standard deviation from investing in the market portfolio is 16 per cent and that from investing in the risk-free security is zero. These risk–return relationships are plotted in Figure 14.1. Note that the return on the market portfolio is represented by R_m and the return on the risk-free security as R_f.

You can see that an investor can invest in any portfolio that falls on the line between points R_f and R_m. For example, if you invest in portfolio X consisting of £500 in the market portfolio and

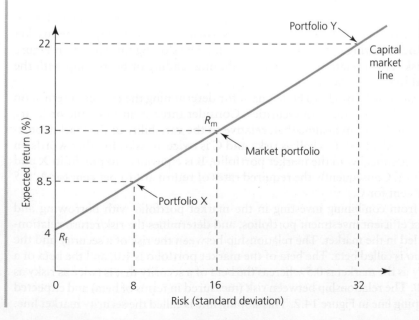

FIGURE 14.1

Risk–return relationship from combining borrowing and lending with the market portfolio

£500 in the risk-free investment, your *expected* return will be 8.5 per cent (£500 at 4 per cent plus £500 at 13 per cent). Note that the standard deviation from investing in portfolio X is

$$\left(\begin{array}{c} 1/2 \times \text{standard deviation of} \\ \text{risk-free security (0)} \end{array}\right) + \left(\begin{array}{c} 1/2 \times \text{standard deviation of} \\ \text{market portfolio (16\%)} \end{array}\right) = 8\% \qquad (14.5)$$

In other words, investing in portfolio X is half as risky as investing in the market portfolio. We can now establish a formula for calculating the *expected* return on portfolios of different levels of risk:

$$\text{expected return} = \frac{\text{risk-free}}{\text{return}} + \left(\text{risk premium} \times \frac{\text{risk of selected portfolio}}{\text{risk of market portfolio}}\right) \qquad (14.6)$$

$$= 4 + (9\% \times 8/16) = 8.5\%$$

Using this formula, we can calculate the expected return for any point along the line R_f to R_m in Figure 14.1. How can you invest in a portfolio that falls on the line above R_m? Such a position is achieved by borrowing and investing your funds in the market portfolio. Suppose you invest £1000 of your own funds and borrow £1000 at the risk-free rate of 4 per cent and invest the combined funds of £2000 in the market portfolio. We shall call this portfolio Y. Your *expected* annual return will be £260 from investing in the market portfolio (£2000 × 13 per cent) less £40 interest on the £1000 loan. Therefore your return will be £220 from investing £1000 of your own funds, i.e. 22 per cent. However, this is the *expected* return, and there is a possibility that the return on the market portfolio could be zero, but you would have to repay the borrowed funds. In other words, by borrowing you increase the variability of your potential returns and therefore the standard deviation. The calculation of the standard deviation for portfolio Y is

$$\frac{(\pounds 2000 \times 16\%) - (\pounds 1000 \times 0\%)}{\pounds 1000} = 32\%$$

We can also use equation (14.6) to calculate the expected return on portfolio Y. It is

$$4\% + (9\% \times 32/16) = 22\%$$

We have now established that an investor can achieve any point along the sloping line in Figure 14.1 by combining lending (i.e. investing in the risk-free security) and investing in the market portfolio or borrowing and investing in the market portfolio. The sloping line shown in Figure 14.1 that indicates the risk return relationship from combining lending or borrowing with the market portfolio is called the capital market line.

The market portfolio can now be used as a benchmark for determining the expected return on *individual* securities, rather than portfolios of securities. Consider three securities – the ordinary shares of companies A, B and C. Let us assume that, relative to the variability of the market portfolio, the risk of security A is identical, B is half as risky and C is twice as risky. In other words, in terms of risk, security A is identical with the market portfolio, B is equivalent to portfolio X and C is equivalent to portfolio Y. Consequently the required rates of return are 13 per cent for A, 8.5 per cent for B and 22 per cent for C.

The returns available from combining investing in the market portfolio with borrowing and lending represent the most efficient investment portfolios, and determines the risk/return relationships for all securities traded in the market. The relationship between the risk of a security and the risk of the market portfolio is called beta. The beta of the market portfolio is 1.0, and the beta of a security that is half as risky as the market is 0.5 whereas the beta of a security that is twice as risky as the market portfolio is 2.0. The relationship between risk (measured in terms of beta) and expected return is shown by the sloping line in Figure 14.2. This sloping line is called the security market line.

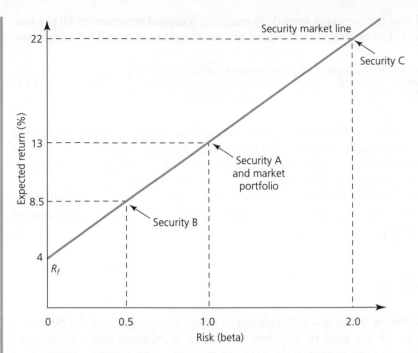

FIGURE 14.2

Risk–return relationship expressed in terms of beta

The model described above is called the capital asset pricing model (CAPM). The equation for the CAPM is the equation for the security market line shown in Figure 14.2, and can be used to establish the expected return on any security. The equation is

$$\begin{matrix} \text{expected} \\ \text{return on a} \\ \text{security} \end{matrix} = \begin{matrix} \text{risk-free} \\ \text{rate} \end{matrix} + \left(\begin{matrix} \text{expected return} \\ \text{on the market} \\ \text{portfolio} \end{matrix} - \begin{matrix} \text{risk-free} \\ \text{rate} \end{matrix} \right) \times \text{beta} \qquad (14.7)$$

Therefore

$$\text{security A} = 4\% + (13\% - 4\%) \times 1.0 = 13\%$$
$$\text{security B} = 4\% + (13\% - 4\%) \times 0.5 = 8.5\%$$
$$\text{security C} = 4\% + (13\% - 4\%) \times 2.0 = 22\%$$

How is beta calculated? For the answer to this question you should consult the business finance literature (see recommended reading at the end of the chapter). Calculating betas in practice is very tedious. Fortunately, it is unnecessary to calculate betas, since their values are published in various risk measurement publications relating to securities traded in financial markets. You should now know how to calculate the required rates of returns for a firm's securities: simply multiply the average risk premium from investing in the market portfolio (9 per cent) by the beta for the security, and add this to the current interest rate on treasury bills.

Weighted average cost of capital

So far we have assumed that firms are financed only by equity finance (i.e. ordinary share capital and retained earnings). However, most companies are likely to be financed by a combination of debt and equity capital. These companies aim to maintain target proportions of debt and equity.

The cost of *new* debt capital is simply the after tax interest cost of raising new debt. Assume that the after tax cost of new debt capital is 6 per cent and the required rate of return on equity capital is 14 per cent and that the company intends to maintain a capital structure of 50 per cent debt and 50 per cent equity. The overall cost of capital for the company is calculated as follows:

$$\left(\begin{array}{c}\text{proportion of debt capital} \\ \times \text{ cost of debt capital} \\ (0.5 \times 6\%)\end{array}\right) + \left(\begin{array}{c}\text{proportion of equity capital} \\ \times \text{ cost of equity capital} \\ (0.5 \times 14\%)\end{array}\right) = 10\% \qquad (14.8)$$

The overall cost of capital is also called the weighted average cost of capital. Can we use the weighted average cost of capital as the discount rate to calculate a project's NPV? The answer is yes, provided that the project is of equivalent risk to the firm's existing assets and the firm intends to maintain its target capital structure of 50 per cent debt and 50 per cent equity.

We have now established how to calculate the discount rate for projects that are of similar risk to the firm's existing assets and to incorporate the financing aspects. It is the weighted average cost of equity and debt capital.

Sensitivity analysis

The aim of sensitivity analysis is not to quantify risk but to assess how responsive the NPV is to changes in the variables which are used to calculate it. Thus it is assumed that risk adjusted discount rates are derived using the approach described in the preceding sections. Figure 14.3 illustrates that the NPV calculation is dependent on several independent variables, all of which are uncertain. The approach requires that the NPVs are calculated under alternative assumptions to determine how sensitive they are to changing conditions.

The application of sensitivity analysis can indicate those variables to which the NPV is most sensitive, and the extent to which these variables may change before the investment results in a negative NPV. In other words, sensitivity analysis indicates why a project might fail. Management should review any critical variables to assess whether or not there is a strong possibility of events occurring which will lead to a negative NPV. Management should also pay particular attention to controlling those variables to which NPV is particularly sensitive, once the decision has been taken to accept the investment. Sensitivity analysis is illustrated with Example 14.4.

FIGURE 14.3

Sensitivity of NPV to changes in independent variables

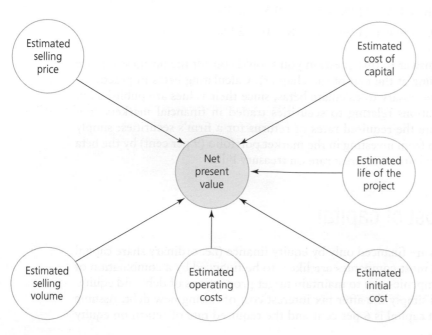

Some of the variables referred to in Example 14.4 to which sensitivity analysis can be applied are as follows.

1 *Sales volume*: The net cash flows will have to fall to £876 040 (£2 000 000/2.283 discount factor) for the NPV to be zero, because it will be zero when the present value of the future cash flows is equal to the investment cost of £2 000 000. As the cash flows are equal each year, the cumulative discount tables in Appendix B can be used. The discount factor for 15 per cent and year 3 is 2.283. If the discount factor is divided into the required present value of £2 000 000, we get an annual cash flow of £876 040. Given that the most likely *net* cash flow is £1 000 000, the *net* cash flow may decline by approximately £124 000 each year (£1million–£876 040) before the NPV becomes zero. Total sales revenue may therefore decline by £372 000 (assuming that net cash flow is 33.1/3 per cent of sales). At a selling price of £30 per unit, this represents 12 400 units, or alternatively we may state that the sales volume may decline by 12.4 per cent before the NPV becomes negative.

2 *Selling price*: When the sales volume is 100 000 units per annum, total annual sales revenue can fall to approximately £2 876 000 (£3 000 000 – £124 000) before the NPV becomes negative (note that it is assumed that total variable costs and units sold will remain unchanged). This represents a selling price per unit of £28.76, or a reduction of £1.24 per unit, which represents a 4.1 per cent reduction in the selling price.

3 *Variable costs*: The total annual variable costs can increase by £124 000 or £1.24 per unit before NPV becomes zero. This represents an increase of 6.2 per cent.

4 *Initial outlay*: The initial outlay can rise by the NPV before the investment breaks even. The initial outlay may therefore increase by £283 000 or 14.15 per cent.

5 *Cost of capital*: We calculate the internal rate of return for the project, which is 23 per cent. Consequently, the cost of capital can increase by 53 per cent before the NPV becomes negative.

The elements to which the NPV appears to be most sensitive are the items with the lowest percentage changes. They are selling price followed by the variable costs, and it is important for the manager to pay particular attention to these items so that they can be carefully monitored.

Sensitivity analysis can take various forms. In our example, for the selected variables, we focused on the extent to which each could change for NPV to become zero. Another form of sensitivity analysis is to examine the impact on NPV of a specified percentage change in a selected variable. For example, what is the impact on NPV if sales volume falls by 10 per cent? A third approach is to examine the impact on NPV of pessimistic, most likely and optimistic estimates for each selected variable.

EXAMPLE 14.4

One of the divisions of the Bothnia Company is considering the purchase of a new machine, and estimates of the most likely cash flows are as follows:

	Year 0 (£)	Year 1 (£)	Year 2 (£)	Year 3 (£)
Initial outlay	–2 000 000			
Cash inflows				
(100 000 units at				
£30 per unit)		3 000 000	3 000 000	3 000 000
Variable costs		2 000 000	2 000 000	2 000 000
Net cash flows	–2 000 000	+1 000 000	+1 000 000	+1 000 000

The cost of capital is 15 per cent and the net present value is £283 000.

Sensitivity analysis has a number of limitations. In particular, the method requires that changes in each key variable be isolated, but management is more interested in the combination of the effect of changes in two or more key variables. Nevertheless, surveys by Pike (1996) and Arnold and Hatzopoulos (2000) indicate that it is the most widely used formal risk management technique being used by approximately 85 per cent of the surveyed firms.

Initiation, authorization and review of projects

The capital investment process should ensure that procedures are in place so that new projects are initiated, investigated and evaluated using the approaches described in this and the previous chapter. It is also necessary to ensure that projects that are accepted contribute to achieving an organization's objectives and support its strategies. In addition, once a project has been authorized procedures should be established for reviewing and controlling new investments. The capital investment process involves several stages including:

1 the search for investment opportunities;
2 initial screening;
3 project authorizations;
4 controlling the capital expenditure during the installation stage;
5 post-completion audit of the cash flows.

Search for investment opportunities

Potential investment projects are not just born – someone has to suggest them. Without a creative search of new investment opportunities, even the most sophisticated appraisal techniques are worthless. A firm's prosperity depends far more on its ability to create investments than on its ability to appraise them. Thus it is important that a firm scans the environment for potential opportunities or takes action to protect itself against potential threats. This process is closely linked to the strategies of an organization. An important task of senior management is therefore to promote a culture that encourages the search for and promotion of new investment opportunities.

Initial screening

During this stage projects are examined and subject to preliminary assessment to ascertain if they are likely to warrant further attention through the application of more sophisticated analysis. Projects that are not considered to warrant further attention are normally discarded. The preliminary assessment involves an examination of whether projects satisfy strategic criteria and conform to initial risk requirements. At this stage projects may also be subject to an assessment as to whether they satisfy simplistic financial criteria, such as meeting required payback periods. For most large firms, those projects that meet the initial screening requirements are included in an annual capital budget, which is a list of projects planned for the coming year. However, it should be noted that the inclusion of a project in the capital budget does not provide an authorization for the final go-ahead for the investment.

Project authorizations

Many organizations require that project proposals are presented in a formalized manner by submitting capital appropriation request forms for each project. These requests include descriptions of the projects, detailed cash flow forecasts, the investment required and a financial appraisal incorporating discounted cash flow analyzes. Because investment decisions are of vital importance appropriation requests are generally submitted for approval to a top management committee. Companies normally set ceilings for investments so that only those projects that exceed the ceiling are submitted to the top management committee. Investments below the ceiling are normally subject to approval at lower management levels.

Controlling the capital expenditure during the installation stage

Comparisons should be made between actual and estimated expenditures at periodic intervals during the installation and construction stage of the project. Reports should be prepared giving details of the percentage completion, over- or under-spending relative to the stage of completion, the estimated costs to complete compared with the original estimate, the time taken compared with the estimate for the current stage of completion, and also the estimated completion date compared with the original estimate. This information will enable management to take corrective cost-saving action such as changing the construction schedule.

SOURCE: ADAPTED FROM MATHIJS BRANTJES; HENK VON EIJE; FRANS EUSMAN AND WOUT PRINS, POST-COMPLETION AUDITING WITHIN HEINEKEN. *MANAGEMENT ACCOUNTING (UK)*, APRIL, 1999, PP. 20–22.

Post-completion auditing (PCA) within Heineken

At Heineken Nederland a PCA is conducted some months after the end of the implementation phase of the investment project. It is still impossible to evaluate whether all the cash flow projections are actually working out; this often depends on various external circumstances. What, however, can be evaluated is whether the project budget was properly estimated, what can be improved in the implementation phase of subsequent investments, how the installation is functioning at that time and whether the expected savings and improvements seem realistic.

It will never be possible to evaluate an investment completely objectively. This leaves room for personal interpretation and perhaps portraying the results in a better light. It is therefore better to separate responsibility for the investment decision from that of the PCA. This means that the line management involved will not conduct the PCA. The staff of the Planning and Control departments are responsible for the PCA. The justification for this internal audit is based on the notion that a professional controller works autonomously and an attempt is made to establish quantifiable objectives which limit the necessary qualitative evaluations. All capital investments are not necessarily subject to a PCA and that business unit managers can be selective. Self-selection bias is, however, reduced because senior management can also ask for a PCA of a specific investment. Finally, as a result of the experiences described, the Executive Board of Heineken NV has, in the context of promoting 'best practices', called for PCAs to be conducted within the entire group worldwide.

Discussion points

1 Why are all capital investments not subject to a PCA?

2 What factors are likely to determine whether an investment will be subject to a PCA?

REAL WORLD VIEWS 14.1

COURTESY OF HEINEKEN INTERNATIONAL

Post-completion audit of cash flows

When the investment is in operation, post-completion audits should be undertaken whereby the actual results are compared with the estimated results that were included in the investment proposal. Whenever possible, actual cash flows plus estimated cash flows for the remainder of the project's life should be compared with the cash flows that were included in the original estimate. However, the feasibility of making such a comparison will depend on the ease and cost of estimating future cash flows.

A major problem is that, except for the very large projects, the portion of cash flows that stem from a specific capital investment is very difficult to isolate. All one can do in such situations is to scrutinize carefully the investment at the approval stage and incorporate the estimated results into departmental operating budgets. Although the results of individual projects cannot be isolated, their combined effect can be examined as part of the conventional periodic performance review.

A post-audit of capital investment decisions is a very difficult task, and any past investment decisions that have proved to be wrong should not be interpreted in isolation. It is important to remind oneself that capital investment decisions are made under uncertainty. For example, a good decision may turn out to be unsuccessful yet may still have been the correct decision in the light of the information and alternatives available at the time. We would agree that a manager should undertake a project that costs £100 000 and has a 0.9 probability of a positive NPV of £20 000 and a 0.1 probability of a negative NPV of £5000. However, if the event with a 0.1 probability occurred, a post-completion audit would suggest that the investment has been undesirable.

Care should be taken to ensure that post-audits are not conducted as recriminatory 'post-mortems'. Adopting such an approach can discourage initiative and produce a policy of over-caution. There is a danger that managers will submit only safe investment proposals. The problem is likely to be reduced if managers know their selections will be fairly judged.

In spite of all the problems a post-audit comparison should be undertaken. A record of past performance and mistakes is one way of improving future performance and ensuring that fewer mistakes are made. In addition, the fact that the proposers of capital investment projects are aware that their estimates will be compared with actual results encourages them to exercise restraint and submit more thorough and realistic appraisals of future investment projects. The survey evidence indicates that post-audits are used by the majority of UK companies. A survey by Arnold and Hatzopoulos (2000) reported that 28 per cent of the surveyed companies always, and a further 59 per cent sometimes, conducted post-audits of major capital expenditure.

SUMMARY

The following items relate to the learning objectives listed at the beginning of the chapter.

● **Explain capital rationing and select the optimum combination of investments when capital is rationed for a single period.**

Capital rationing applies to a situation where there is a constraint on the amount of funds that can be invested during a specific period of time. In this situation the net present value is maximized by adopting the profitability index method (i.e. the present value of cash flows divided by the investment outlay) of ranking and using this ranking to select investments up to the total investment funds that are available for the period.

● **Calculate the incremental taxation payments arising from a proposed investment.**

The cash flows from a project must be reduced by the amount of taxation payable on these cash flows. However, the taxation savings arising from the capital allowances (i.e. annual writing down allowances) reduce the taxation payments. Because taxation payments do not occur at the same time as the associated cash flows, the precise timing of the taxation payments should be identified to calculate NPV. You should refer to the section headed 'Taxation and investment decisions' for an illustration of the computation of the incremental taxation payment.

● **Describe the two approaches for adjusting for inflation when appraising capital projects.**

The net present value can be adjusted by two basic ways to take inflation into account. First, a discount rate can be used, based on the required rate of return, that includes an allowance for inflation. Remember that cash flows must also be adjusted for inflation. Secondly, the anticipated rate of inflation can be excluded from the discount rate, and the cash flows can be expressed in real terms. In other words, the first method discounts nominal cash flows at a nominal discount rate and the second method discounts real cash flows at a real discount rate.

● **Explain how risk-adjusted discount rates are calculated.**

Risk-adjusted discount rates for a firm can be calculated using the capital asset pricing model (CAPM). The CAPM uses beta as a measure of risk. Beta is a measure of the sensitivity of the returns on a firm's securities relative to a proxy market portfolio (e.g. the Financial Times all-share index). The risk-adjusted return is derived by adding a risk premium for a firm's securities to a risk free rate (normally represented by government treasury bills). The risk premium is derived

by estimating the return on the market portfolio over the risk free rate and multiplying this premium by the beta of a firm's shares.

● **Explain how sensitivity analysis can be applied to investment appraisal.**

Sensitivity analysis can take many forms but the most popular form is to independently ascertain the percentage change in each of the variables used to calculate NPV for the NPV to become zero.

● **Describe the initiation, authorization and review procedures for the investment process.**

The capital investment process entails several stages including: (a) the search for investment opportunities; (b) initial screening of the projects; (c) project authorizations; (d) controlling the capital expenditure during the installation stage, and (e) a post-completion audit of the cash flows. You should refer to the end of Chapter 14 for an explanation of each of these stages.

● **Additional learning objective specified in Appendix 14.1.**

The appendix to this chapter includes an additional learning objective: to evaluate mutually exclusive investments with unequal lives. Because this topic does not form part of the curriculum for many courses it is presented in the appendix to this chapter. You should check your course curriculum to ascertain if you need to read Appendix 14.1.

Notes

1 In 2007/8 the profits of UK companies were subject to a corporate tax rate of 30 per cent. For small companies with annual profits of less than £300 000 the corporate tax rate was 20 per cent.

2 Future payments of interest and the principal repayment on maturity are fixed and known with

certainty. Gilt-edged securities, such as treasury bills, are therefore risk-free in nominal terms. However, they are not risk-free in real terms because changes in interest rates will result in changes in the market values.

Appendix 14.1: The evaluation of mutually exclusive investments with unequal lives

ADVANCED READING

The application of the net present value method is complicated when a choice must be made between two or more projects, where the projects have unequal lives. A perfect comparison requires knowledge about future alternatives that will be available for the period of the difference in the lives of the projects that are being considered. Let us look at the situation in Example 14A.1.

In Example 14A.1 it is assumed that both machines produce exactly the same output. Therefore only cash outflows will be considered, because revenue cash inflows are assumed to be the same whichever alternative is selected. Consequently our objective is to choose the alternative with the lower present value of cash outflows. Revenue cash inflows should only be included in the analysis if they differ for each alternative. Suppose we compute the present value (PV) of the cash outflows for each alternative.

| | End of year cash flows (£000) | | | | |
Machine	Year 0	Year 1	Year 2	Year 3	PV at 10%
X	1200	240	240	240	1796.880
Y	600	360	360		1224.960

Machine Y appears to be the more acceptable alternative, but the analysis is incomplete because we must consider what will happen at the end of year 2 if machine Y is chosen. For example, if the life of the task to be performed by the machines is in excess of three years, it will be necessary to replace machine Y at the end of year 2; whereas if machine X is chosen, replacement will be deferred until the end of year 3. We shall consider the following methods of evaluating projects with unequal lives:

1 Evaluate the alternatives over an interval equal to the lowest common multiple of the lives of the alternatives under consideration.

2 Equivalent annual cash flow method by which the cash flows are converted into an equivalent annual annuity.

3 Estimate terminal values for one of the alternatives.

1. Lowest common multiple method

Assume that the life of the task to be performed by the machines is at least six years. Consequently, both machines will be replaced at the end of their useful lives. If machine X is replaced by an identical machine then it will be replaced every three years, whereas machine Y will be replaced every two years. A correct analysis therefore requires that a sequence of decisions be evaluated over a common time horizon so that the analysis of each alternative will be comparable. The common time horizon can be determined by setting the time horizon equal to the lowest common multiple of the

EXAMPLE 14A.1

The Bothnia Company is choosing between two machines, X and Y. They are designed differently but have identical capacity and do exactly the same job. Machine X costs £1 200 000 and will last three years, costing £240 000 per year to run. Machine Y is a cheaper model costing £600 000 but will last only two years and costs £360 000 per year to run. The cost of capital is 10 per cent. Which machine should the firm purchase?

lives of the alternatives under consideration. In Example 14A.1, where the lives of the alternatives are two and three years, the lowest common multiple is six years. The analysis for the sequence of replacements over a six-year period is as follows:

	End-of-year cash flows (£000)						
	0	1	2	3	4	5	6
Sequence of type X machines							
Capital investment	1200			1200			
Operating costs		240	240	240	240	240	240
PV at 10%	−3146.400						
Sequence of type Y machines							
Capital investment	600		600		600		
Operating costs		360	360	360	360	360	360
PV at 10%	−3073.200						

By year 6 machine X is replaced twice and machine Y three times. At this point the alternatives are comparable, and a replacement must be made in year 6 regardless of the initial choice of X or Y. We can therefore compare the present value of the cost of these two sequences of machines. It is preferable to invest in a sequence of type Y machines, since this alternative has the lowest present value of cash outflows.

2. Equivalent annual cash flow method

Comparing projects over a span of time equal to the lowest common multiple of their individual life spans is often tedious. Instead, we can use the second method – the equivalent annual cash flow method. The costs for the different lives of machines X and Y are made comparable if they are converted into an equivalent annuity. The present value of the costs of machine X is £1 796 880 for a three-year time horizon. The equivalent annual cash outflows for the machine can be solved from the following formula:

present value of cash flows = equivalent annual cash flow × annuity factor for N years of R%

(14A.1)

Solving for the equivalent annual cash flow, we have

$$\text{equivalent annual cash flow} = \frac{\text{present value of cash flows}}{\text{annuity factor for } N \text{ years at } R\%} \qquad (14A.2)$$

Using the data for machine X, the equivalent annual cash flow is

$$\frac{£1\ 796\ 880}{2.487} = £722\ 509$$

The annuity factor is obtained from Appendix B for three years and a 10 per cent discount rate.

What does the equivalent annual cash flow represent? Merely that the sequence of machine X cash flows is exactly like a sequence of cash flows of £722 509 a year. Calculating the equivalent annual cash flow for machine Y, you will find that it is £705 622 a year (£1 224 960/1.736). A stream of machine X cash flows is the costlier; therefore we should select machine Y. Using this method, our decision rule is to choose the machine with the lower annual equivalent cost.

Note that when we used the common time horizon method the present value of a sequence of machine Xs was £3 146 400 compared with £3 073 200 for a sequence of machine Ys; a present value cost saving of £73 200 in favour of machine Y. The equivalent annual cash flow saving for machine Y was £16 887 (£722 509 – £705 622). If we discount this saving for a time horizon of six years, the present value is £73 200, the same as the saving we calculated using the lowest common multiple method (note that small differences do exist because of rounding errors).

You should note that the equivalent annual cash flow method should only be used when there is a sequence of identical replacements for each alternative and this process continues until a common time horizon is reached.

3. Estimate terminal values

Consider a situation where machines A and B have lives of six and eight years respectively. Assume that the life of the task to be performed by the machines is ten years. Because the task life is shorter than the lowest common multiple (24 years), we cannot use either of the first two methods. An alternative approach is to assume that each machine will be replaced once (machine X at the end of year 6 and machine Y at the end of year 8) and incorporate estimates of the disposal values into the analysis for both machines at the end of the ten-year task life.

Key terms and concepts

balancing allowance (p. 323)
balancing charge (p. 323)
beta (p. 328)
capital allowances (p. 321)
capital asset pricing model (pp. 329)
capital market line (p. 328)
capital rationing (p. 320)
depreciation tax shields (p. 321)
equivalent annual cash flow method
    (p. 337)

general rate of inflation (p. 325)
hard capital rationing (p. 320)
lowest common multiple method
    (p. 336)
market portfolio (p. 327)
nominal or money rates of return
    (p. 324)
nominal cash flows (p. 324)
profitability index (p. 321)
post-completion audits (p. 334)

real cash flows (p. 324)
real rate of return (p. 324)
risk premium (p. 327)
security market line (p. 328)
sensitivity analysis (p. 330)
soft capital rationing (p. 320)
weighted average cost of capital
    (p. 330)
writing-down allowances (p. 321)

Recommended readings

This chapter has provided an outline of the capital asset pricing model and the calculation of risk-adjusted discount rate. These topics are dealt with in more depth in the business finance literature. You should refer to Brealey and Myers (2006) for a description of the capital asset pricing model and risk-adjusted

discount rates. For a discussion of the differences between company, divisional and project cost of capital and an explanation of how project discount rates can be calculated when project risk is different from average overall firm risk see Pike and Neale (2005).

Key examination points

A common error is for students to include depreciation and apportioned overheads in the DCF analysis. Remember that only incremental cash flows should be included in the analysis. Where a question includes taxation, you should separately calculate the incremental taxable profits and then work out the tax payment. You should then include the tax payment in the DCF analysis. Incremental taxable profits are normally incremental cash flows less capital allowances on the project. To simplify the calculations, questions sometimes indicate that capital allowances should be calculated on a straight-line depreciation method.

Do not use accounting profits instead of taxable profits to work out the tax payment. Taxable profits are calculated

by adding back depreciation to accounting profits and then deducting capital allowances. Make sure that you include any balancing allowance or charge and disposal value in the DCF analysis if the asset is sold.

With inflation, you should discount nominal cash flows at the nominal discount rate. Most questions give the nominal discount rate (also called the money discount rate). You should then adjust the cash flows for inflation. If you are required to choose between alternative projects, check that they have equal lives. If not, use one of the methods described in the Appendix to this chapter.

ASSESSMENT MATERIAL

The review questions are short questions that enable you to assess your understanding of the main topics included in the chapter. The numbers in parentheses provide you with the page numbers to refer to if you cannot answer a specific question.

The review problems are more complex and require you to relate and apply the content to various business problems. The problems are graded by their level of difficulty. Solutions to review problems that are not preceded by the term 'IM' are provided in a separate section at the end of the book. Solutions to problems preceded by the term 'IM' are provided in the *Instructor's Manual* accompanying this book and also on the lecturer's password protected section of the website www.drury-online.com. Additional review problems with fully worked solutions are provided in the *Student's Manual* that accompanies this book.

The website also includes over 30 case problems. A list of these cases is provided on pages 665–7. The Rawhide Company is a case study that is relevant to the introductory stages of a management accounting course.

Review questions

14.1 What is capital rationing? Distinguish between hard and soft capital rationing. *(pp. 320–21)*

14.2 Explain how the optimum investment programme should be determined when capital is rationed for a single period. *(pp. 320–21)*

14.3 How does taxation affect the appraisal of capital investments? *(pp. 321–23)*

14.4 Define writing-down-allowances (also known as depreciation tax shields or capital allowances), balancing allowances and balancing charges. *(pp. 321–23)*

14.5 How does the presence of inflation affect the appraisal of capital investments? *(p. 324)*

14.6 Distinguish between nominal cash flows and real cash flows and nominal discount rates and real discount rates. *(p. 324)*

14.7 Why is it necessary to use risk-adjusted discount rates to appraise capital investments? *(pp. 326–27)*

14.8 Explain how risk-adjusted discount rates are calculated. *(pp. 327–29)*

14.9 How can sensitivity analysis help in appraising capital investments? What are the limitations of sensitivity analysis? *(pp. 330–31)*

14.10 Describe the different forms of sensitivity analysis. *(p. 331)*

14.11 Describe the stages involved in the initiation, authorization and review of projects *(pp. 332–34)*

14.12 Explain what a post-completion audit is and how it can provide useful benefits *(p. 334)*

Review problems

14.13 Intermediate. A five year project has a net present value of $160 000 when it is discounted at 12 per cent. The project includes an annual cash outflow of $50 000 for each of the five years. No tax is payable on projects of this type.

The percentage increase in the value of this annual cash outflow that would make the project no longer financially viable is closest to

a   64%
b   89%
c   113%
d   156%

CIMA P2 Management Accounting: Decision Management

14.14 Advanced. A supermarket is trying to determine the optimal replacement policy for its fleet of delivery vehicles. The total purchase price of the fleet is £220 000.

The running costs and scrap values of the fleet at the end of each year are:

	Year 1	Year 2	Year 3	Year 4	Year 5
Running costs	£110 000	£132 000	£154 000	£165 000	£176 000
Scrap value	£121 000	£88 000	£66 000	£55 000	£25 000

The supermarket's cost of capital is 12 per cent per annum.

Ignore taxation and inflation.

The supermarket should replace its fleet of delivery vehicles at the end of

a   year 1.
b   year 2.
c   year 3.
d   year 4.
e   year 5.

(4 marks)

CIMA Management Accounting – Decision Making

14.15 Advanced. The following data relate to both questions (a) and (b)

A company is considering investing in a manufacturing project that would have a three-year life span. The investment would involve an immediate cash outflow of £50 000 and have a zero residual value. In each of the three years, 4000 units would be produced and sold. The contribution per unit, based on current prices, is £5. The company has an annual cost of capital of 8 per cent. It is expected that the inflation rate will be 3 per cent in each of the next three years.

(a)   The net present value of the project (to the nearest £500) is

a   £4500
b   £5000
c   £5500
d   £6000
e   £6500

(3 marks)

(b)   If the annual inflation rate is now projected to be 4 per cent, the maximum monetary cost of capital for this project to remain viable, is (to the nearest 0.5 per cent)

a   13.0%
b   13.5%
c   14.0%
d   14.5%
e   15.0%

(2 marks)

CIMA Management Accounting – Decision Making

14.16 Advanced: Inflation and taxation. Assume that you have been appointed finance director of Breckall plc. The company is considering investing in the production of an electronic security device, with an expected market life of five years.

The previous finance director has undertaken an analysis of the proposed project; the main features of his analysis are shown below. He has recommended that the project should not be undertaken because the estimated annual accounting rate of return is only 12.3 per cent.

Proposed electronic security device project

	Year 0 (£000)	Year 1 (£000)	Year 2 (£000)	Year 3 (£000)	Year 4 (£000)	Year 5 (£000)
Investment in depreciable fixed assets	4500					
Cumulative investment in working capital	300	400	500	600	700	700
Sales		3500	4900	5320	5740	5320
Materials		535	750	900	1050	900
Labour		1070	1500	1800	2100	1800
Overhead		50	100	100	100	100
Interest		576	576	576	576	576
Depreciation		900	900	900	900	900
		3131	3826	4276	4726	4276
Taxable profit		369	1074	1044	1014	1044
Taxation		129	376	365	355	365
Profit after tax		240	698	679	659	679

Total initial investment is £4 800 000

Average annual after tax profit is £591 000

All the above cash flow and profit estimates have been prepared in terms of present day costs and prices, since the previous finance director assumed that the sales price could be increased to compensate for any increase in costs.

You have available the following additional information:

a   Selling prices, working capital requirements and overhead expenses are expected to increase by 5 per cent per year.

b   Material costs and labour costs are expected to increase by 10 per cent per year.

c   Capital allowances (tax depreciation) are allowable for taxation purposes against profits at 25 per cent per year on a reducing balance basis.

d   Taxation on profits is at a rate of 35 per cent, payable one year in arrears.

e   The fixed assets have no expected salvage value at the end of five years.

f   The company's real after-tax weighted average cost of capital is estimated to be 8 per cent per year, and nominal after-tax weighted average cost of capital 15 per cent per year.

Assume that all receipts and payments arise at the end of the year to which they relate, except those in year 0, which occur immediately.

Required:

a   Estimate the net present value of the proposed project. State clearly any assumptions that you make.   *(13 marks)*

b   Calculate by how much the discount rate would have to change to result in a net present value of approximately zero.   *(4 marks)*

c   Describe how sensitivity analysis might be used to assist in assessing this project. What are the weaknesses of sensitivity analysis in capital investment appraisal? Briefly outline alternative techniques of incorporating risk into capital investment appraisal.   *(8 marks)*

ACCA Level 3 Financial Management

14.17 Advanced: Replacement decision. Ceder Ltd has details of two machines that could fulfil the company's future production plans. Only one of these will be purchased.

The 'standard' model costs £50 000, and the 'de luxe' £88 000, payable immediately. Both machines would require the input of £10 000 working capital throughout their working lives, and both have no expected scrap value at the end of their expected working lives of four years for the standard machine and six years for the de luxe machine.

The forecast pre-tax operating net cash flows (£) associated with the two machines are

	Years hence					
	1	2	3	4	5	6
Standard	20 500	22 860	24 210	23 410		
De luxe	32 030	26 110	25 380	25 940	38 560	35 100

The de luxe machine has only recently been introduced to the market, and has not been fully tested in operating conditions. Because of the higher risk involved, the appropriate discount rate for the de luxe machine is believed to be 14 per cent per year, 2 per cent higher than the discount rate for the standard machine.

The company is proposing to finance the purchase of either machine with a term loan at a fixed interest rate of 11 per cent per year.

Taxation at 35 per cent is payable on operating cash flows one year in arrears, and capital allowances are available at 25 per cent per year on a reducing balance basis.

Required:

a   For both the standard and the de luxe machines calculate:
    (i) payback period;
    (ii) net present value.
    Recommend, with reasons, which of the two machines Ceder Ltd should purchase.
    (Relevant calculations must be shown.)   *(13 marks)*

b   Surveys have shown that the accounting rate of return and payback period are widely used by companies in the capital investment decision process. Suggest reasons for the widespread use of these investment appraisal techniques.   *(6 marks)*

ACCA Level 3 Financial Management

14.18 Advanced: Optimal asset replacement period with inflation. The owner of a taxi company is considering the replacement of his vehicles. He is planning to retire in six years' time and is therefore only concerned with that period of time, but cannot decide whether it is better to replace the vehicles every two years or every three years.

The following data have been estimated (all values at today's price levels):

Purchase cost and trade in values

Taxi cost	£15 000
Trade-in value of taxi:	
after 2 years	£7 000
after 3 years	£4 000

Annual costs and revenues

Vehicle running cost	£20 000 per year
Fares charged to customers	£40 000 per year

Vehicles servicing and repair costs

Vehicle servicing and repair costs depend on the age of the vehicle. In the following table year 1 represents the cost in the first year of the vehicle's ownership; year 2 represents the cost in the second year of ownership, and so on:

Year 1	£500
Year 2	£2500
Year 3	£4000

Inflation

New vehicle costs and trade in-values are expected to increase by 5 per cent per year.
Vehicle running costs and fares are expected to increase by 7 per cent per year.
Vehicle servicing and repair costs are expected to increase by 10 per cent per year.

Required:

Advise the company on the optimum replacement cycle for its vehicles and state the net present value of the opportunity cost of making the wrong decision. Use a discount rate of 12 per cent per year. All workings and assumptions should be shown. Ignore taxation.   *(10 marks)*

CIMA P2 Management Accounting: Decision Management

14.19 Advanced: Single period capital rationing. Banden Ltd is a highly geared company that wishes to expand its operations. Six possible capital investments have been identified, but the company only has access to a total of £620 000. The projects are not divisible and may not be postponed until a future period. After the projects end it is unlikely that similar investment opportunities will occur.

Expected net cash inflows (including salvage value)

Project	Year 1 (£)	2 (£)	3 (£)	4 (£)	5 (£)	Initial Outlay (£)
A	70 000	70 000	70 000	70 000	70 000	246 000
B	75 000	87 000	64 000			180 000
C	48 000	48 000	63 000	73 000		175 000
D	62 000	62 000	62 000	62 000		180 000
E	40 000	50 000	60 000	70 000	40 000	180 000
F	35 000	82 000	82 000			150 000

Projects A and E are mutually exclusive. All projects are believed to be of similar risk to the company's existing capital investments.

Any surplus funds may be invested in the money market to earn a return of 9 per cent per year. The money market may be assumed to be an efficient market.

Banden's cost of capital is 12 per cent per year.

Required:

a Calculate:
  (i) The expected net present value;
  (ii) The expected profitability index associated with each of the six projects, and rank the projects according to both of these investment appraisal methods.
  Explain briefly why these rankings differ. *(8 marks)*

b Give reasoned advice to Banden Ltd recommending which projects should be selected. *(6 marks)*

c A director of the company has suggested that using the company's normal cost of capital might not be appropriate in a capital rationing situation. Explain whether you agree with the director. *(4 marks)*

d The director has also suggested the use of linear or integer programming to assist with the selection of projects. Discuss the advantages and disadvantages of these mathematical programming methods to Banden Ltd. *(7 marks)*

ACCA Level 3 Financial Management

14.20 Advanced: Investment appraisal, expected values and sensitivity analysis. Umunat plc is considering investing £50 000 in a new machine with an expected life of five years. The machine will have no scrap value at the end of five years. It is expected that 20 000 units will be sold each year at a selling price of £3.00 per unit. Variable production costs are expected to be £1.65 per unit, while incremental fixed costs, mainly the wages of a maintenance engineer, are expected to be £10 000 per year. Umunat plc uses a discount rate of 12 per cent for investment appraisal purposes and expects investment projects to recover their initial investment within two years.

Required:

a Explain why risk and uncertainty should be considered in the investment appraisal process. *(5 marks)*

b Calculate and comment on the payback period of the project. *(4 marks)*

c Evaluate the sensitivity of the project's net present value to a change in the following project variables:
  (i) sales volume;
  (ii) sales price;
  (iii) variable cost;
  and discuss the use of sensitivity analysis as a way of evaluating project risk. *(10 marks)*

d Upon further investigation it is found that there is a significant chance that the expected sales volume of 20 000 units per year will not be achieved. The sales manager of Umunat plc suggests that sales volumes could depend on expected economic states that could be assigned the following probabilities:

Economic state	Poor	Normal	Good
Probability	0.3	0.6	0.1
Annual sales volume (units)	17 500	20 000	22 500

Calculate and comment on the expected net present value of the project. *(6 marks)*

ACCA 2.4 Financial Management and Control

IM14.1 Advanced. You have been appointed as chief management accountant of a well-established company with a brief to improve the quality of information supplied for management decision-making. As a first task you have decided to examine the system used for providing information for capital investment decisions. You find that discounted cash flow techniques are used but in a mechanical fashion with no apparent understanding of the figures produced. The most recent example of an investment appraisal produced by the accounting department showed a positive net present value of £35 000 for a five-year life project when discounted at 14 per cent which you are informed 'was the rate charged on the bank loan raised to finance the investment'. You note that the appraisal did not include any consideration of the effects of inflation nor was there any form of risk analysis.

You are required to:

a explain the meaning of a positive net present value of £35 000; *(4 marks)*

b comment on the appropriateness or otherwise of the discounting rate used; *(4 marks)*

c state whether you agree with the treatment of inflation and, if not, explain how you would deal with inflation in investment appraisals; *(6 marks)*

d explain what is meant by 'risk analysis' and describe ways this could be carried out in investment appraisals and what benefits (if any) this would bring. *(6 marks)*

CIMA Stage 3 Management Accounting Techniques Pilot Paper

IM14.2 Intermediate: NPV calculation and taxation.

Data

Tilsley Ltd manufactures motor vehicle components. It is considering introducing a new product. Helen Foster, the production director, has already prepared the following projections for this proposal:

	Year 1 (£000)	2 (£000)	3 (£000)	4 (£000)
Sales	8 750	12 250	13 300	14 350
Direct materials	1 340	1 875	2 250	2 625
Direct labour	2 675	3 750	4 500	5 250
Direct overheads	185	250	250	250
Depreciation	2 500	2 500	2 500	2 500
Interest	1 012	1 012	1 012	1 012
Profit before tax	1 038	2 863	2 788	2 713
Corporation tax @ 30%	311	859	836	814
Profit after tax	727	2 004	1 952	1 899

Helen Foster has recommended to the board that the project is not worthwhile because the cumulative after tax profit over the four years is less than the capital cost of the project.

As an assistant accountant at the company you have been asked by Philip Knowles, the chief accountant, to carry out a full financial appraisal of the proposal. He does not agree with Helen Foster's analysis, and provides you with the following information:

● the initial capital investment and working capital will be incurred at the beginning of the first year. All other receipts and payments will occur at the end of each year;

● the equipment will cost £10 million;

● additional working capital of £1 million;

● this additional working capital will be recovered in full as cash at the end of the four-year period;

● the equipment will qualify for a 25 per cent per annum reducing balance writing down allowance;

● any outstanding capital allowances at the end of the project can be claimed as a balancing allowance;

● at the end of the four-year period the equipment will be scrapped, with no expected residual value;

● the additional working capital required does not qualify for capital allowances, nor is it an allowable expense in calculating taxable profit;

● Tilsley Ltd pays corporation tax at 30 per cent of chargeable profits;

● there is a one-year delay in paying tax;

● the company's cost of capital is 17 per cent.

Task

Write a report to Philip Knowles. Your report should:

a evaluate the project using net present value techniques;

b recommend whether the project is worthwhile;

c explain how you have treated taxation in your appraisal;

d give *three* reasons why your analysis is different from that produced by Helen Foster, the production director.

Notes:

Risk and inflation can be ignored.   *AAT Technicians Stage*

IM14.3 Advanced: Calculation of IRR and incremental yield involving identification of relevant cash flows. LF Ltd wishes to manufacture a new product. The company is evaluating two mutually exclusive machines, the Reclo and the Bunger. Each machine is expected to have a working life of four years, and is capable of a maximum annual output of 150 000 units.

Cost estimates associated with the two machines include:

	Reclo £000	Bunger £000
Purchase price	175	90
Scrap value	10	9
Incremental working capital	40	40
Maintenance (per year)	40 (20 in year 1)	
Supervisor	20	
Allocated central overhead	35	
Labour costs (per unit)	£1.30	
Material costs (per unit)	£0.80	

The Reclo requires 120 square metres of operating space. LF Ltd currently pays £35 per square metre to rent a factory which has adequate spare space for the new product. There is no alternative use for this spare space. £5000 has been spent on a feasibility survey of the Reclo.

The marketing department will charge a fee of £75 000 per year for promoting the product, which will be incorporated into existing plans for catalogues and advertising. Two new salesmen will be employed by the marketing department solely for the new product, at a cost of £22 500 per year each. There are no other incremental marketing costs.

The selling price in year one is expected to be £3.50 per unit, with annual production and sales estimated at 130 000 units throughout the four year period. Prices and costs after the first year are expected to rise by 5 per cent per year. Working capital will be increased by this amount from year one onwards.

Taxation is payable at 25 per cent per year one year in arrears and a writing-down allowance of 25 per cent per year is available on a reducing balance basis.

The company's accountant has already estimated the taxable operating cash flows (sales less relevant labour costs, materials costs etc., but before taking into account any writing-down allowances) of the second machine, the Bunger. These are:

	Bunger – £000			
Year	1	2	3	4
Taxable operating cash flows	50	53	55	59

Required:

a Calculate the expected internal rate of return (IRR) of each of the machines. State clearly any assumptions that you make.
                                        (14 marks)

b Evaluate, using the incremental yield method, which, if either, of the two machines should be selected.   *(6 marks)*

c Explain briefly why the internal rate of return is regarded as a relatively poor method of investment appraisal.   *(5 marks)*
                            ACCA Level 3 Financial Management

IM14.4 Advanced: Net present value calculation for the replacement of a machine and a discussion of the conflict between ROI and NPV. Eckard plc is a large, all-equity financed, divisionalized textile company whose shares are listed on the London Stock Exchange. It has a current cost of capital of 15 per cent. The annual performance of its four divisions is assessed by their return on investment (ROI), i.e. net profit after tax divided by the closing level of capital employed. It is expected that the overall ROI for the company for the year ending 31 December 2000 will

be 18 per cent, with the towelling division having the highest ROI of 25 per cent. The towelling division has a young, ambitious managing director who is anxious to maintain its ROI for the next two years, by which time he expects to be able to obtain a more prestigious job either within Eckard plc or elsewhere. He has recently turned down a proposal by his division's finance director to replace an old machine with a more modern one, on the grounds that the old one has an estimated useful life of four years and should be kept for that period. The finance director has appealed to the main board of directors of Eckard plc to reverse her managing director's decision.

The following estimates have been prepared by the finance director for the new machine:

Investment cost: £256 000, payable on 2 January 2001.

Expected life: four years to 31 December 2004.

Disposal value: equal to its tax written down value on 1 January 2004 and receivable on 31 December 2004.

Expected cash flow savings: £60 000 in 2001, rising by 10 per cent in each of the next three years. These cash flows can be assumed to occur at the end of the year in which they arise.

Tax position: the company is expected to pay 35 per cent corporation tax over the next four years. The machine is eligible for a 25 per cent per annum writing down allowance. Corporation tax can be assumed to be paid 12 months after the accounting year-end on 31 December. No provision for deferred tax is considered to be necessary.

Old machine to be replaced: this would be sold on 2 January 2001 with an accounting net book value of £50 000 and a tax written down value of nil. Sale proceeds would be £40 000, which would give rise to a balancing charge. If retained for a further four years, the disposal value would be zero.

Relevant accounting policies: the company uses the straight-line depreciation method with a full year's depreciation being charged in both the year of acquisition and the year of disposal. The capital employed figure for the division comprises all assets excluding cash.

Requirements

a Calculate the net present value to Eckard plc of the proposed replacement of the old machine by the new one.   *(8 marks)*

b Calculate, for the years 2001 and 2002 only, the effect of the decision to replace the old machine on the ROI of the towelling division.   *(7 marks)*

c Prepare a report for the main board of directors recommending whether the new machine should be purchased. Your report should include a discussion of the effects that performance measurement systems can have on capital investment decisions.
                                        (10 marks)
                              ICAEW P2 Financial Management

IM14.5 Advanced: Determining the optimum replacement period for a fleet of taxis. Eltern plc is an unlisted company with a turnover of £6 million which runs a small fleet of taxis as part of its business. The managers of the company wish to estimate how regularly to replace the taxis. The fleet costs a total of £55 000 and the company has just purchased a new fleet. Operating costs and maintenance costs increase as the taxis get older. Estimates of these costs and the likely resale value of the fleet at the end of various years are presented below.

Year	1 (£)	2 (£)	3 (£)	4 (£)	5 (£)
Operating costs	23 000	24 500	26 000	28 000	44 000
Maintenance costs	6 800	9 200	13 000	17 000	28 000
Resale value	35 000	24 000	12 000	2 000	200

The company's cost of capital is 13 per cent per year.

Required:

a Evaluate how regularly the company should replace its fleet of taxis. Assume all cash flows occur at the year end and are after taxation (where relevant). Inflation may be ignored.   *(10 marks)*

b Briefly discuss the main problems of this type of evaluation.
                                         (4 marks)
                           ACCA Level 3 Financial Management

IM14.6 Advanced: Relevant cash flows and taxation plus unequal lives. Pavgrange plc is considering expanding its operations. The company accountant has produced *pro forma* profit and loss accounts for the next three years assuming that:

(a) The company undertakes no new investment.

(b) The company invests in Project 1.

(c) The company invests in Project 2.

Both projects have expected lives of three years, and the projects are mutually exclusive.

The *pro forma* accounts are shown below:

(a) *No new investment*

Years	1	2	3
	(£000)	(£000)	(£000)
Sales	6500	6950	7460
Operating costs	4300	4650	5070
Depreciation	960	720	540
Interest	780	800	800
Profit before tax	460	780	1050
Taxation	161	273	367
Profit after tax	299	507	683
Dividends	200	200	230
Retained earnings	99	307	453

(b) *Investment in Project 1*

Years	1	2	3
	(£000)	(£000)	(£000)
Sales	7340	8790	9636
Operating costs	4869	5620	6385
Depreciation	1460	1095	821
Interest	1000	1030	1030
Profit before tax	11	1045	1400
Taxation	4	366	490
Profit after tax	7	679	910
Dividends	200	200	230
Retained earnings	(193)	479	680

(c) *Investment in Project 2*

Years	1	2	3
	(£000)	(£000)	(£000)
Sales	8430	9826	11 314
Operating costs	5680	6470	7 230
Depreciation	1835	1376	1 032
Interest	1165	1205	1 205
Profit before tax	(250)	775	1 847
Taxation	0	184	646
Profit after tax	(250)	591	1 201
Dividends	200	200	230
Retained earnings	(450)	391	971

The initial outlay for Project 1 is £2 million and for Project 2 £3½ million.

Tax allowable depreciation is at the rate of 25 per cent on a reducing balance basis. The company does not expect to acquire or dispose of any fixed assets during the next three years other than in connection with Projects 1 or 2. Any investment in Project 1 or 2 would commence at the start of the company's next financial year.

The expected salvage value associated with the investments at the end of three years is £750 000 for Project 1, and £1 500 000 for Project 2.

Corporate taxes are levied at the rate of 35 per cent and are payable one year in arrears.

Pavgrange would finance either investment with a three year term loan at a gross interest payment of 11 per cent per year. The company's weighted average cost of capital is estimated to be 8 per cent per annum.

Required:

  a Advise the company which project (if either) it should undertake. Give the reasons for your choice and support it with calculations.

                                                        (12 marks)

  b What further information might be helpful to the company accountant in the evaluation of these investments? *(3 marks)*

  c If Project 1 had been for four years duration rather than three years, and the new net cash flows of the project (after tax and allowing for the scrap value) for years four and five were £77 000 and (£188 000) respectively, evaluate whether your advice to Pavgrange would change. *(5 marks)*

  d Explain why the payback period and the internal rate of return might not lead to the correct decision when appraising mutually exclusive capital investments.

                                                  (5 marks)

ACCA Level 3 Financial Management

IM14.7 Advanced: Adjusting cash flows for inflation and the calculation of NPV and ROI. The general manager of the nationalized postal service of a small country, Zedland, wishes to introduce a new service. This service would offer same-day delivery of letters and parcels posted before 10am within a distance of 150 kilometres. The service would require 100 new vans costing $8000 each and 20 trucks costing $18 000 each. 180 new workers would be employed at an average annual wage of $13 000 and five managers at average annual salaries of $20 000 would be moved from their existing duties, where they would not be replaced.

Two postal rates are proposed. In the first year of operation letters will cost $0.525 and parcels $5.25. Market research undertaken at a cost of $50 000 forecasts that demand will average 15 000 letters per working day and 500 parcels per working day during the first year, and 20 000 letters per day and 750 parcels per day thereafter. There is a five day working week. Annual running and maintenance costs on similar new vans and trucks are currently estimated in the first year of operation to be $2000 per van and $4000 per truck respectively. These costs will increase by 20 per cent per year (excluding the effects of inflation). Vehicles are depreciated over a five year period on a straight-line basis. Depreciation is tax allowable and the vehicles will have negligible scrap value at the end of five years. Advertising in year one will cost $500 000 and in year two $250 000. There will be no advertising after year two. Existing premises will be used for the new service but additional costs of $150 000 per year will be incurred.

All the above cost data are current estimates and exclude any inflation effects. Wage and salary costs and all other costs are expected to rise because of inflation by approximately 5 per cent per year during the five year planning horizon of the postal service. The government of Zedland will not permit annual price increases within nationalized industries to exceed the level of inflation.

Nationalized industries are normally required by the government to earn at least an annual after tax return of 5 per cent on average investment and to achieve, on average, at least zero net present value on their investments.

The new service would be financed half with internally generated funds and half by borrowing on the capital market at an interest rate of 12 per cent per year. The opportunity cost of capital for the postal service is estimated to be 14 per cent per year. Corporate taxes in Zedland, to which the postal service is subject, are at the rate of 30 per cent for annual profits of up to $500 000 and 40 per cent for the balance in excess of $500 000. Tax is payable one year in arrears. All transactions may be assumed to be on a cash basis and to occur at the end of the year with the exception of the initial investment which would be required almost immediately.

Required:

Acting as an independent consultant prepare a report advising whether the new postal service should be introduced. Include in your report a discussion of other factors that might need to be taken into account before a final decision was made with respect to the introduction of the new postal service. State clearly any assumptions that you make. *(18 marks)*

ACCA Level 3 Financial Management

IM14.8 Advanced: Calculation of discounted payback and NPV incorporating inflation, tax and financing costs. The board of directors of Portand Ltd are considering two *mutually exclusive* investments each of which is expected to have a life of five years. The company does not have the physical capacity to undertake both investments. The first investment is relatively capital intensive whilst the second is relatively labour intensive.

Forecast profits of the two investments are:

Investment 1 (requires four new workers)

			(£000)			
Year	0	1	2	3	4	5
Initial cost	(500)					
Projected sales		400	450	500	550	600
Production costs		260	300	350	450	500
Finance charges		21	21	21	21	21
Depreciation[1]		125	94	70	53	40
Profit before tax		(6)	35	59	26	39
Average profit before tax £30 600						

Investment 2 (requires nine new workers)

			(£000)			
Year	0	1	2	3	4	5
Initial cost	(175)					
Projected sales		500	600	640	640	700
Production costs		460	520	550	590	630
Depreciation[1]		44	33	25	18	14
Profit before tax		(4)	47	65	32	56
Average profit before tax £39 200.						

[1]Depreciation is a tax allowable expense and is at 25 per cent per year on a reducing balance basis. Both investments are of similar risk to the company's existing operations.

Additional information

(i)   Tax and depreciation allowances are payable/receivable one year in arrears. Tax is at 25 per cent per year.

(ii) Investment 2 would be financed from internal funds, which the managing director states have no cost to the company. Investment 1 would be financed by internal funds plus a £150 000, 14 per cent fixed rate term loan.

(iii) The data contains no adjustments for price changes. These have been ignored by the board of directors as both sales and production costs are expected to increase by 9 per cent per year, after year one.

(iv) The company's real overall cost of capital is 7 per cent per year and the inflation rate is expected to be 8 per cent per year for the foreseeable future.

(v)   All cash flows may be assumed to occur at the end of the year unless otherwise stated.

(vi) The company currently receives interest of 10 per cent per year on short-term money market deposits of £350 000.

(vii) Both investments are expected to have negligible scrap value at the end of five years.

Director A favours Investment 2 as it has a larger average profit.

Director B favours Investment 1 which she believes has a quicker discounted payback period, based upon cash flows.

Director C argues that the company can make £35 000 per year on its money market investments and that, when risk is taken into account, there is little point in investing in either project.

Required:

a   Discuss the validity of the arguments of each of Directors A, B and C with respect to the decision to select Investment 1, Investment 2 or neither.   *(7 marks)*

b   Verify whether or not Director B is correct in stating that Investment 1 has the quicker discounted payback period.

    Evaluate which investment, if any, should be selected. All calculations must be shown. Marks will not be deducted for sensible rounding. State clearly any assumptions that you make.   *(14 marks)*

c   Discuss briefly what non-financial factors might influence the choice of investment.   *(4 marks)*

ACCA Level 3 Financial Management

IM14.9 Advanced: Sensitivity analysis and alternative methods of adjusting for risk. Parsifal Ltd is a private company whose ordinary shares are all held by its directors. The chairman has recently been impressed by the arguments advanced by a computer salesman, who has told him that Parsifal will be able to install a fully operational computer system for £161 500. This new system will provide all the data currently being prepared by a local data-processing service. This local service has a current annual cost of £46 000. According to the salesman, annual maintenance costs will be only £2000 and if properly maintained the equipment can be expected to last 'indefinitely'.

The chairman has asked the company accountant to evaluate whether purchase of the computer system is worthwhile. The accountant has spoken to a friend who works for a firm of management consultants. She has told him that Parsifal would probably have to employ two additional members of staff at a total cost of about £15 000 per annum and that there would be increased stationery and other related costs of approximately £4000 per annum if Parsifal purchased the computer system. She also estimates that the useful life of the system would be between 6 and 10 years, depending upon the rate of technological change

and changes in the pattern of the business of Parsifal. The system would have no scrap or resale value at the end of its useful life.

The company accountant has prepared a net present value calculation by assuming that all the annual costs and savings were expressed in real terms and that the company had a real cost of capital of 5 per cent per annum. He chose this course of action because he did not know either the expected rate of inflation of the cash flows or the cost of capital of Parsifal Ltd. All cash flows, except the initial cost of the system, will arise at the end of the year to which they relate.

You are required to:

a   estimate, using the company accountant's assumptions, the life of the system which produces a zero net present value,   *(3 marks)*

b   estimate the internal real rate of return arising from purchase of the computer system, assuming that the system will last:
    (i) for six years, and
    (ii) indefinitely,   *(5 marks)*

c   estimate the value of the annual running costs (maintenance, extra staff, stationery and other related costs) that will produce a net present value of zero, assuming that the system will last for ten years,   *(3 marks)*

d   discuss how the company accountant should incorporate the information from parts (a), (b) and (c) above in his recommendation to the directors of Parsifal Ltd as to whether the proposed computer system should be purchased,   *(7 marks)*

e   discuss how the company accountant could improve the quality of his advice.   *(7 marks)*

Ignore taxation

ICAEW P2 Financial Management

IM14.10 Advanced: Calculation of expected net present value plus a discussion of whether expected values is an appropriate way of evaluating risk. Galuppi plc is considering whether to scrap some highly specialized old plant or to refurbish it for the production of drive mechanisms, sales of which will last for only three years. Scrapping the plant will yield £25 000 immediately, whereas refurbishment will require an immediate outlay of £375 000.

Each drive mechanism will sell for £50 and, if manufactured entirely by Galuppi plc, give a contribution at current prices of £10. All internal company costs and selling prices are predicted to increase from the start of each year by 5 per cent. Refurbishment of the plant will also entail fixed costs of £10 000, £12 500 and £15 000 for the first, second and third years respectively.

Estimates of product demand depend on different economic conditions. Three have been identified as follows:

Economic condition	Probability of occurrence	Demand in the first year (units)
A	0.25	10 000
B	0.45	15 000
C	0.3	20 000

Demand in subsequent years is expected to increase at 20 per cent per annum, regardless of the initial level demanded.

The plant can produce up to 20 000 drive mechanisms per year, but Galuppi plc can supply more by contracting to buy partially completed mechanisms from an overseas supplier at a fixed price of £20 per unit. To convert a partially completed mechanism into the finished product requires additional work amounting, at current prices, to £25 per unit. For a variety of reasons the supplier is only willing to negotiate contracts in batches of 2000 units.

All contracts to purchase the partially completed units must be signed one year in advance, and payment made by Galuppi plc at the start of the year in which they are to be used.

Galuppi plc has a cost of capital of 15 per cent per annum, and you may assume that all cash flows arise at the end of the year, unless you are told otherwise.

Requirements:

a   Determine whether refurbishment of the plant is worthwhile.   *(17 marks)*

b   Discuss whether the expected value method is an appropriate way of evaluating the different risks inherent in the refurbishment decision of Galuppi plc.   *(8 marks)*

ICAEW P2 Financial Management

PART FOUR

PART FOUR

Information for Planning, Control and Performance Measurement

The objective in this section is to consider the implementation of decisions through the planning and control process. Planning involves systematically looking at the future, so that decisions can be made today which will bring the company its desired results. Control can be defined as the process of measuring and correcting actual performance to ensure that plans for implementing the chosen course of action are carried out.

Part Four contains six chapters. Chapter 15 considers the role of budgeting within the planning process and the relationship between the long-range plan and the budgeting process. The budgeting process in profit-oriented organizations is compared with that in non-profit organizations.

Chapters 16–18 are concerned with the control process. To fully understand the role that management accounting control systems play in the control process, it is necessary to be aware of how they relate to the entire array of control mechanisms used by organizations. Chapter 16 describes the different types of controls that are used by companies. The elements of management accounting control systems are described within the context of the overall control process. Chapters 17 and 18 focus on the technical aspects of accounting control systems. They describe the major features of a standard costing system: a system that enables the differences between the planned and actual outcomes to be analyzed in detail. Chapter 17 describes the operation of a standard costing system and explains the procedure for calculating the variances. Chapter 18 examines more complex aspects relating to standard costing.

Chapters 19 and 20 examine the special problems of control and measuring performance of divisions and other decentralized units within an organization. Chapter 19 considers how divisional financial performance measures might be devised which will motivate managers to pursue overall organizational goals. Chapter 20 focuses on the transfer pricing problem and examines how transfer prices can be established that will motivate managers to make optimal decisions and also ensure that the performance measures derived from using the transfer prices represent a fair reflection of managerial performance.

The budgeting process

15

In the previous seven chapters we have considered how management accounting can assist managers in making decisions. The actions that follow managerial decisions normally involve several aspects of the business, such as the marketing, production, purchasing and finance functions, and it is important that management should coordinate these various interrelated aspects of decision-making. If they fail to do this, there is a danger that managers may each make decisions that they believe are in the best interests of the organization when, in fact, taken together they are not; for example, the marketing department may introduce a promotional campaign that is designed to increase sales demand to a level beyond that which the production department can handle. The various activities within a company should be coordinated by the preparation of plans of actions for future periods. These detailed plans are usually referred to as budgets.

Our objective in this chapter is to focus on the planning process within a business organization and to consider the role of budgeting within this process. What do we mean by planning? Planning is the design of a desired future and of effective ways of bringing it about (Ackoff, 1981). A distinction is normally made between short-term planning (budgeting) and long-range planning, alternatively known as strategic or corporate planning. How is long-range planning

LEARNING OBJECTIVES

After studying this chapter, you should be able to:

- explain how budgeting fits into the overall planning and control framework;

- identify and describe the six different purposes of budgeting;

- identify and describe the various stages in the budget process;

- prepare functional and master budgets;

- describe the use of computer-based financial models for budgeting;

- describe the limitations of incremental budgeting;

- describe activity-based budgeting;

- describe zero-base budgeting (ZBB);

- describe the criticisms relating to traditional budgeting.

distinguished from other forms of planning? Sizer (1989) defines long-range planning as a systematic and formalized process for purposely directing and controlling future operations towards desired objectives for periods extending beyond one year. Short-term planning or budgeting, on the other hand, must accept the environment of today, and the physical, human and financial resources at present available to the firm. These are to a considerable extent determined by the quality of the firm's long-range planning efforts.

Stages in the planning process

To help you understand the budgetary process we shall begin by looking at how it fits into an overall general framework of planning, decision-making and control. The framework outlined in Figure 15.1 will be used to illustrate the role of long-term and short-term planning within the overall planning and control process. The first stage involves establishing the objectives of the organization.

Stage 1: Establishing objectives

Establishing objectives is an essential pre-requisite of the planning process. In all organizations employees must have a good understanding of what the organization is trying to achieve. Strategic or long-range planning therefore begins with the specification of the objectives towards which future operations should be directed. The attainment of objectives should be measurable in some way and ideally people should be motivated by them. Johnson and Scholes (2005) distinguish between three different objectives, which form a hierarchy: the 'mission' of an organization, corporate objectives and unit objectives.

The mission of an organization describes in very general terms the broad purpose and reason for an organization's existence, the nature of the business(es) it is in and the customers it seeks to serve and satisfy. It is a visionary projection of the central and overriding concepts on which the organization is based. Objectives tend to be more specific, and represent desired states or results to be achieved.

Corporate objectives relate to the organization as a whole. They are normally measurable and are expressed in financial terms such as desired profits or sales levels, return on capital employed, rates of growth or market share. Corporate objectives are normally formulated by members of the board

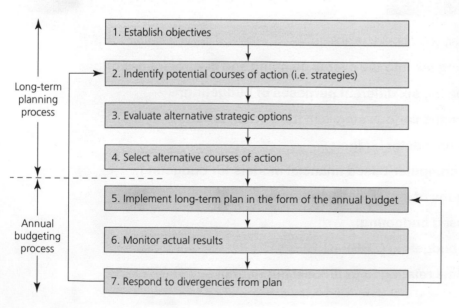

FIGURE 15.1
The role of long- and short-term planning within the planning, decision-making and control process

of directors and handed down to senior managers. It is important that senior managers in an organization understand clearly where their company is going and why and how their own role contributes to the attainment of corporate objectives. Once the overall objectives of the organization have been established they must be broken down into subsidiary objectives relating to areas such as product range, market segmentation, customer service and so on. Objectives must also be developed for the different parts of an organization. Unit objectives relate to the specific objectives of individual units within the organization, such as a division or one company within a holding company. Corporate objectives are normally set for the organization as a whole and are then translated into unit objectives, which become the targets for the individual units. You should note that the expression aims is sometimes used as an alternative to mission and the term goals is synonymous with objectives.

Stage 2: Identify potential strategies

The next stage shown in Figure 15.1 is to identify a range of possible courses of action (or strategies) that might enable the company's objectives to be achieved. The corporate strategy literature advocates that, prior to developing strategies, it is necessary to undertake a strategic analysis to become better informed about the organization's present strategic situation. This involves understanding the company's present position, its strengths and weaknesses and its opportunities and risks.

Having undertaken a strategic analysis, the next stage is to identify alternative strategies. The identification of strategies should take into account the following:

1 the generic strategy to be pursued (i.e. the basis on which the organization will compete or sustain excellence);

2 the alternative directions in which the organization may wish to develop.

An organization should determine the basis on which it will compete and/or sustain a superior level of performance (i.e. the generic strategy that it will follow). The purpose is to ensure that deliberate choices are made regarding the type of competitive advantage it wishes to attain. Porter (1985) has identified three generic strategies that an organization can follow:

1 *cost leadership*, whereby the organization aims to be the lowest cost producer within the industry;

2 *differentiation*, through which the organization seeks some unique dimension in its product/service that is valued by consumers, and which can command a premium price;

3 *focus*, whereby the organization determines the way in which the strategy is focused at particular parts of the market. For example, a product or service may be aimed at a particular buyer group, segment of the product line or smaller geographical area. An organization that adopts a focused strategy aimed at narrow segments of the market to the exclusion of others also needs to determine whether within the segment it will compete through cost leadership or differentiation. Small companies often follow very focused or *niche* strategies by becoming so specialized in meeting the needs of a very small part of the market that they are secure against competition from large organizations.

Porter's view is that any organization seeking a sustainable competitive advantage must select an appropriate generic strategy rather than attempting to be 'all things to all people'.

Having identified the basis on which it will compete, an organization should determine the directions it wishes to take. The company should consider one or more of the following:

1 doing nothing;

2 withdrawing from some markets;

3 selling existing products more effectively in existing markets (market penetration);

4 selling existing products in new markets (market development);

5 developing new products for sale in existing markets (product development);

6 developing new products for sale in new markets (diversification).

Stage 3: Evaluation of strategic options

The alternative strategies should be examined based on the following criteria:[1]

1 *suitability*, which seeks to ascertain the extent to which the proposed strategies fit the situation identified in the strategic analysis. For example, does the strategy exploit the company strengths and environmental opportunities, avoid the weaknesses and counter the environmental threats?

2 *feasibility*, which focuses on whether the strategy can be implemented in resource terms. For example, can the strategy be funded? Can the necessary market position be achieved? Can the company cope with the competitive reactions?

3 *acceptability*, which is concerned with whether a particular strategy is acceptable. For example, will it be sufficiently profitable? Is the level of risk acceptable?

The above criteria represent a broad framework of general criteria against which strategic options can be judged. The criteria narrow down the options to be considered for a detailed evaluation. The evaluation of the options should be based on the approaches described in Chapters 13 and 14 and will not be repeated here. Management should select those strategic options that have the greatest potential for achieving the company's objectives. There could be just one strategy chosen or several.

Stage 4: Select course of action

When management has selected those strategic options that have the greatest potential for achieving the company's objectives, long-term plans should be created to implement the strategies. A **long-term plan** is a statement of the preliminary targets and activities required by an organization to achieve its strategic plans together with a broad estimate for each year of the resources required.

Because long-term planning involves 'looking into the future' for several years ahead the plans tend to be uncertain, general in nature, imprecise and subject to change.

Stage 5: Implementation of the long-term plans

Budgeting is concerned with the implementation of the long-term plan for the year ahead. Because of the shorter planning horizon budgets are more precise and detailed. Budgets are a clear indication of what is expected to be achieved during the budget period whereas long-term plans represent the broad directions that top management intend to follow.

The budget is not something that originates 'from nothing' each year – it is developed within the context of ongoing business and is ruled by previous decisions that have been taken within the long-term planning process. When the activities are initially approved for inclusion in the long-term plan, they are based on uncertain estimates that are projected for several years. These proposals must be reviewed and revised in the light of more recent information. This review and revision process frequently takes place as part of the annual budgeting process, and it may result in important decisions being taken on possible activity adjustments within the current budget period. The budgeting process cannot therefore be viewed as being purely concerned with the current year – it must be considered as an integrated part of the long-term planning process.

Stages 6 and 7: Monitor actual outcomes and respond to divergencies from planned outcomes

The final stages in the decision-making, planning and control process outlined in Figure 15.1 are to compare the actual and the planned outcomes, and to respond to any divergencies from the plan. These stages represent the control process of budgeting, but a detailed discussion of this process will be deferred until Chapter 16. Let us now consider the short-term budgeting process in more detail.

The multiple functions of budgets

Budgets serve a number of useful purposes. They include:

1 *planning* annual operations;
2 *coordinating* the activities of the various parts of the organization and ensuring that the parts are in harmony with each other;
3 *communicating* plans to the various responsibility centre managers;
4 *motivating* managers to strive to achieve the organizational goals;
5 *controlling* activities;
6 *evaluating* the performance of managers.

Let us now examine each of these six factors.

Planning

The major planning decisions will already have been made as part of the long-term planning process. However, the annual budgeting process leads to the refinement of those plans, since managers must produce detailed plans for the implementation of the long-range plan. Without the annual budgeting process, the pressures of day-to-day operating problems may tempt managers not to plan for future operations. The budgeting process ensures that managers do plan for future operations, and that they consider how conditions in the next year might change and what steps they should take now to respond to these changed conditions. This process encourages managers to anticipate problems before they arise, and hasty decisions that are made on the spur of the moment, based on expediency rather than reasoned judgement, will be minimized.

Coordination

The budget serves as a vehicle through which the actions of the different parts of an organization can be brought together and reconciled into a common plan. Without any guidance, managers may each make their own decisions, believing that they are working in the best interests of the organization. For example, the purchasing manager may prefer to place large orders so as to obtain large discounts; the production manager will be concerned with avoiding high stock levels; and the accountant will be concerned with the impact of the decision on the cash resources of the business. It is the aim of budgeting to reconcile these differences for the good of the organization as a whole, rather than for the benefit of any individual area. Budgeting therefore compels managers to examine the relationship between their own operations and those of other departments, and, in the process, to identify and resolve conflicts.

Communication

If an organization is to function effectively, there must be definite lines of communication so that all the parts will be kept fully informed of the plans and the policies, and constraints, to which the organization is expected to conform. Everyone in the organization should have a clear understanding of the part they are expected to play in achieving the annual budget. This process will ensure that the appropriate individuals are made accountable for implementing the budget. Through the budget, top management communicates its expectations to lower level management, so that all members of the organization may understand these expectations and can coordinate their activities to attain them. It is not just the budget itself that facilitates communication – much vital information is communicated in the actual act of preparing it.

Motivation

The budget can be a useful device for influencing managerial behaviour and motivating managers to perform in line with the organizational objectives. A budget provides a standard that under certain circumstances, a manager may be motivated to strive to achieve. However, budgets can also encourage inefficiency and conflict between managers. If individuals have actively participated in preparing the budget, and it is used as a tool to assist managers in managing their departments, it can act as a strong motivational device by providing a challenge. Alternatively, if the budget is dictated from above, and imposes a threat rather than a challenge, it may be resisted and do more harm than good. We shall discuss the dysfunctional motivational consequence of budgets in Chapter 16.

Control

A budget assists managers in managing and controlling the activities for which they are responsible. By comparing the actual results with the budgeted amounts for different categories of expenses, managers can ascertain which costs do not conform to the original plan and thus require their attention. This process enables management to operate a system of management by exception which means that a manager's attention and effort can be concentrated on significant deviations from the expected results. By investigating the reasons for the deviations, managers may be able to identify inefficiencies such as the purchase of inferior quality materials. When the reasons for the inefficiencies have been found, appropriate control action should be taken to remedy the situation.

Performance evaluation

A manager's performance is often evaluated by measuring his or her success in meeting the budgets. In some companies bonuses are awarded on the basis of an employee's ability to achieve the targets specified in the periodic budgets, or promotion may be partly dependent upon a manager's budget record. In addition, the manager may wish to evaluate his or her own performance. The budget thus provides a useful means of informing managers of how well they are performing in meeting targets that they have previously helped to set. The use of budgets as a method of performance evaluation also influences human behaviour, and for this reason we shall consider the behavioural aspects of performance evaluation in Chapter 16.

Conflicting roles of budgets

Because a single budget system is normally used to serve several purposes there is a danger that they may conflict with each other. For instance the planning and motivation roles may be in conflict with each other. Demanding budgets that may not be achieved may be appropriate to motivate maximum performance, but they are unsuitable for planning purposes. For these a budget should be set based on easier targets that are expected to be met.

There is also a conflict between the planning and performance evaluation roles. For planning purposes budgets are set in advance of the budget period based on an anticipated set of circumstances or environment. Performance evaluation should be based on a comparison of actual performance with an adjusted budget to reflect the circumstances under which managers actually operated. In practice, many firms compare actual performance with the original budget (adjusted to the actual level of activity, i.e. a flexible budget), but if the circumstances envisaged when the original budget was set have changed then there will be a planning and evaluation conflict.

The budget period

The conventional approach is that once per year the manager of each budget centre prepares a detailed budget for one year. The budget is divided into either twelve monthly or thirteen four-weekly periods for control purposes. The preparation of budgets on an annual basis has been strongly criticized on the grounds that it is too rigid and ties a company to a 12-month commitment, which can be risky because the budget is based on uncertain forecasts.

An alternative approach is for the annual budget to be broken down by months for the first three months, and by quarters for the remaining nine months. The quarterly budgets are then developed on a monthly basis as the year proceeds. For example, during the first quarter, the monthly budgets for the second quarter will be prepared; and during the second quarter, the monthly budgets for the third quarter will be prepared. The quarterly budgets may also be reviewed as the year unfolds. For example, during the first quarter, the budget for the next three quarters may be changed as new information becomes available. A new budget for a fifth quarter will also be prepared. This process is known as continuous or rolling budgeting, and ensures that a 12-month budget is always available by adding a quarter in the future as the quarter just ended is dropped. Contrast this with a budget prepared once per year. As the year goes by, the period for which a budget is available will shorten until the budget for next year is prepared. Rolling budgets also ensure that planning is not something that takes place once a year when the budget is being formulated. Instead, budgeting is a continuous process, and managers are encouraged to constantly look ahead and review future plans. Furthermore, it is likely that actual performance will be compared with a more realistic target, because budgets are being constantly reviewed and updated. The main disadvantage of a rolling budget is that it can create uncertainty for managers because the budget is constantly being changed.

Irrespective of whether the budget is prepared on an annual or a continuous basis, it is important that monthly or four-weekly budgets be used for *control* purposes.

Administration of the budgeting process

It is important that suitable administration procedures be introduced to ensure that the budget process works effectively. In practice, the procedures should be tailor-made to the requirements of the organization, but as a general rule a firm should ensure that procedures are established for approving the budgets and that the appropriate staff support is available for assisting managers in preparing their budgets.

The budget committee

The budget committee should consist of high-level executives who represent the major segments of the business. Its major task is to ensure that budgets are realistically established and that they are coordinated satisfactorily. The normal procedure is for the functional heads to present their budget to the committee for approval. If the budget does not reflect a reasonable level of performance, it will not be approved and the functional head will be required to adjust the budget and re-submit it for approval. It is important that the person whose performance is being measured should agree that the revised budget can be achieved; otherwise, if it is considered to be impossible to achieve, it will not act as a motivational device. If budget revisions are made, the budgetees should at least feel that they were given a fair hearing by the committee. We shall discuss budget negotiation in more detail later in this chapter.

The budget committee should appoint a budget officer, who will normally be the accountant. The role of the budget officer is to coordinate the individual budgets into a budget for the whole organization, so that the budget committee and the budgetee can see the impact of an individual budget on the organization as a whole.

Accounting staff

The accounting staff will normally assist managers in the preparation of their budgets; they will, for example, circulate and advise on the instructions about budget preparation, provide past information that may be useful for preparing the present budget, and ensure that managers submit their budgets on time. The accounting staff do not determine the content of the various budgets, but they do provide a valuable advisory service for the line managers.

Budget manual

A budget manual should be prepared by the accountant. It will describe the objectives and procedures involved in the budgeting process and will provide a useful reference source for managers responsible for budget preparation. In addition, the manual may include a timetable specifying the order in which the budgets should be prepared and the dates when they should be presented to the budget committee. The manual should be circulated to all individuals who are responsible for preparing budgets.

Stages in the budgeting process

The important stages are as follows:

1 communicating details of budget policy and guidelines to those people responsible for the preparation of budgets;
2 determining the factor that restricts output;
3 preparation of the sales budget;
4 initial preparation of various budgets;
5 negotiation of budgets with superiors;
6 coordination and review of budgets;
7 final acceptance of budgets;
8 ongoing review of budgets.

Let us now consider each of these stages in more detail.

Communicating details of the budget policy

Many decisions affecting the budget year will have been taken previously as part of the long-term planning process. The long-range plan is therefore the starting point for the preparation of the annual budget. Thus top management must communicate the policy effects of the long-term plan to those responsible for preparing the current year's budgets. Policy effects might include planned changes in sales mix, or the expansion or contraction of certain activities. In addition, other important guidelines that are to govern the preparation of the budget should be specified – for example the allowances that are to be made for price and wage increases, and the expected changes in productivity. Also, any expected changes in industry demand and output should be communicated by top management to the managers responsible for budget preparation. It is essential that all managers be made aware of the policy of top management for implementing the long-term plan in the current year's budget so that common guidelines can be established. The process also indicates to the managers responsible for preparing the budgets how they should respond to any expected environmental changes.

Determining the factor that restricts performance

In every organization there is some factor that restricts performance for a given period. In the majority of organizations this factor is sales demand. However, it is possible for production capacity to restrict performance when sales demand is in excess of available capacity. Prior to the preparation of the budgets, it is necessary for top management to determine the factor that restricts performance, since this factor determines the point at which the annual budgeting process should begin.

Preparation of the sales budget

The volume of sales and the sales mix determine the level of a company's operations, when sales demand is the factor that restricts output. For this reason, the sales budget is the most important plan in the annual budgeting process. This budget is also the most difficult plan to produce, because total sales revenue depends on the actions of customers. In addition, sales demand may be influenced by the state of the economy or the actions of competitors.

Initial preparation of budgets

The managers who are responsible for meeting the budgeted performance should prepare the budget for those areas for which they are responsible. The preparation of the budget should be a 'bottom-up' process. This means that the budget should originate at the lowest levels of management and be refined and coordinated at higher levels. The justification for this approach is that it enables managers to participate in the preparation of their budgets and increases the probability that they will accept the budget and strive to achieve the budget targets.

There is no single way in which the appropriate quantity for a particular budget item is determined. Past data may be used as the starting point for producing the budgets, but this does not mean that budgeting is based on the assumption that what has happened in the past will occur in the future. Changes in future conditions must be taken into account, but past information may provide useful guidance for the future. In addition, managers may look to the guidelines provided by top management for determining the content of their budgets. For example, the guidelines may provide specific instructions as to the content of their budgets and the permitted changes that can be made in the prices of purchases of materials and services. For production activities standard costs (see Chapter 17) may be used as the basis for costing activity volumes which are planned in the budget.

Negotiation of budgets

To implement a participative approach to budgeting, the budget should be originated at the lowest level of management. The managers at this level should submit their budget to their superiors for approval. The superior should then incorporate this budget with other budgets for which he or she is responsible and then submit this budget for approval to his or her superior. The manager who is the superior then becomes the budgetee at the next higher level. The process is illustrated in Figure 15.2. Sizer (1989) describes this approach as a two-way process of a top-down statement of objectives and strategies, bottom-up budget preparation and top-down approval by senior management.

The lower-level managers are represented by boxes 1–8. Managers 1 and 2 will prepare their budgets in accordance with the budget policy and the guidelines laid down by top management. The managers will submit their budget to their supervisor, who is in charge of the whole department (department A). Once these budgets have been agreed by the manager of department A, they will be combined by the departmental manager, who will then present this budget to his or her superior (manager of plant 1) for approval. The manager of plant 1 is

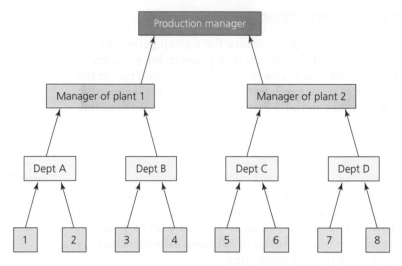

FIGURE 15.2
An illustration of budgets moving up
the organization hierarchy

also responsible for department B, and will combine the agreed budgets for departments A and B before presenting the combined budget to his or her supervisor (the production manager). The production manager will merge the budget for plants 1 and 2, and this final budget will represent the production budget that will be presented to the budget committee for approval.

At each of these stages the budgets will be negotiated between the budgetees and their superiors, and eventually they will be agreed by both parties. Hence the figures that are included in the budget are the result of a bargaining process between a manager and his or her superior. It is important that the budgetees should participate in arriving at the final budget and that the superior does not revise the budget without giving full consideration to the subordinates' arguments for including any of the budgeted items. Otherwise, real participation will not be taking place, and it is unlikely that the subordinate will be motivated to achieve a budget that he or she did not accept.

It is also necessary to be watchful that budgetees do not deliberately attempt to obtain approval for easily attainable budgets, or attempt to deliberately understate budgets in the hope that the budget that is finally agreed will represent an easily attainable target. It is equally unsatisfactory for a superior to impose difficult targets in the hope that an authoritarian approach will produce the desired results. The desired results may be achieved in the short term, but only at the cost of a loss of morale and increased labour turnover in the future.

The negotiation process is of vital importance in the budgeting process, and can determine whether the budget becomes a really effective management tool or just a clerical device. If managers are successful in establishing a position of trust and confidence with their subordinates, the negotiation process will produce a meaningful improvement in the budgetary process and outcomes for the period.

Coordination and review of budgets

As the individual budgets move up the organizational hierarchy in the negotiation process, they must be examined in relation to each other. This examination may indicate that some budgets are out of balance with other budgets and need modifying so that they will be compatible with other conditions, constraints and plans that are beyond a manager's knowledge or control. For example, a plant manager may include equipment replacement in his or her budget when funds are simply not available. The accountant must identify such inconsistencies and bring them to the attention of the appropriate manager. Any changes in the budgets should be made by the responsible managers, and this may require that the budgets be recycled from the bottom to the top for a second or even a third time until all the budgets are coordinated and are acceptable to all the parties involved. During the coordination process, a budgeted profit and loss account, a balance sheet and a cash flow statement should be prepared to ensure that all the parts combine to produce an acceptable whole. Otherwise, further adjustments and budget recycling will be necessary until the budgeted profit and loss account, the balance sheet and the cash flow statement prove to be acceptable.

Final acceptance of the budgets

When all the budgets are in harmony with each other, they are summarized into a master budget consisting of a budgeted profit and loss account, a balance sheet and a cash flow statement. After the master budget has been approved, the budgets are then passed down through the organization to the appropriate responsibility centres. The approval of the master budget is the authority for the manager of each responsibility centre to carry out the plans contained in each budget.

Budget review

The budget process should not stop when the budgets have been agreed. Periodically, the actual results should be compared with the budgeted results. These comparisons should normally be made on a monthly basis and a report sent to the appropriate budgetees in the first week of the following month, so that it has the maximum motivational impact. This will enable management to identify the items that are not proceeding according to plan and to investigate the reasons for the differences. If these differences are within the control of management, corrective action can be taken to avoid similar inefficiencies occurring again in the future. However, the differences may be due to the fact that the budget was unrealistic to begin with, or that the actual conditions during the budget year were different from those anticipated; the budget for the remainder of the year would than be invalid.

During the budget year, the budget committee should periodically evaluate the actual performance and reappraise the company's future plans. If there are any changes in the actual conditions from those originally expected, this will normally mean that the budget plans should be adjusted. This revised budget then represents a revised statement of formal operating plans for the remaining portion of the budget period. The important point to note is that the budgetary process does not end for the current year once the budget has begun; budgeting should be seen as a continuous and dynamic process.

A detailed illustration

Let us now look at an illustration of the procedure for constructing budgets in a manufacturing company, using the information contained in Example 15.1. Note that the level of detail included here is much less than that which would be presented in practice. A truly realistic illustration would fill many pages, with detailed budgets being analyzed in various ways. We shall consider an annual budget, whereas a realistic illustration would analyze the annual budget into twelve monthly periods. Monthly analysis would considerably increase the size of the illustration, but would not give any further insight into the basic concepts or procedures. In addition, we shall assume in this example that the budgets are prepared for only two responsibility centres (namely departments 1 and 2). In practice, many responsibility centres are likely to exist.

EXAMPLE 15.1

The Enterprise Company manufactures two products, known as alpha and sigma. Alpha is produced in department 1 and sigma in department 2. The following information is available for 200X.

Standard material and labour costs:

	(£)
Material X	7.20 per unit
Material Y	16.00 per unit
Direct labour	12.00 per hour

35.20

Overhead is recovered on a direct labour hour basis.

The standard material and labour usage for each product is as follows:

	Model alpha	Model sigma
Material X	10 units	8 units
Material Y	5 units	9 units
Direct labour	10 hours	15 hours

The balance sheet for the previous year end 200X was as follows:

	(£)	(£)	(£)
Fixed assets:			
Land			170 000
Buildings and equipment	1 292 000		
Less depreciation	255 000	1 037 000	1 207 000
Current assets:			
Stocks, finished goods	99 076		
raw materials	189 200		
Debtors	289 000		
Cash	34 000		
	611 276		
Less current liabilities			
Creditors	248 800		362 476
Net assets			1 569 476
Represented by shareholder's interest:			
1 200 000 ordinary shares of £1 each		1 200 000	
Reserves		369 476	
			1 569 476

Other relevant data is as follows for the year 200X:

	Finished product	
	Model alpha	Model sigma
Forecast sales (units)	8500	1600
Selling price per unit	£400	£560
Ending inventory required (units)	1870	90
Beginning inventory (units)	170	85

	Direct material	
	Material X	Material Y
Beginning inventory (units)	8 500	8 000
Ending inventory required (units)	10 200	1 700

	Department 1 (£)	Department 2 (£)
Budgeted variable overhead rates (per direct labour hour):		
Indirect materials	1.20	0.80
Indirect labour	1.20	1.20
Power (variable portion)	0.60	0.40
Maintenance (variable portion)	0.20	0.40
Budgeted fixed overheads		
Depreciation	100 000	80 000
Supervision	100 000	40 000
Power (fixed portion)	40 000	2 000
Maintenance (fixed portion)	45 600	3 196

	(£)
Estimated non-manufacturing overheads:	
Stationery etc. (Administration)	4 000
Salaries	
Sales	74 000
Office	28 000
Commissions	60 000
Car expenses (Sales)	22 000
Advertising	80 000
Miscellaneous (Office)	8 000
	276 000

Budgeted cash flows are as follows:

	Quarter 1 (£)	Quarter 2 (£)	Quarter 3 (£)	Quarter 4 (£)
Receipts from customers	1 000 000	1 200 000	1 120 000	985 000
Payments:				
Materials	400 000	480 000	440 000	547 984
Payments for wages	400 000	440 000	480 000	646 188
Other costs and expenses	120 000	100 000	72 016	13 642

You are required to prepare a master budget for the year 200X and the following budgets:

1 sales budget;

2 production budget;

3 direct materials usage budget;

4 direct materials purchase budget;

5 direct labour budget;

6 factory overhead budget;

7 selling and administration budget;

8 cash budget.

Sales budget

The sales budget shows the quantities of each product that the company plans to sell and the intended selling price. It provides the predictions of total revenue from which cash receipts from customers will be estimated, and it also supplies the basic data for constructing budgets for production costs, and for selling, distribution and administrative expenses. The sales budget is therefore the foundation of all other budgets, since all expenditure is ultimately dependent on the volume of sales. If the sales budget is not accurate, the other budget estimates will be unreliable. We will assume that the Enterprise Company has completed a marketing analysis and that the following annual sales budget is based on the result:

Schedule 1 – Sales budget for year ending 200X

Product	Units sold	Selling price (£)	Total revenue (£)
Alpha	8500	400	3 400 000
Sigma	1600	560	896 000
			4 296 000

Schedule 1 represents the *total* sales budget for the year. In practice, the *total* sales budget will be supported by detailed *subsidiary* sales budgets where sales are analyzed by areas of responsibility, such as sales territories, and into monthly periods analyzed by products.

Production budget and budgeted stock levels

When the sales budget has been completed, the next stage is to prepare the production budget. This budget is expressed in *quantities only* and is the responsibility of the production manager. The objective is to ensure that production is sufficient to meet sales demand and that economic stock levels are maintained. The production budget (schedule 2) for the year will be as follows:

Schedule 2 – Annual production budget

	Department 1 (alpha)	Department 2 (sigma)
Units to be sold	8 500	1600
Planned closing stock	1 870	90
Total units required for sales and stocks	10 370	1690
Less planned opening stocks	170	85
Units to be produced	10 200	1605

The total production for each department should also be analyzed on a monthly basis.

Direct materials usage budget

The supervisors of departments 1 and 2 will prepare estimates of the materials which are required to meet the production budget. The materials usage budget for the year will be as follows:

Schedule 3 – Annual direct material usage budget

	Department 1			Department 2						
	Units	Unit price (£)	Total (£)	Units	Unit price (£)	Total (£)	Total units	Total unit price (£)	Total (£)
Material X	102 000[a]	7.20	734 400	12 840[c]	7.20	92 448	114 840	7.20	826 848
Material Y	51 000[b]	16.00	816 000	14 445[d]	16.00	231 120	65 445	16.00	1 047 120
			1 550 400			323 568			1 873 968

[a]10 200 units production at 10 units per unit of production.
[b]10 200 units production at 5 units per unit of production.
[c]1605 units production at 8 units per unit of production.
[d]1605 units production at 9 units per unit of production.

Direct materials purchase budget

The direct materials purchase budget is the responsibility of the purchasing manager, since it will be he or she who is responsible for obtaining the planned quantities of raw materials to meet the production requirements. The objective is to purchase these materials at the right time at the planned purchase price. In addition, it is necessary to take into account the planned raw material stock levels. The annual materials purchase budget for the year will be as follows:

Schedule 4 – Direct materials purchase budget

	Material X (units)	Material Y (units)
Quantity necessary to meet production requirements as per material usage budget	114 840	65 445
Planned closing stock	10 200	1 700
	125 040	67 145
Less planned opening stock	8 500	8 000
Total units to be purchased	116 540	59 145
Planned unit purchase price	£7.20	£16
Total purchases	£839 088	£946 320

Note that this budget is a summary budget for the year, but for detailed planning and control it will be necessary to analyze the annual budget on a monthly basis.

Direct labour budget

The direct labour budget is the responsibility of the respective managers of departments 1 and 2. They will prepare estimates of the departments' labour hours required to meet the planned production. Where different grades of labour exist, these should be specified separately in the budget. The budget rate per hour should be determined by the industrial relations department. The direct labour budget will be as follows:

Schedule 5 – Annual direct labour budget

	Department 1	Department 2	Total
Budgeted production (units)	10 200	1 605	
Hours per unit	10	15	
Total budgeted hours	102 000	24 075	126 075
Budgeted wage rate per hour	£12	£12	
Total wages	£1 224 000	£288 900	£1 512 900

Factory overhead budget

The factory overhead budget is also the responsibility of the respective production department managers. The total of the overhead budget will depend on the behaviour of the costs of the individual overhead items in relation to the anticipated level of production. The overheads must also be analyzed according to whether they are controllable or non-controllable for the purpose of cost control. The factory overhead budget will be as follows:

Schedule 6 – Annual factory overhead budget
Anticipated activity – 102 000 direct labour hours (department 1)
24 075 direct labour hours (department 2)

	Variable overhead rate per direct labour hour		Overheads		
	Department 1 (£)	Department 2 (£)	Department 1 (£)	Department 2 (£)	Total (£)
Controllable overheads:					
Indirect material	1.20	0.80	122 400	19 260	
Indirect labour	1.20	1.20	122 400	28 890	
Power (variable portion)	0.60	0.40	61 200	9 630	
Maintenance (variable portion)	0.20	0.40	20 400	9 630	
			326 400	67 410	393 810
Non-controllable overheads:					
Depreciation			100 000	80 000	
Supervision			100 000	40 000	
Power (fixed portion)			40 000	2 000	
Maintenance (fixed portion)			45 600	3 196	
			285 600	125 196	410 796
Total overhead			612 000	192 606	804 606
Budgeted departmental overhead rate			£6.00[a]	8.00[b]	

[a] £612 000 total overheads divided by 102 000 direct labour hours.
[b] £192 606 total overheads divided by 24 075 direct labour hours.

The budgeted expenditure for the variable overhead items is determined by multiplying the budgeted direct labour hours for each department by the budgeted variable overhead rate per hour. It is assumed that all variable overheads vary in relation to direct labour hours.

Selling and administration budget

The selling and administration budgets have been combined here to simplify the presentation. In practice, separate budgets should be prepared: the sales manager will be responsible for the selling budget, the distribution manager will be responsible for the distribution expenses and the chief administrative officer will be responsible for the administration budget.

Schedule 7 – Annual selling and administration budget

	(£)	(£)
Selling:		
Salaries	74 000	
Commission	60 000	
Car expenses	22 000	
Advertising	80 000	236 000
Administration:		
Stationery	4 000	
Salaries	28 000	
Miscellaneous	8 000	40 000
		276 000

Departmental budgets

For cost control the direct labour budget, materials usage budget and factory overhead budget are combined into separate departmental budgets. These budgets are normally broken down into twelve separate monthly budgets, and the actual monthly expenditure is compared with the budgeted amounts for each of the items concerned. This comparison is used for judging how effective managers are in controlling the expenditure for which they are responsible. The departmental budget for department 1 will be as follows:

Department 1 – Annual departmental operating budget

	(£)	Budget (£)	Actual (£)
Direct labour (from schedule 5):			
102 000 hours at £12		1 224 000	
Direct materials (from schedule 3):			
102 000 units of material X at £7.20 per unit	734 400		
51 000 units of material Y at £16 per unit	816 000	1 550 400	
Controllable overheads (from schedule 6):			
Indirect materials	122 400		
Indirect labour	122 400		
Power (variable portion)	61 200		
Maintenance (variable portion)	20 400	326 400	
Uncontrollable overheads (from schedule 6):			
Depreciation	100 000		
Supervision	100 000		
Power (fixed portion)	40 000		
Maintenance (fixed portion)	45 600	285 600	
		3 386 400	

Master budget

When all the budgets have been prepared, the budgeted profit and loss account and balance sheet provide the overall picture of the planned performance for the budget period.

Budgeted profit and loss account for the year ending 200X

	(£)	(£)
Sales (schedule 1)		4 296 000
Opening stock of raw materials	189 200	
(from opening balance sheet)		
Purchases (schedule 4)	1 785 408[a]	
	1 974 608	
Less closing stock of raw materials (schedule 4)	100 640[b]	
Cost of raw materials consumed	1 873 968	
Direct labour (schedule 5)	1 512 900	
Factory overheads (schedule 6)	804 606	
Total manufacturing cost	4 191 474	
Add opening stock of finished goods	99 076	
(from opening balance sheet)		
Less closing stock of finished goods	665 984[c]	
	(566 908)	
Cost of sales		3 624 566
Gross profit		671 434
Selling and administration expenses (schedule 7)		276 000
Budgeted operating profit for the year		395 434

[a] £839 088 (X) + £946 320 (Y) from schedule 4.
[b] 10 200 units at £7.20 plus 1700 units at £16 from schedule 4.
[c] 1870 units of alpha valued at £332 per unit, 90 units of sigma valued at £501.60 per unit. The product unit costs are calculated as follows:

	Alpha		Sigma	
	Units	(£)	Units	(£)
Direct materials				
X	10	72.00	8	57.60
Y	5	80.00	9	144.00
Direct labour	10	120.00	15	180.00
Factory overheads:				
Department 1	10	60.00	—	—
Department 2	—	—	15	120.00
		332.00		501.60

Budgeted balance sheet as at 31 December

	(£)	(£)
Fixed assets:		
Land		170 000
Building and equipment	1 292 000	
Less depreciation[a]	435 000	857 000
		1 027 000

Current assets:		
Raw material stock	100 640	
Finished good stock	665 984	
Debtors[b]	280 000	
Cash[c]	199 170	
	1 245 794	
Current liabilities:		
Creditors[d]	307 884	937 910
		1 964 910
Represented by shareholders' interest:		
1 200 000 ordinary shares of £1 each	1 200 000	
Reserves	369 476	
Profit and loss account	395 434	1 964 910

[a]£255 000 + £180 000 (schedule 6) = £435 000.
[b]£289 000 opening balance + £4 296 000 sales – £4 305 000 cash.
[c]Closing balance as per cash budget.
[d]£248 800 opening balance + £1 785 408 purchases + £141 660 indirect materials – £1 876 984 cash.

Cash budgets

The objective of the cash budget is to ensure that sufficient cash is available at all times to meet the level of operations that are outlined in the various budgets. The cash budget for Example 15.1 is presented below and is analyzed by quarters, but in practice monthly or weekly budgets will be necessary. Because cash budgeting is subject to uncertainty, it is necessary to provide for more than the minimum amount required, to allow for some margin of error in planning. Cash budgets can help a firm to avoid cash balances that are surplus to its requirements by enabling management to take steps in advance to invest the surplus cash in short-term investments. Alternatively, cash deficiencies can be identified in advance, and steps can be taken to ensure that bank loans will be available to meet any temporary cash deficiencies. For example, by looking at the cash budget for the Enterprise Company, management may consider that the cash balances are higher than necessary in the second and third quarters of the year, and they may invest part of the cash balance in short-term investments.

The overall aim should be to manage the cash of the firm to attain maximum cash availability and maximum interest income on any idle funds.

Cash budget for year ending 200X

	Quarter 1 (£)	Quarter 2 (£)	Quarter 3 (£)	Quarter 4 (£)	Total (£)
Opening balance	34 000	114 000	294 000	421 984	34 000
Receipts from debtors	1 000 000	1 200 000	1 120 000	985 000	4 305 000
	1 034 000	1 314 000	1 414 000	1 406 984	4 339 000
Payments:					
Purchase of materials	400 000	480 000	440 000	547 984	1 867 984
Payment of wages	400 000	440 000	480 000	646 188	1 966 188
Other costs and expenses	120 000	100 000	72 016	13 642	305 658
	920 000	1 020 000	992 016	1 207 814	4 139 830
Closing balance	114 000	294 000	421 984	199 170	199 170

Final review

The budgeted profit and loss account, the balance sheet and the cash budget will be submitted by the accountant to the budget committee, together with a number of budgeted financial ratios such as the return on capital employed, working capital, liquidity and gearing ratios. If these ratios prove to be acceptable, the budgets will be approved. In Example 15.1 the return on capital employed is approximately 20 per cent, but the working capital ratio (current assets:current liabilities) is over 4:1, so management should consider alternative ways of reducing investment in working capital before finally approving the budgets.

Computerized budgeting

In the past, budgeting was a task dreaded by many management accountants. You will have noted from Example 15.1 that many numerical manipulations are necessary to prepare the budget. In the real world the process is far more complex, and, as the budget is being formulated, it is altered many times since some budgets are found to be out of balance with each other or the master budget proves to be unacceptable.

In today's world, the budgeting process is computerized instead of being primarily concerned with numerical manipulations, the accounting staff can now become more involved in the real planning process. Computer-based financial models normally consist of mathematical statements of inputs and outputs. By simply altering the mathematical statements budgets can be quickly revised with little effort. However, the major advantage of computerized budgeting is that

REAL WORLD VIEWS 15.1

Using Web technology for the budget process

An e-budgeting solution completely automates the development of an organization's budget and forecast. From anywhere in the world, at all times, participants in the process can log through the Internet to access their budget and any pertinent related information so they can work on their plans. Web-based enterprise budgeting systems offer a centrally administered system that provides easy-to-use flexible tools for the end users who are responsible for budgeting. The Web functionality of these applications allows constant monitoring, updates and modelling.

E-budgeting provides the flexibility demanded by modern organizations. For example, the finance department can request across-the-board reallocations of expenditures and model the result immediately. No longer do management accountants have to go back and forth with other managers reinputing data and retallying results. E-budgeting can eliminate the cumbersome accounting tasks of pulling numbers from disparate files, cutting and pasting,

entering and uploading, and constantly performing reconciliation. Also, a Web-based budgeting application lets managers access data from office or home – wherever they happen to be working. It broadens the system's availability to the user community.

When executives at Toronto-Dominion Bank were searching for a new solution capable of handling the bank's enterprise budgeting and planning function, they turned to the Internet. The company selected Clarus Corporation's Web-deployed, enterprise Clarus™ Budget solution. Its accountant stated 'in the past, we have compiled our business plan using hundreds of spreadsheets, and our analysts have spent a disproportionate amount of their time compiling and verifying data from multiple sources. Implementing a Web-based, enterprise-wide budgeting solution will help us to develop our business plans and allow our analysts to be proactive in monitoring quarterly results.'

Discussion point

What impact does e-budgeting have on the management accounting function?

SOURCE: ADAPTED FROM HORNYAK, S. (2000), BUDGETING MADE EASY, MANAGEMENT ACCOUNTING, OCTOBER 1998.

management can evaluate many different options before the budget is finally agreed. Establishing a model enables 'What-if?' analysis to be employed. For example, answers to the following questions can be displayed in the form of a master budget: What if sales increase or decrease by 10 per cent? What if unit costs increase or decrease by 5 per cent? What if the credit terms for sales were reduced from 30 to 20 days?

In addition, computerized models can incorporate actual results, period by period, and carry out the necessary calculations to produce budgetary *control* reports. It is also possible to adjust the budgets for the remainder of the year when it is clear that the circumstances on which the budget was originally set have changed.

Activity-based budgeting

The conventional approach to budgeting works fine for unit level activity costs where the consumption of resources varies proportionately with the volume of the final output of products or services. However, for those indirect costs and support activities where there are no clearly defined input–output relationships, and the consumption of resources does not vary with the final output of products or services, conventional budgets merely serve as authorization levels for certain levels of spending for each budgeted item of expense. Budgets that are not based on well-understood relationships between activities and costs are poor indicators of performance and performance reporting normally implies little more than checking whether the budget has been exceeded. Conventional budgets therefore provide little relevant information for managing the costs of support activities.

With conventional budgeting indirect costs and support activities are prepared on an incremental basis. This means that existing operations and the current budgeted allowance for existing activities are taken as the starting point for preparing the next annual budget. The base is then adjusted for changes (such as changes in product mix, volumes and prices) which are expected to occur during the new budget period. This approach is called incremental budgeting, since the budget process is concerned mainly with the increment in operations or expenditure that will occur during the forthcoming budget period. For example, the allowance for budgeted expenses may be based on the previous budgeted allowance plus an increase to cover higher prices caused by inflation. The major disadvantage of the incremental approach is that the majority of expenditure, which is associated with the 'base level' of activity, remains unchanged. Thus, the cost of non-unit level activities become fixed and past inefficiencies and waste inherent in the current way of doing things is perpetuated.

To manage costs more effectively organizations that have implemented activity-based costing (ABC) have also adopted activity-based budgeting (ABB). The aim of ABB is to authorize the supply of only those resources that are needed to perform activities required to meet the budgeted production and sales volume. Whereas ABC assigns resource expenses to activities and then uses activity cost drivers to assign activity costs to cost objects (such as products, services or customers), ABB is the reverse of this process. Cost objects are the starting point. Their budgeted output determines the necessary activities which are then used to estimate the resources that are required for the budget period. ABB involves the following stages:

1 estimate the production and sales volume by individual products and customers;
2 estimate the demand for organizational activities;
3 determine the resources that are required to perform organizational activities;
4 estimate for each resource the quantity that must be supplied to meet the demand;
5 take action to adjust the capacity of resources to match the projected supply.

The first stage is identical to conventional budgeting. Details of budgeted production and sales volumes for individual products and customer types will be contained in the sales and production budgets. Next, ABC extends conventional budgeting to support activities such as ordering, receiving, scheduling production and processing customers' orders. To implement

ABB a knowledge of the activities that are necessary to produce and sell the products and services and service customers is essential. Estimates of the quantity of activity cost drivers must be derived for each activity. For example, the number of purchase orders, the number of receipts, the number of set-ups and the number of customer orders processed are estimated using the same approach as that used by conventional budgeting to determine the quantity of direct labour and materials that are incorporated into the direct labour and materials purchase budgets. Standard cost data incorporating a bill of activities is maintained for each product indicating the different activities, and the quantity of activity drivers that are required, to produce a specified number of products. Such documentation provides the basic information for building up the activity-based budgets.

The third stage is to estimate the resources that are required for performing the quantity of activity drivers demanded. In particular, estimates are required of each type of resource, and their quantities required, to meet the demanded quantity of activities. For example, if the number of customer orders to be processed is estimated to be 5000 and each order takes 30 minutes processing time then 2500 labour hours of the customer processing activity must be supplied.

Next, the resources demanded (derived from the third stage) are converted into an estimate of the total resources that must be supplied for each type of resource used by an activity. The quantity of resources supplied depends on the cost behaviour of the resource. For flexible resources where the supply can be matched exactly to meet demand, such as direct materials and energy costs, the quantity of resources supplied will be identical to the quantity demanded. For example, if customer processing were a flexible resource exactly 2500 hours would be purchased. However, a more likely assumption is that customer processing labour will be a step cost function in relation to the volume of the activity (see Chapter 2 for a description of step cost functions). Assuming that each person employed is contracted to work 1500 hours per year then 1.67 persons (2500/1500) represents the quantity of resources required, but because resources must be acquired in uneven amounts, two persons must be employed. For other resources, such as equipment, resources will tend to be fixed and committed over a very wide range of volume for the activity. As long as demand is less than the capacity supplied by the committed resource no additional spending will be required.

The final stage is to compare the estimates of the quantity of resources to be supplied for each resource with the quantity of resources that are currently committed. If the estimated demand for a resource exceeds the current capacity additional spending must be authorized within the budgeting process to acquire additional resources. Alternatively, if the demand for resources is less than the projected supply, the budgeting process should result in management taking action to either redeploy or reduce those resources that are no longer required.

Exhibit 15.1 illustrates an activity-based budget for an order receiving process or department. You will see that the budget is presented in a matrix format with the major activities being shown for each of the columns and the resource inputs are listed by rows. The cost driver activity levels are also highlighted. A major feature of ABB is the enhanced visibility arising from showing the outcomes, in terms of cost drivers, from the budgeted expenditure. This information is particularly useful for planning and estimating future expenditure.

Let us now look at how ABB can be applied using the information presented in Exhibit 15.1. Assume that ABB stages one and two as outlined above result in an estimated annual demand of 2800 orders for the processing of the receipt of the standard customers' order activity (column 6 in Exhibit 15.1). For the staff salaries row (that is, the processing of customers' orders labour resource) assume that each member of staff can process on average 50 orders per month, or 600 per year. Therefore 4.67 (2800 orders/600 orders) persons are required for the supply of this resource (that is, stage three as outlined above). The fourth stage converts the 4.67 staff resources into the amount that must be supplied, that is five members of staff. Let us assume that the current capacity or supply of resources committed to the activity is six members of staff at £25 000 per annum, giving a total annual cost of £150 000. Management is therefore made aware that staff resources can be reduced by £25 000 per annum by transferring one member of staff to other activities where staff resources need to be expanded or, more drastically, making them redundant.

EXHIBIT 15.1 Activity-based budget for an order receiving process

Activities →	Handle import goods	Execute express orders	Special Deliveries	Distribution administration	Order receiving (standard products)	Order receiving (non-standard products)	Execute rush orders	Total cost
Resource expense accounts:								
Office supplies								
Telephone expenses								
Salaries								
Travel								
Training								
Total cost								
Activity cost driver → measures	Number of customs documents	Number of customer bills	Number of letters of credit	Number of consignment notes	Number of standard orders	Number of non-standard orders	Number of rush orders	

Some of the other resource expenses (such as office supplies and telephone expenses) listed in Exhibit 15.1 for the processing of customers' order activity represent flexible resources which are likely to vary in the short-term with the number of orders processed. Assuming that the budget for the forthcoming period represents 80 per cent of the number of orders processed during the previous budget period then the budget for those resource expenses that vary in the short-term with the number of orders processed should be reduced by 20 per cent.

With conventional budgeting the budgeted expenses for the forthcoming budget for support activities are normally based on the previous year's budget plus an adjustment for inflation. Support costs are therefore considered to be fixed in relation to activity volume. In contrast, ABB provides a framework for understanding the amount of resources that are required to achieve the budgeted level of activity. By comparing the amount of resources that are required with the amount of resources that are in place, upwards or downwards adjustments can be made during the budget setting phase.

The budgeting process in non-profit-making organizations

The budgeting process in a non-profit-making organization normally begins with the managers of the various activities calculating the expected costs of maintaining current ongoing activities and then adding to those costs any further developments of the services that are considered desirable. For example, the education, health, housing and social services departments of a municipal authority will propose specific activities and related costs for the coming year. These budgets are coordinated by the accounting department into an overall budget proposal.

The available resources for financing the proposed level of public services should be sufficient to cover the total costs of such services. In the case of a municipal authority the resources will be raised by local taxes and government grants. Similar procedures are followed by churches, hospitals, charities and other non-profit-making organizations, in that they produce estimates for undertaking their activities and then find the means to finance them, or reduce the activities to realistic levels so that they can be financed from available financial resources.

One difficulty encountered in non-profit-making organizations is that precise objectives are difficult to define in a quantifiable way, and the actual accomplishments are even more difficult to measure. In most situations outputs cannot be measured in monetary terms. By 'outputs' we mean the quality and amount of the services rendered. In profit-oriented organizations output can be measured in terms of sales revenues. The effect of this is that budgets in non-profit organizations, tend to be mainly concerned with the input of resources (i.e. expenditure), whereas budgets in profit organizations focus on the relationships between inputs (expenditure) and outputs (sales revenue). In non-profit organizations there is not the same emphasis on what was intended to be achieved for a given input of resources. The budgeting process tends to compare what is happening in cash input terms with the estimated cash inputs. In other words, there is little emphasis on measures of managerial performance in terms of the results achieved. The reason for this is that there is no clear relationship between resource inputs and the benefits flowing from the use of these resources.

Line item budgets

The traditional format for budgets in non-profit organizations is referred to as line item budgets. A line item budget is one in which the expenditures are expressed in considerable detail, but the activities being undertaken are given little attention. In other words, line item budgeting shows the nature of the spending but not the purpose. A typical line item budget is illustrated in Exhibit 15.2.

REAL WORLD VIEWS 15.2

The European Union budget cycle

Budgeting is not the sole property of private firms. Hospitals, community organisations, charities and governments also need to plan for their future revenues and costs and thus engage in the preparation of budgets.

The European Union (EU) has twenty-five Members States[1] with plans for further enlargement. While each Member State prepares its own budget, the EU receives funding income from all Member States. This funding (in the region of €110m in 2006) is spent on various items such as developing infrastructure in lesser developed states, common justice systems and social schemes.

The EU has a lengthy budgetary cycle. The cycle commences two years prior to the budget year, in the month of December, with an orientation debate within the European Commission. By the following February a preliminary draft budget is prepared and presented to the European Parliament, European Council and other stakeholders for discussion. Items are debated and prioritised by the Parliament and Council. By November, a work programme is agreed and the budget is finalised. The budget is implemented from January 1st. Once the year is complete the spending activities are completely reviewed by April. Any over or under spending is reviewed and reported on.

Discussion point

As noted, the EU budget cycle commences more than 12 months before the budget year. Is this too long in advance? Might budget estimates be meaningless by the time the budget is implemented?

[1] AS AT 31.12.2006.

EU Parliament building, Brussels
© FRANKY DE MEYER/STOCKPHOTO.COM

SOURCE: EUROPEAN COMMISSION, FINANCIAL PROGRAMMING AND BUDGETING WEBSITE – EC.EUROPA.EU/BUDGET/ BUDGET_DETAIL/INDEX_EN.HTM

EXHIBIT 15.2 Typical line item budget

	Actual 20X2 (£)	Original budget 20X3 (£)	Revised budget 20X3 (£)	Proposed budget 20X4 (£)
Employees	1 292 000	1 400 000	1 441 000	1 830 000
Premises	3 239	12 000	10 800	14 200
Supplies and services	34 735	43 200	44 900	147 700
Transport	25 778	28 500	28 700	30 700
Establishment expenses	123 691	120 000	116 000	158 600
Agency charges	10 120	10 000	9 800	13 300
Financing charges	2 357	2 700	2 800	114 800
Other expenses	1 260	1 350	1 400	1 600
	1 493 180	1 617 750	1 655 400	2 310 900

The amounts in this type of budget are frequently established on the basis of historical costs that have been adjusted for anticipated changes in costs and activity levels. When they are compared with the actual expenditures, line item budgets provide a basis for comparing whether or not the authorized budgeted expenditure has been exceeded or whether underspending has occurred. Note that data for the current year and for the previous year are included to indicate how the proposed budget differs from current spending patterns. However, such line item budgets fail to identify the costs of *activities* and the *programmes* to be implemented. In addition, compliance with line item budgets provides no assurance that resources are used wisely, effectively or efficiently in financing the various activities in a non-profit organization. Planning, programming budgeting systems (PPBS) are intended to overcome these deficiencies. For a description and illustration of PPBS you should refer to Learning Note 15.1 on the open access website accompanying this book (see Preface for details).

Zero-based budgeting

Zero-based budgeting (also known as priority-based budgeting) emerged in the late 1960s as an attempt to overcome the limitations of incremental budgets. This approach requires that all activities are justified and prioritized before decisions are taken relating to the amount of resources allocated to each activity. Besides adopting a 'zero-based' approach zero-base budgeting (ZBB) also focuses on programmes or activities instead of functional departments based on line-items which is a feature of traditional budgeting. Programmes normally relate to various activities undertaken by municipal or government organizations. Examples include extending childcare facilities, improvement of health care for senior citizens and the extension of nursing facilities.

ZBB works from the premise that projected expenditure for existing programmes should start from base zero, with each year's budgets being compiled as if the programmes were being launched for the first time. The budgetees should present their requirements for appropriations in such a fashion that all funds can be allocated on the basis of cost–benefit or some similar kind of evaluative analysis. The cost–benefit approach is an attempt to ensure 'value for money'; it questions long-standing assumptions and serves as a tool for systematically examining and perhaps abandoning any unproductive projects.

ZBB is best suited to discretionary costs and support activities. With discretionary costs management has some discretion as to the amount it will budget for the particular activity in question. Examples of discretionary costs include advertising, research and development and training costs. There is no optimum relationship between inputs (as measured by the costs) and outputs (measured by revenues or some other objective function) for these costs. Furthermore, they are not predetermined by some previous commitment. In effect, management can determine what quantity of service it wishes to purchase and there is no established method for determining the appropriate amount to be spent in particular periods. ZBB has mostly been applied in municipal and government organizations where the predominant costs are of a discretionary nature.

ZBB involves the following three stages:

- a description of each organizational activity in a decision package;
- the evaluation and ranking of decision packages in order of priority;
- allocation of resources based on order of priority up to the spending cut-off level.

Decision packages are identified for each decision unit. Decision units represent separate programmes or groups of activities that an organization undertakes. A decision package represents the operation of a particular programme with incremental packages reflecting different levels of effort that may be expended on a specific function. One package is usually prepared at the 'base' level for each programme. This package represents the minimum level of service or support consistent with the organization's objectives. Service or support higher than the base level is described in one or more incremental packages. For example, managers might be asked to specify the base package in terms of level of service that can be provided at 70 per cent of the current cost level and incremental packages identify higher activity or cost levels.

Once the decision packages have been completed, management is ready to start to review the process. To determine how much to spend and where to spend it, management will rank all packages in order of decreasing benefits to the organization. Theoretically, once management has set the budgeted level of spending, the packages should be accepted down to the spending level based on cost–benefit principles.

The benefits of ZBB over traditional methods of budgeting are claimed to be as follows:

1 Traditional budgeting tends to extrapolate the past by adding a percentage increase to the current year. ZBB avoids the deficiencies of incremental budgeting and represents a move towards the allocation of resources by need or benefit. Thus, unlike traditional budgeting the level of funding is not taken for granted.

2 ZBB creates a questioning attitude rather than one that assumes that current practice represents value for money.

3 ZBB focuses attention on outputs in relation to value for money.

ZBB was first applied in Texas Instruments in 1969. It quickly became one of the fashionable management tools of the 1970s and, according to Phyrr (1976), there were 100 users in the USA in the early 1970s. ZBB never achieved the widespread adoption that its proponents envisaged. The major reason for its lack of success would appear to be that it is too costly and time-consuming. The process of identifying decision packages and determining their purpose, cost and benefits is extremely time-consuming. Furthermore, there are often too many decision packages to evaluate and there is frequently insufficient information to enable them to be ranked.

Research suggests that many organizations tend to approximate the principles of ZBB rather than applying the full-scale approach outlined in the literature. For example, it does not have to be applied throughout the organization. It can be applied selectively to those areas about which management is most concerned and used as a one-off cost reduction programme. Some of the benefits of ZBB can be captured by using priority-based incremental budgets. Priority incremental budgets require managers to specify what incremental activities or changes would occur if their budgets were increased or decreased by a specified percentage (say 10 per cent). Budget allocations are made by comparing the change in costs with the change in benefits. Priority incremental budgets thus represent an economical compromise between ZBB and incremental budgeting.

Criticisms of budgeting

In recent years criticisms of traditional budgeting have attracted much publicity. Indeed, in a series of articles Hope and Fraser (1999a, 1999b, 2001, 2003) have argued that companies should abandon traditional budgeting. They advocate that companies should move beyond budgeting. According to Hope and Fraser (1999a) a number of innovative companies, such as Svenska Handelsbanken (a Swedish bank) and Volvo, are in the process of abandoning traditional budgeting. The major criticism is that the annual budgeting process is incapable of meeting the demands of the competitive environment in the information age. Ekholm and Wallin (2000) and Dugdale and Lyne (2006) have reviewed the literature relating to annual budgets. They have identified the following criticisms relating to the annual budgeting process:

- encouraging rigid planning and incremental thinking;
- being time-consuming;
- producing inadequate variance reports leaving the 'how' and 'why' questions unanswered;
- ignoring key drivers of shareholder value by focusing too much attention on short-term financial numbers;
- being a yearly rigid ritual;
- tying the company to a 12-month commitment, which is risky since it is based on uncertain forecasts;
- meeting only the lowest targets and not attempting to beat the targets;
- spending what is in the budget even if this is not necessary in order to guard against next year's budget being reduced;
- achieving the budget even if this results in undesirable actions.

Ekholm and Wallin conclude that the above criticisms suggest the need for more anticipation, monitoring and empowerment, and less rigid planning and control. The term beyond budgeting is used by Hope and Fraser to relate to alternative approaches that should be used instead of annual budgeting. Rolling forecasts, produced on a monthly or quarterly basis, are suggested as the main alternative to the annual budget. Such rolling forecasts should embrace key performance indicators based on balanced scorecards (see Chapter 22) and should also incorporate exception-based monitoring and benchmarking (see Chapter 21). Rolling forecasts are advocated because they do not have the same compulsory and stifling image when compared with the annual budget. They are also flexible and do not rely on obsolete figures, which should result in a more timely allocation of resources (Gurton, 1990).

Because of the criticisms of budgeting, and the beyond budgeting movement, Dugdale and Lyne (2006) surveyed financial and non-financial managers in 40 UK companies. Their main conclusion was that budgeting is alive and well. All of the companies surveyed used budgets and, generally, both financial and non-financial managers thought they were important for planning, control, performance measurement, coordination and communication. To find out how problematic the respondents viewed their budgets, they were asked whether they agreed with 20 critical propositions. The respondents tended to disagree with the propositions. Ekholm and Wallin also surveyed 168 Finnish companies. They reported that relatively few companies were planning to abandon the annual budget. However, in contrast to the UK findings by Dugdale and Lyne there was strong agreement with many of the criticisms relating to budgeting. Comments by several respondents also indicated that complementary systems, such as rolling forecasts and monitoring systems similar to the balanced scorecard already exist, and are run in parallel with the annual budget.

SUMMARY

The following items relate to the learning objectives listed at the beginning of the chapter.

Explain how budgeting fits into the overall planning and control framework.

The annual budget should be set within the context of longer-term plans, which are likely to exist even if they have not been made explicit. A long-term plan is a statement of the preliminary targets and activities required by an organization to achieve its strategic plans together with a broad estimate for each year of the resources required. Because long-term planning involves 'looking into the future' for several years, the plans tend to be uncertain, general in nature, imprecise and subject to change. Annual budgeting is concerned with the detailed implementation of the long-term plan for the year ahead.

Identify and describe the six different purposes of budgeting.

Budgets are used for the following purposes: (a) planning annual operations; (b) coordinating the activities of the various parts of the organization and ensuring that the parts are in harmony with each other; (c) communicating the plans to the managers of the various responsibility centres; (d) motivating managers to strive to achieve organizational goals; (e) controlling activities; and (f) evaluating the performance of managers.

Identify and describe the various stages in the budget process.

The important stages are as follows: (a) communicating details of the budget policy and guidelines to those people responsible for the preparation of the budgets; (b) determining the factor that restricts output (normally sales volume); (c) preparation of the sales budget (assuming that sales demand is the factor that restricts output); (d) initial preparation of the various budgets; (e) negotiation of budgets with superiors; (f) coordination and review of budgets; (g) final acceptance of budgets; and (h) ongoing review of budgets. Each of the above stages is described in the chapter.

Prepare functional and master budgets.

When all of the budgets have been prepared they are summarized into a master budget consisting in a budgeted profit and loss account, a balance sheet and a cash budget statement. The preparation of functional and master budgets was illustrated using Example 15.1.

Describe the use of computer-based financial models for budgeting.

Computer-based financial models are mathematical statements of the inputs and output relationships that affect the budget. These models allow management to conduct sensitivity analysis to ascertain the effects on the master budget of changes in the original predicted data or changes in the assumptions that were used to prepare the budgets.

Describe the limitations of incremental budgeting.

With incremental budgeting indirect costs and support activities are prepared on an incremental basis. This means that existing operations and the current budgeted allowance for existing activities are taken as the starting point for preparing the next annual budget. The base is then adjusted for changes (such as changes in product mix, volumes and prices) which are expected to occur during the new budget period. When this approach is adopted the concern is mainly with the increment in operations or expenditure that will occur during the forthcoming budget period. The major disadvantage of the incremental approach is that the majority of expenditure, which is associated with the 'base level' of activity, remains unchanged. Thus, past inefficiencies and waste inherent in the current way of doing things are perpetuated.

Describe activity-based budgeting.

With conventional budgeting the budgeted expenses for the forthcoming budget for support activities are normally based on the previous year's budget plus an adjustment for inflation. Support costs are therefore considered to be fixed in relation to activity volume. Activity-based budgeting (ABB) aims to manage costs more effectively by authorizing the supply of only those resources that are needed to perform activities required to meet the budgeted production and sales volume. Whereas ABC assigns resource expenses to activities and then uses activity cost drivers to assign activity costs to cost objects (such as products, services or customers) ABB is the reverse of this process. Cost objects are the starting point. Their budgeted output determines the necessary activities which are then used to estimate the resources that are required for the budget period. ABB involves the following stages: (a) estimate the production and sales volume by individual products and customers; (b) estimate the demand for organizational activities; (c) determine the resources that are required to perform organizational activities; (d) estimate for each resource the quantity that must be supplied to meet the demand; and (e) take action to adjust the capacity of resources to match the projected supply.

● Describe zero-base budgeting (ZBB).

ZBB is a method of budgeting that is mainly used in non-profit organizations but it can also be applied to discretionary costs and support activities in profit organizations. It seeks to overcome the deficiencies of incremental budgeting. ZBB works from the premise that projected expenditure for existing programmes should start from base zero, with each year's budgets being compiled as if the programmes were being launched for the first time. The budgetees should present their requirements for appropriations in such a fashion that all funds can be allocated on the basis of cost–benefit or some similar kind of evaluative analysis. The cost–benefit approach is an attempt to ensure 'value for money'; it questions long-standing assumptions and serves as a tool for systematically examining and perhaps abandoning any unproductive projects.

● Describe the criticisms relating to traditional budgeting

Criticisms relating to traditional budgeting include encouraging rigid planning and incremental thinking, being time-consuming, a failure to encourage continuous improvement, achieving the target even if this results in undesirable actions and being a yearly rigid ritual. The beyond budgeting movement advocates that budgeting should be replaced with rolling forecasts that embrace key performance indicators and also incorporate exception-based monitoring and benchmarking.

Note

1 The criteria specified are derived from Johnson and Scholes (2005).

Key terms and concepts

activity-based budgeting (p. 371)
aims (p. 353)
beyond budgeting (p. 377)
budgeting (p. 354)
budgets (p. 351)
cash budgets (p. 369)
continuous budgeting (p. 357)
corporate objectives (p. 352)
corporate planning (p. 351)
decision package (p. 376)
discretionary costs (p. 375)

generic strategies (p. 353)
goals (p. 353)
incremental budgeting (p. 371)
incremental budgets (p. 375)
line item budgets (p. 374)
long-range planning (p. 351)
long-term plan (p. 354)
management by exception (p. 356)
master budget (p. 361)
mission (p. 352)
objectives (p. 352)

priority based budgets (p. 375)
priority based incremental budgets (p. 376)
rolling budgeting (p. 357)
strategic analysis (p. 353)
strategic planning (p. 351)
strategies (p. 353)
unit objectives (p. 353)
zero-based budgeting (p. 375)

Recommended reading

In this chapter we have provided a very brief summary of the process for selecting alternative strategies. A detailed explanation of strategy formulation can be found in the corporate strategy literature. Predominant texts on this area include Johnson and Scholes (2005) and Thompson (2005). For a more detailed discussion of budgeting in the public sector see Pendlebury (1996). You should refer to Kennedy and Dugdale (1999) for a discussion of the reasons for the dissatisfaction with the budgeting process and suggestions for ways in which they can be eliminated. Other relevant articles relating to the criticisms of budgeting include Ekholm and Wallin (2000), Hope and Fraser (2001) and Dugdale and Lyne (2006).

Key examination points

Examination questions on budgeting frequently require the preparation of functional or cash budgets. A common mistake is to incorrectly deduct closing stocks and add opening stocks when preparing production and material purchase budgets. Examination questions are also set frequently on zero-base budgeting (ZBB). Do make sure that you can describe and discuss the advantages and disadvantages of ZBB. You should refer to the solution to Review problem 15.23 for the application of activity-based budgeting.

ASSESSMENT MATERIAL

The review questions are short questions that enable you to assess your understanding of the main topics included in the chapter. The numbers in parentheses provide you with the page numbers to refer to if you cannot answer a specific question.

The review problems are more complex and require you to relate and apply the content to various business problems. The problems are graded by their level of difficulty. Solutions to review problems that are not preceded by the term 'IM' are provided in a separate section at the end of the book. Solutions to problems preceded by the term 'IM' are provided in the *Instructor's Manual* accompanying this book and also on the lecturer's password protected section of the website www.drury-online.com. Additional review problems with fully worked solutions are provided in the *Student's Manual* that accompanies this book.

The website also includes over 30 case problems. A list of these cases is provided on pages 665–7. Several cases are relevant to the content of this chapter. Examples include Endeavour Twoplise Ltd., Global Ltd. and Integrated Technology Ltd.

Review questions

15.1 Define the term 'budget'. How are budgets used in planning? *(pp. 351–52)*
15.2 Describe the different stages in the planning and control process. *(pp. 352–54)*
15.3 Distinguish between budgeting and long-range planning. How are they related? *(p. 352, p. 354)*
15.4 Describe the different purposes of budgeting. *(pp. 355–56)*
15.5 Explain what is meant by the term 'management by exception'. *(p. 356)*
15.6 Describe how the different roles of budgets can conflict with each other. *(p. 356)*
15.7 Distinguish between continuous and rolling budgets. *(p. 357)*
15.8 Describe the different stages in the budgeting process. *(pp. 358–61)*
15.9 All budgets depend on the sales budget. Do you agree? Explain. *(p. 359)*
15.10 What is a master budget? *(p. 361)*
15.11 Define incremental budgeting. *(p. 371)*
15.12 What are the distinguishing features of activity-based budgeting? *(pp. 371–73)*
15.13 Describe the five different stages that are involved with activity-based-budgeting. *(pp. 371–73)*
15.14 What are the distinguishing features of budgeting in non-profit-making organizations? *(pp. 373–75)*
15.15 What are line item budgets? *(pp. 374–75)*
15.16 How does zero-based budgeting differ from traditional budgeting? *(pp. 375–76)*
15.17 What are discretionary costs? *(pp. 375–76)*
15.18 Distinguish between zero-based budgeting and priority-based incremental budgeting. *(p. 376)*

Review problems

15.19 Basic. D plc operates a retail business. Purchases are sold at cost plus 25 per cent. The management team are preparing the cash budget and have gathered the following data:

1. The budgeted sales are as follows:

Month	£000
July	100
August	90
September	125
October	140

2. It is management policy to hold inventory at the end of each month which is sufficient to meet sales demand in the next half month. Sales are budgeted to occur evenly during each month.

3. Creditors are paid one month after the purchase has been made.

Calculate the entries for purchases that will be shown for August, September and October. *(3 marks)*

CIMA P1 Management Accounting: Performance Evaluation

15.20 Intermediate: Budget preparation and flexible budgets. X Plc manufactures specialist insulating products that are used in both residential and commercial buildings. One of the products, Product W, is made using two different raw materials and two types of labour. The company operates a standard absorption costing system and is now preparing its budgets for the next four quarters. The following information has been identified for Product W:

Sales

Selling price	£220 per unit
Sales demand	
Quarter 1	2250 units
Quarter 2	2050 units
Quarter 3	1650 units
Quarter 4	2050 units
Quarter 5	1250 units
Quarter 6	2050 units

Costs

Materials	
A	5 kgs per unit @ £4 per kg
B	3 kgs per unit @ £7 per kg
Labour	
Skilled	4 hours per unit @ £15 per hour
Semi-skilled	6 hours per unit @ £9 per hour
Annual overheads	£280 000
	40 per cent of these overheads are fixed and the remainder varies with total labour hours. Fixed overheads are absorbed on a unit basis.

Inventory holiday policy

Closing inventory of finished goods	30 per cent of the following quarter's sales demand
Closing inventory of materials	45 per cent of the following quarter's materials usage

The management team are concerned that X Plc has recently faced increasing competition in the market place for Product W. As a consequence there have been issues concerning the availability and costs of the specialised materials and employees needed to manufacture Product W, and there is concern that these might cause problems in the current budget setting process.

a Prepare the following budgets for each quarter for X Plc:
  (i) Production budget in units;
  (ii) Raw material purchases budget in kgs and value for Material B.

(5 Marks)

b X Plc has just been informed that Material A may be in short supply during the year for which it is preparing budgets. Discuss the impact this will have on budget preparation and other areas of X Plc.

(5 Marks)

c Assuming that the budgeted production of Product W was 7,700 units and that the following actual results were incurred for labour and overheads in the year:

Actual production	7250 units
Actual overheads	
Variable	£185 000
Fixed	£105 000
Actual labour costs	
Skilled – £16.25 per hour	£568 750
Semi-skilled – £8 per hour	£332 400

Prepare a flexible budget statement for X Plc showing the total variances that have occurred for the above four costs only.

(5 Marks)

d X Plc currently uses incremental budgeting. Explain how Zero Based Budgeting could overcome the problems that might be faced as a result of the continued use of the current system.

(5 Marks)

e Explain how rolling budgets are used and why they would be suitable for X Plc.

(5 Marks)

CIMA P1 Management Accounting: Performance Evaluation

15.21 Intermediate: Cash budgets. Thorne Co values, advertises and sells residential property on behalf of its customers. The company has been in business for only a short time and is preparing a cash budget for the first four months of 2006. Expected sales of residential properties are as follows.

	2005	2006	2006	2006	2006
Month	December	January	February	March	April
Units sold	10	10	15	25	30

The average price of each property is £180 000 and Thorne Co charges a fee of 3 per cent of the value of each property sold. Thorne Co receives 1 per cent in the month of sale and the remaining 2 per cent in the month after sale. The company has nine employees who are paid on a monthly basis. The average salary per employee is £35 000 per year. If more than 20 properties are sold in a given month, each employee is paid in that month a bonus of £140 for each additional property sold.

Variable expenses are incurred at the rate of 0.5 per cent of the value of each property sold and these expenses are paid in the month of sale. Fixed overheads of £4300 per month are paid in the month in which they arise. Thorne Co pays interest every three months on a loan of £200 000 at a rate of 6 per cent per year. The last interest payment in each year is paid in December.

An outstanding tax liability of £95 800 is due to be paid in April. In the same month Thorne Co intends to dispose of surplus vehicles, with a net book value of £15 000, for £20 000. The cash balance at the start of January 2006 is expected to be a deficit of £40 000.

Required:

a Prepare a monthly cash budget for the period from January to April 2006. Your budget must clearly indicate each item of income and expenditure, and the opening and closing monthly cash balances. *(10 marks)*

b Discuss the factors to be considered by Thorne Co when planning ways to invest any cash surplus forecast by its cash budgets.

(5 marks)

c Discuss the advantages and disadvantages to Thorne Co of using overdraft finance to fund any cash shortages forecast by its cash budgets. *(5 marks)*

ACCA 2.4 Financial Management and Control

15.22 Intermediate: Budget preparation and comments on sales forecasting methods. You have recently been appointed as the management accountant to Alderley Ltd, a small company manufacturing two products, the Elgar and the Holst. Both products use the same type of material and labour but in different proportions. In the past, the company

has had poor control over its working capital. To remedy this, you have recommended to the directors that a budgetary control system be introduced. This proposal has, now, been agreed.

Because Alderley Ltd's production and sales are spread evenly over the year, it was agreed that the annual budget should be broken down into four periods, each of 13 weeks, and commencing with the 13 weeks ending 4 April. To help you in this task, the sales and production directors have provided you with the following information:

1. Marketing and production data

	Elgar	Holst
Budgeted sales for 13 weeks (units)	845	1235
Material content per unit (kilograms)	7	8
Labour per unit (standard hours)	8	5

2. Production labour

The 24 production employees work a 37-hour, five-day week and are paid £8 per hour. Any hours in excess of this involve Alderley in paying an overtime premium of 25 per cent. Because of technical problems, which will continue over the next 13 weeks, employees are only able to work at 95 per cent efficiency compared to standard.

3. Purchasing and opening stocks

The production director believes that raw material will cost £12 per kilogram over the budget period. He also plans to revise the amount of stock being kept. He estimates that the stock levels at the commencement of the budget period will be as follows:

Raw materials	Elgar	Holst
2328 kilograms	163 units	361 units

4. Closing stocks

At the end of the 13-week period closing stocks are planned to change. On the assumption that production and sales volumes for the second budget period will be similar to those in the first period:

 • raw material stocks should be sufficient for 13 days' production;
 • finished stocks of the Elgar should be equivalent to 6 days' sales volume;
 • finished stocks of the Holst should be equivalent to 14 days' sales volume.

Task 1

Prepare in the form of a statement the following information for the 13-week period to 4 April:

a the production budget in units for the Elgar and Holst;
b the purchasing budget for Alderley Ltd in units;
c the cost of purchases for the period;
d the production labour budget for Alderley Ltd in hours;
e the cost of production labour for the period.

Note: Assume a five-day week for both sales and production.

The managing director of Alderley Ltd, Alan Dunn, has also only recently been appointed. He is keen to develop the company and has already agreed to two new products being developed. These will be launched in 18 months' time. While talking to you about the budget, he mentions that the quality of sales forecasting will need to improve if the company is to grow rapidly. Currently, the budgeted sales figure is found by initially adding 5 per cent to the previous year's sales volume and then revising the figure following discussions with the marketing director. He believes this approach is increasingly inadequate and now requires a more systematic approach.

A few days later, Alan Dunn sends you a memo. In that memo, he identifies three possible strategies for increasing sales volume. They are:

 • more sales to existing customers;
 • the development of new markets;
 • the development of new products.

He asks for your help in forecasting likely sales volumes from these sources.

Task 2

Write a brief memo to Alan Dunn. Your memo should:

a identify *four* ways of forecasting future sales volume;
b show how each of your four ways of forecasting can be applied to *one* of the sales strategies identified by Alan Dunn and justify your choice;
c give *two* reasons why forecasting methods might not prove to be accurate.

AAT Technicians Stage

15.23 Advanced: Activity-based budgeting. Flosun plc makes and sells a range of products. Management has carried out an analysis of the total cost of production. The information in Appendix 3.1 reflects this analysis of budgeted costs for the six month period to 30 June 2004. The analysis has identified that the factory is organized in order to permit the operation of three production lines X, Y and Z. Each production line facilitates the production of two or more products. Production line X is only used for the production of products A and B. The products are manufactured in batches on a just-in-time basis in order to fulfil orders from customers. Only one product can be manufactured on the production line at any one time. Materials are purchased and received on a just-in-time basis. Additional information is available for production line X as follows:

(i) Production line machine costs including labour, power, etc., vary in proportion to machine hours.

(ii) Costs incurred for production scheduling, WIP movement, purchasing and receipt of materials are assumed to be incurred in proportion to the number of batches of product which are manufactured. Machine set-up costs vary in proportion to the number of set-ups required and are linked to a batch throughput system.

(iii) Costs for material scheduling systems and design/testing routines are assumed to be incurred by each product in proportion to the total quantity of components purchased and the total number of types of component used respectively. The number of different components designed/tested for products A and B are 12 and 8 respectively.

(iv) Product line development cost is identified with changes in product design and production method. At present such costs for production line X are apportioned 80 per cent:20 per cent to products A and B respectively. Production line maintenance costs are assumed to vary in proportion to the maintenance hours required for each product.

(v) General factory costs are apportioned to each of production lines X, Y and Z in the ratio 25 per cent:30 per cent:45 per cent respectively. Such costs are absorbed by product units at an average rate per unit through each production line.

Required:

a Prepare an activity based budget for production line X for the six month period to 30 June 2004 analyzed into sub-sets for activities which are product unit based, batch based, product sustaining, production line sustaining and factory sustaining.

The budget should show:

(i) Total cost for each activity sub-set grouped to reflect the differing operational levels at which each sub-set is incurred/controlled.

(ii) Average cost per unit for each of products A and B analyzed by activity sub-set. *(24 marks)*

b Discuss the incidence and use of each of the following terms in relation to Flosun plc, giving examples from the question to illustrate your answer:

(i) hierarchy of activities
(ii) cost pools
(iii) cost drivers. *(6 marks)*

c Prepare a sequential set of steps which may be included in an investigation of activities in order to improve company profitability.

This should be a general list of steps and not specifically relating to Flosun plc. *(5 marks)*

ACCA Paper 9 Information for Control and Decision Making

Appendix 3.1
Flosun plc – Budget data six months to 30 June 2004

	Product A	Product B
Material cost per product unit	£60	£45
Production line X – machine hours per unit	0.8	0.5
Production batch size (units)	100	200
Total production (units)	9 000	15 000
Components per product unit (quantity)	20	12
Number of customers	5	10
Number of production line set-ups	15	25
Production line X – maintenance hours	300	150

Cost category	Production line X £	Factory total £
Labour, power, etc.	294 000	
Set-up of machines	40 000	
Production scheduling	29 600	
WIP movement	36 400	
Purchasing and receipt of material	49 500	
Material scheduling system	18 000	
Design/testing routine	16 000	
Production line development	25 000	
Production line maintenance	9 000	
General factory administration		500 000
General factory occupancy		268 000

15.24 Advanced. You are the management accountant of a group of companies and your managing director has asked you to explore the possibilities of introducing a zero-base budgeting system experimentally in one of the operating companies in place of its existing orthodox system. You are required to prepare notes for a paper for submission to the board that sets out:

a how zero-base budgeting would work within the company chosen; *(6 marks)*

b what advantages it might offer over the existing system; *(5 marks)*

c what problems might be faced in introducing a zero-base budgeting scheme; *(5 marks)*

d the features you would look for in selecting the operating company for the introduction in order to obtain the most beneficial results from the experiment. *(4 marks)*

CIMA P3 Management Accounting

15.25 Advanced. Various attempts have been made in the public sector to achieve a more stable, long-term planning base in contrast to the traditional short-term annual budgeting approach, with its emphasis on 'flexibility'.

You are required to:

a explain the deficiencies of the traditional approach to planning which led to the attempts to introduce PPBS (programme budgeting); *(6 marks)*

b give an illustration of how a PPBS plan could be drawn up in respect of one sector of public authority activity; *(8 marks)*

c discuss the problems which have made it difficult in practice to introduce PPBS. *(6 marks)*

CIMA Stage 4: Management Accounting

IM15.1 Intermediate. Outline:

a the objectives of budgetary planning and control systems; *(7 marks)*

b the organization required for the preparation of a master budget. *(10 marks)*

ACCA Level 1 Costing

IM15.2 Intermediate. The preparation of budgets is a lengthy process which requires great care if the ultimate master budget is to be useful for the purposes of management control within an organization.

You are required:

a to identify and to explain briefly the stages involved in the preparation of budgets identifying separately the roles of managers and the budget committee; *(8 marks)*

b to explain how the use of spreadsheets may improve the efficiency of the budget preparation process. *(7 marks)*

CIMA Stage 1 Accounting

IM15.3 Advanced. What is zero-base budgeting and how does it differ from other more traditional forms of budgeting? Discuss the applicability of zero-base budgeting to profit-orientated organizations.

ACCA Level 2 Management Accounting

IM15.4 Advanced. The chief executive of your organization has recently seen a reference to zero-base budgeting. He has asked for more details of the technique.

Management control systems

16

Control is the process of ensuring that a firm's activities conform to its plan and that its objectives are achieved. There can be no control without objectives and plans, since these predetermine and specify the desirable behaviour and set out the procedures that should be followed by members of the organization to ensure that a firm is operated in a desired manner.

Drucker (1964) distinguishes between 'controls' and 'control'. Controls are measurement and information, whereas control means direction. In other words, 'controls' are purely a means to an end; the end is control. 'Control' is the function that makes sure that actual work is done to fulfil the original intention, and 'controls' are used to provide information to assist in determining the control action to be taken. For example, material costs may be greater than budget.

LEARNING OBJECTIVES

After studying this chapter you should be able to:

- describe the three different types of controls used in organizations;
- describe a cybernetic control system;
- distinguish between feedback and feed-forward controls;
- explain the potential harmful side-effects of results controls;
- define the four different types of responsibility centres;
- explain the different elements of management accounting control systems;
- describe the controllability principle and the methods of implementing it;
- describe the different approaches that can be used to determine financial performance targets and discuss the impact of their level of difficulty on motivation and performance;
- describe the influence of participation in the budgeting process;
- distinguish between the three different styles of evaluating performance and identify the circumstances when a particular style is most appropriate.

'Controls' will indicate that costs exceed budget and that this may be because the purchase of inferior quality materials causes excessive wastage. 'Control' is the action that is taken to purchase the correct quality materials in the future to reduce excessive wastage.

'Controls' encompasses all the methods and procedures that direct employees towards achieving the organization objectives. Many different control mechanisms are used in organizations and the management accounting control system represents only one aspect of the various control mechanisms that companies use to control their managers and employees. To fully understand the role that management accounting control systems play in the control process, it is necessary to be aware of how they relate to the entire array of control mechanisms used by organizations.

This chapter begins by describing the different types of controls that are used by companies. The elements of management accounting control systems will then be described within the context of the overall control process.

Control at different organizational levels

Control is applied at different levels within an organization. Merchant (1998) distinguishes between strategic control and management control. Strategic control has an external focus. The emphasis is on how a firm, given its strengths and weaknesses and limitations can compete with other firms in the same industry. We shall explore some of these issues in Chapter 22 within the context of strategic management accounting. In this, and the next four chapters, our emphasis will be on management control systems which consist of a collection of control mechanisms that primarily have an internal focus. The aim of management control systems is to influence employee behaviours in desirable ways in order to increase the probability that an organization's objectives will be achieved.

The terms 'management accounting control systems', 'accounting control systems' and 'management control systems' are often used interchangeably. Both management accounting and accounting control systems refer to the collection of practices such as budgeting, standard costing and periodic performance reporting that are normally administered by the management accounting function. Management control systems represent a broader term that encompasses management accounting/accounting control systems but it also includes other controls such as action, personnel and social controls. These controls are described in the following section.

Different types of controls

Companies use many different control mechanisms to cope with the problem of organizational control. To make sense of the vast number of controls that are used we shall classify them into three categories using approaches that have been adopted by Ouchi (1979) and Merchant (1998). They are:

   1 action (or behavioural) controls;

   2 personnel and cultural (or clan and social) controls;

   3 results (or output) controls.

The terms in parentheses refer to the classification used by Ouchi whereas the other terms refer to the categories specified by Merchant. Because the classifications used by both authors are compatible we shall use the terms interchangeably. You should note that management accounting systems are normally synonymous with output controls whereas management control systems encompass all of the above categories of controls.

Action or behavioural controls

Behavioural controls involve observing the actions of individuals as they go about their work. They are appropriate where cause and effect relationships are well understood, so that if the correct means are followed, the desired outcomes will occur. Under these circumstances effective control can be achieved by having superiors watch and guide the actions of subordinates. For example, if the foreman watches the workers on the assembly line and ensures that the work is done exactly as prescribed then the expected quality and quantity of work should ensue.

Instead of using the term behavioural controls Merchant uses the term action controls. He defines action controls as applying to those situations where the actions themselves are the focus of control. They are usable and effective only when managers know what actions are desirable (or undesirable) and have the ability to make sure that the desirable actions occur (or that the undesirable actions do not occur). Forms of action controls described by Merchant include behavioural constraints, preaction reviews and action accountability.

The aim of *behavioural constraints* is to prevent people from doing things that should not be done. They include physical constraints, such as computer passwords that restrict accessing or updating information sources to authorized personnel, and administrative constraints. Imposing ceilings on the amount of capital expenditure that managers may authorize is an example of an administrative constraint.

Preaction reviews involve the scrutiny and approval of action plans of the individuals being controlled before they can undertake a course of action. Examples include the approval by municipal authorities of plans for the construction of properties prior to building commencing or the approval by a tutor of a dissertation plan prior to the student being authorized to embark on the dissertation.

Action accountability involves defining actions that are acceptable or unacceptable, observing the actions and rewarding acceptable or punishing unacceptable actions. Examples of action accountability include establishing work rules and procedures and company codes of conduct that employees must follow. Line item budgets that were described in the previous chapter are another form of action accountability whereby an upper limit on an expense category is given for the budget period. If managers exceed these limits they are held accountable and are required to justify their actions.

Action controls that focus on *preventing* undesirable behaviour are the ideal form of control because their aim is to prevent the behaviour from occurring. They are preferable to *detection* controls that are applied after the occurrence of the actions because they avoid the costs of undesirable behaviour. Nevertheless, detection controls can still be useful if they are applied in a timely manner so that they can lead to the early cessation of undesirable actions. Their existence also discourages individuals from engaging in such actions.

Personnel, cultural and social controls

Clan and social controls are the second types of controls described by Ouchi. Clan controls are based on the belief that by fostering a strong sense of solidarity and commitment towards organizational goals people can become immersed in the interests of the organization. The main feature of clan controls is the high degree of employee discipline attained through the dedication of each individual to the interests of the whole. Clan controls can be viewed as corporate cultures or a special form of social control such as the selection of people who have already been socialized into adopting particular norms and patterns of behaviour to perform particular tasks. For example, if the only staff promoted to managerial level are those who display a high commitment to the firm's objectives then the need for other forms of controls can be reduced, provided that the managers are committed to achieving the 'right' objectives.

Merchant adopts a similar approach to Ouchi and classifies personnel and cultural controls as a second form of control. He defines personnel controls as helping employees do a good job by building on employees' natural tendencies to control themselves. In particular, they ensure that the employees have the capabilities (in terms of intelligence, qualifications and experience) and the resources needed to do a good job. Merchant identifies three major methods of implementing personnel controls. They are selection and placement, training and job design and the provision of the necessary resources. Selection and placement involves finding the right people to do a specified job. Training can be used to ensure that employees know how to perform the assigned tasks and to make them fully aware of the results and actions that is expected from them. Job design entails designing jobs in such a way that enable employees to undertake their tasks with a high degree of success. This requires that jobs are not made too complex, onerous or badly defined so that employees do not know what is expected of them.

Cultural controls represent a set of values, social norms and beliefs that are shared by members of the organization and that influence their actions. Cultural controls are exercised by individuals over one another – for example, procedures used by groups within an organization to regulate performance of their own members and to bring them into line when they deviate from group norms. It is apparent from the above description that cultural controls are virtually the same as social controls.

Results or output controls

Output or results controls involve collecting and reporting information about the outcomes of work effort. The major advantage of results controls is that senior managers do not have to be knowledgeable about the means required to achieve the desired results or be involved in directly observing the actions of subordinates. They merely rely on output reports to ascertain whether or not the desired outcomes have been achieved. Management accounting control systems can be described as a form of output controls. They are mostly defined in monetary terms such as revenues, costs, profits and ratios such as return on investment. Results measures also include non-accounting measures such as the number of units of defective production, the number of loan applications processed or ratio measures such as the number of customer deliveries on time as a percentage of total deliveries.

Results controls involve the following stages:

1 establishing results (i.e. performance) measures that minimize undesirable behaviour;
2 establishing performance targets;
3 measuring performance;
4 providing rewards or punishment.

Ideally desirable behaviour should improve the performance measure and undesirable behaviour should have a detrimental effect on the measure. A performance measure that is not a good indicator of what is desirable to achieve the organization's objectives might actually encourage employees to take actions that are detrimental to the organization. The term 'What you measure is what you get' can apply whereby employees concentrate on improving the performance measures even when they are aware that their actions are not in the firm's best interests. For example, a divisional manager whose current return on investment (ROI) is 30 per cent might reject a project which yields an ROI of 25 per cent because it will lower the division's average ROI, even though the project has a positive NPV, and acceptance is in the best interests of the organization.

Without the *second-stage* requirement of a pre-set performance target individuals do not know what to aim for. Various research studies suggest that the existence of a clearly defined quantitative target is likely to motivate higher performance than vague statements such as 'do your best'. It is also difficult for employees or their superiors to interpret performance unless actual performance can be compared against predetermined standards.

The *third stage* specified above relates to measuring performance. Ability to measure some outputs effectively constrains the use of results measures. In the previous chapter you will remember that it was pointed out that the outputs in non-profit organizations are extremely difficult to measure and inhibit the use of results controls. Another example relates to measuring the performance of support departments. Consider a personnel department. The accomplishments of the department can be difficult to measure and other forms of control might be preferable. Merchant suggests that to evoke the right behaviours results measures should be precise, objective, timely and understandable.

While 100 per cent accuracy is not essential, measurements should be sufficiently accurate for the purpose required. Measures should also be objective and free from bias. Where performance is self-measured and reported there is a danger that measures will be biased. Objectivity can be increased by performance being measured by people who are independent of the process being measured. Timeliness relates to the time lag between actual performance and the reporting of the results. Significant delays in reporting will result in the measures losing most of their motivational impact and a lengthy delay in taking remedial action when outcomes deviate from target. Finally, measures should be understandable by the individuals whose behaviours are being controlled. If measures are not understandable it is unlikely that managers will know how their actions will effect the measure and there is a danger that the measures will lose their motivational impact.

The *final stage* of results controls involves encouraging employees to achieve organizational goals by having rewards (or punishments) linked to their success (or failure) in achieving the results measures. Organizational rewards include salary increases, bonuses, promotions and recognition. Employees can also derive intrinsic rewards through a sense of accomplishment and achievement. Punishments include demotions, failure to obtain the rewards and possibly the loss of one's job.

Cybernetic control systems

The traditional approach in the management control literature has been to view results controls as a simple cybernetic system. In describing this process authors often use a mechanical model such as a thermostat that controls a central heating system as a resemblance. This process is illustrated in Figure 16.1. You will see that the control system consists of the following elements:

1 The process (the room's temperature) is continually monitored by an automatic regulator (the thermostat).

2 Deviations from a predetermined level (the desired temperature) are identified by the automatic regulator.

3 Corrective actions are started if the output is not equal to the predetermined level. The automatic regulator causes the input to be adjusted by turning the heater on if the temperature falls below a predetermined level. The heater is turned off when the output (temperature) corresponds with the predetermined level.

The output of the process is monitored, and whenever it varies from the predetermined level, the input is automatically adjusted. Emmanuel *et al.* (1990) state that four conditions must be satisfied before any process can be said to be controlled. First, objectives for the process being controlled must exist. Without an aim or purpose control has no meaning. Secondly, the output

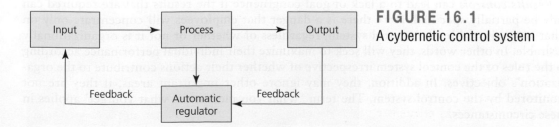

FIGURE 16.1
A cybernetic control system

of the process must be measurable in terms of the dimensions defined by the objectives. In other words, there must be some mechanism for ascertaining whether the process is attaining its objectives. Thirdly, a predictive model of the process being controlled is required so that causes for the non-attainment can be identified and proposed corrective actions evaluated. Finally, there must be a capability for taking action so that deviations from objectives can be reduced. Emmanuel *et al.* stress that if any of these conditions are not met the process cannot be considered to be 'in control'.

Result controls and therefore management accounting controls resemble the thermostat control model. Standards of performance are determined, measurement systems monitor performance, comparisons are made between the standard and actual performance and feedback provides information on the variances. Note that the term variance is used to describe the difference the standard and actual performance of the actions that are being measured.

Feedback and feed-forward controls

The cybernetic system of control described in Figure 16.1 is that of feedback control. Feedback control involves monitoring outputs achieved against desired outputs and taking whatever corrective action is necessary if a deviation exists. In feed-forward control instead of actual outputs being compared against desired outputs, predictions are made of what outputs are expected to be at some future time. If these expectations differ from what is desired, control actions are taken that will minimize these differences. The objective is for control to be achieved before any deviations from desired outputs actually occur. In other words, with feed-forward controls likely errors can be anticipated and steps taken to avoid them, whereas with feedback controls actual errors are identified after the event and corrective action is taken to implement future actions to achieve the desired outputs.

A major limitation of feedback control is that errors are allowed to occur. This is not a significant problem when there is a short time lag between the occurrence of an error and the identification and implementation of corrective action. Feed-forward control is therefore preferable when a significant time lag occurs. The budgeting process is a feed-forward control system. To the extent that outcomes fall short of what is desired, alternatives are considered until a budget is produced that is expected to achieve what is desired. The comparison of actual results with budget, in identifying variances and taking remedial action to ensure that future outcomes will conform with budgeted outcomes is an illustration of a feedback control system. Thus accounting control systems consist of both feedback and feed-forward controls.

Harmful side-effects of controls

Harmful side-effects occur when the controls motivate employees to engage in behaviour that is not organizationally desirable. In this situation the control system leads to a lack of goal congruence. Alternatively, when controls motivate behaviour that is organizationally desirable they are described as encouraging goal congruence.

Results controls can lead to a lack of goal congruence if the results that are required can only be partially specified. Here there is a danger that employees will concentrate only on what is monitored by the control system, regardless of whether or not it is organizationally desirable. In other words, they will seek to maximize their individual performance according to the rules of the control system irrespective of whether their actions contribute to the organization's objectives. In addition, they may ignore other important areas, if they are not monitored by the control system. The term 'What you measure is what you get' applies in these circumstances.

Figure 16.2, derived from Otley (1987) illustrates the problems that can arise when the required results can only be partially specified. You will see that those aspects of behaviour on which subordinates are likely to concentrate to achieve their personal goals (circle B) do not necessarily correspond with those necessary for achieving the wider organizational goals (circle A). In an ideal system the measured behaviour (represented by circle C) should completely cover the area of desired behaviour (represented by circle A). Therefore if a manager maximizes the performance measure, he or she will also maximize his or her contribution to the goals of the organization. In other words, the performance measures encourage goal congruence. In practice, it is unlikely that perfect performance measures can be constructed that measure all desirable organizational behaviour, and so it is unlikely that all of circle C will cover circle A. Assuming that managers desire the rewards offered by circle C, their actual behaviour (represented by circle B) will be altered to include more of circle C and, to the extent that C coincides with A, more of circle A.

However, organizational performance will be improved only to the extent that the performance measure is a good indicator of what is desirable to achieve the firm's goals. Unfortunately, performance measures are not perfect and, as an ideal measure of overall performance, is unlikely to exist. Some measures may encourage goal congruence or organizationally desirable behaviour (the part of circle C that coincides with A), but other measures will not encourage goal congruence (the part of circle C that does not coincide with A). Consequently, there is a danger that subordinates will concentrate only on what is measured, regardless of whether or not it is organizationally desirable. Furthermore, actual behaviour may be modified so that desired results appear to be obtained, although they may have been achieved in an undesirable manner which is detrimental to the firm.

Another harmful side-effect of controls is that they can cause negative attitudes towards the control system. If controls are applied too rigorously they can result in job-related tensions, conflict and a deterioration in relationships with managers. To a certain extent people do not like being subject to controls so that negative attitudes may be unavoidable. Nevertheless, they can be minimized if care is taken in designing control systems. Results controls can cause negative attitudes when targets are set which are considered to be too difficult and unachievable. Performance evaluations are also likely to be considered unfair where managers are held accountable for outcomes over which they have little control.

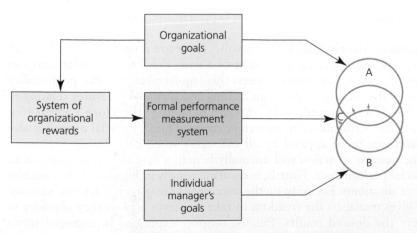

FIGURE 16.2
The measurement and reward process with imperfect measures

A Behaviour necessary to achieve organizational goals
B Behaviour actually engaged in by an individual manager
C Behaviour formally measured by control systems

Advantages and disadvantages of different types of controls

Merchant (1998) suggests that when deciding on the control alternatives managers should start by considering whether *personnel* or *cultural controls* will be sufficient. He suggests that they are worthy of first consideration because they have relatively few harmful side-effects. Also in small organizations they may be completely effective without the need to supplement them with other forms of controls. Merchant concludes that considering personnel/cultural controls first allows managers to consider how reliable these controls are and the extent to which it is necessary to supplement them with other forms of control.

Action controls are the most effective form of control because there is a direct link between the control mechanism and the action and also a high probability that desirable outcomes will occur. They dispense with the need to measure the results and measurement problems do not therefore apply. The major limitation of action controls is that because they are dependent on cause-and-effect work relationships that are well understood they are not feasible in many situations. A second limitation is that they tend to discourage creativity and the ability to adapt to changing circumstances and are therefore likely to be unsuitable in a changing environment.

The major attraction of *results controls* is that they can be applied where knowledge of what actions are desirable is lacking. This situation applies in most organizations. A second attraction of results controls is that their application does not restrict individual autonomy. The focus is on the outcomes thus giving individuals the freedom to determine how they can best achieve the outcomes. Individuals are not burdened with having to follow prescribed rules and procedures.

The major disadvantages of results controls have already been discussed in the previous section. In many cases the results required can only be partially specified, there can be difficulties in separating controllable and uncontrollable factors and measurement problems in the form of precision, objectivity, timeliness and understandability may inhibit their ability to satisfactorily measure performance.

Management accounting control systems

Although output controls predominantly consist of management accounting controls the latter have not been examined in detail. To enable you to understand the role that management accounting control systems play within the overall control process this chapter has initially adopted a broad approach to describing management control systems. We shall now concentrate on management accounting control systems which represent the predominant controls in most organizations.

Why are accounting controls the predominant controls? There are several reasons. First, all organizations need to express and aggregate the results of a wide range of dissimilar activities using a common measure. The monetary measure meets this requirement. Second, profitability and liquidity are essential to the success of all organizations and financial measures relating to these and other areas are closely monitored by stakeholders. It is therefore natural that managers will wish to monitor performance in monetary terms. Third, financial measures also enable a common decision rule to be applied by all managers when considering alternative courses of action. That is, a course of action will normally benefit a firm only if it results in an improvement in its financial performance. Fourth, measuring results in financial terms enables managers to be given more autonomy. Focusing on the outcomes of managerial actions, summarized in financial terms, gives managers the freedom to take whatever actions they consider to be appropriate to achieve the desired results. Finally, outputs expressed in financial terms continue to be effective in uncertain environments even when it is unclear what course of action should be taken. Financial results provide a mechanism to indicate whether the actions benefited the organization.

Responsibility centres

The complex environment in which most businesses operate today makes it virtually impossible for most firms to be controlled centrally. This is because it is not possible for central management to have all the relevant information and time to determine the detailed plans for all the organization. Some degree of decentralization is essential for all but the smallest firms. Organizations decentralize by creating responsibility centres. A responsibility centre may be defined as a unit of a firm where an individual manager is held responsible for the unit's performance. There are four types of responsibility centres. They are:

1 cost or expense centres;
2 revenue centres;
3 profit centres;
4 investment centres.

The creation of responsibility centres is a fundamental part of management accounting control systems. It is therefore important that you can distinguish between the various forms of responsibility centres.

Cost or expense centres

Cost or expense centres are responsibility centres whose managers are normally accountable for only those costs that are under their control. We can distinguish between two types of cost centres – standard cost centres and discretionary cost centres. The main features of standard cost centres are that output can be measured and the input required to produce each unit of output can be specified. Control is exercised by comparing the standard cost (that is, the cost of the inputs that *should* have been consumed in producing the output) with the cost that was *actually* incurred. The difference between the actual cost and the standard cost is described as the variance. Standard cost centres and variance analysis will be discussed extensively in the next chapter.

Standard cost centres are best suited to units within manufacturing firms but they can also be established in service industries such as units within banks, where output can be measured in terms of the number of cheques or the number of loan applications processed, and there are also well defined input–output relationships. Although cost centre managers are not accountable for sales revenues they can affect the amount of sales revenue generated if quality standards are not met and outputs are not produced according to schedule. Therefore quality and timeliness non-financial performance measures are also required besides financial measures.

Discretionary expense centres are those responsibility cost centres where output cannot be measured in financial terms and there are no clearly observable relationships between inputs (the resources consumed) and the outputs (the results achieved). Control normally takes the form of ensuring that actual expenditure adheres to budgeted expenditure for each expense category and also ensuring that the tasks assigned to each centre have been successfully accomplished. Examples of discretionary centres include advertising and publicity and research and development departments. One of the major problems arising in discretionary expense centres is measuring the effectiveness of expenditures. For example, the marketing support department may not have exceeded an advertising budget but this does not mean that the advertising expenditure has been effective. The advertising may have been incorrectly timed, it may have been directed to the wrong audience, or it may have contained the wrong message. Determining the effectiveness and efficiency of discretionary expense centres is one of the most difficult areas of management control.

Revenue centres

Revenue centres are responsibility centres where managers are mainly accountable for financial outputs in the form of generating sales revenues. Typical examples of revenue centres are where regional sales managers are accountable for sales within their regions. Revenue centre managers may also be held accountable for selling expenses, such as salesperson salaries, commissions and order-getting costs. They are not, however, made accountable for the cost of the goods and services that they sell.

Profit centres

Both cost and revenue centre managers have limited decision-making authority. Cost centre managers are accountable only for managing inputs of their centres and decisions relating to outputs are made by other units within the firm. Revenue centres are accountable for selling the products or services but they have no control over their manufacture. A significant increase in managerial autonomy occurs when unit managers are given responsibility for both production and sales. In this situation managers are normally free to set selling prices, choose which markets to sell in, make product-mix and output decisions and select suppliers. Units within an organization whose managers are accountable for both revenues and costs are called profit centres.

Investment centres

Investment centres are responsibility centres whose managers are responsible for both sales revenues and costs and, in addition, have responsibility and authority to make working capital and capital investment decisions. Typical investment centre performance measures include return on investment and economic value added. These measures are influenced by revenues, costs and assets employed and thus reflect the responsibility that managers have for both generating profits and managing the investment base.

Investment centres represent the highest level of managerial autonomy. They include the company as a whole, operating subsidiaries, operating groups and divisions. You will find that many firms are not precise in their terminology and call their investment centres profit centres. Profit and investment centres will be discussed extensively in Chapter 19.

The nature of management accounting control systems

Management accounting control systems have two core elements. The first is the formal planning processes such as budgeting and long-term planning that were described in the previous chapter. These processes are used for establishing performance expectations for evaluating performance. The second is responsibility accounting which involves the creation of responsibility centres. Responsibility centres enable accountability for financial results and outcomes to be allocated to individuals throughout the organization. The objective of responsibility accounting is to accumulate costs and revenues for each individual responsibility centre so that the deviations from a performance target (typically the budget) can be attributed to the individual who is accountable for the responsibility centre. For each responsibility centre the process involves setting a performance target, measuring performance, comparing performance against the target, analyzing the variances and taking action where significant variances exist between actual and target performance. Financial performance targets for profit or investment centres are typically in terms of profits, return on investment or economic value added whereas performance targets for cost centres are defined in terms of costs.

Responsibility accounting is implemented by issuing performance reports at frequent intervals (normally monthly) that inform responsibility centre managers of the deviations from budgets for which they are accountable and are required to take action. An example of a performance report issued to a cost centre manager is presented in the lower section of Exhibit 16.1. You should note that at successively higher levels of management less detailed information is reported. You can see from the upper sections of Exhibit 16.1 that the information is condensed and summarized as the results relating to the responsibility centre are reported at higher levels. Exhibit 16.1 only includes financial information. In addition non-financial measures such as those relating to quality and timeliness may be reported. We shall look at non-financial measures in more detail in Chapter 22.

EXHIBIT 16.1 Responsibility accounting monthly performance reports

Performance report to managing director

		Budget Current month (£)	Budget Year to date (£)	Variance[a] F (A) This month (£)	Variance[a] F (A) Year to date (£)
Managing director	Factory A	453 900	6 386 640	80 000(A)	98 000(A)
	Factory B	X	X	X	X
	Factory C	X	X	X	X
	Administration costs	X	X	X	X
	Selling costs	X	X	X	X
	Distribution costs	X	X	X	X
		2 500 000	30 000 000	400 000(A)	600 000(A)

Performance report to production manager of factory A

Production manager	Works manager's office	X	X	X	X
	Machining department 1	165 600	717 600	32 760(A)	89 180(A)
	Machining department 2	X	X	X	X
	Assembly department	X	X	X	X
	Finishing department	X	X	X	X
		453 900	6 386 640	80 000(A)	98 000(A)

Performance report to head of responsibility centre

Head of responsibility centre	Direct materials	X	X	X	X
	Direct labour	X	X	X	X
	Indirect labour	X	X	X	X
	Indirect materials	X	X	X	X
	Power	X	X	X	X
	Maintenance	X	X	X	X
	Idle time	X	X	X	X
	Other	X	X	X	X
		165 600	717 600	32 760(A)	89 180(A)

[a] F indicates a favourable variance (actual cost less than budgeted cost) and (A) indicates an adverse budget (actual cost greater than budget cost). Note that, at the lowest level of reporting, the responsibility centre head's performance report contains detailed information on operating costs. At successively higher levels of management less detail is reported. For example, the managing director's information on the control of activities consists of examining those variances that represent significant departures from the budget for each factory and functional area of the business and requesting explanations from the appropriate managers.

Responsibility accounting involves:

- distinguishing between those items which managers can control and for which they should be held accountable and those items over which they have no control and for which they are not held accountable (i.e. applying the controllability principle);
- determining how challenging the financial targets should be;
- determining how much influence managers should have in the setting of financial targets.

We shall now examine each of these items in detail.

The controllability principle

Responsibility accounting is based on the application of the controllability principle which means that it is appropriate to charge to an area of responsibility only those costs that are significantly influenced by the manager of that responsibility centre. The controllability principle can be implemented by either eliminating the uncontrollable items from the areas for which managers are held accountable or calculating their effects so that the reports distinguish between controllable and uncontrollable items.

Applying the controllability principle is difficult in practice because many areas do not fit neatly into either controllable and uncontrollable categories. Instead, they are partially controllable. For example, even when outcomes may be affected by occurrences outside a manager's control; such as competitors' actions, price changes and supply shortages, managers can take action to reduce their adverse effects. They can substitute alternative materials where the prices of raw materials change or they can monitor and respond to competitors' actions. If these factors are categorized as uncontrollables managers will be motivated not to try and influence them.

Dealing with the distorting effects of uncontrollable factors before the measurement period

Management can attempt to deal with the distorting effects of uncontrollables by making adjustments either before or after the measurement period. Uncontrollable and controllable factors can be determined prior to the measurement period by specifying which budget line items are to be regarded as controllable and uncontrollable. Uncontrollable items can either be excluded from performance reports or shown in a separate section within the performance report so that they are clearly distinguishable from controllable items. The latter approach has the advantage of drawing managerial attention to those costs that a company incurs to support their activities. Managers may be able to indirectly influence these costs if they are made aware of the sums involved.

How do we distinguish between controllable and uncontrollable items? Merchant suggests that the following general rule should be applied to all employees – 'Hold employees accountable for the performance areas you want them to pay attention to.' Applying this rule explains why some organizations assign the costs of shared resource pools, such as administrative costs relating to personnel and data processing departments, to responsibility centres. Assigning these costs authorizes managers of the user responsibility centres to question the amount of the costs and the quantity and quality of services supplied. In addition, responsibility centres are discouraged from making unnecessary requests for the use of these services when they are aware that increases in costs will be assigned to the users of the services.

Dealing with the distorting effects of uncontrollable factors after the measurement period

Merchant identifies four methods of removing the effects of uncontrollable factors from the results measures after the measurement period and before the rewards are assigned. They are:

1 variance analysis;
2 flexible performance standards;
3 relative performance evaluations;
4 subjective performance evaluations.

Variance analysis seeks to analyze the factors that cause the actual results to differ from predetermined budgeted targets. In particular, variance analysis helps to distinguish between controllable and uncontrollable items and identify those individuals who are accountable for the variances. For example, variances analyzed by each type of cost, and by their price and quantity effects, enables variances to be traced to accountable individuals and also to isolate those variances that are due to uncontrollable factors. Variance analysis will be discussed extensively in Chapters 17 and 18.

REAL WORLD VIEWS 16.1

Autonomous business units in Austrian universities

Large organizations typically have a cost centre structure embedded within their accounting and control systems. Many organizations today use enterprise resource planning (ERP) systems like mySAP[1] to control financial and other resources. ERP systems work with cost and profit centre structures to provide decision making and control information to managers.

In 2002, the Austrian government passed legislation requiring its universities to become more commercially orientated. Annual government grants were replaced by three year grants, with universities given more autonomy to spend money in accordance with the universities' own strategy. The universities were also required to report more frequently to central government. To help university management, all 21 Austrian universities have installed a system called UNI-VERSE – a planning and budgeting system based on mySAP software.

The UNI-VERSE system provides a single ledger for all 21 Austrian universities. Each university in turn has its own cost centres which allow cost centre managers, like faculty heads, track costs in real time. For example, at the University of Vienna, the UNI-VERSE system incorporates more than 400 cost centres, 600 research projects and 200 investment projects. Capturing financial data in such detail permit managers to spot over-spend and take prompt corrective action.

Discussion points

1 Discuss how for example a university business school might have multiple cost centres.

2 Would profit centres be a feature of a university? Can you given an example?

[1]MYSAP IS THE MAIN PRODUCT OF SAP AG, THE NUMBER ONE GLOBAL ERP VENDOR.

The main entrance of the University in Vienna
© GEORGE WITTING/ISTOCKPHOTO.COM

SOURCE: SAP CUSTOMER SUCCESS STORY – UNI-VERSE HTTP://WWW.SAP.COM/INDUSTRIES/HIGHERED/PDF/CS_UNI_VERSE.PDF

Flexible performance standards apply when targets are adjusted to reflect variations in uncontrollable factors arising from the circumstances not envisaged when the targets were set. The most widely used flexible performance standard is to use flexible budgets whereby the uncontrollable volume effects on cost behaviour are removed from the manager's performance reports. Because some costs vary with changes in the level of activity, it is essential when applying the controllability principle to take into account the variability of costs. For example, if the actual level of activity is greater than the budgeted level of activity then those costs that vary with activity will be greater than the budgeted costs purely because of changes in activity. Let us consider the simplified situation presented in Example 16.1.

Assuming that the increase in activity was due to an increase in sales volume greater than that anticipated when the budget was set then the increases in costs arising from the volume change are beyond the control of the responsibility centre manager. It is clearly inappropriate to compare actual *variable* costs of £105 000 from an activity level of 24 000 units with budgeted *variable* costs of £100 000 from an activity level of 20 000 units. This would incorrectly suggest an overspending of £5000. If managers are to be made responsible for their costs, it is essential that they are responsible for performance under the conditions in which they worked, and not for a performance based on conditions when the budget was drawn up. In other words, it is misleading to compare actual costs at one level of activity with budgeted costs at another level of activity. At the end of the period the original budget must be adjusted to the actual level of activity to take into account the impact of the uncontrollable volume change on costs. This procedure is called flexible budgeting. In Example 16.1 the performance report should be as follows:

Budgeted expenditure	Actual expenditure
(flexed to 24 000 units)	(24 000 units)
£120 000	£105 000

The budget is adjusted to reflect what the costs should have been for an actual activity of 24 000 units. This indicates that the manager has incurred £15 000 less expenditure than would have been expected for the actual level of activity, and a favourable variance of £15 000 should be recorded on the performance report, not an adverse variance of £5000, which would have been recorded if the original budget had not been adjusted.

In Example 16.1 it was assumed that there was only one variable item of expense, but in practice the budget will include many different expenses including fixed, semi-variable and variable expenses. You should note that fixed expenses do not vary in the short-term with activity and therefore the budget should remain unchanged for these expenses. The budget should be flexed only for variable and semi-variable expenses.

Budgets may also be adjusted to reflect other uncontrollable factors besides volume changes. Budgets are normally set based on the environment that is anticipated during the budget setting process. If the budget targets are then used throughout the duration of the annual budget period for performance evaluation the managers will be held accountable for uncontrollable factors arising from forecasting errors. To remove the managerial exposure to uncontrollable risks arising from forecasting errors *ex post* budget adjustments can be made whereby the budget is adjusted to the environmental and economic conditions that the manager's actually faced during the period.

EXAMPLE 16.1

An item of expense that is included in the budget for a responsibility centre varies directly in relation to activity at an estimated cost of £5 per unit of output. The budgeted monthly level of activity was 20 000 units and the actual level of activity was 24 000 units at a cost of £105 000.

Relative performance evaluation relates to the situations where the performance of a responsibility centre is evaluated relative to the performance of similar centres within the same company or to similar units outside the organization. To be effective responsibility centres must perform similar tasks and face similar environmental and business conditions with the units that they are being benchmarked against. Such relative comparisons with units facing similar environmental conditions neutralizes the uncontrollable factors because they are in effect held constant when making the relative comparisons. The major difficulty relating to relative performance evaluations is finding benchmark units that face similar conditions and uncertainties.

Instead of making the formal and quantitative adjustments that are a feature of the methods that have been described so far subjective judgements can be made in the evaluation process based on the knowledge of the outcome measures and the circumstances faced by the responsibility centre heads. The major advantage of subjective evaluations is that they can alleviate some of the defects of the measures used by accounting control systems. The disadvantages of subjective evaluations are that they are not objective, they tend not to provide the person being evaluated with a clear indication of how performance has been evaluated, they can create conflict with superiors resulting in a loss of morale and a decline in motivation and they are expensive in terms of management time.

Guidelines for applying the controllability principle

Dealing with uncontrollables represents one of the most difficult areas for the design and operation of management accounting control systems. The following guidelines published by the Report of the Committee of Cost Concepts and Standards in the United States in 1956 still continues to provide useful guidance:

1 If a manager *can control the quantity and price paid* for a service then the manager is responsible for all the expenditure incurred for the service.

2 If the manager *can control the quantity of the service but not the price paid* for the service then only that amount of difference between actual and budgeted expenditure that is due to usage should be identified with the manager.

Responsibility cost control systems in China

Because of the previous lack of effective control of expenditure by the Han Dan Company a system of responsibility accounting and standard costing was introduced in 1990. The basic principles underlying the responsibility cost control system included: (1) setting cost and profit targets (responsibility standards) that take into account market pressures; (2) assigning target costs to various levels of responsibility centre; (3) evaluating performance based on fulfilment of the responsibility targets; and (4) implementing a reward scheme with built-in incentive mechanisms. In order to facilitate performance measurement and evaluation, non-controllable common costs were excluded from the responsibility costs decomposed within primary production factories. Responsibility contracts between factory managers and managers at lower levels must also be signed. Breakdown of the aggregated responsibility targets to all profit centres and their subordinates are conducted by the Department of Finance and Accounting. In addition, the department is responsible for monthly and yearly reporting of the execution results of the responsibility cost control system. It also reports and analyzes the variances between actual outcomes and responsibility targets, and determines the necessary bonus rewards (or penalty) for each responsibility centre in terms of the fulfilment of the cost and profit targets signed by managers. If a responsibility centre or individual worker fails to meet the cost targets specified in the responsibility contracts, all bonus and other benefits relating to the responsibility unit or worker will be forfeited.

Discussion point

What are the limitations of linking bonuses to meeting cost targets?

REAL WORLD VIEWS 16.2

3 If the manager *cannot control either the quantity or the price paid* for the service then the expenditure is uncontrollable and should not be identified with the manager.

An example of the latter situation is when the costs of an industrial relations department are apportioned to a department on some arbitrary basis; such arbitrary apportionments are likely to result in an allocation of expenses that the managers of responsibility centres may not be able to influence. In addition to the above guidelines Merchants's general rule should also be used as a guide – 'Hold employees accountable for the performance areas you want them to pay attention to.'

Setting financial performance targets

There is substantial evidence from a large number of studies that the existence of a defined, quantitative goal or target is likely to motivate higher levels of performance than when no such target is stated. People perform better when they have a clearly defined goal to aim for and are aware of the standards that will be used to interpret their performance. There are three approaches that can be used to set financial targets. They are targets derived from engineering studies of input–output relationships, targets derived from historical data and targets derived from negotiations between superiors and subordinates.

Engineered targets can be used when there are clearly defined and stable input–output relationships such that the inputs required can be estimated directly from product specifications. For example, in a fast-food restaurant for a given output of hamburgers it is possible to estimate the inputs required because there is a physical relationship between the ingredients such as meats, buns, condiments and packaging and the number of hamburgers made. Input–output relationships can also be established for labour by closely observing the processes to determine the quantity of labour that will be required for a given output.

Where clearly defined input–output relationships do not exist other approaches must be used to set financial targets. One approach is to use historical targets derived directly from the results of previous periods. Previous results plus an increase for expected price changes may form the basis for setting the targets or an improvement factor may be incorporated into the estimate, such as previous period costs less a reduction of 10 per cent. The disadvantage of using historical targets is that they may include past inefficiencies or may encourage employees to underperform if the outcome of efficient performance in a previous period is used as a basis for setting a more demanding target in the next period.

Negotiated targets are set based on negotiations between superiors and subordinates. The major advantage of negotiated targets is that they address the information asymmetry gap that can exist between superior and subordinate. This gap arises because subordinates have more information than their superiors on the relationships between outputs and inputs and the constraints that exist at the operating level, whereas superiors have a broader view of the organization as a whole and the resource constraints that apply. Negotiated targets enable the information asymmetry gap to be reduced so that the targets set incorporate the constraints applying at both the operational level and the firm as a whole. You should refer back to the previous chapter for a more detailed discussion of the negotiation process.

The effect of the level of budget difficulty on motivation and performance

The fact that a financial target represents a specific quantitative goal gives it a strong motivational potential, but the targets set must be accepted if managers are to be motivated to achieve higher levels of performance. Unfortunately, it is not possible to specify exactly the optimal degree of difficulty for financial targets, since task uncertainty and cultural, organizational and personality factors all affect an individual manager's reaction to a financial target.

Figure 16.3, derived from Otley (1987), shows the theoretical relationship between budget difficulty, aspiration levels and performance. In Figure 16.3 it is assumed that performance and aspiration levels are identical. Note that the aspiration level relates to the personal goal of the budgetee (that is, the person who is responsible for the budget). In other words, it is the level of performance that they hope to attain. You will see from Figure 16.3 that as the level of budget difficulty is increased both the budgetees' aspiration level and performance increases. However, there becomes a point where the budget is perceived as impossible to achieve and the aspiration level and performance decline dramatically. It can be seen from Figure 16.3 that the budget level that motivates the best level of performance may not be achievable. In contrast, the budget that is expected to be achieved (that is, the expectations budget in Figure 16.3) motivates a lower level of performance.

To motivate the best level of actual performance, demanding budgets should be set and small adverse variances should be regarded as a healthy sign and not as something to be avoided. If budgets are always achieved with no adverse variances, this indicates that the standards are too loose to motivate the best possible results.

Arguments in favour of setting highly achievable budgets

It appears from our previous discussion that tight budgets should be established to motivate maximum performance, although this may mean that the budget has a high probability of not being achieved. However, budgets are not used purely as a motivational device to maximize performance. They are also used for planning purposes and it is most unlikely that tight budgets will be suitable for planning purposes. Why? Tight budgets that have a high probability of not being achieved are most unsuitable for cash budgeting and for harmonizing the company plans in the form of a master budget. Most companies use the same budgets for planning and motivational purposes (Umapathy, 1987). If only one set of budgets is used it is most unlikely that one set can, at the same time, perfectly meet both the planning and the motivational requirements.

Budgets with a high probability of being achieved are widely used in practice. They provide managers with a sense of achievement and self-esteem which can be beneficial to the organization in terms of increased levels of commitment and aspirations. Rewards such as bonuses, promotions and job security are normally linked to budget achievement so that the costs of failing to meet budget targets can be high. The greater the probability of the failure to meet budget targets the greater is the probability that managers will be motivated to distort their performance by engaging in behaviour that will result in the harmful side-effects described earlier in this chapter.

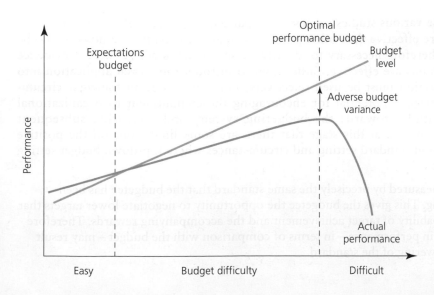

FIGURE 16.3
The effect of budget difficulty on performance.

SOURCE: OTLEY (1987) COPYRIGHT ELSEVIER 1987 REPRODUCED WITH PERMISSION

Participation in the budgeting and target setting process

Participation relates to the extent that subordinates or budgetees are able to influence the figures that are incorporated in their budgets or targets. Participation is sometimes referred to as bottom-up budget setting whereas a non-participatory approach whereby subordinates have little influence on the target setting process is sometimes called top-down budget setting.

Allowing individuals to participate in the setting of performance targets has several advantages. First, individuals are more likely to accept the targets and be committed to achieving them if they have been involved in the target setting process. Second, participation can reduce the information asymmetry gap that applies when standards are imposed from above. Earlier in this chapter it was pointed out that subordinates have more information than their superiors on the relationships between outputs and inputs and the constraints that exist at the operating level whereas the superiors have a broader view of the organization as a whole and the resource constraints that apply. This information sharing process enables more effective targets to be set that attempt to deal with both operational and organizational constraints. Finally, imposed standards can encourage negative attitudes and result in demotivation and alienation. This in turn can lead to a rejection of the targets and poor performance.

Participation has been advocated by many writers as a means of making tasks more challenging and giving individuals a greater sense of responsibility. For many years participation in decision-making was thought to be a panacea for effective organizational effort but this school of thought was later challenged. The debate has never been resolved. The believers have never been able to demonstrate that participation really does have a positive effect on productivity and the sceptics have never been able to prove the opposite (Macintosh, 1985). The empirical studies have presented conflicting evidence on the usefulness of participation in the management process. For every study indicating that participation leads to better attitudes and improved performance, an alternative frequently exists suggesting the opposite.

Because of the conflicting findings relating to the effectiveness of participation research has tended to concentrate on studying how various factors influence the effectiveness of participation. Hopwood (1978) identified the importance of the work situation in determining the appropriateness of participation. He states:

> In highly programmed, environmentally and technologically constrained areas, where speed and detailed control are essential for efficiency, participative approaches may have much less to offer from the point of view of the more economic aspects of organizational effectiveness ... In contrast, in areas where flexibility, innovation and the capacity to deal with unanticipated problems are important, participation in decision-making may offer a more immediate and more narrowly economic payoff than more authoritarian styles.

The evidence from the various studies suggests that participative styles of management will not necessarily be more effective than other styles, and that participative methods should be used with care. It is therefore necessary to identify those situations where there is evidence that participative methods are effective, rather than to introduce universal application into organizations. Participation must be used selectively; but if it is used in the right circumstances, it has an enormous potential for encouraging the commitment to organizational goals, improving attitudes towards the budgeting system, and increasing subsequent performance. Note, however, at this stage that there are some limitations on the positive effects of participation in standard setting and circumstances where top-down budget setting is preferable. They are:

1 Performance is measured by precisely the same standard that the budgetee has been involved in setting. This gives the budgetee the opportunity to negotiate lower targets that increase the probability of target achievement and the accompanying rewards. Therefore an improvement in performance – in terms of comparison with the budget – may result merely from a lowering of the standard.

2 Personality traits of the participants may limit the benefits of participation. For example, the evidence appears to indicate that authoritarians and persons of weak independence needs may well perform better on standards set by a higher authority.

3 Participation by itself is not adequate in ensuring commitment to standards. The manager must also believe that he or she can significantly influence the results and be given the necessary feedback about them.

4 A top-down approach to budget setting is likely to be preferable where a process is highly programmable, and there are clear and stable input–output relationships, so that engineered studies can be used to set the targets. Here there is no need to negotiate targets using a bottom-up process.

Side-effects arising from using accounting information for performance evaluation

Earlier in this chapter we discussed some of the harmful side-effects that can arise from the use of results controls. Some of these effects can be due to the ways in which the output measures are used. A number of studies have been undertaken that examine the side-effects arising from the ways that accounting information is used in performance evaluation. A study of how budgets are used in performance evaluation was undertaken by Hopwood (1976), based on observations in a manufacturing division of a large US company. Three distinct styles of using budget and actual cost information in performance evaluation were observed and were described as follows:

1 Budget-constrained style: Despite the many problems in using accounting data as comprehensive measures of managerial performance, the evaluation is based primarily upon the cost centre head's ability continually to meet the budget on a short-term basis. This criterion of performance is stressed at the expense of other valued and important criteria, and a cost centre head will tend to receive an unfavourable evaluation if his or her actual costs exceed the budgeted costs, regardless of other considerations. Budget data are therefore used in a rigid manner in performance evaluation.

2 Profit-conscious style: The performance of the cost centre head is evaluated on the basis of his or her ability to increase the general effectiveness of his or her unit's operations in relation to the long-term goals of the organization. One important aspect of this at the cost centre level is the head's concern with the minimization of long-run costs. The accounting data must be used with some care and in a rather flexible manner, with the emphasis for performance evaluation in contributing to long-term profitability.

3 Non-accounting style: Accounting data plays a relatively unimportant part in the supervisor's evaluation of the cost centre head's performance.

Emmanuel *et al.* (1990) state that:

The three styles of evaluation are distinguished by the way in which extrinsic rewards are associated with budget achievement. In the rigid (budget constrained) style there is a clear-cut relationship; not achieving budget targets results in punishment, whereas achievement results in rewards. In the flexible (profit conscious) style, the relationship depends on other factors; given good reasons for over-spending, non-attainment of the budget can still result in rewards, whereas the attainment of the budget in undesirable ways may result in punishment. In the non-accounting style, the budget is relatively unimportant because rewards and punishment are not directly associated with its attainment. (Page 179.)

The evidence from Hopwood's study indicated that both the budget-constrained and the profit-conscious styles of evaluation led to a higher degree of involvement with costs than the non-accounting style. Only the profit-conscious style, however, succeeded in attaining this involvement without incurring either emotional costs for the managers in charge of the cost centres or defensive behaviour that was undesirable from the company's point of view.

The budget-constrained style gave rise to a belief that the evaluation was unjust, and caused widespread worry and tension on the job. Hopwood provides evidence of manipulation and undesirable decision behaviour as methods of relieving tension when a budget-constrained style of evaluation is used. In addition, the manager's relationships with the budget-constrained supervisors were allowed to deteriorate, and the rigid emphasis on the short-term budget results also highlighted the interdependent nature of their tasks, so that the immediate instrumental concerns permeated the pattern of social relationships among colleagues. In contrast, Hopwood found that the profit-conscious style avoided these problems, while at the same time it ensured that there was an active involvement with the financial aspects of the operations. A summary of the effect of the three styles of evaluation is given in Exhibit 16.2.

Hopwood's study was based on cost centres having a high degree of interdependence. Rigid measures of performance become less appropriate as the degree of interdependence increases, and therefore the managers used the accounting information in a more flexible manner to ensure that the information remained effective. Otley (1978) replicated Hopwood's study in a British firm that consisted of profit centres with a high degree of independence and where accounting information represented a more adequate basis of performance evaluation. He found no significant differences in the levels of job tension and performance reported by managers evaluated on styles initially used by Hopwood. Three explanations were offered for the differences in results. First, Otley's managers were said to operate more independently of other units within the same organization than Hopwood's managers. Second, Otley's managers were profit centre managers whereas Hopwood's were cost centre managers. Finally, Hopwood's managers operated in a less predictable environment than Otley's.

Otley suggested a style-context framework to reconcile the differences in results between his study and that of Hopwood. The style dimension consisted of a high and low emphasis on budget data in performance evaluation. The context dimension consisted of managerial interdependency[1] (high and low) and task uncertainty[2] (also high and low). Otley's framework suggested that when managers face high levels of interdependency or uncertainty, they may perceive themselves as having less than full control over performance outcomes. Using budget data in a rigid manner in such situations may be dysfunctional for performance, since a rigid use of budget data assumes that most of the factors that have an effect on task outcomes are within the control of the managers being evaluated (Ansari, 1979). On the other hand, Imoisili (1989) suggests that a rigid use of budget data may be more acceptable to managers if they perceive they are able to exercise control over their performance outcomes. This would be the case with tasks characterized by low uncertainty or interdependency. In other words, it is not budget style *per se* that may lead to higher stress or lower performance. Rather, it is the mismatch of budget style and task contexts that may enhance stress or reduce managerial performance (Imoisili, 1989).

EXHIBIT 16.2 Hopwood's findings on the effect of different styles of evaluating budget performance

	Style of evaluation		
	Budget-constrained	Profit-conscious	Non-accounting
Involvement with costs	High	High	Low
Job-related tension	High	Medium	Medium
Manipulation of accounting information	Extensive	Little	Little
Relations with superior	Poor	Good	Good
Relations with colleagues	Poor	Good	Good

Contingency theory

To design effective management accounting control systems it is necessary to consider the circumstances in which they will be used. It should be apparent from this chapter that there is no universally best management accounting control system which can be applied to all organizations. The applicability of a management accounting control system is contingent on the situational factors faced by organizations. This approach is known as the contingency theory approach to management accounting. The situational factors represent the contingent factors (also known as contingent variables or contextual factors). Examples of the contingent factors that have examined in the literature include the external environment faced by organizations, the type of competitive strategy they adopt, organizational structure and the nature of the production process. The aspects of the management accounting control systems that contingency theory research has focused on include dimensions of budgeting (participation, importance of meeting budgets), reliance on accounting information for performance evaluation and dimensions of information (e.g. timeliness and level of aggregation). For example, in this chapter it has been pointed out that the appropriateness of participation is dependent on the nature of the production process. In the previous section it was also suggested that the appropriate style of performance evaluation was influenced by organizational structure and environmental uncertainty.

A considerable amount of literature has emerged focusing on the contingency theory of management accounting. For a detailed summary of this literature your should refer to Learning Note 16.1 on the open access detailed website accompanying this book (see preface for details).

Purposes of management accounting

Throughout this book it is generally assumed that one of the major purposes of management accounting is to aid rational economic decision-making. However, at this stage it is important that you are aware that accounting information can also be used for other purposes that are not necessarily consistent with rational economic behaviour. Managers can find value in accounting information for symbolic purposes even when the information has little or no relation to decision-making. For example, instead of the information actually being used for decision-making or control purposes it may be used as a means of signalling to others inside and outside the organization that decisions are being taken rationally and that managers in an organization are accountable. Accounting information is also used for political purposes. Interested parties use the information to promote their own vested interests to achieve political power or a bargaining position. Finally, accounting information may be used for legitimizing purposes in order to justify and legitimize actions that have already been decided upon rather than the information being used as a decision input. For a more detailed discussion of the different purposes for which accounting information is used you should refer to Learning Note 16.2 on the open access dedicated website.

SUMMARY

The following items relate to the learning objectives listed at the beginning of the chapter.

● Describe the three different types of controls used in organizations.

Three different categories of controls are used – action/behavioural controls, personnel and cultural controls and results/output controls. With action controls the actions themselves are the focus of controls. Personnel controls help employees do a good job by building on employees' natural tendencies to control themselves. They include selection and placement, training and job design. Cultural controls represent a set of values, social norms and beliefs that are shared by members of the organization and that influence their actions. Output or results controls involve collecting and reporting information about the outcomes of work effort.

● Describe a cybernetic control system.

The traditional approach in the management control literature has been to view results controls as a simple cybernetic system. A cybernetic control system resembles the thermostat control model. Standards of performance are determined, measurement systems monitor performance, comparisons are made between the standard and actual performance and feedback provides information on the variances between standard and actual performance of the actions that are being measured.

● Distinguish between feedback and feed-forward controls.

Feedback control involves monitoring outputs achieved against desired outputs and taking whatever corrective action is necessary if a deviation exists. In feed-forward control, instead of actual outputs being compared against desired outputs, predictions are made of what outputs are expected to be at some future time. If these expectations differ from what is desired, control actions are taken that will minimize these differences. The objective is for control to be achieved before any deviations from desired outputs actually occur. The budgeting process is a feed-forward control system. The comparison of actual results with budget, in identifying variances and taking remedial action to ensure future outcomes will conform with budgeted outcomes, is an illustration of a feedback control system.

● Explain the potential harmful side-effects of results controls.

Results controls can promote a number of harmful side-effects. They can lead to a lack of goal congruence when employees seek to achieve the performance targets in a way that is not organizationally desirable. They can also lead to data manipulation and negative attitudes, which can result in a decline in morale and a lack of motivation.

● Define the four different types of responsibility centres.

A responsibility centre may be defined as a unit of a firm where an individual manager is held accountable for the unit's performance. There are four types of responsibility centres – cost or expense centres, revenue centres, profit centres and investment centres. Cost or expense centres are responsibility centres whose managers are normally accountable for only those costs that are under their control. Revenue centres are responsibility centres where managers are accountable only for financial outputs in the form of generating sales revenues. A significant increase in managerial autonomy occurs when unit managers are given responsibility for both production and sales. Units within an organization whose managers are accountable for both revenues and costs are called profit centres. Investment centres are responsibility centres whose managers are responsible for both sales revenues and costs and, in addition, have responsibility and authority to make working capital and capital investment decisions.

● Explain the different elements of management accounting control systems.

Management accounting control systems have two core elements. The first is the formal planning processes such as budgeting and long-term planning. These processes are used for establishing performance expectations for evaluating performance. The second is responsibility accounting, which involves the creation of responsibility centres. Responsibility centres enable accountability for financial results/outcomes to be allocated to individuals throughout the organization. Responsibility accounting involves: (a) distinguishing between those items which managers can control and for which they should be held accountable and those items over which they have no control and for which they are not held accountable; (b) determining how challenging the financial targets should be; and (c) determining how much influence managers should have in the setting of financial targets.

● Describe the controllability principle and the methods of implementing it.

The controllability principle states that it is appropriate to charge to an area of responsibility only those costs that are significantly influenced by the manager of that responsibility centre. The controllability principle can be implemented by either eliminating the uncontrollable items from the areas that managers are held accountable for or calculating their effects so that the reports distinguish between controllable and uncontrollable items.

● Describe the different approaches that can be used to determine financial performance targets and discuss the impact of their level of difficulty on motivation and performance.

There are three approaches that can be used to set financial targets. They involve targets derived from engineering studies of input/output relationships, targets derived from historical data and targets derived from negotiations between superiors and subordinates. Different types of financial performance targets can be set ranging from easily achievable to difficult to achieve. Targets that are considered moderately difficult to achieve (called highly achievable targets) are recommended because they can be used for planning purposes and they also have a motivational impact.

● Describe the influence of participation in the budgeting process.

Participation relates to the extent that budgetees are able to influence the figures that are incorporated in their budgets or targets. Allowing individuals to participate in the setting of performance targets has the following advantages: (a) individuals are more likely to accept the targets and be committed to achieving them if they have been involved in the target setting process;

(b) participation can reduce the information asymmetry gap that applies when standards are imposed from above; and (c) imposed standards can encourage negative attitudes and result in demotivation and alienation. Participation, however, is subject to the following limitations: (a) performance is measured by precisely the same standard that the budgetee has been involved in setting; (b) personality traits of the participants may limit the benefits of participation; and (c) a top-down approach to budget setting is likely to be preferable where a process is highly programmable. Participation must be used selectively; but if it is used in the right circumstances, it has an enormous potential for encouraging the commitment to organizational goals.

● Distinguish between the three different styles of evaluating performance and identify the circumstances when a particular style is most appropriate.

Three distinct styles of performance evaluation have been identified – a budget-constrained style, a profit conscious style and a non-accounting style. With a budget-constrained style, budget data are used in a rigid manner in performance evaluation. A profit-conscious style uses accounting data in a more flexible manner, with the emphasis for performance evaluation on a unit's contribution to long-term profitability. With a non-accounting style, accounting data play a relatively unimportant part in performance evaluation. Using a budget-constrained style when managers face high levels of interdependence or uncertainty is likely to be inappropriate because the rigid use of budget data assumes that most of the factors that have an effect on task outcomes are within the control of the managers being evaluated. In contrast, the rigid use of budget data may be more acceptable where managers perceive that they are able to exercise control over their performance outcomes. This applies where low uncertainty or interdependency characterizes tasks.

Notes

1   Managerial interdependency is the extent to which each manager perceives his or her work-related activities to require the joint or cooperative effort of other managers within the organization.

2   Task uncertainty is the extent to which managers can predict confidently the factors that have effects on their work-related activities.

Key terms and concepts

action controls (p. 389)
aspiration level (p. 403)
behavioural controls (p. 389)
bottom-up budget setting (p. 404)
budget-constrained style (p. 405)
clan controls (p. 389)
contingency theory (p. 407)
control (p. 387)
controllability principle (p. 398)
controls (p. 387)
cost centres (p. 395)
cultural controls (p. 390)
cybernetic system (p. 391)
discretionary expense centres
    (p. 395)

engineered targets (p. 402)
expense centres (p. 395)
ex post budget adjustments (p. 400)
feedback control (p. 392)
feed-forward control (p. 392)
flexible budgets (p. 400)
goal congruence (p. 392)
historical targets (p. 402)
investment centres (p. 396)
management control systems (p. 388)
negotiated targets (p. 402)
non-accounting style (p. 405)
output controls (p. 390)
participation (p. 404)
personnel controls (p. 389)

profit centres (p. 396)
profit-conscious style (p. 405)
relative performance evaluation
    (p. 401)
responsibility accounting (p. 396)
responsibility centre (p. 395)
results controls (p. 390)
revenue centres (p. 396)
social control (p. 389)
standard cost centres (p. 395)
strategic control (p. 388)
subjective judgements (p. 401)
top-down budget setting (p. 404)
variance (pp. 392, 395)
variance analysis (p. 399)

Recommended reading

For a detailed study of the controllability principle you should refer to Merchant (1989). There are a number of important textbooks that specialize in management control. If you wish to study management control in more depth you are recommended to read Merchant (1998). For a discussion of performance measurement in the service industries you should refer to Fitzgerald and Moon (1996).

Key examination points

Essay questions are extensively used in second year management accounting courses. They tend not to be widely used for first year courses. The most frequently examined topic on first year courses is to prepare flexible budgets (see Solutions to Review problem 16.21). If you are required to prepare flexible budgets remember to flex the budget on the basis of target cost for actual output rather than input measures, such as direct labour or input hours. Also questions requiring you to comment on, or redraft performance reports, are frequently set at all levels (e.g. Review problem 16.23). It is important that you distinguish between controllable and non-controllable expenses and stress the need to incorporate non-financial measures. A common error is to compare actual performance with an unflexed budget.

ASSESSMENT MATERIAL

The review questions are short questions that enable you to assess your understanding of the main topics included in the chapter. The numbers in parentheses provide you with the page numbers to refer to if you cannot answer a specific question.

The review problems are more complex and require you to relate and apply the chapter content to various business problems. The problems are graded by their level of difficulty. Solutions to review problems that are not preceded by the term 'IM' are provided in a separate section at the end of the book. Solutions to problems preceded by the term 'IM' are provided in the *Instructor's Manual* accompanying this book and also on the lecturer's password protected section of the website www.drury-online.com. Additional review problems with fully worked solutions are provided in the *Student's Manual* that accompanies this book.

The website also includes over 30 case study problems. A list of these cases is provided on pages 665–7. Several cases are relevant to the content of this chapter. Examples include Airport Complex and Integrated Technology Services Ltd.

Review questions

16.1 Distinguish between 'controls' and 'control'. *(p. 387)*
16.2 Identify and describe three different types of control mechanisms used by companies. *(pp. 388–91)*
16.3 Provide examples of behavioural, action, social, personnel and cultural controls. *(pp. 389–90)*
16.4 Describe the different stages that are involved with output/results controls. *(pp. 390–91)*
16.5 Describe the elements of cybernetic control systems. How do they relate to results/output controls? *(pp. 391–92)*
16.6 Distinguish between feedback and feed-forward controls. Provide an example of each type of control. *(p. 392)*
16.7 Describe some of the harmful side-effects that can occur with output/results controls. *(pp. 392–93)*
16.8 Explain the circumstances when it is appropriate or inappropriate to use personnel/cultural, behavioural/action and results/output controls. *(p. 394)*
16.9 Describe the four different types of responsibility centres. *(pp. 395–96)*
16.10 Explain what is meant by the term 'responsibility accounting'. *(pp. 396–97)*
16.11 What factors must be taken into account when operating a responsibility accounting system? *(p. 398)*
16.12 What is the 'controllability principle'? Describe the different ways in which the principle can be applied. *(pp. 398–402)*
16.13 What are flexible budgets? Why are they preferred to fixed (static budgets)? *(p. 400)*
16.14 What is meant by the term 'aspiration level'? *(p. 403)*
16.15 Describe the effect of the level of budget difficulty on motivation and performance. *(pp. 402–03)*
16.16 Distinguish between participation and top-down budget setting. *(pp. 404–05)*
16.17 Describe the factors influencing the effectiveness of participation in the budget process. *(pp. 404–05)*
16.18 What are the limitations of participation in the budget process? *(pp. 404–05)*

16.19 Distinguish between budget-constrained, profit-conscious and non-accounting styles of performance evaluation. *(p. 405)*
16.20 Under what circumstances is it considered appropriate to use (a) the budget constrained and (b) the profit conscious style of performance evaluation? *(p. 406)*

Review problems

16.21 Intermediate: Performance reporting. M plc designs, manufactures and assembles furniture. The furniture is for home use and therefore varies considerably in size, complexity and value. One of the departments in the company is the Assembly Department. This department is labour intensive; the workers travel to various locations to assemble and fit the furniture using the packs of finished timbers that have been sent to them.

Budgets are set centrally and they are then given to the managers of the various departments who then have the responsibility of achieving their respective targets. Actual costs are compared against the budgets and the managers are then asked to comment on the budgetary control statement. The statement for April for the Assembly Department is shown below.

	Budget	Actual	Variances	
Assembly labour hours	6 400	7 140		
	$	$	$	
Assembly labour	51 970	58 227	6 257	Adverse
Furniture packs	224 000	205 000	19 000	Favourable
Other materials	23 040	24 100	1 060	Adverse
Overheads	62 060	112 340	50 280	Adverse
Total	361 070	399 667	38 597	Adverse

Note: the costs shown are for assembling and fitting the furniture (they do not include time spent travelling to jobs and the related costs). The hours worked by the Manager are not included in the figure given for the assembly labour hours.

The Manager of the Assembly Department is new to the job and has very little previous experience of working with budgets but he does have many years' experience as a supervisor in assembly departments. Based on that experience he was sure that the department had performed well. He has asked for your help in replying to a memo he has just received asking him to 'explain the serious overspending in his department'. He has sent you some additional information about the budget.

1. The budgeted and actual assembly labour costs include the fixed salary of $2050 for the Manager of the Assembly Department. All of the other labour is paid for the hours they work.
2. The cost of furniture packs and other materials is assumed by the central finance office of M plc to vary in proportion to the number of assembly labour hours worked.
3. The budgeted overhead costs are made up of three elements: a fixed cost of $9000 for services from central headquarters, a stepped fixed cost which changes when the assembly hours exceed 7000 hours, and some variable overheads. The variable overheads are assumed to vary in proportion to the number of assembly labour hours. Working papers for the budget showed the impact on the overhead costs of differing amounts of assembly labour hours:

Assembly labour hours	5 000	7 500	10 000
Overhead costs	$54 500	$76 500	$90 000

The actual fixed costs for April were as budgeted.

a Prepare, using the additional information that the Manager of the Assembly Department has given you, a budgetary control statement that would be more helpful to him. *(7 marks)*

b (i) Discuss the differences between the format of the statement that you have produced and that supplied by M plc.

(4 marks)

(ii) Discuss the assumption made by the central office of M plc that costs vary in proportion to assembly labour hours.

(3 marks)

c Discuss whether M plc should change to a system of participative budgeting. *(6 marks)*

CIMA P1 Management Accounting: Performance Evaluation

16.22 Intermediate: Flexible budgets and the motivational role of budgets. Club Atlantic is an all-weather holiday complex providing holidays throughout the year. The fee charged to guests is fully inclusive of accommodation and all meals. However, because the holiday industry is so competitive, Club Atlantic is only able to generate profits by maintaining strict financial control of all activities.

The club's restaurant is one area where there is a constant need to monitor costs. Susan Green is the manager of the restaurant. At the beginning of each year she is given an annual budget which is then broken down into months. Each month she receives a statement monitoring actual costs against the annual budget and highlighting any variances. The statement for the month ended 31 October is reproduced below along with a list of assumptions:

Club Atlantic Restaurant Performance Statement
Month to 31 October

	Actual	Budget	Variance (over)/ under
Number of guest days	11 160	9 600	(1 560)
	(£)	(£)	(£)
Food	20 500	20 160	(340)
Cleaning materials	2 232	1 920	(312)
Heat, light and power	2 050	2 400	350
Catering wages	8 400	7 200	(1 200)
Rent rates, insurance and depreciation	1 860	1 800	(60)
	35 042	33 480	(1 562)

Assumptions:
(a) The budget has been calculated on the basis of a 30-day calendar month with the cost of rents, insurance and depreciation being an apportionment of the fixed annual charge.
(b) The budgeted catering wages assume that:
 (i) there is one member of the catering staff for every 40 guests staying at the complex;
 (ii) the daily cost of a member of the catering staff is £30.
(c) All other budgeted costs are variable costs based on the number of guest days.

Task 1
Using the data above, prepare a revised performance statement using flexible budgeting. Your statement should show both the revised budget and the revised variances. Club Atlantic uses the existing budgets and performance statements to motivate its managers as well as for financial control. If managers keep expenses below budget they receive a bonus in addition to their salaries. A colleague of Susan is Brian Hilton. Brian is in charge of the swimming pool and golf course, both of which have high levels of fixed costs. Each month he manages to keep expenses below budget and in return enjoys regular bonuses. Under the current reporting system, Susan Green only rarely receives a bonus.

At a recent meeting with Club Atlantic's directors Susan Green expressed concern that the performance statement was not a valid reflection of her management of the restaurant. You are currently employed by Hall and Co., the club's auditors, and the directors of Club Atlantic have asked you to advise them whether there is any justification for Susan Green's concern.

At the meeting with the Club's directors, you were asked the following questions:
(a) Do budgets motivate managers to achieve objectives?
(b) Does motivating managers lead to improved performance?
(c) Does the current method of reporting performance motivate Susan Green and Brian Hilton to be more efficient?

Task 2
Write a *brief* letter to the directors of Club Atlantic addressing their question and justifying your answers.

Note: You should make use of the data given in this task plus your findings in Task 1. *AAT Technicians Stage*

16.23 Advanced: Recommendations for improvements to a performance report and a review of the management control system. Your firm has been consulted by the managing director of Inzone plc, which owns a chain of retail stores. Each store has departments selling furniture, tableware and kitchenware. Departmental managers are responsible to a store manager, who is in turn responsible to head office (HO).

All goods for sale are ordered centrally and stores sell at prices fixed by HO. Store managers (aided by departmental managers) order stocks from HO and stores are charged interest based on month-end stock levels. HO appoints all permanent staff and sets all pay levels. Store managers can engage or dismiss temporary workers, and are responsible for store running expenses.

The introduction to Inzone plc's management accounting manual states:

'Budgeting starts three months before the budget year, with product sales projections which are developed by HO buyers in consultation with each store's departmental managers. Expense budgets, adjusted for expected inflation, are then prepared by HO for each store. Inzone plc's accounting year is divided into 13 four-weekly control periods, and the budgeted sales and expenses are assigned to periods with due regard to seasonal factors. The budgets are completed one month before the year begins on 1st January.

'All HO expenses are recharged to stores in order to give the clearest indication of the "bottom line" profit of each store. These HO costs are mainly buying expenses, which are recharged to stores according to their square footage.

'Store reports comparing actual results with budgets are on the desks of HO and store management one week after the end of each control period. Significant variations in performance are then investigated, and appropriate action taken.'

Ms Lewis is manager of an Inzone plc store. She is eligible for a bonus equal to 5 per cent of the amount by which her store's 'bottom-line' profit exceeds the year's budget. However, Ms Lewis sees no chance of a bonus this year, because major roadworks near the store are disrupting trade. Her store report for the four weeks ending 21 June is as follows:

	Actual (£)	Budget (£)
Sales	98 850	110 000
Costs:		
Cost of goods (including stock losses)	63 100	70 200
Wages and salaries	5 300	5 500
Rent	11 000	11 000
Depreciation of store fittings	500	500
Distribution costs	4 220	4 500
Other store running expenses	1 970	2 000
Interest charge on stocks	3 410	3 500
Store's share of HO costs	2 050	2 000
Store profit	7 300	10 800
	98 850	110 000
Stocks held at end of period	341 000	350 000
Store fittings at written down value	58 000	58 000

Requirements:
a Make recommendations for the improvement of Inzone plc's store report, briefly justifying each recommendation.

(11 marks)

b Prepare a report for the managing director of Inzone plc reviewing the company's responsibility delegation, identifying the major strengths and weaknesses of Inzone plc's management control system, and recommending any changes you consider appropriate. *(14 marks)*

ICAEW P2 Management Accounting

16.24 Advanced. 'Responsibility accounting is based on the application of the controllability principle.'
Required:
a Explain the 'controllability' principle and why its application is difficult in practice. *(6 marks)*
b Explain how the management of an organization can attempt to overcome the difficulties inherent in the practical application of the controllability principle. *(8 marks)*

c Explain the following approaches that can be used to set financial targets within an organization:
(i) Engineered approach
(ii) Historical approach
(iii) Negotiated approach. *(6 marks)*
ACCA P3 Performance Measurement

16.25 Advanced. 'A competent management accounting system should endeavour to enhance the performance of a company. It should, in particular, consider the behavioural consequences of the system.'

Required:

a Explain why it is necessary when designing a management accounting system to consider the behavioural consequences of its application. *(5 marks)*

b Explain the potential behavioural issues that may arise in the application of performance monitoring, budgeting and transfer pricing and suggest how problems may be overcome. *(15 marks)*
ACCA P3 Performance Measurement

IM16.1 Intermediate. Explain the meaning of each of the undernoted terms, comment on their likely impact on cash budgeting and profit planning and suggest ways in which any adverse effects of each may be reduced.

a Budgetary slack. *(7 marks)*
b Incremental budgets. *(7 marks)*
c Fixed budgets. *(6 marks)*
ACCA Level 2 Cost and Management Accounting II

IM16.2 Advanced.

a Discuss the use of the following as aids to *each* of planning and control:
(i) rolling budgets
(ii) flexible budgets
(iii) planning and operational variances. *(9 marks)*

b Discuss the extent to which the incidence of budgetary slack is likely to be affected by the use of each of the techniques listed in (a). *(6 marks)*
ACCA Paper 9 Information for Control and Decision Making

IM16.3 Advanced. In the context of budgetary control, certain costs are not amenable to the use of flexible budgets. These include some costs which are often called 'discretionary' (or 'programmed').

You are required to explain:

a the nature of discretionary (or programmed) costs and give *two* examples;

b how the treatment of these costs differs from that of other types of cost in the process of preparing and using budgets for control purposes. *(20 marks)*
CIMA P3 Management Accounting

IM16.4 Advanced.

a In the context of budgeting, provide definitions for *four* of the following terms:
    aspiration level;
    budgetary slack;
    feedback;
    zero-base budgeting;
    responsibility accounting. *(8 marks)*

b Discuss the motivational implications of the level of efficiency assumed in establishing a budget. *(9 marks)*
ACCA Level 2 Management Accounting

IM16.5 Advanced. 'Budgeting is too often looked upon from a purely mechanistic viewpoint. The human factors in budgeting are more important than the accounting techniques. The success of a budgetary system depends upon its acceptance by the company members who are affected by the budgets.'

Discuss the validity of the above statement from the viewpoint of both the planning and the control aspects of budgeting. In the course of your discussion present at least one practical illustration to support your conclusions. *(20 marks)*
ACCA P2 Management Accounting

IM16.6 Advanced. 'The major reason for introducing budgetary control and standard costing systems is to influence human behaviour and to motivate the managers to achieve the goals of the organization. However, the accounting literature provides many illustrations of accounting control systems that fail to give sufficient attention to influencing human behaviour towards the achievement of organization goals.'

You are required:

a To identify and discuss four situations where accounting control systems might not motivate desirable behaviour.

b To briefly discuss the improvements you would suggest in order to ensure that some of the dysfunctional behavioural consequences of accounting control systems are avoided.

IM16.7 Advanced. 'The final impact which any accounting system has on managerial and employee behaviour is dependent not only upon its design and technical characteristics but also in the precise manner in which the resulting information is used' (A. Hopwood, *Accounting and Human Behaviour*).

Discuss this statement in relation to budgeting and standard costing.

IM16.8 Advanced. 'Motivation is the over-riding consideration that should influence management in formulating and using performance measures, and in designing management control systems.'

Discuss this statement in relation to the design and implementation of budgetary control systems.

IM16.9 Advanced.

a Discuss the behavioural arguments for and against involving those members of management who are responsible for the implementation of the budget in the annual budget setting process. *(10 marks)*

b Explain how the methods by which annual budgets are formulated might help to overcome behavioural factors likely to limit the efficiency and effectiveness of the budget. *(7 marks)*

IM16.10 Advanced. An article in *Management Accounting* concluded that there will always be some budgetary padding in any organization.

Requirements:

a As Management Accountant, write a report to your Finance Director, explaining what steps can be taken by you, and by senior management when approving budgets, to minimize budgetary slack. *(8 marks)*

b The Finance Director, having read the report referred to in part (a), discussed the problem with the Managing Director and suggested that appropriate action be taken to reduce budgetary slack.

The Managing Director expressed doubts, stating that in his opinion removing all budget padding could cause considerable problems.

Requirement:

Explain the arguments that can be advanced for accepting some budgetary slack, and the advantages of this to the manager being appraised and to the organization. Discuss whether the budget review and approval process should permit managers to build in some budgetary slack. *(12 marks)*
CIMA Stage 4 Management Accounting Control Systems

IM16.11 Intermediate: Preparation of flexible budgets and an explanation of variances. You have been provided with the following operating statement, which represents an attempt to compare the actual performance for the quarter which has just ended with the budget:

	Budget	Actual	Variance
Number of units sold (000s)	640	720	80
	£000	£000	£000
Sales	1024	1071	47
Cost of sales (all variable)			
Materials	168	144	
Labour	240	288	
Overheads	32	36	
	440	468	(28)
Fixed labour cost	100	94	6
Selling and distribution costs:			
Fixed	72	83	(11)
Variable	144	153	(9)
Administration costs:			
Fixed	184	176	8
Variable	48	54	(6)
	548	560	(12)
Net profit	36	43	7

Required:

a Using a flexible budgeting approach, re-draft the operating statement so as to provide a more realistic indication of the variances and comment briefly on the possible reasons (other than inflation) why they have occurred. *(12 marks)*

b Explain why the original operating statement was of little use to management. *(2 marks)*

c Discuss the problems associated with the forecasting of figures which are to be used in flexible budgeting. *(6 marks)*

ACCA Paper 8 Managerial Finance

IM16.12 Intermediate: Responsibility centre performance reports.

Data

Jim Smith has recently been appointed as the Head Teacher of Mayfield School in Midshire. The age of the pupils ranges from 11 years to 18 years. For many years, Midshire County Council was responsible for preparing and reporting on the school budget. From June, however, these responsibilities passed to the Head Teacher of Mayfield School.

You have recently accepted a part-time appointment as the accountant to Mayfield School, although your previous accounting experience has been gained in commercial organizations. Jim Smith is hoping that you will be able to apply that experience to improving the financial reporting procedures at Mayfield School.

The last budget statement prepared by Midshire County Council is reproduced below. It covers the ten months to the end of May and all figures refer to cash *payments* made.

Midshire County Council Mayfield School
Statement of school expenditure against budget: 10 months ending May

	Expenditure to date	Budget to date	Under/ over spend	Total budget for year
Teachers full-time	1 680 250	1 682 500	2 250 Cr	2 019 000
Teachers part-time	35 238	34 600	638	41 520
Other employee expenses	5 792	15 000	9 208 Cr	18 000
Administrative staff	69 137	68 450	687	82 140
Caretaker and cleaning	49 267	57 205	7 938 Cr	68 646
Resources (books, etc.)	120 673	100 000	20 673	120 000
Repairs and maintenance	458	0	458	0
Lighting and heating	59 720	66 720	7 000 Cr	80 064
Rates	23 826	19 855	3 971	23 826
Fixed assets: furniture and equipment	84 721	100 000	15 279 Cr	120 000
Stationery, postage and phone	1 945	0	1 945	0
Miscellaneous expenses	9 450	6 750	2 700	8 100
Total	2 140 477	2 151 080	10 603 Cr	2 581 296

Task 1

Write a memo to Jim Smith. Your memo should:

a identify *four* weaknesses of the existing statement as a management report;

b include an improved *outline* statement format showing revised column headings and a more meaningful classification of costs which will help Jim Smith to manage his school effectively (figures are not required);

c give *two* advantages of your proposed format over the existing format.

Data

The income of Mayfield School is based on the number of pupils at the school. Jim Smith provides you with the following breakdown of student numbers.

Mayfield School:
Student numbers as at 31 May

School year	Age range	Current number of pupils
1	11–12	300
2	12–13	350
3	13–14	325
4	14–15	360
5	15–16	380
6	16–17	240
7	17–18	220
Total number of students		2175

Jim also provides you with the following information relating to existing pupils:

● pupils move up one school-year at the end of July;

● for those pupils entering year 6, there is an option to leave the school. As a result only 80 per cent of the current school-year 5 pupils go on to enter school-year 6;

● of those currently in school-year 6 only 95 per cent continue into school-year 7;

● pupils currently in school-year 7 leave to go on to higher education or employment;

● the annual income per pupil is £1200 in years 1 to 5 and £1500 in years 6 to 7.

The new year 1 pupils come from the final year at four junior schools. Not all pupils, however, elect to go to Mayfield School. Jim has investigated this matter and derived accurate estimates of the proportion of final year pupils at each of the four junior schools who go on to attend Mayfield School.

The number of pupils in the final year at each of the four junior schools is given below along with Jim's estimate of the proportion likely to choose Mayfield School.

Junior School	Number in final year at 31 May	Proportion choosing Mayfield School
Ranmoor	60	0.9
Hallamshire	120	0.8
Broomhill	140	0.9
Endcliffe	80	0.5

Task 2

a Forecast the number of pupils and the income of Mayfield School for the next year from August to July.

b Assuming expenditure next year is 5 per cent more than the current annual budgeted expenditure, calculate the budgeted surplus or deficit of Mayfield School for next year.

AAT Technicians Stage

IM16.13 Advanced: Comments on an existing performance measurement and bonus system and recommendations for improvement. 1. You are the group management accountant of a large divisionalized group.

There has been extensive board discussion of the existing system of rewarding Divisional General Managers with substantial bonuses based on the comparison of the divisional profit with budget.

The scheme is simple: the divisional profit (PBIT) is compared with the budget for the year. If budget is not achieved no bonus is paid. If budget is achieved a bonus of 20 per cent of salary is earned. If twice budgeted profit is achieved, a bonus of 100 per cent of salary is paid, which is the upper limit of the bonus scheme. Intermediate achievements are calculated *pro rata*.

The Finance Director has been asked to prepare a number of reports on the issues involved, and has asked you to prepare some of these.

He has decided to use the results for Division X as an example on which the various discussions could be based. A schedule of summary available data is given below.

Division X
Summary of management accounting data

	Strategic plan 2001 Prepared Aug 2000	Budget 2001 Prepared Oct 2000	Latest estimate 2001 Prepared April 2001
Sales of units by Division X	35 000	36 000	35 800
Sales	28 000	28 800	28 100
Marginal costs	14 350	15 300	14 900
Fixed factory cost	6 500	6 800	7 200
Product development	2 000	2 000	1 400
Marketing	3 500	3 200	2 600
PBIT	1 650	1 500	2 000

Division X manufactures and sells branded consumer durables in competitive markets. High expenditure is required on product development and advertising, as the maintenance of market share depends on a flow of well-promoted new models.

Reliable statistics on market size are available annually. Based on the market size for 2000, where stronger than anticipated growth had occurred, a revised market estimate of 165 000 units for 2001 is agreed by group and divisional staff in May 2001. This is a significant increase on the estimate of 150 000 units made in May 2000 and used since.

The Divisional General Manager has commented that action now, almost half way through the year, is unlikely to produce significant results during this year. However, had he known last year, at the time of producing the budget, that the market was growing faster, he could have taken the necessary action to maintain the strategic plan market share. The actions would have been:

- cutting prices by £10 per unit below the price at present charged and used in the latest estimate for 2001;
- increasing marketing expenditure by £300 000 compared with the strategic plan.

The Group Managing Director, commenting on the same data, said that the Divisional General Manager could have maintained both strategic plan market share and selling prices by an alternative approach.

The approach, he thought, should have been:

- maintaining expenditure on product development and marketing at 20 per cent of sales over the years;
- spending his time controlling production costs instead of worrying about annual bonuses.

You are required:

  a to analyze and comment on the results of Division X, making appropriate comparisons with Budget, with Plan and with new available data. Present the results in such a form that the Board can easily understand the problems involved; *(17 marks)*

  b to comment on the advantages and problems of the existing bonus system for the Divisional General Manager and the way in which the present bonus scheme may motivate the Divisional General Manager; *(8 marks)*

  c to make specific proposals, showing calculations if appropriate, for an alternative bonus scheme, reflecting your analysis in (a). *(8 marks)*

A non-executive director has commented that he can understand the case for linking executive directors' rewards to group results. He is not convinced that this should be extended to divisional managers, and certainly not to senior managers below this level in divisions and head office.

  d Explain and discuss the case for extending bonus schemes widely throughout the organization. *(7 marks)*
CIMA Stage 4 Management Accounting – Control and Audit

IM16.14 Advanced: Budget use and performance reporting. A new private hospital of 100 beds was opened to receive patients on 2 January though many senior staff members including the supervisor of the laundry department had been *in situ* for some time previously. The first three months were expected to be a settling-in period; the hospital facilities being used to full capacity only in the second and subsequent quarters.

In May the supervisor of the laundry department received her first quarterly performance report from the hospital administrator, together with an explanatory memorandum. Copies of both documents are set out below.

The supervisor had never seen the original budget, nor had she been informed that there would be a quarterly performance report. She knew she was responsible for her department and had made every endeavour to run it as efficiently as possible. It had been made clear to her that there would be a slow build up in the number of patients accepted by the hospital and so she would need only three members of staff, but she had had to take on a fourth during the quarter due to the extra work. This extra hiring had been anticipated for May, not late February.

Rockingham Private Patients Hospital Ltd

MEMORANDUM   30 April

To: All Department Heads/Supervisors

From: Hospital Administrator

Attached is the Quarterly Performance Report for your department. The hospital has adopted a responsibility accounting system so you will be receiving one of these reports quarterly. Responsibility accounting means that you are accountable for ensuring that the expenses of running your department are kept in line with the budget. Each report compares the actual expenses of running your department for the quarter with our budget for the same period. The difference between the actual and forecast will be highlighted so that you can identify the important variations from budget and take corrective action to get back on budget. Any variation in excess of 5 per cent from budget should be investigated and an explanatory memo sent to me giving reasons for the variations and the proposed corrective actions.

Performance report – laundry department
3 months to 31 March

	Actual	Budget	Variation (Over) Under	% Variation
Patient days	8 000	6 500	(1 500)	(23)
Weight of laundry processed (kg)	101 170	81 250	(19 920)	(24.5)
	(£)	(£)	(£)	
Department expenses				
Wages	4 125	3 450	(675)	(19.5)
Supervisor salary	1 490	1 495	5	—
Washing materials	920	770	(150)	(19.5)
Heating and power	560	510	(50)	(10)
Equipment depreciation	250	250	—	—
Allocated administration costs	2 460	2 000	(460)	(23)
Equipment maintenance	10	45	35	78
	9 815	8 520	(1 295)	(15)

Comment: We need to have a discussion about the overexpenditure of the department.

You are required to:

  a discuss in detail the various possible effects on the behaviour of the laundry supervisor of the way that her budget was prepared and the form and content of the performance report, having in mind the published research findings in this area, *(15 marks)*

  b re-draft, giving explanations, the performance report and supporting memorandum in a way which, in your opinion, would make them more effective management tools. *(10 marks)*
ICAEW P2 Management Accounting

IM16.15 Advanced: Advantages and disadvantages of participation and comments on a new performance measurement and evaluation system. Incorporated Finance plc is a finance company having one hundred branch offices in major towns and cities throughout the UK. These offer a variety of hire purchase and loan facilities to personal customers both directly and through schemes operated on behalf of major retailers. The main function of the branches is to sell loans and to ensure that repayments are collected; the head office is responsible for raising the capital required, which it provides to branches at a current rate of interest.

Each year branch managers are invited to provide estimates of the following items for the forthcoming year, as the start of the budgetary process:

    Value of new loans (by category e.g. direct, retail, motor)
    Margin percentage (i.e. loan rate of interest less cost of capital provided by head office)
    Gross margin (i.e. value of new loans × margin percentage)
    Branch operating expenses
    Net margin (i.e. gross margin less operating expenses).

The main branch expenses relate to the cost of sales and administrative staff, and to the cost of renting and maintaining branch premises, but also include the cost of bad debts on outstanding loans.

These estimates are then passed to headquarters by area and regional managers and are used, together with other information such as that relating to general economic conditions, to set an overall company budget. This is then broken down by headquarters into regional figures; regional managers then set the area budgets and area managers finally set branch budgets. However, a common complaint of branch managers is that the budgets they are set often bear little resemblance to the estimates they originally submitted.

Budget targets are set for the five items specified above, with managers receiving a bonus based on the average percentage achievement of all five targets, weighted equally.

Requirements

a Discuss the advantages and disadvantages of allowing managers to participate in budget-setting, and suggest how Incorporated Finance plc should operate its budgetary system.   *(15 marks)*

b The managing director is considering changing the performance evaluation and bonus scheme so that branch managers are set only a net margin target. Prepare a report for him outlining the advantages and disadvantages of making such a change.

(10 marks)

ICAEW P2 Management Accounting

Standard costing and variance analysis 1

In the previous chapter the major features of management accounting control systems have been examined. The different types of controls used by companies were described so that the elements of management accounting control systems could be described within the context of the overall control process. A broad approach to control was adopted and the detailed procedures of financial controls were not examined. In this chapter we shall focus on the detailed financial controls that are used by organizations.

We shall consider a financial control system that enables the deviations from budget to be analyzed in detail, thus enabling costs to be controlled more effectively. This system of control is called standard costing. In particular, we shall examine how a standard costing system operates and how the variances are calculated. Standard costing systems are applied in standard cost centres which were described in the previous chapter. You will recall that the main features of standard cost centres are that output can be measured and the input required to produce each unit of output can be specified. Therefore standard costing is generally applied to manufacturing activities and non-manufacturing activities are not incorporated within the standard costing

LEARNING OBJECTIVES

After studying this chapter, you should be able to:

- **explain how a standard costing system operates;**

- **explain how standard costs are set;**

- **explain the meaning of standard hours produced;**

- **define basic, ideal and currently attainable standards;**

- **identify and describe the purposes of a standard costing system;**

- **calculate labour, material, overhead and sales margin variances and reconcile actual profit with budgeted profit;**

- **identify the causes of labour, material, overhead and sales margin variances;**

- **distinguish between standard variable costing and standard absorption costing.**

tion, the sales variances that are described in this chapter can also be applied in tres. In Chapter 19 we shall look at financial controls that are appropriate for meas-fit and investment centre performance.

dard costs are predetermined costs; they are target costs that should be incurred under cient operating conditions. They are not the same as budgeted costs. A budget relates to an entire activity or operation; a standard presents the same information on a per unit basis. A standard therefore provides cost expectations per unit of activity and a budget provides the cost expectation for the total activity. If the budget output for a product is for 10 000 units and the standard cost is £3 per unit, budgeted cost will be £30 000. We shall see that establishing standard costs for each unit produced enables a detailed analysis to be made of the difference between the budgeted cost and the actual cost so that costs can be controlled more effectively.

In the first part of the chapter (pages 425–36) we shall concentrate on those variances that are likely to be useful for cost control purposes. The final part describes those variances that are required for financial accounting purposes but that are not particularly useful for cost control. If your course does not relate to the disposition of variances for financial accounting purposes, you can omit pages 437–41.

Operation of a standard costing system

Standard costing is most suited to an organization whose activities consist of a series of *common* or *repetitive* operations and the input required to produce each unit of output can be specified. It is therefore relevant in manufacturing companies, since the processes involved are often of a repetitive nature. Standard costing procedures can also be applied in service industries such as units within banks, where output can be measured in terms of the number of cheques or the number of loan applications processed, and there are also well-defined input–output relationships. Standard costing cannot, however, be applied to activities of a non-repetitive nature, since there is no basis for observing repetitive operations and consequently standards cannot be set.

A standard costing system can be applied to organizations that produce many different products, as long as production consists of a series of common operations. For example, if the output from a factory is the result of five common operations, it is possible to produce many different product variations from these operations. It is therefore possible that a large product range may result from a small number of common operations. Thus standard costs should be developed for repetitive operations and product standard costs are derived simply by combining the standard costs from the operations which are necessary to make the product. This process is illustrated in Exhibit 17.1.

It is assumed that the standard costs are £20, £30, £40 and £50 for each of the operations 1 to 4. The standard cost for *product* 100 is therefore £110, which consists of £20 for operation 1, plus £40 and £50 for operations 3 and 4. The standard costs for each of the other products are calculated in a similar manner. In addition, the total standard cost for the total output of each operation for the period has been calculated. For example, six items of operation number 1 have been completed, giving a total standard cost of £120 for this operation (six items at £20 each). Three items of operation 2 have been completed, giving a total standard cost of £90, and so on.

Variances allocated to responsibility centres

You can see from Exhibit 17.1 that different responsibility centres are responsible for each operation. For example, responsibility centre A is responsible for operation 1, responsibility centre B for operation 2, and so on. Consequently, there is no point in comparing the actual cost of *product* 100 with the standard cost of £110 for the purposes of control, since responsibility centres A, C and D are responsible for the variance. None of the responsibility centres is solely answerable for the variance. Cost control requires that responsibility centres be identified with the standard cost for the output achieved. Therefore if the actual costs for responsibility centre A are compared with the standard cost of £120 for the production of the six items (see first row of Exhibit 17.1), the manager of this responsibility centre will be answerable for the full amount of the variance. Only by comparing total actual costs with total standard costs *for each operation or responsibility centre* for a period can control be effectively achieved. A comparison of standard *product* costs (i.e. the columns in Exhibit 17.1) with actual costs that involves several different responsibility centres is clearly inappropriate.

Figure 17.1 provides an overview of the operation of a standard costing system. You will see that the standard costs for the actual output for a particular period are traced to the managers of responsibility centres who are responsible for the various operations. The actual costs for the same period are also charged to the responsibility centres. Standard and actual costs are compared and the variance is reported. For example, if the actual cost for the output of the six items produced in responsibility centre A during the period is £220 and the standard cost is £120 (Exhibit 17.1), a variance of £100 will be reported.

Detailed analysis of variances

The box below the first arrow in Figure 17.1 indicates that the operation of a standard costing system also enables a detailed analysis of the variances to be reported. For example, variances for each responsibility centre can be identified by each element of cost and analyzed according to the price

EXHIBIT 17.1 Standard costs analyzed by operations and products

Responsibility centre	Operation no. and standard cost		Products							Total standard cost	Actual cost
	No.	(£)	100	101	102	103	104	105	106	(£)	
A	1	20	✓	✓		✓	✓	✓	✓	120	
B	2	30			✓		✓			90	
C	3	40	✓		✓			✓		120	
D	4	50	✓	✓	✓				✓	200	
Standard product cost			£110	£100	£90	£50	£60	£50	£70	530	

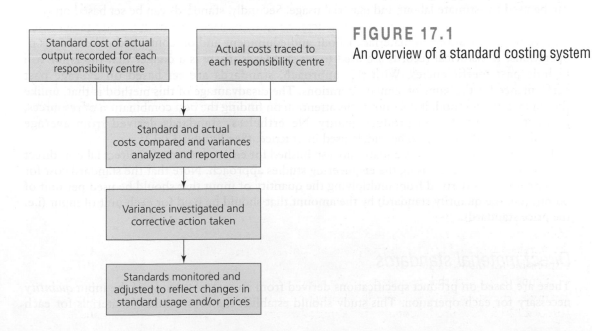

FIGURE 17.1

An overview of a standard costing system

and quantity content. The accountant assists managers by pinpointing where the variances have arisen and the responsibility managers can undertake to carry out the appropriate investigations to identify the reasons for the variance. For example, the accountant might identify the reason for a direct materials variance as being excessive usage of a certain material in a particular process, but the responsibility centre manager must investigate this process and identify the reasons for the excessive usage. Such an investigation should result in appropriate remedial action being taken or, if it is found that the variance is due to a permanent change in the standard, the standard should be changed.

Actual product costs are not required

It is questionable whether the allocation of actual costs to products serves any useful purpose. Because standard costs represent *future* target costs, they are preferable to actual *past* costs for decision-making. Also, the external financial accounting regulations in most countries specify that if standard product costs provide a reasonable approximation of actual product costs, they are acceptable for inventory valuation calculations for external reporting.

There are therefore strong arguments for not producing actual *product* costs when a standard costing system exists, since this will lead to large clerical savings. However, it must be stressed that actual costs must be accumulated periodically for each operation or responsibility centre, so that comparisons can be made with standard costs. Nevertheless, there will be considerably fewer responsibility centres than products, and the accumulation of actual costs is therefore much less time consuming.

Establishing cost standards

Control over costs is best effected through action at the point where the costs are incurred. Hence the standards should be set for the quantities of material, labour and services to be consumed in performing an *operation*, rather than the complete *product* cost standards. Variances from these standards should be reported to show causes and responsibilities for deviations from standard. Product cost standards are derived by listing and adding the standard costs of operations required to produce a particular product. For example, if you refer to Exhibit 17.1 you will see that the standard cost of product 100 is £110 and is derived from the sum of the standard costs of operations 1, 3 and 4.

There are two approaches that can be used to set standard costs. First, past historical records can be used to estimate labour and material usage. Secondly, standards can be set based on engineering studies. With engineering studies a detailed study of each operation is undertaken based on careful specifications of materials, labour and equipment and on controlled observations of operations. If historical records are used to set standards, there is a danger that the latter will include past inefficiencies. With this approach, standards are set based on average past performance for the same or similar operations. The disadvantage of this method is that, unlike the engineering method, it does not focus attention on finding the best combination of resources, production methods and product quality. Nevertheless, standards derived from average historical usage do appear to be widely used in practice. (See Exhibit 17.3.)

Let us now consider how standards are established for each operation for direct labour, direct materials and overheads using the engineering studies approach. Note that the standard cost for each operation is derived from multiplying the quantity of input that should be used per unit of output (i.e. the quantity standard) by the amount that should be paid for each unit of input (i.e. the price standard).

Direct material standards

These are based on product specifications derived from an intensive study of the input *quantity* necessary for each operation. This study should establish the most suitable materials for each product, based on product design and quality policy, and also the optimal quantity that should be used after taking into account any wastage or loss that is considered inevitable in the production process. Material quantity standards are usually recorded on a bill of materials. This describes and states the required quantity of materials for each operation to complete the product. A separate bill of materials is maintained for each product. The standard material product cost is then found by multiplying the standard quantities by the appropriate standard prices.

The standard *prices* are obtained from the purchasing department. The standard material prices are based on the assumption that the purchasing department has carried out a suitable search of alternative suppliers and has selected suppliers who can provide the required quantity of sound quality materials at the most competitive price. Standard prices then provide a suitable base against which actual prices paid for materials can be evaluated.

Direct labour standards

To set labour standards, activities should be analyzed by the different operations. Each operation is studied and an allowed time computed, possibly involving a time and motion study. The normal procedure for such a study is to analyze each operation to eliminate any unnecessary elements and to determine the most efficient production method. The most efficient methods of production, equipment and operating conditions are then standardized. This is followed by time measurements that are made to determine the number of standard hours required by an average worker to complete the job. Unavoidable delays such as machine breakdowns and routine maintenance are included in the standard time. The wage rates are applied to the standard time allowed to determine the standard labour cost for each operation.

Overhead standards

The procedure for establishing standard manufacturing overhead rates for a standard costing system is the same as that which is used for establishing predetermined overhead rates as described in Chapter 3. Separate rates for fixed and variable overheads are essential for planning and control. With traditional costing systems the standard overhead rate will be based on a rate per direct labour hour or machine hour of input.

Fixed overheads are largely independent of changes in activity, and remain constant over wide ranges of activity in the short term. It is therefore inappropriate for short-term cost control purposes to unitize fixed overheads to derive a fixed overhead rate per unit of activity. However, in order to meet the external financial reporting stock valuation requirements, fixed manufacturing overheads must be traced to products. It is therefore necessary to unitize fixed overheads for stock valuation purposes.

The main difference with the treatment of overheads under a standard costing system as opposed to a non-standard costing system is that the product overhead cost is based on the hourly overhead rates multiplied by the *standard hours* (that is, hours which should have been used) rather than the *actual hours* used.

A standard cost card should be maintained for each product and operation. It reveals the quantity of each unit of input that should be used to produce one unit of output. A typical product standard cost card is illustrated in Exhibit 17.2. In most organizations standard cost cards are now stored on a computer. Standards should be continuously reviewed, and, where significant changes in production methods or input prices occur, they should be changed in order to ensure that standards reflect current targets.

Standard hours produced

It is not possible to measure *output* in terms of units produced for a department making several different products or operations. For example, if a department produces 100 units of product X, 200 units of product Y and 300 units of product Z, it is not possible to add the production of these items together, since they are not homogeneous. This problem can be overcome by ascertaining the amount of time, working under efficient conditions, it should take to make each product. This time calculation is called standard hours produced. In other words, standard hours are an *output* measure that can act as a common denominator for adding together the production of unlike items.

Let us assume that the following standard times are established for the production of one unit of each product:

Product X	5 standard hours
Product Y	2 standard hours
Product Z	3 standard hours

This means that it should take five hours to produce one unit of product X under efficient production conditions. Similar comments apply to products Y and Z. The production for the department will be calculated in standard hours as follows:

Product	Standard time per unit produced (hours)	Actual output (units)	Standard hours produced
X	5	100	500
Y	2	200	400
Z	3	300	900
			1800

EXHIBIT 17.2 An illustration of a standard cost card

Date standard set ....   **Product: Sigma**

Direct materials

Operation no.	Item code	Quantity (kg)	Standard price (£)	Department				Totals (£)
				A	B	C	D	
1	5.001	5	3		£15			
2	7.003	4	4			£16		
								31

Direct labour

Operation no.	Standard hours	Standard rate (£)		
1	7	9	£63	
2	8	9	£72	
				135

Factory overhead

Department	Standard hours	Standard rate (£)		
B	7	3	£21	
C	8	4	£32	
				53
Total manufacturing cost per unit (£)				219

Remember that standard hours produced is an output measure, and flexible budget allowances should be based on this. In the illustration we should expect the *output* of 1800 standard hours to take 1800 direct labour hours of *input* if the department works at the prescribed level of efficiency. The department will be inefficient if 1800 standard hours of output are produced using, say, 2000 direct labour hours of input. The flexible budget allowance should therefore be based on 1800 standard hours produced to ensure that no extra allowance is given for the 200 excess hours of input. Otherwise, a manager will obtain a higher budget allowance through being inefficient.

Types of cost standards

The determination of standard costs raises the problem of how demanding the standards should be. Should they represent ideal or faultless performance or should they represent easily attainable performance? Standards are normally classified into three broad categories:

1 basic cost standards;
2 ideal standards;
3 currently attainable standards.

Basic cost standards

Basic cost standards represent constant standards that are left unchanged over long periods. The main advantage of basic standards is that a base is provided for a comparison with actual costs through a period of years with the same standard, and efficiency trends can be established over time. When changes occur in methods of production, price levels or other relevant factors, basic standards are not very useful, since they do not represent *current* target costs. For this reason basic cost standards are seldom used.

Ideal standards

Ideal standards represent perfect performance. Ideal standard costs are the minimum costs that are possible under the most efficient operating conditions. Ideal standards are unlikely to be used in practice because they may have an adverse impact on employee motivation. Such standards constitute goals to be aimed for rather than performance that can currently be achieved.

Currently attainable standard costs

These standards represent those costs that should be incurred under efficient operating conditions. They are standards that are difficult, but not impossible, to achieve. Attainable standards are easier to achieve than ideal standards because allowances are made for normal spoilage, machine breakdowns and lost time. The fact that these standards represent a target that can be achieved under efficient conditions, but which is also viewed as being neither too easy to achieve nor impossible to achieve, provides the best norm to which actual costs should be compared. Attainable standards are equivalent to highly achievable standards described in the previous chapter. For an indication of the types of cost standards that companies actually use you should refer to Exhibit 17.3.

Purposes of standard costing

Standard costing systems are widely used because they provide cost information for many different purposes such as the following.

● Providing a prediction of future costs that can be used for *decision-making purposes*. Standard costs can be derived from either traditional or activity-based costing systems. Because standard costs represent *future* target costs based on the elimination of avoidable inefficiencies they are preferable to estimates based on adjusted past costs which may incorporate inefficiencies. For example, in markets where competitive prices do not exist products may be priced on a bid basis. In these situations standard costs provide more appropriate information because efficient competitors will seek to eliminate avoidable costs. It is therefore unwise to assume that inefficiencies are recoverable within the bid price.

● Providing a *challenging target* which individuals are motivated to achieve. For example research evidence suggests that the existence of a defined quantitative goal or target is likely to motivate higher levels of performance than would be achieved if no such target was set.

● Assisting in *setting budgets* and evaluating managerial performance. Standard costs are particularly valuable for budgeting because a reliable and convenient source of data is provided for converting budgeted production into physical and monetary resource requirements. Budgetary preparation time is considerably reduced if standard costs are available because the standard costs of operations and products can be readily built up into total costs of any budgeted volume and product mix.

● Acting as a *control device* by highlighting those activities which do not conform to plan and thus alerting managers to those situations that may be 'out of control' and in need of corrective action. With a standard costing system variances are analyzed in great detail such as by element of cost, and price and quantity elements. Useful feedback is therefore provided in pinpointing the areas where variances have arisen.

EXHIBIT 17.3 Surveys of company practice

Since its introduction in the early 1900s standard costing has flourished and is now one of the most widely used management accounting techniques. Three independently conducted surveys of USA practice indicate highly consistent figures in terms of adopting standard costing systems. Cress and Pettijohn (1985) and Schwarzbach (1985) report an 85 per cent adoption rate, while Cornick *et al.* (1988), found that 86 per cent of the surveyed firms used a standard costing system. A Japanese survey by Scarborough *et al.* (1991) reported a 65 per cent adoption rate. Surveys of UK companies by Drury *et al.* (1993) and New Zealand companies by Guilding *et al.* (1998) report adoption rates of 76 per cent and 73 per cent respectively.

A CIMA sponsored study of 41 UK manufacturing organizations by Dugdale *et al.* (2006) reported that 30 of the firms employed standard costing. The majority of these firms (26) set standard costs for materials and labour and a smaller majority (20) also set standard overhead costs. They conclude that despite the huge changes in the manufacturing environment standard costing is alive and well.

In relation to the methods to set labour and material standards Drury *et al.* reported the following usage rates:

	Extent of use (%)				
	Never	Rarely	Sometimes	Often	Always
Standards based on design/ engineering studies	18	11	19	31	21
Observations based on trial runs	18	16	36	25	5
Work study techniques	21	18	19	21	21
Average of historic usage	22	11	23	35	9

In the USA Lauderman and Schaeberle (1983) reported that 43 per cent of the respondents used average historic usage, 67 per cent used engineering studies, 11 per cent used trial runs under controlled conditions and 15 per cent used other methods. The results add up to more than 100 per cent because some companies used more than one method.

● Simplifying the task of tracing costs to products for *profit measurement and inventory valuation* purposes. Besides preparing annual financial accounting profit statements most organizations also prepare monthly internal profit statements. If actual costs are used a considerable amount of time is required in tracking costs so that monthly costs can be allocated between cost of sales and inventories. A data processing system is required which can track monthly costs in a resource efficient manner. Standard costing systems meet this requirement You will see from Figure 17.2 that product costs are maintained at standard cost. Inventories and cost of goods sold are recorded at standard cost and a conversion to actual cost is made by writing off all variances arising during the period as a period cost. Note that the variances from standard cost are extracted by comparing actual with standard costs at the responsibility centre level, and not at the product level, so that actual costs are not assigned to individual products.

Variance analysis

It is possible to compute variances simply by committing to memory a series of variance formulae. If you adopt this approach, however, it will not help you to understand what a variance is intended to depict and what the relevant variables represent. In our discussion of each variance we shall therefore concentrate on the fundamental meaning of the variance, so that you can logically deduce the variance formulae as we go along.

All of the variances presented in this chapter are illustrated from the information contained in Example 17.1 on page 426. Note that the level of detail presented is highly simplified. A truly realistic situation would involve many products, operations and responsibility centres but would not give any further insights into the basic concepts or procedures.

Figure 17.3 shows the breakdown of the profit variance (the difference between budgeted and actual profit) into the component cost and revenue variances that can be calculated for a standard variable costing system. We shall now calculate the variances set out in Figure 17.3 using the data presented in Example 17.1.

Material variances

The costs of the materials which are used in a manufactured product are determined by two basic factors: the price paid for the materials, and the quantity of materials used in production. This gives rise to the possibility that the actual cost will differ from the standard cost because the *actual quantity* of materials used will be different from the *standard quantity* and/or that the *actual price* paid will be different from the *standard price*. We can therefore calculate a material usage and a material price variance.

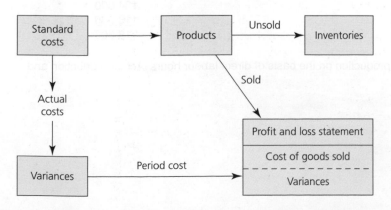

FIGURE 17.2
Standard costs for inventory valuation and profit measurement

EXAMPLE 17.1

Alpha manufacturing company produces a single product, which is known as sigma. The product requires a single operation, and the standard cost for this operation is presented in the following standard cost card:

Standard cost card for product sigma	(£)
Direct materials:	
2 kg of A at £10 per kg	20.00
1 kg of B at £15 per kg	15.00
Direct labour (3 hours at £9 per hour)	27.00
Variable overhead (3 hours at £2 per direct labour hour)	6.00
Total standard variable cost	68.00
Standard contribution margin	20.00
Standard selling price	88.00

Alpha Ltd plan to produce 10 000 units of sigma in the month of April, and the budgeted costs based on the information contained in the standard cost card are as follows:

Budget based on the above standard costs and an output of 10 000 units	(£)	(£)	(£)
Sales (10 000 units of sigma at £88 per unit)			880 000
Direct materials:			
A: 20 000 kg at £10 per kg	200 000		
B: 10 000 kg at £15 per kg	150 000	350 000	
Direct labour (30 000 hours at £9 per hour)		270 000	
Variable overheads (30 000 hours at			
£2 per direct labour hour)		60 000	680 000
Budgeted contribution			200 000
Fixed overheads			120 000
Budgeted profit			80 000

Annual budgeted fixed overheads are £1 440 000 and are assumed to be incurred evenly throughout the year. The company uses a variable costing system for internal profit measurement purposes.

The actual results for April are:

	(£)	(£)
Sales (9000 units at £90)		810 000
Direct materials:		
A: 19 000 kg at £11 per kg	209 000	
B: 10 100 kg at £14 per kg	141 400	
Direct labour (28 500 hours at £9.60 per hour)	273 600	
Variable overheads	52 000	676 000
Contribution		134 000
Fixed overheads		116 000
Profit		18 000

Manufacturing overheads are charged to production on the basis of direct labour hours. Actual production and sales for the period were 9000 units.

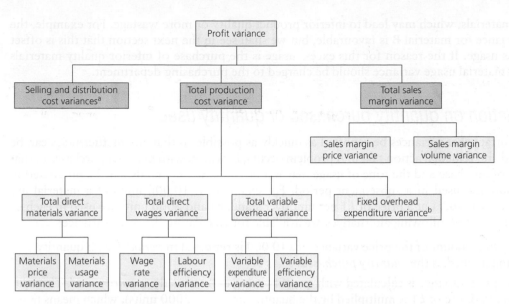

FIGURE 17.3

Variance analysis for a variable costing system

a Selling and distribution cost variances are not presented in this chapter. If activities are of a repetitive nature, standards can be established and variances can be calculated in a similar manner to production cost variances. If standards cannot be established, costs should be controlled by comparing budgeted and actual costs.

b With an absorption costing system, the summary of fixed overhead variances presented in Exhibit 17.5 would replace this box.

Material price variances

The starting point for calculating this variance is simply to compare the standard price per unit of materials with the actual price per unit. You should now read Example 17.1. You will see that the standard price for material A is £10 per kg, but the actual price paid was £11 per kg. The price variance is £1 per kg. This is of little consequence if the excess purchase price has been paid only for a small number of units or purchases. But the consequences are important if the excess purchase price has been paid for a large number of units, since the effect of the variance will be greater.

The difference between the standard material price and the actual price per unit should therefore be multiplied by the quantity of materials purchased. For material A the price variance is £1 per unit; but since 19 000 kg were purchased, the excess price was paid out 19 000 times. Hence the total material price variance is £19 000 adverse. The formula for the material price variance now follows logically:

the **material price variance** is equal to the difference between the standard price (SP) and the actual price (AP) per unit of materials multiplied by the quantity of materials purchased (QP):

$$(SP - AP) \times QP$$

Now refer to material B in Example 17.1. The standard price is £15, compared with an actual price of £14 giving a £1 saving per kg. As 10 100 kg were purchased, the total price variance will be £10 100 (10 100kg at £1). The variance for material B is favourable and that for material A is adverse. The normal procedure is to present the amount of the variances followed by symbols A or F to indicate either adverse or favourable variances.

It is incorrect to assume that the material price variance will always indicate the efficiency of the purchasing department. Actual prices may exceed standard prices because of a change in market conditions that causes a general price increase for the type of materials used. The price variance might therefore be beyond the control of the purchasing department. Alternatively, an adverse price variance may reflect a failure by the purchasing department to seek the most advantageous sources of supply. A favourable price variance might be due to the purchase of inferior quality materials, which may lead to inferior product quality or more wastage. For example, the price variance for material B is favourable, but we shall see in the next section that this is offset by excess usage. If the reason for this excess usage is the purchase of inferior quality materials then the material usage variance should be charged to the purchasing department.

Calculation on quantity purchased or quantity used

It is important that variances be reported as quickly as possible so that any inefficiencies can be identified and remedial action taken. A problem occurs, however, with material purchases in that the time of purchase and the time of usage may not be the same: materials may be purchased in one period and used in a subsequent period. For example, if 10 000 units of a material are purchased in period 1 at a price of £1 per unit over standard and 2000 units are used in each of periods 1 to 5, the following alternatives are available for calculating the price variance:

1   The full amount of the price variance of £10 000 is reported in *period 1* with quantity being defined as the *quantity purchased*.

2   The price variance is calculated with quantity being defined as the *quantity used*. The unit price variance of £1 is multiplied by the quantity used (i.e. 2000 units), which means that a price variance of £2000 will be reported for each of *periods 1 to 5*.

Method 1 is recommended, because the price variance can be reported in the period in which it is incurred, and reporting of the total variance is not delayed until months later when the materials are used. Also, adopting this approach enables corrective action to be taken earlier. For the sake of simplicity we shall assume in Example 17.1 that the actual purchases are identical with the actual usage.

Material usage variance

The starting point for calculating this quantity variance is simply to compare the standard quantity that should have been used with the actual quantity which has been used. Refer again to Example 17.1. You will see that the standard usage for the production of one unit of sigma is 2 kg for material A. As 9000 units of sigma are produced, 18 000 kg of material A should have been used; however, 19 000 kg are actually used, which means there has been an excess usage of 1000 kg.

The importance of this excess usage depends on the price of the materials. For example, if the price is £0.01 per kg then an excess usage of 1000 kg will not be very significant, but if the price is £10 per unit then an excess usage of 1000 kg will be very significant. It follows that to assess the importance of the excess usage, the variance should be expressed in monetary terms.

Should the standard material price per kg or the actual material price per kg be used to calculate the variance? The answer is the standard price. If the *actual* material price is used, the usage variance will be affected by the efficiency of the purchasing department, since any excess purchase price will be assigned to the excess usage. It is therefore necessary to remove the price effects from the usage variance calculation, and this is achieved by valuing the variance at the standard price. Hence the 1000 kg excess usage of material A is multiplied by the standard price of £10 per unit, which gives an adverse usage variance of £10 000. The formula for the variance is:

the material usage variance is equal to the difference between the standard quantity (SQ) required for actual production and the actual quantity (AQ) used multiplied by the standard material price (SP):

$$(SQ - AQ) \times SP$$

For material B you will see from Example 17.1 that the standard quantity is 9000 kg (9000 units × 1 kg), but 10 100 kg have been used. The excess usage of 1100 kg is multiplied by the standard price of £15 per kg, which gives an adverse variance of £16 500. Note that the principles of flexible budgeting described in the previous chapter also apply here, with *standard quantity being based on actual production and not budgeted production*. This ensures that a manager is evaluated under the conditions in which he or she actually worked and not those envisaged at the time the budget was prepared.

The material usage variance is normally controllable by the manager of the appropriate production responsibility centre. Common causes of material usage variances include the careless handling of materials by production personnel, the purchase of inferior quality materials, pilferage, changes in quality control requirements, or changes in methods of production. Separate material usage variances should be calculated for each type of material used and allocated to each responsibility centre.

Joint price usage variance

Note that the analysis of the material variance into the price and usage elements is not theoretically correct, since there may be a joint mutual price/quantity effect. The following information is extracted from Example 17.1 for material A:

1 18 000 kg of material A are required, at a standard price of £10 per kg.
2 19 000 kg are used, at a price of £11 per kg.

The purchasing officer might readily accept responsibility for the price variance of £1 per kg for 18 000kg, but may claim that the extra 1000 kg at £1 is more the responsibility of the production foreman. It may be argued that if the foreman had produced in accordance with the standard then the extra 1000 kg would not have been needed.

The foreman, on the other hand, will accept responsibility for the 1000 kg excess usage at a standard price of £10, but will argue that he should not be held accountable for the additional purchase price of £1 per unit.

One possible way of dealing with this would be to report the joint price/quantity variance of £1000 (1000 kg at £1) separately and not charge it to either manager. In other words, the original price variance of £19 000 would be analyzed as follows:

	(£)
1. Pure price variance (18 000 kg at £1 per kg)	18 000A
2. Joint price/quantity variance (1000 kg at £1 per kg)	1 000A
	19 000A

Most textbooks recommend that the material price variance be calculated by multiplying the difference between the standard and actual prices by the actual quantity, rather than the standard quantity. Adopting this approach results in the joint price/quantity variance being assigned to the materials price variance. This approach can be justified on the ground that the purchasing manager ought to be responsible for the efficient purchase of all material requirements, irrespective of whether or not the materials are used efficiently by the production departments.

Total material variance

From Figure 17.3 you will see that this variance is the total variance before it is analyzed into the price and usage elements. The formula for the variance is:

the total material variance is the difference between the standard material cost (SC) for the actual production and the actual cost (AC):

$$SC - AC$$

For material A the standard material cost is £20 per unit (see Example 17.1), giving a total standard material cost of £180 000 (9000 units × £20). The actual cost is £209 000, and therefore the variance is £29 000 adverse. The price variance of £19 000 plus the usage variance of £10 000 agrees with the total material variance. Similarly, the total material variance for material B is £6400, consisting of a favourable price variance of £10 100 and an adverse usage variance of £16 500.

Note that if the price variance is calculated on the actual quantity *purchased* instead of the actual quantity *used*, the price variance plus the usage variance will agree with the total variance only when the quantity purchased is equal to the quantity which is used in the particular accounting period. Reconciling the price and usage variance with the total variance is merely a reconciliation exercise, and you should not be concerned if reconciliation of the sub-variances with the total variance is not possible.

Wage rate variance

The cost of labour is determined by the price paid for labour and the quantity of labour used. Thus a price and quantity variance will also arise for labour. The price (wage rate) variance is calculated by comparing the standard price per hour with the actual price paid per hour. In Example 17.1 the standard wage rate per hour is £9 and the actual wage rate is £9.60 per hour, giving a wage rate variance of £0.60 per hour. To determine the importance of the variance, it is necessary to ascertain how many times the excess payment of £0.60 per hour is paid. As 28 500 labour hours are used (see Example 17.1), we multiply 28 500 hours by £0.60. This gives an adverse wage rate variance of £17 100. The formula for the wage rate variance is:

> the wage rate variance is equal to the difference between the standard wage rate per hour (SR) and the actual wage rate (AR) multiplied by the actual number of hours worked (AH):

$$(SR - AR) \times AH$$

Note the similarity between this variance and the material price variance. Both variances multiply the difference between the standard price and the actual price paid for a unit of a resource by the actual quantity of resources used.

The wage rate variance is probably the one that is least subject to control by management. In most cases the variance is due to wage rate standards not being kept in line with changes in actual wage rates, and for this reason it is not normally controllable by departmental managers.

Labour efficiency variance

The labour efficiency variance represents the quantity variance for direct labour. The quantity of labour that should be used for the actual output is expressed in terms of *standard hours produced*. In Example 17.1 the standard time for the production of one unit of sigma is three hours. Thus a production level of 9000 units results in an output of 27 000 standard hours. In other words, working at the prescribed level of efficiency, it should take 27 000 hours to produce 9000 units. However, 28 500 direct labour hours are actually required to produce this output, which means that 1500 excess direct labour hours are used. We multiply the excess direct labour hours by the *standard* wage rate to calculate the variance. This gives an adverse variance of £13 500. The formula for calculating the labour efficiency variance is:

> the labour efficiency variance is equal to the difference between the standard labour hours for actual production (SH) and the actual labour hours worked (AH) during the period multiplied by the standard wage rate per hour (SR):

$$(SH - AH) \times SR$$

This variance is similar to the material usage variance. Both variances multiply the difference between the standard quantity and actual quantity of resources consumed by the standard price.

The labour efficiency variance is normally controllable by the manager of the appropriate production responsibility centre and may be due to a variety of reasons. For example, the use of inferior quality materials, different grades of labour, failure to maintain machinery in proper condition, the introduction of new equipment or tools and changes in the production processes will all affect the efficiency of labour. An efficiency variance may not always be controllable by the production foreman; it may be due, for example, to poor production scheduling by the planning department, or to a change in quality control standards.

Total labour variance

From Figure 17.3 you will see that this variance represents the total variance before analysis into the price and quantity elements. The formula for the variance is:

the total labour variance is the difference between the standard labour cost (SC) for the actual production and the actual labour cost (AC):

$$SC - AC$$

SOURCE: SHANK, J. K. AND FISHER, J. (1999), TARGET COSTING AS A STRATEGIC TOOL, *SLOAN MANAGEMENT REVIEW*, FALL, VOL. 41 ISSUE 1, PP. 73–82.
COPYRIGHT 1999 MASSACHUSSETTS INSTITUTE OF TECHNOLOGY. ALL RIGHTS RESERVED. DISTRIBUTED BY TRIBUNE MEDIA SERVICES.

Standard costing at Montclair Papers Division of Mohawk Forest Products

Montclair produces 1500 different products, including Forest Green Carnival. Its standard cost of $2900 per ton is derived from:

- union wage rates for labour costs ('Pattern bargaining' virtually assured comparable labour costs among the major union firms, all of which were unionized);

- standard yield rates for all manufacturing steps, based on latest performance measured against long-standing norms at the Montclair mill;

- current market prices for all purchased components;

- generally accepted industry procedures for building the 'normal' cost of scrap into the standard cost, after deducting the offset for the market value of the scrap generated.

The standards were updated annually for changes in purchase prices, process flows and yield targets. With more than 1500 products manufactured in the mill, more frequent updating was deemed unfeasible.

Manufacturing management accepted that the standard cost represented best practices of the mill and thus was an appropriate basis for monitoring monthly performance. Standard costs were also helpful to simplify calculating the month-end cost of goods sold and the ending inventory for financial

statements. Updated only once a year, the standard cost was stable from month to month. Management viewed this stability as a positive feature in monitoring monthly performance against the annual plan.

REAL WORLD VIEWS 17.1

Discussion points

1   Why do some companies find it inappropriate to implement a standard costing system?

2   Can you think of any other uses of standard costing at Montclair?

© JG PHOTOGRAPHY/ALAMY

In Example 17.1 the actual production was 9000 units, and, with a standard labour cost of £27 per unit, the standard cost is £243 000. The actual cost is £273 600, which gives an adverse variance of £30 600. This consists of a wage rate variance of £17 100 and a labour efficiency variance of £13 500.

Variable overhead variances

A total variable overhead variance is calculated in the same way as the total direct labour and material variances. In Example 17.1 the output is 9000 units and the standard variable overhead cost is £6 *per unit* produced. The standard cost of production for variable overheads is thus £54 000. The actual variable overheads incurred are £52 000, giving a favourable variance of £2000. The formula for the variance is:

> the total variable overhead variance is the difference between the standard variable overheads charged to production (SC) and the actual variable overheads incurred (AC):

$$SC - AC$$

Where variable overheads vary with direct labour or machine hours of *input* the total variable overhead variance will be due to one or both of the following:

1   A *price* variance arising from actual expenditure being different from budgeted expenditure.

2   A *quantity* variance arising from actual direct labour or machine hours of input being different from the hours of input, which *should* have been used.

These reasons give rise to the two sub-variances, which are shown in Figure 17.3: the variable overhead expenditure variance and the variable overhead efficiency variance.

Variable overhead expenditure variance

To compare the actual overhead expenditure with the budgeted expenditure, it is necessary to flex the budget. Because it is assumed in Example 17.1 that variable overheads will vary with direct labour hours of *input* the budget is flexed on this basis. Actual variable overhead expenditure is £52 000, resulting from 28 500 direct labour hours of input. For this level of activity variable overheads of £57 000, which consist of 28 500 input hours at £2 per hour, should have been spent. Spending was £5000 less than it should have been, and the result is a favourable variance.

If we compare the budgeted and the actual overhead costs for 28 500 direct labour hours of input, we shall ensure that any efficiency content is removed from the variance. This means that any difference must be due to actual variable overhead spending being different from the budgeted variable overhead spending. The formula for the variance is:

> the variable overhead expenditure variance is equal to the difference between the budgeted flexed variable overheads (BFVO) for the actual direct labour hours of input and the actual variable overhead costs incurred (AVO):

$$BFVO - AVO$$

Variable overhead represents the aggregation of a large number of individual items, such as indirect labour, indirect materials, electricity, maintenance and so on. The variable overhead variance can arise because the prices of individual items have changed. Alternatively, the variance can also be affected by how efficiently the individual variable overhead items are used. Waste or inefficiency, such as using more kilowatt-hours of power than should have been used will increase the cost of power and, thus, the total cost of variable overhead. The variable overhead expenditure on its own is therefore not very informative. Any meaningful analysis of this variance requires a comparison of the actual expenditure for each individual item of variable overhead expenditure against the budget.

Variable overhead efficiency variance

In Example 17.1 it is assumed that variable overheads vary with direct labour hours of input. The variable overhead efficiency variance arises because 28 500 direct labour hours of input were required to produce 9000 units. Working at the prescribed level of efficiency, it should take 27 000 hours to produce 9000 units of output. Therefore an extra 1500 direct labour hours of input were required. Because variable overheads are assumed to vary with direct labour hours of input, an additional £3000 (1500 hours at £2) variable overheads will be incurred. The formula for the variance is:

the variable overhead efficiency variance is the difference between the standard hours of output (SH) and the actual hours of input (AH) for the period multiplied by the standard variable overhead rate (SR):

$$(SH - AH) \times SR$$

You should note that if it is assumed that variable overheads vary with direct labour hours of input, this variance is identical to the labour efficiency variance. Consequently, the reasons for the variance are the same as those described previously for the labour efficiency variance. If you refer again to Figure 17.3, you will see that the variable overhead expenditure variance (£5000 favourable) plus the variable efficiency variance (£3000 adverse) add up to the total variable overhead variance of £2000 favourable.

Similarities between materials, labour and overhead variances

So far, we have calculated price and quantity variances for direct material, direct labour and variable overheads. You will have noted the similarities between the computations of the three quantity and price variances. For example, we calculated the quantity variances (i.e. material usage, labour efficiency and variable overhead efficiency variances) by multiplying the difference between the standard quantity (SQ) of resources consumed for the actual production and the actual quantity (AQ) of resources consumed by the standard price (SP) per unit of the resource. Thus, the three quantity variances can be formulated as:

$$(SQ - AQ) \times SP$$

Note that the standard quantity is derived from determining the quantity that should be used *for the actual production* for the period so that the principles of flexible budgeting are applied.

The price variances (i.e. material price, wage rate and variable overhead expenditure variances) were calculated by multiplying the difference between the standard price (SP) and the actual price (AP) per unit of a resource by the actual quantity (AQ) of resources acquired/used. The price variances can be formulated as:

$$(SP - AP) \times AQ$$

This can be re-expressed as:

$$(AQ \times SP) - (AQ \times AP)$$

Note that the first term in this formula (with AQ representing actual hours) is equivalent to the budgeted flexed variable overheads that we used to calculate the variable overhead expenditure variance. The last term represents the actual cost of the resources consumed.

We can therefore calculate all the price and quantity variances illustrated so far in this chapter by applying the two formulae outlined above.

Fixed overhead expenditure or spending variance

The final variance shown in Figure 17.3 is the fixed overhead expenditure variance. With a variable costing system, fixed manufacturing overheads are not unitized and allocated to products. Instead, the total fixed overheads for the period are charged as an expense to the period in which they are incurred. Fixed overheads are assumed to remain unchanged in the short term in response to changes in the level of activity, but they may change in response to other factors. For example, price increases may cause expenditure on fixed overheads to increase. The fixed overhead expenditure variance therefore explains the difference between budgeted fixed overheads and the actual fixed overheads incurred. The formula for the fixed overhead expenditure variance is the difference between the budgeted fixed overheads (BFO) and the actual fixed overhead (AFO) spending:

$$BFO - AFO$$

In Example 17.1 budgeted fixed overhead expenditure is £120 000 and actual fixed overhead spending £116 000. Therefore the fixed overhead expenditure variance is £4000. Whenever the actual fixed overheads are less than the budgeted fixed overheads, the variance will be favourable. The total of the fixed overhead expenditure variance on its own is not particularly informative. Any meaningful analysis of this variance requires a comparison of the actual expenditure for each individual item of fixed overhead expenditure against the budget. The difference may be due to a variety of causes, such as changes in salaries paid to supervisors, or the appointment of additional supervisors. Only by comparing individual items of expenditure and ascertaining the reasons for the variances, can one determine whether the variance is controllable or uncontrollable. Generally, this variance is likely to be uncontrollable in the short term.

Sales variances

Sales variances can be used to analyze the performance of the sales function or revenue centres on broadly similar terms to those for manufacturing costs. The most significant feature of sales variance calculations is that they are calculated in terms of profit or contribution margins rather than sales values. Consider Example 17.2.

You will see that when the variances are calculated on the basis of sales *value*, it is necessary to compare the budgeted sales *value* of £110 000 with the actual sales of £120 000. This gives a favourable variance of £10 000. This calculation, however, ignores the impact of the sales effort on profit. The budgeted profit contribution is £40 000, which consists of 10 000 units at £4 per unit, but the actual impact of the sales effort in terms of profit margins indicates a profit contribution of

EXAMPLE 17.2

The budgeted sales for a company are £110 000 consisting of 10 000 units at £11 per unit. The standard cost per unit is £7. Actual sales are £120 000 (12 000 units at £10 per unit) and the actual cost per unit is £7.

£36 000, which consists of 12 000 units at £3 per unit, indicating an adverse variance of £4000. If we examine Example 17.2, we can see that the selling prices have been reduced, and that this has led not only to an increase in the total sales revenue but also to a reduction in total profits. The objective of the selling function is to influence favourably total profits. Thus a more meaningful performance measure will be obtained by comparing the results of the sales function in terms of profit or contribution margins rather than sales revenues. Let us now calculate the sales variances for a standard variable costing system from the information contained in Example 17.1.

Total sales margin variance

Where a variable costing approach is adopted, the total sales *margin* variance seeks to identify the influence of the sales function on the difference between budget and actual profit contribution. In Example 17.1 the budgeted profit contribution is £200 000, which consists of budgeted sales of 10 000 units at a contribution of £20 per unit. This is compared with the contribution from the actual sales volume of 9000 units. Because the sales function is responsible for the sales volume and the unit selling price, but not the unit manufacturing costs, the standard cost of sales and not the actual cost of sales is deducted from the actual sales revenue. The calculation of *actual* contribution for ascertaining the total sales margin variance will therefore be as follows:

	(£)
Actual sales revenue (9000 units at £90)	810 000
Standard variable cost of sales for actual sales volume (9000 units at £68)	612 000
Actual profit contribution margin	198 000

To calculate the total sales margin variance, we compare the budgeted contribution of £200 000 with the actual contribution of £198 000. This gives an adverse variance of £2000 because the actual contribution is less that the budgeted profit contribution.

The formula for calculating the variance is as follows:

the total sales margin variance is the difference between the actual contribution (AC) and the budgeted contribution (BC) (both based on standard unit costs):

$$AC - BC$$

Using the standard cost to calculate both the budgeted and the actual contribution ensures that the production variances do not distort the calculation of the sales variances. The effect of using standard costs throughout the contribution margin calculations means that the sales variances arise because of changes in those variables controlled by the sales function (i.e. selling prices and sales quantity). Figure 17.3 indicates that it is possible to analyze the total sales margin variance into two sub-variances – a sales margin price variance and a sales margin volume variance.

Sales margin price variance

In Example 17.1 the actual selling price is £90 but the budgeted selling price is £88. With a standard unit variable cost of £68, the change in selling price has led to an increase in the contribution margin from £20 per unit to £22 per unit. Because the actual sales volume is 9000 units, the increase in the selling price means that an increased contribution margin is obtained 9000 times, giving a favourable sales margin price variance of £18 000. The formula for calculating the variance is:

the sales margin price variance is the difference between the actual contribution margin (AM) and the standard margin (SM) (both based on standard unit costs) multiplied by the actual sales volume (AV):

$$(AM - SM) \times AV$$

Sales margin volume variance

To ascertain the effect of changes in the sales volume on the difference between the budgeted and the actual contribution, we must compare the budgeted sales volume with the actual sales volume. You will see from Example 17.1 that the budgeted sales are 10 000 units but the actual sales are 9000 units, and to enable us to determine the impact of this reduction in sales volume on profit, we must multiply the 1000 units by the standard contribution margin of £20. This gives an adverse variance of £20 000.

The use of the standard margin (standard selling price less standard cost) ensures that the standard selling price is used in the calculation, and the volume variance will not be affected by any *changes* in the actual selling prices. The formula for calculating the variance is:

the sales margin volume variance is the difference between the actual sales volume (AV) and the budgeted volume (BV) multiplied by the standard contribution margin (SM):

$$(AV - BV) \times SM$$

Difficulties in interpreting sales margin variances

The favourable sales margin price variance of £18 000 plus the adverse volume variance of £20 000 add up to the total adverse sales margin variance of £2000. It may be argued that it is not very meaningful to analyze the total sales margin variance into price and volume components, since changes in selling prices are likely to affect sales volume. Consequently, a favourable price variance will tend to be associated with an adverse volume variance, and vice versa. It may be unrealistic to sell more than the budgeted volume when selling prices have increased.

A further problem with sales variances is that the variances may arise from external factors and may not be controllable by management. For example, changes in selling prices may be the result of a response to changes in selling prices of competitors. Alternatively, a reduction in both selling prices and sales volume may be the result of an economic recession that was not foreseen when the budget was prepared. For control and performance appraisal it may be preferable to compare actual market share with target market share for each product. In addition, the trend in market shares should be monitored and selling prices should be compared with competitors' prices.

Reconciling budgeted profit and actual profit

Top management will be interested in the reason for the actual profit being different from the budgeted profit. By adding the favourable production and sales variances to the budgeted profit and deducting the adverse variances, the reconciliation of budgeted and actual profit shown in Exhibit 17.4 can be presented in respect of Example 17.1.

Example 17.1 assumes that Alpha Ltd produces a single product consisting of a single operation and that the activities are performed by one responsibility centre. In practice, most companies make many products, which require operations to be carried out in different responsibility centres. A reconciliation statement such as that presented in Exhibit 17.4 will therefore normally represent a summary of the variances for many responsibility centres. The reconciliation statement thus represents a broad picture to top management that explains the major reasons for any difference between the budgeted and actual profits.

EXHIBIT 17.4 Reconciliation of budgeted and actual profits for a standard variable costing system

	(£)	(£)	(£)
Budgeted net profit			80 000
Sales variances:			
Sales margin price	18 000F		
Sales margin volume	20 000A	2 000A	
Direct cost variances:			
Material: Price	8 900A		
Usage	26 500A	35 400A	
Labour: Rate	17 100A		
Efficiency	13 500A	30 600A	
Manufacturing overhead variances:			
Fixed overhead expenditure	4 000F		
Variable overhead expenditure	5 000F		
Variable overhead efficiency	3 000A	6 000F	62 000A
Actual profit			18 000

Standard absorption costing

The external financial accounting regulations in most countries require that companies should value inventories at full absorption manufacturing cost. The effect of this is that fixed overheads should be allocated to products and included in the closing inventory valuations. With the variable costing system, fixed overheads are not allocated to products. Instead, the total fixed costs are charged as an expense to the period in which they are incurred. (For a discussion of the differences between variable and absorption costing systems you should refer back to Chapter 7.) With an absorption costing system, an additional fixed overhead variance is calculated. This variance is called a volume variance. In addition, the sales margin variances must be expressed in unit *profit* margins instead of *contribution* margins. These variances are not particularly useful for control purposes. If your course does not relate to the disposition of variances to meet financial accounting requirements, you can omit pages 437–40.

With a standard absorption costing system, predetermined fixed overhead rates are established by dividing annual budgeted fixed overheads by the budgeted annual level of activity. We shall assume that in respect of Example 17.1, budgeted annual fixed overheads are £1 440 000 (£120 000 per month) and budgeted annual activity is 120 000 units (10 000 units per month). The fixed overhead rate *per unit* of output is calculated as follows:

$$\frac{\text{budgeted fixed overheads (£1 440 000)}}{\text{budgeted activity (120 000 units)}} = £12 \text{ per unit of sigma produced}$$

We have noted earlier in this chapter that in most situations more than one product will be produced. Where different products are produced, units of output should be converted to standard hours. In Example 17.1 the output of one unit of sigma requires three direct labour hours. Therefore, the budgeted output in standard hours is 360 000 hours (120 000 × 3 hours). The fixed overhead rate *per standard hour* of output is

$$\frac{\text{budgeted fixed overheads (£1 440 000)}}{\text{budgeted standard hours (360 000)}} = £4 \text{ per standard hour}$$

By multiplying the number of hours required to produce one unit of Sigma by £4 per hour, we also get a fixed overhead allocation of £12 for one unit of Sigma (3 hours × £4). For the remainder of this chapter output will be measured in terms of standard hours produced.

We shall assume that production is expected to occur evenly throughout the year. Monthly budgeted production output is therefore 10 000 units, or 30 000 standard direct labour hours. At the planning stage an input of 30 000 direct labour hours (10 000 × 3 hours) will also be planned as the company will budget at the level of efficiency specified in the calculation of the product standard cost. Thus the budgeted hours of input and the budgeted hours of output (i.e. the standard hours produced) will be the same at the planning stage. In contrast, the *actual* hours of input may differ from the *actual* standard hours of output. In Example 17.1 the actual direct labour hours of input are 28 500, and 27 000 standard hours were actually produced.

With an absorption costing system, fixed overheads of £108 000 (27 000 standard hours of output at a standard rate of £4 per hour) will have been charged to products for the month of April. Actual fixed overhead expenditure was £116 000. Therefore, £8000 has not been allocated to products. In other words, there has been an under-recovery of fixed overheads. Where the fixed overheads allocated to products exceeds the overhead incurred, there will be an over-recovery of fixed overheads. The under- or over-recovery of fixed overheads represents the total fixed overhead variance for the period. The total fixed overhead variance is calculated using a formula similar to those for the total direct labour and total direct materials variances:

the total fixed overhead variance is the difference between the standard fixed overhead charged to production (SC) and the actual fixed overhead incurred (AC):

$$SC \ (£108 \ 000) - AC \ (£116 \ 000) = £8000A$$

Note that the standard cost for the actual production can be calculated by measuring production in standard hours of output (27 000 hours × £4 per hour) or units of output (9000 units × £12 per unit).

The under- or over-recovery of fixed overheads (i.e. the fixed overhead variance) arises because the fixed overhead rate is calculated by dividing *budgeted* fixed overheads by *budgeted* output. If actual output or fixed overhead expenditure differs from budget, an under- or over-recovery of fixed overheads will arise. In other words, the under- or over-recovery may be due to the following:

1 A fixed overhead expenditure variance of £4000 arising from actual *expenditure* (£116 000) being different from budgeted *expenditure* (£120 000).

2 A fixed overhead volume variance arising from actual *production* differing from budgeted production.

Note that the favourable variance of £4000 was explained earlier in this chapter.

Volume variance

This variance seeks to identify the portion of the total fixed overhead variance that is due to actual production being different from budgeted production. In Example 17.1 the standard fixed overhead rate of £4 per hour is calculated on the basis of a normal activity of 30 000 standard hours per month. Only when actual standard hours produced are 30 000 will the budgeted monthly fixed overheads of £120 000 be exactly recovered. Actual output, however, is only 27 000 standard hours. The fact that the actual production is 3000 standard hours less than the budgeted output hours will lead to a failure to recover £12 000 fixed overhead (3000 hours at £4 fixed overhead rate per hour). The formula for the variance is

the volume variance is the difference between actual production (AP) and budgeted production (BP) for a period multiplied by the standard fixed overhead rate (SR):

$$(AP - BP) × SR$$

The volume variance reflects the fact that fixed overheads do not fluctuate in relation to output in the short-term. Whenever actual production is less than budgeted production, the fixed overhead charged to production will be less than the budgeted cost, and the volume variance will be adverse. Conversely, if the actual production is greater than the budgeted production, the volume variance will be favourable.

When the adverse volume variance of £12 000 is netted with the favourable expenditure variance of £4000, the result is equal to the total fixed overhead adverse variance of £8000. It is also possible to analyze the volume variance into two further sub-variances – the volume efficiency variance and the capacity variance.

Volume efficiency variance

If we wish to identify the reasons for the volume variance, we may ask why the actual production was different from the budgeted production. One possible reason may be that the labour force worked at a different level of efficiency from that anticipated in the budget.

The actual number of direct labour hours of input was 28 500. Hence one would have expected 28 500 hours of output (i.e. standard hours produced) from this input, but only 27 000 standard hours were actually produced. Thus one reason for the failure to meet the budgeted output was that output in standard hours was 1500 hours less than it should have been. If the labour force had worked at the prescribed level of efficiency, an additional 1500 standard hours would have been produced, and this would have led to a total of £6000 (£1500 hours at £4 per standard hour) fixed overheads being absorbed. The inefficiency of labour is therefore one of the reasons why the actual production was less than the budgeted production, and this gives an adverse variance of £6000. The formula for the variance is:

the volume efficiency variance is the difference between the standard hours of output (SH) and the actual hours of input (AH) for the period multiplied by the standard fixed overhead rate (SR):

$$(SH - AH) \times SR$$

You may have noted that the physical content of this variance is a measure of labour efficiency and is identical with the labour efficiency variance. Consequently, the reasons for this variance will be identical with those previously described for the labour efficiency variance.

Volume capacity variance

This variance indicates the second reason why the actual production might be different from the budgeted production. The budget is based on the assumption that the direct labour hours of input will be 30 000 hours, but the actual hours of input are 28 500 hours. The difference of 1500 hours reflects the fact that the company has failed to utilize the planned capacity. If we assume that the 1500 hours would have been worked at the prescribed level of efficiency, an additional 1500 standard hours could have been produced and an additional £6000 fixed overhead could have been absorbed. Hence the capacity variance is £6000 adverse. Whereas the volume efficiency variance indicated a failure to utilize capacity *efficiently*, the volume capacity variance indicates a failure to utilize capacity *at all*. The formula is:

the volume capacity variance is the difference between the actual hours of input (AH) and the budgeted hours of input (BH) for the period multiplied by the standard fixed overhead rate (SR):

$$(AH - BH) \times SR$$

A failure to achieve the budgeted capacity may be for a variety of reasons. Machine breakdowns, material shortages, poor production scheduling, labour disputes and a reduction in sales demand are all possible causes of an adverse volume capacity variance.

The volume efficiency variance is £6000 adverse, and the volume capacity variance is also £6000 adverse. When these two variances are added together, they agree with the fixed overhead volume variance of £12 000. Exhibit 17.5 summarizes the variances we have calculated in this section.

You should note that the volume variance and two sub-variances (capacity and efficiency) are sometimes restated in non-monetary terms as follows:

$$\text{production volume ratio} = \frac{\text{standard hours of actual output (27 000)}}{\text{budgeted hours of output (30 000)}} \times 100$$
$$= 90\%$$

$$\text{production efficiency ratio} = \frac{\text{standard hours of actual output (27 000)}}{\text{actual hours worked (28 500)}} \times 100$$
$$= 94.7\%$$

$$\text{capacity usage ratio} = \frac{\text{actual hours worked (28 500)}}{\text{budgeted hours of input (30 000)}} \times 100$$
$$= 95\%$$

Reconciliation of budgeted and actual profit for a standard absorption costing system

The reconciliation of the budgeted and actual profits is shown in Exhibit 17.6. You will see that the reconciliation statement is identical with the variable costing reconciliation statement, apart from the fact that the absorption costing statement includes the fixed overhead volume variance and values the sales margin volume variance at the standard profit margin per unit instead of the contribution per unit. If you refer back to page 426, you will see that the contribution margin for Sigma is £20 per unit sold whereas the profit margin per unit after deducting fixed overhead cost (£12 per unit) is £8. Multiplying the difference in budgeted and actual sales volumes of 1000 units by the standard profit margin gives a sales volume margin variance of £8000. Note that the sales margin price variance is identical for both systems.

EXHIBIT 17.5 Diagram of fixed overhead variances

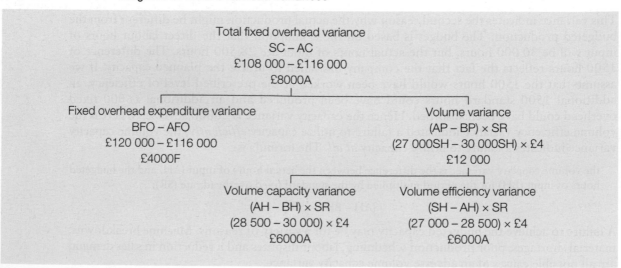

EXHIBIT 17.6 Reconciliation of budgeted and actual profit for a standard absorption costing system

		(£)	(£)	(£)	(£)
Budgeted net profit					80 000
Sales variances:					
Sales margin price			18 000F		
Sales margin volume			8 000A	10 000F	
Direct cost variances:					
Material – Price:	Material A	19 000A			
	Material B	10 100F	8 900A		
– Usage:	Material A	10 000A			
	Material B	16 500A	26 500A	35 400A	
Labour – Rate			17 100A		
Efficiency			13 500A	30 600A	
Manufacturing overhead variances:					
Fixed – Expenditure		4 000F			
Volume		12 000A	8 000A		
Variable – Expenditure		5 000F			
Efficiency		3 000A	2 000F	6 000A	62 000A
Actual profit					18 000

SUMMARY

The following items relate to the learning objectives listed at the beginning of the chapter.

● **Explain how a standard costing system operates.**

Standard costing is most suited to an organization whose activities consist of a series of repetitive operations and the input required to produce each unit of output can be specified. A standard costing system involves the following: (a) the standard costs for the actual output are recorded for each operation for each responsibility centre; (b) actual costs for each operation are traced to each responsibility centre; (c) the standard and actual costs are compared; (d) variances are investigated and corrective action is taken where appropriate; and (e) standards are monitored and adjusted to reflect changes in standard usage and/or prices.

● **Explain how standard costs are set.**

Standards should be set for the quantities and prices of materials, labour and services to be consumed in performing each operation associated with a product. Product standard costs are derived by listing and adding the standard costs of operations required to produce a particular product. Two approaches are used for setting standard costs. First, past historical records can be used to estimate labour and material usage. Secondly, standards can be set based on engineering studies. With engineering studies a detailed study of each operation is undertaken under controlled conditions, based on high levels of efficiency, to ascertain the quantities of labour and materials required. Target prices are then applied based on efficient purchasing to ascertain the standard costs.

● **Explain the meaning of standard hours produced.**

It is not possible to measure output in terms of units produced for a department making several different products or operations. This problem is overcome by ascertaining the amount of time, working under efficient operating conditions, it should take to make each product. This time calculation is called standard hours produced. Standard hours thus represents an output measure that acts as a common denominator for adding together the production of unlike items.

● **Define basic, ideal and currently attainable standards.**

Basic cost standards represent constant standards that are left unchanged over long periods. Ideal standards represent perfect performance. They represent the minimum costs that are possible under the most efficient operating conditions. Currently attainable standards represent those costs that should be incurred under efficient operating conditions. They are standards that are difficult, but not impossible, to achieve. Currently attainable standards are normally recommended for standard costing.

● **Identify and describe the purposes of a standard costing system.**

Standard costing systems can be used for the following purposes: (a) providing a prediction of future costs that can be used for decision-making; (b) providing a challenging target which individuals are motivated to achieve; (c) providing a reliable and convenient source of data for budget preparation; (d) acting as a control device by highlighting those activities that do not conform to plan and thus alerting managers to those situations that may be 'out of control' and in need of corrective action; and (e) simplifying the task of tracing costs to products for profit measurement and inventory valuation purpose.

● **Calculate labour, material, overhead and sales margin variances and reconcile actual profit with budgeted profit.**

To reconcile actual profit with budget profit the favourable variances are added to the budgeted profit and adverse variances are deducted. The end result

should be the actual profit. A summary of the formulae for the computation of the variances is presented in Exhibit 17.7. In each case the formula is presented so that so that a positive variance is favourable and a negative variance unfavourable.

● **Identify the causes of labour, material, overhead and sales margin variances.**

Quantities cost variances arise because the actual quantity of resources consumed exceed actual usage. Examples include excess usage of materials and labour arising from the usage of inferior materials, careless handling of materials and failure to maintain machinery in proper condition. Price variances arise when the actual prices paid for resources exceed the standard prices. Examples include the failure of the purchasing function to seek the most efficient sources of supply or the use of a different grade of labour to that incorporated in the standard costs.

● **Distinguish between standard variable costing and standard absorption costing.**

With a standard variable costing system, fixed overheads are not allocated to products. Sales margin variances are therefore reported in terms of contribution margins and a single fixed overhead variance, that is, the fixed overhead expenditure variance is reported. With a standard absorption costing system, fixed overheads are allocated to products and this process leads to the creation of a fixed overhead volume variance and the reporting of sales margin variances measured in terms of profit margins. The fixed overhead volume variance is not particularly helpful for cost control purposes, but this variance is required for financial accounting purposes.

Key terms and concepts

EXHIBIT 17.7 Summary of the formulae for the computation of the variances

The following variances are reported for both variable and absorption costing systems:

Materials and labour

1   Material price variance   = (standard price per unit of material – actual price) × quantity of materials purchased

2   Material usage variance   = (standard quantity of materials for actual production – actual quantity used) × standard price per unit

3   Total materials cost variance   = (actual production × standard material cost per unit of production) – actual materials cost

4   Wage rate variance   = (standard wage rate per hour – actual wage rate) × actual labour hours worked

5   Labour efficiency variance   = (standard quantity of labour hours for actual production – actual labour hours) × standard wage rate

6   Total labour cost variance   = (actual production × standard labour cost per unit of production) – actual labour cost

Fixed production overhead

7   Fixed overhead expenditure   = budgeted fixed overheads – actual fixed overheads

Variable production overhead

8   Variable overhead expenditure variance   = (budgeted variable overheads for actual input volume – actual variable overhead cost)

9   Variable overhead efficiency variance   = (standard quantity of input hours for actual production – actual input hours) × variable overhead rate

10 Total variable overhead variance   = (actual production × standard variable overhead rate per unit) – actual variable overhead cost

Sales margins

11 Sales margin price variance   = (actual unit contribution margin* – standard unit contribution margin) × actual sales volume

(*Contribution margins are used with a variable standard costing system whereas profit margins are used with an absorption costing system. With both systems, actual margins are calculated by deducting *standard* costs from actual selling price.)

12 Sales margin volume variance   = (actual sales volume – budgeted sales volume) × standard contribution margin

13 Total sales margin variance   = total actual contribution – total budgeted contribution

With a standard absorption costing system the following additional variances can be reported:

14 Fixed overhead volume variance   = (actual production – budgeted production) × standard fixed overhead rate

15 Volume efficiency variance   = (standard quantity of input hours for actual production – actual input hours) × standard fixed overhead rate

16 Volume capacity variance   = (actual hours of input – budgeted hours of input) × standard fixed overhead rate

17 Total fixed overhead variance   = (actual production × standard fixed overhead rate per unit) – actual fixed overhead cost

Key examination points

A common error that students make is to calculate variances based on the original fixed budget. Remember to flex the budget. Therefore the starting point when answering a standard costing question should be to calculate actual production. If more than one product is produced, output should be expressed in standard hours. If standard overhead rates are not given, you can calculate the rates by dividing budgeted fixed and variable overheads by the budgeted output. Remember that output can be measured by units produced or standard hours produced. Make sure you are consistent and use overhead rates per standard hours if production is measured in standard hours, or overhead rates per unit produced if output is measured in terms of units produced. You should always express output in standard hours if the question requires the calculation of overhead efficiency variances. If the question does not specify whether you should calculate the variances on an absorption costing or variable costing basis, choose your preferred method and state the approach you have selected in your answer.

Frequently questions are set that give you the variances but require calculations of actual costs and inputs (see Review problem 17.19). Students who calculate variances simply by committing to memory a series of variance formulae experience difficulties in answering these questions. Make sure you understand how the variances are calculated, and check your answers with the solutions to the Review problems.

ASSESSMENT MATERIAL

The review questions are short questions that enable you to assess your understanding of the main topics included in the chapter. The numbers in parentheses provide you with the page numbers to refer to if you cannot answer a specific question.

The review problems are more complex and require you to relate and apply the content to various business problems. The problems are graded by their level of difficulty. Solutions to review problems that are not preceded by the term 'IM' are provided in a separate section at the end of the book. Solutions to problems preceded by the term 'IM' are provided in the *Instructor's Manual* accompanying this book and also on the lecturer's password protected section of the website www.drury-online.com. Additional review problems with fully worked solutions are provided in the *Student's Manual* that accompanies this book.

The website also includes over 30 case study problems. A list of these cases is provided on pages 665–7. Several cases are relevant to the content of this chapter. Examples include Anjo Ltd., Boston Creamery and the Berkshire Toy Company.

Review questions

17.1 Describe the difference between budgeted and standard costs. *(p. 418)*

17.2 Explain how a standard costing system operates. *(pp. 418–20)*

17.3 Describe how standard costs are established using engineering studies. *(pp. 420–21)*

17.4 What are standard hours produced? What purpose do they serve? *(pp. 421–22)*

17.5 What are basic, ideal and currently attainable standards? Which type of standards are usually adopted? Why? *(p. 423)*

17.6 Describe the different purposes of a standard costing system. *(pp. 423–25)*

17.7 What are the possible causes of (a) material price and (b) material usage variances? *(pp. 428, 429)*

17.8 Explain why it is preferable for the material price variance to be computed at the point of purchase rather than the point of issue. *(p. 428)*

17.9 What are the possible causes of (a) wage rate and (b) labour efficiency variances? *(pp. 430–31)*

17.10 Explain how variable overhead efficiency and expenditure variances are computed. What are the possible causes of each of these variances? *(pp. 432–33)*

17.11 Why are sales variances based on contribution margins rather than sales revenues? *(pp. 434–35)*

17.12 Distinguish between a standard absorption and a standard variable costing system. *(p. 437)*

17.13 What additional variance arises with a standard absorption costing system? Why? *(pp. 437–38)*

17.14 How do sales variances differ between a standard absorption and marginal costing system? *(p. 440)*

17.15 Explain what is meant by a volume variance. Does the volume variance provide any meaningful information for cost control? *(pp. 437–38)*

Review problems

17.16 Basic. Q plc uses standard costing. The details for April were as follows:

Budgeted output	15 000	units
Budgeted labour hours	60 000	hours
Budgeted labour cost	£540 000	
Actual output	14 650	units
Actual labour hours paid	61 500	hours
Productive labour hours	56 000	hours
Actual labour cost	£522 750	

Calculate the ideal time and labour efficiency variances for April

(4 marks)

CIMA P1 Management Accounting: Performance Evaluation

17.17 Basic. A company uses standard absorption costing. The following information was recorded by the company for October:

	Budget	Actual
Output and sales (units)	8 700	8 200
Selling price per unit	£26	£31
Variable cost per unit	£10	£10
Total fixed overheads	£34 800	£37 000

a The sales price variance for October was:
   (i) £38 500 Fav.
   (ii) £41 000 Fav.
   (iii) £41 000 Adverse
   (iv) £65 600 Adverse

b The sales volume profit variance for October was:
   (i) £6 000 Adverse
   (ii) £6 000 Fav.
   (iii) £8 000 Adverse
   (iv) £8 000 Fav.

c The fixed overhead volume variance for October was:
   (i) £2 000 Adverse
   (ii) £2 200 Adverse
   (iii) £2 200 Fav.
   (iv) £4 200 Adverse

CIMA P1 Management Accounting: Performance Evaluation

17.18 Intermediate: Variance analysis and reconciliation of actual and budgeted profit. BS Limited manufactures one standard product and operates a system of variance accounting using a fixed budget. As assistant management accountant, you are responsible for preparing the monthly operating statements. Data from the budget, the standard product cost and actual data for the month ended 31 October are given below.

Using the data given, you are required to prepare the operating statement for the month ended 31 October to show the budgeted profit; the variances for direct materials, direct wages, overhead and sales, each analyzed into causes; and actual profit.

Budgeted and standard cost data:

Budgeted sales and production for the month: 10 000 units

Standard cost for each unit of product:
Direct material:	X:	10 kg at £1 per kg
	Y:	5 kg at £5 per kg
Direct wages:		5 hours at £3 per hour

Fixed production overhead is absorbed at 200 per cent of direct wages

Budgeted sales price has been calculated to give a profit of 20 per cent of sales price

Actual data for month ended 31 October:

Production: 9500 units sold at a price of 10 per cent higher than that budgeted
Direct materials consumed:
X:　96 000 kg at £1.20 per kg
Y:　48 000 kg at £4.70 per kg
Direct wages incurred 46 000 hours at £3.20 per hour
Fixed production overhead incurred £290 000

(30 marks)
CIMA Cost Accounting 2

17.19 Intermediate: Calculation of actual quantities working backwards from variances. The following profit reconciliation statement summarizes the performance of one of SEWs products for March.

	(£)
Budgeted profit	4250
Sales volume variance	850A
Standard profit on actual sales	3400
Selling price variance	4000A
	(600)

Cost variances:	Adverse (£)	Favourable (£)
Direct material price		1000
Direct material usage	150	
Direct labour rate	200	
Direct labour efficiency	150	
Variable overhead expenditure	600	
Variable overhead efficiency	75	
Fixed overhead efficiency		2500
Fixed overhead volume		150
Actual profit	1175	3650
		2475F
		1875

The budget for the same period contained the following data:

Sales volume		1500 units
Sales revenue	£20 000	
Production volume		1500 units
Direct materials purchased		750 kg
Direct materials used		750 kg
Direct material cost	£4 500	
Direct labour hours		1125
Direct labour cost	£4 500	
Variable overhead cost	£2 250	
Fixed overhead cost	£4 500	

Additional information:

- Stocks of raw materials and finished goods are valued at standard cost.
- During the month the actual number of units produced was 1550.
- The actual sales revenue was £12 000.
- The direct materials purchased were 1000 kg.

Required:
a　Calculate
　(i)　the actual sales volume;
　(ii)　the actual quantity of materials used;
　(iii)　the actual direct material cost;
　(iv)　the actual direct labour hours;
　(v)　the actual direct labour cost;
　(vi)　the actual variable overhead cost;
　(vii)　the actual fixed overhead cost.　(19 marks)
b　Explain the possible causes of the direct materials usage variance, direct labour rate variance and sales volume variance.　(6 marks)
CIMA Operational Cost Accounting Stage 2

17.20 Advanced: Performance reporting and variable costing variance analysis. Woodeezer Ltd makes quality wooden benches for both indoor and outdoor use. Results have been disappointing in recent years and a new managing director, Peter Beech, was appointed to raise production volumes. After an initial assessment Peter Beech considered that budgets had been set at levels which made it easy for employees to achieve. He argued that employees would be better motivated by setting budgets which challenged them more in terms of higher expected output.

Other than changing the overall budgeted output, Mr Beech has not yet altered any part of the standard cost card. Thus, the budgeted output and sales for November 2002 was 4,000 benches and the standard cost card below was calculated on this basis:

		£
Wood	25kg at £3.20 per kg	80.00
Labour	4 hours at £8 per hour	32.00
Variable overheads	4 hours at £4 per hour	16.00
Fixed overhead	4 hours at £16 per hour	64.00
		192.00
Selling price		220.00
Standard profit		28.00

Overheads are absorbed on the basis of labour hours and the company uses an absorption costing system. There were no stocks at the beginning of November 2002. Stocks are valued at standard cost.

Actual results for November 2002 were as follows:

		£
Wood	80 000 kg at £3.50	280 000
Labour	16 000 hours at £7	112 000
Variable overhead		60 000
Fixed overhead		196 000
Total production cost (3600 benches)		648 000
Closing stock (400 benches at £192)		76 800
Cost of sales		571 200
Sales (3200 benches)		720 000
Actual profit		148 800

The average monthly production and sales for some years prior to November 2002 had been 3,400 units and budgets had previously been set at this level. Very few operating variances had historically been generated by the standard costs used.

Mr Beech has made some significant changes to the operations of the company. However, the other directors are now concerned that Mr Beech has been too ambitious in raising production targets. Mr Beech had also changed suppliers of raw materials to improve quality, increased selling prices, begun to introduce less skilled labour, and significantly reduced fixed overheads.

The finance director suggested that an absorption costing system is misleading and that a marginal costing system should be considered at some stage in the future to guide decision-making.

Required:
a　Prepare an operating statement for November 2002. This should show all operating variances and should reconcile budgeted and actual profit for the month for Woodeezer Ltd.　(14 marks)
b　In so far as the information permits, examine the impact of the operational changes made by Mr Beech on the profitability of the company. In your answer, consider each of the following:
　(i)　motivation and budget setting; and
　(ii)　possible causes of variances.　(6 marks)
c　Re-assess the impact of your comments in part (b), using a marginal costing approach to evaluating the impact of the operational changes made by Mr Beech.

Show any relevant calculations to support your arguments.

(5 marks)
ACCA 2.4 Financial Management and Control

17.21 Advanced: Comparison of variable and absorption standard costing. Chimera Ltd makes chimes, one of a variety of products. These products pass through several production processes.

The first process is moulding and the standard costs for moulding chimes are as follows:

	Standard costs per unit	(£)
Direct material X	7 kg at £7.00 per kg	49.00
Direct labour	5 hours at £5 per hour	25.00
Overhead (fixed and variable)	5 hours at £6.60 per hour	33.00
		107.00

The overhead allocation rate is based on direct labour hours and comprises an allowance for both fixed and variable overhead costs. With the aid of regression analysis the fixed element of overhead costs has been estimated at £9000 per week, and the variable element of overhead costs has been estimated at £0.60 per direct labour hour. The accounting records do not separate actual overhead costs between their fixed and variable elements.

The moulding department occupies its own premises, and all of the department's overhead costs can be regarded as being the responsibility of the departmental manager.

In week 27 the department moulded 294 chimes, and actual costs incurred were:

Direct material X (2030 kg used)	£14 125
Direct labour (1520 hours worked)	£7 854
Overhead expenditure	£10 200

The 1520 hours worked by direct labour included 40 hours overtime, which is paid at 50 per cent above normal pay rates.

Requirements:

a Prepare a report for the moulding department manager on the results of the moulding department for week 27, presenting information in a way which you consider to be most useful.
(9 marks)

b Discuss the treatment of overheads adopted in your report and describe an alternative treatment, contrasting its use with the method adopted in your report. *(6 marks)*

c Describe the approaches used for determining standards for direct costs and assess their main strengths and weaknesses.
(10 marks)
ICAEW P2 Management Accounting

17.22 Intermediate. A major information source within many businesses is a system of standard costing and variance analysis.

Required:

a Describe briefly four purposes of a system of standard costing.
(4 marks)

b Explain three different levels of performance which may be incorporated into a system of standard costing and comment on how these may relate to the purposes set out in (a) above.
(6 marks)

c Comment on whether standard costing applies in both manufacturing and service businesses and how it may be affected by modern initiatives of continuous performance improvement and cost reduction. *(4 marks)*

d A standard costing system enables variances for direct costs, variable and fixed overheads to be extracted. Identify and briefly discuss some of the complexities and practical problems in calculation which may limit the usefulness of those variances.
(6 marks)
ACCA Paper 8 – Managerial Finance

IM17.1 Intermediate: Flexible budgets and computation of labour and material variances.

a JB plc operates a standard marginal cost accounting system. Information relating to product J, which is made in one of the company departments, is given below:

Product J	Standard marginal product cost Unit (£)
Direct material	
6 kilograms at £4 per kg	24
Direct labour	
1 hour at £7 per hour	7
Variable production overhead[a]	3
	34

[a] Variable production overhead varies with units produced

Budgeted fixed production overhead, per month: £100 000.
Budgeted production for product J: 20 000 units per month.
Actual production and costs for *month* 6 were as follows:

Units of J produced	18 500 (£)
Direct materials purchased and used: 113 500kg	442 650
Direct labour: 17 800 hours	129 940
Variable production overhead incurred	58 800
Fixed production overhead incurred	104 000
	735 390

You are required to:

(i) prepare a columnar statement showing, by element of cost, the:
  (i) original budget;
  (ii) flexed budget;
  (iii) actual;
  (iv) total variances; *(9 marks)*
(ii) subdivide the variances for direct material and direct labour shown in your answer to (a) (i)–(iv) above to be more informative for managerial purposes. *(4 marks)*

b Explain the meaning and use of a 'rolling forecast'. *(2 marks)*
CIMA State 2 Cost Accounting

IM17.2 Intermediate: Reconciliation of standard and actual cost for a variable costing system.

Data

You are employed as the assistant management accountant in the group accountant's office of Hampstead plc. Hampstead recently acquired Finchley Ltd, a small company making a specialist product called the Alpha. Standard marginal costing is used by all the companies within the group and, from 1 August, Finchley Ltd will also be required to use standard marginal costing in its management reports. Part of your job is to manage the implementation of standard marginal costing at Finchley Ltd.

John Wade, the managing director of Finchley, is not clear how the change will help him as a manager. He has always found Finchley's existing absorption costing system sufficient. By way of example, he shows you a summary of its management accounts for the three months to 31 May. These are reproduced below.

Statement of budgeted and actual cost of Alpha Production –
3 months ended 31 May

Alpha production (units)	Actual			Budget		Variance
	10 000			12 000		
	Inputs	(£)	Inputs	(£)		(£)
Materials	32 000 metres	377 600	36 000 metres	432 000		54 400
Labour	70 000 hours	422 800	72 000 hours	450 000		27 200
Fixed overhead absorbed		330 000		396 000		66 000
Fixed overhead unabsorbed		75 000		0		(75 000)
		1 205 400		1 278 000		72 600

John Wade is not convinced that standard marginal costing will help him to manage Finchley. 'My current system tells me all I need to know,' he said. 'As you can see, we are £72 600 below budget which is really excellent given that we lost production as a result of a serious machine breakdown.'

To help John Wade understand the benefits of standard marginal costing, you agree to prepare a statement for the three months ended 31 May reconciling the standard cost of production to the actual cost of production.

Task 1

a Use the budget data to determine:
(i) the standard marginal cost per Alpha; and
(ii) the standard cost of actual Alpha production for the three months to 31 May.

b Calculate the following variances:
(i) material price variance;
(ii) material usage variance;
(iii) labour rate variance;
(iv) labour efficiency variance;
(v) fixed overhead expenditure variance.

c Write a *short* memo to John Wade. Your memo should:
(i) include a statement reconciling the actual cost of production to the standard cost of production;
(ii) give *two* reasons why your variances might differ from those in his original management accounting statement despite using the same basic data;
(iii) *briefly* discuss *one* further reason why your reconciliation statement provides improved management information.

Data

On receiving your memo, John Wade informs you that:

- the machine breakdown resulted in the workforce having to be paid for 12 000 hours even though no production took place;
- an index of material prices stood at 466.70 when the budget was prepared but at 420.03 when the material was purchased.

Task 2

Using this new information, prepare a revised statement reconciling the standard cost of production to the actual cost of production. Your statement should subdivide:

- both the labour variances into those parts arising from the machine breakdown and those parts arising from normal production; and
- the material price variance into that part due to the change in the index and that part arising for other reasons.

Data

Barnet Ltd is another small company owned by Hampstead plc. Barnet operates a job costing system making a specialist, expensive piece of hospital equipment.

Existing system

Currently, employees are assigned to individual jobs and materials are requisitioned from stores as needed. The standard and actual costs of labour and material are recorded for each job. These job costs are totalled to produce the marginal cost of production. Fixed production costs – including the cost of storekeeping and inspection of deliveries and finished equipment – are then added to determine the standard and actual cost of production. Any costs of remedial work are included in the materials and labour for each job.

Proposed system

Carol Johnson, the chief executive of Barnet, has recently been to a seminar on modern manufacturing techniques. As a result, she is considering introducing Just-in-Time stock deliveries and Total Quality Management. Barnet would offer suppliers a long-term contract at a fixed price but suppliers would have to guarantee the quality of their materials.

In addition, she proposes that the workforce is organized as a single team with flexible work practices. This would mean employees helping each other as necessary, with no employee being allocated a particular job. If a job was delayed, the workforce would work overtime without payment in order for the job to be completed on time. In exchange, employees would be guaranteed a fixed weekly wage and time off when production was slack to make up for any overtime incurred.

Cost of quality

Carol has asked to meet you to discuss the implications of her proposals on the existing accounting system. She is particularly concerned to monitor the *cost of quality*. This is defined as the total of all costs incurred in preventing defects plus those costs involved in remedying defects once they have occurred. It is a single figure measuring all the explicit costs of quality that is, those costs collected within the accounting system.

Task 3

In preparation for the meeting, produce *brief* notes. Your notes should:

- a identify *four* general headings (or classifications) which make up the *cost of quality*;
- b give one example of a type of cost likely to be found within each category;
- c assuming Carol Johnson's proposals are accepted, state, with reasons, whether or not:
  - (i) a standard marginal costing system would still be of help to the managers;
  - (ii) it would still be meaningful to collect costs by each individual job;
- d identify *one* cost saving in Carol Johnson's proposals which would not be recorded in the existing costing system.

AAT Technicians Stage

IM17.3 Intermediate: Calculation of labour, material and overhead variances and reconciliation of budgeted and actual profit. You are the management accountant of T plc. The following computer printout shows details relating to April:

	Actual	Budget
Sales volume	4900 units	5000 units
Selling price per unit	£11.00	£10.00
Production volume	5400 units	5000 units
Direct materials		
kgs	10 600	10 000
price per kg	£0.60	£0.50
Direct labour		
hours per unit	0.55	0.50
rate per hour	£3.80	£4.00
Fixed overhead:		
Production	£10 300	£10 000
Administration	£3 100	£3 000

T plc uses a standard absorption costing system.

There was no opening or closing work-in-progress.

Requirements:

a Prepare a statement which reconciles the budgeted profit with the actual profit for April, showing individual variances in as much detail as the above data permit

(20 marks)

b Explain briefly the possible causes of
  (i) the material usage variance;
  (ii) the labour rate variance; and
  (iii) the sales volume profit variance.

(6 marks)

c Explain the meaning and relevance of interdependence of variances when reporting to managers.

(4 marks)

CIMA Stage 2 Operational Cost Accounting

IM17.4 Intermediate: Computation of fixed overhead variances. A manufacturing company has provided you with the following data, which relate to component RYX for the period which has just ended:

	Budget	Actual
Number of labour hours	8 400	7 980
Production units	1 200	1 100
Overhead cost (all fixed)	£22 260	£25 536

Overheads are absorbed at a rate per standard labour hour.

Required:

a (i) Calculate the fixed production overhead cost variance and the following subsidiary variances:
  expenditure
  efficiency
  capacity
  (ii) Provide a summary statement of these four variances.

(7 marks)

b Briefly discuss the possible reasons why adverse fixed production overhead expenditure, efficiency and capacity variances occur.

(10 marks)

c Briefly discuss two examples of interrelationships between the fixed production overhead efficiency variances and the material and labour variances.

(3 marks)

ACCA Paper 8 Managerial Finance

IM17.5 Intermediate: Labour and overhead variances and ex-post wage rate analysis.

Data

The Eastern Division of Countryside Communications plc assembles a single product, the Beta. The Eastern Division has a fixed price contract with the supplier of the materials used in the Beta. The contract also specifies that the materials should be free of any faults. Because of these clauses in the contract, the Eastern Division has no material variances when reporting any differences between standard and actual production.

You have recently accepted the position of assistant management accountant in the Eastern Division. One of your tasks is to report variances in production costs on a four-weekly basis. Fixed overheads are absorbed on the basis of standard labour hours. A colleague provides you with the following data:

Standard costs and budgeted production – four weeks ended 27 November

	Quantity	Unit price	Standard cost per Beta
Material	30 metres	£12.00	£360.00
Labour	10 hours	£5.25	£52.50
Fixed overhead	10 hours	£15.25	£157.50
Standard cost per Beta			£570.00
Budgeted production	1200 Betas	£570.00	£684 000

Actual production – four weeks ended 27 November

	Quantity	Total cost
Actual cost of material	31 200 metres	£374 400
Actual cost of labour	11 440 hours	£59 488
Actual fixed cost overheads		£207 000
Actual cost of actual production		£640 888
Actual production	1040 Betas	

Task 1

a Calculate the following variances:
  (i) the labour rate variance;
  (ii) the labour efficiency variance (sometimes called the utilisation variance);
  (iii) the fixed overhead expenditure variance (sometimes known as the price variance);
  (iv) the fixed overhead volume variance;
  (v) the fixed overhead capacity variance;
  (vi) the fixed overhead efficiency variance (sometimes known as the usage variance).

b Prepare a statement reconciling the standard cost of actual production with the actual cost of actual production.

Data

When the Eastern Division's budget for the four weeks ended 27 November was originally prepared, a national index of labour rates stood at 102.00. In preparing the budget, Eastern Division had allowed for a 5 per cent increase in labour rates. For the actual four weeks ended 27 November, the index stood at 104.04.

Because of this, Ann Green, Eastern Division's production director, is having difficulty understanding the meaning of the labour rate variance calculated in task 1.

Task 2

Write a memo to Ann Green. Your memo should:

a identify the original labour rate before allowing for the 5 per cent increase;

b calculate the revised standard hourly rate using the index of 104.04;

c subdivide the labour rate variance calculated in task 1(a) into that part due to the change in the index and that part arising for other reasons;

d *briefly* interpret the possible meaning of these two subdivisions of the labour rate variance;

e give *two* reasons why the index of labour rates might not be valid in explaining part of the labour rate variance;

f *briefly* explain the meaning of the following variances calculated in task 1 and for *each* variance suggest one reason why it may have occurred;
  (i) the fixed overhead expenditure (or price) variance;
  (ii) the fixed overhead capacity variance;
  (iii) the fixed overhead efficiency (or usage) variance.

AAT Technicians Stage

IM17.6 Calculation of actual input data working back from variances. The following profit reconciliation statement has been prepared by the management accountant of ABC Limited for March:

	(£)
Budgeted profit	30 000
Sales volume profit variance	5 250A
Selling price variance	6 375F
	31 125

Cost variances:

	A (£)	F (£)
Material:		
price	1 985	
usage		400
Labour:		
rate		9 800
efficiency	4 000	
Variable overhead:		
expenditure		1 000
efficiency	1 500	
Fixed overhead:		
expenditure		500
volume	24 500	
	31 985	11 700
		20 285A
Actual profit		10 840

The standard cost card for the company's only product is as follows:

		(£)
Materials	5 litres at £0.20	1.00
Labour	4 hours at £4.00	16.00
Variable overhead	4 hours at £1.50	6.00
Fixed overhead	4 hours at £3.50	14.00
		37.00
Standard profit		3.00
Standard selling price		40.00

The following information is also available:
1. There was no change in the level of finished goods stock during the month.
2. Budgeted production and sales volumes for March were equal.
3. Stocks of materials, which are valued at standard price, decreased by 800 litres during the month.
4. The actual labour rate was £0.28 lower than the standard hourly rate.

Required:
a Calculate the following:
  (i) the actual production/sales volume; (4 marks)
  (ii) the actual number of hours worked; (4 marks)
  (iii) the actual quantity of materials purchased; (4 marks)
  (iv) the actual variable overhead cost incurred; (2 marks)
  (v) the actual fixed overhead cost incurred. (2 marks)

b ABC Limited uses a standard costing system whereas other organizations use a system of budgetary control. Explain the reasons why a system of budgetary control is often preferred to the use of standard costing in non-manufacturing environments.
(9 marks)

CIMA Stage 2 Operational Cost Accounting

IM17.7 Intermediate: Calculation of inputs working backwards from variances. The following data have been collected for the month of April by a company which operates a standard absorption costing system:

Actual production of product EM	600 units
Actual costs incurred:	(£)
Direct material E 660 metres	6 270
Direct material M 200 metres	650
Direct wages 3200 hours	23 200
Variable production overhead (which varied with hours worked)	6 720
Fixed production overhead	27 000
Variances	(£)
Direct material price:	
Material E	330 F
Material M	50 A
Direct material usage:	
Material E	600 A
Material M	nil
Direct labour rate	800 A
Direct labour efficiency	1400 A
Variable production overhead:	
expenditure	320 A
efficiency	400 A
Fixed production overhead:	
expenditure	500 F
volume	2500 F

Opening and closing work in progress figures were identical, so can be ignored.

You are required to:

a prepare for the month of April a statement of total standard costs for product EM; *(3 marks)*

b prepare a standard product cost sheet for one unit of product EM; *(7 marks)*

c calculate the number of units of product EM which were budgeted for April; *(2 marks)*

d state how the material and labour cost standards for product EM would originally have been determined. *(3 marks)*

CIMA Stage 2 Cost Accounting

IM17.8 Advanced: Variance calculations and reconciliation of budgeted and actual profit. Bamfram plc is a well established manufacturer of a specialized product, a Wallop, which has the following specifications for production:

Components	Standard quantity	Standard price (£)
WALS	15	60
LOPS	8	75

The standard direct labour hours to produce a Wallop at the standard wage rate of £10.50 per hour has been established at 60 hours per Wallop.

The annual fixed overhead budget is divided into calendar months with equal production per month. The budgeted annual fixed overheads are £504 000 for the budgeted output of 2400 Wallops per annum.

Mr Jones, a marketing person, is now the managing director of Bamfram plc and must report to the board of directors later this day and he seeks your advice in respect of the following operating information for the month of May:

	(£)	(£)
Sales		504 000
Cost of sales:		
Direct materials	281 520	
Direct labour	112 329	
	393 840	
Fixed production overheads	42 600	436 440
Gross profit		67 560
Administration expenses		11 150
Selling and distribution expenses		17 290
Net profit		39 120

The sales manager informs Mr Jones that despite adverse trading conditions his sales staff have been able to sell 180 Wallops at the expected standard selling price.

The production manager along with the purchasing department manager are also pleased that prices for components have been stable for the whole of the current year and they are able to provide the following information:

Stocks for May are as follows:

	1 May	31 May
Component WALS	600	750
Component LOPS	920	450

The actual number of direct labour hours worked in May was 11 700, considerably less than the production manager had budgeted. Further, the purchasing manager advised that WALS had cost £171 000 at a price of £57 per unit in the month of May and 1000 LOPS had been acquired for £81 000.

Mr Jones, eager to please the board of directors, requests you, as the newly appointed management accountant, to prepare appropriate statements to highlight the following information which is to be presented to the board:

a The standard product cost of a Wallop. *(3 marks)*

b (i) The direct material variances for both price and usage for each component used in the month of May assuming that prices were stable throughout the relevant period.

   (ii) The direct labour efficiency and wage rate variances for the month of May.

   (iii) The fixed production overhead expenditure and volume variances.

   Note: You may assume that during the month of May there is no change in the level of finished goods stocks. *(10 marks)*

c A detailed reconciliation statement of the standard gross profit with the actual gross profit for the month of May. *(4 marks)*

d Draft a brief report for Mr Jones that he could present to the board of directors on the usefulness, or otherwise, of the statement you have prepared in your answer to (c) above. *(5 marks)*

ACCA Level 2 Management Accounting

IM17.9 Advanced: Computation of variances and the reconciliation of budgeted and actual profits for a taxi firm. Tardy Taxis operates a fleet of taxis in a provincial town. In planning its operations for November it estimated that it would carry fare-paying passengers for 40 000 miles at an average price of £1 per mile. However, past experience suggested that the total miles run would amount to 250 per cent of the fare-paid miles. At the beginning of November it employed ten drivers and decided that this number would be adequate for the month ahead.

The following cost estimates were available:

Employment costs of a driver	£1000 per month
Fuel costs	£0.08 per mile run
Variable overhead costs	£0.05 per mile run
Fixed overhead costs	£9000 per month

In November revenue of £36 100 was generated by carrying passengers for 38 000 miles. The total actual mileage was 105 000 miles. Other costs amounted to:

Employment costs of drivers	£9600
Fuel costs	£8820
Variable overhead costs	£5040
Fixed overhead costs	£9300

The saving in the cost of drivers was due to one driver leaving during the month; she was not replaced until early December.

Requirements:

a Prepare a budgeted and actual profit and loss account for November, indicating the total profit variance. *(6 marks)*

b Using a flexible budget approach, construct a set of detailed variances to explain the total profit variance as effectively as possible. Present your analysis in a report to the owner of Tardy Taxis including suggested reasons for the variances. *(14 marks)*

c Outline any further variances you think would improve your explanation, indicating the additional information you would require to produce these. *(5 marks)*

ICAEW P2 Management Accounting

Standard costing and variance analysis 2: further aspects

18

In the previous chapter the principles of a standard costing system and variance analysis were explained. In this chapter we are going to consider further aspects of standard costing. First we shall look at the accounting entries that are necessary to record the variances. Next we shall look at how the material usage variance and sales margin variances can further analyzed. We shall then turn our attention to how variance analysis can be adapted to reflect changes in the environment and the factors that should be taken into account in deciding whether it is worthwhile investigating variances. Finally, we shall consider how standard costing variance analysis can be modified when an ABC system has been implemented.

It is possible the many, or all of the above topics, do not form part of your course curriculum. The accounting entries for recording the variances and the further analysis of the material usage and sales margin variances tend to be only covered on specialist accounting courses. Therefore if you are pursuing a non-specialist accounting course it is likely that you can omit reading those sections of the chapter relating to these topics. The remaining topics tend to be appropriate for both specialist and non-specialist courses but they tend to be covered only on second level courses. It is therefore very important that you refer to your course curriculum to determine which sections within this chapter you should read.

LEARNING OBJECTIVES

After studying this chapter, you should be able to:

- **prepare a set of accounts for a standard costing system;**

- **explain and calculate material mix and yield and sales mix and quantity variances;**

- **explain and calculate planning and operating variances;**

- **explain the factors that influence the decision to investigate a variance and describe the different methods that can be used to determine whether an investigation is warranted;**

- **explain the role of standard costing within an ABC system.**

Recording standard costs in the accounts

If you are not studying for a specialist accounting qualification it is possible that your curriculum may not include the recording of standard costs. You should therefore check whether or not this topic is included in your curriculum to ascertain if you need to read this section. Standard costs can be used for planning, control and decision-making purposes without being entered into the books. However, the incorporation of standard costs into the cost accounting system greatly simplifies the task of tracing costs for inventory valuation and saves a considerable amount of data processing time. For example, if raw material stocks are valued at standard cost, the stock records may be maintained in terms of physical quantities only. The value of raw materials stock may be obtained simply by multiplying the physical quantity of raw materials in stock by the standard cost per unit. This avoids the need to record stocks on a first-in, first-out or average cost basis. The financial accounting regulations in most countries specify that inventory valuations based on standard costs may be included in externally published financial statements, provided the standard costs used are current and attainable. Most companies that have established standard costs therefore incorporate them into their cost accounting recording system.

Variations exist in the data accumulation methods adopted for recording standard costs, but these variations are merely procedural and the actual inventory valuations and profit calculations will be the same whichever method is adopted. In this chapter we shall illustrate a standard absorption costing system that values all inventories at standard cost, and all entries that are recorded in the inventory accounts will therefore be at *standard prices*. Any differences between standard costs and actual costs are debited or credited to variance accounts. Adverse variances will appear as debit balances, since they are additional costs in excess of standard. Conversely, favourable variances will appear as credit balances. Only production variances are recorded, and sales variances are not entered in the accounts.

Let us now consider the cost accounting records, for Example 17.1 (p. 426), which was presented in the previous chapter. The variances recorded in the accounts are those for an absorption costing system, presented in Exhibit 17.6 (p. 441). The appropriate ledger entries are presented in Exhibit 18.1. Each ledger entry and journal entry has been labelled with numbers from 1 to 13 to try to give you a clear understanding of each accounting entry. You will need to refer back to Example 17.1 and Exhibit 17.6 in order to understand the explanation of the accounting procedures.

Purchase of materials

19 000 kg of raw material A at £11 per kg and 10 100 kg of raw material B at £14 per kg were purchased. This gives a total purchase cost of £209 000 for A and £141 400 for B. The standard prices were £10 per kg for A and £5 per kg for B. The accounting entries for material A are:

1. Dr Stores ledger control account (AQ × SP)	190 000	
1. Dr Material price variance account	19 000	
1. Cr Creditors control account (AQ × AP)		209 000

You will see that the stores ledger control account shown in Exhibit 18.1 is debited with the standard price (SP) for the actual quantity purchased (AQ), and the actual price (AP) to be paid is credited to the creditors control account. The difference is the material price variance. The accounting entries for material B are:

2. Dr Stores ledger control account (AQ × SP)	151 500	
2. Cr Material price variance account		10 100
2. Cr Creditors (AQ × AP)		141 400

EXHIBIT 18.1 Accounting entries for a standard costing system

Stores ledger control account

1. Creditors (material A)	190 000	3. Work in progress (material A)	180 000
2. Creditors (material B)	151 500		
		3. Material usage variance (material A)	10 000
		4. Work in progress (material B)	135 000
		4. Material usage variance (material B)	16 500
	341 500		341 500

Creditors control account

2. Material price variance (material B)	10 100	1. Stores ledger control (material A)	190 000
		1. Material price variance (material A)	19 000
		2. Stores ledger control (material B)	151 500

Variance accounts

1. Creditors (material A)	19 000	2. Creditors (material price B)	10 100
3. Stores ledger control (material A usage)	10 000	8. Fixed factory overhead (expenditure)	4 000
4. Stores ledger control (material B usage)	16 500	9. Variable factory overhead (expenditure)	5 000
6. Wages control (wage rate)	17 100		19 100
6. Wages control (lab. effic'y)	13 500	13. Costing P + L a/c (balance)	72 000
8. Fixed factory overhead (volume)	12 000		
9. Variable factory overhead (effic'y)	3 000		
	91 100		91 100

Work in progress control account

3. Stores ledger (material A)	180 000	10. Finished goods stock account	720 000
4. Stores ledger (material B)	135 000		
6. Wages control	243 000		
8. Fixed factory overhead	108 000		
9. Variable factory overhead	54 000		
	720 000		720 000

Wages control account

5. Wages accrued account	273 600	6. WIP	243 000
		6. Wage rate variance	17 100
		6. Labour efficiency variance	13 500
	273 600		273 600

Fixed factory overhead control account

7. Expense creditors	116 000	8. WIP	108 000
8. Expenditure variance	4 000	8. Volume variance	12 000
	120 000		120 000

Variable factory overhead control account

7. Expense creditors	52 000	9. WIP	54 000
9. Expenditure	5 000	9. Efficiency variance	3 000
	57 000		57 000

Finished goods stock control account

10. WIP	720 000	12. Cost of sales	720 000

<table>
<tr><td colspan="4">Cost of sales account</td></tr>
<tr><td>12. Finish goods stock</td><td><u>720 000</u></td><td>13. Costing P + L a/c</td><td><u>720 000</u></td></tr>
</table>

Cost of sales account			
12. Finish goods stock	<u>720 000</u>	13. Costing P + L a/c	<u>720 000</u>

Costing P + L Account			
12. Cost of sales at standard cost	720 000	11. Sales	810 000
13. Variance account (net variances)	72 000		
Profit for period	<u>18 000</u>		
	<u>810 000</u>		<u>810 000</u>

Usage of materials

19 000 kg of A and 10 100 kg of B were actually issued, and the standard usage (SQ) was 18 000 and 9000 kg at standard prices of £10 and £15. The accounting entries for material A are:

3. Dr Work in progress (SQ × SP)	180 000	
3. Dr Material usage variance	10 000	
3. Cr Stores ledger control account (AQ × SP)		190 000

Work in progress is debited with the standard quantity of materials at the standard price and the stores ledger account is credited with the actual quantity issued at the standard price. The difference is the material usage variance. The accounting entries for material B are:

4. Dr Work in progress (SQ × SP)	135 000	
4. Dr Material usage variance	16 500	
4. Cr Stores ledger control account (AQ × SP)		151 500

Direct wages

The actual hours worked were 28 500 hours for the month. The standard hours produced were 27 000. The actual wage rate paid was £9.60 per hour, compared with a standard rate of £9 per hour. The actual wages cost is recorded in the same way in a standard costing system as an actual costing system. The accounting entry for the actual wages paid is:

5. Dr Wages control account	273 600	
5. Cr Wages accrued account		273 600

The wages control account is then cleared as follows:

6. Dr Work in progress (SQ × SP)	243 000	
6. Cr Wages control account		243 000
6. Dr Wage rate variance	17 100	
6. Dr Labour efficiency variance	13 500	
6. Cr Wages control account		30 600

The wages control account is credited and the work in progress account is debited with the standard cost (i.e. standard hours produced times the standard wage rate). The wage rate and labour efficiency variance accounts are debited, since they are both adverse variances and account for the difference between the actual wages cost (recorded as a debit in the wages control account) and the standard wages cost (recorded as a credit in the wages control account).

Manufacturing overhead costs incurred

The actual manufacturing overhead incurred is £52 000 for variable overheads and £116 000 for fixed overheads. The accounting entries for actual overhead *incurred* are recorded in the same way in a standard costing system as in an actual costing system. That is:

7. Dr Factory variable overhead control account	52 000	
7. Dr Factory fixed overhead control account	116 000	
7. Cr Expense creditors		168 000

Absorption of manufacturing overheads and recording the variances

Work in progress is debited with the standard manufacturing overhead cost for the output produced. The standard overhead rates were £4 per standard hour for fixed overhead and £2 per standard hour for variable overheads. The actual output was 27 000 standard hours. The standard fixed overhead cost is therefore £108 000 (27 000 standard hours at £4 per hour) and the variable overhead cost is £54 000. The accounting entries for fixed overheads are:

8. Dr Work in progress (SQ × SP)	108 000	
8. Dr Volume variance	12 000	
8. Cr Factory fixed overhead control account		120 000
8. Dr Factory fixed overhead control account	4 000	
8. Cr Fixed overhead expenditure variance		4 000

You will see that the debit of £108 000 to the work in progress account and the corresponding credit to the factory fixed overhead control account represents the standard fixed overhead cost of production. The difference between the debit entry of £116 000 in the factory fixed overhead control account in Exhibit 18.1 for the *actual* fixed overheads incurred, and the credit entry of £108 000 for the *standard* fixed overhead cost of production is the total fixed overhead variance, which consists of an adverse volume variance of £12 000 and a favourable expenditure variance of £4000. This is recorded as a debit to the volume variance account and a credit to the expenditure variance account. The accounting entries for variable overheads are:

9. Dr Work in progress account (SQ × SP)	54 000	
9. Dr Variable overhead efficiency variance	3 000	
9. Cr Factory variable overhead control account		57 000
9. Dr Factory variable overhead control account	5 000	
9. Cr Variable overhead expenditure variance account		5 000

The same principles apply with variable overheads. The debit to work in progress account and the corresponding credit to the factory variable overhead control account of £54 000 is the standard variable overhead cost of production. The difference between the debit entry of £52 000 in the factory variable overhead account in Exhibit 18.1 for the *actual* variable overheads incurred and the credit entry of £54 000 for the *standard* variable overhead cost of production is the total variable overhead variance, which consists of an adverse efficiency variance of £3000 and a favourable expenditure variance of £5000.

Completion of production

In Exhibit 18.1 the total amount recorded on the debit side of the work in progress account is £720 000. As there are no opening or closing stocks, this represents the total standard cost of production for the period, which consists of 9000 units at £80 per unit. When the completed production is transferred from work in progress to finished goods stock, the accounting entries will be as follows:

10. Dr Finished stock account	720 000	
10. Cr Work in progress account		720 000

Because there are no opening or closing stocks, both the work in progress account and the stores ledger account will show a nil balance.

Sales

Sales variances are not recorded in the accounts, so actual sales of £810 000 for 9000 units will be recorded as:

11. Dr Debtors	810 000	
11. Cr Sales		810 000

As all the production for the period has been sold, there will be no closing stock of finished goods, and the standard cost of production for the 9000 units will be transferred from the finished goods account to the cost of sales account:

12. Dr Cost of sales account	288 000	
12. Cr Finished goods account		288 000

Finally, the cost of sales account and the variance accounts will be closed by a transfer to the costing profit and loss account (the item labelled 13 in Exhibit 18.1). The balance of the costing profit and loss account will be the *actual* profit for the period.

Calculation of profit

To calculate the profit, we must add the adverse variances and deduct the favourable variances from the standard cost of sales, which is obtained from the cost of sales account. This calculation gives the actual cost of sales for the period, which is then deducted from the actual sales to produce the actual profit for the period. The calculations are as follows:

	(£)	(£)	(£)
Sales			810 000
Less standard cost of sales		720 000	
Plus adverse variances:			
Material A price variance	19 000		
Material usage variance	26 500		
Wage rate variance	17 100		
Labour efficiency variance	13 500		
Volume variance	12 000		
Variable overhead efficiency variance	3 000	91 100	
		811 100	
Less favourable variances:			
Material B price variance	10 100		
Fixed overhead expenditure variance	4 000		
Variable overhead expenditure variance	5 000	19 100	
Actual cost of sales			792 000
Actual profit			18 000

Direct materials mix and yield variances

ADVANCED READING

In many industries, particularly of the process type, it is possible to vary the mix of input materials and affect the yield. Where it is possible to combine two or more raw materials, input standards should be established to indicate the target mix of materials required to produce a unit, or a specified number of units, of output. Laboratory and engineering studies are necessary in order to determine the standard mix. The costs of the different material mixes are estimated, and a standard mix is determined based on the mix of materials that minimizes the cost per unit of output but still meets the quality requirements.

By deviating from the standard mix of input materials, operating managers can affect the yield and cost per unit of output. Such deviations can occur as a result of a conscious response to changes in material prices, or alternatively may arise from inefficiencies and a failure to adhere to the standard mix. By computing mix and yield variances, we can provide an indication of the cost of deviating from the standard mix.

Mix variance

The material mix variance arises when the mix of materials used differs from the predetermined mix included in the calculation of the standard cost of an operation. If the mixture is varied so that a larger than standard proportion of more expensive materials is used, there will be an unfavourable variance. When a larger proportion of cheaper materials is included in the mixture, there will be a favourable variance. Consider Example 18.1.

The total input for the period is 100 000 litres, and, using the standard mix, an input of 50 000 litres of X (5/10 × 100 000), 30 000 litres of Y (3/10 × 100 000) and 20 000 litres of Z (2/10 × 100 000) should have been used. However, 53 000 litres of X, 28 000 litres of Y and 19 000 litres of Z were used. Therefore 3000 additional litres of X at a standard price of £7 per litre were substituted for 2000 litres of Y (at a standard price of £5 per litre) and 1000 litres of Z (at a standard price of £2 per litre). An adverse material mix variance of £9000 will therefore be reported. The formula for the material mix variance is as follows:

(actual quantity in standard mix proportions – actual quantity used) × standard price

If we apply this formula, the calculation is as follows:

Actual usage in standard proportions:

		(£)
X = 50 000 litres (5/10 × 100 000) at	£7	350 000
Y = 30 000 litres (3/10 × 100 000) at	£5	150 000
Z = 20 000 litres (2/10 × 100 000) at	£2	40 000
		540 000

Actual usage in actual proportions:

	(£)
X = 53 000 litres at £7	371 000
Y = 28 000 litres at £5	140 000
Z = 19 000 litres at £2	38 000
	549 000
mix variance =	£9 000 A

Note that standard prices are used to calculate the mix variance to ensure that the price effects are removed from the calculation. An adverse mix variance will result from substituting more expensive higher quality materials for cheaper materials. Substituting more expensive materials may result in a boost in output and a favourable yield variance. On the other hand, a favourable mix variance will result from substituting cheaper materials for more expensive materials – but this may not always be in a company's best interests, since the quality of the product may suffer or output might be reduced. Generally, the use of a less expensive mix of inputs will mean the production of fewer units of output than standard. This may be because of excessive evaporation of the input units, an increase in rejects due to imperfections in the lower quality inputs, or other similar factors. To analyze the effect of changes in the quantity of outputs from a given mix of inputs, a yield variance can be calculated. It is important that the standard mix be continuously reviewed and adjusted where necessary, since price changes may lead to a revised standard mix.

Direct materials yield variance

The materials yield variance arises because there is a difference between the standard output for a given level of inputs and the actual output attained. In Example 18.1 an input of 100 000 litres should have given an output of 90 000 litres of product A. (Every 10 litres of input should produce 9 litres of output.) In fact, 92 700 litres were produced, which means that the output was 2700 litres greater than standard. This output is valued at the average standard cost per unit of output, which is calculated as follows:

Each 10 litres of *input* is expected to yield 9 litres of *output*.

The standard cost for this output is £54.

Therefore the standard cost for one litre of *output* = 54 × 1/9 = £6.

The yield variance will be £6 × 2700 = £16 200F. The formula is as follows:

$$\text{(actual yield – standard yield from actual input of material)}$$
$$\times \text{ standard cost per unit of output}$$
$$= \text{(92 700 litres – 90 000 litres)} \times £6 = £16\ 200\text{F}$$

An adverse yield variance may arise from a failure to follow standard procedures. For example, in the steel industry a yield variance may indicate that the practice that was followed for pouring

EXAMPLE 18.1

The Milano company has established the following standard mix for producing 9 litres of product A:

	(£)
5 litres of material X at £7 per litre	35
3 litres of material Y at £5 per litre	15
2 litres of material Z at £2 per litre	4
	£54

A standard loss of 10 per cent of input is expected to occur. Actual input was

	(£)
53 000 litres of material X at £7 per litre	371 000
28 000 litres of material Y at £5.30 per litre	148 400
19 000 litres of material Z at £2.20 per litre	41 800
100 000	£561 200

Actual output for the period was 92 700 litres of product A.

molten metal may have been different from that which was determined as being the most efficient when the standard yield was calculated. Alternatively, the use of inferior quality materials may result in an adverse yield variance.

The material mix variance in Example 18.1 is £9000 adverse, while the material yield variance is £16 200 favourable. There was a trade-off in the material mix, which boosted the yield. This trade-off may have arisen because the prices of materials Y and Z have increased whereas the actual price paid for material X is identical with the standard price. The manager of the production process may have responded to the different relative prices by substituting material X for materials Y and Z. This substitution process has resulted in an adverse mix variance and a favourable yield variance.

Material usage variance

The material usage variance consists of the mix variance and the yield variance. The material usage variance is therefore a favourable variance of £7200, consisting of an adverse mix variance of £9000 and a favourable yield variance of £16 200. To calculate the material usage variance, we compare the standard quantity of materials for the actual production with the actual quantity of materials used and multiply by the standard material prices in the normal way. The calculations are as follows:

Standard quality for actual production at standard prices:

Actual production of 92 700 litres requires an input of 103 000 litres
(92 700 × 10/9), consisting of

	(£)
51 500 litres of X (103 000 × 5/10) at £7 per litre	= 360 500
30 900 litres of Y (103 000 × 3/10) at £5 per litre	= 154 500
20 600 litres of Z (103 000 × 2/10) at £2 per litre	= 41 200
	556 200 (i)

Actual quantity at standard prices:

	(£)
53 000 litres of X at £7 per litre	= 371 000
28 000 litres of Y at £5 per litre	= 140 000
19 000 litres of Z at £2 per litre	= 38 000
	549 000 (ii)
Material usage variance (i) – (ii)	= £7 200 F

Note that the standard quantity for actual production at standard prices can also be calculated by multiplying the actual output by the standard cost per unit of output (92 700 × £6 = £556 200).

Sales mix and sales quantity variances

Where a company sells several different products that have different profit margins, the sales volume margin variance can be divided into a sales quantity (sometimes called a sales yield variance) and sales mix variance. This division is commonly advocated in textbooks. The quantity variance measures the effect of changes in physical volume on total profits, and the mix variance measures the impact arising from the actual sales mix being different from the budgeted sales mix. The variances can be measured either in terms of contribution margins or profit margins. However, contribution margins are recommended because changes in sales volume affect profits by the contribution per unit sold and not the profit per unit sold. Let us now calculate the sales margin mix and quantity variances. Consider Example 18.2.

The total sales margin variance is £4000 adverse, and is calculated by comparing the difference between the budgeted total contribution and the actual contribution. Contribution margins for the three products were exactly as budgeted. The total sales margin for the period therefore consists of a zero sales margin price variance and an adverse sales margin volume variance of £4000. Even though more units were sold than anticipated (22 000 rather than the budgeted 20 000), and budgeted and actual contribution margins were the same, the sales volume variance is £4000 adverse. The reasons for this arises from having sold fewer units of product X, the high margin product, and more units of product Z, which has the lowest margin.

We can explain how the sales volume margin variance was affected by the change in sales mix by calculating the sales margin mix variance. The formula for calculating this variance is:

$$\text{(actual sales quantity} - \text{actual sales quantity in budgeted proportions)} \times \text{standard margin}$$

If we apply this formula, we will obtain the following calculations:

	Actual sales quantity	Actual sales in budgeted proportions	Difference	Standard margin (£)	Sales margin mix variance (£)
Product X	6 000 (27%)	8 800 (40%) =	−2800	20	56 000A
Y	7 000 (32%)	7 700 (35%) =	−700	12	8 400A
Z	9 000 (41%)	5 500 (25%) =	+3500	9	31 500F
	22 000	22 000			32 900A

EXAMPLE 18.2

The budgeted sales for the Milano company for a period were:

	Units	Unit contribution margin (£)	Total contribution (£)
Product X	8 000 (40%)	20	160 000
Y	7 000 (35%)	12	84 000
Z	5 000 (25%)	9	45 000
	20 000		289 000

and the actual sales were:

	Units (£)	Unit contribution margin (£)	Total contribution
Product X	6 000	20	120 000
Y	7 000	12	84 000
Z	9 000	9	81 000
	22 000		285 000

Assumed that actual selling prices and unit costs are identical to standard costs/ prices.
You are required to calculate the sales margin variances.

To compute the sales quantity component of the sales volume variance, we compare the budgeted and actual sales volumes (holding the product mix constant). The formula for calculating the sales quantity variance is:

(actual sales quantity in budgeted proportion – budgeted sales quantity)
× standard margin

Applying this formula gives the following calculations:

	Actual sales in budgeted proportions	Budgeted sales quantity	Difference	Standard margin (£)	Sales margin quantity variance (£)
Product X	8 800 (40%)	8 000 (40%)	+800	20	16 000F
Y	7 700 (35%)	7 000 (35%)	+700	12	8 400F
Z	5 500 (25%)	5 000 (20%)	+500	9	4 500F
	22 000	20 000			28 900F

By separating the sales volume variance into quantity and mix variances, we can explain how the sales volume variance is affected by a shift in the total physical volume of sales and a shift in the relative mix of products. The sales volume quantity variance indicates that if the original planned sales mix of 40 per cent of X, 35 per cent of Y and 25 per cent of Z had been maintained then, for the actual sales volume of 22 000 units, profits would have increased by £28 900. In other words, the sales volume variance would have been £28 900 favourable instead of £4000 adverse. However, because the actual sales mix was not in accordance with the budgeted sales mix, an adverse mix variance of £32 900 occurred. The adverse sales mix variance has arisen because of an increase in the percentage of units sold of product Z, which has the lowest contribution margin, and a decrease in the percentage sold of units of product X, which has the highest contribution margin. An adverse mix variance will occur whenever there is an increase in the percentage sold of units with below average contribution margins or a decrease in the percentage sold of units with above average contribution margins. The division of the sales volume variance into quantity and mix components demonstrates that increasing or maximizing sales volume may not be as desirable as promoting the sales of the most desirable mix of products.

The sales quantity variance is sometimes further divided into a market size and a market share variance. For an explanation of these variances you should refer to Learning Note 18.1 on the dedicated open access website (see Preface for details).

Ex post variance analysis

ADVANCED READING

Standards or plans are normally based on the environment that is anticipated when the targets are set. However, Demski (1977) has argued that if the environment is different from that anticipated, actual performance should be compared with a standard which reflects these changed conditions (i.e. an *ex post* variance analysis approach). Clearly, to measure managerial performance, we should compare like with like and compare actual results with adjusted standards based on the conditions that managers actually operated during the period. Let us now apply this principle to the material price variance. Consider Example 18.3.

The conventional material price variance is £1800 adverse (10 000 units at £0.18). However, this variance consists of an adverse planning variance of £2000 that is due to incorrect estimates of the target buying price and a favourable purchasing efficiency (operational) variance of £200. The planning variance is calculated as follows:

purchasing planning variance

= (original target price − general market price at the time of purchase)
$\qquad$ × quantity purchased

= (£5 − £5.20) × 10 000

= £2000 A

This planning variance is not controllable, but it does provide useful feedback information to management on how successful they are in forecasting material prices, thus helping managers to improve their future estimates of material prices.

The efficiency of the purchasing department is assessed by a purchasing efficiency (operational) variance. This variance measures the purchasing department's efficiency for the conditions that actually prevailed and is calculated as follows:

purchasing efficiency variance

= (general market price − actual price paid) × quantity purchased

= (£5.20 − £5.18) × 10 000

= £200F

Hence the conventional price variance of £1800 adverse can be divided into an *uncontrollable* adverse material planning variance of £2000 and a *controllable* favourable purchasing efficiency variance of £200. This analysis gives a clearer indication of the efficiency of the purchasing function, and avoids including an adverse uncontrollable price variance in performance reports. If an adverse price variance of £1800 is reported, this is likely to lead to dysfunctional motivation effects if the purchasing department have performed the purchasing function efficiently.

In practice, standard prices are often set on an annual basis, with the target representing the average for the year. Price changes will occur throughout the year, and it is unlikely that the actual prices paid for the materials will be equal to the average for the year as a whole even if actual prices are equal to the prices used to set the average standard price. Consequently, with rising prices actual prices will be less than the average earlier in the year (showing favourable variances) and above average standard later in the year (showing adverse variances). This problem can be overcome by calculating separate purchasing planning and efficiency variances.

The same approach as that described above can also be applied to labour, overhead and sales variances. For example, the approach can be applied to usage variances with separate uncontrollable planning and operational usage variances being reported. For a more detailed discussion of *ex post* variance analysis you should refer to Learning Note 18.2 on the open access website. The solution to Review Problem 18.16 also provides a further illustration of *ex post* variance analysis.

EXAMPLE 18.3

The standard cost per unit of raw material was estimated to be £5 per unit. The general market price at the time of purchase was £5.20 per unit and the actual price paid was £5.18 per unit. 10 000 units of the raw materials were purchased during the period.

The investigation of variances

So far in this, and the previous chapter, we have concentrated on variance analysis and reporting. After the variances have been reported management must decide which variances should be investigated. They could adopt a policy of investigating every reported variance. Such a policy would, however, be very expensive and time-consuming, and would lead to investigating some variances that would not result in improvements in operations even if the cause of the variance was determined. If, on the other hand, management do not investigate reported variances, the control function would be ignored. The optimal policy lies somewhere between these two extremes. In other words, the objective is to investigate only those variances that yield benefits in excess of the cost of investigation.

There are several reasons why actual performance might differ from standard performance. A variance may arise simply as a result of an error in measuring the actual outcome. For example, the labour hours for a particular operation may be incorrectly added up or indirect labour costs might be incorrectly classified as a direct labour cost. Unless an investigation leads to an improvement in the accuracy of the recording system, it is unlikely that any benefits will be obtained where the cause is found to be due to measurement errors.

A second cause relates to where frequent changes in prices of inputs occur, resulting in standard prices becoming out of date. Consequently any investigation of price variances will indicate a general change in market prices rather than any efficiencies or inefficiencies in acquiring the resources. Standards can also become out of date where operations are subject to frequent technological changes or fail to take into account learning-curve effects. Investigation of variances falling into this category will provide feedback on the inaccuracy of the standards and highlight the need to update the standard. Where standards are revised, it may be necessary to alter some of the firm's output or input decisions. Ideally, standards ought to be frequently reviewed and, where appropriate, updated in order to minimize variances being reported that are due to standards being out of date.

Variances can also result from inefficient operations due to a failure to follow prescribed procedures, faulty machinery or human errors. Investigation of variances in this category should pinpoint the cause of the inefficiency and lead to corrective action to eliminate the inefficiency being repeated.

Finally, variances can be due to random or chance fluctuations for which no cause can be found. These may occur when a particular process is performed by the same worker under the same conditions, yet performance varies. When no known cause is present to account for this variability, it is said to be due to random or uncontrollable factors. A standard is determined from a series of observations of a particular operation. A representative reading from these observations is chosen to determine a standard. Frequently, the representative reading that is chosen is the average or some other measure of central tendency. The important point to note is that one summary reading has been chosen to represent the standard when in reality a range of outcomes is possible when the process is *under control*. Any observation that differs from the chosen standard when the process is under control can be described as a random uncontrollable variation around the standard.

Any investigation of variances due to random uncontrollable factors will involve a cost, and will not yield any benefits because no assignable cause for the variance is present. Furthermore, those variances arising from assignable causes (such as inaccurate data, out of date standards or out-of-control operations) do not necessarily warrant investigation. For example, such variances may only be worthy of investigation if the benefits expected from the investigation exceed the costs of searching for and correcting the sources of the variance.

Variances may therefore be due to the following causes:

1 random uncontrollable factors when the operation is under control;

2 assignable causes, but with the costs of investigation exceeding the benefits;

3 assignable causes, but with the benefits from investigation exceeding the cost of investigation.

A perfect cost investigation model would investigate only those variances falling in the third category.

Simple rule of thumb cost investigation models

In many companies managers use simple models based on arbitrary criteria such as investigating if the absolute size of a variance is greater than a certain amount or if the variance exceeds the standard cost by some predetermined percentage (say 10 per cent). For example, if the standard usage for a particular component was 10 kilos and the actual output for a period was 1000 components then the variance would not be investigated if actual usage was between 9000 and 11 000 kilos.

The advantages of using simple arbitrary rules are their simplicity and ease of implementation. There are, however, several disadvantages. Simple rule of thumb models do not adequately take into account the statistical significance of the reported variances or consider the costs and benefits of an investigation. For example, investigating all variances that exceed the standard cost by a fixed percentage can lead to investigating many variances of small amounts.

Some of these difficulties can be overcome by applying different percentages or amounts for different expense items as the basis for the investigation decision. For example, smaller percentages might be used as a signal to investigate key expense items, and a higher percentage applied to less important items of expense.

Statistical investigation models

Within a standard costing context statistical control charts can be used to monitor variances. Past observations of an operation when it is under control are used to determine the mean/average usage (i.e. the standard) and standard deviation (σ). Assuming that the past observations approximate a normal distribution then statistical theory indicates that:

> 68.27 per cent of the observations will fall within the range of $\pm 1\sigma$ from the mean
>
> 95.45 per cent of the observations will fall within the range of $\pm 2\sigma$ from the mean

Control limits are now set. For example, if control limits are set based on two standard deviations from the mean then this would indicate 4.55 per cent (100 per cent – 95.45 per cent) of future observations would result from pure chance when the process is *under control*. Similarly if a control limit of one standard deviation is set then 31.73 per cent (100 per cent – 68.27 per cent) of future observations would also result from pure chance when there is no assignable cause is likely to be present. Therefore, with observations one standard deviation from the mean there is a significant probability that the process is under control whereas observations of two standard deviations suggests that there is a high probability that the operation is out of control.

Actual variances are plotted on a control chart (see Figure 18.1). Figure 18.1 shows three control charts, with the outer horizontal lines representing a possible control limit of 2σ, so that all observations outside this range are investigated. You will see that for operation A the process is deemed to be in control because all observations fall within the control limits. For operation B

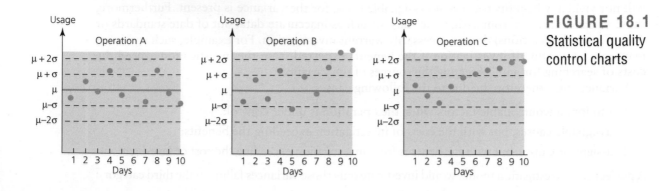

FIGURE 18.1
Statistical quality control charts

the last two observations suggest that the operation is out of control. Therefore both observations should be investigated. With operation C the observations would not prompt an investigation because all the observations are within the control limits. However, the last six observations show a steadily increasing usage in excess of the mean, and the process may be out of control.

Statistical decision models have been extended to incorporate the costs and benefits of investigation. For a description and illustration of these models you should refer to Learning Note 18.3 on the dedicated open access website.

The role of standard costing when ABC has been implemented

For those organizations that have implemented activity-based systems standard costing still has an important role to play in controlling the costs of unit-level activities. Unit-level activities can be defined as those activities that are performed each time a unit of product or service is produced. These activities consume resources in proportion to the number of units produced. For example, if a firm produces 10 per cent more units, it will consume 10 per cent more labour cost, 10 per cent more materials, 10 per cent more machine hours and 10 per cent more energy costs. Expenses in this category include direct labour, direct materials, energy costs and expenses that are consumed in proportion to machine processing times (such as machine maintenance). Therefore traditional variance analysis can be applied for direct labour, direct materials and those variable overheads that vary with output, machine hours and direct labour hours.

Variance analysis is most suited to controlling the costs of unit-level activities but it can also provide meaningful information for managing those overhead costs that are fixed in the short-term but variable in the longer-term if traditional volume-based cost drivers are replaced with activity-based cost drivers that better reflect the causes of resource consumption. Variance analysis, however, cannot be used to manage all overhead costs. It is inappropriate for the control of facility-sustaining (infrastructure) costs because the costs of these resources do not fluctuate in the longer-term according to the demand for them.

Mak and Roush (1994) and Kaplan (1994b) have considered how variance analysis can be applied to incorporate activity costs and cost drivers for those overheads that are fixed in the short term but variable in the long-term. The data presented in Example 18.4 illustrates their ideas relating to ABC overhead variance analysis for a set-up activity. You will see from this example that budgeted fixed costs of £80 000 provide a practical capacity to perform 2000 set-ups during the period. Assuming that the number of set-ups has been identified as the appropriate cost driver a cost of £40 per set-up (£80 000/2000) will be charged to products. Since budgeted capacity usage is 1600 set-ups not all of the capacity provided (2000 set-ups) will be used, and a budgeted cost of unused capacity of £16 000 (400 × £40), will be highlighted during the budget process. The actual number of set-ups performed was 1500 compared with a budget of 1600 and an unexpected capacity utilization variance of £4000 (100 × £40) will be reported at the end of the period. The traditional spending (expenditure) variance is £10 000, being the difference between budgeted and actual fixed costs incurred. We can now reconcile the fixed set-up expenses charged to products with the actual expenses incurred that are recorded in the financial accounts:

	£
Set-up expenses charged to products (1500 × £40)	60 000
Budgeted unused capacity variance (400 × £40)	16 000A
Capacity utilization variance (100 × £40)	4 000A
Expenditure variance	10 000F
Total actual expenses	70 000

The above capacity variances highlight for management attention the £20 000 unused capacity (£16 000 expected and £4000 unexpected) and thus signals the opportunity for actions such as reducing the supply of resources or using the surplus resources to generate additional revenues.

In Example 18.4 it is assumed that the variable set-up costs, such as the cost of supplies used in the set-up activity, varies with the number of set-ups. The variable cost driver rate of £25 per set-up has been calculated by dividing the budgeted variable cost of £40 000 by the budgeted number of set-ups of 1600. Note that the budgeted variable cost per set-up will be £25 for all activity levels. Thus the estimated set-up costs at the practical capacity of 2000 set-ups would be £50 000 (2500 × £25) but the cost per set-up would remain at £25. To calculate the set-up variable cost variance we must flex the budget. The actual number of set-ups performed were 1500 and the flexible budget allowance is £37 500 (1500 × £25). Actual expenditure is £39 000 and therefore an adverse variable cost variance of £1500 will be reported. The reconciliation between the variable set-up expenses charged to products and the actual expenses incurred is as follows:

Variable set-up expenses charged to products	
(1500 × £25)	37 500
Variable overhead variance	1 500A
Total actual expenses	39 000

In Example 18.4 we assumed that the number of set-ups was the cost driver. If set-ups take varying amounts of time they will not represent an homogeneous measure of output and thus may not provide a satisfactory measure of the cost of activity. To overcome this problem it may be preferable to use the number of set-up hours as the cost driver. Let us now assume in Example 18.4 that the cost driver is set-up hours and that the quantity of set-up hours is the same throughout as the number of set-ups. Therefore the variance analysis based on set-up hours will be identical to the variances that were computed when the number of set-ups was the cost driver.

Where cost drivers that capture the duration of the activity are used Mak and Roush (1994) advocate the reporting of separate efficiency variances for each activity. Assume in Example 18.4 that the standard activity level for the actual number of set-ups performed during the period was 1500 hours but the actual number of set-up hours required was 1660. The standard activity level represents the number of set-up hours that should have been required for the actual number of set-ups. The difference between the standard and the actual set-up hours thus arises because of efficiencies/inefficiencies in performing the set-up activities. Assuming that variable costs vary with the number of set-up hours then inefficiency in performing set-up activities has resulted in an extra 160 set-up hours (1660 – 1500) being used thus causing additional spending of £4000 (160 hours × £25). In addition, a favourable variable overhead expenditure variance of £2500 will be reported. This figure is derived in a manner similar to the traditional analysis by deducting the actual variable overhead expenditure of £39 000 from the flexible budget based on actual set-up hours (1660 × £25 = £41 500). Note that the sum of the efficiency variance (£4000A) and

EXAMPLE 18.4

Assume the following information for the set-up activity for a period:

Budget	Actual
Activity level: 1600 set-ups	Total fixed costs: £70 000
Practical capacity supplied: 2000 set-ups	Total variable costs: £39 000
Total fixed costs: £80 000	
Total variable costs: £40 000	Number of set-ups 1500
Cost driver rates (variable): £25 per set-up	
(fixed): £40 per set-up	

the expenditure variance (£2500F) is the same as the variable overhead variance of £1500 reported when the number of set-ups were used as the cost driver.

It is also possible to compute a capacity utilization and efficiency variance for fixed overheads. The efficiency variance is calculated by multiplying the 160 excess set-up hours by the fixed cost driver rate. Therefore an adverse efficiency variance of £6400 (160 × £40) and a favourable capacity utilization variance of £2400 (60 × £40) will be reported. The capacity utilization variance reflects the fact that the actual set-up capacity utilized was 60 hours in excess of the budget (assumed to be 1600 hours) but this was offset by the inefficiency in performing the activity which resulted in 160 hours in excess of requirements being utilized. The sum of the efficiency variance (£6400A) and the revised capacity utilization variance (£2400F) is identical to the capacity utilization variance reported when the number of set-ups was used as the cost driver.

The capacity utilization and efficiency variances relating to activity fixed costs are not particularly useful for short-term cost management. Mak and Roush conclude that they are more useful in a multi-period context whereby recurring adverse capacity variances (unused capacity) indicate the potential cost savings which can result from eliminating excess capacity.

SUMMARY

The following items relate to the learning objectives listed at the beginning of the chapter.

● **Prepare a set of accounts for a standard costing system.**

The method used in the chapter to illustrate the recording of standard costs valued all inventories at standard cost with all entries being recorded in the inventory accounts at standard prices. Any differences between standard costs and actual costs are debited or credited to variance accounts. Adverse variances appear as debit balances and favourable variances as credit balances. The preparation of a set of accounts for a standard costing system was illustrated in Exhibit 18.1.

● **Explain and calculate material mix and yield and sales mix and quantity variances.**

In some production processes it is possible to vary the mix of materials used to make the final product. Any deviations from the standard mix will lead to a materials mix variance. A favourable mix variance will occur when cheaper materials are substituted for more expensive ones. This may not always be in the company's best interest, since product quality may suffer or output may be reduced, leading to an adverse yield variance. The yield variance arises because there is a difference between the standard output for a given level of input and the actual output attained. Part of the sales margin volume variance may be accounted for because the actual sales mix differs from the budgeted sales mix. Calculating a sales margin mix variance can

isolate this element. The remaining part of the sales margin volume variance represents the sales quantity variance. Thus, separating the sales margin volume variance into quantity and mix variances provides an explanation of how the sales volume margin variance is affected by a shift in the total volume of sales and a shift in the relative mix of products. The calculations of the variances were illustrated using Examples 18.1 and 18.2.

● **Explain and calculate planning and operating variances.**

One of the criticisms of standard costing is that standards are normally based on the environment that was anticipated when the targets were set. To overcome this problem, whenever the actual environment is different from the anticipated environment, performance should be compared with a standard that reflects the changed conditions. One possible solution is to extract an uncontrollable planning or forecasting variance and report operating variances based on the changed conditions that applied during the period. The calculations of planning and operating variances were illustrated using Example 18.3.

● **Explain the factors that influence the decision to investigate a variance and describe the different methods that can be used to determine whether an investigation is warranted.**

The decision to investigate a variance should depend on whether the expected benefits are likely to exceed the costs of carrying out the investigation. Variances may be due to: (a) random uncontrollable variations when the variance is under control; (b) assignable causes but the costs of investigation exceed the benefits of investigation; and (c) assignable causes but the benefits from investigation exceed the costs of investigation. The aim should be only to investigate those variances that fall into the latter category. Methods of investigating variances include (a) simple rule of the thumb models and; (b) statistical models that focus on the probability of the variances being out of control.

● **Explain the role of standard costing within an ABC system.**

Within an ABC system variance analysis is most suited to controlling the costs of unit level activities. It can also provide meaningful information for managing those overhead costs that are fixed in the short-term but variable in the longer-term if traditional volume-based cost drivers are replaced with activity-based cost drivers that better reflect the causes of resource consumption. Variance analysis, however, cannot be used to manage all overhead costs. It is inappropriate for the control of facility-sustaining (infrastructure) costs because the cost of these resources does not fluctuate in the longer term according to the demand for them.

Key terms and concepts

assignable causes (p. 463)
ex post variance analysis (p. 461)
material mix variance (p. 457)
materials yield variance (p. 458)
purchasing efficiency variance (p. 462)

purchasing planning variance (p. 462)
random uncontrollable factors (p. 463)
sales margin mix variance (p. 460)
sales margin price variance (p. 460)

sales margin volume variance (p. 460)
sales quantity variance (p. 461)
statistical quality control charts (p. 464)
total sales margin variance (p. 460)

Recommended reading

For a review of the research literature relating to variance investigation models you should refer to Scapens (1991, ch. 6) and Sen (1998). For further reading on ABC variance analysis see Kaplan (1994a) and Mak and Roush (1994, 1996). The future role of standard costing is addressed in the article by Cheatham and Cheatham (1996).

Two articles by Emsley (2000, 2001) describe field studies relating to the role of variance analysis in problem solving.

Key examination points

Questions on mix and yield variances, variance investigation models and calculating planning and operating variance tend to be included only in advanced management accounting examinations. Make sure you understand these topics and attempt the Review problems that relate to these topics. You should compare your answers with the Solutions to the Review problems. Sometimes examination questions require you to discuss the usefulness of standard costing variance analysis in today's business environment and/or the future role of standard costing. These topics are discussed in Learning Notes 18.4 and 18.5 on the dedicated open access website (see Preface for details).

ASSESSMENT MATERIAL

The review questions are short questions that enable you to assess your understanding of the main topics included in the chapter. The numbers in parentheses provide you with the page numbers to refer to if you cannot answer a specific question.

The review problems are more complex and require you to relate and apply the content to various business problems. The problems are graded by their level of difficulty. Solutions to review problems that are not preceded by the term 'IM' are provided in a separate section at the end of the book. Solutions to problems preceded by the term 'IM' are provided in the *Instructor's Manual* accompanying this book and also on the lecturer's password protected section of the website www.drury-online.com. Additional review problems with fully worked solutions are provided in the *Student's Manual* that accompanies this book.

The website also includes over 30 case study problems. A list of these cases is provided on pages 665–7. Several cases are relevant to the content of this chapter. Examples include Anjo Ltd., Boston Creamery and Berkshire Toy Company.

Review questions

18.1 Under what circumstances will a (a) material mix and (b) material yield variances arise? *(pp. 457–58)*

18.2 Distinguish between a sales margin mix and a sales margin quantity variance. *(pp. 459–61)*

18.3 What are planning variances? Why are they separately identified? *(pp. 461–62)*

18.4 Describe the approaches for determining when a variance should be investigated. *(p. 464)*

18.5 Explain why actual performance might differ from standard performance. *(p. 463)*

18.6 When should a standard cost variance be investigated? *(p. 463)*

18.7 What is a statistical control chart? How can it be applied to determining when a variance should be investigated? *(pp. 464–65)*

18.8 How can standard costing be used when ABC has been implemented? *(pp. 465–66)*

18.9 Why is standard costing more suitable for controlling the cost of unit-level activities? *(p. 465)*

Review problems

18.10 Advanced. The following data are to be used to answer questions (a) and (b) below

SW plc manufactures a product known as the TRD100 by mixing two materials. The standard material cost per unit of the TRD100 is as follows:

		£
Material X	12 litres @ £2.50	30
Material Y	18 litres @ £3.00	54

In October 2002, the actual mix used was 984 litres of X and 1230 litres of Y. The actual output was 72 units of TRD100.

a The total material mix variance reported was nearest to
  A £102 (F)   B £49 (F)   C £49 (A)   D £151 (A)

b The total material yield variance reported was nearest to
  A £102 (F)   B £49 (F)   C £49 (A)   D £151 (A)
  CIMA Management Accounting – Performance Management

18.11 Advanced. Company P sells 3 products – R, S and T. Sales information for April 2002 was as follows:

	Budgeted sales units	Budgeted price per unit	Actual sales units	Actual price per unit
R	100	£100	108	£104
S	150	£50	165	£47
T	250	£35	221	£37

The expected size of the market for April was 2500 units. The actual market size was 2650 units.

The market share variance and sales mix variance were:

	Market share variance	Sales mix variance
A	£1490 (A)	£1890 (A)
B	£1575 (F)	£850 (F)
C	£1575 (F)	£315 (A)
D	£1890 (A)	£315 (A)
E	£1890 (A)	£850 (F)

CIMA Management Accounting – Decision Making

18.12 Advanced. The following data relate to both questions (a) and (b)

A company has budgeted to produce and sell 15 000 units per annum of a single product. The budgeted market size for this product is 75 000 units per annum. The budgeted information per unit is as follows:

	£
Selling price	125
Standard cost:	
Direct materials	20
Direct labour	15
Variable overhead	10
Fixed overhead	5
Standard profit	75

In the period covered by the budget, the following actual results were recorded:

Production and sales	13 000 units
Industry sales	10% lower than previously forecast

a The market size variance, calculated on a contribution per unit basis is
  A £40 000 adverse
  B £40 000 favourable
  C £120 000 adverse
  D £120 000 favourable
  E £160 000 adverse

b The market share variance, calculated on a contribution per unit basis is
  A £40 000 adverse
  B £40 000 favourable
  C £120 000 adverse
  D £120 000 favourable
  E £160 000 favourable
  CIMA Management Accounting – Decision Making

18.13 Intermediate: Accounting entries for a standard costing system. Bronte Ltd manufactures a single product, a laminated kitchen unit with a standard cost of £80 made up as follows:

	(£)
Direct materials (15 sq. metres at £3 per sq. metre)	45
Direct labour (5 hours at £4 per hour)	20
Variable overheads (5 hours at £2 per hour)	10
Fixed overheads (5 hours at £1 per hour)	5
	80

The standard selling price of the kitchen unit is £100. The monthly budget projects production and sales of 1000 units. Actual figures for the month of April are as follows:

Sales 1200 units at £102
Production 1400 units
Direct materials 22 000 sq. metres at £4 per sq. metre
Direct wages 6800 hours at £5
Variable overheads £11 000
Fixed overheads £6000

You are required to prepare:

a   a trading account reconciling actual and budgeted profit and showing all the appropriate variances.   (13 marks)
b   ledger accounts in respect of the above transactions.

ICAEW Accounting Techniques *
(*The original examination question did not include part (b).)

18.14 Advanced: Material mix and yield variances. Acca-chem Co plc manufacture a single product, product W, and have provided you with the following information which relates to the period which has just ended:

Standard cost per batch of product W

			Price per kilo (£)	Total (£)
Materials:	Kilos			
	F	15	4	60
	G	12	3	36
	H	8	6	48
		35		144
Less: Standard loss		3		
Standard yield		32		
Labour:		Hours	Rate per hour (£)	
Department P		4	10	40
Department Q		2	6	12
				196

Budgeted sales for the period are 4096 kilos at £16 per kilo. There were no budgeted opening or closing stocks of product W.

The actual materials and labour used for 120 batches were:

			Price per kilo (£)	Total (£)
Materials:	Kilos			
	F	1680	4.25	7 140
	G	1650	2.80	4 620
	H	870	6.40	5 568
		4200		17 328
Less: Actual loss		552		
Actual yield		3648		
Labour:		Hours	Rate per hour (£)	
Department P		600	10.60	6 360
Department Q		270	5.60	1 512
				25 200

All of the production of W was sold during the period for £16.75 per kilo.
Required:

a   Calculate the following material variances:
  – price
  – usage
  – mix
  – yield.   (5 marks)

b   Prepare an analysis of the material mix and price variances for each of the materials used.   (3 marks)
c   Calculate the following labour variances:
  – cost
  – efficiency
  – rate
  for each of the production departments.   (4 marks)
d   Calculate the sales variances.   (3 marks)
e   Comment on your findings to help explain what has happened to the yield variance.   (5 marks)

ACCA Paper 8 Managerial Finance

18.15 Advanced: Sales mix and quantity variances. BRK Co operates an absorption costing system and sells three products, B, R and K which are substitutes for each other. The following standard selling price and cost data relate to these three products:

Product	Selling price per unit	Direct material per unit	Direct labour per unit
B	£14.00	3.00 kg at £1.80 per kg	0.5 hrs at £6.50 per hour
R	£15.00	1.25 kg at £3.28 per kg	0.8 hrs at £6.50 per hour
K	£18.00	1.94 kg at £2.50 per kg	0.7 hrs at £6.50 per hour

Budgeted fixed production overhead for the last period was £81 000. This was absorbed on a machine hour basis. The standard machine hours for each product and the budgeted levels of production and sales for each product for the last period are as follows:

Product	B	R	K
Standard machine hours per unit	0.3 hrs	0.6 hrs	0.8 hrs
Budgeted production and sales (units)	10 000	13 000	9 000

Actual volumes and selling prices for the three products in the last period were as follows:

Product	B	R	K
Actual selling price per unit	£14.50	£15.50	£19.00
Actual production and sales (units)	9 500	13 500	8 500

Required:

a   Calculate the following variances for overall sales for the last period:
  (i)   sales price variance;
  (ii) sales volume profit variance;
  (iii) sales mix profit variance;
  (iv) sales quantity profit variance
  and reconcile budgeted profit for the period to actual sales less standard cost.   (13 marks)
b   Discuss the significance of the sales mix profit variance and comment on whether useful information would be obtained by calculating mix variances for each of these three products.   (4 marks)
c   Describe the essential elements of a standard costing system and explain how quantitative analysis can assist in the preparation of standard costs.   (8 marks)

ACCA 2.4 Financial Management and Control

18.16 Advanced: Planning and operating variances. Linsil has produced the following operating statement reconciling budgeted and actual gross profit for the last three months, based on actual sales of 122 000 units of its single product:

Operating statement	£	£	£
Budgeted gross profit			800 000
Budgeted fixed production overhead			352 000
			1 152 000
Budgeted contribution			
Sales volume contribution variance		19 200	
Sales price variance		(61 000)	
			(41 800)
			1 110 200
Actual sales less standard variable cost of sales			
Planning variances			
Variable cost variances	Favourable	Adverse	
Direct material price		23 570	
Direct material usage	42 090		
Direct labour rate		76 128	
Direct labour efficiency		203 333	
	42 090	303 031	(260 941)

Operational variances			
Variable cost variances		Favourable	Adverse
Direct material price			31 086
Direct material usage		14 030	
Direct labour rate			19 032
Direct labour efficiency		130 133	
		144 163	50 118	94 045
				943 304
Actual contribution				
Budgeted fixed production overhead			(352 000)
Fixed production overhead expenditure variance			27 000
Actual fixed production overhead			(325 000)
Actual gross profit			618 304

The standard direct costs and selling price applied during the three-month period and the actual direct costs and selling price for the period were as follows:

	Standard	Actual
Selling price (£/unit)	31.50	31.00
Direct material usage (kg/unit)	3.00	2.80
Direct material price (£/kg)	2.30	2.46
Direct labour efficiency (hrs/unit)	1.25	1.30
Direct labour rate (£/hr)	12.00	12.60

After the end of the three-month period and prior to the preparation of the above operating statement, it was decided to revise the standard costs retrospectively to take account of the following:

1. A 3 per cent increase in the direct material price per kilogram;
2. A labour rate increase of 4 per cent;
3. The standard for labour efficiency had anticipated buying a new machine leading to a 10 per cent decrease in labour hours; instead of buying a new machine, existing machines had been improved, giving an expected 5 per cent saving in material usage.

Required:

a Using the information provided, demonstrate how each planning and operational variance in the operating statement has been calculated. *(11 marks)*

b Calculate direct labour and direct material variances based on the standard cost data applied during the three-month period. *(4 marks)*

c Explain the significance of separating variances into planning and operational elements, using the operating statement above to illustrate your answer. *(5 marks)*

d Discuss the factors to be considered in deciding whether a variance should be investigated. *(5 marks)*

ACCA 2.4 Financial Management and Control

18.17 Advanced: Traditional and activity-based variance analysis. Frolin Chemicals Ltd produces FDN. The standard ingredients of 1 kg of FDN are:

0.65 kg of ingredient F	@ £4.00 per kg
0.30 kg of ingredient D	@ £6.00 per kg
0.20 kg of ingredient N	@ £2.50 per kg
1.15 kg	

Production of 4000 kg of FDN was budgeted for April. The production of FDN is entirely automated and production costs attributed to FDN production comprise only direct materials and overheads. The FDN production operation works on a JIT basis and no ingredient or FDN inventories are held.

Overheads were budgeted for April for the FDN production operation as follows:

Activity		Total amount
Receipt of deliveries from suppliers	(standard delivery quantity is 460 kg)	£4 000
Despatch of goods to customers	(standard despatch quantity is 100 kg)	£8 000
		£12 000

In April, 4200 kg of FDN were produced and cost details were as follows:

● *Materials used:*
  2840 kg of F, 1210 kg of D and 860 kg of N
  total cost   £20 380

● *Actual overhead costs:*
  12 supplier deliveries (cost £4800) were made, and 38 customer despatches (cost £7800) were processed.

Frolin Chemicals Ltd's budget committee met recently to discuss the preparation of the financial control report for April, and the following discussion occurred:

Chief Accountant: 'The overheads do not vary directly with output and are therefore by definition "fixed". They should be analyzed and reported accordingly.'

Management Accountant: 'The overheads do not vary with output, but they are certainly not fixed. They should be analyzed and reported on an activity basis.'

Requirements:
Having regard to this discussion,

a prepare a variance analysis for FDN production costs in April: separate the material cost variance into price, mixture and yield components; separate the overhead cost variance into expenditure, capacity and efficiency components using consumption of ingredient F as the overhead absorption base; *(11 marks)*

b prepare a variance analysis for FDN production overhead costs in April on an activity basis; *(9 marks)*

c explain how, in the design of an activity-based costing system, you would identify and select the most appropriate activities and cost drivers. *(5 marks)*

CIMA Stage 3 Management Accounting Applications

18.18 Advanced: Investigation of variances. From past experience a company operating a standard cost system has accumulated the following information in relation to variances in its monthly management accounts:

Percentage of total number of variances

1 Its variances fall into two categories:

Category 1: those which are not worth investigating	64
Category 2: those which are worth investigating	36
	100

2 Of Category 2, corrective action has eliminated 70 per cent of the variances, but the remainder have continued.

3 The cost of investigation averages £350 and that of correcting variances averages £550.

4 The average size of any variance not corrected is £525 per month and the company's policy is to assess the present value of such costs at 2 per cent per month for a period of five months.

You are required to:

a prepare *two* decision trees, to represent the position if an investigation is:
  (i) carried out;
  (ii) not carried out; *(12 marks)*

b recommend, with supporting calculations, whether or not the company should follow a policy of investigating variances as a matter of routine; *(3 marks)*

c explain briefly *two* types of circumstance that would give rise to variances in Category 1 and *two* to those in Category 2; *(6 marks)*

d mention any *one* variation in the information used that you feel would be beneficial to the company if you wished to improve the quality of the decision-making rule recommended in (b) above. Explain briefly why you have suggested it. *(4 marks)*

CIMA P3 Management Accounting

18.19 Advanced: (N.B. Relates to material covered in Website Learning Notes 18.4 and 18.5.)

a In high technology small batch manufacture, accountants sometimes take the view that standard costing cannot be applied. The move into high technology is generally accompanied by a shift away from labour-dominated to capital-intensive processes.

You are required to appraise the application of standard costing in the circumstance described above. *(12 marks)*

b In order to secure and direct employee motivation towards the achievement of a firm's goals, it may be considered that budget centres should be created at the lowest defined management level.

You are required to discuss the advantages and disadvantages of creating budget centres at such a level. *(12 marks)*

CIMA Stage 4 Management Accounting – Control and Audit

18.20 Advanced (N.B. Relates to material covered in Website Learning Notes 18.4 and 18.5.) In recent years, writers have argued that standard costing and variance analysis should not be used for cost control and performance evaluation purposes in today's manufacturing world. Its use, they argue, is likely to induce behaviour which is inconsistent with the strategic manufacturing objectives that companies need to achieve in order to survive in today's intensely competitive international economic environment.

Requirements:

a Explain the arguments referred to in the above paragraph concerning the relevance of standard costing and variance analysis. *(10 marks)*

b Explain the arguments in favour of the relevance of standard costing and variance analysis in the modern manufacturing environment. *(8 marks)*

c Suggest methods that might be used by management accountants to control costs and evaluate efficiency as alternatives or complements to standard costing and variance analysis. *(7 marks)*

CIMA Stage 3 Management Accounting Applications

18.21 Advanced.

a The investigation of a variance is a fundamental element in the effective exercise of control through budgetary control and standard costing systems. The systems for identifying the variances may be well defined and detailed yet the procedures adopted to determine whether to pursue the investigation of variances may well not be formalized.

Critically examine this situation, discussing possible effective approaches to the investigation of variances. *(15 marks)*

b Explain the major motivational factors which influence managers in their actions to eliminate variances from budget. *(10 marks)*

CIMA Stage 4 Management Accounting Control and Audit

IM18.1 Advanced. In the new industrial environment, the usefulness of standard costing is being challenged, and new approaches sought.

One approach, pioneered by the Japanese, is to replace standard costs by target costs.

You are required

a to describe the problems associated with standard costing in the new industrial environment; *(6 marks)*

b to explain what target costs are, and how they are developed and used; *(6 marks)*

c to contrast standard and target costs. *(5 marks)*

CIMA Management Accounting Techniques

IM18.2 Advanced. Variance investigation decisions are normally explained in textbooks by simple models, which assume the availability of a significant amount of information.

An example of this approach is:

The managers estimate the probability of any variance being due to a controllable, and therefore correctable, cause at 25 per cent. They estimate the cost of investigating a variance at £1400, and the cost of correcting the cause of a correctable variance at £400. The investigation process is regarded as 100 per cent reliable in that a correctable cause of the variance will be found if it exists.

Managers estimate the loss due to not investigating, and hence not discovering, a correctable cause of the variance, averages 75 per cent of the size of the variance. For example, the loss from the failure to discover a correctable £4000 variance would be £3000.

Requirement:

a Calculate the minimum size of variance that would justify investigation. *(8 marks)*

In addition to the approach described above, alternative approaches exist to decide whether to investigate variances by using criteria related to the absolute size of the variance, and criteria based on the percentage from standard.

Requirement:

b (i) Explain why these approaches are taken rather than the approach described in (a) above.

(ii) Comment on the appropriateness of the alternative approaches described above. *(12 marks)*

CIMA Stage 4 Management Accounting Control Systems

IM18.3 Intermediate: Accounting entries for a standard costing system. Fischer Ltd manufactures a range of chess sets, and operates a standard costing system. Information relating to the Spassky design for the month of March is as follows:

1 Standard costs per 100 sets

	(£)
Raw materials:	
Plaster of Paris, 20kg at £8 per kg	160
Paint, ½ litre at £30 per litre	15
Direct wages, 2½ hours at £10 per hour	25
Fixed production overheads, 400% of direct wages	100
	300

2 Standard selling price per set £3.80

3 Raw materials, work in progress and finished goods stock records are maintained at standard cost.

4 Stock levels at the beginning and end of March were as follows:

	1 March	31 March
Plaster of Paris	2800 kg	2780 kg
Paint	140 litres	170 litres
Finished sets	900 sets	1100 sets

There was no work in progress at either date.

5 Budgeted production and sales during the month were 30 000 sets. Actual sales, all made at standard selling price, and actual production were 28 400 and 28 600 sets respectively.

6 Raw materials purchased during the month were 5400kg of plaster of Paris at a cost of £43 200 and 173 litres of paint at a cost of £5800.

7 Direct wages were 730 hours at an average rate of £11 per hour.

8 Fixed production overheads amounted to £34 120.

Requirement:

Prepare for the month of March:

a the cost ledger accounts for raw materials, work in progress and finished goods; *(10 marks)*

b (i) budget trading statement,

(ii) standard cost trading statement,

(iii) financial trading statement, and

(iv) a reconciliation between these statements identifying all relevant variances. *(14 marks)*

ICAEW Accounting Techniques

IM18.4 Advanced: Mix variances and reconciliation as actual and budgeted profit. A company operates a number of hairdressing establishments which are managed on a franchise arrangement. The franchisor offers support using a PC package which deals with profit budgeting and control information.

Budget extracts of one franchisee for November are shown below analyzed by male and female clients. For the purposes of budget projections average revenue rates are used. At the month end these are compared with the average monthly rates actually achieved using variance analysis. Sales price, sales quantity, sales mix and cost variances are routinely produced in order to compare the budget and actual results.

Staff working in this business are paid on a commission basis in order to act as an incentive to attract and retain clients. The labour rate variance is based on the commission payments, any basic pay is part of the monthly fixed cost.

Budget

	Male	Female
Clients	4000	1000
	(£)	(£)
Average revenue (per client)	7.5	18.0
Average commission (per client)	3.0	10.0
Total monthly fixed cost	£20 000	

Actual results

	Male	Female
Clients	2000	2000
	(£)	(£)
Average revenue (per client)	8.0	20.0
Average commission (per client)	3.5	11.0
Total monthly fixed cost	£24 000	

Required:

a Reconcile the budgeted and actual profit for November by calculating appropriate price, quantity, mix and cost variances, presenting the information in good form. You should adopt a contribution style, with mix variances based on units (i.e. clients).

(10 marks)

b Write a short memorandum to the manager of the business commenting on the result in (a) above. *(4 marks)*

c Comment on the limitations associated with generating sales variances as in (a) above. *(6 marks)*

ACCA Paper 8 Managerial Finance

IM18.5 Advanced: Detailed variance analysis (including revision variances) plus an explanation of the meaning of operating statement variances.
Tungach Ltd make and sell a single product. Demand for the product exceeds the expected production capacity of Tungach Ltd. The holding of stocks of the finished product is avoided if possible because the physical nature of the product is such that it deteriorates quickly and stocks may become unsaleable.

A standard marginal cost system is in operation. Feedback reporting takes planning and operational variances into consideration.

The management accountant has produced the following operating statement for period 9:

Tungach Ltd
Operating Statement – Period 9

	(£)	(£)
Original budgeted contribution		36 000
Revision variances:		
Material usage	9 600(A)	
Material price	3 600(F)	
Wage rate	1 600(F)	4 400(A)
Revised budgeted contribution		31 600
Sales volume variance:		
Causal factor		
Extra capacity	4 740(F)	
Productivity drop	987.5(A)	
Idle time	592.5(A)	
Stock increase	2 370(A)	790(F)
Revised standard contribution		
for sales achieved		32 390
Other variances:		
Material usage	900(F)	
Material price	3 120(A)	
Labour efficiency	1 075(A)	
Labour idle time	645(A)	
Wage rate	2 760(A)	
		6 700(A)
Actual contribution		25 690

(F) = favourable   (A) = adverse

Other data are available as follows:

(i) The original standard contribution per product unit as determined at period 1 was:

	(£)	(£)
Selling price		30
Less: Direct material 1.5 kilos at £8	12	
Direct labour 2 hours at £4.50	9	21
Contribution		9

(ii) A permanent change in the product specification was implemented from period 7 onwards. It was estimated that this change would require 20 per cent additional material per product unit. The current efficient price of the material has settled at £7.50 per kilo.

(iii) Actual direct material used during period 9 was 7800 kilos at £7.90 per kilo. Any residual variances are due to operational problems.

(iv) The original standard wage rate overestimated the degree of trade union pressure during negotiations and was £0.20 higher than the rate subsequently agreed. Tungach Ltd made a short-term operational decision to pay the workforce at £4.60 per hour during periods 7 to 9 in an attempt to minimize the drop in efficiency likely because of the product specification change. Management succeeded in extending the production capacity during period 9 and the total labour hours paid for were 9200 hours. These included 150 hours of idle time.

(v) Budgeted production and sales quantity (period 9)   4000 units
Actual sales quantity (period 9)   4100 units
Actual production quantity (period 9)   4400 units

(vi) Stocks of finished goods are valued at the current efficient standard cost.

Required:

a Prepare detailed figures showing how the material and labour variances in the operating statement have been calculated.

(8 marks)

b Prepare detailed figures showing how the sales volume variance has been calculated for each causal factor shown in the operating statement. *(6 marks)*

c Prepare a report to the management of Tungach Ltd explaining the meaning and relevance of the figures given in the operating statement for period 9. The report should contain specific comments for any two of the sales volume variance causal factors and any two of the 'other variances'. The comments should suggest possible reasons for each variance, the management member likely to be answerable for each variance and possible corrective action. *(8 marks)*

ACCA Level 2 Management Accounting

IM18.6 Advanced: Reconciliation of budgeted and actual profit including operating and planning variances plus an interpretation of the reconciliation statement. Casement Ltd makes windows with two types of frame: plastic and mahogany. Products using the two types of materials are made in separate premises under the supervision of separate production managers.

Data for the three months ended 30 November are shown below.

	Plastic		Mahogany		Totals	
	Budget	Actual	Budget	Actual	Budget	Actual
Sales units	3000	2500	1000	1250	4000	3750
	(£000)	(£000)	(£000)	(000)	(£000)	(£000)
Sales revenue	660	520	340	460	1000	980
Materials	(147)	(120)	(131)	(160)	(278)	(280)
Labour	(108)	(105)	(84)	(85)	(192)	(190)
Fixed production overheads	(162)	(166)	(79)	(83)	(241)	(249)
Sales commissions	(33)	(26)	(17)	(23)	(50)	(49)
Other selling and administration costs					(128)	(133)
Net profit					111	79

Casement Ltd sells to a wide variety of users, so that window sizes and shapes vary widely; consequently a square metre of window is adopted as the standard unit for pricing and costing.

Sales budgets were based on the expectation that the company's share of the regional market in windows would be 12 per cent. The Window Federation's quarterly report reveals that sales in the regional market totalled 25 000 units in the three months ended 30 November. The managing director of Casement Ltd is concerned that the company's sales and profit are below budget; she wants a full analysis of sales variances as well as an analysis of the cost variances which can be obtained from the data.

Labour costs comprise the wages of shop-floor employees who receive a fixed wage for a 40-hour week; no overtime is worked. Production managers receive a fixed monthly salary which is included in production overheads, plus an annual personal performance bonus (excluded from the above data) which is decided by the board of directors at the end of each year. Sales representatives are paid a monthly retainer plus commission of 5 per cent on all sales.

The management of Casement Ltd is keen to improve performance and is reviewing the company's reward structure. One possibility which is under consideration is that the company should adopt a profit-related pay scheme. The scheme would replace all the existing arrangements and would give every employee a basic remuneration equal to 90 per cent of his or her earnings last year. In addition every employee would receive a share in the company's profit; on the basis of the past year's trading this payment would amount to about 17 per cent of basic remuneration for each employee.

Requirements

a Prepare a variance report for the managing director on the results for the quarter ended 30 November, providing market share and market volume (or size) variances, sales mix variance and basic cost variances, from the available information. *(10 marks)*

b Interpret your results in part (a) for the benefit of the managing director. *(7 marks)*

c Examine the issues (excluding taxation) which should be considered by the management of Casement Ltd in relation to the company's reward structure, with particular reference to the proposal to move to a profit-related pay scheme. *(8 marks)*

ICAEW P2 Management Accounting

IM18.7 Advanced: Performance reports for sales and product managers. Zits Ltd makes two models for rotary lawn mowers, the Quicut and the Powacut. The company has a sales director and reporting to her, two product managers, each responsible for the profitability of one of the two models. The company's financial year ended on 31 March. The budgeted and actual results for the two models for the year ended on 31 March are given below:

	Quicut		Powacut		Total	
	Budget	Actual	Budget	Actual	Budget	Actual
Sales units	240	280	120	110	360	390
(000 units)	(£000)	(£000)	(£000)	(000)	(£000)	(£000)
Sales revenue	28 800	32 200	24 000	24 200	52 800	56 400
Costs:						
Variable	9 600	11 480	7 200	6 820	16 800	18 300
Traceable fixed						
manufacturing	8 200	7 600	6 800	6 800	15 000	14 400
Period costs:						
Manufacturing					5 700	6 000
Administration					4 300	4 500
and selling						
					41 800	43 200
Net Profit before Tax					£11 000	£13 200

The accountant had drawn up a series of flexed budgets at the beginning of the year should the actual volume differ from budget. The variable costs were unchanged, but the budgeted fixed costs, assuming a constant sales mix, for the different output ranges were as given below:

Output range	300–360	361–420
(000 units)	(£000)	(£000)
Traceable fixed manufacturing costs	15 000	16 000
Period cost – manufacturing	5 700	6 000
– administration and selling	4 300	4 500
	£25 000	£26 000

The sales director has just received information from the trade association that industry rotary lawn mower sales for the twelve months ended on 31 March were 1.3 million units as against a forecast of 1.0 million.

Requirements:

a Prepare a schedule of variances which will be helpful to the sales director, and a schedule of more detailed variances which will be appropriate to the two product managers who are treated as profit centres. *(16 marks)*

b Discuss the results scheduled in (a) above identifying which of the variances are planning and which are operating variances.

(9 marks)

ICAEW Management Accounting

IM18.8 Advanced: Investigation of variances

a Describe and comment briefly on the basis and limitations of the control chart approach to variance investigation decisions.

(6 marks)

b The following analysis is available for the month of April for Department A:

	(£)
Standard direct material	72 000
Material usage variance	4 500 unfavourable
Material mix variance	2 500 unfavourable

The following estimates have also been made for Department A:

	(£)
Estimated cost of investigating the total material variance	1 000
Estimated cost of correcting the total variance if investigated and found to be out of control	2 000
Estimated cost of permitting out-of-control material variances to continue	10 000

Maximum Probability of a given total variance:

Probability	0.99	0.98	0.96	0.93	0.89	0.85	0.8	0.75
Total								
Variance £000	1	2	3	4	5	6	7	8

You are required to determine, using a payoff table, whether the variance should be investigated. *(6 marks)*

c You are uncertain of the estimated probability in (b). Calculate the probability estimate at which you would be indifferent between investigating and not investigating the variance. *(6 marks)*

d Discuss the use of mathematical models for the variance investigation decision. *(7 marks)*

CIMA Stage 4 Management Accounting Control and Audit

Divisional financial performance measures

19

Large companies produce and sell a wide variety of products throughout the world. Because of the complexity of their operations, it is difficult for top management to directly control operations. It may therefore be appropriate to divide a company into separate self-contained segments or divisions and to allow divisional managers to operate with a great deal of independence. A divisional manager has responsibility for both the production and marketing activities of the division. The danger in creating autonomous divisions is that divisional managers might not pursue goals that are in the best interests of the company as a whole. The objective of this chapter is to consider financial performance measures that aim to motivate managers to pursue those goals that will best benefit the company as a whole. In other words, the objective is to develop performance measures that will achieve goal congruence.

In this chapter we shall focus on financial measures of divisional performance. However, financial measures cannot adequately measure all those factors that are critical to the success of a

LEARNING OBJECTIVES

After studying this chapter, you should be able to:

- distinguish between functional and divisionalized organizational structures;

- explain why it is preferable to distinguish between managerial and economic performance;

- explain the factors that should be considered in designing financial performance measures for evaluating divisional managers;

- explain the meaning of return on investment, residual income and economic value added;

- compute economic value added;

- explain why performance measures may conflict with the net present value decision model;

- identify and explain the approaches that can be used to reduce the dysfunctional consequences of short-term financial measures.

division. Emphasis should also be given to reporting key non-financial measures relating to such areas as competitiveness, product leadership, quality, delivery performance, innovation and flexibility to respond to changes in demand. In particular, performance measures should be developed that support the objectives and competitive strategies of the organization. Divisional financial performance measures should therefore be seen as one of a range of measures that should be used to measure and control divisional performance.

Functional and divisionalized organizational structures

A functional organizational structure is one in which all activities of a similar type within a company are placed under the control of the appropriate departmental head. A simplified organization chart for a functional organizational structure is illustrated in Figure 19.1(a). It is assumed that the company illustrated consists of five separate departments – production, marketing, financial administration, purchasing and research and development. In a typical functional organization none of the managers of the five departments is responsible for more than a part of the process of acquiring the raw materials, converting them into finished products, selling to customers, and administering the financial aspects of this process. For example, the production department is responsible for the manufacture of all products at a minimum cost, and of satisfactory quality, and to meet the delivery dates requested by the marketing department. The marketing department is responsible for the total sales revenue and any costs associated with selling and distributing the products, but not for the total profit. The purchasing department is responsible for purchasing supplies at a minimum cost and of satisfactory quality so that the production requirements can be met.

You will see from Figure 19.1 that the marketing function is a revenue centre and the remaining departments are cost centres. Revenues and costs (including the cost of investments) are combined together only at the chief executive, or corporate level, which is classified as an investment centre.

Let us now consider Figure 19.1(b), which shows a divisionalized organizational structure, which is split up into divisions in accordance with the products which are made. You will see from the diagram that each divisional manager is responsible for all of the operations relating to his or her particular product. To reflect this greater autonomy each division is either an investment centre or a profit centre. To simplify the presentation it is assumed that all of the divisions in Figure 19.1(b) are investment centres (we shall discuss the factors influencing the choice of investment or profit centres later in the chapter). Note that within each division there are multiple cost and revenue centres and also that a functional structure is applied within each division. Figure 19.1(b) shows a simplified illustration of a divisionalized organizational structure. In practice, however, only part of a company may be divisionalized. For example, activities such as research and development, industrial relations, and general administration may be structured centrally on a functional basis with a responsibility for providing services to all of the divisions.

The distinguishing feature between the functional structure (Figure 19.1(a)) and the divisionalized structure (Figure 19.1(b)) is that in the functional structure only the organization as a whole is an investment centre and below this level a functional structure applies throughout. In contrast, in a divisionalized structure the organization is divided into separate investment or profit centres and a functional structure applies below this level. In this chapter we shall focus on financial measures and controls at the profit or investment centre (i.e. divisional) level.

Generally, a divisionalized organizational structure will lead to a decentralization of the decision-making process. For example, divisional managers will normally be free to set selling prices, choose which market to sell in, make product mix and output decisions, and select suppliers (this may include buying from other divisions within the company or from other companies). In a functional organizational structure pricing, product mix and output decisions will be made by central management. Consequently, the functional managers in a centralized organization will have far less independence than divisional managers. One way to express the difference between the two

(a) Functional organizational structure

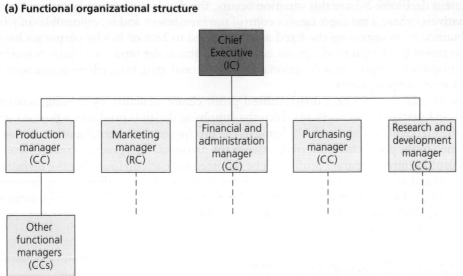

(b) Divisionalized organizational structure

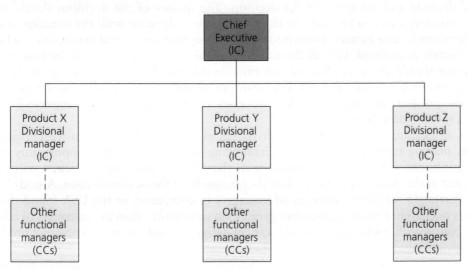

IC = Investment centres, CC = Cost centres, RC = Revenue centres

FIGURE 19.1
A functional and
divisionalized
organizational structure

organizational structures is to say that the divisional managers have profit responsibility. They are responsible for generating revenues, controlling costs and earning a satisfactory return on the capital invested in their operations. The managers of the functional organizational structure do not have profit responsibility. For example, in Figure 19.1(a) the production manager has no control over sources of supply, selling prices, or product mix and output decisions.

Profit centres and investment centres

The creation of separate divisions may lead to the delegation of different degrees of authority; for example, in some organizations a divisional manager may, in addition to having authority to make decisions on sources of supply and choice of markets, also have responsibility for making capital investment decisions. Where this situation occurs, the division is known as an investment centre. Alternatively, where a manager cannot control the investment and is responsible only for the profits obtained from operating the fixed assets assigned to him or her by corporate headquarters, the segment is referred to as a profit centre. In contrast, the term cost centre is used to describe a responsibility centre in a functional organizational structure where a manager is responsible for costs but not profits.

Many firms attempt to simulate a divisionalized profit centre structure by creating separate manufacturing and marketing divisions in which the supplying division produces a product and transfers it to the marketing division, which then sells the product in the external market. Transfer prices are assigned to the products transferred between the divisions. This practice creates pseudo-divisionalized profit centres. Separate profits can be reported for each division, but the divisional managers have limited authority for sourcing and pricing decisions. To meet the true requirements of a divisionalized profit centre, a division should be able to sell the majority of its output to outside customers and should also be free to choose the sources of supply.

Advantages of divisionalization

Divisionalization can improve the decision-making process both from the point of view of the quality of the decision and the speed of the decision. The quality of the decisions should be improved because decisions can be made by the person who is familiar with the situation and who should therefore be able to make more informed judgements than central management who cannot be intimately acquainted with all the activities of the various segments of the business. Speedier decisions should also occur because information does not have to pass along the chain of command to and from top management. Decisions can be made on the spot by those who are familiar with the product lines and production processes and who can react to changes in local conditions in a speedy and efficient manner.

In addition, delegation of responsibility to divisional managers provides them with greater freedom, thus making their activities more challenging and providing the opportunity to achieve self-fulfilment. This process should mean that motivation and efficiency will be increased not just at the divisional manager level but throughout the whole division. A study by Dittman and Ferris (1978) of the attitudes of managers in companies in the USA found that those managers in charge of profit centres had greater job satisfaction than the managers of cost centres. They conclude that wherever possible, system designers ought to try to construct profit centres for organizational units.

Another important reason for adopting a divisionalized structure is that the distribution of decision-making responsibility to divisions frees top management from detailed involvement in day-to-day operations, and enables them to devote more effort to strategic planning. It is also claimed that divisions can provide an excellent training ground for future members of top management by enabling trainee managers to acquire the basic managerial skills and experience in an environment that is less complex than managing the company as a whole.

Disadvantages of divisionalization

If a company is divisionalized, there is a danger that divisions may compete with each other excessively and that divisional managers may be encouraged to take action which will increase their own profits at the expense of the profits of other divisions. This may adversely affect co-operation between the divisions and lead to a lack of harmony in achieving the overall organizational goals of the company. This in turn may lead to a reduction in total company profits.

A further argument against divisionalization is that top management loses some control by delegating decision-making to divisional managers. It is argued that a series of control reports is not as effective as detailed knowledge of a company's activities. However, with a good system of performance evaluation together with appropriate control information, top management should be able to effectively monitor and control operations.

Pre-requisites for successful divisionalization

A divisionalized structure is most suited to companies engaged in several dissimilar activities. The reason is that it is difficult for top management to be intimately acquainted with all the diverse activities of the various segments of the business. On the other hand, when the major activities of a company are closely related, these activities should be carefully coordinated, and this coordination is more easily achieved in a centralized organizational structure. The results from a number of surveys suggest that divisionalization is more common in companies having diversified activities than when single or related activities are undertaken (Ezzamel and Hilton, 1980).

For successful divisionalization it is important that the activities of a division be as independent as possible of other activities. However, Solomons (1965) argues that even though substantial independence of divisions from each other is a necessary condition for divisionalization, if carried to the limit it would destroy the very idea that such divisions are an integral part of any single business. Divisions should be more than investments they should contribute not only to the success of the company but to the success of each other.

According to Solomons, a further condition for the success of divisionalization is that the relations between divisions should be regulated so that no one division, by seeking its own profit, can reduce that of the company as a whole. He states that this is not the same as seeking profit at the expense of other divisions, but the amount that a division adds to its own profit must exceed the loss that it inflicts on another division. Unfortunately, conflicts between divisions do arise, and one of the important tasks of the accountant is to design an accounting control system that will discourage a division from improving its own profit at the expense of the company as a whole.

Distinguishing between the managerial and economic performance of the division

Before discussing the factors to be considered in determining how divisional profitability should be measured, we must decide whether the primary purpose is to measure the performance of the division or that of the divisional manager. The messages transmitted from these two measures may be quite different. For example, a manager may be assigned to an ailing division to improve performance, and might succeed in substantially improving the performance of the division. However, the division might still be unprofitable because of industry factors, such as overcapacity and a declining market. The future of the division might be uncertain, but the divisional manager may well be promoted as a result of the outstanding managerial performance. Conversely, a division might report significant profits but, because of management deficiencies, the performance may be unsatisfactory when the favourable economic environment is taken into account.

If the purpose is to evaluate the divisional manager then only those items directly controllable by the manager should be included in the profitability measure. Thus all allocations of indirect costs, such as central service and central administration costs, which cannot be influenced by divisional managers, ought not to be included in the profitability measure. Such costs can only be controlled where they are incurred; which means that central service managers should be held accountable for them.

Corporate headquarters, however, will also be interested in evaluating a division's economic performance for decision-making purposes, such as expansion, contraction and divestment decisions. In this situation a measure that includes only those amounts directly controllable by the divisional manager would overstate the economic performance of the division. This overstatement occurs because, if the divisions were independent companies, they would have to incur the costs of those services provided by head office. Therefore, to measure the economic performance of the division many items that the divisional manager cannot influence, such as interest expenses, taxes and the allocation of central administrative staff expenses, should be included in the profitability measure.

Alternative divisional profit measures

There are strong arguments for computing two measures of divisional profitability – one to evaluate managerial performance and the other to evaluate the economic performance of the division. In this chapter we shall focus on both these measures. The most common measures of divisional profitability are return on investment (that is, profit as a percentage of the investment in a division) residual income and economic value added. At this stage we shall restrict our attention purely to problems that are encountered with divisional profit measurement before turning our attention to the above three common measures of divisional profitability.

Exhibit 19.1 presents a divisional profit statement. You can see that there are four different profit measures that we can use to measure divisional performance. We shall focus initially on measuring *managerial* performance. The variable short-run contribution margin is inappropriate for performance evaluation, because it does not include fixed costs that are controllable by the divisional manager. For example, a manager may not be motivated to control non-variable labour costs or equipment rentals, since they fall below the variable short-run contribution line and are not included in the performance measure.

The controllable contribution is computed by deducting from total divisional revenues all those costs that are controllable by the division manager. This measure therefore includes controllable fixed costs such as non-variable labour, equipment rental and the cost of utilities. These costs are fixed in the short term, but in the longer term the divisional manager has the option of reducing them by altering the scale of operations or reducing the complexity and diversity of product lines and distribution channels. Where a division is a profit centre, depreciation is not a controllable cost, since the manager does not have authority to make capital investment decisions. Depreciation, however, should be deemed to be a controllable expense for an investment centre in respect of those assets that are controllable by the divisional manager.

Controllable contribution is the most appropriate measure of a divisional manager's performance, since it measures the ability of managers to use the resources under their control effectively. It should not be interpreted in isolation if it is used directly to evaluate the

EXHIBIT 19.1 Alternative divisional profit measures

Sales to outside customers	xxx
Transfers to other divisions	xxx
Total sales revenue	xxx
Less variable costs	xxx
1. *Variable short-run contribution margin*	xxx
Less controllable fixed costs	xxx
2. *Controllable contribution*	xxx
Less non-controllable avoidable costs	xxx
3. *Divisional contribution*	xxx
Less allocated corporate expenses	xxx
4. *Divisional net profit before taxes*	xxx

performance of a divisional manager. Instead, the controllable contribution reported by a division should be evaluated relative to a budgeted performance, so that market conditions can be taken into account.

In practice, it is extremely difficult to distinguish between controllable and non-controllable costs. However, three situations can be identified that will assist us in overcoming this problem. Where a division is completely free to shop around for a service and there is no rule requiring the division to obtain the service from within the company, the expense is clearly controllable. Alternatively, a division may not be free to choose an outside source of supply for the service in question, but it may be able to decide how much of this service is utilized. In this latter situation the quantity is controllable by the division but the price is not. An appropriate solution here is for the division to be charged with the actual quantity at the standard or budgeted cost for the service that has been obtained. Thus any difference between the budget and actual performance would relate solely to excess usage by the division recorded at the standard price. Finally, the division may not be free to decide on either the quantity of the service it utilizes or the price it will be charged. Industrial relations costs may fall into this category. Here the divisions have no choice but to accept an apportioned cost for the benefits they have received (such apportionments may be made for external reporting purposes). In situations like this, the costs charged to the division for the service can only be regarded as a non-controllable item of divisional overhead. Another general rule that can be applied for distinguishing between controllable and non-controllable costs is to follow the guideline suggested by Merchant (1998) – that is, hold managers accountable for those costs that you want them to pay attention to.

Controllable contribution provides an incomplete measure of the *economic* performance of a division, since it does not include those costs that are attributable to the division but which are not controllable by the divisional manager. For example, depreciation of divisional assets, and head office finance and legal staff who are assigned to providing services for specific divisions, would fall into this category. These expenses would be avoidable if a decision were taken to close the division. Those non-controllable expenses that are attributable to a division, and which would be avoidable if the division was closed, are deducted from controllable contribution to derive the divisional contribution. This is clearly a useful figure for evaluating the *economic* contribution of the division, since it represents the contribution that a division is making to corporate profits and overheads. It should not be used, however, to evaluate managerial performance, since it includes costs that are not controllable by divisional managers.

Many companies allocate all corporate general and administrative expenses to divisions to derive a divisional net profit before taxes. From a theoretical point of view, it is difficult to justify such allocations since they tend to be arbitrary and do not have any connection with the manner in which divisional activities influence the level of these corporate expenses. Divisional contribution would therefore seem to be the most appropriate measure of divisions' *economic* performance, since it is not distorted by arbitrary allocations. We have noted, however, that corporate headquarters may wish to compare a division's economic performance with that of comparable firms operating in the same industry. The divisional contribution would overstate the performance of the division, because if the division were independent, it would have to incur the costs of those services performed by head office. The apportioned head office costs are an approximation of the costs that the division would have to incur if it traded as a separate company. Consequently, companies may prefer to use divisional net profit when comparing the economic performance of a division with similar companies.

For the reasons mentioned above, divisional net profit is not a satisfactory measure for evaluating *managerial* performance. Despite the many theoretical arguments against divisional net profit, the empirical evidence indicates that this measure is used widely to evaluate both divisional *economic* and *managerial* performance (Reece and Cool, 1978; Fremgen and Liao, 1981; Ramadan, 1989; Skinner, 1990; Drury *et al.*, 1993, Drury and El-Shishini 2005). In the Fremgen and Liao survey respondents were asked why they allocated indirect costs. The most important managerial performance evaluation reason was to 'remind profit centre managers that indirect costs exist and that profit centre earnings must be adequate to cover a share of these costs'. The counter-argument to this is that if central management wishes to inform managers that divisions must be profitable enough to cover not only their own operations but corporate expenses as well, it is preferable to set a high budgeted controllable contribution target that takes account of these factors. Divisional managers can then concentrate on increasing controllable contribution by focusing on those costs and revenues that are under their control and not be concerned with costs that they cannot control.

A further reason for cost allocations cited in the surveys by Fremgen and Liao and Skinner was that by allocating central overhead costs to divisions, divisional managers are made aware of these costs, so they will exert pressure on central management to minimize the costs of central staff departments. There is also some evidence to suggest that companies hold managers accountable for divisional net profit because this is equivalent to the measure that financial markets focus on to evaluate the performance of the company as a whole (Joseph et al., 1996). Top management therefore require their divisional managers to concentrate on the same measures as those used by financial markets.

A more recent UK study by Drury and El-Shishini (2005) asked the respondents to rank in order of importance the factors influencing organizations to allocate the cost of shared resources to divisions. In rank order the highest rankings were attributed to the following factors:

1 to show divisional managers the total costs of operating their divisions;

2 to make divisional managers aware that such costs exist and must be covered by divisional profits;

3 divisional managers would incur such costs if they were independent units;

4 divisional managers should bear the full business risk as if they were managers of non-divisionalized companies.

Return on investment

Instead of focusing purely on the absolute size of a division's profits, most organizations focus on the return on investment (ROI) of a division. Note that ROI is synonymous with accounting rate of return (ARR) described as an investment appraisal technique in Chapter 13. In Chapter 13 our focus was on future estimates (i.e. an *ex ante* measure) for making investment decisions. In this chapter we are focusing on an historic after-the-event (i.e. *ex post*) performance measure. ROI expresses divisional profit as a percentage of the assets employed in the division. Assets employed can be defined as total divisional assets, assets controllable by the divisional manager or net assets. We shall consider the alternative measures of assets employed later in the chapter.

ROI is the most widely used financial measure of divisional performance. Why? Consider a situation where division A earns a profit of £1 million and division B a profit of £2 million. Can we conclude that Division B is more profitable than Division A? The answer is no, since we should consider whether the divisions are returning a sufficiently high return on the capital invested in the division. Assume that £4 million capital is invested in division A and £20 million in division B. Division A's ROI is 25 per cent (£1m/£4m) whereas the return for division B is 10 per cent (£2m/£20m). Capital invested has alternative uses, and corporate management will wish to ascertain whether the returns being earned on the capital invested in a particular division exceeds the division's opportunity cost of capital (i.e. the returns available from the alternative use of the capital). If, in the above illustration, the return available on similar investments to that in division B is 15 per cent then the economic viability of division B is questionable if profitability cannot be improved. In contrast, the ROI measure suggests that division A is very profitable.

ROI provides a useful overall approximation on the success of a firm's past investment policy by providing a summary measure of the *ex post* return on capital invested. Kaplan and Atkinson (1998) also draw attention to the fact that, without some form of measurement of the *ex post* returns on capital, there is little incentive for accurate estimates of future cash flows during the capital budgeting process.

Another feature of the ROI is that it can be used as a common denominator for comparing the returns of dissimilar businesses, such as other divisions within the group or outside competitors. ROI has been widely used for many years in all types of organizations so that most managers understand what the measure reflects and consider it to be of considerable importance.

Despite the widespread use of ROI, a number of problems exist when this measure is used to evaluate the performance of divisional managers. For example, it is possible that divisional ROI can be increased by actions that will make the company as a whole worse off, and conversely, actions that decrease the divisional ROI may make the company as a whole better off. In other words, evaluating divisional managers on the basis of ROI may not encourage goal congruence. Consider the following example:

	Division X	Division Y
Investment project available	£10 million	£10 million
Controllable contribution	£2 million	£1.3 million
Return on the proposed project	20%	13%
ROI of divisions at present	25%	9%

It is assumed that neither project will result in any changes in non-controllable costs and that the overall cost of capital for the company is 15 per cent. The manager of division X would be reluctant to invest the additional £10 million because the return on the proposed project is 20 per cent, and this would reduce the existing overall ROI of 25 per cent. On the other hand, the manager of division Y would wish to invest the £10 million because the return on the proposed project of 13 per cent is in excess of the present return of 9 per cent, and it would increase the division's overall ROI. Consequently, the managers of both divisions would make decisions that would not be in the best interests of the company. The company should accept only those projects where the return is in excess of the cost of capital of 15 per cent, but the manager of division X would reject a potential return of 20 per cent and the manager of division Y would accept a potential return of 13 per cent. ROI can therefore lead to a lack of goal congruence.

Residual income

To overcome some of the dysfunctional consequences of ROI, the residual income approach can be used. For the purpose of evaluating the performance of *divisional managers*, residual income is defined as controllable contribution less a cost of capital charge on the investment controllable by the divisional manager. For evaluating the *economic performance* of the division residual income can be defined as divisional contribution (see Exhibit 19.1) less a cost of capital charge on the total investment in assets employed by the division. If residual income is used to measure the managerial performance of investment centres, there is a greater probability that managers will be encouraged, when acting in their own best interests, also to act in the best interests of the company. Returning to our previous illustration in respect of the investment decision for divisions X and Y, the residual income calculations are as follows:

	Division X (£)	Division Y (£)
Proposed investment	10 million	10 million
Controllable contribution	2 million	1.3 million
Cost of capital charge (15% of the investment cost)	1.5 million	1.5 million
Residual income	0.5 million	− 0.2 million

This calculation indicates that the residual income of division X will increase and that of division Y will decrease if both managers accept the project. Therefore the manager of division X would invest, whereas the manager of division Y would not. These actions are in the best interests of the company as a whole.

A further reason cited in favour of residual income over the ROI measure is that residual income is more flexible, because different cost of capital percentage rates can be applied to investments that have different levels of risk. Not only will the cost of capital of divisions that have different levels of risk differ – so may the risk and cost of capital of assets within the same division. The residual income measure enables different risk-adjusted capital costs to be incorporated in the calculation, whereas the ROI cannot incorporate these differences.

Residual income suffers from the disadvantages of being an absolute measure, which means that it is difficult to compare the performance of a division with that of other divisions or companies of a different size. For example, a large division is more likely to earn a larger residual income than a small division. To overcome this deficiency, targeted or budgeted levels of residual income should be set for each division that are consistent with asset size and the market conditions of the divisions.

Surveys of methods used by companies to evaluate the performance of divisional managers indicate a strong preference for ROI over residual income. For example, the UK survey by Drury *et al.* (1993) reported that the following measures were used:

	(%)
A target ROI set by the group	55
Residual income	20
A target profit *before* charging interest on investment	61
A target cash flow figure	43

Why is ROI preferred to residual income? Skinner (1990) found evidence to suggest that firms prefer to use ROI because, being a ratio, it can be used for inter-division and inter-firm comparisons. ROI for a division can be compared with the return from other divisions within the group or with whole companies outside the group, whereas absolute monetary measures such as residual income are not appropriate in making such comparisons. A second possible reason for the preference for ROI is that 'outsiders' tend to use ROI as a measure of a company's overall performance. Corporate managers therefore want their divisional managers to focus on ROI so that their performance measure is congruent with outsiders' measure of the company's overall economic performance. A further reason, suggested by Kaplan and Atkinson (1998), is that managers find percentage measures of profitability such as ROI more convenient, since they enable a division's profitability to be compared with other financial measures (such as inflation rates, interest rates, and the ROI rates of other divisions and comparable companies outside the group).

Economic value added (EVA(TM))

During the 1990s residual income has been refined and renamed as economic value added (EVA(TM)) by the Stern Stewart consulting organization and they have registered EVA(TM) as their trademark. An article in an issue of *Fortune* magazine (1993) described the apparent success that many companies had derived from using EVA(TM) to motivate and evaluate corporate and divisional managers. *The Economist* (1997) reported that more than 300 firms world-wide had adopted EVA(TM) including Coca-Cola, AT&T, ICL, Boots and the Burton Group. A UK study by El-Shishini and Drury (2005) reported that 23 per cent of the responding organizations used EVA(TM) to evaluate divisional performance.

The EVA(TM) concept extends the traditional residual income measure by incorporating adjustments to the divisional financial performance measure for distortions introduced by generally accepted accounting principles (GAAP). EVA(TM) can be defined as:

$$\text{EVA}^{(TM)} = \text{Conventional divisional profit} \pm \text{accounting adjustments} - \text{cost of capital charge on divisional assets}$$

Our earlier discussion relating to which of the conventional alternative divisional profit measures listed in Exhibit 19.1 should be used also applies here. There are strong theoretical arguments for using controllable contribution as the conventional divisional profit measure for *managerial* performance and divisional contribution for measuring *economic* performance. Many companies, however, use divisional net profit (after allocated costs) to evaluate both divisional managerial and economic performance.

Adjustments are made to the chosen conventional divisional profit measure in order to replace historic accounting data with a measure that attempts to approximate economic profit and asset values. Stern Stewart have stated that they have developed approximately 160 accounting adjustments that may need to be made to convert the conventional accounting profit into a sound measure of EVA$^{(TM)}$ but they have indicated that most organizations will only need to use about ten of the adjustments. These adjustments result in the capitalization of many discretionary expenditures, such as research and development, marketing and advertising, by spreading these costs over the periods in which the benefits are received. Therefore adopting EVA$^{(TM)}$ should reduce some of the harmful side-effects arising from using financial measures that were discussed in Chapter 16. This is because managers will not bear the full costs of the discretionary expenditures in the period in which they are incurred if the expenses are capitalized. Instead, the cost will be spread across the periods when the benefits from the expenditure are estimated to be received. Also because it is a restatement of the residual income measure, compared with ROI, EVA$^{(TM)}$ is more likely to encourage goal congruence in terms of asset acquisition decisions. By making cost of capital visible

SOURCE: ADAPTED FROM INSTITUTE OF MANAGEMENT & ADMINISTRATION REPORT ON FINANCIAL ANALYSIS PLANNING AND REPORTING, SEPTEMBER, 2002.

How the use of EVA$^{(TM)}$ analysis transformed Armstrong's financial performance

The financial mission of a company should be to invest and create cash flows in excess of the cost of capital. If an investment is announced that is expected to earn in excess of the cost of capital, then the value of the firm will immediately rise by the present value of that excess – as long as the market understands and believes the available projections. The question is: What is the best way to measure this?

Traditional measures of return, such as ROI, actually could unwittingly motivate and reward managers to shrink the value of the company. Therefore, the concept EVA$^{(TM)}$ was developed. In a nutshell, EVA$^{(TM)}$ is designed to measure the degree to which a company's after-tax operating profits exceed – or fall short of – the cost of capital invested in the business. It makes managers think more about the use of capital and the amount of capital in each business.

Armstrong World Industries Inc. is a multibillion-dollar manufacturer and supplier of floor coverings, insulation products, ceiling and wall systems, and installation products. In 1993 the decision was made to discontinue the ROI concept and use EVA for strategic planning, performance measurement, and compensation. EVA$^{(TM)}$ is computed from straightforward adjustments to convert book values on the income statement and balance sheet to an economic basis. Armstrong used about a dozen adjustments.

Armstrong considered EVA$^{(TM)}$ to be the best financial measure for accurately linking accounting measures to stock market value and performance, making it ideal for setting financial targets. Changes in behaviour have become focused on three basic actions: (1) improving profit without more capital; (2) investing in projects earning above the cost of capital; and (3) eliminating operations unable to earn above the cost of capital.

On a higher strategic level, EVA$^{(TM)}$ allowed Armstrong to step back to see where the company was losing value. In what the company called its 'sunken ship' chart it was clear that businesses earning above the cost of capital were providing huge amounts of EVA$^{(TM)}$. However, the ship was being dragged down because of negative EVA$^{(TM)}$ businesses and corporate overhead. By selling or combining negative EVA$^{(TM)}$ businesses and by growing and further reducing costs in its positive EVA$^{(TM)}$ businesses, the company provided the potential to more than double its EVA$^{(TM)}$.

REAL WORLD VIEWS 19.1

Discussion points

1 Can you provide examples of accounting adjustments required to compute EVA$^{(TM)}$?

2 Why is EVA$^{(TM)}$ preferred to ROI?

managers are made aware that capital has a cost and they are thus encouraged to dispose of under-utilized assets that do not generate sufficient income to cover their cost of capital.

Stern Stewart developed EVA^(TM) with the aim of producing an overall financial measure that encourages senior managers to concentrate on the delivery of shareholder value. They consider that the aim of managers of companies, whose shares are traded in the stock market, should be to maximize shareholder value. It is therefore important that the key financial measure that is used to measure divisional or company performance should be congruent with shareholder value. Stern Stewart claim that, compared with other financial measures, EVA^(TM) is more likely to meet this requirement and also to reduce dysfunctional behaviour.

There are a number of issues that apply to ROI, residual income or its replacement EVA^(TM). They concern determining which assets should be included in a division's asset base, and the adjustments that should be made to financial accounting practices to derive managerial information that is closer to economic reality.

Determining which assets should be included in the investment base

We must determine which assets to include in a division's asset base to compute both ROI and EVA^(TM). (Note that for the remainder of the chapter we shall use the term EVA^(TM) to incorporate residual income.) If the purpose is to evaluate the performance of the divisional manager then only those assets that can be directly traced to the division and that are controllable by the divisional manager should be included in the asset base. Assets managed by central headquarters should not be included. For example, if debtors and cash are administered centrally, they should not be included as part of the asset base. On the other hand, if a divisional manager can influence these amounts, they should be included in the investment base. If they were not included, divisional managers could improve their profits by granting over-generous credit terms to customers; they would obtain the rewards of the additional sales without being charged with any cost for the additional capital that would be tied up in debtors.

Any liabilities that are within the control of the division should be deducted from the asset base. The term controllable investment is used to refer to the net asset base that is controllable by divisional managers. Our overall aim in analyzing controllable and non-controllable investment is to produce performance measures that will encourage a manager to behave in the best interests of the organization and also to provide a good approximation of managerial performance. It is therefore appropriate to include in the investment base only those assets that a manager can influence, and any arbitrary apportionments should be excluded.

If the purpose is to evaluate the economic performance of the division, the profitability of the division will be overstated if controllable investment is used. This is because a division could not operate without the benefit of corporate assets such as buildings, cash and debtors managed at the corporate level. These assets would be included in the investment base if the divisions were separate independent companies. Therefore many divisionalized companies allocate corporate assets to divisions when comparing divisional profitability with comparable firms in the same industry.

The impact of depreciation

It is common to find fixed assets valued at either their original cost or their written down value for the purpose of calculating return on investment and EVA^(TM), but both of these valuation methods are weak. Consider, for example, an investment in an asset of £1 million with a life of five years with annual cash flows of £350 000 and a cost of capital of 10 per cent. This investment has a positive NPV of £326 850, and should be accepted. You can see from Exhibit 19.2 that the annual profit is £150 000 when straight line depreciation is used. If the asset is *valued at original cost*, there will be a return of 15 per cent per annum for five years. This will understate the true return, because the economic valuation is unlikely to remain at £1 million each year for five years and then immediately fall to zero. If ROI is based on the *written-down value*, you can see from Exhibit 19.2 that the investment base will decline each year – and, with constant profits, the effect will be to show a steady increase in return on investment. This steady increase in return on investment will suggest an improvement in managerial performance when the economic facts indicate that performance has remained unchanged over the five-year period.

Similar inconsistencies will also occur if the EVA^(TM) method is used. If the asset is valued at the original cost, EVA^(TM) of £50 000 will be reported each year (£150 000 profit – (10 per cent cost of capital × 1 million)). On the other hand, if the cost of capital charge is based on the written-down value of the asset, the investment base will decline each year, and EVA^(TM) will increase.

Exhibit 19.2 serves to illustrate that if asset written-down values are used to determine the division's investment base, managers can improve their ROI or EVA^(TM) by postponing new investments and operating with older assets with low written-down values. In contrast, divisional managers who invest in new equipment will have a lower ROI or EVA^(TM). This situation arises because financial accounting depreciation methods (including the reducing balance method) produce lower profitability measures in the earlier years of an asset's life.

To overcome this problem, it has been suggested that ROI or EVA^(TM) calculations should be based on the original cost (i.e. gross book value) of the assets. When assets are measured at gross book value, managers will have an incentive to replace existing assets with new assets. This is because the increase in the investment base is only the difference between the original cost of the old asset and the purchase cost of the new asset. This difference is likely to be significantly less than the incremental cash flow (purchase cost less sale proceeds of the old asset) of the new asset. Managers may therefore be motivated to replace old assets with new ones that have a negative NPV.

To overcome the problems created by using financial accounting depreciation methods, alternative depreciation models have been recommended. These methods are discussed in Learning Note 19.1 on the dedicated open access website (see Preface for details). The theoretically correct solution to the problem is to value assets at their economic cost (i.e. the present value of future net cash inflows) but this presents serious practical difficulties. An appropriate solution to the practical problems is to value assets at their replacement cost (see Lee, 1996 for a discussion of this topic). Although this method is conceptually distinct from the present value method of valuation, it may provide answers which are reasonable approximations of what would be obtained using a present value approach. In addition, replacement cost is conceptually superior to the historical cost method of asset valuation. It follows that the depreciation charge on controllable investment based on replacement cost is preferable to a charge based on historical cost. The ROI and EVA^(TM) would then be calculated on controllable investment valued at replacement cost.

EXHIBIT 19.2 Profitability measures using straight-line depreciation

	1 (£)	2 (£)	3 (£)	4 (£)	5 (£)
Net cash flow	350 000	350 000	350 000	350 000	350 000
Depreciation	200 000	200 000	200 000	200 000	200 000
Profit	150 000	150 000	150 000	150 000	150 000
Cost of capital (10% of WDV)	100 000	80 000	60 000	40 000	20 000
EVA^(TM)	50 000	70 000	90 000	110 000	130 000
Opening WDV of the asset	1 000 000	800 000	600 000	400 000	200 000
ROI	15%	18.75%	25%	37.5%	75%

The effect of performance measurement on capital investment decisions

ADVANCED READING

Capital investment decisions are the most important decisions that a divisional manager will have to make. We noted in Chapter 13 that these decisions should be taken on the basis of the net present value (NPV) decision rule. The way in which the performance of the divisional manager is measured, however, is likely to have a profound effect on the decisions that he or she will make. There is a danger that, because of the way in which divisional performance is measured, the manager may be motivated to take the wrong decision and not follow the NPV rule. We noted in an earlier example (page 483) that the residual income (or EVA$^{(TM)}$) method of evaluation appeared to encourage a divisional manager to make capital investment decisions that are consistent with the NPV rule, but there is no guarantee that this or any other financial measure will in fact motivate the manager to act in this way. Consider the information presented in Exhibit 19.3, which relates to three mutually exclusive projects: X, Y and Z. Applying the NPV rule, you will see from the information presented that the manager should choose project X in preference to project Z, and should reject project Y.

Profits and return on investment

Divisional managers are likely to estimate the outcomes from alternative investments and choose the investment that maximizes their performance measure. Exhibit 19.4 shows the estimated profits and ROI's for projects X, Y and Z. The calculations in Exhibit 19.4 are based on the net cash flows for each year presented in Exhibit 19.3, less straight-line depreciation of £287 000 per year. The ROI is calculated on the *opening* written-down value at the start of the year. From the calculation in Exhibit 19.4 you will see that a manager who is anxious to improve his or her *short-term* performance will choose project Y if he or she is evaluated on total profits or return on investment, since project Y earns the largest profits and ROI in year 1; but project Y has a negative net present value, and should be rejected. Alternatively, a manager who assesses the impact of the project on his or her performance measure *over the three years* will choose project Z, because this yields the highest total profits and average ROI.

Economic value added (EVA$^{(TM)}$)

Let us now consider whether the EVA$^{(TM)}$ calculations are consistent with the NPV calculations. Exhibit 19.5 presents the estimated EVA$^{(TM)}$ calculations for project X. The total present value of

EXHIBIT 19.3 Mutually exclusive capital projects NPV ranking[1]

	X (£000s)	Y (£000s)	Z (£000s)
Machine cost initial outlay (time zero)	861	861	861
Estimated net cash flow (year 1)	250	390	50
Estimated net cash flow (year 2)	370	250	50
Estimated net cash flow (year 3)	540	330	1100
Estimated net present value at 10% cost of capital[a]	77	(52)	52
Ranking on the basis of NPV	1	3	2

Note
[a] The net present value calculations are to the nearest £000.

EVA[TM] for project X is £77 000 and this is identical with the NPV of project X which was calculated in Exhibit 19.3. EVA[TM] is therefore the long-term counterpart of the discounted NPV. Thus, given that maximizing NPV is equivalent to maximizing shareholder value, then maximizing the present value of EVA[TM] is also equivalent to maximizing shareholder value and Stern Stewart's claim that EVA[TM] is congruent with shareholder value would appear to be justified. Consequently, if divisional managers are evaluated on the basis of the long-run present value of EVA[TM], their capital investment decisions should be consistent with the decisions that would be taken using the NPV rule.

However, there is no guarantee that the short-run EVA[TM] measure will be consistent with the longer-run measure if conventional depreciation methods are used. To ensure consistency with the long-run measure and NPV an adjustment must be made within the EVA[TM] accountancy adjustments so that depreciation is based on economic values and not historic book values. For example, if conventional depreciation is used the EVA[TM] for year 1 for each of the projects will be as follows:

	(£000s)[a]
Project X	(−123)
Project Y	17
Project Z	(−323)

Note
[a] Derived from deducting 10% interest (£86 000) on opening WEV from Year 1 profits shown in Exhibit 19.4.

EXHIBIT 19.4 Estimated profit and ROI from mutually exclusive projects

Profits	X (£000s)	Y (000s)	Z (£000s)
Year 1	(37)	103	(237)
Year 2	83	(37)	(237)
Year 3	253	43	813
Total profits	299	109	339

ROI	X (%)	Y (%)	Z (%)
Year 1	(4.3)	11.9	(27.5)
Year 2	14.5	(6.4)	(41.3)
Year 3	88.1	15.0	283.2
Average	32.8	6.8	71.5

EXHIBIT 19.5 Estimated EVA[TM] calculations for project X[a]

	Year 1 (£000s)	Year 2 (£000s)	Year 3 (£000s)	Total (£000s)
Profit before interest	(37)	83	253	
10% interest on opening written-down value	86	57	29	
EVA[TM]	(123)	26	224	
PV of EVA[TM]	(112)	21	168	77

Note
[a] All calculations are to the nearest £000.

The *short-term* measure of EVA$^{(TM)}$ may lead to acceptance of project Y. In addition, a manager concerned about a possible deterioration in his or her expected EVA$^{(TM)}$ may reject project X even when he or she is aware that acceptance will mean an increase in long-term EVA$^{(TM)}$.

We can therefore conclude that the short-run EVA$^{(TM)}$ measure will be consistent with the longer-run measure if alternative unconventional depreciation methods are used. These methods are described in Learning Note 19.1 on the dedicated open access website for this book (see Preface for details) but they are rarely used because they tend not to conform with generally accepted financial accounting principles. Finally, you should note that to calculate EVA$^{(TM)}$ we must calculate the cost of capital for each division. How should the cost of capital be determined? The answer is that the same rate should be used as that used for capital investment decisions based on the approach outlined in Chapter 14. You will find a more detailed discussion of how the cost of capital can be determined in Learning Note 19.2 on the dedicated website.

Addressing the dysfunctional consequences of short-term financial performance measures

The primary objective of profit-making organizations is to maximize shareholder value. Therefore performance measures should be based on the value created by each division. Unfortunately, direct measures of value creation are not possible because the shares for only the business as a whole are traded on the stockmarket. It is not possible to derive stock market values at the segmental or business unit level of an organization. Instead, most firms use accounting profit or ROI measures as a surrogate for changes in market values.

Unfortunately, using accounting measures such as ROI or EVA$^{(TM)}$ as performance measures can encourage managers to become short-term oriented. For example, it has been shown that in the short term managers can improve both of these measures, by rejecting profitable long-term investments. By not making the investments, they can reduce expenses in the current period and not suffer the lost revenues until future periods. Return on investment and EVA$^{(TM)}$ are short-run concepts that deal only with the current reporting period, whereas managerial performance measures should focus on future results that can be expected because of present actions. Ideally, divisional performance should be evaluated on the basis of economic income by estimating future cash flows and discounting them to their present value. This calculation could be made for a division at the beginning and the end of a measurement period. The difference between the beginning and ending values represents the estimate of economic income.

The main problem with using estimates of economic income to evaluate performance is that it lacks precision and objectivity. It is also inconsistent with external financial accounting information that is used by financial markets to evaluate the performance of the company as a whole. It is likely that corporate managers may prefer their divisional managers to focus on the same financial reporting measures that are used by financial markets to evaluate the company as a whole. A final difficulty with measuring economic income is that the individual that is most knowledgeable and in the best position to provide the cash flow estimates is usually the individual whose performance is being evaluated. Thus, managers will be tempted to bias their estimates.

Various approaches can be used to overcome the short-term orientation that can arise when accounting profit-related measures are used to evaluate divisional performance. One possibility is to improve the accounting measures. EVA$^{(TM)}$ represents such an approach. If you refer back to the formula for calculating EVA$^{(TM)}$ you will see that it is computed by making accounting adjustments to the conventional financial accounting divisional profit calculation. These adjustments, such as capitalizing research and development and advertising expenditure, represent an attempt to approximate economic income. Incorporating a cost of capital charge is also a further attempt to approximate economic income. However, it should be noted that conventional accounting profits are the starting point for calculating EVA$^{(TM)}$ and these are based on historic costs, and not future cash flows, so that EVA$^{(TM)}$ can only provide a rough approximation of economic income.

Another alternative for reducing the short-term orientation, and increasing congruence of accounting measures with economic income is to lengthen the measurement period. The longer the measurement period, the more congruent accounting measures of performance are with economic income. For example, profits over a three-year measurement period are a better indicator of economic income than profits over a six-monthly period. The disadvantage of lengthening the measurement period is that rewards are tied to the performance evaluation, and if they are provided a long time after actions are taken, there is a danger that they will lose much of their motivational effects.

Probably the most widely used approach to mitigate against the dysfunctional consequences that can arise from relying excessively on financial measures is to supplement them with non-financial measures that measure those factors that are critical to the long-term success and profits of the organization. These measures focus on areas such as competitiveness, product leadership, productivity, quality, delivery performance, innovation and flexibility in responding to changes in demand. If managers focus excessively on the short-term, the benefits from improved short-term financial performance may be counter-balanced by a deterioration in the non-financial measures. Such non-financial measures should provide a broad indication of the contribution of a divisional manager's current actions to the long-term success of the organization.

The incorporation of non-financial measures creates the need to link financial and non-financial measures of performance. In particular, there is a need for a balanced set of measures that provide both short-term performance measures and also leading indicators of future financial performance from current actions. The balanced scorecard emerged in the 1990s to meet these requirements. The balanced scorecard will be covered extensively in Chapter 22 but at this stage you should note that the financial performance evaluation measures discussed in this chapter ought to be seen as one of the elements within the balanced scorecard. Divisional performance evaluation should be based on a combination of financial and non-financial measures using the balanced scorecard approach.

SUMMARY

The following items relate to the learning objectives listed at the beginning of the chapter.

● **Distinguish between functional and divisionalized organizational structures.**

A functional structure is one in which all activities of a similar type within a company are placed under the control of a departmental head. The organization as a whole is an investment centre. With a divisionalized structure, the organization is split up into divisions that consist of either investment centres or profit centres. Thus, the distinguishing feature is that in a functional structure only the organization as a whole is an investment centre and below this level a functional structure applies throughout. In contrast, in a divisionalized structure the organization is divided into separate profit or investment centres, and a functional structure applies below this level.

● **Explain why it is preferable to distinguish between managerial and economic performance.**

Divisional economic performance can be influenced by many factors beyond the control of divisional managers. For example, good or bad economic performance may arise mainly from a favourable or unfavourable economic climate faced by the division rather than the specific contribution of the divisional manager. To evaluate the performance of divisional managers an attempt ought to be made to distinguish between the economic and managerial performance.

● **Explain the factors that should be considered in designing financial performance measures for evaluating divisional managers.**

To evaluate the performance of a divisional manager only those items directly controllable by the manager should be included in the divisional managerial performance financial measures. Thus, all allocations of indirect costs, such as those central service and administration costs that cannot be influenced by divisional managers, ought not to be included in the performance measure. Such costs can only be controlled where they are incurred, which means those central service managers should be held accountable for them.

● **Explain the meaning of return on investment (ROI), residual income and economic value added (EVA™).**

ROI expresses divisional profit as a percentage of the assets employed in a division. Residual income is defined as divisional profit less a cost of capital charge on divisional investment (e.g. net assets or total assets). During the 1990s, residual income was refined and renamed as EVA™. It extends the traditional residual income measure by incorporating adjustments to the divisional financial performance measure for distortions introduced by using generally accepted accounting principles that are used for external financial reporting. Thus, EVA™ consists of a divisional profit measure plus or minus the accounting adjustments less a cost of capital charge. All three measures can be used either as measures of managerial or economic performance.

● **Compute economic value added (EVA™).**

EVA™ is computed by starting with a conventional divisional profit measure and (a) adding or deducting adjustments for any distortions to divisional profit measures arising from using generally accepted accounting principles for external reporting, and (b) deducting a cost of capital charge on divisional assets. The measure can be used either as a measure of managerial or economic performance as described

above. Typical accounting adjustments include the capitalization of discretionary expenditures, such as research and development expenditure. A detailed calculation of EVA™ is provided in the solution to Review problem 19.21.

● **Explain why performance measures may conflict with the net present value decision model.**

Divisional managerial and economic performance is normally evaluated using short-term financial criteria whereas investment appraisal decisions using NPV are based on the cash flows over the whole life of the projects. Thus, the way that performance is evaluated can have a profound influence on investment decisions and there is a danger that managers will make decisions on the basis of an investment's impact on the short-term financial performance evaluation criteria rather than using the NPV decision rule. A conflict may arise between the measures because performance measures are short-term, multi-period and historical whereas NPV is a future single period measure over the whole life of the investment.

● **Identify and explain the approaches that can be used to reduce the dysfunctional consequences of short-term financial measures.**

Methods suggested for reducing the dysfunctional consequences include (a) use of improved financial performance measures such as EVA™ that incorporate accounting adjustments that attempt to overcome the deficiencies of conventional accounting measures; (b) lengthen the performance measurement period; and (c) do not rely excessively on accounting measures and incorporate non-financial measures using the balanced scorecard approach described in Chapter 22.

Note

1 This exhibit and subsequent comments were adapted from Flower, J.F. (1977). Measurement of divisional performance, *Readings in Accounting and Business Research, Accounting and Business Research Special Issue*, pp. 121–30.

Key terms and concepts

balanced scorecard (p. 491)
controllable contribution (p. 480)
controllable investment (p. 486)
cost centre (p. 478)
divisional contribution (p. 481)
divisional net profit before taxes
(p. 481)

divisionalized organizational
structure (p. 476)
economic value added (EVA™)
(p. 484)
functional organizational structure
(p. 476)
investment centre (p. 478)

profit centre (p. 478)
residual income (p. 483)
return on investment (ROI) (p. 482)
variable short-run contribution
margin (p. 480)

Recommended reading

You should refer to an article by Keef and Roush (2002) for a discussion of the criticisms of economic value added. Lovata and Costigan (2002) report on a survey relating to the adopters of economic value added. For a theoretical review of economic value added see O'Hanlon and Peasnell (1998). See also Bromwich and Walker (1998) for a discussion of residual income in relation to its past and future. A discussion of the computation of divisional cost of capital is presented in De Bono (1997).

Key examination points

Most examination questions include a comparison of residual income (RI) (or EVA™) and return on investment (ROI). Make sure you can calculate these measures and discuss the merits and deficiencies of RI and ROI. You should emphasize that when evaluating short-term divisional performance, it is virtually impossible to capture in one financial measure all the variables required to measure the performance of a divisional manager. It is also necessary to include in the performance reports other non-financial performance measures.

Examination questions may also require you to compare the change in RI or ROI when the assets are valued at original cost or written-down value (see Review problem 19.20). Note that neither method of valuation is satisfactory (you should therefore pay particular attention to the section on 'The Impact of Depreciation' (see pages 486–87). Economic value added is a recent development and is likely to feature more prominently (instead of residual income) in future examinations. You should refer to the solution to Review problem 19.21 for an illustration of the computation of EVA.

ASSESSMENT MATERIAL

The review questions are short questions that enable you to assess your understanding of the main topics included in the chapter. The numbers in parentheses provide you with the page numbers to refer to if you cannot answer a specific question.

The review problems are more complex and require you to relate and apply the content to various business problems. The problems are graded by their level of difficulty. Solutions to review problems that are not preceded by the term 'IM' are provided in a separate section at the end of the book. Solutions to problems preceded by the term 'IM' are provided in the *Instructor's Manual* accompanying this book and also on the lecturer's password protected section of the website www.drury-online.com. Additional review problems with fully worked solutions are provided in the *Student's Manual* that accompanies this book.

The website also includes over 30 case study problems. A list of these cases is provided on pages 665–7. The EVA(TM) at Ault Foods Case (pp. 669–80) is relevant to this chapter.

Review questions

19.1 Distinguish between a functional and divisionalized organizational structure. *(pp. 467–77)*
19.2 Distinguish between profit centres and investment centres. *(p. 478)*
19.3 What are the advantages and disadvantages of divisionalization? *(pp. 478–79)*
19.4 What are the pre-requisites for successful divisionalization? *(p. 479)*
19.5 Why might it be appropriate to distinguish between the managerial and economic performance of a division? *(pp. 479–80)*
19.6 Describe the four alternative profit measures that can be used to measure divisional performance. Which measures are preferable for (a) measuring divisional *managerial* performance and (b) measuring divisional *economic* performance? *(pp. 480–82)*
19.7 Why is it common practice not to distinguish between managerial and economic performance? *(pp. 481–82)*
19.8 Why is it common practice to allocate central costs to measure divisional managerial performance? *(p. 482)*
19.9 Distinguish between return on investment, residual income and economic value added. *(pp. 482–86)*
19.10 How does the use of return on investment as a performance measure lead to bad decisions? How do residual income and economic value added overcome this problem? *(pp. 483–84)*
19.11 Explain how economic value added is calculated. *(pp. 484–85)*
19.12 Describe the effect of performance measurement on capital investment decisions. *(pp. 488–90)*
19.13 Explain the approaches that can be used to reduce the dysfunctional consequences of short-term financial measures. *(pp. 490–91)*

Review problems

19.14 Intermediate. A company has reported annual operating profits for the year of £89.2m after charging £9.6m for the full development costs of a new product that is expected to last for the current year and two further years. The cost of capital is 13 per cent per annum. The balance sheet for the company

shows fixed assets with a historical cost of £120m. A note to the balance sheet estimates that the replacement cost of these fixed assets at the beginning of the year is £168m. The assets have been depreciated at 20 per cent per year.

The company has a working capital of £27.2m.

Ignore the effects of taxation.

The Ecomonic Valued Added® (EVA(TM)) of the company is closest to

a £64.16m
b £70.56m
c £83.36m
d £100.96m

CIMA P1 Management Accounting: Performance Evaluation

19.15 Intermediate. Division L has reported a net profit after tax of £8.6m for the year ended 30 April 2006. Included in the costs used to calculate this profit are the following items:

● interest payable of £2.3m;
● development costs of £6.3m for a new product that was launched in May 2005, and is expected to have a life of three years;
● advertising expenses of £1.6m that relate to the re-launch of a product in June 2006.

The net assets invested in Division L are £30m.

The cost of capital for Division L is 13 per cent per year.

Calculate the Economic Valued Added® for Division L for the year ended 30 April 2006. *(3 marks)*

CIMA P1 Management Accounting: Performance Evaluation

19.16 Intermediate: Return on investment and residual income. Southe Plc has two divisions, A and B, whose respective performances are under review.

Division A is currently earning a profit of £35 000 and has net assets of £150 000.

Division B currently earns a profit of £70 000 with net assets of £325 000.

South Plc has a current cost of capital of 15 per cent.

Required
a Using the information above, calculate the return on investment and residual income figures for the two divisions under review and comment on your results. *(5 marks)*
b State which method of performance evaluation (i.e. return on investment or residual income) would be more useful when comparing divisional performance and why. *(2 marks)*
c List three general aspects of performance measures that would be appropriate for a service sector company. *(3 marks)*

ACCA Paper 1.2 – Financial Information for Management

19.17 Advanced: ROI and residual income. NCL plc, which has a divisionalized structure, undertakes civil engineering and mining activities. All applications by divisional management teams for funds with which to undertake capital projects require the authorization of the board of directors of NCL plc. Once authorization has been granted to a capital application, divisional management teams are allowed to choose the project for investment.

Under the terms of the management incentive plan, which is currently in operation, the managers of each division are eligible to receive annual bonus payments which are calculated by reference to the return on investment (ROI) earned during each of the first two years by new investments. ROI is calculated using the average capital employed during the year. NCL plc depreciates its investments on a straight-line basis.

One of the most profitable divisions during recent years has been the IOA Division, which is engaged in the mining of precious metals. The management of the IOA Division is currently evaluating three projects relating to the extraction of substance 'xxx' from different areas in its country of operation. The management of the IOA Division has been given approval by the board of directors of NCL plc to spend £24 million on one of the three proposals it is considering (i.e. North, East and South projects).

The following net present value (NPV) calculations have been prepared by the management accountant of the IOA Division.

	North Project		East Project		South Project	
	Net cash inflow/ (outflow) £'000	Present value at 12% £'000	Net cash inflow/ (outflow) £'000	Present value at 12% £'000	Net cash inflow/ (outflow) £'000	Present value at 12% £'000
Year 0	(24 000.0)	(24 000.0)	(24 000.0)	(24 000.0)	(24 000.0)	(24 000.0)
Year 1	6 000.0	5 358.0	11 500.0	10 269.5	12 000.0	10 716.0
Year 2	8 000.0	6 376.0	11 500.0	9 165.5	10 000.0	7 970.0
Year 3	13 500.0	9 612.0	11 500.0	8 188.0	9 000.0	6 408.0
Year 4	10 500.0	6 678.0	–	–	3 000.0	1 908.0
NPV		4 024.0		3 623.0		3 002.0

The following additional information concerning the three projects is available:

1 Each of the above projects has a nil residual value.
2 The life of the East project is three years. The North and South projects are expected to have a life of four years.
3 The three projects have a similar level of risk.
4 Ignore taxation.

Required:

a Explain (with relevant calculations) why the interests of the management of the IOA Division might conflict with those of the board of directors of NCL plc. *(10 marks)*

b Explain how the adoption of residual income (RI) using the annuity method of depreciation might prove to be a superior basis for the management incentive plan operated by NCL plc.

   (N.B. No illustrative calculations should be incorporated into your explanation). *(4 marks)*

The IOA Division is also considering whether to undertake an investment in the West of the country (the West Project). An initial cash outlay investment of £12 million will be required and a net cash inflow amounting to £5 million is expected to arise in each of the four years of the life of the project.

The activities involved in the West project will cause the local river to become polluted and discoloured due to the discharge of waste substances from mining operations.

It is estimated that at the end of year four a cash outlay of £2 million would be required to restore the river to its original colour. This would also clear 90 per cent of the pollution caused as a result of the mining activities of the IOA Division.

The remaining 10 per cent of the pollution caused as a result of the mining activities of the IOA Division could be cleared up by a further cash outlay of £2 million.

c Evaluate the West project and, stating your reasons, comment on whether the board of directors of NCL plc should spend the further £2 million in order to eliminate the remaining 10 per cent of pollution. *(6 marks)*
   (Ignore Taxation).

ACCA P3 Performance Management

19.18 Advanced: Accounting, motivational and ethical issues arising from divisional actions. Within a large group, divisional managers are paid a bonus which can represent a large proportion of their annual earnings. The bonus is paid when the budgeted divisional profit for the financial year is achieved or exceeded.

Meetings of divisional boards are held monthly and attended by the senior management of the division, and senior members of group management.

With the aid of the financial year approaching, there had been discussion in all divisional board meetings of forecast profit for the year, and whether budgeted profit would be achieved. In three board meetings, for divisions which were having difficulty in achieving budgeted profits, the following divisional actions had been discussed. In each case, the amounts involved would have been material in determining whether the division would achieve its budget:

- Division A had severely cut spending on training, and postponed routine re-painting of premises.
- Division B had re-negotiated a contract for consultancy services. It was in the process of installing Total Quality Management (TQM) systems, and had originally agreed to pay progress payments to the consultants, and had budgeted to make these payments. It had re-negotiated that the consultancy would invoice the division with the total cost only when the work was completed in the next financial year.
- Division C had persuaded some major customers to take early delivery, in the current financial year, of products originally ordered for delivery early in the next financial year. This would ensure virtually nil stock at year end.

Requirement:

Discuss the financial accounting, budgeting, ethical and motivational issues which arise from these divisional actions.

Comment on whether any group management action is necessary.

(20 marks)
CIMA Stage 4 Management Accounting Control Systems

19.19 Advanced: Conflict between NPV and performance measurement. Linamix is the chemicals division of a large industrial corporation. George Elton, the divisional general manager, is about to purchase new plant in order to manufacture a new product. He can buy either the Aromatic or the Zoman plant, each of which have the same capacity and expected four year life, but which differ in their capital costs and expected net cash flows, as shown below:

	Aromatic	Zoman
Initial capital investment	£6 400 000	£5 200 000
Net cash flows (before tax)		
2001	£2 400 000	£2 600 000
2002	£2 400 000	£2 200 000
2003	£2 400 000	£1 500 000
2004	£2 400 000	£1 000 000
Net present value (@ 16% p.a.)	£315 634	£189 615

In the above calculations it has been assumed that the plant will be installed and paid for by the end of December 2000, and that the net cash flows accrue at the end of each calendar year. Neither plant is expected to have a residual value after decommissioning costs.

Like all other divisional managers in the corporation, Elton is expected to generate a before tax return on his divisional investment in excess of 16 per cent p.a., which he is currently just managing to achieve. Anything less than a 16 per cent return would make him ineligible for a performance bonus and may reduce his pension when he retires in early 2003. In calculating divisional returns, divisional assets are valued at net book values at the beginning of the year. Depreciation is charged on a straight line basis.

Requirements:

a Explain, with appropriate calculations, why neither return on investment nor residual income would motivate Elton to invest in the process showing the higher net present value. To what extent can the use of alternative accounting techniques assist in reconciling the conflict between using accounting-based performance measures and discounted cash flow investment appraisal techniques? *(12 marks)*

b Managers tend to use post-tax cash flows to evaluate investment opportunities, but to evaluate divisional and managerial performance on the basis of pre-tax profits. Explain why this is so and discuss the potential problems that can arise, including suggestions as to how such problems can be overcome.

(8 marks)

c Discuss what steps can be taken to avoid dysfunctional behaviour which is motivated by accounting-based performance targets.

(5 marks)
ICAEW Management Accounting and Financial Management 2

19.20 Advanced: Calculation and comparison of ROI and RI using straight line and annuity depreciation. Alpha division of a retailing group has five years remaining on a lease for premises in which it sells self-assembly furniture. Management are considering the investment of

£600 000 on immediate improvements to the interior of the premises in order to stimulate sales by creating a more effective selling environment.

The following information is available:

(i) The expected increased sales revenue following the improvements is £500 000 per annum. The average contribution: sales ratio is expected to be 40 per cent.

(ii) The cost of capital is 16 per cent and the division has a target return on capital employed of 20 per cent, using the net book value of the investment at the beginning of the year in its calculation.

(iii) At the end of the five-year period the premises improvements will have a nil residual value.

Required:

a Prepare *two* summary statements for the proposal for years 1 to 5, showing residual income and return on capital employed for each year. Statement 1 should incorporate straight-line depreciation. Statement 2 should incorporate annuity depreciation at 16 per cent. *(12 marks)*

b Management staff turnover at Alpha division is high. The divisions investment decisions and management performance measurement are currently based on the figures for the first year of a proposal.

(i) Comment on the use of the figures from statements 1 and 2 in (a) above as decision-making and management performance measures.

(ii) Calculate the net present value (NPV) of the premises improvement proposal and comment on its compatibility with residual income as a decision-making measure for the proposal's acceptance or rejection *(8 marks)*

c An alternative forecast of the increase in sales revenue per annum from the premises improvement proposal is as follows:

Year:	1	2	3	4	5
Increased sales revenue (£000)	700	500	500	300	200

All other factors remain as stated in the question.

(i) Calculate year 1 values for residual income and return on capital employed where (1) straight-line depreciation and (2) annuity depreciation at 16 per cent are used in the calculations.

(ii) Calculate the net present value of the proposal.

(iii) Comment on management's evaluation of the amended proposal in comparison with the original proposal using the range of measures calculated in (a), (b) and (c). *(10 marks)*

ACCA Level 2 Cost and Management Accounting II

19.21 Advanced: Economic valued added approach to divisional performance measurement. The most recent published results for V plc are shown below:

	Published (£m)
Profit before tax for year ending 31 December	13.6
Summary consolidated balance sheet at 31 December	
Fixed assets	35.9
Current assets	137.2
Less: Current liabilities	(95.7)
Net current assets	41.5
Total assets *less* current liabilities	77.4
Borrowings	(15.0)
Deferred tax provisions	(7.6)
Net assets	54.8
Capital and reserves	54.8

An analyst working for a stockbroker has taken these published results, made the adjustments shown below, and has reported his conclusion that 'the management of V plc is destroying value'.

Analyst's adjustments to profit before tax:

	(£m)
Profit before tax	13.6
Adjustments	
Add: Interest paid (net)	1.6
R&D (Research and Development)	2.1
Advertising	2.3
Amortization of goodwill	1.3
Less: Taxation paid	(4.8)
Adjusted profit	16.1

Analyst's adjustments to summary consolidated balance sheet at 31 December (£m)

Capital and reserves	54.8	
Adjustments		
Add: Borrowings	15.0	
Deferred tax provisions	7.6	
R&D	17.4	Last 7 years' expenditure
Advertising	10.5	Last 5 years' expenditure
Goodwill	40.7	Written off against reserves on acquisitions in previous years
Adjusted capital employed	146.0	
Required return	17.5	12% cost of capital
Adjusted profit	16.1	
Value destroyed	1.4	

The Chairman of V plc has obtained a copy of the analyst's report.

Requirement:

a Explain, as management accountant of V plc, in a report to your Chairman, the principles of the approach taken by the analyst. Comment on the treatment of the specific adjustments to R&D, Advertising, Interest and Borrowings and Goodwill. *(12 marks)*

b Having read your report, the Chairman wishes to know which division or divisions are 'destroying value', when the current internal statements show satisfactory returns on investment (ROIs). The following summary statement is available:

Divisional performance, year ending 31 December

	Division A (Retail) (£m)	Division B (Manufacturing) (£m)	Division C (Services) (£m)	Head office (£m)	Total (£m)
Turnover	81.7	63.2	231.8	–	376.7
Profit before interest and tax	5.7	5.6	5.8	(1.9)	15.2
Total assets *less* current liabilities	27.1	23.9	23.2	3.2	77.4
ROI	21.0%	23.4%	25.0%		

Some of the adjustmnts made by the analyst can be related to specific divisions:

- Advertising relates entirely to Division A (Retail)
- R&D relates entirely to Division B (Manufacturing)
- Goodwill write-offs relate to

Division B (Manufacturing)	£10.3m
Division C (Services)	£30.4m

- The deferred tax relates to

Division B (Manufacturing)	£1.4m
Division C (Services)	£6.2m

- Borrowings and interest, per divisional accounts, are:

	Division A (Retail) (£m)	Division B (Mfg) (£m)	Division C (Services) (£m)	Head office (£m)	Total (£m)
Borrowings	–	6.6	6.9	1.5	15.0
Interest paid/ (received)	(0.4)	0.7	0.9	0.4	1.6

Requirement:

Explain, with appropriate comment, in a report to the Chairman, where 'value is being destroyed'. Your report should include

- a statement of divisional performance,
- an explanation of any adjustments you make,
- a statement and explanation of the assumptions made, and
- comment on the limitations of the answers reached. *(20 marks)*

c The use of ROI has often been criticized as emphasizing short-term profit, but many companies continue to use the measure. Explain the role of ROI in managing business performance, and how the potential problems of short-termism may be overcome. *(8 marks)*

CIMA State 4 Management Accounting Control Systems

19.22 Advanced.

a Explain the meaning of each of the undernoted measures which may be used for divisional performance measurement and investment decision-making. Discuss the advantages and problems associated with the use of each.
(i) Return on capital employed.
(ii) Residual income.
(iii) Discounted future earnings. *(9 marks)*

b   Comment on the reasons why the measures listed in (a) above may give conflicting investment decision responses when applied to the same set of data. Use the following figures to illustrate the conflicting responses which may arise:

Additional investment of £60 000 for a 6 year life with nil residual value.

Average net profit per year: £9000 (after depreciation).

Cost of capital: 14 per cent.

Existing capital employed: £300 000 with ROCE of 20 per cent.

(8 marks)

(Solutions should ignore taxation implications.)

ACCA Level 2 Management Accounting

IM19.1 Advanced. A large organization, with a well-developed cost centre system, is considering the introduction of profit centres and/or investment centres throughout the organisation, where appropriate. As management accountant, you will be providing technical advice and assistance for the proposed scheme.

You are required:

a   to describe the main characteristics and objectives of profit centres and investment centres;   *(4 marks)*

b   to explain what conditions are necessary for the successful introduction of such centres;   *(5 marks)*

c   to describe the main behavioural and control consequences which may arise if such centres are introduced;   *(4 marks)*

d   to compare two performance appraisal measures that might be used if investment centres are introduced.   *(4 marks)*

CIMA Stage 3 Management Accounting Techniques

IM19.2 Advanced. 'In the control of divisional operations within a large company, conflicts often arise between the aims of the organization as a whole and the aspirations of the individual divisions.'

What forms may these conflicts take, and how would you expect the finance function to assist in the resolution of such conflicts?

IM19.3 Advanced. Divisionalized structures are normal in large firms, and occur even when centralized structures would be feasible.

Requirements:

a   Explain and discuss the arguments for divisionalized structures in large firms.   *(6 marks)*

b   Explain the costs and potential inefficiencies of a divisionalized structure.   *(6 marks)*

c   Explain how adoption of a divisionalized structure changes the role of top management and their control of subordinates.

(8 marks)

CIMA Stage 4 Management Accounting Control Systems

IM19.4 Advanced: Establishing a system of divisional performance measurement in a hospital.

a   Briefly explain how the measurement of divisional performance differs when assessing the achievement of strategic targets as distinct from operational targets.   *(5 marks)*

b   J is a hospital which supplies a wide range of healthcare services. The government has created a competitive internal market for healthcare by separating the function of service delivery from purchasing. The government provides funds for local health organizations to identify healthcare needs and to purchase services from different organizations which actually supply the service. The service suppliers are mainly hospitals.

J is service supplier and has established contracts with some purchasing organizations. The healthcare purchasing organizations are free to contract with any supplier for the provision of their healthcare requirements.

Previously, J was organized and controlled on the basis of functional responsibility. This meant that each specialist patient function, such as medical, nursing and pharmacy services, was led by a manager who held operational and financial responsibility for its activities throughout the hospital. J now operates a system of control based on devolved financial accountability. Divisions comprising different functions have been established and are responsible for particular categories of patient care such as general medical or general surgical services. Each division is managed by a senior medical officer.

J's Board recognizes that it exists in a competitive environment. It believes there is a need to introduce a system of divisional appraisal. This measures performance against strategic as well as operational targets, using both financial and non-financial criteria. The Board is concerned to develop a system which improves the motivation of divisional managers. This will encourage them to accept responsibility for achieving strategic as well as operational organizational targets. In particular, the Board wishes to encourage more contractual work to supply services to healthcare purchasing organizations from both within and outside its local geographical area. It is a clear aim of the Board that a cultural change in the management of the organization will result from the implementation of such a system.

Requirement:

Discuss the issues which the Board of J should take into consideration in establishing a system of performance measurement for divisional managers in order to ensure the attainment of its strategic targets.

(15 marks)

CIMA Stage 4 Strategic Management Accounting and Marketing

IM19.5 Advanced: Calculation of NPV and ROI and a discussion as to whether a goal congruence exists. J plc's business is organized into divisions. For operating purposes, each division is regarded as an investment centre, with divisional managers enjoying substantial autonomy in their selection of investment projects. Divisional managers are rewarded via a remuneration package which is linked to a Return on Investment (ROI) performance measure. The ROI calculation is based on the net book value of assets at the beginning of the year. Although there is a high degree of autonomy in investment selection, approval to go ahead has to be obtained from group management at the head office in order to release the finance.

Division X is currently investigating three independent investment proposals. If they appear acceptable, it wishes to assign each a priority in the event that funds may not be available to cover all three. Group finance staff assess the cost of capital to the company at 15 per cent.

The details of the three proposals are:

	Project A (000)	Project B (£000)	Project C (£000)
Initial cash outlay on fixed assets	60	60	60
Net cash inflow in year 1	21	25	10
Net cash inflow in year 2	21	20	20
Net cash inflow in year 3	21	20	30
Net cash inflow in year 4	21	15	40

Ignore tax and residual values.

Depreciation is straight-line over asset life, which is four years in each case.

You are required

a   to give an appraisal of the *three* investment proposals from a divisional and from a company point of view;   *(13 marks)*

b   to explain any divergence between these two points of view and to demonstrate techniques by which the views of both the division and the company can be brought into line.   *(12 marks)*

CIMA Stage 4 Management Accounting Control and Audit

IM19.6 Advanced: Merits and problems associated with three proposed divisional performance measures. Sliced Bread plc is a divisionalized company. Among its divisions are Grain and Bakery. Grain's operations include granaries, milling and dealings in the grain markets; Bakery operates a number of bakeries.

The following data relate to the year ended 30 November:

	Grain (£000)	Bakery (£000)
Sales	44 000	25 900
Gain on sale of plant	—	900
	44 000	26 800
Direct labour	8 700	7 950
Direct materials	25 600	10 200
Depreciation	700	1 100
Divisional overheads	5 300	4 550
Head office costs (allocated)	440	268
	40 740	24 068

	Grain (£000)	Bakery (£000)
Fixed assets (at cost less accumulated depreciation)	7000	9000
Stocks	6350	1800
Trade debtors	4000	2100
Cash at bank	1500	—
Bank overdraft	—	750
Trade creditors	3000	2150

Divisional managements (DMs) are given authority to spend up to £20 000 on capital items as long as total spending remains within an amount provided for small projects in the annual budget. Larger projects, as well as sales of assets with book values in excess of £20 000, must be submitted to central management (CM). All day-to-day operations are delegated to DMs, whose performance is monitored with the aid of budgets and reports.

The basis for appraising DM performance is currently under review. At present divisions are treated as investment centres for DM performance appraisal, but there is disagreement as to whether return on capital employed or residual income is the better measure. An alternative suggestion has been made that DM performance should be appraised on the basis of controllable profit; this measure would exclude depreciation and gains or losses on sale of assets, treating investment in fixed assets as a CM responsibility.

The cost of capital of Sliced Bread plc is 15 per cent per annum.

Requirements

a   Calculate for both divisions the three measures (return on capital employed, residual income and controllable profit) which are being considered by Sliced Bread plc, and state any assumptions or reservations about the data you have used in your calculations.
(5 marks)

b   Examine the merits and problems of Sliced Bread plc's three contemplated approaches to DM performance appraisal, and briefly suggest how CM could determine the required level of performance in each case.
(15 marks)

c   Discuss briefly whether further measures are needed for the effective appraisal of DM performance.
(5 marks)

IM19.7 Advanced: Discussion of residual income and ROI and the problems with using these measures. Indico Ltd is a well established company which has operated in a sound but static market for many years where it has been the dominant supplier. Over the past three years it has diversified into three new product areas which are unrelated to each other and to the original business.

Indico Ltd has organized the operation of its four activities on a divisional basis with four divisional general managers having overall responsibility for all aspects of running each business except for finance. All finance is provided centrally with routine accounting and cash management, including invoicing, debt collection and bill payments, being handled by the Head Office. Head Office operating costs were £1 million in 2000. The total capital employed at mid-2000 amounted to £50 million, of which £20 million was debt capital financed at an average annual interest rate of 10 per cent. Head Office assets comprise 50 per cent fixed assets and 50 per cent working capital. To date, the company has financed its expansion without raising additional equity capital, but it may soon require to do so if further expansion is undertaken. It has estimated that the cost of new equity capital would be 20 per cent per annum. No new investment was undertaken in 2000 pending a review of the performance of each division.

The results for the divisions for the year to 31 December 2000 are as follows:

Division

	A (£m)	B (£m)	C (£m)	D (£m)
Sales	110.0	31.0	18.0	13.0
Trading profit	2.0	1.1	1.2	0.5
Exchange gain (1)	2.0	—	—	—
Profit after currency movement	4.0	1.1	1.2	0.5
Exceptional charge (2)	—	—	(1.8)	—
Profit(loss) after exceptional charges	4.0	1.1	(0.6)	0.5
Group interest charge (3)	(1.1)	(0.3)	(0.2)	(0.1)
Net divisional profit(loss)	2.9	0.8	(0.8)	0.4
Depreciation charged above	3.0	1.0	2.0	0.4
Net assets (at year end)	23.5	9.5	4.0	1.8

1   The exchange gain represents the difference between the original sterling value of an overseas contract and the eventual receipts in sterling.
2   The exceptional charge relates to the closure of a factory in January 2000.
3   Group interest is purely a notional charge from Head Office based on a percentage of sales.

Requirements

a   Calculate the return on investment and residual income for each division, ignoring the Head Office costs and stating any assumptions you consider appropriate. Explain how this information is useful in evaluating divisional performance, and outline the main standards of comparison you would use.
(13 marks)

b   Explain how you would deal with the Head Office costs in measuring divisional performance within Indico Ltd.
(4 marks)

c   Discuss the problems arising from using return on investment and residual income to evaluate a speculative new division operating in a high technology industry. State how you could improve these measures to enable better divisional comparisons to be made.
(8 marks)
ICAEW P2 Management Accounting

IM19.8 Advanced: Performance reporting and a discussion of key measurement issues for a divisionalized company. A recently incorporated power company, set up after the privatization of the electricity and coal industries, owns the following assets:

An electricity generating station, capable of being fuelled either by coal or by oil.

Three coal mines, located some 10 to 20 miles from the generating station, connected to a coal preparation plant.

A coal preparation plant, which takes the coal from the three mines and cleans it into a form suitable for use in the generating plant. As a by-product, a quantity of high quality coal is produced which can be sold on the industrial market. The plant has a rail link to the generating station.

The electricity generated is distributed via power lines owned by a separate company, which has an obligation to provide the distribution service on pre-set terms. The market for electricity is highly competitive with demand varying both by the time of day (in the short-term) and by season of the year (in the medium-term).

The power company is in the process of developing a management accounting system which will be used to provide information to assist in setting electricity tariffs for customers and to hold managers within the company accountable for their performance. Initially there are five main operating units, with a manager responsible for each, namely the generating station, the three coal mines and the coal preparation plant.

Requirements

a   Outline, using pro-forma (i.e. without figures) reports where necessary, the accounting statements you would recommend as a basis for the evaluation of the performance of each of the unit managers.
(10 marks)

b   Discuss the key measurement issues that need to be resolved in designing such a responsibility accounting system.
(8 marks)

c   Explain how the information required for tariff-setting purposes might differ from that used for performance evaluation.
(7 marks)
ICAEW P2 Management Accounting

IM19.9 Advanced: Calculations of residual income using straight line and annuity depreciation.

a   Meldo Division is part of a vertically integrated group where all divisions sell externally and transfer goods to other divisions within the group. Meldo Division management performance is measured using controllable profit before tax as the performance measurement criterion.

(i)   Show the cost and revenue elements which should be included in the calculation of controllable divisional profit before tax.
(3 marks)

(ii) Discuss ways in which the degree of autonomy allowed to Meldo Division may affect the absolute value of controllable profit reported.
(9 marks)

b Kitbul Division management performance is measured using controllable residual income as the performance criterion. Explain why the management of Kitbul Division may make a different decision about an additional investment opportunity where residual income is measured using:

(i) straight-line depreciation or

(ii) annuity depreciation based on the cost of capital rate of the division.

Use the following investment information to illustrate your answer:

Investment of £900 000 with a three year life and nil residual value.

Net cash inflow each year of £380 000.

Cost of capital is 10 per cent. Imputed interest is calculated on the written-down value of the investment at the start of each year. Present value of an annuity of £1 for three years at 10 per cent interest is £2.487. (8 marks)

ACCA Level 2 Cost Accounting II

IM19.10 Advanced: Impact of transactions on divisional performance measures and various issues relating to divisional performance measurement.

Scenario

Frantisek Precision Engineering plc (FPE) is an engineering company which makes tools and equipment for a wide range of applications. FPE has 12 operating divisions, each of which is responsible for a particular product group. In the past, divisional performance has been assessed on the basis of Residual Income (RI). RI is calculated by making a finance charge (at bank base rate + 2 per cent) on net assets (excluding cash) as at the end of the year to each division.

Rapier Management Consultants have recently been engaged to review the management accounting systems of FPE. In regard to the performance evaluation system, Rapier have reported as follows:

RI is a very partial and imperfect performance indicator. What you need is a more comprehensive system which reflects the mission, strategy and technology of each individual division. Further, executives should each be paid a performance bonus linked to an indicator which relates to their own personal effectiveness.

FPE's Directors provisionally accepted the Rapier recommendation and have carried out a pilot scheme in the diving equipment (DE) division. DE division manufactures assorted equipment used by sport and industrial divers. Safety is a critical factor in this sector. Customers will not readily accept new products, design features and technologies, and therefore many remain unexploited.

At the start of 2000, Rapier designed a performance evaluation system for DE division as follows:

Factor	Calculated
Return on Capital Employed (ROCE)	Operating profit for the year divided by book value of net assets (excluding cash) at the end of the year.
Cash conversion period (CCP)	Number of days' debtors plus days' stock minus days' creditors outstanding at the end of the year.
Strategy	Number of new products and major design features (innovations) successfully brought to market.

Under the terms of DEs new performance evaluation system, the bases of bonuses for individual divisional managers are:

ROCE over 10%	Chief Executive, Production Manager, Sales Manager
CCP less than 40 days	Accountant, Office Manager
More than 4 innovations	Chief Executive, Design Manager

DE divisions accounting office currently consists of four employees. The division does not have its own bank account. All main accounting systems are operated by FPE's Head Office. DE's accounting staff draw information from the main accounting system in order to prepare weekly budgetary control reports which are submitted to Head Office. The reports prompt regular visits by Head Office accountants to investigate reported cost variances.

Part One

In November 2000, DE's Accountant predicts that DE's results for 2000 will be as follows:

	2000		End 2000
Sales	£6 900 000	Stock	£530 000
Purchases	£2 920 000	Debtors	£1 035 000
Operating profit	£450 000	Creditors	£320 000
Number of innovations	4	Net assets	£4 800 000

The Accountant further forecasts that in the absence of some change in policy or new investment, the corresponding figures for 2001 and end-2001 will be similar to those shown above for 2000. Upon receiving this forecast, DE division's Chief Executive convenes a meeting of his managers to discuss strategy for the rest of 2000 and for 2001. Several proposals are made, including:

From the Office Manager:

I propose that we immediately dispose of £160 000 of stock at cost and defer a creditor payment of £180 000 due 16 December 2000 until 2 January 2001. The first measure will reduce profit by £16 500 a year from 2001 onwards. The second measure will incur an immediate £2000 penalty.

From the Production Manager:

I recommend we invest £400 000 in new equipment, either immediately or in early 2001. This will increase operation profit by £25 000 per year for eight years and the equipment will have a residual value of £40 000 at the end of its life.

From the Design Manager:

I propose we introduce a new electronic digital depth gauge to the market. This will involve an initial investment of £100 000 in new equipment, either immediately or in early 2001, which will have a life of at least ten years. Sales will have to be on 6 months 'buy or return' credit in order to overcome market resistance. I forecast that the new depth gauge will generate £20 000 extra operating profit per year with purchases, sales, stock and creditors all increasing in proportion.

Requirements:

a Explain the impact of each proposal on the reported performance of DE division in 2000 and 2001, having regard to the new performance evaluation criteria stated in the Scenario. State whether or not each proposal is likely to be acceptable to members of DE management. (15 marks)

b State your views (supported by financial evaluation) on the inherent merits of each proposal, having regard to factors you consider relevant. (10 marks)

Note: Where relevant, you may assume that depreciation is on a straight-line basis and DCF evaluation is carried out using an 8 per cent discount rate and 10-year time horizon.

Part Two

A great deal of management accounting practice (including divisional performance evaluation) can be carried out with varying degrees of sophistication. Many new techniques have been developed in recent years. The degree of sophistication adopted in any case is partly influenced by the imagination and knowledge of the management accountant, and partly by the availability of management information technology.

Requirements:

a In the light of this quotation, state your views on the advantages and disadvantages to FPE of using a firm of consultants to advise on the design of management accounting systems. Explain your opinion on the merits of the statement quoted above. (10 marks)

b Explain the main purpose of divisional organisation and the main features of the management accounting systems that are used to support it. (5 marks)

c Explain the changes that might be required in the management accounting operation of DE division if that division became an independent business. (10 marks)

Part Three

There is nothing inherently wrong with the factors used in DE's new performance evaluation system. The problem is what those factors are used for – in particular, their use as a basis for management remuneration.

For one thing, almost any factor is highly vulnerable to manipulation: for another thing, they can seriously distort business decision making.

Requirements:

Having regard to this statement,

    a explain the strengths and weaknesses of RI and ROCE as divisional business performance indicators as far as FPE is concerned;   *(5 marks)*

    b comment critically on the statement made by Rapier (quoted in the Scenario). In particular, explain the problems connected with linking management pay to performance, and the measures that management accountants might take to deal with these problems;
    (7 marks)

    c explain what JIT philosophy is, in the light of a proposal to adopt just-in-time (JIT) practices in the DE division. Write a report for FPE management on whether or not DE division's Production Manager should be paid a bonus linked to CCP instead of one linked to ROCE (see Scenario), in the light of the proposal to adopt JIT practices in the DE division.   *(13 marks)*

        CIMA State 3 Management Accounting Applications

Transfer pricing in divisionalized companies

20

In the previous chapter alternative financial measures for evaluating divisional performance were examined. However, all of the financial measure outcomes will be significantly affected when divisions transfer goods and services to each other. The established transfer price is a cost to the receiving division and revenue to the supplying division, which means that whatever transfer price is set, will affect the profitability of each division. In addition, this transfer price will also significantly influence each division's input and output decisions, and thus total company profits.

In this chapter we shall examine the various approaches that can be adopted to arrive at transfer prices between divisions. Although our focus will be on transfer pricing between divisions (i.e. profit or investment centres) transfer pricing can also apply between cost centres (typically support/service centres) or from cost centres to profit/investment centres. The same basic principles apply as those that apply between divisions, the only difference being that there is no need for a profit element to be included in the transfer price to reimburse the supplying cost centre. A more rigorous economic analysis of the transfer pricing problem is provided in the Appendix at the end of this chapter.

LEARNING OBJECTIVES

After studying this chapter, you should be able to:

- describe the different purposes of a transfer pricing system;

- identify and describe the five different transfer pricing methods;

- explain why the correct transfer price is the external market price when there is a perfectly competitive market for the intermediate product;

- explain why cost-plus transfer prices will not result in the optimum output being achieved;

- explain the two methods of transfer pricing that have been advocated to resolve the conflicts between the decision-making and performance evaluation objectives;

- describe the additional factors that must be considered when setting transfer prices for multinational transactions.

Purpose of transfer pricing

A transfer pricing system can be used to meet the following purposes:

1 To provide information that motivates divisional managers to make good economic decisions. This will happen when actions that divisional managers take to improve the reported profit of their divisions also improves the profit of the company as a whole.

2 To provide information that is useful for evaluating the managerial and economic performance of the divisions.

3 To intentionally move profits between divisions or locations.

4 To ensure that divisional autonomy is not undermined.

Providing information for making good economic decisions

Goods transferred from the supplying division to the receiving division are known as interme-diate products. The products sold by a receiving division to the outside world are known as final products. The objective of the receiving division is to subject the intermediate product to further processing before it is sold as a final product in the outside market. The transfer price of the intermediate product represents a cost to the receiving division and a revenue to the supplying division. Therefore transfer prices are used to determine how much of the intermediate product will be produced by the supplying division and how much will be acquired by the receiving division. In a centralized company the decision as to whether an intermediate product should be sold or processed further is determined by comparing the incremental cost of, and the revenues from, further processing. In a divisionalized organization structure, however, the manager of the receiving division will treat the price at which the intermediate product is transferred as an incre-mental cost, and this may lead to incorrect decisions being made.

For example, let us assume that the incremental cost of the intermediate product is £100, and the additional further processing costs of the receiving division are £60. The incremental cost of producing the final product will therefore be £160. Let us also assume that the supplying division has a temporary excess capacity which is being maintained in order to meet an expected resurgence in demand and that the market price of the final product is £200. To simplify the illustration, we assume there is no market for the intermediate product. The correct short-term decision would be to convert the intermediate product into the final product. In a centralized company this decision would be taken, but in a divisionalized organization structure where the transfer price for the intermediate product is £150 based on full cost plus a profit margin, the incremental cost of the receiving division will be £210 (£150 + £60). The divisional manager would therefore incorrectly decide not to purchase the intermediate product for further processing. This problem can be overcome if the transfer price is set at the incremental cost of the supplying division, which in this example is £100.

Evaluating divisional performance

When goods are transferred from one division to another, the revenue of the supplying division becomes a cost of the receiving division. Consequently, the prices at which goods are transferred can influence each division's reported profits, and there is a danger that an unsound transfer price will result in a misleading performance measure that may cause divisional managers to believe that the transfer price is affecting their performance rather unfairly. This may lead to disagreement and negative motivational consequences.

Conflict of objectives

Unfortunately, no single transfer price is likely to perfectly serve all of the four specified purposes. They often conflict and managers are forced to make trade-offs. In particular, the decision-making and the performance evaluation purposes may conflict with each other. For example, in some situations the transfer price that motivates the short-run optimal economic decision is marginal cost. If the supplier has excess capacity, this cost will probably equal variable cost. The supplying division will fail to cover any of its fixed costs when transfers are made at variable cost, and will therefore report a loss. Furthermore, if a transfer price equal to variable cost (£100 in the above example) is imposed on the manager of the supplying division, the concept of divisional autonomy and decentralization is undermined. On the other hand, a transfer price that may be satisfactory for evaluating divisional performance (£150 in the above example) may lead divisions to make suboptimal decisions when viewed from the overall company perspective.

Alternative transfer pricing methods

There are five primary types of transfer prices that companies can use to transfer goods and services.

1 Market-based transfer prices: These are usually based on the listed price of an identical or similar products or services, the actual price the supplying division sells the intermediate product to external customers (possibly less a discount that reflects the lower selling costs for inter-group transfers), or the price a competitor is offering.

2 Marginal cost transfer prices: Most accountants assume that marginal cost can be approximated by short-run variable cost which is interpreted as direct costs plus variable indirect costs.

3 Full cost transfer prices: The terms full cost or long-run cost are used to represent the sum of the cost of all of those resources that are committed to a product or service in the long-term. Some firms add an arbitrary mark-up to variable costs in order to cover fixed costs and thus approximate full costs.

4 Cost-plus a mark-up transfer prices: With cost-based transfer prices the supplying divisions do not make any profits on the products or services transferred. Therefore they are not suitable for performance measurement. To overcome this problem a mark-up is added to enable the supplying divisions to earn a profit on inter-divisional transfers.

5 Negotiated transfer prices: In some cases transfer prices are negotiated between the managers of the supplying and receiving divisions. Information about the market prices and marginal or full costs often provide an input into these negotiations, although there is no requirement that they must do so.

Exhibit 20.1 shows the results of surveys of the primary transfer pricing methods used in various countries. This exhibit shows that in the USA transfer prices are used by the vast majority of the firms surveyed. It is apparent from all of the surveys that a small minority (less than 10 per cent) transfer at marginal or variable cost. A significant proportion of firms use each of the other methods with the largest proportions transferring goods or services at market prices or either full cost or full cost plus a mark-up. The following sections describe in detail each of the transfer pricing methods and the circumstances when they are appropriate.

Market-based transfer prices

In most circumstances, where a perfectly competitive market for an intermediate product exists it is optimal for both decision-making and performance evaluation purposes to set transfer prices at competitive market prices. A perfectly competitive market exists where the product is homogeneous and no individual buyer or seller can affect the market prices.

When transfers are recorded at market prices divisional performance is more likely to represent the real economic contribution of the division to total company profits. If the supplying division did not exist, the intermediate product would have to be purchased on the outside market at the current market price. Alternatively, if the receiving division did not exist, the intermediate product would have to be sold on the outside market at the current market price. Divisional profits are therefore likely to be similar to the profits that would be calculated if the divisions were separate organizations. Consequently, divisional profitability can be compared directly with the profitability of similar companies operating in the same type of business.

EXHIBIT 20.1 Surveys of company practice

The studies listed below relate to surveys of transfer pricing practices in the UK and USA. It is apparent from these surveys that variable/marginal costs are not widely used, whereas full cost or full cost plus a mark-up are used extensively. Market price methods are also widely used. Similar findings have also been reported in surveys undertaken in Canada (Tang, 1992) and Australia (Joye and Blayney, 1991).

UK survey (Abu-Serdaneh, 2004)
A survey based on responses from 170 companies reported the percentage of companies that used particular transfer pricing methods to a considerable extent. The percentage usage was as follows:

	%	%
Prevailing market price	16	
Adjusted market price	15	31
Unit full manufacturing cost	24	
Unit full manufacturing cost plus a profit margin	38	62
Unit variable manufacturing cost	2	
Unit variable manufacturing cost plus a profit margin	6	
Unit variable manufacturing cost plus a fixed fee	1	9
Negotiated transfer price		8

The findings indicated that a minority of companies used more than one transfer price.

USA Survey (Borkowski, 1990)

Number of Companies Participating	215
Percentage Using Transfer Prices	89.6%

Percentage using transfers on following bases		
Market price		
Full market price	20.2	
Adjusted market price	12.5	32.7
Negotiated		
To external price	13.6	
To manufacturing costs	3.0	
With no restrictions	6.0	22.6
Full cost		
Standard	14.3	
Actual	7.1	
Plus profit based on cost	14.9	
Plus fixed profit	2.4	
Other	2.4	41.1
Variable cost		
Standard	2.4	
Actual	0.6	
Plus contribution based on cost	0.6	3.6
Total		100.00

In a perfectly competitive market the supplying division should supply as much as the receiving division requires at the current market price, so long as the incremental cost is lower than the market price. If this supply is insufficient to meet the receiving division's demand, it must obtain additional supplies by purchasing from an outside supplier at the current market price. Alternatively, if the supplying division produces more of the intermediate product than the receiving division requires, the excess can be sold to the outside market at the current market price.

Where the selling costs for internal transfers of the intermediate product are identical with those that arise from sales in the outside market, it will not matter whether the supplying division's output is sold internally or externally. To illustrate this we shall consider two alternatives. First, assume initially that the output of the supplying division is sold *externally* and that the receiving division purchases its requirements *externally*. Now consider a second situation where the output of the intermediate product is transferred *internally* at the market price and is not sold on the outside market. You should now refer to Exhibit 20.2. The aim of this diagram is to show that divisional and total profits are not affected, whichever of these two alternatives is chosen.

Exhibit 20.2 illustrates a situation where the receiving division sells 1000 units of the final product in the external market. The incremental costs of the supplying division for the production of 1000 units of the intermediate product are £5000, with a market price for the

EXHIBIT 20.2 Profit impact using market-based transfer prices

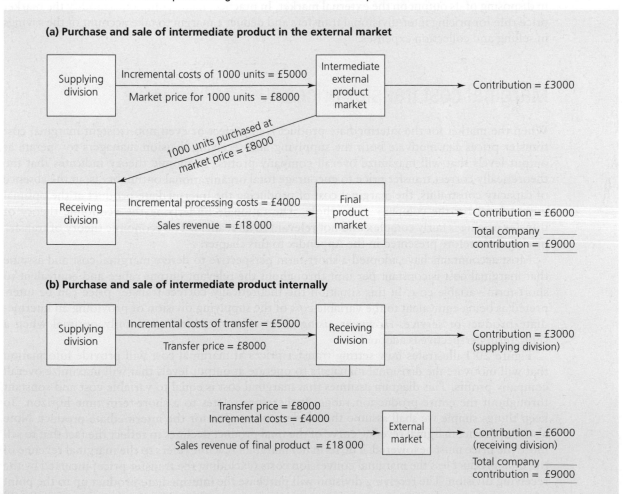

output of £8000. The incremental costs of the receiving division for the additional processing of the 1000 units of the intermediate product are £4000. This output can be sold for £18 000. You will see that it does not matter whether the intermediate product is transferred internally or sold externally – profits of each division and total company profits remain unchanged.

If the supplying division cannot make a profit in the long run at the current outside market price then the company will be better off not to produce the product internally but to obtain its supply from the external market. Similarly, if the receiving division cannot make a long-run profit when transfers are made at the current market price, it should cease processing this product, and the supplying division should be allowed to sell all its output to the external market. Where there is a competitive market for the intermediate product, the market price can be used to allow the decisions of the supplying and receiving division to be made independently of each other.

The effect of selling expenses

In practice, it is likely that total company profits will be different when the intermediate product is acquired internally or externally. The supplying division will incur selling expenses when selling the intermediate product on the external market, but such expenses may not be incurred on inter-divisional transfers. If the transfer price is set at the current market price, the receiving division will be indifferent to whether the intermediate product is obtained internally or externally. However, if the receiving division purchases the intermediate product externally, the company will be worse off to the extent of the selling expenses incurred by the supplying division in disposing of its output on the external market. In practice, many companies modify the market price rule for pricing inter-divisional transfers and deduct a margin to take account of the savings in selling and collection expenses.

Marginal cost transfer prices

When the market for the intermediate product is imperfect or even non-existent marginal cost transfer prices can motivate both the supplying and receiving division managers to operate at output levels that will maximize overall company profits. Economic theory indicates that the theoretically correct transfer price to encourage total organizational optimality is, in the absence of capacity constraints, the marginal cost of producing the intermediate product at the optimal output level for the company as a whole. The rationale underlying the economic theory of transfer pricing is fairly complex and not relevant to all readers. The economic theory of transfer pricing is therefore presented in the Appendix to this chapter.

Most accountants have adopted a short-term perspective to derive marginal cost and assume that marginal cost is constant per unit throughout the relevant output range and equivalent to short-term variable cost. In this situation the theoretically correct transfer price can be interpreted as being equivalent to the variable cost of the supplying division of providing an intermediate product or service. However, using short-term variable cost is only optimal when a short-term perspective is adopted.

Figure 20.1 illustrates how setting transfer prices at marginal cost will provide information that will motivate the divisional managers to operate at output levels that will maximize overall company profits. This diagram assumes that marginal cost is equal to variable cost and constant throughout the entire production range. It therefore relates to a short-term time horizon. To keep things simple we shall assume that there is no market for the intermediate product. Note also that the net marginal revenue curve of the final product declines to reflect the fact that to sell more the price must be lowered. The term net marginal revenue refers to the marginal revenue of the final product less the marginal conversion costs (excluding the transfer price) incurred by the receiving division. The receiving division will purchase the intermediate product up to the point where net marginal revenue equals its marginal costs, as reflected by the transfer price. It will

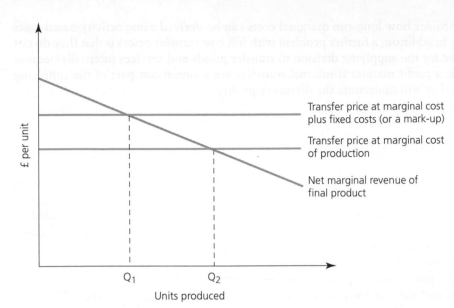

FIGURE 20.1
A comparison of marginal cost and full cost or cost-plus transfer pricing

therefore be the optimal output from the overall company perspective (Q_2) only if the transfer price is set at the marginal cost of the intermediate product or service. If a higher price is set (as indicated by the green line) to cover full cost, or a mark-up is added to marginal cost, then the supplying division will restrict output to the sub-optimal level Q_1.

It is apparent from the surveys of company practice shown in Exhibit 20.1 that less than 10 per cent of the companies transfer goods and services at marginal cost. The major reason for its low use is that when marginal cost is interpreted as being equivalent to variable cost it does not support the profit or investment responsibility structure because it provides poor information for evaluating the performance of either the supplying or receiving divisions. The supplying division will record losses on the capacity allocated to inter-divisional transfers because it bears the full cost of production but only receives revenues that cover variable cost. Conversely the profit of the receiving division will be overstated because it will not bear any of the fixed capacity costs of the supplying division.

A further problem is that marginal costs may not be constant over the entire range of output because step increases in fixed costs can occur. Measuring marginal cost is also difficult in practice beyond a short-term period. The low usage of marginal cost transfer prices suggests that managers reject the short-term interpretation of approximating marginal costs with variable costs. Instead, they view product-related decisions as long-range decisions that must reflect long-run pricing considerations and therefore the appropriate marginal cost to use is long-run marginal cost. We shall examine how long-run marginal cost can be derived later in the chapter.

Full cost transfer prices

Exhibit 20.1 shows that full costs or full cost plus a mark-up are widely used in practice. Their attraction is that, as indicated above, managers view product-related decisions as long-run decisions and therefore require a measure of long-run marginal cost. Full costs attempt to meet this requirement. In addition, they are preferable to short-run variable costs for performance evaluation purposes since the supplying division can recover the full costs of production, although no profit will be obtained on the goods or services transferred.

The major problem with full cost transfer prices is that they are derived from traditional costing systems which, as was pointed out in Chapter 10, can provide poor estimates of long-run marginal costs. Ideally, full cost transfer prices should be derived from an activity-based costing system. We shall consider how long-run marginal costs can be derived using activity-based costs later in the chapter. In addition, a further problem with full cost transfer prices is that they do not provide an incentive for the supplying division to transfer goods and services internally because they do not include a profit margin. If internal transfers are a significant part of the supplying division's business, they will understate the division's profits.

Cost-plus a mark-up transfer prices

Cost-plus a mark-up transfer prices represent an attempt to meet the performance evaluation purpose of transfer pricing by enabling the supplying divisions to obtain a profit on the goods and services transferred. Where full cost is used as the cost base the mark-up is intended to provide a profit margin for the supplying division. Sometimes variable costs are used as the cost base and the mark-up is intended to cover both fixed costs and a profit contribution.

Because they include a margin in excess of either short-run or long-run variable cost, transfer prices based on cost-plus a mark-up will cause inter-divisional transfers to be less than the optimal level for the company as a whole. You will see why if you refer back to Figure 20.1. The green horizontal line in this diagram represents the transfer price and at this price the receiving division manager will restrict output to Q_1 compared to the optimal output level for the company as a whole of Q_2.

A further problem arises if we extend our analysis beyond two divisions to several divisions. If the first division in the process transfers goods to the second division at cost plus 20 per cent, and the goods received from the second division are further processed and transferred at cost plus 20 per cent to a third division, and so on, then the percentage margin becomes enormous by the time a mark-up is added by the final division in the process.

Negotiated transfer prices

The difficulties encountered in establishing a sound system of transfer pricing have led to suggestions that negotiated transfer prices should be used. Negotiated transfer prices are most appropriate in situations where some market imperfections exist for the intermediate product, particularly when there are different selling costs for internal and external sales, or where there exist several different market prices. When there are such imperfections in the market, the respective divisional managers must have the freedom to buy and sell outside the company to enable them to engage in a bargaining process. It is claimed that if this is the case then the friction and bad feeling that may arise from a centrally controlled market transfer price will be eliminated without incurring a mis-allocation of resources.

There are strong arguments for believing that in certain situations, if divisions are allowed to bargain freely with each other, they will usually make decisions that will maximize total company profits – this is of course assuming that managers are competent and know how to use the accounting information. For negotiation to work effectively it is important that managers have equal bargaining power. If the receiving division has many sourcing possibilities for the intermediate product or service, but the supplying division has limited outlets, the bargaining power of the managers will be unequal. Unequal bargaining power can also occur if the transfers are a relatively small proportion of the business for one of the divisions and a relatively large proportion of the business of the other. The manager of the division where transfers are a small proportion of business has considerably more bargaining power because he, or she, will not suffer serious consequences if agreement is not reached on the proposed inter-divisional transfers.

It is important to note that negotiated transfer prices are inappropriate where there is a perfect market for the intermediate product, since in a perfect market situation transfer prices can be based on the competitive market price without the need for the managers to engage in a negotiating process. At the other extreme, where there is no market for the intermediate product, it is most unlikely that managers can engage in meaningful negotiation. Negotiated transfer prices are therefore best suited to situations where there is an imperfect external market for the intermediate product or service. Negotiated transfer prices do, however, suffer from the following limitations:

- because the agreed transfer price can depend on the negotiating skills and bargaining power of the managers involved, the final outcome may not be close to being optimal;
- they can lead to conflict between divisions and the resolution of such conflicts may require top management to mediate;
- measurement of divisional profitability can be dependent on the negotiating skills of managers, who may have unequal bargaining power;
- they are time-consuming for the managers involved, particularly where a large number of transactions are involved.

Even if negotiated prices do not result in an optimum output level, the motivational advantages of giving managers full independence over their input and output decisions may lead to increased profits that outweigh the loss of profits from negotiated non-optimal transfer prices.

Marginal cost plus opportunity cost

Setting transfer prices at the marginal (i.e. incremental) cost of the supplying division per unit transferred plus the opportunity cost per unit of the supplying division is often cited as a general rule that should lead to optimum decisions for the company as a whole. Opportunity cost is defined as the contribution forgone by the supplying division from transferring internally the intermediate product. Assuming that marginal cost is equivalent to variable cost applying this rule, will result in the transfer price being set at the variable cost per unit when there is no market for the intermediate product. Why? If the facilities are dedicated to the production of the intermediate product they will have no alternative use, so the opportunity cost will be zero.

Consider now a situation where is a perfectly competitive external market for the intermediate product. Assume that the market price for the intermediate product is £20 per unit and the variable cost per unit of output is £5. If the supplying division has no spare capacity the contribution forgone from transferring the intermediate product is £15. Adding this to the variable cost per unit will result in the transfer price being set at the market price of £20 per unit. What is the transfer price if the supplying division has temporary spare capacity? In this situation there will be no forgone contribution and the transfer price will be set at the variable cost per unit of £5.

You should have noted that applying the above general rule leads to the same transfer price as was recommended earlier in this chapter. In other words, if there is a perfectly competitive external market for the intermediate product, the market price is the optimal transfer price. When there is no market for the intermediate product, transfers should be made at the marginal cost per unit of output of the intermediate product. Thus, the general rule is merely a restatement of the principles that have been established earlier. The major problem with applying this general rule is that it is difficult to apply in more complex situations such as when there is an imperfect market for the intermediate product.

An illustration of transfer pricing

The data used in Example 20.1 will now be used to illustrate the impact that transfer prices can have on divisional profitability and decision-making. You should now refer to Example 20.1.

At *the full cost plus a mark-up transfer price* of £35 the profit computations for each division will be as follows:

Oslo Division (Supplying division)

Output level (units)	Transfer price revenues	Variable costs	Fixed costs	Total profit/(loss)
1000	35 000	11 000	60 000	(36 000)
2000	70 000	22 000	60 000	(12 000)
3000	105 000	33 000	60 000	12 000
4000	140 000	44 000	60 000	36 000
5000	175 000	55 000	60 000	60 000
6000	210 000	66 000	60 000	84 000

Bergen Division (Receiving division)

Output level (units)	Total revenues	Variable costs	Total cost of transfers	Fixed costs	Total profit/(loss)
1000	100 000	7 000	35 000	90 000	(32 000)
2000	180 000	14 000	70 000	90 000	6 000
3000	240 000	21 000	105 000	90 000	24 000
4000	280 000	28 000	140 000	90 000	22 000
5000	300 000	35 000	175 000	90 000	0
6000	300 000	42 000	210 000	90 000	(42 000)

EXAMPLE 20.1

The Oslo division and the Bergen division are divisions within the Baltic Group. One of the products manufactured by the Oslo division is an intermediate product for which there is no external market. This intermediate product is transferred to the Bergen division where it is converted into a final product for sale on the external market. One unit of the intermediate product is used in the production of the final product. The expected units of the final product which the Bergen division estimates it can sell at various selling prices are as follows:

Net selling price (£)	Quantity sold Units
100	1000
90	2000
80	3000
70	4000
60	5000
50	6000

The costs of each division are as follows:

(£)	Oslo (£)	Bergen (£)
Variable cost per unit	11	7
Fixed costs attributable to the products	60 000	90 000

The transfer price of the intermediate product has been set at £35 based on a full cost plus a mark-up.

The supplying division maximizes profits at an output level of 6000 units whereas the receiving division maximizes profits at an output level of 3000 units. The receiving division will therefore purchase 3000 units from the supplying division. This is because the Bergen division will compare its net marginal revenue with the transfer price and expand output as long as the net marginal revenue of the additional output exceeds the transfer price. Remember that net marginal revenue was defined as the marginal revenue from the sale of the final product less the marginal conversion costs (excluding the transfer price). The calculations are as follows:

Units	Net marginal revenue (£)
1000	93 000 (100 000 – 7000)
2000	73 000 (80 000 – 7000)
3000	53 000 (60 000 – 7000)
4000	33 000 (40 000 – 7000)
5000	13 000 (20 000 – 7000)
6000	–7 000 (0 – 7000)

Faced with a transfer price of £35 000 per 1000 units the Bergen division will not expand output beyond 3000 units because the transfer price paid for each batch exceeds the net marginal revenue.

Let us now look at the profit at the different output levels for the company as a whole. Note that these calculations do not incorporate the transfer price since it represents inter-company trading with the revenue from the supplying division cancelling out the cost incurred by the receiving division.

Whole company profit computations

Output level (units)	Total revenues	Company variable costs	Company fixed costs	Company profit/(loss)
1000	100 000	18 000	150 000	(68 000)
2000	180 000	36 000	150 000	(6 000)
3000	240 000	54 000	150 000	36 000
4000	280 000	72 000	150 000	58 000
5000	300 000	90 000	150 000	60 000
6000	300 000	108 000	150 000	42 000

The profit maximizing output for the company as a whole is 5000 units. Therefore the current transfer pricing system does not motivate the divisional managers to operate at the optimum output level for the company as a whole.

To induce overall company optimality the *transfer price must be set at the marginal cost of the supplying division*, which over the time horizon and output levels under consideration, is the unit variable cost of £11 per unit. Therefore the transfer price for each batch of 1000 units would be £11 000. The receiving division will expand output as long as net marginal revenue exceeds the transfer price. Now look at the net marginal revenue that we calculated for the receiving division. You will see that the net marginal revenue from expanding output from 4000 to 5000 units is £13 000 and the transfer price that the receiving division must pay to acquire this batch of 1000 units is £11 000. Therefore expanding the output will increase the profits of the supplying division. Will the manager of the receiving division be motivated to expand output from 5000 to 6000 units? The answer is no because the net marginal revenue (–£7000) is less than the transfer price of purchasing the 1000 units.

Setting the transfer price at the unit marginal (variable) cost of the supplying division will motivate the divisional managers to operate at the optimum output level for the company as a whole provided that the supplying division manager is instructed to meet the demand of the receiving division at this transfer price. Although the variable cost transfer price encourages overall company optimality it is a poor measure of divisional performance. The supplying division manager will be credited with transfer price revenues of £11 000 per 1000 units. If you look back at the profit computations for the Oslo division you will see that the transfer price revenues will be identical to the variable cost column and therefore a loss equal to the fixed costs of £60 000 will be reported for all output levels. In the short-term the fixed costs are unavoidable and therefore the divisional manager is no worse off since these fixed costs will be still incurred but in the longer-term some, or all of them, may be avoidable and the manager would not wish to produce the intermediate product. The performance measure will overstate the performance of the receiving division because all of the contribution (sales less variable costs) from the sale of the final product will be credited to the manager of the receiving division.

Let us now consider a *full cost transfer price without the mark-up*. We need to estimate unit fixed costs at the planning stage for making decisions relating to output levels. You will also recall from Chapter 3 that it was pointed out that pre-determined fixed overhead rates should be established. Let us assume that the 5000 units optimal output level for the company as a whole is used to determine the fixed overhead rate per unit. Therefore the fixed cost per unit for the intermediate product will be £12 per unit (£60 000 fixed costs/5000 units) giving a full cost of £23 (£11 variable cost plus £12 fixed cost). If the transfer price is set at £23 per unit (i.e. £23 000 per 1000 batch) the receiving division manager will expand output as long as net marginal revenues exceeds the transfer price. If you refer to the net marginal revenue schedule you will see that the receiving division manager will choose to purchase 4000 units. The manager will choose not to expand output to the 5000 units optimal level for the company as a whole because the transfer cost of £23 000 exceeds the net marginal revenue of £13 000. Also at the selected output level of 4000 units the total transfer price revenues of the receiving division will be £92 000 (4000 units at £23) but you will see from the profit calculations for the Oslo division that the total costs are £104 000 (£44 000 + £60 000). Therefore the supplying division will report a loss because all of its fixed costs have not been recovered. Hence the transfer price is suitable for neither performance evaluation nor ensuring that optimal output decisions are made.

Would the managers be able to *negotiate a transfer price* that meets the decision-making and performance evaluation requirements? If the manager of the supplying division cannot avoid the fixed costs in the short-run he or she will have no bargaining power because there is no external market for the intermediate product and would accept any price as long as it is not below variable cost. Meaningful negotiation is not possible. If the fixed costs are avoidable the manager has some negotiating power since he or she can avoid £60 000 by not producing the intermediate product. The manager will try and negotiate a selling price in excess of full cost. If an output level of 5000 units is used to calculate the full cost the unit cost from our earlier calculations was £23 and the manager will try and negotiate a price in excess of £23. If you examine the net marginal revenue of the receiving division you will see that the manager of the receiving division will not expand output to 5000 units if the transfer price is set above £23 per unit. As indicated earlier negotiation is only likely to work when there is an external market for the intermediate market.

We can conclude from this illustration that to ensure overall company optimality the transfer price must be set at the marginal cost of the supplying division. Our analysis has focused on the short term, a period during which we have considered that fixed costs are irrelevant and unavoidable. In the longer term fixed costs are relevant and avoidable and thus represent a marginal cost that should be considered for decision-making. Thus for long-term decisions marginal cost should incorporate avoidable fixed costs but we have noted in earlier chapters that they should not be unitized since this is misleading because it gives the impression that they are variable with output. To incorporate avoidable fixed costs within long-run marginal cost they should be added as a lump-sum to short-run marginal (variable) costs. This is a feature of one of the proposals that we shall look at in the next section.

Proposals for resolving transfer pricing conflicts

Our discussion so far has indicated that in the absence of a perfect market for the intermediate product none of the transfer pricing methods can perfectly meet both the decision-making and performance evaluation requirements and also not undermine divisional autonomy. It has been suggested that if the external market for the intermediate product does not approximate closely those of perfect competition, then if long-run marginal cost can be accurately estimated, transfers at marginal cost should motivate decisions that are optimal from the overall company's perspective. However, transfers at marginal cost are unsuitable for performance evaluation since they do not provide an incentive for the supplying division to transfer goods and services internally. This is because they do not contain a profit margin for the supplying division. Central headquarters intervention may be necessary to instruct the supplying division to meet the receiving division's demand at the marginal cost of the transfers. Thus, divisional autonomy will be undermined. Transferring at cost-plus a mark-up creates the opposite conflict. Here the transfer price meets the performance evaluation requirement but will not induce managers to make optimal decisions.

To resolve the above conflicts the following transfer pricing methods have been suggested:

1 adopt a dual-rate transfer pricing system;
2 transfer at a marginal cost plus a fixed lump-sum fee.

Dual-rate transfer pricing system

Dual-rate transfer pricing uses two separate transfer prices to price each inter-divisional transaction. For example, the supplying division may receive the full cost plus a mark-up on each transaction and the receiving division may be charged at the marginal cost of the transfers. The former transfer price is intended to approximate the market price of the goods or services transferred. Exhibit 20.3, which relates to inter-divisional trading between two divisions in respect of 100 000 units of an intermediate product, is used to illustrate the application of a dual-rate transfer pricing system. You will see that if the transfer price is set at the supplying division's marginal cost of £10 per unit for the intermediate product, the supplying division will be credited with a zero contribution from the transfers, and all of the total contribution of £1 million from inter-divisional trading will be assigned to the receiving division.

Dual-rate transfer pricing can be implemented by setting the transfer price to be charged to the receiving division at the marginal cost of the supplying division (£10 per unit). To keep things simple here, the transfer price that the supplying division receives is set at marginal cost plus 50 per cent, giving a price of £15. It is assumed that the mark-up added will be sufficient to cover the supplying division's fixed costs and also provide a profit contribution. Therefore the receiving division manager will use the marginal cost of the supplying division which should ensure that decisions are made that are optimal from the company's perspective. The transfer price should also meet the performance evaluation requirements of the supplying division since each unit transferred generates a profit. Thus the supplying division manager is motivated to transfer the intermediate product internally. The reported outcomes for each division using the above dual-rate transfer prices, and the information shown in Exhibit 20.3 would be as follows (see p. 514):

EXHIBIT 20.3 Projected financial statement from inter-group trading

	(£)	(£)
Sale of final product: 100 000 units at £50		5 000 000
Marginal costs:		
Supplying division processing costs (100 000 units at £10)	1 000 000	
Receiving division conversion costs (100 000 units at £30)	3 000 000	4 000 000
Total contribution from inter-divisional trading		1 000 000

Supplying division	(£)	Receiving division	(£)
Transfers to the supplying division at £15 (100 000 units at £10 plus 50%)	1 500 000	Sales of the final product at £50 (100 000 units)	5 000 000
Less: marginal processing costs	1 000 000	Less marginal costs: Supplying division transfers (100 000 units at £10)	(1 000 000)
		Conversion costs (100 000 units at £30)	(3 000 000)
Profit contribution	500 000	Profit contribution	1 000 000

Note that the contribution for the company as a whole shown in Exhibit 20.3 is less than the sum of the divisional profits by £500 000, but this can be resolved by a simple accounting adjustment.

Dual-rate transfer prices are not widely used in practice for several reasons. First, the use of different transfer prices causes confusion, particularly when the transfers spread beyond two divisions. Secondly, they are considered to be artificial. Thirdly, they reduce divisional incentives to compete effectively. For example, the supplying division can easily generate internal sales to the receiving divisions when they are charged at marginal cost. This protects them from competition and gives them little incentive to improve their productivity. Finally, top-level managers do not like to double count internal profits because this can result in misleading information and create a false impression of divisional profits. Furthermore, the inter-divisional profits can be considerably in excess of total company profits where a sequence of transfers involves several divisions. At the extreme all of the divisions may report profits when the company as a whole is losing money.

Marginal costs plus a fixed lump-sum fee

A solution that has been proposed where the market for the intermediate product is imperfect or non-existent, and where the supplying division has no capacity constraints, is to price all transfers at the short-run marginal cost and for the supplying division to also charge the receiving division a fixed fee for the privilege of obtaining these transfers at short-run marginal cost. This approach is sometimes described as a two-part transfer pricing system. With this system, the receiving division acquires additional units of the intermediate product at the marginal cost of production. Therefore when it equates its marginal costs with its marginal revenues to determine the optimum profit-maximizing output level, it will use the appropriate marginal costs of the supplying division. The supplying division can recover its fixed costs and earn a profit on the inter-divisional transfers through the fixed fee charged each period. The fixed fee is intended to compensate the supplying division for tying up some of its fixed capacity for providing products or services that are transferred internally. The fixed fee should cover a share of fixed costs of the supplying division and also provide a return on capital. For example, it can be based on the receiving division's budgeted use of the average capacity of the supplying division. Therefore if a particular receiving division plans to use 25 per cent of a supplying division's average capacity, the division would be charged 25 per cent of the fixed costs plus a further charge to reflect the required return on capital. The fixed fee plus the short-run marginal cost represents an estimate of long-run marginal cost.

The advantage of this approach is that transfers will be made at the marginal cost of the supplying division, and both divisions should also be able to report profits from inter-divisional trading. Furthermore, the receiving divisions are made aware, and charged for the full cost of obtaining intermediate products from other divisions, through the two components of the two-part transfer pricing system. It also stimulates planning, communication and coordination amongst the divisions because the supplying and receiving divisions must agree on the capacity requirements in order to determine the bases for the fixed fee.

If you refer back to Example 20.1 you will see that this proposal would result in a transfer price at the short-run marginal (variable) cost of £11 per unit for the intermediate product plus a fixed fee lump-sum payment of £60 000 to cover the fixed costs of the capacity allocated to producing the intermediate product. In addition, a fixed sum to reflect the required return on the capital employed would be added to the £60 000. Adopting this approach the receiving division will use the short-run variable cost to equate with its net marginal revenue and choose to purchase the optimal output level for the company as a whole (5000 units). For longer-term decisions the receiving division will made aware that the revenues must be sufficient to cover the full cost of producing the intermediate product (£11 unit variable cost plus £60 000 fixed costs plus the opportunity cost of capital). When the lump-sum fixed fee is added to the short-run transfer price you will see that the supplying division will report a profit at all output levels.

Kaplan and Cooper (1998) advocate the two-part pricing system approach using an activity-based costing (ABC) system to calculate long-run marginal cost. The short-run element of the marginal cost consists of the cost of the supplying division's unit-level and batch-level activities assigned to the intermediate product or service. You should be able to recall from Chapter 10 that unit-level activities consume resources in proportion to the number of units of production and sales volume and typically include direct labour and material costs. Batch-level activities, such as setting-up a machine or processing a purchase order, are performed each time a batch of goods is produced. Therefore the costs of batch-related activities vary with the number of batches made. They are treated as fixed costs by traditional costing systems.

The fixed fee is added to approximate long-run marginal cost. It consists of an annual fee derived from the product-related and facility-sustaining costs. Remember from Chapter 10 that product-sustaining costs are performed to enable the production and sale of individual products (or services) and include the technical support provided for individual products or services. Facility-sustaining costs are the costs incurred to support a facility's manufacturing process and include general administrative, plant management and property costs. The fixed fee should be based on the user's planned use of the supplying division's products and facilities. For example, if a receiving division plans to use 20 per cent of the average capacity of the supplying division and 30 per cent of the output of a particular product then the fixed fee would be 20 per cent of the facility-sustaining costs plus 30 per cent of the product's sustaining costs.

The prepaid capacity would be reserved for the user paying for that capacity. Kaplan and Atkinson (1998) suggest that the approach has two desirable economic traits. First, in the short-run, transfers will take place at short-run marginal costs (which consist of unit and batch-related costs) as specified by economic theory. Second, managers will be more honest in negotiations at the capacity acquisition stage. If they overstate their estimated requirements in order to ensure adequate capacity for their own use, they will pay a higher fixed fee. Alternatively, if they understate their estimated requirements, to reduce their fixed fee, they may not have sufficient capacity for their needs as the capacity may have been reserved for others who have expressed a willingness to pay for the capacity. When capacity expectations are not realized there is a danger that capacity allocations based on expectations may no longer be assigned to their most profitable current uses. This problem can be overcome by allowing divisions to subcontract with each other so that divisions facing better opportunities can rent the excess capacity from other divisions that they have previously reserved.

Domestic transfer pricing recommendations

This chapter has described the various approaches that can be adopted to arrive at transfer prices for transactions between different units within an organization and the circumstances where they

REAL
WORLD
VIEWS
20.1

How a multinational pharmaceutical company solved its transfer pricing problems using ABC

Teva Pharmaceutical Industries Ltd reorganized its pharmaceutical operations into decentralized cost and profit centres. Teva proposed a transfer pricing system based on marginal costs. But the proposed transfer pricing system generated a storm of controversy. First, some executives observed that the marketing divisions would report extremely high profits because they were being charged for the variable costs only. Second, the operations division would get 'credit' only for the variable expenses. There would be little pressure and motivation to control non-variable expenses. Third, if Teva's plants were less efficient than outside manufacturers of the pharmaceutical products, the marginal cost transfer price would give the marketing divisions no incentive to shift their source of supply. An alternative approach had to be found.

Teva's managers considered, but rejected, several traditional methods for establishing a new transfer pricing system. Market price was not feasible because no market existed for Teva's manufactured and packaged pharmaceutical products that had not been marketed to customers. Senior executives also believed strongly that negotiated transfer prices would lead to endless arguments among managers in the different divisions, which would consume excessive time on non-productive discussions.

Teva solved its transfer pricing problem by using ABC. Transfer prices are calculated in two different procedures. The first one assigns unit and batch-level costs, and the second assigns product-specific and plant-level costs. The marketing divisions are charged for unit-level costs (principally materials and labour) based on the actual quantities of each individual product they acquire. In addition, they are charged batch-level costs based on the actual number of production and packaging batches of each product they order. The product-specific and plant-level expenses are charged to marketing divisions annually in lump sums based on budgeted information.

What about unused capacity? To foster a sense of responsibility among marketing managers for the cost of supplying capacity resources, Teva charges the marketing division that experienced the decline in demand a lump-sum assignment for the cost of maintaining the unused production capacity in an existing line. The assignment of the plant-level costs receives much attention, particularly from the managers of the marketing divisions. They want to verify that these costs do indeed stay 'fixed' and don't creep upward each period. The marketing managers make sure that increases in plant-level costs occur only when they request a change in production capacity.

Marketing managers now distinguish between products that cover all manufacturing costs versus those that cover only the unit and batch-level expenses but not their annual product-sustaining and plant-level expenses. Because of the assignment of unused capacity expenses to the responsible marketing division, the marketing managers incorporate information about available capacity when they make decisions about pricing, product mix and product introduction.

Discussion points

1   How does the transfer pricing system overcome the limitation's of marginal cost transfer pricing?

2   Why is it important that capacity costs are taken into account when making pricing and product mix decisions?

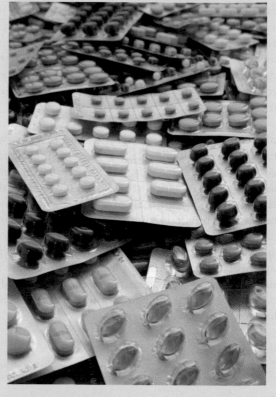

© MARCELO WAIN/ISTOCKPHOTO.COM

SOURCE: ADAPTED FROM KAPLAN, R.S., WEISS, D. AND DESEH, E. (1997) TRANSFER PRICING WITH ABC, *MANAGEMENT ACCOUNTING (USA)*, MAY, PP. 20–8.

are appropriate. The following is a summary of the recommendations that can be derived from our discussion of the different transfer pricing methods:

1 Where a competitive market exists for the intermediate product, the market price (less any adjustments to reflect additional selling and distribution and collection expenses to outside customers) should be used as the transfer price.

2 Where no external market exists for the intermediate product, transfers should be made at the long-run marginal cost of producing a product or delivering a service. The long-run marginal cost should consist of two elements – a short-run marginal cost per unit of the product or service transferred and a fixed lump-sum fee based on the receiving division's budgeted use of the average capacity of the supplying division. The short-run marginal cost per unit plus the lump-sum fixed fee ensures that the receiving division incorporates the full costs of the supplying division's resources required to produce the intermediate product and also motivates the supplying divisions because they are reimbursed for the capacity utilized.

3 Where an imperfect market for the intermediate product or service exists and a small number of products, or transactions, are involved, a negotiated transfer pricing system is likely to be the most suitable method. Here some form of external benchmark price is likely to be available to enable a meaningful bargaining process to take place between the supplying and receiving divisional managers.

4 Where cost-based transfer prices are used standard costs, and not actual costs, per unit of output should be used. If actual costs are used the supplying divisions will be able to pass on the cost of any inefficiencies to the receiving divisions. Using standard costs ensures that the cost of inefficiencies are borne by the supplying divisions.

International transfer pricing

So far we have concentrated on domestic transfer pricing. International transfer pricing is concerned with the prices that an organization uses to transfer products between divisions in different countries. The rise of multinational organizations introduces additional issues that must be considered when setting transfer prices.

When the supplying and the receiving divisions are located in different countries with different taxation rates, and the taxation rates in one country are much lower than those in the other, it would be in the company's interest if most of the profits were allocated to the division operating in the low taxation country. For example, consider an organization that manufactures products in Country A, which has a marginal tax rate of 25 per cent and sells those products to Country B, which has a marginal tax rate of 40 per cent. It is in the company's best interests to locate most of its profits in Country A, where the tax rate is lowest. Therefore it will wish to use the highest possible transfer price so that the receiving division operating in a Country B will have higher costs and report lower profits whereas the supplying division operating in Country A will be credited with higher revenues and thus report the higher profits. In many multinational organizations, the taxation issues outweigh other transfer pricing issues and the dominant consideration in the setting of transfer prices is the minimization of global taxes.

Taxation authorities in each country are aware that companies can use the transfer pricing system to manipulate the taxable profits that are declared in different countries and investigate the transfer pricing mechanisms of companies to ensure that they are not using the transfer pricing system to avoid paying local taxes. For example, in the UK the Income and Corporate Taxes Act 1988, Section 770 and the Finance Act 1998 (Chapter 36 – Schedules 16 and 17) deal with international transfer pricing issues. In an attempt to provide a world-wide consensus on the pricing of international intra-firm transactions the Organization for Economic Co-operation and Development issued a guideline statement in 1995 (OECD, Paris, 1995). This document is important because the taxation authorities in most countries have used it as the basis for regulating transfer pricing behaviour of international intra-firm transactions. The OECD guidelines are based on the arm's-length price principle which relates to the price that would have resulted if the prices actually used had been between two unrelated parties. The arm's-length principle can be implemented using one of the following methods:

1 the comparable uncontrolled price method (which uses externally verified prices of similar transactions involving unrelated prices);

2 the resale price method (which deducts a percentage from the selling price from the final product to allow for profit);

3 the cost-plus method.

The OECD guidelines state that, whenever possible the comparable uncontrolled price method should be used and if there is no market price preference should be given to cost-plus. Where the cost-plus method is used considerable variations in costing practices exist that provide some flexibility for a company to engage in opportunistic behaviour to reduce their taxation burden when determining the cost-plus transfer price. Studies by, Jacob (1996), Harris (1993) and Klassen *et al.* (1993) in the USA and Oyelere and Emmanuel (1998) in the UK found evidence to suggest that multinational enterprises used transfer pricing to shift income between geographical locations in response to changes in taxation rates and rules.

It would appear that multinational companies should use two transfer pricing systems – one for internal purposes based on our discussion in the earlier part of this chapter and another for taxation purposes. However, evidence of two transfer pricing systems is likely to attract the attention of the taxation authorities. It is easier for companies to claim that they are not manipulating profits to evade taxes if they use the same transfer pricing method for taxation and internal purposes. For this reason, and the greater simplicity, multinational companies tend to use the same transfer pricing method for both domestic and international transfers.

REAL WORLD VIEWS 20.2

Transfer pricing: keeping it at arm's length

Not long ago, transfer pricing was a subject for tax administrators and one or two other specialists. But recently, politicians, economists and business people have been waking up to the importance of who pays tax on what in international business transactions between different arms of the same corporation. Globalization is one reason for this interest, the rise of the multinational corporation is another. Once you take on board the fact that more than 60 per cent of world trade takes place within multinational enterprises, the importance of transfer pricing becomes clear.

Consider a profitable UK computer group that buys micro-chips from its own subsidiary in Korea: how much the UK parent pays its subsidiary – the transfer price – will determine how much profit the Korean unit reports and how much local tax it pays. If the parent pays below normal local market prices, the UK tax administrators might not grumble as the profit will be reported at their end, but their Korean counterparts will be disappointed not to have much profit to tax on their side of the operation. If the UK company bought its microchips from an independent company in Korea it would pay the market price, and the supplier would pay taxes on its own profits in the normal way. It is the fact that the various parts of the organization are under some form of common control that is important for the tax authority as this may mean that transfers are not subject to the full play of market forces.

No country – poor, emerging or wealthy – wants its tax base to suffer because of transfer pricing. That is why the OECD has spent so much effort on developing its Transfer Pricing Guidelines. While they help corporations to avoid double taxation, they also help tax administrations to receive a fair share of the tax base of multinational enterprises.

Discussion point

Describe how a multinational company might use its transfer pricing system to reduce global taxes.

SOURCE: ADAPTED FROM NEIGHBOUR, J., TRANSFER PRICING: KEEPING IT AT ARM'S LENGTH, OECD OBSERVER, JAN 2002 PP. 29–30. © OECD 2002, WWW.OECDOBSERVER.ORG

Transfer pricing can also have an impact on import duties and dividend repatriations. Import duties can be minimized by transferring products at low prices to a division located in a country with high import duties. Some countries also restrict the repatriation of income and dividends. By increasing the transfer prices of goods transferred into divisions operating with these restrictions, it is possible to increase the funds repatriated without appearing to violate dividend restrictions.

SUMMARY

The following items relate to the learning objectives listed at the beginning of the chapter.

● **Describe the different purposes of a transfer pricing system.**

Transfer pricing can be used for the following purposes: (a) to provide information that motivates divisional managers to make good economic decisions; (b) to provide information that is useful for evaluating the managerial and economic performance of a division; (c) to intentionally move profits between divisions or locations; and (d) to ensure that divisional autonomy is not undermined.

● **Identify and describe the five different transfer pricing methods.**

The five main transfer pricing methods are (a) market-based transfer prices; (b) marginal cost transfer prices; (c) full cost transfer prices; (d) cost-plus a mark-up transfer prices; and (e) negotiated transfer prices.

● **Explain why the correct transfer price is the external market price when there is a perfectly competitive market for the intermediate product.**

If there is a perfectly competitive market for the intermediate product transfers recorded at market prices are likely to represent the real economic contribution to total company profits. If the supplying division did not exist, the intermediate product would have to be purchased on the outside market at the current market price. Alternatively, if the receiving division did not exist, the intermediate product would have to be sold on the outside market at the current market price. Divisional profits are therefore likely to be similar to the profits that would be calculated if the divisions were separate organizations. For decision-making, if the receiving division does not acquire the intermediate product internally it would be able to acquire the product at the competitive external market price. Similarly, if the supplying division does transfer internally it will be able to sell the product at

the external market price. Thus, the market price represents the opportunity cost of internal transfers.

● **Explain why cost-plus transfer prices will not result in the optimum output being achieved.**

If cost-plus transfer prices are used, the receiving division will determine its optimal output at the point where the marginal cost of its transfers is equal to its net marginal revenue (i.e. marginal revenue less marginal conversion costs, excluding the transfer price). However, the marginal cost of the transfers (i.e. the cost-plus transfer price) will be in excess of the marginal cost of producing the intermediate product for the company as a whole. Thus, marginal cost will be overstated and the receiving division manager will restrict output to the point where net marginal revenue equals the transfer price, rather than the marginal cost to the company of producing the intermediate product.

● **Explain the two methods of transfer pricing that have been advocated to resolve the conflicts between the decision-making and performance evaluation objectives.**

To overcome the decision-making and performance evaluation conflicts that can occur with cost-based transfer pricing two methods have been proposed – a dual-rate transfer pricing system and a two-part transfer pricing system. With a dual rate transfer pricing system the receiving division is charged with the marginal cost of the intermediate product and the supplying division is credited with the full cost per unit plus a profit margin. Therefore, the receiving division should choose the output level at which the marginal cost of the intermediate product is equal to the net marginal revenue of the final product. Also, the supplying division will earn a profit on inter-divisional transfers. Any inter-divisional profits are written off by an accounting adjustment. The two-part transfer pricing system involves transfers being made at the marginal cost per unit of output of the supplying division plus a lump-sum fixed fee charged by the supplying division to the receiving division for the use of the capacity allocated to the intermediate product. This transfer pricing system should also motivate the receiving division to choose the optimal output level and enable the supplying division to obtain a profit on inter-divisional trading.

- **Describe the additional factors that must be considered when setting transfer prices for multinational transactions.**

When divisions operate in different countries, taxation implications can be a dominant influence. The aim is to set transfer prices at levels which will ensure that most of the profits are allocated to divisions operating in low taxation counties. However, taxation authorities in the countries where the divisions are located and the OECD have introduced guidelines and legislation to ensure that companies do not use the transfer prices for taxation manipulation purposes. Transfer pricing can also have an impact on import duties and dividend repatriations.

Import duties can be minimized by transferring products at low prices to a division located in a country with high import duties. Some countries also restrict dividend repatriations. By increasing the transfer prices of the goods transferred into divisions operating with these restrictions, it is possible to increase the funds repatriated without appearing to violate dividend restrictions.

- **Additional learning objective presented in Appendix 20.1: To explain how optimal transfer prices can be determined based on economic theory.**

The theoretically correct transfer price when there are no capacity constraints, is the marginal cost of producing the intermediate product at the optimum output level for the company as a whole. The application of this rule is illustrated with Exhibits 20A.1 and 20A.2 when there is no external market and with Exhibits 20A.3 and 20A.4 when there is an imperfect market for the intermediate product.

Appendix 20.1: Economic theory of transfer pricing

Throughout this chapter it has been pointed out that economic theory indicates that the theoretically correct transfer price to encourage total organizational optimality is, in the absence of capacity constraints, the marginal cost of producing the intermediate product at the optimal output level for the company as a whole. No attempt has been made to explain or illustrate the theory because the explanation is fairly complex and a knowledge of the theory is not essential for you to understand the transfer pricing mechanisms described in this chapter. Indeed, it is unlikely to form part of the curriculum for many readers. However, for those readers pursuing advanced courses for the examinations of the professional accountancy bodies an understanding of economic theory maybe necessary. Questions relating to an understanding of theory are sometimes included in the examinations of the professional accountancy bodies (see for example Questions 20.22–20.23 at the end of the chapter). If you are not pursing the examinations of the professional accountancy bodies, and your curriculum does not require a detailed understanding of economic theory, you may wish to omit this section.

Setting transfer prices when there is no market for the intermediate product

To simplify the presentation we shall initially assume there is no market for the intermediate product. In this situation a responsibility centre may still be classified as a profit or investment centre if it has other activities which involve external sales, and is not dependent on sales revenues only from internal transfers. Besides applying to situations where there is no market for the intermediate product, the theoretically correct transfer price (that is, the marginal cost of producing the intermediate product for the optimal output for the company as a whole) also applies to situations where there is an imperfect market for the intermediate product.

Assuming that there is no market for the intermediate product the optimal output for the company as a whole is the level at which:

$$\left(\begin{array}{c}\text{marginal cost of} \\ \text{supplying division}\end{array}\right) + \left(\begin{array}{c}\text{marginal cost of} \\ \text{receiving division}\end{array}\right) = \left(\begin{array}{c}\text{marginal revenue} \\ \text{of receiving division}\end{array}\right) \quad (20.1)$$

This equation can be re-written as

$$\left(\begin{array}{c}\text{marginal cost of} \\ \text{supplying division}\end{array}\right) = \left(\begin{array}{c}\text{marginal revenue of} \\ \text{receiving division}\end{array}\right) - \left(\begin{array}{c}\text{marginal cost of} \\ \text{receiving division}\end{array}\right) \quad (20.2)$$

The right hand side of equation (20.2) is known as net marginal revenue. This is defined as the marginal revenue derived by the receiving division from the sale of an additional unit less the marginal cost of converting the intermediate product into the final product; so the net marginal revenue therefore excludes the transfer price. The optimum output level can therefore be re-expressed as the output level where

$$\begin{array}{c}\text{marginal cost of} \\ \text{the supplying division}\end{array} = \begin{array}{c}\text{net marginal revenue of} \\ \text{the receiving division}\end{array}$$

This transfer pricing rule is illustrated in Exhibit 20.A1.[1] To simplify the analysis, we shall assume that output can be produced and sold only in 1000-unit batches. You can see that the optimal output level where marginal cost equals net marginal revenue is 7000 units. At this output level profits for the company as a whole are maximized (see column 7). The theoretically correct transfer price for batches of 1000 units is the marginal cost of the supplying division at this output level (i.e. £4000). The receiving division will compare this transfer price with its net marginal revenue (column 6 in Exhibit 20.A1) for each output level, and will be motivated to expand output up to the level where the transfer price equals its net marginal revenue (i.e. 7000 units). The transfer price of £4000 will also induce the supplying division to produce 7000 units. At an output level below 7000 units the supplying division

EXHIBIT 20.A1 Optimum transfer price for an imperfect final market and no market for the intermediate product

Supplying division			Receiving division			
(1)	(2)	(3)	(4)	(5)	(6)	(7)
Units produced	Total cost (£)	Marginal cost (£)	Units produced	Total net revenue (£)[a]	Net marginal revenue (£)	Overall company profit (loss): (5)–(2) (£)
1 000	4 000	4 000	1 000	10 000	10 000	6 000
2 000	7 000	3 000	2 000	19 000	9 000	12 000
3 000	10 000	3 000	3 000	27 000	8 000	17 000
4 000	11 000	1 000	4 000	34 000	7 000	23 000
5 000	13 000	2 000	5 000	40 000	6 000	27 000
6 000	15 000	2 000	6 000	45 000	5 000	30 000
7 000	19 000	4 000	7 000	49 000	4 000	30 000
8 000	24 000	5 000	8 000	52 000	3 000	28 000
9 000	31 000	7 000	9 000	54 000	2 000	23 000
10 000	39 000	8 000	10 000	55 000	1 000	16 000
11 000	48 000	9 000	11 000	55 000	0	7 000
12 000	58 000	10 000	12 000	54 000	−1 000	(4 000)

[a]Net revenue is defined as total revenue from the sale of the final product less the conversion costs incurred. It does not include the transfer price.

will be motivated to expand output, because the transfer price received from the receiving division will be in excess of its marginal cost. However, the supplying division will not be motivated to produce beyond 7000 units, since the marginal cost will be in excess of the transfer price.

The profits for each division at the various output levels based on a transfer price of £4000 per batch of 1000 units are presented in Exhibit 20.A2. You can see that at the optimal transfer price both divisions will arrive at the correct optimal solution. In other words, they will be motivated to operate at output levels that will maximize overall company profits. Note that overall company profits and divisional profits are maximized at an output level of 6000 or 7000 units. This is because marginal cost equals net marginal revenue when output is expanded from 6000 to 7000 units. Overall company profits therefore remain unchanged.

Earlier in this chapter it was pointed out that most accountants assume that marginal cost is constant per unit of output within the relevant output range. In other words, for *short-term* output decisions marginal cost is usually interpreted as being equivalent to variable cost per unit of output.

Assume now that in Exhibit 20.A1 marginal cost is equivalent to variable cost and is £6000 per batch of 1000 units so that the total costs of the supplying division will increase in increments of £6000. In other words, the marginal cost (column 3 in Exhibit 20.A1) would be £6000 for all output levels, and the total cost column would increase in increments of £6000. The optimum output level will be at 5000 units, the level at which marginal cost equals net marginal revenue. Where marginal cost is constant, the marginal cost of producing the intermediate product at the optimum output level will be equivalent to variable cost. Therefore, in the absence of capacity constraints, the theoretically correct transfer price will be equivalent to variable cost per unit of output assuming that marginal cost is constant throughout the entire output range. Applying this rule to Exhibit 20.A1, the correct transfer price is £6000 per batch.

At a transfer price of £6000 per batch the manager of the receiving division will expand output until the transfer price is equal to its net marginal revenue. Hence the receiving division will be motivated to produce 5000 units, which is the optimal output level of the company as a whole. However, the supplying division will be indifferent to the amount it supplies to the receiving division if transfers are priced at a variable cost of £6000 per batch, because it will earn a zero contribution on each batch transferred. On the other hand, all of the total company

EXHIBIT 20.A2 Reported profits at a transfer price of £4000 per batch

Units produced	Supplying division			Receiving division			Total company profit (loss) (£)
	Total cost (£)	Transfer price received (£)	Profit (loss) (£)	Total net revenue (£)	Transfer price paid (£)	Profit (loss) (£)	
1 000	4 000	4 000	0	10 000	4 000	6 000	6 000
2 000	7 000	8 000	1 000	19 000	8 000	11 000	12 000
3 000	10 000	12 000	2 000	27 000	12 000	15 000	17 000
4 000	11 000	16 000	5 000	34 000	16 000	18 000	23 000
5 000	13 000	20 000	7 000	40 000	20 000	20 000	27 000
6 000	15 000	24 000	9 000	45 000	24 000	21 000	30 000
7 000	19 000	28 000	9 000	49 000	28 000	21 000	30 000
8 000	24 000	32 000	8 000	52 000	32 000	20 000	28 000
9 000	31 000	36 000	5 000	54 000	36 000	18 000	23 000
10 000	39 000	40 000	1 000	55 000	40 000	15 000	16 000
11 000	48 000	44 000	(4 000)	55 000	44 000	11 000	7 000
12 000	58 000	48 000	(10 000)	54 000	48 000	6 000	(4 000)

contribution of £10 000 (£40 000 net revenue less £30 000 total cost of the supplying division) arising from inter-divisional trading will be allocated to the receiving division.

This example illustrates the conflicts between the role of a transfer price in motivating optimal decisions and its role in evaluating divisional performance. Where marginal cost is equal to variable costs, the theoretically correct transfer price that motivates optimizing behaviour results in the supplying division earning zero contribution and failing to recover any of its fixed costs on the inter-divisional transfers. Note, however, that where marginal cost is not constant the supplying division will report profits arising from inter-dimensional trading (see Exhibit 20.A2).

Imperfect market for the intermediate product

Where there is an imperfect market for the intermediate product, we can apply the same approach that we used to derive transfer prices when there was no market for the intermediate product. The theoretically correct transfer price, in the absence of capacity constraints, is therefore the marginal cost of producing the intermediate product at the optimal output level for the company as a whole. Consider Exhibit 20.A3.[1]

Column 4 shows the marginal revenue that can be obtained from selling the intermediate product in the external market, and column 6 shows the net marginal revenue from converting the intermediate product into a final product and selling in the external final product market.

To determine the optimal output level, we must allocate the output of the intermediate product between sales in the intermediate product market and the final product market. The sale of the first unit in the intermediate external market gives a marginal revenue (MR) of £40 compared with a net marginal revenue (NMR) of £35 if the first unit is transferred to the receiving division and sold as a final product. Consequently, the first unit of output of the supplying division should be sold in the intermediate external market. The second unit of output should also be sold in the intermediate market because the MR of £37 is in excess of the NMR of £35 if the unit is sold as a final product. The third unit of output of the intermediate product should be sold in the final product market, since the NMR of £35 is in excess of the MR of £34 that can be obtained from selling in the intermediate market. The fourth unit of output yields an MR of £34 if sold in the intermediate market, compared with £33.50 if sold in the final product

EXHIBIT 20.A3 Optimum transfer price for an imperfect intermediate market

	Supplying division			Receiving division	
(1) Units produced	(2) Total cost (£)	(3) Marginal cost (£)	(4) Marginal revenue (£)	(5) Units produced	(6) Net marginal revenue (£)
1	19	19	40 (1)	1	35.00 (3)
2	37	18	37 (2)	2	33.50 (5)
3	54	17	34 (4)	3	32.00 (6)
4	69	15	31 (7)	4	30.50 (8)
5	83	14	28 (10)	5	29.00 (9)
6	98	15	25 (13)	6	27.50 (11)
7	114	16	22	7	26.00 (12)
8	132	18	19	8	24.50
9	152	20	16	9	23.00
10	175	23	13	10	21.50
11	202	27	10	11	20.00
12	234	32	7	12	18.50
13	271	37	4	13	17.00

market. Therefore the fourth unit should be allocated to the intermediate market. The remaining output of the supplying division should be allocated in a similar manner.

The numbers in parentheses in columns 4 and 6 of Exhibit 20.A3 refer to the ranking of the 13 units of output of the supplying division on the basis of MR from the sale of the intermediate product and NMR from the sale of the final product. The allocation of the output of the supplying division based on these rankings is shown in column 3 of Exhibit 20.A4.

We can now determine the optimal output for the company as a whole by comparing the marginal cost of the supplying division (column 2 of Exhibit 20.A4) with the MR/NMR derived from either selling the intermediate product or converting it into a final product for sale (column 4 of Exhibit 20.A4). By comparing these two columns, you will see that the optimal output is 11 units. The twelfth unit should not be produced, because the marginal cost of the supplying division is in excess of the MR/NMR that can be obtained from its most profitable use.

The theoretically correct transfer price is the marginal cost of the supplying division at the optimal output level (i.e. £27). To be more precise, the optimal output level is just in excess of 11 units, and the marginal cost will be between £27 and £27.50 at the optimal output level. In other words, if we were to graph the data in Exhibit 20.A4, the marginal cost and MR/NMR schedules would intersect at a point above £27 and below £27.50. Therefore the transfer price should be set at any point between £27.01 and £27.49.

If you refer to column 4 of Exhibit 20.A3, you will see that if the transfer price is set between £27.01 and £27.49 then the manager of the supplying division will choose to sell the first 5 units of the intermediate product on the external market (this is because marginal revenue is in excess of the transfer price) and transfer the remaining output to the receiving division (this is because the transfer price is in excess of marginal revenue). You will also see that the manager of the supplying division will select an output level of 11 units based on the principle that he or she will not manufacture any units when the marginal cost is in excess of the transfer price.

If the transfer price is set between £27.01 and £27.49, the manager of the receiving division will choose to sell 6 units (see column 6 of Exhibit 20.A3) because NMR is in excess of the transfer price. A transfer price set within this range will therefore induce the supplying division to produce 11 units, sell 5 units to the external market and transfer 6 units to the receiving division; the receiving division will also wish to purchase 6 units from the supplying division. This is identical with the optimal output schedule for the company as a whole shown in Exhibit 20.A4.

EXHIBIT 20.A4 Allocation of output of supplying division between intermediate and external market

(1) Output (units)	(2) Marginal cost of supplying division (£)	(3) Allocation per ranking in Exhibit 21.6	(4) Marginal revenue/ net marginal revenue (£)
1	19	Intermediate market	40.00
2	18	Intermediate market	37.00
3	17	Final market	35.00
4	15	Intermediate market	34.00
5	14	Final market	33.50
6	15	Final market	32.00
7	16	Intermediate market	31.00
8	18	Final market	30.50
9	20	Final market	29.00
10	23	Intermediate market	28.00
11	27	Final market	27.50
12	32	No allocation	26.00

What would be the correct transfer price if the marginal cost per unit of the intermediate product was constant throughout the entire output range (i.e. marginal cost equals variable cost)? The answer is that applying the marginal cost rule will result in the transfer price being set at the variable cost per unit of the supplying division. You can see that if the variable/marginal cost of the supplying division was £29 throughout the entire output schedule in Exhibits 20.A3 and 20.A4 then applying the above procedure would result in the transfer price being set at £29.

Capacity constraints

When there is a capacity constraint, a transfer price based on the marginal cost rule will not ensure that the optimum output levels are achieved. For example, let us assume that in Exhibits 20.A3 and 20.A4 the capacity of the supplying division is restricted to 6 units. You will see from the ranking (see columns 4 and 6 of Exhibit 20.A3) that the scarce capacity of 6 units should be allocated so that 3 units are transferred to the receiving division and 3 units are sold on the intermediate external market. However, column 4 of Exhibit 20.A3 indicates that at a transfer price between £27.01 and £27.49 the supplying division will maximize its own profits by selling 5 units of the intermediate product in the external market and transferring 1 unit to the receiving division. Alternatively, by referring to column 6, you will see that the receiving division will maximize its own profits by taking the entire output of 6 units from the supplying division and selling them as final products.[2] This situation will also apply if the transfer price is set at the marginal cost of the supplying division at the capacity level of 6 units.

Both divisions pursuing their own best interests in isolation will not therefore arrive at the optimal company solution that is, the sale of 3 units of the intermediate product and 3 units of the final product. A conflict occurs because what is in the best interests of a specific division is not in the best interests of the company as a whole. One way of ensuring that the optimal solution is achieved is for central headquarters to obtain information from the supplying and the receiving divisions and to work out the optimal production programme for each division. However, such an approach strikes at the very heart of the transfer price problem, because the optimal production programme has been achieved by an infringement of divisional autonomy.

Summary relating to an imperfect market for the intermediate product

Let us now summarize our findings where there is an imperfect market for the intermediate product. Where the supplying division has no capacity constraints, the theoretically correct transfer price is the marginal cost of producing the intermediate product at the optimal output level for the company as a whole. Where unit marginal cost is constant (and thus equals variable cost) and fixed costs remain unchanged, this rule will give a transfer price equal to the variable cost per unit of the supplying division. However, when capacity constraints apply and the profit maximizing output cannot be achieved, transfer prices based on marginal cost will not ensure that optimal output is achieved, and in this situation it may be necessary for staff at the central headquarters to establish the optimum production programme for each division based on the output derived from a linear programming model. The application of linear programming to management accounting is presented in Chapter 25.

It is difficult to provide a rigorous analysis of transfer pricing in non-diagrammatic form. To overcome this difficulty a number of theoretical transfer pricing models applicable to different situations are presented in diagrammatic form in Learning Note 20.1 on the dedicated open access website (see Preface for details).

Notes

1 Exhibits 20.A1 and 20.A3 are adapted from illustrations first presented by Solomons (1965).

2 The supplying division will obtain marginal revenue in excess of the transfer price of £27.01/£27.49 for the sale of the first five units on the external market and it will not be motivated to follow the optimal company plan for the company as a whole. Similarly, the receiving division will maximize its own profits by accepting all transfers until the net marginal revenue equals the transfer price, and it will therefore wish to sell six units of the final product.

Key terms and concepts

cost-plus a mark-up transfer prices (p. 503)
dual-rate transfer pricing (p. 513)
final products (p. 502)
full cost transfer prices (p. 503)

intermediate products (p. 502)
marginal cost transfer prices (p. 503)
market-based transfer prices (p. 503)
negotiated transfer prices (p. 503)
net marginal revenue (p. 506)

perfectly competitive market (p. 503)
two-part transfer pricing system (p. 514)

Recommended reading

A book authoured by Emmanuel and Mehafdi (1994) focuses exclusively on transfer pricing. For research studies relating primarily to domestic transfer pricing you should refer to Perera *et al.* (2003), Boyns *et al.* (1999) and Chan (1998). Shorter articles by Atkinson and Tyrrall (1997) and Elliott (1998a) provide further insights into international transfer pricing issues and research relating to surveys of international transfer practices is presented in the articles by Elliott (1998b) and Oyelere and Emmanuel (1998).

Key examination points

When discussing a transfer pricing system, you should indicate that the proposed system should motivate managers to make correct decisions, provide a reasonable measure of performance and ensure that divisional autonomy is not undermined. It is not possible for a single transfer price to meet all three of these requirements. Examination questions may also require you to recommend an optimal transfer price. It is particularly important that you understand how optimal transfer prices should be set when there is an imperfect market or no market for the intermediate product.

ASSESSMENT MATERIAL

The review questions are short questions that enable you to assess your understanding of the main topics included in the chapter. The numbers in parentheses provide you with the page numbers to refer to if you cannot answer a specific question.

The review problems are more complex and require you to relate and apply the content to various business problems. The problems are graded by their level of difficulty. Solutions to review problems that are not preceded by the term 'IM' are provided in a separate section at the end of the book. Solutions to problems preceded by the term 'IM' are provided in the *Instructor's Manual* accompanying this book and also on the lecturer's password protected section of the website www.drury-online.com. Additional review problems with fully worked solutions are provided in the *Student's Manual* that accompanies this book.

Review questions

20.1 Distinguish between intermediate products and final products. (*p. 502*)

20.2 Explain the four purposes for which transfer pricing can be used. (*pp. 502–03*)

20.3 Explain why a single transfer pricing method cannot serve all four purposes. (*pp. 502–03*)

20.4 If an external, perfectly competitive market exists for an intermediate product what should be the transfer price? Why? (*pp. 503–06*)

20.5 Define the term 'net marginal revenue'. (*p. 506*)

20.6 If there is no external market for the intermediate product what is the optimal transfer price? Why? (*p. 506*)

20.7 Why are full cost and cost-plus a mark-up transfer prices unlikely to result in the optimum output? (*pp. 507–08*)

20.8 Why are marginal cost transfer prices not widely used in practice? (*p. 507*)

20.9 Why are transfer prices based on full cost widely used in practice? (*pp. 507–08*)

20.10 Discuss the advantages and disadvantages of negotiated transfer prices. (*pp. 508–09*)

20.11 What are the circumstances that favour the use of negotiated transfer prices? (*p. 509*)

20.12 Describe the two proposals that have been recommended for resolving transfer pricing conflicts. (*pp. 513–15*)

20.13 What are the special considerations that must be taken into account with international transfer pricing? (*pp. 517–18*)

20.14 When there is an imperfect market for the intermediate product what is the optimal transfer price? (*p. 523*)

Review problems

20.15 Intermediate. X plc, a manufacturing company, has two divisions: Division A and Division B. Division A produces one type of product, ProdX, which it transfers to Division B and also sells externally. Division B has been approached by another company which has offered to supply 2500 units of ProdX for £35 each.

The following details for Division A are available:

	£
Sales revenue	
Sales to Division B @ £40 per unit	400 000
External sales @ £45 per unit	270 000
Less:	
Variable cost @ £22 per unit	352 000
Fixed costs	100 000
Profit	218 000

If Division B decides to buy from the other company, the impact of the decision on the profits of Division A and X plc, assuming external sales of ProdX cannot be increased, will be

	Division A	X plc
A	£12 500 decrease	£12 500 decrease
B	£15 625 decrease	£12 500 increase
C	£32 500 decrease	£32 500 increase
D	£45 000 decrease	£32 500 decrease
E	£45 000 decrease	£45 000 decrease

(3 marks)
CIMA Management Accounting – Decision Making

20.16 Intermediate. Division A transfers 100 000 units of a component to Division B each year.

The market price of the component is £25.

Division A's variable cost is £15 per unit.

Division A's fixed costs are £500 000 each year.

What price would be credited to Division A for each component that it transfers to Division B under

(i) dual pricing (based on marginal cost and market price)?

(ii) two-part tariff pricing (where the Divisions have agreed that the fixed fee will be £200 000)?

	Dual pricing	Two-part tariff pricing
A	£15	£15
B	£25	£15
C	£15	£17
D	£25	£17
E	£15	£20

(2 marks)
CIMA Management Accounting – Decision Making

20.17 Intermediate. ZP Plc operates two subsidiaries, X and Y. X is a component manufacturing subsidiary and Y is an assembly and final product subsidiary. Both subsidiaries produce one type of output only. Subsidiary Y needs one component from subsidiary X for every unit of Product W produced. Subsidiary X transfers to Subsidiary Y all of the components needed to produce Product W. Subsidiary X also sells components on the external market.

The following budgeted information is available for each subsidiary.

	X	Y
Market price per component	$800	
Market price per unit of W		$1,200
Production costs per component	$600	
Assembly costs per unit of W		$400
Non production fixed costs	$1.5m	$1.3m
External demand	10 000 units	12 000 units
Capacity	22 000 units	
Taxation rates	25%	30%

The production cost per component is 60 per cent variable. The fixed production costs are absorbed based on budgeted output.

X sets a transfer price at marginal cost plus 70 per cent.

Calculate the post tax profit generated by each subsidiary. *(4 marks)*

CIMA P1 Management Accountancy: Performance Evaluation

20.18 Intermediate: Impact on reported profits of variable cost and absorption cost transfer prices. FP sells and repairs photocopiers. The company has operated for many years with two departments, the Sales Department and the Service Department, but the departments had no autonomy. The company is now thinking of restructuring so that the two departments will become profit centres.

The Sales Department

This department sells new photocopiers. The department sells 2000 copiers per year. Included in the selling price is £60 for a one year guarantee. All customers pay this fee. This means that during the first year of ownership if the photocopier needs to be repaired then the repair costs are not charged to the customer. On average 500 photocopiers per year need to be repaired under the guarantee. The repair work is carried out by the Service Department who, under the proposed changes, would charge the Sales Department for doing the repairs. It is estimated that on average the repairs will take three hours each and that the charge by the Service Department will be £136 500 for the 500 repairs.

The Service Department

This department has two sources of work; the work needed to satisfy the guarantees for the Sales Department and repair work for external customers. Customers are charged at full cost plus 40 per cent. The details of the budget for the next year for the Service Department revealed standard costs of:

Parts	at cost
Labour	£15 per hour
Variable overheads	£10 per labour hour
Fixed overheads	£22 per labour hour

The calculation of these standards is based on the estimated maximum market demand and includes the expected 500 repairs for the Sales Department. The average cost of the parts needed for a repair is £54. This means that the charge to the Sales Department for the repair work, including the 40 per cent mark-up, will be £136 500.

Proposed Change

It has now been suggested that FP should be structured so that the two departments become profit centres and that the managers of the Departments are given autonomy. The individual salaries of the managers would be linked to the profits of their respective departments.

Budgets have been produced for each department on the assumption that the Service Department will repair 500 photocopiers for the Sales Department and that the transfer price for this work will be calculated in the same way as the price charged to external customers.

However the manager of the Sales Department has now stated that he intends to have the repairs done by another company, RS, because they have offered to carry out the work for a fixed fee of £180 per repair and this is less than the price that the Sales Department would charge.

Required:

a   Calculate the individual profits of the Sales Department and the Service Department, and of FP as a whole from the guarantee scheme if:

(i) The repairs are carried out by the Service Department and are charged at full cost plus 40 per cent;

(ii) The repairs are carried out by the Service Department and are charged at marginal cost;

(iii) The repairs are carried out by RS. *(8 marks)*

b   (i) Explain, with reasons, why a 'full cost plus' transfer pricing model may not be appropriate for FP. *(3 marks)*

(ii) Comment on other issues that the managers of FP should consider if they decide to allow RS to carry out the repairs. *(4 marks)*

c   Briefly explain the advantages and disadvantages of structuring the departments as profit centres. *(5 marks)*

CIMA P1 Management Accounting: Performance Evaluation

20.19 Advanced: Determining optimal transfer prices for three different scenarios. Manuco Ltd has been offered supplies of special ingredient Z at a transfer price of £15 per kg by Helpco Ltd which is part of the same group of companies. Helpco Ltd processes and sells special ingredient Z to customers external to the group at £15 per kg. Helpco Ltd bases its transfer price on cost plus 25 per cent profit mark-up. Total cost has been estimated as 75 per cent variable and 25 per cent fixed.

Required:

Discuss the transfer prices at which Helpco Ltd should offer to transfer special ingredient Z to Manuco Ltd in order that group profit maximizing decisions may be taken on financial grounds in each of the following situations:

(i) Helpco Ltd has an external market for all of its production of special ingredient Z at a selling price of £15 per kg. Internal transfers to Manuco Ltd would enable £1.50 per kg of variable packing cost to be avoided.

(ii) Conditions are as per (i) but Helpco Ltd has production capacity for 3000 kg of special ingredient Z for which no external market is available.

(iii) Conditions are as per (ii) but Helpco Ltd has an alternative use for some of its spare production capacity. This alternative use is equivalent to 2000 kg of special ingredient Z and would earn a contribution of £6000. *(13 marks)*

ACCA Paper 9 Information for Control and Decision Making

20.20 Impact of cost-plus transfer price on decision making and divisional profits. Enormous Engineering (EE) plc is a large multidivisional engineering company having interests in a wide variety of product markets. The Industrial Products Division (IPD) sells component parts to consumer appliance manufacturers, both inside and outside the company. One such part, a motor unit, it sells solely to external customers, but buys the motor itself internally from the Electric Motor Division. The Electric Motor Division (EMD) makes the motor to IPD specifications and it does not expect to be able to sell it to any other customers.

In preparing the 2001 budgets IPD estimated the number of motor units it expects to be able to sell at various prices as follows:

Price (ex works) (£)	Quantity sold (units)
50	1000
40	2000
35	3000
30	4000
25	6000
20	8000

It then sought a quotation from EMD, who offered to supply the motors at £16 each based on the following estimate:

	(£)
Materials and bought-in parts	2
Direct labour costs	4
Factory overhead (150% of direct labour costs)	6
Total factory cost	12
Profit margin (33⅓% on factory cost)	4
Quoted price	£16

Factory overhead costs are fixed. All other costs are variable.

Although it considered the price quoted to be on the high side, IPD nevertheless believed that it could still sell the completed unit at a profit because it incurred costs of only £4 (material £1 and direct labour £3) on each unit made. It therefore placed an order for the coming year.

On reviewing the budget for 2001 the finance director of EE noted that the projected sales of the motor unit were considerably less than those for the previous year, which was disappointing as both divisions concerned were working well below their capacities. On making enquiries he was told by IPD that the price reduction required to sell more units would reduce rather than increase profit and that the main problem was the high price charged by EMD. EMD stated that they required the high price in order to meet their target profit margin for the year, and that any reduction would erode their pricing policy.

You are required to:

a   develop tabulations for each division, and for the company as a whole, that indicate the anticipated effect of IPD selling the motor unit at each of the prices listed, *(10 marks)*

b   (i) show the selling price which IPD should select in order to maximize its own divisional profit on the motor unit, *(2 marks)*

(ii) show the selling price which would be in the best interest of EE as a whole, *(2 marks)*

(iii) explain why this latter price is not selected by IPD, *(1 mark)*

c state:

(i) what changes you would advise making to the transfer pricing system so that it will motivate divisional managers to make better decisions in future, *(5 marks)*

(ii) what transfer price will ensure overall optimality in this situation. *(5 marks)*

ICAEW Management Accounting

20.21 Advanced: Calculating the effects of a transfer pricing system on divisional and company profits. Division A of a large divisionalized organization manufactures a single standardized product. Some of the output is sold externally whilst the remainder is transferred to Division B where it is a subassembly in the manufacture of that division's product. The unit costs of Division A's product are as follows:

	(£)
Direct material	4
Direct labour	2
Direct expense	2
Variable manufacturing overheads	2
Fixed manufacturing overheads	4
Selling and packing expense – variable	1
	15

Annually 10 000 units of the product are sold externally at the standard price of £30.

In addition to the external sales, 5000 units are transferred annually to Division B at an internal transfer charge of £29 per unit. This transfer price is obtained by deducting variable selling and packing expense from the external price since this expense is not incurred for internal transfers.

Division B incorporates the transferred-in goods into a more advanced product. The unit costs of this product are as follows:

	(£)
Transferred-in item (from Division A)	29
Direct material and components	23
Direct labour	3
Variable overheads	12
Fixed overheads	12
Selling and packing expense – variable	1
	80

Division B's manager disagrees with the basis used to set the transfer price. He argues that the transfers should be made at variable cost plus an agreed (minimal) mark-up since he claims that his division is taking output that Division A would be unable to sell at the price of £30.

Partly because of this disagreement, a study of the relationship between selling price and demand has recently been made for each division by the company's sales director. The resulting report contains the following table:

Customer demand at various selling prices:

Division A			
Selling price	£20	£30	£40
Demand	15 000	10 000	5000
Division B			
Selling price	£80	£90	£100
Demand	7 200	5 000	2800

The manager of Division B claims that this study supports his case. He suggests that a transfer price of £12 would give Division A a reasonable contribution to its fixed overheads while allowing Division B to earn a reasonable profit. He also believes that it would lead to an increase of output and an improvement in the overall level of company profits.

You are required:

a to calculate the effect that the transfer pricing system has had on the company's profits, and *(16 marks)*

b to establish the likely effect on profits of adopting the suggestion by the manager of Division B of a transfer price of £12.

(6 marks)

ACCA Level 2 Management Accounting

20.22 Advanced: Setting an optimal transfer price when there is an intermediate imperfect market. Memphis plc is a multi-division firm operating in a wide range of activities. One of its divisions, Division A, produces a semi-finished product Alpha, which can be sold in an outside market. It can also be sold to Division B, which can use it in manufacturing its finished product Beta. Assume also that the marginal cost of each division is a rising linear function of output, and that the goal for Memphis plc is to maximize its total profits. Relevant information about both divisions is given below.

Output of Alpha (units)	Total cost of Alpha (£000)	Revenue from outside selling of Alpha (£000)	Net marginal revenue of Beta (£000)
60	112	315	47
70	140	350	45
80	170	380	43
90	203	405	40
100	238	425	36
110	275	440	33
120	315	450	30
130	359	455	25

You are required to calculate the optimal transfer price for Alpha and the optimal activity level for each division. *(10 marks)*

ICAEW Management Accounting

20.23 Advanced: Calculation of optimal selling price using calculus and the impact of using the imperfect market price as the transfer price. AB Ltd has two Divisions – A and B. Division A manufactures a product called the aye and Division B manufactures a product called the bee. Each bee uses a single aye as a component. A is the only manufacturer of the aye and supplies both B and outside customers.

Details of A's and B's operations for the coming period are as follows:

	Division A	Division B
Fixed costs	£7 500 000	£18 000 000
Variable costs per unit	£280	£590*
Capacity – units	30 000	18 000

*Note: Excludes transfer costs

Market research has indicated that demand for AB Ltd's products from outside customers will be as follows in the coming period:

● the aye: at unit price £1000 no ayes will be demanded but demand will increase by 25 ayes with every £1 that the unit price is reduced below £1000;

● the bee: at unit price £4000 no bees will be demanded, but demand will increase by 10 bees with every £1 that the unit price is reduced below £4000.

Requirements:

a Calculate the unit selling price of the bee (accurate to the nearest £) that will maximize AB Ltd's profit in the coming period.

(10 marks)

b Calculate the unit selling price of the bee (accurate to the nearest £) that is likely to emerge if the Divisional Managers of A and B both set selling prices calculated to maximize Divisional profit from sales to outside customers and the transfer price of ayes going from A to B is set at 'market selling price'. *(10 marks)*

c Explain why your answers to parts (a) and (b) are different, and propose changes to the system of transfer pricing in order to ensure that AB Ltd is charging its customers at optimum prices.

(5 marks)

CIMA Stage 3 Management Accounting Applications

20.24 Advanced. P plc is a multi-national conglomerate company with manufacturing divisions, trading in numerous countries across various continents. Trade takes place between a number of the divisions in different countries, with partly-completed products being transferred between them. Where a transfer takes place between divisions trading in different countries, it is the policy of the Board of P plc to determine centrally the appropriate transfer price without reference to the divisional managers concerned. The Board of plc justifies this policy to divisional managers on the grounds that its objective is to maximize the conglomerate's post-tax profits and that the global position can be monitored effectively only from the Head Office.

Requirements:

a Explain and critically appraise the possible reasoning behind P plc's policy of centrally determining transfer prices for goods traded between divisions operating in different countries.

(10 marks)

b   Discuss the ethical implications of P plc's policy of imposing transfer prices on its overseas divisions in order to maximize post-tax profits.   *(10 marks)*

CIMA Stage 4 Strategic Management Accounting and Marketing

IM20.1 Advanced. Exel Division is part of the Supeer Group. It produces a basic fabric which is then converted in other divisions within the group. The fabric is also produced in other divisions within the Supeer Group and a limited quantity can be purchased from outside the group. The fabric is currently charged out by Exel Division at total actual cost plus 20 per cent profit mark-up.

a   Explain why the current transfer pricing method used by Exel Division is unlikely to lead to:

(i)   maximization of group profit and

(ii)   effective divisional performance measurement.   *(6 marks)*

b   If the supply of basic fabric is insufficient to meet the needs of the divisions who convert it for sale outside the group, explain a procedure which should lead to a transfer pricing and deployment policy for the basic fabric for group profit maximization.

(6 marks)

c   Show how the procedure explained in (b) may be in conflict with other objectives of transfer pricing and suggest how this conflict may be overcome.   *(5 marks)*

ACCA Level 2 – Cost and Management Accounting II

IM20.2 Advanced: Discussion of transfer price where there is an external market for the intermediat product. Fabri Division is part of the Multo Group. Fabri Division produces a single product for which it has an external market which utilizes 70 per cent of its production capacity. Gini Division, which is also part of the Multo Group requires units of the product available from Fabri Division which it will then convert and sell to an external customer. Gini Division's requirements are equal to 50 per cent of Fabri Division's production capacity. Gini Division has a potential source of supply from outside the Multo Group. It is not yet known if this source is willing to supply on the basis of (i) only supplying *all* of Gini Division's requirements or (ii) supplying any part of Gini Division's requirements as requested.

a   Discuss the transfer pricing method by which Fabri Division should offer to transfer its product to Gini Division in order that group profit maximization is likely to follow.

You may illustrate your answer with figures of your choice.

(14 marks)

b   Explain ways in which (i) the degree of divisional autonomy allowed and (ii) the divisional performance measure in use by Multo Group may affect the transfer pricing policy of Fabri Division.   *(6 marks)*

ACCA Level 2 Cost and Management Accounting II

IM20.3 Advanced.

a   Spiro Division is part of a vertically integrated group of divisions allocated in one country. All divisions sell externally and also transfer goods to other divisions within the group. Spiro Division performance is measured using profit before tax as a performance measure.

(i)   Prepare an outline statement which shows the costs and revenue elements which should be included in the calculation of divisional profit before tax.   *(4 marks)*

(ii)   The degree of autonomy which is allowed to divisions may affect the absolute value of profit reported.

Discuss the statement in relation to Spiro Division.   *(6 marks)*

b   Discuss the pricing basis on which divisions should offer to transfer goods in order that corporate profit maximizing decisions should take place.   *(5 marks)*

ACCA Paper 9 Information for Control and Decision Making

IM20.4 Advanced.

a   The transfer pricing method used for the transfer of an intermediate product between two divisions in a group has been agreed at standard cost plus 30 per cent profit markup. The transfer price may be altered after taking into consideration the planning and operational variance analysis at the transferor division.

Discuss the acceptability of this transfer pricing method to the transferor and transferee divisions.   *(5 marks)*

b   Division A has an external market for product X which fully utilizes its production capacity.

Explain the circumstances in which division A should be willing to transfer product X to division B of the same group at a price which is less than the existing market price.   *(5 marks)*

c   An intermediate product which is converted in divisions L, M and N of a group is available in limited quantities from other divisions within the group and from an external source. The total available quantity of the intermediate product is insufficient to satisfy demand. Explain the procedure which should lead to a transfer pricing and deployment policy resulting in group profit maximization.

(5 marks)

ACCA Paper 9 Information for Control and Decision Making

IM20.5 Advanced: Resolving a transfer price conflict. Alton division (A) and Birmingham division (B) are two manufacturing divisions of Conglom plc. Both of these divisions make a single standardized product; A makes product I and B makes product J. Every unit of J requires one unit of I. The required input of I is normally purchased from division A but sometimes it is purchased from an outside source.

The following table gives details of selling price and cost for each product:

	Product I (£)	Product J (£)
Established selling price	<u>30</u>	<u>50</u>
Variable costs		
Direct material	8	5
Transfers from A	—	30
Direct labour	5	3
Variable overhead	<u>2</u>	<u>2</u>
	15	40
Divisional fixed cost (per annum)	£500 000	£225 000
Annual outside demand with current selling prices (units)	100 000	25 000
Capacity of plant (units)	130 000	30 000
Investment in division	£6 625 000	£1 250 000

Division B is currently achieving a rate of return well below the target set by the central office. Its manager blames this situation on the high transfer price of product I. Division A charges division B for the transfers of I at the outside supply price of £30. The manager of division A claims that this is appropriate since this is the price 'determined by market forces'. The manager of B has consistently argued that intra group transfers should be charged at a lower price based on the costs of the producing division plus a 'reasonable' mark-up.

The board of Conglom plc is concerned about B's low rate of return and the divisional manager has been asked to submit proposals for improving the situation. The board has now received a report from B's manager in which he asks the board to intervene to reduce the transfer price charged for product I. The manager of B also informs the board that he is considering the possibility of opening a branch office in rented premises in a nearby town, which should enlarge the market for product J by 5000 units per year at the existing price. He estimates that the branch office establishment costs would be £50 000 per annum.

You have been asked to write a report advising the board on the response that it should make to the plans and proposals put forward by the manager of division B. Incorporate in your report a calculation of the rates of return currently being earned on the capital employed by each division and the changes to these that should follow from an implementation of any proposals that you would recommend.

(22 marks)

ACCA Level 2 Management Accounting

IM20.6 Advanced: Apportionment of company profit to various departments. AB Limited which buys and sells machinery has three departments:

New machines (manager, Newman)

Second-hand machines (manager, Handley)

Repair workshops (manager, Walker)

In selling new machines Newman is often asked to accept an old machine in part exchange. In such cases the old machine is disposed of by Handley.

The workshops do work both for outside customers and also for the other two departments. Walker charges his outside customers for materials at cost and for labour time at £8 per hour. This £8 is made up as follows:

Per hour (£)		
Fixed costs	2.00	(10 000 budgeted hours per annum)
Variable costs	4.50	
Profit	1.50	
	£8.00	

AB Limited wishes to go over to a profit centre basis of calculations so as to be able to reward its three managers according to their results. It wishes to assess the situation in the context of the following transaction:

Newman sold to PQ Limited a new machine at list price of £16 000, the cost of which to AB Limited was £12 000.

To make the sale, however, Newman had to allow PQ Limited £5000 for its old machine in part exchange.

PQ Limited's old machine was in need of repair before it could be re-sold and Newman and Handley were agreed in their estimate of those repairs as £50 in materials and 100 hours of workshop's labour time. That estimate was proved to be correct when the workshops undertook the repair.

At the time of taking PQ Limited's machine in part exchange Handley would have been able to buy a similar machine from other dealers for £3700 without the need for any repair. When the machine had been repaired he sold it to ST Limited for £4200.

You are required to:

a show how you would calculate the profit contribution for each of the three departments from the above transaction.

b re-calculate the profit contribution for each department if there were the following alternative changes of circumstances:
  (i) When the workshops came to repair the old machine they found that they required an extra 50 hours of labour time because of a fault not previously noticed.
  (ii) Before deciding on the figure he would allow PQ Limited for their old machine, Newman asks Walker to estimate the cost of repairs. This estimate is £50 in materials and 100 hours of workshops labour time. When, however, workshops came to repair the old machine, it took them 50 per cent longer than estimated.

c recommend briefly how to deal with the following situations in the context of profit centre calculation:
  (i) The manufacturer of the new machines allows AB Limited £200 per machine for which AB Limited undertakes to do all warranty repairs. Over the year the total cost of repairs under warranty exceeds the amount allowed by the supplier.
  (ii) Although 4000 hours of workshop time were budgeted to be reserved for the other two departments, their load increases over the year by 20 per cent (at standard efficiency). The load from outside customers, however, stays as budgeted.

(25 marks)
CIMA P3 Management Accounting

IM20.7 Advanced: Computation of three different transfer prices and the extent to which each price encourages goal congruence. English Allied Traders plc has a wide range of manufacturing activities, principally within the UK. The company operates on the divisionalized basis with each division being responsible for its own manufacturing, sales and marketing, and working capital management. Divisional chief executives are expected to achieve a target 20 per cent return on sales.

A disagreement has arisen between two divisions which operate on adjacent sites. The Office Products Division (OPD) has the opportunity to manufacture a printer using a new linear motor which has recently been developed by the Electric Motor Division (EMD). Currently there is no other source of supply for an equivalent motor in the required quantity of 30 000 units a year, although a foreign manufacturer has offered to supply up to 10 000 units in the coming year at a price of £9 each. EMD's current selling price for the motor is £12. Although EMD's production line for this motor is currently operating at only 50 per cent of its capacity, sales are encouraging and EMD confidently expects to sell 100 000 units in 2001, and its maximum output of 120 000 units in 2002.

EMD has offered to supply OPD's requirements for 2001 at a transfer price equal to the normal selling price, less the variable selling and distribution costs that it would not incur on this internal order. OPD responded by offering an alternative transfer price of the standard variable manufacturing cost plus a 20 per cent profit margin. The two divisions have been unable to agree, so the corporate operations director has suggested a third transfer price equal to the standard full manufacturing cost plus 15 per cent. However, neither divisional chief executive regards such a price as fair.

EMD's 2001 budget for the production and sale of motors, based on its standard costs for the forecast 100 000 units sales, but excluding the possible sales to OPD, is as follows:

	(£000)
Sales Revenue (100 000 units at £12.00 each)	1200
Direct Manufacturing Costs	
Bought-in materials	360
Labour	230
Packaging	40
Indirect Manufacturing Costs	
Variable overheads	10
Line production managers	30
Depreciation	
Capital equipment	150
Capitalized development costs	60
Total manufacturing costs	880
Sales and Distribution Costs	
Salaries of sales force	50
Carriage	20
General Overhead	50
Total costs	1000
Profit	200

Notes

1 The costs of the sales force and indirect production staff are not expected to increase up to the current production capacity.

2 General overhead includes allocations of divisional administrative expenses and corporate charges of £20 000 specifically related to this product.

3 Depreciation for all assets is charged on a straight line basis using a five year life and no residual value.

4 Carriage is provided by an outside contractor.

Requirements

a Calculate each of the three proposed transfer prices and comment on how each might affect the willingness of EMD's chief executive to engage in inter-divisional trade. *(10 marks)*

b Outline an alternative method of setting transfer prices which you consider to be appropriate for this situation, and explain why it is an improvement on the other proposals. *(5 marks)*

ICAEW P2 Management Accounting and Financial Management 2

IM20.8 Advanced: Optimal output and transfer price where the market for the intermediate product is imperfect. Engcorp and Flotilla are UK divisions of Griffin plc, a multinational company. Both divisions have a wide range of activities. You are an accountant employed by Griffin plc and the Finance Director has asked you to investigate a transfer pricing problem.

Engcorp makes an engine, the Z80, which it has been selling to external customers at £1350 per unit. Flotilla wanted to buy Z80 engines to use in its own production of dories; each dory requires one engine. Engcorp would only sell if Flotilla paid £1350 per unit. The managing director of Engcorp commented:

'We have developed a good market for this engine and £1350 is the current market price. Just because Flotilla is not efficient enough to make a profit is no reason for us to give a subsidy.'

Flotilla has now found that engines suitable for its purpose can be bought for £1300 per unit from another manufacturer. Flotilla is preparing to buy engines from this source.

From information supplied by the divisions you have derived the following production and revenue schedules which are applicable over the capacity range of the two divisions:

| | Engcorp's data for Z80 engines | | | Flotilla's data for dories | |
Annual number of units	Total manufacturing cost (£000)	Total revenue from outside sales (£000)	Total cost of producing dories excluding engine costs (£000)	Total revenue from sales of dories (£000)
100	115	204	570	703
200	185	362	1120	1375
300	261	486	1670	2036
400	344	598	2220	2676
500	435	703	2770	3305
600	535	803	3320	3923
700	645	898	3870	4530
800	766	988	4420	5126

Requirements

a Ignoring the possibility that Flotilla could buy engines from another manufacturer, calculate to the nearest 100 units:
  (i) the quantity of Z80 production that would maximize profits for Griffin plc, and
  (ii) the consequent quantity of Z80 units that would be sold to external customers and the quantity that would be transferred to Flotilla. *(8 marks)*

b Explain the issues raised by the problems of transfer pricing between Engcorp and Flotilla, and discuss the advantages and disadvantages of the courses of action which could be taken. *(10 marks)*

c Discuss the major considerations in setting transfer prices for a profit-maximizing international group. *(7 marks)*

ICAEW P2 Management Accounting

IM20.9 Advanced: Calculation of optimum selling price using calculus as the effect of using the imperfect market price as the transfer price. HKI plc has an Engineering Division and a Motorcycle Division. The Engineering Division produces engines which it sells to 'outside' customers and transfers to the Motorcycle Division. The Motorcycle Division produces a powerful motorbike called the 'Beast' which incorporates an HKI engine in its design.

The Divisional Managers have full control over the commercial policy of their respective Divisions and are each paid 1 per cent of the profit that is earned by their Divisions as an incentive bonus.

Details of the Engineering Division's production operation for the next year are expected to be as follows:

Annual fixed costs	£3 000 000
Variable cost per engine	£350

Details of the Motorcycle Division's production operation for the next year are expected to be as follows:

Annual fixed costs	£50 000
Variable cost per Beast	£700*

*Note: this figure excludes transfer costs

Both Divisions have significant surplus capacity.

Market research has indicated that demand from 'outside' customers for HKI plcs products is as follows:

● 9000 engines are sold at a unit selling price of £700; sales change by an average of 10 engines for each £1 change in the selling price per engine;

● 1000 Beasts are sold at a unit selling price of £2200; sales change by an average of 125 Beasts for each £100 change in the selling price per Beast.

It is established practice for the Engineering Division to transfer engines to the Motorcycle Division at 'market selling price'.

You are required

a to calculate the unit selling price of the Beast (accurate to the nearest penny) that should be set in order to maximize HKI plc's profit; *(7 marks)*

b to calculate the selling price of the Beast (accurate to the nearest penny) that is likely to emerge if the Engineering Division Manager sets a market selling price for the engine which is calculated to maximize profit from engine sales to outside customers. You may assume that both Divisional Managers are aware of the information given above. Explain your reasoning and show your workings; *(8 marks)*

c to explain why you agree or disagree with the following statement made by the Financial Director of HKI plc:

  'Pricing policy is a difficult area which offers considerable scope for dysfunctional behaviour. Decisions about selling prices should be removed from the control of Divisional Managers and made the responsibility of a Head Office department.'

(12 marks)
CIMA Stage 4 Management Accounting – Decision Making

PART FIVE

PART FIVE

Cost Management and Strategic Management Accounting

In Part Four the major features of traditional management accounting control systems and the mechanisms that can be used to control costs were described. The focus was on comparing actual results against a pre-set standard (typically the budget), identifying and analyzing variances and taking remedial action to ensure that future outcomes conform with budgeted outcomes. Traditional cost control systems tend to be based on the preservation of the *status-quo* and the ways of performing existing activities are not reviewed. The emphasis is on cost containment rather than cost reduction. In contrast, cost management focuses on cost reduction rather than cost containment. Chapter 21 examines the various approaches that fall within the area of cost management.

During the late 1980s criticisms of traditional management accounting practices were widely publicized and new approaches were advocated which are more in tune with today's competitive and business environment. In particular, strategic management accounting has been identified as a way forward. However, there is still no comprehensive framework as to what constitutes strategic management accounting. Chapter 22 examines the elements of strategic management accounting and describes the different contributions that have been made to its development. In addition, recent developments that seek to incorporate performance measurement within the strategic management process are described.

Cost management

21

In Chapters 16–18 the major features of traditional management accounting control systems and the mechanisms that can be used to control costs were described. The focus was on comparing actual results against a pre-set standard (typically the budget), identifying and analyzing variances and taking remedial action to ensure that future outcomes conform with budgeted outcomes. Traditional cost control systems tend to be based on the preservation of the *status quo* and the ways of performing existing activities are not reviewed. The emphasis is on cost containment rather than cost reduction.

Cost management focuses on cost reduction and continuous improvement and change rather than cost containment. Indeed, the term cost reduction could be used instead of cost management

LEARNING OBJECTIVES

After studying this chapter, you should be able to:

- distinguish between the features of a traditional management accounting control system and cost management;

- explain life-cycle costing and describe the typical pattern of cost commitment and cost incurrence during the three stages of a product's life cycle;

- describe the target costing approach to cost management;

- describe tear-down analysis, value engineering and functional analysis;

- distinguish between target costing and *kaizen* costing;

- describe activity-based cost management;

- distinguish between value added and non-value added activities;

- explain the purpose of a cost of quality report;

- describe how value chain analysis can be used to increase customer satisfaction and manage costs more effectively;

- explain the role of benchmarking within the cost management framework;

- outline the main features of a just-in-time philosophy.

but the former is an emotive term. Therefore cost management is preferred. Whereas traditional cost control systems are routinely applied on a continuous basis, cost management tends to be applied on an *ad hoc* basis when an opportunity for cost reduction is identified. Also many of the approaches that are incorporated within the area of cost management do not necessarily involve the use of accounting techniques. In contrast, cost control relies heavily on accounting techniques.

Cost management consists of those actions that are taken by managers to reduce costs, some of which are prioritized on the basis of information extracted from the accounting system. Other actions, however, are undertaken without the use of accounting information. They involve process improvements, where an opportunity has been identified to perform processes more effectively and efficiently, and which have obvious cost reduction outcomes. It is important that you are aware of all the approaches that can be used to reduce costs even if these methods do not rely on accounting information. You should also note that although cost management seeks to reduce costs, it should not be at the expense of customer satisfaction. Ideally, the aim is to take actions that will both reduce costs and enhance customer satisfaction.

Life-cycle costing

ADVANCED READING

Traditional management accounting control procedures have focused primarily on the manufacturing stage of a product's life cycle. Pre-manufacturing costs, such as research and development and design and post-manufacturing abandonment and disposal costs are treated as period costs. Therefore they are not incorporated in the product cost calculations, nor are they subject to the conventional management accounting control procedures.

Life-cycle costing estimates and accumulates costs over a product's entire life cycle in order to determine whether the profits earned during the manufacturing phase will cover the costs incurred during the pre- and post-manufacturing stages. Identifying the costs incurred during the different stages of a product's life cycle provides an insight into understanding and managing the total costs incurred throughout its life cycle. In particular, life-cycle costing helps management to understand the cost consequences of developing and making a product and to identify areas in which cost reduction efforts are likely to be most effective.

Most accounting systems report on a period-by-period basis, and product profits are not monitored over their life cycles. In contrast, product life-cycle reporting involves tracing costs and revenues on a product-by-product basis over several calendar periods throughout their life cycle. A failure to trace all costs to products over their life cycles hinders management's understanding of product profitability, because a product's actual life-cycle profit is unknown. Consequently, inadequate feedback information is available on the success or failure in developing new products.

Figure 21.1 illustrates a typical pattern of cost commitment and cost incurrence during the three stages of a product's life cycle – the planning and design stage, the manufacturing stage and the service and abandonment stage. Committed or locked-in costs are those costs that have not been incurred but that will be incurred in the future on the basis of decisions that have already been made. Costs are incurred when a resource is used or sacrificed. Costing systems record costs only when they have been incurred. It is difficult to significantly alter costs after they have been committed. For example, the product design specifications determine a product's material and labour inputs and the production process. At this stage costs become committed and broadly determine the future costs that will be incurred during the manufacturing stage.

You will see from Figure 21.1 that approximately 80 per cent of a product's costs are *committed* during the planning and design stage. At this stage product designers determine the product's design and the production process. In contrast, the majority of costs are *incurred* at the manufacturing stage, but they have already become locked-in at the planning and design stage and are difficult to alter.

It is apparent from Figure 21.1 that cost management can be most effectively exercised during the planning and design stage and not at the manufacturing stage when the product design and processes have already been determined and costs have been committed. At this latter stage the focus is more on cost containment than cost management. An understanding of life-cycle costs

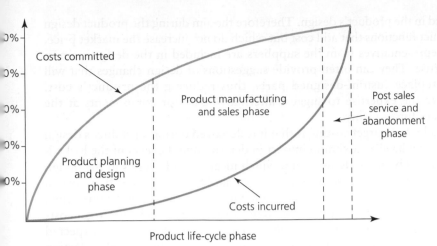

FIGURE 21.1
Product life-cycle phases: relationship between costs committed and costs incurred

and how they are committed and incurred at different stages throughout a product's life cycle led to the emergence of target costing, a technique that focuses on managing costs during a product's planning and design phase.

Target costing

In Chapter 11 we briefly looked at target costing as a mechanism for determining selling prices. We shall now consider how target costing can be used as a cost management tool. Target costing involves the following stages:

Stage 1: Determine the target price which customers will be prepared to pay for the product.

Stage 2: Deduct a target profit margin from the target price to determine the target cost.

Stage 3: Estimate the actual cost of the product.

Stage 4: If estimated actual cost exceeds the target cost investigate ways of driving down the actual cost to the target cost.

Target costing is a customer-oriented technique that is widely used by Japanese companies and which has recently been adopted by companies in Europe and the USA. The first stage requires market research to determine the customers' perceived value of the product based on its functions and its attributes (i.e. its functionality), its differentiation value relative to competing products and the price of competing products. The target profit margin depends on the planned return on investment for the organization as a whole and profit as a percentage of sales. This is then decomposed into a target profit for each product which is subsequently deducted from the target price to give the target cost. The target cost is compared with the predicted actual cost. If the predicted actual cost is above the target cost intensive efforts are made to close the gap so that the predicted cost equals the target cost.

A major feature of target costing is that a team approach is adopted to achieve the target cost. The team members include designers, engineers, purchasing, manufacturing, marketing and management accounting personnel. Their aim is to achieve the target cost specified for the product at the prescribed level of functionality and quality. The discipline of a team approach ensures that no particular group is able to impose their functional preferences. For example, design engineers pursuing their flair for design may design into products features that increase a product's costs but which customers do not value, or features that require the use of unique parts when alternative designs requiring standardized parts may meet customer requirements. Similarly, without a multi-functional team approach a marketing emphasis might result in the introduction of product features that customers find attractive, but not essential, and so they are not prepared to pay to have them included in the product's design. Therefore the aim during the product design process is to eliminate product functions that add cost but which do not increase the market price.

In some organizations representatives from the suppliers are included in the design team in order to obtain their expertise. They can often provide suggestions of design changes that will enable standard parts to replace custom-designed parts, thus reducing the product's cost. Alternatively, suppliers have the expertise to suggest alternative parts or components at the lowest cost for a given level of functionality.

The major advantage of adopting target costing is that it is deployed during a product's design and planning stage so that it can have a maximum impact in determining the level of the locked-in costs. It is an iterative process with the design team, which ideally should result in the design team continuing with its product and process design attempts until it finds designs that give an expected cost that is equal or less than the target cost. If the target cost cannot be attained then the product should not be launched. Design teams should not be allowed to achieve target costs by eliminating desirable product functions. Thus, the aim is to design a product with an expected cost that does not exceed target cost and that also meets the target level of functionality. Design teams use tear-down analysis and value engineering to achieve the target cost.

Tear-down analysis

Tear-down analysis (also known as reverse engineering) involves examining a competitor's product in order to identify opportunities for product improvement and/or cost reduction. The competitor's product is dismantled to identify its functionality and design and to provide insights about the processes that are used and the cost to make the product. The aim is to benchmark provisional product designs with the designs of competitors and to incorporate any observed relative advantages of the competitor's approach to product design.

Value engineering

Value engineering (also known as value analysis) is a systematic interdisciplinary examination of factors affecting the cost of a product or service in order to devise means of achieving the specified purpose at the required standard of quality and reliability at the target cost. The aim of value engineering is to achieve the assigned target cost by (i) identifying improved product designs that reduce the product's cost without sacrificing functionality and/or (ii) eliminating unnecessary functions that increase the product's costs and for which customers are not prepared to pay extra.

Value engineering requires the use of functional analysis. This process involves decomposing the product into its many elements or attributes. For example, in the case of automobiles, functions might consist of style, comfort, operability, reliability, quality, attractiveness and many others (Kato, 1993). A price, or value, for each element is determined which reflects the amount the customer is prepared to pay. To obtain this information companies normally conduct surveys and interviews with customers. The cost of each function of a product is compared with the benefits perceived by the customers. If the cost of the function exceeds the benefit to the customer, then the function should be either eliminated, modified to reduce its cost, or enhanced in terms of its perceived value so that its value exceeds the cost. Also by focusing on the product's functions, the design team will often consider components that perform the same function in other products, thus increasing the possibility of using standard components and reducing costs.

The need for accurate cost measurement systems

It is important that target costing is supported by an accurate cost system. In particular, cost drivers should be established that are the significant determinants of the costs of the activities so that cause-and-effect allocations are used. Arbitrary cost allocations should be avoided. If arbitrary cost allocations are used the allocation base will not be a significant determinant of cost. Let us assume that an arbitrary allocation base, say direct labour hours, is used to allocate support costs to products. To reduce the projected cost towards the target cost the target costing team will be motivated to focus on reducing direct labour hours. Why? Because this will result in a smaller proportion of the support costs being assigned to the product. However, the support costs incurred by the organization will not be reduced because there is no cause-and-effect relationship between direct labour hours and the resulting costs. Therefore the target costing exercise will merely result in a reduction in the costs that are allocated to the product but organizational costs will not be reduced. In contrast, if cause-and-effect allocation bases (i.e. cost drivers) are established, reductions in cost driver usage should be followed by a reduction in organizational support costs.

Therefore it is very important that cost systems use cost drivers that are the determinants of costs so that they will motivate designers to take actions that will reduce organizational costs. Decisions taken at the design stage lead to the committed usage of cost drivers which can be difficult to change in the future.

An illustration of target costing

Example 21.1 is used to illustrate the target costing process. You will have noted from reading the information presented in this example that the projected cost of the product is £700 compared with a target cost of £560. To achieve the target cost the company establishes a project team to undertake an intense target costing exercise. Example 21.1 indicates that the end result of the target costing exercise is a projected cost of £555 which is marginally below the target cost of £560. Let us now look at how the company has achieved the target cost and also how the costs shown in Example 21.1 have been derived.

In response to the need to reduce the projected cost the project team starts by purchasing similar types of camcorders from its main competitors and undertaking a tear-down analysis. This process involves dismantling the camcorders to provide insights into potential design improvements for the new camcorder that will be launched. Value engineering is also undertaken with the project team working closely with the design engineers. Their objective is to identify new designs that will accomplish the same functions at a lower cost and also to eliminate any functions that are deemed to be unnecessary. This process results in a simplified design, the reduction in the number of parts and the replacement of some customized parts with standard parts. The outcome of the tear-down analysis and value engineering activities is a significant reduction in the projected direct materials, labour and rework costs, but the revised cost estimates still indicate that the projected cost exceeds the target cost.

Next the team engages in functional analysis. They identify the different elements, functions and attributes of the camcorder and potential customers are interviewed to ascertain the values that they place on each of the functions. This process indicates that several functions that have been included in the prototype are not valued by customers. The team therefore decide to eliminate these functions. The functional analysis results in further cost reductions being made, principally in the areas of materials and direct labour assembly costs but the revised cost estimates still indicate that the target cost has not been attained.

The team now turn their attention to redesigning the production and support processes. They decide to redesign the ordering and receiving process by reducing the number of suppliers and working closely with a smaller number of suppliers. The suppliers are prepared to enter into contractual arrangements whereby they are periodically given a pre-determined production schedule and in return they will inspect the shipments and guarantee quality prior to delivery. In addition, the marketing, distribution and customer after-sales services relating to the product are subject to an intensive review, and process improvements are made that result in further reductions in costs that are attributable to the camcorder. The projected cost after undertaking all of the above activities is £555 compared with the target cost of £560 and at this point the target costing exercise is concluded.

Having described the target costing approach that the Digital Electronics Company has used let us now turn our attention to the derivation of the projected costs shown in Example 21.1. The projected cost for direct materials prior to the target costing exercise is £390 but value engineering and the functional analysis have resulted in a reduction in the number of parts that are required to manufacture the camcorder. The elimination of most of the unique parts, and the use of standard parts that the company currently purchases in large volumes, also provides scope for further cost savings. The outcome of the redesign process is a direct material cost of £325.

The simplified product design enables the assembly time to be reduced thus resulting in the reduction of direct labour costs from £100 to £80. The direct machine costs relate to machinery that will be used exclusively for the production of the new product. The estimated cost of acquiring, maintaining and operating the machinery throughout the product's life cycle is £6 million. This is divided by the projected lifetime sales volume of the camera (300 000 units) giving a unit cost of £20. However, it has not been possible to reduce the unit cost because the

EXAMPLE 21.1 Expected costs for various safety stocks

The Digital Electronics Company manufactures cameras and video equipment. It is in the process of introducing the world's smallest and lightest camcorder with HD and SD recording modes. The company has undertaken market research to ascertain the customers' perceived value of the product based on its special features and a comparison with competitors' products. The results of the survey, and a comparison of the new camcorder with competitors' products and market prices, have been used to establish a target selling price and projected lifetime volume. In addition, cost estimates have been prepared based on the proposed product specification. The company has set a target profit margin of 30 per cent on the proposed selling price and this has been deducted from the target selling price to determine the target cost. The following is a summary of the information that has been presented to management:

Projected lifetime sales volume	300 000 units
Target selling price	£800
Target profit margin (30% of selling price)	£240
Target cost (£800 – £240)	£560
Projected cost	£700

The excess of the projected cost over the target cost results in an intensive target costing exercise. After completing the target costing exercise the projected cost is £555 which is marginally below the target cost of £560. The analysis of the projected cost before and after the target costing exercise is as follows:

	Before		After	
	(£)	(£)	(£)	(£)
Manufacturing cost				
Direct material (bought in parts)	390		325	
Direct labour	100		80	
Direct machining costs	20		20	
Ordering and receiving	8		2	
Quality assurance	60		50	
Rework	15		6	
Engineering and design	10	603	8	491
Non-manufacturing costs				
Marketing	40		25	
Distribution	30		20	
After-sales service and warranty costs	27	97	19	64
Total cost		700		555

machinery costs are committed, and fixed, and the target costing exercise has not resulted in a change in the predicted lifetime volume.

Prior to the target costing exercise 80 separate parts were included in the product specification. The estimated number of orders placed for each part throughout the product's life cycle is 150 and the predicted cost per order for the order and receiving activity is £200. Therefore the estimated lifetime costs are £2.4 million (80 parts × 150 orders × £200 per order) giving a unit cost of £8 (£2.4 million/300 000 units). The simplified design, and the parts standardization arising from the functional analysis and the value engineering activities, have enabled the number of parts to be reduced to 40. The redesign of the ordering and receiving process has also enabled the number of orders and the ordering cost to be reduced (the former from 150 to 100 and the latter from £200 to £150 per order). Thus the projected lifetime ordering and receiving costs after the target costing exercise are £600 000 (40 parts × 100 orders × £150 per order) giving a revised unit cost of £2 (£600 000/300 000 units).

Quality assurance involves inspecting and testing the camcorders. Prior to the target costing exercise the projected cost was £60 (12 hours at £5 per hour) but the simplified design means that the camcorder will be easier to test resulting in revised cost of £50 (10 hours at £5 per hour). Rework costs of £15 represent the average rework costs per camcorder. Past experience with manufacturing similar products suggests that 10 per cent of the output will require rework. Applying this rate to the estimated total lifetime volume of 300 000 camcorders results in 30 000 camcorders requiring rework at an estimated average cost of £150 per reworked camcorder. The total lifetime rework cost is therefore predicted to be £4.5 million (30 000 × £150) giving an average cost per unit of good output of £15 (£4.5 million/300 000). Because of the simplified product design the rework rate and the average rework cost will be reduced. The predicted rework rate is now 5 per cent and the average rework cost will be reduced from £150 to £120. Thus, the revised estimate of the total lifetime cost is £1.8 million (15 000 reworked units at £120 per unit) and the projected unit cost is £6 (£1.8 million/300 000 units).

The predicted total lifetime engineering and design costs and other product sustaining costs are predicted to be £3 million giving a unit cost of £10. The simplified design and reduced number of parts enables the lifetime cost to be reduced by 20 per cent, to £2.4 million, and the unit cost to £8. The planned process improvements have also enabled the predicted marketing, distribution and after-sales service costs to be reduced. In addition, the simplified product design and the use of fewer parts has contributed to the reduction to the after-sales warranty costs. However, to keep our example brief the derivation of the non-manufacturing costs will not be presented, other than to note that the company uses an activity-based-costing system. All costs are assigned using cost drivers that are based on established cause-and-effect relationships.

Kaizen costing

In addition to target costing *kaizen* costing is widely used by Japanese organizations as a mechanism for reducing and managing costs. *Kaizen* is the Japanese term for making improvements to a process through small incremental amounts, rather than through large innovations. The major difference between target and *kaizen* costing is that target costing is normally applied during the design stage whereas *kaizen* costing is applied during the manufacturing stage of the product life cycle. With target costing the focus is on the product, and cost reductions are achieved primarily through product design. In contrast, *kaizen* costing focuses on the production processes and cost reductions are derived primarily through the increased efficiency of the production process. Therefore the potential cost reductions are smaller with kaizen costing because the products are already in the manufacturing stage of their life cycles and a significant proportion of the costs will have become locked-in.

The aim of *kaizen* costing is to reduce the cost of components and products by a pre-specified amount. Monden and Hamada (1991) describe the application of *kaizen* costing in a Japanese automobile plant. Each plant is assigned a target cost reduction ratio and this is applied to the previous year's actual costs to determine the target cost reduction. *Kaizen* costing relies heavily on employee empowerment. They are assumed to have superior knowledge about how to improve processes because they are closest to the manufacturing processes and customers and are likely to have greater insights into how costs can be reduced. Thus, a major feature of *kaizen* costing is that workers are given the responsibility to improve processes and reduce costs. Unlike target costing it is not accompanied by a set of techniques or procedures that are automatically applied to achieve the cost reductions.

Activity-based management

The early adopters of activity-based costing (ABC) used it to produce more accurate product (or service) costs but it soon became apparent to the users that it could be extended beyond purely product costing to a range of cost management applications. The terms activity-based management (ABM) or activity-based cost management (ABCM) are used to describe the cost management applications of ABC. To implement an ABM system only the first three of the four stages described in Chapter 10 for designing an activity-based product costing system are required. They are:

1 identifying the major activities that take place in an organization (i.e. activity analysis);

2 assigning costs to cost pools/cost centres for each activity;

3 determining the cost driver for each major activity.

Thus, firms can omit the final stage of assigning activity costs to products and adopt ABC solely for cost management without activity-based product costing. Where a firm does use an activity-based system for both cost management and product costing it may choose to create a large number of activity cost pools to monitor the costs of the many different activities but aggregate the pools so that a smaller number is used for product costing purposes.

ABM views the business as a set of linked activities that ultimately add value to the customer. It focuses on managing the business on the basis of the activities that make up the organization. ABM is based on the premise that activities consume costs. Therefore by managing activities costs will be managed in the long term. Managing activities requires an understanding of what factors cause activities to be performed and what causes activity costs to change. The goal of ABM is to enable customer needs to be satisfied while making fewer demands on organizational resources (i.e. cost reduction). Besides providing information on what activities are performed, ABM provides information on the cost of activities, why the activities are undertaken, and how well they are performed.

Traditional budget and control reports analyze costs by types of expense for each responsibility centre. In contrast, ABM analyzes costs by activities and thus provides management with information on why costs are incurred and the output from the activity (in terms of cost drivers). Exhibit 21.1 illustrates the difference between the conventional analysis and the activity-based analysis in respect of customer order processing. The major differences are that the ABM approach reports by *activities* whereas the traditional analysis is by *departments*. Also ABM reporting is by sub-activities but traditional reporting is by expense categories. Another distinguishing feature of ABM reporting is that it often reports information on activities that cross departmental boundaries. For example, different production departments and the distribution department might undertake customer processing activities. They may resolve customer problems by expediting late deliveries. The finance department may assess customer credit worthiness and the remaining customer processing activities might be undertaken by the customer service department. Therefore the total cost of the customer processing activity could be considerably in excess of the costs that are assigned to the customer service department. However, to simplify the presentation it is assumed in Exhibit 21.1 that the departmental and activity costs are identical but if the cost of the customer order processing activity was found to be, say, three times the amount assigned to the customer service department, this would be important information because it may change the way in which the managers view the activity. For example, the managers may give more attention to reducing the costs of the customer processing activity.

It is apparent from an examination of Exhibit 21.1 that the ABM approach provides more meaningful information. It gives more visibility to the cost of undertaking the activities that make up the organization and may raise issues for management action that are not highlighted by the traditional analysis. For example, why is £90 000 spent on resolving customer problems? Attention-directing information such as this is important for managing the cost of the activities.

Johnson (1990) suggests that knowing costs by activities is a catalyst that eventually triggers the action necessary to become competitive. Consider a situation where salespersons, as a result

SOURCE: ADAPTED FROM NARAYANAN, V.G. AND SARKAR, R.G., THE IMPACT OF ACTIVITY-BASED COSTING ON MANAGERIAL DECISIONS AT INSTEEL INDUSTRIES: A FIELD STUDY, JOURNAL OF ECONOMICS AND MANAGEMENT STRATEGY, VOL.11, NO.2, SUMMER 2002, PP. 257–288.

The impact of ABC at Insteel Industries

REAL WORLD VIEWS 21.1

In 1996 Insteel Industries decided to implement ABC at the Andrews, South Carolina plant. The ABC team analyzed Andrews's operations and identified 12 business processes involving a total of 146 activities. The ABC study revealed that the 20 most expensive activities accounted for 87 per cent of Andrew's total physical and people resource of $21.4 million. Within the top 20 activities, almost $5 million pertained to quality-related activities such as reactive maintenance, management of by-products and scrap, and preventive maintenance. The analysis also revealed that material-handling costs, including freight costs, consumed $4.6 million. Activities were further classified into value-added and non-value-added. Nearly $4.9 million was spent on non-value-added activities such as reactive maintenance, dealing with scrap, moving materials, reworking products and managing customer complaints. Those activities, within the 20 most expensive, were targeted for cost reduction and process improvement.

Separate teams were formed for managing quality costs, material handling, and preventive maintenance. The company estimates that within a year of the first ABC study, $1.8 million had been saved in quality costs, mainly through a reduction of scrap and reactive maintenance costs. Freight costs were reduced $555,000 in a year in the Andrews plant alone. Non-value-added activities were reduced from 22 per cent of activity costs to 17 per cent.

Insteel focused on freight because delivering products to customers represented 16 per cent of the total people and physical resources cost at the Andrews plant. As a part of the ABC study, Insteel started tracking freight cost per pound shipped. This directed attention to ways in which these costs could be reduced. In 1997, by changing the layout of boxes within each truck, the Andrews plant was able to ship 7400 pounds more per truckload than in 1996. This represented a 20 per cent reduction in freight expense.

When Insteel realized how much they were actually incurring in quality costs, the team probed deeper into understanding better what was causing the quality costs to be incurred and for suggesting steps to reduce them. Insteel realized that certain foreign suppliers of rods were lower in price but supplied poorer-quality rods that caused breakdowns in Insteel's manufacturing process. The lower price of those suppliers did not compensate for the quality costs. Insteel switched to higher-quality rod suppliers. Insteel also realized that smaller-diameter wire products were more likely to break and disrupt the manufacturing process. Insteel migrated its product mix to more large-diameter wire products. Such initiatives led to reduction in quality costs from $6.7 million in 1996 to $4.9 million in 1997.

It is hard to estimate how much of these savings would have been realized had Insteel not conducted an ABC analysis. The activity analysis gave them an appreciation of the scope and quantified the magnitude of the improvement potential, thereby allowing them to prioritize among various process improvement possibilities. Clearly ABC served as a focusing device at Insteel by providing cost data by activity rather than by department, directing attention to the top 20 activities, and by labeling some of them as non-value-added activities.

Discussion points

1 How might activity costs for Insteel differ from departmental costs?

2 What approaches can be used to identify the activities undertaken by Insteel?

accordance with the production schedule and also guaranteeing their quality by inspecting them prior to delivery. The end result might be the elimination, or a permanent reduction, of the storing, purchasing and inspection activities. These activities are non-value added activities since they represent an opportunity for cost reduction without reducing the products' service potentials to customers.

A distinguishing feature of business process re-engineering is that it involves radical and dramatic changes in processes by abandoning current practices and reinventing completely new methods of performing business processes. The focus is on major changes rather than marginal improvements. A further example of business process re-engineering is moving from a traditional functional plant layout to a just-in-time cellular product layout and adopting a just-in-time philosophy. Adopting a just-in-time (JIT) system and philosophy has important implications for cost management and performance reporting. It is therefore important that you understand the nature of such systems and how they differ from traditional systems, but rather than deviating at this point from our discussion of cost management the description of a JIT system will be deferred until the end of the chapter.

Cost of quality

To compete successfully in today's global competitive environment companies are becoming 'customer-driven' and making customer satisfaction an overriding priority. Customers are demanding ever-improving levels of service regarding cost, quality, reliability, delivery and the choice of innovative new products. Quality has become one of the key competitive variables in

SOURCE: ADAPTED FROM BRINKMAN, S.L. AND APPELBAUM, M.A. (1994), THE QUALITY COST REPORT: IT IS ALIVE AND WELL AT GILROY FOODS, *MANAGEMENT ACCOUNTING (USA)*, SEPTEMBER, PP. 61–65.

REAL WORLD VIEWS 21.2

The quality cost report at Gilroy Foods

Prepared monthly, Gilroy's Quality Cost Report (QCR) is divided into two parts: a narrative and the data. We consider the narrative to be as important as the data. It is divided into two sections: an Executive Summary and the Monthly Topic. The Executive Summary discusses monthly results in total and highlights major factors contributing to quality costs. The Monthly Topic addresses ideas for improvement, implemented improvements, areas needing attention, explanation of prior events and other areas prime for management focus.

For the data part we currently include nearly 40 items in our QCR segregated into the four cost categories, and the list is growing. Month and year-to-date numbers are included and expressed as a percent of sales. Prior year-to-date numbers and a variance column comparing this year vs. last are also shown.

It is our opinion that our report understates quality costs in spite of our best efforts. Nonetheless, we feel the Total Quality Cost Report is superior to traditional accounting information for several reasons:

- It clearly segregates costs and identifies them as non-value added, which allows the organization to focus on the reduction or elimination of those items.

- It is a true barometer for the current health of the company because the cost data are not embedded in cost of sales, which can mask current performance.

- Because of the segregation of costs into prevention, appraisal, internal failure and external failure categories, the impact is magnified, and the focus is improved.

- It provides a target that can be shared with the entire company that really measures progress of the total quality programme in concrete terms.

Discussion points

1 What are the benefits of including a narrative within the QCR?

2 Explain why the QCR might understate quality costs.

both service and manufacturing organizations and this has created the need for management accountants to become more involved in the provision of information relating to the quality of products and services and activities that produce them. In the UK quality related costs have been reported to range from 5 per cent to 15 per cent of total company sales revenue (Plunkett et al., 1985). Eliminating inferior quality by implementing quality improvement initiatives can therefore result in substantial cost savings and higher revenues.

Total quality management (TQM), a term used to describe a situation where all business functions are involved in a process of continuous quality improvement, has been adopted by many companies. TQM has broadened, from its early concentration on the statistical monitoring of manufacturing processes, to a customer-oriented process of continuous improvement that focuses on delivering products or services of consistent high quality in a timely fashion. In the past most European and American companies considered quality to be an additional cost of manufacturing, but recently they have begun to realize that quality saves money. The philosophy of emphasizing production volume over quality resulted in high levels of stocks at each production stage in order to protect against shortages caused by inferior quality at previous stages and excessive expenditure on inspection, rework, scrap and warranty repairs. Companies discovered that it was cheaper to produce the items correctly the first time rather than wasting resources by making substandard items that have to be detected, reworked, scrapped or returned by customers.

Management accounting systems can help organizations achieve their quality goals by providing a variety of reports and measures that motivate and evaluate managerial efforts to improve quality. These include financial and non-financial measures. Many companies are currently not aware of how much they are spending on quality because they are incurred across many different departments and not accumulated as a separate cost object within the costing system. Managers need to know the costs of quality and how they are changing over time. A cost of quality report should be prepared to indicate the total cost to the organization of producing products or services that do not conform with quality requirements. Four categories of costs should be reported.

1 Prevention costs are the costs incurred in preventing the production of products that do not conform to specification. They include the costs of preventive maintenance, quality planning and training and the extra costs of acquiring higher quality raw materials.

2 Appraisal costs are the costs incurred to ensure that materials and products meet quality conformance standards. They include the costs of inspecting purchased parts, work in process and finished goods, quality audits and field tests.

3 Internal failure costs are the costs associated with materials and products that fail to meet quality standards. They include costs incurred before the product is despatched to the customer, such as the costs of scrap, repair, downtime and work stoppages caused by defects.

4 External failure costs are the costs incurred when products or services fail to conform to requirements or satisfy customer needs after they have been delivered. They include the costs of handling customer complaints, warranty replacement, repairs of returned products and the costs arising from a damaged company reputation. Costs within this category can have a dramatic impact on future sales.

Exhibit 21.2 presents a typical cost of quality report. Note that some of the items in the report will have to be estimated. For example, included in the external failure costs category is the forgone contribution from lost sales arising from poor quality. This cost is extremely difficult to estimate. Nevertheless, the lost contribution can be substantial and it is preferable to include an estimate rather than omit it from the report. By expressing each category of costs as a percentage of sales revenues comparisons can be made with previous periods, other organizations and divisions within the same group. Such comparisons can highlight problem areas. For example, comparisons of external failure costs with other companies can provide an indication of the current level of customer satisfaction.

The cost of quality report can be used as an attention-directing device to make the top management of a company aware of how much is being spent on quality-related costs. The report can also draw management's attention to the possibility of reducing total quality costs by a wiser allocation of costs among the four quality categories. For example, by spending more on the prevention costs, the amount of spending in the internal and external failure categories can be substantially reduced, and therefore total spending can be lowered. Also, by designing quality into the products and processes, appraisal costs can be reduced, since far less inspection is required.

Prevention and appraisal costs are sometimes referred to as the costs of quality conformance or compliance and internal and external failure costs are also known as the costs of non-conformance or non-compliance. Costs of compliance are incurred with the intention of eliminating the costs of failure. They are discretionary in the sense that they do not have to be incurred whereas costs of non-compliance are the result of production imperfections and can only be reduced by increasing compliance expenditure. The optimal investment in compliance costs is when total costs of quality reach a minimum. This can occur when 100 per cent quality compliance has not been achieved. It is virtually impossible to measure accurately all quality costs (particularly the lost contribution from forgone sales) and determine the optimal investment in conformance costs. However, some people argue that a failure to achieve 100 per cent quality compliance is non-optimal and that a zero-defects policy is optimal. With a zero-defects policy the focus is on continuous improvement with the ultimate aim of achieving zero-defects and eliminating all internal and external failure costs.

EXHIBIT 21.2 Cost of quality report

	(£000s)	% of sales (£100 million)
Prevention costs		
Quality training	1000	
Supplier reviews	300	
Quality engineering	400	
Preventive maintenance	500	
	2 200	2.2
Appraisal costs		
Inspection of materials received	500	
Inspection of WIP and completed units	1000	
Testing equipment	300	
Quality audits	800	
	2 600	2.6
Internal failure costs		
Scrap	800	
Rework	1000	
Downtime due to quality problems	600	
Retesting	400	2 800	2.8
External failure costs		
Returns	2000	
Recalls	1000	
Warranty repairs	800	
Handling customer complaints	500	
Foregone contribution from lost sales	3000	
	7 300	7.3
	14 900	14.9

A zero-defects policy does not use percentages as the unit of measurement because a small percentage defect rate can result in a large number of defects. For example, a 1 per cent defect rate from an output of 1 million units results in 10 000 defective units. To overcome this problem the attainment of a zero-defects goal is measured in parts per million (PPM) so that seemingly small numbers can be transferred into large numbers. Thus, instead of reporting a 1 per cent defect rate, a measure of 10 000 PPM is more likely to create pressure for action and highlight the trend in defect rates. Cost of quality reports provide a useful summary of quality efforts and progress to top management, but at lower management levels non-financial quality measures provide more timely and appropriate target measures for quality improvement. These measures will be discussed in the next chapter.

Besides using non-financial measures statistical quality control charts are used as a mechanism for distinguishing between random and non-random variations in operating processes. A control chart is a graph of a series of successive observations of operations taken at regular intervals of time to test whether a batch of produced items is within pre-set tolerance limits. Usually samples from a particular production process are taken at hourly or daily intervals. The mean, and sometimes the range, of the sampled items are calculated and plotted on a quality control chart (see Figure 21.2). Each observation is plotted relative to pre-set points on the expected distribution. Only observations beyond specified pre-set control limits are regarded as worthy of investigation.

The control limits are based on a series of past observations of a process when it is under control, and thus working efficiently. It is assumed that the past observations can be represented by a normal distribution. The past observations are used to estimate the population mean and the population standard deviation. Assuming that the distribution of possible outcomes is normal, then, when the process is under control, we should expect

68.27 per cent of the observation to fall within the range $+1\sigma$ from the mean;

95.45 per cent of the observation to fall within the range $+2\sigma$ from the mean.

Control limits are now set. For example, if control limits are set based on two standard deviations from the mean then this would indicate 4.55 per cent (100 per cent − 95.45 per cent) of future observations would result from pure chance when the process is under control. Therefore there is a high probability that an observation outside the 2σ control limits is out of control.

Figure 21.2 shows three control charts, with the outer horizontal lines representing a possible control limit of 2σ, so that all observations outside this range are investigated. You will see that for operation A the process is deemed to be in control because all observations fall within the control limits. For operation B the last two observations suggest that the operation is out of control. Therefore both observations should be investigated. With operation C the observations would not prompt an investigation because all the observations are within the control limits. However, the last six observations show a steadily increasing usage in excess of the mean, and the process may be out of control. Statistical procedures (called casum procedures) that consider the trend in recent usage as well as daily usage can also be used.

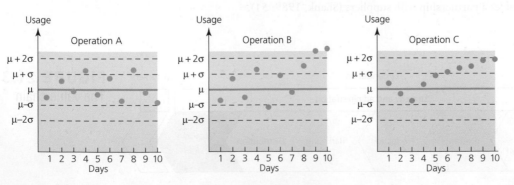

FIGURE 21.2
Statistical quality control charts

Cost management and the value chain

Increasing attention is now being given to value-chain analysis as a means of increasing customer satisfaction and managing costs more effectively. The value chain is illustrated in Figure 21.3. It is the linked set of value-creating activities all the way from basic raw material sources for component suppliers through to the ultimate end-use product or service delivered to the customer. A value-chain analysis is used to analyze, coordinate and optimize linkages in the value chain. Coordinating the individual parts of the value chain together creates the conditions to improve customer satisfaction, particularly in terms of cost efficiency, quality and delivery. A firm which performs the value chain activities more efficiently, and at a lower cost, than its competitors will gain a competitive advantage. Therefore it is necessary to understand how value chain activities are performed and how they interact with each other. The activities are not just a collection of independent activities but a system of inter-dependent activities in which the performance of one activity affects the performance and cost of other activities.

The linkages in the value chain express the relationships between the performance of one activity and its effects on the performance of another activity. A linkage occurs when interde-pendence exists between activities and the higher the interdependence between activities the greater is the required coordination. Thus, it is appropriate to view the value chain from the customer's perspective, with each link being seen as the customer of the previous link. If each link in the value chain is designed to meet the needs of its customers, then end-customer satis-faction should ensue. Furthermore, by viewing each link in the value chain as a supplier–customer relationship, the opinions of the customers can be used to provide useful feedback information on assessing the quality of service provided by the supplier. Opportunities are thus identified for improving activities throughout the entire value chain.

Shank and Govindarajan (1992) argue that traditional management accounting adopts an internal focus which, in terms of the value chain, starts too late and stops too soon. Starting cost analysis with purchases misses all the opportunities for exploiting linkages with the firm's suppliers and stopping cost analysis at the point of sale eliminates all opportunities for exploiting linkages with customers. Shank (1989) illustrates how an American automobile company failed to use the value chain approach to exploit links with suppliers and enhance profitability. The company had made significant internal savings from introducing JIT manufacturing techniques, but, at the same time, price increases from suppliers more than offset these internal cost savings. A value chain perspective revealed that 50 per cent of the firm's costs related to purchases from parts suppliers. As the automobile company reduced its own need for buffer stocks, it placed major new strains on the manufacturing responsiveness of suppliers. The increase in the suppliers' manufacturing costs was greater than the decrease in the automobile company's internal costs. Shank states:

> For every dollar of manufacturing cost the assembly plants saved by moving towards JIT management concepts, the suppliers' plant spent much more than one dollar extra because of schedule instability arising from the introduction of JIT. Because of its narrow value added perspective, the auto company had ignored the impact of its changes on its suppliers' costs. Management had ignored the idea that JIT involves a partnership with suppliers (Shank, 1989: 51).

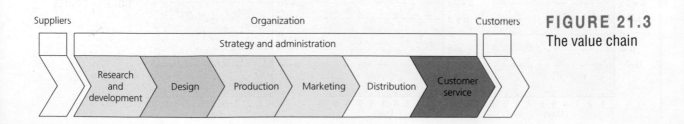

FIGURE 21.3
The value chain

SOURCE: ADAPTED FROM DEKKER, H.C. (2003), VALUE CHAIN ANALYSIS IN INTERFIRM RELATIONSHIPS: A FIELD STUDY, *MANAGEMENT ACCOUNTING RESEARCH*, VOL. 14, NO. 1, PP. 1–23.

Value chain analysis in interfirm relationships

The following presents extracts from a case study on the use of an ABC cost model by a large UK retail firm (Sainsburys) and a group of suppliers for supporting their supply chain management practices. This cost model was based on the principles of value chain analysis and integrated cost information across the supply chain. It was used to improve supply chain operations by performing benchmark analyses, strategic what-if analyses and cost monitoring. The model was used to identify opportunities to reduce supply chain costs.

To be able to analyze the supply chain costs, cost and cost driver data were required from both Sainsbury and suppliers. Suppliers were free to choose whether or not they would participate in this initiative. When they decided to participate, they were required to deliver cost data and cost driver quantities to Sainsbury for feeding the supplier section of the model.

Benchmarking was used to compare suppliers' activity costs with the average of their network. In addition, cost comparisons were made between networks, regions and store types. By clustering suppliers into different networks the most important differences between their operations were eliminated, as suppliers within a network performed fairly comparable activities. The most important measure for the benchmark analysis was the cost per cost driver (i.e. the cost driver rate), as this measure could be compared directly with other suppliers. The benchmark analysis revealed the suppliers' relative performance against the network average. When a supplier deviated significantly from the average, the Logistics Operations department would initiate a discussion with the supplier to find out the cause(s) of the difference, by analyzing the underlying activities, and to assess whether and how performance could be improved. In addition, as suppliers in different networks faced no competition, comparing the costs of their activities and analyzing the differences in their operations could be used to transfer efficient supply chain practices across networks.

Strategic what-if analyses were performed to analyze the effects of changes in the supply chain on supply chain costs. When, for example, as a result of a benchmark analysis, Sainsbury and a supplier developed ideas or scenarios for improving supply chain processes, the model was used to calculate the expected changes in costs of each scenario.

REAL WORLD VIEWS 21.3

Discussion points

1 What kinds of activities might be included in the benchmark analysis?

2 What cost drivers might be used within the benchmark analysis?

© FERRUCCIO/ALAMY

Managing linkages in the value chain is also the central idea of the concept of supply chain management. By examining potential linkages with suppliers and understanding supplier costs it may be possible for the buying organization to change its activities in order to reduce the supplier's costs. For example, cost generating activities in the supplying organizations are often triggered by purchasing parameters (e.g. design specifications, lot size, delivery schedule, number of shipments, design changes and level of documentation). However, the buying organization can only be sensitive to these issues if it understands how supplier costs are generated (Seal *et al.*, 1999). In many organizations materials purchased from suppliers account for more than 60 per cent of total manufacturing costs (Drury *et al.*, 1993) and therefore managing supply chain costs has become a critical element in overall cost management. Because of this some companies have established strategic supply partnerships. Seal *et al.* (1999) describe the attempt at a strategic supply partnership between two UK companies and how the buying company was seeking information sharing and research and development collaboration with the supplier for strategic components. In return the supplier was wishing to develop a higher level of cooperation and trust. Such developments represent an attempt to apply cost management throughout the entire value chain.

Similarly, by developing linkages with customers mutually beneficial relationships can be established. For example, Shank and Govindarajan (1992), drawing off research by Hergert and Morris (1989) point out that some container producers in the USA have constructed manufacturing facilities near beer breweries and deliver the containers through overhead conveyers directly onto the customers' assembly lines. This practice results in significant cost reductions for both the container producers and their customers by expediting the transport of empty containers, which are bulky and heavy.

Benchmarking

In order to identify the best way of performing activities and business processes organizations are turning their attention to benchmarking, which involves comparing key activities with best practices found within and outside the organization. External benchmarking attempts to identify an activity, such as customer order processing, that needs to be improved and finding a non-rival organization that is considered to represent world-class best practice for the activity and studying how it performs the activity. The objective is to find out how the activity can be improved and ensure that the improvements are implemented. In contrast, with internal benchmarking different business units within an organization that perform the same activities are compared. The unit that is considered to represent best practice becomes the target to achieve.

Benchmarking is cost beneficial since an organization can save time and money avoiding mistakes that other companies have made and/or the organization can avoid duplicating the efforts of other companies. The overall aim should be to find and implement best practice.

Environmental cost management

Environmental cost management is becoming increasingly important in many organizations. There are several reasons for this. First, environmental costs can be large for some industrial sectors. For example, Ranganathan and Ditz (1996) reported that Amoco's environmental costs at its Yorktown refinery were at least 22 per cent of operating costs. Second, regulatory requirements involving huge fines for non-compliance have increased significantly over the past decade. Therefore, selecting the least costly method of compliance has become a major objective. Third, society is demanding that companies focus on becoming more environmentally friendly. Companies are finding that becoming a good social citizen and being environmentally responsible improves their image and enhances their ability to sell their products and services. These developments have created the need for companies to develop a system of measuring, reporting and monitoring environmental costs.

According to Epstein and Roy (1997) many companies cannot identify their total environmental costs and do not recognize that they can be controlled and reduced. In most cost accounting systems, environmental costs are hidden within general overheads and are either not allocated to cost objects, or they are allocated on an arbitrary basis within the allocation of general overheads. Thus, crucial relationships are not identified between environmental costs and the responsible products, processes and underlying activities. For example, Ranganathan and Ditz point out that the principal environmental issue facing Spectrum Glass, a major manufacturer of specialty sheet glass, is the use and release of cadmium. It discovered that only one product (Ruby red glass) was responsible for all of its cadmium emissions but the cost accounting system allocated a portion of this cost to all products. This process resulted in ruby red glass being undercosted and other products being overcosted.

Environmental costs should be accumulated by separate cost pools, analyzed by appropriate categories and traced to the products or processes that caused the costs using ABC concepts. Knowledge of the amount and categories of environmental costs, and their causes, provides the information that managers need to not only manage environmental costs more effectively by process redesign but to also reduce the pollutants emitted to the environment.

Hansen and Mendoza (1999) point out that environmental costs are incurred because poor environmental quality exists and thus are similar in nature to quality costs discussed earlier in this chapter. They advocate that an environmental cost report should be periodically produced, based on the principles of a cost of quality report (see Exhibit 21.2) to indicate the total environmental costs to the organization associated with the creation, detection, remedy and prevention of environmental degradation. Adopting a similar classification as that used for quality costs, the following four categories of environmental costs can be reported:

1 **Environmental prevention costs** are the costs of activities undertaken to prevent the production of waste that could cause damage to the environment. Examples include the costs associated with the design and operation of processes to reduce contaminants, training employees, recycling products and obtaining certification relating to meeting the requirements of international and national standards.

2 **Environmental detection costs** are the costs incurred to ensure that a firm's activities, products and processes conform to regulatory laws and voluntary standards. Examples include inspection of products and processes to ensure regulatory compliance, auditing environmental activities and performing contamination tests.

3 **Environmental internal failure costs** are the costs incurred from performing activities that have produced contaminants and waste that have not been discharged into the environment. Such costs are incurred to eliminate or reduce waste to levels that comply with regulatory requirements. Examples include the costs of disposing of toxic materials and recycling scrap.

4 **Environmental external failure costs** are the costs incurred on activities performed after discharging waste into the environment. Examples include the costs of cleaning up contaminated soil, restoring land to its natural state and cleaning up oil spills and waste discharges. Clearly this category of costs has the greatest impact on a company in terms of adverse publicity.

The environmental cost report should be similar in format to the cost of quality report (see Exhibit 21.2) with each category of costs expressed as a percentage of sales revenues (or operating costs) so that comparisons can be made with previous periods, other organizations and divisions within the same group. The environmental cost report should be used as an attention-directing device to make top management aware of how much is being spent on environmental costs and the relative amount in each category. The report also draws management's attention to those areas that have the greatest potential for cost reduction. The same principles as those described for quality cost reporting also apply. That is, investing more in prevention and detection activities has the potential to significantly reduce environmental failure costs. A major limitation of environmental cost reports is that they only report those environmental costs for which the company is responsible. The report does not include costs that are caused by a firm but borne by society. Examples include losing land for recreational use and damaging ecosystems from solid waste disposal. Attempts should be made to develop non-financial and/or qualitative measures that draw attention to how an organization is contributing to becoming environmentally responsible and a good social citizen.

In addition to the approaches described above, the environmental consequences of products should be evaluated using the life-cycle costing approach described at the beginning of this chapter. In other words, the environmental consequences should be managed at the planning and design stage and not at the manufacturing stage when a substantial proportion of the environmental costs and outcomes will already have been determined. Finally, you should note at this point that incorporating an environmental perspective within a balanced scorecard framework has been adopted by some companies to link their environmental strategy to concrete performance measures. The balanced scorecard framework requires that within the scorecard the environmental objectives are clearly specified and that these objectives should be translated into specific performance measures. In addition, within the scorecard, firms should describe the major initiatives for achieving each objective and also establish targets for each performance measure. For feedback reporting, actual performance measures should also be added. The balanced scorecard framework is described in the next chapter.

Just-in-time systems

Earlier in this chapter it was pointed out that re-organizing business processes and adopting a just-in-time (JIT) system was an illustration of business process engineering but so far a JIT system has not been explained. Given that implementing a JIT system is a mechanism for reducing non-value added costs and long-run costs it is important that you understand the nature of such a system and its cost management implications.

The success of Japanese firms in international markets in the 1980s and 1990s generated interest among many Western companies as to how this success was achieved. The implementation of just-in-time (JIT) production methods was considered to be one of the major factors contributing to this success. The JIT approach involves a continuous commitment to the pursuit of excellence in all phases of manufacturing systems design and operations. The aims of JIT are to produce the required items, at the required quality and in the required quantities, at the precise time they are required. In particular, JIT seeks to achieve the following goals:

- elimination of non-value added activities;
- zero inventory;
- zero defects;
- batch sizes of one;
- zero breakdowns;
- a 100 per cent on-time delivery service.

The above goals represent perfection, and are most unlikely to be achieved in practice. They do, however, offer targets, and create a climate for continuous improvement and excellence. Let us now examine the major features of a JIT manufacturing philosophy.

Elimination of non-value added activities

JIT manufacturing is best described as a philosophy of management dedicated to the elimination of waste. Waste is defined as anything that does not add value to a product. The lead or cycle time involved in manufacturing and selling a product consists of process time, inspection time, move time, queue time and storage time. Of these five steps, only process time actually adds value to the product. All the other activities add cost but no value to the product, and are thus deemed non-value added processes within the JIT philosophy. According to Berliner and Brimson (1988), process time was less than 10 per cent of total manufacturing lead time in many organizations in the USA in the 1980s. Therefore 90 per cent of the manufacturing lead time associated with a product added costs, but no value, to the product. By adopting a JIT philosophy and focusing on reducing lead times, it is claimed that total costs can be significantly reduced. The ultimate goal of JIT is to convert raw materials to finished products with lead times equal to processing times, thus eliminating all non-value added activities.

Factory layout

The first stage in implementing JIT manufacturing techniques is to rearrange the production process away from a batch production functional layout towards a product layout using flow lines. With a functional plant layout products pass through a number of specialist departments that normally contain a group of similar machines. Products are processed in large batches so as to minimize the set-up times when machine settings are changed between processing batches of different products. Batches move via different and complex routes through the various departments, travelling over much of the factory floor before they are completed. Each process normally involves a considerable amount of waiting time. In addition, much time is taken transporting items from one process to another. A further problem is that it is not easy at any point in time to determine what progress has been made on individual batches. Therefore detailed cost accumulation records are necessary to track work in progress. The consequences of this complex routing process are high work in progress stock levels, long manufacturing cycle times and high material handling costs.

The JIT solution is to reorganize the production process by dividing the many different products that an organization makes into families of similar products or components. All of the products in a particular group will have similar production requirements and routings. Production is rearranged so that each product family is manufactured in a well-defined production cell based on flow line principles. In a product flow line, specialist departments containing *similar* machines no longer exist. Instead groups of *dissimilar* machines are organized into product or component family flow lines that function like an assembly line. For each product line the machines are placed close together in the order in which they are required by the group of products to be processed. Items in each product family can now move, one at a time, from process to process more easily, thereby reducing work in progress stocks and lead times. The ideal layout of each flow line is normally U-shaped. This layout, which is called cellular manufacturing.

JIT manufacturing aims to produce the right parts at the right time, only when they are needed, and only in the quantity needed. This philosophy has resulted in a pull manufacturing system, which means that parts move through the production system based on end-unit demand, focusing on maintaining a constant flow of components rather than batches of WIP. With the pull system, work on components does not commence until specifically requested by the next process. JIT techniques aim to keep the materials moving in a continuous flow with no stoppages and no storage.

The pull system is implemented by monitoring the consumption of parts at each operation stage and using various types of visible signalling systems (known as *Kanbans*) to authorize production and movement of the part to the using location. The producing cell cannot run the parts until authorized to do so. The signalling mechanism usually involves the use of *Kanban* containers. These containers hold materials or parts for movement from one work centre to another. The capacity of *Kanban* containers tends to vary from two to five units. They are just big enough to permit the production line to operate smoothly despite minor interruptions to individual work centres within the cell. To illustrate how the system works consider three machines forming part of a cell where the parts are first processed by machine A before being further processed on machine B and then machine C. The *Kanbans* are located between the machines. As long as the *Kanban* container is not full, the worker at machine A continues to produce parts, placing them in the *Kanban* container. When the container is full the worker stops producing and recommences when a part has been removed from the container by the worker operating machine B. A similar process applies between the operations of machines B and C. This process can result in idle time within certain locations within the cell, but the JIT philosophy considers that it is more beneficial to absorb short-run idle time rather than add to inventory during these periods. During idle time the workers perform preventive maintenance on the machines.

With a pull system problems arising in any part of the system will immediately halt the production line because work centres at the earlier stages will not receive the pull signal (because the *Kanban* container is full) if a problem arises at a later stage. Alternatively, work centres at a later stage will not have their pull signal answered (because of empty *Kanban* containers) when problems arise with work centres at the earlier stages of the production cycle. Thus attention is drawn immediately to production problems so that appropriate remedial action can be taken. This is deemed to be preferable to the approach adopted in a traditional manufacturing system where large stock levels provide a cushion for production to continue.

In contrast, the traditional manufacturing environment is based on a push manufacturing system. With this system, machines are grouped into work centres based on the similarity of their functional capabilities. Each manufactured part has a designated routing, and the preceding process supplies parts to the subsequent process without any consideration being given to whether the next process is ready to work on the parts or not. Hence the use of the term 'push-through system'.

Batch sizes of one

Set-up time is the amount of time required to adjust equipment settings and to retool for a different product. Long set-up and changeover times make the production of batches with a small number of units uneconomic. However, the production of large batches leads to substantial throughput delays and the creation of high inventory levels. Throughput delays arise because several lengthy production runs are required to process larger batches through the factory. A further problem with large batches is that they often have to wait for lengthy periods before they are processed by the next process or before they are sold. The JIT philosophy is to reduce and eventually eliminate set-up times. For example, by investing in advanced manufacturing technologies some machine settings can be adjusted automatically instead of manually. Alternatively, some set-up times can be eliminated entirely by redesigning products so that machines do not have to be reset each time a different product has to be made.

If set-up times are approaching zero, this implies that there are no advantages in producing in batches. Therefore the optimal batch size can be one. With a batch size of one, the work can flow smoothly to the next stage without the need for storage and to schedule the next machine to accept this item. In many situations set-up times will not be approaching zero, but by significantly reducing set-up times, small batch sizes will be economical. Small batch sizes, combined with short throughput times, also enable a firm to adapt more readily to short-term fluctuations in market demand and respond faster to customer requests, since production is not dependent on long planning lead times.

JIT purchasing arrangements

The JIT philosophy also extends to adopting JIT purchasing techniques, whereby the delivery of materials immediately precedes their use. By arranging with suppliers for more frequent deliveries, stocks can be cut to a minimum. Considerable savings in material handling expenses can be obtained by requiring suppliers to inspect materials before their delivery and guaranteeing their quality. This improved service is obtained by giving more business to fewer suppliers and placing longer-term purchasing orders. Therefore the supplier has an assurance of long-term sales, and can plan to meet this demand. Thus, a critical component of JIT purchasing is that strong relationships are established with suppliers.

Companies that have implemented JIT purchasing techniques claim to have substantially reduced their investment in raw materials and work in progress stocks. Other advantages include a substantial saving in factory space, large quantity discounts, savings in time from negotiating with fewer suppliers and a reduction in paperwork arising from issuing blanket long-term orders to a few suppliers rather than individual purchase orders to many suppliers.

JIT and management accounting

Management accountants in many organizations have been strongly criticized because of their failure to alter the management accounting system to reflect the move from a traditional manufacturing to a just-in-time manufacturing system. Conventional management accounting systems can encourage behaviour that is inconsistent with a just-in-time manufacturing philosophy. Management accounting must support just-in-time manufacturing by monitoring, identifying and communicating to decision-makers any delay, error and waste in the system. Modern management accounting systems are now placing greater emphasis on providing information on supplier reliability, set-up times, throughput cycle times, percentage of deliveries that are on time and defect rates. All of these measures are critical to supporting a just-in-time manufacturing philosophy and are discussed in more detail in the next chapter.

Because JIT manufacturing systems result in the establishment of production cells that are dedicated to the manufacturing of a single product or a family of similar products many of the support activities can be directly traced to the product dedicated cells. Thus, a high proportion of costs can be directly assigned to products. Therefore the benefits from implementing ABC product costing may be lower in JIT organizations.

SUMMARY

The following items relate to the learning objectives listed at the beginning of the chapter.

● **Distinguish between the features of a traditional management accounting control system and cost management.**

A traditional management accounting control system tends to be based on the preservation of the status quo and the ways of performing existing activities are not reviewed. The emphasis is on cost containment rather than cost reduction. Cost management focuses on cost reduction rather than cost containment. Whereas traditional cost control systems are routinely applied on a continuous basis, cost management tends to be applied on an *ad-hoc* basis when an opportunity for cost reduction is identified. Also many of the approaches that are incorporated within the area of cost management do not involve the use of accounting techniques. In contrast, cost control relies heavily on accounting techniques.

● **Explain life-cycle costing and describe the typical pattern of cost commitment and cost incurrence during the three stages of a product's life cycle.**

Life-cycle costing estimates and accumulates costs over a product's entire life cycle in order to determine whether the profits earned during the manufacturing phase will cover the costs incurred during the pre- and post-manufacturing stages. Three stages of a product's life cycle can be identified – the planning and design stage, the manufacturing stage and the service and abandonment stage. Approximately 80 per cent of a product's costs are committed during the planning and design stage. At this stage product designers determine the product's design and the production process. In contrast, the majority of costs are incurred at the manufacturing stage, but they have already become locked-in at the planning and design stage and are difficult to alter. Cost management can be most effectively exercised during the planning and design stage and not at the manufacturing stage when the product design and processes have already been determined and costs have been committed.

● Describe the target costing approach to cost management.

Target costing is a customer-oriented technique that is widely used by Japanese companies and which has recently been adopted by companies in Europe and the USA. The first stage requires market research to determine the target selling price for a product. Next a standard or desired profit margin is deducted to establish a target cost for the product. The target cost is compared with the predicted actual cost. If the predicted actual cost is above the target cost intensive efforts are made to close the gap. Value engineering and functional analysis are used to drive the predicted actual cost down to the target cost. The major advantage of adopting target costing is that it is deployed during a product's design and planning stage so that it can have a maximum impact in determining the level of the locked-in costs.

● Describe tear-down analysis, value engineering and functional analysis.

Tear-down analysis involves examining a competitor's product in order to identify opportunities for product improvement and/or cost reduction. The aim of value engineering is to achieve the assigned target cost by (a) identifying improved product designs that reduce the product's cost without sacrificing functionality and/or (b) eliminating unnecessary functions that increase the product's costs and for which customers are not prepared to pay extra. Value engineering requires the use of functional analysis. This involves decomposing the product into its many elements or attributes. A value for each element is determined which reflects the amount the customer is prepared to pay. The cost of each function of a product is compared with the benefits perceived by the customers. If the cost of the function exceeds the benefit to the customer, then the function is either eliminated, modified to reduce its cost, or enhanced in terms of its perceived value so that its value exceeds the cost.

● Distinguish between target costing and *kaizen* costing.

The major difference between target and *kaizen* costing is that target costing is normally applied during the design stage whereas *kaizen* costing is applied during the manufacturing stage of the product life cycle. With target costing, the focus is on the product and cost reductions are achieved primarily through product design. In contrast, *kaizen* costing focuses on the production processes and cost reductions are derived primarily through the increased efficiency of the production process. The aim of *kaizen* costing is to reduce the cost of components and products by a pre-specified amount. A major feature is that workers are given the responsibility to improve processes and reduce costs.

● Describe activity-based cost management.

Activity-based management (ABM) focuses on managing the business on the basis of the activities that make up the organization. It is based on the premise that activities consume costs. Therefore, by managing activities, costs will be managed in the long term. The goal of ABM is to enable customer needs to be satisfied while making fewer demands on organization resources. Knowing the cost of activities enables those activities with the highest cost to be highlighted so that they can be prioritized for detailed studies to ascertain whether they can be eliminated or performed more efficiently.

● Distinguish between value added and non-value added activities.

To identify and prioritize the potential for cost reduction using ABM, many organizations have found it useful to classify activities as either value added or non-value added. A value added activity is an activity that customers perceive as adding usefulness to the product or service they purchase whereas a non-value added activity is an activity where there is an opportunity for cost reduction without reducing the product's service potential to the customer. Taking action to reduce or eliminate non-value added activities is given top priority because by doing so the organization permanently reduces the cost it incurs without reducing the value of the product to the customer.

● Explain the purpose of a cost of quality report.

A cost of quality report indicates the total cost to the organization of producing products or services that do not conform with quality requirements. Quality costs are analyzed by four categories for reporting purposes (prevention, appraisal, and internal and external failure costs). The report draws management's attention to the possibility of reducing total quality costs by a wiser allocation of costs among the four quality categories.

● **Describe how value chain analysis can be used to increase customer satisfaction and manage costs more effectively.**

Increasing attention is now being given to value chain analysis as a means of increasing customer satisfaction and managing costs more effectively. The value chain is the linked set of value-creating activities all the way from basic raw material sources from component suppliers through to the ultimate end-use product or service delivered to the customer. Understanding how value chain activities are performed and how they interact with each other creates the conditions to improve customer satisfaction, particularly in terms of cost efficiency, quality and delivery.

● **Explain the role of benchmarking within the cost management framework.**

Benchmarking involves comparing key activities with world-class best practices by identifying an activity that needs to be improved, finding a non-rival organization that is considered to represent world-class best practice for the activity, and studying how it performs the activity. The objective is to establish how the activity can be improved and ensure that the improvements are implemented. The outcome should be reduced costs for the activity or process or performing the activity more effectively, thus increasing customer satisfaction.

● **Outline the main features of a just-in-time philosophy.**

Many companies seek to eliminate and/or reduce the costs of non-value added activities by introducing just-in-time (JIT) systems. The aims of a JIT system are to produce the required items, at the required quality and in the required quantities, at the precise time they are required. In particular, JIT aims to eliminate waste by minimizing inventories and reducing cycle or throughput times (i.e. the time elapsed from when customers place an order until the time when they receive the desired product or service). Adopting a JIT manufacturing system involves moving from a batch production functional layout to a cellular flow line manufacturing system. The JIT philosophy also extends to adopting JIT purchasing techniques, whereby the delivery of materials immediately precedes their use. By arranging with suppliers for more frequent deliveries, stocks can be cut to a minimum.

Key terms and concepts

activity-based cost management (p. 544)
activity-based management (p. 544)
appraisal costs (p. 549)
batch production functional layout (p. 557)
benchmarking (p. 554)
business process re-engineering (p. 547)
cellular manufacturing (p. 557)
committed costs (p. 538)
costs of non-compliance (p. 550)
costs of non-conformance (p. 550)
costs of quality compliance (p. 550)
costs of quality conformance (p. 550)
cost of quality report (p. 549)

environmental detection costs (p. 550)
environmental external failure costs (p. 550)
environmental internal failure costs (p. 550)
environmental prevention costs (p. 555)
external failure costs (p. 549)
functional analysis (p. 540)
internal failure costs (p. 549)
just-in-time (JIT) production methods (p. 550)
kaizen costing (p. 543)
Kanbans (p. 557)
life-cycle costing (p. 538)
locked-in costs (p. 538)

non-value added activity (p. 546)
prevention costs (p. 549)
product flow line (p. 557)
pull manufacturing system (p. 557)
push manufacturing system (p. 558)
reverse engineering (p. 540)
statistical quality control charts (p. 550)
supply chain management (p. 554)
target costing (p. 539)
tear-down analysis (p. 540)
total quality management (p. 549)
value added activity (p. 546)
value analysis (p. 540)
value-chain analysis (p. 550)
value engineering (p. 540)
zero-defects policy (p. 550)

Recommended reading

You should refer to Kato (1993) and Tani *et al*. (1994) for a description of target costing in Japanese companies. For a survey of target costing in Dutch firms you should refer to Dekker and Smidt (2003). A more detailed description of activity-based cost management can be found in Chapter 8 of Kaplan and Cooper (1998). For a description of the application of value chain analysis to cost management see Shank and Govindarajan (1992). See also McNair *et al*. (2001) for a discussion of a value creation model.

Key examination points

Much of the content of this chapter relates to relatively new topics. Therefore fewer examination questions have been set by the professional examining bodies on the content of this chapter. The questions that follow provide an illustration of the type of questions that have been set.

It is likely that most of the questions that will be set on cost management topics will be essays and will require students to demonstrate that they have read widely on the various topics covered in this chapter. Questions set are likely to be open-ended and there will be no ideal answer.

ASSESSMENT MATERIAL

The review questions are short questions that enable you to assess your understanding of the main topics included in the chapter. The numbers in parentheses provide you with the page numbers to refer to if you cannot answer a specific question.

The review problems are more complex and require you to relate and apply the content to various business problems. The problems are graded by their level of difficulty. Solutions to review problems that are not preceded by the term 'IM' are provided in a separate section at the end of the book. Solutions to problems preceded by the term 'IM' are provided in the *Instructor's Manual* accompanying this book and also on the lecturer's password protected section of the website www.drury-online.com. Additional review problems with fully worked solutions are provided in the *Student's Manual* that accompanies this book.

Review questions

21.1 How does cost management differ from traditional management accounting control systems? *(pp. 537–38)*
21.2 What are committed (locked-in) costs? *(p. 538)*
21.3 Explain the essential features of life-cycle costing. *(pp. 538–39)*
21.4 Describe the stages involved with target costing. Describe how costs are reduced so that the target cost can be achieved. *(pp. 539–41)*
21.5 What is *kaizen* costing? *(pp. 543–44)*
21.6 What are the distinguishing features of activity based management? *(pp. 544–46)*
21.7 Distinguish between value added and non-value added activities. *(p. 546)*
21.8 What is business process re-engineering? *(pp. 547–48)*
21.9 Identify and discuss the four kinds of quality costs that are included in a cost of quality report. Give examples of costs that fall within each category. *(p. 549)*
21.10 Discuss the value of a cost of quality report. *(p. 550)*
21.11 Describe what is meant by a zero-defects policy. *(p. 550)*
21.12 Explain what is meant by value-chain analysis. Illustrate how value-chain analysis can be applied. *(pp. 552–54)*
21.13 Explain how benchmarking can be used to manage costs and improve activity performance. What are the major features of a just-in-time manufacturing philosophy? *(p. 554, pp. 556–59)*
21.14 Distinguish between a pull and push manufacturing system. *(pp. 557–58)*
21.15 What are the essential features of just-in-time purchasing arrangements? *(pp. 558–59)*

Review problems

21.16 Advanced: Cost of quality reporting. Burdoy plc has a dedicated set of production facilities for component X. A just-in-time system is in place such that no stock of materials; work-in-progress or finished goods are held.

At the beginning of period 1, the planned information relating to the production of component X through the dedicated facilities is as follows:

(i) Each unit of component X has input materials: 3 units of material A at £18 per unit and 2 units of material B at £9 per unit.
(ii) Variable cost per unit of component X (excluding materials) is £15 per unit worked on.
(iii) Fixed costs of the dedicated facilities for the period: £162 000.
(iv) It is anticipated that 10 per cent of the units of X worked on in the process will be defective and will be scrapped.

It is estimated that customers will require replacement (free of charge) of faulty units of component X at the rate of 2 per cent of the quantity invoiced to them in fulfilment of orders.

Burdoy plc is pursuing a total quality management philosophy. Consequently all losses will be treated as abnormal in recognition of a zero defect policy and will be valued at variable cost of production.

Actual statistics for each periods 1 to 3 for component X are shown in Appendix 3.1. No changes have occurred from the planned price levels for materials, variable overhead or fixed overhead costs.

Required:
  a Prepare an analysis of the relevant figures provided in Appendix 3.1 to show that the period 1 actual results were achieved at the planned level in respect of (i) quantities and losses and (ii) unit cost levels for materials and variable costs. *(5 marks)*
  b Use your analysis from (a) in order to calculate the value of the planned level of each of internal and external failure costs for period 1. *(3 marks)*
  c Actual free replacements of component X to customers were 170 units and 40 units in periods 2 and 3 respectively. Other data relating to periods 2 and 3 is shown in Appendix 3.1.
  Burdoy plc authorized additional expenditure during periods 2 and 3 as follows:
  Period 2: Equipment accuracy checks of £10 000 and staff training of £5000.
  Period 3: Equipment accuracy checks of £10 000 plus £5000 of inspection costs; also staff training costs of £5000 plus £3000 on extra planned maintenance of equipment.
  Required:
  (i) Prepare an analysis for EACH of periods 2 and 3 which reconciles the number of components invoiced to customers with those worked-on in the production process. The analysis should show the changes from the planned quantity of process losses and changes from the planned quantity of replacement of faulty components in customer hands;
  (All relevant working notes should be shown) *(8 marks)*
  (ii) Prepare a cost analysis for EACH of periods 2 and 3 which shows actual internal failure costs, external failure costs, appraisal costs and prevention costs; *(6 marks)*
  (iii) Prepare a report which explains the meaning and inter-relationship of the figures in Appendix 3.1 and in the analysis in (a), (b) and (c) (i)/(ii). The report should also give examples of each cost type and comment on their use in the monitoring and progressing of the TQM policy being pursued by Burdoy plc. *(13 marks)*

Appendix 3.1
Actual statistics for component X

	Period 1	Period 2	Period 3
Invoiced to customers (units)	5 400	5 500	5 450
Worked-on in the process (units)	6 120	6 200	5 780
Total costs:			
Materials A and B (£)	440 640	446 400	416 160
Variable cost of production (£)			
(excluding material cost)	91 800	93 000	86 700
Fixed cost (£)	162 000	177 000	185 000

ACCA Paper 9 Information for Control and Decision Making

21.17 Advanced: Calculation of total savings from introducing a JIT system and determination of optimal selling price. X Ltd manufactures and distributes three types of car (the C1, C2 and C3). Each type of car has its own production line. The company is worried by extremely difficult market conditions and forecasts losses for the forthcoming year.

Current operations
The budgeted details for next year are as follows:

	C1 £	C2 £	C3 £
Direct materials	2 520	2 924	3 960
Direct labour	1 120	1 292	1 980
Total direct cost per car	3 640	4 216	5 940
Budgeted production (cars)	75 000	75 000	75 000
Number of production runs	1 000	1 000	1 500
Number of orders executed	4 000	5 000	5 600
Machine hours	1 080 000	1 800 000	1 680 000

Annual overheads

	Fixed £000	Variable £
Set ups	42 660	13 000 per production run
Materials handling	52 890	4 000 per order executed
Inspection	59 880	18 000 per production run
Machining	144 540	40 per machine hour
Distribution and warehousing	42 900	3 000 per order executed

Proposed JIT system
Management has hired a consultant to advise them on how to reduce costs. The consultant has suggested that the company adopts a just-in-time (JIT) manufacturing system. The introduction of the JIT system would have the following impact on costs (fixed and variable):

Direct labour	Increase by 20%
Set ups	Decrease by 30%
Materials handling	Decrease by 30%
Inspection	Decrease by 30%
Machining	Decrease by 15%
Distribution and warehousing	Eliminated

Required:
a Based on the budgeted production levels, calculate the total annual savings that would be achieved by introducing the JIT system. *(6 marks)*

The following table shows the price/demand relationship for each type of car per annum.

C1		C2		C3	
Price £	Demand	Price £	Demand	Price £	Demand
5000	75 000	5750	75 000	6500	75 000
5750	65 000	6250	60 000	6750	60 000
6000	50 000	6500	45 000	7750	45 000
6500	35 000	7500	35 000	8000	30 000

Required:
b Assuming that X Ltd adopts the JIT system and that the revised variable overhead cost per car remains constant (as per the proposed JIT system budget), calculate the profit-maximizing price and output level for each type of car. *(12 marks)*

Investigations have revealed that some of the fixed costs are directly attributable to the individual production lines and could be avoided if a line is closed down for the year. The specific fixed costs for each of the production lines, expressed as a percentage of the total fixed costs, are:

C1	4%
C2	5%
C3	8%

Required:
c Determine the optimum production plan for the forthcoming year (based on the JIT cost structure and the prices and output levels you recommended in answer to requirement (b)). *(4 marks)*
d Write a report to the management of X Ltd which explains the conditions that are necessary for the successful implementation of a JIT manufacturing system. *(8 marks)*
CIMA Management Accounting – Decision Making

21.18 Advanced: Traditional and activity-based budget statements and life-cycle costing. The budget for the Production, Planning and Development Department of Obba plc, is currently prepared as part of a traditional budgetary planning and control system. The analysis of costs by expense type for the period ended 30 November 2000 where this system is in use is as follows:

Expense type	Budget %	Actual %
Salaries	60	63
Supplies	6	5
Travel cost	12	12
Technology cost	10	7
Occupancy cost	12	13

The total budget and actual costs for the department for the period ended 30 November 2000 are £1 000 000 and £1 060 000 respectively.

The company now feels that an Activity Based Budgeting approach should be used. A number of activities have been identified for the Production, Planning and Development Department. An investigation has indicated that total budget and actual costs should be attributed to the activities on the following basis:

	Budget %	Actual %
Activities		
1. Routing/scheduling – new products	20	16
2. Routing/scheduling – existing products	40	34
3. Remedial re-routing/scheduling	5	12
4. Special studies – specific orders	10	8
5. Training	10	15
6. Management & administration	15	15

Required:
a (i) Prepare *two* budget control statements for the Production Planning and Development Department for the period ended 30 November 2000 which compare budget with actual cost and show variances using
  1 a traditional expense based analysis and
  2 an activity based analysis. *(6 marks)*
  (ii) Identify and comment on *four* advantages claimed for the use of Activity Based Budgeting over traditional budgeting using the Production Planning and Development example to illustrate your answer. *(12 marks)*
  (iii) Comment on the use of the information provided in the activity based statement which you prepared in (i) in activity based performance measurement and suggest additional information which would assist in such performance measurement. *(8 marks)*
b Other activities have been identified and the budget quantified for the three months ended 31 March 2001 as follows:

Activities	Cost Driver Unit basis	Units of Cost Driver	Cost (£000)
Product design	design hours	8 000	2000 (see note 1)
Purchasing	purchase orders	4 000	200
Production	machine hours	12 000	1500 (see note 2)
Packing	volume (cu.m.)	20 000	400
Distribution	weight (kg)	120 000	600

Note 1: this includes all design costs for new products released this period.

Note 2: this includes a depreciation provision of £300 000 of which £8000 applies to 3 months' depreciation on a straight line basis for a new product (NPD). The remainder applies to other products.

New product NPD is included in the above budget. The following additional information applies to NPD:

(i) Estimated total output over the product life cycle: 5000 units (4 years life cycle).
(ii) Product design requirement: 400 design hours
(iii) Output in quarter ended 31 March 2001: 250 units
(iv) Equivalent batch size per purchase order: 50 units
(v) Other product unit data: production time 0.75 machine hours: volume 0.4 cu. metres; weight 3 kg.

Required:
Prepare a unit overhead cost for product NPD using an activity based approach which includes an appropriate share of life cycle costs using the information provided in (b) above. *(9 marks)*
ACCA Paper Information for Control and Decision Making

21.19 Advanced. The implementation of budgeting in a world class manufacturing environment may be affected by the impact of (i) a total quality ethos (ii) a just-in-time philosophy and (iii) an activity based focus.

Briefly describe the principles incorporated in EACH of (i) to (iii) and discuss ways in which each may result in changes in the way in which budgets are prepared as compared to a traditional incremental budgeting system. *(15 marks)*
ACCA Paper 9 Information for Control and Decision Making

21.20 Advanced. New techniques are often described as contributing to cost reduction, but when cost reduction is necessary it is not obvious that such new approaches are used in preference to more established approaches. Three examples are:

new technique	compared with	established approach
(a) benchmarking		interfirm comparison
(b) activity based budgeting		zero base budgeting
(c) target costing		continuous cost improvement

You are required, for two of the three newer techniques mentioned above:

- to explain its objectives
- to explain its workings
- to differentiate it from the related approach identified
- to explain how it would contribute to a cost reduction programme. *(20 marks)*
CIMA Stage 4 Management Accounting – Control and Audit

21.21 Advanced.
'ABC is still at a relatively early stage of its development and its implications for process control may in the final analysis be more important than its product costing implications. It is a good time for every organization to consider whether or not ABC is appropriate to its particular circumstances.'
J. Innes & F. Mitchell, *Activity Based Costing, A Review with Case Studies*, CIMA, 1990.

You are required:

a to contrast the feature of organizations which would benefit from ABC with those which would not; *(8 marks)*
b to explain in what ways ABC may be used to manage costs, and the limitations of these approaches; *(11 marks)*
c to explain and to discuss the use of target costing to control product costs. *(6 marks)*
CIMA Stage 4 Management Accounting – Control and Audit

21.22 Advanced. You are Financial Controller of a medium-sized engineering business. This business was family-owned and managed for many years but has recently been acquired by a large group to become its Engineering Division.

The first meeting of the management board with the newly appointed Divisional Managing Director has not gone well.

He commented on the results of the division:

- Sales and profits were well below budget for the month and cumulatively for the year, and the forecast for the rest of the year suggested no improvement.
- Working capital was well over budget.
- Even if budget were achieved the return on capital employed was well below group standards.

He proposed a Total Quality Management (TQM) programme to change attitudes and improve results.

The initial responses of the managers to these comments were:

- The Production Director said there was a limit to what was possible with obsolete machines and facilities and only a very short-term order book.
- The Sales Director commented that it was impossible to get volume business when deliveries and quality were unreliable and designs out of date.
- The Technical Director said that there was little point in considering product improvements when the factory could not be bothered to update designs and the sales executives were reluctant to discuss new ideas with new potential customers.

You have been asked to prepare reports for the next management board meeting to enable a more constructive discussion.

You are required:

a to explain the critical success factors for the implementation of a programme of Total Quality Management. Emphasize the factors that are crucial in changing attitudes from those quoted; *(11 marks)*
b to explain how you would measure quality cost, and how the establishment of a system of measuring quality costs would contribute to a TQM programme. *(9 marks)*
CIMA Stage 4 Management Accounting – Control and Audit

21.23 Advanced. At a recent board meeting of Spring plc, there was a heated discussion on the need to improve financial performance. The Production Director argued that financial performance could be improved if the company replaced its existing absorption costing approach with an activity-based costing system. He argued that this would lead to better cost control and increased profit margins. The Managing Director agreed that better cost control could lead to increased profitability, but informed the meeting that he believed that performance needed to be monitored in both financial and non-financial terms. He pointed out that sales could be lost due to poor product quality or a lack of after-sales service just as easily as by asking too high a price for Spring plc's products. He suggested that while the board should consider introducing activity-based costing, it should also consider ways in which the company could monitor and assess performance on a wide basis.

Required:

a Describe the key features of activity-based costing and discuss the advantages and disadvantages of adopting an activity-based approach to cost accumulation. *(14 marks)*
b Explain the need for the measurement of organizational and managerial performance, giving examples of the range of financial and non-financial performance measures that might be used. *(11 marks)*
ACCA 2.4 Financial Management and Control

IM21.1 Advanced. Your managing director, after hearing a talk at a branch meeting on just-in-time (JIT) manufacturing would like the management to consider introducing JIT at your unit which manufactures typewriters and also keyboards for computing systems.

You are required as the assistant management accountant, to prepare a discussion paper for circulation to the directors and senior management, describing just-in-time manufacturing, the likely benefits which would follow its introduction and the effect its introduction would probably have on the cost accounting system. *(13 marks)*
CIMA Stage 2 Cost Accounting

IM21.2 Advanced.

a Life Cycle Costing normally refers to costs incurred by the user of major capital equipment over the whole of the useful equipment life. Explain the determination and calculation of these costs and the problems in their calculation. *(8 marks)*
b In the strategy and marketing literature there is continual discussion of the product life cycle.

You are required to explain, for *each* of the *four* stages of the product life cycle,

- start-up
- growth
- maturity
- harvest,

which system of product costing would be most useful for decision making and control, and why.

Explain briefly in your answer possible alternative organizational structures at each stage in the life cycle. *(12 marks)*
CIMA Stage 4 Management Accounting – Control and Audit

IM21.3 Advanced. Kaplan ('Relevance Regained', *Management Accounting*, September 1988) states the view that the 'time-honoured traditions of cost accounting' are 'irrelevant, misleading and wrong'. Variance analysis, product costing and operational control are cited as examples of areas where information provided by management accountants along traditional lines could well fail to meet today's needs of management in industry.

You are required to
a state what you consider to be the main requirements for effective operational control and product costing in modern industry; *(10 marks)*
b identify which 'traditional cost accounting' methods in the areas quoted in (a) *may be considered* to be failing to supply the appropriate information to management, and explain why; *(9 marks)*
c recommend changes to the 'traditional cost accounting' methods and information which would serve to meet the problems identified in (b). *(6 marks)*
CIMA Stage 4 Management Accounting – Control and Audit

IM21.4 Advanced. A company is proposing the introduction of an activity-based costing (ABC) system as a basis for much of its management accounting information.
a Briefly describe how ABC is different from a traditional absorption approach to costing and explain why it was developed. *(8 marks)*
b Discuss the advantages and limitations of this 'approach based on activities' for management accounting information in the context of:
(i) preparing plans and budgets
(ii) monitoring and controlling operations
(iii) decision-making, for example, product deletion decisions. *(12 marks)*
ACCA Paper 8 Managerial Finance

IM21.5 Advanced. 'Japanese companies that have used just-in-time (JIT) for five or more years are reporting close to a 30 per cent increase in labour productivity, a 60 per cent reduction in inventories, a 90 per cent reduction in quality rejection rates, and a 15 per cent reduction in necessary plant space. However, implementing a just-in-time system does not occur overnight. It took Toyota over twenty years to develop its system and realize significant benefits from it.' *Source:* Sumer C. Aggrawal, *Harvard Business Review* (9/85)

Requirements:
a Explain how the benefits claimed for JIT in the above quotation are achieved and why it takes so long to achieve those benefits. *(15 marks)*
b Explain how management information systems in general (and management accounting systems in particular) should be developed in order to facilitate and make best use of JIT. *(10 marks)*
CIMA Stage 3 Management Accounting Applications

IM21.6 Advanced: Feedback control theory and product quality measurement.
a In control theory, a 'feedback control' mechanism is one which supplies information to determine whether corrective action should be taken to re-establish control of a system.

You are required to:
(i) illustrate by means of a diagram how the feedback mechanism operates within a control system, adding a commentary describing how the system functions; *(9 marks)*
(ii) distinguish 'feedforward' from 'feedback' control, giving two examples of each from within management accounting. *(4 marks)*

b Achievement of a high standard of product quality has become a major issue in modern manufacturing industry.

In support of programmes aimed at achieving acceptable quality standards, some companies have introduced detailed 'quality cost' measurement schemes.

In others, the philosophy has been that no measurement procedures should be devoted especially to the measurement of quality costs: quality cost schemes designed to measure performance in this area are considered to add to administrative burdens; in reality 'quality' should be the expected achievement of the required product specification.
(i) set out a classification of quality costs which would be useful for reporting purposes. Give examples of actual costs which would be represented in each classification; *(7 marks)*
(ii) discuss the reality of the differences of philosophy expressed in the opening statement. Do they represent fundamental differences or may they be reconciled? *(5 marks)*
CIMA Stage 4 Management Accounting – Control and Audit

IM21.7 Advanced: Financial evaluation of implementing a quality management programme. Bushworks Ltd convert synthetic slabs into components AX and BX for use in the car industry. Bushworks Ltd is planning a quality management programme at a cost of £250 000. The following information relates to the costs incurred by Bushworks Ltd both before and after the implementation of the quality management programme:

1 *Synthetic slabs*
Synthetic slabs cost £40 per hundred. On average 2.5 per cent of synthetic slabs received are returned to the supplier as scrap because of deterioration in stores. The supplier allows a credit of £1 per hundred slabs for such returns. In addition, on receipt in stores, checks to ensure that the slabs received conform to specification costs £14 000 per annum.

A move to a just-in-time purchasing system will eliminate the holding of stocks of synthetic slabs. This has been negotiated with the supplier who will deliver slabs of guaranteed design specification for £44 per hundred units, eliminating all stockholding costs.

2 *Curing/moulding process*
The synthetic slabs are issued to a curing/holding process which has variable conversion costs of £20 per hundred slabs input. This process produces sub-components A and B which have the same cost structure. Losses of 10 per cent of input to the process because of incorrect temperature control during the process are sold as scrap at £5 per hundred units. The quality programme will rectify the temperature control problem thus reducing losses to 1 per cent of input to the process.

3 *Finishing process*
The finishing process has a bank of machines which perform additional operations on type A and B sub-components as required and converts them into final components AX and BX respectively. The variable conversion costs in the finishing process for AX and BX are £15 and £25 per hundred units respectively. At the end of the finishing process 15 per cent of units are found to be defective. Defective units are sold for scrap at £10 per hundred units. The quality programme will convert the finishing process into two dedicated cells, one for each of component types AX and BX. The dedicated cell variable costs per hundred sub-components A and B processed will be £12 and £20 respectively. Defective units of components AX and BX are expected to fall to 2.5 per cent of the input to each cell. Defective components will be sold as scrap as at present.

4 *Finished goods*
A finished goods stock of components AX and BX of 15 000 and 30 000 units respectively is held throughout the year in order to allow for customer demand fluctuations and free replacement of units returned by customers due to specification faults. Customer returns are currently 2.5 per cent of components delivered to customers. Variable stock holding costs are £15 per thousand component units.

The proposed dedicated cell layout of the finishing process will eliminate the need to hold stocks of finished components, other than sufficient to allow for the free replacement of those found to be defective in customer hands. This stock level will be set at one month's free replacement to customers which is estimated at 500 and 1000 units for types AX and BX respectively. Variable stockholding costs will remain at £15 per thousand component units.

5 *Quantitative data*

Some preliminary work has already been carried out in calculating the number of units of synthetic slabs, sub-components A and B and components AX and BX which will be required both before and after the implementation of the quality management programme, making use of the information in the question. Table 1 summarizes the relevant figures.

Table 1

	Existing situation		Amended situation	
	Type A/AX (units)	Type B/BX (units)	Type A/AX (units)	Type B/BX (units)
Sales	800 000	1 200 000	800 000	1 200 000
Customer returns	20 000	30 000	6 000	12 000
Finished goods delivered	820 000	1 230 000	806 000	1 212 000
Finished process losses	144 706	217 059	20 667	31 077
Input to finishing process	964 706	1 447 059	826 667	1 243 077
		2 411 765		2 069 744
Curing/moulding losses		267 974		20 907
Input to curing/moulding		2 679 739		2 090 651
Stores losses		68 711		—
Purchase of synthetic slabs		2 748 450		2 090 651

Required:

a Evaluate and present a statement showing the net financial benefit or loss per annum of implementing the quality management programme, using the information in the question and the data in Table 1.
   (All relevant workings must be shown)   *(27 marks)*

b Explain the meaning of the terms internal failure costs, external failure costs, appraisal costs and prevention costs giving examples of each.   *(8 marks)*

Strategic management
accounting

22

During the late 1980s and early 1990s criticisms of traditional management accounting practices were widely publicized and new approaches were advocated which are more in tune with today's competitive and business environment. In particular, strategic management accounting has been identified as a way forward. However, there is still no comprehensive framework as to what constitutes strategic management accounting. In this chapter we shall examine the elements of strategic management accounting and describe the different contributions that have been made to its development.

One of the elements of strategic management accounting involves the provision of information for the formulation of an organization's strategy and managing strategy implementation. To encourage behaviour that is consistent with an organization's strategy, attention is now being given to developing an integrated framework of performance measurement that can be used to clarify, communicate and manage strategy. In the latter part of this chapter recent developments that seek to incorporate performance measurement within the strategic management process are described.

LEARNING OBJECTIVES

After studying this chapter, you should be able to:

- describe the different elements of strategic management accounting;

- describe three competitive strategies that a firm can adopt to achieve sustainable competitive advantage and explain how they influence management accounting practices;

- describe the balanced scorecard;

- explain each of the four perspectives of the balanced scorecard;

- provide illustrations of performance measures for each of the four perspectives;

- explain how the balanced scorecard links strategy formulation to financial outcomes.

What is strategic management accounting?

For many years strategic management accounting has been advocated as a potential area of development that would enhance the future contribution of management accounting. In the late 1980s the UK Chartered Institute of Management Accountants commissioned an investigation to review the current state of development of management accounting. The findings were published in a report entitled *Management Accounting: Evolution not Revolution*, authoured by Bromwich and Bhimani (1989). In the report, and a follow-up report (*Management Accounting: Pathways to Progress*, 1994) Bromwich and Bhimani drew attention to strategic management accounting as an area for future development. Despite the publicity that strategic management accounting has received there is still no comprehensive conceptual framework of what strategic management accounting is (Tomkins and Carr, 1996). For example, Coad (1996) states:

> Strategic management accounting is an emerging field whose boundaries are loose and, as yet, there is no unified view of what it is or how it might develop. The existing literature in the field is both disparate and disjointed (Coad, 1996: 392)

Innes (1998) defines strategic management accounting as the provision of information to support the strategic decisions in organizations. Strategic decisions usually involve the longer-term, have a significant effect on the organization and, although they may have an internal element, they also have an external element. Adopting this definition suggests that the provision of information that supports an organization's major long-term decisions, such as the use of activity-based costing information for providing information relating to product mix, introduction and abandonment decisions falls within the domain of strategic management accounting. This view is supported by Cooper and Kaplan (1988) who state that strategic accounting techniques are designed to support the overall competitive strategy of the organization, principally by the power of using information technology to develop more refined product and service costs. Various writers have suggested that other management accounting techniques that fall within the domain of strategic management accounting are target costing, life-cycle costing and activity-based management (see Chapter 21 for a discussion of these techniques).

Other writers, however, have adopted definitions that emphasize that strategic management accounting is externally focused. Simmonds (1981, 1982), who first coined the term strategic management accounting, views it as the provision and analysis of management accounting data about a business and its competitors which is of use in the development and monitoring of the strategy of that business. He views profits as emerging not from internal efficiencies but from the firm's competitive position in its markets. More recently, Bromwich (1990), a principal advocate of strategic management accounting, has provided the following definition:

> The provision and analysis of financial information on the firm's product markets and competitors' costs and cost structures and the monitoring of the enterprise's strategies and those of its competitors in these markets over a number of periods (Bromwich, 1990: 28).

The Chartered Institute of Management Accountants (CIMA) in the UK defines strategic management accounting as:

> A form of management accounting in which emphasis is placed on information which relates to factors external to the firm, as well as non-financial information and internally generated information (CIMA Official Terminology, 2005: 54).

Because of the lack of consensus on what constitutes strategic management accounting Lord (1996) reviewed the literature and identified several strands that have been used to characterize strategic management accounting. They include:

1 The extension of traditional management accounting's internal focus to include external information about competitors.

2 The relationship between the strategic position chosen by a firm and the expected emphasis on management accounting (i.e. accounting in relation to strategic positioning).

3 Gaining competitive advantage by analyzing ways to decrease costs and/or enhance the differentiation of a firm's products, through exploiting linkages in the value chain and optimizing cost drivers.

Let us now examine each of the above characteristics in more detail.

External information about competitors

Much of the early work relating to strategic management accounting can be attributed to the writings of Simmonds (1981, 1982 and 1986). He argued that management accounting should be more outward looking and should help the firm evaluate its competitive position relative to the rest of the industry by collecting data on costs and prices, sales volumes and market shares, and cash flows and resources availability for its main competitors. To protect an organization's strategic position and determine strategies to improve its future competitiveness managers require information that indicates by whom, by how much and why they are gaining or being beaten. This information provides advance warning of the need for a change in competitive strategy. Competitive information is available from public sources such as company annual reports, press, official institutions and informal sources (e.g. sales personnel, analyzing competitors' products, industry specialists, consultants, etc.).

Simmonds also stressed the importance of the learning curve (see Chapter 23) as a means of obtaining strategic advantage by forecasting cost reductions and consequently selling price reductions of competitors. He also drew attention to the importance of early experience with a new product as a means of conferring an unbeatable lead over competitors. The leading competitor should be able to reduce its selling price for the product (through the learning curve effect) which should further increase its volume and market share and eventually force some lagging competitors out of the industry.

An organization may also seek to gain strategic advantage by its pricing policy. Here the management accounting function can assist by attempting to assess each major competitor's cost structure and relate this to their prices. In particular, Simmonds suggests that it may be possible to assess the cost–volume–profit relationship of competitors in order to predict their pricing responses. He states:

> Clearly, competitor reactions can substantially influence the outcome of a price move. Moreover, likely reactions may not be self-evident when each competitor faces a different cost–volume–profit situation. Competitors may not follow a price lead nor even march in perfect step as they each act to defend or build their own positions. For an adequate assessment of the likelihood of competitor price reactions, then, some calculation is needed of the impact of possible price moves on the performance of individual competitors. Such an assessment in turn requires an accounting approach that can depict both competitor cost–volume–profit situations and their financial resources (Simmonds: 1982: 207).

Besides dealing with costs and prices Simmonds focused on volume and market share. By monitoring movements in market share for its major products, an organization can see whether it is gaining or losing position, and an examination of relative market shares will indicate the strength of different competitors. Including market-share details in management accounting reports helps to make management accounting more strategically relevant. Competitor information may be obtained through public, formal sources, such as published reports and the business press, or through informal channels, such as the firm's salesforce, its customers and its suppliers.

Simmonds (1981) also suggested some changes and additions to traditional management accounting reporting systems in order to include the above information. Market share statements could be incorporated into management accounts. In addition, budgets could be routinely presented in a strategic format with columns for Ourselves, Competitor A, Competitor B, etc. According to Ward (1992) very few firms regularly report competitor information.

Accounting in relation to strategic positioning

Various classifications of strategic positions that firms may choose have been identified in the strategic management literature. Porter (1985) suggests that a firm has a choice of three generic strategies in order to achieve sustainable competitive advantage. They are:

- *cost leadership*, whereby an enterprise aims to be the lowest-cost producer within the industry thus enabling it to compete on the basis of lower selling prices rather than providing unique products or services. The source of this competitive advantage may arise from factors such as economies of scale, access to favourable raw materials prices and superior technology (Langfield-Smith, 1997).

- *differentiation*, whereby the enterprise seeks to offer products or services that are considered by its customers to be superior and unique relative to its competitors. Examples include the quality or dependability of the product, after-sales service, the wide availability of the product and product flexibility (Langfield-Smith, 1997).

- *focus*, which involves seeking advantage by focusing on a narrow segment of the market that has special needs that are poorly served by other competitors in the industry. Competitive advantage is based on either cost leadership or product differentiation.

Miles and Snow (1978) distinguish between *defenders* and *prospectors*. Defenders operate in relatively stable areas, have limited product lines and employ a mass production routine technology. They compete through making operations efficient through cost, quality and service leadership, and engage in little product/market development. Prospectors compete through new product innovations and market development and are constantly looking for new market opportunities. Hence, they face a more uncertain task environment.

The accounting literature suggests that firms will place more emphasis on particular accounting techniques, depending on which strategic position they adopt. For example, Porter (1980) suggested that tight cost controls are more appropriate when a cost leadership strategy is followed. Simons (1987) found that business units that follow a defender strategy tend to place a greater emphasis on the use of financial measures (e.g., short-term budget targets) for compensating financial managers. Prospector firms placed a greater emphasis on forecast data and reduced importance on cost control. Ittner *et al.* (1997) also found that the use of non-financial measures for determining executive's bonuses increases with the extent to which firms follow an innovation-oriented prospector strategy. Shank (1989) stresses the need for management accounting to support a firm's competitive strategies, and illustrates how two different competitive strategies – cost leadership and product differentiation – demand different cost analysis perspectives. For example, carefully engineered product cost standards are likely to be a very important management control tool for a firm that pursues a cost leadership strategy in a mature commodity business. In contrast, carefully engineered manufacturing cost standards are likely to be less important for a firm following a product differentiation strategy in a market-driven, rapidly changing and fast-growing business. A firm pursuing a product differentiation strategy is likely to require more information than a cost leader about new product innovations, design cycle times, research and development expenditures and marketing cost analysis. Exhibit 22.1 illustrates some potential differences in cost management emphasis, depending on the primary strategic thrust of the firm.

Gaining competitive advantage using value-chain analysis

Porter (1985) advocated using value-chain analysis (see Chapter 21) to gain competitive advantage. The aim of value chain analysis is to find linkages between value-creating activities which result in lower cost and/or enhanced differentiation. These linkages can be within the firm or between the firm and its suppliers, and customers. The value chain comprises five primary activities and a number of support activities. The primary activities are defined sequentially as inbound logistics, operations, outbound logistics, marketing and sales and

EXHIBIT 22.1 Relationship between strategies and cost management emphasis

	Product differentiation	Cost leadership
Role of standard costs in assessing performance	Not very important	Very important
Importance of such concepts as flexible budgeting for manufacturing cost control	Moderate to low	High to very high
Perceived importance of meeting budgets	Moderate to low	High to very high
Importance of marketing cost analysis	Critical to success	Often not done at all on a formal basis
Importance of product cost as an input to pricing decisions	Low	High
Importance of competitor cost analysis	Low	High

Source: Shank (1989) Strategic cost management: New wine, or just new bottles? *Journal of Management Accounting Research* (1): 47–65.

services. The secondary activities exist to support the primary activities and include the firm's infrastructure, human resource management, technology and procurement. Costs and assets are assigned to each activity in the value chain. The cost behaviour pattern of each activity depends on a number of causal factors which Porter calls cost drivers. These cost drivers operate in an interactive way and it is management's success in coping with them which determines the cost structure.

Strategic cost analysis also involves identifying the value chain and the operation of cost drivers of competitors in order to understand relative competitiveness. Porter advocates that organizations should use this information to identify opportunities for cost reduction, either by improving control of the cost drivers or reconfiguring the value chain. The latter involves deciding on those areas of the value chain where the firm has a comparative advantage and those which it should source to suppliers. It is essential that the cost reduction performance of both the organization and its principal competitors is continually monitored if competitive advantage is to be sustained.

You may be able to remember the illustration in the previous chapter relating to how an American automobile company failed to use the value chain approach to exploit links with suppliers and enhance profitability. The company had made significant internal savings from introducing JIT manufacturing techniques, but, at the same time, price increases from suppliers more than offset these internal cost savings. A value chain perspective revealed that 50 per cent of the firm's costs related to purchases from parts suppliers. As the automobile company reduced its own need for buffer stocks, it placed major new strains on the manufacturing responsiveness of suppliers. The increase in the suppliers' manufacturing costs was greater than the decrease in the automobile company's internal costs. Shank (1989) states:

> For every dollar of manufacturing cost the assembly plants saved by moving towards JIT management concepts, the suppliers' plant spent much more than one dollar extra because of schedule instability arising from the introduction of JIT. Because of its narrow value added perspective, the auto company had ignored the impact of its changes on its suppliers' costs. Management had ignored the idea that JIT involves a partnership with suppliers (Shank, 1989: 51).

Other contributions to strategic management accounting

In this section we shall briefly consider further approaches to strategic management accounting which have not been included within Lord's classification of the literature. Bromwich (1990) has attempted to develop strategic management accounting to consider the benefits which products offer to customers, and how these contribute to sustainable competitive advantage. Bromwich sought to compare the relative cost of product attributes or characteristics with what the customer is willing to pay for them. Products are seen as comprising a package of attributes which they offer to customers. It is these attributes that actually constitute commodities, and which appeal to customers so that they buy the product. The attributes might include a range of quality elements (such as operating performance variables, reliability and warranty arrangements, physical features – including the degree of finish and trim, and service factors – such as the assurance of supply and after-sales service). A firm's market share depends on the match between the attributes provided by its products and consumers' tastes and on the supply of attributes by competitors. Bromwich argues that it is the product attributes which need to be the subject of appropriate analysis. The purpose of the analysis should be to attribute those costs which are normally treated as product costs to the benefits they provide to the consumer for each of those attributes which are believed to be of strategic importance. By matching costs with benefits firms can compare whether revenues generated from the benefits exceed their costs.

Bromwich concludes that information about a number of demand and cost factors appertaining to attributes possessed by a firm's products and those of its rivals is needed for optimal decision-making. Management accountants can play an important role here in costing the characteristics provided and in monitoring and reporting on these costs regularly. Similarly, they need to be involved in determining the cost of any package of attributes which is being considered for introduction to the market because deciding to provide a product with a particular configuration of attributes or characteristics requires the organization to achieve this at a competitive cost level.

Roslender (1995) has identified target costing as falling within the domain of strategic management accounting. The justification for this is the external focus and that it is a market driven approach to product pricing and cost management. In addition it involves the diffusion of management accounting information throughout the organization and the active involvement of staff from across a broad spectrum of management functions. Their aim is to achieve the target cost which involves identifying, valuing and costing product attributes using functional analysis and examining cost reduction opportunities throughout the entire value chain. For a detailed explanation of target costing you should refer back to Chapter 21.

Surveys of strategic management accounting practices

Little research has been undertaken on the extent to which companies use strategic management accounting practices. A notable exception is a survey undertaken by Guilding *et al.* (2000). The survey consisted of a sample of 312 large companies comprising 63 from the UK, 127 from the USA and 124 from New Zealand.

Guilding *et al.* acknowledge the difficulty in identifying what are generally accepted as constituting strategic management accounting practices. Based on a review of the literature they identified 12 strategic management accounting practices. The criteria that they used for identifying the practices were that they must exhibit one or more of the following characteristics: environmental or marketing orientation; focus on competitors; and long-term, forward-looking orientation. The average usage of the identified practices and their perceived merits are reported in Exhibit 22.2. You will see that attribute costing is one of the 12 identified practices. This practice, based on the views promoted by Bromwich (1990) was described in the previous section. Three of the 12 listed practices; namely quality costing (involving the use of cost of quality reports), life-cycle costing and target costing were described in the previous chapter. Although some of the remaining eight practices have been described in this chapter they can be subject to different interpretations and definitions. The following represent the definitions of these eight terms given to the respondents participating in the survey:

- *Competitive position monitoring* The analysis of competitor positions within the industry by assessing and monitoring trends in competitor sales, market share, volume, unit costs and return on sales. This information can provide a basis for the assessment of a competitor's market strategy.

- *Strategic pricing* The analysis of strategic factors in the pricing decision process. These factors may include: competitor price reaction; price elasticity; market growth; economies of scale and experience.

- *Competitor performance appraisal based on published financial statements* The numerical analysis of a competitor's published statements as part of an assessment of the competitor's key sources of competitive advantage.

- *Competitor cost assessment* The provision of regularly updated estimates of a competitor's costs based on, for example, appraisal of facilities, technology, economies of scale. Sources include direct observation, mutual suppliers, mutual customers and ex-employees.

- *Strategic costing* The use of cost data based on strategic and marketing information to develop and identify superior strategies that will sustain a competitive advantage.

- *Value-chain costing* An activity-based costing approach where costs are allocated to activities required to design, procure, produce, market, distribute and service a product or service.

- *Brand value monitoring* The financial valuation of a brand through the assessment of brand strength factors such as: leadership; stability; market; internationality; trend; support; and protection combined with historical brand profits.

- *Brand value budgeting* The use of brand value as a basis for managerial decisions on the allocation of resources to support/enhance a brand position, thus placing attention on management dialogue on brand issues.

EXHIBIT 22.2 Usage and perceived merit of strategic management accounting practices

Strategic management accounting practice	Average usage score[a]	Ranking	Average perceived merit score[b]	Ranking
Competitive position monitoring	4.99	1	5.73	1
Strategic pricing	4.54	2	5.45	2
Competitor performance appraisal based on published financial statements	4.42	3	5.31	3
Competitor cost assessment	4.07	4	5.27	4
Strategic costing	3.49	5	4.91	5
Quality costing	3.22	6	4.29	6
Target costing	3.12	7	3.94	8
Value-chain costing	3.04	8	4.27	7
Brand value monitoring	2.73	9	3.38	11
Life-cycle costing	2.60	10	3.58	9
Attribute costing	2.33	11	3.49	10
Brand value budgeting	2.32	12	3.33	12

Notes

[a]All items scored on a Likert scale where 1 denotes used 'not at all' and 7 denotes used 'to a great extent'.

[b]All items scored on a Likert scale where 1 denotes 'not at all helpful' and 7 denotes 'helpful to a great extent'.

It is apparent from Exhibit 22.2 that the three competitor accounting practices and strategic pricing are the most popular strategic management accounting practices. They all have average scores above the mid-point on the seven-point scale for the 'not at all/to a large extent' used measure. You will also see from Exhibit 22.2 that the usage rates for the remaining eight strategic management accounting practices are below the mid-point of the '1–7' measurement scale used, thus suggesting that these practices are not widely used by the responding organizations.

In terms of the perceived merit of the 12 practices, the rankings shown in Exhibit 22.2 are similar to those reported for the extent of usage. Guilding *et al.* conclude that while usage rates for most of the practices appraised scored relatively lowly, two factors suggest that it would be inappropriate to dismiss their potential. First, for all of the strategic management accounting practices appraised, the perceived merit scores are significantly greater than the usage rate scores. Secondly, for the eight strategic management accounting practices where relatively low usage rates were observed, three (strategic costing, quality costing and value-chain costing) scored above the mid-point with respect to perceived merit. These observations suggest that there is a gap between what is needed and what is reported by an accounting system.

Guilding *et al.* also examined the familiarity of practising accountants with the term 'strategic management accounting'. The responses suggest that there was negligible use of the term in organizations and practising accountants have a limited appreciation of what the term means. This reinforces Tomkins and Carr's (1996) claim, made in an academic context, that strategic management accounting is ill-defined.

The balanced scorecard

A more recent contribution to strategic management accounting that emphasizes the role of management accounting in formulating and supporting the overall competitive strategy of an organization is the balanced scorecard. The balanced scorecard seeks to encourage behaviour that is consistent with an organization's strategy. It comprises of on an integrated framework of performance measurements that aim to clarify, communicate and manage strategy implementation. The financial performance measures that have been described in Chapters 16–19 tend to be used primarily as a financial control mechanism whereas the balanced scorecard integrates both financial and non-financial measures and incorporates performance measurement within the strategic management process.

Prior to the 1980s management accounting control systems tended to focus mainly on financial measures of performance. The inclusion of only those items that could be expressed in monetary terms motivated managers to focus excessively on cost reduction and ignore other important variables which were necessary to compete in the global competitive environment that emerged during the 1980s. Product quality, delivery, reliability, after-sales service and customer satisfaction became key competitive variables but none of these were given sufficient importance measured by the traditional management accounting performance measurement system.

During the 1980s much greater emphasis was given to incorporating into the management reporting system those non-financial performance measures that provided feedback on the key variables that are required to compete successfully in a global economic environment. However, a proliferation of performance measures emerged. This resulted in confusion when some of the measures conflicted with each other and it was possible to enhance one measure at the expense of another. It was also not clear to managers how the non-financial measures they were evaluated on contributed to the whole picture of achieving success in financial terms. According to Kaplan and Norton (2001a) previous performance measurement systems that incorporated non-financial measurements used *ad hoc* collections of such measures, more like checklists of measures for managers to keep track of and improve than a comprehensive system of linked measurements.

The need to integrate financial and non-financial measures of performance and identify key performance measures that link measurements to strategy led to the emergence of the balanced scorecard. The balanced scorecard was devised by Kaplan and Norton (1992) and refined in later publications (Kaplan and Norton, 1993, 1996a, 1996b, 2001a, 2001b). Therefore the following discussion is a summary of Kaplan and Norton's writings on this topic. They use the diagram reproduced in Figure 22.1 to illustrate how the balanced scorecard translates strategy into tangible objectives and linked performance measures.

Figure 22.1 emphasizes that the balanced scorecard philosophy creates a strategic focus by translating an organisation's vision and strategy into operational objectives and performance measures for the following four perspectives:

1　Financial perspective (How do we look to shareholders?)

2　Customer perspective (How do customers see us?)

3　Internal business perspective (What must we excel at?)

4　Learning and growth perspective (Can we continue to improve and create value?)

The balanced scorecard is a strategic management technique for communicating and evaluating the achievement of the mission and strategy of the organization. Kaplan and Norton define strategy as:

> Choosing the market and customer segments the business unit intends to serve, identifying the critical internal and business processes that the unit must excel at to deliver the value propositions to customers in the targeted market segments, and selecting the individual and organizational capabilities required for the internal and financial objectives.

You will see by referring to Figure 22.1 that strategy is implemented by specifying the major objectives for each of the four perspectives and translating them into specific performance measures, targets and initiatives. There may be one or more objectives for each perspective and one or more performance measures linked to each objective. Only the critical performance measures are incorporated in the scorecard. To minimize information overload and avoid a proliferation of measures each perspective ought to comprise four to five separate measures. Thus, the scorecard can provide *top* management with a fast but comprehensive view of the organizational unit (i.e. a division/strategic business unit). Let us now examine each of the four

SOURCE: KAPLAN AND NORTON, THE BALANCED SCORECARD: TRANSLATING STRATEGY INTO ACTION. COPYRIGHT © 1996 BY THE HARVARD BUSINESS SCHOOL PUBLISHING CORPORATION: ALL RIGHTS RESERVED.

FIGURE 22.1
The balanced scorecard

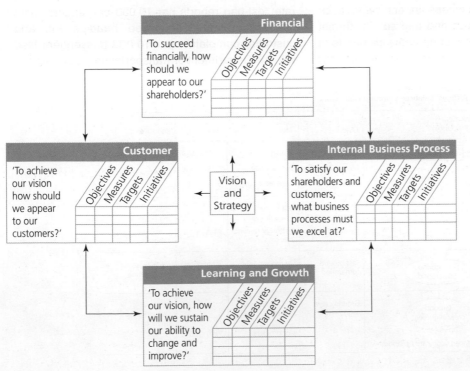

REAL WORLD VIEWS 22.1

How Southwest Airlines developed its balanced scorecard analysis

© STEVEN WIDOFF/ALAMY

Southwest Airlines set 'operating efficiency' as its strategic theme. The four perspectives embodied in the balanced scorecard were linked together by a series of relatively simple questions and answers:

Financial: What will drive operating efficiency? *Answer:* More customers on fewer planes.

Customer: How will we get more customers on fewer planes? *Answer:* Attract targeted segments of customers who value price and on-time arrivals.

Internal: What must our internal focus be? *Answer:* Fast aircraft turnaround time.

Learning: How will our people accomplish fast turnaround? *Answer:* Educate and compensate the ground crew regarding how they contribute to the firm's success. Also, use the employee stockholder programme.

The chart below shows how Southwest used this framework to lay out its balanced scorecard model. The first column of the chart contains the 'strategy map', that illustrates the cause-and-effect relationships between strategic objectives. The Objectives column shows what each strategy must achieve and what is critical to its success. The Measurement column shows how success in achieving each strategy will be measured and tracked. The Target column spells out the level of performance or rate of improvement that is needed. The Initiative column

contains key action programmes required to achieve objectives. Note that all of the measures, targets and initiatives are all aligned to each objective.

The company extended the effort to the department level, and the degree of development varied between departments. The goal was to identify key performance measures in each segment for the operating personnel. Some of the non-financial metrics that have emerged on a departmental level include: load factor (percentage of seats occupied); utilization factors on aircraft and personnel; on-time performance; available seat miles; denied-boarding rate; lost-bag reports per 10 000 passengers; flight cancellation rate; employee head count; and customer complaints per 10 000 passengers filed with the Department of Transportation.

Southwest Airlines' Balanced Scorecard Framework

Strategic Theme: Operating Efficiency	Objectives	Measurement	Target	Initiative
Financial — Profitability; Fewer planes; More customers	Profitability	Market value	30% CAGR	
	More customers	Seat revenue	20% CAGR	
	Fewer planes	Plane lease cost	5% CAGR	
Customer — Flight is on time; Lowest prices	Flight is on time	FAA on time arrival rating	#1	Quality management
	Lowest prices	Customer ranking (market survey)	#1	Customer loyalty program
Internal — Fast ground turnaround	Fast ground turnaround	On ground time	30 minutes	Cycle time optimization
		On time departure	90%	
Learning — Ground crew alignment	Ground crew alignment	% Ground crew trained	Yr. 1 70%	ESOP Ground crew training
		% Ground crew stockholders	Yr. 3 90% Yr. 5 100%	

(Source: Balanced Scorecard Collaborative)

SOURCE: ADAPTED FROM INSTITUTE OF MANAGEMENT & ADMINISTRATION REPORT ON FINANCIAL ANALYSIS PLANNING AND REPORTING, JULY 2002.

perspectives. The following discussion presents generic core objectives and measures applicable to each perspective. In practice each organization will customize the objectives and performance measures to fit their own specific strategies.

The financial perspective

The financial perspective specifies the financial performance objectives anticipated from pursing the organization's strategy and also the economic consequences of the outcomes expected from achieving the objectives specified from the other three perspectives. Therefore the objectives and measures from the other perspectives should be selected to ensure that the financial outcomes will be achieved. Kaplan and Norton state that they have observed three core financial themes that drive the business strategy: revenue growth and mix, cost reduction and asset utilization.

Generic objectives and possible measures for these themes are shown in Exhibit 22.3. Typical *revenue growth* objectives for a business pursuing a growth strategy include increasing the number of new products, developing new customers and markets and changing to a more profitable product or service mix. Once the objectives have been determined performance measures should be established that are linked to each objective. Possible measures are listed against each objective in Exhibit 22.3. They are percentage revenues from new products, percentage revenues from new customers/markets and growth of sales in the targeted segments.

The *cost reduction* objectives may include reduction in unit product costs and a reduction in selling and general and administration costs. Thus the percentage reduction in costs per unit of output for the selected cost objects and the percentage to total revenues of selling and administrative costs represent possible performance measures.

Exhibit 22.3 lists the improvement of *asset utilization* as the major objective of the asset utilization theme. Financial performance measures such as return on investment and economic value-added that were described in Chapter 19 provide overall outcome measures of success for the overall financial objectives of revenue growth, cost reduction and asset utilization.

The customer perspective

The customer perspective should identify the customer and market segments in which the business unit will compete. The customer perspective underpins the revenue element for the financial perspective objectives. Therefore the achievement of customer objectives should ensure that target revenues will be generated. Exhibit 22.4 lists five typical core or generic objectives. They are:

EXHIBIT 22.3 Financial perspective objectives and measures

Objectives	Measures
Revenue growth:	
Increase the number of new products	Percentage of revenues from new products
Develop new customers and markets	Percentage of revenues from new customers/markets
Change to a more profitable product (or service) mix	Sales growth percentage for targeted segments
Cost reduction:	
Reduce product/service cost per unit	Percentage reduction in cost per unit
Reduce selling/general administration costs	Percentage to total revenues of selling and administration costs
Asset utilization:	
Improve asset utilization	Return on investment
	Economic value-added

increasing market share, increasing customer retention, increasing customer acquisition, increasing customer satisfaction and increasing customer profitability. Typical core measures for these objectives (see Exhibit 22.4) are respectively: percentage market share, percentage growth of business with existing customers, number of new customers or total sales to new customers, ratings from customer satisfaction surveys and profitability analysis by customer segments. The first four measures relate to the means required to achieve customer profitability but they do not measure the outcome. Customer profitability measures meet this requirement. In other words, a company does not want just satisfied customers, it also wants profitable customers.

Kaplan and Norton state that there is also a need to focus on customer value propositions that represent the attributes that drive core objectives and measures relating to the customer perspective. They identify common product/service attributes as encompassing the functionality of the products/services, their price and quality, and for the customer dimension they identify the delivery time attribute. Focusing on these attributes has the potential to increase customer value and thus have a favourable impact on the core objectives. Typical objectives relating to the above attributes are listed in Exhibit 22.4. They are respectively: improve product functionality, decrease price relative to competitors, improve quality and improve delivery time. Possible measures for these objectives include, respectively, customer surveys satisfaction scores relating to product functionality, price relative to competitors, percentage of returns from customers and percentage of on-time deliveries.

The internal business perspective

The internal business perspective requires that managers identify the critical internal processes for which the organization must excel in implementing its strategy. Critical processes should be identified that are required to achieve the organization's customer and financial objectives. Kaplan and Norton identify a generic process value chain that provides guidance for companies applying the internal process perspective. The process value chain consists of three processes: the innovation process, the operations process and the post-sales process.

In the *innovation process*, managers research the needs of customers and then create the products or services that will meet those needs. It represents the long wave of value creation in which companies first identify new markets, new customers, and the emerging and latent needs of existing customers. Then continuing on this long wave of value creation companies design and develop new products and services that enable them to reach these new markets and customers. Typical objectives for the innovation process are listed in Exhibit 22.5. They are increasing the number of new products, developing new markets and customers and decreasing the time taken to develop new products. Supporting performance measures are, respectively: percentage of sales

EXHIBIT 22.4 Customer perspective objectives and measures

Objectives	Measures
Core:	
Increase market share	Percentage market share
Increase customer retention	Percentage growth in business from existing customers
Increase customer acquisition	Total sales to new customers
Increase customer satisfaction	Customer survey satisfaction ratings
Increase customer profitability	Customer profitability analysis
Customer value propositions:	
Improve product functionality	Customer survey product functionality rating scores
Decrease price relative to competitors	Price relative to competitors
Improve product/service quality	Percentage returns from customers
Improve delivery time	Percentage on-time deliveries

from new products (also new product introductions versus competitors), percentage of sales from new markets and development cycle time (e.g. time to the market).

The *operations process* represents the short wave of value creation. It is concerned with producing and delivering existing products and services to customers. Objectives of the operation process listed in Exhibit 22.5 include, increasing process efficiency, increasing process quality, decreasing process cost and decreasing process time. Historically, the operations process has been the major focus of most of an organization's performance measurement system and many possible measures exist. Typical measures associated with each of the objectives for the operations process are listed in Exhibit 22.5.

Process efficiency measures tend to focus on output/input measures such as the production efficiency ratio (standard hours of output/actual hours of input) or capacity measures such as the capacity usage ratio (actual hours utilized/budgeted hours to be utilized). Quality measures include total quality costs as a percentage of sales derived from the cost of quality report (see Chapter 21), process parts per million defect rates, percentage of defective units and percentage of processes under statistical control. Process cost measures include unit cost trend measures relating to key processes and cycle time measures have evolved that support the objective of decreasing process time.

The total manufacturing cycle time consists of the sum of processing time, inspection time, wait time and move time. Only processing time adds value, and the remaining activities are non-value-added activities. The aim is to reduce the time spent on non-value added activities and thus minimize manufacturing cycle time. A measure of cycle time that has been adopted is manufacturing cycle efficiency (MCE):

$$ MCE = \frac{\text{processing time}}{\text{processing time} + \text{inspection time} + \text{wait time} + \text{move time}} $$

The generic performance measures that have been illustrated above relate to manufacturing operations but similar measures can be adopted for service companies. For example, many customers are forced to queue to receive a service. Companies that can eliminate waiting time for a service will find it easier to attract customers. The time taken to process mortgage and loan applications by financial institutions can take a considerable time period involving a considerable amount of non-value-added

EXHIBIT 22.5 Internal business perspective objectives and measures

Objectives	Measures
Innovation:	
Increase the number of new products	Percentage of sales from new products
	New product introductions versus competitors
Develop new markets and customers	Percentage of sales from new markets
Decrease the time taken to develop new products	Development cycle time (time to the market)
Operations:	
Increase process efficiency	Output/inputs ratios
Increase process quality	Total quality costs as a percentage of sales
	Percentage of defective output
Decrease process cost	Unit cost trends
Decrease process time	Manufacturing cycle efficiency
Post-sales service:	
Increase service quality	Percentage of customer requests that are handled with a single call
Increase service efficiency	Output/inputs ratios
Decrease service time	Cycle time in resolving customer problems
Decrease service cost	Unit cost trends

waiting time. Thus, reducing the time to process the applications enhances customer satisfaction and creates the potential for increasing sales revenues. Therefore service companies should also develop cycle time measures that support their specific customer processing activity objectives.

The *post-sales service process* represents the final item in the process value chain for the operations process perspective. It focuses on how responsive the organization is to customers after the product or service has been delivered. Post-sales services include warranty and repair activities, treatment of defects and returns and the process and administration of customer payments. Increasing quality, increasing efficiency and decreasing process time and cost are also objectives that apply to the post-sales service. Performance can be measured by some of the time, quality and cost measurements that have been suggested for the operations process. For example, service quality can be measured by first-pass yields defined as the percentage of customer requests that are handled with a single service call, rather than requiring multiple calls to resolve the problem. Increasing efficiency can be measured by appropriate output/input ratios and decreasing process time can be measured by cycle time where the process starts with the receipt of a customer request and ends with the ultimate resolution of the problem. Finally, the trend in unit costs can be used to measure the key post-sale service processes.

The learning and growth process

To ensure that an organization will continue to have loyal and satisfied customers in the future and continue to make excellent use of its resources, the organization and its employees must keep learning and developing. Hence there is a need for a perspective that focuses on the capabilities that an organization needs to create long-term growth and improvement. This perspective stresses the importance of organizations investing in their infrastructure (people, systems and organizational procedures) to provide the capabilities that enable the accomplishment of the other three perspectives' objectives. Kaplan and Norton have identified three major enabling factors for this perspective. They are: employee capabilities, information systems capabilities and the organizational climate for motivation, empowerment and alignment. Thus this perspective has three major core objectives: increase employee capabilities, increase information system capabilities and increase motivation, empowerment and alignment. The objectives and associated performance measures for this perspective are listed in Exhibit 22.6.

Core measures for the *employee capabilities* objective are concerned with employee satisfaction, employee retention and employee productivity. Many companies periodically measure employee satisfaction using surveys to derive employee satisfaction ratings. Employee retention can be measured by the annual percentage of key staff that resigns and many different methods can be used to measure employee productivity. A generic measure of employee productivity that

EXHIBIT 22.6 Learning and growth perspective objectives and measures

Objectives	Measures
Increase employee capabilities	Employee satisfaction survey ratings
	Annual percentage of key staff leaving
	Sales revenue per employee
Increase information system capabilities	Percentage of processes with real time feedback capabilities
	Percentage of customer-facing employees having on-line access to customer and product information
Increase motivation, empowerment and alignment	Number of suggested improvements per employee
	Number of suggestions implemented per employee
	Percentage of employees with personal goals aligned to the balanced scorecard
	Percentage of employees who achieve personal goals

can be applied throughout the organization and compared with different divisions is the sales revenue per employee.

For employees to be effective in today's competitive environment they need accurate and timely information on customers, internal processes and the financial consequences of their decisions. Measures of *strategic information system capabilities* suggested by Kaplan and Norton include percentage of processes with real time quality, cycle time and cost feedback capabilities available and the percentage of customer-facing employees having on-line access to customer and product information.

The number of suggested improvements per employee and the number of suggestions implemented per employee are proposed measures relating to the objective having *motivated and empowered employees*. Suggested measures relating to the objective of increasing individual and organizational alignment are the percentage of employees with personal goals aligned to the balanced scorecard and the percentage of employees who achieve personal goals.

Targets and initiatives

Look at Figure 22.1. You will see that, besides objectives and measures, targets and initiatives are also incorporated in the balanced scorecard. Target values should be should be established for the measures associated with each objective. In addition, the major initiatives for each objective should be described. For feedback reporting actual performance measures can also be added. There is also evidence to indicate that the balanced scorecard approach is linked to incentive compensation schemes. Epstein and Manzoni (1998) reported that 60 per cent of the 100 large USA organizations surveyed linked the balanced scorecard approach to incentive pay for their senior executives. Failure to change the reward system may result in managers continuing to focus on short-term financial performance at the expense of concentrating on the strategic objectives of the scorecard.

Cause-and-effect relationships

A critical assumption of the balanced scorecard is that each performance measure is part of a cause-and-effect relationship involving a linkage from strategy formulation to financial outcomes. Measures of organizational learning and growth are assumed to be the drivers of the internal business processes. The measures of these processes are in turn assumed to be the drivers of measures of customer perspective, while these measures are the driver of the financial perspective. The assumption that there is a cause-and-effect relationship is necessary because it allows the measurements relating to the non-financial perspectives to be used to predict future financial performance. In this context, Kaplan and Norton (1996b) indicate that the chain of cause-and-effect relationships encompasses all four perspectives of the balanced scorecard such that economic value added (see Chapter 19) may be an outcome measure for the financial perspective. The driver of this measure could be an expansion of sales from existing customers. This expansion may be achieved by enhancing customers' loyalty by meeting their preference from on-time delivery. Thus, the improved on-time delivery is expected to lead to higher customer loyalty which in turn leads to higher financial performance. The on-time delivery is part of the internal process perspective and to achieve it the business needs to achieve short cycle time in operating processes and the short cycle time can be achieved by training the employees, this goal being part of the learning and growth perspective.

The balanced scorecard thus consists of two types of performance measures. The first consists of lagging measures. These are the outcome measures that mostly fall within the financial perspective and are the results of past actions. These measures generally do not incorporate the effect of decisions when they are made. Instead, they show the financial impact of the decisions as their impact materializes and this can be long after the decisions were made. The second are leading measures that are the drivers of future financial performance. They cause the outcome. These tend to be the non-financial measures relating to the customer, internal business process and learning and growth perspectives.

Benefits and limitations of the balanced scorecard approach

The following is a summary of the major benefits that can be attributed to the balanced scorecard approach:

1 The scorecard brings together in a single report four different perspectives on a company's performance that relate to many of the disparate elements of the company's competitive agenda such as becoming customer oriented, shortening response time, improving quality, emphasizing team-work, reducing new product launch times and managing for the long-term. Many organizations collect some performance measures relating to each of the four perspectives but they are typically presented in several different large reports that often prove to be unhelpful because they suffer from information overload.

2 The approach provides a comprehensive framework for translating company's strategic goals into a coherent set of performance measures by developing the major goals for the four perspectives and then translating these goals into specific performance measures.

3 The scorecard helps managers to consider all the important operational measures together. It enables managers see whether improvements in one area may have been at the expense of another.

4 The approach improves communications within the organization and promotes the active formulation and implementation of organizational strategy by making it highly visible through the linkage of performance measures to business unit strategy.

The balanced scorecard has also been subject to frequent criticisms. Most of them question the assumption of the cause-and-effect relationship on the grounds that they are too ambiguous and lack a theoretical underpinning or empirical support. The empirical studies that have been undertaken have failed to provide evidence on the underlying linkages between non-financial data and future financial performance (American Accounting Association Financial Accounting Standards Committee, 2002). Other criticisms relate to the omission of important perspectives, the most notable being the environmental/impact on society perspective (see Chapter 21) and an employee perspective. It should be noted, however, that Kaplan and Norton presented the four perspectives as a suggested framework rather than a constraining straitjacket. There is nothing to

EXHIBIT 22.7 Surveys of practice relating to balanced scorecard usage

Surveys indicate that even though the balanced scorecard did not emerge until the early 1990s it is now widely used in many countries throughout the world. A USA survey by Silk (1998) estimated that 60 per cent of Fortune 1000 firms have experimented with the balanced scorecard. In the UK a survey of 163 manufacturing companies (annual sales turnover in excess of £50 million) by Zuriekat (2005) reported that 30 per cent had implemented the balanced scorecard. Other studies in mainland Europe indicate significant usage. Pere (1999) reported a 31 per cent usage rate of companies in Finland with a further 30 per cent in the process of implementing it. In Sweden Kald and Nilsson (2000) reported that 27 per cent of major Swedish companies have implemented the approach. Oliveras and Amat (2002) report widespread usage in Spain and and Speckbacher et al. (2003) report a usage rate of 24 per cent in German-speaking countries (Germany, Austria and Switzerland). Major companies adopting the balanced scorecard include KPMG Peat Marwick, Allstate Insurance and AT&T (Chow et al., 1997).

In terms of the perspectives used Malmi (2001) conducted a study involving semi-structured interviews in 17 companies in Finland. He found that 15 companies used the four perspectives identified by Kaplan and Norton and two companies added a fifth – an employee's perspective. The UK study by Zuriekat (2005) reported that virtually all of the balanced scorecard respondents used the financial, customer and internal business process perspectives. Other perspectives used were learning and growth, employee, supplier and the environment. The respective percentage usage rates for the balance scorecard adopters were 39 per cent, 45 per cent, 65 per cent and 26 per cent. The study also reported that 35 per cent of the adopters linked their reward systems to the balanced scorecard. A study by Olve et al. (2000) found that 15–20 performance measures are customarily used.

prevent companies adding additional perspectives to meet their own requirements but they must avoid the temptation of creating too many perspectives and performance measures since one of the major benefits of the balanced scorecard is its conciseness and clarity of presentation.

Our discussion relating to the core objectives and measures of the four perspectives has concentrated mainly on the manufacturing organizations. The balance scorecard, however, has been widely adopted in service organizations. Exhibit 22.8 provides an illustration of potential balanced scorecard performance measures for different types of service organizations. You will also find it appropriate at this point to refer to Exhibit 22.7 which summarizes surveys of practice relating to the usage of the balanced scorecard. For a discussion of an alternative system of performance measurement in service organizations you should refer to Learning Note 22.1 on the open access website (see Preface for details).

EXHIBIT 22.8 Potential scorecard measures in different business sectors

	Generic	Health care	Airlines	Banking
Financial Strength (Looking Back)	Market share Revenue growth Operating profits Return on equity Stock market performance Growth in margin	Patient census Unit profitability Funds raised for capital improvements Cost per care Per cent of revenue – new programmes	Revenue/cost per available passenger mile Mix of freight Mix of full fare to discounted Average age of fleet Available seat miles and related yields	Outstanding loan balances Deposit balances Non-interest income
Customer Service & Satisfaction (Looking from the outside in)	Customer satisfaction Customer retention Quality customer service Sales from new products/services	Patient satisfaction survey Patient retention Patient referral rate Admittance or discharge timeliness Medical plan awareness	Lost bag reports per 10 000 passengers Denied boarding rate Flight cancellation rate Customer complaints filed with the DOT	Customer retention Number of new customers Number of products per customer Face time spent between loan officers and customers
Internal Operating Efficiency (Looking from the inside out)	Delivery time Cost Process quality Error rates on shipments Supplier satisfaction	Weekly patient complaints Patient loads Breakthroughs in treatments and medicines Infection rates Readmission rate Length of stay	Load factors (percentage of seats occupied) Utilization factors on aircraft and personnel On-time performance	Sales calls to potential customers Thank you calls or cards to new and existing customers Cross selling statistics
Learning and Growth (Looking ahead)	Employee skill level Training availability Employee satisfaction Job retention Amount of overtime worked Amount of vacation time taken	Training hours per caregiver Number of peer reviewed papers published Number of grants awarded (NIH) Referring MDs Employee turnover rate	Employee absenteeism Worker safety statistics Performance appraisals completed Training programme hours per employee	Test results from training knowledge of product offerings, sales and service Employee satisfaction survey

SOURCE: LEAUBY AND WENTZEL, 2002

SUMMARY

The following items relate to the learning objectives listed at the beginning of the chapter.

● **Describe the different elements of strategic management accounting.**

Despite the publicity that strategic management accounting has received there is still no comprehensive conceptual framework of what strategic management accounting is. Because of the lack of consensus on what constitutes strategic management accounting the elements that have been identified in the literature to characterize strategic management accounting have been described. Three elements can be identified: (a) the extension of traditional management accounting's internal focus to include external information about competitors; (b) the relationship between the strategic position chosen by a firm and the expected emphasis on management accounting; and (c) gaining competitive advantage by analyzing ways to decrease costs and/or enhance the differentiation of a firm's products, through exploiting linkages in the value chain and optimizing cost drivers. Some authors have adopted a broader view of strategic management accounting that encompasses activity-based costing, target costing and the cost management approaches described in the previous chapter.

● **Describe three competitive strategies that a firm can adopt to achieve sustainable competitive advantage and explain how they influence management accounting practices.**

Porter suggests that a firm has a choice of three generic strategies to achieve sustainable competitive advantage. A firm adopting a cost leadership strategy seeks to be the lowest-cost producer within the industry thus enabling it to compete on the basis of lower selling prices. A differentiation strategy applies when a firm seeks to offer products or services that are considered by its customers to be superior and unique relative to its competitors. Finally, a firm can adopt a focus strategy, which involves focusing on a narrow segment of the market that has special needs that are poorly served by other competitors. More emphasis is likely to be given to cost controls (e.g. standard costing) in firms pursing a low cost strategy whereas firms following a product differentiation strategy are likely to have a greater need for information about new product innovations, design cycle times and marketing cost analysis.

● **Describe the balanced scorecard.**

Recent developments in performance evaluation have sought to integrate financial and non-financial measures and assist in clarifying, communicating and managing strategy. The balanced scorecard attempts to meet these requirements. It requires that managers view the business from the following four different perspectives: (a) customer perspective (how do customers see us?); (b) internal business process perspective (what must we excel at?); (c) learning and growth perspective (can we continue to improve and create value?), and (d) financial perspective (how do we look to shareholders?). Organizations should articulate the major goals for each of the four perspectives and then translate these goals into specific performance measures. Each organization must decide what are its critical performance measures. The choice will vary over time and should be linked to the strategy that the organization is following.

● **Explain each of the four perspectives of the balanced scorecard.**

The financial perspective provides objectives and associated performance measures relating to the financial outcomes of past actions. Thus, it provides feedback on the success of pursuing the objectives identified for the other three perspectives. In the customer perspective managers identify the customer and market segments in which the businesses unit will compete. Obectives and performance measures should be developed within this perspective that track a business unit's ability to create satisfied and loyal customers in the targeted segments. They relate to market share, customer retention, new customer acquisition, customer satisfaction and customer profitability. In the internal business perspective, managers identify the critical internal processes for which the organization must excel in implementing its strategy. The internal business process objectives and measures should focus on the internal processes that will have the greatest impact on customer satisfaction and achieving the organization's financial objectives. The principal internal business processes include the innovation processes, operation processes and post-service sales processes. The final perspective on the balanced scorecard identifies the infrastructure that the business must build to create long-term growth and improvement. The following three categories have been identified as falling within this perspective: employee capabilities, information system capabilities and motivation, empowerment and alignment.

● **Provide illustrations of performance measures for each of the four perspectives.**

Within the financial perspective examples include economic value added and residual income. Market share and customer satisfaction ratings are generic measures within the customer perspective. Typical internal business perspective measures include percentage of sales from new products (innovation processes), cycle time measures such as manufacturing cycle efficiency (operation processes) and percentage returns from customers (post-service sales processes). Measures of employee satisfaction represent generic measures within the learning and growth satisfaction.

● **Explain how the balanced scorecard links strategy formulation to financial outcomes.**

The balanced scorecard philosophy translates an organization's vision and strategy into operational objectives and performance measures for each of the four perspectives. Each performance measure is part of a cause-and-effect relationship involving a linkage from strategy formulation to financial outcomes. Measures of organizational learning and growth are assumed to be the drivers of the internal business processes. The measures of these processes are in turn assumed to be the drivers of measures of customer perspective, while these measures are the driver of the financial perspective. Measurements relating to the non-financial perspectives are assumed to be predictors of future financial performance.

Key terms and concepts

balanced scorecard (p. 576)
brand value budgeting (p. 575)
brand value monitoring (p. 575)
capacity usage ratio (p. 581)
competitive position monitoring
   (p. 575)
competitor cost assessment (p. 575)
competitor performance appraisal
   (p. 575)
customer perspective (p. 577)
customer value propositions (p. 580)

financial perspective (p. 577)
internal business process perspective
   (p. 577)
lagging measures (p. 583)
leading measures (p. 583)
learning and growth perspective
   (p. 577)
learning curve (p. 571)
manufacturing cycle efficiency
   (MCE) (p. 581)
production efficiency ratio (p. 581)

strategic costing (p. 575)
strategic management accounting
   (p. 570)
strategic pricing (p. 575)
target costing (p. 574)
value-chain analysis (p. 572)
value-chain costing (p. 575)

Recommended reading

For a more detailed discussion of the elements of strategic management accounting you should refer to the articles by Lord (1996) or Roslender (1995, 1996), and Roslender and Hart (2002, 2003). Research relating to a survey of strategic management accounting practices is presented in Guilding *et al.* (2000). Kaplan and Norton designed the balanced scorecard and in their writings they describe its development and the experiences of companies that have implemented it. This chapter has summarized Kaplan and Norton's writings but for a more

detailed description of their work you should refer to the books they have written on the balance scorecard – *Translating Strategy into Action: The Balance Scorecard* (1996b) and *The Strategy-Focused Organization* (2001a). See also Kaplan and Norton (2001b) and Epstein and Manzoni (1998) for shorter articles on the balanced scorecard. You should refer to the writings of Norreklit (2000, 2003) for a critique of the balanced scorecard. For a broader description of performance measurement linked to strategy you should refer to Simons (1998).

Key examination points

Strategic management accounting and the balanced scorecard are relatively new topics so they have not been extensively examined in the past. Consequently fewer past examination questions are included in this chapter. Strategic management accounting can be viewed as incorporating a wide range of topics. In addition, other approaches to performance measurement have been examined that do not

adopt a balanced scorecard perspective. Therefore some questions are included that do not relate directly to the chapter content. However, where questions are set on performance measurement you should try and adopt a balanced scorecard approach by emphasizing the need to integrate financial and non-financial measures and link performance measurement to an organization's strategies.

ASSESSMENT MATERIAL

The review questions are short questions that enable you to assess your understanding of the main topics included in the chapter. The numbers in parentheses provide you with the page numbers to refer to if you cannot answer a specific question.

The review problems are more complex and require you to relate and apply the content to various business problems. The problems are graded by their level of difficulty. Solutions to review problems that are not preceded by the term 'IM' are provided in a separate section at the end of the book. Solutions to problems preceded by the term 'IM' are provided in the *Instructor's Manual* accompanying this book and also on the lecturer's password protected section of the website www.drury-online.com. Additional review problems with fully worked solutions are provided in the *Student's Manual* that accompanies this book.

The website also includes over 30 case study problems. A list of these cases is provided on pages 665–7. The Brunswick Plastics case is relevant to the content of this chapter.

Review questions

22.1 Provide a definition of strategic management accounting. *(p. 570)*
22.2 Describe the three major strands of strategic management accounting that can be identified from the literature. *(pp. 570–73)*
22.3 How do different competitive strategies influence the emphasis that is given to particular management accounting techniques? *(p. 572)*
22.4 What is the purpose of a balanced scorecard? *(p. 577)*
22.5 Describe the four perspectives of the balanced scorecard. *(pp. 579–83)*
22.6 Explain the differences between lag measures and lead measures. *(p. 583)*
22.7 Explain what is meant by cause-and-effect relationships within balanced scorecard. *(p. 583)*
22.8 Discuss the benefits and limitations of the balanced scorecard. *(pp. 584–85)*
22.9 Identify and describe the core objectives of the customer perspective. *(pp. 579–80)*
22.10 Describe the three principal internal business processes that can be included within the internal business perspective. *(pp. 580–82)*
22.11 What is manufacturing cycle efficiency? *(p. 581)*
22.12 Describe three principal categories within the learning and growth perspective. *(pp. 582–83)*
22.13 Provide examples of performance measures within each of the four perspectives of the balanced scorecard. *(pp. 579–83)*

Review problems

22.14 Advanced: Financial and non-financial performance measures. BS Ltd provides consultancy services to small and medium sized businesses. Three types of consultants are employed offering administrative, data processing and marketing advice respectively. The consultants work partly on the client's premises and partly in BS Ltd premises, where chargeable development work in relation to each client contract will be undertaken. Consultants spend some time negotiating with potential clients attempting to secure contracts from them. BS Ltd has recently implemented a policy change which allows for a number of follow-up (remedial) hours at the client's premises after completion of the contract in order to eliminate any problems which have arisen in the initial stages of operation of the system.

Contract negotiation and remedial work hours are not charged directly to each client. BS Ltd carries out consultancy for new systems and also to offer advice on existing systems which a client may have introduced before BS Ltd became involved. BS Ltd has a policy of retaining its consultancy staff at a level of 60 consultants on an ongoing basis.

Additional information for the year ended 30 April is as follows:
(i) BS Ltd invoices clients £75 per chargeable consultant hour.
(ii) Consultant salaries are budgeted at an average per consultant of £30 000 per annum. Actual salaries include a bonus for hours in excess of budget paid for at the budgeted average rate per hour.
(iii) Sundry operating costs (other than consultant salaries) were budgeted at £3 500 000. Actual was £4 100 000.
(iv) BS Ltd capital employed (start year) was £6 500 000.
(v) Table 1 shows an analysis of sundry budgeted and actual quantitative data.

Required:
a (i) Prepare an analysis of actual consultancy hours for the year ended 30 April which shows the increase or decrease from the standard/allowed non-chargeable hours. This increase or decrease should be analyzed to show the extent to which it may be shown to be attributable to a change from standard in: 1. standard chargeable hours; 2. remedial advice hours; 3. contract negotiation hours; 4. other non-chargeable hours.
(13 marks)

(ii) Calculate the total value of each of 1 to 4 in (a) above in terms of chargeable client income per hour. *(4 marks)*

b BS Ltd measure business performance in a number of ways. For each of the undernoted measures, comment on the performance of BS Ltd using quantitative data from the question and your answer to (a) to assist in illustrating your answer:
(i) Financial performance
(ii) Competitive performance
(iii) Quality of service
(iv) Flexibility
(v) Resource utilization
(vi) Innovation. *(18 marks)*

Table 1: BS Ltd Sundry statistics for year ended 30 April

	Budget	Actual
Number of consultants:		
Administration	30	23
Data processing	12	20
Marketing	18	17
Consultants hours analysis:		
contract negotiation hours	4 800	9 240
remedial advice hours	2 400	7 920
other non-chargeable hours	12 000	22 440
general development work hours (chargeable)	12 000	6 600
customer premises contract hours	88 800	85 800
Gross hours	120 000	132 000
Chargeable hours analysis:		
new systems	70%	60%
existing systems advice	30%	40%
Number of clients enquiries received:		
new systems	450	600
existing systems advice	400	360
Number of client contracts worked on:		
new systems	180	210
existing systems advice	300	288
Number of client complaints	5	20
Contracts requiring remedial advice	48	75

ACCA Paper 9 Information for Control and Decision Making

22.15 Advanced: Financial and non-financial performance measurement in a service organization. The owners of *The Eatwell Restaurant* have diversified business interests and operate in a wide range of commercial areas. Since buying the restaurant in 1997 they have carefully recorded the data below.

Recorded Data for The Eatwell Restaurant (1998–2001)

	1998	1999	2000	2001
Total meals served	3 750	5 100	6 200	6 700
Regular customers attending weekly	5	11	15	26
Number of items on offer per day	4	4	7	9
Reported cases of food poisoning	4	5	7	7
Special theme evenings introduced	0	3	9	13
Annual operating hours with no customers	380	307	187	126
Proposals submitted to cater for special events	10	17	29	38
Contracts won to cater for special events	2	5	15	25
Complimentary letters from satisfied customers	0	4	3	6
Average number of customers at peak times	18	23	37	39
Average service delay at peak time (mins)	32	47	15	35
Maximum seating capacity	25	25	40	40
Weekly opening hours	36	36	40	36
Written complaints received	8	12	14	14
Idle time	570	540	465	187
New meals introduced during the year	16	8	27	11
Financial Data	£	£	£	£
Average customer spend on wine	3	4	4	7
Total Turnover	83 000	124 500	137 000	185 000
Turnover from special events	2 000	13 000	25 000	55 000
Profit	11 600	21 400	43 700	57 200
Value of food wasted in preparation	1 700	1 900	3 600	1 450
Total turnover of all restaurants in locality	895 000	1 234 000	980 000	1 056 000

Required:

a Assess the overall performance of the business and submit your comments to the owners. They wish to compare the performance of the restaurant with their other business interests and require your comments to be grouped into the key areas of performance such as those described by Fitzgerald and Moon. (see Learning Note 22.1 on the website) *(14 marks)*

b Identify any additional information that you would consider of assistance in assessing the performance of *The Eatwell Restaurant* in comparison with another restaurant. Give reasons for your selection and explain how they would relate to the key performance area categories used in (a). *(6 marks)*

ACCA Paper 3.3 Performance Management

22.16 Advanced. CM Limited was formed ten years ago to provide business equipment solutions to local businesses. It has separate divisions for research, marketing, product design, technology and communication services, and now manufactures and supplies a wide range of business equipment (copiers, scanners, printers, fax machines and similar items).

To date it has evaluated its performance using monthly financial reports that analyze profitability by type of equipment.

The Managing Director of CM Limited has recently returned from a course on which it had been suggested that the 'Balanced Scorecard' could be a useful way of measuring performance.

Required:

a Explain the 'Balanced Scorecard' and how it could be used by CM Limited to measure its performance. *(13 marks)*

While on the course, the Managing Director of CM Limited overheard someone mention how the performance of their company had improved after they introduced 'Benchmarking'.

Required:

b Explain 'Benchmarking' and how it could be used to improve the performance of CM Limited. *(12 marks)*

CIMA Management Accounting – Performance Management

22.17 Advanced. The concept of Generic Strategies was established by Professor Michael Porter during the 1980s. He stated that a company

must choose one of these strategies in order to compete and gain sustainable competitive advantage. In addition to assessing the source of competitive advantage, Porter also explained that it was necessary to identify the target for the organization's products or services. This involved distinguishing between whether the target was broad and covered the majority of the overall market, or narrow and concentrated on a small but profitable part of it.

Requirements:

a Critically appraise the value of Porter's Generic Strategy model for strategic planning purposes. *(12 marks)*

b Explain how the theoretical principles of the Experience Curve may be applied to determine a generic strategy for a company. *(8 marks)*

CIMA Stage 4 Strategic Management Accountancy and Marketing

22.18 Advanced: Performance measurement in non-profit organizations.

a The absence of the profit measure in Not for Profit (NFP) organizations causes problems for the measurement of their efficiency and effectiveness.

You are required to explain:

(i) why the absence of the profit measure should be a cause of the problems referred to *(9 marks)*

(ii) how these problems extend to activities within business entities which have a profit motive. Support your answer with examples. *(4 marks)*

b A public health clinic is the subject of a scheme to measure its efficiency and effectiveness. Amongst a number of factors, the 'quality of care provided' has been included as an aspect of the clinic's service to be measured. Three features of 'quality of care provided' have been listed:

Clinic's adherence to appointment times
Patients' ability to contact the clinic and make appointments without difficulty
The provision of a comprehensive patient health monitoring programme.

You are required to:

(i) suggest a set of quantitative measures which can be used to identify the effective level of achievement of each of the features listed; *(9 marks)*

(ii) indicate how these measures could be combined into a single 'quality of care' measure. *(3 marks)*

CIMA Stage 4 Management Accounting – Control and Audit

22.19 Intermediate. ZY is an airline operator. It is implementing a balanced scorecard to measure the success of its strategy to expand its operations. It has identified two perspectives and two associated objectives. They are:

Perspective	Objective
Growth	Fly to new destinations
Internal capabilities	Reduce time between touch down and take off

(i) For the 'growth perspective' of ZY, recommend a performance measure and briefly justify your choice of the measure by explaining how it will reflect the success of the strategy. *(2 marks)*

(ii) For the 'internal capabilities perspective' of ZY, state data that you would gather and explain how this could be used to ensure the objective is met. *(2 marks)*

CIMA P1 Management Accounting: Performance Evaluation

22.20 Advanced. You are responsible for managing the preparation of all revenue and cost budgets for a motor component manufacturer. You are aware that the external environment has a significant impact on the business activity and financial performance of your company and that the current information systems are underdeveloped and ineffective in this respect.

Required:

a Identify which aspects of the external environment you are likely to consider and give reasons for your choice. *(10 marks)*

b Identify where you might find the relevant sources of information. *(5 marks)*

c Suggest how an external environment information system could be introduced into your company. *(5 marks)*

ACCA P3 Performance Measurement

IM22.1 Advanced. Management accounting practice has traditionally focused on techniques to assist organizational decision-making and cost control. In concentrating on the internal environment, the management accounting function has been criticized for not addressing the needs of senior management to enable effective strategic planning. In particular, the criticism has focused on inadequate provision of information which analyzes the organization's exposure to environmental change and its progress towards the achievement of corporate objectives.

Requirement:

Explain how Strategic Management Accounting can provide information which meets the requirements of senior managers in seeking to realize corporate objectives. *(20 marks)*

CIMA Stage 4 Strategic Management Accountancy and Marketing

IM22.2 Advanced. The new manufacturing environment is characterized by more flexibility, a readiness to meet customers' requirements, smaller batches, continuous improvements and an emphasis on quality.

In such circumstances, traditional management accounting performance measures are, at best, irrelevant and, at worst, misleading.

You are required:

a to discuss the above statement, citing specific examples to support or refute the views expressed; *(10 marks)*

b to explain in what ways management accountants can adapt the services they provide to the new environment. *(7 marks)*

CIMA Stage 3 Management Accounting Techniques

IM22.3 Advanced. Research on Performance Measurement in Service Businesses, reported in *Management Accounting*, found that 'performance measurement often focuses on easily quantifiable aspects such as cost and productivity whilst neglecting other dimensions which are important to competitive success'.

You are required:

a to explain what 'other dimensions' you think are important measures of performance; *(8 marks)*

b to describe what changes would be required to traditional information systems to deal with these 'other dimensions'. *(9 marks)*

CIMA Stage 3 Management Accounting

IM22.4 Advanced. The 'Balanced Scorecard' approach aims to provide information to management to assist strategic policy formulation and achievement. It emphasises the need to provide the user with a set of information which addresses all relevant areas of performance in an objective and unbiased fashion.

Requirements

(i) Discuss in general terms the main types of information which would be required by a manager to implement this approach to measuring performance; and

(ii) comment on three specific examples of performance measures which could be used in a company in a service industry, for example a firm of consultants. *(10 marks)*

CIMA Stage 4 Strategic Financial Management

IM22.5 Advanced: Design and discussion of key performance indicators for DIY outlets and regional companies. Duit plc has recently acquired Ucando Ltd which is a regional builders' merchants/DIY company with three outlets all within a radius of 40 miles. Duit plc is building up its national coverage of outlets. Duit plc has set up regional companies each with its own board of directors responsible to the main board situated in London.

It is expected that eventually each regional company will have between 10 and 20 outlets under its control. A regional company will take over control of the three Ucando Ltd outlets. Each outlet will have its own manager, and new ones have just been appointed to the three Ucando Ltd outlets.

The outlets' managers will be allowed to hire and fire whatever staff they need and the introduction of a head count budget is being considered by Head Office. Each outlet manager is responsible for his own sales policy, pricing, store layout, advertising, the general running of the outlet and the purchasing of goods for resale, subject to the recommendations below. Duit plc's policy is that all outlet managers have to apply to the regional board for all items of capital expenditure greater than £500, while the regional board can sanction up to £100 000 per capital expenditure project.

The outlets will vary in size of operations, and this will determine the number of trade sales representatives employed per outlet. There will be a minimum of one trade sales representative per outlet under the direction of the outlet manager. Each manager and representative will be entitled to a company car.

Outlet sales are made to both retail and trade on either cash or credit terms. Debtor and cash control is the responsibility of regional office. Cash received is banked locally, and immediately credited to the Head Office account. Credit sales invoices are raised by the outlet with a copy sent to regional office. Within each outlet it is possible to identify the sales origin, e.g. timber yard, saw mill, building supplies, kitchen furniture, etc.

Timber for resale is supplied to an outlet on request from stocks held at regional office or direct from the ports where Duit (Timber Importers) Ltd has further stocks. Duit Kitchens Ltd provides kitchen furniture that the outlets sell. Duit plc also has a small factory making windows, doors and frames which are sold through the outlets. When purchasing other products for resale, the outlet is requested to use suppliers with which Head Office has negotiated discount buying arrangements. All invoices for outlet purchases and overheads are passed by the respective outlet manager before being paid by regional office. In existing Duit outlets a perpetual inventory system is used, with a complete physical check once a year.

Information concerning last year's actual results for one of Ucando Ltd's outlets situated at Birport is given below:

Birport DIY outlet
Trading and profit and loss account for year to 31 March

	(£)	(£)
Sales (1)		1 543 000
Less Cost of sales		1 095 530
Prime gross margin (29%)		447 470
Less:		
Wages (2)	87 400	
Salaries (3)	45 000	
Depreciation:		
equipment (4)	9 100	
buildings	3 500	
vehicles (3 cars)	6 500	
Vehicle running expenses	6 170	
Leasing of delivery lorry	6 510	
Lorry running expenses	3 100	
Energy costs	9 350	
Telephone/stationery	9 180	
Travel and entertaining	3 490	
Commission on sales	7 770	
Bad debts written off	9 440	
Advertising	25 160	
Repairs	6 000	
Rates, insurance	13 420	
Sundry expenses	10 580	
Delivery expenses	7 400	269 070
Net profit		£178 400
(11.56%)		

Position at 31 March	
	(£)
Debtors	100 900
Stock	512 000

Notes:

(1) Sales can be identified by till code–cash/credit, trade/retail, timber, kitchen furniture, frames, heavy building supplies, light building supplies, sawmill etc.

(2) Workforce distributed as follows: timber yard (3), sawmill (1), sales (7), general duties (1), administration (3).

(3) Paid to sales representatives (2), assistant manager, manager.

(4) Equipment used in sales area, sawmill, yard.

Requirements:

a Describe a cost centre, a profit centre and an investment centre and discuss the problems of and benefits from using them for management accounting purposes. *(7 marks)*

b Suggest key performance indicators which can be used either individually or jointly by each member of the management team for the regional outlet network, i.e. those in the regional office, the outlets and their departments, in a responsibility reporting system for their evaluation purposes. *(6 marks)* c Justify the key performance indicators that you have suggested in (b) incorporating, where appropriate, reference to whether the individuals or entities are being treated as cost, profit or investment centres. *(6 marks)*

d Design a pro forma monthly report without figures which can be used by both the outlet manager for his management and control needs and by the regional board to evaluate the outlet. The report can include two or more sections if you wish. Provide a brief explanation for the format chosen. *(6 marks)*

Note: The manufacturing companies and the importing company report direct to the main board. *ICAEW Management Accounting*

IM22.6 Advanced: Financial and non-financial performance measures.
Scotia Health Consultants Ltd provides advice to clients in medical, dietary and fitness matters by offering consultation with specialist staff.

The budget information for the year ended 31 May is as follows:
(i) Quantitative data as per Appendix.
(ii) Clients are charged a fee per consultation at the rate of: medical £75; dietary £50 and fitness £50.
(iii) Health foods are recommended and provided only to dietary clients at an average cost to the company of £10 per consultation. Clients are charged for such health foods at cost plus 100 per cent mark-up.
(iv) Each customer enquiry incurs a variable cost of £3, whether or not it is converted into a consultation.
(v) Consultants are *each* paid a fixed annual salary as follows: medical £40 000; dietary £28 000; fitness £25 000.
(vi) Sundry other fixed cost: £300 000.

Actual results for the year to 31 May incorporate the following additional information:
(i) Quantitative data as per Appendix.
(ii) A reduction of 10 per cent in health food costs to the company per consultation was achieved through a rationalization of the range of foods made available.
(iii) Medical salary costs were altered through dispensing with the services of two full-time consultants and sub-contracting outside specialists as required. A total of 1900 consultations were sub-contracted to outside specialists who were paid £50 per consultation.
(iv) Fitness costs were increased by £80 000 through the hire of equipment to allow sophisticated cardio-vascular testing of clients.
(v) New computer software has been installed to provide detailed records and scheduling of all client enquiries and consultations. This software has an annual operating cost (including depreciation) of £50 000.

Required:
a Prepare a statement showing the financial results for the year to 31 May in tabular format. This should show:
(i) the budget and actual gross margin for each type of consultation and for the company
(ii) the actual net profit for the company
(iii) the budget and actual margin (£) per consultation for each type of consultation. (Expenditure for each expense heading should be shown in (i) and (ii) as relevant.) *(15 marks)*

b Suggest ways in which each of the undernoted performance measures (1 to 5) could be used to supplement the financial results calculated in (a). You should include relevant quantitative analysis from the Appendix below for each performance measure:
1. Competitiveness; 2 Flexibility; 3. Resource utilization;
4. Quality; 5. Innovation. *(20 marks)*

Appendix
Statistics relating to the year ended 31 May

	Budget	Actual
Total client enquiries:		
new business	50 000	80 000
repeat business	30 000	20 000
Number of client consultations:		
new business	15 000	20 000
repeat business	12 000	10 000
Mix of client consultations:		
medical	6 000	5 500
		(note 1)
dietary	12 000	10 000
fitness	9 000	14 500
Number of consultants employed:		
medical	6	4
		(note 1)
dietary	12	12
fitness	9	12
Number of client complaints:	270	600

Note 1: Client consultations *includes* those carried out by outside specialists. There are now four full-time consultants carrying out the remainder of client consultations.

ACCA Paper 9 Information for Control and Decision Making

PART SIX

The Application of Quantitative Methods to Management Accounting

In this Part we examine the application of quantitative methods to various aspects of management accounting. Chapter 23 examines the contribution of mathematical and statistical techniques in determining cost behaviour patterns for cost–volume–profit analysis and the planning and control of costs and revenues. Chapter 24 concentrates on the application of quantitative models to determine the optimum investment in inventories and Chapter 25 looks at the application of linear programming to decision-making and planning and control activities.

Rather than delaying the chapters on the application of quantitative techniques to management accounting until Part Six you may prefer to read Chapter 23 immediately after reading Chapter 8 on cost–volume–profit analysis. Chapter 24 is self-contained and may be assigned to follow any of the chapters in Part Four. Chapter 25 should be read only after you have studied Chapter 9.

Cost estimation and cost behaviour

23

Determining how cost will change with output or other measurable factors of activity is of vital importance for decision-making, planning and control. The preparation of budgets, the production of performance reports, the calculation of standard costs and the provision of relevant costs for pricing and other decisions all depend on reliable estimates of costs and distinguishing between fixed and variable costs, at different activity levels.

Unfortunately, costs are not easy to predict, since they behave differently under different circumstances. For example, direct labour can be classified as a variable cost where a company uses casual labour hired on a daily basis so that the employment of labour can be exactly matched to meet the production requirements. In contrast, direct labour may be classified as a step-fixed cost for activities where a fixed number of people are employed and this number is maintained even when there is a temporary reduction in the quantity of the activity used. Depreciation is often quoted as a non-variable cost (also known as a fixed cost), but it may well be variable if asset value declines in direct proportion to usage. Therefore we cannot generalize by categorizing direct labour as a variable cost and depreciation as a non-variable cost.

LEARNING OBJECTIVES

After studying this chapter, you should be able to:

● **identify and describe the different methods of estimating costs;**

● **calculate regression equations using the high–low, scattergraph and least-squares techniques;**

● **explain, calculate and interpret the coefficient of determination test of reliability;**

● **explain the meaning of the term correlation coefficient;**

● **identify and explain the six steps required to estimate cost functions from past data;**

● **describe the learning curve and compute the average and incremental labour hours for different output levels.**

Many costs are fairly easy to classify as purely variable (e.g. direct materials), fixed (e.g. rental of equipment), or step-fixed (e.g. labour costs) but others fall into a mixed-cost category (also known as semi-variable costs). In Chapter 2 it was pointed out that a semi-variable cost is a cost that has both a fixed and variable component. For example, the cost of maintenance is a semi-variable cost consisting of planned maintenance that is undertaken whatever the activity, and a variable element that is directly related to activity. Thus, it is the semi-variable costs that we need to separate into their fixed and variable categories.

Frequently the only information that is available for a semi-variable cost is the cost of the activity and a measure of activity usage. For example, records may only be available for the total cost of the maintenance activity for a given period and the number of maintenance hours used during that period. To separate the total cost into its fixed and variable elements it is necessary to use one of the techniques described in this chapter.

Whether a cost is fixed or variable with respect to a particular activity measure or cost driver is also affected by the length of the time span under consideration. The longer the time span the more likely the cost will be variable. For example, maintenance staff salaries are likely to be fixed in the short run and will thus remain unchanged when the volume of maintenance hours changes. However, in the long run, maintenance salaries are likely to vary with the maintenance time required. If maintenance activity expands, extra staff will be appointed but, if activity contracts, staff will be redeployed or made redundant. It is therefore important to specify the length of the time period under consideration when predicting costs for different activity levels.

The importance of accurately estimating costs and the complexity of cost behaviour means that accountants must use increasingly sophisticated techniques. Advances in information technology have made it possible for more sophisticated techniques to be used for estimating costs, even by small businesses. These development have led to an increasing awareness of the important potential of mathematical and statistical techniques for estimating costs, and it is the aim of this chapter to provide an understanding of these techniques.

Some non-mathematical techniques will also be explained so that you can assess the additional benefits that can be obtained from using the more sophisticated techniques. We shall then examine the effect of experience on cost, which is normally referred to as the learning curve. The emphasis in this chapter will be on manufacturing costs, and we shall consider various techniques for estimating how these costs change with activity; similar techniques, however, can be applied to non-manufacturing costs that change with activity.

A major objective of this chapter is to ascertain the activity measure or cost driver that exerts the major influence of the cost of a particular activity. A cost driver can be defined as any factor whose change causes a change in the total cost of an activity. Examples of cost drivers include direct labour hours, machine hours, units of output and number of production run set-ups. Throughout this chapter the terms cost-driver' and 'activity measure' will be used synonymously.

General principles applying to estimating cost functions

Before we consider the various methods that are appropriate for estimating costs, we need to look at some of the terms that will be used. A regression equation identifies an estimated relationship between a dependent variable (cost) and one or more independent variables (i.e. an activity measure or cost driver) *based on past observations*. When the equation includes only one independent variable, it is referred to as simple regression and it is possible in this situation to plot the regression equation on a graph as a regression line. When the equation includes two or more independent variables, it is referred to as multiple regression. If there is only one independent variable and the relationship is linear, the regression line can be described by the equation for a straight line:

$$y = a + bx$$

Assuming that we wish to express the relationship between the dependent variable (cost) and the independent variable (activity), then:

y = total cost for the period at an activity level of x

a = total non-variable (fixed) cost for the period

b = average variable cost per unit of activity

x = volume of activity levels or cost driver for the period

If non-variable (fixed) costs for a particular period are £5000, the average unit variable cost is £1, and direct labour hours represent the cost driver, then:

$$\text{total cost} = £5000 + [£1 \times \text{direct labour hours } (x)]$$

or

$$y = a + bx$$

so that

$$y = £5000 + £1x$$

The term cost function is also used to refer to a regression equation that describes the relationship between a dependent variable and one or more independent variables. Cost functions are normally estimated from past cost data and activity levels. Cost estimation begins with measuring *past* relationships between total costs and the potential drivers of those costs. The objective is to use past cost behaviour patterns as an aid to predicting future costs. Any expected changes of circumstances in the future will require past data to be adjusted in line with future expectations.

There is a danger that cost functions derived from past data may be due to a spurious correlation in the data which can end at any time without warning. High correlation is only likely to continue if the relationship between the variables is economically plausible. Cost functions should not be derived solely on the basis of past observed statistical relationships. The nature of the observed statistical relationship should make sense and be economically plausible. If these conditions do not exist one cannot be confident that the estimated relationship will be repeated when the cost function is used to predict outcomes using a different set of data.

Economic plausibility exists when knowledge of operations or logic implies that a cause-and-effect relationship may exist. For example, the number of component parts is a potential cost driver for material handling costs since the greater the number of parts the higher the material handling costs. Logic suggests that a potential cause-and-effect relationship exists.

Cost estimation methods

The following approaches to cost estimation will be examined:

1 engineering methods;
2 inspection of the accounts method;
3 graphical or scattergraph method;
4 high–low method;
5 least-squares method.

These approaches differ in terms of the costs of undertaking the analysis and the accuracy of the estimated cost functions. They are not mutually exclusive and different methods may be used for different cost categories.

Engineering methods

Engineering methods of analyzing cost behaviour are based on the use of engineering analyzes of technological relationships between inputs and outputs – for example methods study, work sampling and time and motion studies. The approach is appropriate when there is a physical relationship between costs and the cost driver. The procedure when undertaking an engineering study is to make an analysis based on *direct* observations of the underlying physical quantities required for an activity and then to convert the final results into cost estimates. Engineers, who are familiar with the technical requirements, estimate the quantities of materials and the labour and machine hours required for various operations; prices and rates are then applied to the physical measures to obtain the cost estimates. The engineering method is useful for estimating costs of repetitive processes where input–output relationships are clearly defined. For example, this method is usually satisfactory for estimating costs that are usually associated with direct materials, labour and machine time, because these items can be directly observed and measured. However, the engineering method is not a method that can be used for separating semi-variable costs into their fixed and variable elements.

The engineering method is not restricted to manufacturing activities – time and motion studies can also be applied to well-structured administrative and selling activities such as typing, invoicing and purchasing. It is not generally appropriate, however, for estimating costs that are difficult to associate directly with individual units of output, such as many types of overhead costs, since these items cannot easily be directly observed and measured.

Inspection of the accounts

The inspection of accounts method requires that the departmental manager and the accountant inspect each item of expenditure within the accounts for a particular period, and then classify each item of expense as a wholly fixed, wholly variable or a semi-variable cost. A single average *unit* cost figure is selected for the items that are categorized as variable, whereas a single *total* cost for the period is used for the items that are categorized as fixed. For semi-variable items the departmental manager and the accountant agree on a cost function that appears to best describe the cost behaviour. The process is illustrated in Example 23.1.

Note that repairs and maintenance have been classified as a semi-variable cost consisting of a variable element of £0.50 per unit of output plus £5000 non-variable cost. A check on the *total* cost calculation indicates that the estimate of a unit variable cost of £24.50 will give a total variable cost of £245 000 at an output level of 10 000 units. The non-variable costs of £50 000 are added to this to produce an estimated total cost of £295 000. The cost function is therefore $y = 50\,000 + £24.50x$. This cost function is then used for estimating total cost centre costs at other output levels.

You will see from this example that the analysis of costs into their variable and non-variable elements is very subjective. Also, the latest cost details that are available from the accounts will normally be used, and this may not be typical of either past or future cost behaviour. Whenever possible, cost estimates should be based on a series of observations. Cost estimates based on this method involve individual and often arbitrary judgements, and they may therefore lack the precision necessary when they are to be used in making decisions that involve large sums of money and that are sensitive to measurement errors.

Graphical or scattergraph method

This method involves plotting on a graph the total costs for each activity level. The total cost is represented on the vertical (Y axis) and the activity levels are recorded on the horizontal (X axis).

A straight line is fitted to the scatter of plotted points by visual approximation. Figure 23.1 illustrates the procedure using the data presented in Example 23.2.

You will see by referring to Figure 23.1 that the maintenance costs are plotted for each activity level, and a straight line is drawn through the middle of the data points as closely as possible so that the distances of observations above the line are equal to the distances of observations below the line.

The point where the straight line in Figure 23.1 cuts the vertical axis (i.e. £240) represents the non-variable costs, item a in the regression formula $y = a + bx$. The unit variable cost b in the regression formula is found by observing the differences between any two points on the straight line (see the dashed line in Figure 23.1 for observations of 160 and 240 hours) and completing the following calculations:

$$\frac{\text{difference in cost}}{\text{difference in activity}} = \frac{£720 - £560}{240 \text{ hours} - 160 \text{ hours}} = £2 \text{ per hour}$$

This calculation is based on a comparison of the changes in costs that can be observed on the straight line between activity levels of 160 and 240 hours. This gives a regression formula.

$$y = £240 + £2x$$

If x is assigned a value of 100 hours then

$$y = 240 + (2 \times 100) = £440$$

EXAMPLE 23.1

The following cost information has been obtained from the latest monthly accounts for an output level of 10 000 units for a cost centre.

	(£)
Direct materials	100 000
Direct labour	140 000
Indirect labour	30 000
Depreciation	15 000
Repairs and maintenance	10 000
	295 000

The departmental manager and the accountant examine each item of expense and analyze the expenses into their variable and non-variable elements. The analysis might be as follows:

	Unit variable cost (£)	Total non-variable cost (£)
Direct materials	10.00	
Direct labour	14.00	
Indirect labour		30 000
Depreciation		15 000
Repairs and maintenance	0.50	5 000
	24.50	50 000

The graphical method is simple to use, and it provides a useful visual indication of any lack of correlation or erratic behaviour of costs. However, the method suffers from the disadvantage that the determination of exactly where the straight line should fall is subjective, and different people will draw different lines with different slopes, giving different cost estimates. To overcome this difficulty, it is preferable to determine the line of best fit mathematically using the least-squares method.

High–low method

The high–low method consists of selecting the periods of highest and lowest activity levels and comparing the changes in costs that result from the two levels. This approach is illustrated in Example 23.3.

The non-variable (fixed) cost can be estimated at any level of activity (assuming a constant unit variable cost) by subtracting the variable cost portion from the total cost. At an activity level of 5000 units the total cost is £22 000 and the total variable cost is £10 000 (5000 units at

EXAMPLE 23.2

The total maintenance costs and the machine hours for the past ten four-weekly accounting periods were as follows:

Period	Machine hours x	Maintenance cost y
1	400	960
2	240	880
3	80	480
4	400	1200
5	320	800
6	240	640
7	160	560
8	480	1200
9	320	880
10	160	440

You are required to estimate the regression equation using the graphical method.

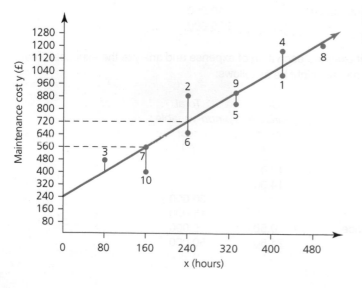

FIGURE 23.1
Graph of maintenance costs at different activity levels

£2 per unit). The balance of £12 000 is therefore assumed to represent the non-variable cost. The cost function is therefore:

$$y = £12\ 000 + £2x$$

The method is illustrated in Figure 23.2, with points A and B representing the lowest and highest output levels, and TC_1 and TC_2 representing the total cost for each of these levels. The other crosses represent past cost observations for other output levels. The straight (blue) line joining the observations for the lowest and highest activity levels represent the costs that would be estimated for each activity level when the high–low method is used.

You will see from this illustration that the method ignores all cost observations other than the observations for the lowest and highest activity levels. Unfortunately, cost observations at the extreme ranges of activity levels are not always typical of normal operating conditions, and therefore may reflect abnormal rather than normal cost relationships. Figure 23.2 indicates how the method can give inaccurate cost estimates when they are obtained by observing only the highest and lowest output levels. It would obviously be more appropriate to incorporate all of the available observations into the cost estimate, rather than to use only two extreme observations.

The lower straight (green) line, using the graphical or scattergraph approach described in the previous section, incorporates all of the observations. It is likely to provide a better estimate of the cost function than a method that relies on only two observations. The high–low method cannot therefore be recommended.

EXAMPLE 23.3

The monthly recordings for output and maintenance costs for the past 12 months have been examined and the following information has been extracted for the lowest and highest output levels:

	Volume of production (units)	Maintenance costs (£)
Lowest activity	5 000	22 000
Highest activity	10 000	32 000

The variable cost per unit is calculated as follows:

$$\frac{\text{difference in cost}}{\text{difference in activity}} = \frac{£10\ 000}{5000} = £2 \text{ variable cost per unit of output}$$

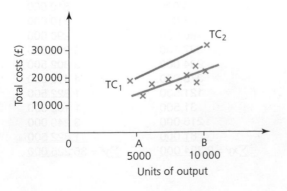

FIGURE 23.2
High–low method

The least-squares method

This method determines mathematically the regression line of best fit. It is based on the principle that the sum of the squares of the vertical deviations from the line that is established using the method is less than the sum of the squares of the vertical deviations from any other line that might be drawn. The regression equation for a straight line that meets this requirement can be found from the following two equations by solving for a and b:

$$a = \frac{\sum y}{n} - \frac{b\sum x}{n} \tag{23.1}$$

$$b = \frac{n\sum xy - \sum x \sum y}{n\sum x^2 - (\sum x)^2} \tag{23.2}$$

where n is the number of observations and $\sum$ represents the sum of the variables specified in the above formulae.

Exhibit 23.1 is used to illustrate the **least-squares method**. It is assumed that past information is available for total maintenance cost and machine hours used. We can now insert the data derived from Exhibit 23.1 into the above formulae but do note spreadsheet packages have regression routines that will perform these calculations. You should also note that examination questions generally provide you with formulae 23.1 and 23.2 and the associated values for the variables shown in Exhibit 23.1. Therefore it is most unlikely that you will be required to compute the values shown in Exhibit 23.1.

Applying the above formulae 23.1 and 23.2 we must first calculate the value of 'b' using formula 23.2:

$$b = \frac{12(2\ 394\ 000) - (1\ 260)(19\ 800)}{12(163\ 800) - (1\ 260)^2} = 3\ 780\ 000/378\ 000 = £10$$

$$a = \frac{19\ 800}{12} - \frac{(10)(1\ 260)}{12} = £600$$

EXHIBIT 23.1 Past observations of maintenance costs

Hours x	Maintenance cost y (£)	x^2	xy	y^2
90	1 500	8 100	135 000	2 250 000
150	1 950	22 500	292 500	3 802 500
60	900	3 600	54 000	810 000
30	900	900	27 000	810 000
180	2 700	32 400	486 000	7 290 000
150	2 250	22 500	337 500	5 062 500
120	1 950	14 400	234 000	3 802 500
180	2 100	32 400	378 000	4 410 000
90	1 350	8 100	121 500	1 822 500
30	1 050	900	31 500	1 102 500
120	1 800	14 400	216 000	3 240 000
60	1 350	3 600	81 000	1 822 500
$\sum x = 1260$	$\sum y = 19\ 800$	$\sum x^2 = 163\ 800$	$\sum xy = 2\ 394\ 000$	$\sum y^2 = 36\ 225\ 000$

We can now use the above cost function ($y = £600 + £10x$) to predict the cost incurred at different activity levels, including those for which we have no past observations. For example, at an activity level of 100 hours the cost prediction is £600 non-variable cost, plus £1000 variable cost (100 hours × £10). The regression line and the actual observations (represented by the dots) are recorded in Figure 23.3. The closer the vertical distances of the plotted actual observations are to the straight line the more reliable is the estimated cost function in predicting cost behaviour. In other words, the closer the observations are to the line the stronger the relationship between the independent variable (machine hours in our example) and the dependent variable (i.e. total maintenance cost).

Tests of reliability

In Exhibit 23.1 the cost function was derived using machine hours as the activity measure/cost driver. However a number of other potential cost drivers exist, such as direct labour hours, units of output and number of production runs. Various tests of reliability can be applied to see how reliable potential cost drivers are in predicting the dependent variable. The most simplistic approach is to plot the data for each potential cost driver and examine the distances from the straight line derived from a visual fit (using the graphical method) or the least squares regression equation. A more sophisticated approach is to compute the coefficient of variation (known as r^2). The coeffeicient of variation is the square of the correlation coefficient (known as r). It is a goodness of fit measure that indicates how well the predicted values of the dependent variable (i.e. the estimated cost observations represented by y), based on the chosen independent variable (i.e. machine hours (x) in our example shown in Exhibit 23.1), matches the actual cost observations (Y). In particular, the coefficient of variation measures the percentage variation in the dependent variable that is explained by the independent variable.

When you are required to calculate the coefficient of determination most examination questions provide you with the following formula for the correlation coefficient (r):

$$r = \frac{n\sum xy - \sum x \sum y}{\sqrt{(n\sum x^2 - (\sum x)^2)(n\sum y^2 - (\sum y)^2)}} \qquad (23.3)$$

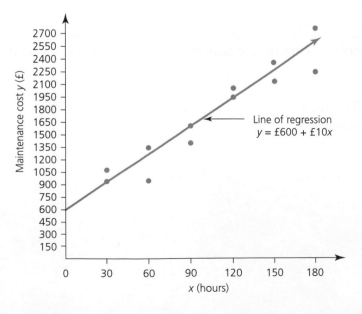

FIGURE 23.3

Regression line $y = 600 + 10x$ compared with actual observations

Applying the data derived from Exhibit 23.1 to formula 23.3:

$$R \text{ (correlation coefficient)} = \frac{12(2\ 394\ 000) - (1\ 260)(19\ 800)}{\sqrt{[12(163\ 800) - (1\ 260)^2][12 \times 36\ 225\ 000)(19\ 800)^2]}}$$

$$= \frac{3\ 780\ 000}{4\ 015\ 654} = 0.941$$

so that r^2 (the coefficient of determination) = $(0.941)^2 = 0.8861$

You should note that the values computed in Exhibit 23.1 are normally provided in examination questions. What does a coefficient of determination of 0.8861 mean? In percentage terms it means that 88.61 per cent of the variation in total cost is explained by variations in the activity base (cost driver) and the remaining 11.39 per cent is explained by either random variation, or random variation plus the combined effect that other omitted explanatory variables, have on the dependent variable (total cost). Therefore, the higher the coefficient of variation the stronger is the relationship between the independent and the dependent variable.

The correlation coefficient (r) represents the degree of association between two variables, such a cost and activity. If the degree of association between two variables is very close it will be almost possible to plot the observations on a straight line, and r and r^2 will be very near to 1. In this situation a very strong positive association exists between activity and costs, as illustrated in Figure 23.4. A positive correlation exists when an increase in one variable is associated with an increase in the other variable and a negative correlation exists when an increase in one variable is associated with a decrease in the other variable. Alternatively, the costs may be so randomly distributed that there is little or no correlation between costs and the activity base selected. Thus r and r^2 will be near to zero. An illustration of the situation where no correlation exists is shown in Figure 23.5.

Relevant range and non-linear cost functions

It may be very misleading to use a cost estimation equation (cost function) to estimate the total costs for ranges of activities outside the range of observations that were used to establish the cost function. This is because a cost function is normally only valid within the range of the actual observations that were used to establish the equation.

You will see from Figure 23.6 that in the past the company has operated only between activity levels x_1 and x_2 (this represents the actual observations). A cost equation developed from this information may provide satisfactory cost estimates for activity levels between x_1 and x_2, but it

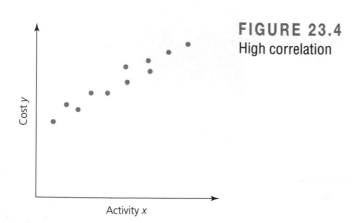

FIGURE 23.4
High correlation

Cost y

Activity x

may not do so for activity levels outside this range of observations. For example, the dashed line that meets the vertical axis at A might represent a cost equation that has been developed from these observations; the dashed line will represent a satisfactory estimate of total cost only between activity levels x_1 and x_2. However, any extrapolation of the dashed line outside the range of observations may result in an unsatisfactory estimate of total cost.

You will remember that in Chapter 8 it was stressed that linear cost functions may only apply over the relevant production range (i.e. between activity levels x_1, and x_2 in Figure 23.6), and that over a very wide range of activity a curvilinear (non-linear) relationship may exist, similar to the curved line BC in Figure 23.6. It therefore follows that the extrapolation of the dashed line represents an unsatisfactory estimate outside the relevant range if a curvilinear relationship exists.

In practice, the problem of extrapolation may not occur, since the majority of decisions are normally taken within the relevant operating range over which the firm has had experience of operating in the past. However, if decisions are to be based on cost information that is projected beyond the relevant range, the cost estimates must be used with care.

To determine whether a curvilinear relationship exists, the observations should be plotted on a graph, so that a simple examination of the graph may indicate whether or not such relationships exist. Indeed, it is a good idea always to prepare graphs and look carefully at the plotted data to ensure that some of the important requirements of cost estimation are not violated – blind reliance on mathematical techniques can be very dangerous.

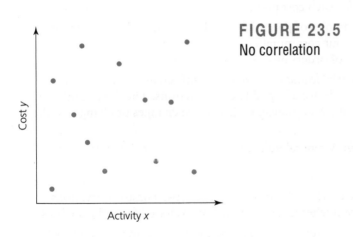

FIGURE 23.5
No correlation

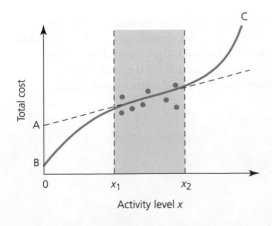

FIGURE 23.6
Effect of extrapolation costs

A summary of the steps involved in estimating cost functions

We can now summarize the stages involved in the estimation of a cost function based on the analysis of past data. They are:

1 Select the dependent variable y (the cost variable) to be predicted.
2 Select the potential cost drivers.
3 Collect data on the dependent variable and cost drivers.
4 Plot the observations on a graph.
5 Estimate the cost function.
6 Test the reliability of the cost function.

It may be necessary to undertake each of these stages several times for different potential cost drivers before an acceptable cost function can be identified.

1 *Select the dependent variable y*: The choice of the cost (or costs) to be predicted will depend upon the purpose of the cost function. If the purpose is to estimate the indirect costs of a production or activity cost centre then all indirect costs associated with the production (activity) centre that are considered to have the same cause-and-effect relationship with the potential costs drivers should be grouped together. For example, if some overheads are considered to be related to performing production set-ups and others are related to machine running hours then it may be necessary to establish two cost pools: one for set-up-related costs and another for machine-related costs. A separate cost function would be established for each cost pool.

2 *Select potential cost drivers*: Examples of potential cost drivers include direct labour hours, machine hours, direct labour cost, number of units of output, number of production run set-ups, number of orders processed and weight of materials.

3 *Collect data on the dependent variable and cost drivers*: A sufficient number of past observations must be obtained to derive acceptable cost functions. The data should be adjusted to reflect any changes of circumstance, such as price changes or changes in the type of equipment used.

4 *Plot the observations on a graph*: A general indication of the relationship between the dependent variable and the cost driver can be observed from the graph. The graph will provide a visual indication as to whether a linear cost function can approximate the cost behaviour and also highlight extreme or abnormal observations. These observations should be investigated to ascertain whether they should be excluded from the analysis.

5 *Estimate the cost function*: The cost function should be estimated using the approaches described in this chapter.

6 *Test the reliability of the cost function*: The reliability of the cost function should be tested. The cost function should be plausible. Cost functions should not be derived solely on the basis of observed past statistical relationships. Instead, they should be used to confirm or reject beliefs that have been developed from a study of the underlying process. The nature of the statistical relationship should be understood and make economic sense.

Cost estimation when the learning effect is present

ADVANCED READING

Difficulties occur in estimating costs when technological changes take place in the production process: past data is not then very useful for estimating costs. For example, changes in the efficiency of the labour force may render past information unsuitable for predicting future labour costs. A situation like this may occur when workers become more familiar with the tasks that they perform, so that less labour time is required for the production of each unit. The phenomenon has been observed in a number of manufacturing situations, and is known as the learning-curve effect. From the experience of aircraft production during World War II, aircraft manufacturers found that the rate of improvement was so regular that it could be reduced to a formula, and the labour hours required could be predicted with a high degree of accuracy from a learning curve. Based on this information, experiments have been undertaken in other industries with learning curves, and these experiments also indicate some regularity in the pattern of a worker's ability to learn a new task.

The first time a new operation is performed, both the workers and the operating procedures are untried. As the operation is repeated, the workers become more familiar with the work, labour efficiency increases and the labour cost per unit declines. This process continues for some time, and a regular rate of decline in cost per unit can be established at the outset. This rate of decline can then be used in predicting future labour costs. The learning process starts from the point when the first unit comes off the production line. From then on, each time cumulative production is doubled, the average time taken to produce each unit of cumulative production will be a certain percentage of the average time per unit of the previous cumulative production.

An application of the 80 per cent learning curve is presented in Exhibit 23.2, which shows the labour hours required on a sequence of six orders where the cumulative number of units is doubled for each order. The first unit was completed on the first order in 2000 hours; for each subsequent order the *cumulative production* was doubled (see column 3), so that the average hours per unit were 80 per cent of the average hours per unit of the previous *cumulative production*. For example, the *cumulative average time* shown in column 4 for each unit of output is calculated as follows:

order number 1 = 2000 hours
2 = 1600 hours (80% × 2000)
3 = 1280 hours (80% × 1600)
4 = 1024 hours (80% × 1280)
5 = 819 hours (80% × 1024)
6 = 655 hours (80% × 819)

EXHIBIT 23.2 Labour hours for 80 per cent learning curve

| (1) Order no. | Number of units | | Cumulative hours | | Hours for each order | |
	(2) Per order	(3) Cumulative production	(4) Per unit	(5) Total (3) × (4)	(6) Total	(7) Per unit (6) ÷ (2)
1	1	1	2000	2 000	2000	2000
2	1	2	1600	3 200	1200	1200
3	2	4	1280	5 120	1920	960
4	4	8	1024	8 192	3072	768
5	8	16	819	13 104	4912	614
6	16	32	655	20 960	7856	491

Exhibit 23.2 provides information for specific quantities only. No information is available for other quantities such as 10, 20 or 30 units, although such information could be obtained either graphically or mathematically.

Graphical method

The quantities for the average time per unit of cumulative production (column 4 of Exhibit 23.2) are presented in graphical form in Figure 23.7. The entries in column 4 are plotted on the graph for each level of cumulative production, and a line is drawn through these points. (You should note that more accurate graphs can be constructed if the observations are plotted on log-log graph paper.)

The graph shows that the average time per unit declines rapidly at first and then more slowly, until eventually the decline is so small that it can be ignored. When no further improvement is expected and the regular efficiency level is reached, the situation is referred to as the **steady-state production level**. The cumulative average hours per unit is 953 hours for 10 units and 762 hours for 20 units. To obtain the total number of hours, we merely multiply the average number of hours by the cumulative quantity produced, which gives 9530 total hours for 10 units and 15 240 total hours for 20 units.

Mathematical method

The learning curve can be expressed in equation form as:

$$Y_x = aX^b \tag{23.4}$$

where Y_x is defined as the average time per unit of cumulative production to produce X units, a is the time required to produce the first unit of output and X is the number of units of output under consideration. The exponent b is defined as the ratio of the logarithm of the learning curve improvement rate (e.g. 0.8 for an 80 per cent learning curve) divided by the logarithm of 2. The improvement exponent can take on any value between −1 and zero. For example, for an 80 per cent learning curve

$$b = \frac{\log 0.8}{\log 2} = \frac{-0.2231}{0.6931} = -0.322$$

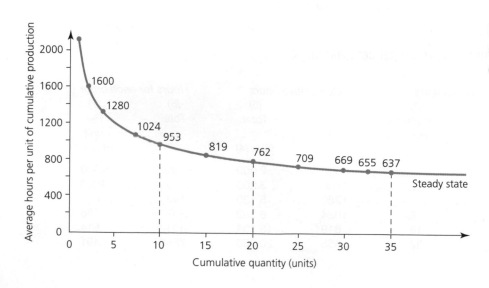

FIGURE 23.7
80 per cent learning curve

The average time taken per unit of cumulative production to produce 10 and 20 units can therefore be calculated as follows:

$$Y_{10} = 2000 \times 10^{-0.322}$$
$$= 2000 \times 0.476431$$
$$= \underline{953}$$

and

$$Y_{20} = 2000 \times 20^{-0.322}$$
$$= 2000 \times 0.381126$$
$$= \underline{762}$$

A computation of the exponent values may be made by using either logarithm tables or a calculator with exponent functions.

Estimating incremented hours and incremental cost

Incremental hours cannot be determined directly from the learning-curve graph or formula, since the results are expressed in terms of average hours per unit of cumulative production. It is possible, however, to obtain incremental hours by examining the differences between total hours for various combinations of cumulative hours. For example, assume that for Exhibit 23.2 the company has completed orders such that cumulative production is 4 units and that an enquiry has been received for an order of 6 units. We can calculate the incremental hours for these 6 units as follows:

Total hours if an additional 6 units are produced (10 × 953)	9530
(cumulative production will be 10 units)	
Total hours for the first 4 units (4 × 1280)	5120
Hours required for 6 units after completion of 4 units	= 4410

Note that the total hours are calculated by taking the average hours per unit of cumulative production and multiplying by the cumulative production. The incremental hours for 6 units are obtained by taking the difference between the total time required for 10 units and the time required for 4 units.

Let us assume that the company completes the order for the 6 units and then receives a new order for an additional 10 units. How many labour hours will be needed? The cumulative quantity is now 20 units (10 already completed plus 10 now on order). The estimated hours for the 10 new units are calculated as follows:

Total hours for first 20 units (20 × 762)	15 240
Total hours for first 10 units (10 × 953)	9 530
Hours required for 10 units after completion of 10 units	5 710

The learning curve can be used to estimate labour costs and those other costs which vary in direct proportion to labour costs. Note that the learning effect only applies to direct labour costs and those variable overheads that are a direct function of labour hours of input. It does not apply to material costs, non-variable costs or items that vary with output rather than input.

SUMMARY

The following items relate to the learning objectives listed at the beginning of the chapter.

● **Identify and describe the different methods of estimating costs.**

The following approaches can be used to estimate costs: (a) engineering methods; (b) inspection of accounts method; (c) graphical or scattergraph method; (d) high-low method; (e) least squares method; and (f) multiple regression analysis. With engineering studies a detailed study of each operation is undertaken under controlled conditions, based on high levels of efficiency, to ascertain the quantities of labour and materials required. Target prices are then applied based on efficient purchasing to ascertain the standard costs. The engineering method is most appropriate for estimating direct costs for repetitive processes where input–output relationships are clearly defined. The inspection of accounts method requires that a subjective estimate is made of the fixed and variable elements for each item of expenditure within the accounts for a particular period. The remaining four methods are described below.

● **Calculate regression equations using high–low, scattergraph and least-squares techniques.**

The high-low method consists of selecting the periods of highest and lowest activity levels and comparing the changes in costs that result from these two levels. The variable cost per unit is derived by dividing the difference in cost between the two levels by the differences in activity. Fixed costs are computed by deducting the derived variable cost from total cost at either the lowest or highest output level (see Example 23.3 for an illustration of the calculations). The scattergraph method involves plotting on a graph the total cost for each observed activity level. A straight line is drawn through the middle of the scatter of points so that the distances of observations below the line are equal to the distances above the line. The variable cost per unit is derived from the straight line by dividing the difference in cost by the difference in activity. The intercept gives the estimated fixed cost (see Example 23.2 and Figure 23.1 for an illustration of the computations). The least squares method determines mathematically the line of best fit. It is based on the principle that the sum of the squares of the vertical deviations from the line that is established using this method is less than the sum of the squares of the vertical deviations from any other line that might be drawn (see Exhibit 23.1 for an illustration of the computations). Because this method uses all of the observations and determines the line of best fit mathematically it is considered superior to the high–low or scattergraph methods.

● **Explain, calculate and interpret the coefficient of variation test of reliability.**

Various tests of reliability can be applied to ascertain how reliable potential independent variables (i.e. cost drivers) are in predicting the dependent variable (i.e. the actual cost observations). One such test is the coefficient of variation (r^2). It is a goodness of fit measure that indicates how well the predicted values of the dependent variable, based on the chosen independent variable, matches the actual cost observations. In particular, the coefficient of variation measures the percentage variation in the dependent variable that is explained by the independent variable. You should refer to Exhibit 23.1 and formula 23.3 for an illustration of the calculation of the coefficient of determination.

● **Explain the meaning of the term correlation coefficient.**

The correlation coefficient measures the degree of association between two variables. If the degree of association between the two variables is very close it will almost be possible to plot the relationship on a straight line and the correlation coefficient will be very close to 1. A positive correlation exists when an increase in one variable is associated with an increase in the other variable whereas a negative correlation exists when an increase/decrease in one variable is associated with a decrease/increase in the other variable. Alternatively, zero correlation exists where there is little or no association between two variables.

● **Identify and explain the six steps required to estimate cost functions from past data.**

The following six steps are required: (a) select the cost (dependent) variable to be predicted; (b) select potential cost drivers (i.e. the causes of costs); (c) collect data on the dependent variable and the selected cost driver; (d) plot the observations on a graph; (e) estimate the cost function; and (f) test the reliability of the cost function.

● **Describe the learning curve and compute the average and incremental labour hours for different output levels.**

If the labour content per unit is expected to decline, as workers become more familiar with a process, learning curve principles can be applied. Previous experience in some industries has found that the rate of improvement was so regular that it could be reduced to a formula, and that the labour hours required could be predicted with a high degree of accuracy from a learning curve. The learning curve is based on the principle that the learning process starts from the point when the first unit comes off the production line. From then on, each time cumulative production is doubled, the average time taken to produce each unit of cumulative production will be a certain percentage (often assumed to be 80 per cent) of the average time per unit of the previous cumulative

production. See Exhibit 23.2 for an illustration of the application of the learning curve.

● **Additional learning objective presented in Appendix 23.1.**

Appendix 23.1 includes an additional learning objective: to describe multiple regression analysis and indicate the circumstances when it should be used. The least-squares regression method described in the main body of the chapter assumes that total costs are determined by one variable only (i.e. activity). Multiple regression can be used when it is considered that total costs are determined by more than one variable. Thus, if a single activity measure is found to be unreliable, and other variables are considered to significantly influence total costs, multiple regression analysis should be used.

Appendix 23.1: Multiple regression analysis

ADVANCED READING

The least-squares regression equation was based on the assumption that total cost was determined by one activity-based variable only. However, other variables besides activity are likely to influence total cost. A certain cost may vary not only with changes in the hours of operation but also with the weight of the product being made, temperature changes or other factors. With simple least-squares regression, only one factor is taken into consideration; but with multiple regression, several factors are considered in combination. As far as possible, all the factors related to cost behaviour should be brought into the analysis so that costs can be predicted and controlled more effectively.

The equation for simple regression can be expanded to include more than one independent variable. If there are two independent variables and the relationship is assumed to be linear, the regression equation will be

$$y = a + b_1 x_1 + b_2 x_2$$

Item a represents the non-variable cost item. Item b_1 represents the average change in y resulting from a unit change in x_1, assuming that x_2 and all the unidentified items remain constant. Similarly, b_2 represents the average change in y resulting from a unit change in x_2 assuming that x_1 remains constant.

Multiple regression analysis is based on the assumption that the independent variables are not correlated with each other. When the independent variables are highly correlated with each other, it is very difficult, and sometimes impossible, to separate the effects of each of these variables on the dependent variable. This occurs when there is a simultaneous movement of two or more independent variables in the same direction and at approximately the same rate. This condition is called **multicollinearity**. Multicollinearity can be found in a variety of ways. One way is to measure the correlation between the independent variables. Generally, a coefficient of correlation between independent variables greater than 0.70 indicates multicollinearity.

Key terms and concepts

activity measure (p. 596)
coefficient of determination, r_2 (p. 604)
coefficient of variation (p. 603)
correlation coefficient, r (p. 603, p. 610)
cost driver (p. 596)
cost function (p. 597)

dependent variable (p. 597)
engineering methods (p. 598)
goodness-of-fit (p. 603)
high–low method (p. 600)
independent variable (p. 597)
inspection of accounts method (p. 598)
learning curve (p. 607)

learning-curve effect (p. 607)
least-squares method (p. 602)
multicollinearity (p. 611)
multiple regression (p. 596)
regression equation (p. 596)
simple regression (p. 596)
steady-state production level (p. 608)
tests of reliability (p. 603)

Recommended reading

This chapter has provided an introduction to the various cost estimation techniques. For a more detailed discussion of these

techniques you should refer to Chapter 4 of Scapens (1991) and Chapters 4 and 5 of Kaplan and Atkinson (1989).

Key examination points

In recent years emphasis has switched from calculation to interpretation. Do make sure you can interpret regression equations and explain the meaning of the various statistical tests of reliability. Different formulae can be used to calculate regression equations and r^2 but the formulae specified in the chapter should be given. The examiner will have set the question assuming you will use the formula. Do not worry if you are unfamiliar with the

formula. All that is necessary is for you to enter the figures given in the question into it.

Remember with learning curves that only labour costs and variable overheads that vary with labour costs are subject to the learning effect. A common requirement is for you to calculate the incremental hours per order. Make sure that you understand columns 6 and 7 of Exhibit 23.2.

ASSESSMENT MATERIAL

The review questions are short questions that enable you to assess your understanding of the main topics included in the chapter. The numbers in parentheses provide you with the page numbers to refer to if you cannot answer a specific question.

The review problems are more complex and require you to relate and apply the content to various business problems. The problems are graded by their level of difficulty. Solutions to review problems that are not preceded by the term 'IM' are provided in a separate section at the end of the book. Solutions to problems preceded by the term 'IM' are provided in the *Instructor's Manual* accompanying this book and also on the lecturer's password protected section of the website www.drury-online.com. Additional review problems with fully worked solutions are provided in the *Student's Manual* that accompanies this book.

The website also includes over 30 case study problems. A list of these cases is provided on pages 665–7. The Beta Company is a case study that is relevant to the content of this chapter.

Review questions

23.1 Explain what is meant by the term 'cost function'. *(p. 597)*
23.2 Under what circumstances can the engineering method be used to estimate costs. *(p. 598)*
23.3 Describe the high–low method. *(pp. 600–01)*
23.4 What is the major limitation of the high–low method? *(p. 601)*
23.5 Describe how the scattergraph method is used to analyze costs into their fixed and variable elements. *(pp. 598–600)*
23.6 Describe the least-squares method. Why is this method better than the high–low and scattergraph methods? *(pp. 602–03)*
23.7 When is multiple regression required to explain cost behaviour? *(p. 611)*
23.8 Describe the steps that should be followed in estimating cost functions. *(p. 606)*
23.9 Why is a scattergraph a useful first step in estimating cost functions? *(p. 606)*
23.10 Describe what is meant by the learning curve effect. *(p. 607)*
23.11 Define the steady-state production level. *(p. 608)*
23.12 Describe what is meant by 'goodness of fit'. *(p. 603)*
23.13 Explain the meaning of coefficient of variation. *(p. 603)*

Review problems

23.14 Basic. A hospital's records show that the cost of carrying out health checks in the last five accounting periods have been as follows:

Period	Number of patients seen	Total cost $
1	650	17 125
2	940	17 800
3	1260	18 650
4	990	17 980
5	1150	18 360

Using the high–low method and ignoring inflation, the estimated cost of carrying out health checks on 850 patients in period 6 is

a $17 515.
b $17 570.
c $17 625.
d $17 680.   *CIMA – Management Accounting Fundamentals*

23.15 Basic. M plc uses time series analysis and regression techniques to estimate future sales demand. Using these techniques, it has derived the following trend equation:

$$y = 10\,000 + 4200x$$
where y is the total sales units; and
x is the time period

It has also derived the following seasonal variation index values for each of the quarters using the multiplicative (proportional) seasonal variation model:

Quarter	Index value
1	120
2	80
3	95
4	105

The total sales units that will be forecast for time period 33, which is the first quarter of year 9, are

a   138 720
b   148 720
c   176 320
d   178 320
    CIMA Management Accounting – Performance Management

23.16 Basic. Brisbane Limited has recorded the following sales information for the past six months:

Month	Advertising expenditure £000	Sales revenue £000
1	1.5	30
2	2	27
3	1.75	25
4	3	40
5	2.5	32
6	2.75	38

The following has also been calculated:

Σ(Advertising expenditure) = £13 500
Σ(Sales revenue) = £192 000
Σ(Advertising expenditure × Sales revenue) = £447 250 000
Σ(Sales revenue²) = £6 322 000 000
Σ(Advertising expenditure²) = £32 125 000

What is the value of b, i.e. the gradient of the regression line (see formulae 23.1 and 23.2)?

a   0.070
b   0.086
c   8.714
d   14.286   *ACCA – Financial Information for Management*

23.17 Advanced: Cost estimation using linear regression. Albatross Plc, the Australian subsidiary of a British packaging company, is preparing its budget for the year to 30 June 2001. In respect of fuel oil consumption, it is desired to estimate an equation of the form $y = a + bx$, where y is the total expense at an activity level x, a is the fixed expense and b is the rate of variable cost.

The following data relates to the year ending 30 June 2000:

Month	Machine hours (£000)	Fuel oil expense (£000)	Month	Machine hours (£000)	Fuel oil expense (£000)
July	34	640	January	26	500
August	30	620	February	26	500
September	34	620	March	31	530
October	39	590	April	35	550
November	42	500	May	43	580
December	32	530	June	48	680

The annual total and monthly average figures for the year ending 30 June 2000 were as follows:

	Machine hours (000)	Fuel oil expense ($)
Annual total	420	6840
Monthly average	35	570

You are required to:

a estimate fixed and variable elements of fuel oil expense from the above data by both the following methods:
 (i) high and low points (4 marks)
 (ii) least-squares regression analysis (8 marks)
b compare briefly the methods used in (a) above in relation to the task of estimating fixed and variable elements of a semi-variable cost; (7 marks)
c accepting that the coefficient of determination arising from the data given in the question is approximately 0.25, interpret the significance of this fact. (6 marks)

ICAEW Management Accounting

23.18 Intermediate. PT has discovered that when it employs a new test engineer there is a learning curve with a 75 per cent rate of learning that exists for the first 12 customer assignments. A new test engineer completed her first customer assignment in six hours.

Calculate the time that she should take for her 7th assignment to the nearest 0.1 hours.

Note: The index for a 75 per cent learning curve is –0.415.

(2 marks)

CIMA P2 Management Accounting: Decision Management

23.19 Intermediate. FH is an electronics company that has developed a new product for the video conferencing market. The product has successfully completed its testing phase and FH has now produced the first four production units. The first unit took three hours of labour time and the total time for the first four units was 8.3667 hours.

Calculate the learning curve improvement rate (rate of learning) to the nearest 0.1 per cent.

(3 marks)

CIMA P2 Management Accounting: Decision Management

23.20 Advanced: Learning curves. Velo Racers has designed a radically new concept in racing bikes with the intention of selling them to professional racing teams. The estimated cost and selling price of the first bike to be manufactured and assembled is as follows:

	£
Materials	1000
Assembly Labour (50 hours at £10 per hour)	500
Fixed Overheads (200 per cent of Assembly labour)	1000
Profit (20 per cent of total cost)	500
Selling Price	3000

Velo Racers plans to sell all bikes at total cost plus 20 per cent and the material cost per bike will remain constant irrespective of the number sold.

Velo Racers' management expects the assembly time to gradually improve with experience and has estimated an 80 per cent learning curbe.

A racing team has approached the company and asked for the following quotations:

1. If we were to purchase the first bike assembled, and immediately put in an order for the second, what would be the price of the second bike?
2. If we waited until you had sold two bikes to another team, and then ordered the third and fourth bikes to be assembled, what would be the average price of the third and fourth bikes?

3. If we decided to immediately equip our entire team with the new bike, what would be the price per bike if we placed an order for the first eight to be assembled?

Required:

a Explain Learning Curve Theory and in particular the concept of cumulative average time. (4 marks)
b Provide detailed price quotations for each of the three enquiries outlined above. (6 marks)
c Identify the major areas within management accounting where learning curve theory is likely to have consequences and suggest potential limitations of this theory. (10 marks)

ACCA P3 Performance Management

23.21 Advanced: Calculation of learning rate and contract completion using the learning curve. Maxmarine plc builds boats. Earlier this year the company accepted an order for 15 specialized 'Crest' boats at a fixed price of £100 000 each. The contract allows four months for building and delivery of all the boats and stipulates a penalty of £10 000 for each boat delivery late.

The boats are built using purchased components and internally manufactured parts, all of which are readily available. However, there is only a small team of specialized technicians and boatyard space is limited, so that only one boat can be built at a time. Four boats have now been completed and as Maxmarine plc has no previous experience of this particular boat the building times have been carefully monitored as follows:

Boat number	Completion time (days)
1	10.0
2	8.1
3	7.4
4	7.1

Maxmarine plc has 23 normal working days in every month and the first four boats were completed with normal working.

Management is now concerned about completing the contract on time.

The management accountant's estimate of direct costs per boat, excluding labour costs, is as follows:

	(£000)
Purchased components	40
Manufactured parts	15
Other direct expenses	5
	60

Direct labour costs are £2500 per day for the normal 23 working days per month. Additional weekend working days at double the normal pay rates can be arranged up to a maximum of seven days per month (making 30 possible working days per month in total).

Overheads will be allocated to the contract at a rate of £3000 per normal working day and no overheads will be allocated for overtime working.

Requirements:

a Using the completion time information provided, calculate the learning rate showing full workings. (6 marks)
b Discuss the limitations of the learning curve in this type of application. (6 marks)
c Calculate whether it would be preferable for Maxmarine plc to continue normal working or to avoid penalties by working weekends. Support your calculations with any reservations or explanations you consider appropriate. (13 marks)

ICAEW Management Accounting

23.22 Advanced. The theory of the experience curve is that an organization may increase its profitability through obtaining greater familiarity with supplying its products or services to customers. This reflects the view that profitability is solely a function of market share.

Requirement:
Discuss the extent to which the application of experience curve theory can help an organization to prolong the life cycle of its products or services.

(20 marks)

CIMA Stage 4 Strategic Management Accounting and Marketing

IM23.1 Intermediate. Discuss the conditions that should apply if linear regression analysis is to be used to analyze cost behaviour.

(6 marks)

ACCA Level 2 Management Accounting

IM23.2 Intermediate.

a Briefly discuss the problems that occur in constructing cost estimation equations for estimating costs at different output levels.

(7 marks)

b Describe four different cost estimation methods and for each method discuss the limitations and circumstances in which you would recommend their use.

(18 marks)

IM23.3 Intermediate. Explain the 'learning curve' and discuss its relevance to setting standards.

(5 marks)

ACCA Level 2 Management Accounting

IM23.4 Advanced.

a Comment on factors likely to affect the accuracy of the analysis of costs into fixed and variable components.

(8 marks)

b Explain how the analysis of costs into fixed and variable components is of use in planning, control and decision-making techniques used by the management accountant.

(9 marks)

ACCA Level 2 Management Accounting

IM23.5 Advanced: Comparison of independent variables for cost estimates. Abourne Ltd manufactures a microcomputer for the home use market. The management accountant is considering using regression analysis in the annual estimate of total costs. The following information has been produced for the 12 months ended 31 December:

Month	Total cost Y (£)	Output, X_1 (numbers)	Number of employees, X_2 (numbers)	Direct labour hours, X_3 (hours)
1	38 200	300	28	4 480
2	40 480	320	30	4 700
3	41 400	350	30	4 800
4	51 000	500	32	5 120
5	52 980	530	32	5 150
6	60 380	640	35	5 700
7	70 440	790	41	7 210
8	32 720	250	41	3 200
9	75 800	820	41	7 300
10	71 920	780	39	7 200
11	68 380	750	38	6 400
12	33 500	270	33	3 960
	$\Sigma Y =$ 637 200	$\Sigma X_1 =$ 6 300	$\Sigma X_2 =$ 420	$\Sigma X_3 =$ 65 220

Additionally:

$\Sigma Y^2 = 36\ 614.05 \times 10^6$
$\Sigma X_1^2 = 3.8582 \times 10^6$
$\Sigma X_2^2 = 14\ 954$
$\Sigma X_3^2 = 374.423 \times 10^6$
$\Sigma X_1 Y = 373.537\ 4 \times 10^6$
$\Sigma X_2 Y = 22.812\ 84 \times 10^6$
$\Sigma X_3 Y = 3692.277\ 4 \times 10^6$

The management accountant wants to select the best independent variable $(X_1, X_2$ or $X_3)$ to help in future forecasts of total production costs using an ordinary least-squares regression equation. He is also considering the alternatives of using the Hi-Lo and multiple regression equations as the basis for future forecasts.

You are required to:

a Identify which one of the three independent variables $(X_1, X_2$ or $X_3)$ given above is likely to be the least good estimator of total costs (Y). Give your reasons, but do not submit any calculations.

(3 marks)

b Compute separately, for the remaining two independent variables, the values of the two parameters α and β for each regression line. Calculate the coefficient of determination (R^2) for each relationship.

(6 marks)

c State, with reasons, which one of these independent variables should be used to estimate total costs in the future given the results of (b) above.

(3 marks)

d Devise the two equations which could be used, using the Hi-Lo technique, instead of the two regression lines computed in (b) above and comment on the differences found between the two sets of equations.

(5 marks)

e Comment critically on the use of Hi-Lo and ordinary least-squares regression as forecasting and estimating aids using the above results as a basis for discussion. In addition, comment on the advantages and problems of using multiple regression for forecasting and estimating; and state whether, in your opinion, the management accountant should consider using it in the present circumstances.

(8 marks)

Note: The following formulae can be used to answer the above question.

$$\beta = \frac{\Sigma xy - n\bar{x}\bar{y}}{\Sigma x^2 - n\bar{x}^2}$$

$$\alpha = \bar{y} - \beta\bar{x}$$

$$R^2 = \frac{\alpha\Sigma y + \beta\Sigma xy - n\bar{y}^2}{\Sigma y^2 - n\bar{y}^2}$$

$$Se = \sqrt{\frac{\Sigma y^2 - \alpha\Sigma y - \beta\Sigma xy}{n-2}}$$

$$s\beta = \frac{Se}{\sqrt{\Sigma x^2 - nx^2}}$$

ICAEW P2 Management Accounting

IM23.6 Advanced: Calculation of co-efficient of determination. A management accountant is analyzing data relating to retail sales on behalf of marketing colleagues. The marketing staff believe that the most important influence upon sales is local advertising undertaken by the retail store. The company also advertises by using regional television areas. The company owns more than 100 retail outlets, and the data below relate to a sample of 10 representative outlets.

Outlet number	Monthly sales (£000)	Local advertising by the retail store (£000 per month)	Regional advertising by the company (£000 per month)
	y	x_1	x_2
1	220	6	4
2	230	8	6
3	240	12	10
4	340	12	16
5	420	2	18
6	460	8	20
7	520	16	26
8	600	15	30
9	720	14	36
10	800	20	46

The data have been partly analyzed and the intermediate results are available below.

Σy	= 4550	Σy_2	= 2 451 300	$\Sigma x_2 y$	= 58 040
Σx_1	= 113	Σx_1^2	= 1 533	$\Sigma x_1 y$	= 121 100
Σx_2	= 212	Σx_2^2	= 6 120	$\Sigma x_1 x_2$	= 2 780

You are required to examine closely, using co-efficients of determination, the assertion that the level of sales varies more with movements in the level of local advertising than with changes in the level of regional company advertising.

(8 marks)

Note that the co-efficient of determination for y and x_1 may be calculated from

$$r^2 = \frac{n\Sigma x_1 y - \Sigma x_1 \Sigma y}{\left(n\Sigma x_1^2 - (\Sigma x_1)^2\right) \times \left(n\Sigma y^2 - (\Sigma y)^2\right)}$$

CIMA Stage 3 Management Accounting Techniques

IM23.7 Advanced: Estimates of sales volume and revenues using regression analysis and calculation of optimum price using differential calculus. The Crispy Biscuit Company (CBC) has developed a new variety of biscuit which it has successfully test marketed in different parts of the country. It has, therefore, decided to go ahead with full-scale production and is in the process of commissioning a production line located in a hitherto unutilized part of the main factory building. The new line will be capable of producing up to 50 000 packets of new biscuit each week.

The factory accountant has produced the following schedule of the expected unit costs of production at various levels of output:

	Production level (packets per week)				
	(10 000)	(20 000)	(30 000)	(40 000)	(50 000)
Unit costs (pence)					
Labour (1)	20.0	15.0	13.3	12.5	12.0
Materials	8.0	8.0	8.0	8.0	8.0
Machine costs (2)	8.0	5.0	4.0	3.5	3.2
Total direct costs	36.0	28.0	25.3	24.0	23.2
Factory overhead (3)	9.0	7.0	6.3	6.0	5.8
Total costs	45.0	35.0	31.6	30.0	29.0

(1) The labour costs represent the cost of the additional labour that would require to be taken on to operate the new line.
(2) Machine costs include running costs, maintenance costs and depreciation.
(3) Factory overhead costs are fixed for the factory overall but are allocated to cost centres at 25 per cent of total direct costs.

In addition to establishing product acceptability, the test marketing programme also examined the likely consumer response to various selling prices. It concluded that the weekly revenue likely to be generated at various prices was as follows:

Retail price	Revenue to CBC
£0.62	£15 190
£0.68	£14 960
£0.78	£11 310
£0.84	£10 500
£0.90	£10 350
£0.98	£4 900

The above prices represent the prices at which the product was test marketed, but any price between £0.60 and £0.99 is a possibility. The manufacturer receives 50 per cent of the retail revenue.

Requirements
a Estimate the variable costs of producing the new biscuit, using any simple method (such as the high–low method). *(3 marks)*
b Using linear regression, estimate the relationship between the price charged by CBC and the expected demand. *(6 marks)*
c Using the above estimates, calculate the optimum price and evaluate how sensitive your solution is to changes in this price. *(8 marks)*
d Outline the practical problems faced in attempting to derive a unit cost for a new product. *(8 marks)*

ICAEW P2 Management Accounting

The question provided the following formula for answering this question:

$$b = \frac{\sum(x-\bar{x})(y-\bar{y})}{\sum(x-\bar{x})^2} \text{ or } \frac{n\sum xy - \sum x \sum y}{n\sum x^2 - (\sum x)^2}$$

$$\text{and } a = \bar{y} - b\bar{x}$$

IM23.8 Advanced: Learning curves. Present a table of production times showing the following columns for E. Condon Ltd, which produces up to 16 units while experiencing a 90 per cent learning curve, the first unit requiring 1000 hours of production time:
(1) units produced,
(2) total production time (hours),
(3) average production time per unit in each successive lot (hours),
(4) cumulative average production time per unit (hours), and
(5) percentage decline in (4). *(10 marks)*

ICAEW Management Accounting

IM23.9 Advanced: The application of the learning curve to determine target cash flows. Leano plc is investigating the financial viability of a new product X. Product X is a short life product for which a market has been identified at an agreed design specification. It is not yet clear whether the market life of the product will be six months or 12 months.

The following estimated information is available in respect of product X:
(i) Sales should be 10 000 units per month in batches of 100 units on a just-in-time production basis. An average selling price of £1200 per batch of 100 units is expected for a six month life cycle and £1050 per batch of 100 units for a 12 month life cycle.
(ii) An 80 per cent learning curve will apply in months 1 to 7 (inclusive), after which a steady state production time requirement will apply, with labour time per batch stabilising at that of the final batch in month 7. Reductions in the labour requirement will be achieved through natural labour turnover. The labour requirement for the first batch in month 1 will be 500 hours at £5 per hour.
(iii) Variable overhead is estimated at £2 per labour hour.
(iv) Direct material input will be £500 per batch of product X for the first 200 batches. The next 200 batches are expected to cost 90 per cent of the initial batch cost. All batches thereafter will cost 90 per cent of the batch cost for each of the second 200 batches.
(v) Product X will incur directly attributable fixed costs of £15 000 per month.
(vi) The initial investment for the new product will be £75 000 with no residual value irrespective of the life of the product.

A target cash inflow required over the life of the product must be sufficient to provide for:
(a) the initial investment plus 33⅓ per cent thereof for a six month life cycle, or
(b) the initial investment plus 50 per cent thereof for a 12 month life cycle.

Note: learning curve formula:

$$y = ax^b$$

where
y = average cost per batch
a = cost of initial batch
x = total number of batches
b = learning factor (=−0.3219 for 80 per cent learning rate)

Required:
a Prepare detailed calculations to show whether product X will provide the target cash inflow over six months and/or 12 months. *(17 marks)*
b Calculate the initial batch labour hours at which the cash inflow achieved will be exactly equal to the target figure where a six month life cycle applies. It has been determined that the maximum labour and variable overhead cost at which the target return will be achieved is £259 000. All other variables remain as in part (a). *(6 marks)*
c Prepare a report to management which:
(i) explains why the product X proposal is an example of a target costing/pricing situation; *(3 marks)*
(ii) suggests specific actions which may be considered to improve the return on investment where a six month product cycle is forecast; *(6 marks)*
(iii) comments on possible factors which could reduce the rate of return and which must, therefore, be avoided. *(3 marks)*

ACCA Paper 9 Information for Control and Decision Making

IM23.10 Advanced: Application of learning curve to determine the incremental costs for different production batches. Limitation plc commenced the manufacture and sale of a new product in the fourth quarter of 2000. In order to facilitate the budgeting process for quarters 1 and 2 of 2001, the following information has been collected:
(i) Forecast production/sales (batches of product):

quarter 4,	2000	30 batches
quarter 1,	2001	45 batches
quarter 2,	2001	45 batches

(ii) It is estimated that direct labour is subject to a learning curve effect of 90 per cent. The labour cost of batch 1 of quarter 4, 2000 was £600 (at £5 per hour). The labour output rates from the commencement of production of the product, after adjusting for learning effects, are as follows:

Total produced (batches)	Overall average time per batch (hours)
15	79.51
30	71.56
45	67.28
60	64.40
75	62.25
90	60.55
105	59.15
120	57.96

Labour hours worked and paid for will be adjusted to eliminate spare capacity during each quarter. All time will be paid for at £5 per hour.

(iii) Direct material is used at the rate of 200 units per batch of product for the first 20 batches of quarter 4, 2000. Units of material used per batch will fall by 2 per cent of the original level for each 20 batches thereafter as the learning curve effect improves the efficiency with which the material is used. All material will be bought at £1.80 per unit during 2001. Delivery of the total material requirement for a quarter will be made on day one of the quarter. Stock will be held in storage capacity hired at a cost of £0.30 per quarter per unit held in stock. Material will be used at an even rate throughout each quarter.

(iv) Variable overhead is estimated at 150 per cent of direct labour cost during 2001.

(v) All units produced will be sold in the quarter of production at £1200 per batch.

Required:

a   Calculate the labour hours requirement for the second batch and the sum of the labour hours for the third and fourth batches produced in quarter 4, 2000.   (3 marks)

b   Prepare a budget for each of quarters 1 and 2, 2001 showing the contribution earned from the product. Show all relevant workings.   (14 marks)

c   The supplier of the raw material has offered to deliver on a 'just-in-time' basis in return for a price increase to £1.90 per unit in quarter 1, 2001 and £2 per unit thereafter.

   (i) Use information for quarters 1 and 2, 2001 to determine whether the offer should be accepted on financial grounds.

   (ii) Comment on other factors which should be considered before a final decision is reached.   (8 marks)

d   Limitation plc wish to prepare a quotation for 12 batches of the product to be produced at the start of quarter 3, 2001.

   Explain how the learning curve formula $y=ax^b$ may be used in the calculation of the labour cost of the quotation. Your answer should identify each of the variables y, a, x and b. No calculations are required.   (5 marks)

ACCA Level 2 Cost and Management Accounting II

Quantitative models for the planning and control of stocks

24

Investment in stocks represents a major asset of most industrial and commercial organizations, and it is essential that stocks be managed efficiently so that such investments do not become unnecessarily large. A firm should determine its optimum level of investment in stocks – and, to do this, two conflicting requirements must be met. First, it must ensure that stocks are sufficient to meet the requirements of production and sales; and, secondly, it must avoid holding surplus stocks that are unnecessary and that increase the risk of obsolescence. The optimal stock level lies somewhere between these two extremes. Our objective in this chapter is to examine the application of quantitative models for determining the optimum investment in stocks, and describe the alternative methods of scheduling material requirements. We shall also consider the economic order quantity and the level at which stocks should be replenished. We shall concentrate here on manufacturing firms, but the same basic analysis can also be applied to merchandising companies and non-profit organizations.

LEARNING OBJECTIVES

After studying this chapter, you should be able to:

- justify which costs are relevant and should be included in the calculation of the economic order quantity (EOQ);

- calculate the EOQ using the formula and tabulation methods;

- determine whether or not a company should purchase larger quantities in order to take advantage of quantity discounts;

- calculate the optimal safety stock when demand is uncertain;

- describe the ABC classification method;

- describe materials requirement planning (MRP) systems;

- explain just-in-time purchasing.

Why do firms hold stocks?

There are three general reasons for holding stocks; the transactions motive, the precautionary motive and the speculative motive. The transactions motive occurs whenever there is a need to hold stocks to meet production and sales requirements, and it is not possible to meet these requirements instantaneously. A firm might also decide to hold additional amounts of stocks to cover the possibility that it may have underestimated its future production and sales requirements or the supply of raw materials may be unreliable because of uncertain events affecting the supply of materials. This represents a precautionary motive, which applies only when future demand is uncertain.

When it is expected that future input prices may change, a firm might maintain higher or lower stock levels to *speculate* on the expected increase or decrease in future prices. In general, quantitative models do not take into account the speculative motive. Nevertheless, management should be aware that optimum stock levels do depend to a certain extent on expected price movements. For example, if prices of input factors are expected to rise significantly, a firm should consider increasing its stocks to take advantage of a lower purchase price. However, this decision should be based on a comparison of future cost savings with the increased costs due to holding additional stocks.

Where a firm is able to predict the demand for its inputs and outputs with perfect certainty and where it knows with certainty that the prices of inputs will remain constant for some reasonable length of time, it will have to consider only the transactions motive for holding stocks. To simplify the introduction to the use of models for determining the optimum investment in stocks, we shall begin by considering some quantitative models which incorporate only the transactions motive for holding stocks.

Relevant costs for quantitative models under conditions of certainty

The relevant costs that should be considered when determining optimal stock levels consist of holding costs and ordering costs. Holding costs usually consist of the following:

1 opportunity cost of investment in stocks;
2 incremental insurance costs;
3 incremental warehouse and storage costs;
4 incremental material handling costs;
5 cost of obsolescence and deterioration of stocks.

The relevant holding costs for use in quantitative models should include only those items that will vary with the levels of stocks. Costs that will not be affected by changes in stock levels are not relevant costs. For example, in the case of warehousing and storage only those costs should be included that will vary with changes in the number of units ordered. Salaries of storekeepers, depreciation of equipment and fixed rental of equipment and buildings are often irrelevant because they are unaffected by changes in stock levels.

To the extent that funds are invested in stocks, there is an opportunity cost of holding them. This opportunity cost is reflected by the required return that is lost from investing in stocks rather than some alternative investment. The opportunity cost should be applied only to those costs that vary with the number of units purchased. The relevant holding costs for other items such as material handling, obsolescence and deterioration are difficult to estimate, but we shall see that these costs are unlikely to be critical to the investment decision. Normally, holding costs are expressed as a percentage rate per pound of average investment.

Ordering costs usually consist of the clerical costs of preparing a purchase order, receiving deliveries and paying invoices. Ordering costs that are common to all stock decisions are not relevant, and only the incremental costs of placing an order are used in formulating the quantitative models.

The costs of acquiring stocks through buying or manufacturing are not a relevant cost to be included in the quantitative models, since the acquisition costs remain unchanged, irrespective of the order size or stock levels, unless quantity discounts are available. (We shall discuss the effect of quantity discounts later in this chapter.) For example, it does not matter in terms of acquisition cost whether total annual requirements of 1000 units at £10 each are purchased in one 1000-unit batch, ten 100-unit batches or one hundred 10-unit batches; the acquisition cost of £10 000 will remain unchanged. The acquisition cost is not therefore a relevant cost, but the ordering and holding costs will change in relation to the order size, and these will be relevant for decision-making models.

Determining the economic order quantity

If we assume certainty, the optimum order will be determined by those costs that are affected by either the quantity of stocks held or the number of orders placed. If more units are ordered at one time, fewer orders will be required per year. This will mean a reduction in the ordering costs. However, when fewer orders are placed, larger average stocks must be maintained, which leads to an increase in holding costs. The problem is therefore one of trading off the costs of carrying large stocks against the costs of placing more orders. The optimum order size is the order quantity that will result in the total amount of the ordering and holding costs being minimized. This optimum order size is known as the economic order quantity (EOQ); it can be determined by tabulating the total costs for various order quantities, by a graphical presentation or by using a formula. All three methods are illustrated using the information given in Example 24.1.

Tabulation method

It is apparent from Example 24.1 that a company can choose to purchase small batches (e.g. 100 units) at frequent intervals or large batches (e.g. 10 000 units) at infrequent intervals. The annual relevant costs for various order quantities are set out in Exhibit 24.1.

You will see that the economic order quantity is 400 units. At this point the total annual relevant costs are at a minimum.

Graphical method

The information tabulated in Exhibit 24.1 is presented in graphical form in Figure 24.1 for every order size up to 800 units. The vertical axis represents the relevant annual costs for the

EXAMPLE 24.1

A company purchases a raw material from an outside supplier at a cost of £9 per unit. The total annual demand for this product is 40 000 units, and the following additional information is available.

	(£)	(£)
Required annual return on investment in stocks (10% × £9)	0.90	
Other holding costs per unit	0.10	
Holding costs per unit		1.00
Cost per purchase order:		
Clerical costs, stationery, postage, telephone etc.		2.00
You are required to determine the optimal order quantity.		

investment in stocks, and the horizontal axis can be used to represent either the various order quantities or the average stock levels; two scales are actually shown on the horizontal axis so that both items can be incorporated. You will see from the graph that as the average stock level or the order quantity increases, the holding cost also increases. Alternatively, the ordering costs decline as stock levels and order quantities are increased. The total cost line represents the summation of both the holding and the ordering costs.

Note that the total cost line is at a minimum for an order quantity of 400 units and occurs at the point where the ordering cost and holding cost curves intersect. That is, the economic order quantity is found at the point where the holding costs equal the ordering costs. It is also interesting to note from the graph (see also Exhibit 24.1) that the total relevant costs are not particularly sensitive to changes in the order quantity. For example, if you refer to Exhibit 24.1 you will see that a 25 per cent change in the order quantity from 400 units to either 300 or 500 units leads to an increase in annual costs from £400 to £410 or £416, an increase of 2.5 per cent or 4 per cent. Alternatively, an increase of 50 per cent in the order quantity from 400 units to 600 units leads to an increase in annual costs from £400 to £434 or 8.5 per cent.

EXHIBIT 24.1 Relevant costs for various order quantities

Order quantity	100	200	300	400	500	600	800	10 000
Average stock in units[a]	50	100	150	200	250	300	400	5 000
Number of purchase orders[b]	400	200	133	100	80	67	50	4
Annual holding costs[c]	£50	£100	£150	£200	£250	£300	£400	£5 000
Annual ordering cost	£800	£400	£266	£200	£160	£134	£100	£8
Total relevant cost	£850	£500	£416	£400	£410	£434	£500	£5 008

[a] If there are no stocks when the order is received and the units received are used at a constant rate, the average stock will be one-half of the quantity ordered. Even if a minimum safety stock is held, the average stock relevant to the decision will still be one-half of the quantity order, because the minimum stock will remain unchanged for each alternative order quantity.
[b] The number of purchase orders is ascertained by dividing the total annual demand of 40 000 units by the order quantity.
[c] The annual holding cost is ascertained by multiplying the average stock by the holding cost of £1 per unit.

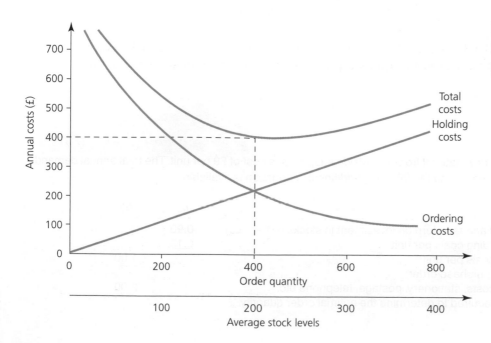

FIGURE 24.1
Economic order quantity graph

Formula method

The economic order quantity can be found by applying a formula that incorporates the basic relationships between holding and ordering costs and order quantities. These relationships can be stated as follows: the number of orders for a period is the total demand for that item of stock for the period (denoted by D) divided by the quantity ordered in units (denoted by Q). The total ordering cost is obtained by multiplying the number of orders for a period by the ordering cost per order (denoted by O), and is given by the formula:

$$\frac{\text{total demand for period}}{\text{quantity ordered}} \times \text{ordering cost per order} = \frac{DO}{Q}$$

Assuming that holding costs are constant per unit, the total holding cost for a period will be equal to the average stock for the period, which is represented by the quantity ordered divided by two ($Q/2$), multiplied by the holding cost per unit (denoted by H); it is therefore given by:

$$\frac{\text{quantity ordered}}{2} \times \text{holding cost per unit} = \frac{QH}{2}$$

The total relevant cost (TC) for any order quantity can now be expressed as

$$TC = \frac{DO}{Q} + \frac{QH}{2}$$

We can determine a minimum for this total cost function by differentiating the above formula with respect to Q and setting the derivative equal to zero.[1] We then get the economic order quantity Q:

$$Q = \sqrt{\left(\frac{2\,DO}{H}\right)}$$

or

$$Q = \sqrt{\left(\frac{2 \times \text{total demand for period} \times \text{cost per order}}{\text{holding cost per unit}}\right)}$$

If we apply this formula to Example 24.1, we have

$$Q = \sqrt{\left(\frac{2 \times 40\,000 \times 2}{1}\right)} = 400 \text{ units}$$

Assumptions of the EOQ formula

The calculations obtained by using the EOQ model should be interpreted with care, since the model is based on a number of important assumptions. One of these is that the holding cost per unit will be constant. While this assumption might be correct for items such as the funds invested in stocks, other costs might increase on a step basis as stock levels increase. For example, additional storekeepers might be hired as stock levels reach certain levels. Alternatively, if stocks decline, it may be that casual stores labour may be released once stocks fall to a certain critical level.

Another assumption that we made in calculating the total holding cost is that the average balance in stock was equal to one-half of the order quantity. If a constant amount of stock is not used per day, this assumption will be violated; there is a distinct possibility that seasonal and cyclical factors will produce an uneven usage over time. Despite the fact that much of the data used in the model represents approximations, calculation of the EOQ is still likely to be useful. If you examine Figure 24.1, you will see that the total cost curve tends to flatten out, so that total cost may not be significantly affected if some of the underlying assumptions are violated or if there are minor variations in the cost predictions. For example, assume that the cost per order in Example 24.1 was predicted to be £4 instead of the correct cost of, say, £2. The cost of this error would be as follows:

$$\text{revised EOQ} = \sqrt{\left(\frac{2\,DO}{H}\right)} = \sqrt{\left(\frac{2 \times 40\,000 \times 4}{1}\right)} = 565$$

TC for revised EOQ but using the correct ordering cost $= \dfrac{DO}{Q} + \dfrac{QH}{2}$

$$= \frac{40\,000 \times 2}{565} + \frac{565 \times 1}{2} = £425$$

TC for original EOQ of 400 units based on actual ordering cost

$$= \frac{40\,000 \times 2}{400} + \frac{400 \times 1}{2} = £400$$

$$\therefore \text{cost of prediction error} = £25$$

The cost of the prediction error of £25 represents an error of 6 per cent from the optimal financial result. Similarly, if the holding cost was predicted to be £2 instead of the correct cost of £1, the calculations set out above could be repeated to show a cost of prediction error of approximately 6 per cent.

Application of the EOQ model in determining the optimum lot size for a production run

The economic order quantity formula can be adapted to determine the optimum length of the production runs when a set-up cost is incurred only once for each batch produced. Set-up costs include incremental labour, material, machine down-time, and other ancillary costs of setting up facilities for production. The objective is to find the optimum number of units that should be manufactured in each production run, and this involves balancing set-up costs against stock holding costs. To apply the EOQ formula to a production run problem, we merely substitute set-up costs for the production runs in place of the purchase ordering costs.

To illustrate the formula let us assume that the annual sales demand D for a product is 9000 units. Labour and other expenditure in making adjustments in preparation for a production run require a set-up cost S of £90. The holding cost is £2 per unit per year. The EOQ model can be used for determining how many units should be scheduled for each production run to secure the lowest annual cost. The EOQ formula is modified to reflect the circumstances: the symbol O (ordering costs) is replaced by the symbol S (set-up cost). Using the formula:

$$Q = \sqrt{\left(\frac{2\,DS}{H}\right)} = \sqrt{\left(\frac{2 \times 9000 \times 90}{2}\right)} = 900$$

With an annual demand of 9000 units and an optimum production run of 900 units, 10 production runs will be required throughout the year. If we assume there are 250 working days throughout the course of the year, this will mean that production runs are undertaken at 25-day intervals. If demand is uniform throughout the year, 36 units will be demanded per working day (i.e. 9000 units annual demand divided by 250 working days). To determine the point when the production run should be started, we need to ascertain the number of days required for a production run. Let us assume it is five. So during this period, 180 units (five days at 36 units per day) will be demanded before any of the production run is available to meet demand. If we assume that no safety stock is required, we can establish that a production run should be started when the stock level reaches 180 units. This situation should occur 25 days after the start of the previous production run. The process is illustrated in Figure 24.2.

Quantity discounts

Circumstances frequently occur where firms are able to obtain quantity discounts for large purchase orders. Because the price paid per unit will not be the same for different order sizes, this must be taken into account when the economic order quantity is determined. However, the basic EOQ formula can still be used as a starting point for determining the optimum quantity to order. Buying in larger consignments to take advantage of quantity discounts will lead to the following savings:

1 A saving in purchase price, which consists of the total amount of discount for the period.
2 A reduction in the total ordering cost because fewer orders are placed to take advantage of the discounts.

These cost savings must, however, be balanced against the increased holding cost arising from higher stock levels when larger quantities are purchased. To determine whether or not a discount is worthwhile, the benefits must be compared with the additional holding costs. Consider the information presented in Example 24.2.

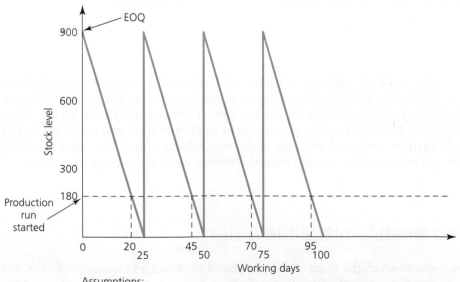

FIGURE 24.2
EOQ model and length of production run

Assumptions:
EOQ = 900 units; length of production run = 5 days;
point where production run started = 180 units;
usage per day = 36 units; length of production run = 5 days.
Production run started on days 20, 45, 70, 95 etc.

EXAMPLE 24.2

A company purchases a raw material from an outside supplier at a cost of £7 per unit. The total annual demand for this product is 9000 units. The holding cost is £4 per unit and the ordering cost is £5 per order. A quantity discount of 3 per cent of the purchase price is available for orders in excess of 1000 units. Should the company order in batches of 1000 units and take advantage of quantity discounts?

The starting point is to calculate the economic order quantity and then to decide whether the benefits exceed the costs if the company moves from the EOQ point and purchases larger quantities to obtain the discounts. The procedure is as follows:

$$\text{EOQ} = \sqrt{\left(\frac{2 \times 9000 \times 5}{4}\right)} = 150 \text{ units}$$

The savings available to the firm if it purchases in batches of 1000 units instead of batches of 150 units are as follows:

	(£)
1 Saving in purchase price	1890
(3% of annual purchase cost of £63 000)	
2 Saving in ordering cost	
$\dfrac{DO}{Q_d} - \dfrac{DO}{Q} = \dfrac{9000 \times 5}{1000} - \dfrac{9000 \times 5}{150}$	255
(Q_d represents the quantity order to obtain the discount and Q represents EOQ)	
Total savings	2145

The additional holding cost if the larger quantity is purchased is calculated as

$$\frac{(Q_d - Q)H}{2} = \frac{(1000 - 150) \times £4}{2} = £1700$$

The additional savings of £2145 exceed the additional costs, and the firm should adopt the order quantity of 1000 units. If larger discounts are available, for example by purchasing in batches of 2000 units, a similar analysis should be applied that compares the savings from purchasing in batches of 2000 units against purchasing in batches of 1000 units. The amount of the savings should then be compared with the additional holding costs. Note that the EOQ formula serves as a starting point for comparing the savings against the costs of a change in order size.

Determining when to place the order

To determine the point at which the order should be placed to obtain additional stocks (i.e. the re-order point), we must ascertain the time that will elapse between placing the order and the actual delivery of the stocks. This time period is referred to as the lead time. In a world of certainty the re-order point will be the number of days/weeks lead time multiplied by the daily/weekly usage during the period. For materials, components and supplies the re-order point is the point in time when the purchase requisition is initiated and the order is sent to the supplier. For the finished goods stock of a manufacturer the re-order point is the level of finished goods stock at which the production order should be issued.

If we assume that an annual usage of a raw material is 6000 units and the weekly usage is constant then if there are 50 working weeks in a year, the weekly usage will be 120 units. If the lead time is two weeks, the order should be placed when stocks fall to 240 units. The economic order quantity can indicate how frequently the stocks should be purchased. For example, if the EOQ is 600 then, with an annual demand of 6000 units, ten orders will be placed every five weeks. However, with a lead time of two weeks, the firm will place an order three weeks after the first delivery when the stock will have fallen to 240 units (600 units EOQ less three weeks usage at 120 units per week). The order will then be repeated at five-weekly intervals. The EOQ model can therefore under certain circumstances be used to indicate when to replenish stocks and the amount to replenish. This process is illustrated in Figure 24.3(a).

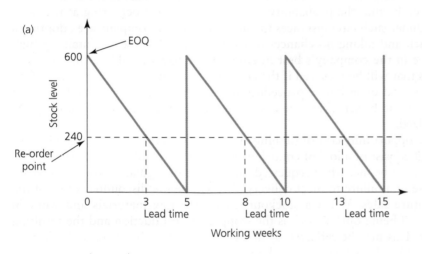

FIGURE 24.3
Behaviour of stocks under conditions of certainty and uncertainty: (a) demand known with certainty: (b) demand not known with certainty and role of safety stocks

Assumptions:
EOQ = 600 units; lead time = 2 weeks; usage per week = 120 units;
Re-order point 240 units; order placed at end of weeks 3, 8, 13 etc.

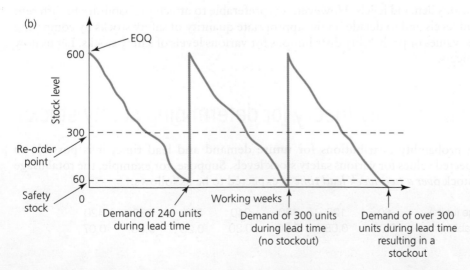

Uncertainty and safety stocks

ADVANCED READING

In practice, demand or usage of stocks is not known with certainty. In addition, there is usually a degree of uncertainty associated with the placement of an order and delivery of the stocks. To protect itself from conditions of uncertainty, a firm will maintain a level of safety stocks for raw materials, work in progress and finished goods stocks. Thus safety stocks are the amount of stocks that are carried in excess of the expected use during the lead time to provide a cushion against running out of stocks because of fluctuations in demand. For example, a firm that sets its re-order point on the assumption that the average lead time will be two weeks with an average weekly usage of 120 units will re-order when stocks fall to 240 units. However, the firm will run out of stock if actual demand increases to 140 units per week or if the lead time is three weeks. A firm might respond to this possibility by setting a re-order point of 420 units based on a *maximum usage* of 140 units per week and a lead time of three weeks. This will consist of a re-order point based on *expected usage* and lead time of 240 units (two weeks at 120 units) plus the balance of 180 units *safety stocks* to cover the possibility that lead time and expected usage will be greater than expected. Thus when demand and lead time are uncertain the re-order point is computed by adding the safety stock to the average usage during the average lead time.

In this illustration the safety stock was calculated on the basis of maximum demand and delivery time. It may well be that the probability of both these events occurring at the same time is extremely low. Under such circumstances the managers of the company are adopting a very risk-averse approach and taking no chances of running out of stock. Maintaining high safety stocks may not be in the company's best interests if the cost of holding the excessive stocks exceeds the costs that will be incurred if the company runs out of stock. It is therefore desirable to establish a sound quantitative procedure for determining an acceptable level of safety stocks. The level should be set where the cost of a stockout plus the cost of holding the safety stocks are minimized.

Stockout costs are the opportunity cost of running out of stock. In the case of finished goods the opportunity cost will consist of a loss of contribution if customers take their business elsewhere because orders cannot be met when requested. In the case of regular customers who are permanently lost because of a failure to meet delivery, this will be the discounted value of the lost contribution on future sales. When a stockout occurs for raw materials and work in progress stocks, the cost of being out of stock is the stoppage in production and the resulting inefficiencies that occur. This may be reflected by an estimate of the labour costs of idle time assuming that sales are *not* lost because of the stockout. Clearly, stockout costs are very difficult to estimate.

Once the stockout costs have been estimated, the costs of holding safety stocks should be compared for various demand levels. However, it is preferable to attach probabilities to different potential demand levels and to decide on the appropriate quantity of safety stocks by comparing the expected cost values or probability distributions for various levels of safety stocks. Let us now illustrate this process.

The use of probability theory for determining safety stocks

By constructing probability distributions for future demand and lead time, it is possible to calculate the expected values for various safety stock levels. Suppose, for example, the total usage for an item for stock *over a two-week lead time* is expected to be as follows:

Usage (units)	60	120	180	240	300	360	420
Probability	0.07	0.08	0.20	0.30	0.20	0.08	0.07

The average usage during the two week lead time is 240 units, and it is assumed that the lead time is known with certainty. If the firm carries no safety stock, the re-order point will be set at 240 units (i.e. average usage during the lead time), and there will be no stockouts if actual usage is 240 units or less. However, if usage during the lead time period proves to be 300 units instead of 240 there will be a stockout of 60 units, and the probability of this occurring is 0.20. Alternatively, if usage is 360 or 420 units, there will be stockouts of 120 units and 180 units respectively with associated probabilities of 0.08 and 0.07. By maintaining a safety stock of 180 units (420 units – 240 units), the firm ensures that a stockout will *not* occur.

Assuming we estimate stockout costs of £5 per unit and a holding cost of £1 per unit for the period, we can calculate the expected stockout cost, holding cost and total cost for various levels of safety stock. This information is presented in Exhibit 24.2. Note that if the re-order point is set at 360 units a stockout will only occur if usage is 420 units. Alternatively, if the re-order point is set at 300 units there will be a stockout of 60 units if usage is 360 units (probability = 0.08) and 120 units if usage is 420 units (probability = 0.07).

You will see that a safety stock of 60 units represents the level at which total expected costs are at their lowest. Hence a re-order point of 300 units will be set, consisting of the average usage during the lead time of 240 units plus a safety stock of 60 units.

A re-order point of 300 units with an uncertain demand is illustrated in Figure 24.3(b) for demands of 240, 300 and over 300 units during the lead time period. Note that the declines in stock levels do not fall on a straight line when demand is uncertain. If the probability distributions for each two-weekly period are expected to remain unchanged throughout the year, this safety stock (60 units) should be maintained.

However, if demand is expected to vary throughout the year, the calculations presented in Exhibit 24.2 must be repeated for the probability distributions for each period in which the probability distribution changes. The safety stock should then be adjusted prior to the commencement of each period.

Because of the difficulty in estimating the cost of a stockout, some firms might prefer not to use quantitative methods to determine the level of safety stocks. Instead, they might specify a maximum probability of running out of stock. If the firm in our illustration does not wish the probability of a stockout to exceed 10 per cent, it will maintain a safety stock of 120 units and a re-order point of 360 units. A stockout will then occur only if demand is in excess of 360 units; the probability of such an occurrence is 7 per cent.

EXHIBIT 24.2 Expected costs for various safety stocks

Average usage (units)	Safety stock (units)	Re-order point (units)	Stockout (units)	Stockout cost (£5 per unit)	Probability	Expected stockout cost (£)	Holding cost[a] (£)	Total expected cost (£)
240	180	420	0	0	0	0	180	180
240	120	360	60	300	0.07	21	120	141
240	60	300	120	600	0.07	42		
			60	300	0.08	24		
						66	60	126
240	0	240	180	900	0.07	63		
			120	600	0.08	48		
			60	300	0.20	60		
						171	0	171

[a]To simplify the analysis, it is assumed that a safety stock is maintained throughout the period. The average safety stock will therefore be equal to the total of the safety stock.

Control of stock through classification

In large firms it is quite possible for tens of thousands of different items to be stored. It is clearly impossible to apply the techniques outlined in this chapter to all of these. It is therefore essential that stocks be classified into categories of importance so that a firm can apply the most elaborate procedures of controlling stocks only to the most important items. The commonest procedure is known as the ABC classification method. This is illustrated in Exhibit 24.3.

The ABC method requires that an estimate be made of the total purchase cost for each item of stock for the period. The sales forecast is the basis used for estimating the quantities of each item of stock to be purchased during the period. Each item is then grouped in decreasing order of annual purchase cost. The top 10 per cent of items in stock in terms of annual purchase cost are categorized as A items, the next 20 per cent as B items and the final 70 per cent as C items. If we assume there are 10 000 stock items then the top 1000 items in terms of annual purchase costs will be classified as A items, and so on. In practice, it will be unnecessary to estimate the value of many of the 7000 C items, since their annual purchase cost will be so small it will be obvious that they will fall into the C category.

You will see from Exhibit 24.3 that 10 per cent of all stock items (i.e. the A items) represents 73 per cent of the total cost; 20 per cent of the items (B items) represent 19 per cent of the total cost; and 70 per cent of the items (C items) represent 8 per cent of the total cost. It follows that the greatest degree of control should be exerted over the A items, which account for the high investment costs, and it is the A category items that are most appropriate for the application of the quantitative techniques discussed in this chapter. For these items an attempt should be made to maintain low safety stocks consistent with avoiding high stockout costs. Larger orders and safety stocks are likely to be a feature of the C-category items. Normally, re-order points for these items will be determined on a subjective basis rather than using quantitative methods, the objective being to minimize the expense in controlling these items. The control of B-category

EXHIBIT 24.3 ABC Classification of stocks

Stage 1. For each item in stock multiply the estimated usage for a period by the estimated unit price to obtain the total purchase cost:

Item	Estimated usage	Unit price (£)	Total purchase cost (£)
1	60 000	1.00	60 000
2	20 000	0.05	1 000
3	1 000	0.10	100
4	10 000	0.02	200
5	100 000	0.01	1 000
6	80 000	2.00	160 000

(This list is continued until all items in stock are included.)

Stage 2. Group all the above items in descending order of purchase price and then divide into class A (top 10 per cent), class B (next 20 per cent) and then class C (bottom 70 per cent). The analysis might be as follows:

	Number of items in stock		Total cost	
	No	%	Amount (£)	%
Class A	1 000	10	730 000	73
Class B	2 000	20	190 000	19
Class C	7 000	70	80 000	8
	10 000	100	1 000 000	100

items is likely to be based on quantitative methods, but they are unlikely to be as sophisticated as for the A-category items.

The percentage value of total cost for the A, B and C categories in Exhibit 24.3 is typical of most manufacturing companies. In practice, it is normal for between 10 per cent and 15 per cent of the items in stock to account for between 70 per cent and 80 per cent of the total value of purchases. At the other extreme, between 70 per cent and 80 per cent of the items in stock account for approximately 10 per cent of the total value. The control of stock levels is eased considerably if it is concentrated on that small proportion of stock items that account for most of the total cost.

Other factors influencing the choice of order quantity

Shortage of future supplies

For various reasons, a firm may depart from quantitative models that provide estimates of the economic order quantity and the re-order point. A company may not always be able to rely on future supplies being available if the major suppliers are in danger of experiencing a strike. Alternatively, future supplies may be restricted because of import problems or transportation difficulties. In anticipation of such circumstances a firm may over-order so that stocks on hand will be sufficient to meet production while future supplies are restricted.

Future price increases

When a supplier announces a price increase that will be effective at some future date, it may be in a firm's interest to buy in excess of its immediate requirements before the increase becomes effective. Indeed, in times of rapid inflation firms might have an incentive to maintain larger stocks than would otherwise be necessary.

Obsolescence

Certain types of stocks are subject to obsolescence. For example, a change in technology may make a particular component worthless. Alternatively, a change in fashion may cause a clothes retailer to sell stocks at considerably reduced prices. Where the probability of obsolescence is high or goods are of a perishable nature, frequent purchases of small quantities and the maintenance of low stocks may be appropriate, even when the EOQ formula may suggest purchasing larger quantities and maintaining higher stock levels.

Steps to reduce safety stocks

When demand is uncertain, higher safety stocks are likely to be maintained. However, safety stocks may be reduced if the purchasing department can find new suppliers who will promise quicker and more reliable delivery. Alternatively, pressure may be placed on existing suppliers for faster delivery. The lower the average delivery time, the lower will be the safety stock that a firm needs to hold, and the total investment in stocks will be reduced.

Materials requirement planning

The discussion so far in this chapter has assumed that the replenishment of stocks and the determination of re-order points and order quantities (i.e. the EOQ) for each item of material occurs independently of other items. However, in complex manufacturing environments the demand for material purchases is dependent on the volume of the planned output of components and sub-components which include the raw materials that must be purchased. Materials requirement planning (MRP) originated in the early 1960s as a computerized approach for coordinating the planning of materials acquisition and production. The major feature of MRP is that it first involves an estimation of the quantity and timing of finished goods demanded and then uses this to determine the requirements for components/sub-components at each of the prior stages of production. This provides the basis for determining the quantity and timing of purchased materials and any bought-in components.

Figure 24.4 provides an overview of the approach. You can see that the top-level items represent three finished goods items (FG1, FG2 and FG3). The MRP system determines the requirements for each product into its components (or sub-components) and these are further separated into second, third and so on levels of sub-components, until at the lowest level of the hierarchy only purchased items (i.e. direct materials, DM) exist. For both FG1 and FG2 purchased raw materials are used to produce components before production of the end finished product. You should also note that in Figure 24.4 both FG1 and FG2 require the same sub-component (SC1), which in turn require the same direct materials (DM1).

The operation of an MRP system involves the following:

1 A *master production schedule*: This schedule is the starting point for MRP. It specifies both the timing, and quantity demanded of each of the top-level finished goods items.

2 A *bill of materials file*, which specifies the components/sub-components and materials required for each finished product.

3 A *master parts file* containing planned lead times of all items to be purchased and internally produced components.

4 An *inventory file* for each item of material and component/sub-component containing details of the current balance available, scheduled orders and items allocated to production but not yet drawn from stocks.

The aim of MRP is to generate a planned coordinated schedule of materials requirements for a specified time period for each item of material after taking into account scheduled receipts, projected target stock levels and items already allocated to production but not yet drawn from stocks. The EOQ model can be used within MRP systems to determine economic quantity sizes to be purchased provided that the major assumption of the EOQ model of constant demand broadly applies.

Finally, you should note that after its introduction in the 1960s, materials requirement planning was later extended to the management of all manufacturing resources. In particular, it focuses on machine capacity planning and labour scheduling as well as materials requirement

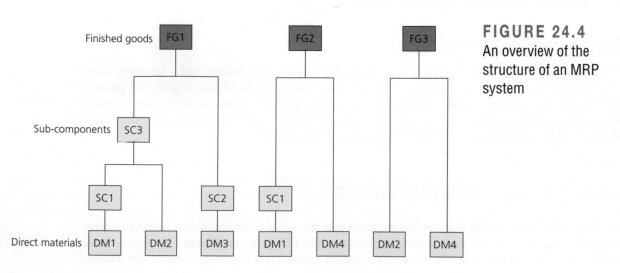

FIGURE 24.4
An overview of the structure of an MRP system

planning. This extended system is known as manufacturing resource planning or MRP II. The term MRP I is used to describe materials requirement planning.

Just-in-time purchasing arrangements

In Chapter 21 the JIT manufacturing philosophy was described. It was pointed out that the goals of JIT included eliminating non-value added activities (such as some of the activities related to purchasing), a batch size of one, and zero inventories. To achieve these goals, JIT firms have extended the JIT philosophy to the purchasing function and the management of materials requirements.

JIT purchasing techniques seek to ensure that the delivery of materials immediately precedes their use. By arranging with suppliers for more frequent deliveries, stocks can be cut to a minimum. JIT purchasing also normally requires suppliers to inspect materials before their delivery and guarantee their quality. This can result in considerable savings in material handling expenses. This improved service is obtained by giving more business to fewer suppliers and placing long-term purchase orders. Therefore the supplier has an assurance of long-term sales, and can plan to meet this demand. For JIT purchasing to be successful close cooperation with suppliers, including providing them with planned production schedules, is essential. Thus, a major feature of JIT purchasing is that suppliers are not selected on the basis of price alone. Performance in terms of the quality of the components and materials supplied, the ability to always deliver as needed and a commitment to JIT purchasing are also of vital importance.

Companies that have implemented JIT purchasing techniques claim to have substantially reduced their investment in raw materials and work in progress stocks. Other advantages include significant quantity discounts, savings in time from negotiating with fewer suppliers and a reduction in clerical work from issuing long-term orders to a few suppliers rather than individual purchase orders to many suppliers.

Finally, you should note that the proponents of JIT claim that by giving more business to a few high quality suppliers and placing long-term purchasing orders results in a dramatic decline in ordering costs. They also claim that holding costs, in terms of maintaining stock levels, has been seriously underestimated in the past. How will a reduction in the ordering cost and an increase in the holding cost per unit affect the EOQ? If you refer back to the EOQ formula you will see that a decrease in the ordering cost reduces the numerator and the increase in the carrying cost increases the denominator so that the EOQ declines. Therefore under JIT purchasing EOQ supports more frequent purchases of lower quantities.

SUMMARY

The following items relate to the learning objectives listed at the beginning of the chapter.

● **Justify which costs are relevant and should be included in the calculation of the economic order quantity (EOQ).**

The relevant costs that should be considered when determining the EOQ consist of holding costs and ordering costs. The relevant holding costs should include only those items that will vary with the levels of stocks. Examples include the opportunity cost in terms of the return that is lost from the capital tied up in stocks and incremental insurance, material handling and warehousing and storage costs. Ordering costs usually consist of the incremental clerical costs of preparing a purchase order, receiving deliveries and paying invoices. The purchase price is not normally a relevant cost since the cost per unit will be the same, irrespective of the order size. Note that special techniques can be applied to incorporate quantity discounts.

● Calculate the EOQ using the tabulation and formula methods.

The tabulation method merely involves listing the ordering and holding costs for each potential order quantity over a selected period. The order costs are computed by multiplying the number of orders by the incremental cost per order. To compute the holding costs the average stock level is multiplied by the holding cost per unit. Assuming constant usage, average stock levels are derived by dividing the potential order quantities by 2. The computation of the EOQ using both methods was illustrated using Example 24.1.

● Determine whether or not a company should purchase larger quantities in order to take advantage of quantity discounts.

To ascertain whether larger quantities should be purchased the sum of the savings in purchase price arising from the discounts and the reduced ordering costs arising from fewer purchases are compared with the additional holding costs resulting from the increased stock levels associated with the larger order quantity. The computation was illustrated using Example 24.2.

● Calculate the optimal safety stock when demand is uncertain.

Potential alternative levels of safety stock are added to estimated average usage for a particular period to derive potential re-order points. The expected cost, based on probabilities of demand, is determined for each potential re-order point. The optimal safety stock is represented by the safety stock associated with the re-order point that has the lowest expected cost. The analysis should include stockout costs (i.e. the opportunity cost of running out of stock). The computation of the optimal safety stock was illustrated in Exhibit 24.2.

● Describe the ABC classification method.

The ABC method classifies stocks into categories of importance so that the most elaborate procedures of controlling stocks can be applied to the most important items. The ABC classification method requires that an estimate be made of the total purchase cost for each item in stock for a period. Each item is then grouped in decreasing order in terms of their purchase cost for the period. The top 10 per cent of items in stock in terms of the purchase cost for the period are classified as 'A' items. The next 20 per cent as 'B' items and the final 30 per cent as 'C' items. It is generally found that the 'A' items can account for over 70 per cent of the total purchase cost for a period. The most sophisticated procedures for planning and controlling stocks are applied to the 'A' items.

● Describe materials requirement planning (MRP) systems.

The EOQ model assumes that the demand for each item of material occurs independently of other activities. However, in complex manufacturing environments the demand for material purchases is not independent. It is dependent on the volume of the planned output of components and sub-components which include the raw materials that must be purchased. The major feature of MRP is that it first involves an estimation of the quantity and timing of finished goods demanded and then uses this to determine the requirements for components/sub-components at each of the prior stages of production. This provides the basis for determining the quantity and timing of purchased materials and any bought-in components. The aim of MRP is to generate a planned coordinated schedule of materials requirements for a specified time period for each item of material.

● Explain just-in-time purchasing.

The JIT philosophy also extends to adopting JIT purchasing techniques, whereby the delivery of materials immediately precedes their use. By arranging with suppliers for more frequent deliveries, stocks can be cut to a minimum. This improved service is obtained by giving more business to fewer suppliers and placing long-term purchase orders. For JIT purchasing to be successful close cooperation with suppliers is essential.

Note

1 The steps are as follows;

$$TC = \frac{DO}{Q} + \frac{QH}{2}$$

$$\frac{dTC}{dQ} = \frac{-DO}{Q^2} + \frac{H}{2}$$

set

$$\frac{dTC}{dQ} = 0 : \frac{H}{2} - \frac{DO}{Q^2} = 0$$

$$HQ^2 = 2DO = 0$$

$$Q^2 = \frac{2DO}{H}$$

Therefore

$$Q = \sqrt{\left(\frac{2DO}{H}\right)}$$

Key terms and concepts

ABC classification method (p. 630)
cost of prediction error (p. 624)
economic order quantity (EOQ) (p. 620)
holding costs (p. 620)
just-in-time purchasing techniques (p. 633)

lead time (p. 626)
manufacturing resource planning (p. 633)
materials requirements planning (MRP) (p. 632)
ordering costs (p. 620)
precautionary motive (p. 620)

re-order point (p. 626)
safety stocks (p. 628)
speculative motive (p. 620)
stockout costs (p. 628)
transactions motive (p. 620)

Recommended reading

For a more detailed review of stock control models see Samuels *et al.* (1998) and Wilkes (1989).

Key examination points

A common mistake is to unitize fixed ordering and holding costs and include these costs in the EOQ formula. The EOQ should be calculated using variable unit costs. The EOQ formula does not include the cost of purchasing materials, since it is assumed that the cost per unit is the same for all order quantities. If the question includes quantity discounts, you should adopt the approach illustrated in this chapter.

The EOQ formula should not be used when the purchase cost per unit varies with the quantity ordered. Instead, you should prepare a schedule of the relevant costs for different order quantities. For an illustration of this approach see the answer to Review problem 24.17.

You should also ensure that you can cope with problems where future demand is uncertain. Compare your answers with Review problems 24.20 and 24.21. Sometimes examination questions (see Review Problem 24.13) require you to calculate maximum, minimum and re-order stock levels. You should use the following formulae:

Re-order level = Maximum usage × maximum lead time
Minimum stock level = Re-order level – average usage during average lead time
Maximum stock level = Re-order level + EOQ – minimum usage for the minimum lead time

ASSESSMENT MATERIAL

The review questions are short questions that enable you to assess your understanding of the main topics included in the chapter. The numbers in parentheses provide you with the page numbers to refer to if you cannot answer a specific question.

The review problems are more complex and require you to relate and apply the chapter content to various business problems. The problems are graded by their level of difficulty. Solutions to review problems that are not preceded by the term 'IM' are provided in the *Instructor's Manual* accompanying this book and also on the lecturer's password protected section of the website www.drury-online.com Additional review problems with fully worked solutions are provided in the *Student's Manual* that accompanies this book.

Review questions

24.1 What are holding costs? Provide some examples. *(p. 620)*

24.2 What are ordering costs? Provide some examples. *(p. 620)*

24.3 What determines which holding and ordering costs should be included in the economic order quantity calculation? *(pp. 620–21)*

24.4 What are the assumptions underlying the economic order quantity? *(pp. 623–24)*

24.5 Define lead time. *(p. 626)*

24.6 Explain what is meant by the re-order point. *(p. 626)*

24.7 What are stockout costs? Provide some examples. *(p. 628)*

24.8 Explain how safety stocks are used to deal with demand uncertainty. *(pp. 628–29)*

24.9 Describe the ABC classification method. What purposes does it serve? *(pp. 630–31)*

24.10 Describe the other factors, besides the economic order quantity, that should be taken into account when choosing an order quantity. *(p. 631)*

24.11 What are the main features of materials requirements planning? *(pp. 631–33)*

24.12 What are the essential features of just-in-time purchasing arrangements? *(p. 633)*

Review problems

24.13 Basic. A domestic appliance retailer with multiple outlets stocks a popular toaster known as the Autocrisp 2000, for which the following information is available:

Average sales	75 per day
Maximum sales	95 per day
Minimum sales	50 per day
Lead time	12–18 days
Re-order quantity	1750

(i) Based on the data above, at what level of stocks would a replenishment order be issued?

a 1050.
b 1330.
c 1710.
d 1750.

(ii) Based on the data above, what is the maximum level of stocks possible?

a 1750.
b 2860.
c 3460.
d 5210.

CIMA Stage 1 Cost Accounting

24.14 Basic: Calculation of EOQ. One of the components used by K Ltd is ordered from a specialist supplier. The daily usage for this component and the time between placing and receiving an order (the lead time) can vary as follows:

Maximum usage	750 per day
Average usage	580 per day
Minimum usage	450 per day
Maximum lead time	15 days
Average lead time	12 days
Minimum lead time	8 days

Calculate the number of units that can be ordered at the re-order level if, as a result of storage problems, the company cannot allow stock to rise above 15 000 units. *(3 marks)*

CIMA Management Accounting Fundamentals

24.15 Basic: Calculation of number of orders and holding costs. N Ltd's Chief Executive believes the company is holding excessive stocks and has asked for the Management Accountant to carry out an investigation.

Information on the two stock items is given below:

Stock item	Purchase price $ per unit	Administration cost $ per order	Demand units	Holding cost per year % of purchase price
G	200	80	15 000 per year	13.33
H	25	28	2 800 per year	8.00

The company's stock ordering policy is based on the Economic Order Quantity (EOQ).

Required:

a Determine the number of orders per year that the company will place for item G *(3 marks)*

b Determine the annual holding cost of the stock of item H *(3 marks)*

CIMA Management Accounting Fundamentals

24.16 Intermediate: Calculation of EOQ. A business currently order 1000 units of product X at a time. It has decided that it may be better to use the Economic Order Quantity method to establish an optimal reorder quantity.

Information regarding stocks is given below:

Purchase price	£15/unit
Fixed cost per order	£200
Holding cost	8 per cent of the purchase price per annum
Annual demand	12 000 units

Current annual total stock costs are £183 000, being the total of the purchasing, ordering and holding costs of product X.

Required:

a Calculate the Economic Order Quantity *(2 marks)*

b Using your answer to (a) above calculate the revised annual total stock costs of product X and so establish the difference compared to the current ordering policy. *(4 marks)*

ACCA Paper 1.2 – Financial Information for Management

24.17 Intermediate: Calculation of optimum order size. A company is reviewing its stock policy, and has the following alternatives available for the evaluation of stock number 12 789:

(i) Purchase stock twice monthly, 100 units
(ii) Purchase monthly, 200 units
(iii) Purchase every three months, 600 units
(iv) Purchase six monthly, 1200 units
(v) Purchase annually, 2400 units.

It is ascertained that the purchase price per unit is £0.80 for deliveries up to 500 units. A 5 per cent discount is offered by the supplier on the whole order where deliveries are 501 up to 1000, and 10 per cent reduction on the total order for deliveries in excess of 1000.

Each purchase order incurs administration costs of £5.

Storage, interest on capital and other costs are £0.25 per unit of average stock quantity held.

You are required to advise management on the optimum order size.

(9 marks)
AAT

24.18 Intermediate: Relevant costs and cost of prediction error. The annual demand for an item of raw materials is 4000 units and the purchase price is expected to be £90 per unit. The incremental cost of processing an order is £135 and the cost of storage is estimated to be £12 per unit.

a   What is the optimal order quantity and the total relevant cost of this order quantity?
b   Suppose that the £135 estimate of the incremental cost of processing an order is incorrect and should have been £80. Assume that all other estimates are correct. What is the cost of this prediction error, assuming that the solution to part (a) is implemented for one year?
c   Assume at the start of the period that a supplier offers 4000 units at a price of £86. The materials will be delivered immediately and placed in the stores. Assume that the incremental cost of placing this order is zero and the original estimate of £135 for placing an order for the economic batch size is correct. Should the order be accepted?
d   Present a performance report for the purchasing officer, assuming that the budget was based on the information presented in (a) and the purchasing officer accepted the special order outlined in (c).

24.19 Advanced: Relevant costs and calculation of optimum batch size. Pink Ltd is experiencing some slight problems concerning two stock items sold by the company.

The first of these items is product Exe which is manufactured by Pink. The annual demand for Exe of 4000 units, which is evenly spread throughout the year, is usually met by production taking place four times per year in batches of 1000 units. One of the raw material inputs to product Exe is product Dee which is also manufactured by Pink. Product Dee is the firms major product and is produced in large quantities throughout the year. Production capacity is sufficient to meet in full *all* demands for the production of Dees.

The standard costs of products Exe and Dee are:

Standard costs – per unit

	Product	
	Exe	Dee
	(£)	(£)
Raw materials – purchased from external suppliers	13	8
– Dee standard cost	22	–
Labour – unskilled	7	4
– skilled	9	5
Variable overheads	5	3
Fixed overheads	4	2
Standard cost	£60	£22

Included in the fixed overheads for Exe are the set-up costs for each production run. The costs of each set-up, which apply irrespective of the size of the production run, are:

Costs per set-up

		(£)
(i)	Labour costs – skilled labour	66
(ii)	Machine parts	70
	Total	£136

The 'Machine parts' relate to the cost of parts required for modifications carried out to the machine on which Exe is produced. The parts can be used for only one run, irrespective of run length, and are destroyed by replacement on reinstatement of the machine. There are no set-up costs associated with Dee.

The cost of financing stocks of Exe is 15 per cent p.a. Each unit of Exe in stock requires 0.40 square metres of storage space and units *cannot* be stacked on top of each other to reduce costs. Warehouse rent is £20 p.a. per square metre and Pink is only required to pay for storage space actually used.

Pink is not working to full capacity and idle-time payments are being made to all grades of labour except unskilled workers. Unskilled labour is not guaranteed a minimum weekly wage and is paid only for work carried out.

The second stock item causing concern is product Wye. Product Wye is purchased by Pink for resale and the 10 000 unit annual demand is again spread evenly throughout the year. Incremental ordering costs are £100 per order and the normal unit cost is £20. However the suppliers of Wye are now offering quantity discounts for large orders. The details of these are:

Quantity ordered	Unit price (£)
Up to 999	20.00
1000 to 1999	19.80
2000 and over	19.60

The purchasing manager feels that full advantage should be taken of discounts and purchases should be made at £19.60 per unit using orders for 2000 units or more. Holding costs for Wye are calculated at £8.00 per unit per year and this figure will not be altered by any change in the purchase price per unit.

Required:

a   Show the optimum batch size for the production of Exes. If this differs from the present policy, calculate the annual savings to be made by Pink Ltd from pursuing the optimal policy. Briefly explain the figures incorporated in your calculations. (The time taken to carry out a production run may be ignored.)

(10 marks)

b   Advise Pink Ltd on the correct size of order for the purchase of Wyes. *(6 marks)*
c   Briefly describe two major limitations, or difficulties inherent in the practical application, of the model used in (a) to determine the optimum batch size. *(4 marks)*

ACCA P2 Management Accounting

24.20 Advanced: Safety stocks and probability theory. A company has determined that the EOQ for its only raw material is 2000 units every 30 days. The company knows with certainty that a four-day lead time is required for ordering. The following is the probability distribution of estimated usage of the raw material for the month.

Usage (units)	1800	1900	2000	2100	2200	2300	2400	2500
Probability	0.06	0.14	0.30	0.16	0.13	0.10	0.07	0.04

Stockouts will cost the company £10 per unit, and the average monthly holding cost is £1 per unit.

a   Determine the optimal safety stock.
b   What is the probability of being out of stock?

24.21 Advanced: Safety stocks, uncertain demand and quantity discounts. Kattalist Ltd is a distributor of an industrial chemical in the north east of England. The chemical is supplied in drums which have to be stored at a controlled temperature.

The company's objective is to maximize profits, and it commenced business on 1 October.

The managing director's view:

The company's managing director wishes to improve stock holding policy by applying the economic order quantity model. Each drum of the chemical costs £50 from a supplier and sells for £60. Annual demand is estimated to be for 10 000 drums, which the managing director assumes to be evenly distributed over 300 working days. The cost of delivery is estimated at £25 per order and the annual variable holding cost per drum at £45 plus 10 per cent of purchase cost. Using these data the managing director calculates the economic order quantity and proposes that this should be the basis for purchasing decisions of the industrial chemical in future periods.

The purchasing manager's view:
Written into the contract of the company's purchasing manager is a clause that he will receive a bonus (rounded to the nearest £1) of 10 per cent of the amount by which total annual inventory holding and order costs before such remuneration are below £10 000. Using the same assumptions as the managing director, the purchasing manager points out that in making his calculations the managing director has not only ignored his bonus but also the fact that suppliers offer quantity discounts on purchase orders. In fact, if the order size is 200 drums or above, the price per drum for an entire consignment is only £49.90, compared to £50 when an order is between 100 and 199 drums; and £50.10 when an order is between 50 and 99 drums.

The finance director's view.
The company's finance director accepts the need to consider quantity discounts and pay a bonus, but he also feels the managing director's approach is too simplistic. He points out that there is a lead time for an order of three days and that demand has not been entirely even over the past year. Moreover, if the company has no drums in stock, it will lose specific orders as potential customers will go to rival competitors in the region to meet their immediate needs.

To support his argument the finance director summarizes the evidence from salesmen's records over the past year, which show the number of drums demanded during the lead times were as follows:

Drums demanded during 3-day lead time	Number of times each quantity of drums was demanded
106	4
104	10
102	16
100	40
98	14
96	14
94	2

In the circumstances, the managing director decides he should seek further advice on what course of action he should take.

Requirements:
a   Calculate the economic order quantity as originally determined by the company's managing director.   *(1 mark)*
b   Calculate the optimum economic order quantity, applying the managing director's assumptions and after allowing for the purchasing manager's bonus and for supplier quantity discounts, but without using an expected value approach.   *(3 marks)*
c   Adopting the financial director's assumptions and an expected value approach, and assuming that it is a condition of the supplier's contract that the order quantity is to be constant for all orders in the year, determine the expected level of safety (i.e. buffer) stock the company should maintain. For this purpose, use the figures for the economic order quantity you have derived in answering (b). Show all workings and state any assumptions you make.   *(5 marks)*
d   As an outside consultant, write a report to the managing director on the company's stock ordering and stock holding policies, referring where necessary to your answers to (a)–(c). The report should *inter alia* refer to other factors he should consider when taking his final decisions on stock ordering and stock holding policies.   *(9 marks)*

Note: Ignore taxation.

(Total 18 marks)
ICAEW Management Accounting and Financial Management Part Two

IM24.1 Intermediate: Calculation of EOQ and frequency at ordering. A company is planning to purchase 90 800 units of a particular item in the year ahead. The item is purchased in boxes, each containing 10 units of the item, at a price of £200 per box. A safety stock of 250 boxes is kept.

The cost of holding an item in stock for a year (including insurance, interest and space costs) is 15 per cent of the purchase area. The cost of placing and receiving orders is to be estimated from cost data collected relating to similar orders, where costs of £5910 were incurred on 30 orders. It should be assumed that ordering costs change in proportion to the number of orders placed. 2 per cent should be added to the above ordering costs to allow for inflation.

Required:
Calculate the order quantity that would minimize the cost of the above item, and determine the required frequency of placing orders, assuming that usage of the item will be even over the year.   *(8 marks)*
ACCA Foundation Stage Paper 3

IM24.2 Intermediate: Calculation of EOQ. Sandy Lands Ltd carries an item of inventory in respect of which the following data apply:

fixed cost of ordering per batch	£10
expected steady quarterly volume of sales	3125 units
cost of holding one unit in stock for one year	1

You are required to:
(i)   calculate the minimum annual cost of ordering and stocking the item;   *(4 marks)*
(ii) calculate to the nearest whole number of units the optimal batch size if the expected steady quarterly volume of sales
        first falls to 781 units and
        second rises to 6250 units
      and to state the relationship between the rates of change of sales and the optimal batch size;   *(4 marks)*
(iii) explain the basis of the derivation of the formula for the optimal batch size which is given in the table of formulae.   *(4 marks)*
ICAEW Management Accounting

IM24.3 Intermediate: Calculation of EOQ and a make or buy decision. A company is considering the possibility of purchasing from a supplier a component it now makes. The supplier will provide the components in the necessary quantities at a unit price of £9. Transportation and storage costs would be negligible.

The company produces the component from a single raw material in economic lots of 2000 units at a cost of £2 per unit. Average annual demand is 20 000 units. The annual holding cost is £0.25 per unit and the minimum stock level is set at 400 units. Direct labour costs for the component are £6 per unit, fixed manufacturing overhead is charged at a rate of £3 per unit based on a normal activity of 20 000 units. The company also hires the machine on which the components are produced at a rate of £200 per month.

Should the company make the component?

IM24.4 Intermediate: Calculation of minimum purchase cost when cost per unit is not constant. A company is reviewing the purchasing policy for one of its raw materials as a result of a reduction in production requirement. The material, which is used evenly throughout the year, is used in only one of the company's products, the production of which is currently 12 000 units per annum. Each finished unit of the product contains 0.4kg of the material. 20 per cent of the material is lost in the production process. Purchases can be made in multiples of 500kg, with a minimum purchase order quantity of 1000kg.

The cost of the raw material depends upon the purchase order quantity as follows:

Order quantity (kg)	Cost per kg (£)
1000	1.00
1500	0.98
2000	0.965
2500	0.95
3000 and above	0.94

Costs of placing and handling each order are £90, of which £40 is an apportionment of costs which are not expected to be affected in the short term by the number of orders placed. Annual holding costs of stock are £0.90 per unit of average stock, of which only £0.40 is expected to be affected in the short term by the amount of stock held.

The lead time for the raw materials is one month, and a safety stock of 250kg is required.

Required:
a   Explain, and illustrate from the situation described above, the meaning of the terms 'variable', 'semivariable' and 'fixed' costs.   *(8 marks)*
b   Calculate the annual cost of pursuing alternative purchase order policies and thus advise the company regarding the purchase order quantity for the material that will minimize cost.   *(14 marks)*
ACCA Level 1 Costing

IM24.5 Advanced: Evaluation of an increase in order size incorporating quantity discounts. Whirlygig plc manufactures and markets automatic dishwashing machines. Among the components which it purchases each year from external suppliers for assembly into the finished article are window units, of which it uses 20 000 units per annum.

It is considering buying in larger amounts in order to claim quantity discounts. This will lower the number of orders placed but raise the administrative and other costs of placing and receiving orders. Details of actual and expected ordering and carrying costs are given in the table below:

	Actual	Proposed
O = Ordering cost per order	£31.25	£120
P = Purchase price per item	£6.25	£6.00
I = (annual) Inventory holding cost (as a percentage of the purchase price)	20%	20%

To implement the new arrangements will require reorganization costs estimated at £10 000 which can be wholly claimed as a business expense for tax purposes in the tax year before the system comes into operation. The rate of corporate tax is 33 per cent, payable with a one-year delay.

Required:

a Determine the change in the economic order quantity (EOQ) caused by the new system. *(4 marks)*

b Calculate the payback period for the proposal and comment on your results. *(10 marks)*

c Briefly discuss the suitability of the payback method for evaluating investments of this nature. *(6 marks)*

ACCA Paper 8 Managerial Finance

IM24.6 Advanced: Quantity discounts and calculation of EOQ. Wagtail Ltd uses the 'optimal batch size' model (see below) to determine optimal levels of raw materials. Material B is consumed at a steady, known rate over the company's planning horizon of one year; the current usage is 4000 units per annum. The costs of ordering B are invariant with respect to order size; clerical costs of ordering have been calculated at £30 per order. Each order is checked by an employee engaged in using B in production who earns £5 per hour irrespective of his output. The employee generates a contribution of £4 per hour when not involved in materials checks and the stock check takes five hours. Holding costs amount to £15 per unit per annum.

The supplier of material B has very recently offered Wagtail a quantity discount of £0.24 a unit on the current price of £24, for all orders of 400 or more units of B.

You are required to:

a calculate the optimal order level of material B, ignoring the quantity discount; *(3 marks)*

b evaluate whether the quantity discount offered should be taken up by Wagtail; *(5 marks)*

c explain how uncertainties in materials usage and lead time may be incorporated into the analysis. *(8 marks)*

Note: Ignore taxation.

ICAEW P2 Financial Management

IM24.7 Advanced: Calculation of EOQ and a comparison of relevant purchasing costs of different suppliers. Mr Evans is a wholesaler who buys and sells a wide range of products, one of which is the Laker. Mr Evans sells 24 000 units of the Laker each year at a unit price of £20. Sales of the Laker normally follow an even pattern throughout the year but to protect himself against possible deviations Mr Evans keeps a minimum stock of 1000 units. Further supplies of the Laker are ordered whenever the stock falls to this minimum level and the time lag between ordering and delivery is small enough to be ignored.

At present, Mr Evans buys all his supplies of Lakers from May Ltd, and usually purchases them in batches of 5000 units. His most recent invoice from May Ltd was as follows:

	(£)
Basic price: 5000 Lakers at £15 per unit	75 000
Delivery charge: Transport at £0.50 per unit	2 500
Fixed shipment charge per order	1 000
	78 500

In addition, Mr Evans estimates that each order he places costs him £500, comprising administrative costs and the cost of sample checks. This cost does not vary with the size of the order.

Mr Evans stores Lakers in a warehouse which he rents on a long lease for £5 per square foot per annum. Warehouse space available exceeds current requirements and, as the lease cannot be cancelled, spare capacity is sublet on annual contracts at £4 per square foot per annum. Each unit of Laker in stock requires two square feet of space. Mr Evans estimates that other holding costs amount to £10 per Laker per annum.

Mr Evans has recently learnt that another supplier of Lakers, Richardson Ltd, is willing, unlike May Ltd, to offer discounts on large orders. Richardson Ltd sells Lakers at the following prices:

Order size	Price per unit (£)
1–2999	15.25
3000–4999	14.50
5000 and over	14.25

In other respects (i.e. delivery charges and the time between ordering and delivery) Richardson Ltd's terms are identical to those of May Ltd.

You are required to:

a calculate the optimal re-order quantity for Lakers and the associated annual profit Mr Evans can expect from their purchase and sale, assuming that he continues to buy from May Ltd, *(10 marks)*

b prepare calculations to show whether Mr Evans should buy Lakers from Richardson Ltd rather than from May Ltd and, if so, in what batch sizes, *(8 marks)*

c explain the limitations of the methods of analysis you have used. *(7 marks)*

Ignore taxation.

ICAEW Elements of Financial Decisions

IM24.8 Advanced: Calculation of EOQ and discussion of safety stocks. A company needs to hold a stock of item X for sale to customers.

Although the item is of relatively small value per unit, the customers' quality control requirements and the need to obtain competitive supply tenders at frequent intervals result in high procurement costs.

Basic data about item X are as follows:

Annual sales demand (d) over 52 weeks	4095 units
Cost of placing and processing a purchase order (procurement costs, C_p)	£48.46
Cost of holding one unit for one year (C_h)	£4.00
Normal delay between placing purchase order and receiving goods	3 weeks

You are required to:

a calculate
(i) the economic order quantity for item X,
(ii) the frequency at which purchase orders would be placed, using that formula,
(iii) the total annual procurement costs and the total annual holding costs when the EOQ is used; *(6 marks)*

b explain why it might be unsatisfactory to procure a fixed quantity of item X at regular intervals if it were company policy to satisfy all sales demands from stock and if
(i) the rate of sales demand could vary between 250 and 350 units per four-week period or
(ii) the delivery delay on purchases might vary between 3 and 5 weeks suggesting in each case what corrective actions might be taken; *(6 marks)*

c describe in detail a fully-developed stock control system for item X (or other fast-moving items), designed to ensure that stock holdings at all times are adequate but not excessive. Illustrate your answer with a freehand graph, not to scale. *(8 marks)*

CIMA Stage 4 Financial Management

IM24.9 Advanced: Calculation of EOQ, safety stocks and stockholding costs where demand is uncertain. The financial controller of Mexet plc is reviewing the company's stock management procedures. Stock has gradually increased to 25 per cent of the company's total assets and, with finance costs at 14 per cent per annum, currently costs the company £4.5 million per year, including all ordering and holding costs.

Demand for the company's major product is not subject to seasonal fluctuations. The product requires £6 million of standard semi-finished goods annually which are purchased in equal quantities from three separate suppliers at a cost of £20 per unit. Three suppliers are used to prevent problems that could result from industrial disputes in a single supplier.

Stock costs £2 per unit per year to hold, including insurance costs and financing costs, and each order made costs £100 fixed cost and £0.10 per unit variable cost. There is a lead time of one month between the placing of an order and delivery of the goods. Demand fluctuation for the company's finished products results in the following probability distribution of monthly stock usage.

Usage per month	19 400	23 000	25 000	27 000	30 000
Probability	0.10	0.22	0.36	0.20	0.12

The cost per unit of running out of stock is estimated to be £0.4.

Required:

a Calculate the economic order quantity for the semi-finished goods.
(3 marks)

b Determine what level of safety stock should be kept for these goods.
(8 marks)

c Calculate the change in annual stock management costs that would result if the goods were bought from only one supplier. Assume that no quantity discounts are available.
(5 marks)

d The financial controller feels that JIT (just in time) stock management might be useful for the company, but the three suppliers will only agree to this in return for an increase in unit price.

Explain the possible advantages and disadvantages of JIT, and briefly discuss whether or not Mexet should introduce it.
(9 marks)

ACCA Level 3 Financial Management

IM24.10 Advanced: Calculation of stockholding costs, costs of stockouts when demand is uncertain and a discussion of JIT. Rainbow Ltd is a manufacturer which uses alkahest in many of its products. At present the company has an alkahest plant on a site close to the company's main factory. A summary of the alkahest plants budget for the next year is shown below.

Production	300 0000 litres of alkahest
Variable manufacturing costs	£840 000
Fixed manufacturing costs	£330 000

The budget covers costs up to and including the cost of piping finished alkahest to the main factory. At the main factory alkahest can be stored at a cost of £20 per annum per thousand litres, but additional costs arise in storage because alkahest evaporates at a rate of 5 per cent per annum. Production of alkahest is adjusted to meet the demands of the main factory; in addition safety stocks of 60 000 litres are maintained in case of disruption of supplies.

The alkahest plant has a limited remaining life and has been fully depreciated. The management of Rainbow Ltd is considering whether the plant should be retained for the time being or should be closed immediately. On closure the equipment would be scrapped and the site sold for £400 000. Employees would be redeployed within the company and supplies of alkahest would be bought from an outside supplier.

Rainbow Ltd has found that Alchemy plc can supply all its alkahest requirements at £370 per thousand litres. Transport costs of £30 per thousand litres would be borne by Rainbow Ltd. There would be administration costs of £15 000 per year, in addition to order costs of £60 for each delivery. It has been decided that if purchases are made from Alchemy plc the safety stock will be increased to 100 000 litres.

Rainbow Ltd has 250 working days in each year and a cost of capital of 15 per cent per annum. The company's current expectations for demand and costs apply for the foreseeable future.

Requirements:

a Calculate the total annual costs of the options available to Rainbow Ltd for its supply of alkahest and interpret the results for management.
(10 marks)

b Calculate the expected annual stock-outs in litres implied by a safety stock of 100 000 litres and calculate the stock-out cost per litre at which it would be worthwhile to increase safety stock from 100 000 litres to 120 000 litres, under the following assumptions:

(i) for any delivery there is a 0.8 probability that lead time will be 5 days and a 0.2 probability that lead time will be 10 days, and

(ii) during the lead time for any delivery there is a 0.5 probability that Rainbow Ltd will use alkahest at the rate of 10 000 litres per day and a 0.5 probability that the company will use alkahest at the rate of 14 000 litres per day.
(6 marks)

c Explain the requirements for the successful adoption of a just-in-time inventory policy and discuss the relative costs and benefits of just-in-time policies compared with economic-order-quantity policies.
(9 marks)

ICAEW P2 Management Accounting

The application of linear programming to management accounting

25

In Chapter 9 we considered how accounting information should be used to ensure that scarce resources are efficiently allocated. To refresh your memory you should now refer back to Example 9.2 to ascertain how the optimum production programme was determined. You will see that where a scarce resource exists, that has alternative uses, the contribution per unit should be calculated for each of these uses. The available capacity of this resource is then allocated to the alternative uses on the basis of the contribution per scarce resource.

Where more than one scarce resource exists, the optimum production programme cannot easily be established by the process described in Chapter 9. In such circumstances there is a need to resort to linear programming techniques to establish the optimum production programme. Our objective in this chapter is to examine how linear programming techniques can be applied to determine the optimum production programme in situations where more than one scarce resource exists. Initially we shall assume that only two products are produced so that the optimum output can be determined using a two dimensional graph. Where more than two products are produced the optimal output cannot easily be determined using the graphical method. Instead, the optimal output can be determined using a non-graphical approach that is known as the simplex method.

Linear programming is a topic that is often included in second level cost and management accounting courses but recently some professional accountancy examining bodies have incorporated this topic (normally based on the graphical approach) in first level courses. You should therefore check your course content to ascertain if you will need to read this chapter.

LEARNING OBJECTIVES

After studying this chapter you should be able to:

- describe the situations when it may be appropriate to use linear programming;

- explain the circumstances when the graphical method can be used;

- use graphical linear programming to find the optimum output levels;

- formulate the initial linear programming model using the simplex method;

- explain the meaning of the term shadow prices.

Linear programming

Linear programming is a powerful mathematical technique that can be applied to the problem of rationing limited facilities and resources among many alternative uses in such a way that the optimum benefits can be derived from their utilization. It seeks to find a feasible combination of output that will maximize or minimize the objective function. The objective function refers to the quantification of an objective, and usually takes the form of maximizing profits or minimizing costs. Linear programming may be used when relationships can be assumed to be linear and where an optimal solution does in fact exist.

To comply with the linearity assumption, it must be assumed that the contribution per unit for each product and the utilization of resources per unit are the same whatever quantity of output is produced and sold within the output range being considered. It must also be assumed that units produced and resources allocated are infinitely divisible. This means that an optimal plan that suggests we should produce 94.38 units is possible. However, it will be necessary to interpret the plan as a production of 94 units.

Let us now apply this technique to the problem outlined in Example 25.1, where there is a labour restriction plus a limitation on the availability of materials and machine hours. The contributions per scarce resource are as follows:

	Product Y (£)	Product Z (£)
Labour	2.33 (£14/6 hours)	2.00 (£16/8 hours)
Material	1.75 (£14/8 units)	4.00 (£16/4 units)
Machine capacity	3.50 (£14/4 hours)	2.67 (£16/6 hours)

EXAMPLE 25.1 Multiple resource constraint problem

The LP company currently makes two products. The standards per unit of product are as follows:

Product Y	(£)	(£)	Product Z	(£)	(£)
Product Y			Product Z		
Standard selling price		110	Standard selling price		118
Less standard costs:			Less standard costs:		
Materials (8 units at £4)	32		Materials (4 units at £4)	16	
Labour (6 hours at £10)	60		Labour (8 hours at £10)	80	
Variable overhead			Variable overhead		
(4 machine hours at £1)	4		(6 machine hours at £1)	6	
		96			102
Contribution		14	Contribution		16

During the next accounting period, the availability of resources are expected to be subject to the following limitations:

Labour	2880 hours
Materials	3440 units
Machine capacity	2760 hours

The marketing manager estimates that the maximum sales potential for product Y is limited to 420 units. There is no sales limitation for product Z. You are asked to advise how these limited facilities and resources can best be used so as to gain the optimum benefit from them.

This analysis shows that product Y yields the largest contribution per labour hour, and product Z yields the largest contribution per unit of scarce materials, but there is no clear indication of how the quantity of scarce resources should be allocated to each product. Linear programming should be used in such circumstances.

The procedure is first, to formulate the problem algebraically, with Y denoting the number of units of product Y and Z the number of units of product Z that are manufactured by the company. Secondly, we must specify the objective function, which in this example is to maximize contribution (denoted by C), followed by the input constraints. We can now formulate the linear programming model as follows:

$$\text{Maximize } C = 14Y + 16Z \text{ subject to}$$
$$8Y + 4Z \leqslant 3440 \text{ (material constraint)}$$
$$6Y + 8Z \leqslant 2880 \text{ (labour constraint)}$$
$$4Y + 6Z \leqslant 2760 \text{ (machine capacity constraint)}$$
$$0 \leqslant Y \leqslant 420 \text{ (maximum and minimum sales limitation)}$$
$$Z \geqslant 0 \text{ (minimum sales limitation)}$$

In this model, 'maximize C' indicates that we wish to maximize contribution with an unknown number of units of Y produced, each yielding a contribution of £14 per unit, and an unknown number of units of Z produced, each yielding a contribution of £16. The labour constraint indicates that six hours of labour are required for each unit of product Y that is made, and eight hours for each unit of product Z. Thus (6 hours $\times$ Y) + (8 hours $\times$ Z) cannot exceed 2880 hours. Similar reasoning applies to the other inputs.

Because linear programming is nothing more than a mathematical tool for solving constrained optimization problems, nothing in the technique itself ensures that an answer will 'make sense'. For example, in a production problem, for some very unprofitable product, the optimal output level may be a negative quantity, which is clearly an impossible solution. To prevent such non-sensical results, we must include a non-negativity requirement, which is a statement that all variables in the problem must be equal to or greater than zero. We must therefore add to the model in our example the constraint that Y and Z must be greater than or equal to zero, i.e. $Z \geqslant 0$ and $0 \leqslant Y \leqslant 420$. The latter expression indicates that sales of Y cannot be less than zero or greater than 420 units. The model can be solved graphically, or by the Simplex method. When no more than two products are manufactured, the graphical method can be used, but this becomes impracticable where more than two products are involved, and it is then necessary to resort to the Simplex method.

Graphical method

Taking the first *constraint for the materials* input $8Y + 4Z \leqslant 3440$ means that we can make a maximum of 860 units of product Z when production of product Y is zero. The 860 units is arrived at by dividing the 3440 units of materials by the four units of material required for each unit of product Z. Alternatively, a maximum of 430 units of product Y can be made (3440 units divided by eight units of materials) if no materials are allocated to product Z. We can therefore state that

$$\text{when } Y = 0, Z = 860$$
$$\text{when } Z = 0, Y = 430$$

These items are plotted in Figure 25.1, with a straight line running from $Z = 0$, $Y = 430$ to $Y = 0$, $Z = 860$. Note that the vertical axis represents the number of units of Y produced and the horizontal axis the number of units of Z produced.

The area to the left of line $8Y + 4Z \leq 3440$ contains all possible solutions for Y and Z in this particular situation, and any point along the line connecting these two outputs represents the maximum combinations of Y and Z that can be produced with not more than 3440 units of materials. Every point to the right of the line violates the material constraint.

The *labour constraint* $6Y + 8Z \leq 2880$ indicates that if production of product Z is zero, then a maximum of 480 units of product Y can be produced (2880/6), and if the output of Y is zero then 360 units of Z (2880/8) can be produced. We can now draw a second line $Y = 480, Z = 0$ to $Y = 0, Z = 360$, and this is illustrated in Figure 25.2. The area to the left of line $6Y + 8Z \leq 2880$ in this figure represents all the possible solutions that will satisfy the labour constraint.

The *machine input constraint* is represented by $Z = 0, Y = 690$ and $Y = 0, Z = 460$, and the line indicating this constraint is illustrated in Figure 25.3. The area to the left of the line $4Y + 6Z \leq 2760$ in this figure represents all the possible solutions that will satisfy the machine capacity constraint.

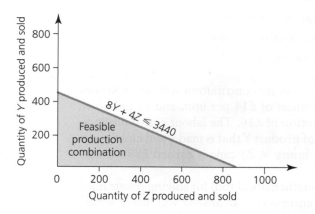

FIGURE 25.1
Constraint imposed by limitations of materials

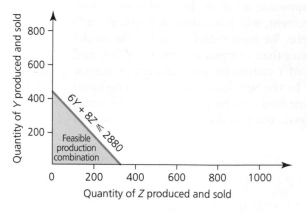

FIGURE 25.2
Constraint imposed by limitations of labour

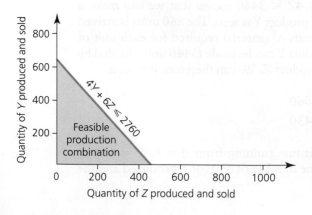

FIGURE 25.3
Constraint imposed by machine capacity

The final constraint is that the *sales output* of product Y cannot exceed 420 units. This is represented by the line $Y \leq 420$ in Figure 25.4, and all the items below this line represent all the possible solutions that will satisfy this sales limitation.

It is clear that any solution that is to fit *all* the constraints must occur in the shaded area ABCDE in Figure 25.5, which represents Figures 25.1–25.4 combined together. The point must now be found within the shaded area *ABCDE* where the contribution C is the greatest. The maximum will occur at one of the corner points ABCDE. The objective function is $C = 14Y + 16Z$, and a random contribution value is chosen that will result in a line for the objective function falling within the area *ABCDE*.

If we choose a random total contribution value equal to £2240, this could be obtained from producing 160 units (£2240/£14) of Y at £14 contribution per unit or 140 units of Z (£2240/£16) at a contribution of £16 per unit. We can therefore draw a line Z = 0, Y = 160 to Y = 0, Z = 140. This is represented by the dashed line in Figure 25.5. Each point on the dashed line represents all the output combinations of Z and Y that will yield a total contribution of £2240. The dashed line

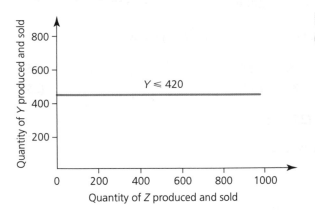

FIGURE 25.4
Constraint imposed by sales limitation of product Y

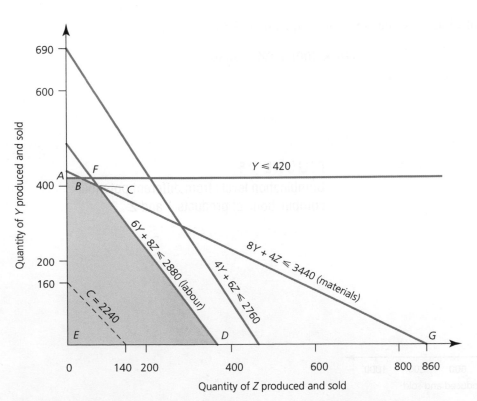

FIGURE 25.5
Combination of Figures
25.1–25.4

is extended to the right until it touches the last corner of the boundary *ABCDE*. This is the optimal solution and is at point *C*, which indicates an output of 400 units of *Y* (contribution £5600) and 60 units of *Z* (contribution £960), giving a total contribution of £6560.

The logic in the previous paragraph is illustrated in Figure 25.6. The shaded area represents the feasible production area *ABCDE* that is outlined in Figure 25.5, and parallel lines represent possible contributions, which take on higher values as we move to the right. If we assume that the firm's objective is to maximize total contribution, it should operate on the highest contribution curve obtainable. At the same time, it is necessary to satisfy the production constraints, which are indicated by the shaded area in Figure 25.6. You will see that point *C* indicates the solution to the problem, since no other point within the feasible area touches such a high contribution line.

It is difficult to ascertain from Figure 25.5 the exact output of each product at point *C*. The optimum output can be determined exactly by solving the simultaneous equations for the constraints that intersect at point *C*:

$$8Y + 4Z = 3440 \tag{25.1}$$
$$6Y + 8Z = 2880 \tag{25.2}$$

We can now multiply equation (25.1) by 2 and equation (25.2) by 1, giving

$$16Y + 8Z = 6880 \tag{25.3}$$
$$6Y + 8Z = 2880 \tag{25.4}$$

Subtracting equation (25.4) from equation (25.3) gives

$$10Y = 4000$$

and so

$$Y = 400$$

We can now substitute this value for *Y* onto equation (25.3), giving

$$(16 \times 400) + 8Z = 6880$$

and so

$$Z = 60$$

FIGURE 25.6

Combination levels from different potential combinations of products *Y* and *Z*

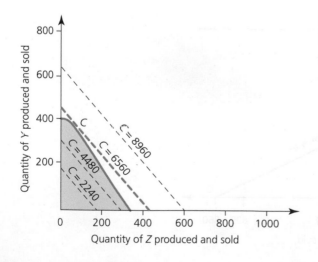

You will see from Figure 25.5 that the constraints that are binding at point C are materials and labour. It might be possible to remove these constraints and acquire additional labour and materials resources by paying a premium over and above the existing acquisition cost. How much should the company be prepared to pay? To answer this question, it is necessary to determine the optimal use from an additional unit of a scarce resource.

We shall now consider how the optimum solution would change if an additional unit of materials were obtained. You can see that if we obtain additional materials, the line $8Y + 4Z \leqslant 3440$ in Figure 25.5 will shift upwards and the revised optimum point will fall on line CF. If one extra unit of materials is obtained, the constraints $8Y + 4Z \leqslant 3440$ and $6Y + 8Z \leqslant 2880$ will still be binding, and the new optimum plan can be determined by solving the following simultaneous equations:

$$8Y + 4Z = 3441 \text{ (revised materials constraint)}$$
$$6Y + 8Z = 2880 \text{ (unchanged labour constraint)}$$

The revised optimal output when the above equations are solved is 400.2 units of Y and 59.85 units of Z. Therefore the planned output of product Y should be increased by 0.2 units, and planned production of Z should be reduced by 0.15 units. This optimal response from an independent marginal increase in a resource is called the marginal rate of substitution. The change in contribution arising from obtaining one additional unit of materials is as follows:

	(£)
Increase in contribution from Y (0.2 × £14)	2.80
Decrease in contribution of Z (0.15 × £16)	(2.40)
Increase in contribution	0.40

Therefore the value of an additional unit of materials is £0.40. The value of an independent marginal increase of scarce resource is called the opportunity cost or shadow price. We shall be considering these terms in more detail later in the chapter. You should note at this stage that for materials purchased in excess of 3440 units the company can pay up to £0.40 over and above the present acquisition cost of materials of £4 and still obtain a contribution towards fixed costs from the additional output.

From a practical point of view, it is not possible to produce 400.2 units of Y and 59.85 units of Z. Output must be expressed in single whole units. Nevertheless, the output from the model can be used to calculate the revised optimal output if additional units of materials are obtained. Assume that 100 additional units of materials can be purchased at £4.20 per unit from an overseas supplier. Because the opportunity cost (£0.40) is in excess of the additional acquisition cost of £0.20 per unit (£4.20 – £4), the company should purchase the extra materials. The marginal rates of substitution can be used to calculate the revised optimum output. The calculation is

Increase Y by 20 units (100 × 0.2 units)

Decrease Z by 15 units (100 × 0.15 units)

Therefore the revised optimal output is 420 outputs (400 + 20) of Y and 35 units (60 – 15) of Z. You will see later in this chapter that the substitution process outlined above is applicable only within a particular range of material usage.

We can apply the same approach to calculate the opportunity cost of labour. If an additional labour hour is obtained, the line $6Y + 8Z \leqslant 2880$ in Figure 25.5 will shift to the right, and the revised optimal point will fall on line CG. The constraints $8Y + 4Z \leqslant 3440$ and $6Y + 8Z \leqslant 2880$ will still be binding, and the new optimum plan can be determined by solving the following simultaneous equations:

$$8Y + 4Z = 3440 \text{ (unchanged materials constraint)}$$
$$6Y + 8Z = 2881 \text{ (revised labour constraint)}$$

The revised optimal output when the above equations are solved is 399.9 units of Y and 60.2 units of Z. Therefore the planned output of product Y should be decreased by 0.1 units and planned production of Z should be increased by 0.2 units. The opportunity cost of a scarce labour hour is

	(£)
Decrease in contribution from Y (0.1 × £14)	(1.40)
Increase in contribution from Z (0.2 × £16)	3.20
Increase in contribution (opportunity cost)	1.80

Simplex method

ADVANCED READING

Where more than two products can be manufactured using the scarce resources available, the optimum solution cannot easily be established from the graphical method. An alternative is a non-graphical solution known as the Simplex method. This method also provides additional information on opportunity costs and marginal rates of substitution that is particularly useful for decision-making, and also for planning and control.

The Simplex method involves many tedious calculations, but there are standard spreadsheet packages that will complete the task within a few minutes. The aim of this chapter is not therefore to delve into these tedious calculations but to provide you with an understanding of how the simplex linear programming model should be formulated for an input into a spreadsheet package and also how to interpret the optimal solution from the output from the spreadsheet package. However, if you are interested in how the optimal solution is derived you should refer to Learning Note 25.1 on the open access website (see preface for details) but do note that examination questions do not require you to undertake the calculations. They merely require you to formulate the initial model and interpret the output derived from the model. Example 25.1 is now used to illustrate the Simplex method.

To apply the Simplex method, we must first formulate a model that does not include any *inequalities*. This is done by introducing what are called slack variables to the model. Slack variables are added to a linear programming problem to account for any constraint that is unused at the point of optimality, and one slack variable is introduced for each constraint. In our example, the company is faced with constraints on materials, labour, machine capacity and maximum sales for product Y. Therefore S_1 is introduced to represent unused material resources, S_2 represents unused labour hours, S_3 represents unused machine capacity and S_4 represents unused potential sales output. We can now express the model for Example 25.1 in terms of equalities rather than inequalities:

$$\text{Maximize } C = 14Y + 16Z$$

subject to

$$8Y + 4Z + S_1 = 3440 \text{ (materials constraint)}$$
$$6Y + 8Z + S_2 = 2880 \text{ (labour constraint)}$$
$$4Y + 6Z + S_3 = 2760 \text{ (machine capacity constraint)}$$
$$1Y + S_4 = 420 \text{ (sales constraint for product Y)}$$

For labour (6 hours × Y) + (8 hours × Z) plus any unused labour hours (S_2) will equal 2880 hours when the optimum solution is reached. Similar reasoning applies to the other production constraints. The sales limitation indicates that the number of units of Y sold plus any shortfall on maximum demand will equal 420 units.

We shall now express all the above equations in matrix form (sometimes described as in tableau form), with the slack variables on the left-hand side:

Initial matrix

Quantity	Y	Z	
$S_1 = 3440$	−8	−4	(1) (material constraint)
$S_2 = 2880$	−6	−8	(2) (labour constraint)
$S_3 = 2760$	−4	−6	(3) (machine hours constraint)
$S_4 = 420$	−1	0	(4) (sales constraint)
$C = 0$	+14	+16	(5) contribution

Note that the quantity column in the matrix indicates the resources available or the slack that is not taken up when production is zero. For example, the S_1 row of the matrix indicates that 3440 units of materials are available when production is zero. Column Y indicates that eight units of materials, six labour hours and four machine hours are required to produce one unit of product Y, and this will reduce the potential sales of Y by one. You will also see from column Y that the production of one unit of Y will yield £14 contribution. Similar reasoning applies to column Z. Note that the entry in the contribution row (i.e. the C row) for the quantity column is zero because this first matrix is based on nil production, which gives a contribution of zero.

The Simplex method involves the application of matrix algebra to generate a series of matrices until a final matrix emerges that represents the optimal solution based on the initial model. The final matrix containing the optimal solution is shown below.

Final matrix

Quantity	S_1	S_2	
$Y = 400$	$-\frac{1}{5}$	$+\frac{1}{10}$	(1)
$Z = 60$	$+\frac{3}{20}$	$-\frac{1}{5}$	(2)
$S_3 = 800$	$-\frac{1}{10}$	$+\frac{4}{5}$	(3)
$S_4 = 20$	$+\frac{1}{5}$	$-\frac{1}{10}$	(4)
$C = 6560$	$-\frac{2}{5}$	$-1\frac{4}{5}$	(5)

Interpreting the final matrix

The final matrix can be interpreted using the same approach that was used for the initial matrix but the interpretation is more complex. The contribution row (equation 5) of the final matrix contains only negative items, which signifies that the optimal solution has been reached. The quantity column for any products listed on the left hand side of the matrix indicates the number of units of the product that should be manufactured when the optimum solution is reached. 400 units of Y and 60 units of Z should therefore be produced, giving a total contribution of £6560. This agrees with the results we obtained using the graphical method. *When an equation appears for a slack variable, this indicates that unused resources exist.* The final matrix therefore indicates that the optimal plan will result in 800 unused machine hours (S_3) and an unused sales potential of 20 units for product Y (S_4). The fact that there is no equation for S_1 and S_2 means that these are the inputs that are fully utilized and that limit further increases in output and profit.

The S_1 column (materials) of the final matrix indicates that the materials are fully utilized. (*Whenever resources appear as column headings in the final matrix, this indicates that they are fully utilized.*) So, to obtain a unit of materials, the column for S_1 indicates that we must alter the optimum production programme by increasing production of product Z by $\frac{3}{20}$ of a unit and decreasing production of product Y by $\frac{1}{5}$ of a unit. The effect of removing one scarce unit of material from the production process is summarized in Exhibit 25.1.

Look at the machine capacity column of Exhibit 25.1. If we increase production of product Z by $\frac{3}{20}$ of a unit then more machine hours will be required, leading to the available capacity being reduced by $\frac{9}{10}$ of an hour. Each unit of product Z requires six machine hours, so $\frac{3}{20}$ of a unit will require $\frac{9}{10}$ of an hour ($\frac{3}{20} \times 6$). Decreasing production of product Y by $\frac{1}{5}$ unit will release $\frac{4}{5}$ of a machine hour, given that one unit of product Y requires four machine hours. The overall effect of this process is to reduce the available machine capacity by $\frac{1}{10}$ of a machine hour. Similar principles apply to the other calculations presented in Exhibit 25.1.

Let us now reconcile the information set out in Exhibit 25.1 with the materials column (S_1) of the final matrix. The S_1 column of the final matrix indicates that to release one unit of materials from the optimum production programme we should increase the output of product Z by $\frac{3}{20}$, and decrease product Y by $\frac{1}{5}$ of a unit. This substitution process will lead to the unused machine capacity being reduced by $\frac{1}{10}$ of a machine hour, an increase in the unfulfilled sales demand of product Y (S_4) by $\frac{1}{5}$ of a unit and a reduction in contribution of £$\frac{2}{5}$. All this information is obtained from column S_1 of the final matrix, and Exhibit 25.1 provides the proof. Note that Exhibit 25.1 also proves that the substitution process that is required to obtain an additional unit of materials releases exactly 1 unit. In addition, Exhibit 25.1 indicates that the substitution process for labour gives a net effect of zero, and so no entries appear in the S_1 column of the final matrix in respect of the labour row (i.e. S_2).

The contribution row of the final matrix contains some vital information for the accountant. The figures in this row represent opportunity costs (also known as shadow prices) for the scarce factors of materials and labour. For example, the reduction in contribution from the loss of one unit of materials is £$\frac{2}{5}$ (£0.40) and from the loss of one labour hour is £$1\frac{4}{5}$ (£1.80). Our earlier studies have indicated that this information is vital for decision-making, and we shall use this information again shortly to establish the relevant costs of the resources.

The proof of the opportunity costs can be found in Exhibit 25.1. From the contribution column we can see that the loss of one unit of materials leads to a loss of contribution of £0.40.

Substitution process when additional resources are obtained

Management may be able to act to remove a constraint which is imposed by the shortage of a scarce resource. For example, the company might obtain substitute materials or it may purchase the materials from an overseas supplier. A situation may therefore occur where resources additional to those included in the model used to derive the optimum solution are available. In such circumstances the marginal rates of substitution specified in the final matrix can indicate the optimum use of the additional resources. However, when additional resources are available it is necessary to *reverse* the signs in the final matrix. The reason is that the removal of one unit of

EXHIBIT 25.1 The effect of removing 1 unit of material from the optimum production programme

	S_3 Machine capacity	S_4 Sales of Y	S_1 Materials	S_2 Labour	Contribution (£)
Increase product Z by $\frac{3}{20}$ of a unit	$-\frac{9}{10}(\frac{3}{20} \times 6)$	–	$-\frac{3}{5}(\frac{3}{20} \times 4)$	$-1\frac{1}{5}(\frac{3}{20} \times 8)$	$+2\frac{2}{5}(\frac{3}{20} \times 16)$
Decrease product Y by $\frac{1}{5}$ of a unit	$+\frac{4}{5}(\frac{1}{5} \times 4)$	$+\frac{1}{5}$	$+1\frac{3}{5}(\frac{1}{5} \times 8)$	$+1\frac{1}{5}(\frac{1}{5} \times 6)$	$-2\frac{4}{5}(\frac{1}{5} \times 14)$
Net effect	$-\frac{1}{10}$	$+\frac{1}{5}$	$+1$	Nil	$-\frac{2}{5}$

materials from the optimum production programme requires that product Z be increased by $\frac{3}{20}$ of a unit and product Y decreased by $\frac{1}{5}$ of a unit. If we then decide to return released materials to the optimum production programme, we must reverse this process – that is, increase product Y by $\frac{1}{5}$ of a unit and reduce product Z by $\frac{3}{20}$ of a unit. The important point to remember is that *when considering the response to obtaining additional resources over and above those specified in the initial model, the signs of all the items in the final matrix must be reversed.*

We can now establish how we should best use an additional unit of scarce materials. Inspection of the final matrix indicates that product Y should be increased by $\frac{1}{5}$ of a unit and product Z reduced by $\frac{3}{20}$, giving an additional contribution of £0.40. Note that this is identical with the solution we obtained using the graphical method.

Note that this process will lead to an increase in machine hours of $\frac{1}{10}$ hour (S_3) and a decrease in potential sales of product Y by $\frac{1}{5}$ (S_4). Similarly, if we were to obtain an additional labour hour, we should increase production of Z by $\frac{1}{5}$ of a unit and decrease production of product Y by $\frac{1}{10}$ of a unit, which would yield an additional contribution of £1.80. These are the most efficient uses that can be obtained from additional labour and material resources. From a practical point of view, decisions will not involve the use of fractions; for example, the LP company considered here might be able to obtain 200 additional labour hours; the final matrix indicates that optimal production plan should be altered by increasing production of product Z by 40 units (200 × $\frac{1}{5}$ of a unit) and decreasing production of product Y by 20 units. This process will lead to machine capacity being reduced by 160 hours and potential sales of product Y being increased by 20 units.

Note that examination questions often present the final matrix in a different format to the approach illustrated in this chapter. You should refer to the Key examination points section at the end of the chapter for an explanation of how you can reconcile the alternative approaches.

Uses of linear programming

Calculation of relevant costs

The calculation of relevant costs is essential for decision-making. When a resource is scarce, alternative uses exist that provide a contribution. An opportunity cost is therefore incurred whenever the resource is used. The relevant cost for a scarce resource is calculated as

$$\text{acquisition cost of resource} + \text{opportunity cost}$$

When more than one scarce resource exists, the opportunity cost should be established using linear programming techniques. Note that the opportunity costs of materials and labour are derived from the final row (monetary figures expressed in fractions) of the third and final matrix. Let us now calculate the relevant costs for the resources used by the LP company. The costs are as follows:

materials	= £4.40 (£4 acquisition cost plus £0.40 opportunity cost)
labour	= £11.80 (£10 acquisition cost plus £1.80 opportunity cost)
variable overheads	= £1.00 (£1 acquisition cost plus zero opportunity cost)
fixed overheads	= nil

Because variable overheads are assumed to vary in proportion to machine hours, and because machine hours are not scarce, no opportunity costs arise for variable overheads. Fixed overheads have not been included in the model, since they do not vary in the short term with changes in activity. The relevant cost for fixed overheads is therefore zero.

Selling different products

Let us now assume that the company is contemplating selling a modified version of product Y (called product L) in a new market. The market price is £160 and the product requires ten units input of each resource. Should this product L be manufactured? Conventional accounting information does not provide us with the information necessary to make this decision. Product L can be made only by restricting output of Y and Z, because of the input constraints, and we need to know the opportunity costs of releasing the scarce resources to this new product. Opportunity costs were incorporated in our calculation of the relevant costs for each of the resources, and so the relevant information for the decision is as follows:

	(£)	(£)
Selling price of product L		160
Less relevant costs:		
Materials (10 × 4.40)	44	
Labour (10 × 11.80)	118	
Variable overhead (10 × 1.00)	10	
Contribution		172
		(−12)

Total planned contribution will be reduced by £12 for each unit produced of product L.

Maximum payment for additional scarce resources

Opportunity costs provide important information in situations where a company can obtain additional scarce resources, but only at a premium. How much should the company be prepared to pay? For example, the company may be able to remove the labour constraint by paying overtime. The final matrix indicates that the company can pay up to an additional £1.80 over and above the standard wage rate for each hour worked in excess of 2880 hours and still obtain a contribution from the use of this labour hour. The total contribution will therefore be improved by any additional payment below £1.80 per hour. Similarly, LP will improve the total contribution by paying up to £0.40 in excess of the standard material cost for units obtained in excess of 3440 units. Hence the company will increase short-term profits by paying up to £11.80 for each additional labour hour in excess of 2880 hours and up to £4.40 for units of material that are acquired in excess of 3440 units.

Control

Opportunity costs are also important for cost control. For example, material wastage is reflected in an adverse material usage variance. The responsibility centre should therefore be identified not only with the acquisition cost of £4 per unit but also with the opportunity cost of £0.40 from the loss of one scarce unit of materials. This process highlights the true cost of the inefficient usage of scarce resources and encourages responsibility heads to pay special attention to the control of scarce factors of production. This approach is particularly appropriate where a firm has adopted an optimized production technology (OPT) strategy (see Chapter 9) because variance arising from bottleneck operations will be reported in terms of opportunity cost rather than acquisition cost.

Capital budgeting

Linear programming can be used to determine the optimal investment programme when capital rationing exists. This topic tends not to form part of the management accounting curriculum for most courses. You should refer to Learning Note 25.2 if you wish to study how linear programming can be used in capital investment appraisal.

Sensitivity analysis

ADVANCED READING

Opportunity costs are of vital importance in making management decisions, but production constraints do not exist permanently, and therefore opportunity costs cannot be regarded as permanent. There is a need to ascertain the range over which the opportunity cost applies for each input. This information can be obtained from the final matrix. For materials we merely examine the negative items for column S_1 in the final matrix and divide each item into the quantity column as follows:

$$Y = 400/(-\tfrac{1}{5}) = -2000$$
$$S_3 = 800/(-\tfrac{1}{10}) = -8000$$

The number closest to zero in this calculation (namely −2000) indicates by how much the availability of materials used in the model can be reduced. Given that the model was established using 3440 units of materials, the lower limit of the range is 1440 units (3440 − 2000). The upper limit is determined in a similar way. We divide the positive items in column S_4 into the quantity column as follows:

$$Z = 60/\tfrac{3}{20} = 400$$
$$S_4 = 20/\tfrac{1}{5} = 100$$

The lower number in the calculation (namely 100) indicates by how much the materials can be increased. Adding this to the 3440 units of materials indicates that the upper limit of the range is 3540 units. The opportunity cost and marginal rates of substitution for materials therefore apply over the range of 1440 to 3540 units.

Let us now consider the logic on which these calculations are based. The lower limit is determined by removing materials from the optimum production programme. We have previously established from the final matrix and Exhibit 25.1 that removing one unit of material from the optimum production programme means that product Y will be reduced by $\tfrac{1}{5}$ and machine capacity will be reduced by $\tfrac{1}{10}$ of an hour. Since the final matrix indicates an output of 400 units of product Y, this reduction can only be carried out 2000 times (400/$\tfrac{1}{5}$) before the process must stop. Similarly, 800 hours of machine capacity are still unused, and the reduction process can only be carried out 8000 times (800/$\tfrac{1}{10}$) before the process must stop. Given the two constraints on reducing materials, the first constraint that is reached is the reduction of product Y. The planned usage of materials can therefore be reduced by 2000 units before the substitution process must stop. The same reasoning applies (with the signs reversed) in understanding the principles for establishing the upper limit of the range.

Similar reasoning can be applied to establish that the opportunity cost and marginal rates of substitution apply for labour hours over a range of 2680 to 3880 hours. For any decisions based on scarce inputs outside the ranges specified a revised model must be formulated and a revised final matrix produced. From this matrix revised opportunity costs and marginal rates of substitution can be established.

SUMMARY

The following items relate to the learning objectives listed at the beginning of the chapter.

● **Describe the situations when it may be appropriate to use linear programming.**

Conventional limiting factor analysis (see Chapter 9) should be used when there is only one scarce factor. Linear programming can be used to determine the production programme that maximizes total contribution when there is more than one scarce input factor.

● **Explain the circumstances when the graphical method can be used.**

The graphical method can be used with two products. Where more than two products are involved the simplex method should be used.

● **Use graphical linear programming to find the optimum output levels.**

Production/sales quantities for one of the two products are labelled on the horizontal axis and the vertical axis is used for the other product. Combinations of the maximum output (based on the two products) from fully utilizing each resource, and any sales volume limitations, are plotted on the graph. A series of contribution lines are plotted based on the potential output levels for each product that will achieve a selected total contribution. The optimum output levels are derived at the point where the feasible production region touches the highest contribution line. The process is illustrated in Figure 25.5 using the data presented in Example 25.1.

● **Formulate the initial linear programming model using the Simplex method.**

Assuming that the objective function is to maximize total contribution the objective function should initially be specified expressed in terms of the contributions per unit for each product. Next the constraints should be listed in equation form with slack variables introduced to ensure that model is specified in terms of equalities rather than inequalities. The initial matrix is prepared by converting the linear programming model into a matrix format. The process is illustrated using Example 25.1.

● **Explain the meaning of the term shadow prices.**

The Simplex method of linear programming generates shadow prices (also known as opportunity costs) for each of those scarce resources that are fully utilized in the optimum production programme. The shadow prices represent the reduction in total contribution that will occur from the loss of one unit of a scarce resource. Conversely, they represent the increase in total contribution that will occur if an additional unit of the scarce resource can be obtained.

Key terms and concepts

linear programming (p. 642)
marginal rate of substitution (p. 647)
objective function (p. 642)

opportunity cost (p. 647)
shadow price (p. 647)
Simplex method (p. 648)

slack variables (p. 648)

Key examination points

A common error is to state the objective function in terms of profit per unit. This is incorrect, because the fixed cost per unit is not constant. The objective function should be expressed in terms of contribution per unit. You should note that there are several ways of formulating the matrices for a linear programming model. The approach adopted in this chapter was to formulate the first matrix with positive contribution signs and negative signs for the slack variable equations. The optimal solution occurs when the signs in the contribution row are all negative. Sometimes examination questions are set that adopt the opposite procedure. That is, the signs are the reverse of the approach presented in this chapter.

For an illustration of how to cope with this situation you should refer to the answers to Review problem 25.14. A more recent approach is to present the output from the model as a computer printout. You should refer to the solution to Review problem 25.15 to make sure you understand this approach.

Most examination questions include the final matrix and require you to interpret the figures. You may also be required to formulate the initial model. It is most unlikely that you will be required to complete the calculations and prepare the final matrix. However, you may be asked to construct a graph and calculate the marginal rates of substitution and opportunity costs.

ASSESSMENT MATERIAL

The review questions are short questions that enable you to assess your understanding of the main topics included in the chapter. The numbers in parentheses provide you with the page numbers to refer to if you cannot answer a specific question.

The review problems are more complex and require you to relate and apply the content to various business problems. The problems are graded by their level of difficulty. Solutions to review problems that are not preceded by the term 'IM' are provided in a separate section at the end of the book. Solutions to problems preceded by the term 'IM' are provided in the *Instructor's Manual* accompanying this book and also on the lecturer's password protected section of the website www.drury-online.com. Additional review problems with fully worked solutions are provided in the *Student's Manual* that accompanies this book.

Review questions

25.1 Describe the situations when it may be appropriate to use linear programming. *(pp. 641–43)*

25.2 Explain what is meant by the term 'objective function'. *(p. 642)*

25.3 What is the feasible production area? *(p. 654)*

25.4 What is the marginal rate of substitution? *(p. 647)*

25.5 Explain what is meant by the term 'shadow price'. *(p. 647)*

25.6 Explain the circumstances when it is appropriate to use the Simplex method. *(p. 648)*

25.7 What are slack variables? *(p. 648)*

25.8 Provide illustrations of how the information derived from linear programming can be applied to a variety of management accounting problems. *(pp. 651–52)*

25.9 Explain how sensitivity analysis can be applied to the output of a linear programming model. *(p. 653)*

Review problems

25.10 Intermediate. The following graph relates to a linear programming problem:

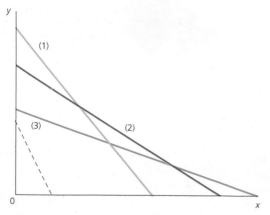

The objective is to maximize contribution and the dotted line on the graph depicts this function. There are three constraints which are all of the 'less than or equal to' type which are depicted on the graph by the three solid lines labelled (1), (2) and (3).

At which of the following intersections is contribution maximized?

a Constraints (1) and (2)
b Constraints (2) and (3)
c Constraints (1) and (3)
d Constraint (1) and the *x*-axis

ACCA – Financial Information for Management

25.11 Intermediate. Taree Limited uses linear programming to establish the optimal production plan for the production of its two products, A and U, given that it has the objective of minimizing costs. The following graph has been established bearing in mind the various constraints of the business. The clear area indicates the feasible region.

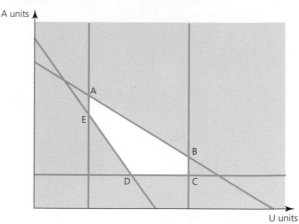

Which points are most likely to give the optimal solution?

a A and B only
b A, B and C only
c D and E only
d B, D and E only.

ACCA – Financial Information for Management

25.12 Intermediate. A company uses linear programming to establish an optimal production plan in order to maximize profit.

The company finds that the next year materials and labour are likely to be in short supply.

Details of the company's products are as follows:

	A £	B £
Materials (at £2 per kg)	6	8
Labour (at £6 per hour)	30	18
Variable overheads (at £1 per hour)	5	3
Variable cost	41	29
Selling price	50	52
Contribution	9	23

There are only 30 000 kg of material and 36 000 labour hours available. The company also has an agreement to supply 1000 units of product A which must be met.

Required:

a Formulate the objective function and constraint equations for this problem. *(4 marks)*

b Plot the constraints on a suitable graph and determine the optimal production plan. *(6 marks)*

ACCA – Financial Information for Management

25.13 Advanced: Optimal output and calculation of shadow prices using graphical approach. Brass Ltd produces two products, the Masso and the Russo. Budgeted data relating to these products on a unit basis for August are as follows:

	Masso (£)	Russo (£)
Selling price	150	100
Materials	80	30
Salesmen's commission	30	20

Each unit of product incurs costs of machining and assembly. The total capacity available in August is budgeted to be 700 hours of machining and 1000 hours of assembly, the cost of this capacity being fixed at £7000 and £10 000 respectively for the month, whatever the level of usage made of it. The number of hours required in each of these departments to complete one unit of output is as follows:

	Masso	Russo
Machining	1.0	2.0
Assembly	2.5	2.0

Under the terms of special controls recently introduced by the government in accordance with EEC requirements, selling prices are fixed and the maximum permitted output of either product in August is 400 units (i.e. Brass Ltd may produce a maximum of 800 units of product). At the present controlled selling prices the demand for the products exceeds this considerably.

You are required:

a to calculate Brass Ltd's optimal production plan for August, and the profit earned, *(10 marks)*

b to calculate the value to Brass Ltd of an independent marginal increase in the available capacity for each of machining and assembly, assuming that the capacity of the other department is not altered and the output maxima continue to apply, *(10 marks)*

c to state the principal assumptions underlying your calculations in (a) above, and to assess their general significance. *(5 marks)*

ICAEW Management Accounting

25.14 Advanced: Optimal output with a single limiting factor and interpretation of a final matrix.

Hint: Reverse the signs in the final matrix.

a Corpach Ltd manufactures three products for which the sales maxima, for the forthcoming year, are estimated to be:

Product 1	Product 2	Product 3
£57 500	£96 000	£125 000

Summarized unit cost data are as follows:

	Product 1 (£)	Product 2 (£)	Product 3 (£)
Direct material cost	10.00	9.00	7.00
Variable processing costs	8.00	16.00	10.00
Fixed processing costs	2.50	5.00	4.00
	£20.50	30.00	£21.00

The allocation of fixed processing costs has been derived from last year's production levels and the figures may need revision if current output plans are different.

The established selling prices are:

Product 1	Product 2	Product 3
£23.00	£32.00	£25.00

The products are processed on machinery housed in three buildings:

Building A contains type A machines on which 9800 machine hours are estimated to be available in the forthcoming year. The fixed overheads for this building are £9800 p.a.

Building B1 contains type B machines on which 10 500 machine hours are estimated to be available in the forthcoming year.

Building B2 also contains type B machines and again 10 500 machine hours are estimated to be available in the forthcoming year.

The fixed overheads for the B1 and B2 buildings are, in total, £11 200 p.a.

The times required for one unit of output for each product on each type of machine, are as follows:

	Product 1	Product 2	Product 3
Type A machines	1 hour	2 hours	3 hours
Type B machines	1.5 hours	3 hours	1 hour

Assuming that Corpach Ltd wishes to maximize its profits for the ensuing year, you are required to determine the optimal production plan and the profit that this should produce. *(9 marks)*

b Assume that, before the plan that you have prepared in part (a) is implemented, Corpach Ltd suffers a major fire which completely destroys building B2. The fire thus reduces the availability of type B machine time to 10 500 hours p.a. and the estimated fixed overhead for such machines, to £8200. In all other respects the conditions set out, in part (a) to this question, continue to apply.

In his efforts to obtain a revised production plan the company's accountant makes use of a linear programming computer package. This package produces the following optimal tableau:

Z	X1	X2	X3	S1	S2	S3	S4	S5	
0	0	0	0	0.5	1	0	0.143	−0.429	1 150
0	0	1	0	−0.5	0	0	−0.143	0.429	1 850
0	0	0	0	0	0	1	−0.429	0.286	3 800
0	0	0	1	0	0	0	0.429	−0.286	1 200
0	1	0	0	1	0	0	0	0	2 500
1	0	0	0	1.5	0	0	2.429	0.714	35 050

In the above: Z is the total contribution,

$X1$ is the budgeted output of product 1,
$X2$ is the budgeted output of product 2,
$X3$ is the budgeted output of product 3,
$S1$ is the unsatisfied demand for product 1,
$S2$ is the unsatisfied demand for product 2,
$S3$ is the unsatisfied demand for product 3,
$S4$ is the unutilized type A machine time,
$S5$ is the unutilized type B machine time.

and

The tableau is interpreted as follows:

Optimal plan – Make 2500 units of Product 1,
      1850 units of Product 2,
      1200 units of Product 3,
Shadow prices – Product 1 £1.50 per unit,
 Type A Machine Time £2.429 per hour,
 Type B Machine Time £0.714 per hour.

Explain the meaning of the shadow prices and consider how the accountant might make use of them. Calculate the profit anticipated from the revised plan and comment on its variation from the profit that you calculated in your answer to part (a). *(9 marks)*

c Explain why linear programming was not necessary for the facts as set out in part (a) whereas it was required for part (b). *(4 marks)*

ACCA Level 2 Management Accounting

25.15 Advanced: Interpretation of the linear programming solution. Woodalt plc has two automated machine groups X and Y, through which timber is passed in order to produce two models of an item of sports equipment. The models are called 'Traditional' and 'Hightech'.

The following forecast information is available for the year to 31 December 2001:

		'Traditional'	'Hightech'
(i)	Maximum sales potential (units)	6000	10 000
(ii)	Equipment unit data:		
	Selling price	£100	£90
	Machine time: group X (hours)	0.5	0.3
	group Y (hours)	0.4	0.45

(iii) Machine groups *X* and *Y* have maximum operating hours of 3400 and 3840 respectively. The sports equipment production is the sole use available for the production capacity.

(iv) The maximum quantity of timber available is 34 000 metres. Each product unit requires four metres of timber. Timber may be purchased in lengths as required at £5 per metre.

(v) Variable machine overhead cost for machine groups *X* and *Y* is estimated at £25 and £30 per machine hour respectively.

(vi) All units are sold in the year in which they are produced.

A linear programme of the situation has been prepared in order to determine the strategy which will maximize the contribution for the year to 31 December 2001 and to provide additional decision making information. Appendix 3.1 shows a print-out of the solution to the LP model.

Required:

a   Formulate the mathematical model from which the input to the LP programme would be obtained.   *(4 marks)*

b   Using the linear programme solution in Appendix 3.1 where appropriate, answer the following in respect of the year to 31 December 2001:

   (i)   State the maximum contribution and its distribution between the two models;   *(3 marks)*

   (ii) Explain the effect on contribution of the limits placed on the availability of timber and machine time;   *(3 marks)*

   (iii) In addition to the sports equipment models, Woodalt plc has identified additional products which could earn contribution at the rate of £20 and £30 per machine hour for machine groups *X* and *Y* respectively. Such additional products would be taken up only to utilize any surplus hours not required for the sports equipment production.
   Prepare figures which show the additional contribution which could be obtained in the year to 31 December 2001 from the additional sales outlets for each of machine groups *X* and *Y*;
                                                                (4 marks)

   (iv) Explain the sensitivity of the plan to changes in contribution per unit for each sports equipment product type;   *(2 marks)*

   (v) Woodalt plc expects to be able to overcome the timber availability constraint. All other parameters in the model remain unchanged. (*The additional products suggested in (iii) above do not apply.*)
   Calculate the increase in contribution which this would provide;   *(2 marks)*

   (vi) You are told that the amended contribution maximizing solution arising from (v) will result in the production and sale of the 'Traditional' product being 3600 units.
   Determine how many units of the 'Hightech' product will be produced and sold.   *(2 marks)*

c   Suggest ways in which Woodalt plc may overcome the capacity constraints which limit the opportunities available to it in the year to 31 December 2001. Indicate the types of cost which may be incurred in overcoming each constraint.   *(6 marks)*

d   Explain why Woodalt plc should consider each of the following items before implementing the profit maximizing strategy indicated in Appendix 3.1:
   (i)   Product specific costs;
   (ii) Customer specific costs;
   (iii) Life cycle costs.
   Your answer should include relevant examples for each of (i) to (iii).
                                                                (9 marks)

Appendix 3.1
Forecast strategy evaluation for the year to 31 December 2001

Target Cell (Max) (£)

Cell	Name	Final Value
C2	Contribution	444 125

Adjustable Cells (Units)

Cell	Name	Final Value
A1	Traditional	4250
B1	Hightech	4250

Adjustable Cells (Units and £)

Cell	Name	Final Value	Reduced Cost	Objective Coefficient	Allowable Increase	Allowable Decrease
A1	Traditional	4250	0	55.50	26.17	6.50
B1	Hightech	4250	0	49.00	6.50	15.70

Constraints (Quantities and £)

Cell	Name	Final Value	Shadow Price	Constraint R.H. Side	Allowable Increase	Allowable Decrease
C3	Timber	34 000	9.8125	34 000	1733.33	6800
C4	Machines X	3 400	32.5	3 400	850	850
C5	Machines Y	3 612.5	0	3 840	IE+30	227.5

ACCA Paper 9 Information for Control and Decision Making

IM25.1 Intermediate: Optimal output using the graphical approach. G Limited, manufacturers of superior garden ornaments, is preparing its production budget for the coming period. The company makes four types of ornament, the data for which are as follows:

Product	Pixie (£ per unit)	Elf (£ per unit)	Queen (£ per unit)	King (£ per unit)
Direct materials	25	35	22	25
Variable overhead	17	18	15	16
Selling price	111	98	122	326
Direct labour hours:	*Hours per unit*	*Hours per unit*	*Hours per unit*	*Hours per unit*
Type 1	8	6	—	—
Type 2	—	—	10	10
Type 3	—	—	5	25

Fixed overhead amounts to £15 000 per period.

Each type of labour is paid £5 per hour but because of the skills involved, an employee of one type cannot be used for work normally done by another type.

The maximum hours available in each type are:

Type 1	8 000 hours
Type 2	20 000 hours
Type 3	25 000 hours

The marketing department judges that, at the present selling prices, the demand for the products is likely to be:

Pixie	Unlimited demand
Elf	Unlimited demand
Queen	1500 units
King	1000 units

You are required:

a   to calculate the product mix that will maximize profit, and the amount of the profit;   *(14 marks)*

b   to determine whether it would be worthwhile paying Type 1 Labour for overtime working at time and a half and, if so, to calculate the extra profit for each 1000 hours of overtime;
                                                                (2 marks)

c   to comment on the principles used to find the optimum product mix in part (a), pointing out any possible limitations;   *(3 marks)*

d   to explain how a computer could assist in providing a solution for the data shown above.   *(3 marks)*

CIMA Stage 3 Management Accounting Techniques

IM25.2 Advanced: Optimal output using the graphical approach and the impact of an increase in capacity. A company makes two products, *X* and *Y*. Product *X* has a contribution of £124 per unit and product *Y* £80 per unit. Both products pass through two departments for processing and the times in minutes per unit are:

	Product X	Product Y
Department 1	150	90
Department 2	100	120

Currently there is a maximum of 225 hours per week available in department 1 and 200 hours in department 2. The company can sell all it can produce of *X* but EEC quotas restrict the sale of *Y* to a maximum of 75 units per week.

The company, which wishes to maximize contribution, currently makes and sells 30 units of *X* and 75 units of *Y* per week.

The company is considering several possibilities including

(i) altering the production plan if it could be proved that there is a better plan than the current one;

(ii) increasing the availability of either department 1 or department 2 hours. The extra costs involved in increasing capacity are £0.5 per hour for each department;

(iii) transferring some of their allowed sales quota for Product Y to another company. Because of commitments the company would always retain a minimum sales level of 30 units.

You are required to

a calculate the optimum production plan using the existing capacities and state the extra contribution that would be achieved compared with the existing plan; (8 marks)

b advise management whether they should increase the capacity of either department 1 or department 2 and, if so, by how many hours and what the resulting increase in contribution would be over that calculated in the improved production plan; (7 marks)

c calculate the minimum price per unit for which they could sell the rights to their quota, down to the minimum level, given the plan in (a) as a starting point. (5 marks)

CIMA Stage 3 Management Accounting Techniques

IM25.3 Advanced: Maximizing profit and sales revenue using the graphical approach. Goode, Billings and Prosper plc manufactures two products, Razzle and Dazzle. Unit selling prices and variable costs, and daily fixed costs are:

	Razzle (£)	Dazzle (£)
Selling price per unit	20	30
Variable costs per unit	8	20
Contribution margin per unit	12	10
Joint fixed costs per day	£60	

Production of the two products is restricted by limited supplies of three essential inputs: Raz, Ma, and Taz. All other inputs are available at prevailing prices without any restriction. The quantities of Raz, Ma, and Taz necessary to produce single units of Razzle and Dazzle, together with the total supplies available each day, are:

	kg per unit required		Total available
	Razzle	Dazzle	(kg per day)
Raz	5	12.5	75
Ma	8	10	80
Taz	2	0	15

William Billings, the sales director, advises that any combination of Razzle and/or Dazzle can be sold without affecting their market prices. He also argues very strongly that the company should seek to maximize its sales revenues subject to a minimum acceptable profit of £44 per day in total from these two products.

In contrast, the financial director, Silas Prosper, has told the managing director, Henry Goode, that he believes in a policy of profit maximization at all times.

You are required to:

a calculate:
   (i) the profit and total sales revenue per day, assuming a policy of profit maximization, (10 marks)
   (ii) the total sales revenue per day, assuming a policy of sales revenue maximization subject to a minimum acceptable profit of £44 per day, (10 marks)

b suggest why businessmen might choose to follow an objective of maximizing sales revenue subject to a minimum profit constraint. (5 marks)

(Total 25 marks)
ICAEW Management Accounting

IM25.4 Advanced: Optimal output and shadow prices using the graphical approach. Usine Ltd is a company whose objective is to maximize profits. It manufactures two speciality chemical powders, gamma and delta, using three processes: heating, refining and blending. The powders can be produced and sold in infinitely divisible quantities.

The following are the estimated production hours for each process per kilo of output for each of the two chemical powders during the period 1 June to 31 August:

	Gamma (hours)	Delta (hours)
Heating	400	120
Refining	100	90
Blending	100	250

During the same period, revenues and costs per kilo of output are budgeted as

	Gamma (£ per kilo)	Delta (£ per kilo)
Selling price	16 000	25 000
Variable costs	12 000	17 000
Contribution	4 000	8 000

It is anticipated that the company will be able to sell all it can produce at the above prices, and that at any level of output fixed costs for the three month period will total £36 000.

The company's management accountant is under the impression that there will only be one scarce factor during the budget period, namely blending hours, which cannot exceed a total of 1050 hours during the period 1 June to 31 August. He therefore correctly draws up an optimum production plan on this basis.

However, when the factory manager sees the figures he points out that over the three month period there will not only be a restriction on blending hours, but in addition the heating and refining hours cannot exceed 1200 and 450 respectively during the three month period.

Requirements:

a Calculate the initial production plan for the period 1 June to 31 August as prepared by the management accountant, assuming blending hours are the only scarce factor. Indicate the budgeted profit or loss, and explain why the solution is the optimum. (4 marks)

b Calculate the optimum production plan for the period 1 June to 31 August, allowing for both the constraint on blending hours and the additional restrictions identified by the factory manager, and indicate the budgeted profit or loss. (8 marks)

c State the implications of your answer in (b) in terms of the decisions that will have to be made by Usine Ltd with respect to production during the period 1 June to 31 August after taking into account all relevant costs. (2 marks)

d Under the restrictions identified by the management accountant and the factory manager, the shadow (or dual) price of one extra hour of blending time on the optimum production plan is £27.50. Calculate the shadow (or dual) price of one extra hour of refining time. Explain how such information might be used by management, and in so doing indicate the limitations inherent in the figures. (6 marks)

Note: Ignore taxation.

Show all calculations clearly.

ICAEW Management Accounting and Financial Management I Part Two

IM25.5 Advanced: Formulation of initial tableau and interpretation of final tableau. The Alphab Group has five divisions A, B, C, D and E. Group management wish to increase overall group production capacity per year by up to 30 000 hours. Part of the strategy will be to require that the minimum increase at any one division must be equal to 5 per cent of its current capacity. The maximum funds available for the expansion programme are £3 000 000.

Additional information relating to each division is as follows:

Division	Existing capacity (hours)	Investment cost per hour (£)	Average contribution per hour (£)
A	20 000	90	12.50
B	40 000	75	9.50
C	24 000	100	11
D	50 000	120	8
E	12 000	200	14

A linear programme of the plan has been prepared in order to determine the strategy which will maximize additional contribution per annum and to provide additional decision-making information. The Appendix to this question shows a print-out of the LP model of the situation.

Required:

a Formulate the mathematical model from which the input to the LP programme would be obtained. *(6 marks)*

b Use the linear programme solution in the Appendix in order to answer the following:

(i) State the maximum additional contribution from the expansion strategy and the distribution of the extra capacity between the divisions. *(3 marks)*

(ii) Explain the cost to the company of providing the minimum 5 per cent increase in capacity at each division. *(3 marks)*

(iii) Explain the effect on contribution of the limits placed on capacity and investment. *(2 marks)*

(iv) Explain the sensitivity of the plan to changes in contribution per hour. *(4 marks)*

(v) Group management decide to relax the 30 000 hours capacity constraint. All other parameters of the model remain unchanged. Determine the change in strategy which will then maximize the increase in group contribution. You should calculate the increase in contribution which this change in strategy will provide. *(6 marks)*

(vi) Group management wish to decrease the level of investment while leaving all other parameters of the model (as per the Appendix) unchanged.

Determine and quantify the change in strategy which is required indicating the fall in contribution which will occur. *(6 marks)*

c Explain the limitations of the use of linear programming for planning purposes. *(5 marks)*

Appendix
Divisional investment evaluation
Optimal solution – detailed report

Variable	Value
1 DIV A	22 090.91
2 DIV B	2 000.00
3 DIV C	1 200.00
4 DIV D	2 500.00
5 DIV E	2 209.09

	Constraint	Type	RHS	Slack	Shadow price
1	Max. Hours	<=	30 000.00	0.00	11.2727
2	DIV A	>=	1 000.00	21 090.91	0.0000
3	DIV B	>=	2 000.00	0.00	–2.7955
4	DIV C	>=	1 200.00	0.00	–1.6364
5	DIV D	>=	2 500.00	0.00	–4.9091
6	DIV E	>=	600.00	1 609.09	0.0000
7	Max. Funds	<=	3 000 000.00	0.00	0.0136

Objective function value=359 263.6

Sensitivity Analysis of Objective Function Coefficients

Variable	Current coefficient	Allowable minimum	Allowable maximum
1 DIV A	12.50	10.7000	14.0000
2 DIV B	9.50	–Infinity	12.2955
3 DIV C	11.00	–Infinity	12.6364
4 DIV D	8.00	–Infinity	12.9091
5 DIV E	14.00	12.5000	27.7778

Sensitivity Analysis of Right-hand Side Values

	Constraint	Type	Current value	Allowable minimum	Allowable maximum
1	Max. Hours	<=	30 000.00	18 400.00	31 966.67
2	DIV A	>=	1 000.00	–Infinity	22 090.91
3	DIV B	>=	2 000.00	0.00	20 560.00
4	DIV C	>=	1 200.00	0.00	18 900.00
5	DIV D	>=	2 500.00	0.00	8 400.00
6	DIV E	>=	600.00	–Infinity	2 209.09
7	Max. Funds	<=	3 000 000.00	2 823 000.00	5 320 000.00

Note: RHS=Right-hand side

ACCA Paper 9 Information for Control and Decision Making

IM25.6 Formulation of initial tableau and interpretation of final tableau using the simplex method.

a The Argonaut Company makes three products, Xylos, Yo-yos and Zicons. These are assembled from two components, Agrons and Bovons, which can be produced internally at a variable cost of £5 and £8 each respectively. A limited quantity of each of these components may be available for purchase from an external supplier at a quoted price which varies from week to week.

The production of Agrons and Bovons is subject to several limitations. Both components require the same three production processes (L, M and N), the first two of which have limited availabilities of 9600 minutes per week and 7000 minutes per week respectively. The final process (N) has effectively unlimited availability but for technical reasons must produce at least one Agron for each Bovon produced. The processing times are as follows:

Process	L	M	N
Time (mins) required to produce			
1 Agron	6	5	7
1 Bovon	8	5	9

The component requirements of each of the three final products are:

Product	Xylo	Yo-yo	Zicon
Number of components required			
Agrons	1	1	3
Bovons	2	1	2

The ex-factory selling prices of the final products are given below, together with the standard direct labour hours involved in their assembly and details of other assembly costs incurred:

Product	Xylo	Yo-yo	Zicon
Selling price	£70	£60	£150
Direct labour hours used	6	7	16
Other assembly costs	£4	£5	£15

The standard direct labour rate is £5 per hour. Factory overhead costs amount to £4350 per week and are absorbed to products on the basis of the direct labour costs incurred in their assembly. The current production plan is to produce 100 units of each of the three products each week.

Requirements:

(i) Present a budgeted weekly profit and loss account, by product, for the factory. *(4 marks)*

(ii) Formulate the production problem facing the factory manager as a linear program:

(1) assuming there is no external availability of Agrons and Bovons; *(5 marks)*

and

(2) assuming that 200 Agrons and 300 Bovons are available at prices of £10 and £12 each respectively. *(4 marks)*

b In a week when no external availability of Agrons and Bovons was expected, the optimal solution to the linear program and the shadow prices associated with each constraint were as follows:

Production of Xylos	50 units
Production of Yo-yos	0 units; shadow price £2.75
Production of Zicons	250 units

Shadow price associated with:

Process L	£0.375 per minute
Process M	£0.450 per minute
Process N	£0.000 per minute
Agron availability	£9.50 each
Bovon availability	£13.25 each

If sufficient Bovons were to become available on the external market at a price of £12 each, a revised linear programming solution indicated that only Xylos should be made.

Requirement:

Interpret this output from the linear program in a report to the factory manager. Include calculations of revised shadow prices in your report and indicate the actions the manager should take and the benefits that would accrue if the various constraints could be overcome. *(12 marks)*

ICAEW P2 Management Accounting

IM25.7 Advanced: Formulation of an initial tableau and interpretation of a final tableau using the simplex method.

Hint: Reverse the signs and ignore entries of 0 and 1.

The Kaolene Co. Ltd has six different products all made from fabricated steel. Each product passes through a combination of five production operations: cutting, forming, drilling, welding and coating.

Steel is cut to the length required, formed into the appropriate shapes, drilled if necessary, welded together if the product is made up of more than one part, and then passed through the coating machine. Each operation is separate and independent, except for the cutting and forming operations, when, if needed, forming follows continuously after cutting. Some products do not require every production operation.

The output rates from each production operations, based on a standard measure for each product, are set out in the tableau below, along with the total hours of work available for each operation. The contribution per unit of each product is also given. It is estimated that three of the products have sales ceilings and these are also given below:

Products	X_1	X_2	X_3	X_4	X_5	X_6
Contribution per unit (£)	5.7	10.1	12.3	9.8	17.2	14.0
Output rate per hour:						
Cutting	650	700	370	450	300	420
Forming	450	450	—	520	180	380
Drilling	—	200	380	—	300	—
Welding	—	—	380	670	400	720
Coating	500	—	540	480	600	450
Maximum sales units (000)	—	—	150	—	20	70

	Cutting	Forming	Drilling	Welding	Coating
Production hours available	12 000	16 000	4000	4000	16 000

The production and sales for the year were found using a linear programming algorithm. The final tableau is given below.

Variables X_7 to X_{11} are the slack variables relating to the production constraints, expressed in the order of production. Variables X_{12} to X_{14} are the slack variables relating to the sales ceilings of X_3, X_5 and X_6 respectively.

After analysis of the above results, the production manager believes that further mechanical work on the cutting and forming machines costing £200 can improve their hourly output rates as follows:

Products	X_1	X_2	X_3	X_4	X_5	X_6
Cutting	700	770	410	500	330	470
Forming	540	540	—	620	220	460

The optimal solution to the new situation indicates the shadow prices of the cutting, drilling and welding sections to be £59.3, £14.2 and £71.5 per hour respectively.

Requirements:

a Explain the meaning of the seven items ringed in the final tableau.
(9 marks)

b Show the range of values within which the following variables or resources can change without changing the optimal mix indicated in the final tableau
  (i) c_4: contribution of X4
  (ii) b_5: available coating time. *(4 marks)*

c Formulate the revised linear programming problem taking note of the revised output rates for cutting and forming. *(5 marks)*

d Determine whether the changes in the cutting and forming rates will increase profitability. *(3 marks)*

e Using the above information discuss the usefulness of linear programming to managers in solving this type of problem.
(4 marks)

ICAEW P2 Management Accounting

X_1	X_2	X_3	X_4	X_5	X_6	X_7	X_8	X_9	X_{10}	X_{11}	X_{12}	X_{13}	X_{14}	Variable in basic solution	Value of variable in basic solution
1	0	−1.6	−0.22	−0.99	0	10.8	0	−3.0	−18.5	0	0	0	0	X_1	43 287.0 units
0	0	−0.15	−0.02	0.12	0	−1.4	1	−0.3	0.58	0	0	0	0	X_8	15 747.81 hours
0	1	0.53	0	0.67	0	0	0	3.33	0	0	0	0	0	X_2	13 333.3 units
0	0	1.9	1.08	1.64	1	0	0	0	12	0	0	0	0	X_6	48 019.2 units
0	0	0.06	0.01	0	0	−1.3	0	0.37	0.63	1	0	0	0	X_{11}	150 806.72 hours
0	0	1	0	0	0	0	0	0	0	0	1	0	0	X_{12}	150 000.0 units
0	0	0	0	1	0	0	0	0	0	0	0	1	0	X_{13}	20 000.0 units
0	0	−1.9	−1.0	−1.6	0	0	0	0	−12	0	0	0	1	X_{14}	21 980.8 units
0	0	10.0	4	6.83	0	61.7	0	16.0	62.1	0	0	0	0	$(Z_i - C_i)$	£1 053 617.4

CASE STUDIES

Case studies available from the website

EVA(TM) at Ault Foods Limited

The dedicated website for this book includes over 30 case studies. Both students and lecturers can download these case studies from the open access website. The authors of the cases have provided teaching notes for each case and these can be downloaded only by lecturers from the password protected lecturer's section of the website.

The cases generally cover the content of several chapters and contain questions to which there is no ideal answer. They are intended to encourage independent thought and initiative and to relate and apply the content of this book to more uncertain situations. They are also intended to develop critical thinking and analytical skills.

Details relating to the cases that are available from the website are listed on the following pages. One example case is included at the end of this section. The teaching note for this case is also available on the website.

CASE STUDIES AVAILABLE FROM THE WEBSITE

Airport Complex Peter Nordgaard and Carsten Rhode, Copenhagen Business School
A general case providing material for discussion of several aspects involved in the management control of a service company, which is mainly characterized by mass services.

Anjo Ltd Lin Fitzgerald, Loughborough University Business School
Variance analysis that provides the opportunity to be used as a role playing exercise.

Baldwin Bicycle Company R. N. Anthony and J. S. Reece
Relevant cost analysis and strategic accounting.

Berkshire Threaded Fasteners Company John Shank, The Amos Tuck School of Business Administration Dartmouth College
Cost analysis for dropping a product, for pricing, for product mix and product improvement.

Berkshire Toy Company D. Crawford and E.G. Henry, State University of New York (SUNY) at Oswego
Variance analysis, performance evaluation, responsibility accounting and the balanced scorecard.

Blessed Farm Partnership Rona O'Brien, Sheffield Hallam University
Strategic decision-making, evaluation of alternatives, ethics, sources of information.

Boston Creamery John Shank, The Amos Tuck School of Business Administration Dartmouth College
Management control systems, profit planning, profit variance analysis and flexible budgets.

Brunswick Plastics Anthony Atkinson, University of Waterloo and adapted by John Shank, The Amos Tuck School of Business Administration Dartmouth College
Relevant cost analysis for a new product, short-run versus strategic considerations, pricing considerations.

Chadwick's Department Store Lewis Gordon, Liverpool John Moores University
The application of budget-building techniques and spreadsheet skills to a retail-sector situation.

Company A Mike Tayles, University of Hull Business School and Paul Walley, Warwick Business School
Evaluation of a product costing system and suggested performance measures to support key success factors.

Company B Mike Tayles, University of Hull Business School and Paul Walley, Warwick Business School
The impact of a change in manufacturing strategy and method upon product costing and performance measurement systems.

Danfoss Drives Dan Otzen, Copenhagen Business School
The linkage between operational management and management accounting/control of a company including a discussion of the operational implications of JIT for management accounting.

Dumbellow Ltd Stan Brignall, Aston Business School
Marginal costing versus absorption costing, relevant costs and cost–volume–profit analysis.

Edit 4U Ltd Rona O'Brien, Sheffield Hallam University
The case study explores and evaluates the role of management accounting information in a small business context.

Electronic Boards plc John Innes, University of Dundee and Falconer Mitchell, University of Edinburgh
A general case that may be used at an introductory stage to illustrate the basics of management accounting and the role it can play within a firm.

Endeavour Twoplise Ltd Jayne Ducker, Antony Head, Brenda McDonnell, Sheffield Hallam University and Susan Richardson, Sheffield University
Functional budget and master budget construction, budgetary control and decision-making.

Fleet Ltd Lin Fitzgerald, Loughborough University Business School
Outsourcing decision involving relevant costs and qualitative factors.

Fosters Construction Ltd Deryl Northcott, Auckland University of Technology
Capital investment appraisal, relevant cash flows, taxation, inflation, uncertainty, post-audits.

Global Ltd Susan Richardson, Sheffield University
Cash budgeting, links between cash and profit, pricing/bidding, information system design and behavioural aspects of management control.

Hardhat Ltd Stan Brignall, Aston Business School
Cost–volume–profit analysis.

High Street Reproduction Furniture Ltd Jayne Ducker, Antony Head, Rona O'Brien, Sheffield Hallam University and Sue Richardson, Sheffield University
Relevant costs, strategic decision-making and limiting factors.

Integrated Technology Services (UK) Ltd Mike Johnson, University of Dundee
An examination of the planning and control framework of an information services business which provides outsourced computing support services to large industrial and government organizations.

Kinkead Equipment Ltd John Shank, The Amos Tuck School of Business Administration Dartmouth College
Profit variance analysis that emphasizes how variance analysis should be redirected to consider strategic issues.

Lynch Printers Peter Clarke, University College Dublin
Cost-plus pricing within the context of correctly forecasting activity for a forthcoming period in order to determine the overhead rates. The case illustrates that a company can make a loss even when an anticipated profit margin is added to all jobs.

Majestic Lodge John Shank, The Amos Tuck School of Business Administration Dartmouth College
Relevant costs and cost–volume–profit analysis.

Maxcafe Ltd Colin Drury, University of Huddersfield.
Design of management accounting control systems.

Merrion Products Ltd Peter Clarke, University College Dublin
Cost–volume–profit analysis, relevant costs and limiting factors.

Mestral Robin Roslender, Heriot-Watt University, Edinburgh
The different roles and purposes of management accounting.

Moult Hall Jayne Ducker, Antony Head, Brenda McDonnell, Sheffield Hallam University and Susan Richardson, Sheffield University
Organizational objectives, strategic decision-making, evaluation of alternatives, relevant costs, debating the profit ethos, break-even analysis.

Oak City R.W. Ingram, W.C. Parsons, University of Alabama and W.A. Robbins, Attorney, Pearson and Sutton
Cost allocation in a government setting to determine the amount of costs that should be charged to business for municipal services. The case also includes ethical considerations.

Quality Shopping Rona O'Brien, Sheffield Hallam University
Departmental budget construction, credit checking, environmental issues, behavioural issues and management control systems.

Rawhide Development Company Bill Doolin, Deryl Northcott, Auckland University of Technology
Capital investment appraisal involving relevant cash flows, uncertainty, application of spreadsheet tools and social considerations.

Reichard Maschinen, GmbH Professor John Shank, The Amos Tuck School of Business Administration Dartmouth College
Relevant costs and pricing decisions.

Rogatec Ltd Jayne Ducker, Antony Head, Brenda McDonnell, Sheffield Hallam University and Susan Richardson, Sheffield University
Standard costing and variance analysis, budgets, ethics, sources of information.

Sheridan Carpet Company James S. Reece
Pricing decision, strategic cost analysis.

Southern Paper Inc – ERP in Spain Martin Quinn, Dublin City University
Control issues faced by internal accounting functions with ERP systems.

The Beta Company Peter Clarke, University College Dublin
Cost estimation involving regression analysis and relevant costs.

Traditions Ltd Jayne Ducker, Antony Head, Brenda McDonnell, Sheffield Hallam University and Susan Richardson, Sheffield University
Relevant cost analysis relating to a discontinuation decision and budgeting.

EXAMPLE CASE:
EVA^(TM) AT AULT FOODS LIMITED

Angela Skubovius, Professor Sarah C. Mavrinac, and Henry Fiorillo prepared this case solely to provide material for class discussion. The authors do not intend to illustrate either effective or ineffective handling of a managerial situation. The authors may have disguised certain names and other identifying information to protect confidentiality.

IVEY

Richard Ivey School of Business
The University of Western Ontario

Ivey Management Services prohibits any form of reproduction, storage or transmittal without its written permission. This material is not covered under authorization from CanCopy or any reproduction rights organization. To order copies or request permission to reproduce materials, contact Ivey Publishing, Ivey Management Services, c/o Richard Ivey School of Business, The University of Western Ontario, London, Ontario, Canada, N6A 3K7; phone (519) 661-3208; fax (519) 661-3882; e-mail cases@ivey.uwo.ca. Copyright © 1998 Ivey Management Services. One-time permission to reproduce Ivey cases granted by Ivey Management Services on September 6th, 2007.

Version: (A) 1999-07-029

As chief financial officer of Ault Foods Limited, John Hamilton was responsible for enhancing shareholder value through the development and implementation of innovative financial strategies. To accomplish his mission, Hamilton relied heavily on the company's capital budgeting programs, costing systems, and performance measurement tools. One of Hamilton's most valuable tools was the company's EVA^(TM) (Economic Value Added) system, a system that he had helped install some six months after the company's initial public offering. Hamilton believed that the system had markedly improved his ability to track the company's asset utilization and to evaluate its performance capabilities.

On a crisp October day in the fall of 1996, Hamilton was compiling the data he would need to run a divisional EVA^(TM) analysis. Graham Freeman, Ault's chief executive officer, had asked him to present this analysis to the company's board of directors at its next meeting. Freeman hoped that when the board members became aware of the divisions' EVA^(TM) trends, they would finally begin to appreciate the benefits of spinning off some of the company's less profitable divisions. He firmly believed that a spinoff of at least one division would significantly boost the company's growth potential and bolster the confidence of Ault's shareholder base.

Hamilton wondered if pruning one of the company's divisions really was the best strategy for value creation. If it were, he wondered which of the divisions should be divested first. He hoped the EVA^(TM) analysis would give him the insights he needed.

Company history

Ault Foods Limited (Ault) traced its history to the year 1891 when Jack Ault opened his first small cheese factory in Cass Bridge, Ontario. Run as a small family operation, the company grew modestly over the years until in 1968 it was acquired by John Labatt Limited, one of Canada's largest consumer conglomerates. Between 1968 and the late 1980s, Labatt invested in or acquired an additional 20 dairy operations, ultimately becoming one of the largest milk and dairy producers in Canada.

As Labatt entered the 1990s, its conglomerate structure became unwieldy and shareholders encouraged company management to divest itself of unrelated acquisitions. The dairy businesses were among the first to be spunoff and on May 7, 1993, Ault Foods Limited, a combination of some 14 Labatt dairy acquisitions, emerged as a publicly traded corporation. With the offering, Ault immediately became the largest fully-integrated dairy producer in Canada, with almost

3000 employees, 28 distribution depots and 15 plants in Ontario and Quebec. Ault shares began trading at $15.50 and quickly broke through the $18.00 mark.

The Ault offering was conceived and launched with tremendous optimism on the part of both the company management and its investors on Bay Street. With independence from Labatt came a new strategic vision for the company and the dairy industry at large. Ever since assuming command, Freeman had worked to position the company as the 'dairy that would change the industry as a value-added producer.' His strategic mission was to generate supra-competitive returns by positioning the company as the high technology, premium producer in a commodity business. The premium niche would be realized through investments in research and development (R&D) and through innovative product extensions.

R&D was a priority at Ault and during the early 1990s the company produced a number of new technologies and products. Among its many R&D accomplishments, the company listed the development of: 1) Lactantia PurFiltre, a premium milk boasting a longer shelf life than other milks, 2) Cheestrings™, individually wrapped 'stringable' cheese snacks, 3) Dairylight, an all-natural dairy ingredient providing a low-calorie alternative to butterfat, and 4) Olivina margarine, an olive oil based product that contained the highest level of cholesterol reducing mono-unsaturates of any margarine in the world.

Despite the enthusiasm that defined its offering and despite its R&D capability, the company began to experience serious difficulties after six months of public trading. By the summer of 1996, earnings had fallen from $1.35 per share in 1994 to just under $0.70 per share. (For annual financial data, see **Exhibit 1**.) Over the same period, share price drifted down from a high of $18.87 to a price below $16.00 per share. (See **Exhibit 2** for data on share price movements.) On top of this, Ault faced a continuing price war in the fluid milk market, increasing competitive pressure from a new multinational competitor in the ice cream area, legal battles over its new 'premium' milk product, and an increasingly unhappy shareholder base. Summing up the company's position and prospects, Irene Nattel, a securities analyst at RBC Dominion Securities in Montreal wrote, 'Life is not a lot of fun for Ault right now.'[1]

Despite these difficulties, some of the company's largest investors remained confident. Mike Palmer, an analyst with Equity Research Associates, never faltered in his enthusiasm for the stock. In a 1995 report, for example, he wrote:

> Fluid milk is a lousy business and Ault's attempt to decommoditize it through the launch of Lactantia PurFiltre, has been a mixed success. Nevertheless, management is committed to improving shareholder returns and there are ample opportunities to do so. ... The stock is cheap and will go higher.[2]

Other investors, like Keith Graham of the Ontario Teachers' Pension Plan Board (Teachers') were less sanguine. Describing his impression of Ault and its performance over the years, Keith said:

> We were all very favorably disposed towards Ault when it first went public. One reason why we found the stock so attractive was because we believed the company was undervalued, but Freeman is also a charismatic leader and we were convinced that the company had real earnings power. But sometime in late 1994 or 1995, the company lost its momentum. Its competitive strength was shaken by the entry of Unilever, by Beatrice's restructuring, and by the fluid milk wars. It just lost its strategic position. We had to ask ourselves, 'Will management be able to do what's necessary to repair the damage? Will they do the right thing?' Obviously, we decided 'No'.[3]

In July, 1996, Ault posted another in a series of disappointing earnings announcements. Earnings per share (EPS) for the fourth quarter fiscal year 1996 were 72 per cent below those posted the previous year. Earnings per share for the full year were 50 per cent lower than posted earnings in fiscal year 1995. In the wake of this announcement and the various sell recommendations being launched by industry analysts, Teachers' began unwinding its position.

When word of Teachers' sale reached Ault management, Freeman knew that dramatic action was required not only to boost share price and corporate performance but also to reassure the company's remaining shareholders. He was convinced that divestiture represented Ault's best option. Unfortunately, he also knew the Ault board would resist any effort that reduced the size of the company. When Freeman had entered into tentative discussion with Nestlé over the sale

EXHIBIT 1 Financial statements[1]

Consolidated statement of earnings and retained earnings for the years ended
April 27, 1996 and April 29, 1995 in thousands of dollars

	1996	1995
Net sales	$1 346 505	$1 292 706
Cost of Sales, selling and administration expenses	1 267 536	1 199 852
Research and development[2]	9 247	8 883
Depreciation and amortization[3]	37 215	33 023
Earnings before the undernoted	$32 507	$50 948
Interest expense, net	11 691	10 233
Unusual items	0	15 800
Earnings before income taxes	$20 816	$24 915
Income taxes		
Current	10 951	12 245
Deferred	(2 576)	(1 939)
Net earnings	$12 441	$14 609
Retained earnings, beginning of year	$19 195	$16 412
Dividends	12 122	11 826
Retained earnings, end of year	$19 514	$19 195
Net earnings per common share	$0.68	$0.80

Consolidated balance sheet as at April 27, 1996 and April 29, 1995
in thousands of dollars

	1996	1995
Assets		
Current assets		
Cash	$2 944	$1 927
Accounts receivable	35 417	74 691
Inventories	173 114	155 152
Prepaid expenses	18 896	30 646
Income and other taxes receivable	5 394	927
Investments and other[4]	$123 696	$121 506
Fixed assets, net	$249 828	$254 405
Total assets	$609 289	$639 254
Liabilities and shareholders' equity		
Current liabilities		
Bank Debt	$13 774	$25 810
Accounts payable and accrued charges	132 382	157 212
Long-term debt due within one year	475	475
Long-term debt	$134 288	$125 031
Deferred income tax	$42 105	$45 231
Shareholders' equity		
Share capital	$266 751	$266 300
Retained earnings	19 514	19 195
Total liabilities and shareholders' equity	$609 289	$639 254

[1] All numbers have been altered slightly from actual.
[2] Ault Foods Limited expensed $7.233, $7.923 and $6.847 million in Research & Development costs during the fiscal years 1994, 1993, and
 1992 respectively.
[3] Includes an annual goodwill amortization charge of $2 914 000.
[4] These investment figures include $82 704 and $85 618 in unamortized goodwill for 1996 and 1995, respectively. Accumulated goodwill
 amortization totalled approximately $15.4 million in 1996 and $12.5 million in 1995.

SOURCE: COMPANY DOCUMENTS.

EXHIBIT 2 Share price movements

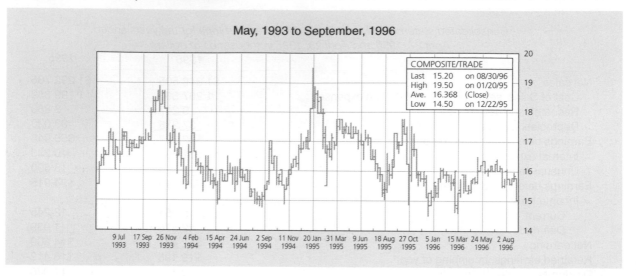

May, 1993 to September, 1996

COMPOSITE/TRADE
Last 15.20 on 08/30/96
High 19.50 on 01/20/95
Ave. 16.368 (Close)
Low 14.50 on 12/22/95

9 Jul 1993 · 17 Sep 1993 · 26 Nov 1993 · 4 Feb 1994 · 15 Apr 1994 · 24 Jun 1994 · 2 Sep 1994 · 11 Nov 1994 · 20 Jan 1995 · 31 Mar 1995 · 9 Jun 1995 · 18 Aug 1995 · 27 Oct 1995 · 5 Jan 1996 · 15 Mar 1996 · 24 May 1996 · 2 Aug 1996

SOURCE: BLOOMBERG L.P.

of the Frozen Division, board members had reacted with alarm. Most of the company's directors were sure that divestiture would not only depress earnings in the short term but also seriously impair the company's growth potential over the long term. They made it crystal clear that they would never entertain a downsizing strategy without clear illustration of its value creating potential.

Ault's business line-up

The Ault structure included two main operating groups, the Refrigerated and Frozen Products and the Cheese and Butter Products groups, each of which supported a number of distinct product divisions. When Labatt acquired its various dairy businesses, there had been few apparent synergies between any of them other than that they were dairy-related. In 1996, however, there was one common trait uniting almost all of Ault's operations. Virtually all faced shrinking markets and demand levels. Only a few of the cheese and ice cream operations had consistently posted stable earnings. (See **Exhibit 3** for financial information by segment.)

Refrigerated and Frozen Products Group

The Refrigerated and Frozen Products group included three key product divisions: Fluid Milk, Cultured Products, and Ice Cream and Novelty Products.

Fluid Milk Ault processed and distributed fluid milk throughout the two Canadian provinces of Ontario and Quebec. While most of the company's sales were made through large supermarket chains under the Sealtest brand name, the company also packaged milk under the Royal Oak, Copper Cliff and Dallaire labels. The efficiency, productivity and competitive pricing offered by Ault had allowed the company to realize a 23 per cent market share in Quebec and a full 31 per cent share in Ontario. Competitors in the Ontario market included two long-time producers: Beatrice and Neilson, which boasted market shares of 31 per cent and 21 per cent, respectively, as well as Natrel and Dairyworld, two more recent entrants who were expanding beyond their original market areas. In Quebec the only formidable competitor was Natrel, operating with a 70 per cent share of the market.

While fluid milk products were a staple of the Ault product lineup and had consistently generated at least one third of company revenues, milk margins had suffered throughout the early 1990s, as consumption continued to fall from its peak in the mid-1980s. The period from 1985 to 1995 witnessed a full 10 per cent decrease in milk consumption. While there were a variety of demographic explanations for this demand shift, Graham Freeman believed that the decline in consumption was due at least in part to consumers' switch to lower priced soda.

In addition to these disappointing demand trends, Ault also had to contend with a market that, since 1994, had become increasingly competitive. Natrel and Dairyworld had entered the market from Quebec and British Columbia, respectively; Agropur, a fluid milk processor had begun a national expansion; and Beatrice, in its attempts to divest its fluid milk business, had helped escalate a price war that had reduced margins to rock bottom. Industry analysts speculated that the price war would continue at least until Beatrice had solved its debt problems and finally found a willing buyer for this division. Beatrice had reportedly been looking to divest itself of its milk operations for a number of years but had found little interest.

Late in 1994, in response to the mounting pressure on fluid milk margins and in keeping with its high technology strategy, Ault introduced Lactantia PurFiltre, a new premium milk product that featured a more stringent filtering of bacteria and a fresher taste and longer shelf life. Having invested over $31 million in PurFiltre's development and introduction, Ault management was relying heavily on this value-added product to boost sagging earnings. By the spring of 1995,

EXHIBIT 3 Segment financial data[1]

Estimates of earnings and retained earnings by product segment for the year ended April 27, 1996 in thousands of dollars

| | Refrigerated and Frozen Products | | | Cheese and Butter Products | |
	Fluid Milk	Cultured	Ice Cream	Industrial	Intern'l
Net sales	$477 834	$79 639	$166 518	$560 263	$62 251
Cost of Sales, selling and administration[2]	460 434	76 916	152 042	522 379	55 765
Research and Development	4 384	133	1 223	3 398	109
Depreciation and amortization[3]	15 824	2 637	5 514	11 916	1 324
Earnings before the undernoted	($2 808)	($47)	$7 739	$22 570	$5 053
Interest expense, net	3 627	604	1 264	5 576	620
Income taxes Current			1 897	7 832	1 222
Deferred			(447)	(1 842)	(287)
Net earnings	($6 435)	($651)	$5 025	$11 004	$3 498

Identifiable assets and liabilities by product segment as of April 27, 1996 in thousands of dollars

| | Refrigerated and Frozen Products | | | Cheese and Butter Products | |
	Fluid Milk	Cultured	Ice Cream	Industrial	Intern'l
Assets					
Current assets					
Cash	$1 045	$174	$364	$1 225	$136
Accounts receivable	12 568	2 095	4 380	14 737	1 637
Inventories	30 988	10 587	52 338	74 198	5 003
Prepaid expenses	4 932	1 822	2 718	6 782	2 642
Income and other taxes receivable	1 267	0	1 236	2 244	647
Investments and other	43 896	7 316	15 297	51 468	5 719
Fixed assets, net	88 656	14 776	30 895	103 950	11 551
Accounts payable and accrued charges	46 977	7 831	16 372	55 084	6 118

[1]All numbers have been altered slightly from actual.
[2]Includes $17 million in corporate overhead charges allocated on basis of sales.
[3]Includes goodwill amortization charge allocated on basis of net fixed assets.

SOURCE: GENERATED BY CASEWRITERS.

PurFiltre had realized a retail penetration rate in Quebec of about 85 per cent and management was hoping to recover all its investment costs during the first year of sales. In Ontario, however, Ault had difficulty obtaining shelf space in leading supermarket chains. By June of 1995, retail penetration rates were still less than 50 per cent. Ault was effectively shut out of the Loblaw's grocery chain in large part because of the threat Lactantia posed to the Neilson products which were produced and distributed by Loblaw's owner, Weston's. Compounding the distribution problems were a host of legal problems that were raised as a result of Beatrice's claims of false advertising. By the fall of 1996, the Lactantia PurFiltre product still had not generated the sales forecasted in Ontario and earnings continued to suffer.

While current performance levels were disappointing, there was some suggestion that future performance could be worse still. Trade talks were currently under way which would decide which treaty, the GATT (General Agreement on Tariffs and Trade) agreement or the NAFTA (North American Free Trade Agreement) would most affect the dairy industry. If NAFTA were upheld, import/export restrictions would rapidly be abolished creating an entirely new source of competition for the Canadian producer.

Cultured Products, Juice and Drinks   While fluid milk products constituted almost one third of the company's sales, cultured products, juice and drinks accounted for less than 10 per cent. Chief among the product lineup were Sealtest Light 'n Lively yogurts, Florida Squeezed orange juice, Sealtest lemonade, and Sealtest dips and sour creams. Ault had a reasonable position in the yogurt market, holding a 16 per cent market share in Ontario. However, in the sour cream and cottage cheese product markets, Ault was consistently positioned as number one or two in the market. Despite its evident leadership, and while touted in the industry press as a true product innovator, Ault never realized substantial profits from this product line. The intense price competition, oversupply and the rapid entry of private label brands into the market ensured that the cultured, juice, and drinks division never operated above break-even.

Ice Cream and Novelty Products   The ice cream and novely products lineup was a major source of Ault's growth and financial profitability. As Canada's only full-line ice cream producer and distributor, Ault enjoyed a national category market share of well over 30 per cent. Underpinning this market position were such brand names as Haagen-Dazs, Eskimo Pie, Drumstick, Oh Henry! and Sealtest Parlour, Canada's best-selling premium brand.

While clearly a dominant force in this market. Ault saw its position severely challenged in 1996 by the entry of Unilever, a multinational competitor with over $46 billion in sales worldwide. Unilever had ensured rapid market dominance by entering through the acquisition of Beatrice's ice cream division rather than through its own start-up. At the time of the acquisition, Unilever had announced publicly that its strategic intent was to expand its ice cream business worldwide to realize a number one position in every national market.

The competitive pricing pressures wrought by Unilever, coupled with the market's natural seasonality and heavy inventory requirements, had damaged Ault's earnings power in this area. Industry analysts speculated that while Ault's ice cream business had generated an estimated $6 million in EBIT (earnings before interest and tax), Ault would achieve little more than break-even returns in 1996 and 1997.

Cheese and Butter Products Group

Ault's Cheese and Butter Products group consisted of two operating divisions: the Industrial and the International Divisions.

Industrial   Ault's Industrial Division specialized in the conversion of industrial-grade milk products into whey powders, milk powders, and consumer cheeses and butter. Operating out of seven plants in Ontario and Quebec, the division processed more than 500 million litres of milk each year and had earned the position as the largest butter producer in Canada years before. The division served not only end-use consumers through convenience stores and supermarkets but also a variety of companies in the food service and food processing industries as well. To all of these customers, Ault offered such products as Black Diamond, Lactantia, Balderson, and Plum Hollow cheeses, Lactantia and New Dundee butters, and Olivina and La Croissantiere margarines.

Historically, Ault had performed well in this market and the early 1990s offered no real exception. Lactantia was the largest selling butter brand and Black Diamond was the second-largest cheese brand in Canada. The division was finding still greater success with its new snackfood innovations like Cheestrings™, which were breaking new ground and building record market share. By the spring of 1996, the product had realized a full 72 per cent market share in the cheese snack market. This success was one reason why Ault's Industrial Division was such a consistent contributor to company profits.

In conversation with the casewriters, Graham Freeman commented on the history and potential of this division.

> You will recall that this division was Ault's first. Our company founder started with the manufacture of cheese products and made a true success of it. The business is still a success, and I believe it has the potential to create real value for shareholders. One reason why the business is so strong is because we focused so much of our R&D talents on it. We really zeroed in on the potential we saw there and we generated very favourable results in both manufacturing and formulation yield applications.

Despite the evident success of this division with Ault consumers, the market was competitive. Butter consumption was declining drastically, while private label brands were making real inroads into major food retailing outlets. Raw material was also becoming increasingly difficult to obtain. Ault operated under a government-regulated milk supply system that severely regulated the availability of both table and industrial milk. The stated objective of the regulation was to ensure stable revenues for dairy farmers and to maintain balance between supply and demand. The government attempted to achieve these goals by setting the price paid to farmers and limiting the amount of milk that processors were allowed to purchase.

In the mid-1990s, Quebec held 47 per cent of the national industrial milk quota while Ontario held 31 per cent. Recent quota reductions had limited the amounts of raw material available for cheese production and Ault, like its competitors, was beginning to feel the impact. One of Ault's responses to the quota cuts was to acquire the cheese assets of Schneider Corporation in November of 1995. These assets represented a full $80 million in annual sales. With the acquisition of Schneider, the milk quota owned by Ault that had been used for lower-value export butter and skim milk powder, became available for use in higher-margin cheese made under the Schneider label.

International Established in 1992, Ault's International Division was dedicated to marketing Ault's proprietary technologies and product innovations through licensing agreements across the world. A recent licensing coup had been realized when Golden Vale Food Products Inc. of Ireland licensed the Cheestrings™ cheese snacks line for sale in the United Kingdom. The division also provided consulting services to international customers and pursued joint ventures and partnership arrangements with established dairy companies where Ault's technical expertize could add value.

Most of the division's trading activities were conducted through the trading arm of Lovell and Christmas, a trading division acquired by Ault in fiscal year 1995, and focused on the sale of specialty cheeses, pre-blended ice cream mixes, infant formula, milk and whey powder, and other dairy products. During fiscal year 1996, sales were made in more than 35 countries. An increasing penetration of markets in the United States, South America, and Asia was expected in 1997.

EVA^(TM) at Ault

With such a vast array of businesses operating in such a complex business environment, management often had difficulty understanding the impact of each division's performance on the financial condition of the company overall. In the spring of 1993, recognizing his need for more detailed performance data, Freeman asked his staff to launch an EVA™ experiment. He had been introduced to the EVA™ concept several months before and it appeared to be a logical tool for identifying which divisions were creating, and which were destroying, value for Ault's shareholders. The company eventually adopted EVA™ late in 1993 under the direction of Douglas Shields, John Hamilton's predecessor as chief financial officer.

With the help of Ernst & Young, a management consulting firm, Ault's executives spent the remainder of 1993 examining the EVA™ performance of a range of different Ault businesses and training divisional managers in the effective use of EVA$^{(TM)}$. In 1994, management expanded the program to encourage the achievement of quarterly EVA$^{(TM)}$ goals. These goals were established during management planning meetings and were based on tough negotiations between Freeman and his division leaders. EVA$^{(TM)}$ calculations also became a familiar part of capital budgeting and post-investment review processes.

In the summer of 1996, Ault expanded its EVA$^{(TM)}$ program yet again. In an attempt to tie management's interests even more closely to shareholders', Ault instituted an EVA$^{(TM)}$-based bonus plan. The plan was to be implemented in two phases. In 1996, it was to run alongside the existing earnings-based bonus plan. After this experimental year, during which the plan was to be further studied and refined, the EVA$^{(TM)}$ focused plan was to replace the earnings plan altogether.

It was this last, motivational use that most intrigued John Hamilton. In an interview with the casewriter, he said:

> Back in 1994 and 1995, our key challenge was to link the income statement and the balance sheet. For too long, we had focused almost exclusively on the income statement. We were earnings driven. Cash and capital were free. Sure, we did some serious capital budgeting and we imposed a twenty per cent hurdle rate on all major projects. But once the project was approved, no one thought about the capital again. By installing the EVA$^{(TM)}$ bonus system, we really focused our attention on both the income statement and the balance sheet simultaneously. We really focused on our use of assets and ways to maximize their value.

Late in the summer of 1996, Hamilton and his team completed their annual EVA$^{(TM)}$ analysis for the company as a whole. The results were disappointing: the company had again failed to realize a positive EVA$^{(TM)}$. (See **Exhibit 4** for corporate EVA$^{(TM)}$ calculations.) Still more unfortunately, the analysis hadn't made clear either the source of Ault's financial difficulties or its opportunities. Hamilton and Freeman agreed then that more specific divisional analyzes would be needed to determine the real drivers of value at Ault.

As soon as Freeman learned of the Teachers' sale, he asked Hamilton to step up the analysis and to present his findings and recommendations to the board at its next meeting a week hence. Hamilton knew that if his presentation were to have any influence, he would have to start from scratch, explaining to the board what EVA$^{(TM)}$ was, how it worked, and why it was useful to Ault. Then, he would have to walk through the divisional calculations step by step, making comments about the strengths and weaknesses of each division, before he made any recommendations about sale.

Hamilton also knew that before he could present any of this to the board, he would have to work through all the calculations to be certain in his own mind that it was appropriate to base a divestiture decision on EVA$^{(TM)}$ numbers. He pulled out the documents (see **Exhibit 5**) he had compiled years ago to describe the EVA$^{(TM)}$ concept and its calculations to Graham Freeman and set to work.

The formula for generating the EVA$^{(TM)}$ measure is simply:

$$\text{EVA}^{(TM)} = \text{Net Operating Profit After Tax} - \text{Required Return on Assets} \qquad (1)$$

where

$$\text{Required Return on Assets} = \text{Assets Employed} \times \text{Cost of Capital} \qquad (2)$$

Note that the manager's goal is to increase EVA$^{(TM)}$. Consequently, moving from a negative EVA$^{(TM)}$ to a less negative EVA$^{(TM)}$ should be seen as progress.

How does it Increase Shareholder Value?

EVA$^{(TM)}$ analyses can be used not only to assess the performance of the organization or individual but also to identify opportunities for performance improvement. There are four general ways to increase EVA$^{(TM)}$ performance:

1 increase profitability, e.g., by increasing sales or by minimizing variable costs
2 improve operating efficiency and use of assets
3 rationalize and/or exiting unrewarding businesses, i.e. reduce the asset base, or
4 reduce the cost of capital.

The Uses and Benefits of EVA(TM)

One of the great features of EVA(TM) is its simplicity. Virtually any employee in the organization can understand the EVA(TM) concept and its importance. Consequently, EVA(TM) can be used as a powerful motivational and communications tool.

EXHIBIT 4 Corporate EVA(TM) performance calculations

(All data in 000s)

1. Economic Book Value (EBV) Capital Calculation – Operating Approach

	1996	1995
Assets		
Operating Cash	$2 944	$1 927
Accounts Receivable	35 417	74 691
Inventories	173 114	155 152
Prepaid Expenses	18 896	30 646
Income and Other Taxes Receivable	5 394	927
Total Current Assets	$235 765	$263 343
Less: Accounts Payable	(132 382)	(157 212)
Net Working Capital	$103 383	$106 131
Investments and Other	$123 696	$121 506
Accumulated Amortized Goodwill	15 443	12 529
Net Property, Plant and Equipment	249 828	254 405
Accumulated Research and Development[1], Net	17 205	15 985
EBV Capital	$509 555	$510 556

2. Net Operating Profit After Tax (NOPAT) Calculation – Operating Approach

	1996	1995
Earnings before Unusual Items, Interest and Tax	$32 507	$50 948
Research and Development Add Back	9 247	8 883
Less: Amortization of Acc. R&D Expenses[2]	(8 027)	(7 505)
Goodwill Amortization Add Back	2 914	2 914
Adjusted Net Operating Profit before the Undernoted	$36 641	$55 240
Unusual Items	0	15 800
Adjusted Net Operating Profit before Tax	$36 641	$39 440
Cash Operating Taxes[3]	13 003	14 059
Adjusted Net Operating Profit After Tax (NOPAT)	$23 638	$25 381

3. EVA(TM) Calculation

EVA(TM) = NOPAT − (EBV Capital × WACC)

1996	1995
EVA(TM) = $23 638 − ($509 555 × 0.10)	EVA(TM) = $25 381 − ($510 556 × 0.10)
EVA(TM) = $23 638 − $50 956	EVA(TM) = $25 381 − $51 056
EVA(TM) = ($27 318)	EVA(TM) = ($25 675)

[1]Although R&D was recognized as an expense in Ault's financial statements, Ault management recognized R&D expenditures as a legitimate investment in Ault's future product line-up. Consequently, R&D figures were included as an amortizable asset in EVA(TM) calculations. In an attempt to generate conservative estimates of R&D value, Hamilton used a straight-line five year amortization schedule.
[2]R&D was amortized at the rate of 20 per cent per annum. For 1996, the amortization figure was $8027, i.e., 20 per cent × ($9247 + $8883 + $7233 + $7923 + $6847).
[3]The corporate income tax rate was approximately 40 per cent. Hamilton estimated cash taxes as equal to EBIT × the tax rate.

SOURCE: GENERATED BY CASEWRITERS.

EXHIBIT 5   The principles of EVA(TM)[1]

SOURCE: COMPILED BY CASEWRITERS

What is EVA(TM)?

The term EVA(TM), or Economic Value Added, refers to a specific accounting calculation that has recently been developed as a guide for managers running complex organizations. In simple terms, EVA(TM) is a measure of 'economic profit,' calculated as net operating profit after tax less a charge for capital employed. Like accounting profit calculations, economic profit calculations, or EVA(TM) calculations, are used to provide a summary of the financial 'success' or 'failure' of the company over some period of time. However, economic profits can be distinguished from accounting profits in that they include this charge for the company's use of capital. That is, a positive EVA(TM) is not realized until **all** the costs of doing business, like the cost of using capital, have been tallied.

EVA(TM) is a particularly useful tool for divisionalized companies which often have a difficult time estimating the profitability of individual businesses. Because it encourages managers to continually assess and maximize the use of divisional assets, EVA(TM) can also be a useful vehicle for individual performance measurement and motivation. Any incentive scheme which encourages managers to maximize their EVA(TM) will enhance the probability that managers are working in the best interest of shareholders.

Note
[1] Parts of this note are excerpted from the Ivey Business School Note 9A96B043, 'Note on Economic Value Added,' prepared by John Manning and John McCartney under the supervision of Professor James E. Hatch.

The EVA(TM) figure is also a powerful representation of corporate performance. As such, EVA(TM) makes irrelevant a number of other corporate measures that simply don't offer as clear and unbiased a signal of performance as this 'residual income' figure. If a manager relies on EVA(TM), he or she does not need to review copious reports or reams of numbers to understand his or her company's financial position. The power of EVA(TM) is derived from its focus on shareholder value and its expression of performance as a relative term. Recall that EVA(TM) calculations generate positive profits only after deducting a cost for the use of capital. Consequently, performance is measured *relative* to the capital base or set of resources the manager used to measure the profits. EVA(TM) links the operating returns to the assets that were used to generate those returns.

The learning which flows from EVA(TM) analyzes can be extremely insightful and can allow the manager not only to pinpoint areas of weakness in performance but also to easily identify solutions or programs for improvements. EVA's(TM) use in multi-businesses stems from the fact that it can help to assess divisional contributors to, or detractors from, overall profitability.

Note that EVA(TM) adopters tend to have greater asset dispositions and faster asset turns. The market value to book value measure of EVA(TM) adopters also tend to be 60 per cent higher than non-adopters. According to *The Quest for Value*, Stern, Stewart & Co's description of EVA(TM), equity market values tend to be more highly correlated with annual EVA(TM) levels than with most other performance measures of return on equity, cash flow growth, EPS growth, or growth in sales or capital.

Shortcomings

Although the EVA(TM) tool offers real benefits it also, like any tool, has its limitations and weaknesses. Chief among these weaknesses is EVA's(TM) single period focus. EVA(TM) is a period measure. Its value can be calculated only for a single period at a time. Consequently, EVA(TM) cannot capture all the long-term implications of decision making. Of course, it is possible to run a number of annual EVA(TM) forecasts and then reduce the results using discounting techniques, but it is not a simple or perfect process.

Of course, reliance on any single measure can be dangerous. Too strict a reliance on EVA(TM) can distract the manager from other pertinent business issues such as customer satisfaction, productivity, or levels of innovation and learning. At times, in an attempt to boost EVA(TM), managers might also divest the company of certain businesses or divisions that are not truly underperforming. As with any other tool used, business sense and prudent judgment must be used.

How does EVA(TM) Work?

The three key figures or components of the EVA(TM) calculation are: NOPAT, EBV Capital, and the firm's cost of capital. NOPAT is the annual cash flow that is available to cover costs of raising all equity and debt capital on an after-tax basis. EBV (Economic Book Value) Capital is an estimate of total capital utilized by a firm for a period, including debt and equity. The cost of capital is the appropriate risk-adjusted rate applied to the division or entity.

To generate the NOPAT and EBV Capital figures, adjustments must be made to both the traditional capital employed and the operating profit figures. The purpose of these adjustments is to ensure that the numbers accurately reflect the base upon which shareholders expect to earn their returns and the cash flow from the company's activities. According to Stern, Stewart & Co., the developers of the EVA(TM) tool, there are over 160 different adjustments that can be made. Which ones are used by any given company will depend on its industry, technology and value-creation process.

Application to Ault

Like other divisionalized businesses, Ault should find substantial value in the EVA(TM) performance approach. As suggested above, Ault can find applications for EVA(TM) in performance measurement, compensation, business re-engineering, corporate finance, divestiture planning, and resource allocation processes. Ault should also find the EVA(TM) tool useful for divisional comparisons.

Now may be an especially appropriate time for Ault to adopt the EVA(TM) tool. The EVA(TM) calculations generated for the consolidated Ault corporation suggest that the company faces a number of performance challenges. In 1994, Ault earned an EVA(TM) of negative $11 million. Indeed, it appears that Ault has returned a negative EVA(TM) since 1992. This negative performance trend has clearly impacted share valuation. The current market value of Ault shares is $15.75, only 88 per cent of Ault's equity book value. If Ault continues to generate returns below the cost of capital, there is a strong possibility that the stock will come under additional pressure. Note that the EVA(TM) of competitors Ben & Jerry's, Dean Foods, Agropur, and Beatrice was approximately $2 million, $21 million, $0, and negative $6 million.

At this time, we would strongly recommend the adoption of EVA(TM) techniques and investment in fuller divisional analysis of EVA(TM) trends. To conduct such an analysis, we recommend the use of the following three accounting adjustments:

- use of cash tax v. statutory tax rates,
- add back of goodwill amortization amounts, and
- add back of research and development expenses.

Notes

1 Nattel, Irene, 'Consumer Products Review: Eat, Drink and Be Merry', RBC Dominion Securities, Montreal, January, 1996

2 Palmer, Michael, 'Ault', Equity Research Associates, Toronto, Ontario, June, 1995

3 Personal Communications

Suggested questions

The questions below are suggested by the author of this book and were not included in the original version of the case study.

1 Assume you are Hamilton. Explain to the board what EVA(TM) is, how it works, what its shortcomings are and why it is likely to be useful to Ault.

2 Calculate divisional EVA(TM) performance figures for 1996 and explain your calculations to the board.

3 Compare EVA(TM) with other alternative measures of divisional performance.

4 Explain how you think cost of capital ought to be derived for computing divisional EVA$^{(TM)}$.

5 Explain how EVA$^{(TM)}$ relates to shareholder value.

6 Examine the strengths and weaknesses of each of Ault's divisions. What do you conclude about the performance capabilities and value of Ault's divisions? Is divisional divesture an appropriate course of action? What role do the EVAs$^{(TM)}$ that you have calculated play in the decision.

BIBLIOGRAPHY

Abernethy, M.A., Lillis, A.M., Brownell, P. and Carter, P. (2001) Product diversity and costing system design: field study evidence, *Management Accounting Research*, **12**(3), 261–80.

Abu-Serdaneh, J. (2004) Transfer pricing in UK manufacturing companies, PhD dissertation, University of Huddersfield.

Accounting Standards Committee (1988) Accounting for Stocks and Work in Progress (SSAP 9).

Ackoff, R.L. (1981) *Creating the Corporate Future*, Wiley.

Adelberg, A. (1986) Resolving conflicts in intracompany transfer pricing, *Accountancy*, November, 86–9.

Ahmed, M.N. and Scapens, R.W. (1991) Cost allocation theory and practice: the continuing debate, in *Issues in Management Accounting* (eds D. Ashton, T. Hopper and R.W. Scapens), Prentice-Hall, 39–60.

Ahmed, M.N. and Scapens, R.W. (2000) Cost allocation in Britain: towards an institutional analysis, *The European Accounting Review*, **9**(?), 159–204.

Al-Omiri, M. and Drury, C. (2007), A survey of the factors influencing the choice of product costing systems in UK organizations, *Management Accounting Research,* **18**(4).

American Accounting Association (1957) *Accounting and Reporting Standards for Corporate Financial Statements and Preceding Statements and Supplements*, 4.

American Accounting Association (1966) *A Statement of Basic Accounting Theory*, American Accounting Association.

Amey, L.R. (1975) Tomkins on residual income, *Journal of Business Finance and Accounting*, **2**(1), Spring, 55; 68.

Ansari, S. (1979) Towards an open system approach to budgeting, *Accounting, Organisations and Society*, **4**(3), 149–61.

Anthony, R.N. and Young, D.W. (1988) *Management Control in Non-Profit Organizations*, R.D. Irwin.

Armitage, H.M. and Nicholson, R. (1993) Activity based costing: a survey of Canadian practice, Issue Paper No. 3, Society of Management Accountants of Canada.

Arnold, G.C. and Hatzopoulos, P.D. (2000) The theory–practice gap in capital budgeting: evidence from the United Kingdom, *Journal of Business Finance and Accounting*, **27**(5) and (6), June/July, 603–26.

Ask, U. and Ax, C. (1992) Trends in the Development of Product Costing Practices and Techniques – A Survey of Swedish Manufacturing Industry, Paper presented at the 15th Annual Congress of the European Accounting Association, Madrid.

Ask, U., Ax, C. and Jonsson, S. (1996) Cost management in Sweden: from modern to post-modern, in Bhimani, A. (ed.) *Management Accounting: European Perspectives*, Oxford, Oxford University Press, 199–217.

Atkinson, M. and Tyrrall, D. (1997) International transfer pricing: the taxman cometh, *Management Accounting (UK)*, December, 32–4.

Ballas, A. and Venieris, G. (1996) A survey of management accounting practices in Greek firms, in Bhimani, A. (ed.) *Management Accounting: European Perspectives*, Oxford, Oxford University Press, 123–39.

Banerjee, J. and Kane, W. (1996) Report on CIMA/JBA survey, *Management Accounting*, October, **30**, 37.

Barbato, M.B., Collini, P. and Quagli, C. (1996) Management accounting in Italy, in Bhimani, A. (ed.) *Management Accounting: European Perspectives*, Oxford, Oxford University Press, 140–163.

Barrett, M.E. and Fraser, L.B. (1977) Conflicting roles in budget operations, *Harvard Business Review*, July–August, 137–46.

Barton, T.L., Shenkir, W.G. and Hess, J.E. (1995) *CPA Journal*, June, 65(6), 48–50.

Baxter, W.T. and Oxenfeldt, A.R. (1961) Costing and pricing: the cost accountant versus the economist, *Business Horizons*, Winter, 77–90; also in *Studies in Cost Analysis*, 2nd edn (ed. D. Solomons) Sweet and Maxwell (1968), 293–312.

Berliner, C. and Brimson, J.A. (1988) *Cost Management for Today's Advanced Manufacturing*, Harvard Business School Press.

Bierman, H., Fouraker, I.E. and Jaedicke, R.K. (1977) A use of probability and statistics in performance evaluation, in *Contemporary Cost Accounting and Control*, (ed. G.J. Benston) Dickenson Publishing.

Bjornenak T. (1997a) Diffusion and accounting: the case of ABC in Norway, *Management Accounting Research*, 8(1), 317.

Bjornenak T. (1997b) Conventional wisdom and accounting practices, *Management Accounting Research*, 8(4), 367–82.

Blayney, P. and Yokoyama, I. (1991) Comparative analysis of Japanese and Australian cost accounting and management practices, Working paper, University of Sydney, Australia.

Boer, G. (1990) Contribution margin analysis: no longer relevant/ strategic cost management: the new paradigm, *Journal of Management Accounting Research (USA)*, Fall, 24–7.

Boland, R. (1979) Causality and information system requirements, *Accounting, Organisations and Society*, 4(4), 259–72.

Boons, A., Roozen, R.A. and Weerd, R.J. de (1994) Kosteninformatie in de Nederlandse Industrie, in *Relevantie methoden en ontwikkelingen* (Rotterdam: Coopers and Lybrand).

Borkowski, S.C. (1990) Environmental and organizational factors affecting transfer pricing: a survey, *Journal of Management Accounting Research*, 2, 78–99.

Bower, J.L. (1970) *Managing the Resource Allocation Process*, Division of Research, Graduate School of Business Administration, Harvard University.

Boyns, T., Edwards, J.R. and Emmanuel, C. (1999) A longitudinal study of the determinants of transfer pricing change, *Management Accounting Research*, 10(2), 85–108.

Brantjes, M., von Eije, H., Eusman, F. and Prins, W. (1999) Post-completion auditing within Heineken, *Management Accounting (UK)*, April, 20–2.

Brealey, R.A. and Myers, S.C. (2006) *Principles of Corporate Finance*, McGraw-Hill, New York.

Brierley, J.A., Cowton, C.J. and Drury, C. (2001) Research into product costing practice: a European perspective, *The European Accounting Review*, 10(2), 215–56.

Brinkman, S.L. and Appelbaum, M.A. (1994) The quality cost report: It is alive and well at Gilroy Foods, *Management Accounting (USA)*, September, 61–5.

Bromwich, M. (1990) The case for strategic management accounting: the role of accounting information for strategy in competitive markets, *Accounting, Organisations and Society*, 1, 27–46.

Bromwich, M. and Walker, M. (1998) Residual income past and future, *Management Accounting Research*, 9(4), 392–419.

Bromwich, M. and Bhimani, A. (1989) *Management Accounting: Evolution not Revolution*, Chartered Institute of Management Accountants.

Bromwich, M. and Bhimani, A. (1994) *Management Accounting: Pathways to Progress*, Chartered Institute of Management Accountants.

Brounen, D., de Jong, A. and Koedijk, K. (2004) Corporate Finance in Europe: confronting theory with practice, *Financial Management*, 33(4), 71–101.

Brownell, P. (1981) Participation in budgeting, locus of control and organisational effectiveness, *The Accounting Review*, October, 944–58.

Bruggeman, W., Slagmulder, R. and Waeytens, D. (1996) Management accounting changes; the Belgian experience, in Bhimani, A. (ed.) *Management Accounting: European Perspectives*, Oxford, Oxford University Press, 1–30.

Burchell, S., Clubb, C., Hopwood, A.G., Hughes, J. and Jahapier, J. (1980) The roles of accounting in organizations and society, *Accounting, Organisations and Society*, 1, 5–27.

Burrows, G.H. (1994) Allocations and common costs in long-run investment and pricing decisions: An historical perspective, *Abacus*, 30(1), 50–64.

Cats-Baril, W.L. *et al.* (1986) Joint Product Costing, *Management Accounting (USA)*, September, 41–5.

Chan, C.W. (1998) Transfer pricing negotiation outcomes and the impact of negotiator mixed-motives and culture: empirical evidence from the US and Australia, *Management Accounting Research*, 9(2), 139–61.

Chandler, A.D., Jr. (1962) *Strategy and Structure: Chapters in the History of the Industrial Enterprise*, Cambridge, MA: MIT Press.

Charles, I. (1985a) The economics approach to transfer price, *Accountancy*, June, 110–12.

Charles, I. (1985b) Transfer-price solution where market exists, *Accountancy*, July, 96.

Chartered Institute of Management Accountants (2000) *Management Accounting: Official Terminology*, CIMA.

Cheatham, C.B. and Cheatham, L.R. (1996) Redesigning cost systems: Is standard costing obsolete?, *Accounting Horizons*, December, 23–31.

Chenhall, R.H. (2003) Management control system design within its organizational context: findings from contingency-based research and directions for the future, *Accounting, Organizations and Society*, 28, 127–68.

Chenhall, R.H. and Langfield-Smith, K. (1998a) Adoption and benefits of management accounting practices: an Australian perspective, *Management Accounting Research*, 9(1), 120.

Chenhall, R.H. and Langfield-Smith, K. (1998b) The relationship between strategic priorities, management techniques and management accounting: An empirical investigation using a systems approach, *Accounting, Organisations and Society*, 23(3), 243–64.

Chenhall, R.H. and Morris, D. (1985) The impact of structure, environment and interdependence on the perceived usefulness of management accounting systems, *The Accounting Review*, 1, 16–35.

Chow, C., Haddad, K. and Williamson, J. (1997) Applying the Balanced Scorecard to Small Companies, *Management Accounting*, August, 21–7.

Chow, C.W. (1983) The effect of job standards, tightness and compensation schemes on performance: an exploration of linkages, *The Accounting Review*, October, 667–85.

Chua, W.F. (1988) Interpretive sociology and management accounting research: a critical review, *Accounting, Auditing Accountability Journal*, 1(1), 59–79.

Clarke, P.J. (1992) Management Accounting Practices and Techniques in Irish Manufacturing Firms, The 15th Annual Congress of the European Accounting Association, Madrid, Spain.

Clarke, P. (1995) Management accounting practices and techniques in Irish manufacturing companies, Working paper, Trinity College, Dublin.

Coad, A. (1996) Smart work and hard work: explicating a learning orientation in strategic management accounting, *Management Accounting Research*, 7(4), 387–408.

Cohen, M.D., March, J.G. and Olsen, J.P. (1972) A garbage can model of organizational change. *Administrative Science Quarterly*, March, 1–25.

Collins, F. (1978) The interaction of budget characteristics and personality variables with budget response attitudes, *The Accounting Review*, April, 324–35.

Cooper, D.J. (1980) Discussion of 'Towards a Political Economy of Accounting', *Accounting, Organisations, and Society*, 5(1), 161–6.

Cooper, D.J., Hayes, D. and Wolf, F. (1981) Accounting in organised anarchies: understanding and designing accounting systems in ambiguous situations, *Accounting, Organisations and Society*, 6(3) 175–91.

Cooper, R. (1990a) Cost classifications in unit-based and activity-based manufacturing cost systems, *Journal of Cost Management*, Fall, 4–14.

Cooper, R. (1990b) Explicating the logic of ABC, *Management Accounting*, November, 5860.

Cooper, R. (1996) Costing techniques to support corporate strategy: evidence from Japan, *Management Accounting Research*, 7, 219–46.

Cooper, R. (1997) Activity-Based Costing: Theory and Practice, in Brinker, B.J. (ed.), *Handbook of Cost Management*, Warren, Gorham and Lamont, B1–B33.

Cooper, R. and Kaplan, R.S. (1987) How cost accounting systematically distorts product costs, in *Accounting and Management: Field Study Perspectives* (eds W.J. Bruns and R.S. Kaplan), Harvard Business School Press, Ch. 8.

Cooper, R. and Kaplan, R.S. (1988) Measure costs right: make the right decisions, *Harvard Business Review*, September/October, 96–103.

Cooper, R. and Kaplan, R.S. (1991) *The Design of Cost Management Systems: Text, Cases and Readings*, Prentice-Hall.

Cooper, R. and Kaplan, R.S. (1992) Activity based systems: measuring the costs of resource usage, *Accounting Horizons*, September, 1–13.

Cornick, M., Cooper, W. and Wilson, S. (1988) How do companies analyse overhead?, *Management Accounting*, June, 41–3.

Coughlan, P. and Darlington, J. (1993) As fast as the slowest operations: the theory of constraints, *Management Accounting (UK)*, June, 14–17.

Covaleski, M. and Dirsmith, M. (1980) Budgeting as a Means for Control and Loose Coupling in Nursing Services (unpublished), Pennsylvania State University.

Cress, W. and Pettijohn, J. (1985) A survey of budget-related planning and control policies and procedures, *Journal of Accounting Education*, 3, Fall, 61–78.

Currie, W. (1990) Strategic management of advanced manufacturing technology, *Management Accounting*, October, 50–2.

Currie, W. (1991a) Managing technology: a crisis in management accounting, *Management Accounting*, February, 24–7.

Currie, W. (1991b) Managing production technology in Japanese industry, *Management Accounting*, June, 28–9, July/August, 36–8.

Cyert, R.M. and March, J.G. (1969) *A Behavioural Theory of the Firm*, Prentice-Hall.

Darlington, J., Innes, J., Mitchell, F. and Woodward, J. (1992) Throughput accounting: the Garrett Automative experience, *Management Accounting (UK)*, April, 32–5, 38.

Davenport, T.H. (2000) *Mission Critical: Realising the promise of Enterprise Systems*, Boston, Harvard Business School Press.

DeBono, J. (1997) Divisional cost of equity capital, *Management Accounting (UK)*, November, 40–1.

Dekker, H.C. (2003) Value chain analysis in interfirm relationships: a field study, *Management Accounting Research*, 14(1), 1–23.

Dekker, H. and Smidt, P. (2003) A survey of the adoption and use of target costing in Dutch firms, *International Journal of Production Economics*, 84(3), 293–306.

Demski, J.S. (1968) Variance analysis using a constrained linear model, in *Studies in Cost Analysis*, 2nd edn (ed. D. Solomons), Sweet and Maxwell.

Demski, J.S. (1977) Analysing the effectiveness of the traditional standard costing variance model, in *Contemporary Cost Accounting and Control* (ed. G.J. Benston), Dickenson Publishing.

Dhavale, D.G. (1989) Product costing in flexible manufacturing systems, *Journal of Management Accounting Research* (USA), Fall, 66–88.

Dirsmith, M.W. and Jablonsky, S.F. (1979) MBO, political rationality and information inductance, *Accounting, Organisations and Society*, 1, 39–52.

Dittman, D.A. and Ferris, KR. (1978) Profit centre: a satisfaction generating concept, *Accounting and Business Research*, 8(32), Autumn, 242–5.

Drucker, P.F. (1964) Controls, control and management, in *Management Controls: New Directions in Basic Research* (eds C.P. Bonini, R. Jaedicke and H. Wagner), McGraw-Hill.

Drury, C. (1998) *Costing: An Introduction*, International Thomson Business Press, Ch. 3.

Drury, C. (2003) *Cost and Management Accounting: An introduction*, Thomson Learning.

Drury, C. and El-Shishini, H. (2005) *Divisional performance measurement,* Chartered Institute of Management Accountants.

Drury, C. and Tayles, M. (1994) Product costing in UK manufacturing organisations, *The European Accounting Review*, 3(3), 443–69.

Drury, C. and Tayles, M. (2000) *Cost system design and profitability analysis in UK companies*, Chartered Institute of Management Accountants.

Drury, C. and Tayles M. (2005) Explicating the design of overhead absorption procedures in UK organizations, *British Accounting Review*, 37(1), 47–84.

Drury, C. and Tayles, M. (2006) Profitability analysis in UK organizations: An exploratory study, *British Accounting Review*, 38(4), 405–25.

Drury, C., Braund, S., Osborne, P. and Tayles, M. (1993) A survey of management accounting practices in UK manufacturing companies, ACCA Research Paper, Chartered Association of Certified Accountants.

Dugdale, D. (1989) Contract accounting and the SSAP, *Management Accounting*, June, 624.

Dugdale, D. and Jones, T.C. (1998) Throughput accounting: transformation practices?, *British Accounting Review*, 30(3), 203–20.

Dugdale, D., Jones, T.C. and Green, S. (2006) *Contemporary management accounting practices in UK manufacturing companies*, Chartered Institute of Management Accountants.

Dugdale, D. and Lyne, S. (2006), Are budgets still needed?, *Financial Management*, November, 32–35.

Earl, M.J. and Hopwood, A.G. (1981) From management information to information management, in *The Information Systems Environment* (ed. Lucas, H.C. Jr. *et al.*), Amsterdam, Holland.

Egginton, D. (1995) Divisional performance measurement: residual income and the asset base, *Management Accounting Research*, September, 201–22.

Ekholm, B-G. and Wallin, J. (2000) Is the annual budget really dead?, *The European Accounting Review*, **9**(4), 519–39.

Elliott, J. (1998a) International transfer pricing: the consultative document, *Management Accounting (UK)*, March, 34–5.

Elliott, J. (1998b) International transfer pricing: a survey of UK and non-UK groups, *Management Accounting (UK)*, November, 48–50.

Elphick, C. (1983) A new approach to cost allocations, *Management Accounting*, December, 22–5.

El-Shishini, H. and Drury, C. (2001) Divisional performance measurement in UK companies, Paper presented to the Annual Congress of the European Accounting Association, Athens.

Emmanuel, C. and Mehafdi, M. (1994) *Transfer Pricing*, Academic Press.

Emmanuel, C.R. and Otley, D. (1976) The usefulness of residual income, *Journal of Business Finance and Accounting*, **13**(4), Winter, 43–52.

Emmanuel, C., Otley, D. and Merchant, K. (1990) *Accounting for Management Control*, International Thomson Business Press.

Emore, J.R. and Ness, J.A. (1991) The slow pace of meaningful changes in cost systems, *Journal of Cost Management for the Manufacturing Industry*, Winter, 36–45.

Emsley, D. (2000) Variance analysis and performance: two empirical studies, *Accounting, Organisations and Society*, **25**, 1–12.

Emsley, D. (2001) Redesigning variance analysis for problem solving, *Management Accounting Research*, **12**(1), 21–40.

Epstein, M. and Manzoni, J.F. (1998) Implementing corporate strategy: From tableaux de bord to balanced scorecards, *European Management Journal*, **16**(2), 190–203.

Epstein, M. and Roy, M.J. (1997) Environmental management to improve corporate profitability, *Journal of Cost Management*, November–December, 26–34.

Evans, H. and Ashworth, G. (1996) Survey conclusions: wakeup to the competition, *Management Accounting* (UK), May, 16–18.

Ezzamel, M. and Hart, H. (1987) *Advanced Management Accounting: An Organisational Emphasis*. London, Cassell.

Ezzamel, M.A. and Hilton, K. (1980) Divisionalization in British industry: a preliminary study, *Accounting and Business Research*, Summer, 197–214.

Feldman, M.S. and March, J.G. (1981) Information in organizations as signal and symbol, *Administrative Science Quarterly*, **26**(2), 171–86.

Fielden, J. and Robertson, J. (1980) The content of a value for money review of performance audit, *Public Finance and Accounting*, November, 23–5.

Fisher, I. (1930) *The Theory of Interest*, Macmillan.

Fisher, J. (1995) Contingency-based research on management control systems: Categorization by level of complexity, *Journal of Accounting Literature*, **14**, 24–53.

Fitzgerald, L., Johnston, R., Silvestro, R. and Steele, A. (1989) Management control in service industries, *Management Accounting*, April, 44–6.

Fitzgerald, L., Johnston, R., Brignall, T.J., Silvestro, R. and Voss, C. (1991) *Performance Measurement in Service Businesses*, Chartered Institute of Management Accountants.

Fitzgerald, L. and Moon, P. (1996) *Performance Management in Service Industries*, Chartered Institute of Management Accountants.

Flower, J. (1973) *Computer Models for Accountants*, Haymarket, Chs 4, 5.

Foster, G. and Horngren, C.T. (1988) Cost accounting and cost management in a JIT environment, *Journal of Cost Management for the Manufacturing Industry*, Winter, 4–14.

Franklin, L. (1998) Taxation and the capital expenditure decision, *Management Accounting (UK)*, November, 44–6.

Fremgen, J.M. and Liao, S.S. (1981) The Allocation of Corporate Indirect Costs, National Association of Accountants, New York.

Friedman, A.L. and Lynne, S.R. (1995) *Activity-based Techniques: The Real Life Consequences*, Chartered Institute of Management Accountants.

Friedman, A.L. and Lynne, S.R. (1997) Activity-based techniques and the death of the beancounter, *The European Accounting Review*, **6**(1), 19–44.

Friedman, A.L. and Lynne, S.R. (1999) *Success and Failure of Activity-based Techniques: A long-term perspective*, Chartered Institute of Management Accountants.

Galloway, D. and Waldron, D. (1988) Throughput accounting – 1: the need for a new language for manufacturing, *Management Accounting*, November, 34–5.

Gardiner, S.C. (1993) Measures of product attractiveness and the theory of constraints. *International Journal of Retail and Distribution*, **21**(7), 37–40.

Gibson, B. (1990) Determining meaningful sales relational (mix) variances, *Accounting and Business Research*, Winter, 35–40.

Goetz, B. (1949) *Management Planning and Control: A Managerial Approach to Industrial Accounting*, McGraw-Hill, p. 142.

Goldratt, E.M. and Cox, J. (1984) *The Goal*, London, Gower.

Goldratt, E.M. and Cox, J. (1992) *The Goal* (2nd edn), London, Gower.

Gordon, L.A. and Narayanan, V.K. (1984) Management accounting systems, perceived environmental uncertainty and organizational structure: an empirical investigation, *Accounting, Organizations and Society*, Vol. 9, No. 1, pp 33–47.

Gould, J.R. (1964) Internal pricing on firms when there are costs of using an outside market, *Journal of Business*, 37(1), January, 61–7.

Govindarajan, V. (1984) Appropriateness of accounting data in performance evaluation: an empirical evaluation of environmental uncertainty as an intervening variable, *Accounting, Organisations and Society*, 9(2), 125–36.

Govindarajan, V. (1988) A contingency approach to strategy implementation at the business unit level: integrating administrative mechanisms with strategy, *Academy of Management Journal*, 33, 828–53.

Govindarajan, V. and Gupta, A.K. (1985) Linking control systems to business unit strategy: Impact on performance, *Accounting, Organisations and Society*, 10(1), 51–66.

Granlund, M. and Lukka, K. (1998) It's a small world of management accounting practices, *Journal of Management Accounting Research*, 10, 151–79.

Granlund, M. and Malmi, T. (2002) Moderate impact of ERPS on management accounting: a lag or permanent outcome?, *Management Accounting Research*, 13 (3), 299–321.

Green, F.B. and Amenkhienan, F.E. (1992) Accounting innovations: A cross sectional survey of manufacturing firms, *Journal of Cost Management for the Manufacturing Industry*, Spring 58–64.

Guilding, C., Craven, K.S. and Tayles, M. (2000) An international comparison of strategic management accounting practices, *Management Accounting Research*, 11(1), 113–35.

Guilding, C., Drury, C. and Tayles, M. (2005) An empirical investigation of the importance of cost-plus pricing, *Managerial Auditing Journal*, 20 (2), 125–37.

Guilding, C., Lamminmaki, D. and Drury, C. (1998) Budgeting and standard costing practices in New Zealand and the United Kingdom, *The International Journal of Accounting*, 33(5), 41–60.

Gul, F.A. and Chia, Y.M. (1994) The effects of management accounting systems, perceived environmental uncertainty and decentralization on managerial performance: A test of threeway interaction, *Accounting, Organizations and Society*, 19(4/5), 413–26.

Gurton, A. (1990), Bye bye budget: the annual budget is dead, *Accountancy*, March, 60.

Hansen, D.R. and Mendoza, R. (1999) Costos de Impacto Ambiental: Su Medicion, Asignacion, y Control, *INCAE Revista*, Vol. X, No. 2, 1999.

Hansen, D.R. and Mowen, M. (2000) *Management Accounting*, South Western Publishing, Chapter 12.

Harris, D.G. (1993) The impact of US tax law revision on multinational corporations' capital location and income shifting decisions, *Journal of Accounting Research*, 31 (Supplement), 111–39.

Hedberg, B. and Jonsson, S. (1978) Designing semi-confusing information systems for organizations in changing environments, *Accounting, Organisations and Society*, 1, 47–64.

Hergert, M. and Morris, D. (1989) Accounting data for value chain analysis, *Strategic Management Journal*, 10, 175–88.

Hiromoto, T. (1991) Restoring the relevance of management accounting, *Journal of Management Accounting Research*, 3, 1–15.

Hirshleifer, J. (1956) On the economies of transfer pricing, *Journal of Business*, July, 172–84.

Hirst, M.K. (1981) Accounting information and the evaluation of subordinate performance, *The Accounting Review*, October, 771–84.

Hirst, M.K. (1987) The effects of setting budget goals and task uncertainty on performance: a theoretical analysis, *The Accounting Review*, October, 774–84.

Hofstede, G.H. (1968) *The Game of Budget Control*, Tavistock.

Holton, M. (1998) Implementing ABC in a service driven business – DHL Worldwide Express, in Innes, J. (ed.), *Handbook of Management Accounting*, Gee, Chapter 23.

Holzer, H.P. and Norreklit, H. (1991) Some thoughts on the cost accounting developments in the United States, *Management Accounting Research*, March, 3–13.

Hope, J. and Fraser, R. (1999a), Beyond budgeting: Building a new management model for the information age, *Management Accounting*, January, 16–21.

Hope, J. and Fraser, R. (2001) Figures of Hate, *Financial Management*, February, 22–5.

Hope, J. and Fraser, R. (1999b), Take it away, *Accountancy*, May, 66–67.

Hope, J. and Fraser, R. (2003), Who needs budgets? *Harvard Business Review*, February, 42–48.

Hopper, T.M., Storey, J. and Willmott, H. (1987) Accounting for accounting: towards the development of a dialectical view, *Accounting, Organisations and Society*, 12(5) 437–56.

Hopper, T., Kirkham, L., Scapens, R.W. and Turley, S. (1992) Does financial accounting dominate management accounting – A research note, *Management Accounting Research*, 3(4), 307–11.

Hopwood, A.G. (1976) *Accountancy and Human Behaviour*, Prentice-Hall.

Hopwood, A.G. (1978) Towards an organisational perspective for the study of accounting and information systems, *Accounting, Organisations and Society*, 3(1), 3–14.

Horngren, C.T. (1967) Process costing in perspective: forget FIFO, *Accounting Review*, July.

Horngren, C.T. (1990) Contribution margin analysis: no longer relevant/strategic cost management: the new paradigm, *Journal of Management Accounting Research* (USA), Fall, 21–4.

Horngren, G.T. and Sorter, G.H. (1962) Asset recognition and economic attributes: the relevant costing approach, *The Accounting Review*, 37, July, 394, also in *Contemporary Cost Accounting and Control*, (ed G.J. Benston), Dickenson (1977), 462–74.

Hornyak, S. (2000) Budgeting made easy, in Reeve, J.M. (ed.), *Readings and Issues in Cost Management*, South Western College Publishing, 341–6.

Imoisili, O.A. (1989) The role of budget data in the evaluation of managerial performance, *Accounting, Organizations and Society*, 14(4), 325–35.

Innes, J. (1998) Strategic Management Accounting, in Innes, J. (ed.), *Handbook of Management Accounting*, Gee, Ch. 2.

Innes, J. and Mitchell, F. (1991) ABC: A survey of CIMA members, *Management Accounting*, October, 28–30.

Innes, J. and Mitchell, F. (1992) A review of activity based costing practice, in *Handbook in Management Accounting Practice* (ed. C. Drury), Butterworth-Heinemann, Ch. 3.

Innes, J. and Mitchell, F. (1995a) A survey of activity-based costing in the UK's largest companies, *Management Accounting Research*, June, 137–54.

Innes, J. and Mitchell, F. (1995b) Activity-based costing, in *Issues in Management Accounting* (eds D. Ashton, T. Hopper and R.W. Scapens), Prentice-Hall, 115–36.

Innes, J. and Mitchell, F. (1997) The application of activity-based costing in the United Kingdom's largest financial institutions, *The Service Industries Journal*, 17(1), 190–203.

Innes, J., Mitchell, F. and Sinclear, D. (2000) Activity-based costing in the UK's largest companies: a comparison of 1994 and 1999 survey results, *Management Accounting Research*, 11(3), 349–62.

Israelsen, P., Anderson, M., Rohde, C. and Sorensen, P.E. (1996) Management accounting in Denmark: theory and practice, in Bhimani, A. (ed.) *Management Accounting: European Perspectives*, Oxford, Oxford University Press, 3153.

Ittner, C.D., Larcker, D.F. and Rajan, M.V. (1997) The choice of performance measures in annual bonus contracts, *The Accounting Review*, 72(2), 231–55.

Jacob, J. (1996) Taxes and transfer pricing: income shifting and the volume of intrafirm transfers, *Journal of Accounting Research*, 34(2), 301–15.

Jaedicke R.K. and Robichek, A.A. (1964) Cost–volume–profit analysis under conditions of uncertainty, *The Accounting Review*, 39(4), October, 917–26; also in *Studies in Cost Analysis* (ed. D. Solomons), Sweet and Maxwell (1968); also in *Cost Accounting, Budgeting and Control* (ed. W.E. Thomas), 192–210, South Western Publishing Company.

Johnson, G. and Scholes, K. (1999) *Exploring Corporate Strategy*, Prentice-Hall.

Johnson, G. and Scholes, K. (2005) *Exploring Corporate Strategy*, Prentice-Hall.

Johnson, H.T. (1990) Professors, customers and value: bringing a global perspective to management accounting education, in *Performance Excellence in Manufacturing and Services Organizations* (ed. P. Turney), American Accounting Association.

Johnson, H.T. and Kaplan, R.S. (1987) *Relevance Lost: The Rise and Fall of Management Accounting*, Harvard Business School Press.

Jones, T.C. and Dugdale, D. (1998) Theory of constraints: transforming ideas?, *British Accounting Review*, **30**(1), 73–92.

Jones, T.C. and Dugdale, D. (2002) The ABC bandwagon and the juggernaut of modernity, *Accounting, Organizations and Society*, **27**, 121–63.

Joseph, N., Turley, S., Burns, J., Lewis, L., Scapens, R.W. and Southworth, A. (1996) External financial reporting and management information: A survey of UK management accountants, *Management Accounting Research* **7**(1), 73–94.

Joshi, P.L. (1998) An explanatory study of activity-based costing practices and benefits in large size manufacturing companies in India, *Accounting and Business Review*, **5**(1), 65–93.

Joye, M.P. and Blayney, P.J. (1990) Cost and management accounting practice in Australian manufacturing companies: survey results, Monograph No. 7, University of Sydney.

Joye, M.P. and Blayney, P.J. (1991) Strategic management accounting survey, Monograph No. 8, University of Sydney.

Kald, M. and Nilsson, F. (2000) Performance measurement at Nordic companies, *European Management Journal*, **1**, 113–27.

Kaplan, R.S. (1975) The significance and investigation of cost variances: survey and extensions, *Journal of Accounting Research*, **13**(2), Autumn, 311–37, also in *Contemporary Issues in Cost and Managerial Accounting* (eds H.R. Anton, P.A. Firmin and H.D. Grove), Houghton Mifflin (1978).

Kaplan, R.S. (1982) *Advanced Management Accounting*, Prentice-Hall.

Kaplan, R.S. (1990) Contribution margin analysis: no longer relevant/strategic cost management: the new paradigm, *Journal of Management Accounting Research* (USA), Fall, 2–15.

Kaplan, R.S. (1994a) Management accounting (1984–1994): development of new practice and theory, *Management Accounting Research*, September and December, 247–60.

Kaplan, R.S. (1994b) Flexible budgeting in an activity-based costing framework, *Accounting Horizons*, June, 104–109.

Kaplan, R.S. and Atkinson, A.A. (1989) *Advanced Management Accounting*, Prentice-Hall.

Kaplan, R.S. and Atkinson, A.A. (1998) *Advanced Management Accounting*, Prentice-Hall, Ch. 3

Kaplan, R.S. and Cooper, R. (1998) *Cost and Effect: Using Integrated Systems to Drive Profitability and Performance*, Harvard Business School Press.

Kaplan, R.S. and Norton, D.P. (1992) The balanced scorecard: measures that drive performance, *Harvard Business Review*, Jan–Feb, 71–9.

Kaplan, R.S. and Norton, D.P. (1993) Putting the balanced scorecard to work, *Harvard Business Review*, September–October, 134–47.

Kaplan, R.S. and Norton, D.P. (1996a) Using the balanced scorecard as a strategic management system, *Harvard Business Review*, Jan–Feb, 75–85.

Kaplan, R.S. and Norton, D.P. (1996b) *The Balanced Scorecard: Translating strategy into action*, Harvard Business School Press.

Kaplan, R.S. and Norton, D.P. (2001a) *The Strategy-focused Organization*, Harvard Business School Press.

Kaplan, R.S. and Norton, D.P. (2001b) Balance without profit, *Financial Management*, January, 23–6.

Kaplan, R.S. and Norton, D.P. (2001c) Transforming the balanced scorecard from performance measurement to strategic management: Part 1, *Accounting Horizons*, March, 87–104.

Kaplan, R.S. and Norton, D.P. (2001d) Transforming the balanced scorecard from performance measurement to strategic management: Part 2, *Accounting Horizons*, June, 147–60.

Kaplan R.S., Weiss, D. and Deseh, E. (1997) Transfer pricing with ABC, *Management Accounting (USA)*, 20–8.

Kato, Y. (1993) Target costing support systems: lessons from leading Japanese companies, *Management Accounting Research*, March, 33–48.

Keef, S. and Roush, M. (2002) Does MVA measure up?, *Financial Management*, January, 20–1.

Kelly, M. and Pratt, M. (1992) Purposes and paradigms of management accounting: beyond economic reductionism, *Accounting Education*, **1**(3), 225–46.

Kenis, I. (1979) The effects of budgetary goal characteristics on managerial attitudes and performance, *The Accounting Review*, October, 707–21.

Kennedy, A. and Dugdale, D. (1999) Getting the most from budgeting, *Management Accounting (UK)*, February, 22–4.

Khandwalla, P.N. (1972) The effects of different types of competition on the use of management controls, *Journal of Accounting Research*, Autumn, 275–85.

Klassan, K., Lang, M. and Wolfson, M. (1993) Geographic income shifting by multinational corporations in response to tax rate changes, *Journal of Accounting Research*, **31**(Supplement), 141–73.

Langfield-Smith, K. (1997) Management control systems and strategy: a critical review, *Accounting, Organizations and Society*, **22**, 207–32.

Lauderman, M. and Schaeberle, F.W. (1983) The cost accounting practices of firms using standard costs, *Cost and Management* (Canada), July/August, 21–5.

Leauby, B.A. and Wentzel, K. (2002) Know the score: The balanced scorecard approach to strategically assist clients, *Pennsylvania CPA Journal*, Spring, 29–32.

Lee, J.Y. and Jacobs, B.G. (1993) How process and activity-based cost analysis meets the needs of a small manufacturer, *CMA Magazine* (Canada), **67**(3), 15–19.

Lee, T.A. (1996) *Income and Value Measurement*, Thomson Business Press.

Licata, M.P., Strawser, R.H. and Welker, R.B. (1986) A note on participation in budgeting and locus of control, *The Accounting Review*, January, 112–17.

Lindblom, C.E. (1959) The science of 'Muddling Through', *Public Administration Review*, Summer, 79–88.

Lister, R. (1983) Appraising the value of post-audit procedures, *Accountancy Age*, 20 October, 40.

Lord, B.R. (1996) Strategic management accounting: the emperor's new clothes? *Management Accounting Research*, 7(3), 347–66.

Lovata, L.M. and Costigan, M.L. (2002) Empirical analysis of adopters of economic value added, *Management Accounting Research*, **13**(2), 251–72.

Lucas, M.R. (2003) Pricing decisions and the neoclassical theory of the firm, *Management Accounting Research*, 14(3), 201–18.

Lukka, K. and Granlund, M. (1996) Cost accounting in Finland: Current practice and trends of development, *The European Accounting Review*, 5(1), 1–28.

Lukka, K. and Granlund, M. (2002) The fragmented communication structure within the accounting academia: the case of activity-based costing genres, *Accounting, Organizations and Society*, **27**, 165–90.

Macintosh, N.B. (1985) *The Social Software of Accounting and Information Systems*, Wiley.

Macintosh, N.B. (1994) *Management Accounting and Control Systems: An Organisational and Behavioural Approach*, Wiley.

Mak, Y.T. and Roush, M.L. (1994) Flexible budgeting and variance analysis in an activity-based costing environment, *Accounting Horizons*, June, 93–104.

Mak, Y.T. and Roush, M.L. (1996) Managing activity costs with flexible budgets and variance analysis, *Accounting Horizons*, September, 141–6.

Malmi, T. (1997) Balance scorecards in Finnish companies: a research note, *Management Accounting Research*, **12**(2), 207–20.

Malmi, T. (2001) Balanced scorecards in Finnish companies: a research note, *Management Accounting Research*, Vol. 12, No. 2, pp 207–20.

Manes, R.P. (1983) Demand elasticities: supplements to sales budget variance reports, *The Accounting Review*, January, 143–56.

Mauriel, J. and Anthony, R.N. (1986) Mis-evaluation of investment centre performance, *Harvard Business Review*, March/April, 98–105.

McGowan, A.S. and Klammer, T.P. (1997) Satisfaction with activity-based cost management, *Journal of Management Accounting Research*, 9, 217–38.

McNair, C.J., Polutnik, L. and Silvi, R. (2001) Cost management and value creation, *European Accounting Review*, **10**(1), 33–50.

Merchant, K.A. (1989) *Rewarding Results: Motivating Profit Center Managers*, Harvard Business School Press.

Merchant, K.A. (1990) How challenging should profit budget targets be? *Management Accounting*, November, 46–8.

Merchant, K.A. (1998) *Modern Management Control Systems: Text and Cases*, Prentice-Hall, New Jersey.

Merchant, K.A. and Shields, M.D. (1993) When and why to measure costs less accurately to improve decision making, *Accounting Horizons*, June, 76–81.

Mia, L. (1989) The impact of participation in budgeting and job difficulty on managerial performance and work motivation: a research note, *Accounting, Organisations and Society*, 14(4), 347–57.

Milani, K. (1975) The relationship of participation in budget setting to industrial supervisor performance and attitudes: a field study, *The Accounting Review*, April, 274–84.

Miles, R.E. and Snow, C.C. (1978) *Organizational Strategies, Structure and Process*, New York, McGraw-Hill.

Mills, R.W. (1988) Pricing decisions in UK manufacturing and service companies, *Management Accounting*, November, 38–9.

Monden, Y. and Hamada, K. (1991) Target costing and Kaizen costing in Japanese automobile companies, *Journal of Management Accounting Research*, Autumn, 16–34.

Moon, P. and Fitzgerald, L. (1996) *Performance Measurement in Service Industries: Making it Work*, Chartered Institute of Management Accountants, London.

Moore, P.G. and Thomas, H. (1991) *The Anatomy of Decisions*, Penguin.

Narayanan, V.G. and Sarkar, R.G. (2002) The impact of activity-based costing on managerial decisions at Insteel industries: A field study, *Journal of Economics and Management Strategy*, 11(2), 257–88.

Neale, C.W. and Holmes, D. (1988) Post-completion audits: The costs and benefits, *Management Accounting*, 66(3), 27–31.

Neale, C.W. and Holmes, D. (1991) *Post-completion Auditing*, Pitman.

Neighbour, J. (2002) Transfer pricing: keeping it at arm's length, *OECD Observer*, January, 29–30.

Nicholls, B. (1992) ABC in the UK – a status report, *Management Accounting*, May, 22–3.

Norreklit, H. (2000) The balance on the balanced scorecard – a critical analysis of some of its assumptions, *Management Accounting Research*, Vol. 11, No. 1, pp 65–88.

Norreklit, H. (2003) The balanced scorecard: what is the score? A rhetorical analysis of the balanced scorecard, *Accounting, Organizations and Society*, 28, 591–619.

O'Hanlon, J.O. and Peasnell, K. (1998) Wall's Street's contribution to management accounting: the Stern Stewart EVA® financial management system, *Management Accounting Research*, 9(4), 421–44.

Oliveras, E. and Amat, O. (2002) The balanced scorecard assumptions and the drivers of business growth, Paper presented at the 25th Annual Congress of the European Accounting Association, Copenhagan, Denmark.

Olve, N., Roy, J. and Wetter, M. (2000) *Performance Drivers: A Practical Guide to Using the Balanced Scorecard*, John Wiley & Sons.

Osni, M. (1973) Factor analysis of behavioural variables affecting budgetary stock, *The Accounting Review*, 535–48.

Otley, D.T. (1978) Budget use and managerial performance, *Journal of Accounting Research*, 16(1), Spring, 122–49.

Otley, D.T. (1980) The contingency theory of management accounting: achievement and prognosis, *Accounting, Organizations and Society*, 5(4), 413–28.

Otley, D.T. (1987) *Accounting Control and Organizational Behaviour*, Heinemann.

Ouchi, W.G. (1979) A conceptual framework for the design of organizational control mechanisms, *Management Science*, 833–48.

Oyelere, P.B. and Emmanuel, C.R. (1998) International transfer pricing and income shifting: evidence from the UK, *The European Accounting Review*, 7(4), 623–35.

Pendlebury, M.E. (1994) Management accounting in local government, *Financial Accountability & Management*, May, 117–29.

Pendlebury, M. (1996) Management accounting in local government, in *Handbook of Management Accounting Practice* (ed. C. Drury), Butterworth-Heinemann, London.

Pere, T. (1999) How the execution of strategy is followed in large organisations located in Finland, Masters Thesis (Helsinki School of Economics and Business Administration).

Perera, S., McKinnon, J.L. and Harrison, G.L. (2003) Diffusion of transfer pricing innovation in the context of commercialization – a longitudinal study of government trading enterprises, *Management Accounting Research*, 14(2),140–64.

Perrin, J. (1987) The costs and joint products of English teaching hospitals, *Financial Accountability and Management*, 3(2), 209–30.

Pfeffer, J. and Salancik, G.R. (1974) Organisational decision making as a political process: the case of a university budget, *Administrative Science Quarterly*, June, 135–50.

Phyrr, P.A. (1976) Zero-based budgeting – where to use it and how to begin, *S.A.M. Advanced Management Journal*, Summer, 5.

Pike, R.H. (1996) A longitudinal study of capital budgeting practices, *Journal of Business Finance and Accounting*, **23**(1), 79–92.

Pike, R. and Neale, B. (2005) *Corporate Finance and Investment*, Prentice-Hall Europe.

Plunkett, J.J., Dale, B.G. and Tyrrell, R.W. (1985) *Quality Costs*, London, Department of Trade and Industry.

Porter, M. (1980) *Competitive strategy techniques analysing industries and competitors*, New York, Free Press.

Porter, M. (1985) *Competitive Advantage*, New York, Free Press.

Puxty, A.G. (1993) *The Social and Organisational Context of Management Accounting*, Academic Press.

Puxty, A.G. and Lyall, D. (1990) *Cost Control into the 1990s: A Survey of Standard Costing and Budgeting Practices in the UK*, Chartered Institute of Management Accountants; see also *Management Accounting*, February, 1990, 445.

Ramadan, S.S. (1989) The rationale for cost allocation: A study of UK companies, *Accounting and Business Research*, Winter, 31–7.

Ranganathan, J. and Ditz, D. (1996) Environmental accounting: a tool for better management, *Management Accounting*, February, 38–40.

Reece, J.S. and Cool, W.R. (1978) Measuring investment centre performance, *Harvard Business Review*, May/June 29–49.

Roslender, R. (1992) *Sociological Perspectives on Modern Accountancy*, Routledge.

Roslender, R. (1995) Accounting for strategic positioning: Responding to the crisis in management accounting, *British Journal of Management*, **6**, 45–57.

Roslender, R. (1996) Relevance lost and found: Critical perspectives on the promise of management accounting, *Critical Perspectives on Accounting*, **7**(5), 533–61.

Roslender, R. and Hart, S.J. (2002) Integrating management accounting and marketing in the pursuit of competitive advantage: the case for strategic management accounting, *Critical Perspectives on Accounting*, **13**(2), 255–77.

Roslender, R. and Hart, S.J. (2003) In search of strategic management accounting: theoretical and field study perspectives, *Management Accounting Research*, **14**(3), 255–80.

Saez-Torrecilla, A., Fernandez-Fernandez, A., Texeira-Quiros, J. and Vaquera-Mosquero, M. (1996) Management accounting in Spain: trends in thought and practice, in Bhimani, A. (ed.) *Management Accounting: European Perspective 3*, Oxford, Oxford University Press, 180–90.

Salkin, G. and Kornbluth, J. (1973) *Linear Programming in Financial Planning*, Prentice-Hall, Ch. 7.

Samuels, J.M., Wilkes, F.M. and Brayshaw, R.E. (1998) *Management of Company Finance*, Chapman and Hall.

Scapens, R., Jazayeri, M. and Scapens, J. (1998) SAP: Integrated information systems and the implications for management accountants, *Management Accounting (UK)*, September, 46–8.

Scapens, R.W. (1991) *Management Accounting: A Review of Recent Developments*, Macmillan.

Scarborough, P.A., Nanni, A. and Sakurai, M. (1991) Japanese management accounting practices and the effects of assembly and process automation, *Management Accounting Research*, **2**, 27–46.

Scherrer, G. (1996) Management accounting: a German perspective, in Bhimani, A. (ed.), *Management Accounting: European Perspectives*, Oxford, Oxford University Press, 100–22.

Schiff, M. and Lewin, A.Y. (1970) The impact of people on budgets, *The Accounting Review*, April, 259–68.

Schwarzbach, H.R. (1985) The impact of automation on accounting for direct costs, *Management Accounting* (USA), **67**(6), 45–50.

Seal, W., Cullen, J., Dunlop, D., Berry, T. and Ahmed, M. (1999) Enacting a European supply chain: a case study on the role of management accounting, *Management Accounting Research*, **10**(3), 303–22.

Sen, P.K. (1998) Another look at cost variance investigation, *Accounting Horizons*, February, 127–37.

Shank, J.K. (1989) Strategic cost management: new wine or just new bottles?, *Journal of Management Accounting Research* (USA), Fall, 47–65.

Shank, J. and Govindarajan, V. (1992) Strategic cost management: the value chain perspective, *Journal of Management Accounting Research*, **4**, 179–97.

Shields, M.D. (1995) An empirical analysis of firms' implementation experiences with activity-based costing, *Journal of Management Accounting Research*, **7**, Fall, 148–66.

Shim, E. and Stagliano, A. (1997) A survey of US manufacturers on implementation of ABC, *Journal of Cost Management*, March/ April, 39–41.

Silk, S. (1998) Automating the balanced scorecard, *Management Accounting*, May, 38–44.

Simmonds, K. (1981) Strategic management accounting, *Management Accounting*, **59**(4), 26–9.

Simmonds, K. (1982) Strategic management accounting for pricing: a case example, *Accounting and Business Research*, **12**(47), 206–14.

Simmonds, K. (1986) The accounting assessment of competitive position, *European Journal of Marketing, Organisations and Society*, **12**(4), 357–74.

Simon, H.A. (1959) Theories of decision making in economics and behavioural science, *The American Economic Review*, June, 233–83.

Simons, R. (1987) Accounting control systems and business strategy, *Accounting, Organizations and Society*, **12**(4), 357–74.

Simons, R. (1998) *Performance Measurement and Control Systems for Implementing Strategy: Text and cases*, Prentice-Hall.

Simons, R. (1999) *Performance Measurement and Control Systems for Implementing Strategy*, Prentice-Hall, New Jersey.

Sizer, J. (1989) *An Insight into Management Accounting*, Penguin, Chs 11, 12.

Sizer, J. and Mottram, G. (1996) Successfully evaluating and controlling investments in advanced manufacturing technology, in *Management Accounting Handbook* (ed. C. Drury), Butterworth-Heinemann.

Skinner, R.C. (1990) The role of profitability in divisional decision making and performance, *Accounting and Business Research*, Spring, 135–41.

Slater, K. and Wootton, C. (1984) *Joint and By-product Costing in the UK*, Institute of Cost and Management Accounting.

Soin, K., Seal, W. and Cullen, J. (2002) ABC and organizational change: an institutional perspective, *Management Accounting Research*, **13**(2), 151–72.

Solomons, D. (1965) *Divisional Performance: Measurement and Control*, R.D. Irwin.

Speckbacher, G., Bischof, J. and Pfeiffer, T. (2003) A Descriptive Analysis on the Implementation of Balanced Scorecards in German-Speaking Countries, *Management Accounting Research*, **14**(4), 361–88.

Stedry, A. and Kay, E. (1966) The effects of goal difficulty on performance: a field experiment, *Behavioural Science*, November, 459–70.

Stewart, G.B. (1991) *The Quest for Value: A Guide for Senior Managers*, Harper Collins, New York.

Stewart, G.B. (1994) EVA(TM): Fact and Fantasy, *Journal of Applied Corporate Finance*, Summer, 71–84.

Stewart, G.B. (1995) EVA(TM) works But not if you make common mistakes, *Fortune*, 1 May, 81–2.

Tang, R. (1992) Canadian transfer pricing in the 1990s, *Management Accounting* (USA), February.

Tani, T., Okano, H., Shimizu, N., Iwabuchi, Y, Fukuda, J. and Cooray, S. (1994) Target cost management in Japanese companies: current state of the art, *Management Accounting Research*, **5**(1), 67–82.

Thompson, J.D. (1967) *Organisations in Action*, McGraw-Hill.

Thompson, J.D. and Tuden, A. (1959) Strategies, structures and processes of organizational decision, in *Comparative Studies in Administration* (eds Thompson, J.D. *et al.*), University of Pittsburg Press.

Thompson, J.L. (2005) *Strategic Management*, Thomson Learning, London.

Tomkins, C. (1973) *Financial Planning in Divisionalised Companies*, Haymarket, Chs 4 and 8.

Tomkins, C. (1975) Another look at residual income, *Journal of Business Finance and Accounting*, **2**(1), Spring 39–54.

Tomkins, C. and Carr, C. (1996) Editorial in Special Issue of Management Accounting Research: Strategic Management Accounting, *Management Accounting Research*, **7**(2), 165–7.

Tomkins, C. and McAulay, L. (1996) Modelling fair transfer prices where no market guidelines exist, in *Management Accounting Handbook* (ed. C. Drury), Butterworth-Heinemann, Ch. 16.

Trahan, E.A. and Gitman, L.J. (1995) Bridging the theory–practice gap in corporate finance: A survey of chief finance officers, *The Quarterly Review of Economics and Finance*, **35**(1), Spring, 73–87.

Trenchard, P.M. and Dixon, R. (2003) The clinical allocation of joint blood product costs, *Management Accounting Research*, **14**(2), 165–76.

Turney, P. (1993) *Common Cents: The ABC Performance Breakthrough*, Cost Technology, Hillsboro, Oregon, USA.

Umapathy, S. (1987) *Current Budgeting Practices in U.S. Industry: The State of the Art*, New York, Quorum.

Virtanen, K., Malmi, T., Vaivio, J. and Kasanen, E. (1996) Drivers of management accounting in Finland, in Bhimani, A. (ed.) *Management Accounting: European Perspectives*, Oxford, Oxford University Press, 218–41.

Vroom, V.H. (1960) *Some Personality Determinants of the Effects of Participation*, Prentice-Hall.

Ward, K. (1992) Accounting for marketing strategies, in *Management Accounting Handbook* (ed. C. Drury), Butterworth-Heinemann, Ch. 7.

Watson, D.H. and Baumler, J.V. (1975) Transfer pricing: a behavioural context, *Accounting Review*, 50(3), July, 466–74.

Wetnight, R.B. (1958) Direct costing passes the future benefit test, *NAA Bulletin*, 39, August, 84.

Weick, K.E. (1969) *The Social Psychology of Organising*, Addison Wesley.

Wildavsky, A. (1974) *The Politics of Budgetary Process*, Little Brown.

Wilkes, F.M. (1989) *Operational Research: Analysis and Applications*, McGraw-Hill.

Wilson, R.M. and Chua, W.E. (1993) *Management Accounting: Method and Meaning*, International Thomson Business Press, Ch. 7.

Woodward, J. (1965) *Industrial Organization; Theory and Practice*, Oxford University Press.

Yoshikawa, T., Innes, J., Mitchell, F. and Tanaka, M. (1993) *Contemporary Cost Management*, Chapman and Hall.

Young, P. H. (1985) *Cost Allocation: Methods, Principles, Applications*, Amsterdam: North Holland.

Zuriekat, M. (2005) Performance measurement systems: An examination of the influence of contextual factors and their impact on performance with specific emphasis on the balanced scorecard approach, PhD dissertation, University of Huddersfield.

APPENDICES

Appendix A: Present value of £1 after n years $= £1(1+k)^n$

Years hence	1%	2%	4%	6%	8%	10%	12%	14%	15%	16%
1	0.990	0.980	0.962	0.943	0.926	0.909	0.893	0.877	0.870	0.862
2	0.980	0.961	0.925	0.890	0.857	0.826	0.797	0.769	0.756	0.743
3	0.971	0.942	0.889	0.840	0.794	0.751	0.712	0.675	0.658	0.641
4	0.961	0.924	0.855	0.792	0.735	0.683	0.636	0.592	0.572	0.552
5	0.951	0.906	0.822	0.747	0.681	0.621	0.567	0.519	0.497	0.476
6	0.942	0.888	0.790	0.705	0.630	0.564	0.507	0.456	0.432	0.410
7	0.933	0.871	0.760	0.665	0.583	0.513	0.452	0.400	0.376	0.354
8	0.923	0.853	0.731	0.627	0.540	0.467	0.404	0.351	0.327	0.305
9	0.914	0.837	0.703	0.592	0.500	0.424	0.361	0.308	0.284	0.263
10	0.905	0.820	0.676	0.558	0.463	0.386	0.322	0.270	0.247	0.227
11	0.896	0.804	0.650	0.527	0.429	0.350	0.287	0.237	0.215	0.195
12	0.887	0.788	0.625	0.497	0.397	0.319	0.257	0.208	0.187	0.168
13	0.879	0.773	0.601	0.469	0.368	0.290	0.229	0.182	0.163	0.145
14	0.870	0.758	0.577	0.442	0.340	0.263	0.205	0.160	0.141	0.125
15	0.861	0.743	0.555	0.417	0.315	0.239	0.183	0.140	0.123	0.108
16	0.853	0.728	0.534	0.394	0.292	0.218	0.163	0.123	0.107	0.093
17	0.844	0.714	0.513	0.371	0.270	0.198	0.146	0.108	0.093	0.080
18	0.836	0.700	0.494	0.350	0.250	0.180	0.130	0.095	0.081	0.069
19	0.828	0.686	0.475	0.331	0.232	0.164	0.116	0.083	0.070	0.060
20	0.820	0.673	0.456	0.312	0.215	0.149	0.104	0.073	0.061	0.051

Years hence	18%	20%	22%	24%	25%	26%	28%	30%	35%
1	0.847	0.833	0.820	0.806	0.800	0.794	0.781	0.769	0.741
2	0.718	0.694	0.672	0.650	0.640	0.630	0.610	0.592	0.549
3	0.609	0.579	0.551	0.524	0.512	0.500	0.477	0.455	0.406
4	0.516	0.482	0.451	0.423	0.410	0.397	0.373	0.350	0.301
5	0.437	0.402	0.370	0.341	0.328	0.315	0.291	0.269	0.223
6	0.370	0.335	0.303	0.275	0.262	0.250	0.227	0.207	0.165
7	0.314	0.279	0.249	0.222	0.210	0.198	0.178	0.159	0.122
8	0.266	0.233	0.204	0.179	0.168	0.157	0.139	0.123	0.091
9	0.225	0.194	0.167	0.144	0.134	0.125	0.108	0.094	0.067
10	0.191	0.162	0.137	0.116	0.107	0.099	0.085	0.073	0.050
11	0.162	0.135	0.112	0.094	0.086	0.079	0.066	0.056	0.037
12	0.137	0.112	0.092	0.076	0.069	0.062	0.052	0.043	0.027
13	0.116	0.093	0.075	0.061	0.055	0.050	0.040	0.033	0.020
14	0.099	0.078	0.062	0.049	0.044	0.039	0.032	0.025	0.015
15	0.084	0.065	0.051	0.040	0.035	0.031	0.025	0.020	0.011
16	0.071	0.054	0.042	0.032	0.028	0.025	0.019	0.015	0.008
17	0.060	0.045	0.034	0.026	0.023	0.020	0.015	0.012	0.006
18	0.051	0.038	0.028	0.021	0.018	0.016	0.012	0.009	0.005
19	0.043	0.031	0.023	0.017	0.014	0.012	0.009	0.007	0.003
20	0.037	0.026	0.019	0.014	0.012	0.010	0.007	0.005	0.002

Appendix B: Present value of an annuity of £1 received annually for n years $= \frac{£1}{K}\left(1 - \frac{1}{(1+K)^n}\right)$

Years hence	1%	2%	4%	6%	8%	10%	12%	14%	15%	16%	18%
1	0.990	0.980	0.962	0.943	0.926	0.909	0.893	0.877	0.870	0.862	0.847
2	1.970	1.942	1.886	1.833	1.783	1.736	1.690	1.647	1.626	1.605	1.566
3	2.941	2.884	2.775	2.673	2.577	2.487	2.402	2.322	2.283	2.246	2.174
4	3.902	3.808	3.630	3.465	3.312	3.170	3.037	2.914	2.855	2.798	2.690
5	4.853	4.713	4.452	4.212	3.993	3.791	3.605	3.433	3.352	3.274	3.127
6	5.795	5.601	5.242	4.917	4.623	4.355	4.111	3.889	3.784	3.685	3.498
7	6.728	6.472	6.002	5.582	5.206	4.868	4.564	4.288	4.160	4.039	3.812
8	7.652	7.325	6.733	6.210	5.747	5.335	4.968	4.639	4.487	4.344	4.078
9	8.566	8.162	7.435	6.802	6.247	5.759	5.328	4.946	4.772	4.607	4.303
10	9.471	8.983	8.111	7.360	6.710	6.145	5.650	5.216	5.019	4.833	4.494
11	10.368	9.787	8.760	7.887	7.139	6.495	5.937	5.453	5.234	5.029	4.656
12	11.255	10.575	9.385	8.384	7.536	6.814	6.194	5.660	5.421	5.197	4.793
13	12.134	11.343	9.986	8.853	7.904	7.103	6.424	5.842	5.583	5.342	4.910
14	13.004	12.106	10.563	9.295	8.244	7.367	6.628	6.002	5.724	5.468	5.008
15	13.865	12.849	11.118	9.712	8.559	7.606	6.811	6.142	5.847	5.575	5.092
16	14.718	13.578	11.652	10.106	8.851	7.824	6.974	6.265	5.954	5.669	5.162
17	15.562	14.292	12.166	10.477	9.122	8.022	7.120	6.373	6.047	5.749	5.222
18	16.398	14.992	12.659	10.828	9.372	8.201	7.250	6.467	6.128	5.818	5.273
19	17.226	15.678	13.134	11.815	9.604	8.365	7.366	6.550	6.198	5.877	5.316
20	18.046	16.351	13.590	11.470	9.818	8.514	7.469	6.623	6.259	5.929	5.353

Years hence	20%	22%	24%	25%	26%	28%	30%	35%	36%	37%
1	0.833	0.820	0.806	0.800	0.794	0.781	0.769	0.741	0.735	0.730
2	1.528	1.492	1.457	1.440	1.424	1.392	1.361	1.289	1.276	1.263
3	2.106	2.042	1.981	1.952	1.923	1.868	1.816	1.696	1.673	1.652
4	2.589	2.494	2.404	2.362	2.320	2.241	2.166	1.997	1.966	1.935
5	2.991	2.864	2.745	2.689	2.635	2.532	2.436	2.220	2.181	2.143
6	3.326	3.167	3.020	2.951	2.885	2.759	2.643	2.385	2.339	2.294
7	3.605	3.416	3.242	3.161	3.083	2.937	2.802	2.508	2.455	2.404
8	3.837	3.619	3.421	3.329	3.241	3.076	2.925	2.598	2.540	2.485
9	4.031	3.786	3.566	3.463	3.366	3.184	3.019	2.665	2.603	2.544
10	4.192	3.923	3.682	3.571	3.465	3.269	3.092	2.715	2.649	2.587
11	4.327	4.035	3.776	3.656	3.544	3.335	3.147	2.752	2.683	2.618
12	4.439	4.127	3.851	3.725	3.606	3.387	3.190	2.779	2.708	2.641
13	4.533	4.203	3.912	3.780	3.656	3.427	3.223	2.799	2.727	2.658
14	4.611	4.265	3.962	3.824	3.695	3.459	3.249	2.814	2.740	2.670
15	4.675	4.315	4.001	3.859	3.726	3.483	3.268	2.825	2.750	2.679
16	4.730	4.357	4.033	3.887	3.751	3.503	3.283	2.834	2.757	2.685
17	4.775	4.391	4.059	3.910	3.771	3.518	3.295	2.840	2.763	2.690
18	4.812	4.419	4.080	3.928	3.786	3.529	3.304	2.844	2.767	2.693
19	4.844	4.442	4.097	3.942	3.799	3.539	3.311	2.848	2.770	2.696
20	4.870	4.460	4.110	3.954	3.808	3.546	3.316	2.850	2.772	2.698

ANSWERS TO REVIEW PROBLEMS

Chapter 2

2.15 a. SV (or variable if direct labour can be matched exactly to output)
  b. F
  c. F
  d. V
  e. F (Advertising is a discretionary cost. See Chapter 15 (the budgeting process) for an explanation of this cost.)
  f. SV
  g. F
  h. SF
  i. V

2.16 Answer = D

2.17 Answer = D

2.18 Answer = B

2.19 See the description of cost behaviour in Chapter 2 for the answer to these questions. In particular the answer should provide graphs for fixed costs, variable costs, semi-fixed costs and semi-variable costs.

2.20 See Chapter 2 for the answer to this question.

2.21 a. See 'Functions of management accounting' in Chapter 1 for the answer to this question. In particular your answer should stress that the cost accountant provides financial information for stock valuation purposes and also presents relevant information to management for decision-making and planning and cost control purposes. For example, the cost accountant provides information on the costs and revenues of alternative courses of action to assist management in selecting the course of action which will maximize future cash flows. By coordinating plans together in the form of budgets and comparing actual performance with plans the accountant can pinpoint those activities which are not proceeding according to plan.
  b. i. Direct costs are those costs which can be traced to a cost objective. If the cost objective is a sales territory then *fixed* salaries of salesmen will be a direct cost. Therefore the statement is incorrect.
    ii. Whether a cost is controllable depends on the level of authority and time span being considered. For example, a departmental foreman may have no control over the number of supervisors employed in his department but this decision may be made by his superior. In the long term such costs are controllable.
    iii. This statement is correct. See 'Sunk costs' in Chapter 2 for an explanation of why this statement is correct.

2.22 See Chapter 2 for the answer to this question.

2.23 Cost information is required for the following purposes:
  a. costs for stock valuation and profit measurement;
  b. costs for decision-making;
  c. costs for planning and control.
  For the alternative measures of cost that might be appropriate for each of the above purposes see Chapter 2.

2.24 i. See Chapter 2 for a definition of opportunity cost and sunk cost.
  ii. *Opportunity cost:* If scarce resources such as machine hours are required for a special contract then the cost of the contract should include the lost profit that would have been earned on the next best alternative. This should be recovered in the contract price.
    Sunk cost: The original cost of equipment used for a contract is a sunk cost and should be ignored. The change in the resale value resulting from the use of the equipment represents the relevant cost of using the equipment.
  iii. The significance of opportunity cost is that relevant costs do not consist only of future cash outflows associated directly with a particular course of action. Imputed costs must also be included.
    The significance of sunk costs is that past costs are not relevant for decision-making.

2.25 See Chapter 2 for an explanation of the terms avoidable costs and unavoidable costs and Chapter 3 for an explanation of cost centres. A cost unit is a unit of product or service for which costs are ascertained. In a manufacturing organization a cost unit will be a unit of output produced within a cost centre. In a service organization, such as an educational establishment, a cost unit might be the cost per student.

2.26 a. i. Schedule of annual mileage costs

	5000 miles (£)	10 000 miles (£)	15 000 miles (£)	30 000 miles (£)
Variable costs:				
Spares	100	200	300	600
Petrol	380	760	1140	2280
Total variable cost	480	960	1440	2880
Variable cost per mile	0.096	0.096	0.096	0.096
Fixed costs				
Depreciation[a]	2000	2000	2000	2000
Maintenance	120	120	120	120
Vehicle licence	80	80	80	80
Insurance	150	150	150	150
Tyres[b]	—	—	75	150
	2350	2350	2425	2500
Fixed cost per mile	0.47	0.235	0.162	0.083
Total cost	2830	3310	3865	5380
Total cost per mile	0.566	0.331	0.258	0.179

Notes
[a]Annual depreciation = $\dfrac{\text{£5500 (cost)} - \text{£1500 (trade-in price)}}{2 \text{ years}} = \text{£2000}$

[b]At 15 000 miles per annum tyres will be replaced once during the two-year period at a cost of £150. The average cost per year is £75.
At 30 000 miles per annum tyres will be replaced once each year.

  Comments
  Tyres are a semi-fixed cost. In the above calculations they have been regarded as a step fixed cost. An alternative approach would be to regard the semi-fixed cost as a variable cost by dividing £150 tyre replacement by 25 000 miles. This results in a variable cost per mile of £0.006.
    Depreciation and maintenance cost have been classified as fixed costs. They are likely to be semi-variable costs, but in the absence of any additional information they have been classified as fixed costs.
  ii. See Figure 2.26.

iii. The respective costs can be obtained from the vertical
dashed lines in the graph (Figure 2.26).

b. The *cost per mile* declines as activity increases. This is because
the majority of costs are fixed and do not increase when
mileage increases. However, *total cost* will increase with
increases in mileage.

FIGURE 2.26 *The step increase in fixed cost is assumed to occur at an
annual mileage of 12 500 and 25 000 miles, because tyres are
assumed to be replaced at this mileage*

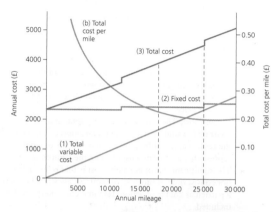

2.27 a. i. For an explanation of sunk and opportunity costs see
Chapter 2. The down payment of £5000 represents a sunk
cost. The lost profit from subletting the shop of £1600 p.a.
((£550 × 12) – £5000) is an example of an opportunity
cost. Note that only the £5000 additional rental is included
in the opportunity cost calculation. (The £5000 sunk cost
is excluded from the calculation.)

ii. The relevant information for running the shop is:

	(£)
Net sales	100 000
Costs (£87 000 – £5000 sunk cost)	82 000
	18 000
Less opportunity cost from subletting	1 600
Profit	16 400

The above indicates that £16 400 additional profits will be
obtained from using the shop for the sale of clothing. It is
assumed that Mrs Johnson will not suffer any other loss of
income if she devotes half her time to running the shop.

b. The CIMA terminology defines a notional cost as
'A hypothetical cost taken into account in a particular situation
to represent a benefit enjoyed by an entity in respect of which
no actual expense is incurred.' Examples of notional cost
include:

i. Interest on capital to represent the notional cost of using
an asset rather than investing the capital elsewhere.

ii. Including rent as a cost for premises owned by the
company so as to represent the lost rent income resulting
from using the premises for business purposes.

Chapter 3

3.14 Overhead absorbed (£714 000) = Actual hours (119 000) ×
Pre-determined overhead rate.
Pre-determined overhead rate = £714 000/119 000 = £6.
Budgeted overheads (£720 000) = Budgeted machine hours ×
Budgeted overhead rate (£6).
Budgeted machine hours = £720 000/£6 = 120 000 hours.
Answer = C

3.15 Budgeted machine hour rate = $3.60 ($180 000/50 000 hours)
Standard machine hours per unit = 1.25 (50 000 hours/
40 000 units)

	$
Overheads incurred	178 080
Overheads absorbed (38 760 units × 1.25 hours × $3.60) =	174 420
Under absorbed overheads	3 660

Answer = B

3.16

	£
Absorbed overheads (4 500 units × £8)	36 000
Over absorbed overheads	(6 000)
Actual overheads incurred	30 000

Answer = A

3.17 Answer = D

3.18 Because production is highly automated it is assumed that
overheads will be most closely associated with machine hours. The
pre-determined overhead rate will therefore be £18 derived from
dividing budgeted overheads (£180 000) by the budgeted machine
hours (10 000). Therefore the answer is B.

3.19

Direct materials	10 650
Direct labour	3 260
Prime cost	13 910
Production overhead (140 × $8.50)	1 190
Non-manufacturing overheads and profit (60% × $13 910)	8 346
Estimated price	23 446

Answer = C

3.20 a.

	Total	Departments				
		A	B	C	X	Y
	(£)	(£)	(£)	(£)	(£)	(£)
Rent and rates[a]	12 800	6 000	3 600	1 200	1200	800
Machine insurance[b]	6 000	3 000	1 250	1 000	500	250
Telephone charges[c]	3 200	1 500	900	300	300	200
Depreciation[b]	18 000	9 000	3 750	3 000	1500	750
Supervisors' salaries[d]	24 000	12 800	7 200	4 000		
Heat and light[a]	6 400	3 000	1 800	600	600	400
	70 400					
Allocated		2 800	1 700	1 200	800	600
		38 100	20 200	11 300	4900	3000
Reapportionment of X		2 450 (50%)	1 225 (25%)	1 225 (25%)	(4900)	
Reapportionment of Y		600 (20%)	900 (30%)	1 500 (50%)		(3000)
		£41 150	£22 325	£14 025		
Budgeted D.L. hours[e]		3 200	1 800	1 000		
Absorption rates		£12.86	£12.40	£14.02		

Notes

[a]Apportioned on the basis of floor area.

[b]Apportioned on the basis of machine value.

[c]Should be apportioned on the basis of the number of telephone points or estimated usage.
This information is not given and an alternative arbitrary method of apportionment should be
chosen. In the above analysis telephone charges have been apportioned on the basis of floor
area.

[d]Apportioned on the basis of direct labour hours.

[e]Machine hours are not given but direct labour hours are. It is assumed that the examiner
requires absorption to be on the basis of direct labour hours.

b.

	Job 123	Job 124
	(£)	(£)
Direct material	154.00	108.00
Direct labour:		
Department A	76.00	60.80
Department B	42.00	35.00
Department C	34.00	47.60
Total direct cost	306.00	251.40
Overhead:		
Department A	257.20	205.76
Department B	148.80	124.00
Department C	140.20	196.28
Total cost	852.20	777.44
Profit	284.07	259.15

c. Listed selling price   1136.27   1036.59

Note

Let SP represent selling price.

Cost + 0.25SP = SP

Job 123: £852.20 + 0.25SP = 1SP

            0.75SP = £852.20

            Hence SP = £1136.27

For Job 124:   0.75SP = £777.44

            Hence SP = £1036.59

d. For the answer to this question see sections on materials recording procedure and pricing the issues of materials in Chapter 4.

3.21 a. i. Calculation of budgeted overhead absorption rates:

Apportionment of overheads to production departments

	Machine shop (£)	Fitting section (£)	Canteen (£)	Machine maintenance section (£)	Total (£)
Allocated overheads	27 660	19 470	16 600	26 650	90 380
Rent, rates, heat and light[a]	9 000	3 500	2 500	2 000	17 000
Depreciation and insurance of equipment[a]	12 500	6 250	2 500	3 750	25 000
	49 160	29 220	21 600	32 400	132 380
Service department apportionment					
Canteen[b]	10 800	8 400	(21 600)	2 400	—
Machine maintenance section	24 360	10 440	—	(34 800)	—
	84 320	48 060	—	—	132 380

Calculation of absorption bases

		Machine shop		Fitting section	
Product	Budgeted production	Machine hours per product	Total machine hours	Direct labour cost per product (£)	Total direct wages (£)
X	4200 units	6	25 200	12	50 400
Y	6900 units	3	20 700	3	20 700
Z	1700 units	4	6 800	21	35 700
			52 700		106 800

Budgeted overhead absorption rates

Machine shop

$$\frac{\text{budgeted overheads}}{\text{budgeted machine hours}} = \frac{£84\ 320}{£52\ 700}$$

$$= £1.60 \text{ per machine hour}$$

Fitting section

$$\frac{\text{budgeted overheads}}{\text{budgeted direct wages}} = \frac{48\ 060}{106\ 800}$$

$$= 45\% \text{ of direct wages}$$

Notes

[a]Rents, rates, heat and light are apportioned on the basis of floor area. Depreciation and insurance of equipment are apportioned on the basis of book value.

[b]Canteen costs are reapportioned according to the number of employees. Machine maintenance section costs are reapportioned according to the percentages given in the question.

ii. The budgeted manufacturing overhead cost for producing one unit of product X is as follows:

	(£)
Machine shop: 6 hours at £1.60 per hour	9.60
Fittings section: 45% of £12	5.40
	15.00

b. The answer should discuss the limitations of blanket overhead rates and actual overhead rates. See 'Blanket overhead rates' and 'Budgeted overhead rates' in Chapter 3 for the answer to this question.

3.22 a. The calculation of the overhead absorption rates are as follows:

Forming department machine hour rate = £6.15 per machine hour (£602 700/98 000 hours)

Finishing department labour hour rate = £2.25 per labour hour (£346 500/154 000 hours)

The forming department is mechanized, and it is likely that a significant proportion of overheads will be incurred as a consequence of employing and running the machines. Therefore a machine hour rate has been used. In the finishing department several grades of labour are used. Consequently

the direct wages percentage method is inappropriate, and the direct labour hour method should be used.

b. The decision should be based on a comparison of the incremental costs with the purchase price of an outside supplier if spare capacity exists. If no spare capacity exists then the lost contribution on displaced work must be considered. The calculation of incremental costs requires that the variable element of the total overhead absorption rate must be calculated. The calculation is:

Forming department variable machine hour rate = £2.05 (£200 900/98 000 hours)

Finishing department variable direct labour hour rate = £0.75 (£115 500/154 000 hours)

The calculation of the variable costs per unit of each component is:

	A (£)	B (£)	C (£)
Prime cost	24.00	31.00	29.00
Variable overheads: Forming	8.20	6.15	4.10
Finishing	2.25	7.50	1.50
Variable unit manufacturing cost	34.45	44.65	34.60
Purchase price	£30	£65	£60

On the basis of the above information, component A should be purchased and components B and C manufactured. This decision is based on the following assumptions:

i. Variable overheads vary in proportion to machine hours (forming department) and direct labour hours (finishing department).

ii. Fixed overheads remain unaffected by any changes in activity.

iii. Spare capacity exists.

For a discussion of make-or-buy decisions see Chapter 9.

c. Production overhead absorption rates are calculated in order to ascertain costs per unit of output for stock valuation and profit measurement purposes. Such costs are inappropriate for decision-making and cost control. For an explanation of this see the section in Chapter 3 titled 'Different costs for different purposes'.

3.23 a. i.

	Machining (£)	Finishing (£)	Assembly (£)	Materials handling (£)	Inspection (£)
Initial cost	400 000	200 000	100 000	100 000	50 000
Reapportion:					
Materials handling	30 000	25 000	35 000	(100 000)	10 000
	430 000	225 000	135 000	—	60 000
Inspection	12 000 (20%)	18 000 (30%)	27 000 (45%)	3 000 (5%)	(60 000)
	442 000	243 000	162 000	3 000	—
Materials handling	900 (30%)	750 (25%)	1 050 (45%)	(3 000)	300 (10%)
	442 900	243 750	163 050	—	300
Inspection	60 (20%)	90 (30%)	135 (45%)	15 (5%)	(300)
	442 960	243 840	163 185	(15)	
	5	4	6		
	442 965	243 844	163 191		

ii. Let

x = material handling

y = inspection

$x = 100\ 000 + 0.05y$

$y = 50\ 000 + 0.1x$

Rearranging the above equations:

$x - 0.05y = 100\ 000$ (1)

$-0.1x + y = 50\ 000$ (2)

Multiply equation (1) by 1 and equation (2) by 10:

$x - 0.05y = 100\ 000$

$-x + 10y = 500\ 000$

Adding the above equations:

$9.95y = 600\ 000$

$y = 60\ 301$

Substituting for y in equation (1):

$x - 0.05 \times 60\ 301 = 100\ 000$

$x = 103\ 015$

Apportioning the values of x and y to the production departments in the agreed percentages:

	Machining (£)		Finishing (£)		Assembly (£)
Initial cost	400 000		200 000		100 000
(x) Materials handling	(0.3) 30 905	(0.25)	25 754	(0.35)	36 055
(y) Inspection	(0.2) 12 060	(0.3)	18 090	(0.45)	27 136
	442 965		243 844		163 191

b. Reapportioning production service department costs is necessary to compute product costs for stock valuation purposes in order to meet the financial accounting requirements. However, it is questionable whether arbitrary apportionments of fixed overhead costs provides useful information for decision-making. Such apportionments are made to meet stock valuation requirements, and they are inappropriate for decision-making, cost control and performance reporting.

An alternative treatment would be to adopt a variable costing system and treat fixed overheads as period costs. This would eliminate the need to reapportion service department fixed costs. A more recent suggestion is to trace support/service department costs to products using an activity-based costing system (ABCS). For a description of ABCS you should refer to Chapter 10.

c. For the answer to this question see 'Under- and over-recovery of overheads'.

Chapter 4

4.10 Production will be charged at the most recent (higher prices) resulting in lower profits and stocks will consist of the earlier (lower prices). Therefore answer = A.

4.11 a. Purchases are 460 units and issues are 420 units resulting in a closing stock of 40 units. Therefore closing stock valuation = 40 units at the latest purchase price ($1.90) = $76. Therefore answer = D

b. Answer = C (see outcomes for Example 4.1 in the text)

4.12 Answer = D

4.13 In the financial accounts there is a total stock decrease of £2900 (£1000 materials and £1900 finished goods) and a decrease of £3200 in the costs accounts (£1200 materials and £2000 finished goods). Since a stock decrease represents an increase in cost of goods sold and a decrease in profits the cost accounting profit will be £300 less than the financial accounting profit. In other words, the financial accounting profit will be £300 greater than the cost accounting profit.
Answer = A

4.14 The cost of goods sold will be debited with £100 000 (1000 units at £100). Included within this figure will be £55 000 for conversion costs (1000 units at £55). Conversion costs actually incurred were £60 000. Assuming that an adjustment is made at the end of each month for conversion costs that have not been applied £5000 will be debited in April resulting in the cost of sales account having a debit balance of £105 000 (£100 000 + £5000). Therefore the answer is C.

4.15 a. i. Stores ledger card – FIFO method

Date	Receipts			Issues			Balance	
	Qty	Price (£)	Value (£)	Qty	Price (£)	Value (£)	Qty	Value (£)
1 April							40	400
4 April	140	11	1540				180	1940
10 April				40	10	400		
				50	11	550		
				90		950	90	990
12 April	60	12	720				150	1710
13 April				90	11	990		
				10	12	120		
				100		1110	50	600
16 April	200	10	2000				250	2600
21 April				50	12	600		
				20	10	200	180	1800
				70		800		
23 April				80	10	800	100	1000
26 April	50	12	600				150	1600
29 April				60	10	600	90	1000

ii. Stores ledger card – LIFO method

Date	Receipts			Issues			Balance	
	Qty	Price (£)	Value (£)	Qty	Price (£)	Value (£)	Qty	Value (£)
1 April							40	400
4 April	140	11	1540				180	1940
10 April				90	11	990	90	950
12 April	60	12	720				150	1670
13 April				60	12	720		
				40	11	440		
				100		1160	50	510
16 April	200	10	2000				250	2510
21 April				70	10	700	180	1810
23 April				80	10	800	100	1010
26 April	50	12	600				150	1610
29 April				50	12	600		
				10	10	100		
				60		700	90	910

b. Cost of material used in April: LIFO – £4260; FIFO – £4350

c. The weighted-average method determines the issue price by dividing the total value by the number of units in stock. This will tend to smooth out price fluctuations and the closing stock valuation will fall between that resulting from the FIFO and LIFO methods. In times of rising prices the cost of sales figure will be higher than FIFO but lower than LIFO.

4.16 a.

Stores ledger control account

(£)		(£)
Opening balances b/f	24 175	Materials issued:
Creditors – materials		Work in progress control 26 350
purchased	76 150	Production overhead
		control 3 280
		Closing stock c/f 70 695
	£100 325	£100 325

Wages control account

(£)		(£)
Direct wages:		WIP 15 236
Wages accrued a/c	17 646	Capital equipment a/c 2 670
Employees'		Factory overhead
contributions a/c	4 364	(idle time) 5 230
Indirect wages:		Factory overhead
Wages accrued a/c	3 342	(indirect wages) 4 232
Employees'		
contributions a/c	890	
Balances (Wages		
accrued a/c)	1 126	
	27 368	27 368

Work in progress control account

(£)		(£)
Opening balance b/f	19 210	Finished goods
Stores ledger – materials		control – cost of goods
issued	26 350	transferred 62 130
Wages control direct		Closing stock c/f 24 360
wages	15 236	
Production overhead		
control:		
overhead absorbed		
(15 236 × 150%)	22 854	
Profit and loss a/c:		
stock gain[a]	2 840	
	£86 490	£86 490

Finished goods control account

(£)		(£)
Opening balance b/f	34 164	Profit and loss a/c:
Working in progress:		cost of sales 59 830
cost of goods sold	62 130	Closing stock c/f
		(difference) 36 464
	£96 294	£96 294

Production overhead control account

	(£)		(£)
Prepayments b/f	2 100	Work in progress:	
Stores ledger:		absorbed overheads	
materials issued for		(15 236 × 150%)	22 854
repairs	3 280	Capital under	
Wages control:		construction a/c:	
idle time of direct		overheads absorbed	
workers	5 230	(2670 × 150%)	4 005
Wages control: indirect		Profit and loss a/c:	
workers' wages		underabsorbed	
(3342 + 890)	4 232	overhead balance	183
Cash/creditors:			
other overheads			
incurred	12 200		
	£27 042		£27 042

Profit and loss account

	(£)		(£)
Cost of goods sold	59 830	Sales	75 400
Gross profit c/f	15 570		
	£75 400		75 400
Selling and distribution		Gross profit b/f	15 570
overheads	5 240	Stock gainª:	
Production overhead		WIP control	2 840
control:			
underabsorbed			
overhead	183		
Net profit c/f	12 987		
	£18 410		£18 410

Note

ªThe stock gain represents a balancing figure. It is assumed that the stock gain arises from the physical count of closing stocks at the end of the period.

Note that value of materials transferred between batches will be recorded in the subsidiary records, but will not affect the control (total) accounts.

b. i.   Large increase in raw material stocks. Is this due to maintaining uneconomic stock levels or is it due to an anticipated increase in production to meet future demand?

 ii.   WIP stock gain.

 iii. Idle time, which is nearly 25 per cent of the total direct wages cost.

 iv.   The gross direct wages are £22 010 (£17 646 + £4364), but the allocation amounts to £23 136 (£15 236 + £5230 + £2670).

c.   Stocks are valued at the end of the period because they represent unexpired costs, which should not be matched against sales for the purpose of calculating profits. Stocks represent unexpired costs, which must be valued for inclusion in the balance sheet. Manufacturing expense items such as factory rent are included in the stock valuations because they represent resources incurred in transforming the materials into a more valuable finished product. The UK financial accounting regulations (SSAP 9) states that 'costs of stocks (and WIP) should comprise those costs which have been incurred in bringing the product to its present location and condition, including all related production overheads.'

4.17 a.   See 'Accounting entries for a JIT manufacturing system' in Chapter 4 for the answer to this question. The answer should point out that a backflush accounting system is a simplified and less accurate system that works backwards when allocating costs between the cost of goods sold and inventories. It is appropriate for a JIT system when the value of stocks and WIP are of insignificant value.

 b. i.   The journal entries and the ledger accounts are as follows:

	Dr	Cr
	£	£
1. Raw materials inventory a/c	5 575 000	
Creditors		5 575 000
2. Conversion costs	4 883 000	
Bank		1 735 000
Creditors		3 148 000
3. Finished goods inventory	10 080 000	
Raw materials inventory a/c		5 460 000
Conversion costs: – labour		1 722 000
– overheads		2 898 000
4. Cost of sales (206 000 × £48)	9 888 000	
Finished goods inventory		9 888 000

Raw materials inventory

1. Creditors	£5 575 000	3. Finished goods	£5 460 000
		Balance c/fwd	£115 000
	£5 575 000		£5 575 000

Finished goods inventory

3. Raw materials	£5 460 000	4. Cost of sales	£9 888 000
Conversion		Balance c/fwd	£192 000
costs	£4 620 000		
	£10 080 000		£10 080 000

Conversion costs

2. Bank	£1 735 000	3. Finished goods	£4 620 000
Creditors	£3 148 000	Balance c/fwd	£263 000
	£4 883 000		£4,883,000

Cost of sales

4. Finished goods	£9 888 000	To Profit and Loss a/c	£9 888 000
	£9 888 000		£9 888 000

The inventory balances as at 30 November 2005 are:

	£
Raw materials account	115,000
Finished goods account	192,000
	307,000

Note that the balance of the conversion costs account will be transferred to the profit and loss account at the end of the period.

 b. ii. In a perfect JIT system stocks of raw materials and finished goods would be zero. In other words, completed units would be identical to sales (206 000 units) resulting in zero finished good stocks. In practice, the system approximately meets the requirements of a perfect JIT system since finished goods stock (4000 units) is approximately 2 per cent of the units sold.

Chapter 5

5.12

	Units
Opening stock	400
Input	3000
	3400
Closing stock	(200)
Actual losses (normal + abnormal)	(400)
Output	2800

Answer = A

5.13 The input cost consists of materials of £9000 plus conversion costs of £13 340 giving a total of £22 340.

Cost per unit =

$$\frac{\text{Input cost (£22 340) less scrap value of normal loss (100 × £3)}}{\text{Expected output (2000 × 0.95 = 1900 units)}}$$

= £11.60

Answer = B

5.14 Input = Opening WIP (2000 units) + Material input (24 000) = 26 000

Output = Completed units (19 500) + Closing WIP (3000) + Normal Loss (2400) = 24 900

Abnormal Loss = 1100 units (Balance of 26 000 – 24 900)

Equivalent units (FIFO)

	Completed units less Opening WIP equiv. units	Closing WIP equiv. units	Abnormal loss equiv. units	Total equiv. units
Materials	17 500 (19 500 – 2000)	3000 (100%)	1100 (100%)	21 600
Conversion	18 700 (19 500 – 800)	1350 (45%)	1100 (100%)	21 150

It is assumed that losses are detected at the end of the process and that the answer should adopt the short-cut method and ignore the normal loss in the cost per unit calculations.

Answer = C

5.15 a. The debit side (input) indicates that 4 000 units were input into the process but the output recorded on the credit side is 3850 units thus indicating that the balance must represent an abnormal loss of 150 units. The accounting entries for abnormal losses are to debit the abnormal loss account and credit the process account. Therefore the answer is A.

b. and c.

The calculation of the closing WIP value and the cost of finished goods is as follows:

Cost element	Total cost ($)	Completed units	Abnormal loss equivalent units	Closing WIP equivalent units	Total equivalent units	Cost per unit ($)	Closing WIP ($)
Materials[1]	15 300	2750	150	700	3600	4.25	2 975.00
Labour	8 125	2750	150	350	3250	2.50	875.00
Production overhead	3 498	2750	150	280	3180	1.10	308.00
	27 923					7.85	4 158.00
				Finished goods (2750 × $7.85)			21 587.50
				Abnormal loss (150 × $7.85)			1 177.50
							27 923.00

Note

[1]£16 000 materials less £700 scrap value of the normal loss. The above computation is based on the short-cut method described in the Appendix of Chapter 5.

Therefore the answer is B for part both parts (b) and (c).

5.16

Completed units less opening WIP equivalent units	4000 (4100 less 40% × 250 units)
Abnormal loss	275
Closing WIP	45 (150 × 30%)
Equivalent units	4320

It is assumed that the short-cut method (see Appendix 5.1) will be used in respect of normal losses.

Answer = C

5.17 The normal loss is 180 units (10 per cent of 1800 units) and the actual loss is 180 units. Therefore there are no abnormal losses in process. It is assumed that the sale proceeds from the normal loss relates primarily to the materials input. Hence the sales proceeds are deducted from materials in the unit cost calculation. Assuming that losses occur prior to the WIP stage of completion it is appropriate to use the short cut method to compute the unit costs. The calculations are as follows:

Cost element	Total cost (£)	Completed units	WIP equiv. units	Total equiv. units	Cost per unit (£)
Materials	484 000[a]	1920	500	2420	200
Labour	322 320[b]	1920	450	2370	136
Overheads	156 880[b]	1920	200	2120	74
					410

Notes:
[a]Opening WIP plus current cost less sales value of normal loss
[b]Opening WIP plus current cost

Cost of completed production = 1920 units × £410 = £787 200

5.18

Process 1 account

	(kg)	(£)		(kg)	(£)
Material	3000	750	Normal loss (20%)	600	120
Labour		120	Transfer to process 2	2300	1150
Process plant time		240	Abnormal loss	100	50
General overhead (120/£204 × £357)		210			
	3000	1320		3000	1320

$$\text{cost per unit} = \frac{\text{cost of production less scrap value of normal loss}}{\text{expected output}}$$

$$= \frac{£1320 - £120}{2400 \text{ kg}} = £0.50$$

Process 2 account

	(kg)	(£)		(kg)	(£)
Previous process cost	2300	1150	Normal loss	430	129
Materials	2000	800	Transfer to finished stock	4000	2400
Labour		84			
General overhead (£84/£204 × £357)		147			
Process plant time		270			
		2451			
Abnormal gain (130 kg at £0.60)	130	78			
	4430	2529		4430	2529

$$\text{cost per unit} = \frac{£2451 - £129}{3870 \text{ kg}} = £0.60$$

Finished stock account

	(£)
Process 2	2400

Normal loss account (income due)

	(£)		(£)
Process 1 normal loss	120	Abnormal gain account	39
Process 2 normal loss	129	Balance or cash received	230
Abnormal loss account	20		
	269		269

Abnormal loss account

	(£)		(£)
Process 1	50	Normal loss account (100 × £0.20)	20
		Profit and loss account	30
	50		50

Abnormal gain account

	(£)		(£)
Normal loss account (Loss of income 130 × £0.30)	39	Process 2	78
Profit and loss account	39		
	78		78

5.19 a.

Fully complete production	= Input (36 000) – Closing WIP (8000)
	= 28 0000 kg
Normal loss	= 2800 (10% × 28 000 kg)
Abnormal loss	= 800 (Actual loss (3600) – 2800)
Good output	= 24 400 (28,000 – 3600)

b. The short-cut method described in Chapter 5 is used to compute the unit costs. This method allocates the normal loss between completed units, WIP and the abnormal loss. Because the units actually lost are fully complete it is likely that losses are detected on completion. Therefore the short-cut method is not theoretically correct. Nevertheless the computations suggest that it was the examiner's intention that the question should be answered using the short-cut method. The revised answer is as follows:

	Completed units	Abnormal loss	WIP	Total equiv. units	Cost per unit	WIP
	(£)				(£)	(£)
Previous process cost	166 000	24 400	800	8000	33 200	5.00	40 000
Conversion cost	73 000	24 400	800	4000	29 200	2.50	10 000
	230 000					7.50	50 000
Completed units (24 400 × £7.50)							183 000
Abnormal loss (800 × £7.50)							6 000
							239 000

Distillation process account

	(kg)	(£)		(kg)	(£)
Input from mixing	36 000	166 000	Finished goods	24 400	183 000
Labour		43 800	Abnormal loss	800	6 000
Overheads		29 200	Normal loss	2 800	—
			Closing WIP	8 000	50 000
	36 000	239 000		36 000	239 000

c. If the scrapped production had a resale value the resale value would be credited to the process account (thus reducing the cost of the process account). The accounting entries would be as follows:

Dr Cash
Cr Process Account (with sales value of normal loss)
Cr Abnormal Loss Account (with sales value of abnormal loss)

5.20 a. It is assumed that the normal loss occurs at the start of the process and should be allocated to completed production and closing WIP. It is also assumed that process 2 conversion costs are not incurred when losses occur. Therefore losses should not be allocated to conversion costs.

Statement of input and output (units)

Input		Output	
Opening WIP	1 200	Completed output	105 400
Transferred from Process 1	112 000	WIP	1 600
		Normal loss (5% × 112 000)	5 600
		Abnormal loss (balance)	600
	113 200		113 200

Since the loss occurs at the start of the process it should be allocated over all units that have reached this point. Thus the normal loss should be allocated to all units of output. This can be achieved by adopting the short-cut method described in Chapter 5 whereby the normal loss is not included in the unit cost statement.

Calculation of cost per unit and cost of completed production (FIFO method)

	Current costs (£)	Completed units less opening WIP equiv. units	Abnormal loss	Closing WIP equiv. units	Current total equiv. units	Cost per unit (£)
Previous process cost	187 704					
Materials	47 972					
	235 676	104 200 (105 400 − 1200)	600	1600	106 400	2.215
Conversion costs	63 176	104 800 (105 400 − 600)	—	1200	106 000	0.596
	298 852					2.811

	(£)	(£)
Cost of completed production:		
Opening WIP (given)	3 009	
Previous process cost and materials (104 200 × £2.215)	230 803	
Conversion cost (104 800 × £0.596)	62 461	296 273
Abnormal Loss (600 × £2.215)		1 329
Closing WIP:		
Previous process cost and materials (1600 × £2.215)	3 544	
Conversion costs (1200 × £0.596)	715	4 259
		301 861

Process 2 account

	(£)		(£)
Opening WIP	3 009	Transfer to finished goods	296 273
Transfers from Process 1	187 704	Abnormal loss	1 329
Raw materials	47 972	Closing WIP	4 259
Conversion costs	63 176		
	301 861		301 861

b. If the loss occurs at the end of the process then the normal loss should only be charged to those units that have reached the end of the process. In other words, the cost of normal losses should not be allocated to closing WIP. To meet this requirement a separate column for normal losses is incorporated into the unit cost statement and the normal loss equivalent units are included in the calculation of total equivalent units. The cost of the normal loss should be calculated and added to the cost of completed production. For an illustration of the approach see 'Losses in process and partially completed units' in the appendix to Chapter 5.

Chapter 6

6.10

Joint costs to be allocated = $140 000 less by product revenues
(3000 × $6) = $122 000
Sales value of X = $125 000 (2500 × $50)
Sales value of Y = $210 000 (3500 × $60)
Total sales value = $335 000
Costs allocated to X = ($125 000/$335 000 × $122 000) + $24 000
= $69 522
Costs allocated to Y = ($210 000/335 000 × $122 000) + $46 000
= $122 478

6.11 a.

	Product X (£)	Material B (£)
Apportionment of joint costs (W1)	35 400	106 200
Further processing costs	18 000	—
	53 400	106 200
Sales (W2)	50 400	180 000
Profit/(loss)	(3 000)	73 800
Profit/(loss) per kg (W3)	(0.33)	2.46

Workings:
(W1) X = (£141 600/40 000 kg) × 10 000 kg
     B = (£141 600/40 000 kg) × 30 000 kg
(W2) X = 9000 kg at £5.60, B = 30 000 × £6
(W3) X = £3000/9000 kg, B = £73 800/30 000 kg

b. The answer should stress that a joint products costs cannot be considered in isolation from those of other joint products. If product X was abandoned the joint costs apportioned to X would still continue and would have to be absorbed by material B. Therefore no action should be taken on product X without also considering the implications for material B. Note that the process as a whole is profitable. The decision to discontinue product X should be based on a comparison of those costs which would be avoidable if X were discontinued with the lost sales revenue from product X. Joint costs apportionments are appropriate for stock valuation purposes but not for decision-making purposes.

c. An alternative method is to apportion joint costs on the basis of net realizable value at split-off point. The calculations are as follows:

	Sales value	Costs beyond split-off point	Net-realizable value at split-off point	Joint cost apportionment
Product X	50 400	18 000	32 400	21 600 (W1)
Material A	180 000	—	180 000	120 000 (W2)
			212 400	141 600

Workings:
(W1) (£32 400/£212 400) × £141 600
(W2) (£180 000/£212 400) × £141 600

The revised profit calculation for product X is:

	(£)
Sales	50 400
Less Joint costs	21 600
Processing costs	18 000
	39 600
Profit	10 800
Profit per kg	£1.20 (£10 800/9000 kg)

Apportionment methods based on sales value normally ensure that if the process as a whole is profitable, then each of the joint products will be shown to be making a profit. Consequently it is less likely that incorrect decisions will be made.

6.12 a. Operating statement for October 2000

	(£)	(£)
Sales: Product A (80 000 × £5) =	400 000	
Product B (65 000 × £4) =	260 000	
Product C (75 000 × £9) =	675 000	1 335 000
Operating costs	1 300 000	
Less closing stock[a]	200 000	
		1 100 000
Profit		235 000

Note
[a]Production for the period (kg):

	A	B	C	Total
Sales requirements	80 000	65 000	75 000	
Closing stock	20 000	15 000	5 000	
Production	100 000	80 000	80 000	260 000

Cost per kg = 260 000 kg = $\dfrac{£1\,300\,000}{260\,000}$ = £5 per kg

Therefore
Closing stock = 40 000 kg at £5 per kg

b. Evaluation of refining proposal

	A	B	C	Total (£)
Incremental revenue per kg (£)	12	10	11.50	
Variable cost per kg (£)	4	6	12.00	
Contribution per kg (£)	8	4	(0.50)	
Monthly production (kg)	100 000	80 000	80 000	
Monthly contribution (£)	800 000	320 000	(40 000)	1 080 000
Monthly fixed overheads (specific to B)		360 000		360 000
Contribution to refining general fixed costs (£)	800 000	(40 000)	(40 000)	720 000
Refining general fixed overheads				700 000
Monthly profit				20 000

1. It is more profitable to sell C in its unrefined state and product B is only profitable in its refined state if monthly sales are in excess of 90 000 kg (£360 000 fixed costs/£4 contribution per unit).

2. If both products B and C are sold in their unrefined state then the refining process will yield a profit of £100 000 per month (£800 000 product A contribution less £700 000 fixed costs).

3. The break-even point for the refining process if only product A were produced is 87 500 kg (£700 000 fixed costs/£8 contribution per unit). Consequently if sales of A declined by 12½ per cent, the refining process will yield a loss. Note that 80 000 kg of A were sold in October.

6.13 a.

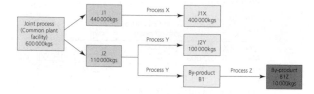

b. i. *Physical units allocation basis*

	Product J1X Total (£000)	Cost per unit[b]	Product J2Y Total (£000)	Cost per unit[b]
Joint costs[a]	440	1.100	110	1.100
Further processing costs	410	1.025	135	1.350
By-product net revenues	—	0.000	(5)	(0.050)
Total cost	850	2.125	240	2.400
Sales	970	2.425	450	4.500
Manufacturing profit	120	0.300	210	2.100

Notes

[a]Apportioned 440 000 : 110 000 kg

[b]Divided by 400 000 kg for J1X and 100 000 kg for J2Y

ii. *Net realizable value allocation basis*

	Product J1X Total (£000)	Cost per unit[a]	Product J2Y Total (£000)	Cost per unit[b]
Joint costs	350	0.875	200	2.000
Further processing costs	410	1.025	135	1.350
By-product net revenues	—	0.000	(5)	(0.050)
Total cost	760	1.900	330	3.300
Sales	970	2.425	450	4.500
Manufacturing profit	210	0.525	120	1.200

Notes

[a]Divided by 400 000 kg for J1X and 100 000 kg for J2Y

[b]Net realizable values are calculated as follows:

Product J1X: Sales (£970 000) – Further processing costs (£410 000) = £560 000.

Product J2Y: Sales (£450 000) + By-product net revenue (£5000) – Further processing costs (£135 000) = £320 000. Joint costs are therefore apportioned in the ratio of £560 000 : £320 000.

For comments on the above two methods of joint cost allocations see 'Methods of allocating joint costs' in Chapter 6.

c. i. The answer requires a comparison of the incremental revenues with the incremental costs of further processing. It is assumed that direct materials, direct labour and variable overheads are incremental costs. Note that the order represents 10 per cent of the current volume of J2Y.

The extra costs of 10 000 kg of of J2Y are as follows:

10% of common facility variable costs		50 000
10% of finishing process (Y)		13 000
		63 000
Net revenue from J2Y:		
Sales (10 000 kg at £4)	40 000	
Net revenue from sale of 1000 kg of by-product B1Z (£1500 – (10% × £7000))	800	40 800
Shortfall		22 200

It would appear that by itself the order is not justifiable because there is a £22 000 shortfall. By itself a minimum selling price of £6.22 (£4 + £22 200/10 000 kg) is required to break-even. However, production of 10 000 kg of J2Y will result in an extra output of 40 000 kg of J1. To convert J1 into J1X incremental further processing costs of £38 500 (10 per cent of J1X current incremental costs of £338 500) will be incurred. For the offer to be justifiable the extra output of J1X must generate sales revenue in excess of £60 700 (£38 500 incremental costs plus £22 200 shortfall from the order). This represents a minimum selling price of approximately £1.51 per kg (£60 700/40 000 kg) compared with the current market price of £2.425.

ii. The following should be included in the answer:

i. Does the company have sufficient capacity to cope with the 10 per cent increase in output? If not the opportunity cost of the lost output should be incorporated in the above analysis.

ii. Are any of the fixed overheads incremental costs?

iii. Direct labour is assumed to be an incremental cost. Is this correct or can the existing labour force cope with the extra output from the order?

iv. What are the long-run implications? At the present selling price the order should be viewed as a one time special short-term order. For a more detailed discussion of the issues involved here you should refer to 'Special pricing decisions' in Chapter 9.

Chapter 7

7.13 Fixed overhead = £250 per unit

Inventories decreased by 300 units resulting in an extra £75 000 (300 × £250) being charged as a production cost with an absorption costing system. Therefore profits will be £75 000 lower with an absorption costing system (i.e. Answer = B)

7.14 The profit difference is due to the fixed overheads being incorporated in the stock movements with the absorption costing system.

Profit difference = £9750 (£60 150 – £50 400)

Fixed overheads in stock movement = £9750

Physical stock movement = 1500 units

Fixed overhead rate per unit = £9750/1500 units = £6.50

Answer = D

7.15 a. Fixed overheads per unit = $15 000/10 000 units = $1.50

Production exceeds sales so that absorption costing will be greater than the marginal costing profit by the amount of fixed overheads included in the increase in inventories. Therefore the absorption profit will exceed the marginal costing profit by $750 (500 units × $1.50). Answer = (iii)

	$	$
Sales (10 300 × $6.40)		65 920
Cost of sales:		
Variable costs (10 300 × $3.60)	37 080	
Fixed overheads (10 300 × $1.50)	15 450	
	52 530	
Under-absorbed fixed overheads ($15 700 – $15 000)	700	53 230
Profit		12 690

Answer = ii.

7.16

Calculation of product cost	(£)
Materials	10
Labour	2
Variable production cost	12
Variable distribution cost	1
Total variable cost	13
Fixed overhead (£10 000/1000 units)	10
Total costs	23

The product costs for stock valuation purposes are as follows:

Variable costing   £12 (variable production cost)

Absorption costing   £22 (variable production cost + fixed manufacturing overhead)

It is assumed that all of the fixed overhead relates to production. Note that the distribution cost is per unit *sold* and not per unit *produced*.

a.   i.   *Variable costing*

	t_1	t_2	t_3
Opening stock	1 200	1 200	1 200
Production	12 000	12 000	12 000
	13 200	13 200	13 200
Closing stock	1 200	1 200	1 200
Cost of sales	12 000	12 000	12 000
Sales at £25 per unit	25 000	25 000	25 000
Gross profit	13 000	13 000	13 000
Distribution costs	1 000	1 000	1 000
Fixed labour costs	5 000	5 000	5 000
Fixed overhead costs	5 000	5 000	5 000
Net profit	£2 000	£2 000	£2 000
Total profit £6000			

Absorption costing

	t_1 (£)	t_2 (£)	t_3 (£)
Opening stock	2 200	2 200	2 200
Production	22 000	22 000	22 000
	24 200	24 200	24 200
Closing stock	2 200	2 200	2 200
Cost of sales	22 000	22 000	22 000
Sales at £25 per unit	25 000	25 000	25 000
Gross profit	3 000	3 000	3 000
Distribution cost	1 000	1 000	1 000
Net profit	£2 000	£2 000	£2 000
Total profit £6000			

   ii.   *Variable costing*

	t_1 (£)	t_2 (£)	t_3 (£)
Opening stock	1 200	7 200	4 800
Production	18 000	9 600	8 400
	19 200	16 800	13 200
Closing stock	7 200	4 800	1 200
Cost of sales	12 000	12 000	12 000
Sales at £25 per unit	25 000	25 000	25 000
Gross profit	13 000	13 000	13 000
Distribution costs	1 000	1 000	1 000
Fixed labour costs	5 000	5 000	5 000
Fixed overhead costs	5 000	5 000	5 000
Net profit	£2 000	£2 000	£2 000
Total profit £6000			

Absorption costing

	t_1 (£)	t_2 (£)	t_3 (£)
Opening stock	2 200	13 200	8 800
Production	33 000	17 600	15 400
	35 200	30 800	24 200
Under-/(over) recovery	(5 000)	2 000	3 000
	30 200	32 800	27 200
Closing stock	13 200	8 800	2 200
Cost of sales	17 000	24 000	25 000
Sales at £25 per unit	25 000	25 000	25 000
Gross profit	8 000	1 000	—
Distribution cost	1 000	1 000	1 000
Net profit	£7 000	—	£(1 000)
Total profit £6 000			

iii.   *Variable costing*

	t_1 (£)	t_2 (£)	t_3 (£)
Opening stock	1 200	7 200	4 800
Production	12 000	12 000	12 000
	13 200	19 200	16 800
Closing stock	7 200	4 800	1 200
Cost of sales	6 000	14 400	15 600
Sales at £25 per unit	12 500	30 000	32 500
Gross profit	6 500	15 600	16 900
Distribution costs	500	1 200	1 300
Fixed labour costs	5 000	5 000	5 000
Fixed overhead costs	5 000	5 000	5 000
Net profit	£(4 000)	£4 400	£5 600
Total profit £6000			

Absorption costing

	t_1 (£)	t_2 (£)	t_3 (£)
Opening stock	2 200	13 200	8 800
Production	22 000	22 000	22 000
	24 200	35 200	30 800
Closing stock	13 200	8 800	2 200
Cost of sales	11 000	26 400	28 600
Sales at £25 per unit	12 500	30 000	32 500
Gross profit	1 500	3 600	3 900
Distribution cost	500	1 200	1 300
Net profit	£1 000	£2 400	£2 600
Total profit £6000			

b.   For the answer to this question see Chapter 7: Note that profits are identical for both systems in (i), since production equals sales. In (ii) and (iii) profits are higher with absorption costing when production exceeds sales, whereas profits are higher with variable costing when production is less than sales. Taking the three periods as a whole there is no change in the level of opening stock in t_1 compared with the closing stock in t_3, so that the disclosed profit for the three periods is the same under both systems. Also note that the differences in profits disclosed in (a) (ii) and (a) (iii) is accounted for in the fixed overheads included in the stock valuation changes.

Chapter 8

8.11   BEP = Fixed costs/PV ratio

PV ratio = Contribution/Sales = £275 000/£500 000 = 0.55

BEP = £165 000/0.55 = £300 000

Answer = D

8.12   Contribution/sales (%) = (0.33 × 40% Aye) + (0.33 × 50% Bee) + (0.33 × ? Cee) = 48%

Cee = 54% (Balancing figure)

The total contribution/sales ratio for the revised sales mix is:

(0.40 × 40% Aye) + (0.25 × 50% Bee) + (0.35 × 54% Cee) = 47.4%

Answer = C

8.13   a.   Budgeted contribution per unit = $11.60 – $3.40 – (5% × $11.60) = $7.62

Break-even point (units) = ($430 500 + 198 150)/ $7.62 = 82 500 units

Break-even point (sales value) = 82 500 × $11.60 = $957 000

Budgeted sales = $1 044 000 (90 000 × $11.60)

Margin of safety ($) = $1 044 000 – $957 000 = $87 000

Margin of safety (%) = $87 000/$1 044 000 = 8.33%

Answer = B

b.   Budgeted contribution per unit = $12.25 – $3.40 – (8% × $12.25) = $7.87

Break-even point (units) = ($430 500 + 198 150)/ $7.87 = 79 879 units

Answer = C

8.14 Break-even point (units) $= 5220 - (19.575\% \times 5220) =$
4198 units

Fixed costs $=$ Contribution at the
break-even point
$= 4198 \times £42 \times 40\%$
$= £70\,526$

Answer $= B$

8.15 Weighted average contribution/sales ratio $=$

$$\frac{(30\% \times 2) + (20\% \times 5) + (25\% \times 3)}{10} = 23.5\%$$

Break-even sales $=$ Fixed costs (£100 000)/contribution to sales
ratio (0.235)
$= £425\,532$

Answer $= C$

8.16 i. $p =$ total sales revenue
$q =$ total cost (fixed cost + variable cost)
$r =$ total variable cost
$s =$ fixed costs at the specific level of activity
$t =$ total loss at the specific level of activity
$u =$ total profit at that level of activity
$v =$ total contribution at the specific level of activity
$w =$ total contribution at a lower level of activity
$x =$ level of activity of output sales
$y =$ monetary value of cost and revenue function for level of
activity

ii. At event m the selling price per *unit* decreases, but it remains
constant. Note that p is a straight line, but with a lower
gradient above m compared with below m.

At event n there is an increase in fixed costs equal to the
dotted line. This is probably due to an increase in capital
expenditure in order to expand output beyond this point. Also
note that at this point the variable cost per unit declines as
reflected by the gradient of the variable cost line. This might be
due to more efficient production methods associated with
increased investment in capital equipment.

iii. Break-even analysis is of limited use in a multi-product
company, but the analysis can be a useful aid to the
management of a small single product company. The following
are some of the main benefits:

a. Break-even analysis forces management to consider the
functional relationship between costs, revenue and activity,
and gives an insight into how costs and revenue change
with changes in the level of activity.

b. Break-even analysis forces management to consider the
fixed costs at various levels of activity and the selling price
that will be required to achieve various levels of output.

You should refer to Chapter 8 for a discussion of more specific
issues of break-even analysis. Break-even analysis can be a useful
tool, but it is subject to a number of assumptions that restrict its
usefulness (see, especially, 'Cost–volume–profit analysis
assumptions').

8.17

The budgeted contribution is £6.5 million (Budgeted fixed costs
plus budgeted profit
Contribution from product X = £1.5 million
Contribution from product Y = £2 million
Required contribution from product Z = £3 million
Therefore, given that the C/S ratio for Z is 0.25, sales revenue of
£12 million is required to obtain a contribution of £3 million.

8.18 *Preliminary calculations:*

	Sales (units)	Profit/(loss)
November	30 000	£40 000
December	35 000	£60 000
Increase	5 000	£20 000

An increase in sales of 5000 units increases contribution (profits)
by £20 000. Therefore contribution is £4 per unit. Selling price is
£10 per unit (given) and variable cost per unit will be £6.

At £30 000 unit sales:

Contribution	minus Fixed costs	= Profit
£120 000	minus ?	= £40 000

∴ Fixed costs $= £80\,000$

The above information can now be plotted on a graph.
A break-even chart or a profit–volume graph could be constructed.
A profit–volume graph avoids the need to calculate the profits since
the information can be read directly from the graph. (See Figure 1
for a break-even chart and Figure 2 for a profit–volume graph.)

a. i. Fixed costs = £80 000.
   ii. Variable cost per unit = £6.
   iii. Profit–volume =

$$\frac{\text{Contribution per unit (£4)}}{\text{Selling price per unit (£10)}} \times 100 = 40\%$$

   iv. Break-even point = 20 000 units.
   v. The margin of safety represents the difference between
      actual or expected sales volume and the break-even point.
      Therefore the margin of safety will be different for each
      month's sales. For example, the margin of safety in
      November is 10 000 units (30 000 units – 20 000 units).
      The margin of safety can be read from Figure 2 for various
      sales levels.

b. and c. See the sections on 'The accountants'
          cost–volume–profit model' and 'Cost–volume–profit
          analysis assumptions' in Chapter 8 for the answers.

FIGURE 1 *Break-even chart*

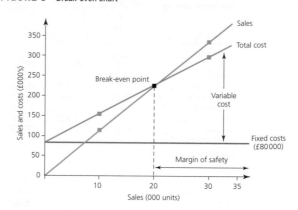

FIGURE 2 *Profit–volume graph*

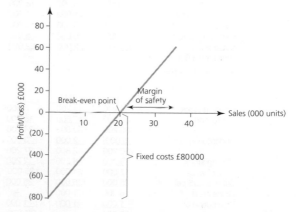

8.19 a.

	August (£)	September (£)	Change (£)
Sales	80 000	90 000	10 000
Cost of sales	50 000	55 000	5 000
Selling and distribution	8 000	9 000	1 000
Administration	15 000	15 000	Nil

The only activity measure that is given is sales revenue. An increase in sales of £10 000 results in an increase in cost of sales of £5000 and an increase in selling and distribution costs of £1000. It is therefore assumed that the increase is attributable to variable costs and variable cost of sales is 50 per cent of sales and variable selling and distribution costs are 10 per cent of sales.

Fixed costs are derived by deducting variable costs from total costs for either month. The figures for August are used in the calculations below:

	Total cost (£)	Variable cost (£)	Fixed cost (Balance) (£)
Cost of sales	50 000	40 000	10 000
Selling and distribution	8 000	8 000	Nil
Administration	15 000	Nil	15 000
			25 000

Total cost = £25 000 fixed costs + variable costs (60 per cent of sales)

b. The following items are plotted on the graph (Figure 3):

	Variable cost	Total cost
Zero sales	Nil	£25 000 fixed cost
£80 000 sales	£48 000 (60%)	£73 000
£90 000 sales	£54 000 (60%)	£79 000
£50 000 sales	£30 000 (60%)	£55 000
£100 000 sales	£60 000	£85 000

Break-even point

$$= \frac{\text{Fixed costs (£25 000)}}{\text{Contribution to sales ratio (0.40)}} = £62\ 500 \text{ sales}$$

FIGURE 3 Contribution break-even graph

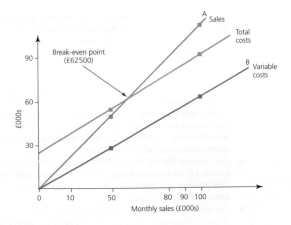

Area of contribution = Area AOB

c.

		(£)
Actual sales = 1.3 × Break-even sales (£62 500)	=	81 250
Contribution (40% of sales)	=	32 500
Fixed costs	=	25 000
Monthly profit	=	7 500
Annual profit	=	90 000

d.

		(£)
Annual contribution from single outlet (£32 500 × 12)	=	390 000
Contribution to cover lost sales (10%)	=	39 000
Specific fixed costs	=	100 000
Total contribution required		529 000

Required sales = £529 000/0.4 = £1 322 500

e. The answer should draw attention to the need for establishing a sound system of budgeting and performance reporting for each of the different outlets working in close conjunction with central office. The budgets should be merged together to establish a master budget for the whole company.

8.20 a. Let x = number of units of output
Total cost for 30 000 units or less = £50 000 + 5x) where 5 = variable cost per unit)
Total cost for more than 30 000 units = £100 000 + 5x

b.

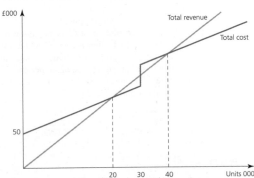

c. There are two break-even points resulting in the production plan being profitable only between 20 000 and 30 000 units and above 40 000 units. The production plan should be set based on these considerations.

8.21 $$\text{Break-even point} = \frac{\text{Fixed costs}}{\text{Contribution per unit}}$$

Product X	25 000 units (£100 000/£4)
Product Y	25 000 units (£200 000/£8)
Company as a whole	57 692 units (£300 000/£5.20[a])

Note:
[a]Average contribution per unit

$$= \frac{(70\ 000 \times £4) + (30\ 000 \times £8)}{100\ 000 \text{ units}}$$

$$= £5.20$$

The sum of the product break-even points is less than the break-even point for the company as a whole. It is incorrect to add the product break-even points because the sales mix will be different from the planned sales mix. The sum of the product break-even points assumes a sales mix of 50 per cent to X and 50 per cent to Y. The break-even point for the company as a whole assumes a planned sales mix of 70 per cent to X and 30 per cent to Y. CVP analysis will yield correct results only if the planned sales mix is equal to the actual sales mix.

8.22 a. $$\text{BEP} = \frac{400\ 000 \text{ (fixed costs)} \times £1\ 000\ 000 \text{ (sales)}}{£420\ 000 \text{ (contribution)}}$$

$$= 952\ 380$$

b. i.

	(£)	(£)
Revised selling price		9.00
Less variable costs:		
Direct materials	1.00	
Direct labour	3.50	
Variable overhead	0.60	
Delivery expenses	0.50	
Sales commission (2% of selling price)	0.18	
		5.78
Contribution per unit		3.22

Number of units sold	140 000
Total contribution (140 000 × 3.22)	450 800
Fixed costs	400 000
Profit from proposal (i)	50 800

ii.

Desired contribution	= 480 000
Contribution per unit for present proposal	= 3.22
Required units to earn large profit	= 149 068

c. i. The variable cost of selling to the mail order firm is:

	(£)
Direct material	1.00
Direct labour	3.50
Variable overhead	0.60
Delivery expenses	nil
Sales commission	nil
Additional package cost	0.50
	5.60

To break even, a contribution of £1.20 is required (60 000 fixed cost/50 000 units sold). Therefore selling price to break even is £6.80 (£5.60 + £1.20).

ii. To earn £50 800 profit, a contribution of £110 800 (£60 000 + £50 800) is required.
That is, a contribution of £2.22 per unit is required. Therefore required selling price is £7.82 (£5.60 + £2.22).

iii. To earn the target profit of £80 000, a contribution of £140 000 is required. That is, £2.80 per unit. Therefore required selling price = £8.40 (£5.60 + £2.80).

d. Contribution per unit is £3.22 per (B)

Unit sold	160 000
Total contribution	£515 200
Fixed costs	£430 000
Profit	£85 200

Chapter 9

9.15 Based on the contribution per limiting factor (materials) the rankings are products (iii), (ii) and (i). Minimum demand requirements for product (i) = 8000 kg leaving a balance of 27 000 kg to be allocated as follows:
Product (iii) maximum demand = 2000
Product (ii) maximum output from the unallocated materials = 3000 units (15 000kg/5kg)
Answer = B (with a minimum demand of 1000 units for product (i).

9.16 The 400 labour hours unused capacity has zero relevant cost. The remaining 100 hours can be obtained from diverting production from product X. The relevant cost of this alternative consists of the labour cost (100 hours × £12) plus the lost contribution from the use of these labour hours (100/2 × £4 = £200), giving a total of £1400 (see 'Determining the relevant costs of direct labour' in Chapter 9 for an explanation of this point). In other words, the relevant cost is the lost contribution before deducting unavoidable labour costs. The other alternative is to work overtime resulting in an additional (relevant) cost of £1800 (100 hours at £18 per hour). Therefore it is cheaper to divert labour hours from the production of product X.
Therefore answer = C

9.17 The original purchase price is a sunk cost and therefore not a relevant cost. The relevant cost of the materials in stock is $1000 (100 reams at $10 net realizable value). An additional 150 reams must be purchased for $3900 (150 × $26) resulting in a relevant cost of $4900.
Answer = B

9.18 Incremental cost of new employees = £40 000 × 4 = £160 000
Supervision is not an incremental cost.
Incremental costs of retraining
= £15 000 + £100 000 replacement cost = £115 000
Retraining is the cheaper alternative and therefore the relevant cost of the contract is £115 000.
Answer = B

9.19 Specific (avoidable) fixed overheads per division = £262.5 × 60%
= £157.5/3 = £52.5

The specific fixed costs are deducted from the divisional contributions to derive the following contributions (£000's) to general fixed costs:

Division A = £17.5
Division B = £157.5
Division C = £22.5

Only divisions A and B should remain open since they both provide positive contributions to general fixed costs.
Answer = B

9.20 With throughput accounting direct labour and all overheads are assumed to be a fixed cost and contribution consists of sales less variable costs. The contribution per bottleneck minute is:

W = £17.66 (£159/9)
X = £13.00 (£130/10)
Y = £17.14 (£120/7)

The rankings are W, Y and X.

9.21 a.

	North East (£)	South coast (£)
Material X from stock (i)	19 440	
Material Y from stock (ii)		49 600
Firm orders of material X (iii)	27 360	
Material X not yet ordered (iv)	60 000	
Material Z not yet ordered (v)		71 200
Labour (vi)	86 000	110 000
Site management (vii)	—	—
Staff accommodation and travel for site management (viii)	6 800	5 600
Plant rental received (ix)	(6000)	—
Penalty clause (x)		28 000
	193 600	264 400
Contract price	288 000	352 000
Net benefit	94 400	87 600

b. i. If material X is not used on the North East contract the most beneficial use is to use it as a substitute material thus avoiding future purchases of £19 440 (0.9 × 21 600). Therefore by using the stock quantity of material X the company will have to spend £19 440 on the other materials.

ii. Material Y is in common use and the company should not dispose of it. Using the materials on the South coast contract will mean that they will have to be replaced at a cost of £49 600 (£24 800 × 2). Therefore the future cash flow impact of taking on the contract is £49 600.

iii. It is assumed that with firm orders for materials it is not possible to cancel the purchase. Therefore the cost will occur whatever future alternative is selected. The materials will be used as a substitute material if they are not used on the contract and therefore, based on the same reasoning as note (i) above, the relevant cost is the purchase price of the substitute material (0.9 × £30 400).

iv. The material has not been ordered and the cost will only be incurred if the contract is undertaken. Therefore additional cash flows of £60 000 will be incurred if the company takes on the North East contract.

v. The same principles apply here as were explained in note (iv) and additional cash flows of £71 200 will be incurred only if the company takes on the South coast contract.

vi. It is assumed that labour is an incremental cost and therefore relevant.

vii. The site management function is performed by staff at central headquarters. It is assumed that the total company costs in respect of site management will remain unchanged in the short term whatever contracts are taken on. Site management costs are therefore irrelevant.

viii. The costs would be undertaken only if the contracts are undertaken. Therefore they are relevant costs.

ix. If the North East contract is undertaken the company will be able to hire out surplus plant and obtain a £6000 cash inflow.

x. If the South coast contract is undertaken the company will have to withdraw from the North East contract and incur a penalty cost of £28 000.

xi. The headquarter costs will continue whichever alternative is selected and they are not relevant costs.

xii. It is assumed that there will be no differential cash flows relating to notional interest. However, if the interest costs associated with the contract differ then they would be relevant and should be included in the analysis.

xiii. Depreciation is a sunk cost and irrelevant for decision-making.

9.22 a. i.

Product	A (£)	B (£)	C (£)
Selling price	15	12	11
Less variable costs:			
Materials	(5)	(4)	(3)
Labour	(3)	(2)	(1.5)
Variable overhead (1)	(3.50)	(2)	(1.5)
Contribution	3.50	4	5

Note:

(1) Fixed overheads are apportioned to products on the basis of sales volume and the remaining overheads are variable with output.

ii.

Product	B (£)	C (£)
Selling price	12	9.50
Less variable costs:		
Materials	(4)	(3)
Labour	(2)	(1.80)
Variable overhead	(2)	(1.50)
Contribution	4	3.20

b. i.

Product	A	B	C	Total
Total contribution	350 000	480 000	400 000	1 230 000
Less fixed costs:				
Labour				(220 000)
Fixed administration				(900 000)
Profit				110 000

ii.

Product	B	C	Total
Total contribution[a]	480 000	576 000	1 056 000
Less fixed costs:			
Labour[b]			(160 000)
Fixed administration[c]			(850 000)
Profit			46 000

Notes:

[a]B = 120 000 units × £4 contribution,

C = 18 000 units × £3.20 contribution.

[b](25% × £320 000 for B) plus (25% × £160 000 × 2 for C).

[c]Fixed administration costs will decline by $\frac{1}{6}$ of the amount apportioned to Product A (100/300 × £900 000). Therefore fixed overheads will decline from £900 000 to £850 000.

c. Product A should not be eliminated even though a loss is reported for this product. If Product A is eliminated the majority of fixed costs allocated to it will still continue and will be borne by the remaining products. Product A generates a contribution of £350 000 towards fixed costs but the capacity released can be used to obtain an additional contribution from Product C of £176 000 (£576 000 − £400 000). This will result in a net loss in contribution of £174 000. However, fixed cost savings of £110 000 (£50 000 administration apportioned to Product A plus £100 000 labour for A less an extra £40 000 labour for Product C) can be obtained if Product A is abandoned. Therefore there will be a net loss in contribution of £64 000 (£174 000 − £110 000) and profits will decline from £110 000 to £64 000.

9.23 The following information represents a comparison of alternatives 1 and 2 with the sale of material XY.

Alternative 1: Conversion versus immediate sale	(£)	(£)	(£)
1. Sales revenue (900 units at £400 per unit			360 000
Less Relevant costs:			
2. Material XY opportunity cost		21 000	
3. Material A (600 units at £90)		54 000	
4. Material B (1000 units at £45)		45 000	
5. Direct labour:			
Unskilled (5000 hrs at £6)	30 000		
Semi-skilled	nil		
Highly skilled (5000 hrs at £17)	85 000	115 000	
6. Variable overheads (15 000 hrs at £1)		15 000	
7. Selling and delivery expenses		27 000	
Advertising		18 000	
8. Fixed overheads		—	295 000
Excess of relevant revenues			65 000

Alternative 2: Adaptation versus immediate sale			
9. Saving on purchase of sub-assembly:			
Normal spending (1200 units at £900)		1 080 000	
Revised spending (900 units at £950)		855 000	225 000
Less relevant costs:			
2. Material XY opportunity cost		21 000	
10. Material C (1000 units at £55)		55 000	
5. Direct labour:			
Unskilled (4000 hrs at £6)	24 000		
Semi-skilled	nil		
Skilled (4000 hrs at £16)	64 000	88 000	
6. Variable overheads (9000 hrs at £1)		9 000	
8. Fixed overheads		nil	173 000
Net relevant savings			52 000

Notes:

1. There will be additional sales revenue of £360 000 if alternative 1 is chosen.

2. Acceptance of either alternative 1 or 2 will mean a loss of revenue of £21 000 from the sale of the obsolete material XY. This is an opportunity cost, which must be covered whichever alternative is chosen. The original purchase cost of £75 000 for material XY is a sunk cost and is irrelevant.

3. Acceptance of alternative 1 will mean that material A must be replaced at an additional cost of £54 000.

4. Acceptance of alternative 1 will mean that material B will be diverted from the production of product Z. The excess of relevant revenues over relevant cost for product Z is £180 and each unit of product Z uses four units of material. The lost contribution (excluding the cost of material B which is incurred for both alternatives) will therefore be £45 for each unit of material B that is used in converting the raw materials into a specialized product.

5. Unskilled labour can be matched exactly to the company's production requirements. The acceptance of either alternative 1 or 2 will cause the company to incur additional unskilled labour costs of £6 for each hour of unskilled labour that is used. It is assumed that the semi-skilled labour would be retained and that there would be sufficient excess supply for either alternative at no extra cost to the company. In these circumstances semi-skilled labour will not have a relevant cost. Skilled labour is in short supply and can only be obtained by reducing production of product L, resulting in a lost contribution of £24 or £6 per hour of skilled labour. We have already established that the relevant cost for labour that is in short supply is the hourly labour cost plus the lost contribution per hour, so the relevant labour cost here will be £16 per hour.

6. It is assumed that for each direct labour hour of input variable overheads will increase by £1. As each alternative uses additional direct labour hours, variable overheads will increase, giving a relevant cost of £1 per direct labour hour.

7. As advertising selling and distribution expenses will be different if alternative 1 is chosen, these costs are clearly relevant to the decision.

8. The company's fixed overheads will remain the same whichever alternative is chosen, and so fixed overheads are not a relevant cost for either alternative.

9. The cost of purchasing the sub-assembly will be reduced by £225 000 if the second alternative is chosen, and so these savings are relevant to the decision.

10. The company will incur additional variable costs of £55 for each unit of material C that is manufactured, so the fixed overheads for material C are not a relevant cost.

When considering a problem such as this one, there are many different ways in which the information may be presented. The way in which we have dealt with the problem here is to compare each of the two stated alternatives with the other possibility of selling off material XY for its scrap value of £21 000. The above answer sets out the relevant information, and shows that of the three possibilities alternative 1 is to be preferred.

An alternative presentation of this information, which you may prefer, is as follows:

	Sale of obsolete materials for scrap	Alternative 1	Alternative 2
Relevant revenues less relevant costs	£21 000	£86 000	£73 000

Difference = £65 000

Difference = £13 000
(£86 000 – £73 000)

We show here *the sale of the obsolete materials as a separate alternative*, and so the opportunity cost of material XY, amounting to £21 000 (see item 2 in the answer) is not included in either alternative 1 or 2, since it is brought into the analysis under the heading 'Sale of obsolete materials for scrap' in the above alternative presentation. Consequently, in both alternatives 1 and 2 the relevant revenues less relevant costs figure is increased by £21 000. The differences between alternative 1 and 2 and the sale of the obsolete materials are still, however, £65 000 and £52 000 respectively, which gives an identical result to that obtained in the above solution.

9.24 a. *Preliminary calculations*

Variable costs are quoted per acre, but selling prices are quoted per tonne. Therefore, it is necessary to calculate the planned sales revenue per acre. The calculation of the selling price and contribution per acre is as follows:

	Potatoes	Turnips	Parsnips	Carrots
(a) Yield per acre in tonnes	10	8	9	12
(b) Selling price per tonne	£100	£125	£150	£135
(c) Sales revenue per acre, (a) × (b)	£1000	£1000	£1350	£1620
(d) Variable cost per acre	£470	£510	£595	£660
(e) Contribution per acre (a) (i)	£530	£490	£755	£960

i. Profit statement for current year

	Potatoes	Turnips	Parsnips	Carrots	Total
(a) Acres	25	20	30	25	
(b) Contribution per acre	£530	£490	£755	£960	
(c) Total contribution (a × b)	£13 250	£9800	£22 650	£24 000	£69 700
			Less fixed costs		£54 000
			Profit		£15 700

ii. Profit statement for recommended mix

	Area A (45 acres)		Area B (55 acres)		
	Potatoes	Turnips	Parsnips	Carrots	Total
(a) Contribution per acre	£530	£490	£755	£960	
(b) Ranking	1	2	2	1	
(c) Minimum sales requirements in acres[a]		5	4		
(d) Acres allocated[b]	40			51	
(e) Recommended mix (acres)	40	5	4	51	
(f) Total contribution, (a) × (e)	£21 200	£2450	£3020	£48 960	£75 630
			Less fixed costs		£54 000
			Profit		£21 630

Notes:

[a]The minimum sales requirement for turnips is 40 tonnes, and this will require the allocation of 5 acres (40 tonnes/8 tonnes yield per acre). The minimum sales requirement for parsnips is 36 tonnes, requiring the allocation of 4 acres (36 tonnes/9 tonnes yield per acre).

[b]Allocation of available acres to products on basis of a ranking that assumes that acres are the key factor.

b. i. Production should be concentrated on carrots, which have the highest contribution per acre (£960).

	(£)
ii. Contribution from 100 acres of carrots	
(100 × £960)	96 000
Fixed overhead	54 000
Profit from carrots	42 000

iii.

$$\text{Break-even point in acres for carrots} = \frac{\text{fixed costs (£54 000)}}{\text{contribution per acre (£960)}}$$

$$= 56.25 \text{ acres}$$

Contribution in sales value for carrots
= £91 125 (56.25 acres at £1620 sales revenue per acre).

9.25 a. Roadstar requires 0.16 hours (1hour/6.25 units) and Everest 0.2 hours (1hour/5units) in the finishing department. A total of 38 000 hours are required to meet the demand (150 000 units of Roadstar × 0.16 hours plus 70 000 units of Everest × 0.2 hours). Therefore the finishing department hours are a bottleneck or limiting factor resource.

	Roadstar	Everest
Contribution per unit (£)	100 (200 – 100)	120 (280 – 160)
Hours per limiting factor	0.16	0.2
Contribution per limiting factor (£)	625	600

Ride should produce Roadstar until it has met the total demand and use any remaining hours to produce Everest. Thus 24 000 hours will be allocated to Roadstar (150 000 × 0.16 hours) and the remaining 6 000 hours to Everest. This will enable 30 000 units of Everest (6 000/0.2 hours) to be produced. The profit for the period is:

	(£000's)
Roadstar contribution	15 000 (150 000 × £100)
Everest contribution	3 600 (30 000 × £120)
Total contribution	18 600
Fixed costs	4 050
Profit	14 550

b.

	Roadstar	Everest
Selling price – material cost (£)	120	180
Bottleneck hours utilized	0.16	0.20
Return per factory hour (£)	750 (£120/0.16)	900 (£180/0.2)
Cost per factory hour (£)	295 (£8 850 000/30 000)	295
Throughput accounting ratio (£)	2.54 (£750/£295)	3.05 (£900/£295)

Note:

That the cost per factory hour consists of total fixed costs (£4 800 000 + £4 050 000) divided by the hours available in the finishing department.

c. Since Everest has the highest throughput ratio Ride should produce Everest until it has met the total demand and use any remaining hours to produce Roadstar. Thus 14 000 hours will be allocated to Everest (70 000 × 0.2 hours) and the remaining 16 000 hours to Roadstar. This will enable 100 000 units of Roadstar (16 000/0.16 hours) to be produced. The profit for the period is:

	(£000's)
Roadstar throughput return	12 000 (100 000 × £120)
Everest throughput return	12 600 (70 000 × £180)
Total throughput return	24 600
Fixed costs	8 850
Profit	15 750

d. Contribution and throughput accounting differ in terms of their definition of variable cost. Contribution treats direct materials, direct labour and variable overheads as variable costs whereas throughput accounting assumes that only direct materials represent variable costs. Throughput accounting is more short-term oriented and assumes that direct labour and variable overheads cannot be avoided within a very short-term period (e.g. one month). In contrast, contribution assumes that the short-term represents a longer period than that assumed with throughput accounting and thus classifies direct labour and overheads as variable within this period (typically less than one year). The different interpretation of variable costs results in the contribution (selling price less material cost) used in throughput accounting being higher than that using the conventional analysis based on relevant cost principles. This is apparent from the question with the variable overheads of £4 800 000 being treated as variable in part (a) but fixed in the very short-term in part (b) where throughput accounting is applied.

It is apparent from the above discussion that the different interpretations of variable costs can yield different contributions per unit of bottleneck resource and thus result in a different recommended optimal product mix. Care must therefore be exercised in deciding which approach to use when they result in different optimal product mixes.

Chapter 10

10.19 Cost driver rates are as follows:

Receiving/inspection etc. = £1 400 000/5000 = £280 per requisition
Production scheduling/machine set-up = £1 200 000/800 = £1500
per set-up

	W (£)	X (£)	Y (£)
Direct costs	80.00	75.00	65.00
Receiving/inspection[a]	33.60	33.60	31.11
Production scheduling[a]	36.00	26.00	25.00
Total cost per unit	149.60	134.60	121.11
Selling price	200.00	183.00	175.00
Profit per unit	50.40	48.40	53.89

Notes:

[a](Number of units of activity used by each product × Cost driver rate)/units produced
e.g. Product W for receiving/ inspection = (1200 × £280)/10 000 = £33.60

10.20 Budgeted number of batches per product:

D = 1000 (100 000/100)
R = 2000 (100 000/50)
P = 2000 (50 000/25)
    5000

Budgeted machine set-ups:

D = 3 000 (1000 × 3)
R = 8 000 (2000 × 4)
P = 12 000 (2000 × 6)
    23 000

Budgeted cost per set-up = £150 000/23 000 = £6.52
Budgeted set-up cost per unit of R = (£6.52 × 4)/50 = £0.52
Answer = A

10.21 The answer to the question should describe the two-stage overhead allocation process and indicate that most cost systems use direct labour hours in the second stage. In today's production environment direct labour costs have fallen to about 10 per cent of total costs for many firms and it is argued that direct labour is no longer a suitable base for assigning overheads to products. Using direct labour encourages managers to focus on reducing direct labour costs when they represent only a small percentage of total costs.

Approaches which are being adopted include:

i. Changing from a direct labour overhead-recovery rate to recovery methods based on machine time. The justification for this is that overheads are caused by machine time rather than direct labour hours and cost.

ii. Implementing activity-based costing systems that use many different cost drivers in the second stage of the two-stage overhead allocation procedure.

The answer should then go on to describe the benefits of ABC outlined in Chapter 10. Attention should also be drawn to the widespread use of direct labour hours by Japanese companies. According to Hiromoto[1] Japanese companies allocate overhead costs using the direct labour cost/hours to focus design engineers' attention on identifying opportunities to reduce the products' labour content. They use direct labour to encourage designers to make greater use of technology because this frequently improves long-term competitiveness by increasing quality, speed and flexibility of manufacturing.

Notes:

[1]Hiromoto, T. (1988) 'Another hidden edge – Japanese management accounting', *Harvard Business Review*, July/ August, pp. 22–6.

10.22 a. Large-scale service organizations have a number of features that have been identified as being necessary to derive significant benefits from the introduction of ABC:

i. They operate in a highly competitive environment;

ii. They incur a large proportion of indirect costs that cannot be directly assigned to specific cost objects;

iii. Products and customers differ significantly in terms of consuming overhead resources;

iv. They market many different products and services. Furthermore, many of the constraints imposed on manufacturing organizations, such as also having to meet

financial accounting stock valuation requirements, or a reluctance to change or scrap existing systems, do not apply. Many service organizations have only recently implemented cost systems for the first time. This has occurred at the same time as when the weaknesses of existing systems and the benefits of ABC systems were being widely publicized. These conditions have provided a strong incentive for introducing ABC systems.

b. The following may create problems for the application of ABC:

i. Facility sustaining costs (such as property rents etc.) represent a significant proportion of total costs and may only be avoidable if the organization ceases business. It may be impossible to establish appropriate cost drivers;

ii. It is often difficult to define products where they are of an intangible nature. Cost objects can therefore be difficult to specify;

iii. Many service organizations have not previously had a costing system and much of the information required to set up an ABC system will be nonexistent. Therefore introducing ABC is likely to be expensive.

c. The uses for ABC information for service industries are similar to those for manufacturing organizations:

i. It leads to more accurate product costs as a basis for pricing decisions when cost-plus pricing methods are used;

ii. It results in more accurate product and customer profitability analysis statements that provide a more appropriate basis for decision-making;

iii. ABC attaches costs to activities and identifies the cost drivers that cause the costs. Thus ABC provides a better understanding of what causes costs and highlights ways of performing activities more effectively by reducing cost driver transactions. Costs can therefore be managed more effectively in the long term. Activities can also be analyzed into value added and non-value added activities and by highlighting the costs of non-value added activities attention is drawn to areas where there is a potential for cost reduction without reducing the products' service potentials to customers.

d. The following aspects would be of most interest to a regulator:

i. The costing method used (e.g. Marginal, traditional full cost or ABC). This is of particular importance to verify whether or not reasonable prices are being set and that the organization is not taking advantage of its monopolistic situation. Costing information is also necessary to ascertain whether joint costs are fairly allocated so that cross-subsidization from one service to another does not apply;

ii. Consistency in costing methods from period to period so that changes in costing methods are not used to distort pricing and profitability analysis;

iii. In many situations a regulator may be interested in the ROI of the different services in order to ensure that excessive returns are not being obtained. A regulator will therefore be interested in the methods and depreciation policy used to value assets and how the costs of assets that are common to several services (e.g. corporate headquarters) are allocated. The methods used will influence the ROI of the different services.

10.23 a.

Total machine hours = (120 × 4 hrs) + (100 × 3 hrs) + (80 × 2 hrs) + (120 × 3 hrs) = 1300 hrs

$$\text{Machine hour overhead rate} = \frac{£10\,430 + £5250 + £3600 + £2100 + £4620}{1300\text{ hrs}}$$

= £20 per machine hour

Product	A (£)	B (£)	C (£)	D (£)
Direct material	40	50	30	60
Direct labour	28	21	14	21
Overheads at £20 per machine hour	80	60	40	60
	148	131	84	141
Units of output	120	100	80	120
Total cost	£17 760	£13 100	£6720	£16 920

b.

Costs	(£)	Cost driver	Cost driver transactions	Cost per unit (£)
Machine department	10 430	Machine hours	1300 hours	8.02
Set-up costs	5 250	Production runs	21	250
Stores receiving	3 600	Requisitions raised	80 (4 × 20)	45
Inspection/quality control	2 100	Production runs	21	100
Materials handling	4 620	Number of orders executed	42	110

Note:

Number of production runs = Total output (420 units)/20 units per set-up.

Number of orders executed = Total output (420 units)/10 units per order.

The total costs for each product are computed by multiplying the cost driver rate per unit by the quantity of the cost driver consumed by each product.

	A	B	C	D
Prime costs	8 160 (£68 × 120)	7 100	3520	9 720
Set ups	1 500 (£250 × 6)	1 250 (£250 × 5)	1000	1 500
Stores/receiving	900 (£45 × 20)	900	900	900
Inspection/quality	600 (£100 × 6)	500	400	600
Handling despatch	1 320 (£110 × 12)	1 100 (£110 × 10)	880	1 320
Machine dept cost[a]	3 851	2 407	1284	2 888
Total costs	16 331	13 257	7984	16 928

Note:

[a]A = 120 units × 4 hrs × £8.02: B = 100 units × 3 hrs × £8.02

c. Cost per unit

Costs from (a)	148.00	131.00	84.00	141.00
Costs from (b)	136.09	132.57	99.80	141.07
Difference	(11.91)	1.57	15.80	0.07

Product A is over-costed with the traditional system. Products B and C are under-costed and similar costs are reported with Product D. It is claimed that ABC more accurately measures resources consumed by products. Where cost-plus pricing is used, the transfer to an ABC system will result in different product prices. If activity-based costs are used for stock valuations then stock valuations and reported profits will differ.

10.24 a. i. Direct labour overhead rate

$$= \frac{\text{total overheads (£1 848 000)}}{\text{total direct labour hours (88 000)}}$$

$$= £21 \text{ per direct labour hour}$$

Product costs

Product	X (£)	Y (£)	Z (£)
Direct labour	8	12	6
Direct materials	25	20	11
Overhead[a]	28	42	21
Total cost	61	74	38

Note:

[a]X = 1⅓ hours × £21

Y = 2 hours × £21

Z = 1 hour × £21

ii. Materials handling

Overhead rate

$$= \frac{\text{receiving department overheads (£435 000)}}{\text{direct material cost (£1 238 000)}} \times 100$$

$$= 35.14\% \text{ of direct material cost}$$

Machine hour overhead rate

$$= \frac{\text{other overheads (£1 413 000)}}{76\ 000 \text{ machine hours}}$$

$$= £18.59 \text{ per machine hour}$$

Product costs

Product	X (£)	Y (£)	Z (£)
Direct labour	8.00	12.00	6.00
Direct materials	25.00	20.00	11.00
Materials handling overhead	8.78 (£25 × 35.14%)	7.03 (£20 × 35.14%)	3.87 (£11 × 35.14%)
Other overheads[a] (machine hour basis)	24.79	18.59	37.18
Total cost	66.57	57.62	58.05

Note:

[a]X = 1⅓ × £18.59

Y = 1 × £18.59

Z = 2 × £18.59

b. The cost per transaction or activity for each of the cost centres is as follows:

Set-up cost

Cost per setup

$$= \frac{\text{setup cost (£30 000)}}{\text{number of production runs (30)}} = £1000$$

Receiving

Cost per receiving order

$$= \frac{\text{receiving cost (£435 000)}}{\text{number of orders (270)}} = £1611$$

Packing

Cost per packing order

$$= \frac{\text{packing cost (£250 000)}}{\text{number of orders (32)}} = £7812$$

Engineering

Cost per production order

$$= \frac{\text{engineering cost (£373 000)}}{\text{number of production orders (50)}} = £7460$$

The total set-up cost for the period was £30 000 and the cost per transaction or activity for the period is £1000 per set-up. Product X required three production runs, and thus £3000 of the set-up cost is traced to the production of product X for the period. Thus the cost per set-up per unit produced for product X is £0.10 (£3000/30 000 units).

Similarly, product Z required 20 set-ups, and so £20 000 is traced to product Z. Hence the cost per set-up for product Z is £2.50 (£20 000/8000 units).

The share of a support department's cost that is traced to each unit of output for each product is therefore calculated as follows:

$$\text{cost per transaction} \times \frac{\text{number of transactions per product}}{\text{number of units produced}}$$

The unit standard costs for products X, Y and Z using an activity-based costing system are

	X	Y	Z
Direct labour	£8.00	£12.00	£6.00
Direct materials	25.00	20.00	11.00
Machine overhead[a]	13.33	10.00	20.00
Set-up costs	0.10	0.35	2.50
Receiving[b]	0.81	2.82	44.30
Packing[c]	2.34	1.17	19.53
Engineering[d]	3.73	3.73	23.31
Total manufacturing cost	53.31	50.07	126.64

Notes:

[a]Machine hours × machine overhead rate (£760 000/76 000 hrs)

[b]X = (£1611 × 15)/30 000

Y = (£1611× 35)/20 000

Z = (£1611× 220)/8000

[c]X = (£7812 × 9)/30 000

Y = (£7812 × 3)/20 000

Z = (£7812 × 20)/8000

[d]X = (£7460 × 15)/30 000

Y = (£7460 × 10)/20 000

Z = (£7460 × 25)/8000

c. The traditional product costing system assumes that products consume resources in relation to volume measures such as direct labour, direct materials or machine hours. The activity-based system recognizes that some overheads are unrelated to production volume, and uses cost drivers that are independent of production volume. For example, the activity-based system assigns the following percentage of costs to product Z, the low volume product:

Set-up-related costs	66.67%
	(20 out of 30 set-ups)
Delivery-related costs	62.5%
	(20 out of 32 deliveries)
Receiving costs	81.5%
	(220 out of 270 receiving orders)
Engineering-related costs	50%
	(25 out of 50 production orders)

In contrast, the current costing system assigns the cost of the above activities according to production volume, measured in machine hours. The total machine hours are

Product X 40 000 (30 000 × 1⅓)
Product Y 20 000 (20 000 × 1)
Product Z 16 000 (8 000 × 2)
        76 000

Therefore 21 per cent (16 000/76 000) of the non-volume-related costs are assigned to product Z if machine hours are used as the allocation base. Hence the traditional system undercosts the low-volume product, and, on applying the above approach, it can be shown that the high-volume product (product X) is overcosted. For example, 53 per cent of the costs (40 000/76 000) are traced to product X with the current system, whereas the activity-based system assigns a much lower proportion of non-volume-related costs to this product.

10.25

a.

Cost pool	Cost (£)	Number of drivers	Cost driver rate
Production set-ups	105 000	300 set-ups	£350 per set-up
Product testing	300 000	1500 test	£200 per test
Component supply and storage	25 000	500 component orders	£50 per order
Customer orders and delivery	112 500	1000 customer orders	£112.50 per order

b.

Production of product ZT3	= (100 × 60) + (60 × 50)
	= 9000 units per year
Number of production runs	= 10 set-ups (9000/90)
Number of product tests	= 10 set-ups × 4 = 40 tests
Number of component orders	= Number of production runs = 10 orders
Number of customer orders	= 160 orders (100 + 60)
Number of direct labour hours required for ZT3	= 9000 × 10/60 hours
	= 1500 hours
General overheads absorption rate	= £3 per direct labour hour (£900 000/33 000 hours)

Activity	Cost driver rate	Number of drivers	Annual cost (£)
Set-ups	£350 per set-up	10	3 500
Product testing	£200 per test	40 tests	8 000
Components supply	£50 per order	10 orders	500
Customer supply	£112.50 per order	160 orders	18 000
			30 000
General overheads	1500 hours at £3 per direct labour hour		4 500
Total annual overhead cost			34 500

Total unit cost	£
Components	1.00
Direct labour (10/60 × £7.80)	1.30
Overheads (£34 500/9000)	3.83
Total cost	6.13
Profit mark-up (40%)	2.45
Selling price	8.58

c. See 'A comparison of traditional and ABC systems', 'The emergence of ABC systems' and 'Volume-based and non-volume-based cost drivers' in Chapter 10 for the answer to this question.

10.26

a. i.
Direct labour hour overhead rate = Total overheads (£12 000 000)/Total direct labour hours (500 000) = £24

	Sunshine (£)	Roadster (£)	Fireball (£)
Direct labour at £5 per hour	1 000 000	1 100 000	400 000
Materials	800 000 (£400 per unit)	960 000 (£600 per unit)	360 000 (£900 per unit)
Overheads at £24 per hour	4 800 000	5 280 000	1 920 000
Total cost	6 600 000	7 340 000	2 680 000
Sales revenue	8 000 000	9 600 000	3 200 000
Profit	1 400 000	2 260 000	520 000
Total cost per unit	3 300	4 587.5	6 700
Selling price per unit	4 000	6 000	8 000
Profit per unit	700	1 412.5	1 300

Total profit = £4 180 000

ii.

The cost driver rates are as follows:

Deliveries to retailers £2,400,000/250 = £9,600
Set-ups £6,000,000/100 = £60,000
Deliveries inwards £3,600,000/800 = £4,500

	Sunshine (£)	Roadster (£)	Fireball (£)
Direct labour at £5 per hour	1 000 000	1 100 000	400 000
Materials	800 000 (£400 per unit)	960 000 (£600 per unit)	360 000 (£900 per unit)
Overheads: Deliveries	960 000 (100 × £9 600)	768 000 (80 × £9 600)	672 000 (70 × £9 600)
Set-ups	2 100 000 (35 × £60 000)	2 400 000 (40 × £60 000)	1 500 000 (25 × £60 000)
Purchasing	1 800 000 (400 × £4 500)	1 350 000 (300 × £4 500)	450 000 (100 × £4 500)
Total cost	6 660 000	6 578 000	3 382 000
Sales revenue	8 000 000	9 600 000	3 200 000
Profit/(loss)	1 340 000	3 022 000	(182 000)
Total cost per unit	3 330	4 111.25	8 455
Selling price per unit	4 000	6 000	8 000
Profit/(loss) per unit	670	1 888.75	(455)

Total profit = £4 180 000

b. i.

The report should include the following points:

● The direct costs are identical for both costing methods.
● Direct labour is a relatively minor cost but the existing method that allocates overhead costs on the basis of direct labour hours overstates their importance.
● The existing method is based on the assumption that there is a cause-and-effect relationship between overheads and labour hours. This assumption appears to be unlikely based on the information given in the question. If this assumption is incorrect then misleading results will be reported.
● ABC attempts to allocate overheads based on using several different cost drivers rather than the single base used with the existing method.
● ABC seeks to assign overheads based on cause-and-effect cost drivers. The accuracy of the reported ABC product costs depends on the extent to which the cause-and-effect assumption is correct.
● For additional comments see 'A comparison of traditional and ABC systems' and 'Volume-based and non-volume-based cost drivers' in Chapter 10.

ii.

The comment by the finance director is incorrect since Fireball is profitable with the existing system but unprofitable with the ABC system. The message from the two systems can have a significant impact on overall profits. The reason for the difference in product profits is that Fireball has the lowest volume but it makes the greatest relative demand on the three activities identified by the ABC system. Because Fireball uses a lower proportion of direct labour hours than the other products the existing system allocates a lower share of overheads to Fireball.

The marketing director argues that incremental costs are required for the pricing decision. It is important to distinguish between short-term and long-term incremental costs. ABC seeks to report long-term incremental costs. If decisions are based on short-term incremental cost opportunities will be lost to reduce capacity and the longer-term incremental costs will remain unchanged. ABC recognises that longer-term incremental costs can be reduced by making decisions that ensure that activities should be undertaken only where incremental revenues exceed long-term incremental costs. It is important that facility-sustaining costs are omitted from the costs reported by the ABC system since they are neither short-term nor long-term incremental costs.

The managing director is correct that the cost per activity should not remain constant over the longer term. Attempts should be made to reduce the costs of activities and improve their efficiency. Thus ABC reported costs should be reviewed and revised at periodic intervals. Also some costs (i.e. facility sustaining costs) do not change with activity and are not variable with any activity measure. Such costs should be excluded from the reported costs or reported separately as facility sustaining costs.

The chairman is correct that the profitability analysis based on maintaining the same product mix will yield the same total profits. However, different profits/losses are reported by products and making future decisions on the basis of ABC information compared with the existing system should result in a different product mix and therefore have an impact on total future profits. For example, assuming that the costs reported by the ABC system are all based on cause-and-effect relationships then a decision may be made to discontinue production of Fireball. This is not apparent with the existing system. However, it is important that decisions should not be based solely on financial factors and non-financial factors should also be taken into account.

Chapter 11

11.13 Profits will be increased up to the point where marginal cost equals marginal revenue (see Chapter 2 for a definition of marginal cost and marginal revenue). The following schedule shows the calculation of marginal cost and marginal revenues for different output levels.

Demand Units	Selling Price per unit £	Total Revenue £	Marginal Revenue £	Cost per unit £	Total Cost £	Marginal Cost £
		units × unit selling price		units × cost per unit		
1100	48	52 800	52 800	22	24 200	24 200
1200	46	55 200	2 400	21	25 200	1 000
1300	45	58 500	3 300	20	26 000	800
1400	42	58 800	300	19	26 600	600

Marginal cost exceeds marginal revenue at output levels above 1300 units. Therefore profits are maximized at an output level of 1300 units and a selling price of £45 per unit.

11.14 a. Variable cost plus 20% = £30 × 1.20 = £36
Total cost plus 20% = £37 × 1.20 = £44.40
Advantages of variable costs include that it avoids arbitrary allocations, identifies short-term relevant costs, simplicity and mark-up can be increased to provide a contribution to fixed costs and profit. The disadvantages are that it represents only a partial cost, it is short-term oriented and ignores price/demand relationships.

Advantages of total cost include that it attempts to include all costs, reduces the possibility that fixed costs will not be covered and simplicity. The disadvantages are that total cost is likely to involve some arbitrary apportionments and the price/demand relationship is ignored.

b. See 'Pricing policies' in Chapter 11 for the answer to this question. The answer should point out that price skimming is likely to lead to a higher initial price whereas a pricing penetration policy is likely to lead to a lower initial price.

11.15 a. The question states that fixed manufacturing costs are absorbed into the unit costs by a charge of 200 per cent of variable cost. Therefore unit variable cost is one third of total unit cost.

Contribution per processing hour

	Product A (£)	Product B (£)	Product C (£)
Selling price	20	31	39
Variable cost	6	8	10
Production contribution	14	23	29
Contribution per processing hour	14	23	14.50
Ranking	3	1	2

Optimal programme

	Output	Hours used	Contribution (£)
Product B	8000	8000	184 000
C	2000	4000	58 000
A	1500	1500	21 000
			263 000

Existing programme

	Output	Hours used	Contribution (£)
Product A	6000	6000	84 000
B	6000	6000	138 000
C	750	1500	21 750
			243 750

Contribution and profits will increase by £19 250 if the optimal production programme is implemented. An additional hour of processing would be used to increase product A by one unit, thus increasing contribution by £14. Therefore the shadow price (or opportunity cost) of one scarce processing hour is £14.

Capacity is limited to 13 500 hours. It is therefore necessary to allocate output on the basis of marginal contribution per hour. Products A and B each require 1 processing hour, whereas product C requires 2 processing hours. To simplify the calculations, hours are allocated in 2000 blocks. Consequently, the allocation of the first 2000 hours will yield a marginal contribution of £37 000 from A, £52 000 from B and £29 500 from C. Note that an output of 2000 units of C will require 4000 processing hours, and will yield a contribution of £59 000. Therefore the contribution from 2000 hours will be £29 500. In other words, the marginal contributions for A and B in the above schedule are expressed in terms of blocks of 2000 hours, whereas the marginal contribution for C is expressed in terms of blocks of 4000 hours. To express the marginal contribution of C in terms of blocks of 2000 hours, it is necessary to divide the final column of the above schedule by 2.

Processing hours are allocated as follows:

	Hours		Marginal contribution (£)
Product B	first	2000	52 000
B	next	2000	48 000
B	2 000		44 000
B	2 000		40 000
A	2 000		37 000
B	2 000		36 000
A	1 500	(balance)	24 250[a]
	13 500		281 250

Note
[a]3500 × (£23.50 − £6) − £37 000 = £24 250

The optimum output is £10 000 units of product B at a selling price of £30 and 3500 units of A at a selling price of £23.50, and contribution will be maximized at £281 250. It is assumed that it is company policy to change selling prices only in steps of £1.

(b)

		Product A	
Demand	Price (£)	Total contribution (£000)	Marginal contribution (£000)
2 000	24.50	37	37
4 000	23.50	70	33
6 000	22.50	99	29
8 000	21.50	124	25
10 000	20.50	145	21
12 000	19.50	162	17
14 000	18.50	175	13

Product B

Demand	Price (£)	Total contribution (£000)	Marginal contribution (£000)
2 000	34	52	52
4 000	33	100	48
6 000	32	144	44
8 000	31	184	40
10 000	30	220	36
12 000	29	252	32
14 000	28	280	28

Product C

Demand	Price (£)	Total contribution (£000)	Marginal contribution (£000)
2 000	39.50	59	59
4 000	39.00	116	57
6 000	38.50	171	55
8 000	38.00	224	53
10 000	37.50	275	51
12 000	37.00	324	49
14 000	36.50	371	47

11.16 a. The part of the question concerning the total cost model relates to material that is covered in Chapter 23. The cost model formula is a simple linear equation denoted by $y = a + bx$, where 'a' represents the total fixed costs and 'b' the variable cost per unit. With the current model total fixed costs are £5 000 and variable cost is £0.6 per unit sold. The revised model has lower fixed costs (£4 750) but a higher variable cost per unit sold (£0.8). Therefore, the estimated total cost for the revised model is lower at lower output levels, but higher at higher output levels compared with the existing model.

The revenue function describes a non-linear downward sloping demand curve where it is necessary to lower the selling price in order to sell more units. The revised model relates to a lower initial selling price (£19 instead of £20) but a slower decline in price as the units sold increase. In other words, the revised model depicts a lower price elasticity of demand (see Learning Note 11.1 on the open access website for a description of elasticity of demand). Therefore, the revised model generates lower total revenue estimates at low sales volumes, but higher total revenues at high sales volumes compared with the current model.

b. i. The optimal output level can be determined based on using differential calculus to ascertain the output level where marginal cost equals marginal revenue. See Appendix 11.1 for a description of this approach. Alternatively, revenue and cost estimates can be prepared for potential output levels and the profits compared at different output levels in order to establish the profit maximising output. See case B in Example 11.2 and the answer to problem 11.13 for an illustration of this approach.

ii. The model should represent estimates based on efficient performance to achieve the optimum output level based on the expected environment faced by the business. However, if business conditions change the model should be updated to reflect the changing conditions. Managerial performance should be based on a comparison of actual performance with a revised model that depicts the business conditions faced by managers during the period.

c. Cost and revenue models are frequently derived from past data based on conditions that a business has faced in the past. The past can only be an adequate predictor of the future if conditions remain unchanged. However, if past technological, marketing and environmental factors change the cost and revenue models must be adjusted to reflect these changes. The cost models used in (a) assume constant fixed costs and unit variable costs but step functions can occur and variable costs per unit may only be constant within a certain relevant output range. Such factors should be taken into account to improve the validity of the model. You should refer to 'The economist's model' and 'The accountant's cost-volume-profit model' in Chapter 8 for a more detailed discussion of these issues.

The revenue model is extremely difficult to apply in practice because of the difficulty of estimating demand at different price levels. See Learning Note 11.1 on the open access website for a discussion of the difficulties in applying economic pricing models in practice. The revenue model is also very simplistic since it assumes that price is the only factor that determines demand. To improve the validity of the model other factors such as the nature of the competition, the influence of advertising, credit terms offered and the quality of the after sales service should be incorporated in the model.

11.17 a. *New machine not leased*

Marginal cost per unit = materials (£2) + piecework rate (£0.50)

+ royalties (£0.50)

= £3

So total cost function = £50 000 fixed costs + £3x

If the selling price is £5, sales demand will be zero. To increase demand by 1 unit, selling price must be reduced by £0.01/1000 units or £0.00001.

Therefore the maximum selling price attainable for an output of x units is £5 – £0.00001x

Therefore

$$P = 5 - £0.00001x$$

$$TR = x(5 - 0.00001x)$$

$$= 5x - 0.00001x^2$$

$$MR = \frac{dTR}{dx} = 5 - 0.00002x$$

Marginal cost = £3

So the optimum output is where MC = MR
i.e. $3 = 5 - 0.00002x$

That is,

$$0.00002x = 2$$

Therefore $x = 100 000$ units (optimum output level)

Selling price at optimum level = $5 - 0.00001 \times 100 000$

= £4

Maximum profit is TR – TC

TR = £400 000 (100 000 × £4)

TC = £350 000 (100 000 × £3) + (£50 000 FC)

Profit = £50 000

New machine leased

Revised total cost function = £165 000 + £2x

Note that fixed costs increase by £115 000

Optimal output is where MC = MR
i.e., $2 = 5 - 0.00002x$

That is,

$$0.00002x = 3$$

Therefore $x = 150 000$ units (optimum output level)

Selling price at optimum output level = $5 - 0.00001 \times 150 000$

= £3.50

Maximum profit is TR – TC

TR = £525 000 (150 000 × £3.50)

TC = £465 000 (150 000 × £2) + £165 000

Profit = £60 000

The new machine should be hired, since profit will increase by £10 000. In order to obtain the maximum profit, a price of £3.50 per unit should be charged, which will produce a demand of 150 000 units.

b. i.

$$P = 100 - 2Q$$

$$TR = Q(100 - 2Q)$$

$$= 100Q - 2Q^2$$

$$MR = \frac{dTR}{dQ} = 100 - 4Q$$

Total cost function $= Q^2 + 10Q + 500$

$$MC = \frac{dTC}{dQ} = 2Q = 10$$

The optimal output level is where MC = MR, i.e.

$$2Q + 10 = 100 - 4Q$$

So

$$6Q = 90$$

$$Q = 15$$

Therefore, optimal output level is 15 000 units.
Substituting into the demand function

$$P = 100 - 2Q:$$

$$P = 100 - 2 \times 15$$

$$P = £70 \text{ per unit optimum selling price}$$

Profit = TR − TC

TR = 1050 (15 units × £70)

TC = $\underline{875}$ ($15^2 + (10 \times 15) + 500$)

Profit = $\underline{175}$

So the maximum profit = £175 000

ii.

$$TR = 100Q - 2Q^2$$

Total revenue will be maximized when MR = 0
MR = 100 − 4Q (see b(i))
So the total revenue is maximized where 100 − 4Q = 0
Q = 25 (i.e. 25 000 units)

Substituting into the demand function:

$$P = 100 - 2Q$$

$$= 100 - 2 \times 25$$

$$= £50 \text{ per unit}$$

Total sales revenue will be £1 250 000 (25 000 units × £50)

Loss = TR − TC

TR = £1 250 000

TC = $\underline{£1\ 375\ 000}$ ($25^2 + (10 \times 25) + 500$)

Loss = $\underline{(£125\ 000)}$

Summary of results

	Output level (units)	Selling price	Total revenue	Total profit (loss)
(i) Profit maximization	15 000	£70	£1 050 000	£175 000
(ii) Sales maximization	25 000	£50	£1 125 000	(£125 000)

11.18 The question relates to the pricing of customized products in a price setting firm. Generally the marginal cost approach to pricing refers to using variable cost as the cost base to determine cost-plus selling prices. However, marginal cost can also be viewed as representing short-run incremental costs which are normally interpreted to represent direct labour and material costs. In contrast, absorption costs include a share of fixed overheads and are normally considered to represent an estimate of the resources that are committed to producing a product in the long-term. A full description of variable (marginal) and absorption costing is provided in Chapter 7. The discussion of the second part of the question should incorporate issues discussed in the sections relating to short-run and long-run pricing decisions faced by a price setting firm. In particular, the answer should draw attention to the fact that adopting a policy of accepting business at a price that exceeds variable cost is appropriate only for one time special orders and is only justifiable if certain conditions as specified in the text are met.

In the long-run firms can adjust the supply of virtually all of their resources. Therefore a product or service should be priced to cover all of the resources that committed to it. Thus absorption costing principles should be used for determining the cost base for long-run decisions when using cost-plus pricing for customized products.

11.19 a. Short-run profits are maximized at the output level where marginal revenue equals marginal cost. The optimum selling price is that which corresponds to the optimal output level (see Figure 11.3 in Learning Note 11.1 on the website). From Figure 11.3 you will see that, with imperfect competition (no pricing decision is necessary with perfect competition), firms are faced with a downward-sloping demand curve. The highest selling price will apply to the first unit sold, but Figure 11.3 indicates that it is unlikely that this will be at the point where marginal revenue equals marginal cost.

b. The objective is to maximize total contribution not unit contribution. Contribution per unit sold is the difference between marginal revenue and marginal cost. It is unlikely that contribution per unit will remain constant over the entire range of output. In Chapter 8 we noted that variable cost per unit and selling price per unit may change in relation to output. With a downward-sloping demand curve, marginal revenue will decline, thus causing contribution per unit to decline as output is increased. From Figure 11.3 in Learning Note 11.1 we can see that profit is maximized where MR = MC. This is not at the point where unit contribution (difference between marginal revenue and marginal cost) is the greatest.

c. Joint costs are allocated on an arbitrary basis, and costs that include arbitrary allocations are inappropriate for product, project or divisional comparisons. Performance should be judged on the basis of comparisons between controllable costs and revenues. With profit centres, measures such as controllable residual income should be used, whereas contribution should be used for comparing products.

d. This statement presumably refers to the use of cost-plus pricing methods. If prices are set completely on a cost-plus basis then accounting information will determine the selling price. Consequently, the marketing and production people might feel that they have no influence in determining selling prices with pricing dominated by a concern for recovering full costs. If cost-plus pricing is used in a rigid way then marketing and production people may well consider the statement in the question to be correct. Cost information should be used in a flexible manner, and is one of several variables that should be used in determining selling prices. If this approach is adopted then the statement in the question will be incorrect.

e. Management accounting should not be constrained by the requirements of external reporting. The emphasis should be on assembling financial information so as to help managers make good decisions and to plan and control activities effectively. In Chapter 9 we noted that there are strong arguments for adopting a system of variable costing in preference to absorption costing. If management accounts were consistent with SSAP 9 then the financial information might motivate managers to make wrong decisions.

f. All costs must be covered in the long run if a firm is to be profitable. Therefore the objective should be to recover R and D expenditure in the long-run. R and D expenditure should be regarded as a pool of fixed costs to which products should generate sufficient contribution. Giant Steps Ltd should not rely on a policy of recovering R and D in relation to expenditure on each individual product. Price/demand relationships for some products might mean that the associated R and D cannot be recovered, while other products might be able to recover more than their fair share. Once a product is launched, only the incremental costs are relevant to the pricing decision. The objective should be to obtain a selling price in excess of relevant short-run costs and to provide a contribution to fixed costs and profit. R and D should be regarded as part of the pool of fixed costs to be recovered.

Chapter 12

12.11

Expected income with advertising = (£200 000 × 0.95) + (£70 000 × 0.05) = £193 500

Expected income without advertising = (£200 000 × 0.7) + (£70 000 × 0.3) = £161 000

The maximum amount the company should pay for advertising is the increase in expected value of £32 500.
Therefore the answer is A.

12.12

Expected value of new building = (0.8 × £2 million) + (0.2 × £1 million) – £1 million = £0.8 million

Expected value of upgrade = (0.7 × £2 million) + (0.3 × £1 million – upgrade (?) = £1.7 million – upgrade

Cost of upgrade to make the company financially indifferent = £0.9 million (1.7 – 0.8 million)
Answer = B

12.13

Selling price expected value = (£20 × 25%) + (£25 × 40%) + £30 × 35%) = £25.50

Variable cost expected value = (£8 × 20%) + (£10 × 50%) + (£12 × 30%) = £10.20

Expected unit contribution = £15.30

Expected total contribution = £15.30 × 1 000 units = £15 300

Answer = D

12.14

The unit contribution must be £13.50 for the total contribution to exceed £13 500. The following selling prices and unit contributions meet this requirement:

Selling price (£)	Variable cost (£)	Joint probability
25	8	0.08 (.4 × .2)
25	10	0.20 (.4 × .5)
30	8	0.07 (.35 × .2)
30	10	0.175 (.35 × .50)
30	12	0.105 (.35 × .30)
		0.63

Answer = C

12.15

The contributions for the different output and demand levels are as follows:

	Sales demand (in batches)		
	10	11	12
Output (batches): 10	£500	£500	£500
11	£480	£550	£550
12	£460	£530	£600

The regret table (expressed in terms of contributions) for each output level based on the different demand levels is as follows:

	Sales demand (in batches)			
Decision	10	11	12	Maximum regret
Produce 10 batches	£0a	£50b	£100	£100
Produce 11 batches	£20c	£0a	£50	£50
Produce 12 batches	£40d	£20	£0a	£40

Notes:
aMaximum contribution is obtained where production matches sales demand thus resulting in a zero regret.
bIf a decision is made to produce 10 batches and sales demand is 11 batches a contribution of £500 will be obtained. However, for a demand of 11 batches contribution is maximized with an output of 11 units (£550). Therefore the maximum regret is £50.
cIf a decision is made to produce 11 batches and sales demand is 10 batches a contribution of £480 will be obtained. However, for a demand of 10 batches contribution is maximized with an output of 10 units (£500). Therefore the maximum regret is £20.
dIf a decision is made to produce 12 batches and sales demand is 10 batches a contribution of £460 will be obtained. However, for a demand of 10 batches contribution is maximized with an output of 10 units (£500). Therefore the maximum regret is £40.
The output level that minimizes the maximum regret is 12 batches. Therefore 12 batches should be produced.

12.16

a. There are two possible selling prices and three possible direct material costs for each selling price. The calculation of unit contributions are as follows:

	£15 sales price			£24 sales price		
	No purchasing contract	Contract (40 000 kg)	Contract (60 000 kg)	No purchasing contract	Contract (40 000 kg)	Contract (60 000 kg)
Selling price	15	15	15	24	24	24
Material cost	(8)	(7.50)	(7)	(8)	(7.50)	(7)
Other variable cost	(5)	(5)	(5)	(5)	(5)	(5)
Unit contribution	£2	2.5	3	£11	11.50	12

The realizable value from the sale of excess materials is as follows:

	16 000 kg and over	Less than 16 000 kg
Sales price	2.90	2.40
Less selling, delivery and insurance costs	0.90	0.90
Realizable value per kg	£2.00	£1.50

Statement of outcomes

Sales quantities (000)	Total contribution (£000)	Fixed costs (£000)	Profit/(loss) on sale of materials (£000)	Profit (£000)	Probability	Expected value (£000)
Sales price of £15 (no contract)						
20	40	50	—	–10	0.1	–1
30	60	50	—	10	0.6	6
40	80	50	—	30	0.3	9
						14
Sales price of £15 (40 000 kg contract)						
20	50	50	—	—	0.1	—
30	75	50	—	25	0.6	15
40	100	50	—	50	0.3	15
						30
Sales price of £15 (60 000 kg contract)						
20	60	50	–30a	–20	0.1	–2
30	90	50	—	40	0.6	24
40	120	50	—	70	0.3	21
						43
Sales price of £24 (no contract)						
8	88	160	—	–72	0.1	–7.2
16	176	160	—	16	0.3	4.8
20	220	160	—	60	0.3	18.0
24	264	160	—	104	0.3	31.2
						46.8
Sales price of £24 (40 000 kg contract)						
8	92	160	–42b	–110	0.1	–11.0
16	184	160	–18b	6	0.3	1.8
20	230	160	—	70	0.3	21.0
24	276	160	—	116	0.3	34.8
						46.6
Sales price of £24 (60 000 kg contract)						
8	96	160	–66	–130	0.1	–13
16	192	160	–42	–10	0.3	–3
20	240	160	–30	50	0.3	15
24	288	160	–24	104	0.3	31.2
						30.2

Notes
aSales quantity of 20 000 units results in 40 000 kg being used. Therefore 20 000 kg of the raw material are sold at a realizable value of £2 per kg. The cost of acquiring the raw materials is £3.50 per kg. Consequently 20 000 kg are sold at a loss of £1.50 per kg.
b24 000 kg sold at a loss of £1.75 per kg.

b. i. The highest expected value of profits occurs when the sales price is £24 with no contract for the supply of raw materials.

ii. In order to minimize the effect of the worst outcome then the sales price should be £15 and a contract to purchase 40 000 kg entered into.

iii. Applying Central's own 'Desirability' measure, the best choice is a sales price of £15 combined with entering into a contract of 60 000 kg. The 'Desirability' measure is calculated as follows:

Strategy		Expected monetary value (£000)	Worst outcome (£000)	'Desirability'
Price per unit	Contract			L + 3E
£15	none	14	–10	32
£15	40 000 kg	30	0	90
£15	60 000 kg	43	–20	109
£24	none	46.8	–72	68.4
£24	40 000 kg	46.6	–110	29.8
£24	60 000 kg	30.2	–130	–39.4

c. i. Other factors to be considered are:

(A) The reliability of future supplies of raw materials might be subject to uncertainty. In this situation it may be preferable to operate at a lower production volume and sales.

(B) If there is spare production capacity then the labour cost might not be a relevant cost. More information is required regarding the alternative use of the labour if a lower production volume is selected.

ii. For a discussion of the expected value approach see Chapter 12. The criteria of pessimism in (b) (ii) focuses on the least desirable outcome. The 'desirability' measure is an attempt to formalize the importance of the two relevant measures to a particular decision-maker by attaching a weighting to the expected value and the worst possible outcome. It may be better to compare the probability distributions rather than using summary measures of the distributions.

12.17 a. Chemical X is added at the rate of 1 kg per 100 kg of waste. Therefore the possible requirements for chemical X are 500 000 kg (50 million of waste at 1 kg per 100 kg of waste), 380 000 and 300 000. The cost of purchasing chemical X is calculated as follows:

Demand (000kg)	Cost per kg (£)	Total cost (£000)
High advance order of 500 000 kg		
500	1.00	500
380	1.00 + 0.25 = 1.25	475
300	1.00 + 0.60 = 1.60	480
Medium advance order of 380 000 kg		
500	1.20 − 0.10 = 1.10	550
380	1.20	456
300	1.20 + 0.25 = 1.45	435
Low advance order of 300 000 kg		
500	1.40 − 0.15 = 1.25	625
380	1.40 − 0.10 = 1.30	494
300	1.40	420

Aluminium is extracted at 15 per cent of waste input thus resulting in the following extraction levels:

	High	Medium	Low
Aluminium extracted (000 kg)	7500	5700	4500
Contribution at 30% of £0.65 per kg (£000)	1462.5	1111.5	877.5

The net contribution is calculated as follows:

Advance order of chemical X	Level of waste	Probability	Contribution (excluding X) (£000)	Chemical X cost (£000)	Net contribution (£000)
High	High	0.30	1462.5	500	962.5
	Medium	0.50	1111.5	475	636.5
	Low	0.20	877.5	480	397.5
Medium	High	0.30	1462.5	550	912.5
	Medium	0.50	1111.5	456	655.5
	Low	0.20	877.5	435	442.5
Low	High	0.30	1462.5	625	837.5
	Medium	0.50	1111.5	494	617.5
	Low	0.20	877.5	420	457.5

b. The expected value for each advance order is calculated as follows:

High chemical X advance order = (£962.5 × 0.30) + (636.5 × 0.50) + (397.5 × 0.2) = £686 500

Medium chemical X advance order = (£912.5 × 0.30) + (655.5 × 0.50) + (442.5 × 0.2) = £690 000

Low chemical X advance order = (£837.5 × 0.30) + (617.5 × 0.50) + (457.5 × 0.2) = £651 500

Adopting the expected value rule the medium advance order for chemical X should be entered into.

c. The maximax technique is based on the assumption that the best payoff (i.e. the highest contribution) will occur for each alternative. Based on this criterion the high advance order will be selected because it yields the largest possible net contribution of £962 500. This indicates a risk seeking preference by management. Note also that the high advance order has a 20 per cent probability that the worst possible outcome of £397 500 will occur.

The maximin strategy assumes that the worst possible outcome will occur and that the decision-maker should choose the largest possible payoff under this assumption. The worst possible outcomes are as follows:

High advance order = £397 500
Medium advance order = £442 500
Low advance order = £457 500

Adopting the maximin strategy the low advance order should be selected. This approach indicates a risk averse attitude.

d. Assuming perfect information a perfect prediction of the level of demand would be obtained. If the high level of waste is the outcome the high advance order will be made because this gives the highest contribution for the high level of waste. Similarly, if the medium level of waste is the outcome the medium advance order will be made because this gives the highest contribution for the medium level of waste. Finally, if the low level of waste is the outcome the highest contribution will be derived from a low advance order.

When the decision to employ the consultant is made, it is not known which level of waste will be predicted and therefore the best estimates that high, medium and low levels of waste will be predicted are 0.3, 0.5 and 0.2. Therefore the expected value of perfect information will be as follows:

Consultant's advice	Chemical X advance order	Contribution (£000)	Probability	(£000)
High waste	high	962.5	0.30	288.75
Medium waste	medium	655.5	0.50	327.75
Low waste	low	457.5	0.20	91.50
				708.00
Expected value without consultant's advice				690.00
Hence the maximum payable to consultant =				18.00

e. Imperfect information recognizes that the consultant's information may not give a 100 per cent perfect prediction. Probabilites are attached to the likelihood that the consultant will be correct or incorrect. Revised probabilities of a given waste level based on the combined effect of the original probabilities of waste available for reprocessing and the probability of the actual waste level given the content of a particular report from the consultant are then calculated. These revised probabilities measure the probability of a particular level of waste being available given a high, medium or low forecast. The expected value is then calculated and therefore the maximum sum payable to the consultant for the information. The major problem is that it is necessary to predict in advance the likelihood that the consultant's forecast will be correct or incorrect.

12.18 a. i. See the decision tree shown in Figure Q12.18.

ii. 1. The assumption underlying the maximin technique is that the worst outcome will occur. The decision-maker should select the outcome with the largest possible payoff assuming the worst possible outcome occurs. From the decision tree we can see that the payoffs for the worst possible outcomes are as follows:

	Payoff (£000)
Hire of machine 200	55
Hire of machine 300	45
Hire of machine 600	38.5
Do not franchise	90

The decision is not to franchise using the maximum criterion.

2. The expected values for each alternative (see Figure Q12.18) are as follows:

	(£000)
Hire of machine 200	87.0
Hire of machine 300	101.0
Hire of machine 600	99.0
Do not franchise	90.0

The company will maximize the expected value of the contributions if it hires the 300 batch machine.

3. The probability of a contribution of less than £100 000 for each alternative can be found by adding the joint

probabilities from payoffs of less than £100 000. The probabilities are as follows:

Hire of machine 200	= 0.85
Hire of machine 300	= 0.55
Hire of machine 600	= 0.65
Do not franchise	= 1.00

The company should hire the 300 machine adopting this decision criterion.

FIGURE Q12.18

b. The approaches in part (a) enable uncertainty to be incorporated into the analysis and for decisions to be based on range of outcomes rather than a single outcome. This approach should produce better decisions in the long run. The main problem with this approach is that only a few selected outcomes with related probabilities are chosen as being representative of the entire distribution of possible outcomes. The approach also gives the impression of accuracy, which is not justified. Comments on the specific methods used in (a) are as follows:

Maximin: Enables an approach to be adopted which minimizes risk. The main disadvantage is that such a risk-averse approach will not result in decisions that will maximize long-run profits.

Expected value: For the advantages of this approach see 'Expected value' in Chapter 12. The weaknesses of expected value are as follows:

i. It ignores risk. Decisions should not be made on expected value alone. It should be used in conjunction with measures of dispersion.

ii. It is a long-run average payoff. Therefore it is best suited to repetitive decisions.

iii. Because it is an average, it is unlikely that the expected value will occur.

Probability of earning an annual contribution of less than £100 000: This method enables decision-makers to specify their attitude towards risk and return and choose the alternative that meets the decision-makers risk–return preference. It is unlikely that this approach will be profit-maximizing or result in expected value being maximized.

Chapter 13

13.13

Time	Cash flow (£000)	Discount factor at 8%	Present value (£000)
0	(20 000)	1.0	(20 000)
1–4	3 000	3.312	9 936
5–8	7 000	2.435 (5.747 –3.312)	17 045
10	(10 000)	0.463	(4 630)
		NPV	2 351

Note that the discount factors for periods 1–4 and 5–8 are derived from the annuity tables since the cash flows are constant per period for the time period involved.

Answer = D

13.14 Applying formula 13.5 shown in Chapter 13:

$$IRR = 10\% + \left(\frac{383}{383 - (-246)}\right)(15\% - 10\%)$$

$$IRR = 10\% + \left(\frac{383}{383 + 246}\right) \times 5\%$$

$$IRR = 10\% + \left(\frac{383}{629}\right) \times 5\%$$

$$IRR = 10\% + 3\% = 13\%$$

Answer = B

13.15 The annual percentage rate (APR) is 12.68%, which is based on annual payments.

Monthly interest rate = $\sqrt[12]{1.1268} - 1 = 0.01$ so that $r = 1\%$

In other words a monthly interest rate compounded for 12 periods at 1 per cent is equivalent to an annual rate of 12.68 per cent. This is derived from using the compound interest formula used in the chapter = $(1 + 0.01)^{12} - 1 = 0.1268 = 12.68\%$

To determine the future value of an annuity where a constant amount is invested each period the future value

$$= A\left[\frac{(1+r)^n - 1}{r}\right]$$ where r is the rate of interest per period

and A is the annuity amount.

$$\text{Future value} = 50 \times \left[\frac{1.01^{13 \times 12} - 1}{.01}\right] = £18\,610$$

Answer = D

13.16 Because the investment is a constant amount each period we can use the annuity future value formula shown in the answer to question 13.15:

$$\text{Future value} = A\left[\frac{(1+r)^n - 1}{r}\right]$$ where r is the rate of interest per

period and A is the annuity amount.

$$£7000 = A \times \left[\frac{1.005^{12 \times 5} - 1}{.005}\right]$$

$£7000 = 69.77A$

$A = £100.33$

Answer = C

13.17 The loan represents the present value of a series of repayments over a three year period. Since the payments are constant per period we can use the following annuity present value formula:

$$\text{Present value} = \frac{A}{r}\left[1 - \frac{1}{(1+r)^n}\right]$$

where A is the annuity amount and r is the interest rate per period. The annual interest rate must be converted to a monthly rate since we are dealing with monthly repayments.

Monthly interest rate = $\sqrt[12]{1.10} - 1 = .0079$ (i.e. 0.79%)

Present value (2000) $= \dfrac{A}{0.0079}\left[1 - \dfrac{1}{1.0079^{36}}\right]$

$2000 = \dfrac{A}{0.0079}(0.2467)$

$2000\,(0.0079) = 0.2467A$

$A = 15.8/.2467 = £64.04$

Answer = B

13.18 a. Applying the formula shown in question 13.15:

Future value $= 50 \times \left[\dfrac{1.01^{10\times12} - 1}{0.01}\right] = £11\,501.94$

We must now compound forward a further 5 years at an annual rate of 15%:

£11 501.95 × $(1.15)^5$ = £23 134.53

b. i.

Loan 1

APR of 9.38% results in a monthly rate of $^{12}\sqrt{1.0938} =$
1.0075 so that $r = .0075$ (i.e. .75%)

The loan represents the present value of a series of repayments over a three year period. Since the payments are constant per period we can use the following annuity present value formula:

Present value $= \dfrac{A}{r}\left[1 - \dfrac{1}{(1+r)^n}\right]$

where A is the annuity amount and r is the interest rate per period.

Present value (2000) $= \dfrac{A}{0.0075}\left[1 - \dfrac{1}{1.0075^{36}}\right]$

$2000 = \dfrac{A}{0.0075}(0.23585)$

$2000\,(0.0075) = 0.23585A$

$A = 15/.23585 = £63.60$

Loan 2

APR of 12.68% results in a monthly rate of
$^{12}\sqrt{1.1268} = 1.01$ so that $r = .01$ (i.e. 1%)

Present value (2000) $= \dfrac{A}{0.01}\left[1 - \dfrac{1}{1.01^{24}}\right]$

$2000 = \dfrac{A}{.01}(0.2124)$

$2000\,(.01) = 0.2124A$

$A = 20/.2124 = £94.16$

ii.

Loan 1 total amount repaid = £63.60 × 36 = £2289.60
Loan 2 total amount repaid = £94.16 × 24 = £2259.84

Loan 2 is the slightly cheaper loan

13.19 a. i. Average capital invested

$= \dfrac{£50\,000 + £10\,000}{2} = £30\,000$

For an explanation of why the project's scrap value is added to the initial cost to calculate the average capital employed, you should refer to note 1 at the end of Chapter 13.

Note that the mid-point of the project's life is two years and the written down value at the end of year 2 is £30 000.
Average annual profit (Project A)

$= \dfrac{£25\,000 + £20\,000 + £15\,000 + £10\,000}{4}$

$= £17\,500$

Average annual profit (Project B)

$= \dfrac{£10\,000 + £10\,000 + £14\,000 + £26\,000}{4}$

$= £15\,000$

Average annual return:

A $58.33\%\ \left(\dfrac{£17\,500}{£30\,000} \times 100\right)$

B $50\%\ \left(\dfrac{£15\,000}{£30\,000} \times 100\right)$

ii. Payback period:

Project A 1.5 years $\left(1 + \dfrac{£15\,000}{£30\,000}\right)$

Project B 2.4 years $\left(2 + \dfrac{£10\,000}{£24\,000}\right)$

iii.

Year	Project A Cash inflows (W1) (£)	Project B Cash inflows (W1) (£)	Discount factor	Project A PV (£)	Project B PV (£)
1	35 000	20 000	0.909	31 815	18 180
2	30 000	20 000	0.826	24 780	16 520
3	25 000	24 000	0.751	18 775	18 024
4	20 000	36 000	0.683	13 660	24 588
4	10 000	10 000	0.683	6 830	6 830
				95 860	84 142
		Investment cost		(50 000)	(50 000)
		NPV		45 860	34 142

Workings:
(W1) Cash flows = Profit + depreciation.
Note that the estimated resale value is included as a year 4 cash inflow.

b. See Chapter 13 for the answer to this section of the problem.
c. Project A is recommended because it has the highest NPV and also the shortest payback period.

13.20 a. Project A = 3 years $+ \dfrac{350 - 314}{112} = 3.32$ years

Project B = 3.0 years

Project C = 2.00 years

b. Accounting rate of return = average profit/average investment

Project A = 79/175 = 45%

Project B = 84/175 = 48%

Project C = 70/175 = 40%

Note that average profit = (sum of cash flows – investment cost)/project's life.

c. The report should include:
i. NPVs of each project (project A = £83 200 (W1), project B = £64 000 (W2), project C = £79 000 (W3). A simple description of NPV should also be provided. For example, the NPV is the amount over and above the cost of the project which could be borrowed, secure in the knowledge that the cash flows from the project will repay the loan.
ii. The following rankings are based on the different evaluation procedures:

Project	IRR	Payback	ARR	NPV
A	2	3	2	1
B	3	2	1	3
C	1	1	3	2

iii. A discussion of each of the above evaluation procedures.
iv. IRR is subject to the following criticisms:
1. Multiple rates of return can occur when a project has unconventional cash flows.
2. It is assumed that the cash flows received from a project are re-invested at the IRR and not the cost of capital.
3. Inability to rank mutually exclusive projects.
4. It cannot deal with different sized projects. For example, it is better to earn a return of 35 per cent on £100 000 than 40 per cent on £10 000.

Note that the above points are explained in detail in Chapter 13.

v. Payback ignores cash flows outside the payback period, and it also ignores the timing of cash flows within the payback period. For example, the large cash flows for project A are ignored after the payback period. This method may be appropriate for companies experiencing liquidity problems who wish to recover their initial investment quickly.

vi. Accounting rate of return ignores the timing of cash flows, but it is considered an important measure by those who believe reported profits have a significant impact on share prices.

vii. NPV is generally believed to be the theoretically correct evaluation procedure. A positive NPV from an investment is supposed to indicate the increase in the market value of the shareholders' funds, but this claim depends upon the belief that the share price is the discounted present value of the future dividend stream. If the market uses some other method of valuing shares then a positive NPV may not represent the increase in market value of shareholders' funds. Note that the cash flows have been discounted at the company's cost of capital. It is only suitable to use the company's cost of capital as the discount rate if projects A, B and C are equivalent to the average risk of all the company's existing projects. If they are not of average risk then project risk-adjusted discount rates should be used.

viii. The projects have assumed unequal lives. It is assumed that the equipment will not be replaced. If the equipment is to be replaced, it will be necessary to consider the projects over a common time horizon using the techniques described for projects with unequal lives in the appendix to Chapter 14.

ix. It is recommended that NPV method is used and project A should be selected.

d. Stadler prefers project C because it produces the highest accounting profit in year 3. Stadler is assuming that share prices are influenced by short-run reported profits. This is in contrast with theory, which assumes that the share price is the discounted present value of the future dividend stream. Stadler is also assuming that the market only has access to reported historical profits and is not aware of the future benefits arising from the projects. The stock market also obtains company information on future prospects from sources other than reported profits. For example, press releases, chairman's report and signals of future prosperity via increased dividend payments.

Workings

(W1) Project A = (100 × 0.8333) + (110 × 0.6944) + (104 × 0.5787) + (112 × 0.4823) + (138 × 0.4019) + (160 × 0.3349) + (180 × 0.2791) – £350

(W2) Project B = (40 × 0.8333) + (100 × 0.6944) + (210 × 0.5787) + (260 × 0.4823) + (160 × 0.4019) – £350

(W3) Project C = (200 × 0.8333) + (150 × 0.6944) + (240 × 0.5787) + (40 × 0.4823) – £350

13.21 a.

	Discount 10%	factors 20%	Project X NPV at 10% (£000)	Project X NPV at 20% (£000)	Project Y NPV at 10% (£000)	Project Y NPV at 20% (£000)
Year 0	1.000	1.000	(200.00)	(200.00)	(200.00)	(200.00)
1	0.9091	0.8333	31.82	29.16	198.19	181.66
2	0.8264	0.6944	66.11	55.55	8.26	6.94
3	0.7513	0.5787	67.62	52.08	7.51	5.79
4	0.683	0.4823	51.22	36.17	2.73	1.93
5	0.6209	0.4019	12.42	8.04	1.87	1.21
			29.19	(19.00)	18.56	(2.47)

Using the interpolation method, the IRRs are:

Project X = 10% + [29.19/(29.19 + 19.00)] × 10%
= 16.05%

Project Y = 10% + [18.56/(18.56 + 2.47)] × 10%
= 18.83%

b. The projects are mutually exclusive, and conflicting rankings occur. Where conflicting rankings occur, the NPV method will indicate the correct rankings (see Chapter 13 for an explanation). Therefore project X should be undertaken, since it yields the larger NPV at a discount rate of 10 per cent.

c. For the answer to this question see 'Comparison of net present value and internal rate of return' in Chapter 13.

d. The cost of capital at which project Y would be preferred to project X can be ascertained by calculating the IRR on the incremental investment X – Y.

Year	0 (£000)	1 (£000)	2 (£000)	3 (£000)	4 (£000)	5 (£000)
Project X cash flows	–200	35	80	90	75	20
Project Y cash flows	–200	218	10	10	4	3
Project X – Y	0	–183	+70	+80	+71	+17

The IRR on the incremental investment X – Y is 13 per cent. Therefore if the cost of capital were in excess of 13 per cent, the decision in (b) would be reversed (assuming that one of the projects has a positive NPV). Alternatively, the discount rate can be found by constructing a graph for the NPVs at different discount rates. You can see from the graph shown in Figure Q13.21 that project Y has a higher NPV for discount rates above 13 per cent.

FIGURE Q13.21

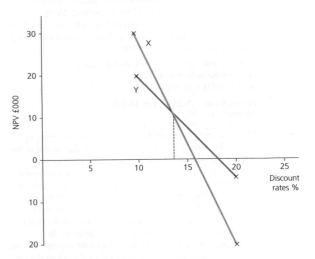

Chapter 14

14.13 Let CF = the revised increase in annual cash flows. Assuming that the other items remain constant NPV will be zero when:

CF × 3.605 = £160 000
CF = £44 382

Percentage increase in annual cash flows = £44 382/£50 000
= 0.8876
Answer = B

14.14

	Replacement Periods 1 (£000)	2 (£000)	3 (£000)	4 (£000)	5 (£000)
Cash outflows at end of year:					
1	11 (100 – 121)	–110	–110	–110	–110
2		–44 (132 – 88)	–132	–132	–132
3			–88 (154 – 66)	–154	–154
4				–110 (165 – 55)	–165
5					–151 (176 – 25)
Present value of outflows	9.83	133.30	266.09	383.04	503.64
Purchase cost	220.00	220.00	220.00	220.00	220.00
Present value	210.17	353.30	486.09	603.04	723.64
Annuity factor	0.893	1.690	2.402	3.037	3.605
Equivalent annual cost	235.35	209.05	202.37	198.56	200.73

The lowest equivalent annual cost is £198 560. Therefore the fleet should be replaced at the end of four years so the answer is D.

14.15 a. It is assumed that the cost of capital is a nominal rate. The NPV can be calculated by discounting real cash flows at the real discount rate or nominal cash flows at the nominal discount rate. The real discount rate

$(1 + \text{real discount rate})$ is $(1 + \text{nominal rate})/(1 + \text{anticipated inflation rate}) = 0.0485 \, (1.08/1.03 - 1)$.

The annual cash flows in current prices are £20 000 (£5 × 4000 units).

NPV based on real cash flows and the real discount rate:

$(£20\,000)/(1.0485) + (20\,000)/(1.0485)^2 + (20\,000)/(1.0485)^3 - £50\,000 = £4640$

NPV based on discounting nominal cash flows at the nominal discount rate:

$(£20\,000 \times 1.03)/1.08 + (£20\,000 \times 1.03^2)/1.08^2 + (£20\,000 \times 1.03^3)/1.08^3 - £50\,000 = £4640$

Answer = A

b. NPV will be zero where:

Annual cash flows (£20 000) × Annuity discount factor = Investment outlay (£50 000)
Annuity discount factor = 2.5 (£50 000/20 000)

For a three year life the annuity tables indicate a factor of 2.531 for 9 per cent and 2.487 for 10 per cent. Using interpolation a factor of 2.5 is equivalent to 9.7 per cent. Note that this is a real discount rate (based on using real cash flows). To convert to a nominal (monetary rate):

$(1 + \text{nominal rate}) = (1 + \text{real discount rate}) \times (1 + \text{anticipated inflation rate})$
$= (1 + .097) \times (1.04) = 1.141$

Nominal rate = 1.141 − 1 = 14.1%
Answer = C

14.16 a. The NPV calculations can be adjusted in two basic ways to account for inflation. Real cash flows can be discounted at the real discount rate or inflation adjusted cash flows can be discounted at a discount rate which incorporates a premium for inflation. It is only appropriate to leave the cash flows in terms of present-day prices and discount these cash flows at the real cost of capital when all the cash flows are expected to increase at the general level of inflation. The cash flows in the question are subject to different levels of inflation. In particular, capital allowances are based on the original cost and do not change in line with changing prices. Therefore the cash flows should be adjusted for inflation and discounted at a cost of capital which incorporates a premium for inflation. The inflation adjusted revenues, expenses and taxation liabilities are:

Year	1	2	3	4	5
Sales at 5% inflation (W1)	3675	5402	6159	6977	6790
Materials at 10% inflation	(588)	(907)	(1198)	(1537)	(1449)
Labour at 10% inflation	(1177)	(1815)	(2396)	(3075)	(2899)
Overheads at 5% inflation	(52)	(110)	(116)	(122)	(128)
Capital allowances (W2)	(1125)	(844)	(633)	(475)	(1423)
Taxable profits	733	1726	1816	1768	891
Taxation at 35%	256	604	636	619	312

The interest payments are not included because they are taken into account when the cash flows are discounted.

Workings

(W1) Year 1 = £3500 (1.05), year 2 = £4900 (1.05)², year 3 = £5320 (1.05)³, year 4 = £5740 (1.05)⁴, year 5 = £5320 (1.05)⁵. The same approach is used to calculate the inflation adjusted cash flows for the remaining items.

(W2) 25% writing down allowances on £4500 with a balancing allowance in year 5.

The cash flow estimates and NPV calculation are as follows:

Year	0	1	2	3	4	5	6
Inflows							
Sales	—	3675	5402	6159	6977	6790	—
Outflows							
Materials	—	588	907	1198	1537	1449	—
Labour	—	1177	1815	2396	3075	2899	—
Overheads	—	52	110	116	122	128	—
Fixed assets	4500						
Working capital (W1)	300	120	131	144	156	(851)	—
Taxation			256	604	636	619	312
Total outflows	4800	1937	3219	4458	5526	4244	312
Net cash flows	(4800)	1738	2183	1701	1451	2546	(312)
Discount factors at 15%		0.870	0.756	0.658	0.572	0.497	0.432
Present values	(4800)	1512	1650	1119	830	1265	(135)

The NPV is £1 441 000 and it is therefore recommended that the project should be undertaken. Note that the interest cost is already incorporated in the DCF calculation and should not be included in the cash flows when calculating present values.

Workings

(W1) It is assumed that the working capital is released at the end of the project. Year 1 = 400 (1.05) − 300, year 2 = 500 (1.05)² − 420, and so on.

b. Calculating the IRR will produce an NPV of zero. NPV is £1 441 000 at a 15 per cent discount rate. In order to use the interpolation method to calculate the IRR, it is necessary to ascertain a negative NPV. At a discount rate of 30 per cent the NPV is

Year	Cash flow (£000)	Discount factor	PV (£000)
0	(4800)	1.0000	(4800)
1	1738	0.7692	1337
2	2183	0.5917	1292
3	1701	0.4552	774
4	1451	0.3501	508
5	2546	0.2693	686
6	(312)	0.2071	(65)
			(268)

Using the interpolation method, the IRR is

$$15\% + \frac{1441}{1441 - (-205)} \times 15\% = 28\%$$

c. See 'Sensitivity analysis' in Chapter 14 for a description and discussion of the weaknesses of sensitivity analysis. Other traditional techniques include the use of probability distributions to calculate expected net present value and standard deviation, simulation and certainty equivalents. More recent techniques include portfolio theory and the capital asset pricing model. Theorists would suggest that risk should be incorporated into the analysis by discounting the expected value of a project's cash flows at a risk-adjusted discount rate using the capital asset pricing model.

14.17 a. The tax liability calculations are

	Standard (£)			
Year	1	2	3	4
Operating cash flows	20 500	22 860	24 210	23 410
Capital allowance	12 500	9 375	7 031	21 094 (W1)
	8 000	13 485	17 179	2 316
Taxation (35%)	2 800	4 720	6 013	811

	De-luxe (£)					
Year	1	2	3	4	5	6
Operating cash flows	32 030	26 110	25 380	25 040	38 560	35 100
Capital allowance	22 000	16 500	12 375	9 281	6 961	20 883 (W1)
	10 030	9 610	13 005	16 659	31 599	14 217
Taxation (35%)	3 511	3 363	4 552	5 831	11 060	4 976

The NPV calculations are

	Standard (£)					
Year	0	1	2	3	4	5
Fixed assets	(50 000)					
Working capital	(10 000)				10 000 (W3)	
Operating cash flows		20 500	22 860	24 210	23 410	
Taxation (W2)	—	—	(2 800)	(4 720)	(6 013)	(811)
	(60 000)	20 500	20 060	19 490	27 397	(811)
Discount factor (12%)		0.893	0.797	0.712	0.636	0.567
Present values	(60 000)	18 307	15 988	13 877	17 424	(460)

Payback period is approximately three years
Net present value is £5136

De-luxe (£)

Year	0	1	2	3	4	5	6	7
Fixed assets	(88 000)							
Working capital	(10 000)						10 000	(W3)
Operating cash flows		32 030	26 110	25 380	25 940	38 560	35 100	
Taxation (W2)	–	–	(3 511)	(3 363)	(4 552)	(5 831)	(11 060)	(4976)
	(98 000)	32 030	22 599	22 017	21 388	32 729	34 040	(4976)
Discount factor (14%)		0.877	0.769	0.675	0.592	0.519	0.456	0.400
Present values	(98 000)	28 090	17 379	14 861	12 662	16 986	15 522	(1990)

Payback period is approximately four years
Net present value is £5510

Workings

(W1) Final-year balancing allowance.

(W2) It is assumed that the capital allowance for the purchase of the asset is included in t_1 accounts, which are submitted to the Inland Revenue, and the cash flow effect arises in t_2.

(W3) It is assumed that the working capital is realized immediately the project ends.

The de-luxe model has the largest NPV, but the projects have unequal lives and this factor needs to be taken into account. One method of doing this is to convert the cash flows into an equivalent annual cash flow with NPVs of £5136 for the standard machines and £5510 for the de-luxe machines. The following formula is used to calculate the equivalent annual cash flow:

$$\frac{\text{NPV}}{\text{annuity factor for N years at R\%}}$$

$$\text{Standard} = \frac{5136}{3.605} = £1425$$

$$\text{De-luxe} = \frac{5510}{4.288} = £1285$$

The cash flow effects are for five years for the standard machine and seven years for the de-luxe machine. Therefore the annuity factors are for five years at 12 per cent and seven years at 14 per cent respectively. The equivalent annual cash flow for the standard machine indicates that a sequence of cash flows from this machine is exactly like a sequence of cash flows of £1425 per year. Note that the equivalent annual cash flow method is based on the assumption that reinvestment takes place over a period of 12 years (the common denominator of four years and six years) or infinity.

As the standard machine has the higher equivalent annual cash flow, it is recommended that this machine be purchased.

b. Possible reasons for the widespread use of accounting rate of return and payback include:

1. Simple to calculate and widely understood.
2. Appropriate for small projects which do not warrant detailed appraisal.
3. They are often used as initial screening tools and supplementary to a DCF analysis.
4. Return on capital employed (ROCE) is a widely used measure by outsiders to judge company performance and ROCE is also a popular measure for evaluating a divisional manager's performance. Managers might also consider it appropriate to judge individual projects on the same well-known criterion.
5. Payback might be appropriate for companies experiencing liquidity problems who wish to recover their investment quickly.
6. Lack of understanding of more sophisticated techniques.

14.18 It is assumed that the discount rate given in the question relates to a nominal rate.

2-year plan

Year		Cashflow	Discount Factor	Present Value
		£		£
2	Replacement	8 000 × 1.05² 8 820	.797	7 030
3	Servicing	500 × 1.10³ 666	.712	474
4	Servicing	2 500 × 1.10⁴ 3 660		
	Replacement	8 000 × 1.05⁴ 9 724		
		13 384	.636	8 512
5	Servicing	500 × 1.10⁵ 805	.567	456
6	Servicing	2 500 × 1.10⁶ 4 429		
	Trade in Value	7 000 × 1.05⁶ (9 381)		
		(4 952)	.507	(2 511)
				13 961

3-year plan

Year		Cashflow	Discount Factor	Present Value
		£		£
3	Servicing	4 000 × 1.10³ 5 324		
	Replacement	11 000 × 1.05³ 12 734		
		18 058	.712	12 857
4	Servicing	500 × 1.10⁴ 732	.636	466
5	Servicing	2 500 × 1.10⁵ 4 026	.567	2 283
6	Servicing	4 000 × 1.10⁶ 7 086		
	Trade In Value	4 000 × 1.05⁶ (5 360)		
		1 726	.507	875
				16 481

The above values exclude the non-relevant costs.

The two year replacement is recommended because it has £2 420 lower NPV. Thus the opportunity cost of making the wrong investment is £2 420.

14.19 a. *Calculations of expected net present value and profitability indices*

Project A
NPV (£70 000 × 3.605) – £246 000 = £6350

$$\text{Profitability index} = \frac{\text{present value of cash inflows}}{\text{initial outlay}} = \frac{252\,350}{246\,000} = 1.026$$

Project B
NPV (£75 000 × 0.893) + (£87 000 × 0.797) + (£64 000 × 0.712) – £180 000 = £1882

$$\text{Profitability index} = \frac{181\,882}{180\,000} = 1.010$$

Project C
NPV (£48 000 × 1.69) + (£63 000 × 0.712) + (£73 000 × 0.636) – £175 000 = (£2596)

$$\text{Profitability index} = \frac{172\,404}{175\,000} = 0.985$$

Project D
NPV (£62 000 × 3.037) – £180 000 = £8294

$$\text{Profitability index} = \frac{188\,294}{180\,000} = 1.046$$

Project E
NPV (£40 000 × 0.893) + (£50 000 × 0.797) + (£60 000 × 0.712) + (£70 000 × 0.636) + (£40 000 × 0.567) – £180 000 = £5490

$$\text{Profitability index} = \frac{185\,490}{180\,000} = 1.031$$

Project F
NPV 5 (£35 000 × 0.893) + (£82 000 × 1.509) – £150 000 = £4993

$$\text{Profitability index} = \frac{154\,993}{150\,000} = 1.033$$

Project rankings	NPV	PI
1	D	D
2	A	F
3	E	E
4	F	A
5	B	B
6	C	C

The rankings differ because NPV is an absolute measure whereas the profitability index is a relative measure that takes into account the different investment cost of each project.

b. The objective is to select a combination of investments that will maximize NPV subject to a total capital outlay of £620 000. Projects A and E are mutually exclusive and project C has a negative NPV. The following are potential combinations of projects:

Projects	Expected NPV (£)	Total expected NPV (£)	Total Outlay (£)
A, B, D	6350 + 1882 + 8294	16 526	606 000
A, B, F	6350 + 1882 + 4993	13 225	576 000
A, D, F	6350 + 8294 + 4993	19 637	576 000
B, D, E	1882 + 8294 + 5490	15 666	540 000
B, D, F	1882 + 8294 + 4993	15 169	510 000
D, E, F	8294 + 5490 + 4993	18 777	510 000

Note that it is not possible to combine four projects within the constraints outlined above and that expected NPV cannot be increased by combining two projects. Accepting projects A, D and F will maximize NPV. This combination will require a total capital outlay of £576 000, and the unused funds will be invested to yield a return of 9 per cent. The risk-adjusted discount rate for the investment will also be 9 per cent. Therefore the NPV of funds invested in the money market will be zero.

c. Where a company rejects projects with positive NPVs because of capital rationing, the IRR forgone on the most profitable project that has been rejected represents the opportunity cost of capital. For a more detailed explanation of this point see 'Capital rationing' in Chapter 14. Therefore the director is correct in stating that the company's cost of capital might not be appropriate.

d. *Advantages of mathematical programming:*
   i. Ability to solve complex problems incorporating the effects of complex interactions.
   ii. Speed in solving the problem using computer facilities.
   iii. The output from the model can highlight the key constraints to which attention should be directed.
   iv. Sensitivity analysis can be applied. The effects of changes in the variables can be speedily tested.

   Disadvantages of mathematical programming:
   i. Divisibility of projects may not be realistic, and integer programming may have to be used.
   ii. Constraints are unlikely to be completely fixed and precise, as implied in the mathematical models.
   iii. Not all the relevant information can be quantified.
   iv. All the information for the model may not be available. For example, it may not be possible to specify the constraints of future periods.
   v. All the relationships contained within the formulation may not be linear.
   vi. All the potential investment opportunities may not be identified and included in the analysis.
   vii. The linear programming formulation assumes that all the project's cash flows are certain, and therefore it cannot incorporate uncertainty. The solution produced can only be considered optimal given this restrictive assumption.

14.20 a. Because future cash flows are uncertain there is a need to express how NPV calculations might be affected by the level of uncertainty. NPV calculations are normally based on the most likely cash flows and if uncertainty is not taken into account there is a danger that managers might place too much confidence in the results of the investment appraisal. When the level of uncertainty is incorporated into the analysis managers may reject projects with positive high NPVs because the cash flows are subject to very high levels of uncertainty. Alternatively, other projects with lower NPVs, and lower uncertainty, may be deemed to be more attractive.

b.

Annual cash flows = 20 000 × (£3 − £1.65) − £10 000
= £17 000

Payback period = £50 000/£17 000
= 2.94 years (assuming that the cash flows occur evenly throughout the year).

The company uses a payback period of two years and since the project has a payback of nearly three years it will be rejected using the payback method. The answer should also describe the deficiencies of the payback (see Chapter 13 for an outline of the disadvantages of the payback method).

c.

NPV = Annual cash flows (£17 000) × 3.605 discount factor − investment outlay (£50 000) = £11 285.

Sales volume sensitivity analysis

Let SV = Sales volume

NPV will be zero when:
(1.35SV − £10 000)3.605 = £50 000
4.86675 SV − £36 050 = £50 000
SV = 17 681 units

This represents a decrease of 2 319 units (i.e. 11.6%)

Selling price sensitivity analysis

Let SP = Selling price

NPV will be zero when:
((20 000SP − (£1.65 × 20 000))3.605 − (£10 000 × 3.605) = £50 000
72 100SP − £118 965 − £36 050 = £50 000
72100SP = £205 015
SP = £2.843 (A decrease of 15.7 pence or 5.2%)

Unit variable cost sensitivity analysis

Let VC = Variable cost

NPV will be zero when:
((£20 000 × £3) − 20 000VC))3.605 − (£10 000 × 3.605) = £50 000
£216 300 − 72 100VC − £36 050 = £50 000
72 100VC = £130 250
VC = £1.8065 (An increase of 15.7 pence or 9.5%).

For a discussion of the use of sensitivity analysis for investment appraisal see 'Sensitivity Analysis' in Chapter 14. In particular, the answer should describe the objectives and limitations of sensitivity analysis.

d.

Expected value of sales volume = (17 500 × 0.3) + (20 000 × 0.6) + (22 500 × 0.1) = 19 500 units
Expected NPV = (19 500 × £1.35 × 3.605) − (£10 000 × 3.605) − £50 000 = £8 852

The project still has a positive expected NPV and should be adopted based on the expected value of the cash flows. However, the expected value is based on using the weighted average of the potential cash flows and is thus unlikely to occur in practice. An examination of the probability distribution indicates that positive NPVs will occur for the normal and good economic states. If the poor economic state occurs the NPV will be as follows:

(17 500 × £1.35 × 3.605) − (£10 000 × 3.605) − £50 000 = (£882)

Thus there is a 30 per cent chance that the project will yield a negative NPV and a 70 per cent chance that the project will yield a positive NPV. It is possible that managers may consider a 30 per cent risk of a negative NPV to be unacceptable. The decision is likely to depend on the managers' attitude towards risk, the current profitability of the company and how the cash flows correlate with existing activities. Assigning probabilities to the potential outcomes has produced useful information that may help managers to make better investment decisions. The disadvantage of this approach is that the estimates of the probabilities of future economic states are likely to be subject to a high degree of uncertainty and subjectivity.

Chapter 15

15.19 All figures are £000

Month	Sales	Cost of sales	Opening inventory	Closing inventory	Purchases	Paid
July	100	80	40	36	76	
August	90	72	36	50	86	76
September	125	100	50	56	106	86
October	140	112	56			106

15.20 a.

Production Budget in units

	Quarter 1	Quarter 2	Quarter 3	Quarter 4	Total
Required by sales	2 250	2 050	1 650	2 050	8 000
Plus required closing inventory	615	495	615	375	375
less opening inventory	−675	−615	−495	−615	−675
Production Budget	2 190	1 930	1 770	1 810	7 700

Raw Materials purchases budget

Material B	Quarter 1 kg	Quarter 2 kg	Quarter 3 kg	Quarter 4 kg	Total kg
Required by production	6 570	5 790	5 310	5 430	23 100
Plus required closing inventory	2 605.50	2 389.50	2 443.50	2 011.50	2 011.50
less opening inventory	−2 956.50	−2 605.50	−2 389.50	−2 443.50	−2 956.50
Material Purchases Budget	6 219	5 574	5 364	4 998	22 155
Value	£43 533	£39 018	£37 548	£34 986	£155 085

b. If material A is in short supply the company will need to obtain an alternative source of supply or find a substitute material. If they are unable to do this they will need to use limiting factor analysis (see Chapter 9) to determine the optimum output level. In this situation sales will not be the limiting factor and the production budget will become the key budget factor in the budget preparation process.

c. It is assumed that the flexible budget statement does not require the inclusion of direct materials. The statement is as follows:

Operating Statement

	Fixed Budget	Flexed Budget	Actual	Flexible Budget Variance
Activity	7 700	7 250	7 250	
Overheads	£	£	£	£
Variable	168 000	158 182	185 000	26 818 advance
Fixed	112 000	112 000	105 000	7 000 favourable
Labour				
Skilled	462 000	435 000	568 750	133 750 adverse
Semi-skilled	415 800	391 500	332 400	59 100 favourable
	1 157 800	1 096 682	1 191 150	94 468 adverse

Note that the fixed and variable overheads for the fixed budget are respectively £112 000 (40% × £240 000) and £168 000 (60% × £240 000). The variable overhead rate per unit of output is £21.818 (£168 000/7 700 units). This rate per unit is multiplied by 7 250 units to obtain the flexible budget allowance for variable overheads.

d. See 'Zero-base Budgeting'(ZBB) in Chapter 15 for the answer to this question. In particular, the answer should point out that with incremental budgeting the budget process uses the previous year's budget or actual results and adjusts for anticipated changes in the budget period. Thus past inefficiencies are incorporated in the budget. In contrast, ZBB starts from base zero and requires each cost element to be specifically justified as if the budgeted activities were being undertaken for the first time.

e. See 'The Budget Process' in Chapter 15 for the answer to this question. The answer should point out that rolling budgets are particularly useful when it is difficult to forecast future costs/activities accurately. Given that the company is experiencing an increase in competition and a shortage of raw materials it may need to react speedily to these factors in terms of competitive responses and sourcing alternative supplies. In these circumstances rolling budgets may be preferable.

15.21 a. The cash budget for January to April is as follows:

	January £	February £	March £	April £
Receipts				
Cash fees	18 000	27 000	45 000	54 000
Credit fees	36 000	36 000	54 000	90 000
Sale of assets				20 000
Total receipts	54 000	63 000	99 000	164 000
Payments				
Salaries	26 250	26 250	26 250	26 250
Bonus			6 300	12 600
Expenses	9 000	13 500	22 500	27 000
Fixed overheads	4 300	4 300	4 300	4 300
Taxation				95 800
Interest			3 000	
Total payments	39 550	44 050	62 350	165 950
Net cash flow	14 450	18 950	36 650	(1 950)
Opening balance	(40 000)	(25 550)	(6 600)	30 050
Closing balance	(25 550)	(6 600)	30 050	28 100

Workings

Month	December	January	February	March	April
Units sold	10	10	15	25	30
Sales value (£000)	1 800	1 800	2 700	4 500	5 400
Cash fees at 1% (£)	18 000	18 000	27 000	45 000	54 000
Credit fees at 2% (£)	36 000	36 000	54 000	90 000	108 000
Variable costs at 0.5% (£)		9 000	13 500	22 500	27 000

Monthly salary cost = (35 000 × 9)/12 = £26 250
Bonus for March = (25 − 20) × 140 × 9 = £6 300
Bonus for April = (30 − 20) × 140 × 9 = £12 600

b. It is apparent from the monthly sales volume that seasonal variations exist. It would appear that sales are lower in winter and increase in spring. Cash deficits occur in January and February but surpluses occur in March and April. Therefore any cash surpluses are likely to be temporary and any investment of surplus cash should be on a short-term basis in risk free securities or bank deposits that can be quickly converted to cash. The specific investments selected will depend on the size of the amount available, the yield offered, the risk involved and any penalties for early withdrawal. Also since the company operates in a competitive and high risk industry and has been in business for only a short period of time it may have difficulty in obtaining long-term sources of finance. Thus future investments may have to be financed by internal finance. It is therefore important that cash surpluses are easily accessible when there is a need for future investment.

c. The cash budget indicates that in two of the four months the company has a cash deficit. Even though the company has a bank loan of £200 000 it is likely that the short-term deficits will be financed by a bank overdraft. The major advantage of an overdraft is that it is flexible and can be adjusted (up to the amount of the overdraft) to the level of the deficits and not used when surpluses exist. Thus the company will only have to pay interest on the amount of the overdraft facility that is actually used. Also the interest will be at a variable rate linked to market rates. In contrast, interest is payable on a bank loan even when it does not require it. Thus an overdraft is likely to be cheaper than a bank loan. The disadvantages of overdrafts are that the interest rate fluctuates and may only be available if the company provides some form of security (e.g. a floating charge on the company's assets or a personal guarantee from the company's owners).

15.22

Task 1
Alderley Ltd Budget Statements 13 weeks to 4 April

a. Production Budget

	Elgar units	Holst units
Budgeted sales volume	845	1235
Add closing stock[a]	78	1266
Less Opening stock	(163)	(361)
Units of production	760	1140

b. Material Purchases Budget

	Elgar kg	Holst kg	Total kg
Material consumed	5320 (760 × 7)	9120 (1140 × 8)	14 440
Add raw material closing stock[b]			2 888
Less raw material opening stock			(2 328)
Purchases (kg)			15 000

c. Purchases (£) (1500 × £12) £180 000

d. Production Labour Budget

	Elgar hours	Holst hours	Total hours
Standard hours produced[c]	6080	5700	11 780
Productivity adjustment (5/95 × 11 780)			620
Total hours employed			12 400
Normal hours employed[d]			11 544
Overtime hours			856

e. Labour cost

	£
Normal hours (11 544 × £8)	92 352
Overtime (856 × £8 × 125%)	8 560
Total	100 912

Notes:

[a]Number of days per period = 13 weeks × 5 days = 65

Stock: Elgar = (6/65) × 845 = 78, Holst = (14/65) × 1235 = 266

[b](13/65) × (5320 + 9120) = 2888

[c]Elgar 760 × 8 hours = 6080, Holst 1140 × 5 hours = 5700

[d]24 employees × 37 hours × 13 weeks = 11 544

Task 2

a. Four ways of forecasting future sales volume are:

  i. Where the number of customers is small it is possible to interview them to ascertain what their likely demand will be over the forecasting period.

  ii. Produce estimates based on the opinion of executives and sales personnel. For example, sales personnel may be asked to estimate the sales of each product to their customers, or regional sales managers may estimate the total sales for each of their regions.

  iii. Market research may be necessary where it is intended to develop new products or new markets. This may involve interviews with existing and potential customers in order to estimate potential demand.

  iv. Estimates involving statistical techniques that incorporate general business and market conditions and past growth in sales.

b. Interviewing customers and basing estimates on the opinions of sales personnel are likely to be more appropriate for existing products and customers involving repeat sales. Market research is appropriate for new products or markets and where the market is large and anticipated revenues are likely to be sufficient to justify the cost of undertaking the research.

Statistical estimates derived from past data are likely to be appropriate where conditions are likely to be stable and past demand patterns are likely to be repeated through time. This method is most suited to existing products or markets where sufficient data is available to establish a trend in demand.

c. The major limitation of interviewing customers is that they may not be prepared to divulge the information if their future plans are commercially sensitive. There is also no guarantee that the orders will be placed with Alderley Ltd. They may place their orders with competitors.

Where estimates are derived from sales personnel there is a danger that they might produce over-optimistic estimates in order to obtain a favourable performance rating at the budget setting stage. Alternatively, if their future performance is judged by their ability to achieve the budgeted sales they may be motivated to underestimate sales demand.

Market research is expensive and may produce unreliable estimates if inexperienced researchers are used. Also small samples are often used which may not be indicative of the population and this can result in inaccurate estimates.

Statistical estimates will produce poor demand estimates where insufficient past data is available, demand is unstable

over time and the future environment is likely to be significantly different from the past. Statistical estimates are likely to be inappropriate for new products and new markets where past data is unavailable.

15.23 a. Activity based budget for six months ending 30 June 2004

	Product A 9000 units		Product B 15 000 units		Total
Production	Per unit (£)	Total (£000)	Per unit (£)	Total (£000)	£000
Product unit-based					
Materials[a]	60.000	540.0	45.000	675.0	1 215.0
Labour, power etc.[b]	16.000	144.0	10.000	150.0	294.0
	76.000	684.0	55.000	825.0	1 509.0
Batch based					
Production scheduling					29.6
WIP movement					36.4
Purchasing and receipt					49.5
Sub-total[c]		63.0		52.5	115.5
Machine set-up[d]		15.0		25.0	40.0
	8.667	78.0	5.167	77.5	155.5
Product sustaining					
Material scheduling[e]		9.0		9.0	18.0
Design/testing[f]		9.6		6.4	16.0
	2.067	18.6	1.027	15.4	34.0
Product line sustaining					
Product line development[g]		20.0		5.0	25.0
Product line maintenance[h]		6.0		3.0	9.0
	2.889	26.0	0.533	8.0	34.0
Factory sustaining					
General factory administration[i]					125.0
General factory occupancy[j]					67.0
	8.000	72.0	8.000	120.0	192.0
Totals	97.623	878.6	69.727	1 045.9	1 924.5

Notes

[a]Output × material cost per unit given in the question.

[b]Machine hours = (9000 × 0.8) + (15 000 × 0.5) = 14 700

  Rate per hour = (£294 000/14 700) = £20

  Product A = 0.8 hours × £20

[c]Product batches required = (9000/100) + (15 000/200) = 165

  Cost per batch = £115 500/165 = £700

  Assigned to product A = 90 batches at £700 = £63 000

[d]Cost per set up = £40 000/40 = £1000 per set up

  Assigned to product A = 15 set ups × £1000

[e]Components purchased = 180 000 for product A (9000 × 20) and 180 000 for product B

  (15 000 × 12) resulting in equal costs being allocated to each product.

[f]Design and testing allocated in the ratio 12 : 8 as given in the question.

[g]Allocated 80% and 20% as indicated in the question.

[h]Production line maintenance cost per maintenance hour = £9000/450 = £20

  Allocated to product A = 300 hours at £20 per hour = £6000

[i]£768 000 × 25% = £192 000/number of units (24 000) = £8 per unit

  Allocated to A = £72 000 (9000 units × £8)

  b. See 'activity hierarchies' and 'designing ABC systems' in Chapter 10 for the answer to this question. Note that cost pools are also known as cost centres. An explanation of cost pools can be found in Chapter 3.

  c. Steps include:

    ● Ascertaining what activities are being carried out and investigate whether they are necessary.

    ● Ascertaining how effectively are the activities carried out and investigate ways of performing activities more effectively.

    ● Identify value-added and non-value-added activities and give priority to reducing non-value-added activities.

    ● Benchmark (see Chapter 21) activities against best practice.

15.24 a. See 'Zero-base budgeting' in Chapter 15 for the answer to this question. In particular the answer should stress that the first stage should be to explicitly state the objectives that each part of the organization is trying to achieve. The activities for achieving these objectives should be described in a decision package. A decision package should consist of a base package, which would normally represent a minimum level of activity, plus incremental packages for higher levels of activity and costs. The packages are then evaluated and ranked in order of their decreasing benefits. A cut-off point is determined by the budgeted spending level, and packages are allocated according to their ranking until the budgeted spending level is reached.

  b. For the answer to this question see 'Zero-base budgeting' in Chapter 15.

c. The problems that might be faced in introducing a zero-base budgeting scheme are:

i. Implementation of zero-base budgeting might be resisted by staff. Traditional incremental budgeting tends to protect the empire that a manager has built. Zero-base budgeting challenges this empire, and so there is a strong possibility that managers might resist the introduction of such a system.

ii. There is a need to combat a feeling that current operations are efficient.

iii. The introduction of zero-base budgeting is time-consuming, and management may lack the necessary expertise.

iv. Lack of top-management support.

d. Beneficial results are likely to be obtained from a company with the following features:

i. A large proportion of the expenditure is of a discretionary nature.

ii. Management and employees of the company are unlikely to be resistant to change.

iii. Suitable output measures can be developed.

iv. A senior manager is employed who has some experience from another organization of implementing zero-base budgeting.

15.25 a. See 'The budgeting process in non-profit organizations' in Chapter 15 for the answer to this question. In particular, the answer should cover the following points:

i. Insufficient strategic thinking and long-term planning. The annual budgeting process based on short-term plans was frequently used for policy planning. Allocation of resources should be based on a long-term planning process and not the annual budgeting process.

ii. Traditional approaches failed to identify the costs of activities and the programmes to be implemented.

iii. Traditional approaches tend to be based on incremental budgeting rather than considering alternative ways of achieving objectives.

iv. Emphasis tended to be on separate planning for each department rather than focusing on activities or functions necessary to achieve organizational objectives.

b. See 'Planning, programming budgeting systems' in Learning Note 15.1 on the website for an illustration of PPBS.

c. Problems that have made PPBS difficult to introduce include:

i. PPBS cuts across departmental activities and focuses on programmes rather than departments. Consequently, the system does not focus on traditional lines of authority and there is a tendency for heads of departments to be resistant to such changes.

ii. Difficulty in matching programme structure to the organization's structure for the purpose of cost control (see 'Planning, programming budgeting systems' in Learning Note 15.1 for an explanation of this).

iii. Difficulty in defining objectives and stating objectives in quantitative terms. It *is* extremely difficult to measure the output of *services* and compare actual accomplishments with planned accomplishments.

Chapter 16

16.21 a. The assembly labour, furniture packs and other materials are assumed to vary with assembly labour hours. Therefore a cost per assembly labour hour is calculated for each of these items and the flexible budget allowance is derived by multiplying the cost per hour by 7 140 hours for each element of cost. There is no change in step fixed costs when output is increases from 7 500 to 10 000 hours so variable costs represent the increase in total costs. Therefore the variable cost per assembly hour is $5.40 (($90 000 – $76 500)/2 500 increase in assembly hours). The total variable cost at an output of 7 500 units is $40 500 (7 500 × $5.40) so the balance of $36 000 represents the fixed

cost and stepped fixed cost. Given that the share of central fixed costs is $9 000 the remaining $27 000 represent stepped fixed costs. The flexible budget allowance for variable overheads is $38 556 (7 140 hours × $5.40 per hour). The following budget statement provides more meaningful information:

	Original Budget	Flexed Budget	Actual	Variance	
Assembly labour hours	6 400	7 140	7 140		
Variable costs	$	$	$	$	
Assembly labour	49 920	55 692	56 177	485	Adv
Furniture packs	224 000	249 900	205 000	44 900	Fav
Other materials	23 040	25 704	24 100	1 604	Fav
Variable Overheads	34 560	38 556	76 340	37 784	Adv
Total Variable costs	331 520	369 852	361 617	8 235	Fav
Departmental Fixed costs					
Manager	2 050	2 050	2 050	–	
Overheads	18 500	27 000	27 000	–	
Total Departmental Fixed costs	20 550	29 050	29 050	–	
Central costs	9 000	9 000	9 000	–	
	361 070	407 902	399 667	8 235	Fav

b. i. The revised statement is more helpful to management because it:

● It compares 'like with like.' That is, it compares the manager's performance based on the actual activity level and not the level of activity anticipated when the budget was set. Thus it is more appropriate to compare a manager's performance with a flexed budget rather than a fixed budget;

● It distinguishes between controllable and non-controllable items;

● It distinguishes between fixed and variable costs.

ii. It is assumed that all variable costs vary in relation to assembly hours but some, or all costs, may vary with other factors. For example, assembly and fitting may vary with size, complexity and value. Therefore the company should investigate the extent to which costs vary with other cost drivers and flex the budget on the basis of what causes the variations in costs.

c. The answer should describe the benefits and limitations of budgeting as outlined in the section in Chapter 16 titled 'Participation in the budgeting and target setting process.'

16.22

Task 1:

Performance Statement – Month to 31 October

Number of guest days = Original budget	9 600
Flexed budget	11 160

	Flexed budget (£)	Actual (£)	Variance (£)
Controllable expenses			
Food (1)	23 436	20 500	2936F
Cleaning materials (2)	2 232	2 232	U
Heat, light and power (3)	2 790	2 050	740F
Catering staff wages (4)	8 370	8 400	30A
	36 828	33 182	3646F
Non-controllable expenses			
Rent, rates, insurance and depreciation (5)	1 860	1 860	0

Notes:
(1) £20 160/9600 × 11 160.
(2) £1920/9600 × 11 160.
(3) £2400/9600 × 11 160.
(4) £11 160/40 × £30.
(5) Original fixed budget based on 30 days but October is a 31-day month (£1800/30 × 31).

Task 2:

a. See the sections on the multiple functions of budgets (motivation) in Chapter 15, and 'Setting financial performance targets' in Chapter 16 for the answers to this question.

b. Motivating managers ought to result in improved performance. However, besides motivation, improved performance is also dependent on managerial ability, training, education and the existence of a favourable environment. Therefore motivating managers is not guaranteed to lead to improved performance.

c. The use of a fixed budget is unlikely to encourage managers to become more efficient where budgeted expenses are variable with activity. In the original performance report actual expenditure for 11.160 guest days is compared with budgeted expenditure for 9600 days. It is misleading to compare actual costs at one level of activity with budgeted costs at another level of activity. Where the actual level of activity is above the budgeted level adverse variances are likely to be reported for variable cost items. Managers will therefore be motivated to reduce activity so that favourable variances will be reported. Therefore it is not surprising that Susan Green has expressed concern that the performance statement does not reflect a valid reflection of her performance. In contrast, most of Brian Hilton's expenses are fixed and costs will not increase when volume increases. A failure to flex the budget will therefore not distort his performance.

To motivate, challenging budgets should be set and small adverse variances should normally be regarded as a healthy sign and not something to be avoided. If budgets are always achieved with no adverse variances this may indicate that undemanding budgets may have been set which are unlikely to motivate best possible performance. This situation could apply to Brian Hilton who always appears to report favourable variances.

16.23 a. Recommendations are as follows:
   i. For cost control and managerial performance evaluation, expenses should be separated into their controllable and non-controllable categories. Two separate profit calculations should be presented: controllable profit, which is appropriate for measuring managerial performance, and a 'bottom-line' net profit, which measures the economic performance of each store rather than the manager.
   ii. The report should be based on an ex-post basis. In other words, if the environment is different from that when the original budget was set, actual performance should be compared with a budget that reflects any changed conditions. For example, the budget should be adjusted to reflect the effect of the roadworks.
   iii. Actual expenses should be compared with flexed budgets and not the original budget.
   iv. Each store consists of three departments. The report should therefore analyze gross profits by departments. Selling prices and the cost of goods sold are beyond the control of the stores' managers, but each departmental manager can influence sales volume. An analysis of gross profits by departments and a comparison with previous periods should provide useful feedback on sales performance and help in deciding how much space should be allocated to each activity.
   v. Stock losses should be minimized. Such losses are controllable by departmental managers. The cost of stock losses should therefore be monitored and separately reported.
   vi. The budget should include cumulative figures to give an indication of trends, performance to date and the potential annual bonus.
   vii. Any imputed interest charges should be based on economic values of assets and not historic costs.
b. The report should include a discussion of the following:
   i. *Review of delegation policies:* Head office purchases the goods for sale, fixes selling prices, appoints permanent staff and sets pay levels. Stores managers are responsible for stores' running expenses, employment of temporary staff and control of stocks.

   Purchasing is centralized, thus enabling the benefits of specialized buying and bulk purchasing to be obtained. Purchasing policies are coordinated with expected sales by consultation between head office buyers and stores and departmental managers. It is wise to make stores managers responsible for controlling stocks because they are in the best position to assess current and future demand.

Managers are responsible for sales volume but they cannot fix selling prices. There are strong arguments for allowing stores to set selling prices, and offer special discounts on certain goods. Central management may wish to retain some overall control by requiring proposed price changes beyond certain limits referred to them for approval. There are also strong arguments for allowing the stores' managers to appoint permanent staff. The stores' managers are likely to be in a better position to be able to assess the abilities necessary to be a successful member of their own team.

   ii. *Strengths of the management control system:*
      1. Sales targets are set after consultation between head office and the departmental managers.
      2. The budgets are prepared well in advance of the start of the budget year, thus giving adequate time for consultation.
      3. Performance reports are available one week after the end of the period.
      4. Budgets are adjusted for seasonal factors.
      5. Significant variations in performance are investigated and appropriate action is taken.
   iii. *Weaknesses of the management control system:*
      1. There is no consultation in the setting of expense budgets.
      2. Actual costs are compared with a fixed budget and not a flexible budget.
      3. Costs are not separated into controllable and non-controllable categories.
      4. Budgets are set on an incremental basis with budgets set by taking last year's base and adjusting for inflation.
      5. Budgets are not revised for control purposes. Targets set for the original budget before the start of the year may be inappropriate for comparison with actual expenses incurred towards the end of the budget year.
      6. Using a budget that does not include ex-post results and that is not linked to controllable profit is likely to be demotivating, and results in managers having little confidence in the budget system.
   iv. *Recommendations:*
      1. Compare actual costs with a flexed budget.
      2. The performance report should separate costs into controllable and uncontrollable categories, and controllable profit should be highlighted. Any bonus payments should be related to controllable profit and not 'bottom-line' profits.
      3. Introduce monthly or quarterly rolling budgets.
      4. Ensure that the stores managers participate in setting the budget and accept the target against which they will be judged.
      5. Set targets using a zero-base approach.
      6. Consider extending the bonus scheme to departmental managers.

16.24 a. For the answer to this question see 'Controllability principle' in Chapter 16. The answer should describe the controllability principle and outline the difficulties in practice of distinguishing between controllable and non-controllable items.
b. The answer should draw off the material in Chapter 16 relating to dealing with distorting effects before and after the measurement period. Within the latter category the answer should discuss variance analysis, flexible performance standards, relative performance evaluations and subjective performance evaluations. In addition the answer should incorporate aspects of the section in Chapter 16 titled 'Guidelines for applying the controllability principle.'
c. You should refer to 'Establishing cost targets' in Chapter 17 for the answers to the first two items and 'Negotiation of budgets' in Chapter 15 for the answer to the third item

16.25 a. Management accounting control systems are essentially concerned with encouraging individuals within an organization to alter their behaviour so that the overall aims of the organization are effectively attained. Aspects of accounting control systems that influence human behaviour include the setting of goals, encouraging individuals to accomplish these goals, motivating desirable performance, evaluating performance and suggesting when corrective action must be taken. If attention is not given to the behavioural aspects, and how individuals respond to accounting control systems, harmful side-effects can occur and individuals may be motivated to engage in behaviour that is not organizationally desirable (see 'Harmful side-effects of controls' in Chapter 16 for a more detailed explanation.

b. For performance monitoring the answer should draw off the content presented in the sections on 'Results or output controls' and 'Harmful side-effects of controls' in Chapter 16. In particular, the answer should draw attention to the negative behavioural consequences arising from:

- The difficulties in measuring performance of responsibility centres;
- Distinguishing between controllable and non-controllable items;
- Difficulty in measuring key variables that are not easy to quantify (e.g. enhancing customer satisfaction);
- Problems in ensuring that the system encourages goal congruence (Figure 16.2 could be used as an illustration);
- Concentrating on achieving the performance measures rather than what needs to be achieved (e.g. rejecting activities that result in a decline in the existing ROI even when acceptance is in the best interests of the organization);
- Over-emphasis on short-term results at the expense of long-term results.

Behavioural issues relating to budgeting include negative behavioural consequences arising from:

- Negative effects from imposed budgets without any participation;
- Inappropriate levels of budget difficulty (e.g. being either too difficult or easily attainable);
- Inappropriate style of budget evaluation (e.g. adoption of a budget constrained style);
- At the budgetary control stage a failure to distinguish between controllable and non-controllable activities and to apply the principles of flexible budgeting and *ex-post* budget adjustments.

In terms of transfer pricing behavioural issues relate to the fact that a transfer pricing system attempts to achieve a number of conflicting objectives – encouraging managers to make sound decisions, providing appropriate information for performance measurement and enhancing divisional autonomy. In the section titled 'Purposes of transfer pricing' you will find an explanation of how behavioural issues can arise in relation to a failure to achieve each of these objectives.

Chapter 17

17.16 Idle time variance = Unproductive hours (5500) × Standard wage rate (£540 000/60 000 hours) = £49 500 Adverse

Labour efficiency variance = (standard productive hours – actual productive hours) × standard wage rate
[(14 650 × 60 000 hours/15 000 units) – 56 000] × £9
= £23 400 Favourable

17.17 a.

Sales price variance = (Actual margin – budgeted margin) × actual sales volume
(£17 – £12) × 8200 = £41 000 Favourable
(Answer = (ii))
Note that fixed overhead rate per unit is £4 (£34 800/8700)

b.

Sales volume = (Actual sales volume – budgeted sales volume) × Standard margin
(8200 – 8700) × £12 = 6 000 Adverse
(Answer = (i))

c.

Fixed overhead volume = (Actual production – budgeted production) × standard fixed overhead rate
(8200 – 8700) × £4 = £2000 Adverse
(Answer = (i))

17.18 1. *Preliminary calculations*
The standard product cost and selling price are calculated as follows:

	(£)
Direct materials	
X (10 kg at £1)	10
Y (5 kg at £5)	25
Direct wages (5 hours × £3)	15
Fixed overhead (5 hours × 200% of £3)	30
Standard cost	80
Profit (20/(100 – 20)) × £80	20
Selling price	100

The actual profit for the period is calculated as follows:

	(£)	(£)
Sales (9500 at £110)		1 045 000
Direct materials: X	115 200	
Y	225 600	
Direct wages (46 000 × £3.20)	147 200	
Fixed overhead	290 000	778 000
Actual profit		267 000

It is assumed that the term 'using a fixed budget' refers to the requirement to reconcile the budget with the original fixed budget.

	(£)	(£)
Material price variance:		
(standard price – actual price)		
× actual quantity		
X: (£1 – £1.20) × 96 000	19 200 A	
Y: (£5 – £4.70) × 48 000	14 440 F	4800 A
Material usage variance:		
(standard quantity – actual quantity)		
× standard price		
X: (9500 × 10 = 95 000 – 96 000) × £1	1 000 A	
Y: (9500 × 5 = 47 500 – 48 000) × £5	2 500 A	3500 A

The actual materials used are in standard proportions. Therefore there is no mix variance.

	(£)	(£)
Wage rate variance:		
(standard rate – actual rate) × actual hours		
(£3 – £3.20) × 46 000	9 200 A	
Labour efficiency variance:		
(standard hours – actual hours) × standard rate		
(9500 × 5 = 47 500 – 46 000) × £3	4 500 F	4 700 A
Fixed overhead expenditure:		
budgeted fixed overheads – actual fixed overheads		
(10 000 × £30 = £300 000 – £290 000)		10 000 F
Volume efficiency variance:		
(standard hours – actual hours) × fixed		
overhead rate (47 500 – 46 000) × £6	9 000 F	
Volume capacity variance:		
(actual hours – budgeted hours) × fixed		
overhead rate (46 000 – 50 000) × £6	24 000 A	15 000 A
Sales margin price variance:		
(actual margin – standard margin) × actual		
sales volume (£30 – £20) × 9500	95 000 F	
Sales margin volume variance:		
(actual sales volume – budgeted sales volume)		
× Standard margin		
(9500 – 10 000) × £20	10 000 A	85 000 F
Total variance		67 000 F

	(£)
Budgeted profit (10 000 units at £20)	200 000
Add favourable variances (see above)	67 000
Actual profit	267 000

17.19 a. i. A fixed overhead volume variance only occurs with an absorption costing system. The question indicates that a volume variance has been reported. Therefore the company must operate an absorption costing system and report the sales volume variance in terms of profit margins, rather than contribution margins.

Budgeted profit margin = Budgeted profit
(£4250)/Budgeted volume (1500 units)
= £2.83

Adverse sales volume variance in units = £850/£2.83
= 300 units

Therefore actual sales volume was 300 units below
budgeted sales volume

Actual sales volume = 1200 units (1500 units – 300 units)

ii. Standard quantity of material used per units of output:

Budgeted usage (750 kg)/Budgeted production (1500 units)
= 0.5 kg

Standard price = Budgeted material cost (£4500)/Budgeted
usage (750 kg) = £6

Material usage variance = (Standard quantity – Actual
Quantity) Standard price
£150A = (1550 × 0.5 kg = 775 kg – AQ) £6
– £150 = 4650 – 6AQ
6AQ = 4800

Actual quantity used = 800 kg

iii.

Material price variance = (Standard price – Actual price) ×
Actual purchases
£1000F = (£6 – Actual price) × 1000 kg
£1000F = £6000 – 1000AP
1000AP = £5000
AP = £5 per kg

Actual material cost = 1000 kg × £5 = £5000

iv. Standard hours per unit of output = $\dfrac{\text{Budgeted hours (1125)}}{\text{Budgeted output (1500 units)}}$

= 0.75 hours

Standard wage rate = Budgeted labour cost
(£4500)/Budgeted hours (1125) = £4
Labour efficiency variance = (Standard hours – Actual
hours) × Standard rate
£150A = (1550 × 0.75 = 1162.5 – Actual hours) × £4
– £150 = £4650 – 4AH
4AH = £4800

Actual hours = 1200

v.

Total labour variance = Standard cost – Actual cost
(£200A + £150A)   = (1550 × 0.75 hrs × £4) –
Actual cost
£350A = £4650 – Actual cost

Actual cost = £5000

vi.

Standard variable overhead cost per unit

= $\dfrac{\text{Budgeted variable overheads (2250)}}{\text{Budgeted output (1500 units)}}$

= £1.50 hours

Total variable overhead variance = Standard cost – Actual
cost
(£600A + £75A) = (1550 × £1.50 = £2325) – Actual cost
£675A = £2325 – Actual cost

Actual cost = £3000

vii.

Fixed overhead expenditure variance = Budgeted cost –
Actual cost
£2500F = £4500 – Actual cost

Actual cost = £2000

b. See Chapter 17 for an explanation of the causes of the direct
material usage, direct labour rate and sales volume variances.

17.20 a. The variances shown below have been calculated using the
formulae presented in Exhibit 17.7.

Budgeted profit (4000 × £28)		112 000
Sales Volume Profit Variance (3200 – 4000) £28		(22 400)A
Standard profit on actual sales		89 600
Sales margin price variance		
[(£225 – £192) – (£220 – £192)] × 3200		16 000F
		105 600

Cost variances

		Fav	Adv
Material Usage	[(3600 × 25) – 80 000] £3.2	32 000	
Material Price	(3.2 – 3.5) 80 000		24 000
Labour efficiency	[(4 × 3600) – 16 000)] £8		12 800
Labour rate	(8 – 7) 16 000	16 000	
Var O/H eff	[(4 × 3600) – 16 000)] £4		6 400
Var O/H exp	(£4 × 16 000) – 60 000	4 000	
Fixed O/H exp	(256 000 – 196 000)	60 000	
Fixed O/H eff	[(4 × 3600) – 16 000)] £16		25 600
Fixed O/H capacity	[16 000 – (4 × 4000)] £16	nil	
		112 000	68 800
Actual profit			43 200
			148 800

b. It appears that in the past budgets have been set based on easily
attainable standards but apart from output the standard costs
have remained unchanged. It is possible that cost targets
therefore reflect easily attainable standards that may not
provide sufficient motivation to implement cost efficiencies. In
terms of output a challenging target has been set that is
significantly in excess of past output. Not surprisingly this
output has not been met and it is possible that such a difficult
target may have a detrimental impact on the motivation of the
sales staff that are responsible for achieving the extra output. In
terms of the managers responsible for the cost variances they
are not affected by the more challenging output levels because
flexible budgeting principles are applied whereby cost
variances are based on the actual output achieved.

The adverse sales volume variance reflects the fact that a
very demanding budget has been set with the budget being
increased from the previous average volume of 3400 benches
to 4000 benches. The sales price and sales volume variance
may be inter-related and the increase in price may explain why
actual sales of 3200 benches were lower than the previous
average of 3400 benches.

Better quality materials have been purchased and this has
not been reflected in the standards. This may have contributed
to the favourable material price variance. The use of lower
skilled labour may account for the favourable wage rate
variance but this may also explain the adverse labour efficiency
variance. Because new labour has been introduced there may
be an initial learning effect. The adverse labour efficiency also
accounts for the overhead efficiency variances. The value of the
fixed overhead efficiency variance is questionable for control
purposes (i.e. it is a sunk cost) and variable overheads may not
vary proportionately with labour hours. The fixed overhead
expenditure variance is very large and requires further
investigation because discretionary expenditure may have been
extensively reduced and this may have a detrimental long-term
impact.

c. Adopting a marginal costing approach will result in the
budgeted profit being identical (£112 000) to the marginal
costing profit since budgeted output equals budgeted sales. The
only differences in the variances calculated in (a) relate to the
sales volume margin variance and the fixed overhead volume
variances. The sales volume variance will now be expressed in
terms of unit contribution margin (800 units at £92 = £73 600
Adverse) compared with an adverse variance of £22 400 with
absorption costing. With the marginal costing system fixed
overheads are not unitized and assigned to the products so
volume capacity and efficiency variances do not apply. The
marginal costing reconciliation statement will be as follows:

	£
Budgeted profit	112 000
Sales volume contribution margin variance	(73 600) A
Standard contribution on sales	38 400
Sales margin price variance (unchanged)	16 000F
Cost variances excluding fixed overhead volume variances (£43 200 + £25 600)	68 800F
Actual profit	123 200

Note that the marginal costing profit is £25 600 lower than the absorption costing profit because closing stocks are now restated at variable cost (400 × £128 = £51 200) instead of absorption cost (£76 800). Therefore, one of the reasons for the increase in profit achieved by the new managing director shown in part (a) relates to the increase in stock levels of 400 units that has enabled fixed overheads of £25 600 to be included in the closing stock and deferred as an expense to the next period. Marginal costing advocates that such costs are period costs. The revised statement shows a truer picture of the impact of failing to achieve the budgeted sales volume with an adverse variance of £73 600 being reported compared with a variance of £22 400 with the absorption costing profit. Nevertheless, it should be noted that there has been a significant improvement on average past profits of £56 800 (3400 units at a contribution of £92 per unit less fixed costs of £256 000). However, £60 000 of this has been due to a decrease in fixed costs. It can be concluded that the absorption costing profit statement tends to overstate the impact of the actions implemented on the profit for the period.

17.21 a.

			(£)
Standard cost for actual production (W1)			31 638
Material variances:	Favourable	Adverse	
	(£)	(£)	
Price (W2)	85		
Usage (W3)	196		
Labour variances:			
Rate (W4)		154	
Overtime (W4)		100	
Efficiency (W5)		250	
Variable overhead efficiency (W6)		30	
Overhead expenditure variance (W7)	__	288	
	281	822	541A
Actual cost			32 179

Workings

(W1) Variable cost per unit:	(£)
Direct materials	49
Direct labour	25
Variable overhead	3
	77

Standard cost for actual production:		
Variable cost	22 638	(294 × £77)
Fixed cost	9 000	
	31 638	

Note that the above calculation is based on a variable costing basis, with fixed costs treated as a period cost.
(W2) Material price variance: [£7 − (£14 125/2030)] × 2030 = £85F
(W3) Material usage variance: [(294 × 7 = 2058) − 2030] × £7 = £196F
(W4) Wage rate variance: [£5 − (£7854/1520)] × 1520 = £254A
    £100 of the variance is due to overtime (40 hrs at £2.50)
(W5) Labour efficiency: [(294 × 5 = 1470) − 1520] × £5 = £250A
(W6) Variable overhead efficiency: [(294 × 5 = 1470) − 1520] × £0.60 = £30A
(W7) Overhead expenditure: [£9000 + (1520 × £0.60)] − £10 200 = £288A

b. A variable costing approach has been adopted in (a). Therefore the fixed overheads are not unitized and included in the product costs. Consequently, a fixed overhead volume variance does not arise. With a variable costing system, the fixed overhead volume variance is not considered to be of economic significance, since fixed overheads are a sunk cost. The fixed overhead expenditure variance should be calculated, because actual expenditure may be different from budget, and is therefore of economic significance. It is not possible to separate the expenditure variance into the fixed and variable elements from the information given in the question. In practice, the variances should be separated, since this will provide more useful control information. Note that the variable overhead efficiency variance is included with the labour variances, since this is due to labour efficiency.

An alternative presentation would have been to calculate the variances based on an absorption costing system. This approach would result in the following additional variances:

Volume capacity [1520 − (300(W1) × 5)] × £6	=	£120 F
Volume efficiency [(294 × 5 = 1470) − 1520] × £6	=	£300 A
Volume variance		180 A

The revised report is as follows:

	(£)
Standard cost for actual production (294 × £107)	31 458

	Favourable	Adverse	
Variances calculated in (a)		541	
Volume capacity	120		
Volume efficiency	__	300	
Actual cost	120	841	721A
			32 179

Note that fixed overheads are now unitized and charged to production at £30 per unit. This approach is necessary for external reporting, but is questionable for cost control. The amounts attached to the volume capacity and efficiency variances have no economic significance because the fixed overheads are a sunk cost.
Working
(W1) Budgeted fixed overheads are £9000 and the budgeted rate per unit is £30. Therefore budgeted production is 300 units (9000/30).

c. For a description of the approaches see 'Establishing cost standards' in Chapter 17 and 'Engineering methods' Chapter 23. Note that the approaches outlined in Chapter 17 also refer to engineering methods. If the product has been produced in the past the standard quantity can be estimated from historical records. The limitation of this approach is that standard quantities might be set that incorporate existing inefficiencies. Any adjustments from the historical standard are likely to be resisted unless inducements are offered. The advantage of using historical records is that it avoids the intensive and expensive studies of operations (e.g. time and motion studies) which are associated with engineering methods. Operatives may also be hostile to a standard costing system if time and motion studies are employed to set standard times.

The advantage of engineering methods is that the most efficient methods of operating are established and rigorous scientific methods are used to set standards. This might result in tight standards that are not internalized by the budgetees. It is therefore important that production staff participate in setting the standards.

It is normally possible to set reliable quantity standards, but this is unlikely to be the case with price standards. Price changes are normally due to external factors that are beyond the control of the purchasing officer (for materials) or the personnel officer (for wages rates). It is likely that price variances are due to incorrect forecasts rather than purchasing performance. Nevertheless, feedback information should be produced indicating the ability of the purchasing officer to predict future prices. This feedback might help to improve the accuracy of future forecasts of material prices.

A major problem in setting standards is that future changes might occur that were not envisaged when the standard was set. It is therefore important that standards be reviewed frequently and changes made. Wherever possible, variances should be split into planning and operational variances.

17.22 a. See 'purposes of standard costing' in Chapter 17 for the answer to this question.

b. See 'Types of cost standards' in Chapter 17 for the answer. Currently attainable standards are generally considered to be appropriate for meeting all of the purposes specified in (a).

c. Standard costing is best suited to manufacturing organizations but it can be applied to activities within service organizations where output can be measured and there are clearly defined input/output relationships. For a discussion of how standard costing might be affected by modern initiatives see 'criticisms of standard costing' and 'future role of standard costing' in Learning Notes 18.4 and 18.5 on the website.

d. The answer to this question could discuss the problem of the joint price/usage variance (see Chapter 17) and the limitations of fixed overhead variances for cost control purposes (see also Chapter 17). In addition, the answer could question the linking of direct labour hours to overhead variances since overheads may be caused by cost drivers other than direct labour.

Chapter 18

18.10 a.

Material	Actual mix (litres)	Standard mix (litres)	Difference	Standard price (£)	Variance (£)
X	984	885.6 (40%)	98.4A	2.50	246.0A
Y	1230	1328.4 (60%)	98.4F	3.00	295.2F
	2214	2214.0			49.2F

Answer = B

b. Expected output = 73.8 units (2314/30)
Actual output = 72 units
Standard cost per unit of output = £84
Yield variance = 1.8 units × £84 = £151.20A

Answer = D

18.11 Budgeted average price = [(£100 × 100) + (£50 × 150) + (£35 × 250)]/500 = £52.50

The market share variance is calculated as follows:
(Actual market share – budgeted market share) ×
(Actual industry volume × budgeted average selling price)
(494/2650 – 500/2500) × (2650 × £52.50) = £1890A

Sales mix variance calculation:

Product	Actual sales (units)	Actual sales in budgeted mix	Difference	Budgeted price (£)	Variance (£)
R	108	98.8 (20%)	9.2F	100	920F
S	165	148.2 (30%)	16.8F	50	840F
T	221	247.0 (50%)	26.0A	35	910A
	494	494.0			850F

Answer = E

18.12 a. Market size variance = (Budgeted market share percentage) × (Actual industry sales – budgeted industry sales) × budgeted contribution
= (15 000/75 000) × (10% × 75 000) × £80 = £120 000A

Answer = C

b. The market share variance is calculated as follows:
(Actual market share – budgeted market share) ×
(Actual industry volume × budgeted average contribution)
[(13 000/67 500) – 0.20] (67 500 × £80) = £40 000A

Answer = A

18.13 a. Material price:
(standard price – actual price) × actual quantity
(£3 – £4) × 22 000   = £22 000 A

Material usage:
(standard quantity – actual quantity) × standard price ((1400 × 15 = 21 000) – 22 000) × £3   = 3000 A

Wage rate:
(standard rate – actual rate) × actual hours
(£4 – £5) × 6800   = £6800 A

Labour efficiency:
((1400 × 5 = 7000) – 6800) × £4   = £800 F

Fixed overhead expenditure:
(budgeted fixed overheads – actual fixed overheads) (1000 × £5 = £5000 – £6000)   = £1000 A

Volume efficiency:
(standard hrs – actual hrs) × FOAR
(1400 × 5 = 7000 – 6800) × £1   = 200 F

Volume capacity:
(actual hrs – budgeted hrs) × FOAR
(6800 – 5000) × £1   = £1800 F

Variable overhead efficiency:
(standard hrs – actual hrs) × VOAR
(7000 – 6800) × £2   = £400 F

Variable overhead expenditure:
(flexed budgeted variable overheads – actual variable overheads) (6800 × £2 – £11 000)   = £2600 F

Sales margin price:
(actual margin – standard margin) ×
actual sales volume
(£102 – £80 = £22 – £20) × 1200   = £2400 F

Sales margin volume:
(actual sales – budgeted sales) × standard margin (1200 – 1000) × £20   = 4000 F

Reconciliation of budgeted and actual profit

			(£)
Budgeted profit			20 000
	Adverse (£)	Favourable (£)	
Sales margin price		2 400	
Sales margin volume		4 000	
Material price	22 000		
Material usage	3 000		
Wage rate	6 800		
Labour efficiency		800	
Fixed overhead expenditure	1 000		
Fixed overhead efficiency		200	
Fixed overhead capacity		1 800	
Variable overhead expenditure		2 600	
Variable overhead efficiency		400	
	32 800	12 200	
Net adverse variance			20 600
Actual profit/(loss)			(600)

b.

Stores ledger control account

Creditors	66 000	WIP	63 000
		Material usage variance	3 000
	66 000		66 000

Variance accounts

Creditors	22 000	Wages control	
Stores ledger		(labour efficiency)	800
(material usage)	3 000	Fixed overhead (volume)	2 000
Wages control (wage rate)	6 800	Variable overhead	
Fixed overhead		(expenditure)	2 600
(expenditure)	1 000	Variable overhead	
		(efficiency)	400
		Costing P + L a/c (balance)	27 000
	32 800		32 800

Costing P + L account

Cost of sales	96 000	Sales	122 400
Variance account		Loss for period	600
(net variances)	27 000		
	123 000		123 000

WIP control account

Stores ledger	63 000	Finished goods stock	112 000
Wages control	28 000		
Fixed factory overhead	7 000		
Variable factory overhead	14 000		
	112 000		112 000

Wages control account

Wages accrued account	34 000	WIP	28 000
Labour efficiency variance	800	Wage rate variance	6 800
	34 800		34 800

Fixed factory overhead account

Expense creditors	6 000	WIP	7 000
Volume variance	2 000	Expenditure variance	1 000
	8 000		8 000

Variable factory overhead account

Expense creditors	11 000	WIP	14 000
Expenditure variance	2 600		
Efficiency variance	400		
	14 000		14 000

Finished goods stock

WIP	112 000	Cost of sales	96 000
		Closing stock c/fwd	16 000
	112 000		112 000

Cost of sales account

Finished goods stock	96 000	Cost P + L a/c	96 000

18.14 a.

	(£)	(£)
(i) Actual quantity at actual prices (given)		17 328
(ii) Actual quantity in actual mix at standard prices		
F 1680 × £4	6720	
G 1650 × £3	4950	
H 870 × £6	5220	16 890
(iii) Actual quantity in standard mix at standard prices		
F (4200 × 15/35 = 1800) × £4	7200	
G (4200 × 12/35 = 1440) × £3	4320	
H (4200 × 8/35 = 960) × £6	5760	17 280

Material price variance
= (Standard price – Actual price) Actual quantity
= (Actual quantity × Standard price) – Actual cost
= (ii) – (i)   438A
Mix variance = (iii) – (ii)   390F
Yield variance = (Actual yield – Standard yield for actual
input) × standard cost per unit of output
= (3648 – (4200/35 × 32 = 3840)) × £4.50
(i.e. £144/32)   864A
Material usage variance = Mix variance (£390F) + Yield
variance (£864A)   474A
or Standard cost for actual output (3648 × £4.50 = £16 416)
– Actual quantity at standard prices (£16 890)
= £474A

b. *Mix variances*

	Total	F	G	H
Standard mix		1800	1440	960
Actual usage		1680	1650	870
Difference		120	210	90
Standard price		£4	£3	£6
Variance	390F	£480F	£630A	£540F
Price variances				
Standard price (£)		4.00	3.00	6.00
Actual price (£)		4.25	2.80	6.40
Actual quantity used		1680	1650	870
Variance	438A	420A	330F	348A

c. *Labour cost variance*

(Standard cost for actual production) – (Actual cost)
Department P (120 batches × £40 = £4800 – £6360)   £1560A
Department Q (120 × £12 = £1440 – £1512)   £72A

Labour efficiency variance

(Standard hours for actual production – Actual hours) × Standard rate
Department P (120 batches × 4 hours = 480 hours – 600 hours)
× £10   £1200A
Department Q (120 × 2 hours = 240 hours – 270 hours) × £6   £180A

Labour rate variance

(Standard rate – Actual rate) × Actual hours
Department P (£10 – £10.60) × 600   £360A
Department Q (£6 – £5.60) × 270   £108F

d. *Total sales margin variance*

(Actual margin) – (Budgeted margin)
(3648 kg at (£16.75 – £6.125ᵃ)) – (4096 kg at (£16 – £6.125))   £1688A

Sales volume variance

(Actual sales volume – Budgeted sales volume) × Standard margin
(3648 – 4096) at (£16 – £6.125)   £4424A

Sales margin price variance

(Actual margin – Standard margin) × Actual sales volume
((£16.75 – £6.125) – (£16 – £6.125)) × 3648   £2736F

Note
ᵃthe standard cost per kg sold is £196/32 kg = £6.125

e. The answer should indicate that a different mix of the materials from the standard mix was used. Less of materials F and H and more of the lower cost material G were used compared with the standard mix. This may explain the adverse yield variance. Also the purchase price for material G was less than standard which may indicate the purchase of poorer quality materials which may have had an adverse impact on the yield.

18.15 a. The company uses a standard costing system. Therefore sales variances will be expressed in profit margins rather than contribution margins. The calculations of the standard profits per unit are as follows:

Budgeted machine hours = (10 000 × 0.3) + (13 000 × 0.6) + (9 000 × 0.8) = 18 000 hours
Overhead absorption rate = 81 000/18 000 = £4.50 per machine hour

Product	B(£)	R(£)	K(£)
Direct material	5.40 (3 × 1.80)	4.10 (1.25 × 3.28)	4.85 (1.94 × 2.50)
Direct labour	3.25 (0.5 × 6.50)	5.20 (0.8 × 6.50)	4.55 (0.7 × 6.50)
Fixed production overhead	1.35 (0.3 × 4.50)	2.70 (0.6 × 4.50)	3.60 (0.8 × 4.50)
Standard cost	10.00	12.00	13.00
Selling price	14.00	15.00	18.00
Standard profit	4.00	3.00	5.00

(1) Budgeted sales quantity in standard mix at standard profit margins

Product	Quantity	Standard profit	£
B	10 000	£4	40 000
R	13 000	£3	39 000
K	9 000	£5	45 000
	32 000		124 000

(2) Actual sales quantity in actual mix at actual profit margins (i.e. actual selling price – standard cost)

		Actual selling price	
Product	Quantity	less standard cost	£
B	9 500	(14.5 – 10.0)	42 750
R	13 500	(15.5 – 12.0)	47 250
K	8 500	(19.0 – 13.0)	51 000
	31 500		141 000

(3) Actual sales quantity in actual mix at standard profit margins

Product	Quantity	Standard profit	£
B	9 500	£4	38 000
R	13 500	£3	40 500
K	8 500	£5	42 500
	31 500		121 000

(4) Actual sales quantity in standard mix at standard profit margins

Product	Quantity	Standard profit	£
B	9 843.75 (10/32)	£4	39 375
R	12 796.875 (13/32)	£3	38 390
K	8 859.375 (9/32)	£5	44 297
	31 500		122 062

	£	£
Sales margin price variance (2 – 3)		20 000 (F)
Sales margin mix variance (3 – 4)	1 062 (A)	
Sales margin quantity variance (4 – 1)	1 938 (A)	
Sales margin volume variance (3 – 1)		3 000 (A)
Total sales margin variance (2 – 1)		17 000 (F)

Reconciliation	£	£	£
Budgeted sales at standard profit			124 000
Sales price variance		20 000 (F)	
Sales mix profit variance	1 062 (A)		
Sales quantity profit variance	1 928 (A)		
Sales volume profit variance		3 000 (A)	
			17 000 (F)
Actual sales at actual prices less standard cost			141 000

b. The sales margin mix variance explains how much of sales volume margin variance is due to a change in sales mix. For example, the adverse sales margin mix of £1062 calculated in (a) indicates that the actual sales mix contained a greater proportion of low margin products and a lower proportion of high margin products than the planned budgeted proportions. The following schedule shows the impact of the change in sales mix:

Product	Standard mix	Actual mix	Difference	Standard profit	£
B	9 844	9 500	(344)	£4	1 376 (A)
R	12 797	13 500	703	£3	2 109 (F)
K	8 859	8 500	(359)	£5	1 795 (A)
	31 500	31 500			1 062 (A)

It can be seen that more of the lowest margin product (product R) than the budgeted mix were sold. In contrast, the actual sales mix contained a lower proportion of the higher margin products.

The sales margin mix variance is of significance only when there is an identifiable relationship between the products and these relationships are incorporated into the planning process. Where relationships between products are not expected, the mix variance does not provide meaningful information, since it incorrectly suggests that a possible cause of the sales margin variance arises from a change in the mix.

c. For the answer to this question see 'Operation of a standard costing system' and 'Establishing cost standards' in Chapter 17. In particular, the answer should describe the different stages outlined in Figure 17.1.

18.16 a. The revised standards are as follows:

Direct material price = £2.30 × 1.03 = £2.369 per kg.
Direct material usage = 3 × 0.95 = £2.85 kg. per unit
Wage rate = £12 × 1.04 = £12.48 per hour
Labour usage = 1.25/0.9 = 1.3888 hours per unit

Price/rate variances

Planning variance = (Original standard price – revised standard price) × actual quantity
Material price = (£2.30 – £2.369) × (122 000 × 2.80 = 341 600) = £23 570 (A)
Wage rate = (£12 – £12.48) × (1.30 × 122 000 = 158 600) = £76 128 (A)
Operational variance = (Revised standard price – actual price) × actual quantity
Material price = (£2.369 – £2.46) × 341 600 = £31 086 (A)
Wage rate = (£12.48 – £12.60) × 158 600 = £19 032 (A)

Quantity variances

Planning variance = (Original standard quantity – revised standard quantity) × standard price
Material usage = [(122 000 × 3 = 366 000) – (122 000 × 2.85 = 347 700)] × £2.30 = £42 090 (F)
Labour efficiency = [(122 000 × 1.25 = 152 500) – (122 000 × 1.3888 = 169 444)] × £12 = £203 333 (A)
Operational variance = (Revised standard quantity – actual quantity) × standard price
Material usage = (122 000 × 2.85 = 347 700 – 341 600) × £2.30 = £14 030 (F)
Labour efficiency = (122 000 × 1.3888 = 169 444.44 – 158 600) × £12 = £130 133 (F)

b. The direct labour and material variances based on the standard cost data applied through the period consists of the sum of the planning and operational variances:

Material price = £23 570 + £31 086 = £54 656 (A)
Wage rate = £76 128 + £19 032 = £95 160
Material usage = £42 090 + £14 030 = £56 120 (F)
Labour efficiency = £203 333 – £130 133 = £73 200 (A)

c. The variances calculated in (b) are based on the circumstances envisaged when the standards were originally set. When the circumstances have changed actual performance should be compared with a standard that reflects the changed conditions. If the standards are not changed the reported variances will include uncontrollable planning variances. For example, in (b) an adverse labour efficiency variance of £73 200 is reported but the approach adopted in (a) highlights that it consists of an adverse planning variance of £203 333 and a favourable operational variance of £130 133. Thus a different picture emerges when the variances are separated into uncontrollable planning variances and controllable operational variances. Attention is also directed for the need to update the standards.

d. See 'Investigation of variances' in Chapter 18 for the answer to this question.

18.17 a. Standard cost of materials per kg of output (0.65 kg × £4) + (0.3 kg × £6) + (0.2 kg × £2.50) = £4.90
Standard overhead rate = £12 000/Budgeted standard quantity of ingredient F (4000 × 0.65) = £4.6154 per kg of ingredient F
Standard overhead rate per kg of output of FDN = 0.65 kg × £4.6154 = £3

	(£)
Standard cost of actual output:	
Materials (4200 × £4.90)	20 580
Overheads (4200 × £3)	12 600
	34 180
Actual cost of output	
Materials	20 380
Overheads (£7800 + £4800)	12 600
	32 980

Variance calculations

Material price variance = (Standard price – Actual price)Actual quantity
= (Standard price × Actual quantity) – Actual cost
= (£4 × 2840) + (£6 × 1210) + (£2.50 × 860)
= £20 770 – £20 380   390A

Material yield variance = (Actual yield – Standard yield) × Standard material cost per unit of output
= (4200 – 4910 materials used/1.15) × £4.90   341A

Material mix variance
(Actual quantity in actual mix at standard prices) – (Actual quantity in standard mix at standard prices)

			(£)	
F	(4910 × 0.65/1.15 = 2775 – 2840) × £4		260A	
D	(4910 × 0.30/1.15 = 1281 – 1210) × £6		426F	
N	(4910 × 0.20/1.15 = 854 – 860) × 2.50		15A	151F

Overhead efficiency variance = (Standard quantity of ingredient F – Actual quantity) × standard overhead rate per kg of ingredient F
= (4200 × 0.65 = 2730 – 2840) × £4.6154   508A

Overhead capacity variance = (Budgeted input of ingredient F – Actual input) × standard overhead rate per kg of ingredient F
= (4000 × 0.65 = 2600 – 2840) × £4.6154   1108A

Overhead expenditure = Budgeted cost (£12 000) – Actual cost (£12 600)   600A

Reconciliation of standard cost and actual cost of output

	(£)	(£)
Standard cost of actual production		33 180
Material variances		
Material price variance	390F	
Material yield variance	341A	
Material mix variance	151F	200F
Overhead variances:		
Overhead efficiency	508A	
Overhead capacity	1108A	
Overhead expenditure	600A	Nil
Actual cost		32 980

b.

Standard number of deliveries (4000 × 1.15 kg)/460 kg	10
Standard cost per supplier delivery (£4000/10)	£400
Standard number of despatches to customers (4000/100)	40
Standard cost per customer despatch (£8000/40)	£200
Actual output exceeds budgeted output by 5 per cent (4200/4000)	

Activity-based costing reconciliation statement

		(£)
Standard cost for actual output:		
Deliveries (1.05 × 10 deliveries = 10.5 × £400 per delivery)	4200	
Despatches (1.05 × 40 despatches = 42 × £200 per despatch)	8400	12 600
Activity usage variance		
Deliveries (10.5 – 12) × £400	600A	
Despatches (42 – 38) × £200	800F	200F
Activity expenditure variances		
Deliveries (12 × £400 = £4800 – £4800)	Nil	
Despatches (38 × £200 = £7600 – £7800)	200A	200A
Actual overheads		12 600

Note that the expenditure variance has been flexed. An alternative presentation would be to work in whole numbers only since 10.5 deliveries is not feasible.

c. See 'Designing ABC systems' in Chapter 10 for the answer to this question. In particular, the answer should stress the need to interview the employees engaged on the activities to ascertain what causes the activities.

18.18 a. i. *Decision tree if an investigation is carried out*

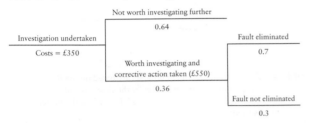

It is assumed that the £550 correction cost applies to all variances that the initial investigation indicates are worthy of further investigation. The expected cost if the investigation is carried out is:

$$£350 + 0.36 × £550 \text{ (corrective action)}$$
$$+ 0.36 × 0.3 × £2476^a \text{ (continuing variance)} = £815$$

Note
^{a}£2476 represents the PV of £525 for 5 months at 2% (£525 × 4.7135) for variances that are not eliminated.

ii. *Decision tree if an investigation is not carried out*

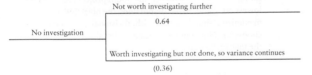

The expected cost if no investigation is undertaken is:

$$0.36 × £525 × 4.7135 = £891$$

b. Applying the expected value decision rule, the company should follow a policy of investigating variances as a matter of routine. The expected cost of investigation is £815, compared with an expected cost if no investigation is undertaken of £891. On average, the benefits from investigation are £75 per variance.

c. Examples of category 1 variances include:
  i. The variance is due to random uncontrollable factors and is under control. (See 'Random uncontrollable factors' in Chapter 18 for an explanation.)
  ii. Where the cause is obvious (e.g. a machine fault) and future action has been taken to remedy the situation.
  Examples of category 2 variances include:
  i. Excessive usage of materials and labour due possibly to wrong working practices on a repetitive operation which is likely to continue if not corrected.
  ii. Where the variance is significant and exceeds a specified percentage of standard usage.

d. The above analysis assumes that the average variance is £525 and additional costs of £525 in excess of standard continue for five months. Presumably, working practices are changed every five months. Costs of investigation and corrective action are £350 and £550 irrespective of the amount of the variance. It would therefore be appropriate to determine the value of variances which justify investigation. Let x = savings per month. The expected cost of investigation is equal to the expected cost of no investigation where:

$$£350 + (0.36 × £550) + (0.36 × 0.3 × 4.7135x) = 0.36 × 4.7135x$$
$$x = £461$$

Only variances in excess of £461 should be investigated.

18.19 a. See 'Criticisms of standard costing' and 'The future role of standard costing' in Learning Notes 18.4 and 18.5 on the website for the answer to this question.

b. The creation of budget centres at the lowest defined management level would enable managers to participate in the budget setting process. Lower level managers would therefore be involved in the budget negotiation process, and this should improve communication with their superiors and create a greater awareness of the need for the activities of the budget centres to be in congruence with the goals of the organization. By participating in the process, it is claimed that managers will be more committed and strive to achieve their budgets. The creation of budget centres should also improve a manager's attitude towards the budget system. In particular, the potential for improved communication and the acceptance of budgets as relevant standards to achieve should lead to improved motivation.

Creating budget centres at lower levels will place greater administrative demands on operating the system and lengthen the budget preparation period.

In addition, the cost of reporting will be increased. Whether or not the additional benefits exceed the additional costs is likely to depend on the circumstances of the company. For example, in an environment where an organization faces considerable uncertainty or where an organization undertakes a diverse range of activities, decentralization and the creation of budget centres at lower levels might be preferable. However, where the activities of an organization can be programmed in detail and close coordination and swift reaction is necessary it might be preferable not to create budget centres at lower levels. In particular, if the activities of budget centres are heavily dependent on the activities of other centres, there is a greater likelihood that the benefits from increased motivation will not outweigh the administrative and coordination difficulties.

18.20 For the answer to these questions see 'Criticisms of standard costing' and 'The future role of standard costing' in Learning Notes 18.4 and 18.5 on the website. In part (c) the answer should also include a discussion of the role of non-financial measures. See the section on operation processes in Chapter 22 for a discussion of non-financial measures in non-manufacturing organizations. The answer could also include a discussion of activity-based management. This topic is covered in Chapter 21.

18.21 a. For the answer to this question see 'Investigation of variances' in Chapter 18. In particular the answer should explain that variances may be due to several causes, and not all are worthy of investigation. In addition the answer should stress the possible approaches to investigating variances:
  i. *Use of rule of thumb percentages:* For example, all variances in excess of 10 per cent of standard cost might be investigated. This approach ignores the costs and benefits of investigation.
  ii. *Use of statistical quality control charts:* Control limits are set using an analysis of historical results to indicate suitable confidence intervals. This method utilizes a statistical probability approach of not investigating a variance unless there is a high probability that the process is out of control.
  iii. *Use of a statistical decision theory approach:* This approach is described in Learning Note 18.3 on the website.
  It is unlikely that statistical decision theory can be applied in practice, because of the difficulty in estimating costs and benefits of investigation. Nevertheless, the approach provides a

suitable model that gives a manager an insight into the important factors that should be considered when deciding whether or not to investigate a variance. Experience and an understanding of the model is likely to be the best way of establishing whether or not investigation is worthwhile.

b. See Chapter 16 for the answer to this question.

i. The level of budget difficulty is likely to have a motivational influence on a manager's actions to eliminate variances. If a manager believes a target to be unattainable, he or she is unlikely to strive to eliminate variances. (See 'The effect of budget difficulty on motivation and performance' in Chapter 16.)

ii. Managers may manipulate information in order to avoid adverse variances. This is most likely to occur if a budget-constrained style of performance evaluation is used. Genuine performance improvements are most likely to occur if a profit-conscious style of evaluation is used. For a detailed discussion of styles of evaluation see 'Side effects from using accounting information in performance evaluation' in Chapter 16.

iii. Managers are most likely to strive to eliminate variances if they accept the budget and this becomes a motivational target. Budget acceptance is more likely to be achieved by participation and not by imposed budgets. See 'Participation in the budgeting and target setting process' in Chapter 16 for a more detailed discussion of the influence of participation on acceptance of budgets.

iv. The extent to which performance appraisal, future promotion and cash bonuses are tied to meeting the budget will provide a major motivation stimulus to meeting the budget. However, if too much stress is placed on meeting the budget, there is a danger that over-generous budgets will be sought or information will be distorted so as to avoid adverse variances.

v. Performance reports comparing actual with budget should be provided soon after the end of the budget period (weekly or monthly). A manager is more likely to be motivated to eliminate variances if feedback reports are timely and understandable. A climate of failure and punishment should be avoided, and the emphasis should be on *helping* managers to eliminate adverse variances.

Chapter 19

19.14

	£m
Profit	89.20
Add back:	
Current depreciation (120 × 20%)	24.00
Development costs ((£9.60 × 2/3)	6.40
Less: Replacement depreciation (£168 × 20%)	33.60
Adjusted profit	86.00
Less: Cost of capital charge (13% × £168)[a]	21.84
EVA	64.16

Note:

[a]13% × [Fixed assets (£168 − £33.6) + Working capital (£27.2) + Development costs (£6.4)]

Answer = A

19.15

	£m	£m
Net profit after tax		8.6
Add:		
Interest	2.3	
Development costs	6.3	
Advertising	1.6	10.2
Less development costs (1/3)		(2.1)
		16.7
Less cost of capital charge (£30m × 13%)		(3.9)
EVA		12.8

19.16 a. Return on investment (ROI)

Division A	£
Profit	35 000
Net assets	150 000

Return on investment = 35 000/150 000 = 23.3%

Division B	£
Profit	70 000
Net assets	325 000

Return on investment = 70 000/325 000% = 21.5%

Residual income (RI)

Division A = £35 000 − (150 000 × 0.15) = £12 500
Division B = £70 000 − (325 000 × 0.15) = £21 250

Division A has a higher ROI but a lower residual income.

b. Return on investment would be the better measure when comparing divisions as it is a relative measure (i.e. based on percentage returns)

c. Appropriate aspects of performance include:

- competitiveness;
- financial performance;
- quality of service;
- flexibility;
- innovation;
- resource utilization efficiency.

19.17 a.
Divisional management bonuses are based on the ROI obtained for each of the first two years by the new investment. The ROI calculations for the first two years for each of the projects are as follows:

Project		North	East	South
Year 1	Cashflow	6 000.0	11 500.0	12 000.0
	Depreciation	(6 000.0)	(8 000.0)	(6,000.0)
	Profit/(loss)	nil	3 500.0	6 000.0
	Average invested capital	21 000.0	20 000.0	21 000.0
	Return on Investment (ROI)	nil	17.50%	28.57%
Year 2	Cashflow	8 000.0	11 500.0	10 000.0
	Depreciation	(6 000.0)	(8 000.0)	(6 000.0)
	Profit	2 000.0	3 500.0	4 000.0
	Average invested capital	15 000.0	12 000.0	15 000.0
	Return on Investment (ROI)	13.33%	29.17%	26.67%

It can be seen that the South project yields the highest ROI over the two year period. Therefore divisional management are likely to choose this project since it maximizes the performance rating and bonus. However, the South project generates the lowest NPV and, based on pursuing the objective of maximizing shareholder wealth, divisional management should choose the North project because it has the highest NPV. Thus the management incentive plan is encouraging dysfunctional behaviour by adopting a short-term focus which is detrimental to the organizations as a whole. Ideally performance measures should encourage behaviour that motivates managers to take decisions that are in the long-term interests of the organizations as a whole.

b. The answer to this question should explain how residual income is more likely to overcome some of the dysfunctional consequences of ROI. You should refer to the section on residual income in Chapter 19 for an explanation of the issues involved. For an explanation of how annuity depreciation might prove to be superior you should refer to Learning Note 19.1 on the open access website. In particular, your answer should point out that annuity depreciation can only produce a short-term measure that will lead to decisions that are consistent with the NPV rule when net cash flows are constant each year (e.g. the East project).

c. The following NPV calculation discounts the cash flows at 12 per cent based on the assumption that the project has similar risk characteristics to the projects outlined in (a). The NPV of the project without the environmental expenditure is £3 185 million (£5 million annual cash flow × 3.037 cumulative discount factor less the initial investment outlay of £12 million).

The NPVs for the two alternative environmental expenditures are as follows:

Environmental expenditure	£2m	£4m
NPV before environmental expenditure	3.185m	3.185m
Year 4 expenditure (£2m × 0.636 discount factor)	(1.272m)	
Year 4 expenditure (£4m × 0.636 discount factor)		(2.544m)
NPV	1.913m	0.641m

The project has a positive NPV for both levels of environmental expenditure. There is a decline in NPV of £1.272m if the highest level of environmental expenditure is incurred. Therefore management must decide whether a loss on £1.272m is outweighed by pursing socially responsible policies and enhancing their image as a socially responsible organization. Pursuing such a policy has the potential for enhancing longer-term benefits that may be difficult to quantify or specify.

19.18 *Division A*

Both items represent discretionary expenditure. Management can choose to determine whatever is deemed necessary to spend on these activities but the amount of expenditure should seek to maximize long-term profitability. The proposed actions are likely to harm long-term profitability but they will have a beneficial short-term effect on the divisional performance measure. There are no financial accounting issues involved and, although the published accounts are likely to be slightly misleading, there would not be any problem in getting the accounts externally audited. Divisional management are, however, manipulating the budget for their own benefit at the expense of the long-term success of the organization. They are therefore engaging in unethical behaviour.

Division B

This action is an attempt to defer expenditure. The cost of consultancy services received to date should, however, be accrued and provided for in the current year's accounts for the division. This would prevent the divisional management from enhancing the profit for the current period and thus affect the bonuses. A failure to make a provision would be in breach of financial accounting regulations. If management does not make the provision it will be acting in an unethical manner and if the accountant becomes aware of the circumstances it is his, or her, professional duty to insist that the provision is made. Failure to do so would be classed as unethical behaviour. If no provision is made next year's budgeted expenses should be increased to reflect the deferred expenditure. As with division A the divisional managers are motivated to manipulate the results to achieve the budget.

Division C

Financial accounting regulations require that revenues are recognized at the point of delivery. Therefore the action does not contravene financial accounting regulations and there should be no problems with the audit of the accounts. However, future profitability may be impaired because stocks will be very low at the end of the year. This may result in a loss in future profits arising from lost sales from a failure to meet demand and also a loss of customer goodwill. The behaviour is therefore unethical and also requires that some existing customers become involved in the collusion. The motivational desire to obtain the bonus is causing the dysfunctional behaviour.

Comment on whether group management action is necessary

None of the actions are illegal but it is questionable whether managers should be able to earn bonuses arising from the actions. On the other hand divisions have been created to enhance managerial autonomy and any interference by corporate top management will undermine divisional autonomy. Some dysfunctional behaviour is likely to apply with all performance measurement systems and, as long as major dysfunctional consequences do not arise, it could be argued that the actions should be tolerated as part of the costs of decentralization. Non-interference also ensures that the motivational benefits arising from divisional autonomy are not eroded. If major dysfunctional consequences do arise from the current system then it will be necessary for central management to take appropriate action to reduce the harmful side effects. For a discussion of potential actions see 'Addressing the dysfunctional consequences of short-term financial measures' in Chapter 19.

19.19 a. The annual ROI and residual income calculations for each plant are as follows:

	2001	2002	2003	2004	Total
Aromatic					
(1) Net cash flow (£m)	2.4	2.4	2.4	2.4	9.6
(2) Depreciation	1.6	1.6	1.6	1.6	
(3) Profit	0.8	0.8	0.8	0.8	3.2
(4) Cost of capital (16% of 6)	(1.02)	(0.77)	(0.51)	(0.26)	
(5) Residual income	(0.22)	0.03	0.29	0.54	
(6) Opening WDV of asset	6.4	4.8	3.2	1.6	
(7) ROI (Row 3/Row 6)	12.5%	16.67%	25%	50%	
Zoman					
(1) Net cash flow	2.6	2.2	1.5	1.0	7.3
(2) Depreciation	1.3	1.3	1.3	1.3	
(3) Profit	1.3	0.9	0.2	(0.3)	2.1
(4) Cost of capital (16%)	(0.83)	(0.62)	(0.42)	(0.21)	
(5) Residual income	0.47	0.28	(0.22)	(0.51)	
(6) Opening WDV of asset	5.2	3.9	2.6	1.3	
(7) ROI	25%	23%	7.7%	(23%)	

The answer should indicate:

i. Over the whole life of the project both ROI and residual income (RI) favour the Aromatic plant. The average ROI and RI figures are 25 per cent and £0.16m (£0.64m/4) for the Aromatic plant and 20 per cent and £0.005m (£0.02m/4) for the Zoman plant. The ROI calculations are based on expressing the average profits as a percentage of the average investment (defined as one half of the initial capital investment).

ii. An explanation that Mr Elton will favour the Zoman plant because it yields a higher ROI and RI over the first two years. Mr Elton will probably focus on a two-year time horizon because of his personal circumstances, since choosing the Aromatic plant is likely to result in him losing his bonus. Therefore he will choose the plant with the lower NPV and there will be a lack of goal congruence.

iii. Suggestions as to how alternative accounting techniques can assist in reconciling the conflict between accounting performance measures and DCF techniques:

1. Avoiding short-term evaluations and evaluating performance at the end of the project's life. Thus bonuses would be awarded with hindsight;

2. Use alternative asset valuations other than historic cost (e.g. replacement cost);

3. Choose alternative depreciation methods that are most consistent with NPV calculations (e.g. annuity depreciation);

4. Incorporate a range of variables (both financial and non-financial when evaluating managerial performance) that give a better indication of future results that can be expected from current actions.

b. Managers may use pre-tax profits to evaluate divisional performance because it is assumed that taxation is non-controllable. Taxation payable is based on total group profits and present and past capital expenditure rather than individual divisional profitability. After tax cash flows are used to appraise capital investments because the focus is on decision-making and accepting those projects that earn a return in excess of the investors' opportunity cost of capital. To do this IRRs and NPVs should be based on after-tax cash flows.

The following potential problems can arise:

i. Managers may ignore the taxation impact at the decision-making stage because it is not considered when evaluating their performance;

ii. Confusion and demotivation can occur when different criteria are used for decision-making and performance evaluation.

Possible solutions include evaluating divisional profitability after taxes or evaluating performance based on a comparison of budgeted and actual cash flows. Adopting the latter approach is an attempt to ensure that the same criteria is used for decision-making and performance evaluation.

c. Steps that can be taken to avoid dysfunctional behaviour include:

i. Not placing too much emphasis on short-term performance measures and placing greater emphasis on the long term by adopting a profit-conscious style of evaluation.

ii. Focusing on controllable residual income or economic value added combined with asset valuations derived from depreciation models that are consistent with NPV calculations (see Learning Note 19.1 on the website). Alternatively, performance evaluation might be based on a comparison of budgeted and actual cash flows. The budgeted cash flows should be based on cash flows that are used to appraise capital investments.

iii. Supplementing financial performance measures with non-financial measures when evaluating performance (see 'Addressing the dysfunctional consequences of short-term financial measures' in Chapter 19).

19.20 a. *Summary statement I (Straight-line depreciation)*

Year	1	2	3	4	5
	(£000)	(£000)	(£000)	(£000)	(£000)
Investment at start of year	600	480	360	240	120
Net cash flow (40% of sales)	200	200	200	200	200
Less: depreciation	120	120	120	120	120
Net profit	80	80	80	80	80
Less: interest on capitalᵃ	96	76.8	57.6	38.4	19.2
Residue income	(16)	3.2	22.4	41.6	60.8
ROCEᵇ	13.3%	16.7%	22.2%	33.3%	66.7%

Notes

ᵃ16% of investment at the start of the year.

ᵇNet profit expressed as a percentage of the investment at the start of the year.

Calculation of annuity depreciation

	(1)	(2)	(3) = (1) − (2)	(4) = (4) − (3)
		16% interest		
	Annual	on capital	Capital	Capital
Year	repayment	outstanding	repayment	outstanding
	(£000)	(£000)	(£000)	(£000)
0				600.0
1	183.24	96.0	87.24	512.76
2	183.24	82.04	101.20	411.56
3	183.24	65.85	117.39	294.17
4	183.24	47.07	136.17	158.00
5	183.24	25.28	158.00	—

For an explanation of the calculations see Learning Note 19.1 on the website. Note that the annual repayment is determined by dividing the investment of £600 000 by the cumulative discount factor for five years at 16 per cent (3.274 shown in Appendix B).

Summary statement 2 (Annuity depreciation)

Year	1	2	3	4	5
	(£000)	(£000)	(£000)	(£000)	(£000)
Investment at start of year	600	512.76	411.56	294.17	158.00
Net cash flow	200	200	200	200	200
Depreciation	87.24	101.20	117.39	136.17	158.00
Net profit	112.76	98.80	82.61	63.83	42.0
Imputed interest	96.00	82.04	65.85	47.07	25.28
Residual income	16.76	16.76	16.76	16.76	16.72
ROCE	18.8%	19.3%	20.1%	21.7%	26.6%

b. i. Management are motivated to focus only on the outcomes of the first year for any new project because of the criterion used for performance measurement and investment decisions. When straight-line depreciation is used residual income is negative and the ROCE of 13.3 per cent is less than the target return of 20 per cent. Therefore if the focus is only on the performance measures for the first year the project will be rejected even though residual income and ROCE rise steadily throughout the five-year period.

When annuity depreciation is used residual income is positive and constant for each year of the project's life and therefore the proposal would be accepted if the residual income method is used. ROCE is 18.8 per cent and this is less than the target return of 20 per cent and the project would be rejected using this method. However, ROCE ranges from 18.8 per cent to 26.6 per cent when annuity depreciation is used, compared with 13.3 per cent to 66.7 per cent with straight-line depreciation. Therefore, when compared with straight-line depreciation annuity depreciation does not distort ROCE to the same extent.

ii. NPV = £200 000 × cumulative discount factor for 5 years at 16% (3.274) − Investment outlay (£600 000)
= £54 800

The project has a positive NPV and should be accepted. Residual income is the long-run counterpart of NPV. The present value of residual income of £16 760 per year for 5 years discounted at 16 per cent is approximately £54 800. When cash flows are constant and the annuity method of depreciation is used residual income will also be constant. For a more detailed discussion of the relationship between residual income and NPV see Learning Note 19.1 on the website.

c. i.

	Year 1 (straight-line depreciation) (£000)	Year 1 (annuity depreciation) (£000)
Investment at beginning of year	600	600
Net cash flow (40% × £700 000)	280	280
Less:		
Depreciation (see part (a))	(120)	(87.3)
Profit	160	192.7
Less:		
Interest on capital	(96)	(96)
Residual income	64	96.7
ROCE	26.7%	32.1%

ii. *Discounted cash flow approach:*

Year	Physical	Discount factor at 16%	DCF
	(£000)		(£000)
0	(600)	1.000	(600)
1	280	0.862	241.36
2	200	0.743	148.60
3	200	0.641	128.20
4	120	0.552	66.24
5	80	0.476	38.08
		NPV	22.48

iii. Adopting the criteria used by management both projects yield a positive residual income and a ROCE in excess of the target return in the first year using either straight-line or annuity methods of depreciation. The project therefore will be accepted. The project also has a positive NPV and, in this situation, the criteria used by management will be consistent with the NPV decision model. The decline in NPV reflects the fact that sales revenue has declined over the five-year period.

19.21 a. The answer to this question should include much of the content included in the section entitled 'Economic value added' in Chapter 19. In addition, the answer should include the following points:

i. Some of the revenue expenditure, such as research and development and advertising, provide future benefits over several years but financial accounting requirements often require such expenditure to be written off in the year in which they are incurred. This understates the value added during a particular period.

ii. The profits computed to meet financial accounting requirements do not take into account the cost of equity finance provided by the shareholders. The only cost of capital that is taken into account is interest on borrowed funds (i.e. the cost of debt finance). Profits should reflect the cost of both debt and equity finance.

iii. A better measure of the managers' ability to create value is to adjust the traditional financial statements for those expenses that are likely to provide benefits in future periods. The economic value added measure attempts to meet this requirement.

The following comments relate to the treatment of specific adjustments:

Research and development

The expenditure of £2.1 million is added back because it represents an investment that will yield future benefits. Therefore it should be capitalized and allocated to the future periods based on the benefits received in the particular period. The expenditure of £17.4m is added back based on the assumption that the company is continuing to benefit from such expenditures that have previously been written off against profits. There should be an element of this expenditure written off as depreciation based on the value that has been eroded during the period.

Advertising

Advertising expenditure adds value by supporting future sales arising from increasing customer awareness and brand loyalty. Based on the same justification as research and development expenditure, advertising should be capitalized for the EVA calculation and added back to profits. The £10.5m added back in the balance sheet reflects the costs incurred in building up future income. Some of this cost should be depreciated based on the value of future benefits eroded during the period.

Interest and borrowings

The aim is to ascertain whether value is being added for the shareholders in the sense of whether the funds invested in the business generate a return in excess of the opportunity cost of capital (see Chapter 14). To do this a profit figure is calculated that initially does not include any charges for the cost of capital. Interest on borrowings is therefore added back to avoid the situation where the cost of capital on debt finance is included in the traditional profit calculation whereas the cost of equity capital is not. To ascertain the total source of funds invested in the business borrowings are added back to the capital base in the balance sheet. The required return (i.e. the opportunity cost of capital) of £17.5m on the resulting capital base is calculated and compared with the adjusted profit of £16.1m generated from the funds. This comparison captures the cost of both debt and equity and indicates that value added is a negative figure.

Goodwill

Goodwill refers to the price paid for the business in excess of the current cost of net assets. Goodwill payments should therefore add value to the company. Hence the amount written off is added back to profits since it represents part of the intangible asset value of the business. The cumulative write off of £40.7m is added back in order to provide a more realistic value of the capital base from which a return should be generated. This is because it represents an element of the value of the business. The value of goodwill should be regularly reviewed and the amount eroded written off against profits.

b. *Revised divisional profit statements*

	Division A (£m)	Division B (£m)	Division C (£m)	Head office (£m)	Total (£m)
Profit before interest and tax	5.7	5.6	5.8	(1.9)	15.2
Add back:					
Advertising	2.3				2.3
Research and development		2.1			2.1
Goodwill[a]		0.3	1.0		1.3
Allocation of head office expenses[b]	(0.4)	(0.3)	(1.2)	1.9	
Less tax paid[c]	(2.0)	(1.6)	(1.2)		(4.8)
Revised profit	5.6	6.1	4.4		16.1

Revised balance sheet

	Division A (£m)	Division B (£m)	Division C (£m)	Head office (£m)	Total (£m)
Total assets less current liabilities	27.1	23.9	23.2	3.2	77.4
Add back:					
Advertising	10.5				10.5
Research and development		17.4			17.4
Goodwill		10.3	30.4		40.7
Head office net assets[d]	0.7	0.5	2.0	(3.2)	
Revised capital base	38.3	52.1	55.6		146.0
Cost of capital at 12% of revised capital base	4.6	6.2	6.7		17.5
Revised profit	5.6	6.1	4.4		16.1
Value added	1.0	(0.1)	(2.3)		(1.4)

Notes

[a]Allocated on the same basis as previous goodwill write-offs (10.3/40.7 to Division B and 30.4/40.7 to Division C

[b]Apportioned on the basis of divisional turnover. Ideally head office costs should be allocated to divisions on the basis of the benefits received by the divisions.

[c]Allocated on the basis of profits before interest and tax less head office allocated costs plus interest received less interest paid. The outcome of this calculation is £5.7m for Division A, £4.6m for Division B and £3.7m for Division C and tax is allocated pro-rata to these figures.

[d]Arbitrary allocation on the basis of sales revenue adopting the same allocation base as that used for head office expenses.

The above analysis suggests that value is being 'destroyed' in Division C and to a minor extent in Division B. Division A is adding value. This is not apparent from the initial presentation which indicates a ROCE of 25 per cent (£5.6m/£23.2m) for Division C. The limitations of the analysis include:

i. The use of arbitrary apportionments to allocate head office expenses, the tax liability and head office net assets to the business.

ii. The assumption that the same cost of capital is applicable to all divisions.

iii. The use of historical asset values rather than economic values.

iv. The failure to distinguish between managerial and economic divisional performance. The analysis focuses on the economic performance of the divisions.

c. See 'Return on investment' and the discussion of the survey evidence within the section entitled 'Residual income' in Chapter 19 for the answer to this question. For a discussion of how the problems of short-termism might be overcome see 'Addressing the dysfunctional consequences of short-term financial measures' in Chapter 19.

19.22 a. For the answer to this question see 'Return on investment' and 'Residual income' and 'The effect of performance measurement on capital investment decisions' in Chapter 19. Note that discounted future earnings are the equivalent to discounted future profits.

b. The existing ROCE is 20 per cent and the estimated ROCE on the additional investment is 15 per cent (£9000/£60 000). The divisional manager will therefore reject the additional investment, since adding this to the existing investments will result in a decline in the existing ROCE of 20 per cent.

The residual income on the additional investment is £600 (£9000 average profit for the year less an imputed interest charge of 14% × £6000 = £8400). The manager will accept the additional investment, since it results in an increase in residual income.

If the discounted future earnings method is used, the investment would be accepted, since it will yield a positive figure for the year (that is, £9000 × 3.889 discount factor).

Note that the annual future cash flows are £19 000 (£9000 net profit plus £10 000 depreciation provision). The project has a 6-year life. The annual cash inflow must be in excess of £15 428 (£60 000/3.889 annuity factor – 6 years at 14%) if the investment is to yield a positive NPV. If annual cash flows are £19 000 each year for the next 6 years, the project should be accepted.

The residual income and discounted future earnings methods of evaluation will induce the manager to accept the investment. These methods are consistent with the correct economic evaluation using the NPV method. If ROCE is used to evaluate performance, the manager will incorrectly reject the investment. This is because the manager will only accept projects that yield a return in excess of the current ROCE of 20 per cent.

Note that the above analysis assumes that the cash flows/profits are constant from year to year.

Chapter 20

20.15 The loss of contribution (profits) in Division A from lost internal sales of 2500 units at £18 (£40 – £22) is £45 000.

The impact on the whole company is that the external purchase cost is £87 500 (2500 × £35) compared with the incremental cost of manufacture of £55 000 (2500 × £22). Therefore the company will be worse off by £32 500.

Answer = D

20.16 The dual market price in respect of Division A will be the market price of £25. The two-part tariff transfer price per unit is the marginal cost of £15.
Answer = B

20.17 Variable cost of the component = $360 (60% of $600)
Transfer price = (1.7 × $360) = $612

	X($)	Y ($)
External sales (10 000 × $800)	8 000 000	
Internal sales (12 000 × $612)	7 344 000	
External sales (12 000 × $1 200)		14 400 000
Production costs: (22 000 × $600)	(13 200 000)	
Transfer costs (12 000 × $612)		(7 344 000)
Assembly costs (12 000 × $400)		(4 800 000)
Non-production costs	(1 500 000)	(1 300 000)
Profit	644 000	956 000
Tax	(161 000)	(286 800)
Profit after tax	483 000	669 200

20.18 a. The calculation of the transfer price is as follows:

	£ per repair	Total cost for 500 repairs (£)
Parts	54	
Labour	45	
Variable cost	30	
Marginal cost	129	64 500
Fixed overhead	66	33 000
Total cost	195	97 500
Mark-up (40%)	78	39 000
Selling price	273	136 500

Impact of transfers at 40% mark-up

	Sales Dept. (£)	Service Dept. (£)	FP
Sales	120 000	136 500	120 000
Costs	136 500	97 500	97 500
Profit/(Loss)	(16 500)	39 000	22 500

Impact of transfers at marginal cost

	Sales Dept. (£)	Service Dept. (£)	FP
Sales	120 000	64 500	120 000
Costs	64 500	97 500	97 500
Profit/(Loss)	55 500	(33 000)	22 500

Impact if repairs carried out by RS

	Sales Dept. (£)	Service Dept. (£)	FP
Sales	120 000	0	120 000
Costs	90 000	(33 000)	123 000
Profit/(Loss)	30 000	(33 000)	(3 000)

b. i. The full cost transfer price is encouraging the manager of the sales department manager to contract the repairs out at a cost per repair of £180 because the transfer price has been set at £273 per repair. FP is worse off as a result of the transfers because the marginal cost per repair is £129. Therefore the purchase cost exceeds the marginal cost by £51 per repair or £25 500 for 500 repairs. If the transfer price is set at marginal cost the sales department will choose for the repairs to be undertaken internally but the service department will earn zero contribution for the repairs. A possible solution would be to set the transfer price at the external repair cost of £180. This will enable the service department to obtain a contribution of £51 per repair (£25 500 for 500 repairs) towards the fixed costs of £33 000 and a loss of £7500, instead of £33 000, will be reported by the service department. In the long term consideration should be given to outsourcing the repairs if the decision enables the fixed costs of the service department to be reduced by £33 000. See 'Cost-plus a mark-up transfer prices' for additional comments relating to this transfer pricing method.

ii. Issues to consider include the quality of the repairs carried out by RS, the time period that applies for which the purchase cost is applicable, the extent to which other suppliers are available (otherwise FP may be at the mercy of the supplier), the extent to which the fixed costs of the service department are avoidable and the alternative uses of the released capacity.

c. See 'Advantages and disadvantages' of divisionalization in Chapter 19 for items that are relevant for answering this question.

20.19 a. The proposed transfer price of £15 is based on cost plus 25 per cent implying that the total cost is £12. This comprises £9 variable cost (75%) and £3 fixed cost. The general transfer pricing guideline described in Chapter 20 can be applied to this question. That is the transfer price that should be set at marginal cost plus opportunity. It is assumed in the first situation that transferring internally will result in Helpco having a lost contribution of £6 (£15 external market price less £9 variable cost for the external market). The marginal cost of the transfer is £7.50 (£9 external variable cost less £1.50 packaging costs not required for internal sales). Adding the opportunity cost of £6 gives a transfer price of £13.50 per kg. This is equivalent to applying the market price rule where the transfer price is set at the external market price (£15) less selling costs avoided (£1.50) by transferring internally.

b. For the 3000 kg where no external market is available the opportunity cost will not apply and transfers should be at the variable cost of £7.50. The remaining output should be transferred at £13.50 as described above.

c. The lost contribution for the 2000 kg is £3 per kg (£6000/2000 kg) giving a transfer price of £10.50 (£7.50 variable cost plus £3 opportunity cost). The remaining 1000 kg for which there is no external market should be transferred at £7.50 variable cost and the balance for which there is an external market transferred at £13.50.

20.20 a. The effects on each division and the company as a whole of selling the motor unit at each possible selling price are presented in the following schedules:

i. EM division

Output level (units)	Total revenues (£)	Variable costs (£)	Total contribution (£)
1000	16 000	6 000	10 000
2000	32 000	12 000	20 000
3000	48 000	18 000	30 000
4000	64 000	24 000	40 000
6000	96 000	36 000	60 000
8000	128 000	48 000	**80 000**

ii. IP division

Output level (units)	Total revenues (£)	Variable costs (£)	Total cost of transfers (£)	Total contribution (£)
1000	50 000	4 000	16 000	30 000
2000	80 000	8 000	32 000	40 000
3000	105 000	12 000	48 000	**45 000**
4000	120 000	16 000	64 000	40 000
6000	150 000	24 000	96 000	30 000
8000	160 000	32 000	128 000	nil

iii. Enormous Engineering plc

Output level (units)	Total revenues (£)	Variable costs (EMD) (£)	Variable costs (IPD) (£)	Total contribution (£)
1000	50 000	6 000	4 000	40 000
2000	80 000	12 000	8 000	60 000
3000	105 000	18 000	12 000	75 000
4000	120 000	24 000	16 000	80 000
6000	150 000	36 000	24 000	**90 000**
8000	160 000	48 000	32 000	80 000

The above schedules indicate that EM division maximizes profits at an output of 8000 units, whereas IP division maximizes profits at an output level of 3000 units. Profits are maximized for the company as a whole at an output level of 6000 units.

b. i. Based on the tabulation in (a), IPD should select a selling price of £35 per unit. This selling price produces a maximum divisional contribution of £45 000.

ii. The company as a whole should select a selling price of £25 per unit. This selling price produces a maximum company contribution of £90 000.

iii. If IPD selected a selling price of £25 per unit instead of £35 per unit, its overall marginal revenue would increase by £45 000 but its marginal cost would increase by £60 000.

Consequently it is not in IPD's interest to lower the price from £35 to £25 when the transfer price of the intermediate product is set at £16.

c. i. Presumably profit centres have been established so as to provide a profit incentive for each division and to enable divisional managers to exercise a high degree of divisional autonomy. The maintenance of divisional autonomy and the profitability incentive can lead to sub-optimal decisions. The costs of sub-optimization may be acceptable to a certain extent in order to preserve the motivational advantages which arise with divisional autonomy.

Within the EE group, EMD has decision-making autonomy with respect to the setting of transfer prices. EMD sets transfer prices on a full cost-plus basis in order to earn a target profit. The resulting transfer price causes IPD to restrict output to 3000 units, which is less than the group optimum. The cost of this sub-optimal decision is £15 000 (£90 000 – £75 000). A solution to the problem is to set the transfer price at the variable cost per unit of the supplying division. This transfer price will result in IPD selecting the optimum output level, but will destroy the profit incentive for the EM division. Note that fixed costs will not be covered and there is no external market for the intermediate product.

Possible solutions to achieving the motivational and optimality objectives include:
1. operating a dual transfer pricing system;
2. lump sum payments.
See 'Proposals for resolving transfer pricing conflicts' in Chapter 20 for an explanation of the above items.

ii. Where there is no market for the intermediate product and the supplying division has no capacity constraints, the correct transfer price is the marginal cost of the supplying division for that output at which marginal cost equals the receiving division's net marginal revenue from converting the intermediate product. When unit variable cost is constant and fixed costs remain unchanged, this rule will result in a transfer price which is equal to the supplying division's unit variable cost. Therefore the transfer price will be set at £6 per unit when the variable cost transfer pricing rule is applied. IPD will then be faced with the following marginal cost and net marginal revenue schedule:

Output level (units)	Marginal cost of transfers (£)	Net marginal revenue of IPD (£)
1000		
2000	6 000	26 000
3000	6 000	21 000
4000	6 000	11 000
6000	12 000	22 000
8000	12 000	2 000

IPD will select an output level of 6000 units and will not go beyond this because NMR < marginal cost. This is the optimal output for the group, but the profits from the sale of the motor unit will accrue entirely to the IP division, and the EM division will make a loss equal to the fixed costs.

20.21 a. The variable costs per unit of output for sales *outside* the company are £11 for the intermediate product and £49 [£10(A) + £39(B)] for the final product. Note that selling and packing expenses are not incurred by the supplying division for the transfer of the intermediate product. It is assumed that the company has sufficient capacity to meet demand at the various selling prices.

Optimal output of intermediate product for sale on external market

Selling price (£)	20	30	40
Unit contribution (£)	9	19	29
Demand (units)	15 000	10 000	5 000
Total contribution (£)	135 000	190 000	145 000

Optimal output is 10 000 units at a selling price of £30.

Optimal output for final product

Selling price (£)	80	90	100
Unit contribution (£)	31	41	51
Demand (units)	7 200	5 000	2 800
Total contribution (£)	223 200	205 000	142 800

Optimal output is 7200 units at a selling price of £80.

Optimal output of Division B based on a transfer price of £29

Division B will regard the transfer price as a variable cost. Therefore total variable cost per unit will be £68 (£29 + £39), and Division B will calculate the following contributions:

Selling price (£)	80	90	100
Unit contribution (£)	12	22	32
Demand (units)	7 200	5 000	2 800
Total contribution (£)	86 400	110 000	89 600

The manager of Division B will choose an output level of 5000 units at a selling price of £90. This is sub-optimal for the company as a whole. Profits for the *company as a whole* from the sale of the final product are reduced from £223 200 (7200 units) to £205 000 (5000 units). The £205 000 profits would be allocated as follows:

Division A £95 000 [5000 units at (£29 – £10)]
Division B £110 000

b. At a transfer price of £12, the variable cost per unit produced in Division B will be £51 (£12 + £39). Division B will calculate the following contributions:

Selling price (£)	80	90	100
Unit contribution (£)	29	39	49
Demand (units)	7 200	5 000	2 800
Total contribution (£)	208 800	195 000	137 200

The manager of Division B will choose an output level of 7200 units and a selling price of £80. This is the optimum output level for the company as a whole. Division A would obtain a contribution of £14 400 [7200 × (£12 – £10)] from internal transfers of the intermediate product, whereas Division B would obtain a contribution of £208 800 from converting the intermediate product and selling as a final product. Total contribution for the company as a whole would be £223 200. Note that Division A would also earn a contribution of £190 000 from the sale of the intermediate product to the external market.

20.22 Schedule 1: *Calculation of marginal cost, marginal revenue and net marginal revenue*

Output of Alpha (units)	Alpha marginal cost (£000)	Alpha marginal revenues[a,b] (£000)	Beta net marginal revenue[a] (£000)
0–10	<28	65 (1)	57 (3)
10–20	<28	60 (2)	55 (4/5)
20–30	<28 [c]	55 (4/5)	53 (6)
30–40	<28	50 (8)	51 (7)
40–50	<28	45 (11/12)	49 (9)
50–60	<28	40	47 (10)
60–70	28	35	45 (11/12)
70–80	30	30	43 (13)
80–90	33	25	40
90–100	35	20	36
100–110	37	15	33
110–120	40	10	30
120–130	44	5	25

Notes

[a]The numbers in parentheses represent the descending order of ranking of marginal revenue/net marginal revenue for Alpha and Beta.

[b]The question indicates that the marginal revenue function for Alpha decreases in increments of £5000 for each 10 units increase in sales value of Alpha for output levels from 60 to 130 units. This implies that the total revenue and marginal revenue function of Alpha can be computed from this information on the basis of a £5000 decline in marginal revenue for each 10 units of output.

[c]The marginal cost per 10 units of Alpha increases as output expands. This implies that the marginal cost per 10 units of Alpha is less than £28 000 for output of less than 60 units.

[d]The NMR of Beta declines as output rises, thus suggesting an imperfect final product market. The implication of this is that NMR is in excess of £47 000 for increments of 10 units sales of Beta at less than 50 units. The NMR for the first 50 units sales of

Beta has been estimated based on the information given in the question. We shall see that the accuracy of the estimates for output levels below 60 units is not critical for calculating the optimum transfer price and activity level.

The output of Alpha is allocated between the sale of the intermediate product on the external market and the transfer of the intermediate product for sale as a final product on the basis of the ranking indicated in the parentheses in Schedule 1. The allocation is presented in the following schedule:

Schedule 2: Allocation of output of Alpha

(1) Output of Alpha (units)	(2) Alpha marginal cost (£000)	(3) Allocation per ranking in Schedule 1[a]	(4) Marginal revenue or NMR[b]
0–10	<28	Alpha	65
10–20	<28	Alpha	60
20–30	<28	Beta	57
30–40	<28	Beta	55
40–50	<28	Alpha	55
50–60	<28	Beta	53
60–70	28	Beta	51
70–80	30	Alpha	50
80–90	33	Beta	49
90–100	35	Beta	47
100–110	37	Beta	45
110–120	40	Alpha	45
120–130	44	no allocation (MR/NMR < MC)	43

Notes
[a]Alpha refers to sale of Alpha as an intermediate product. Beta refers to the transfer of Alpha internally for conversion to Beta and sale in the final product market.
[b]Appropriate MR/NMR per ranking in Schedule 1.

Conclusions
The optimal output level is 120 units. Below this output level MR > MC, but beyond 120 units MC > MR. To induce the output of 120 units, the transfer price should be set at £44 so as to prevent the receiving division from requesting a further 10 units, which will yield an NMR of £43. Examination of Schedule 2 indicates that 70 units should be transferred internally for sale as a final product and 50 units of the intermediate product sold externally. A transfer price of £44 will result in both divisions arriving at this production plan independently. Therefore, the optimal transfer price is the marginal cost of the supplying division for that output at which marginal cost equals the sum of the receiving division's net marginal revenue from using the intermediate product and the marginal revenue from the sale of the intermediate product – in other words, where column 2 equals column 4 in Schedule 2.

20.23 a. The starting point to answering this question is to ascertain whether the capacity of the supplying division is sufficient to meet the demand from both the external market and the receiving division. To increase demand by one unit of Aye the selling price must be reduced by £0.04 (£1/25 units). Thus the maximum selling price for an output of x units is:

SP = £1000 – £0.04x
Total revenue for an output of x units = £1000x – £0.0x^2
Marginal revenue = dTR/dx = £1000 – £0.08x
Marginal cost = variable cost = £280

At the optimum output level where MR = MC:
£1000 – 0.08x = £280
x = 9000 units

The highest selling price at which the optimum output can be sold is: SP = £1000 – £0.04 (9000) = £640. This leaves 21 000 units spare capacity for Division A. Therefore Division A can meet the maximum output for Bee of 18 000 units without restricting sales and a forgone contribution from Aye. The maximum selling price for Bee for output of x units is:

SP = £4000 – £0.10x
Total revenue for an output of x units = £4000x – £0.10x^2
Marginal revenue = dTR/dx = £4000 – £0.20x
Marginal costs = £280 + £590 = £870

At the optimum output level where MR = MC:
£4000 – £0.20x = £870
x = 15 650 units

The highest selling price at which the optimum output can be sold is: SP = £4000 – 0.10 (15 650) = £2435. The contributions at the optimal selling prices are:

Division A = £ 3 240 000 [9000 × (£640 – £280)]
Division B = £24 492 250 [15 650 × (£2435 – £870)]
Group = £27 732 250

b. If Division A sets the transfer price at the optimum selling price of £640 the variable cost per unit of output for producing Bee will be £1230 (£640 + £590).

MR of Division B = £4000 – £0.20x (See part (a))

The optimum output level is where:

£4000 – £0.20x = £1230
x = 13 850 units

The optimum selling price is:

£4000 – £0.10 (13 850) = £2615

c. The revised contributions if the transfer price is set at £640 will be as follows:

		(£)
Division A:	External sales [9000 × (£640 – £280)]	3 240 000
	Internal transfers [13 850 × (£640 – £280)]	4 986 000
Division B:	External sales [13 850 × (£2615 – £1230)]	19 182 250
Total contribution		27 408 250

Setting the transfer price at the market price results in an increase in total contribution of Division A and a decline in the total contribution of Division B. The contribution for the group as a whole declines by £324 000.

As a result of the increase in the transfer price Division B's marginal cost increases and it will therefore restrict output and set a higher selling price. Where the market for the intermediate product is imperfect, the optimal transfer price is the marginal cost of producing the intermediate product at the optimum output level for the group as a whole. Since marginal cost per unit is constant and equal to variable cost, the optimum transfer price is variable cost. If the transfer price is set at variable cost the receiving division will have a cost function identical to that specified in (a) and will set the selling price at the optimum output for the group as a whole.

20.24 a. See 'International transfer pricing' in Chapter 20 for the answer to this question. Besides the ethical issues and legal considerations other criticisms relate to the distortions in the divisional profit reporting system. Also divisional autonomy will be undermined if the transfer prices are imposed on the divisional managers.

b. The ethical limitations relate to multinational companies using the transfer pricing system to reduce the amount paid in custom duties, taxation and the manipulation of dividends remitted. Furthermore, using the transfer prices for these purposes is likely to be illegal, although there is still likely to be some scope for manipulation that is within the law. It is important that multinational companies are seen to be acting in a socially responsible manner. Any bad publicity relating to using the transfer pricing system purely to avoid taxes and custom duties will be very harmful to the image of the organization. Nevertheless tax management and the ability to minimize corporate taxes is an important task for management if it is to maximize shareholder value. Thus it is important that management distinguish between tax avoidance and tax evasion. Adopting illegal practices is not acceptable and management must ensure that their transfer pricing policies do not contravene the regulations and laws of the host counties in which they operate.

Chapter 21

21.16 a. i.

	Units
Components worked on in the process	6120
Less: planned defective units	612
replacements to customers (2% × 5400)	108
Components invoiced to customers	5400

Therefore actual results agree with planned results.

ii. Planned component cost = (3 × £18 for material A) + (2 × £9 for material B) + £15 variable cost = £87

Comparing with the data in the appendix:

Materials = £440 640/6120 = £72

Variable overhead = £91 800/6120 = £15

This indicates that prices were at the planned levels.

b. Internal failure costs = £53 244 (612 units × £87)

External failure costs = £9396 (108 units × £87)

c. i.

	Period 2 (units)	Period 3 (units)
Components invoiced to customers	5500	5450
Planned replacement (2%)	110	109
Unplanned replacements	60 (170 – 110)	−69 (40 – 109)
Components delivered to customers	5670	5490
Planned process defects (10% of worked on in the process)	620	578
Unplanned defects (difference to agree with final row)	−90	−288
Components worked on in the process	6200	5780

ii.

	Period 2 (£)	Period 3 (£)
Internal failure costs	46 110 (620 – 90) × £87	25 230 (578 – 288) × £87
External failure costs	14 790 (110 + 60) × £87	3 480 (109 – 69) × £87
Appraisal costs	10 000	15 000
Prevention costs	5 000	8 000

iii. The following points should be included in the report:

1. Insufficient detail is provided in the statistics shown in the appendix thus resulting in the need to for an improvement in reporting.
2. The information presented in (c) i. indicates that free replacements to customers were 60 greater than planned in period 2 but approximately 70 less than planned in period 3. In contrast, the in process defects were 90 less than planned (approximately 15%) in period 2 and 288 less than plan (approximately 50%) in period 3.
3. Internal failures costs show a downward trend from periods 1–3 with a substantial decline in period 3. External failure costs increased in period 2 but declined significantly in period 3.
4. The cost savings arising in periods 2 and 3 are as follows:

	Period 2 (£)	Period 3 (£)
Increase/decrease from previous period:		
Internal failure costs	−7134 (£53 244 − £46 110)	−20 880 (£46 110 − £25 230)
External failure costs	+5394 (£9396 − £14 790)	−11 310 (£14 790 − £3480)
Total decrease	−1740	−32 190

The above savings should be compared against the investment of £10 000 appraisal costs and £5000 prevention costs for period 2 and £15 000 and £8000 respectively in period 3. It can be seen that the costs exceed the savings in period 2 but the savings exceeded the costs in period 3. There has also been an increase in the external failure costs from period 1 to period 2. Investigations should be made relating to the likely time lag from incurring prevention/appraisal costs and their subsequent benefits.

5. The impact on customer goodwill from the reduction in replacements should also be examined.

21.17 a. The annual cost savings are as follows:

	£000
Direct labour 0.2 (£1120 + £1292 + £1980) × 75 000	+65 880
Variable set-ups (30% × £13 000) × 3500	−13 650
Variable materials handling (30% × 4000 × 14 600)	−17 520
Variable inspection (30% × £18 000 × 3500)	−18 900
Variable machining (15% × £40 × 4 560 000)	−27 360
Variable distribution and warehousing (£3000 × 14 600)	−43 800
Fixed costs [30% (£42 660 + £52 890 + £59 880) + (15% × £144 540) + £42 900]	−111 210
Total savings	166 560

b. The total variable overhead costs allocated to each product is as follows:

	C1 (£000)	C2 (£000)	C3 (£000)
Set-up costs at £9100 per production run	9 100	9 100	13 650
Materials handling at £2800 per order	11 200	14 000	15 680
Inspection at £12 600 per production run	12 600	12 600	18 900
Machining at £34 per machine hour	36 720	61 200	57 120
	69 620	96 900	105 350
Total output (000's)	75	75	75
Variable overhead per car (£)	928.26	1 292.00	1 404.67
Direct materials	2 520.00	2 924.00	3 960.00
Direct labour	1 344.00	1 550.40	2 376.00
Total variable cost per car	4 792.26	5 766.40	7 740.67

The above variable costs per car are now used to derive the following contributions for various price/demand levels:

Selling price (£)	Demand	Unit contribution (£)	Total contribution (£000)
C1 Car			
5000	75 000	207.74	15 581
5750	65 000	957.74	62 253
6000	50 000	1207.74	60 387
6500	35 000	1707.74	59 771
C2 Car			
5750	75 000	−16.40	−1 230
6250	60 000	483.60	29 016
6500	45 000	733.60	33 012
7500	35 000	1733.60	60 676
C3 Car			
6500	75 000	−1240.67	−93 050
6750	60 000	−990.67	−59 440
7750	45 000	9.33	420
8000	30 000	259.33	7 780

The profit maximizing price and output levels are £5750 and 65 000 demand for C1, £7500 and 35 000 for C2 and £8000 and 30 000 for C3.

c.

(£000)	C1 (£000)	C2 (£000)	C3
Total contribution	62 253	60 676	7 780
Avoidable fixed costs	9 266	11 583	18 533
Contribution to general fixed costs and profit	52 987	49 093	−10 753

The above analysis suggests (ignoring any qualitative factors) that C3 should be discontinued and that C1 and C2 are produced.

d. The report should include the following points:

1 The need for smooth and uniform production rates and the need to avoid fluctuations in production rates since this will lead to excess work in progress.
2 A description of the pull/ kanban system.
3 The need to ensure a cell production layout and that workers have multiple skills.
4 Focus on eliminating non-value added activities.
5 Focus on routine and preventative maintenance to avoid machine downtime.
6 Focus on reducing set-up times to a minimum.
7 Establishment of JIT purchasing arrangements accompanied by establishing close relationships with suppliers.

21.18 a. i. Performance report for period ending 30 November
(Traditional analysis)
Expenses

	Budget (£)	Actual (£)	Variance (£)
Salaries	600 000	667 800	67 800A
Supplies	60 000	53 000	7 000F
Travel cost	120 000	127 200	7 200A
Technology cost	100 000	74 200	25 800F
Occupancy cost	120 000	137 800	17 800A
Total	1 000 000	1 060 000	60 000A

Performance report for period ending 30 November
(Activity-based analysis)
Activities

	(£)	(£)	(£)
Routing/scheduling – new products	200 000	169 600	30 400F
Routing/scheduling – existing products	400 000	360 400	39 600F
Remedial re-routing/scheduling	50 000	127 200	77 200A
Special studies – specific orders	100 000	84 800	15 200F
Training	100 000	159 000	59 000A
Management and administration	150 000	159 000	9 000A
Total	1 000 000	1 060 000	60 000A

ii. See 'Activity-based budgeting' in Chapter 15 for the answer to this question. In particular, the answer should stress:

i. The enhanced visibility of activity-based budgeting (ABB) by focusing on outcomes (activities) rather than a listing by expense categories.

ii. The cost of activities are highlighted thus identifying high cost non-value added activities that need to be investigated.

iii. ABB identifies resource requirements to meet the demand for activities whereas traditional budgeting adopts an incremental approach.

iv. Excess resources are identified that can be eliminated or redeployed.

v. ABB enables more realistic budgets to be set.

vi. ABB avoids arbitrary cuts in specific budget areas in order to meet overall financial targets.

vii. It is claimed that ABB leads to increased management commitment to the budget process because it enables management to focus on the objectives of each activity and compare the outcomes with the costs that are allocated to the activity.

iii. The ABB statement shows a comparison of actual with budget by activities. All of the primary value-adding activities (i.e. the first, second and fourth activities in the budget statement) have favourable variances. Remedial rerouting is a non-value added activity and has the highest adverse variance. Given the high cost, top priority should be given to investigating the activity with a view to eliminating it, or to substantially reducing the cost by adopting alternative working practices. Training and management and administration are secondary activities which support the primary activities. Actual training expenditure exceeds budget by 50 per cent and the reason for the over-spending should be investigated.

For each activity it would be helpful if the costs were analyzed by expense items (such as salaries, supplies, etc.) to pinpoint the cost build up of the activities and to provide clues indicating why an overspending on some activities has occurred.

Cost driver usage details should also be presented in a manner similar to that illustrated in Exhibit 15.1 in Chapter 15. Many organizations that have adopted ABC have found it useful to report budgeted and actual cost driver rates. The trend in cost driver rates is monitored and compared with similar activities undertaken within other divisions where a divisionalized structure applies. As indicated in Chapter 15, care must be taken when interpreting cost driver rates.

For additional points to be included in the answer see 'Activity-based management' in Chapter 21.

b. The cost driver rates are as follows:

Product design = £250 per design hour (£2m/8000 hours)
Purchasing = £50 per purchase order (£200 000/4000 orders)
Production (excluding depreciation) = £100 per machine hour ((£1 500 000 – £300 000)/12 000 hours)
Packing = £20 per cubic metre (£400 000/20 000)
Distribution = £5 per kg (£600 000/120 000)

The activity-based overhead cost per unit is as follows:

		(£)
Product design	(400 design hours at £250 per hour = £100 000 divided by life-cycle output of 5000 units)	20.00
Purchasing	(5 purchase orders at 50 units per order costing a total of £250 for an output of 250 units)	1.00
Production	(0.75 machine hours at £100 per machine hour)	75.00
Depreciation	(Asset cost over life cycle of 4 years = 16 quarters' depreciation at £8000 per quarter divided by life-cycle output of 5000 units)	25.60
Packing	(0.4 cubic metres at £20)	8.00
Distribution	(3 kg at £5)	15.00
Total cost		144.60

21.19 See 'Cost of quality', 'Just-in-time systems' and 'Activity-based management' in Chapter 21 for the answer to this question. You should also refer to 'Activity-based budgeting' in Chapter 15. All of the approaches seek to eliminate waste and therefore when the principles are applied to budget preparation there should be a move away from incremental budgeting to the resources that are required to meet budgeted demand. For an explanation of this point see 'Activity-based budgeting' in Chapter 15. Within the budgeting process a total quality ethos would result in a move towards a zero-defects policy when the budgets are prepared. There would be reduced budget allocations for internal and external failure costs and an increase in the allocation for prevention and appraisal costs. The just-in-time philosophy would result in a substantial budgeted reduction in stocks and establishing physical targets that support JIT systems, such as manufacturing cycle efficiency and set-up times. See 'Operation processes' and 'Cycle time measures' in Chapter 22 for an explanation of some of the performance targets that are appropriate for JIT systems. The activity-based focus should result in the implementation of activity-based budgeting (see Chapter 15).

21.20 Benchmarking is a continuous process that involves comparing business processes and activities in an organization with those in other companies that represent world-class best practices in order to see how processes and activities can be improved. The comparison involves both financial and non-financial indicators.

Two different approaches are adopted in most organizations. Cost-driven bench-marking involves applying the principles of benchmarking from a distance and comparing some aspects of performance with those of competitors, usually using intermediaries such as consultants. The outcome of the exercise is cost reduction. The second approach involves process-driven benchmarking. It is a process involving the philosophy of continuous improvement. The focus is not necessarily on competitors but on a benchmarking partner. The aim is to obtain a better understanding of the processes and questions the reason why things take place, how they take place and how often they take place. The outcome should be superior performance through the strengthening of processes and business behaviour.

Inter-firm comparisons place much greater emphasis on the use of financial data and mostly involve comparisons at the company or strategic business unit level rather than at the business process or activity level. Inter-firm comparisons tend to compare data derived from published financial accounts whereas benchmarking also makes use of both internal and external data.

Benchmarking contributes to cost reduction by highlighting those areas where performance is inferior to competitors and where opportunities for cost reduction exist (e.g. elimination of non-value added activities or more efficient ways of carrying out activities).

Activity-based budgeting (ABB) is an extension of ABC applied to the preparation of budgets. It focuses on the costs of activities necessary to produce and sell products and services by assigning costs to separate activity cost pools. The cause and effect criterion based on cost drivers is used to establish budgets for each cost pool.

ABB involves the following stages:

1. Determining the budgeted cost (i.e. the cost driver rate) of performing each unit of activity for all major activities.
2. Determining the required resources for each individual activity to meet sales and production requirements.
3. Computing the budgeted cost for each activity.

Note that ABB focuses on budgets for the cost of activities rather than functional departments.

Zero-base budgeting tends to be used more as a one-off cost reduction programme. The emphasis is on functional responsibility areas, rather than individual activities, with the aim of justifying all costs from a zero base.

Activity analysis is required prior to implementing ABB. This process can help to identify non-value added activities that may be candidates for elimination or performing the activities in different ways with less resources. Activity performance measures can be established that enable the cost per unit of activity to be monitored and used as a basis for benchmarking. This information should highlight those activities where there is a potential for performing more efficiently by reducing resource consumption and future spending.

See 'Target costing' in Chapter 21 for an explanation of the objectives and workings of target costing.

Continuous cost improvement is a process whereby a firm gradually reduces costs without attempting to achieve a specific target. Target costing is emphasized more at a product's design and development stage whereas continuous cost improvement occurs throughout a product's life. The principles of target costing can also be applied to cost reduction exercises for existing products. Where this approach is applied there is little difference between the two methods. Both approaches clearly focus on reducing costs throughout a product's life cycle but target costing emphasizes cost reduction at the design and development stage. At this stage there is a greater potential for reducing costs throughout the product life cycle.

21.21 a. The factors influencing the preferred costing system are different for every firm. The benefits from implementing ABC are likely to be influenced by the level of competition, the number of products sold, the diversity of the product range and the proportion of overheads and direct costs in the cost structure. Companies operating in a more competitive environment have a greater need for more accurate cost information, since competitors are more likely to take advantage of any errors arising from the use of distorted cost information generated by a traditional costing system. Where a company markets a small number of products special studies can be undertaken using the decision-relevant approach. Problems do not arise in determining which product or product combinations should be selected for undertaking special studies. Increased product diversity arising from the manufacture and sale of low-volume and high-volume products favours the use of ABC systems. As the level of diversity increases so does the level of distortion reported by traditional costing systems. Finally, organizations with a large proportion of overheads and a low proportion of direct costs are likely to benefit from ABC, because traditional costing systems can be relied upon only to report accurately direct product costs. Distorted product costs are likely to be reported where a large proportion of overheads are related to product variety rather than volume.

b. For a more detailed answer to this question you should refer to 'Activity-based management' in Chapter 21. In particular, the answer should draw attention to the fact that ABM attaches costs to activities and identifies the cost drivers that cause the costs. Thus ABM provides a better understanding of what causes costs, and highlights ways of performing activities more efficiently by reducing cost driver transactions.

Costs can therefore be managed more effectively in the long run. Activities can be analyzed into value added and non-value added activities and by highlighting the costs of non-value added activities attention is drawn to areas where there is an opportunity for cost reduction, without reducing the products' service potentials to customers.

Finally, the cost of unused activity capacity is reported for each activity, thus drawing attention to where capacity can be reduced or utilized more effectively to expand future profitability.

c. See 'Target Costing' in Chapter 21 for the answer to this question.

21.22 a. Total quality management (TQM) is a term that is used to describe a situation where all business functions are involved in a process of continuous quality improvement. The critical success factors for the implementation of TQM are:

i. The focus should be on customer needs. This should not just represent the final customer. All sections within a company should be seen as a potential customer of a supplying section and a potential supplier of services to other sections.

ii. Everyone within the organization should be involved in TQM. Senior management should provide the commitment that creates the culture needed to support TQM.

iii. The focus should be on continuous improvement. Continuous improvement seeks to eliminate non-value activities, produce products and provide services with zero defects and simplify business processes. All employees, rather than just management, should be involved in the process since employees involved in the processes are often the source of the best ideas.

iv. The aim should be to design quality into the product and the production process. This requires a close working relationship between sales, production, distribution and research.

v. Senior management should promote the required culture change by promoting a climate for continuous improvement rather than imposing blame for a failure to achieve static targets.

vi. An effective performance measurement system that measures continuous improvement from the customer's perspective should be introduced. Simple non-financial measures involving real time reporting should be seen as a vital component of the performance measurement system.

vii. Existing rewards and performance measurements should be reviewed to ensure that they encourage, rather than discourage, quality improvements.

viii. Appropriate training and education should be given so that everyone is aware of the aims of TQM.

b. For the answer to this question you should refer to 'Cost of quality' in Chapter 21. In particular the answer should describe the different categories of cost that are included in a Cost of Quality Report and indicate how the report can be used to draw management's attention to the possibility of reducing total quality costs by a wiser allocation of costs between the different categories.

21.23 a. The key features of ABC are described in Chapter 10. In particular, you should refer to 'A comparison of traditional and ABC systems' and 'Volume-based and non-volume based cost drivers'. The question refers to both activity-based product costing and activity-based cost management. In terms of the former, ABC should generate more accurate product costs for pricing and profitability analysis (see Chapter 10). For the cost management benefits of ABC see 'Activity-based management' in Chapter 21.

b. The measurement of organizational and management performance represents part of the management control process within an organization. Actual performance is compared with planned performance and where actual performance deviates adversely from planned performance action is taken in order to achieve planned performance. Financial performance measures (profit, ROI, residual income and EVA) are described in Chapter 19. The answer should draw attention for the need to also incorporate non-financial measures. For a discussion of this issue see 'Addressing the dysfunctional consequences of short-term financial measures' in Chapter 19. In addition, the balanced scorecard should be described (see Chapter 22). Examples of the range of financial and non-financial measures are provided in the section on the balanced scorecard in Chapter 22.

Chapter 22

22.14 a.

	Original budget based on 120 000 gross hours	Standard hours based on actual gross hours	Actual hours	Variance (hours)	Variance (£) at £75 per hour
Gross hours	120 000	132 000	132 000		
Contract negotiation	4 800 (4%)	5 280 (4%)	9 240 (7%)	3 960A	297 000A
Remedial advice	2 400 (2%)	2 640 (2%)	7 920 (6%)	5 280A	396 000A
Other non-chargeable	12 000 (10%)	13 200 (10%)	22 440 (17%)	9 240A	693 000A
Chargeable hours	100 800 (84%)	110 880 (84%)	92 400 (70%)	18 480A	1 386 000A

There was a capacity gain over budget of 10 080 (110 880 – 100 800) hours at a client value of £756 000 (10 080 hours at £75) but because all of this was not converted into actual chargeable hours there was a net fall in chargeable hours compared with the original budget of 8400 (100 800 – 92 400) hours at a client value of £630 000.

b. *Financial performance*

Profit statement and financial ratios for year ending 30 April

	Budget (£000)	Actual (£000)
Revenue from client contracts (chargeable hours × £75)	7560	6930
Costs:		
Consultant salaries	1800	1980
Sundry operating costs	3500	4100
	5300	6080
Net profit	2260	850
Capital employed	6500	6500
Financial ratios:		
Net profit: Turnover	29.9%	12.3%
Turnover: Capital employed	1.16 times	1.07 times
Net profit: Capital employed	34.8%	13.1%

The above figures indicate a poor financial performance for the year. The statement in (a) indicates an increase in gross hours from 120 000 to 132 000 hours providing the potential for 110 880 chargeable hours compared with the budget of 100 800 hours. This should have increased fee income by £756 000 (10 080 × £75). However, of the potential 110 880 hours there were only 92 400 chargeable hours resulting in a shortfall of 18 480 hours at a lost fee income of £1 386 000. The difference between these two monetary figures of £630 000 represents the difference between budgeted and actual revenues.

Competitiveness

Competitiveness should be measured in terms of market share and sales growth. Sales are less than budget but the offer of free remedial advice to clients presumably represents the allocation of staff time to improve longer term competitiveness even though this has had an adverse impact on short-term profit.

Competitiveness may also be measured in terms of the relative success/failure in obtaining business from clients. The data shows that the budgeted uptake from clients is 40 per cent for new systems and 75 per cent for existing systems compared with actuals of 35 per cent and 80 per cent respectively. For new systems worked on there is a 16.7 per cent increase compared with the budget whereas for existing systems advice actual is 4 per cent less than budget.

Quality

The data indicate that client complaints were four times the budgeted level and that the number of clients requiring remedial advice was 75 compared with a budgeted level of 48. These items should be investigated.

Flexibility

Flexibility relates to the responsiveness to customer enquiries. For BS Ltd this relates to its ability to cope with changes in volume, delivery speed and the employment of staff who are able to meet changing customer demands. The company has retained 60 consultants in order to increase its flexibility in meeting demand. The data given show a change in the mix of consultancy specialists that may reflect an attempt to respond to changes in the marketing mix. The ratio of new systems to existing systems advice has changed and this may indicate a flexible response to market demands.

Resource utilization

The budget was based on chargeable hours of 84 per cent of gross hours but the actual percentage was 70 per cent (see part (a)). There was an increased level of remedial advice (6 per cent of gross hours compared with 2 per cent in the budget) and this may represent an investment with the aim of stimulating future demand.

Innovation

Innovation relates to the ability of the organization to provide new and better quality services. The company has established an innovative feature by allowing free remedial advice after completion of a contract. In the short term this is adversely affecting financial performance but it may have a beneficial long-term impact. The answer to part (a) indicates that remedial advice exceeded the adjusted budget by 5280 hours. This should be investigated to establish whether or not this was a deliberate policy decision.

Other points

Only budgeted data were given in the question. Ideally, external benchmarks ought to be established and the trend monitored over several periods rather than focusing only on a single period.

22.15 a.
The key areas of performance referred to in the question are listed in Learning Note 22.1 – financial, competitiveness, quality of service, flexibility, resource utilization and innovation.

Financial

- There has been a continuous growth in sales turnover during the period – increasing by 50% in 1999, 10% in 2000 and 35% in 2001.
- Profits have increased at a higher rate than sales turnover – 84% in 1999, 104% in 2000 and 31% in 2001.
- Profit margins (profit/sales) have increased from 14% in 1998 to 31% in 2001.

Competitiveness

Market share (total turnover/total turnover of all restaurants) has increased from 9.2% in 1998 to 17.5% in 2001. The proposals submitted to cater for special events has increased from 2 in 1998 to 38 in 2002. This has also been accompanied by an increase in the percentage of contracts won which has increased over the years (20% in 1998, 29% in 1999, 52% in 2000 and 66% in 2001). Although all of the above measures suggest good performance in terms of this dimension the average service delay at peak times increased significantly in 2001. This area requires investigating.

Quality of service

The increasing number of regular customers attending weekly suggests that they are satisfied with the quality of service. Other factors pointing to a high level quality of service are the increase in complimentary letters from satisfied customers. Conversely the number of letters of complaints and reported cases of food poisoning have not diminished over the years. Therefore the performance measures do not enable a definitive assessment to be made on the level of quality of service.

Innovation/flexibility

Each year the restaurant has attempted to introduce a significant number of new meals. There has also an increase each year in the number of special theme evenings introduced and the turnover from special events has increased significantly over the years. These measures suggest that the restaurant has been fairly successful in terms of this dimension.

Resource utilization

The total meals served have increased each year. Idle time and annual operating hours with no customers have also decreased significantly each year. There has also been an increase in the average number of customers at peak times. The value of food wasted has varied over the years but was at the lowest level in 2001. All of the measures suggest that the restaurant has been particularly successful in terms of this dimension.

b. *Financial*

Details of the value of business assets are required to measure profitability (e.g. return on investment). This is important because the seating capacity has been increased. This may have resulted in an additional investment in assets and there is a need to ascertain whether an adequate return has been generated. Analysis of expenditure by different categories (e.g. food, drinks, wages, etc.) is required to compare the trend in financial ratios (e.g. expense categories as a percentage of sales) and with other restaurants.

Competitiveness

Comparison with other restaurants should be made in respect of the measures described in (a) such as percentage of seats occupied and average service delay at peak times.

Quality of service

Consider using mystery shoppers (i.e. employment of outsiders) to visit this and competitor restaurants to assess the quality of service relative to competitors and to also identify areas for improvement.

Innovation/flexibility

Information relating to the expertise of the staff and their ability to perform multi-skill activities is required to assess the ability of the restaurant to cope with future demands.

Resource utilization

Data on the number of employees per customer served, percentage of tables occupied at peak and non-peak times would draw attention to areas where there may be a need to improve resource utilization.

22.16 a. See 'The balanced scorecard' in Chapter 22 for the answer to this question. In particular, the answer should describe the four different perspectives of the balanced scorecard, the assumed cause-and-effect relationships and also provide illustrations of performance measures applicable to CM Ltd.

b. See 'Benchmarking' in Chapter 21 for the answer to this question. The answer should stress the need to identify important activities or processes that may be common to other organizations (e.g. dispatching, invoicing or ordering activities) and to compare these activities with an organization that is considered to be a world leader in undertaking these activities.

22.17 a. For an explanation of the generic strategies identified by Porter you should refer to the section on identifying potential strategies in Chapter 15. The value of Porter's work could be criticized on the grounds that it is too general. For example, being the lowest cost producer and selling at the lowest prices in the industry does not guarantee success. There are many other factors besides selling prices and a low cost structure that can have an affect on the success of an organization. Differentiation can take many different forms. Also the tastes of customers and the availability of alternative products are factors that will influence the level of sales. In addition, the pricing policy will influence the extent of competitive advantage.

b. For an explanation of how the experience curve can affect a firm's cost structure you should refer to 'Cost estimation when the learning effect is present' in Chapter 23. The experience curve can be used as a means of obtaining strategic advantage by forecasting cost reductions and consequently selling price reductions of competitors. Early experience with a new product can provide a means of conferring an unbeatable lead over competitors. Through the experience curve the leading competitor should be able to reduce its selling price for the product which should further increase its volume and market share and eventually force some lagging competitors out of the industry. Exploiting the principles of the experience curve can ensure that a firm has the lowest costs in the industry and therefore adopt a strategy of cost leadership in terms of Porter's generic strategy model.

22.18 a. i. Efficiency measures focus on the relationship between outputs and inputs. Optimum efficiency levels are achieved by maximizing the output from a given input or minimizing the resources used in order to achieve a particular output. Measures of effectiveness attempt to measure the extent to which the outputs of an organization achieve the latter's goals. An organization can be efficient but not effective. For example, it can use resources efficiently but fail to achieve its goals.

In organizations with a profit motive, effectiveness can be measured by return on investment. Inputs and outputs can be measured. Outputs represent the quality and amount of service offered. In profit-orientated organizations output can be measured in terms of sales revenues. This provides a useful proxy measure of the quality and amount of services offered. In non-profit-making organizations outputs cannot be easily measured in monetary terms. Consequently, it is difficult to state the objectives in quantitative terms and thus measure the extent to which objectives are being achieved.

If it is not possible to produce a statement of a particular objective in measurable terms, the objectives should be stated with sufficient clarity that there is some way of judging whether or not they have been achieved. However, the focus will tend to be on subjective judgements rather than quantitative measures of effectiveness. Because of the difficulty in measuring outputs, efficiency measures tend to focus entirely on input measures such as the amount of spending on services or the cost per unit of input.

ii. Similar problems to those of measuring effectiveness and efficiency in non-profit-making organizations arise in measuring the performance of non-manufacturing activities in profit-orientated organizations. This is because it is extremely difficult to measure the output of non-manufacturing activities. For a discussion of the problems that arise when measuring the performance of non-manufacturing activities see Learning Note 16.1 (Effectiveness and Efficiency Tests).

b. i. *Adherence to appointment times*

1. Percentage meeting appointment times.
2. Percentage within 15 minutes of appointment time.
3. Percentage more than 15 minutes late.
4. Average delay in meeting appointments.

Ability to contact and make appointments

It is not possible to obtain data on all those patients who have had difficulty in contacting the clinic to make appointments. However, an indication of the difficulties can be obtained by asking a sample of patients at periodic intervals to indicate on a scale (from no difficulty to considerable difficulty) the difficulty they experienced when making appointments. The number of complaints received and the average time taken to establish telephone contact with the clinic could also provide an indication of the difficulty patients experience when making appointments.

Monitoring programme

1. Comparisons with programmes of other clinics located in different regions.

2. Questionnaires asking respondents to indicate the extent to which they are aware of monitoring facilities currently offered.
3. Responses on level of satisfaction from patients registered on the programme.
4. Percentage of population undertaking the programme.

ii. Combining the measures into a 'quality of care' measure requires that weights be attached to each selected performance measure. The sum of the performance measures multiplied by the weights would represent an overall performance measure. The problems with this approach are that the weights are set subjectively, and there is a danger that staff will focus on those performance measures with the higher weighting and pay little attention to those with the lower weighting.

22.19 i. The percentage of occupancy on flights to new destinations should provide feedback on how successful this policy is in terms of meeting the growth objective.

ii. Measures of baggage loading/unloading times, aircraft cleaning times and fuel loading times can be used to implement a policy of continuous improvement and thus contribute to the achievement of the internal capabilities objective.

22.20 a. The following aspects of the external environment should be considered:

● Existing and future customer and markets: Existing and future customers/markets should be identified and an assessment made relating to the extent that their current and future needs are being met. Information relating to market shares for the major products/services, percentage growth in business from existing customers, total sales to new customers and customer satisfaction ratings should be gathered and appropriate actions taken now in order to achieve long-term competitive advantage;

● Competitors: See 'External information about competitors' in Chapter 22 for items that are relevant to competitor information;

● Suppliers: Information should be obtained concerning present and potential suppliers relating to their prices, quality of service/materials provided, delivery reliability and their financial viability;

● Environmental and legal aspects: Information should be gathered on the environmental and legal issues that the company must address (e.g. vehicle emission requirements). Attempts should be made to develop measures that draw attention to how the organization is contributing to becoming environmentally responsible and a good social citizen. For a more detailed discussion of environmental aspects see 'Environmental cost management' in Chapter 21;

● The economic environment: Information is required on the future economic environment that the organization will face (e.g. the government's transport policy). Also information should be provided on the trend in inflation, interest and foreign exchange rates and issues relating to import and export restrictions. These aspects are likely to have a significant impact on the business.

b. Sources of information include:

● Market research undertaken or commissioned by the company and information that is generally available within the public domain (e.g. trade and industry reports);

● Government reports on industrial sectors;

● Government statistics (economic indicators, consumer spending, inflation rates, interest rates etc.);

● Various sources of information that can be accessed from the internet, newspapers, trade magazines etc.

● Suppliers' price lists and brochures.

c. An appropriate individual should be made responsible for identifying the information required, designing a system for capturing the data and determining the information that is to be provided to different parties within the organization.

Information should be provided only to the appropriate people. Only relevant information should be provided and information overload avoided. Alternative means of disseminating the information should be evaluated (e.g. e-mail, special reports, meetings etc.). Feedback should be obtained on the information provided and the reporting system should be periodically reviewed and updated.

Chapter 23

23.14

Low	650 patients	$17 125
High	1260 patients	18 650
Difference	610 patients	1 525

Variable cost per patient = $1525/610 = $2.50
Total fixed cost using 650 patients = Total cost ($17 125) − variable cost (650 × $2.50) = $15 500
Estimated cost for 850 patients = Variable costs (850 × $2.50) + $15 500 = $17 625

Answer = C

23.15

Trend value = 10 000 = (4200 × 33) = 148 600
Seasonal variation index value = 120
Forecasted unit sales = 148 600 × 120% = 178 320

Answer = D

23.16 It is assumed that advertising generates sales. Therefore advertising is the independent variable and sales revenue the dependent variable. Applying formula 23.2 (see Chapter 23) which was provided in the examination paper:

$$b = \frac{(6 \times 447\ 250\ 000) - (13\ 500 \times 192\ 000)}{(6 \times 32\ 150\ 000) - (13\ 500)^2} = 8.714$$

Answer = C

23.17 a. i. *High- and low-point method*

	Machine hours 000s	Fuel oil expenses (£000's)
High point (June 2000)	48	680
Low point (January 2000)	26	500
Difference	22	180

Variable cost per machine hour £8.182 (£180/22)
Substituting for January 2000

	(£000's)
Variable cost (26 × £8.182) =	212.73
Fixed Cost (difference)	287.27
Total cost	500.00

The total cost equation is $y = 287.27 + 8.182x$

ii. *Least-squares regression method*

	Hours x	Fuel oil y	x^2	xy
July	34	640	1 156	21 760
August	30	620	900	18 600
September	34	620	1 156	21 080
October	39	590	1 521	23 010
November	42	500	1 764	21 000
December	32	530	1 024	16 960
January	26	500	676	13 000
February	26	500	676	13 000
March	31	530	961	16 430
April	35	550	1 225	19 250
May	43	580	1 849	24 940
June	48	680	2 304	32 640
	$\Sigma x = 420$	$\Sigma y = 6840$	$\Sigma x^2 = 15\ 212$	$\Sigma xy = 241\ 670$
	$\bar{x} = 35$	$\bar{y} = 570$		

$$\Sigma y = Na + bx \quad (1)$$
$$\Sigma xy = \Sigma xa + b\Sigma x^2 \quad (2)$$

Substituting from the above table:

$$6840 = 12a + 420b \quad (1)$$
$$241\ 670 = 420a + 15\ 212b \quad (2)$$

Multiply equation (1) by 35 (= 420/12):

$$239\,400 = 420a + 14\,700 \qquad (3)$$

Subtract equation (3) from equation (2):

$$2270 = 512b, \text{ and so } b = 2270/512 = 4.4336$$

Substitute in equation (1), giving

$$6840 = 12a + 420 \times 4.4336, \text{ so } a = \frac{6840 - 1862.112}{12}$$

$$= 414.824$$

$$y = 414.82 + 4.43x$$

b. For the answer to this question see Chapter 23.

c. An r^2 calculation of 0.25 means that 75 per cent of the total variation of y from its mean is not caused by variations in x (machine hours). This means that a large proportion of changes in fuel oil expenses do not result from changes in machine hours. The cost must depend on factors other than machine hours. Other measures of activity might be examined in order to test whether they are closely related to changes in costs. If other measures do not yield a close approximation then this might indicate that cost is dependent on several variables. In these circumstances multiple regression techniques should be used.

23.18 Applying the formula $Y_x = aX^b$ described in Chapter 23 where Y^x is the cumulative average time to produce x units, a is the time required to produce the first unit (6 hours), the exponent b is –0.415 for a 75 per cent learning curve and X is the number of units of output under consideration. The average times per unit of cumulative production are:

6 assignments = 6 hours × $6^{-0.415}$ = 6 × 0.4754 = 2.8525 hours
7 assignments = 6 hours × $7^{-0.415}$ = 6 × 0.4459 = 2.6757 hours
Total time for 6 assignments = 17.115 hours (6 × 2.8525)
Total time for 7 assignments = 18.730 hours (7 × 2.6757)

Therefore the time taken to produce the seventh unit is 1.615 hours

23.19 The answer to this question requires knowledge of mathematical relationships that apply to the learning curve. You will see from Exhibit 23.2 in the text that the average time for producing 4 units is 0.64 of the time for producing the first unit (1280/2000). The average learning rate is $\sqrt{0.64}$ = 0.8 or 80%. The average time for producing eight units is 0.512 of the time for producing the first unit (1024/2000). Therefore the average learning rate is $\sqrt[3]{(0.512)}$ = 0.8.

Applying the same principles to the question the average time per unit for 4 units is 2.0917 hours (8.3667/4 units). Therefore the average time for producing 4 units is 0.697 of the time for producing the first unit (2.0917/3). The average learning rate is 83.5 per cent ($\sqrt{0.697}$).

23.20 a. See Chapter 23 for an explanation of learning curve theory. The average time per unit of cumulative production is assumed to decrease by a constant percentage every time output doubles. Cumulative average time refers to the average time per unit for all of the units produced for a specific output level, from and including the first unit made.

b.

(1) Number of bikes	(2) Cumulative average time (hours)	(3) Total time (hours) (Col.1 × Col.2)	(4) Incremental time (hours)
1	50	50	50
2	40 (50 × 0.8)	80	30
4	32 (40 × 0.8)	128	48
8	25.6	204.8	76.8

Quotation 1	£
Materials	1000
Labour (30 × 10)	300
Overheads	600
Total cost	1900
Profit (20%)	380
Selling Price	2280

Quotation 2	£
Materials	2000
Labour (48 × 10)	480
Overheads	960
Total cost	3440
Profit (20%)	688
Selling Price	4128

4128/2 = £2064 Per Bike

Quotation 3	£
Materials	8 000
Labour (204.8 × 10)	2 048
Overheads	4 096
Total cost	14 144
Profit (20%)	2 828.8
Selling Price	16 972.8

16 972.8/8 = £2121.6 Per Bike

c. Learning curve theory is applicable to:

● Setting standard labour times within a standard costing system and the use of these changing standards up to the steady-state production level for variance analysis and budgeting;
● Work scheduling to enable inputs to be more accurately predicted thus enabling more accurate customer delivery schedules to be determined;
● Preparing better cost predictions to enable price quotations to be prepared.

Limitations of the learning curve include:

● Learning curve data relating to an appropriate learning rate may be difficult to obtain;
● Staff may resist scheduling and targets based on declining standard times;
● Different percentage learning rates may apply rather than a constant percentage rate throughout the entire learning curve;
● Changes in production techniques and labour turnover may result in the learning rate not being maintained.

23.21 a.

Cumulative production (boats)	Completion time (days)	Cumulative time (days)	Average time (days)
1	10.0	10.0	10.0
2	8.1	18.1	9.05 (18.1/2)
3	7.4	25.5	8.50 (25.5/3)
4	7.1	32.6	8.15 (32.6/4)

As production doubles from one to two boats, average time falls to 90.5 per cent of the time for producing the first boat. As production doubles from two to four boats, average time falls to 90.06 per cent (8.15/9.05) of the previous average. The objective is to calculate the *average* learning rate. You should now refer to Exhibit 23.2 in Chapter 23. You can see that the average time for producing four units is 0.64 of the time for producing the first unit (1280/2000). The average learning rate is $\sqrt{(0.64)}$ = 0.8 or 80%. The average time for producing eight units is 0.512 of the time for producing the first unit (1024/2000). The average learning rate is $\sqrt[3]{(0.512)}$ = 0.8. Similarly, the average time for producing 16 units is 0.4095 of the time for producing the first unit (819/2000). The average learning rate is $\sqrt[4]{(0.4095)}$ = 0.80. In Exhibit 23.2 the learning rate remained constant at 80 per cent throughout, and it was therefore unnecessary to calculate the average learning rate.

Applying the approach outlined above, the average time for four boats is 0.815 of the time for the first boat, thus indicating an average learning rate of $\sqrt{(0.815)}$ = 0.903 or 90.3%.

An alternative approach is to use the learning curve equation:

$$y_x = ax^b$$

where y_x is defined as the cumulative average time required to produce x units, a is the time required to produce the first unit of output and x is the number of units of output under consideration. The exponent b is defined as the ratio of the logarithm of the learning curve improvement rate to the logarithm of 2. Therefore:

$$y^4 = 10 \times 4^b$$
$$8.15 = 10 \times 4^b$$
$$4^b = 0.815$$

Our objective is to calculate the exponent function that, when multiplied by 4, equals 0.815. A trial-and-error approach is now adopted:

exponent function for 80% learning curve = −0.322 (see Chapter 24)
exponent function for 90% learning curve = −0.152 (log 0.9/log 2)
exponent function for 91% learning curve = −0.136 (log 0.91/log 2)

$$4^{-0.322} = 0.64$$
$$4^{-0.152} = 0.810$$
$$4^{-0.136} = 0.828$$

The average learning rate is between 90 per cent and 91 per cent.

b. The following points should be discussed:
  i. Only four observations have been used, and this might be insufficient to establish an average learning rate for the production of 15 boats.
  ii. It is assumed that working methods, equipment and staff will remain constant. Improvements in working procedures, staff changes or absenteeism might affect the learning rate.
  iii. Uncertainty as to when the learning process will stop. If the learning process stops before the steady-state phase is reached then the assumption that the learning rate will continue might result in inaccurate estimates.
  iv. The learning rate may not be constant throughout the process, and the use of an average learning rate might result in inaccurate estimates for different output levels.

c. Materials, other direct expenses and overheads will remain unchanged irrespective of whether the boats are completed in normal time (possibly involving penalties) or working weekends. Overheads appear to be fixed since they are allocated on the basis of *normal* working days. The total times required, assuming a 90 per cent learning rate, are as follows:

Average time for 15 boats = $y_{15} = 10 \times 15^{-0.152}$ = 6.6257 days
Total time for 15 boats = 15×6.6257 = 99.4 days
Total time for 14 boats = $14 \times 10 \times 14^{-0.152}$ = 93.7 days
Total time for 13 boats = $13 \times 10 \times 13^{-0.152}$ = 88.0 days

The contract is for 4 months (therefore 92 working days are available without overtime or 120 days with overtime) and penalties are charged at £10 000 per boat late. Thirteen boats can be delivered within the contract period. To complete 15 boats within the contract period, it will be necessary to work 7.4 days (99.4 days − 92 days) overtime. If overtime is not worked, two boats will incur a penalty. Without overtime, the total labour cost plus penalties will be:

(99.4 days × £2500 = £248 500) + (2 × £10 000) = £268 500
With overtime, the total labour cost will be:

(92 days × £2500 = £230 000) + (7.4 days × 5000) = £267 000
It is assumed that payments can be made for part days only. It is slightly cheaper to work overtime and avoid the penalty cost. Another possibility is to complete 14 boats using overtime and deliver 1 boat late:

Cost for 14 boats = (92 days × £2500) +
  (1.7 days × £5000)   = £238 500
Cost for 15th boat = (5.7 days × £2500) +
  (1 × £10 000)   = £ 24 250
                                     £262 750

The most profitable alternative is to deliver one boat late. Other factors to be considered include:
i. the four factors outlined in part (b);

ii. the possibility of bad weather affecting production times;
iii. the effect on customer goodwill and the possibility of not obtaining future orders if the contract is not completed on time;
iv. the promise of overtime work might induce the workforce to slow down in order to obtain overtime work.

23.22 The experience curve states that the cost of production will decrease as greater experience is gained with a product or process. Although cost reduction will be a function of the learning curve the experience curve covers a greater number of areas such as product innovation and management skills. The experience curve can be used as a means of obtaining strategic advantage by forecasting cost reductions and consequently the selling price reductions of competitors. Early experience with a new product can provide a means of conferring an unbeatable lead over competitors. Through the experience curve the leading competitor should be able to reduce its selling price for the product which should further increase its volume and market share and eventually force some lagging competitors out of the industry. Exploiting the principles of the experience curve can ensure that a firm has the lowest costs in the industry. It is therefore important that managers are aware of their organization's position on the experience curve at the strategic planning stage.

By exploiting the cost reductions of the experience curve a firm can lower its selling prices and thus extend a product's life cycle by stimulating demand from existing customers and/or enticing new customers by price reductions. Furthermore, a knowledge of an organization's experience curve relative to that of its competitors will allow it to maximize market share and prolong the life cycle of its products or services.

A favourable position on the experience curve via product innovation and management skills will enable a firm to take appropriate steps to ensure that its products are competitive and prolong their profitable lives. In particular, it will enable managers to modify existing products and introduce new products that ensures that the organization is at the forefront of product development. This will help to delay the decline in demand for its products and prolong their life cycles. Also the experience of managers will enable them to react to environmental and technological changes so that the organization remains competitive. It will thus be able to respond effectively to changes in demand for its products and take steps to prolong their life cycles.

Chapter 24

24.13 i.
Re-order level = Maximum usage × Maximum lead time
  = 95 × 18 = 1710

Answer = C

ii.
Maximum stock = Re-order level + Re-order quantity − Minimum usage during minimum lead time
  = 1710 + 1750 − (50 × 12)
  = 2860

Answer = B

24.14
Re-order level = Maximum usage (750) × Maximum lead time (15 days) = 11 250 units
Minimum stock reduction before an order is received = 11 250 − (450 × 8days) = 7 650 units
Maximum order size = 15 000 − 7 650 = 7 350 units

Answer = 7 350 units

24.15 a.
EOQ = √(2 × 15 000 × 80)/(0.1333 × 200) = 300 units
Number of orders per year = 15 000/300 = 50 orders

b.

$$EOQ = \sqrt{(2 \times 2\,800 \times 28)/(25 \times .08)} = 280 \text{ units}$$
$$\text{Holding cost} = 280/2 \times £2 = \$280$$

24.16 a.

$$EOQ = \sqrt{(2 \times 12\,000 \times 200)/(£15 \times 0.08)} = 2\,000 \text{ units}$$

b. Revised stock costs

	£
Purchase costs (12 000 × £15)	180 000
Order costs $\dfrac{12\,000}{2\,000} \times 200$	1 200
Holding costs $\dfrac{2\,000}{2} \times 15 \times 0.08$	1 200
	182 400
Original stock costs	183 000
Saving	600

24.17 The purchase cost is not constant per unit. It is therefore not possible to use the EOQ formula. Instead the following schedule of costs should be prepared:

Evaluation of optimum order size

Size of order	No. of orders	Annual purchase cost (WI) (£)	Storage cost (£)	Admin. cost (£)	Total cost (£)
2400	1	1728 (£0.72)	300	5	2033
1200	2	1728 (£0.72)	150	10	1888
600	4	1824 (£0.76)	75	20	1919
200	12	1920 (£0.80)	25	60	2005
100	24	1920 (£0.80)	12.50	120	2052.50

It is recommended that two orders be placed per year for 1200 units.

	(£)
Calculation of cost 2(1200 × £0.80 − 10%)	= £1728
Add: Storage, average quantity held 600 × £0.25	= 150
Add two orders placed per annum × £5	= 10
	£1888

Workings (W1) Annual demand of 2400 units × unit purchase cost

24.18 a.

$$EOQ = \sqrt{\left(\frac{2DO}{H}\right)} = \sqrt{\frac{2 \times 4000 \times 135}{12}} = 300$$

The relevant cost is

$$\text{holding cost} + \text{ordering cost} = \frac{300 \times 12}{2} + \frac{4000 \times 135}{300} = 3600$$

b.

$$\text{Revised EOQ} = \sqrt{\left(\frac{2 \times 4000 \times 80}{12}\right)} = 231$$

The relevant cost is

$$\text{holding cost} + \text{ordering cost} = \frac{231 \times 12}{2} + \frac{4000 \times 80}{231} = 2772$$

The relevant cost using the original EOQ of 300 units but with an incremental ordering cost of £80 is

$$\frac{300 \times 12}{2} + \frac{4000 \times 80}{300} = 2867$$

Cost of prediction error = £95 (£2867 − £2772)

c. The annual costs of purchasing, ordering and holding the materials consist of:

Special offer at £86:

holding cost + ordering cost + purchase cost

$$\frac{4000 \times 12}{2} + 0 = 4000 \times 86 = £368\,000$$

Normal price of £90:

$$\frac{300 \times 12}{2} + \frac{4000 \times 135}{300} + 4000 \times 90 = \underline{£363\,600}$$

Additional cost of specific offer £4 400

Therefore the purchase of 4000 units at £86 is not recommended.

d.

	Budget (£)	Actual (£)	Variance (£)
Material cost	360 000	344 000	16 000F
	(4000 × £90)	(4000 × £86)	
Ordering cost	1800	0	1 800F
$\left(\frac{D}{Q} \times O\right)$			17 800F

It can be seen that favourable variances would appear on the performance report, and goal congruence would not exist. The performance evaluation system conflicts with the EOQ decision model. This is because the purchasing officer is not charged for the use of capital but the EOQ model includes a charge for the use of capital. Therefore if an imputed capital charge is not included in the performance report, there is a danger that goal congruence will not exist. The revised performance report including a capital charge is shown below:

	Budget (£)	Actual (£)	Variance (£)
Material cost	360 000	344 000	16 000F
Ordering cost	1 800	0	1 800F
Holding cost	1 800	24 000	22 200A
			4 400A

24.19 a. The question requires the calculation of the optimum number of units to be manufactured in each production run in order to secure the lowest annual cost. In Chapter 24 we noted that the formula for the optimum number of units to be manufactured (Q) is as follows:

$$Q = \sqrt{\left(\frac{2DS}{H}\right)}$$

where D = total demand for period, S = set-up costs, H = holding cost per unit. The set-up costs and holding cost per unit to be used in the formula are relevant or incremental costs. Those costs that will not change as a result of changes in the number of units manufactured in each batch should not be included in the analysis. These costs include:

i. Skilled labour costs. (Skilled labour is being paid idle time. Its total cost will not alter as a result of the current decision.)
ii. Fixed overheads. (These costs are independent of the batch size.)

Therefore the relevant cost of producing product Exe is as follows:

			(£)
Raw materials – external suppliers			13
– Dee standard cost:	Raw materials	8	
	Unskilled labour	4	
	Variable overheads	3	15
Unskilled labour			7
Variable overheads			5
Incremental cost of production			40

The relevant decision variables for the formula are as follows:
Annual demand of Exe (D) = 4000 units
Set-up costs (S) = £70 (skilled labour of £66 is not an incremental cost)
Annual holding costs = £14 [cost of storage (£8) plus cost of capital tied up in stocks (£6)]
Storage cost per unit (0.40 m² × £20) = £8
Incremental interest tied up in each unit of Exe stock (15% × £40 incremental cost of Exe) = £6
Applying the above figures to the formula, we have:

$$Q = \sqrt{\left(\frac{2 \times 4000 \times £70}{£14}\right)}$$

$$= 200 \text{ units}$$

	(£)
Cost of current policy	
Set-up costs (4 production runs at £70)	280
Holding costs (average stocks × unit holding cost)	
$\frac{1000}{2} \times £14$	7000
Total cost	7280
Cost of optimum policy	
Set-up costs [(4000/200) production runs at £70]	1400
Holding costs (average stocks × unit holding cost)	
$\frac{200}{2} \times £14$	1400
Total cost	2800
Annual savings (£7280 − £2800)	£4480

b.

$$Q = \sqrt{\left(\frac{DO}{H}\right)}$$

where D = annual demand, O = incremental ordering cost per order, H = holding cost per unit. For producing Wye:

$$Q = \sqrt{\left(\frac{2 \times 10\,000 \times £100}{£8}\right)} = 500 \text{ units}$$

Buying in larger quantities in order to take advantage of bulk discounts results in the following savings:

i. a saving in purchase price for the period consisting of the total amount of the discount for the period;

ii. a reduction in total ordering cost because of fewer orders being placed to take advantage of bulk discounts.

The above cost savings must be compared with the increased holding costs resulting from higher stock levels.

We now compare the cost savings with the increased holding costs from increasing the quantity purchased from the EOQ of 500 units to the lowest purchase quantity at which Wye can be purchased at £19.80 per unit (i.e. 1000 units):

	(£)
Savings in purchase price (10 000 annual purchases at £0.20)	2000
Saving in ordering cost[a]	
$\frac{DO}{Q_d} - \frac{DO}{Q} = \frac{10\,000 \times 100}{1000} - \frac{10\,000 \times 100}{500}$	1000
Total savings	3000

Note

[a] Q_d represents quantity ordered to obtain discount and Q represents EOQ.

The additional holding cost if the larger quantity is purchased is calculated as follows:

$$\frac{(Q_d - Q)H}{2} = \frac{(1000 - 500) \times £8}{2} = £2000$$

Therefore a saving of £1000 is made if the firm purchases in quantities of 1000 units at a price of £19.80 per unit.

We now follow the same procedure in order to determine whether it would be better to purchase in quantities of 2000 units:

	(£)
Savings in purchase price (10 000 annual purchases at £0.40)	4000
Saving in ordering cost	
$\frac{DO}{Q_d} - \frac{DO}{Q} = \frac{10\,000 \times 100}{2000} - \frac{10\,000 \times 100}{500}$	1500
Total savings	5500

The additional holding cost if we purchase in 2000-unit quantities instead of 500-unit quantities is as follows:

$$\frac{(Q_d - Q)H}{[2]} = \frac{(2000 - 500) \times £8}{2} = £6000$$

Therefore an additional £500 will be incurred if the firm purchases in 2000-unit batches compared with purchasing in 500-unit batches.

The above analysis indicates that Pink should purchase in batches of 1000 units at a price of £19.80 per unit.

c. Limitations include the following:

i. It is very difficult to obtain relevant data. Incremental holding, ordering and set-up costs are very difficult to estimate in practice. In addition, many of the fixed costs that were excluded in the analysis may not be fixed over the whole range of output. Some fixed costs may increase in steps as the quantity purchased is increased.

ii. Model assumes certainty. A more sophisticated approach is required where the demand and the cost structure are uncertain.

iii. Model assumes that demand is constant throughout the year. In practice, there may be seasonal variations in demand throughout the year.

24.20 a.

Safety stock	Stockout	Stockout cost at £10 (£)	Probability	Expected cost (£)	Total (£)
500	0	0	0	0	0
400	100	1000	0.04	40	40
300	200	2000	0.04	80	
	100	1000	0.07	70	150
200	300	3000	0.04	120	
	200	2000	0.07	140	
	100	1000	0.10	100	360
100	400	4000	0.04	160	
	300	3000	0.07	210	
	200	2000	0.10	200	
	100	1000	0.13	130	700
0	500	5000	0.04	200	
	400	4000	0.07	280	
	300	3000	0.10	300	
	200	2000	0.13	260	
	100	1000	0.16	160	1200

Safety stock	Stockout cost (£)	Holding cost (£)	Total cost (£)
0	1200	0	1200
100	700	100	800
200	360	200	560
300	150	300	450
400	40	400	440
500	0	500	500

The optimal safety stock is 400 units.

b. The probability of being out of stock at an optimal safety stock of 400 units is 0.04.

24.21 a.

$$\text{EOQ} = \sqrt{\frac{2DO}{H}} = \sqrt{\frac{2 \times 10\,000 \times 25}{(45 + 5)}} = 100 \text{ units}$$

b. Without any discount prices the EOQ =

$$\sqrt{\frac{2 \times 10\,000 \times 25}{(45 + 5.01)}} = 99.99 \text{ units}$$

Thus it is preferable to purchase 100 units at £50 rather than pay £50.10 for purchasing 99 units. To ascertain whether it is worthwhile increasing the purchase quantity from 100 to 200 units we must compare the total costs at each of these quantities:

	(£)
Total costs with a reorder quantity of 100 units	
Annual holding cost (100/2 × £50)	2 500
Annual ordering costs (10 000/100 × £25)	2 500
	5 000
Purchasing manager's bonus (10% × £5000)	500
Annual purchase cost (10 000 × £50)	500 000
Total annual costs	505 500
Total costs with a reorder quantity of 200 units	
Annual holding costs (200/2 × £49.99)	4 999
Annual ordering costs (10 000/200 × £25)	1 250
	6 249
Purchasing manager's bonus (10% × (£10 000 − £6249))	375
Annual purchase cost (10 000 × £49.90)	499 000
Total annual costs	505 624

The optimal order quantity is still 100 units.

c. The probability distribution of demand over the three day lead time is as follows:

Demand lead time	Frequency	Probability	Expected value
106	4	0.04	4.24
104	10	0.10	10.40
102	16	0.16	16.32
100	40	0.40	40.00
98	14	0.14	13.72
96	14	0.14	13.44
94	2	0.02	1.88
	100	1.00	100.00

It is assumed that the reorder point will be set at 100 units (expected value). The expected costs for various levels of safety stock are as follows:

Safety stock (units)	Reorder point (units)	Stockout per order (units)	Stockout per year[a] (units)	Probability of stockout	Expected stockout cost[b] (£)	Holding cost[c] (£)	Total expected cost[d] (£)
6	106	0	0	0	0	270	270
4	104	2	200	0.04	80	180	260
2	102	2	200	0.10	200		
		4	400	0.04	160	90	450
0	100	2	200	0.16	320		
		4	400	0.10	400		
		6	600	0.04	240	0	960

Notes

[a]During the year 100 orders will be made (10 000 units annual demand/EOQ of 100 units). Stockout per year in units is calculated by multiplying the stockouts per order by 100 orders;

[b]Expected stockout costs = Annual stockout in units × probability of stockout × £10 lost contribution

[c]Holding cost = Safety stock × (Holding cost of £50 – saving of 10% on purchasing manager's bonus)

[d]It is assumed that stockout costs are equal to the lost contribution on the lost sales.

Conclusion

Costs are minimized if a safety stock of 4 units is maintained.

d. The following items should be included in the report:
   i. The disadvantages of ordering from only one supplier (e.g. vulnerability of disruption of supplies due to strikes/production difficulties or bankruptcy);
   ii. Failure to seek out cheap or alternative sources of supply;
   iii. It is assumed no large price increases are anticipated that will justify holding additional stocks or that the stocks are not subject to deterioration or obsolescence;
   iv. It is assumed that lead time will remain unchanged. However, investigations should be made as to whether this, or other suppliers, can guarantee a shorter lead time;
   v. The need to ascertain the impact on customer goodwill if a stockout occurs. The answer to (c) assumes that the company will merely lose the contribution on the sales and long-term sales will not be affected if a stockout occurs.

Chapter 25

25.10 The feasible output area is the area to the left where constraints (1) and (3) intersect. To determine the optimal output level at which profits are maximized the objective function dotted line is extended to the right by a series of parallel lines. These lines take on higher total contribution levels as they are moved to the right. The aim is to determine the highest contribution attainable within the feasible region. This will occur at the point where constraint 1 intersects with the x-axis.
Answer = D

25.11 Where the objective function is to minimize total costs the potential optimal solutions will be at the points closest to the origin that fall within the feasible region. Therefore the optimal solution will be at either points E or D. Note that total costs are lower for E compared with A since E and A entail the same output of U units but E has a lower output of A units.
Answer = C

25.12 a. Objective is to maximize profit:
Let a = the number of units of A to be produced
Let b = the number of units of B to be produced
Objective function: $9a + 23b$

Constraints:
Non-negativity	$b \geq 0$
Minimum requirement of A	$a \geq 1000$
Materials	$3a + 4b \leq £\,30\,000$
Labour	$5a + 3b \leq £\,36\,000$

b.

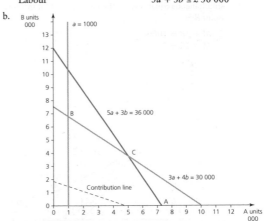

The feasible output region is ABC. To determine the contribution line, a random total contribution is selected. It is easier to establish a random contribution if it is based on a common denominator for the objective function $9a + 23b$. If a random contribution of £41 400 is selected this could be obtained by producing 4600 units of A (£41 400/£9) or 1800 units of B (£41 400/£23). The objective function line for a total contribution of £41 400 is therefore drawn from 4600 units of A and 1800 units of B. This is represented by the dashed line in the diagram. To determine the optimal output level at which profits are maximized, the objective function dashed line is extended to the right by a series of parallel lines. These lines take on higher total contribution levels as they are moved to the right. The aim is to determine the highest contribution attainable within the feasible region. This will occur at the point B. At this point the equations $a = 1000$ and $3a + 4b = 30\,000$ are the binding constraints. Given that $a = 1000$ we can determine the value for b in the second equation:

$3(1000) + 4b = 30\,000$
so that, $b = 6750$.

Therefore the optimal production plan is to produce 1000 units of A and 6750 units of B.

25.13 a. Let M = number of units of Masso produced and sold.
Let R = number of units of Russo produced and sold.
The linear programming model is as follows:
Maximize $Z = 40M + 50R$ (production contributions)
subject to

$M + 2R$	≤ 700 (machining capacity)
$2.5M + 2R$	≤ 1000 (assembly capacity)
M	≤ 400 (maximum output of Masso constraint)
R	≤ 400 (maximum output of Russo constraint)
M	≥ 0
R	≥ 0

The constraints are plotted on the graph as follows:

Machining constraint: line from ($M = 700$, $R = 0$) to ($R = 350$, $M = 0$)
Assembly constraint: line from ($M = 400$, $R = 0$) to ($R = 500$, $M = 0$)
Output of Masso constraint: line from $M = 400$
Output of Russo constraint: line from $R = 400$

At the optimum point (B in the graph) the output mix is as follows:

	(£)
200 units of Masso at a contribution of £40 per unit =	8 000
250 units of Russo at a contribution of £50 per unit =	12 500
Total contribution	20 500
Less fixed costs (£7000 + £10 000)	17 000
Profit	3 500

The optimum output can be determined exactly by solving the simultaneous equations for the constraints that intersect at point B:

$$2.5M + 2R = 1000 \quad (1)$$
$$M + 2R = 700 \quad (2)$$

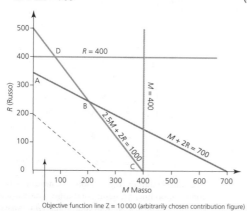

Objective function line Z = 10 000 (arbitrarily chosen contribution figure)
Feasible region = OABC

Subtract equation (2) from equation (1):

$$1.5M = 300$$
$$M = 200$$

Substituting in equation (1):

$$2.5 \times 200 + 2R = 1000$$
$$R = 250$$

b. *Machining capacity*
If we obtain additional machine hours, the line $M + 2R = 700$ will shift upward. Therefore the revised optimum point will fall on the line BD. If one extra machine hour is obtained, the constraints $M + 2R = 700$ and $2.5M + 2R$ will still be binding and the new optimal plan can be determined by solving the following equations:

$$M + 2R = 701 \text{ (revised machining constraint)}$$
$$2.5M + 2R = 1000 \text{ (unchanged assembly constraint)}$$

The values for M and R when the above equations are solved are $M = 199.33$ and $R = 250.83$.

Therefore Russo is increased by 0.83 units and Masso is reduced by 0.67 units and the change in contribution will be as follows:

		(£)
Increase in contribution from Russo (0.83 × £50)	=	41.50
Decrease in contribution from Masso (0.67 × 40)	=	(26.80)
	Increase in contribution	14.70

Hence the value of an independent marginal increase in machine capacity is £14.70 per hour.
Assembly capacity
With an additional hour of assembly capacity, the new optimal plan will be given by the solution of the following equations:

$$M + 2R = 700 \text{ (unchanged machining constraint)}$$
$$2.5M + 2R = 1001 \text{ (revised assembly constraint)}$$

The values for M and R when the above equations are solved are $M = 200.67$ and $R = 249.67$. Therefore Masso is increased by 0.67 units and Russo is decreased by 0.33 units, and the change in contribution will be as follows:

		(£)
Increase in contribution from Masso (0.67 × £40)	=	26.80
Decrease in contribution from Russo (0.33 × £50)	=	(16.50)
	Increase in contribution	10.30

Hence the value of an independent marginal increase in assembly capacity is £10.30 per hour.
c. The assumptions underlying the above calculations are:
i. linearity over the whole output range for costs, revenues and quantity of resources used;
ii. divisibility of products (it is assumed that products can be produced in fractions of units);
iii. divisibility of resources (supplies of resources may only be available in specified multiples);
iv. the objectives of the firm (it is assumed that the single objective of a firm is to maximize short-term contribution);
v. all of the available opportunities for the use of the resources have been included in the linear programming model.

25.14 a.

	Product 1	Product 2	Product 3	Total
Maximum sales value (£)	57 500	96 000	125 000	
Unit selling price (£)	23	32	25	
Maximum demand (units)	2 500	3 000	5 000	
Hours required on type A machine	2 500 (2500 × 1)	6 000 (3000 × 2)	15 000 (5000 × 3)	23 500
Hours required on type B machine	3 750 (2500 × 1½)	9 000 (3000 × 3)	5 000 (5000 × 1)	17 750

We now compare the machine capacity available with the machine hours required to meet the maximum sales so as to determine whether or not production is a limiting factor.

	Machine type A	Machine type B
Hours required (see above)	23 500	17 750
Hours available	9 800	21 000

Because hours required are in excess of hours available for machine type A, but not for machine type B, it follows that machine type A is the limiting factor. Following the approach illustrated in Example 9.2 in Chapter 9, we calculate the contribution per limiting factor. The calculations are as follows:

	Product 1	Product 2	Product 3
Unit contribution (£)	5	7	8
Contribution per hour of type A machine time (£)	5 (5/1)	3.50 (7/2)	2.67 (8/3)
Ranking	1	2	3

The optimal allocation of type A machine hours based on the above ranking is as follows:

Production	Machine hours used	Balance of machine hours available
2500 units of product 1	2500	7300 (9800 – 2500)
3000 units of product 2	6000	1300 (7300 – 6000)
433 units of product 3	1300	—

The 433 units of product 3 are obtained by dividing the 1300 unused machine hours by the 3 machine hours required for each unit of product 3. The proposed production programme results in the following calculation of total profit:

	(£)
2500 units of product 1 at £5 per unit contribution	12 500
3000 units of product 2 at £7 per unit contribution	21 000
433 units of product 3 at £8 per unit contribution	3 464
Total contribution	36 964
Less fixed overheads	21 000
Profit	15 964

b. There are several ways of formulating the tableau for a linear programming model. The tableau from the computer package can be reproduced as follows:

	Quantity	S1	S4	S5
S2	1 150	−0.5	−0.143	0.429
X2	1 850	0.5	0.143	−0.429
S3	3 800		0.429	−0.286
X3	1 200		−0.429	0.286
X1	2 500	−1	0	0
C	35 050	−1.5	−2.429	−0.714

In Chapter 25 the approach adopted was to formulate the first tableau with positive contribution signs and negative signs for the slack variable equations. The optimal solution occurs when the signs in the contribution row are all negative. The opposite procedure has been applied with the tableau presented in the question. Therefore the signs have been reversed in the above tableau to ensure that it is in the same format as that presented in Chapter 25. Note that an entry of 1 in the tableau presented in the question signifies the product or slack variable that is to be entered in each row of the above tableau.

The total contribution is £35 050, consisting of:

2500 units of product 1 at a contribution of £5 per unit
1850 units of product 2 at a contribution of £7 per unit
1200 units of product 3 at a contribution of £8 per unit

The revised fixed overheads are £18 000, resulting in a total profit of £17 050. This is higher than the profit before the fire (£15 964) because the fixed overheads saved by the fire exceed the lost contribution.

The shadow prices (or opportunity costs) for S4 indicate that if an additional type A machine hour can be acquired then profits will increase by £2.429 by increasing production of product 3 by 0.429 units and reducing production of product 2 by 0.143 units. Similarly, if an additional Type B machine hour can be acquired, then profits will increase by £0.714 by increasing production of product 2 by 0.429 units and reducing production of product 3 by 0.286 units. An extra unit of demand for product 1 will yield a contribution of £5, but, in order to obtain the resources, it is necessary to sacrifice half a unit of product 2. This will result in a loss of contribution of £3.50 (½ × £7). Therefore the net gain is £1.50.

The shadow prices indicate the premium over and above the present acquisition costs that the company should be willing to pay in order to obtain extra hours of machine time. The shadow price for product 1 indicates the upper limit to advertising or promotional expenses that should be incurred in order to stimulate demand by one further unit.

c. In part A there was only one limiting factor. In Chapter 25 we noted that the optimal solution can be derived by using the contribution per key factor approach whenever there is only one production constraint. Where more than one limiting factor exists then it is necessary to use linear programming to determine the optimal production programme.

25.15 a. Traditional (T) contribution per unit = £55.50 (£100 − (0.5 × £25 + 0.4 × £30 overheads + £20 timber))
Hightech (H) contribution per unit = £49
The linear programming model is as follows:
Maximize 55.5T + 49H (contribution)
Where

$$0.5T + 0.3H = 3400 \text{ (capacity X)}$$
$$0.4T + 0.45H = 3840 \text{ (capacity Y)}$$
$$4T + 4H = 34\ 000 \text{ (timber available)}$$

subject to 0 ≤ T ≤ 6000 and 0 ≤ H ≤ 10 000

b. i. The maximum contribution is shown as £444 125 and is derived as follows:

Traditional = 4250 units × £55.50 = £235 875
Hightech = 4250 units × £49.00 = £208 250

ii. The shadow prices indicate the extra contribution that can be obtained for each extra metre of timber (£9.8125) or additional machine group X hour (£32.50). Machine group Y has a zero shadow price because there is still some available capacity (slack) which has not been utilized (3840 hours available − 3612.5 hours allocated = 227.5 unused hours).

iii. There is no surplus capacity for machine group X and 227.5 hours surplus capacity for machine group Y giving an additional contribution of £6825 (227.5 hours × £30 = £6825).

iv. The adjustable cells table show the sensitivity of the plan to changes in the contribution per unit of each product. For the 'Traditional' product the contribution would have to be greater than £81.67 (i.e. an increase of £26.17) or less than £49 (i.e. a decrease of £6.50) for a change in the planned sales mix to occur. For the 'Hightech' product the contribution would have to exceed £55.50 (i.e. an increase of £6.50) or be less than £33.30 (i.e. a decrease of £15.70) for a change in the planned sales mix to occur.

v. For each additional metre an extra contribution of £9.8125 can be obtained but the parameters of the existing model indicate that this applies only for an extra 1733.33 metres of timber. The additional contribution from an extra 1733.33 metres of timber is £17 008 (1733.33 × £9.8125).

vi. A total of 35 733.33 metres (34 000 + 1733.33) will be allocated to production. The timber requirements for producing 'Hightech' are 14 400 metres resulting in 21 333.33 metres (35 733.33 − 14 400) being available for 'Traditional'. This will result in the production of 5333.33 units of 'Traditional'.

c. The following should be considered as a means of overcoming the capacity constraints:

● Investigate alternative sources of supply for the timber. Such supplies may only be obtainable at additional costs (e.g. purchasing from overseas suppliers).

● Increase the operating hours of the machinery. This may result in additional overtime payments to operators or require the appointment of extra staff.

● Increase the output per machine hour. This may result in additional labour payments and an increase in maintenance costs.

● Acquire additional machinery. To ascertain whether this is worthwhile, a capital investment appraisal should be undertaken that incorporates the cash flow consequences over the whole life of the machinery.

● Sub-contract some of the production to outside companies. This is likely to be more expensive than the internal incremental production costs and may also create quality control problems.

d. Only variable costs are included in the model. Therefore product specific (avoidable) fixed costs are not taken into account. Such costs may be relevant if they are avoidable or involve step functions. Examples include staff dedicated to a single product such as marketing costs attributable to only one of the products.

Customer specific costs may differ between customers. For example distribution costs may vary according to the location of customers or some customers may rely on many small volume frequent orders whereas others may rely on large volume infrequent orders. The costs of servicing the latter category of customers are likely to be less than the former.

Life cycle costs represent the costs incurred over a product's life cycle from the introduction, growth, maturity and decline stages. Costs may vary at the different stages. If one of the products is at the introductory stage it may incur additional marketing costs in order to promote it. Thus costs may differ between the two products if they are subject to different stages within their life cycles.

INDEX